military		militar
music		
noun		
nautica		
onesel		
pejora		
photo		
plural		
politi		
possessive		
past participle	*pp*	participio pasado
preposition	*prep*	preposición
present participle	*pres p*	participio de presente
pronoun	*pron*	pronombre
past tense	*pt*	tiempo pasado
railroad	*Rail*	ferrocarril
religion	*Relig*	religión
school	*Schol*	enseñanza
singular	*sing*	singular
someone	*s. o.*	alguien
something	*sth*	algo
technical	*Tec*	técnico
university	*Univ*	universidad
verb	*vb*	verbo
intransitive verb	*vi*	verbo intransitivo
pronominal verb	*vpr*	verbo pronominal
transitive verb	*vt*	verbo transitivo
transitive & intransitive verb	*vti*	verbo transitivo e intransitivo

Oxford Spanish Minidictionary
Diccionario Oxford Mini

Spanish–English • English–Spanish
español-inglés • inglés-español

Diccionario Oxford Mini

TERCERA EDICIÓN

español–inglés
inglés–español

OXFORD
UNIVERSITY PRESS

Oxford Spanish Minidictionary

THIRD EDITION

Spanish–English
English–Spanish

OXFORD
UNIVERSITY PRESS

OXFORD
UNIVERSITY PRESS

Great Clarendon Street, Oxford OX2 6DP

Oxford University Press is a department of the University of Oxford.
It furthers the University's objective of excellence in research, scholarship,
and education by publishing worldwide in

Oxford New York

Auckland Cape Town Dar es Salaam Hong Kong Karachi Kuala Lumpur
Madrid Melbourne Mexico City Nairobi New Delhi Shanghai Taipei
Toronto

With offices in
Argentina Austria Brazil Chile Czech Republic France Greece
Guatemala Hungary Italy Japan South Korea Poland Portugal
Singapore Switzerland Thailand Turkey Ukraine Vietnam

Published in the United States
by Oxford University Press Inc., New York

British Library Cataloguing in Publication Data
Data available

Library of Congress Cataloging in Publication Data
Data available

ISBN 978-0-19-861043-4

ISBN 978-0-19-861046-5 (Spanish cover edition)

10 9 8 7 6 5 4 3

Typeset by Interactive Sciences Ltd, Gloucester
Printed and bound in Italy by
Legoprint S.p.A.

Contents/Índice

Proprietary terms

This dictionary includes some words which have, or are asserted to have, proprietary status as trademarks. Their inclusion does not imply that they have acquired for legal purposes a non-proprietary or general significance, nor any other judgement concerning their legal status. In cases where the editorial staff have some evidence that a word has proprietary status this is indicated in the entry for that word by the symbol ®, but no judgement concerning the legal status of such words is made or implied thereby.

Marcas registradas

Este diccionario incluye algunas palabras que son o pretenden ser marcas registradas. Cuando al editor le consta que una palabra es una marca registrada, esto se indica por medio del símbolo ®. No debe atribuirse ningún valor jurídico ni a la presencia ni a la ausencia de tal designación.

Contributors/Colaboradores

Third Edition/Tercera edición

Nicholas Rollin
Carol Styles Carvajal

Second Edition/Segunda edición

Editors/Editores
Carol Styles Carvajal
Michael Britton
Jane Horwood

Phrasefinder/Índice temático de frases
Idoia Noble
Neil and Roswitha Morris

Data input/Entrada de datos
Susan Wilkin

First Edition/Primera edición

Editor/Editora
Christine Lea

Introduction

This new edition of the *Oxford Spanish Minidictionary* is designed as an effective and practical reference tool for the student, adult learner, traveller, and business professional.

The wordlist has been revised and updated to reflect recent additions to both languages. The *Phrasefinder* section has been expanded. It aims to provide the user with the confidence to communicate in the most commonly encountered social situations such as travel, shopping, eating out, and organizing leisure activities.

Another valuable feature of the dictionary is the special status given to more complex grammatical words which provide the basic structure of both languages. Boxed entries in the text for these *function words* provide extended treatment, including notes to warn of possible pitfalls.

The dictionary has an easy-to-use, streamlined layout. Bullets separate each new part of speech within an entry. Nuances of sense or usage are pinpointed by indicators or by typical collocates with which the word frequently occurs. Extra help is given in the form of symbols to mark the register of words and phrases. An exclamation mark [!] indicates colloquial language, and a cross [✖] indicates slang.

Each English headword is followed by its phonetic transcription between slashes. The symbols used are those of the International Phonetic Alphabet. Pronunciation is also shown for derivatives and compounds where it is not easily deduced from that of a headword. The rules for the pronunciation of Spanish are given on pages xii–xiii.

The swung dash (~) is used to represent a headword or that part of a headword preceding the vertical bar (|).

In both English and Spanish only irregular plurals are given. Normally Spanish nouns and adjectives ending in an unstressed vowel form the plural by adding s (e.g. *libro*, *libros*). Nouns and adjectives ending in a stressed vowel or a consonant add es (e.g. *rubí*, *rubíes*, *pared*, *paredes*). An accent on the final syllable is not required when es is added (e.g. *nación*, *naciones*). Final *z* becomes *ces* (e.g. *vez*, *veces*).

Spanish nouns and adjectives ending in o form the feminine by changing the final *o* to *a* (e.g. *hermano*, *hermana*). Most Spanish nouns and adjectives ending in anything other than final *o* do not have a separate feminine form, with the exception of those denoting nationality etc.; these add a to the masculine singular form (e.g. *español*, *española*). An accent on the penultimate syllable is then not required (e.g. *inglés*, *inglesa*). Adjectives ending in *án*, *ón*, or *or* behave like those denoting nationality, with the following exceptions: *inferior*, *mayor*, *mejor*, *menor*, *peor*, *superior*, where the feminine has the same form as the masculine. Spanish verb tables will be found at the end of the book.

The Spanish alphabet

In Spanish *ñ* is considered a separate letter and in the Spanish–English section, therefore, is alphabetized after *ny*.

Introducción

Esta nueva edición del *Minidiccionario de Oxford* ha sido concebida a fin de proporcionar una herramienta de referencia práctica y eficaz al estudiante, joven y adulto, al viajero y a la persona de negocios.

Se ha revisado la lista de palabras con el objeto de incorporar nuevos términos en ambos idiomas. La sección central contiene una *Lista temática de frases*, que se ha ampliado, destinada a que el usuario adquiera la confianza necesaria para comunicarse en las situaciones más normales de la vida diaria, como las que se encuentran al viajar, hacer compras, comer fuera y organizar actividades recreativas.

Otro valioso aspecto del diccionario es la importancia especial que se da a palabras con una función más compleja dentro de la gramática y que proveen la estructura básica de ambos idiomas. Estos *vocablos clave* están contenidos en recuadros dentro del texto, donde se les da un tratamiento amplio y se incluyen notas para advertir sobre posibles escollos.

El diccionario tiene una presentación clara y es fácil de usar. Símbolos distintivos separan las diferentes categorías gramaticales dentro de cada entrada. Los matices de sentido y de uso se muestran con precisión mediante indicadores o por colocaciones típicas con las que la palabra se usa frecuentemente. Se encuentra ayuda adicional en los signos que indican el registro idiomático de las palabras y frases. Un signo de exclamación [!] señala el uso coloquial y una cruz [x] el uso argot.

Cada palabra cabeza de artículo en inglés va seguida de su transcripción fonética entre barras oblicuas. Los símbolos que se usan son los del Alfabeto Fonético Internacional. También aparece la pronunciación de derivados y nombres compuestos cuando no es posible deducirla de la palabra cabeza de artículo. Las reglas sobre pronunciación inglesa se encuentran en la página xiv.

La tilde (~) se emplea para sustituir la palabra cabeza de artículo o aquella parte de tal palabra que precede a la barra vertical (|).

Tanto en inglés como en español se dan los plurales solamente si son irregulares. Para formar el plural regular en inglés se añade la letra s al sustantivo singular, pero se añade es cuando se trata de una palabra que termina en *ch*, *sh*, *s*, *ss*, *us*, *x*, *o*, *z* (p.ej. *sash*, *sashes*). En el caso de una palabra que termine en *y* precedida por una consonante, la y se transforma en *ies* (p.ej. *baby*, *babies*). Para formar el tiempo pasado y el participio pasado se añade *ed* al infinitivo de los verbos regulares ingleses (p.ej. *last*, *lasted*). En el caso de los verbos ingleses que terminan en e muda se añade sólo la *d* (p.ej. *move*, *moved*). En el caso de los verbos ingleses que terminan en *y*, se debe cambiar la *y* por *ied* (p.ej. *carry*, *carried*). Los verbos irregulares se encuentran en el diccionario por orden alfabético remitidos al infinitivo, y también en la lista que aparece en las últimas páginas del diccionario.

Pronunciation of Spanish

Vowels

a between pronunciation of *a* in English *cat* and *arm*

e like *e* in English *bed*

i like *ee* in English *see* but a little shorter

o like *o* in English *hot* but a little longer

u like *oo* in English *too*

y when a vowel is as Spanish **i**

Consonants

b (1) in initial position or after a nasal consonant is like English *b*
(2) in other positions is between English *b* and English *v*

c (1) before **e** or **i** is like *th* in English *thin*. In Latin American Spanish is like English *s*.
(2) in other positions is like *c* in English *cat*

ch like *ch* in English *chip*

d (1) in initial position, after nasal consonants and after **l** is like English *d*
(2) in other positions is like *th* in English *this*

f like English *f*

g (1) before **e** or **i** is like *ch* in Scottish *loch*
(2) in initial position is like *g* in English *get*
(3) in other positions is like (2) but a little softer

h silent in Spanish but see also **ch**

j like *ch* in Scottish *loch*

k like English *k*

l like English *l* but see also **ll**

ll like *lli* in English *million*

m like English *m*

n like English *n*

ñ like *ni* in English *opinion*

p like English *p*

q like English *k*

r rolled or trilled

s like *s* in English *sit*

t like English *t*

v (1) in initial position or after a nasal consonant is like English *b*
(2) in other positions is between English b and English *v*

w like Spanish **b** or **v**

x like English *x*

y like English *y*

z like *th* in English *thin*

Pronunciación inglesa

Símbolos fonéticos

Vocales y diptongos

iː	*see*	ɔː	*saw*	eɪ	*page*	ɔɪ	*join*
ɪ	*sit*	ʊ	*put*	əʊ	*home*	ɪə	*near*
e	*ten*	uː	*too*	aɪ	*five*	eə	*hair*
æ	*hat*	ʌ	*cup*	aɪə	*fire*	ʊə	*poor*
ɑː	*arm*	ɜː	*fur*	aʊ	*now*		
ɒ	*got*	ə	*ago*	aʊə	*flour*		

Consonantes

p	*pen*	tʃ	*chin*	s	*so*	n	*no*
b	*bad*	dʒ	*June*	z	*zoo*	ŋ	*sing*
t	*tea*	f	*fall*	ʃ	*she*	l	*leg*
d	*dip*	v	*voice*	ʒ	*measure*	r	*red*
k	*cat*	θ	*thin*	h	*how*	j	*yes*
g	*got*	ð	*then*	m	*man*	w	*wet*

El símbolo ˈ precede a la sílaba sobre la cual recae el acento tónico.

Aa

a *preposición*

Note that **a** followed by **el** becomes **al**, e.g. **vamos al cine**

····➤ (*dirección*) to. **fui a México** I went to Mexico. **muévete a la derecha** move to the right

····➤ (*posición*) **se sentaron a la mesa** they sat at the table. **al lado del banco** next to the bank. **a orillas del río** on the banks of the river

····➤ (*distancia*) **queda a 5 km** it's 5 km away. **a pocos metros de aquí** a few meters from here

····➤ (*fecha*) **hoy estamos a 5** today is the 5th. **¿a cuánto estamos?**, (*LAm*) **¿a cómo estamos?** what's the date?

····➤ (*hora, momento*) at. **a las 2** at 2 o'clock. **a fin de mes** at the end of the month. **a los 21 años** at the age of 21; (*después de*) after 21 years

····➤ (*precio*) **¿a cómo están las peras?** how much are the pears? **están a 3 euros el kilo** they're 3 euros a kilo. **salen a 15 euros cada uno** they work out at 15 euros each.

····➤ (*medio, modo*) **fuimos a pie** we went on foot. **hecho a mano** hand made. **pollo al horno** (*LAm*) roast chicken

····➤ (*cuando precede al objeto directo de persona*) *no se traduce*. **conocí a Juan** I met Juan. **quieren mucho a sus hijos** they love their children very much

····➤ (*con objeto indirecto*) to. **se lo di a Juan** I gave it to Juan. **le vendí el coche a mi amigo** I sold my friend the car, I sold the car to my friend. **se lo compré a mi madre** I bought it from my mother; (*para*) I bought it for my mother

➡ Cuando la preposición **a** se emplea precedida de ciertos verbos como **empezar, faltar, ir, llegar** etc., ver bajo el respectivo verbo

ábaco *m* abacus

abadejo *m* pollack

abadía *f* abbey

abajo *adv* (down) below; (*dirección*) down(wards); (*en casa*) downstairs. ● *int* down with. ~ **de** (*LAm*) under(neath). **calle** ~ down the street. **el** ~ **firmante** the undersigned. **escaleras** ~ down the stairs. **la parte de** ~ the bottom (part). **más** ~ further down

abalanzarse [10] *vpr* rush (**hacia** towards)

abanderado *m* standard-bearer; (*Mex, en fútbol*) linesman

abandon|ado *adj* abandoned; (*descuidado*) neglected; (persona) untidy. ~**ar** *vt* leave (un lugar); abandon (persona, cosa). ● *vi* give

a

up. **~arse** *vpr* give in; (*descuidarse*) let o.s. go. **~o** *m* abandonment; (*estado*) neglect
abani|car 7 *vt* fan. **~co** *m* fan
abaratar *vt* reduce
abarcar 7 *vt* put one's arms around, embrace; (*comprender*) embrace
abarrotar *vt* overfill, pack full
abarrotes *mpl* (*LAm*) groceries; (*tienda*) grocer's shop
abast|ecer 11 *vt* supply. **~ecimiento** *m* supply; (*acción*) supplying. **~o** *m* supply. **no dar ~o** be unable to cope (**con** with)
abati|do *adj* depressed. **~miento** *m* depression
abdicar 7 *vt* give up. ● *vi* abdicate
abdom|en *m* abdomen. **~inal** *adj* abdominal
abec|é *m* I alphabet, ABC. **~edario** *m* alphabet
abedul *m* birch (tree)
abej|a *f* bee. **~orro** *m* bumblebee
aberración *f* aberration
abertura *f* opening
abeto *m* fir (tree)
abierto *pp véase* ABRIR. ● *adj* open
abism|al *adj* abysmal; (*profundo*) deep. **~ar** *vt* throw into an abyss; (*fig, abatir*) humble. **~arse** *vpr* be absorbed (**en** in), be lost (**en** in). **~o** *m* abyss; (*fig, diferencia*) world of difference
ablandar *vt* soften.**~se** *vpr* soften
abnega|ción *f* self-sacrifice. **~do** *adj* self-sacrificing
abochornar *vt* embarrass. **~se** *vpr* feel embarrassed
abofetear *vt* slap
aboga|cía *f* law. **~do** *m* lawyer, solicitor; (*ante tribunal superior*) barrister (*Brit*), attorney (*Amer*).
abolengo *m* ancestry
aboli|ción *f* abolition. **~cionismo** *m* abolitionism. **~cionista** *m & f* abolitionist. **~r** 24 *vt* abolish
abolla|dura *f* dent. **~r** *vt* dent
abolsado *adj* baggy
abomba|do *adj* convex; (*LAm, atontado*) dopey. **~r** *vt* make convex. **~rse** *vpr* (*LAm, descomponerse*) go bad
abominable *adj* abominable
abona|ble *adj* payable. **~do** *adj* paid. ● *m* subscriber. **~r** *vt* pay; (*en agricultura*) fertilize. **~rse** *vpr* subscribe.
abono *m* payment; (*estiércol*) fertilizer; (*a un periódico*) subscription
aborda|ble *adj* reasonable; (*persona*) approachable. **~je** *m* boarding. **~r** *vt* tackle (un asunto); approach (una persona); (*Naut*) come alongside; (*Mex, Aviac*) board
aborigen *adj & m* native
aborrec|er 11 *vt* loathe. **~ible** *adj* loathsome. **~ido** *adj* loathed. **~imiento** *m* loathing
abort|ar *vi* have a miscarriage. **~ivo** *adj* abortive. **~o** *m* miscarriage; (*voluntario*) abortion. **hacerse un ~o** have an abortion
abotonar *vt* button (up). **~se** *vpr* button (up)
abovedado *adj* vaulted
abrasa|dor *adj* burning. **~r** *vt* burn. **~rse** *vpr* burn
abraz|ar *vt* 10 embrace. **~arse** *vpr* embrace. **~o** *m* hug. **un fuerte ~o de** (*en una carta*) with best wishes from
abre|botellas *m invar* bottle-

opener. ~**cartas** *m invar* paper-knife. ~**latas** *m invar* tin opener (*Brit*), can opener

abrevia|ción *f* abbreviation; (*texto abreviado*) abridged text. ~**do** *adj* brief; (texto) abridged. ~**r** *vt* abbreviate; abridge (texto); cut short (viaje etc). ● *vi* be brief. ~**tura** *f* abbreviation

abrig|ado *adj* (lugar) sheltered; (persona) well wrapped up. ~**ador** *adj* (*Mex, ropa*) warm. ~**ar** 12 *vt* shelter; cherish (esperanza); harbour (duda, sospecha). ~**arse** *vpr* (take) shelter; (*con ropa*) wrap up. ~**o** *m* (over)coat; (*lugar*) shelter

abril *m* April. ~**eño** *adj* April

abrillantar *vt* polish

abrir (*pp* **abierto**) *vt/i* open. ~**se** *vpr* open; (*extenderse*) open out; (el tiempo) clear

abrochar *vt* do up; (*con botones*) button up

abruma|dor *adj* overwhelming. ~**r** *vt* overwhelm

abrupto *adj* steep; (*áspero*) harsh

abrutado *adj* brutish

absentismo *m* absenteeism

absolución *f* (*Relig*) absolution; (*Jurid*) acquittal

absolut|amente *adv* absolutely, completely. ~**o** *adj* absolute. **en** ~**o** (not) at all. ~**orio** *adj* of acquittal

absolver 2 (*pp* **absuelto**) *vt* (*Relig*) absolve; (*Jurid*) acquit

absor|bente *adj* absorbent; (*fig, interesante*) absorbing. ~**ber** *vt* absorb. ~**ción** *f* absorption. ~**to** *adj* absorbed

abstemio *adj* teetotal. ● *m* teetotaller

absten|ción *f* abstention. ~**erse** 40 *vpr* abstain, refrain (**de** from)

abstinencia *f* abstinence

abstra|cción *f* abstraction. ~**cto** *adj* abstract. ~**er** 41 *vt* abstract. ~**erse** *vpr* be lost in thought. ~**ído** *adj* absent-minded

absuelto *adj* (*Relig*) absolved; (*Jurid*) acquitted

absurdo *adj* absurd. ● *m* absurd thing

abuche|ar *vt* boo. ~**o** *m* booing

abuel|a *f* grandmother. ~**o** *m* grandfather. ~**os** *mpl* grandparents

ab|ulia *f* apathy. ~**úlico** *adj* apathetic

abulta|do *adj* bulky. ~**r** *vt* (*fig, exagerar*) exaggerate. ● *vi* be bulky

abunda|ncia *f* abundance. **nadar en la** ~**ncia** be rolling in money. ~**nte** *adj* abundant, plentiful. ~**r** *vi* be plentiful

aburguesarse *vpr* become middle-class

aburri|do *adj* (*con estar*) bored; (*con ser*) boring. ~**dor** *adj* (*LAm*) boring. ~**miento** *m* boredom; (*cosa pesada*) bore. ~**r** *vt* bore. ~**rse** *vpr* get bored

abus|ar *vi* take advantage. ~**ar de la bebida** drink too much. ~**ivo** *adj* excessive. ~**o** *m* abuse

acá *adv* here. ~ **y allá** here and there. **de** ~ **para allá** to and fro. **de ayer** ~ since yesterday. **más** ~ nearer

acaba|do *adj* finished; (*perfecto*) perfect. ● *m* finish. ~**r** *vt/i* finish. ~**rse** *vpr* finish; (*agotarse*) run out; (*morirse*) die. ~**r con** put an end to. ~**r de** (+ *infinitivo*) have just (+ *pp*). ~ **de llegar** he has just arrived. ~**r por** (+ *infinitivo*) end up (+ *gerundio*). **¡se acabó!** that's it!

acabóse *m*. **ser el** ~ be the end, be the limit

acad|emia *f* academy. **~émico** *adj* academic
acallar *vt* silence
acalora|do *adj* heated; (persona) hot. **~rse** *vpr* get hot; (*fig, excitarse*) get excited
acampar *vi* camp
acantilado *m* cliff
acapara|r *vt* hoard; (*monopolizar*) monopolize. **~miento** *m* hoarding; (*monopolio*) monopolizing
acariciar *vt* caress; (animal) stroke; (idea) nurture
ácaro *m* mite
acarre|ar *vt* transport; (desgracias etc) cause. **~o** *m* transport
acartona|do *adj* (piel) wizened. **~rse** *vpr* (*ponerse rígido*) go stiff; (piel) become wizened
acaso *adv* maybe, perhaps. • *m* chance. **~ llueva mañana** perhaps it will rain tomorrow. **por si ~** (just) in case
acata|miento *m* compliance (**de** with). **~r** *vt* comply with
acatarrarse *vpr* catch a cold, get a cold
acaudalado *adj* well off
acceder *vi* agree; (*tener acceso*) have access
acces|ible *adj* accessible; (persona) approachable. **~o** *m* access, entry; (*Med, ataque*) attack
accesorio *adj* & *m* accessory
accident|ado *adj* (terreno) uneven; (*agitado*) troubled; (persona) injured. **~al** *adj* accidental. **~arse** *vpr* have an accident. **~e** *m* accident
acci|ón *f* (*incl Jurid*) action; (*hecho*) deed; (*Com*) share. **~onar** *vt* work. • *vi* gesticulate. **~onista** *m* & *f* shareholder
acebo *m* holly (tree)
acech|ar *vt* lie in wait for. **~o** *m* spying. **al ~o** on the look-out
aceit|ar *vt* oil; (*Culin*) add oil to. **~e** *m* oil. **~e de oliva** olive oil. **~te de ricino** castor oil. **~era** *f* cruet; (*para engrasar*) oilcan. **~ero** *adj* oil. **~oso** *adj* oily
aceitun|a *f* olive. **~ado** *adj* olive. **~o** *m* olive tree
acelera|dor *m* accelerator. **~r** *vt* accelerate; (*fig*) speed up, quicken
acelga *f* chard
acent|o *m* accent; (*énfasis*) stress. **~uación** *f* accentuation. **~uar** **21** *vt* stress; (*fig*) emphasize. **~uarse** *vpr* become noticeable
acepción *f* meaning, sense
acepta|ble *adj* acceptable. **~ción** *f* acceptance; (*éxito*) success. **~r** *vt* accept
acequia *f* irrigation channel
acera *f* pavement (*Brit*), sidewalk (*Amer*)
acerca de *prep* about
acerca|miento *m* approach; (*fig*) reconciliation. **~r** **7** *vt* bring near. **~rse** *vpr* approach
acero *m* steel. **~ inoxidable** stainless steel
acérrimo *adj* (*fig*) staunch
acert|ado *adj* right, correct; (*apropiado*) appropriate. **~ar** **1** *vt* (*adivinar*) get right, guess. • *vi* get right; (*en el blanco*) hit. **~ar a** happen to. **~ar con** hit on. **~ijo** *m* riddle
achacar **7** *vt* attribute
achacoso *adj* sickly
achaque *m* ailment
achatar *vt* flatten
achicar **7** *vt* make smaller; (*fig, fam, empequeñecer*) belittle; (*Naut*)

bale out. **~rse** *vpr* become smaller; (*humillarse*) be intimidated

achicharra|r *vt* burn; (*fig*) pester. **~rse** *vpr* burn

achichincle *m & f* (*Mex*) hanger-on

achicopalado *adj* (*Mex*) depressed

achicoria *f* chicory

achiote *m* (*LAm*) annatto

achispa|do *adj* tipsy. **~rse** *vpr* get tipsy

achulado *adj* cocky

acicala|do *adj* dressed up. **~r** *vt* dress up. **~rse** *vpr* get dressed up

acicate *m* spur

acidez *f* acidity; (*Med*) heartburn

ácido *adj* sour. ● *m* acid

acierto *m* success; (*idea*) good idea; (*habilidad*) skill

aclama|ción *f* acclaim; (*aplausos*) applause. **~r** *vt* acclaim; (*aplaudir*) applaud

aclara|ción *f* explanation. **~r** *vt* lighten (colores); (*explicar*) clarify; (*enjuagar*) rinse. ● *vi* (el tiempo) brighten up. **~rse** *vpr* become clear. **~torio** *adj* explanatory

aclimata|ción *f* acclimatization, acclimation (*Amer*). **~r** *vt* acclimatize, acclimate (*Amer*). **~rse** *vpr* become acclimatized, become acclimated (*Amer*)

acné *m* acne

acobardar *vt* intimidate. **~se** *vpr* lose one's nerve

acocil *m* (*Mex*) freshwater shrimp

acog|edor *adj* welcoming; (ambiente) friendly. **~er** **14** *vt* welcome; (*proteger*) shelter; (*recibir*) receive. **~erse** *vpr* take refuge. **~ida** *f* welcome; (*refugio*) refuge

acolcha|do *adj* quilted. **~r** *vt* quilt, pad

acomedido *adj* (*Mex*) obliging

acomet|er *vt* attack; (*emprender*) undertake. **~ida** *f* attack

acomod|ado *adj* well off. **~ador** *m* usher. **~adora** *f* usherette. **~ar** *vt* arrange; (*adaptar*) adjust. ● *vi* be suitable. **~arse** *vpr* settle down; (*adaptarse*) conform

acompaña|miento *m* accompaniment. **~nte** *m & f* companion; (*Mus*) accompanist. **~r** *vt* go with; (*hacer compañía*) keep company; (*adjuntar*) enclose

acondicionar *vt* fit out; (*preparar*) prepare

aconseja|ble *adj* advisable. **~do** *adj* advised. **~r** *vt* advise. **~rse** *vpr*. **~rse con** consult

acontec|er **11** *vi* happen. **~imiento** *m* event

acopla|miento *m* coupling; (*Elec*) connection. **~r** *vt* fit; (*Elec*) connect; (*Rail*) couple

acorazado *adj* armour-plated. ● *m* battleship

acord|ar **2** *vt* agree (upon); (*decidir*) decide; (*recordar*) remind. **~arse** *vpr* remember. **~e** *adj* in agreement; (*Mus*) harmonious. ● *m* chord

acorde|ón *m* accordion. **~onista** *m & f* accordionist

acordona|do *adj* (lugar) cordoned off; (zapatos) lace-up. **~r** *vt* lace (up); (*rodear*) cordon off

acorralar *vt* round up (animales); corner (personas)

acortar *vt* shorten; cut short (permanencia). **~se** *vpr* get shorter

acos|ar *vt* hound; (*fig*) pester. **~o** *m* pursuit; (*fig*) pestering

acostar **2** *vt* put to bed; (*Naut*) bring alongside. ● *vi* (*Naut*) reach

a

land. **~se** *vpr* go to bed; (*echarse*) lie down. **~se con** (*fig*) sleep with

acostumbra|do *adj* (*habitual*) usual. **~do a** used to. **~r** *vt* get used. **me ha ~do a levantarme por la noche** he's got me used to getting up at night. ● *vi.* **~r** be accustomed to. **acostumbro a comer a la una** I usually have lunch at one o'clock. **~rse** *vpr* become accustomed, get used

acota|ción *f* (*nota*) margin note (*en el teatro*) stage direction; (*cota*) elevation mark. **~miento** *m* (*Mex*) hard shoulder

acrecentar **1** *vt* increase. **~se** *vpr* increase

acredita|do *adj* reputable; (*Pol*) accredited. **~r** *vt* prove; accredit (diplomático); (*garantizar*) guarantee; (*autorizar*) authorize. **~rse** *vpr* make one's name

acreedor *adj* worthy (**de** of). ● *m* creditor

acribillar *vt* (*a balazos*) riddle (**a** with); (*a picotazos*) cover (**a** with); (*fig, a preguntas etc*) bombard (**a** with)

acr|obacia *f* acrobatics. **~obacias aéreas** aerobatics. **~óbata** *m & f* acrobat. **~obático** *adj* acrobatic

acta *f* minutes; (*certificado*) certificate

actitud *f* posture, position; (*fig*) attitude, position

activ|ar *vt* activate; (*acelerar*) speed up. **~idad** *f* activity. **~o** *adj* active. ● *m* assets

acto *m* act; (*ceremonia*) ceremony. **en el ~** immediately

act|or *m* actor. **~riz** *f* actress

actuación *f* action; (*conducta*) behaviour; (*Theat*) performance

actual *adj* present; (asunto) topical. **~idad** *f* present; (*de asunto*) topicality. **en la ~idad** (*en este momento*) currently; (*hoy en día*) nowadays. **~idades** *fpl* current affairs. **~ización** *f* modernization. **~izar** **10** *vt* modernize. **~mente** *adv* now, at the present time

actuar **21** *vi* act. **~ de** act as

acuarel|a *f* watercolour. **~ista** *m & f* watercolourist

acuario *m* aquarium. **A~** Aquarius

acuartelar *vt* quarter, billet; (*mantener en cuartel*) confine to barracks

acuático *adj* aquatic

acuchillar *vt* slash; stab (persona)

acuci|ante *adj* urgent. **~ar** *vt* urge on; (*dar prisa a*) hasten. **~oso** *adj* keen

acudir *vi.* **~ a** go to; (*asistir*) attend; turn up for (a una cita); (*en auxilio*) go to help

acueducto *m* aqueduct

acuerdo *m* agreement. ● *vb véase* **ACORDAR**. **¡de ~!** OK! **de ~ con** in accordance with. **estar de ~** agree. **ponerse de ~** agree

acuesto *vb véase* **ACOSTAR**

acumula|dor *m* accumulator. **~r** *vt* accumulate. **~rse** *vpr* accumulate

acunar *vt* rock

acuñar *vt* mint, coin

acupuntura *f* acupuncture

acurrucarse **7** *vpr* curl up

acusa|do *adj* accused; (*destacado*) marked. ● *m* accused. **~r** *vt* accuse; (*mostrar*) show; (*denunciar*) denounce; acknowledge (recibo)

acuse *m.* **~ de recibo** acknowledgement of receipt

acus|ica *m & f* **!** telltale. **~ón** *m*

! telltale

acústic|a *f* acoustics. **~o** *adj* acoustic

adapta|ble *adj* adaptable. **~ción** *f* adaptation. **~dor** *m* adapter. **~r** *vt* adapt; (*ajustar*) fit. **~rse** *vpr* adapt o.s.

adecua|do *adj* suitable. **~r** *vt* adapt, make suitable

adelant|ado *adj* advanced; (niño) precocious; (reloj) fast. **por ~ado** in advance.. **~amiento** *m* advance(ment); (*Auto*) overtaking. **~ar** *vt* advance, move forward; (*acelerar*) speed up; put forward (reloj); (*Auto*) overtake. ● *vi* advance, go forward; (reloj) gain, be fast. **~arse** *vpr* advance, move forward; (reloj) gain; (*Auto*) overtake. **~e** *adv* forward. ● *int* come in!; (*¡siga!*) carry on! **más ~e** (*lugar*) further on; (*tiempo*) later on. **~o** *m* advance; (*progreso*) progress

adelgaza|miento *m* slimming. **~r** **10** *vt* make thin; lose (kilos). ● *vi* lose weight; (*adrede*) slim. **~rse** *vpr* lose weight; (*adrede*) slim

ademán *m* gesture. **en ~ de** as if to. **ademanes** *mpl* (*modales*) manners.

además *adv* besides; (*también*) also; (*lo que es más*) what's more. **~ de** besides

adentr|arse *vpr*. **~arse en** penetrate into; study thoroughly (tema etc). **~o** *adv* in(side). **~ de** (*LAm*) in(side). **mar ~o** out at sea. **tierra ~o** inland

adepto *m* supporter

aderez|ar **10** *vt* flavour (bebidas); (*condimentar*) season; dress (ensalada). **~o** *m* flavouring; (*con condimentos*) seasoning; (*para ensalada*) dressing

adeud|ar *vt* owe. **~o** *m* debit

adhe|rir **4** *vt/i* stick. **~rirse** *vpr* stick; (*fig*) follow. **~sión** *f* adhesion; (*fig*) support. **~sivo** *adj & m* adhesive

adici|ón *f* addition. **~onal** *adj* additional. **~onar** *vt* add

adicto *adj* addicted. ● *m* addict; (*seguidor*) follower

adiestra|do *adj* trained. **~miento** *m* training. **~r** *vt* train. **~rse** *vpr* practise

adinerado *adj* wealthy

adiós *int* goodbye!; (*al cruzarse con alguien*) hello!

adit|amento *m* addition; (*accesorio*) accessory. **~ivo** *m* additive

adivin|anza *f* riddle. **~ar** *vt* foretell; (*acertar*) guess. **~o** *m* fortuneteller

adjetivo *adj* adjectival. ● *m* adjective

adjudica|ción *f* award. **~r** **7** *vt* award. **~rse** *vpr* appropriate. **~tario** *m* winner of an award

adjunt|ar *vt* enclose. **~o** *adj* enclosed; (*auxiliar*) assistant. ● *m* assistant

administra|ción *f* administration; (*gestión*) management. **~dor** *m* administrator; (*gerente*) manager. **~dora** *f* administrator; manageress. **~r** *vt* administer. **~tivo** *adj* administrative

admira|ble *adj* admirable. **~ción** *f* admiration. **~dor** *m* admirer. **~r** *vt* admire; (*sorprender*) amaze. **~rse** *vpr* be amazed

admi|sibilidad *f* admissibility. **~sible** *adj* acceptable. **~sión** *f* admission; (*aceptación*) acceptance. **~tir** *vt* admit; (*aceptar*) accept

adobar *vt* (*Culin*) pickle; (*condimentar*) marinade

a

adobe *m* sun-dried brick
adobo *m* pickle; (*condimento*) marinade
adoctrinar *vt* indoctrinate
adolecer 11 *vi.* ~ **de** suffer from
adolescen|cia *f* adolescence. ~**te** *adj* adolescent. ● *m & f* teenager, adolescent
adonde *adv* where
adónde *adv* where?
adop|ción *f* adoption. ~**tar** *vt* adopt. ~**tivo** *adj* adoptive; (hijo) adopted; (patria) of adoption
adoqu|ín *m* paving stone; (*imbécil*) idiot. ~**inado** *m* paving. ~**inar** *vt* pave
adora|ción *f* adoration. ~**r** *vt* adore
adormec|er 11 *vt* send to sleep; (*fig, calmar*) calm, soothe. ~**erse** *vpr* fall asleep; (un miembro) go to sleep. ~**ido** *adj* sleepy; (un miembro) numb
adormilarse *vpr* doze
adorn|ar *vt* adorn (**con, de** with). ~**o** *m* decoration
adosar *vt* lean (**a** against); (*Mex, adjuntar*) to enclose
adqui|rir 4 *vt* acquire; (*comprar*) purchase. ~**sición** *f* acquisition; (*compra*) purchase. ~**sitivo** *adj* purchasing
adrede *adv* on purpose
adrenalina *f* adrenalin
aduan|a *f* customs. ~**ero** *adj* customs. ● *m* customs officer
aducir 47 *vt* allege
adueñarse *vpr* take possession
adul|ación *f* flattery. ~**ador** *adj* flattering. ● *m* flatterer. ~**ar** *vt* flatter
ad|ulterar *vt* adulterate. ~**ulterio** *m* adultery
adulto *adj & m* adult, grown-up
advenedizo *adj & m* upstart
advenimiento *m* advent, arrival; (*subida al trono*) accession
adverbio *m* adverb
advers|ario *m* adversary. ~**idad** *f* adversity. ~**o** *adj* adverse, unfavourable
advert|encia *f* warning. ~**ir** 4 *vt* warn; (*notar*) notice
adviento *m* Advent
adyacente *adj* adjacent
aéreo *adj* air; (foto) aerial; (ferrocarril) overhead
aeróbico *adj* aerobic
aerodeslizador *m* hovercraft
aero|ligero *m* microlight. ~**lito** *m* meteorite. ~**moza** *f* (*LAm*) flight attendant. ~**puerto** *m* airport. ~**sol** *m* aerosol
afab|ilidad *f* affability. ~**le** *adj* affable
afamado *adj* famous
af|án *m* hard work; (*deseo*) desire. ~**anador** *m* (*Mex*) cleaner. ~**anar** *vt* ⊠ pinch ⊡. ~**anarse** *vpr* strive (**en, por** to)
afear *vt* disfigure, make ugly; (*censurar*) censure
afecta|ción *f* affectation. ~**do** *adj* affected. ~**r** *vt* affect
afect|ivo *adj* sensitive. ~**o** *m* (*cariño*) affection. ● *a.* ~**o a** attached to. ~**uoso** *adj* affectionate. **con un ~uoso saludo** (*en cartas*) with kind regards. **suyo ~ísimo** (*en cartas*) yours sincerely
afeita|do *m* shave. ~**dora** *f* electric razor. ~**r** *vt* shave. ~**rse** *vpr* shave, have a shave
afeminado *adj* effeminate. ● *m* effeminate person
aferrar *vt* grasp. ~**se** *vpr* to

cling (**a** to)
afianza|miento *m* (*refuerzo*) strengthening; (*garantía*) guarantee. **~rse** 10 *vpr* become established
afiche *m* (*LAm*) poster
afici|ón *f* liking; (*conjunto de aficionados*) fans. **por ~ón** as a hobby. **~onado** *adj* keen (**a** on), fond (**a** of). ● *m* fan. **~onar** *vt* make fond. **~onarse** *vpr* take a liking to
afila|do *adj* sharp. **~dor** *m* knife-grinder. **~r** *vt* sharpen
afilia|ción *f* affiliation. **~do** *adj* affiliated. **~rse** *vpr* become a member (**a** of)
afín *adj* similar; (*contiguo*) adjacent; (personas) related
afina|ción *f* (*Auto, Mus*) tuning. **~do** *adj* (*Mus*) in tune. **~dor** *m* tuner. **~r** *vt* (*afilar*) sharpen; (*Auto, Mus*) tune. **~rse** *vpr* become thinner
afincarse 7 *vpr* settle
afinidad *f* affinity; (*parentesco*) relationship by marriage
afirma|ción *f* affirmation. **~r** *vt* make firm; (*asentir*) affirm. **~rse** *vpr* steady o.s. **~tivo** *adj* affirmative
aflicción *f* affliction
afligi|do *adj* distressed. **~r** 14 *vt* distress. **~rse** *vpr* distress o.s.
aflojar *vt* loosen; (*relajar*) ease. ● *vi* let up. **~se** *vpr* loosen
aflu|encia *f* flow. **~ente** *adj* flowing. ● *m* tributary. **~ir** 17 *vi* flow (**a** into)
afónico *adj* hoarse
aforismo *m* aphorism
aforo *m* capacity
afortunado *adj* fortunate, lucky
afrancesado *adj* Frenchified
afrenta *f* insult; (*vergüenza*) disgrace
África *f* Africa. **~ del Sur** South Africa
africano *adj & m* African
afrodisíaco *adj & m* aphrodisiac
afrontar *vt* bring face to face; (*enfrentar*) face, confront
afuera *adv* out(side) **¡~!** out of the way! **~ de** (*LAm*) outside. **~s** *fpl* outskirts
agachar *vt* lower. **~se** *vpr* bend over
agalla *f* (*de los peces*) gill. **~s** *fpl* (*fig*) guts
agarradera *f* (*LAm*) handle
agarr|ado *adj* (*fig, fam*) mean. **~ar** *vt* grasp; (*esp LAm*) take; (*LAm, pillar*) catch. **~arse** *vpr* hold on; (*fam, reñirse*) have a fight. **~ón** *m* tug; (*LAm, riña*) row
agarrotar *vt* tie tightly; (el frío) stiffen; garotte (un reo). **~se** *vpr* go stiff; (*Auto*) seize up
agasaj|ado *m* guest of honour. **~ar** *vt* look after well. **~o** *m* good treatment
agazaparse *vpr* crouch
agencia *f* agency. **~ de viajes** travel agency. **~ inmobiliaria** estate agency (*Brit*), real estate agency (*Amer*). **~rse** *vpr* find (out) for o.s.
agenda *f* diary (*Brit*), appointment book (*Amer*); (*programa*) agenda
agente *m* agent; (*de policía*) policeman. ● *f* agent; (*de policía*) policewoman. **~ de aduanas** customs officer. **~ de bolsa** stockbroker
ágil *adj* agile
agili|dad *f* agility. **~zación** *f* speeding up. **~zar** *vt* speed up
agita|ción *f* waving; (*de un lí-*

a

quido) stirring; (*intranquilidad*) agitation. **~do** *adj* (el mar) rough; (*fig*) agitated. **~dor** *m* (*Pol*) agitator

agitar *vt* wave; shake (botellas etc); stir (líquidos); (*fig*) stir up. **~se** *vpr* wave; (el mar) get rough; (*fig*) get excited

aglomera|ción *f* agglomeration; (*de tráfico*) traffic jam. **~r** *vt* amass. **~rse** *vpr* form a crowd

agnóstico *adj* & *m* agnostic

agobi|ante *adj* (trabajo) exhausting; (calor) oppressive. **~ar** *vt* weigh down; (*fig, abrumar*) overwhelm. **~o** *m* weight; (*cansancio*) exhaustion; (*opresión*) oppression

agolparse *vpr* crowd together

agon|ía *f* death throes; (*fig*) agony. **~izante** *adj* dying; (luz) failing. **~izar** 10 *vi* be dying

agosto *m* August. **hacer su ~** feather one's nest

agota|do *adj* exhausted; (*todo vendido*) sold out; (libro) out of print. **~dor** *adj* exhausting. **~miento** *m* exhaustion. **~r** *vt* exhaust. **~rse** *vpr* be exhausted; (existencias) sell out; (libro) go out of print

agracia|do *adj* attractive; (*que tiene suerte*) lucky. **~r** *vt* make attractive

agrada|ble *adj* pleasant, nice. **~r** *vt/i* please. **esto me ~** I like this

agradec|er 11 *vt* thank (persona); be grateful for (cosa). **~ido** *adj* grateful. **¡muy ~ido!** thanks a lot! **~imiento** *m* gratitude

agrado *m* pleasure; (*amabilidad*) friendliness

agrandar *vt* enlarge; (*fig*) exaggerate. **~se** *vpr* get bigger

agrario *adj* agrarian, land; (*política*) agricultural

agrava|nte *adj* aggravating. ● *f* additional problem. **~r** *vt* aggravate; (*aumentar el peso*) make heavier. **~rse** *vpr* get worse

agravi|ar *vt* offend; (*perjudicar*) wrong. **~o** *m* offence

agredir 24 *vt* attack. **~ de palabra** insult

agrega|do *m* aggregate; (*diplomático*) attaché. **~r** 12 *vt* add; appoint (persona). **~rse** *vpr* to join

agres|ión *f* aggression; (*ataque*) attack. **~ividad** *f* aggressiveness. **~ivo** *adj* aggressive. **~or** *m* aggressor

agreste *adj* country; (terreno) rough

agriar *regular, o raramente* 20 *vt* sour. **~se** *vpr* turn sour; (*fig*) become embittered

agr|ícola *adj* agricultural. **~icultor** *m* farmer. **~icultura** *f* agriculture, farming

agridulce *adj* bitter-sweet; (*Culin*) sweet-and-sour

agrietar *vt* crack. **~se** *vpr* crack; (piel) chap

agrio *adj* sour. **~s** *mpl* citrus fruits

agro|nomía *f* agronomy. **~pecuario** *adj* farming

agrupa|ción *f* group; (*acción*) grouping. **~r** *vt* group. **~rse** *vpr* form a group

agruras *fpl* (*Mex*) heartburn

agua *f* water; (*lluvia*) rain; (*marea*) tide; (*vertiente del tejado*) slope. **~ abajo** downstream. **~ arriba** upstream. **~ bendita** holy water. **~ corriente** running water. **~ de colonia** eau de cologne. **~ dulce** fresh water. **~ mineral con gas** fizzy mineral water. **~ mineral sin gas** still mineral water. **~ potable**

drinking water. ~ **salada** salt water. **hacer** ~ (*Naut*) leak. **se me hizo** ~ **la boca** (*LAm*) my mouth watered

aguacate *m* avocado pear; (*árbol*) avocado pear tree

aguacero *m* downpour, heavy shower

aguado *adj* watery; (*Mex, aburrido*) boring

agua|fiestas *m & f invar* spoilsport, wet blanket. **~mala** *f* (*Mex*), **~mar** *m* jellyfish. **~marina** *f* aquamarine

aguant|ar *vt* put up with, bear; (*sostener*) support. ● *vi* hold out. **~arse** *vpr* restrain o.s. **~e** *m* patience; (*resistencia*) endurance

aguar 15 *vt* water down

aguardar *vt* wait for. ● *vi* wait

agua|rdiente *m* (cheap) brandy. **~rrás** *m* turpentine, turps ▯

agud|eza *f* sharpness; (*fig, perspicacia*) insight; (*fig, ingenio*) wit. **~izar** 10 *vt* sharpen. **~izarse** *vpr* (enfermedad) get worse. **~o** *adj* sharp; (ángulo, enfermedad) acute; (voz) high-pitched

agüero *m* omen. **ser de mal** ~ be a bad omen

aguijón *m* sting; (*vara*) goad

águila *f* eagle; (*persona perspicaz*) astute person; (*Mex, de moneda*) heads. **¿~ o sol?** heads or tails?

aguileño *adj* aquiline

aguinaldo *m* Christmas box; (*LAm, paga*) Christmas bonus

aguja *f* needle; (*del reloj*) hand; (*de torre*) steeple. **~s** *fpl* (*Rail*) points

agujer|ear *vt* make holes in. **~o** *m* hole

agujetas *fpl* stiffness; (*Mex, de zapatos*) shoe laces. **tener** ~ be stiff

aguzado *adj* sharp

ah *int* ah!, oh!

ahí *adv* there. ~ **nomás** (*LAm*) just there. **de** ~ **que** that is why. **por** ~ that way; (*aproximadamente*) thereabouts

ahija|da *f* god-daughter, godchild. **~do** *m* godson, godchild. **~dos** *mpl* godchildren

ahínco *m* enthusiasm; (*empeño*) insistence

ahog|ado *adj* (*en el agua*) drowned; (*asfixiado*) suffocated. **~ar** 12 *vt* (*en el agua*) drown; (*asfixiar*) suffocate; put out (fuego). **~arse** *vpr* (*en el agua*) drown; (*asfixiarse*) suffocate. **~o** *m* breathlessness; (*fig, angustia*) distress

ahondar *vt* deepen. ● *vi* go deep. ~ **en** (*fig*) examine in depth. **~se** *vpr* get deeper

ahora *adv* now; (*hace muy poco*) just now; (*dentro de poco*) very soon. ~ **bien** however. ~ **mismo** right now. **de** ~ **en adelante** from now on, in future. **por** ~ for the time being

ahorcar 7 *vt* hang. **~se** *vpr* hang o.s.

ahorita *adv* (*esp LAm fam*) now. ~ **mismo** right now

ahorr|ador *adj* thrifty. **~ar** *vt* save. **~arse** *vpr* save o.s. **~o** *m* saving. **~os** *mpl* savings

ahuecar 7 *vt* hollow; fluff up (colchón); deepen (la voz)

ahuizote *m* (*Mex*) scourge

ahuma|do *adj* (*Culin*) smoked; (*de colores*) smoky. **~r** *vt* (*Culin*) smoke; (*llenar de humo*) fill with smoke. ● *vi* smoke. **~rse** *vpr* become smoky; (comida) acquire a smoky taste

ahuyentar *vt* drive away; banish (pensamientos etc)

a

aimará *adj & m* Aymara. ● *m & f* Aymara indian

airado *adj* annoyed

aire *m* air; (*viento*) breeze; (*corriente*) draught; (*aspecto*) appearance; (*Mus*) tune, air. ~ **acondicionado** air-conditioning. **al** ~ **libre** outdoors. **darse** ~**s** give o.s. airs. ~**ar** *vt* air; (*ventilar*) ventilate; (*fig, publicar*) make public. ~**arse** *vpr.* **salir para** ~**arse** go out for some fresh air

airoso *adj* graceful; (*exitoso*) successful

aisla|do *adj* isolated; (*Elec*) insulated. ~**dor** *adj* (*Elec*) insulating. ~**nte** *adj* insulating. ~**r** 23 *vt* isolate; (*Elec*) insulate

ajar *vt* crumple; (*estropear*) spoil

ajedre|cista *m & f* chess-player. ~**z** *m* chess

ajeno *adj* (*de otro*) someone else's; (*de otros*) other people's; (*extraño*) alien

ajetre|ado *adj* hectic, busy. ~**o** *m* bustle

ají *m* (*LAm*) chilli; (*salsa*) chilli sauce

aj|illo *m* garlic. **al** ~**illo** cooked with garlic. ~**o** *m* garlic. ~**onjolí** *m* sesame

ajuar *m* furnishings; (*de novia*) trousseau; (*de bebé*) layette

ajust|ado *adj* right; (vestido) tight. ~**ar** *vt* fit; (*adaptar*) adapt; (*acordar*) agree; settle (una cuenta); (*apretar*) tighten. ● *vi* fit. ~**arse** *vpr* fit; (*adaptarse*) adapt o.s.; (*acordarse*) come to an agreement. ~**e** *m* fitting; (*adaptación*) adjustment; (*acuerdo*) agreement; (*de una cuenta*) settlement

al = **a** + **el**

ala *f* wing; (*de sombrero*) brim. ● *m & f* (*deportes*) winger

alaba|nza *f* praise. ~**r** *vt* praise

alacena *f* cupboard (*Brit*), closet (*Amer*)

alacrán *m* scorpion

alambr|ada *f* wire fence. ~**ado** *m* (*LAm*) wire fence. ~**e** *m* wire. ~**e de púas** barbed wire

alameda *f* avenue; (*plantío de álamos*) poplar grove

álamo *m* poplar. ~ **temblón** aspen

alarde *m* show. **hacer** ~ **de** boast of

alarga|do *adj* long. ~**dor** *m* extension. ~**r** 12 *vt* lengthen; stretch out (mano etc); (*dar*) give, pass. ~**rse** *vpr* get longer

alarido *m* shriek

alarm|a *f* alarm. ~**ante** *adj* alarming. ~**ar** *vt* alarm, frighten. ~**arse** *vpr* be alarmed. ~**ista** *m & f* alarmist

alba *f* dawn

albacea *m & f* executor

albahaca *f* basil

albanés *adj & m* Albanian

Albania *f* Albania

albañil *m* builder; (*que coloca ladrillos*) bricklayer

albarán *m* delivery note

albaricoque *m* apricot. ~**ro** *m* apricot tree

albedrío *m* will. **libre** ~ free will

alberca *f* tank, reservoir; (*Mex, piscina*) swimming pool

alberg|ar 12 *vt* (*alojar*) put up; (vivienda) house; (*dar refugio*) shelter. ~**arse** *vpr* stay; (*refugiarse*) shelter. ~**ue** *m* accommodation; (*refugio*) shelter. ~**ue de juventud** youth hostel

albino *adj & m* albino

albóndiga *f* meatball, rissole

albornoz *m* bathrobe

alborot|ado *adj* excited; (*aturdido*) hasty. **~ador** *adj* rowdy. ● *m* trouble-maker. **~ar** *vt* disturb, upset. ● *vi* make a racket. **~arse** *vpr* get excited; (el mar) get rough. **~o** *m* row, uproar

álbum *m* (*pl* **~es** *o* **~s**) album

alcachofa *f* artichoke

alcald|e *m* mayor. **~esa** *f* mayoress. **~ía** *f* mayoralty; (*oficina*) mayor's office

alcance *m* reach; (*de arma, telescopio etc*) range; (*déficit*) deficit

alcancía *f* money-box; (*LAm, de niño*) piggy bank

alcantarilla *f* sewer; (*boca*) drain

alcanzar 10 *vt* (*llegar a*) catch up; (*coger*) reach; catch (un autobús); (bala etc) strike, hit. ● *vi* reach; (*ser suficiente*) be enough. **~ a** manage

alcaparra *f* caper

alcázar *m* fortress

alcoba *f* bedroom

alcoh|ol *m* alcohol. **~ol desnaturalizado** methylated spirits, meths. **~ólico** *adj & m* alcoholic. **~olímetro** *m* Breathalyser . **~olismo** *m* alcoholism

alcornoque *m* cork-oak; (*persona torpe*) idiot

aldaba *f* door-knocker

aldea *f* village. **~no** *adj* village. ● *m* villager

alea|ción *f* alloy. **~r** *vt* alloy

aleatorio *adj* uncertain

aleccionar *vt* instruct

aledaños *mpl* outskirts

alega|ción *f* allegation; (*LAm, disputa*) argument. **~r** 12 *vt* claim; (*Jurid*) plead. ● *vi* (*LAm*) argue. **~ta** *f* (*Mex*) argument. **~to** *m* plea

alegoría *f* allegory

alegr|ar *vt* make happy; (*avivar*) brighten up. **~arse** *vpr* be happy; (*emborracharse*) get merry. **~e** *adj* happy; (*achispado*) merry, tight. **~ía** *f* happiness

aleja|do *adj* distant. **~miento** *m* removal; (*entre personas*) estrangement; (*distancia*) distance. **~r** *vt* remove; (*ahuyentar*) get rid of; (*fig, apartar*) separate. **~rse** *vpr* move away

alemán *adj & m* German

Alemania *f* Germany. **~ Occidental** (*historia*) West Germany. **~ Oriental** (*historia*) East Germany

alenta|dor *adj* encouraging. **~r** 1 *vt* encourage. ● *vi* breathe

alerce *m* larch

al|ergia *f* allergy. **~érgico** *adj* allergic

alero *m* (*del tejado*) eaves

alerta *adj* alert. **¡~!** look out! **estar ~** be alert; (*en guardia*) be on the alert. **~r** *vt* alert

aleta *f* wing; (*de pez*) fin

aletarga|do *adj* lethargic. **~r** 12 *vt* make lethargic. **~rse** *vpr* become lethargic

alet|azo *m* (*de un ave*) flap of the wings; (*de un pez*) flick of the fin. **~ear** *vi* flap its wings, flutter

alevosía *f* treachery

alfab|ético *adj* alphabetical. **~etizar** 10 *vt* alphabetize; teach to read and write. **~eto** *m* alphabet. **~eto Morse** Morse code

alfalfa *f* alfalfa

alfar|ería *m* pottery. **~ero** *m* potter

alféizar *m* (window)sill

alférez *m* second lieutenant

alfil *m* (*en ajedrez*) bishop

a

alfile|r *m* pin. **~tero** *m* pincushion; (*estuche*) pin-case
alfombr|a *f* (*grande*) carpet; (*pequeña*) rug, mat. **~ado** *adj* (*LAm*) carpeted. **~ar** *vt* carpet. **~illa** *f* rug, mat; (*Med*) type of measles
alforja *f* saddle-bag
algarabía *f* hubbub
algas *fpl* seaweed
álgebra *f* algebra
álgido *adj* (*fig*) decisive
algo *pron* something; (*en frases interrogativas, condicionales*) anything. ● *adv* rather. **¿~ más?** anything else? **¿quieres tomar ~?** would you like a drink?; (*de comer*) would you like something to eat?
algod|ón *m* cotton. **~ón de azúcar** candy floss (*Brit*), cotton candy (*Amer*). **~ón hidrófilo** cotton wool. **~onero** *adj* cotton. ● *m* cotton plant
alguacil *m* bailiff
alguien *pron* someone, somebody; (*en frases interrogativas, condicionales*) anyone, anybody
algún *véase* ALGUNO
alguno *adj* (*delante de nombres masculinos en singular* **algún**) some; (*en frases interrogativas, condicionales*) any; (*pospuesto al nombre en frases negativas*) at all. **no tiene idea alguna** he hasn't any idea at all. **alguna que otra vez** from time to time. **algunas veces, alguna vez** sometimes. ● *pron* one; (*en plural*) some; (*alguien*) someone
alhaja *f* piece of jewellery; (*fig*) treasure. **~s** *fpl* jewellery
alharaca *f* fuss
alhelí *m* wallflower
alia|do *adj* allied. ● *m* ally. **~nza** *f* alliance; (*anillo*) wedding ring. **~r** [20] *vt* combine. **~rse** *vpr* be combined; (*formar una alianza*) form an alliance
alias *adv & m* alias
alicaído *adj* (*fig, débil*) weak; (*fig, abatido*) depressed
alicates *mpl* pliers
aliciente *m* incentive; (*de un lugar*) attraction
alienado *adj* mentally ill
aliento *m* breath; (*ánimo*) courage
aligerar *vt* make lighter; (*aliviar*) alleviate, ease; (*apresurar*) quicken
alijo *m* (*de contrabando*) consignment
alimaña *f* pest. **~s** *fpl* vermin
aliment|ación *f* diet; (*acción*) feeding. **~ar** *vt* feed; (*nutrir*) nourish. ● *vi* be nourishing. **~arse** *vpr* feed (**con, de** on). **~icio** *adj* nourishing. **productos** *mpl* **~icios** foodstuffs. **~o** *m* food. **~os** *mpl* (*Jurid*) alimony
alinea|ción *f* alignment; (*en deportes*) line-up. **~r** *vt* align, line up
aliñ|ar *vt* (*Culin*) season; dress (ensalada). **~o** *m* seasoning; (*para ensalada*) dressing
alioli *m* garlic mayonnaise
alisar *vt* smooth
alistar *vt* put on a list; (*Mil*) enlist. **~se** *vpr* enrol; (*Mil*) enlist; (*LAm, prepararse*) get ready
alivi|ar *vt* lighten; relieve (dolor, etc); (*arg, hurtar*) steal, pinch [I]. **~arse** *vpr* (dolor) diminish; (persona) get better. **~o** *m* relief
aljibe *m* tank
allá *adv* (over) there. **¡~ él!** that's his business! **~ fuera** out there. **~ por 1970** back in 1970. **el más ~** the beyond. **más ~** further on. **más ~ de** beyond. **por ~** that way

allana|miento *m*. **~miento (de morada)** breaking and entering; (*LAm, por la autoridad*) raid. **~r** *vt* level; remove (obstáculos); (*fig*) iron out (dificultades etc); break into (una casa); (*LAm, por la autoridad*) raid

allega|do *adj* close. ● *m* close friend; (*pariente*) close relative. **~r** [12] *vt* collect

allí *adv* there; (*tiempo*) then. **~ fuera** out there. **por ~** that way

alma *f* soul; (*habitante*) inhabitant

almac|én *m* warehouse; (*LAm, tienda*) grocer's shop; (*de un arma*) magazine. **~enes** *mpl* department store. **~enaje** *m* storage; (*derechos*) storage charges. **~enar** *vt* store; stock up with (provisiones)

almanaque *m* almanac

almeja *f* clam

almendr|a *f* almond. **~ado** *adj* almond-shaped. **~o** *m* almond tree

alm|íbar *m* syrup. **~ibarar** *vt* cover in syrup

almid|ón *m* starch. **~onado** *adj* starched; (*fig, estirado*) starchy

almirante *m* admiral

almizcle *m* musk. **~ra** *f* muskrat

almohad|a *f* pillow. **consultar con la ~a** sleep on it. **~illa** *f* small cushion. **~ón** *m* large pillow, bolster

almorranas *fpl* haemorrhoids, piles

alm|orzar [2] & [10] *vt* (*a mediodía*) have for lunch; (*desayunar*) have for breakfast. ● *vi* (*a mediodía*) have lunch; (*desayunar*) have breakfast. **~uerzo** *m* (*a mediodía*) lunch; (*desayuno*) breakfast

alocado *adj* scatter-brained

aloja|miento *m* accommodation. **~r** *vt* put up. **~rse** *vpr* stay

alondra *f* lark

alpaca *f* alpaca

alpargata *f* canvas shoe, espadrille

alpin|ismo *m* mountaineering, climbing. **~ista** *m & f* mountaineer, climber. **~o** *adj* Alpine

alpiste *m* birdseed

alquil|ar *vt* (*tomar en alquiler*) hire (vehículo), rent (piso, casa); (*dar en alquiler*) hire (out) (vehículo), rent (out) (piso, casa). **se alquila** to let (*Brit*), for rent (*Amer.*) **~er** *m* (*acción — de alquilar un piso etc*) renting; (*— de alquilar un vehículo*) hiring; (*precio — por el que se alquila un piso etc*) rent; (*— por el que se alquila un vehículo*) hire charge. **de ~er** for hire

alquimi|a *f* alchemy. **~sta** *m* alchemist

alquitrán *m* tar

alrededor *adv* around. **~ de** around; (*con números*) about. **~es** *mpl* surroundings; (*de una ciudad*) outskirts

alta *f* discharge

altaner|ía *f* (*arrogancia*) arrogance. **~o** *adj* arrogant, haughty

altar *m* altar

altavoz *m* loudspeaker

altera|ble *adj* changeable. **~ción** *f* change, alteration. **~r** *vt* change, alter; (*perturbar*) disturb; (*enfadar*) anger, irritate. **~rse** *vpr* change, alter; (*agitarse*) get upset; (*enfadarse*) get angry; (comida) go off

altercado *m* argument

altern|ar *vt/i* alternate. **~arse** *vpr* take turns. **~ativa** *f* alternative. **~ativo** *adj* alternating. **~o** *adj* alternate; (*Elec*) alternating

Alteza *f* (*título*) Highness

altibajos *mpl* (*de terreno*) unevenness; (*fig*) ups and downs
altiplanicie *f*, **altiplano** *m* high plateau
altisonante *adj* pompous
altitud *f* altitude
altiv|ez *f* arrogance. **~o** *adj* arrogant
alto *adj* high; (persona, edificio) tall; (voz) loud; (*fig, elevado*) lofty; (*Mus*) (nota) high(-pitched); (*Mus*) (voz, instrumento) alto; (horas) early. • *adv* high; (*de sonidos*) loud(ly). • *m* height; (*de un edificio*) top floor; (*viola*) viola; (*voz*) alto; (*parada*) stop. • *int* halt!, stop! **en lo ~ de** on the top of. **tiene 3 metros de ~** it is 3 metres high
altoparlante *m* (*esp LAm*) loudspeaker
altruis|mo *m* altruism. **~ta** *adj* altruistic. • *m & f* altruist
altura *f* height; (*Aviac, Geog*) altitude; (*de agua*) depth; (*fig, cielo*) sky. **a estas ~s** at this stage. **tiene 3 metros de ~** it is 3 metres high
alubia *f* (haricot) bean
alucinación *f* hallucination
alud *m* avalanche
aludi|do *adj* in question. **darse por ~do** take it personally. **no darse por ~do** turn a deaf ear. **~r** *vi* mention
alumbra|do *adj* lit. • *m* lighting. **~miento** *m* lighting; (*parto*) childbirth. **~r** *vt* light
aluminio *m* aluminium (*Brit*), aluminum (*Amer*)
alumno *m* pupil; (*Univ*) student
aluniza|je *m* landing on the moon. **~r** **10** *vi* land on the moon
alusi|ón *f* allusion. **~vo** *adj* allusive
alza *f* rise. **~da** *f* (*de caballo*) height; (*Jurid*) appeal. **~do** *adj* raised; (*Mex, soberbio*) vain; (precio) fixed. **~miento** *m* (*Pol*) uprising. **~r** **10** *vt* raise, lift (up); raise (precios). **~rse** *vpr* (*Pol*) rise up
ama *f* lady of the house. **~ de casa** housewife. **~ de cría** wetnurse. **~ de llaves** housekeeper
amab|ilidad *f* kindness. **~le** *adj* kind; (*simpático*) nice
amaestra|do *adj* trained. **~r** *vt* train
amag|ar **12** *vt* (*mostrar intención de*) make as if to; (*Mex, amenazar*) threaten. • *vi* threaten; (algo bueno) be in the offing. **~o** *m* threat; (*señal*) sign; (*Med*) symptom
amainar *vi* let up
amalgama *f* amalgam. **~r** *vt* amalgamate
amamantar *vt/i* breast-feed; (animal) to suckle
amanecer *m* dawn. • *vi* dawn; (persona) wake up. **al ~** at dawn, at daybreak. **~se** *vpr* (*Mex*) stay up all night
amanera|do *adj* affected. **~rse** *vpr* become affected
amansar *vt* tame; break in (un caballo); soothe (dolor etc). **~se** *vpr* calm down
amante *adj* fond. • *m & f* lover
amapola *f* poppy
amar *vt* love
amara|je *m* landing on water; (*de astronave*) splash-down. **~r** *vi* land on water; (astronave) splash down
amarg|ado *adj* embittered. **~ar** **12** *vt* make bitter; embitter (persona). **~arse** *vpr* become bitter. **~o** *adj* bitter. **~ura** *f* bitterness
amariconado *adj* **!** effe-

minate
amarill|ento *adj* yellowish; (tez) sallow. **~o** *adj & m* yellow
amarra|s *fpl*. **soltar las ~s** cast off. **~do** *adj* (*LAm*) mean. **~r** *vt* moor; (*esp LAm, atar*) tie. **~rse** *vpr LAm* tie up
amas|ar *vt* knead; (*acumular*) to amass. **~ijo** *m* dough; (*acción*) kneading; (*fig, fam, mezcla*) hotch-potch
amate *m* (*Mex*) fig tree
amateur *adj & m & f* amateur
amazona *f* Amazon; (*jinete*) horsewoman
ámbar *m* amber
ambici|ón *f* ambition. **~onar** *vt* aspire to. **~onar ser** have an ambition to be. **~oso** *adj* ambitious. • *m* ambitious person
ambidextro *adj* ambidextrous. • *m* ambidextrous person
ambient|ar *vt* give an atmosphere to. **~arse** *vpr* adapt o.s. **~e** *m* atmosphere; (*entorno*) environment
ambig|üedad *f* ambiguity. **~uo** *adj* ambiguous
ámbito *m* sphere; (*alcance*) scope
ambos *adj & pron* both
ambulancia *f* ambulance
ambulante *adj* travelling
ambulatorio *m* out-patients' department
amedrentar *vt* frighten, scare. **~se** *vpr* be frightened
amén *m* amen. • *int* amen! **en un decir ~** in an instant
amenaza *f* threat. **~r** **10** *vt* threaten
amen|idad *f* pleasantness. **~izar** **10** *vt* brighten up. **~o** *adj* pleasant
América *f* America. **~ Central** Central America. **~ del Norte** North America. **~ del Sur** South America. **~ Latina** Latin America
american|a *f* jacket. **~ismo** *m* Americanism. **~o** *adj* American
amerita|do *adj* (*LAm*) meritorious. **~r** *vt* (*LAm*) deserve
amerizaje *m véase* AMARAJE
ametralla|dora *f* machine-gun. **~r** *vt* machine-gun
amianto *m* asbestos
amig|a *f* friend; (*novia*) girl-friend; (*amante*) lover. **~able** *adj* friendly. **~ablemente** *adv* amicably
am|ígdala *f* tonsil. **~igdalitis** *f* tonsillitis
amigo *adj* friendly. • *m* friend; (*novio*) boyfriend; (*amante*) lover. **ser ~ de** be fond of. **ser muy ~s** be close friends
amilanar *vt* daunt. **~se** *vpr* be daunted
aminorar *vt* lessen; reduce (velocidad)
amist|ad *f* friendship. **~ades** *fpl* friends. **~oso** *adj* friendly
amn|esia *f* amnesia. **~ésico** *adj* amnesiac
amnist|ía *f* amnesty. **~iar** **20** *vt* grant an amnesty to
amo *m* master; (*dueño*) owner
amodorrarse *vpr* feel sleepy
amoldar *vt* mould; (*adaptar*) adapt; (*acomodar*) fit. **~se** *vpr* adapt
amonestar *vt* rebuke, reprimand; (*anunciar la boda*) publish the banns
amoniaco, **amoníaco** *m* ammonia
amontonar *vt* pile up; (*fig, acumular*) accumulate. **~se** *vpr* pile up; (gente) crowd together

a

amor *m* love. **~es** *mpl* (*relaciones amorosas*) love affairs. **~ propio** pride. **con mil ~es, de mil ~es** with (the greatest of) pleasure. **hacer el ~** make love. **por (el) ~ de Dios** for God's sake

amoratado *adj* purple; (*de frío*) blue

amordazar 10 *vt* gag; (*fig*) silence

amorfo *adj* amorphous, shapeless

amor|ío *m* affair. **~oso** *adj* loving; (cartas) love; (*LAm*), *encantador*) cute

amortajar *vt* shroud

amortigua|dor *adj* deadening. • *m* (*Auto*) shock absorber. **~r** 15 *vt* deaden (ruido); dim (luz); cushion (golpe); tone down (color)

amortiza|ble *adj* redeemable. **~ción** *f* (*de una deuda*) repayment; (*de bono etc*) redemption. **~r** 10 *vt* repay (una deuda)

amotinar *vt* incite to riot. **~se** *vpr* rebel; (*Mil*) mutiny

ampar|ar *vt* help; (*proteger*) protect. **~arse** *vpr* seek protection; (*de la lluvia*) shelter. **~o** *m* protection; (*de la lluvia*) shelter. **al ~o de** under the protection of

amperio *m* ampere, amp !

amplia|ción *f* extension; (*photo*) enlargement. **~r** 20 *vt* enlarge, extend; (*photo*) enlarge

amplifica|ción *f* amplification. **~dor** *m* amplifier. **~r** 7 amplify

ampli|o *adj* wide; (*espacioso*) spacious; (ropa) loose-fitting. **~tud** *f* extent; (*espaciosidad*) spaciousness; (*espacio*) space

ampolla *f* (*Med*) blister; (*de medicamento*) ampoule, phial

ampuloso *adj* pompous

amputar *vt* amputate; (*fig*) delete

amueblar *vt* furnish

amuleto *m* charm, amulet

amuralla|do *adj* walled. **~r** *vt* build a wall around

anacr|ónico *adj* anachronistic. **~onismo** *m* anachronism

anales *mpl* annals

analfabet|ismo *m* illiteracy. **~o** *adj & m* illiterate

analgésico *adj* analgesic. • *m* painkiller

an|álisis *m invar* analysis. **~álisis de sangre** blood test. **~alista** *m & f* analyst. **~alítico** *adj* analytical. **~alizar** 10 *vt* analyze

an|alogía *f* analogy. **~álogo** *adj* analogous

anaranjado *adj* orangey

an|arquía *f* anarchy. **~árquico** *adj* anarchic. **~arquismo** *m* anarchism. **~arquista** *adj* anarchistic. • *m & f* anarchist

anat|omía *f* anatomy. **~ómico** *adj* anatomical

anca *f* haunch; (*parte superior*) rump; (*fam, nalgas*) bottom. **en ~s** (*LAm*) on the crupper

ancestro *m* ancestor

ancho *adj* wide; (ropa) loose-fitting; (*fig*) relieved; (*demasiado grande*) too big; (*ufano*) smug. • *m* width; (*Rail*) gauge. **~ de banda** bandwidth. **tiene 3 metros de ~** it is 3 metres wide

anchoa *f* anchovy

anchura *f* width; (*medida*) measurement

ancian|o *adj* elderly, old. • *m* elderly man, old man. **~a** *f* elderly woman, old woman. **los ~os** old people

ancla *f* anchor. **echar ~s** drop anchor. **levar ~s** weigh anchor. **~r** *vi* anchor

andad|eras *fpl* (*Mex*) baby-walker. **~or** *m* baby-walker
Andalucía *f* Andalusia
andaluz *adj & m* Andalusian
andamio *m* platform. **~s** *mpl* scaffolding
and|anzas *fpl* adventures. **~ar** 25 *vt* (*recorrer*) cover, go. • *vi* walk; (máquina) go, work; (*estar*) be; (*moverse*) move. **~ar a caballo** (*LAm*) ride a horse. **~ar en bicicleta** (*LAm*) ride a bicycle. **¡anda!** go on!, come on! **~ar por** be about. **~arse** *vpr* (*LAm, en imperativo*) **¡andate!** go away! • *m* walk. **~ariego** *adj* fond of walking
andén *m* platform
Andes *mpl*. **los ~** the Andes
andin|o *adj* Andean. **~ismo** *m* (*LAm*) mountaineering, climbing. **~ista** *m & f* (*LAm*) mountaineer, climber
andrajo *m* rag. **~so** *adj* ragged
anduve *vb véase* **ANDAR**
anécdota *f* anecdote
anecdótico *adj* anecdotal
anegar 12 *vt* flood. **~se** *vpr* be flooded, flood
anejo *adj véase* **ANEXO**
an|emia *f* anaemia. **~émico** *adj* anaemic
anest|esia *f* anaesthesia; (*droga*) anaesthetic. **~esiar** *vt* anaesthetize. **~ésico** *adj & m* anaesthetic. **~esista** *m & f* anaesthetist
anex|ar *vt* annex. **~o** *adj* attached. • *m* annexe
anfibio *adj* amphibious. • *m* amphibian
anfiteatro *m* amphitheatre; (*en un teatro*) upper circle
anfitri|ón *m* host. **~ona** *f* hostess

ángel *m* angel; (*encanto*) charm
angelical *adj*, **angélico** *adj* angelic
angina *f*. **~ de pecho** angina (pectoris). **tener ~s** have tonsillitis
anglicano *adj & m* Anglican
angl|icismo *m* Anglicism. **~ófilo** *adj & m* Anglophile. **~ohispánico** *adj* Anglo-Spanish. **~osajón** *adj & m* Anglo-Saxon
angosto *adj* narrow
angu|ila *f* eel. **~la** *f* elver, baby eel
ángulo *m* angle; (*rincón, esquina*) corner; (*curva*) bend
angusti|a *f* anguish. **~ar** *vt* distress; (*inquietar*) worry. **~arse** *vpr* get distressed; (*inquietarse*) get worried. **~oso** *adj* anguished; (*que causa angustia*) distressing
anhel|ar *vt* (+ *nombre*) long for; (+ *verbo*) long to. **~o** *m* (*fig*) yearning
anidar *vi* nest
anill|a *f* ring. **~o** *m* ring. **~o de boda** wedding ring
ánima *f* soul
anima|ción *f* (*de personas*) life; (*de cosas*) liveliness; (*bullicio*) bustle; (*en el cine*) animation. **~do** *adj* lively; (sitio etc) busy. **~dor** *m* host. **~dora** *f* hostess; (*de un equipo*) cheerleader
animadversión *f* ill will
animal *adj* animal; (*fig, fam, torpe*) stupid. • *m* animal; (*fig, fam, idiota*) idiot; (*fig, fam, bruto*) brute
animar *vt* give life to; (*dar ánimo*) encourage; (*dar vivacidad*) liven up. **~se** *vpr* (*decidirse*) decide; (*ponerse alegre*) cheer up. **¿te animas a ir al cine?** do you feel like going to the cinema?
ánimo *m* soul; (*mente*) mind; (*valor*) courage; (*intención*) inten-

tion. ¡~! come on!, cheer up! **dar ~s** encourage

animos|idad *f* animosity. **~o** *adj* brave; (*resuelto*) determined

aniquilar *vt* annihilate; (*acabar con*) ruin

anís *m* aniseed; (*licor*) anisette

aniversario *m* anniversary

anoche *adv* last night, yesterday evening

anochecer 11 *vi* get dark. **anochecí en Madrid** I was in Madrid at dusk. • *m* nightfall, dusk. **al ~** at nightfall

anodino *adj* bland

an|omalía *f* anomaly. **~ómalo** *adj* anomalous

an|onimato *m* anonymity. **~ónimo** *adj* anonymous; (*sociedad*) limited. • *m* (*carta*) anonymous letter

anormal *adj* abnormal. • *m & f* ! idiot. **~idad** *f* abnormality

anota|ción *f* (*nota*) note; (*acción de poner notas*) annotation. **~r** *vt* (*poner nota*) annotate; (*apuntar*) make a note of; (*LAm*) score (un gol)

anquilosa|miento *m* (*fig*) paralysis. **~rse** *vpr* become paralyzed

ansi|a *f* anxiety, worry; (*anhelo*) yearning. **~ar** 20 *vt* long for. **~edad** *f* anxiety. **~oso** *adj* anxious; (*deseoso*) eager

antag|ónico *adj* antagonistic. **~onismo** *m* antagonism. **~onista** *m & f* antagonist

antaño *adv* in days gone by

antártico *adj & m* Antarctic

ante *prep* in front of, before; (*frente a*) in the face of; (*en vista de*) in view of. • *m* elk; (*piel*) suede. **~anoche** *adv* the night before last. **~ayer** *adv* the day before yesterday. **~brazo** *m* forearm

antece|dente *adj* previous. • *m* antecedent. **~dentes** *mpl* history, background. **~dentes penales** criminal record. **~der** *vt* precede. **~sor** *m* predecessor; (*antepasado*) ancestor

antelación *f* (advance) notice. **con ~** in advance

antemano *adv*. **de ~** beforehand

antena *f* antenna; (*radio, TV*) aerial

antenoche *adv* (*LAm*) the night before last

anteoj|eras *fpl* blinkers. **~o** *m* telescope. **~os** *mpl* binoculars; (*LAm, gafas*) glasses, spectacles. **~os de sol** sunglasses

ante|pasados *mpl* forebears, ancestors. **~poner** 34 *vt* put in front (**a** of); (*fig*) put before, prefer. **~proyecto** *m* preliminary sketch; (*fig*) blueprint

anterior *adj* previous; (*delantero*) front. **~idad** *f*. **con ~idad** previously. **con ~idad a** prior to

antes *adv* before; (*antiguamente*) in the past; (*mejor*) rather; (*primero*) first. **~ de** before. **~ de ayer** the day before yesterday. **~ de que** + *subjuntivo* before. **~ de que llegue** before he arrives. **cuanto ~, lo ~ posible** as soon as possible

anti|aéreo *adj* anti-aircraft. **~biótico** *adj & m* antibiotic. **~ciclón** *m* anticyclone

anticip|ación *f*. **con ~ación** in advance. **con media hora de ~ación** half an hour early. **~ado** *adj* advance. **por ~ado** in advance. **~ar** *vt* bring forward; advance (dinero). **~arse** *vpr* be early. **~o** *m* (*dinero*) advance; (*fig*) foretaste

anti|conceptivo *adj & m* contraceptive. ~ **de emergencia** morning-after pill. ~**congelante** *m* antifreeze

anticua|do *adj* old-fashioned. ~**rio** *m* antique dealer

anticuerpo *m* antibody

antídoto *m* antidote

anti|estético *adj* ugly. ~**faz** *m* mask

antig|ualla *f* old relic. ~**uamente** *adv* formerly; (*hace mucho tiempo*) long ago. ~**üedad** *f* antiquity; (*objeto*) antique; (*en un empleo*) length of service. ~**uo** *adj* old; (ruinas) ancient; (mueble) antique

Antillas *fpl*. **las** ~ the West Indies

antílope *m* antelope

antinatural *adj* unnatural

antip|atía *f* dislike; (*cualidad de antipático*) unpleasantness. ~**ático** *adj* unpleasant, unfriendly

anti|semita *m & f* anti-Semite. ~**séptico** *adj & m* antiseptic. ~**social** *adj* antisocial

antítesis *f invar* antithesis

antoj|adizo *adj* capricious. ~**arse** *vpr* fancy. **se le** ~**a un caramelo** he fancies a sweet. ~**itos** *mpl* (*Mex*) snacks bought at street stands. ~**o** *m* whim; (*de embarazada*) craving

antología *f* anthology

antorcha *f* torch

ántrax *m* anthrax

antro *m* (*fig*) dump, hole. ~ **de perversión** den of iniquity

antrop|ología *f* anthropology. ~**ólogo** *m* anthropologist

anua|l *adj* annual. ~**lidad** *f* annuity. ~**lmente** *adv* yearly. ~**rio** *m* yearbook

anudar *vt* tie, knot. ~**se** *vpr* tie

anula|ción *f* annulment, cancellation. ~**r** *vt* annul, cancel. ● *adj* (dedo) ring. ● *m* ring finger

anunci|ante *m & f* advertiser. ~**ar** *vt* announce; advertise (producto comercial); (*presagiar*) be a sign of. ~**o** *m* announcement; (*para vender algo*) advertisement, advert [!]; (*cartel*) poster

anzuelo *m* (fish)hook; (*fig*) bait. **tragar el** ~ swallow the bait

añadi|dura *f* addition. **por** ~**dura** in addition. ~**r** *vt* add

añejo *adj* (vino) mature

añicos *mpl*. **hacer(se)** ~ smash to pieces

año *m* year. ~ **bisiesto** leap year. ~ **nuevo** new year. **al** ~ per year, a year. **¿cuántos** ~**s tiene?** how old is he? **tiene 5** ~**s** he's 5 (years old). **el** ~ **pasado** last year. **el** ~ **que viene** next year. **entrado en** ~**s** elderly. **los** ~**s 60** the sixties

añora|nza *f* nostalgia. ~**r** *vt* miss

apabulla|nte *adj* overwhelming. ~**r** *vt* overwhelm

apacible *adj* gentle; (clima) mild

apacigua|r [15] *vt* pacify; (*calmar*) calm; relieve (dolor etc). ~**rse** *vpr* calm down

apadrinar *vt* sponsor; be godfather to (a un niño)

apag|ado *adj* extinguished; (color) dull; (aparato eléctrico, luz) off; (persona) lifeless; (sonido) muffled. ~**ar** [12] *vt* put out (fuego, incendio); turn off, switch off (aparato eléctrico, luz); quench (sed); muffle (sonido). ~**arse** *vpr* (fuego, luz) go out; (sonido) die away. ~**ón** *m* blackout

apalabrar *vt* make a verbal agreement; (*contratar*) engage

apalear *vt* winnow (grano); beat

a

(alfombra, frutos, persona)

apantallar *vt* (*Mex*) impress

apañar *vt* (*arreglar*) fix; (*remendar*) mend; (*agarrar*) grasp, take hold of. **~se** *vpr* get along, manage

apapachar *vt* (*Mex*) cuddle

aparador *m* sideboard; (*Mex, de tienda*) shop window

aparato *m* apparatus; (*máquina*) machine; (*doméstico*) appliance; (*teléfono*) telephone; (*radio, TV*) set; (*ostentación*) show, pomp. **~so** *adj* showy, ostentatious; (caída) spectacular

aparca|miento *m* car park (*Brit*), parking lot (*Amer*). **~r** **7** *vt/i* park

aparear *vt* mate (animales).**~se** *vpr* mate

aparecer **11** *vi* appear. **~se** *vpr* appear

aparej|ado *adj*. **llevar ~ado, traer ~ado** mean, entail. **~o** *m* (*avíos*) equipment; (*de caballo*) tack; (*de pesca*) tackle

aparent|ar *vt* (*afectar*) feign; (*parecer*) look. • *vi* show off. **~a 20 años** she looks like she's 20. **~e** *adj* apparent

apari|ción *f* appearance; (*visión*) apparition. **~encia** *f* appearance; (*fig*) show. **guardar las ~encias** keep up appearances

apartado *adj* separated; (*aislado*) isolated. • *m* (*de un texto*) section. **~ (de correos)** post-office box, PO box

apartamento *m* apartment, flat (*Brit*)

apart|ar *vt* separate; (*alejar*) move away; (*quitar*) remove; (*guardar*) set aside. **~arse** *vpr* leave; (*quitarse de en medio*) get out of the way; (*aislarse*) cut o.s. off. **~e** *adv* apart; (*por separado*) separately; (*además*) besides. • *m* aside; (*párrafo*) new paragraph. **~e de** apart from. **dejar ~e** leave aside. **eso ~e** apart from that

apasiona|do *adj* passionate; (*entusiasta*) enthusiastic; (*falto de objetividad*) biased. • *m*. **~do de** lover. **~miento** *m* passion. **~r** *vt* excite. **~rse** *vpr* be mad (**por** about); (*ser parcial*) become biased

ap|atía *f* apathy. **~ático** *adj* apathetic

apea|dero *m* (*Rail*) halt. **~rse** *vpr* get off

apechugar **12** *vi*. **I** **~ con** put up with

apedrear *vt* stone

apeg|ado *adj* attached (**a** to). **~o** *m* **I** attachment. **tener ~o a** be fond of

apela|ción *f* appeal. **~r** *vi* appeal; (*recurrir*) resort (**a** to). • *vt* (*apodar*) call. **~tivo** *m* (nick)name

apellid|ar *vt* call. **~arse** *vpr* be called. **¿cómo te apellidas?** what's your surname? **~o** *m* surname

apelmazarse *vpr* (lana) get matted

apenar *vt* sadden; (*LAm, avergonzar*) embarrass. **~se** *vpr* be sad; (*LAm, avergonzarse*) be embarrassed

apenas *adv* hardly, scarcely; (*Mex, sólo*) only. • *conj* (*esp LAm, en cuanto*) as soon as. **~ si** **I** hardly

ap|éndice *m* appendix. **~endicitis** *f* appendicitis

apergaminado *adj* (piel) wrinkled

aperitivo *m* (*bebida*) aperitif; (*comida*) appetizer

aperos *mpl* implements; (*de labranza*) agricultural equipment; (*LAm, de un caballo*) tack

a

apertura *f* opening
apesadumbrar *vt* upset. **~se** *vpr* sadden
apestar *vt* infect. ● *vi* stink (**a** of)
apet|ecer 11 *vi*. **¿te ~ece una copa?** do you fancy a drink? do you feel like a drink?. **no me ~ece** I don't feel like it. **~ecible** *adj* attractive. **~ito** *m* appetite; (*fig*) desire. **~itoso** *adj* appetizing
apiadarse *vpr* feel sorry (**de** for)
ápice *m* (*nada, en frases negativas*) anything. **no ceder un ~** not give an inch
apilar *vt* pile up
apiñar *vt* pack in. **~se** *vpr* (*personas*) crowd together; (*cosas*) be packed tight
apio *m* celery
aplacar 7 *vt* placate; soothe (*dolor*)
aplanar *vt* level. **~ calles** (*LAm fam*) loaf around
aplasta|nte *adj* overwhelming. **~r** *vt* crush. **~rse** *vpr* flatten o.s.
aplau|dir *vt* clap, applaud; (*fig*) applaud. **~so** *m* applause; (*fig*) praise
aplaza|miento *m* postponement. **~r** 10 *vt* postpone; defer (*pago*)
aplica|ble *adj* applicable. **~ción** *f* application. **~do** *adj* (*persona*) diligent. **~r** 7 *vt* apply. ● *vi* (*LAm, a un puesto*) apply (for). **~rse** *vpr* apply o.s.
aplom|ado *adj* composed. **~o** *m* composure
apocado *adj* timid
apocar 7 *vt* belittle (*persona*). **~se** *vpr* feel small
apodar *vt* nickname
apodera|do *m* representative. **~rse** *vpr* seize
apodo *m* nickname
apogeo *m* (*fig*) height
apolilla|do *adj* moth-eaten. **~rse** *vpr* get moth-eaten
apolítico *adj* non-political
apología *f* defence
apoltronarse *vpr* settle o.s. down
apoplejía *f* stroke
aporrear *vt* hit, thump; beat up (*persona*)
aport|ación *f* contribution. **~ar** *vt* contribute. **~e** *m* (*LAm*) contribution
aposta *adv* on purpose
apostar¹ 2 *vt/i* bet
apostar² *vt* station. **~se** *vpr* station o.s.
apóstol *m* apostle
apóstrofo *m* apostrophe
apoy|ar *vt* lean (**en** against); (*descansar*) rest; (*asentar*) base; (*reforzar*) support. **~arse** *vpr* lean, rest. **~o** *m* support
apreci|able *adj* appreciable; (*digno de estima*) worthy. **~ación** *f* appreciation; (*valoración*) appraisal. **~ar** *vt* value; (*estimar*) appreciate. **~o** *m* appraisal; (*fig*) esteem
apremi|ante *adj* urgent, pressing. **~ar** *vt* urge; (*obligar*) compel; (*dar prisa a*) hurry up. ● *vi* be urgent. **~o** *m* urgency; (*obligación*) obligation
aprender *vt/i* learn. **~se** *vpr* learn
aprendiz *m* apprentice. **~aje** *m* learning; (*período*) apprenticeship
aprensi|ón *f* apprehension; (*miedo*) fear. **~vo** *adj* apprehensive, fearful
apresar *vt* seize; (*capturar*) capture

a

aprestar *vt* prepare. **~se** *vpr* prepare

apresura|do *adj* in a hurry; (*hecho con prisa*) hurried. **~r** *vt* hurry. **~rse** *vpr* hurry up

apret|ado *adj* tight; (*difícil*) difficult; (*tacaño*) stingy, mean. **~ar** **1** *vt* tighten; press (botón); squeeze (persona); (*comprimir*) press down. • *vi* be too tight. **~arse** *vpr* crowd together. **~ón** *m* squeeze. **~ón de manos** handshake

aprieto *m* difficulty. **verse en un ~** be in a tight spot

aprisa *adv* quickly

aprisionar *vt* trap

aproba|ción *f* approval. **~r** **2** *vt* approve (of); pass (examen). • *vi* pass

apropia|ción *f* appropriation. **~do** *adj* appropriate. **~rse** *vpr*. **~rse de** appropriate, take

aprovecha|ble *adj* usable. **~do** *adj* (*aplicado*) diligent; (*ingenioso*) resourceful; (*oportunista*) opportunist. **bien ~do** well spent. **~miento** *m* advantage; (*uso*) use. **~r** *vt* take advantage of; (*utilizar*) make use of. • *vi* make the most of it. **¡que aproveche!** enjoy your meal! **~rse** *vpr*. **~rse de** take advantage of

aprovisionar *vt* provision (**con**, **de** with). **~se** *vpr* stock up

aproxima|ción *f* approximation; (*proximidad*) closeness; (*en la lotería*) consolation prize. **~damente** *adv* roughly, approximately. **~do** *adj* approximate, rough. **~r** *vt* bring near; (*fig*) bring together (personas). **~rse** *vpr* come closer, approach

apt|itud *f* suitability; (*capacidad*) ability. **~o** *adj* (*capaz*) capable; (*adecuado*) suitable

apuesta *f* bet

apuesto *m* handsome. • *vb véase* APOSTAR [1]

apuntalar *vt* shore up

apunt|ar *vt* aim (arma); (*señalar*) point at; (*anotar*) make a note of, note down; (*inscribir*) enrol; (*en el teatro*) prompt. • *vi* (*con un arma*) to aim (**a** at). **~arse** *vpr* put one's name down; score (triunfo, tanto etc). **~e** *m* note; (*bosquejo*) sketch. **tomar ~s** take notes

apuñalar *vt* stab

apur|ado *adj* difficult; (*sin dinero*) hard up; (*LAm, con prisa*) in a hurry. **~ar** *vt* (*acabar*) finish; drain (vaso etc); (*causar vergüenza*) embarrass; (*LAm, apresurar*) hurry. **~arse** *vpr* worry; (*LAm, apresurarse*) hurry up. **~o** *m* tight spot, difficult situation; (*vergüenza*) embarrassment; (*estrechez*) hardship, want; (*LAm, prisa*) hurry

aquejar *vt* afflict

aquel *adj* (*f* **aquella**, *mpl* **aquellos**, *fpl* **aquellas**) that; (*en plural*) those

aquél *pron* (*f* **aquélla**, *mpl* **aquéllos**, *fpl* **aquéllas**) that one; (*en plural*) those

aquello *pron* that; (*asunto*) that business

aquí *adv* here. **de ~** from here. **de ~ a 15 días** in a fortnight's time. **~ mismo** right here. **de ~ para allá** to and fro. **de ~ que** that is why. **hasta ~** until now. **por ~** around here

aquietar *vt* calm (down)

árabe *adj* & *m* & *f* Arab; (*lengua*) Arabic

Arabia *f* Arabia. **~ Saudita**, **~ Saudí** Saudi Arabia

arado *m* plough. **~r** *m* ploughman

arancel *m* tariff; (*impuesto*) duty. **~ario** *adj* tariff

arándano *m* blueberry

arandela *f* washer

araña *f* spider; (*lámpara*) chandelier. **~r** *vt* scratch

arar *vt* plough

arbitra|je *m* arbitration; (*en deportes*) refereeing. **~r** *vt/i* arbitrate; (*en fútbol etc*) referee; (*en tenis etc*) umpire

arbitr|ariedad *f* arbitrariness. **~ario** *adj* arbitrary. **~io** *m* (free) will

árbitro *m* arbitrator; (*en fútbol etc*) referee; (*en tenis etc*) umpire

árbol *m* tree; (*eje*) axle; (*palo*) mast. **~ genealógico** family tree. **~ de Navidad** Christmas tree

arbol|ado *m* trees. **~eda** *f* wood

arbusto *m* bush

arca *f* (*caja*) chest. **~ de Noé** Noah's ark

arcada *f* arcade; (*de un puente*) arch; (*náuseas*) retching

arcaico *adj* archaic

arce *m* maple (tree)

arcén *m* (*de autopista*) hard shoulder; (*de carretera*) verge

archipiélago *m* archipelago

archiv|ador *m* filing cabinet. **~ar** *vt* file (away). **~o** *m* file; (*de documentos históricos*) archives

arcilla *f* clay

arco *m* arch; (*Elec, Mat*) arc; (*Mus, arma*) bow; (*LAm, en fútbol*) goal. **~ iris** rainbow

arder *vi* burn; (*LAm, escocer*) sting; (*fig, de ira*) seethe. **estar que arde** be very tense

ardid *m* trick, scheme

ardiente *adj* burning

ardilla *f* squirrel

ardor *m* heat; (*fig*) ardour; (*LAm, escozor*) smarting. **~ de estómago** heartburn

arduo *adj* arduous

área *f* area

arena *f* sand; (*en deportes*) arena; (*en los toros*) (bull)ring. **~ movediza** quicksand

arenoso *adj* sandy

arenque *m* herring. **~ ahumado** kipper

arete *m* (*LAm*) earring

Argel *m* Algiers. **~ia** *f* Algeria

Argentina *f* Argentina

argentino *adj* Argentinian, Argentine. • *m* Argentinian

argolla *f* ring. **~ de matrimonio** (*LAm*) wedding ring

arg|ot *m* slang. **~ótico** *adj* slang

argucia *f* cunning argument

argüir 19 *vt* (*probar*) prove, show; (*argumentar*) argue. • *vi* argue

argument|ación *f* argument. **~ar** *vt/i* argue. **~o** *m* argument; (*de libro, película etc*) story, plot

aria *f* aria

aridez *f* aridity, dryness

árido *adj* arid, dry. **~s** *mpl* dry goods

Aries *m* Aries

arisco *adj* unfriendly

arist|ocracia *f* aristocracy. **~ócrata** *m & f* aristocrat. **~ocrático** *adj* aristocratic

aritmética *f* arithmetic

arma *f* arm, weapon; (*sección*) section. **~ de fuego** firearm, **~s de destrucción masiva** weapons of mass destruction. **~da** *f* navy; (*flota*) fleet. **~do** *adj* armed (**de** with). **~dura** *f* armour; (*de gafas etc*) frame; (*Tec*) framework. **~mentismo** *m* build up of arms.

a

~mento *m* arms, armaments; (*acción de armar*) armament. **~r** *vt* arm (**de** with); (*montar*) put together. **~r un lío** kick up a fuss

armario *m* cupboard; (*para ropa*) wardrobe (*Brit*), closet (*Amer*)

armatoste *m* huge great thing

armazón *m & f* frame(work)

armiño *m* ermine

armisticio *m* armistice

armonía *f* harmony

armónica *f* harmonica, mouth organ

armoni|oso *adj* harmonious. **~zar** 10 *vt* harmonize. ● *vi* harmonize; (personas) get on well (**con** with); (colores) go well (**con** with)

arn|és *m* armour. **~eses** *mpl* harness

aro *m* ring, hoop

arom|a *m* aroma; (*de flores*) scent; (*de vino*) bouquet. **~ático** *adj* aromatic

arpa *f* harp

arpía *f* harpy; (*fig*) hag

arpillera *f* sackcloth, sacking

arpón *m* harpoon

arquear *vt* arch, bend. **~se** *vpr* arch, bend

arque|ología *f* archaeology. **~ológico** *adj* archaeological. **~ólogo** *m* archaeologist

arquero *m* archer; (*LAm, en fútbol*) goalkeeper

arquitect|o *m* architect. **~ónico** *adj* architectural. **~ura** *f* architecture

arrabal *m* suburb; (*barrio pobre*) poor area. **~es** *mpl* outskirts. **~ero** *adj* suburban; (*de modales groseros*) common

arraiga|do *adj* deeply rooted. **~r** 12 *vi* take root. **~rse** *vpr* take root; (*fig*) settle

arran|car 7 *vt* pull up (planta); pull out (diente); (*arrebatar*) snatch; (*Auto*) start. ● *vi* start. **~carse** *vpr* pull out. **~que** *m* sudden start; (*Auto*) start; (*fig*) outburst

arras *fpl* security; (*en boda*) coins

arrasar *vt* level, smooth; raze to the ground (edificio etc); (*llenar*) fill to the brim. ● *vi* (*en deportes*) sweep to victory; (*en política*) win a landslide victory

arrastr|ar *vt* pull; (*por el suelo*) drag (along); give rise to (consecuencias). ● *vi* trail on the ground. **~arse** *vpr* crawl; (*humillarse*) grovel. **~e** *m* dragging; (*transporte*) haulage. **estar para el ~e** 1 be done in

arre *int* gee up! **~ar** *vt* urge on

arrebat|ado *adj* (*irreflexivo*) impetuous. **~ar** *vt* snatch (away); (*fig*) win (over); captivate (corazón etc). **~arse** *vpr* get carried away. **~o** *m* (*de cólera etc*) fit; (*éxtasis*) ecstasy

arrech|ar *vt* (*LAm fam, enfurecer*) to infuriate. **~arse** *vpr* get furious. **~o** *adj* furious

arrecife *m* reef

arregl|ado *adj* neat; (*bien vestido*) well-dressed; (*LAm, amañado*) fixed. **~ar** *vt* arrange; (*poner en orden*) tidy up; sort out (asunto, problema etc); (*reparar*) mend. **~arse** *vpr* (*solucionarse*) get sorted out; (*prepararse*) get ready; (*apañarse*) manage, make do; (*ponerse de acuerdo*) come to an agreement. **~árselas** manage, get by. **~o** *m* (*incl Mus*) arrangement; (*acción de reparar*) repair; (*acuerdo*) agreement; (*solución*) solution. **con**

~**o a** according to

arrellanarse *vpr* settle o.s. (**en** into)

arremangar 12 *vt* roll up (mangas); tuck up (falda). ~**se** *vpr* roll up one's sleeves

arremeter *vi* charge (**contra** at); (*atacar*) attack

arremolinarse *vpr* mill about; (el agua) to swirl

arrenda|dor *m* landlord. ~**dora** *f* landlady. ~**miento** *m* renting; (*contrato*) lease; (*precio*) rent. ~**r** 1 *vt* (*dar casa en alquiler*) let; (*dar cosa en alquiler*) hire out; (*tomar en alquiler*) rent. ~**tario** *m* tenant

arreos *mpl* tack

arrepenti|miento *m* repentance, regret. ~**rse** 4 *vpr* (*retractarse*) to change one's mind; (*lamentarse*) be sorry. ~**rse de** regret; repent of (pecados)

arrest|ar *vt* arrest, detain; (*encarcelar*) imprison. ~**o** *m* arrest; (*encarcelamiento*) imprisonment

arriar 20 *vt* lower (bandera, vela)

arriba *adv* up; (*dirección*) up(wards); (*en casa*) upstairs. ● *int* up with; (*¡levántate!*) up you get!; (*¡ánimo!*) come on! **¡~ España!** long live Spain! ~ **de** (*LAm*) on top of. ~ **mencionado** aforementioned. **calle** ~ up the street. **de** ~ **abajo** from top to bottom. **de 10 euros para** ~ over 10 euros. **escaleras** ~ upstairs. **la parte de** ~ the top part. **los de** ~ those at the top. **más** ~ higher up

arrib|ar *vi* (barco) reach port; (*esp LAm, llegar*) arrive. ~**ista** *m & f* social climber. ~**o** *m* (*esp LAm*) arrival

arriero *m* muleteer

arriesga|do *adj* risky; (person) daring. ~**r** 12 *vt* risk; (*aventurar*) venture. ~**rse** *vpr* take a risk

arrim|ar *vt* bring close(r). ~**arse** *vpr* come closer, approach

arrincona|do *adj* forgotten; (*acorralado*) cornered. ~**r** *vt* put in a corner; (*perseguir*) corner (*arrumbar*) put aside. ~**rse** *vpr* become a recluse

arroba *f* (*Internet*) at (@); measure of weight

arrocero *adj* rice

arrodillarse *vpr* kneel (down)

arrogan|cia *f* arrogance; (*orgullo*) pride. ~**te** *adj* arrogant; (*orgulloso*) proud

arroj|ar *vt* throw; (*emitir*) give off, throw out; (*producir*) produce. ● *vi* (*esp LAm, vomitar*) throw up. ~**arse** *vpr* throw o.s. ~**o** *m* courage

arrollar *vt* roll (up); (*atropellar*) run over; (*vencer*) crush

arropar *vt* wrap up; (*en la cama*) tuck up. ~**se** *vpr* wrap (o.s.) up

arroy|o *m* stream; (*de una calle*) gutter. ~**uelo** *m* small stream

arroz *m* rice. ~ **con leche** rice pudding. ~**al** *m* rice field

arruga *f* (*en la piel*) wrinkle, line; (*en tela*) crease. ~**r** 12 *vt* wrinkle; crumple (papel); crease (tela). ~**rse** *vpr* (la piel) become wrinkled; (tela) crease, get creased

arruinar *vt* ruin; (*destruir*) destroy. ~**se** *vpr* (persona) be ruined

arrullar *vt* lull to sleep. ● *vi* (palomas) coo

arrumbar *vt* put aside

arsenal *m* (*astillero*) shipyard; (*de armas*) arsenal; (*fig*) mine

arsénico *m* arsenic

arte *m* (*f en plural*) art; (*habilidad*) skill; (*astucia*) cunning. **bellas** ~**s** fine arts. **con** ~ skilfully. **malas**

a

~**s** trickery. **por amor al ~** for the fun of it

artefacto *m* device

arteria *f* artery; (*fig, calle*) main road

artesan|al *adj* craft. **~ía** *f* handicrafts. **objeto** *m* **de ~ía** traditional craft object. **~o** *m* artisan, craftsman

ártico *adj* Arctic. **Á~** *m*. **el Á~** the Arctic

articula|ción *f* joint; (*pronunciación*) articulation. **~do** *adj* articulated; (lenguaje) articulate. **~r** *vt* articulate

artículo *m* article. **~s** *mpl* (*géneros*) goods. **~ de exportación** export product. **~ de fondo** editorial, leader

artífice *m & f* artist; (*creador*) architect

artifici|al *adj* artificial. **~o** *m* (*habilidad*) skill; (*dispositivo*) device; (*engaño*) trick

artiller|ía *f* artillery. **~o** *m* artilleryman, gunner

artilugio *m* gadget

artimaña *f* trick

art|ista *m & f* artist. **~ístico** *adj* artistic

artritis *f* arthritis

arveja *f* (*LAm*) pea

arzobispo *m* archbishop

as *m* ace

asa *f* handle

asado *adj* roast(ed) • *m* roast (meat), joint; (*LAm, reunión*) barbecue. **~o a la parrilla** grilled meat; (*LAm*) barbecued meat

asalariado *adj* salaried. • *m* employee

asalt|ante *m* attacker; (*de un banco*) robber. **~ar** *vt* storm (fortaleza); attack (persona); raid (banco etc); (*fig*) (duda) assail; (*fig*) (idea etc) cross one's mind. **~o** *m* attack; (*robo*) robbery; (*en boxeo*) round

asamblea *f* assembly; (*reunión*) meeting

asar *vt* roast. **~se** *vpr* be very hot. **~ a la parrilla** grill; (*LAm*) barbecue. **~ al horno** (*sin grasa*) bake; (*con grasa*) roast

asbesto *m* asbestos

ascend|encia *f* descent; (*LAm, influencia*) influence. **~ente** *adj* ascending. **~er** **1** *vt* promote. • *vi* go up, ascend; (cuenta etc) come to, amount to; (*ser ascendido*) be promoted. **~iente** *m & f* ancestor; (*influencia*) influence

ascens|ión *f* ascent; (*de grado*) promotion. **día** *m* **de la A~ión** Ascension Day. **~o** *m* ascent; (*de grado*) promotion

ascensor *m* lift (*Brit*), elevator (*Amer*). **~ista** *m & f* lift attendant (*Brit*), elevator operator (*Amer*)

asco *m* disgust. **dar ~** be disgusting; (*fig, causar enfado*) be infuriating. **estar hecho un ~** be disgusting. **me da ~** it makes me feel sick. **¡qué ~!** how disgusting! **ser un ~** be disgusting

ascua *f* ember. **estar en ~s** be on tenterhooks

asea|do *adj* clean; (*arreglado*) neat. **~r** *vt* (*lavar*) wash; (*limpiar*) clean; (*arreglar*) tidy up

asedi|ar *vt* besiege; (*fig*) pester. **~o** *m* siege

asegura|do *adj & m* insured. **~dor** *m* insurer. **~r** *vt* secure, make safe; (*decir*) assure; (*concertar un seguro*) insure; (*preservar*) safeguard. **~rse** *vpr* make sure

asemejarse *vpr* be alike

asenta|do *adj* situated; (*arraigado*) established. **~r** **1** *vt* place; (*asegurar*) settle; (*anotar*) note down; (*Mex, afirmar*) state. **~rse** *vpr* settle; (*estar situado*) be situated; (*esp LAm, sentar cabeza*) settle down

asentir **4** *vi* agree (**a** to). **~ con la cabeza** nod

aseo *m* cleanliness. **~s** *mpl* toilets

asequible *adj* obtainable; (precio) reasonable; (persona) approachable

asesin|ar *vt* murder; (*Pol*) assassinate. **~ato** *m* murder; (*Pol*) assassination. **~o** *m* murderer; (*Pol*) assassin

asesor *m* adviser, consultant. **~ar** *vt* advise. **~arse** *vpr*. **~arse con** consult. **~ía** *f* consultancy; (*oficina*) consultant's office

asfalt|ado *adj* asphalt. **~ar** *vt* asphalt. **~o** *m* asphalt

asfixia *f* suffocation. **~nte** *adj* suffocating. **~r** *vt* suffocate. **~rse** *vpr* suffocate

así *adv* (*de esta manera*) like this, like that. ● *adj* such. **~ ~** so-so. **~ como** just as. **~ como ~**, (*LAm*) **~ nomás** just like that. **~ ... como** both ... and. **~ pues** so. **~ que** so; (*en cuanto*) as soon as. **~ sea** so be it. **~ y todo** even so. **aun ~** even so. **¿no es ~?** isn't that right? **si es ~** if that is the case. **y ~ (sucesivamente)** and so on

Asia *f* Asia

asiático *adj & m* Asian

asidero *m* handle; (*fig, pretexto*) excuse

asidu|amente *adv* regularly. **~o** *adj & m* regular

asiento *m* seat; (*en contabilidad*) entry. **~ delantero** front seat. **~ trasero** back seat

asignar *vt* assign; allot (porción, tiempo etc)

asignatura *f* subject. **~ pendiente** (*en enseñanza*) failed subject; (*fig*) matter still to be resolved

asil|ado *m* inmate; (*Pol*) refugee. **~o** *m* asylum; (*fig*) shelter; (*de ancianos etc*) home. **pedir ~o político** ask for political asylum

asimétrico *adj* asymmetrical

asimila|ción *f* assimilation. **~r** *vt* assimilate

asimismo *adv* also; (*igualmente*) in the same way, likewise

asir **45** *vt* grasp

asist|encia *f* attendance; (*gente*) people (present); (*en un teatro etc*) audience; (*ayuda*) assistance. **~encia médica** medical care. **~enta** *f* (*mujer de la limpieza*) charwoman. **~ente** *m & f* assistant. **~ente social** social worker. **~ido** *adj* assisted. **~ir** *vt* assist, help. ● *vi*. **~ir a** attend, be present at

asm|a *f* asthma. **~ático** *adj & m* asthmatic

asno *m* donkey; (*fig*) ass

asocia|ción *f* association; (*Com*) partnership. **~do** *adj* associated; (socio) associate. ● *m* associate. **~r** *vt* associate; (*Com*) take into partnership. **~rse** *vpr* associate; (*Com*) become a partner

asolar **1** *vt* devastate

asomar *vt* show. ● *vi* appear, show. **~se** *vpr* (persona) lean out (**a, por** of); (cosa) appear

asombr|ar *vt* (*pasmar*) amaze; (*sorprender*) surprise. **~arse** *vpr* be amazed; (*sorprenderse*) be surprised. **~o** *m* amazement, surprise.

~oso *adj* amazing, astonishing
asomo *m* sign. **ni por ~** by no means
aspa *f* cross, X-shape; (*de molino*) (windmill) sail. **en ~** X-shaped
aspaviento *m* show, fuss. **~s** *mpl* gestures. **hacer ~s** make a big fuss
aspecto *m* look, appearance; (*fig*) aspect
aspereza *f* roughness; (*de sabor etc*) sourness
áspero *adj* rough; (sabor etc) bitter
aspersión *f* sprinkling
aspiración *f* breath; (*deseo*) ambition
aspirador *m*, **aspiradora** *f* vacuum cleaner
aspira|nte *m & f* candidate. **~r** *vt* breathe in; (máquina) suck up. ● *vi* breathe in; (máquina) suck. **~r a** aspire to
aspirina *f* aspirin
asquear *vt* sicken. ● *vi* be sickening. **~se** *vpr* be disgusted
asqueroso *adj* disgusting
asta *f* spear; (*de la bandera*) flagpole; (*cuerno*) horn. **a media ~** at half-mast. **~bandera** *f* (*Mex*) flagpole
asterisco *m* asterisk
astilla *f* splinter. **~s** *fpl* firewood
astillero *m* shipyard
astringente *adj & m* astringent
astr|o *m* star. **~ología** *f* astrology. **~ólogo** *m* astrologer. **~onauta** *m & f* astronaut. **~onave** *f* spaceship. **~onomía** *f* astronomy. **~ónomo** *m* astronomer
astu|cia *f* cleverness; (*ardid*) cunning trick. **~to** *adj* astute; (*taimado*) cunning
asumir *vt* assume
asunción *f* assumption. **la A~** the Assumption
asunto *m* (*cuestión*) matter; (*de una novela*) plot; (*negocio*) business. **~s** *mpl* **exteriores** foreign affairs. **el ~ es que** the fact is that
asusta|dizo *adj* easily frightened. **~r** *vt* frighten. **~rse** *vpr* be frightened
ataca|nte *m & f* attacker. **~r** **7** *vt* attack
atad|o *adj* tied. ● *m* bundle. **~ura** *f* tie
ataj|ar *vi* take a short cut; (*Mex, en tenis*) pick up the balls. ● *vt* (*LAm, agarrar*) catch. **~o** *m* short cut
atañer **22** *vt* concern
ataque *m* attack; (*Med*) fit, attack. **~ al corazón** heart attack. **~ de nervios** fit of hysterics
atar *vt* tie. **~se** *vpr* tie up
atarantar *vt* (*LAm*) fluster. **~se** *vpr* (*LAm*) get flustered
atardecer **11** *vi* get dark. ● *m* dusk. **al ~** at dusk
atareado *adj* busy
atasc|ar **7** *vt* block; (*fig*) hinder. **~arse** *vpr* get stuck; (tubo etc) block. **~o** *m* blockage; (*Auto*) traffic jam
ataúd *m* coffin
atav|iar **20** *vt* dress up. **~iarse** *vpr* dress up, get dressed up. **~ío** *m* dress, attire
atemorizar **10** *vt* frighten. **~se** *vpr* be frightened
atención *f* attention; (*cortesía*) courtesy, kindness; (*interés*) interest. **¡~!** look out!. **llamar la ~** attract attention, catch the eye; **prestar ~** pay attention
atender **1** *vt* attend to; (*cuidar*) look after. ● *vi* pay attention

atenerse 40 *vpr* abide (**a** by)

atentado *m* (*ataque*) attack; (*afrenta*) affront (**contra** to). **~ contra la vida de uno** attempt on s.o.'s life

atentamente *adv* attentively; (*con cortesía*) politely; (*con amabilidad*) kindly. **lo saluda ~** (*en cartas*) yours faithfully

atentar *vi.* **~ contra** threaten. **~ contra la vida de uno** make an attempt on s.o.'s life

atento *adj* attentive; (*cortés*) polite; (*amable*) kind

atenua|nte *adj* extenuating. • *f* extenuating circumstance. **~r** 21 *vt* attenuate; (*hacer menor*) diminish, lessen

ateo *adj* atheistic. • *m* atheist

aterciopelado *adj* velvety

aterra|dor *adj* terrifying. **~r** *vt* terrify

aterriza|je *m* landing. **~je forzoso** emergency landing. **~r** 10 *vt* land

aterrorizar 10 *vt* terrify

atesorar *vt* hoard; amass (fortuna)

atesta|do *adj* packed, full up. • *m* sworn statement. **~r** *vt* fill up, pack; (*Jurid*) testify

atestiguar 15 *vt* testify to; (*fig*) prove

atiborrar *vt* fill, stuff. **~se** *vpr* stuff o.s.

ático *m* attic

atina|do *adj* right; (*juicioso*) wise, sensible. **~r** *vt/i* hit upon; (*acertar*) guess right

atizar 10 *vt* poke; (*fig*) stir up

atlántico *adj* Atlantic. **el (océano) A~** the Atlantic (Ocean)

atlas *m* atlas

atl|eta *m & f* athlete. **~ético** *adj* athletic. **~etismo** *m* athletics

atmósfera *f* atmosphere

atole *m* (*LAm*) boiled maize drink

atolladero *m* bog; (*fig*) tight corner

atolondra|do *adj* scatter-brained; (*aturdido*) stunned. **~r** *vt* fluster; (*pasmar*) stun. **~rse** *vpr* get flustered

at|ómico *adj* atomic. **~omizador** *m* spray, atomizer

átomo *m* atom

atónito *m* amazed

atonta|do *adj* stunned; (*tonto*) stupid. **~r** *vt* stun. **~rse** *vpr* get confused

atorar *vt* (*esp LAm*) to block; (*Mex, sujetar*) secure. **~se** *vpr* (*esp LAm, atragantarse*) choke; (*atascarse*) get blocked; (puerta) get jammed

atormentar *vt* torture. **~se** *vpr* worry, torment o.s.

atornillar *vt* screw on

atosigar 12 *vt* pester

atraca|dor *m* mugger; (*de banco*) bank robber. **~r** 7 *vt* dock; (*arrimar*) bring alongside; hold up (banco); mug (persona). • *vi* (barco) dock

atracci|ón *f* attraction. **~ones** *fpl* entertainment, amusements

atrac|o *m* hold-up, robbery. **~ón** *m.* **darse un ~ón** stuff o.s. (**de** with)

atractivo *adj* attractive. • *m* attraction; (*encanto*) charm

atraer 41 *vt* attract

atragantarse *vpr* choke (**con** on). **la historia se me atraganta** I can't stand history

atrancar 7 *vt* bolt (puerta). **~se**

a

vpr get stuck

atrapar *vt* catch; (*encerrar*) trap

atrás *adv* back; (*tiempo*) previously, before. **años ~** years ago. **~ de** (*LAm*) behind. **dar un paso ~** step backwards. **hacia ~, para ~** backwards

atras|ado *adj* behind; (reloj) slow; (*con deudas*) in arrears; (país) backward. **llegar ~ado** (*esp LAm*) arrive late. **~ar** *vt* put back (reloj); (*demorar*) delay, postpone. ● *vi* (reloj) be slow. **~arse** *vpr* be late; (reloj) be slow; (*quedarse atrás*) fall behind. **~o** *m* delay; (*de un reloj*) slowness; (*de un país*) backwardness. **~os** *mpl* (*Com*) arrears

atravesa|do *adj* lying across. **~r** **1** *vt* cross; (*traspasar*) go through (*poner transversalmente*) lay across. **~rse** *vpr* lie across; (*en la garganta*) get stuck, stick

atrayente *adj* attractive

atrev|erse *vpr* dare. **~erse con** tackle. **~ido** *adj* daring; (*insolente*) insolent. **~imiento** *m* daring; (*descaro*) insolence

atribu|ción *f* attribution. **~ciones** *fpl* authority. **~uir** **17** *vt* attribute; confer (función). **~irse** *vpr* claim

atribulado *adj* afflicted

atributo *m* attribute

atril *m* lectern; (*Mus*) music stand

atrocidad *f* atrocity. **¡qué ~!** how awful!

atrofiarse *vpr* atrophy

atropell|ado *adj* hasty. **~ar** *vt* knock down; (*por encima*) run over; (*empujar*) push aside; (*fig*) outrage, insult. **~arse** *vpr* rush. **~o** *m* (*Auto*) accident; (*fig*) outrage

atroz *adj* appalling; (*fig*) atrocious

atuendo *m* dress, attire

atún *m* tuna (fish)

aturdi|do *adj* bewildered; (*por golpe*) stunned. **~r** *vt* bewilder; (golpe) stun; (ruido) deafen

auda|cia *f* boldness, audacity. **~z** *adj* bold

audi|ble *adj* audible. **~ción** *f* hearing; (*prueba*) audition. **~encia** *f* audience; (*tribunal*) court; (*sesión*) hearing

auditor *m* auditor. **~io** *m* audience; (*sala*) auditorium

auge *m* peak; (*Com*) boom

augur|ar *vt* predict; (cosas) augur. **~io** *m* prediction. **con nuestros mejores ~ios para** with our best wishes for. **mal ~** bad omen

aula *f* class-room; (*Univ*) lecture room

aull|ar **23** *vi* howl. **~ido** *m* howl

aument|ar *vt* increase; magnify (imagen). ● *vi* increase. **~o** *m* increase; (*de sueldo*) rise

aun *adv* even. **~ así** even so. **~ cuando** although. **más ~** even more. **ni ~** not even

aún *adv* still, yet. **~ no ha llegado** it still hasn't arrived, it hasn't arrived yet

aunar **23** *vt* join. **~se** *vpr* join together

aunque *conj* although, (even) though

aúpa *int* up! **de ~** wonderful

aureola *f* halo

auricular *m* (*de teléfono*) receiver. **~es** *mpl* headphones

aurora *f* dawn

ausen|cia *f* absence. **en ~cia de** in the absence of. **~tarse** *vpr* leave. **~te** *adj* absent. ● *m & f* absentee; (*Jurid*) missing person. **~tismo** *m* (*LAm*) absenteeism

auspici|ador *m* sponsor. **~ar** *vt* sponsor. **~o** *m* sponsorship; (*signo*) omen. **bajo los ~s de** sponsored by

auster|idad *f* austerity. **~o** *adj* austere

austral *adj* southern

Australia *m* Australia

australiano *adj & m* Australian

Austria *f* Austria

austriaco, **austríaco** *adj & m* Austrian

aut|enticar **7** authenticate. **~enticidad** *f* authenticity. **~éntico** *adj* authentic

auto *m* (*Jurid*) decision; (*orden*) order; (*Auto, fam*) car. **~s** *mpl* proceedings

auto|abastecimiento *m* self-sufficiency. **~biografía** *f* autobiography

autobús *m* bus. **en ~** by bus

autocar *m* (long-distance) bus, coach (*Brit*)

autocontrol *m* self-control

autóctono *adj* indigenous

auto|determinación *f* self-determination. **~didacta** *adj* self-taught. • *m & f* self-taught person. **~escuela** *f* driving school. **~financiamiento** *m* self-financing

autógrafo *m* autograph

autómata *m* robot

autom|ático *adj* automatic. • *m* press-stud. **~atización** *f* automation

automotor *m* diesel train

autom|óvil *adj* motor. • *m* car. **~ovilismo** *m* motoring. **~ovilista** *m & f* driver, motorist

aut|onomía *f* autonomy. **~onómico** *adj*, **~ónomo** *adj* autonomous

autopista *f* motorway (*Brit*), freeway (*Amer*)

autopsia *f* autopsy

autor *m* author. **~a** *f* author(ess)

autori|dad *f* authority. **~tario** *adj* authoritarian

autoriza|ción *f* authorization. **~do** *adj* authorized, official; (*opinión etc*) authoritative. **~r** **10** *vt* authorize

auto|rretrato *m* self-portrait. **~servicio** *m* self-service restaurant. **~stop** *m* hitch-hiking. **hacer ~stop** hitch-hike

autosuficiente *adj* self-sufficient

autovía *f* dual carriageway

auxili|ar *adj* auxiliary; (*profesor*) assistant. • *m & f* assistant. • *vt* help. **~o** *m* help. **¡~o!** help! **en ~o de** in aid of. **pedir ~o** shout for help. **primeros ~os** first aid

Av. *abrev* (**Avenida**) Ave

aval *m* guarantee

avalancha *f* avalanche

avalar *vt* guarantee

aval|uar *vt* **21** (*LAm*) value. **~úo** *m* valuation

avance *m* advance; (*en el cine*) trailer. **avances** *mpl* (*Mex*) trailer

avanzar **10** *vt* move forward. **~ la pantalla** scroll up. • *vi* advance

avar|icia *f* avarice. **~icioso** *adj*, **~iento** *adj* greedy; (*tacaño*) miserly. **~o** *adj* miserly. • *m* miser

avasallar *vt* dominate

Avda. *abrev* (**Avenida**) Ave

ave *f* bird. **~ de paso** (*incl fig*) bird of passage. **~ de rapiña** bird of prey

AVE - Alta Velocidad Española A high-speed train service linking Madrid, Seville and Huelva via Cadiz, established in 1992 in time for the international exhibition, Expo 92 in Seville. Lines under construction include: Madrid-Barcelona, with an extension to France, and Barcelona-Valencia. An Ave service linking Madrid and Galicia is planned.

avecinarse *vpr* approach
avejentar *vt* age
avellan|a *f* hazelnut. **~o** *m* hazel (tree)
avemaría *f* Hail Mary
avena *f* oats
avenida *f* (*calle*) avenue
avenir 53 *vt* reconcile. **~se** *vpr* come to an agreement; (*entenderse*) get on well (**con** with)
aventaja|do *adj* outstanding. **~r** *vt* be ahead of; (*superar*) surpass
avent|ar 1 *vt* fan; winnow (grano etc); (*Mex, lanzar*) throw; (*Mex, empujar*) push. **~arse** *vpr* (*Mex*) throw o.s.; (*atreverse*) dare. **~ón** *m* (*Mex*) ride, lift (*Brit*)
aventur|a *f* adventure. **~a amorosa** love affair. **~ado** *adj* risky. **~ero** *adj* adventurous. • *m* adventurer
avergonzar 10 & 16 *vt* shame; (*abochornar*) embarrass. **~se** *vpr* be ashamed; (*abochornarse*) be embarrassed
aver|ía *f* (*Auto*) breakdown; (*en máquina*) failure. **~iado** *adj* broken down. **~iarse** 20 *vpr* break down
averigua|ción *f* inquiry; (*Mex, disputa*) argument. **~r** 15 *vt* find out. • *vi* (*Mex*) argue
aversión *f* aversion (**a, hacia, por** to)
avestruz *m* ostrich
avia|ción *f* aviation; (*Mil*) air force. **~dor** *m* (*piloto*) pilot
av|ícola *adj* poultry. **~icultura** *f* poultry farming
avidez *f* eagerness, greed
ávido *adj* eager, greedy
avinagra|do *adj* sour. **~rse** *vpr* go sour; (*fig*) become embittered
avi|ón *m* aeroplane (*Brit*), airplane (*Amer*); (*Mex, juego*) hopscotch. **~onazo** *m* (*Mex*) plane crash
avis|ar *vt* warn; (*informar*) notify, inform; call (médico etc). **~o** *m* warning; (*comunicación*) notice; (*LAm, anuncio, cartel*) advertisement; (*en televisión*) commercial. **estar sobre ~o** be on the alert. **sin previo ~o** without prior warning
avisp|a *f* wasp. **~ado** *adj* sharp. **~ero** *m* wasps' nest; (*fig*) mess. **~ón** *m* hornet
avistar *vt* catch sight of
avivar *vt* stoke up (fuego); brighten up (color); arouse (interés, pasión); intensify (dolor). **~se** *vpr* revive; (*animarse*) cheer up; (*LAm, despabilarse*) wise up
axila *f* armpit, axilla
axioma *m* axiom
ay *int* (*de dolor*) ouch!; (*de susto*) oh!; (*de pena*) oh dear! **¡~ de ti!** poor you!
aya *f* governess, child's nurse
ayer *adv* yesterday. • *m* past. **antes de ~** the day before yesterday. **~ por la mañana**, (*LAm*) **~ en la mañana** yesterday morning
ayuda *f* help, aid. **~ de cámara** valet. **~nta** *f*, **~nte** *m* assistant; (*Mil*) adjutant. **~r** *vt* help
ayun|ar *vi* fast. **~as** *fpl*. **estar en**

~as have had nothing to eat or drink; (*fig, fam*) be in the dark. **~o** *m* fasting

ayuntamiento *m* town council, city council; (*edificio*) town hall

azabache *m* jet

azad|a *f* hoe. **~ón** *m* (large) hoe

azafata *f* air hostess

azafate *m* (*LAm*) tray

azafrán *m* saffron

azahar *m* orange blossom; (*del limonero*) lemon blossom

azar *m* chance; (*desgracia*) misfortune. **al ~** at random. **por ~** by chance. **~es** *mpl* ups and downs

azaros|amente *adv* hazardously. **~o** *adj* hazardous, risky; (vida) eventful

azorar *vt* embarrass. **~rse** *vpr* be embarrassed

Azores *fpl*. **las ~** the Azores

azotador *m* (*Mex*) caterpillar

azot|ar *vt* whip, beat; (*Mex, puerta*) slam. **~e** *m* whip; (*golpe*) smack; (*fig, calamidad*) calamity

azotea *f* flat roof

azteca *adj & m & f* Aztec

> *i* **Aztecas** A Náhuatl-speaking people who in the fourteenth century established a brilliant and tyrannical civilization in central and southern Mexico. Its capital was Tenochtitlán, built on reclaimed marshland, and which became Mexico City. The Aztec empire collapsed in 1521 after defeat by the Spaniards led by Hernán Cortés.

az|úcar *m & f* sugar. **~ucarado** *adj* sweet, sugary. **~ucarar** *vt* sweeten. **~ucarero** *m* sugar bowl

azucena *f* (white) lily

azufre *m* sulphur

azul *adj & m* blue. **~ado** *adj* bluish. **~ marino** navy blue

azulejo *m* tile

azuzar [10] *vt* urge on, incite

> *i* **Año Nuevo** See ▷**NOCHEVIEJA**

Bb

bab|a *f* spittle. **~ear** *vi* drool, slobber; (niño) dribble. **caérsele la ~a a uno** be delighted. **~eo** *m* drooling; (*de un niño*) dribbling. **~ero** *m* bib

babor *m* port. **a ~** to port, on the port side

babosa *f* slug

babosada *f* (*Mex*) drivel

babos|ear *vt* slobber over; (niño) dribble over. • *vi* (*Mex*) day dream. **~o** *adj* slimy; (*LAm, tonto*) silly

babucha *f* slipper

baca *f* luggage rack

bacalao *m* cod

bache *m* pothole; (*fig*) bad patch

bachillerato *m* school-leaving examination

bacteria *f* bacterium

bagaje *m*. **~ cultural** cultural knowledge; (*de un pueblo*) cultural heritage

bahía *f* bay

bail|able *adj* dance. **~aor** *m* Flamenco dancer. **~ar** *vt/i* dance. **ir a ~ar** go dancing. **~arín** *m* dancer.

b

~arina *f* dancer; (*de ballet*) ballerina. **~e** *m* dance; (*actividad*) dancing. **~e de etiqueta** ball

baja *f* drop, fall; (*Mil*) casualty. **~ por maternidad** maternity leave. **darse de ~** take sick leave. **~da** *f* slope; (*acto de bajar*) descent; (*camino*) way down. **~r** *vt* lower; (*llevar abajo*) get down; go down (escalera); bow (la cabeza). • *vi* go down; (temperatura, precio) fall. **~rse** *vpr* pull down (pantalones). **~r(se) de** get out of (coche); get off (autobús, caballo, tren, bicicleta)

bajeza *f* vile deed

bajío *m* shallows; (*de arena*) sandbank; (*LAm, terreno bajo*) low-lying area

bajo *adj* low; (*de estatura*) short, small; (cabeza, ojos) lowered; (*humilde*) humble, low; (*vil*) vile, low; (voz) low; (*Mus*) deep. • *m* lowland; (*Mus*) bass. • *adv* quietly; (volar) low. • *prep* under. **~ cero** below zero. **~ la lluvia** in the rain. **los ~s** (*LAm*) ground floor (*Brit*), first floor (*Amer*); **los ~s fondos** the underworld

bajón *m* sharp drop; (*de salud*) sudden decline

bala *f* bullet; (*de algodón etc*) bale. (*LAm, en atletismo*) shot. **como una ~** like a shot. **lanzamiento de ~** (*LAm*) shot put

balada *f* ballad

balan|ce *m* balance; (*documento*) balance sheet; (*resultado*) outcome. **~cear** *vt* balance. **~cearse** *vpr* swing. **~ceo** *m* swinging. **~cín** *m* rocking chair; (*de niños*) seesaw. **~za** *f* scales; (*Com*) balance

balar *vi* bleat

balazo *m* (*disparo*) shot; (*herida*) bullet wound

balboa *f* (*unidad monetaria panameña*) balboa

balbuc|ear *vt/i* stammer; (niño) babble. **~eo** *m* stammering; (*de niño*) babbling. **~ir** 24 *vt/i* stammer; (niño) babble

balcón *m* balcony

balda *f* shelf

balde *m* bucket. **de ~** free (of charge). **en ~** in vain

baldío *adj* (terreno) waste

baldosa *f* (floor) tile; (*losa*) flagstone

bale|ar *adj* Balearic. • **las (Islas) B~ares** the Balearics, the Balearic Islands. • *vt* (*LAm*) to shoot. **~o** *m* (*LAm, tiroteo*) shooting

balero *m* (*Mex*) cup and ball toy; (*rodamiento*) bearing

balido *m* bleat; (*varios sonidos*) bleating

balística *f* ballistics

baliza *f* (*Naut*) buoy; (*Aviac*) beacon

ballena *f* whale

ballet /ba'le/ (*pl* **~s**) *m* ballet

balneario *m* spa; (*con playa*) seaside resort

balompié *m* soccer, football (*Brit*)

bal|ón *m* ball. **~oncesto** *m* basketball. **~onmano** *m* handball. **~onvolea** *m* volleyball

balotaje *m* (*LAm*) voting

balsa *f* (*de agua*) pool; (*plataforma flotante*) raft

bálsamo *m* balsam; (*fig*) balm

i

balseros The name given to illegal immigrants who try to enter a country in small boats or on rafts. It applies particularly to Cubans who try to enter the US by sailing to

Florida and to immigrants attempting to enter Spain by crossing the Straits of Gibraltar.

baluarte *m* (*incl fig*) bastion
bambalina *f* drop curtain. **entre ~s** behind the scenes
bambole|ar *vi* sway. **~arse** *vpr* sway; (mesa etc) wobble; (barco) rock. **~o** *m* swaying; (*de mesa etc*) wobbling; (*de barco*) rocking
bambú *m* (*pl* **~es**) bamboo
banal *adj* banal. **~idad** *f* banality
banan|a *f* (*esp LAm*) banana. **~ero** *adj* banana. **~o** *m* (*LAm*) banana tree
banc|a *f* banking; (*conjunto de bancos*) banks; (*en juegos*) bank; (*LAm, asiento*) bench. **~ario** *adj* bank, banking. **~arrota** *f* bankruptcy. **hacer ~arrota, ir a la ~arrota** go bankrupt. **~o** *m* (*asiento*) bench; (*Com*) bank; (*bajío*) sandbank; (*de peces*) shoal
banda *f* (*incl Mus, Radio*) band; (*Mex, para el pelo*) hair band; (*raya ancha*) stripe; (*cinta ancha*) sash; (*grupo*) gang, group. **~ sonora** sound-track. **~da** *f* (*de pájaros*) flock; (*de peces*) shoal
bandeja *f* tray
bandejón *m* (*Mex*) central reservation (*Brit*), median strip (*Amer*)
bander|a *f* flag. **~illa** *f* banderilla. **~ear** *vt* stick the banderillas in. **~ero** *m* banderillero. **~ín** *m* pennant, small flag
bandido *m* bandit
bando *m* edict, proclamation; (*facción*) camp, side. **~s** *mpl* banns. **pasarse al otro ~** go over to the other side
bandolero *m* bandit
bandoneón *m* large accordion
banjo *m* banjo
banquero *m* banker
banquete *m* banquet; (*de boda*) wedding reception
banquillo *m* bench; (*Jurid*) dock; (*taburete*) footstool
bañ|ador *m* (*de mujer*) swimming costume; (*de hombre*) swimming trunks. **~ar** *vt* bath (niño); (*Culin, recubrir*) coat. **~arse** *vpr* go swimming, have a swim; (*en casa*) have a bath. **~era** *f* bath (tub). **~ista** *m & f* bather. **~o** *m* bath; (*en piscina, mar etc*) swim; (*cuarto*) bathroom; (*LAm, wáter*) toilet; (*bañera*) bath(tub); (*capa*) coat(ing)
baqueano (*LAm*), **baquiano** *m* guide
bar *m* bar
baraja *f* pack of cards. **~r** *vt* shuffle; juggle (cifras etc); consider (posibilidades); (*Mex, explicar*) explain
baranda, **barandilla** *f* rail; (*de escalera*) banisters
barat|a *f* (*Mex*) sale. **~ija** *f* trinket. **~illo** *m* junk shop; (*géneros*) cheap goods. **~o** *adj* cheap. ● *adv* cheap(ly)
barba *f* chin; (*pelo*) beard
barbacoa *f* barbecue; (*carne*) barbecued meat
barbari|dad *f* atrocity; (*fam, mucho*) awful lot ⓘ. **¡qué ~dad!** how awful! **~e** *f* barbarity; (*fig*) ignorance. **~smo** *m* barbarism
bárbaro *adj* barbaric, cruel; (*bruto*) uncouth; (*fam, estupendo*) terrific ⓘ ● *m* barbarian. **¡qué ~!** how marvellous!
barbear *vt* (*Mex, lisonjear*) suck up to
barbecho *m*. **en ~** fallow
barber|ía *f* barber's (shop). **~o** *m*

barber; (*Mex, adulador*) creep
barbilla *f* chin
barbitúrico *m* barbiturate
barbudo *adj* bearded
barca *f* (small) boat. **~ de pasaje** ferry. **~za** *f* barge
barcelonés *adj* of Barcelona, from Barcelona. • *m* native of Barcelona
barco *m* boat; (*navío*) ship. **~ cisterna** tanker. **~ de vapor** steamer. **~ de vela** sailing boat. **ir en ~** go by boat
barda *f* (*Mex*) wall; (*de madera*) fence
barítono *adj & m* baritone
barman *m* (*pl* **~s**) barman
barniz *m* varnish; (*para loza etc*) glaze; (*fig*) veneer. **~ar** **10** *vt* varnish; glaze (loza etc)
barómetro *m* barometer
bar|ón *m* baron. **~onesa** *f* baroness
barquero *m* boatman
barquillo *m* wafer; (*Mex, de helado*) ice-cream cone
barra *f* bar; (*pan*) loaf of French bread; (*palanca*) lever; (*de arena*) sandbank; (*LAm, de hinchas*) supporters. **~ de labios** lipstick
barrabasada *f* mischief, prank
barraca *f* hut; (*vivienda pobre*) shack, shanty
barranco *m* ravine, gully; (*despeñadero*) cliff, precipice
barrer *vt* sweep; thrash (rival)
barrera *f* barrier. **~ del sonido** sound barrier
barriada *f* district; (*LAm, barrio marginal*) slum
barrial *m* (*LAm*) quagmire
barrida *f* sweep; (*LAm, redada*) police raid
barrig|a *f* belly. **~ón** *adj*, **~udo** *adj* pot-bellied
barril *m* barrel
barrio *m* district, area. **~s bajos** poor quarter, poor area. **el otro ~** (*fig, fam*) the other world. **~bajero** *adj* vulgar, common
barro *m* mud; (*arcilla*) clay; (*arcilla cocida*) earthenware
barroco *adj* Baroque. • *m* Baroque style
barrote *m* bar
bartola *f*. **tirarse a la ~** take it easy
bártulos *mpl* things. **liar los ~** pack one's bags
barullo *m* racket; (*confusión*) confusion. **a ~** galore
basar *vt* base. **~se** *vpr*. **~se en** be based on
báscula *f* scales
base *f* base; (*fig*) basis, foundation. **a ~ de** thanks to; (*mediante*) by means of; (*en una receta*) mainly consisting of. **~ de datos** database. **partiendo de la ~ de, tomando como ~** on the basis of
básico *adj* basic
basílica *f* basilica
básquetbol, **basquetbol** *m* (*LAm*) basketball

bastante

• *adjetivo/pronombre*

····▸ (*suficiente*) enough. **¿hay ~s sillas?** are there enough chairs? **ya tengo ~** I have enough already

····▸ (*mucho*) quite a lot. **vino ~ gente** quite a lot of people came. **tiene ~s amigos** he has quite a lot of friends **¿te gusta?- sí, ~** do you like it?

— yes, quite a lot

● *adverbio*

....➤ (*suficientemente*) enough. **no has estudiado ~** you haven't studied enough. **no es lo ~ inteligente** he's not clever enough (**como para** to)

....➤ **bastante** + *adjetivo/adverbio* (*modificando la intensidad*) quite, fairly. **parece ~ simpático** he looks quite friendly. **es ~ fácil de hacer** it's quite easy to do. **canta ~ bien** he sings quite well

....➤ **bastante** *con verbo* (*considerablemente*) quite a lot. **el lugar ha cambiado ~** the place has changed quite a lot

bastar *vi* be enough. **¡basta!** that's enough! **basta con decir que** suffice it to say that. **basta y sobra** that's more than enough

bastardilla *f* italics

bastardo *adj* & *m* bastard

bastidor *m* frame; (*Auto*) chassis. **~es** *mpl* (*en el teatro*) wings. **entre ~es** behind the scenes

basto *adj* coarse. **~s** *mpl* (*naipes*) clubs

bast|ón *m* walking stick; (*de esquí*) ski pole. **~onazo** *m* blow with a stick; (*de mando*) staff of office

basur|a *f* rubbish, garbage (*Amer*); (*en la calle*) litter. **~al** *m* (*LAm, lugar*) rubbish dump. **~ero** *m* dustman (*Brit*), garbage collector (*Amer*); (*sitio*) rubbish dump; (*Mex, recipiente*) dustbin (*Brit*), garbage can (*Amer*)

bata *f* dressing-gown; (*de médico etc*) white coat; (*esp LAm, de baño*) bathrobe

batahola *f* (*LAm*) pandemonium

batall|a *f* battle. **~a campal** pitched battle. **de ~a** everyday. **~ador** *adj* fighting. ● *m* fighter. **~ar** *vi* battle, fight. **~ón** *m* battalion.

batata *f* sweet potato

bate *m* bat. **~ador** *m* batter; (*cricket*) batsman. **~ar** *vi* bat

batería *f* battery; (*Mus*) drums. ● *m* & *f* drummer. **~ de cocina** kitchen utensils, pots and pans

baterista *m* & *f* drummer

batido *adj* beaten; (nata) whipped. ● *m* batter; (*bebida*) milk shake. **~ra** *f* (food) mixer

batir *vt* beat; break (récord); whip (nata). **~ palmas** clap. **~se** *vpr* fight

batuta *f* baton. **llevar la ~** be in command, be the boss

baúl *m* trunk

bauti|smal *adj* baptismal. **~smo** *m* baptism, christening. **~zar** 10 *vt* baptize, christen. **~zo** *m* christening

baya *f* berry

bayeta *f* cloth

bayoneta *f* bayonet

baza *f* (*naipes*) trick; (*fig*) advantage. **meter ~** interfere

bazar *m* bazaar

bazofia *f* revolting food; (*fig*) rubbish

beato *adj* blessed; (*piadoso*) devout; (*pey*) overpious

bebé *m* baby

beb|edero *m* drinking trough; (*sitio*) watering place. **~edizo** *m* potion; (*veneno*) poison. **~edor** *m* heavy drinker. **~er** *vt/i* drink. **~ida** *f* drink. **~ido** *adj* drunk

beca *f* grant, scholarship. **~do** *m* (*LAm*) scholarship holder, scholar.

~r [7] *vt* give a scholarship to. **~rio** *m* scholarship holder, scholar

beige /beis, beʒ/ *adj & m* beige

béisbol *m*, (*Mex*) **beisbol** *m* baseball

belén *m* crib, nativity scene

belga *adj & m & f* Belgian

Bélgica *f* Belgium

bélico *adj*, **belicoso** *adj* warlike

bell|eza *f* beauty. **~o** *adj* beautiful. **~as artes** *fpl* fine arts

bellota *f* acorn

bemol *m* flat. **tener (muchos) ~es** be difficult

bend|ecir [46] (*pero imperativo* **bendice**, *futuro, condicional y pp regulares*) *vt* bless. **~ición** *f* blessing. **~ito** *adj* blessed; (*que tiene suerte*) lucky; (*feliz*) happy

benefactor *m* benefactor

benefic|encia *f* charity. **de ~encia** charitable. **~iar** *vt* benefit. **~iarse** *vpr* benefit. **~iario** *m* beneficiary; (*de un cheque etc*) payee. **~io** *m* benefit; (*ventaja*) advantage; (*ganancia*) profit, gain. **~ioso** *adj* beneficial

benéfico *adj* beneficial; (*de beneficencia*) charitable

ben|evolencia *f* benevolence. **~évolo** *adj* benevolent

bengala *f* flare. **luz** *f* **de ~** flare

benigno *adj* kind; (*moderado*) gentle, mild; (tumor) benign

berberecho *m* cockle

berenjena *f* aubergine (*Brit*), eggplant (*Amer*)

berr|ear *vi* (animales) bellow; (niño) bawl. **~ido** *m* bellow; (*de niño*) bawling

berrinche *m* temper; (*de un niño*) tantrum

berro *m* watercress

besamel(a) *f* white sauce

bes|ar *vt* kiss. **~arse** *vpr* kiss (each other). **~o** *m* kiss

bestia *f* beast; (*bruto*) brute; (*idiota*) idiot. **~ de carga** beast of burden. **~l** *adj* bestial, animal; (*fig, fam*) terrific. **~lidad** *f* (*acción brutal*) horrid thing; (*insensatez*) stupidity

besugo *m* red bream

besuquear *vt* cover with kisses

betabel *f* (*Mex*) beetroot

betún *m* (*para el calzado*) shoe polish

biberón *m* feeding-bottle

Biblia *f* Bible

bibliografía *f* bibliography

biblioteca *f* library; (*mueble*) bookcase. **~ de consulta** reference library. **~rio** *m* librarian

bicarbonato *m* bicarbonate

bicho *m* insect, bug; (*animal*) small animal, creature. **~ raro** odd sort

bici *f* [!] bike. **~cleta** *f* bicycle. **ir en ~cleta** cycle. **~moto** (*LAm*) moped

bidé, bidet /bi'ðeɪ/ *m* bidet

bidón *m* drum, can

bien *adv* well; (*muy*) very, quite; (*correctamente*) right; (*de buena gana*) willingly. ● *m* good; (*efectos*) property. **¡~!** fine!, OK!, good! **~... (o) ~** either... or. **¡está ~!** fine!, alright!; (*basta*) that is enough!. **más ~** rather. **¡muy ~!** good! **no ~** as soon as. **¡qué ~!** marvellous!, great! [!]. **si ~** although

bienal *adj* biennial

bien|aventurado *adj* fortunate. **~estar** *m* well-being. **~hablado** *adj* well-spoken. **~hechor** *m* benefactor. **~intencionado** *adj* well-meaning

bienio *m* two year-period

bienvenid|a *f* welcome. **dar la ~a a uno** welcome s.o. **~o** *adj* welcome. **¡~o!** welcome!

bifurca|ción *f* junction. **~rse** 7 *vpr* fork; (*rail*) branch off

b|igamia *f* bigamy. **~ígamo** *adj* bigamous. ● *m* bigamist

bigot|e *m* moustache. **~ón** *adj* (*Mex*), **~udo** *adj* with a big moustache

bikini *m* bikini

bilingüe *adj* bilingual

billar *m* billiards

billete *m* ticket; (*de banco*) (bank) note (*Brit*), bill (*Amer*). **~ de ida y vuelta** return ticket (*Brit*), round-trip ticket (*Amer*). **~ sencillo** single ticket (*Brit*), one-way ticket (*Amer*). **~ra** *f*, **~ro** *m* wallet, billfold (*Amer*)

billón *m* billion (*Brit*), trillion (*Amer*)

bi|mensual *adj* fortnightly, twice-monthly. **~mestral** *adj* two-monthly. **~mestre** two-month period. **~motor** *adj* twin-engined. ● *m* twin-engined plane

binoculares *mpl* binoculars

bi|ografía *f* biography. **~ográfico** *adj* biographical

bi|ología *f* biology. **~ológico** *adj* biological. **~ólogo** *m* biologist

biombo *m* folding screen

biopsia *f* biopsy

bioterrorismo *m* bioterrorism

biplaza *m* two-seater

biquini *m* bikini

birlar *vt* ! steal, pinch !

bis *m* encore. **¡~!** encore! **vivo en el 3 ~** I live at 3A

bisabuel|a *f* great-grandmother. **~o** *m* great-grandfather. **~os** *mpl* great-grandparents

bisagra *f* hinge

bisiesto *adj*. **año** *m* **~** leap year

bisniet|a *f* great-granddaughter. **~o** *m* great-grandson. **~os** *mpl* great-grandchildren

bisonte *m* bison

bisoño *adj* inexperienced

bisté, **bistec** *m* steak

bisturí *m* scalpel

bisutería *f* imitation jewellery, costume jewellery

bitácora *f* binnacle

bizco *adj* cross-eyed

bizcocho *m* sponge (cake)

bizquear *vi* squint

blanc|a *f* white woman; (*Mus*) minim. **~o** *adj* white; (tez) fair. ● *m* white; (*persona*) white man; (*espacio*) blank; (*objetivo*) target. **dar en el ~o** hit the mark. **dejar en ~o** leave blank. **pasar la noche en ~o** have a sleepless night. **~ura** *f* whiteness

blandir 24 *vt* brandish

bland|o *adj* soft; (carácter) weak; (*cobarde*) cowardly; (carne) tender. **~ura** *f* softness; (*de la carne*) tenderness

blanque|ar *vt* whiten; whitewash (paredes); bleach (tela); launder (dinero). ● *vi* turn white. **~o** *m* whitening; (*de dinero*) laundering

blasón *m* coat of arms

bledo *m*. **me importa un ~** I couldn't care less

blinda|je *m* armour (plating). **~r** *vt* armour(-plate)

bloc *m* (*pl* **~s**) pad

bloque *m* block; (*Pol*) bloc. **en ~** en bloc. **~ar** *vt* block; (*Mil*) blockade; (*Com*) freeze. **~o** *m* blockade; (*Com*) freezing

blusa *f* blouse

b

bob|ada *f* silly thing. **decir ~adas** talk nonsense. **~ería** *f* silly thing

bobina *f* reel; (*Elec*) coil

bobo *adj* silly, stupid. • *m* idiot, fool

boca *f* mouth; (*fig, entrada*) entrance; (*de buzón*) slot; (*de cañón*) muzzle. **~ abajo** face down. **~ arriba** face up

bocacalle *f* junction. **la primera ~ a la derecha** the first turning on the right

bocad|illo *m* (filled) roll; (*fam, comida ligera*) snack. **~o** *m* mouthful; (*mordisco*) bite; (*de caballo*) bit

boca|jarro. a ~jarro point-blank. **~manga** *f* cuff

bocanada *f* puff; (*de vino etc*) mouthful; (*ráfaga*) gust

bocata *f* sandwich

bocatería *f* sandwich bar

bocaza *m & f invar* big-mouth

boceto *m* sketch; (*de proyecto*) outline

bochinche *m* row; (*alboroto*) racket. **~ro** *adj* (*LAm*) rowdy

bochorno *m* sultry weather; (*fig, vergüenza*) embarrassment. **¡qué ~!** how embarrassing!. **~so** *adj* oppressive; (*fig*) embarrassing

bocina *f* horn; (*LAm, auricular*) receiver. **tocar la ~** sound one's horn. **~zo** *m* toot

boda *f* wedding

bodeg|a *f* cellar; (*de vino*) wine cellar; (*LAm, almacén*) warehouse; (*de un barco*) hold. **~ón** *m* cheap restaurant; (*pintura*) still life

bodoque *m & f* (*fam, tonto*) thickhead; (*Mex, niño*) kid

bofes *mpl* lights. **echar los ~** slog away

bofet|ada *f* slap; (*fig*) blow. **~ón** *m* punch

boga *f* (*moda*) fashion. **estar en ~** be in fashion, be in vogue. **~r** 12 *vt* row. **~vante** *m* (*crustáceo*) lobster

Bogotá *f* Bogotá

bogotano *adj* from Bogotá. • *m* native of Bogotá

bohemio *adj & m* Bohemian

bohío *m* (*LAm*) hut

boicot *m* (*pl* **~s**) boycott. **~ear** *vt* boycott. **~eo** *m* boycott. **hacer un ~** boycott

boina *f* beret

bola *f* ball; (*canica*) marble; (*mentira*) fib; (*Mex, reunión desordenada*) rowdy party; (*Mex, montón*). **una ~ de** a bunch of; (*Mex, revolución*) revolution; (*Mex, brillo*) shine

boleadoras (*LAm*) *fpl* bolas

bolear *vt* (*Mex*) polish, shine

bolera *f* bowling alley

bolero *m* (*baile, chaquetilla*) bolero; (*fig, fam, mentiroso*) liar; (*Mex, limpiabotas*) bootblack

bole|ta *f* (*LAm, de rifa*) ticket; (*Mex, de notas*) (school) report; (*Mex, electoral*) ballot paper. **~taje** *m* (*Mex*) tickets. **~tería** *f* (*LAm*) ticket office; (*de teatro, cine*) box office. **~tero** *m* (*LAm*) ticket-seller

boletín *m* bulletin; (*publicación periódica*) journal; (*de notas*) report

boleto *m* (*esp LAm*) ticket; (*Mex, de avión*) (air) ticket. **~ de ida y vuelta**, (*Mex*) **~ redondo** return ticket (*Brit*), round-trip ticket (*Amer*). **~ sencillo** single ticket (*Brit*), one-way ticket (*Amer*)

boli *m* [I] Biro (P), ball-point pen

boliche *m* (*juego*) bowls; (*bolera*) bowling alley

bolígrafo *m* Biro (P), ball-point pen

bolillo *m* bobbin; (*Mex, pan*) (bread) roll
bolívar *m* (*unidad monetaria venezolana*) bolívar
Bolivia *f* Bolivia
boliviano *adj* Bolivian. ● *m* Bolivian; (*unidad monetaria de Bolivia*) boliviano
boll|ería *f* baker's shop. **~o** *m* roll; (*con azúcar*) bun
bolo *m* skittle; (*Mex, en bautizo*) coins. **~s** *mpl* (*juego*) bowling
bols|a *f* bag; (*Mex, bolsillo*) pocket; (*Mex, de mujer*) handbag; (*Com*) stock exchange; (*cavidad*) cavity. **~a de agua caliente** hot-water bottle. **~illo** *m* pocket. **de ~illo** pocket. **~o** *m* (*de mujer*) handbag. **~o de mano, ~o de viaje** (overnight) bag
bomba *f* bomb; (*máquina*) pump; (*noticia*) bombshell. **~ de aceite** (*Auto*) oil pump. **~ de agua** (*Auto*) water pump. **pasarlo ~** have a marvellous time
bombachos *mpl* baggy trousers, baggy pants (*Amer*)
bombarde|ar *vt* bombard; (*desde avión*) bomb. **~o** *m* bombardment; (*desde avión*) bombing. **~ro** *m* (*avión*) bomber
bombazo *m* explosion
bombear *vt* pump
bombero *m* fireman. **cuerpo** *m* **de ~s** fire brigade (*Brit*), fire department (*Amer*)
bombilla *f* (light) bulb; (*LAm, para mate*) pipe for drinking maté
bombín *m* pump; (*fam, sombrero*) bowler (hat) (*Brit*), derby (*Amer*)
bombo *m* (*tambor*) bass drum. **a ~ y platillos** with a lot of fuss
bomb|ón *m* chocolate; (*Mex, malvavisco*) marshmallow. **~ona** *f* gas cylinder
bonachón *adj* easygoing; (*bueno*) good-natured
bonaerense *adj* from Buenos Aires. ● *m* native of Buenos Aires
bondad *f* goodness; (*amabilidad*) kindness; (*del clima*) mildness. **tenga la ~ de** would you be kind enough to. **~oso** *adj* kind
boniato *m* sweet potato
bonito *adj* nice; (*mono*) pretty. **¡muy ~!, ¡qué ~!** that's nice!, very nice!. ● *m* bonito
bono *m* voucher; (*título*) bond. **~ del Tesoro** government bond
boñiga *f* dung
boqueada *f* gasp. **dar la última ~** be dying
boquerón *m* anchovy
boquete *m* hole; (*brecha*) breach
boquiabierto *adj* open-mouthed; (*fig*) amazed, dumbfounded. **quedarse ~** be amazed
boquilla *f* mouthpiece; (*para cigarillos*) cigarette-holder; (*filtro de cigarillo*) tip
borbotón *m*. **hablar a borbotones** gabble. **salir a borbotones** gush out
borda|do *adj* embroidered. ● *m* embroidery. **~r** *vt* embroider
bord|e *m* edge; (*de carretera*) side; (*de plato etc*) rim; (*de un vestido*) hem. **al ~e de** on the edge of; (*fig*) on the brink of. ● *adj* (*Esp fam*) stroppy. **~ear** *vt* go round; (*fig*) border on. **~illo** *m* kerb (*Brit*), curb (*esp Amer*)
bordo. **a ~** on board
borla *f* tassel
borrach|era *f* drunkenness. **pegarse una ~era** get drunk. **~ín** *m* drunk; (*habitual*) drunkard. **~o** *adj* drunk. ● *m* drunkard. **estar ~o** be

b

drunk. **ser ~o** be a drunkard

borrador *m* rough draft; (*de contrato*) draft; (*para la pizarra*) (black)board rubber; (*goma*) eraser

borrar *vt* rub out; (*tachar*) cross out; delete (información)

borrasc|a *f* depression; (*tormenta*) storm. **~oso** *adj* stormy

borrego *m* year-old lamb; (*Mex, noticia falsa*) canard

borrico *m* donkey; (*fig, fam*) ass

borrón *m* smudge; (*de tinta*) inkblot. **~ y cuenta nueva** let's forget about it!

borroso *adj* blurred; (*fig*) vague

bos|coso *adj* wooded. **~que** *m* wood, forest

bosquej|ar *vt* sketch; outline (plan). **~o** *m* sketch; (*de plan*) outline

bosta *f* dung

bostez|ar 10 *vi* yawn. **~o** *m* yawn

bota *f* boot; (*recipiente*) wineskin

botana *f* (*Mex*) snack, appetizer

botánic|a *f* botany. **~o** *adj* botanical. ● *m* botanist

botar *vt* launch; bounce (pelota); (*esp LAm, tirar*) throw away. ● *vi* bounce

botarate *m* irresponsible person; (*esp LAm, derrochador*) spendthrift

bote *m* boat; (*de una pelota*) bounce; (*lata*) tin, can; (*vasija*) jar. **~ de la basura** (*Mex*) rubbish bin (*Brit*), trash can (*Amer*). **~ salvavidas** lifeboat. **de ~ en ~** packed

botella *f* bottle

botica *f* chemist's (shop) (*Brit*), drugstore (*Amer*). **~rio** *m* chemist (*Brit*), druggist (*Amer*)

botijo *m* earthenware jug

botín *m* half boot; (*de guerra*) booty; (*de ladrones*) haul

botiquín *m* medicine chest; (*de primeros auxilios*) first aid kit

bot|ón *m* button; (*yema*) bud; (*LAm, insignia*) badge. **~ones** *m invar* bellboy (*Brit*), bellhop (*Amer*)

bóveda *f* vault

boxe|ador *m* boxer. **~ar** *vi* box. **~o** *m* boxing

boya *f* buoy; (*corcho*) float. **~nte** *adj* buoyant

bozal *m* (*de perro etc*) muzzle; (*de caballo*) halter

bracear *vi* wave one's arms; (*nadar*) swim, crawl

bracero *m* seasonal farm labourer

braga(s) *f(pl)* panties, knickers (*Brit*)

bragueta *f* flies

bram|ar *vi* bellow. **~ido** *m* bellowing

branquia *f* gill

bras|a *f* ember. **a la ~a** grilled. **~ero** *m* brazier

brasier *m* (*Mex*) bra

Brasil *m.* **(el) ~** Brazil

brasile|ño *adj & m* Brazilian. **~ro** *adj & m* (*LAm*) Brazilian

bravío *adj* wild

brav|o *adj* fierce; (*valeroso*) brave; (mar) rough. **¡~!** *int* well done! bravo! **~ura** *f* ferocity; (*valor*) bravery

braz|a *f* fathom. **nadar a ~a** swim breast-stroke. **~ada** *f* (*en natación*) stroke. **~alete** *m* bracelet; (*brazal*) arm-band. **~o** *m* arm; (*de caballo*) foreleg; (*rama*) branch. **~o derecho** right-hand man. **del ~o** arm in arm

brea *f* tar, pitch

brebaje *m* potion; (*pej*) concoction

brecha *f* opening; (*Mil*) breach; (*Med*) gash. **~ generacional** generation gap. **estar en la ~** be in the thick of it

brega *f* struggle. **andar a la ~** work hard

breva *f* early fig

breve *adj* short. **en ~** soon, shortly. **en ~s momentos** soon. **~dad** *f* shortness

brib|ón *m* rogue, rascal. **~onada** *f* dirty trick

brida *f* bridle

brigad|a *f* squad; (*Mil*) brigade. **~ier** *m* brigadier (*Brit*), brigadier-general (*Amer*)

brill|ante *adj* bright; (*lustroso*) shiny; (persona) brilliant. ● *m* diamond. **~ar** *vi* shine; (*centellear*) sparkle. **~o** *m* shine; (*brillantez*) brilliance; (*centelleo*) sparkle. **sacar ~o** polish. **~oso** *adj* (*LAm*) shiny

brinc|ar **7** *vi* jump up and down. **~o** *m* jump. **dar un ~o, pegar un ~o** jump

brind|ar *vt* offer. ● *vi*. **~ar por** toast, drink a toast to. **~is** *m* toast

br|ío *m* energy; (*decisión*) determination. **~ioso** *adj* spirited; (*garboso*) elegant

brisa *f* breeze

británico *adj* British. ● *m* Briton, British person

brocha *f* paintbrush; (*para afeitarse*) shaving-brush

broche *m* clasp, fastener; (*joya*) brooch; (*Mex, para el pelo*) hairslide (*Brit*), barrete (*Amer*)

brocheta *f* skewer; (*plato*) kebab

brócoli *m* broccoli

brom|a *f* joke. **~a pesada** practical joke. **en ~a** in fun. **ni de ~a** no way. **~ear** *vi* joke. **~ista** *adj* fond of joking. ● *m & f* joker

bronca *f* row; (*reprensión*) telling-off; (*LAm, rabia*) foul mood. **dar ~ a uno** bug s.o.

bronce *m* bronze; (*LAm*) brass. **~ado** *adj* bronze; (*por el sol*) tanned. **~ar** *vt* tan (piel). **~arse** *vpr* get a suntan

bronquitis *f* bronchitis

brot|ar *vi* (*plantas*) sprout; (*Med*) break out; (líquido) gush forth; (lágrimas) well up. **~e** *m* shoot; (*Med*) outbreak

bruces: **de ~** face down(wards). **caer de ~** fall flat on one's face

bruj|a *f* witch. **~ería** *f* witchcraft. **~o** *m* wizard, magician. ● *adj* (*Mex*) broke

brújula *f* compass

brum|a *f* mist; (*fig*) confusion. **~oso** *adj* misty, foggy

brusco *adj* (*repentino*) sudden; (persona) brusque

Bruselas *f* Brussels

brusquedad *f* roughness; (*de movimiento*) abruptness

brut|al *adj* brutal. **~alidad** *f* brutality; (*estupidez*) stupidity. **~o** *adj* ignorant; (*tosco*) rough; (peso, sueldo) gross

bucal *adj* oral; (lesión) mouth

buce|ar *vi* dive; (*nadar*) swim under water. **~o** *m* diving; (*natación*) underwater swimming

bucle *m* ringlet

budín *m* pudding

budis|mo *m* Buddhism. **~ta** *m & f* Buddhist

buen *véase* **BUENO**

buenaventura *f* good luck; (*adivinación*) fortune

bueno *adj* (*delante de nombre mas-*

b

culino en singular **buen**) good; (*agradable*) nice; (tiempo) fine. ● *int* well!; (*de acuerdo*) OK!, very well! **¡buena la has hecho!** you've gone and done it now! **¡buenas noches!** good night! **¡buenas tardes!** (*antes del atardecer*) good afternoon!; (*después del atardecer*) good evening! **¡~s días!** good morning! **estar de buenas** be in a good mood. **por las buenas** willingly. **¡qué bueno!** (*LAm*) great!

Buenos Aires *m* Buenos Aires

buey *m* ox

búfalo *m* buffalo

bufanda *f* scarf

bufar *vi* snort

bufete *m* (*mesa*) writing-desk; (*despacho*) lawyer's office

buf|o *adj* comic. **~ón** *adj* comical. ● *m* buffoon; (*Historia*) jester

buhardilla *f* attic; (*ventana*) dormer window

búho *m* owl

buhonero *m* pedlar

buitre *m* vulture

bujía *f* (*Auto*) spark plug

bulbo *m* bulb

bulevar *m* avenue, boulevard

Bulgaria *f* Bulgaria

búlgaro *adj & m* Bulgarian

bull|a *f* noise. **~icio** *m* hubbub; (*movimiento*) bustle. **~icioso** *adj* bustling; (*ruidoso*) noisy

bullir 22 *vi* boil; (*burbujear*) bubble; (*fig*) bustle

bulto *m* (*volumen*) bulk; (*forma*) shape; (*paquete*) package; (*maleta etc*) piece of luggage; (*protuberancia*) lump

buñuelo *m* fritter

BUP *abrev* (**Bachillerato Unificado Polivalente**) secondary school education

buque *m* ship, boat

burbuj|a *f* bubble. **~ear** *vi* bubble; (vino) sparkle

burdel *m* brothel

burdo *adj* rough, coarse; (excusa) clumsy

burgu|és *adj* middle-class, bourgeois. ● *m* middle-class person. **~esía** *f* middle class, bourgeoisie

burla *f* taunt; (*broma*) joke; (*engaño*) trick. **~r** *vt* evade. **~rse** *vpr*. **~rse de** mock, make fun of

burlesco *adj* (*en literatura*) burlesque

burlón *adj* mocking

bur|ocracia *f* bureaucracy; (*Mex, funcionariado*) civil service. **~ócrata** *m & f* bureaucrat; (*Mex, funcionario*) civil servant. **~ocrático** *adj* bureaucratic; (*Mex*) (empleado) government

burro *adj* stupid; (*obstinado*) pigheaded. ● *m* donkey; (*fig*) ass

bursátil *adj* stock-exchange

bus *m* bus

busca *f* search. **a la ~ de** in search of. ● *m* beeper

buscador *m* search engine

buscapleitos *m & f invar* (*LAm*) trouble-maker

buscar 7 *vt* look for. ● *vi* look. **buscársela** ask for it; **ir a ~ a uno** fetch s.o.

búsqueda *f* search

busto *m* bust

butaca *f* armchair; (*en el teatro etc*) seat

buzo *m* diver

buzón *m* postbox (*Brit*), mailbox (*Amer*)

Cc

C/ *abrev* (**Calle**) St, Rd
cabal *adj* exact; (*completo*) complete. **no estar en sus ~es** not be in one's right mind
cabalga|dura *f* mount, horse. **~r** 12 *vt* ride. • *vi* ride, go riding. **~ta** *f* ride; (*desfile*) procession
caballa *f* mackerel
caballerango *m* (*Mex*) groom
caballeresco *adj* gentlemanly. **literatura** *f* **caballeresca** books of chivalry
caballer|ía *f* mount, horse. **~iza** *f* stable. **~izo** *m* groom
caballero *m* gentleman; (*de orden de caballería*) knight; (*tratamiento*) sir. **~so** *adj* gentlemanly
caballete *m* (*del tejado*) ridge; (*para mesa*) trestle; (*de pintor*) easel
caballito *m* pony. **~ del diablo** dragonfly. **~ de mar** sea-horse. **~s** *mpl* (*carrusel*) merry-go-round
caballo *m* horse; (*del ajedrez*) knight; (*de la baraja española*) queen. **~ de fuerza** horsepower. **a ~** on horseback
cabaña *f* hut
cabaret /kaba're/ *m* (*pl* **~s**) night-club
cabecear *vi* nod off; (*en fútbol*) head the ball; (caballo) toss its head
cabecera *f* (*de la cama*) headboard; (*de la mesa*) head; (*en un impreso*) heading
cabecilla *m* ringleader
cabello *m* hair. **~s** *mpl* hair
caber 28 *vi* fit (**en** into). **no cabe duda** there's no doubt
cabestr|illo *m* sling. **~o** *m* halter
cabeza *f* head; (*fig, inteligencia*) intelligence. **andar de ~** have a lot to do. **~da** *f* nod. **dar una ~da** nod off. **~zo** *m* butt; (*en fútbol*) header
cabida *f* capacity; (*extensión*) area; (*espacio*) room. **dar ~ a** have room for, accommodate
cabina *f* (*de pasajeros*) cabin; (*de pilotos*) cockpit; (*electoral*) booth; (*de camión*) cab. **~ telefónica** telephone box (*Brit*), telephone booth (*Amer*)
cabizbajo *adj* crestfallen
cable *m* cable
cabo *m* end; (*trozo*) bit; (*Mil*) corporal; (*mango*) handle; (*en geografía*) cape; (*Naut*) rope. **al ~ de** after. **de ~ a rabo** from beginning to end. **llevar a ~** carry out
cabr|a *f* goat. **~iola** *f* jump, skip. **~itilla** *f* kid. **~ito** *m* kid
cábula *m* (*Mex*) crook
cacahuate, (*Mex*) **cacahuete** *m* peanut
cacalote *m* (*Mex*) crow
cacao *m* (*planta y semillas*) cacao; (*polvo*) cocoa; (*fig*) confusion
cacarear *vt* boast about. • *vi* (gallo) crow; (gallina) cluck
cacería *f* hunt. **ir de ~** go hunting
cacerola *f* saucepan, casserole
cacharro *m* (earthenware) pot; (*coche estropeado*) wreck; (*cosa inútil*) piece of junk; (*chisme*) thing. **~s** *mpl* pots and pans
cachear *vt* frisk
cachemir *m*, **cachemira** *f* cashmere

cacheo *m* frisking
cachetada *f* (*LAm*) slap
cache|te *m* slap; (*esp LAm, mejilla*) cheek. **~tear** *vt* (*LAm*) slap. **~tón** *adj* (*LAm*) chubby-cheeked
cachimba *f* pipe
cachiporra *f* club, truncheon
cachivache *m* piece of junk. **~s** *mpl* junk
cacho *m* bit, piece; (*LAm, cuerno*) horn
cachondeo *m* ⊡ joking, joke
cachorro *m* (*perrito*) puppy; (*de león, tigre*) cub
cachucha *f* (*Mex*) cup
caciqu|e *m* cacique, chief; (*Pol*) local political boss; (*hombre poderoso*) tyrant. **~il** *adj* despotic. **~ismo** *m* despotism
caco *m* thief
cacofonía *f* cacophony
cacto *m*, **cactus** *m invar* cactus
cada *adj invar* each, every. **~ uno** each one, everyone. **uno de ~ cinco** one in five. **~ vez más** more and more
cadáver *m* corpse
cadena *f* chain; (*TV*) channel. **~ de fabricación** production line. **~ de montañas** mountain range. **~ perpetua** life imprisonment
cadera *f* hip
cadete *m* cadet
caduc|ar ⑦ *vi* expire. **~idad** *f*. **fecha** *f* **de ~idad** sell-by date. **~o** *adj* outdated
cae|r ㉙ *vi* fall. **dejar ~r** drop. **este vestido no me ~ bien** this dress doesn't suit me. **hacer ~r** knock over. **Juan me ~ bien** I like Juan. **su cumpleaños cayó en martes** his birthday fell on a Tuesday. **~rse** *vpr* fall (over). **se le cayó** he dropped it
café *m* coffee; (*cafetería*) café; (*Mex, marrón*) brown. ● *adj*. **color ~** coffee-coloured. **~ con leche** white coffee. **~ cortado** coffee with a little milk. **~ negro** (*LAm*) expresso. **~ solo** black coffee
cafe|ína *f* caffeine. **~tal** *m* coffee plantation. **~tera** *f* coffee-pot. **~tería** *f* café. **~tero** *adj* coffee
caíd|a *f* fall; (*disminución*) drop; (*pendiente*) slope. **~o** *adj* fallen

> **i** **cafetería** In Spain, a place to have a coffee or other drinks, pastries and cakes. *Cafeterías* are frequently combined with *bares* and are very similar. However, *cafeterías* are usually smarter, and serve a wider variety of dishes.

caigo *vb véase* CAER
caimán *m* cayman, alligator
caj|a *f* box; (*de botellas*) case; (*ataúd*) coffin; (*en tienda*) cash desk; (*en supermercado*) check-out; (*en banco*) cashier's desk. **~a de ahorros** savings bank. **~a de cambios** gearbox. **~a de caudales**, **~a fuerte** safe. **~a negra** black box. **~a registradora** till. **~ero** *m* cashier. **~ero automático** cash dispenser. **~etilla** *f* packet. **~ita** *f* small box. **~ón** *m* (*de mueble*) drawer; (*caja grande*) crate; (*LAm, ataúd*) coffin; (*Mex, en estacionamiento*) parking space. **ser de ~ón** be obvious. **~uela** *f* (*Mex*) boot (*Brit*), trunk (*Amer*)
cal *m* lime
cala *f* cove
calaba|cín *m*, **|cita** *f* (*Mex*) courgette (*Brit*), zucchini (*Amer*). **~za** *f* pumpkin; (*fig, fam, idiota*) idiot.

dar ~zas a uno give s.o. the brush-off
calabozo *m* prison; (*celda*) cell
calado *adj* soaked. **estar ~ hasta los huesos** be soaked to the skin. ● *m* (*Naut*) draught
calamar *m* squid
calambre *m* cramp
calami|dad *f* calamity, disaster. **~toso** *adj* calamitous
calaña *f* sort
calar *vt* soak; (*penetrar*) pierce; (*fig, penetrar*) see through; rumble (persona); sample (fruta). **~se** *vpr* get soaked; (zapatos) leak; (*Auto*) stall
calavera *f* skull; (*Mex, Auto*) tail light
calcar 7 *vt* trace; (*fig*) copy
calcet|a *f*. **hacer ~** knit. **~ín** *m* sock
calcetín *m* sock
calcinar *vt* burn
calcio *m* calcium
calcomanía *f* transfer
calcula|dor *adj* calculating. **~dora** *f* calculator. **~r** *vt* calculate; (*suponer*) reckon, think; (*imaginar*) imagine
cálculo *m* calculation; (*Med*) stone
caldear *vt* heat, warm. **~se** *vpr* get hot
caldera *f* boiler
calderilla *f* small change
caldo *m* stock; (*sopa*) clear soup, broth
calefacción *f* heating. **~ central** central heating
caleidoscopio *m* kaleidoscope
calendario *m* calendar; (*programa*) schedule
calent|ador *m* heater. **~amiento** *m* warming; (*en deportes*) warm-up. **~ar** 1 *vt* heat; (*templar*) warm. **~arse** *vpr* get hot; (*templarse*) warm up; (*LAm, enojarse*) get mad. **~ura** *f* fever, (high) temperature. **~uriento** *adj* feverish
calibr|ar *vt* calibrate; (*fig*) weigh up. **~e** *m* calibre; (*diámetro*) diameter; (*fig*) importance
calidad *f* quality; (*condición*) capacity. **en ~ de** as
calidez *f* (*LAm*) warmth
cálido *adj* warm
caliente *adj* hot; (habitación, ropa) warm; (*LAm, enojado*) angry
califica|ción *f* qualification; (*evaluación*) assessment; (*nota*) mark. **~do** *adj* (*esp LAm*) qualified; (*mano de obra*) skilled. **~r** 7 *vt* qualify; (*evaluar*) assess; mark (examen etc). **~r de** describe as, label
cáliz *m* chalice; (*en botánica*) calyx
caliz|a *f* limestone. **~o** *adj* lime
calla|do *adj* quiet. **~r** *vt* silence; keep (secreto); hush up (asunto). ● *vi* be quiet, keep quiet, shut up ‼. **~rse** *vpr* be quiet, keep quiet, shut up ‼ **¡cállate!** be quiet!, shut up! ‼
calle *f* street, road; (*en deportes, autopista*) lane. **~ de dirección única** one-way street. **~ mayor** high street, main street. **de ~** everyday. **~ja** *f* narrow street. **~jear** *vi* hang out on the streets. **~jero** *adj* street. ● *m* street plan. **~jón** *m* alley. **~ón sin salida** dead end. **~juela** *f* back street, side street
call|ista *m & f* chiropodist. **~o** *m* corn, callus. **~os** *mpl* tripe. **~osidad** *f* callus
calm|a *f* calm. **¡~a!** calm down!. **en ~a** calm. **perder la ~a** lose

one's composure. **~ante** *m* tranquilizer; (*para el dolor*) painkiller. **~ar** *vt* calm; (*aliviar*) soothe. • *vi* (viento) abate. **~arse** *vpr* calm down; (viento) abate. **~o** *adj* calm. **~oso** *adj* calm; (*fam, flemático*) slow

calor *m* heat; (*afecto*) warmth. **hace ~** it's hot. **tener ~** be hot. **~ía** *f* calorie. **~ífero** *adj* heat-producing. **~ífico** *adj* calorific

calumni|a *f* calumny; (*oral*) slander; (*escrita*) libel. **~ar** *vt* slander; (*por escrito*) libel. **~oso** *adj* slanderous; (cosa escrita) libellous

caluroso *adj* warm; (clima) hot

calv|a *f* bald head; (*parte sin pelo*) bald patch. **~icie** *f* baldness. **~o** *adj* bald

calza *f* wedge

calzada *f* road; (*en autopista*) carriageway

calza|do *adj* wearing shoes. • *m* footwear, shoe. **~dor** *m* shoehorn. **~r** 10 *vt* put shoes on; (*llevar*) wear. **¿qué número calza Vd?** what size shoe do you take? • *vi* wear shoes. **~rse** *vpr* put on

calz|ón *m* shorts. **~ones** *mpl* shorts; (*LAm, ropa interior*) panties. **~oncillos** *mpl* underpants

cama *f* bed. **~ de matrimonio** double bed. **~ individual** single bed. **guardar ~** stay in bed

camada *f* litter

camafeo *m* cameo

camaleón *m* chameleon

cámara *f* (*aposento*) chamber; (*fotográfica*) camera. **~ fotográfica** camera. **a ~ lenta** in slow motion

camarad|a *m & f* colleague; (*de colegio*) schoolfriend; (*Pol*) comrade. **~ería** *f* camaraderie

camarer|a *f* chambermaid; (*de restaurante etc*) waitress. **~o** *m* waiter

camarógrafo *m* cameraman

camarón *m* shrimp

camarote *m* cabin

cambi|able *adj* changeable; (*Com etc*) exchangeable. **~ante** *adj* variable; (persona) moody. **~ar** *vt* change; (*trocar*) exchange. • *vi* change. **~ar de idea** change one's mind. **~arse** *vpr* change. **~o** *m* change; (*Com*) exchange rate; (*moneda menuda*) (small) change; (*Auto*) gear. **en ~o** on the other hand

camello *m* camel

camellón *m* (*Mex*) traffic island

camerino *m* dressing room

camilla *f* stretcher

camin|ante *m* traveller. **~ar** *vt/i* walk. **~ata** *f* long walk. **~o** *m* road; (*sendero*) path, track; (*dirección, ruta*) way. **~o de** towards, on the way to. **abrir ~o** make way. **a medio ~o, a la mitad del ~o** half-way. **de ~o** on the way

cami|ón *m* truck, lorry; (*Mex, autobús*) bus. **~onero** *m* lorry-driver; (*Mex, de autobús*) bus driver. **~oneta** *f* van; (*LAm, coche familiar*) estate car

i

Camino de Santiago A pilgrimage route since the Middle Ages across north-western Spain to Santiago de Compostela in Galicia. The city was founded at a place where a shepherd is said to have discovered the tomb of St James the Apostle, and its cathedral reputedly houses the saint's relics.

camis|a *f* shirt. **~a de fuerza** strait-jacket. **~ería** *f* shirtmaker's.

~**eta** *f* T-shirt; (*ropa interior*) vest. ~**ón** *m* nightdress

camorra *f* ⓘ row. **buscar** ~ look for a fight

camote *m* (*LAm*) sweet potato

campamento *m* camp. **de** ~ *adj* camping

campan|a *f* bell. ~**ada** *f* stroke. ~**ario** *m* bell tower, belfry. ~**illa** *f* bell

campaña *f* campaign

campe|ón *adj & m* champion. ~**onato** *m* championship

campes|ino *adj* country. • *m* peasant. ~**tre** *adj* country

camping /'kampin/ *m* (*pl* ~**s**) camping; (*lugar*) campsite. **hacer** ~ go camping

camp|iña *f* countryside. ~**o** *m* country; (*agricultura, fig*) field; (*de fútbol*) pitch; (*de golf*) course. ~**osanto** *m* cemetery

camufla|je *m* camouflage. ~**r** *vt* camouflage

cana *f* grey hair, white hair. **peinar** ~**s** be getting old

Canadá *m*. **el** ~ Canada

canadiense *adj & m & f* Canadian

canal *m* (*incl TV*) channel; (*artificial*) canal; (*del tejado*) gutter. ~ **de la Mancha** English Channel. ~ **de Panamá** Panama Canal. ~**ón** *m* (*horizontal*) gutter; (*vertical*) drainpipe

canalla *f* rabble. • *m* (*fig, fam*) swine. ~**da** *f* dirty trick

canapé *m* sofa, couch; (*Culin*) canapé

Canarias *fpl*. **las (islas)** ~ the Canary Islands, the Canaries

canario *adj* of the Canary Islands. • *m* native of the Canary Islands; (*pájaro*) canary

canast|a *f* (large) basket ~**illa** *f* small basket; (*para un bebé*) layette. ~**illo** *m* small basket. ~**o** *m* (large) basket

cancela|ción *f* cancellation. ~**r** *vt* cancel; write off (deuda)

cáncer *m* cancer. **C**~ Cancer

cancha *f* court; (*LAm, de fútbol, rugby*) pitch, ground

canciller *m* chancellor; (*LAm, ministro*) Minister of Foreign Affairs

canci|ón *f* song. ~**ón de cuna** lullaby. ~**onero** *m* song-book

candado *m* padlock

candel|a *f* candle. ~**abro** *m* candelabra. ~**ero** *m* candlestick

candente *adj* (*rojo*) red-hot; (*fig*) burning

candidato *m* candidate

candidez *f* innocence; (*ingenuidad*) naivety

cándido *adj* naive

candil *m* oil lamp. ~**ejas** *fpl* footlights

candor *m* innocence; (*ingenuidad*) naivety

canela *f* cinnamon

cangrejo *m* crab. ~ **de río** crayfish

canguro *m* kangaroo. • *m & f* (*persona*) baby-sitter

caníbal *adj & m & f* cannibal

canica *f* marble

canijo *adj* weak; (*Mex, terco*) stubborn; (*Mex, intenso*) incredible

canilla *f* (*LAm*) shinbone

canino *adj* canine. • *m* canine (tooth)

canje *m* exchange. ~**ar** *vt* exchange

cano *adj* grey. **de pelo** ~ grey-haired

canoa *f* canoe

C

can|ónigo *m* canon. **~onizar** 10 *vt* canonize

canoso *adj* grey-haired

cansa|do *adj* tired; (*que cansa*) tiring. **~dor** (*LAm*) tiring. **~ncio** *m* tiredness. **~r** *vt* tire; (*aburrir*) bore. • *vi* be tiring; (*aburrir*) get boring. **~rse** *vpr* get tired

canta|nte *adj* singing. • *m & f* singer. **~or** *m* Flamenco singer. **~r** *vt/i* sing. **~rlas claras** speak frankly. • *m* singing; (*poema*) poem

cántaro *m* pitcher. **llover a ~s** pour down

cante *m* folk song. **~ flamenco, ~ jondo** Flamenco singing

cantera *f* quarry

cantidad *f* quantity; (*número*) number; (*de dinero*) sum. **una ~ de** lots of

cantimplora *f* water-bottle

cantina *f* canteen; (*Rail*) buffet; (*LAm, bar*) bar

cant|inela *f* song. **~o** *m* singing; (*canción*) chant; (*borde*) edge; (*de un cuchillo*) blunt edge. **~o rodado** boulder; (*guijarro*) pebble. **de ~o** on edge

canturre|ar *vt/i* hum. **~o** *m* humming

canuto *m* tube

caña *f* (*planta*) reed; (*del trigo*) stalk; (*del bambú*) cane; (*de pescar*) rod; (*de la bota*) leg; (*vaso*) glass. **~ de azúcar** sugar-cane. **~da** *f* ravine; (*camino*) track; (*LAm, arroyo*) stream

cáñamo *m* hemp. **~ indio** cannabis

cañ|ería *f* pipe; (*tubería*) piping. **~o** *m* pipe, tube; (*de fuente*) jet. **~ón** *m* (*de pluma*) quill; (*de artillería*) cannon; (*de arma de fuego*) barrel; (*desfiladero*) canyon. **~onera** *f* gunboat

caoba *f* mahogany

ca|os *m* chaos. **~ótico** *adj* chaotic

capa *f* layer; (*de pintura*) coat; (*Culin*) coating; (*prenda*) cloak; (*más corta*) cape; (*en geología*) stratum

capaci|dad *f* capacity; (*fig*) ability. **~tar** *vt* qualify, enable; (*instruir*) train

caparazón *m* shell

capataz *m* foreman

capaz *adj* capable, able

capcioso *adj* sly, insidious

capellán *m* chaplain

caperuza *f* hood; (*de bolígrafo*) cap

capilla *f* chapel

capital *adj* capital, very important. • *m* (*dinero*) capital. • *f* (*ciudad*) capital. **~ de provincia** county town. **~ino** *adj* (*LAm*) of/from the capital. **~ismo** *m* capitalism. **~ista** *adj & m & f* capitalist. **~izar** 10 *vt* capitalize

capit|án *m* captain; (*de pesquero*) skipper. **~anear** *vt* lead, command; skipper (pesquero); captain (un equipo)

capitel *m* (*de columna*) capital

capitulaci|ón *f* surrender. **~ones** *fpl* marriage contract

capítulo *m* chapter; (*de serie*) episode

capó *m* bonnet (*Brit*), hood (*Amer*)

capón *m* (*pollo*) capon

caporal *m* (*Mex*) foreman

capot|a *f* (*de mujer*) bonnet; (*Auto*) folding top; (*de cochecito*) hood. **~e** *m* cape; (*Mex, de coche*) bonnet (*Brit*), hood (*Amer*)

capricho *m* whim. **~so** *adj* capricious, whimsical

Capricornio *m* Capricorn
cápsula *f* capsule
captar *vt* harness (agua); grasp (sentido); capture (atención); win (confianza); (*radio*) pick up
captura *f* capture. **~r** *vt* capture
capucha *f* hood
capullo *m* bud; (*de insecto*) cocoon
caqui *m* khaki
cara *f* face; (*de una moneda*) heads; (*de un objeto*) side; (*aspecto*) look, appearance; (*descaro*) cheek. **~ a** facing. **~ a ~** face to face. **~ dura** *véase* CARADURA. **~ o cruz** heads or tails. **dar la ~ a** face up to. **hacer ~ a** face. **tener mala ~** look ill. **volver la ~** look the other way
carabela *f* caravel
carabina *f* carbine; (*fig, fam, señora*) chaperone
caracol *m* snail; (*de mar*) winkle; (*LAm, concha*) conch; (*de pelo*) curl. **¡~es!** Good Heavens!. **~a** *f* conch
carácter *m* (*pl* **caracteres**) character; (*índole*) nature. **con ~ de** as
característic|a *f* characteristic. **~o** *adj* characteristic, typical
caracteriza|do *adj* characterized; (*prestigioso*) distinguished. **~r** 10 *vt* characterize
caradura *f* cheek, nerve. • *m & f* cheeky person
caramba *int* good heavens!
carambola *f* (*en billar*) cannon; (*Mex, choque múltiple*) pile-up. **de ~** by pure chance
caramelo *m* sweet (*Brit*), candy (*Amer*); (*azúcar fundido*) caramel
caraqueño *adj* from Caracas
carátula *f* (*de disco*) sleeve (*Brit*), jacket (*Amer*); (*de video*) case; (*de libro*) cover; (*Mex, del reloj*) face
caravana *f* caravan; (*de vehículos*) convoy; (*Auto*) long line, traffic jam; (*remolque*) caravan (*Brit*), trailer (*Amer*); (*Mex, reverencia*) bow
caray *int* ! good heavens!
carb|ón *m* coal; (*para dibujar*) charcoal. **~ de leña** charcoal. **~oncillo** *m* charcoal. **~onero** *adj* coal. • *m* coal-merchant. **~onizar** 10 *vt* (*fig*) burn (to a cinder). **~ono** *m* carbon
carbura|dor *m* carburettor. **~nte** *m* fuel
carcajada *f* guffaw. **reírse a ~s** roar with laughter. **soltar una ~** burst out laughing
cárcel *f* prison, jail
carcelero *m* jailer
carcom|er *vt* eat away; (*fig*) undermine. **~erse** *vpr* be eaten away; (*fig*) waste away
cardenal *m* cardinal; (*contusión*) bruise
cardiaco, **cardíaco** *adj* cardiac, heart
cardinal *adj* cardinal
cardo *m* thistle
carear *vt* bring face to face (personas); compare (cosas)
care|cer 11 *vi*. **~cer de** lack. **~cer de sentido** not to make sense. **~ncia** *f* lack. **~nte** *adj* lacking
care|ro *adj* pricey. **~stía** *f* (*elevado*) high cost
careta *f* mask
carey *m* tortoiseshell
carga *f* load; (*fig*) burden; (*acción*) loading; (*de barco, avión*) cargo; (*de tren*) freight; (*de arma*) charge; (*Elec, ataque*) charge; (*obligación*) obligation. **llevar la ~ de algo** be responsible for sth. **~da** *f* (*Mex,*

Pol) supporters. **~do** *adj* loaded; (*fig*) burdened; (atmósfera) heavy; (café) strong; (pila) charged. **~mento** *m* load; (*acción*) loading; (*de un barco*) cargo. **~r** 12 *vt* load; (*fig*) burden; (*Elec, atacar*) charge; fill (pluma etc). ● *vi* load. **~r con** carry. **~rse** *vpr* (pila) charge. **~rse de** to load s.o. down with

cargo *m* (*puesto*) post; (*acusación*) charge. **a ~ de** in the charge of. **hacerse ~ de** take responsibility for. **tener a su ~** be in charge of

carguero *m* (*Naut*) cargo ship

caria|do *adj* decayed. **~rse** *vpr* decay

caribeño *adj* Caribbean

caricatura *f* caricature

caricia *f* caress; (*a animal*) stroke

caridad *f* charity. **¡por ~!** for goodness sake!

caries *f invar* tooth decay; (*lesión*) cavity

cariño *m* affection; (*caricia*) caress. **~ mío** my darling. **con mucho ~** (*en carta*) with love from. **tener ~ a** be fond of. **tomar ~ a** become fond of. **~so** *adj* affectionate

carisma *m* charisma

caritativo *adj* charitable

cariz *m* look

carmesí *adj & m* crimson

carmín *m* (*de labios*) lipstick; (*color*) red

carnal *adj* carnal. **primo ~** first cousin

carnaval *m* carnival. **~esco** *adj* carnival

carne *f* meat; (*Anat, de frutos, pescado*) flesh. **~ de cerdo** pork. **~ de cordero** lamb. **~ de gallina** goose pimples. **~ molida** (*LAm*), **~ picada** mince (*Brit*), ground beef (*Amer*). **~ de ternera** veal. **~ de vaca** beef. **me pone la ~ de gallina** it gives me the creeps. **ser de ~ y hueso** be only human

carné, carnet *m* card. **~ de conducir** driving licence (*Brit*), driver's license (*Amer*) **~ de identidad** identity card. **~ de manejar** (*LAm*) driving license (*Brit*), driver's license (*Amer*). **~ de socio** membership card

carnero *m* ram

carnicer|ía *f* butcher's (shop); (*fig*) massacre. **~o** *adj* carnivorous. ● *m* butcher

carnívoro *adj* carnivorous. ● *m* carnivore

carnoso *adj* fleshy; (pollo) meaty

caro *adj* expensive. ● *adv* dear, dearly. **costar ~ a uno** cost s.o. dear.

carpa *f* carp; (*LAm, tienda*) tent

carpeta *f* folder, file. **~zo** *m*. **dar ~zo a** shelve

carpinter|ía *f* carpentry. **~o** *m* carpinter, joiner

carraspe|ar *vi* clear one's throat. **~ra** *f*. **tener ~ra** have a frog in one's throat

carrera *f* run; (*prisa*) rush; (*concurso*) race; (*estudios*) degree course; (*profesión*) career; (*de taxi*) journey

carreta *f* cart. **~da** *f* cartload

carrete *m* reel; (*película*) film

carretear *vi* (*LAm*) taxi

carretera *f* road. **~ de circunvalación** bypass, ring road. **~ nacional** A road (*Brit*), highway (*Amer*)

carretilla *f* wheelbarrow

carril *m* lane; (*Rail*) rail

carrito *m* (*en supermercado, para equipaje*) trolley (*Brit*), cart (*Amer*)

carro *m* cart; (*LAm, coche*) car;

(*Mex, vagón*) coach. ~ **de combate** tank. ~**cería** *f* (*Auto*) bodywork

carroña *f* carrion

carroza *f* coach, carriage; (*en desfile de fiesta*) float

carruaje *m* carriage

carrusel *m* merry-go-round

cart|a *f* letter; (*lista de platos*) menu; (*lista de vinos*) list; (*mapa*) map; (*naipe*) card. ~**a blanca** free hand. ~**a de crédito** letter of credit. ~**a verde** green card. ~**earse** *vpr* correspond

cartel *m* poster; (*letrero*) sign. ~**era** *f* hoarding; (*en periódico*) listings; (*LAm en escuela, oficina*) notice board (*Brit*), bulletin board (*Amer*). **de** ~ celebrated

carter|a *f* wallet; (*de colegial*) satchel; (*para documentos*) briefcase; (*LAm, de mujer*) handbag (*Brit*), purse (*Amer*). ~**ista** *m & f* pickpocket

cartero *m* postman, mailman (*Amer*)

cartílago *m* cartilage

cartilla *f* first reading book. ~ **de ahorros** savings book. **leerle la** ~ **a uno** tell s.o. off

cartón *m* cardboard

cartucho *m* cartridge

cartulina *f* card

casa *f* house; (*hogar*) home; (*empresa*) firm. ~ **de huéspedes** boarding-house. ~ **de socorro** first aid post. **ir a** ~ go home. **salir de** ~ go out

casaca *f* jacket

casado *adj* married. **los recién** ~**s** the newly-weds

casa|mentero *m* matchmaker. ~**miento** *m* marriage; (*ceremonia*) wedding. ~**r** *vt* marry. ~**rse** *vpr* get married

cascabel *m* small bell; (*de serpiente*) rattle

cascada *f* waterfall

casca|nueces *m invar* nutcrackers. ~**r** **7** *vt* crack (nuez, huevo); (*pegar*) beat. ~**rse** *vpr* crack

cáscara *f* (*de huevo, nuez*) shell; (*de naranja*) peel; (*de plátano*) skin

cascarrabias *adj invar* grumpy

casco *m* helmet; (*de cerámica etc*) piece, fragment; (*cabeza*) scalp; (*de barco*) hull; (*envase*) empty bottle; (*de caballo*) hoof; (*de una ciudad*) part, area

cascote *m* piece of rubble. ~**s** *mpl* rubble

caserío *m* country house; (*poblado*) hamlet

casero *adj* home-made; (*doméstico*) domestic; (*amante del hogar*) home-loving; (reunión) family. ● *m* owner; (*vigilante*) caretaker

caseta *f* hut; (*puesto*) stand. ~ **de baño** bathing hut

casete *m & f* cassette

casi *adv* almost, nearly; (*en frases negativas*) hardly. ~ ~ very nearly. ~ **nada** hardly any. **¡~ nada!** is that all? ~ **nunca** hardly ever

casill|a *f* hut; (*en ajedrez etc*) square; (*en formulario*) box; (*compartimento*) pigeonhole. ~ **electrónica** e-mail address. ~**ero** *m* pigeonholes; (*compartimento*) pigeonhole

casino *m* casino; (*club social*) club

caso *m* case. **el** ~ **es que** the fact is that. **en** ~ **de** in the event of. **en cualquier** ~ in any case, whatever happens. **en ese** ~ in that case. **en todo** ~ in any case. **en último** ~ as a last resort. **hacer** ~ **de** take notice of. **poner por** ~ suppose

caspa *f* dandruff
casquivana *f* flirt
cassette *m & f* cassette
C **casta** *f* (*de animal*) breed; (*de persona*) descent; (*grupo social*) caste
castaña *f* chestnut
castañetear *vi* (dientes) chatter
castaño *adj* chestnut; (ojos) brown. • *m* chestnut (tree)
castañuela *f* castanet
castellano *adj* Castilian. • *m* (*persona*) Castilian; (*lengua*) Castilian, Spanish. **~parlante** *adj* Castilian-speaking, Spanish-speaking. **¿habla Vd ~?** do you speak Spanish?

> i
> **castellano** In Spain the term *castellano*, rather than *español*, refers to the Spanish language as opposed to Catalan, Basque etc. The choice of word has political overtones; *castellano* has separatist connotations and *español* is considered neutral. In Latin America *castellano* is another term for Spanish.

castidad *f* chastity
castig|ar 12 *vt* punish; (*en deportes*) penalize. **~o** *m* punishment; (*en deportes*) penalty
castillo *m* castle
cast|izo *adj* traditional; (*puro*) pure. **~o** *adj* chaste
castor *m* beaver
castrar *vt* castrate
castrense *m* military
casual *adj* chance, accidental. **~idad** *f* chance, coincidence. **dar la ~idad** happen. **de ~idad, por ~idad** by chance. **¡qué ~idad!** what a coincidence!. **~mente** *adv* by chance; (*precisamente*) actually
cataclismo *m* cataclysm
catador *m* taster
catalán *adj & m* Catalan
catalizador *m* catalyst
cat|alogar 12 *vt* catalogue; (*fig*) classify. **~álogo** *m* catalogue
Cataluña *f* Catalonia
catamarán *m* catamaran
catapulta *f* catapult
catar *vt* taste, try
catarata *f* waterfall, falls; (*Med*) cataract
catarro *m* cold
cat|ástrofe *m* catastrophe. **~astrófico** *adj* catastrophic
catecismo *m* catechism
cátedra *f* (*en universidad*) professorship, chair; (*en colegio*) post of head of department
catedral *f* cathedral
catedrático *m* professor; (*de colegio*) teacher, head of department
categ|oría *f* category; (*clase*) class. **de ~oría** important. **de primera ~oría** first-class. **~órico** *adj* categorical
cat|olicismo *m* catholicism. **~ólico** *adj* (Roman) Catholic • *m* (Roman) Catholic
catorce *adj & m* fourteen
cauce *m* river bed; (*fig, artificial*) channel
caucho *m* rubber
caudal *m* (*de río*) volume of flow; (*riqueza*) wealth. **~oso** *adj* (río) large
caudillo *m* leader
causa *f* cause; (*motivo*) reason; (*Jurid*) trial. **a ~ de, por ~ de** because of. **~r** *vt* cause
cautel|a *f* caution. **~oso** *adj* cautious, wary
cauterizar 10 *vt* cauterize

cautiv|ar *vt* capture; (*fig, fascinar*) captivate. **~erio** *m*, **~idad** *f* captivity. **~o** *adj & m* captive

cauto *adj* cautious

cavar *vt/i* dig

caverna *f* cave, cavern

caviar *m* caviare

cavidad *f* cavity

caza *f* hunting; (*con fusil*) shooting; (*animales*) game. • *m* fighter. **andar a (la) ~ de** be in search of. **~ mayor** game hunting. **dar ~** chase, go after. **ir de ~** go hunting/shooting. **~dor** *m* hunter. **~dora** *f* jacket. **~r** 10 *vt* hunt; (*con fusil*) shoot; (*fig*) track down; (*obtener*) catch, get

caz|o *m* saucepan; (*cucharón*) ladle. **~oleta** *f* (small) saucepan. **~uela** *f* casserole

cebada *f* barley

ceb|ar *vt* fatten (up); bait (anzuelo); prime (arma de fuego). **~o** *m* bait; (*de arma de fuego*) charge

ceboll|a *f* onion. **~eta** *f* spring onion (*Brit*), scallion (*Amer*). **~ino** *m* chive

cebra *f* zebra

cece|ar *vi* lisp. **~o** *m* lisp

cedazo *m* sieve

ceder *vt* give up; (*transferir*) transfer. • *vi* give in; (*disminuir*) ease off; (*romperse*) give way, collapse. **ceda el paso** give way (*Brit*), yield (*Amer*)

cedro *m* cedar

cédula *f* bond. **~ de identidad** identity card

CE(E) *abrev* **(Comunidad (Económica) Europea)** E(E)C

ceg|ador *adj* blinding. **~ar** 1 & 12 *vt* blind; (*tapar*) block up. **~arse** *vpr* be blinded (**de** by). **~uera** *f* blindness

ceja *f* eyebrow

cejar *vi* give way

celada *f* ambush; (*fig*) trap

cela|dor *m* (*de cárcel*) prison warder; (*de museo etc*) security guard. **~r** *vt* watch

celda *f* cell

celebra|ción *f* celebration. **~r** *vt* celebrate; (*alabar*) praise. **~rse** *vpr* take place

célebre *adj* famous

celebridad *f* fame; (*persona*) celebrity

celest|e *adj* heavenly; (vestido) pale blue. **azul ~e** sky-blue. **~ial** *adj* heavenly

celibato *m* celibacy

célibe *adj* celibate

celo *m* zeal; (*de las hembras*) heat; (*de los machos*) rut; (*cinta adhesiva*) Sellotape (P) (*Brit*), Scotch (P) tape (*Amer*). **~s** *mpl* jealousy. **dar ~s** make jealous. **tener ~s** be jealous

celofán *m* cellophane

celoso *adj* conscientious; (*que tiene celos*) jealous

celta *adj & m* (*lengua*) Celtic. • *m & f* Celt

célula *f* cell

celular *adj* cellular. • *m* (*LAm*) mobile, cellphone

celulosa *f* cellulose

cementerio *m* cemetery

cemento *m* cement; (*hormigón*) concrete; (*LAm, cola*) glue

cena *f* dinner; (*comida ligera*) supper

cenag|al *m* marsh, bog; (*fig*) tight spot. **~oso** *adj* boggy

cenar *vt* have for dinner; (*en cena ligera*) have for supper. • *vi* have dinner; (*tomar cena ligera*) have supper

c

cenicero *m* ashtray
ceniza *f* ash
censo *m* census. ~ **electoral** electoral roll
censura *f* censure; (*de prensa etc*) censorship. ~**r** *vt* censure; censor (prensa etc)
centavo *adj & m* hundredth; (*moneda*) centavo
centell|a *f* flash; (*chispa*) spark. ~**ar**, ~**ear** *vi* sparkle
centena *f* hundred. ~**r** *m* hundred. **a** ~**res** by the hundred. ~**rio** *adj* centenarian. ● *m* centenary; (*persona*) centenarian
centeno *m* rye
centésim|a *f* hundredth. ~**o** *adj* hundredth
cent|ígrado *adj* centigrade, Celsius. ● *m* centigrade. ~**igramo** *m* centigram. ~**ilitro** *m* centilitre. ~**ímetro** *m* centimetre
céntimo *adj* hundredth. ● *m* cent
centinela *f* sentry
centolla *f*, **centollo** *m* spider crab
central *adj* central. ● *f* head office. ~ **de correos** general post office. ~ **eléctrica** power station. ~ **nuclear** nuclear power station. ~ **telefónica** telephone exchange. ~**ita** *f* switchboard
centraliza|ción *f* centralization. ~**r** **10** *vt* centralize
centrar *vt* centre
céntrico *adj* central
centrífugo *adj* centrifugal
centro *m* centre. ~ **comercial** shopping centre (*Brit*), shopping mall (*Amer*). ~ **de llamadas** call centre
Centroamérica *f* Central America
centroamericano *adj & m* Central American
ceñi|do *adj* tight. ~**r** **5** & **22** *vt* take (corona); (vestido) cling to. ~**rse** *vpr* limit o.s. (**a** to)
ceñ|o *m* frown. **fruncir el** ~**o** frown. ~**udo** *adj* frowning
cepill|ar *vt* brush; (*en carpintería*) plane. ~**o** *m* brush; (*en carpintería*) plane. ~**o de dientes** toothbrush
cera *f* wax
cerámic|a *f* ceramics; (*materia*) pottery; (*objeto*) piece of pottery. ~**o** *adj* ceramic
cerca *f* fence; (*de piedra*) wall. ● *adv* near, close. ~ **de** *prep* close to, close up, closely
cercan|ía *f* nearness, proximity. ~**ías** *fpl* vicinity. **tren** *m* **de** ~**ías** local train. ~**o** *adj* near, close.
cercar **7** *vt* fence in, enclose; (gente) surround; (*asediar*) besiege
cerciorar *vt* convince. ~**se** *vpr* make sure
cerco *m* (*asedio*) siege; (*círculo*) ring; (*LAm, valla*) fence; (*LAm, seto*) hedge
cerdo *m* pig; (*carne*) pork
cereal *m* cereal
cerebr|al *adj* cerebral. ~**o** *m* brain; (*persona*) brains
ceremoni|a *f* ceremony. ~**al** *adj* ceremonial. ~**oso** *adj* ceremonious
cerez|a *f* cherry. ~**o** *m* cherry tree
cerill|a *f* match. ~**o** *m* (*Mex*) match
cern|er **1** *vt* sieve. ~**erse** *vpr* hover. ~**idor** *m* sieve
cero *m* nought, zero; (*fútbol*) nil (*Brit*), zero (*Amer*); (*tenis*) love; (*persona*) nonentity
cerquillo *m* (*LAm, flequillo*) fringe (*Brit*), bangs (*Amer*)
cerra|do *adj* shut, closed; (*espa-*

cio) shut in, enclosed; (cielo) overcast; (curva) sharp. **~dura** *f* lock; (*acción de cerrar*) shutting, closing. **~jero** *m* locksmith. **~r** **1** *vt* shut, close; (*con llave*) lock; (*cercar*) enclose; turn off (grifo); block up (agujero etc). ● *vi* shut, close. **~rse** *vpr* shut, close; (herida) heal. **~r con llave** lock

cerro *m* hill

cerrojo *m* bolt. **echar el ~** bolt

certamen *m* competition, contest

certero *adj* accurate

certeza, **certidumbre** *f* certainty

certifica|do *adj* (carta etc) registered. ● *m* certificate. **~r** **7** *vt* certify

certitud *f* certainty

cervatillo, **cervato** *m* fawn

cerve|cería *f* beerhouse, bar; (*fábrica*) brewery. **~za** *f* beer. **~za de barril** draught beer. **~za rubia** lager

cesa|ción *f* cessation, suspension. **~nte** *adj* redundant. **~r** *vt* stop. ● *vi* stop, cease; (*dejar un empleo*) resign. **sin ~r** incessantly

cesárea *f* caesarian (section)

cese *m* cessation; (*de un empleo*) dismissal. **~ del fuego** (*LAm*) ceasefire

césped *m* grass, lawn

cest|a *f* basket. **~o** *m* basket. **~o de los papeles** waste-paper basket

chabacano *adj* common; (chiste etc) vulgar. ● *m* (*Mex, albaricoque*) apricot

chabola *f* shack. **~s** *fpl* shanty town

cháchara *f* **!** chatter; (*Mex, objetos sin valor*) junk

chacharear *vt* (*Mex*) sell. ● *vi* **!** chatter

chacra *f* (*LAm*) farm

chal *m* shawl

chalado *adj* **!** crazy

chalé *m* house (with a garden), villa

chaleco *m* waistcoat, vest (*Amer*). **~ salvavidas** life-jacket

chalet *m* (*pl* **~s**) house (with a garden), villa

chalote *m* shallot

chamac|a *f* (*esp Mex*) girl. **~o** *m* (*esp Mex*) boy

chamarra *f* sheepskin jacket; (*Mex, chaqueta corta*) jacket

chamb|a *f* (*Mex, trabajo*) work. **por ~a** by fluke. **~ear** *vi* (*Mex, fam*) work

champán *m*, **champaña** *m & f* champagne

champiñón *m* mushroom

champú *m* (*pl* **~es** *o* **~s**) shampoo

chamuscar **7** *vt* scorch

chance *m* (*esp LAm*) chance

chancho *m* (*LAm*) pig

chanchullo *m* **!** swindle, fiddle **!**

chanclo *m* clog; (*de caucho*) rubber overshoe

chándal *m* (*pl* **~s**) tracksuit

chantaje *m* blackmail. **~ar** *vt* blackmail

chanza *f* joke

chapa *f* plate, sheet; (*de madera*) plywood; (*de botella*) metal top; (*carrocería*) bodywork; (*LAm cerradura*) lock. **~do** *adj* plated. **~do a la antigua** old-fashioned. **~do en oro** gold-plated

chaparro *adj* (*LAm*) short, squat

chaparrón *m* downpour

chapopote *m* (*Mex*) tar

chapotear *vi* splash

chapucero *adj* (persona) slapdash; (trabajo) shoddy

chapulín *m* (*Mex*) locust; (*saltamontes*) grasshopper

chapurrar, **chapurrear** *vt* have a smattering of, speak a little

chapuza *f* botched job; (*trabajo ocasional*) odd job

chaquet|a *f* jacket. **cambiar de ~a** change sides. **~ón** *m* three-quarter length coat

charc|a *f* pond, pool. **~o** *m* puddle, pool

charcutería *f* delicatessen

charla *f* chat; (*conferencia*) talk. **~dor** *adj* talkative. **~r** *vi* [!] chat. **~tán** *adj* talkative. • *m* chatterbox; (*vendedor*) cunning hawker; (*curandero*) charlatan

charol *m* varnish; (*cuero*) patent leather. **~a** *f* (*Mex*) tray

charr|a *f* (*Mex*) horsewoman, cowgirl. **~o** *m* (*Mex*) horseman, cowboy

chascar [7] *vt* crack (látigo); click (lengua); snap (dedos). • *vi* (madera) creak. **~ con la lengua** click one's tongue

chasco *m* disappointment

chasis *m* (*Auto*) chassis

chasqu|ear *vt* crack (látigo); click (lengua); snap (dedos). • *vi* (madera) creak. **~ con la lengua** click one's tongue. **~ido** *m* crack; (*de la lengua*) click; (*de los dedos*) snap

chatarra *f* scrap iron; (*fig*) scrap

chato *adj* (nariz) snub; (objetos) flat. • *m* wine glass

chav|a *f* (*Mex*) girl, lass. **~al** *m* [!] boy, lad. **~o** *m* (*Mex*) boy, lad.

checa|da *f* (*Mex*) check; (*Mex, Med*) checkup. **~r** [7] *vt* (*Mex*) check; (*vigilar*) check up on. **~r tarjeta** clock in

checo *adj* & *m* Czech. **~slovaco** *adj* & *m* (*History*) Czechoslovak

chelín *m* shilling

chelo *m* cello

cheque *m* cheque. **~ de viaje** traveller's cheque. **~ar** *vt* check; (*LAm*) check in (equipaje). **~o** *m* check; (*Med*) checkup. **~ra** *f* cheque-book

chévere *adj* (*LAm*) great

chica *f* girl; (*criada*) maid, servant

chicano *adj* & *m* Chicano, Mexican-American

> **Chicano** *Chicanos* are Mexican Americans, descendants of Mexican immigrants living in US. For long looked down by Americans of European descent, Chicanos have found a new pride in their origins and culture. There are numerous Chicano radio stations and many universities and colleges now offer courses in Chicano studies.

chícharo *m* (*Mex*) pea

chicharra *f* cicada; (*timbre*) buzzer

chichón *m* bump

chicle *m* chewing-gum

chico *adj* [!] small; (*esp LAm, de edad*) young. • *m* boy. **~s** *mpl* children

chicoria *f* chicory

chifla|do *adj* [!] crazy, daft. **~r** *vt* whistle at, boo. • *vi* (*LAm*) whistle; ([!], *gustar mucho*) **me chifla el chocolate** I'm mad about chocolate. **~rse** *vpr* be mad (**por** about)

chilango *adj* (*Mex*) from Mexico City

chile *m* chilli

Chile *m* Chile
chileno *adj & m* Chilean
chill|ar *vi* scream, shriek; (ratón) squeak; (cerdo) squeal. **~ido** *m* scream, screech. **~ón** *adj* noisy; (colores) loud; (sonido) shrill
chimenea *f* chimney; (*hogar*) fireplace
chimpancé *m* chimpanzee
china *f* Chinese (woman)
China *f* China
chinche *m* drawing-pin (*Brit*), thumbtack (*Amer*); (*insecto*) bedbug; (*fig*) nuisance. **~eta** *f* drawing-pin (*Brit*), thumbtack (*Amer*)
chinela *f* slipper
chino *adj* Chinese; (*Mex rizado*) curly. ● *m* Chinese (man); (*Mex, de pelo rizado*) curly-haired person
chipriota *adj & m & f* Cypriot
chiquero *m* pen; (*LAm, pocilga*) pigsty (*Brit*), pigpen (*Amer*)
chiquillo *adj* childish. ● *m* child, kid ⊡
chirimoya *f* custard apple
chiripa *f* fluke
chirri|ar ⓴ *vi* creak; (frenos) screech; (pájaro) chirp. **~do** *m* creaking; (*de frenos*) screech; (*de pájaros*) chirping
chis *int* sh!, hush!; (*fam, para llamar a uno*) hey!, psst!
chism|e *m* gadget, thingumajig ⊡; (*chismorreo*) piece of gossip. **~es** *mpl* things, bits and pieces. **~orreo** *m* gossip. **~oso** *adj* gossipy. ● *m* gossip
chisp|a *f* spark; (*pizca*) drop; (*gracia*) wit; (*fig*) sparkle. **estar que echa ~a(s)** be furious. **~eante** *adj* sparkling. **~ear** *vi* spark; (*lloviznar*) drizzle; (*fig*) sparkle. **~orrotear** *vt* throw out sparks; (fuego) crackle; (aceite) spit
chistar *vi*. **ni chistó** he didn't say a word. **sin ~** without saying a word
chiste *m* joke, funny story. **tener ~** be funny
chistera *f* top hat
chistoso *adj* funny
chiva|rse *vpr* tip-off; (niño) tell. **~tazo** *m* tip-off. **~to** *m* informer; (*niño*) telltale
chivo *m* kid; (*LAm, macho cabrío*) billy goat
choca|nte *adj* shocking; (*Mex desagradable*) unpleasant. **~r** ⑦ *vt* clink (vasos); (*LAm*) crash (vehículo). **¡chócala!** give me five! ● *vi* collide, hit. **~r con**, **~r contra** crash into
choch|ear *vi* be gaga. **~o** *adj* gaga; (*fig*) soft
choclo *m* (*LAm*) corn on the cob
chocolate *m* chocolate. **tableta *f* de ~** bar of chocolate
chófer, (*LAm*) **chofer** *m* chauffeur; (*conductor*) driver
cholo *adj & m* (*LAm*) half-breed
chopo *m* poplar
choque *m* collision; (*fig*) clash; (*eléctrico*) shock; (*Auto, Rail etc*) crash, accident; (*sacudida*) jolt
chorizo *m* chorizo
chorro *m* jet, stream; (*caudal pequeño*) trickle; (*fig*) stream. **a ~** (avión) jet. **a ~s** (*fig*) in abundance
chovinista *adj* chauvinistic. ● *m & f* chauvinist
choza *f* hut
chubas|co *m* shower. **~quero** *m* raincoat, anorak
chuchería *f* trinket
chueco *adj* (*LAm*) crooked

c

chufa *f* tiger nut
chuleta *f* chop
chulo *adj* cocky; (*bonito*) lovely (*Brit*), neat (*Amer*); (*Mex, atractivo*) cute. ● *m* tough guy; (*proxeneta*) pimp
chup|ada *f* suck; (*al helado*) lick; (*al cigarro*) puff. **~ado** *adj* skinny; (*fam, fácil*) very easy. **~ar** *vt* suck; puff at (cigarro etc); (*absorber*) absorb. **~ete** *m* dummy (*Brit*), pacifier (*Amer*). **~ón** *m* sucker; (*LAm*) dummy (*Brit*), pacifier (*Amer*); (*Mex, del biberón*) teat
churrasco *m* barbecued steak
churro *m* fritter; ⊡ mess
chut|ar *vi* shoot. **~e** *m* shot
cianuro *m* cyanide
cibernética *f* cibernetics
cicatriz *f* scar. **~ar** 10 *vt/i* heal. **~arse** *vpr* heal
cíclico *adj* cyclic(al)
ciclis|mo *m* cycling. **~ta** *adj* cycle. ● *m & f* cyclist
ciclo *m* cycle; (*de películas, conciertos*) season; (*de conferencias*) series
ciclomotor *m* moped
ciclón *m* cyclone
ciego *adj* blind. ● *m* blind man, blind person. **a ciegas** in the dark
cielo *m* sky; (*Relig*) heaven; (*persona*) darling. **¡~s!** good heavens!, goodness me!
ciempiés *m invar* centipede
cien *adj* a hundred. **~ por ~** one hundred per cent
ciénaga *f* bog, swamp
ciencia *f* science; (*fig*) knowledge. **~s** *fpl* (*Univ etc*) science. **~s empresariales** business studies. **a ~ cierta** for certain
cieno *m* mud
científico *adj* scientific. ● *m* scientist
ciento *adj & m* a hundred, one hundred. **~s de** hundreds of. **por ~** per cent
cierre *m* fastener; (*acción de cerrar*) shutting, closing; (*LAm, cremallera*) zip, zipper (*Amer*)
cierto *adj* certain; (*verdad*) true. **estar en lo ~** be right. **lo ~ es que** the fact is that. **no es ~** that's not true. **¿no es ~?** isn't that right? **por ~** by the way. **si bien es ~ que** although
ciervo *m* deer
cifra *f* figure, number; (*cantidad*) sum. **en ~** coded, in code. **~do** *adj* coded. **~r** *vt* code; place (esperanzas)
cigala *f* crayfish
cigarra *f* cicada
cigarr|illera *f* cigarette box; (*de bolsillo*) cigarette case. **~illo** *m* cigarette. **~o** *m* (*cigarrillo*) cigarette; (*puro*) cigar
cigüeña *f* stork
cilantro *m* coriander
cil|índrico *adj* cylindrical. **~indro** *m* cylinder
cima *f* top; (*fig*) summit
cimbr|ear *vt* shake. **~earse** *vpr* sway. **~onada** *f*, **~onazo** *m* (*LAm*) jolt; (*de explosión*) blast
cimentar 1 *vt* lay the foundations of; (*fig, reforzar*) strengthen
cimientos *mpl* foundations
cinc *m* zinc
cincel *m* chisel. **~ar** *vt* chisel
cinco *adj & m* five; (*en fechas*) fifth
cincuent|a *adj & m* fifty; (*quincuagésimo*) fiftieth. **~ón** *adj* in his fifties
cine *m* cinema; (*local*) cinema (*Brit*), movie theater (*Amer*). **~asta** *m & f*

film maker (*Brit*), movie maker (*Amer*). **~matográfico** *adj* film (*Brit*), movie (*Amer*)

cínico *adj* cynical. ● *m* cynic

cinismo *m* cynicism

cinta *f* ribbon; (*película*) film (*Brit*), movie (*Amer*); (*para grabar, en carreras*) tape. **~ aislante** insulating tape. **~ métrica** tape measure. **~ virgen** blank tape

cintur|a *f* waist. **~ón** *m* belt. **~ón de seguridad** safety belt. **~ón salvavidas** lifebelt

ciprés *m* cypress (tree)

circo *m* circus

circuito *m* circuit; (*viaje*) tour. **~ cerrado** closed circuit. **corto ~** short circuit

circula|ción *f* circulation; (*vehículos*) traffic. **~r** *adj* circular. ● *vi* circulate; (líquidos) flow; (*conducir*) drive; (*caminar*) walk; (autobús) run

círculo *m* circle. **~ vicioso** vicious circle. **en ~** in a circle

circunci|dar *vt* circumcise. **~sión** *f* circumcision

circunferencia *f* circumference

circunflejo *m* circumflex

circunscri|bir (*pp* **circunscrito**) *vt* confine. **~birse** *vpr* confine o.s. (a to). **~pción** *f* (*distrito*) district. **~pción electoral** constituency

circunspecto *adj* circumspect

circunstancia *f* circumstance

circunv|alar *vt* bypass. **~olar** *vt* **2** circle

cirio *m* candle

ciruela *f* plum. **~ pasa** prune

ciru|gía *f* surgery. **~jano** *m* surgeon

cisne *m* swan

cisterna *f* tank, cistern

cita *f* appointment; (*entre chico y chica*) date; (*referencia*) quotation. **~ a ciegas** blind date. **~ flash** speed dating. **~ción** *f* quotation; (*Jurid*) summons. **~do** *adj* aforementioned. **~r** *vt* make an appointment with; (*mencionar*) quote; (*Jurid*) summons. **~rse** *vpr* arrange to meet

cítara *f* zither

ciudad *f* town; (*grande*) city. **~ balneario** (*LAm*) coastal resort. **~ perdida** (*Mex*) shanty town. **~ universitaria** university campus. **~anía** *f* citizenship; (*habitantes*) citizens. **~ano** *adj* civic. ● *m* citizen, inhabitant

cívico *adj* civic

civil *adj* civil. ● *m & f* civil guard; (*persona no militar*) civilian

civiliza|ción *f* civilization. **~r** **10** *vt* civilize. **~rse** *vpr* become civilized

civismo *m* community spirit

clam|ar *vi* cry out, clamour. **~or** *m* clamour; (*protesta*) outcry. **~oroso** *adj* noisy; (*éxito*) resounding

clandestino *adj* clandestine, secret; (periódico) underground

clara *f* (*de huevo*) egg white

claraboya *f* skylight

clarear *vi* dawn; (*aclarar*) brighten up

clarete *m* rosé

claridad *f* clarity; (*luz*) light

clarifica|ción *f* clarification. **~r** **7** *vt* clarify

clar|ín *m* bugle. **~inete** *m* clarinet. **~inetista** *m & f* clarinettist

clarividen|cia *f* clairvoyance; (*fig*) far-sightedness. **~te** *adj* clairvoyant; (*fig*) far-sighted

claro *adj* clear; (*luminoso*) bright;

(colores) light; (líquido) thin. ● *m* (*en bosque etc*) clearing; (*espacio*) gap. ● *adv* clearly. ● *int* of course! **¡~ que sí!** yes, of course! **¡~ que no!** of course not!

clase *f* class; (*tipo*) kind, sort; (*aula*) classroom. **~ media** middle class. **~ obrera** working class. **~ social** social class. **dar ~s** teach

clásico *adj* classical; (*típico*) classic. ● *m* classic

clasifica|ción *f* classification; (*deportes*) league. **~r** **7** *vt* classify

claustro *m* cloister; (*Univ*) staff

claustrof|obia *f* claustrophobia. **~óbico** *adj* claustrophobic

cláusula *f* clause

clausura *f* closure

clava|do *adj* fixed; (*con clavo*) nailed. **es ~do a su padre** he's the spitting image of his father. ● *m* (*LAm*) dive. **~r** *vt* knock in (clavo); stick in (cuchillo); (*fijar*) fix; (*juntar*) nail together

clave *f* key; (*Mus*) clef; (*instrumento*) harpsichord. **~cín** *m* harpsichord

clavel *m* carnation

clavícula *f* collarbone, clavicle

clav|ija *f* peg; (*Elec*) plug. **~o** *m* nail; (*Culin*) clove

claxon /ˈklakson/ *m* (*pl* **~s**) horn

clemencia *f* clemency, mercy

clementina *f* tangerine

cleptómano *m* kleptomaniac

clerical *adj* clerical

clérigo *m* priest

clero *m* clergy

clic *m*: **hacer ~ en** to click on

cliché *m* cliché; (*Foto*) negative

cliente *m* customer; (*de médico*) patient; (*de abogado*) client. **~la** *f* clientele, customers; (*de médico*) patients

clim|a *m* climate; (*ambiente*) atmosphere. **~ático** *adj* climatic. **~atizado** *adj* air-conditioned

clínic|a *f* clinic. **~o** *adj* clinical

cloaca *f* drain, sewer

clon *m* clone

cloro *m* chlorine

club *m* (*pl* **~s** *o* **~es**) club

coacci|ón *f* coercion. **~onar** *vt* coerce

coagular *vt* coagulate; clot (sangre); curdle (leche). **~se** *vpr* coagulate; (sangre) clot; (leche) curdle

coalición *f* coalition

coarta|da *f* alibi. **~r** *vt* hinder; restrict (libertad etc)

cobard|e *adj* cowardly. ● *m* coward. **~ía** *f* cowardice

cobert|izo *m* shed. **~ura** *f* covering; (*en radio, TV*) coverage

cobij|a *f* (*Mex, manta*) blanket. **~as** *fpl* (*LAm, ropa de cama*) bedclothes. **~ar** *vt* shelter. **~arse** *vpr* (take) shelter. **~o** *m* shelter

cobra *f* cobra

cobra|dor *m* collector; (*de autobús*) conductor. **~r** *vt* collect; (*ganar*) earn; charge (precio); cash (cheque); (*recuperar*) recover. ● *vi* be paid

cobr|e *m* copper. **~izo** *adj* coppery

cobro *m* collection; (*de cheque*) cashing; (*pago*) payment. **presentar al ~** cash

coca|ína *f* cocaine. **~lero** *adj* (of) coca farming. ● *n* coca farmer

cocción *f* cooking; (*Tec*) firing

coc|er **2** & **9** *vt/i* cook; (*hervir*) boil; (*Tec*) fire. **~ido** *m* stew

coche *m* car, automobile (*Amer*); (*de tren*) coach, carriage; (*de bebé*) pram (*Brit*), baby carriage (*Amer*). **~-cama** sleeper. **~ fúnebre** hearse. **~ restaurante** dining-car. **~s de choque** dodgems. **~ra** *f* garage; (*de autobuses*) depot

cochin|ada *f* dirty thing. **~o** *adj* dirty, filthy. • *m* pig

cociente *m* quotient. **~ intelectual** intelligence quotient, IQ

cocin|a *f* kitchen; (*arte*) cookery, cuisine; (*aparato*) cooker. **~a de gas** gas cooker. **~a eléctrica** electric cooker. **~ar** *vt/i* cook. **~ero** *m* cook

coco *m* coconut; (*árbol*) coconut palm; (*cabeza*) head; (*que mete miedo*) bogeyman. **comerse el ~** think hard

cocoa *f* (*LAm*) cocoa

cocodrilo *m* crocodile

cocotero *m* coconut palm

cóctel *m* (*pl* **~s** *o* **~es**) cocktail

cod|azo *m* nudge (with one's elbow). **~ear** *vt/i* elbow, nudge. **~earse** *vpr* rub shoulders (**con** with)

codici|a *f* greed. **~ado** *adj* coveted, sought after. **~ar** *vt* covet. **~oso** *adj* greedy

código *m* code. **~ de la circulación** Highway Code

codo *m* elbow; (*dobladura*) bend. **~ a ~** side by side. **hablar (hasta) por los ~s** talk too much

codorniz *m* quail

coeficiente *m* coefficient. **~ intelectual** intelligence quotient, IQ

coerción *f* constraint

coetáneo *adj & m* contemporary

coexist|encia *f* coexistence. **~ir** *vi* coexist

cofradía *f* brotherhood

cofre *m* chest; (*Mex, capó*) bonnet (*Brit*), hood (*Amer*)

coger **14** *vt* (*esp Esp*) take; catch (tren, autobús, pelota, catarro); (*agarrar*) take hold of; (*del suelo*) pick up; pick (frutos etc); (*LAm, vulgar*) to screw. **~se** *vpr* trap, catch; (*agarrarse*) hold on

cogollo *m* (*de lechuga etc*) heart; (*brote*) bud

cogote *m* nape; (*LAm, cuello*) neck

cohech|ar *vt* bribe. **~o** *m* bribery

cohe|rente *adj* coherent. **~sión** *f* cohesion

cohete *m* rocket

cohibi|do *adj* shy; (*inhibido*) awkward; (*incómodo*) awkward. **~r** *vt* inhibit; (*incomodar*) make s.o. feel embarrassed. **~rse** *vpr* feel inhibited

coima *f* (*LAm*) bribe

coincid|encia *f* coincidence. **dar la ~encia** happen. **~ir** *vt* coincide

coje|ar *vt* limp; (mueble) wobble. **~ra** *f* lameness

coj|ín *m* cushion. **~inete** *m* small cushion

cojo *adj* lame; (mueble) wobbly. • *m* lame person

col *f* cabbage. **~es de Bruselas** Brussel sprouts

cola *f* tail; (*fila*) queue; (*para pegar*) glue. **a la ~** at the end. **hacer ~** queue (up) (*Brit*), line up (*Amer*)

colabora|ción *f* collaboration. **~dor** *m* collaborator. **~r** *vi* collaborate

colada *f* washing. **hacer la ~** do the washing

colador *m* strainer

colapso *m* collapse; (*fig*) standstill

colar 2 *vt* strain; pass (moneda falsa etc). • *vi* (líquido) seep through; (*fig*) be believed. **~se** *vpr* slip; (*en una cola*) jump the queue; (*en fiesta*) gatecrash

colch|a *f* bedspread. **~ón** *m* mattress. **~oneta** *f* air bed; (*en gimnasio*) mat

colear *vi* wag its tail; (asunto) not be resolved. **vivito y coleando** alive and kicking

colecci|ón *f* collection. **~onar** *vt* collect. **~onista** *m & f* collector

colecta *f* collection

colectivo *adj* collective

colega *m & f* colleague

colegi|al *m* schoolboy. **~ala** *f* schoolgirl. **~o** *m* school; (*de ciertas profesiones*) college. **~o mayor** hall of residence

cólera *m* cholera. • *f* anger, fury. **montar en ~** fly into a rage

colérico *adj* furious, irate

colesterol *m* cholesterol

coleta *f* pigtail

colga|nte *adj* hanging. • *m* pendant. **~r** 2 & 12 *vt* hang; hang out (ropa lavada); hang up (abrigo etc); put down (teléfono). • *vi* hang; (*teléfono*) hang up. **~rse** *vpr* hang o.s. **dejar a uno ~do** let s.o. down

colibrí *m* hummingbird

cólico *m* colic

coliflor *f* cauliflower

colilla *f* cigarette end

colina *f* hill

colinda|nte *adj* adjoining. **~r** *vt* border (**con** on)

colisión *f* collision, crash; (*fig*) clash

collar *m* necklace; (*de perro*) collar

colmar *vt* fill to the brim; try (paciencia); (*fig*) fulfill. **~ a uno de atenciones** lavish attention on s.o.

colmena *f* beehive, hive

colmillo *m* eye tooth, canine (tooth); (*de elefante*) tusk; (*de carnívoro*) fang

colmo *m* height. **ser el ~** be the limit, be the last straw

coloca|ción *f* positioning; (*empleo*) job, position. **~r** 7 *vt* put, place; (*buscar empleo*) find work for. **~rse** *vpr* find a job

Colombia *f* Colombia

colombiano *adj & m* Colombian

colon *m* colon

colón *m* (*unidad monetaria de Costa Rica y El Salvador*) colon

colon|ia *f* colony; (*comunidad*) community; (*agua de colonia*) cologne; (*Mex, barrio*) residential suburb. **~ia de verano** holiday camp. **~iaje** *m* (*LAm*) colonial period. **~ial** *adj* colonial. **~ialista** *m & f* colonialist. **~ización** *f* colonization. **~izar** 10 colonize. **~o** *m* colonist, settler; (*labrador*) tenant farmer

coloqui|al *adj* colloquial. **~o** *m* conversation; (*congreso*) conference

color *m* colour. **de ~** colour. **en ~(es)** (fotos, película) colour. **~ado** *adj* (*rojo*) red. **~ante** *m* colouring. **~ear** *vt/i* colour. **~ete** *m* blusher. **~ido** *m* colour

colosal *adj* colossal; (*fig, fam, magnífico*) terrific

columna *f* column; (*en anatomía*) spine. **~ vertebral** spinal column; (*fig*) backbone

columpi|ar *vt* swing. **~arse** *vpr* swing. **~o** *m* swing

coma *f* comma; (*Mat*) point. • *m*

(*Med*) coma

comadre *f* (*madrina*) godmother; (*amiga*) friend. **~ar** *vi* gossip

comadreja *f* weasel

comadrona *f* midwife

comal *m* (*Mex*) griddle

comand|ancia *f* command. **~ante** *m & f* commander. **~o** *m* command; (*Mil, soldado*) commando; (*de terroristas*) cell

comarca *f* area, region

comba *f* bend; (*juguete*) skipping-rope; (*de viga*) sag. **saltar a la ~** skip. **~rse** *vpr* bend; (viga) sag

combat|e *m* combat; (*pelea*) fight. **~iente** *m* fighter. **~ir** *vt/i* fight

combina|ción *f* combination; (*enlace*) connection; (*prenda*) slip. **~r** *vt* combine; put together (colores)

combustible *m* fuel

comedia *f* comedy; (*cualquier obra de teatro*) play; (*LAm, telenovela*) soap (opera)

comedi|do *adj* restrained; (*LAm, atento*) obliging. **~rse** **5** *vpr* show restraint

comedor *m* dining-room; (*restaurante*) restaurant

comensal *m* companion at table, fellow diner

comentar *vt* comment on; discuss (tema); (*mencionar*) mention. **~io** *m* commentary; (*observación*) comment. **~ios** *mpl* gossip. **~ista** *m & f* commentator

comenzar **1** & **10** *vt/i* begin, start

comer *vt* eat; (*a mediodía*) have for lunch; (*esp LAm, cenar*) have for dinner; (*corroer*) eat away; (*en ajedrez*) take. ● *vi* eat; (*a mediodía*) have lunch; (*esp LAm, cenar*) have dinner. **dar de ~ a** feed. **~se** *vpr* eat (up)

comerci|al *adj* commercial; (ruta) trade; (nombre, trato) business. ● *m* (*LAm*) commercial, ad. **~ante** *m* trader; (*de tienda*) shopkeeper. **~ar** *vi* trade (**con** with, **en** in); (*con otra persona*) do business. **~o** *m* commerce; (*actividad*) trade; (*tienda*) shop; (*negocios*) business

comestible *adj* edible. **~s** *mpl* food. **tienda de ~s** grocer's (shop) (*Brit*), grocery (*Amer*)

cometa *m* comet. ● *f* kite

comet|er *vt* commit; make (falta). **~ido** *m* task

comezón *m* itch

comicios *mpl* elections

cómico *adj* comic; (*gracioso*) funny. ● *m* comic actor; (*humorista*) comedian

comida *f* food; (*a mediodía*) lunch; (*esp LAm, cena*) dinner; (*acto*) meal

comidilla *f*. **ser la ~ del pueblo** be the talk of the town

comienzo *m* beginning, start

comillas *fpl* inverted commas

comil|ón *adj* greedy. **~ona** *f* feast

comino *m* cumin. **(no) me importa un ~** I couldn't care less

comisar|ía *f* police station. **~io** *m* commissioner; (*deportes*) steward

comisión *f* assignment; (*organismo*) commission, committee; (*Com*) commission

comisura *f* corner. **~ de los labios** corner of the mouth

comité *m* committee

como *prep* as; (*comparación*) like. ● *adv* about. ● *conj* as. **~ quieras** as you like. **~ si** as if

cómo *adverbio*

····➤ how. **¿~ se llega?** how do you get there? **¿~ es de alto?** how tall is it? **sé ~ pasó** I know how it happened

! Cuando **cómo** va seguido del verbo **llamar** se traduce por *what*, p. ej. **¿~ te llamas?** *what's your name?*

····➤ **cómo** + *ser* (*sugiriendo descripción*) **¿~ es su marido?** what's her husband like?; (*físicamente*) what does her husband look like? **no sé ~ es la comida** I don't know what the food's like

····➤ (*por qué*) why. **¿~ no actuaron antes?** why didn't they act sooner?

····➤ (*pidiendo que se repita*) sorry?, pardon? **¿~? no te escuché** sorry? I didn't hear you

····➤ (*en exclamaciones*) **¡~ llueve!** it's really pouring! **¡~! ¿que no lo sabes?** what! you mean you don't know? **¡~ no!** of course!

cómoda *f* chest of drawers

comodidad *f* comfort. **a su ~** at your convenience

cómodo *adj* comfortable; (*conveniente*) convenient

comoquiera *conj.* **~ que sea** however it may be

compacto *adj* compact; (*denso*) dense; (líneas etc) close

compadecer **11** *vt* feel sorry for. **~se** *vpr.* **~se de** feel sorry for

compadre *m* godfather; (*amigo*) friend

compañ|ero *m* companion; (*de trabajo*) colleague; (*de clase*) classmate; (*pareja*) partner. **~ía** *f* company. **en ~ía de** with

compara|ble *adj* comparable. **~ción** *f* comparison. **~r** *vt* compare. **~tivo** *adj & m* comparative

comparecer **11** *vi* appear

comparsa *f* group. ● *m & f* (*en el teatro*) extra

compartim(i)ento *m* compartment

compartir *vt* share

compás *m* (*instrumento*) (pair of) compasses; (*ritmo*) rhythm; (*división*) bar (*Brit*), measure (*Amer*); (*Naut*) compass. **a ~** in time

compasi|ón *f* compassion, pity. **tener ~ón de** feel sorry for. **~vo** *adj* compassionate

compatib|ilidad *f* compatibility. **~le** *adj* compatible

compatriota *m & f* compatriot

compendio *m* summary

compensa|ción *f* compensation. **~ción por despido** redundancy payment. **~r** *vt* compensate

competen|cia *f* competition; (*capacidad*) competence; (*poder*) authority; (*incumbencia*) jurisdiction. **~te** *adj* competent

competi|ción *f* competition. **~dor** *m* competitor. **~r** **5** *vi* compete

compinche *m* accomplice; (*fam, amigo*) friend, mate **!**

complac|er **32** *vt* please. **~erse** *vpr* be pleased. **~iente** *adj* obliging; (marido) complaisant

complej|idad *f* complexity. **~o** *adj & m* complex

complement|ario *adj* complementary. **~o** *m* complement; (*Gram*) object, complement

complet|ar *vt* complete. **~o** *adj* complete; (*lleno*) full; (*exhaustivo*) comprehensive

complexión *f* build

complica|ción *f* complication; (*esp AmL, implicación*) involvement. **~r** 7 *vt* complicate; involve (persona). **~rse** *vpr* become complicated; (*implicarse*) get involved

cómplice *m & f* accomplice

complot *m* (*pl* **~s**) plot

compon|ente *adj* component. • *m* component; (*miembro*) member. **~er** 34 *vt* make up; (*Mus, Literatura etc*) write, compose; (*esp LAm, reparar*) mend; (*LAm*) set (hueso); settle (estómago). **~erse** *vpr* be made up; (*arreglarse*) get better. **~érselas** manage

comporta|miento *m* behaviour. **~rse** *vpr* behave. **~rse mal** misbehave

composi|ción *f* composition. **~tor** *m* composer

compostura *f* composure; (*LAm, arreglo*) repair

compota *f* stewed fruit

compra *f* purchase. **~ a plazos** hire purchase. **hacer la(s) ~(s)** do the shopping. **ir de ~s** go shopping. **~dor** *m* buyer. **~r** *vt* buy. **~venta** *f* buying and selling; (*Jurid*) sale and purchase contract. **negocio** *m* **de ~venta** secondhand shop

compren|der *vt* understand; (*incluir*) include. **~sión** *f* understanding. **~sivo** *adj* understanding

compresa *f* compress; (*de mujer*) sanitary towel

compr|esión *f* compression. **~imido** *adj* compressed. • *m* pill, tablet. **~imir** *vt* compress

comproba|nte *m* proof; (*recibo*) receipt. **~r** *vt* check; (*demostrar*) prove

comprom|eter *vt* compromise; (*arriesgar*) jeopardize. **~eterse** *vpr* compromise o.s.; (*obligarse*) agree to; (novios) get engaged. **~etido** *adj* (situación) awkward, delicate; (autor) politically committed. **~iso** *m* obligation; (*apuro*) predicament; (*cita*) appointment; (*acuerdo*) agreement. **sin ~iso** without obligation

compuesto *adj* compound; (persona) smart. • *m* compound

computa|ción *f* (*esp LAm*) computing. **curso** *m* **de ~ción** computer course. **~dor** *m*, **computadora** *f* computer. **~r** *vt* calculate. **~rizar**, **computerizar** 10 *vt* computerize

cómputo *m* calculation

comulgar 12 *vi* take Communion

común *adj* common; (*compartido*) joint. **en ~** in common. **por lo ~** generally. • *m* **el ~ de** most

comunal *adj* communal

comunica|ción *f* communication. **~do** *m* communiqué. **~do de prensa** press release. **~r** 7 *vt* communicate; (*informar*) inform; (*LAm, por teléfono*) put through. **está ~ndo** (teléfono) it's engaged. **~rse** *vpr* communicate; (*ponerse en contacto*) get in touch. **~tivo** *adj* communicative

comunidad *f* community. **~ de vecinos** residents' association. **C~ (Económica) Europea** European (Economic) Community. **en ~** together

Comunidad Autónoma

In 1978 Spain was divided into *comunidades autónomas* or *autonomías*, which have far greater powers than the old

C

regiones. The *comunidades autónomas* are: Andalusia, Aragon, Asturias, Balearic Islands, the Basque Country, Canary Islands, Cantabria, Castilla y León, Castilla-La Mancha, Catalonia, Extremadura, Galicia, Madrid, Murcia, Navarre, La Rioja, Valencia and the North African enclaves of Ceuta and Melilla.

comunión *f* communion; (*Relig*) (Holy) Communion

comunis|mo *m* communism. **~ta** *adj & m & f* communist

con *prep* with; (+ *infinitivo*) by. **~ decir la verdad** by telling the truth. **~ que** so. **~ tal que** as long as

concebir 5 *vt/i* conceive

conceder *vt* concede, grant; award (premio); (*admitir*) admit

concej|al *m* councillor. **~ero** *m* (*LAm*) councillor. **~o** *m* council

concentra|ción *f* concentration; (*Pol*) rally. **~r** *vt* concentrate; assemble (personas). **~rse** *vpr* concentrate

concep|ción *f* conception. **~to** *m* concept; (*opinión*) opinion. **bajo ningún ~to** in no way

concerniente *adj*. **en lo ~ a** with regard to

concertar 1 *vt* arrange; agree (upon) (plan)

concesión *f* concession

concha *f* shell; (*carey*) tortoiseshell

conciencia *f* conscience; (*conocimiento*) awareness. **~ limpia** clear conscience. **~ sucia** guilty conscience. **a ~ de que** fully aware that. **en ~** honestly. **tener ~ de** be aware of. **tomar ~ de** become aware of. **~r** *vt* make aware. **~rse** *vpr* become aware

concientizar 10 *vt* (*esp LAm*) make aware. **~se** *vpr* become aware

concienzudo *adj* conscientious

concierto *m* concert; (*acuerdo*) agreement; (*Mus, composición*) concerto

concilia|ción *f* reconciliation. **~r** *vt* reconcile. **~r el sueño** get to sleep. **~rse** *vpr* gain

concilio *m* council

conciso *m* concise

conclu|ir 17 *vt* finish; (*deducir*) conclude. ● *vi* finish, end. **~sión** *f* conclusion. **~yente** *adj* conclusive

concord|ancia *f* agreement. **~ar** 2 *vt* reconcile. ● *vi* agree. **~e** *adj* in agreement. **~ia** *f* harmony

concret|amente *adv* specifically, to be exact. **~ar** *vt* make specific. **~arse** *vpr* become definite; (*limitarse*) confine o.s. **~o** *adj* concrete; (*determinado*) specific, particular. **en ~o** definite; (*concretamente*) to be exact; (*en resumen*) in short. ● *m* (*LAm, hormigón*) concrete

concurr|encia *f* concurrence; (*reunión*) audience. **~ido** *adj* crowded, busy. **~ir** *vi* meet; ; (*coincidir*) agree. **~ a** (*asistir a*) attend

concurs|ante *m & f* competitor, contestant. **~ar** *vi* compete, take part. **~o** *m* competition; (*ayuda*) help

cond|ado *m* county. **~e** *m* earl, count

condena *f* sentence. **~ción** *f* condemnation. **~do** *m* convicted person. **~r** *vt* condemn; (*Jurid*) convict

condensa|ción *f* condensation.

~r *vt* condense
condesa *f* countess
condescende|ncia *f* condescension; (*tolerancia*) indulgence. **~r** **1** *vi* agree; (*dignarse*) condescend
condici|ón *f* condition. **a ~ón de (que)** on condition that. **~onal** *adj* conditional. **~onar** *vt* condition
condiment|ar *vt* season. **~o** *m* seasoning
condolencia *f* condolence
condominio *m* joint ownership; (*LAm, edificio*) block of flats (*Brit*), condominium (*esp Amer*)
condón *m* condom
condonar *vt* (*perdonar*) reprieve; cancel (deuda)
conducir **47** *vt* drive (vehículo); carry (electricidad, gas, agua). ● *vi* drive; (*fig, llevar*) lead. **¿a qué conduce?** what's the point? **~se** *vpr* behave
conducta *f* behaviour
conducto *m* pipe, tube; (*en anatomía*) duct. **por ~ de** through. **~r** *m* driver; (*jefe*) leader; (*Elec*) conductor
conduzco *vb véase* CONDUCIR
conectar *vt/i* connect
conejo *m* rabbit
conexión *f* connection
confabularse *vpr* plot
confecci|ón *f* (*de trajes*) tailoring; (*de vestidos*) dressmaking. **~ones** *fpl* clothing, clothes. **de ~ón** ready-to-wear. **~onar** *vt* make
confederación *f* confederation
conferencia *f* conference; (*al teléfono*) long-distance call; (*Univ*) lecture. **~ en la cima, ~ (en la) cumbre** summit conference. **~nte** *m & f* lecturer
conferir **4** *vt* confer; award (premio)
confes|ar **1** *vt/i* confess. **~arse** *vpr* confess. **~ión** *f* confession. **~ionario** *m* confessional. **~or** *m* confessor
confeti *m* confetti
confia|do *adj* trusting; (*seguro de sí mismo*) confident. **~nza** *f* trust; (*en sí mismo*) confidence; (*intimidad*) familiarity. **~r** **20** *vt* entrust. ● *vi*. **~r en** trust
confiden|cia *f* confidence, secret. **~cial** *adj* confidential. **~te** *m* confidant. ● *f* confidante
configur|ación *f* configuration. **~ar** *vt* to configure
conf|ín *m* border. **~ines** *mpl* outermost parts. **~inar** *vt* confine; (*desterrar*) banish
confirma|ción *f* confirmation. **~r** *vt* confirm
confiscar **7** *vt* confiscate
confit|ería *f* sweet-shop (*Brit*), candy store (*Amer*). **~ura** *f* jam
conflict|ivo *adj* difficult; (época) troubled; (*polémico*) controversial. **~o** *m* conflict
confluencia *f* confluence
conform|ación *f* conformation, shape. **~ar** *vt* (*acomodar*) adjust. ● *vi* agree. **~arse** *vpr* conform. **~e** *adj* in agreement;(*contento*) happy, satisfied; (*según*) according (**con** to). **~e a** in accordance with, according to. ● *conj* as. ● *int* OK!. **~idad** *f* agreement; (*tolerancia*) resignation. **~ista** *m & f* conformist
conforta|ble *adj* comfortable. **~nte** *adj* comforting. **~r** *vt* comfort
confronta|ción *f* confrontation. **~r** *vt* confront
confu|ndir *vt* (*equivocar*) mistake,

C

confuse; (*mezclar*) mix up, confuse; (*turbar*) embarrass. **~ndirse** *vpr* become confused; (*equivocarse*) make a mistake. **~sión** *f* confusion; (*vergüenza*) embarrassment. **~so** *adj* confused; (*borroso*) blurred

congela|do *adj* frozen. **~dor** *m* freezer. **~r** *vt* freeze

congeniar *vi* get on

congesti|ón *f* congestion. **~onado** *adj* congested. **~onarse** *vpr* become congested

congoja *f* distress; (*pena*) grief

congraciarse *vpr* ingratiate o.s.

congratular *vt* congratulate

congrega|ción *f* gathering; (*Relig*) congregation. **~rse** 12 *vpr* gather, assemble

congres|ista *m & f* delegate, member of a congress. **~o** *m* congress, conference. **C~o** Parliament. **C~o de los Diputados** Chamber of Deputies

cónico *adj* conical

conífer|a *f* conifer. **~o** *adj* coniferous

conjetura *f* conjecture, guess. **~r** *vt* conjecture, guess

conjuga|ción *f* conjugation. **~r** 12 *vt* conjugate

conjunción *f* conjunction

conjunto *adj* joint. ● *m* collection; (*Mus*) band; (*ropa*) suit, outfit. **en ~** altogether

conjurar *vt* exorcise; avert (peligro). ● *vi* plot, conspire

conllevar *vt* to entail

conmemora|ción *f* commemoration. **~r** *vt* commemorate

conmigo *pron* with me

conmo|ción *f* shock; (*tumulto*) upheaval. **~ cerebral** concussion. **~cionar** *vt* shock. **~ver** 2 *vt* shake; (*emocionar*) move

conmuta|dor *m* switch; (*LAm, de teléfonos*) switchboard. **~r** *vt* exchange

connota|ción *f* connotation. **~do** *adj* (*LAm, destacado*) distinguished. **~r** *vt* connote

cono *m* cone

conoc|edor *adj & m* expert. **~er** 11 *vt* know; (*por primera vez*) meet; (*reconocer*) recognize, know. **se conoce que** apparently. **dar a ~er** make known. **~erse** *vpr* know o.s.; (dos personas) know each other; (*notarse*) be obvious. **~ido** *adj* well-known. ● *m* acquaintance. **~imiento** *m* knowledge; (*sentido*) consciousness. **sin ~imiento** unconscious. **tener ~imiento de** know about

conozco *vb véase* **CONOCER**

conque *conj* so

conquista *f* conquest. **~dor** *adj* conquering. ● *m* conqueror; (*de América*) conquistador. **~r** *vt* conquer, win

consabido *adj* usual, habitual

Conquistadores The collective term for the succession of explorers, soldiers and adventurers who, from the sixteenth century onward led the settlement and exploitation of Spain's Latin American colonies.

consagra|ción *f* consecration. **~r** *vt* consecrate; (*fig*) devote. **~rse** *vpr* devote o.s.

consanguíneo *m* blood relation

consciente *adj* conscious

consecuen|cia *f* consequence; (*coherencia*) consistency. **a ~cia de** as a result of. **~te** *adj* consistent

consecutivo *adj* consecutive

conseguir **5** & **13** *vt* get, obtain; (*lograr*) manage; achieve (objetivo)

consej|ero *m* adviser; (*miembro de consejo*) member. **~o** *m* piece of advice; (*Pol*) council. **~o de ministros** cabinet

consenso *m* assent, consent

consenti|do *adj* (niño) spoilt. **~miento** *m* consent. **~r** **4** *vt* allow; spoil (niño). ● *vi* consent

conserje *m* porter, caretaker. **~ría** *f* porter's office

conserva *f* (*mermelada*) preserve; (*en lata*) tinned food. **en ~** tinned (*Brit*), canned. **~ción** *f* conservation; (*de alimentos*) preservation

conservador *adj* & *m* (*Pol*) conservative

conservar *vt* keep; preserve (alimentos). **~se** *vpr* keep; (costumbre) survive

conservatorio *m* conservatory

considera|ble *adj* considerable. **~ción** *f* consideration; (*respeto*) respect. **de ~ción** serious. **de mi ~ción** (*LAm*, *en cartas*) Dear Sir. **~do** *adj* considerate; (*respetado*) respected. **~r** *vt* consider; (*respetar*) respect

consigna *f* order; (*para equipaje*) left luggage office (*Brit*), baggage room (*Amer*); (*eslogan*) slogan

consigo *pron* (*él*) with him; (*ella*) with her; (*Ud*, *Uds*) with you; (*uno mismo*) with o.s.

consiguiente *adj* consequent. **por ~** consequently

consist|encia *f* consistency. **~ente** *adj* consisting (**en** of); (*firme*) solid; (*LAm*, *congruente*) consistent. **~ir** *vi*. **~ en** consist of; (*radicar en*) be due to

consola|ción *f* consolation. **~r** **2** *vt* console, comfort. **~rse** *vpr* console o.s.

consolidar *vt* consolidate. **~se** *vpr* consolidate

consomé *m* clear soup, consommé

consonante *adj* consonant. ● *f* consonant

consorcio *m* consortium

conspira|ción *f* conspiracy. **~dor** *m* conspirator. **~r** *vi* conspire

consta|ncia *f* constancy; (*prueba*) proof; (*LAm*, *documento*) written evidence. **~nte** *adj* constant. **~r** *vi* be clear; (*figurar*) appear, figure; (*componerse*) consist. **hacer ~r** state; (*por escrito*) put on record. **me ~ que** I'm sure that. **que conste que** believe me

constatar *vt* check; (*confirmar*) confirm

constipa|do *m* cold. ● *adj*. **estar ~do** have a cold; (*LAm*, *estreñido*) be constipated. **~rse** *vpr* catch a cold

constitu|ción *f* constitution; (*establecimiento*) setting up. **~cional** *adj* constitutional. **~ir** **17** *vt* constitute; (*formar*) form; (*crear*) set up, establish. **~irse** *vpr* set o.s. up (**en** as). **~tivo** *adj*, **~yente** *adj* constituent

constru|cción *f* construction. **~ctor** *m* builder. **~ir** **17** *vt* construct; build (edificio)

consuelo *m* consolation

consuetudinario *adj* customary

cónsul *m* & *f* consul

consulado *m* consulate

consult|a *f* consultation. **horas** *fpl* **de ~a** surgery hours. **obra** *f* **de ~a** reference book. **~ar** *vt* consult. **~orio** *m* surgery

consumar *vt* complete; commit (crimen); carry out (robo); consummate (matrimonio)

consum|ición *f* consumption; (*bebida*) drink; (*comida*) food. **~ición mínima** minimum charge. **~ido** *adj* (persona) skinny, wasted. **~idor** *m* consumer. **~ir** *vt* consume. **~irse** *vpr* (persona) waste away; (vela, cigarillo) burn down; (líquido) dry up. **~ismo** *m* consumerism. **~o** *m* consumption; (*LAm, en restaurante etc*) (*bebida*) drink; (*comida*) food. **~o mínimo** minimum charge

contab|ilidad *f* book-keeping; (*profesión*) accountancy. **~le** *m & f* accountant

contacto *m* contact. **ponerse en ~ con** get in touch with

conta|do *adj*. **al ~** cash. **~s** *adj pl* few. **tiene los días ~s** his days are numbered. **~dor** *m* meter; (*LAm, persona*) accountant

contagi|ar *vt* infect (persona); pass on (enfermedad); (*fig*) contaminate. **~o** *m* infection; (*directo*) contagion. **~oso** *adj* infectious; (*por contacto directo*) contagious

contamina|ción *f* contamination, pollution. **~r** *vt* contaminate, pollute

contante *adj*. **dinero** *m* **~** cash

contar **2** *vt* count; tell (relato). **se cuenta que** it's said that. ● *vi* count. **~ con** rely on, count on. **~se** *vpr* be included (**entre** among)

contempla|ción *f* contemplation. **sin ~ciones** unceremoniously. **~r** *vt* look at; (*fig*) contemplate

contemporáneo *adj & m* contemporary

conten|er **40** *vt* contain; hold (respiración). **~erse** *vpr* contain o.s. **~ido** *adj* contained. ● *m* contents

content|ar *vt* please. **~arse** *vpr.* **~arse con** be satisfied with, be pleased with. **~o** *adj* (*alegre*) happy; (*satisfecho*) pleased

contesta|ción *f* answer. **~dor** *m*. **~ automático** answering machine. **~r** *vt/i* answer; (*replicar*) answer back

contexto *m* context

contienda *f* conflict; (*lucha*) contest

contigo *pron* with you

contiguo *adj* adjacent

continen|tal *adj* continental. **~te** *m* continent

continu|ación *f* continuation. **a ~ación** immediately after. **~ar** **21** *vt* continue, resume. ● *vi* continue. **~idad** *f* continuity. **~o** *adj* continuous; (*frecuente*) continual. **corriente** *f* **~a** direct current

contorno *m* outline; (*de árbol*) girth; (*de caderas*) measurement. **~s** *mpl* surrounding area

contorsión *f* contortion

contra *prep* against. **en ~** against. ● *m* cons. ● *f* snag. **llevar la ~** contradict

contraata|car **7** *vt/i* counterattack. **~que** *m* counter-attack

contrabaj|ista *m & f* double-bass player. **~o** *m* double-bass; (*persona*) double-bass player

contraband|ista *m & f* smuggler. **~o** *m* contraband

contracción *f* contraction

contrad|ecir **46** *vt* contradict. **~icción** *f* contradiction. **~ictorio** *adj* contradictory

contraer **41** *vt* contract. **~ matri-**

monio marry. **~se** *vpr* contract
contralto *m* counter tenor. • *f* contralto
contra|mano. **a ~** in the wrong direction. **~partida** *f* compensation. **~pelo**. **a ~** the wrong way
contrapes|ar *vt* counterweight. **~o** *m* counterweight
contraproducente *adj* counterproductive
contrari|a *f*. **llevar la ~a** contradict. **~ado** *adj* upset; (*enojado*) annoyed. **~ar** 20 *vt* upset; (*enojar*) annoy. **~edad** *f* setback; (*disgusto*) annoyance. **~o** *adj* contrary (**a** to); (dirección) opposite. **al ~o** on the contrary. **al ~o de** contrary to. **de lo ~o** otherwise. **por el ~o** on the contrary. **ser ~o a** be opposed to, be against
contrarrestar *vt* counteract
contrasentido *m* contradiction
contraseña *f* (*palabra*) password; (*en cine*) stub
contrast|ar *vt* check, verify. • *vi* contrast. **~e** *m* contrast; (*en oro, plata*) hallmark
contratar *vt* contract (servicio); hire, take on (empleados); sign up (jugador)
contratiempo *m* setback; (*accidente*) mishap
contrat|ista *m & f* contractor. **~o** *m* contract
contraven|ción *f* contravention. **~ir** 53 *vt* contravene
contraventana *f* shutter
contribu|ción *f* contribution; (*tributo*) tax. **~ir** 17 *vt/i* contribute. **~yente** *m & f* contributor; (*que paga impuestos*) taxpayer
contrincante *m* rival, opponent
control *m* control; (*vigilancia*) check; (*lugar*) checkpoint. **~ar** *vt* control; (*vigilar*) check. **~arse** *vpr* control s.o.
controversia *f* controversy
contundente *adj* (arma) blunt; (argumento) convincing
contusión *f* bruise
convalec|encia *f* convalescence. **~er** 11 *vi* convalesce. **~iente** *adj & m & f* convalescent
convalidar *vt* recognize (título)
convenc|er 9 *vt* convince. **~imiento** *m* conviction
convenci|ón *f* convention. **~onal** *adj* conventional
conveni|encia *f* convenience; (*aptitud*) suitability. **~ente** *adj* suitable; (*aconsejable*) advisable; (*provechoso*) useful. **~o** *m* agreement. **~r** 53 *vt* agree. • *vi* agree (**en** on); (*ser conveniente*) be convenient for, suit; (*ser aconsejable*) be advisable
convento *m* (*de monjes*) monastery; (*de monjas*) convent
conversa|ción *f* conversation. **~ciones** *fpl* talks. **~r** *vi* converse, talk
conver|sión *f* conversion. **~so** *adj* converted. • *m* convert. **~tible** *adj* convertible. • *m* (*LAm*) convertible. **~tir** 4 *vt* convert. **~tirse** *vpr*. **~tirse en** turn into; (*Relig*) convert
convic|ción *f* conviction. **~to** *adj* convicted
convida|do *m* guest. **~r** *vt* invite
convincente *adj* convincing
conviv|encia *f* coexistence; (*de parejas*) life together. **~ir** *vi* live together; (*coexistir*) coexist
convocar 7 *vt* call (huelga, elecciones); convene (reunión); summon (personas)
convulsión *f* convulsion
conyugal *adj* marital, conjugal; (vida) married

cónyuge *m* spouse. **~s** *mpl* married couple
coñac *m* (*pl* **~s**) brandy
coopera|ción *f* cooperation. **~r** *vi* cooperate. **~nte** *m & f* voluntary aid worker. **~tiva** *f* cooperative. **~tivo** *adj* cooperative
coordinar *vt* coordinate
copa *f* glass; (*deportes, fig*) cup; (*de árbol*) top. **~s** *fpl* (*naipes*) hearts. **tomar una ~** have a drink
copia *f* copy. **~ en limpio** fair copy. **sacar una ~** make a copy. **~r** *vt* copy
copioso *adj* copious; (lluvia, nevada etc) heavy
copla *f* verse; (*canción*) folksong
copo *m* flake. **~ de nieve** snowflake. **~s de maíz** cornflakes
coquet|a *f* flirt; (*mueble*) dressing-table. **~ear** *vi* flirt. **~o** *adj* flirtatious
coraje *m* courage; (*rabia*) anger
coral *adj* choral. • *m* coral; (*Mus*) chorale
coraza *f* cuirass; (*Naut*) armour-plating; (*de tortuga*) shell
coraz|ón *m* heart; (*persona*) darling. **sin ~ón** heartless. **tener buen ~ón** be good-hearted. **~onada** *f* hunch; (*impulso*) impulse
corbata *f* tie, necktie (*esp Amer*). **~ de lazo** bow tie
corche|a *f* quaver. **~te** *m* fastener, hook and eye; (*gancho*) hook; (*paréntesis*) square bracket
corcho *m* cork. **~lata** *f* (*Mex*) (crown) cap
corcova *f* hump
cordel *m* cord, string
cordero *m* lamb
cordial *adj* cordial, friendly. • *m* tonic. **~idad** *f* cordiality, warmth
cordillera *f* mountain range
córdoba *m* (*unidad monetaria de Nicaragua*) córdoba
cordón *m* string; (*de zapatos*) lace; (*cable*) cord; (*fig*) cordon. **~ umbilical** umbilical cord
coreografía *f* choreography
corista *f* (*bailarina*) chorus girl
cornet|a *f* bugle; (*Mex, de coche*) horn. **~ín** *m* cornet
coro *m* (*Mus*) choir; (*en teatro*) chorus
corona *f* crown; (*de flores*) wreath, garland. **~ción** *f* coronation. **~r** *vt* crown
coronel *m* colonel
coronilla *f* crown. **estar hasta la ~** be fed up
corpora|ción *f* corporation. **~l** *adj* (castigo) corporal; (trabajo) physical
corpulento *adj* stout
corral *m* farmyard. **aves** *fpl* **de ~** poultry
correa *f* strap; (*de perro*) lead; (*cinturón*) belt
correc|ción *f* correction; (*cortesía*) good manners. **~to** *adj* correct; (*cortés*) polite
corrector ortográfico *m* spell checker
corre|dizo *adj* running. **nudo** *m* **~dizo** slip knot. **puerta** *f* **~diza** sliding door. **~dor** *m* runner; (*pasillo*) corridor; (*agente*) agent, broker. **~dor de coches** racing driver
corregir **5** & **14** *vt* correct
correlación *f* correlation
correo *m* post, mail; (*persona*) courier; (*LAm, oficina*) post office. **~s** *mpl* post office. **~ electrónico**

e-mail. **echar al ~** post

correr *vt* run; (*mover*) move; draw (cortinas). • *vi* run; (agua, electricidad etc) flow; (tiempo) pass. **~se** *vpr* (*apartarse*) move along; (colores) run

correspond|encia *f* correspondence. **~er** *vi* correspond; (*ser adecuado*) be fitting; (*contestar*) reply; (*pertenecer*) belong; (*incumbir*) fall to. **~erse** *vpr* (*amarse*) love one another. **~iente** *adj* corresponding

corresponsal *m* correspondent

corrid|a *f* run. **~a de toros** bullfight. **de ~a** from memory. **~o** *adj* (*continuo*) continuous

corriente *adj* (agua) running; (monedas, publicación, cuenta, año) current; (*ordinario*) ordinary. • *f* current; (*de aire*) draught; (*fig*) tendency. • *m* current month. **al ~** (*al día*) up-to-date; (*enterado*) aware

corr|illo *m* small group. **~o** *m* circle

corroborar *vt* corroborate

corroer 24 & 37 *vt* corrode; (*en geología*) erode; (*fig*) eat away

corromper *vt* corrupt, rot (materia). **~se** *vpr* become corrupted; (materia) rot; (alimentos) go bad

corrosi|ón *f* corrosion. **~vo** *adj* corrosive

corrupción *f* corruption; (*de materia etc*) rot

corsé *m* corset

corta|do *adj* cut; (carretera) closed; (leche) curdled; (*avergonzado*) embarrassed; (*confuso*) confused. • *m* coffee with a little milk. **~dura** *f* cut. **~nte** *adj* sharp; (viento) biting; (frío) bitter. **~r** *vt* cut; (*recortar*) cut out; (*aislar, separar, interrumpir*) cut off. • *vi* cut; (novios) break up. **~rse** *vpr* cut o.s.; (leche etc) curdle; (*fig*) be embarrassed. **~rse el pelo** have one's hair cut. **~rse las uñas** cut one's nails. **~uñas** *m invar* nail-clippers

corte *m* cut; (*de tela*) length. **~ de luz** power cut. **~ y confección** dressmaking. • *f* court; (*LAm, tribunal*) Court of Appeal. **hacer la ~** court. **las C~s** the Spanish parliament. **la C~ Suprema** the Supreme Court

cortej|ar *vt* court. **~o** *m* (*de rey etc*) entourage. **~o fúnebre** cortège, funeral procession

cortés *adj* polite

cortesía *f* courtesy

corteza *f* bark; (*de queso*) rind; (*de pan*) crust

cortijo *m* farm; (*casa*) farmhouse

cortina *f* curtain

corto *adj* short; (*apocado*) shy. **~ de** short of. **~ de alcances** dim, thick. **~ de vista** short-sighted. **a la corta o a la larga** sooner or later. **quedarse ~** fall short; (*subestimar*) underestimate. **~circuito** *m* short circuit.

Coruña *f*. **La ~** Corunna

cosa *f* thing; (*asunto*) business; (*idea*) idea. **como si tal ~** just like that; (*como si no hubiera pasado nada*) as if nothing had happened. **decirle a uno cuatro ~s** tell s.o. a thing or two

cosecha *f* harvest; (*de vino*) vintage. **~r** *vt* harvest

coser *vt* sew; sew on (botón); stitch (herida). • *vi* sew. **~se** *vpr* stick to s.o.

cosmético *adj* & *m* cosmetic

cósmico *adj* cosmic

cosmo|polita *adj* & *m* & *f* cosmopolitan. **~s** *m* cosmos

cosquillas *fpl*. **dar ~** tickle. **hacer ~** tickle. **tener ~** be ticklish

costa *f* coast. **a ~ de** at the expense of. **a toda ~** at any cost

costado *m* side

costal *m* sack

costar 2 *vt* cost. ● *vi* cost; (*resultar difícil*) to be hard. **~ caro** be expensive. **cueste lo que cueste** at any cost

costarricense *adj & m*, **costarriqueño** *adj & m* Costa Rican

cost|as *fpl* (*Jurid*) costs. **~e** *m* cost. **~ear** *vt* pay for; (*Naut*) sail along the coast

costero *adj* coastal

costilla *f* rib; (*chuleta*) chop

costo *m* cost. **~so** *adj* expensive

costumbre *f* custom; (*de persona*) habit. **de ~** usual; (*como adv*) usually

costur|a *f* sewing; (*línea*) seam; (*confección*) dressmaking. **~era** *f* dressmaker. **~ero** *m* sewing box

cotejar *vt* compare

cotidiano *adj* daily

cotille|ar *vt* gossip. **~o** *m* gossip

cotiza|ción *f* quotation, price. **~r** 10 *vt* (*en la bolsa*) quote. ● *vi* pay contributions. **~rse** *vpr* fetch; (*en la bolsa*) stand at; (*fig*) be valued

coto *m* enclosure; (*de caza*) preserve. **~ de caza** game preserve

cotorr|a *f* parrot; (*fig*) chatterbox. **~ear** *vi* chatter

coyuntura *f* joint

coz *f* kick

cráneo *m* skull

cráter *m* crater

crea|ción *f* creation. **~dor** *adj* creative. ● *m* creator. **~r** *vt* create

crec|er 11 *vi* grow; (*aumentar*) increase; (río) rise. **~ida** *f* (*de río*) flood. **~ido** *adj* (persona) grown-up; (número) large, considerable; (plantas) fully-grown. **~iente** *adj* growing; (luna) crescent. **~imiento** *m* growth

credencial *f* document. ● *adj*. **cartas** *fpl* **~es** credentials

credibilidad *f* credibility

crédito *m* credit; (*préstamo*) loan. **digno de ~** reliable

credo *m* creed

crédulo *adj* credulous

cre|encia *f* belief. **~er** 18 *vt/i* believe; (*pensar*) think. **~o que no** I don't think so, I think not. **~o que sí** I think so. **no ~o** I don't think so. **¡ya lo ~o!** I should think so!. **~erse** *vpr* consider o.s. **no me lo ~o** I don't believe it. **~íble** *adj* credible

crema *f* cream; (*Culin*) custard; (*LAm*, *de la leche*) cream. **~ batida** (*LAm*) whipped cream. **~ bronceadora** sun-tan cream

cremallera *f* zip (*Brit*), zipper (*Amer*)

crematorio *m* crematorium

crepitar *vi* crackle

crepúsculo *m* twilight

crespo *adj* frizzy; (*LAm*, *rizado*) curly. ● *m* (*LAm*) curl

cresta *f* crest; (*de gallo*) comb

creyente *m* believer

cría *f* breeding; (*animal*) baby animal. **las ~s** the young

cria|da *f* maid, servant. **~dero** *m* (*de pollos etc*) farm; (*de ostras*) bed; (*de plantas*) nursery. ● *m* servant. **~dor** *m* breeder. **~nza** *f* breeding. **~r** 20 *vt* suckle; grow (plantas); breed (animales); (*educar*) bring up

(*Brit*), raise (*esp Amer*). **~rse** *vpr* grow up
criatura *f* creature; (*niño*) baby
crim|en *m* (serious) crime; (*asesinato*) murder; (*fig*) crime. **~inal** *adj* & *m* & *f* criminal
crin *f* mane
crío *m* child
criollo *adj* Creole; (*LAm, música, comida*) traditional. ● *m* Creole; (*LAm, nativo*) Peruvian, Chilean etc
crisantemo *m* chrysanthemum
crisis *f invar* crisis
crispar *vt* twitch; (*fam, irritar*) annoy. **~le los nervios a uno** get on s.o.'s nerves
cristal *m* crystal; (*Esp, vidrio*) glass; (*Esp, de una ventana*) pane of glass. **limpiar los ~es** (*Esp*) clean the windows. **~ino** *adj* crystalline; (*fig*) crystal-clear. **~izar** **10** crystallize. **~izarse** *vpr* crystallize
cristian|dad *f* Christendom. **~ismo** *m* Christianity. **~o** *adj* Christian. **ser ~o** be a Christian. ● *m* Christian
cristo *m* crucifix
Cristo *m* Christ
criterio *m* criterion; (*discernimiento*) judgement; (*opinión*) opinion
cr|ítica *f* criticism; (*reseña*) review. **~iticar** **7** *vt* criticize. **~ítico** *adj* critical. ● *m* critic
croar *vi* croak
crom|ado *adj* chromium-plated. **~o** *m* chromium, chrome
crónic|a *f* chronicle; (*de radio, TV*) report; (*de periódico*) feature. **~ deportiva** sport section. **~o** *adj* chronic
cronista *m* & *f* reporter
crono|grama *m* schedule, timetable. **~logía** *f* chronology
cron|ometrar *vt* time. **~ómetro** *m* (*en deportes*) stop-watch
croqueta *f* croquette
cruce *m* crossing; (*de calles, carreteras*) crossroads; (*de peatones*) (pedestrian) crossing
crucial *adj* crucial
crucifi|car **7** *vt* crucify. **~jo** *m* crucifix
crucigrama *m* crossword (puzzle)
crudo *adj* raw; (*fig*) harsh. ● *m* crude (oil)
cruel *adj* cruel. **~dad** *f* cruelty
cruji|do *m* (*de seda, de hojas secas*) rustle; (*de muebles*) creak. **~r** *vi* (seda, hojas secas) rustle; (muebles) creak
cruz *f* cross; (*de moneda*) tails. **~ gamada** swastika. **la C~ Roja** the Red Cross
cruza|da *f* crusade. **~r** **10** *vt* cross; exchange (palabras). **~rse** *vpr* cross; (*pasar en la calle*) pass each other. **~rse con** pass
cuaderno *m* exercise book; (*para apuntes*) notebook
cuadra *f* (*caballeriza*) stable; (*LAm, distancia*) block
cuadrado *adj* & *m* square
cuadragésimo *adj* fortieth
cuadr|ar *vt* square. ● *vi* suit; (cuentas) tally. **~arse** *vpr* (*Mil*) stand to attention; (*fig*) dig one's heels in. **~ilátero** *m* quadrilateral; (*Boxeo*) ring
cuadrilla *f* group; (*pandilla*) gang
cuadro *m* square; (*pintura*) painting; (*Teatro*) scene; (*de números*) table; (*de mando etc*) panel; (*conjunto del personal*) staff. **~ de distribución** switchboard. **a ~s, de ~s** check. **¡qué ~!, ¡vaya un ~!**

what a sight!

cuadrúpedo *m* quadruped

cuádruple *adj & m* quadruple

cuajar *vt* congeal (sangre); curdle (leche); (*llenar*) fill up. ● *vi* (nieve) settle; (*fig, fam*) work out. **cuajado de** full of. **~se** *vpr* coagulate; (sangre) clot; (leche) curdle

cual *pron.* **el ~, la ~ etc** (*animales y cosas*) that, which; (*personas, sujeto*) who, that; (*personas, objeto*) whom. ● *adj* (*LAm, qué*) what. **~ si** as if. **cada ~** everyone. **lo ~** which. **por lo ~** because of which. **sea ~ sea** whatever

cuál *pron* which; (*LAm, qué*) what

cualidad *f* quality

cualquiera *adj* (*delante de nombres* **cualquier,** *pl* **cualesquiera**) any. ● *pron* (*pl* **cualesquiera**) anyone, anybody; (*cosas*) whatever, whichever. **un ~** a nobody. **una ~** a slut

cuando *adv* when. ● *conj* when; (*si*) if. **~ más** at the most. **~ menos** at the least. **aun ~** even if. **de ~ en ~** from time to time

cuándo *adv & conj* when. **¿de ~ acá?, ¿desde ~?** since when? **¡~ no!** (*LAm*) as usual!, typical!

cuant|ía *f* quantity; (*extensión*) extent. **~ioso** *adj* abundant. **~o** *adj* as much ... as, as many ... as. ● *pron* as much as, as many as. ● *adv* as much as. **~o antes** as soon as possible. **~o más, mejor** the more the merrier. **en ~o** as soon as. **en ~o a** as for. **por ~o** since. **unos ~os** a few, some

cuánto *adj* (*interrogativo*) how much?; (*interrogativo en plural*) how many?; (*exclamativo*) what a lot of! ● *pron* how much?; (*en plural*) how many? ● *adv* how much. **¿~ mides?** how tall are you? **¿~ tiempo?** how long? **¡~ tiempo sin verte!** it's been a long time! **¿a ~s estamos?** what's the date today? **un Sr. no sé ~s** Mr So-and-So

cuáquero *m* Quaker

cuarent|a *adj & m* forty; (*cuadragésimo*) fortieth. **~ena** *f* (*Med*) quarantine. **~ón** *adj* about forty

cuaresma *f* Lent

cuarta *f* (*palmo*) span

cuartel *m* (*Mil*) barracks. **~ general** headquarters

cuarteto *m* quartet

cuarto *adj* fourth. ● *m* quarter; (*habitación*) room. **~ de baño** bathroom. **~ de estar** living room. **~ de hora** quarter of an hour. **estar sin un ~** be broke. **y ~** (a) quarter past

cuarzo *m* quartz

cuate *m* (*Mex*) twin; (*amigo*) friend; (**[!]**, *tipo*) guy

cuatro *adj & m* four. **~cientos** *adj & m* four hundred

Cuba *f* Cuba

cuba|libre *m* rum and Coke (P). **~no** *adj & m* Cuban

cúbico *adj* cubic

cubículo *m* cubicle

cubiert|a *f* cover; (*neumático*) tyre; (*Naut*) deck. **~o** *adj* covered; (cielo) overcast. ● *m* place setting, piece of cutlery; (*en restaurante*) cover charge. **a ~o** under cover

cubilete *m* bowl; (*molde*) mould; (*para los dados*) cup

cubis|mo *m* cubism. **~ta** *adj & m & f* cubist

cubo *m* bucket; (*Mat*) cube

cubrecama *m* bedspread

cubrir (*pp* **cubierto**) *vt* cover; fill

(vacante). **~se** *vpr* cover o.s.; (*ponerse el sombrero*) put on one's hat; (el cielo) cloud over, become overcast

cucaracha *f* cockroach

cuchar|a *f* spoon. **~ada** *f* spoonful. **~adita** *f* teaspoonful. **~illa**, **~ita** *f* teaspoon. **~ón** *m* ladle

cuchichear *vi* whisper

cuchill|a *f* large knife; (*de carnicero*) cleaver; (*hoja de afeitar*) razor blade. **~ada** *f* stab; (*herida*) knife wound. **~o** *m* knife

cuchitril *m* (*fig*) hovel

cuclillas: **en ~** *adv* squatting

cuco *adj* shrewd; (*mono*) pretty, nice. ● *m* cuckoo

cucurucho *m* cornet

cuello *m* neck; (*de camisa*) collar. **cortar(le) el ~ a uno** cut s.o.'s throat

cuenc|a *f* (*del ojo*) (eye) socket; (*de río*) basin. **~o** *m* hollow; (*vasija*) bowl

cuenta *f* count; (*acción de contar*) counting; (*cálculo*) calculation; (*factura*) bill; (*en banco, relato*) account; (*de collar*) bead. **~ corriente** current account, checking account (*Amer*). **dar ~ de** give an account of. **darse ~ de** realize. **en resumidas ~s** in short. **por mi propia ~** on my own account. **tener en ~** bear in mind

cuentakilómetros *m invar* milometer

cuent|ista *m & f* story-writer; (*de mentiras*) fibber. **~o** *m* story; (*mentira*) fib, tall story. **~ de hadas** fairy tale. ● *vb véase* **CONTAR**

cuerda *f* rope; (*más fina*) string; (*Mus*) string. **~ floja** tightrope. **dar ~ a** wind up (un reloj)

cuerdo *adj* (persona) sane; (acción) sensible

cuerno *m* horn

cuero *m* leather; (*piel*) skin; (*del grifo*) washer. **~ cabelludo** scalp. **en ~s (vivos)** stark naked

cuerpo *m* body

cuervo *m* crow

cuesta *f* slope, hill. **~ abajo** downhill. **~ arriba** uphill. **a ~s** on one's back

cuestión *f* matter; (*problema*) problem; (*cosa*) thing

cueva *f* cave

cuida|do *m* care; (*preocupación*) worry. **¡~do!** watch out!. **tener ~do** be careful. **~doso** *adj* careful. **~r** *vt* look after. ● *vi*. **~r de** look after. **~rse** *vpr* look after o.s. **~rse de** be careful to

culata *f* (*de revólver, fusil*) butt. **~zo** *m* recoil

culebr|a *f* snake. **~ón** *m* soap opera

culinario *adj* culinary

culminar *vi* culminate

culo *m* [I] bottom; (*LAm vulg*) arse (*Brit vulg*), ass (*Amer vulg*)

culpa *f* fault. **echar la ~** blame. **por ~ de** because of. **tener la ~** be to blame (**de** for). **~bilidad** *f* guilt. **~ble** *adj* guilty. ● *m & f* culprit. **~r** *vt* blame (**de** for)

cultiv|ar *vt* farm; grow (plantas); (*fig*) cultivate. **~o** *m* farming; (*de plantas*) growing

cult|o *adj* (persona) educated. ● *m* cult; (*homenaje*) worship. **~ura** *f* culture. **~ural** *adj* cultural

culturismo *m* body-building

cumbre *f* summit

cumpleaños *m invar* birthday

cumplido *adj* perfect; (*cortés*) polite. ● *m* compliment. **de ~** courc d

tesy. **por ~** out of a sense of duty. **~r** *adj* reliable

cumpli|miento *m* fulfilment; (*de ley*) observance; (*de orden*) carrying out. **~r** *vt* carry out; observe (ley); serve (condena); reach (años); keep (promesa). **hoy cumple 3 años** he's 3 (years old) today. ● *vi* do one's duty. **por ~r** as a mere formality. **~rse** *vpr* expire; (*realizarse*) be fulfilled

cuna *f* cradle; (*fig, nacimiento*) birthplace

cundir *vi* spread; (*rendir*) go a long way

cuneta *f* ditch

cuña *f* wedge

cuñad|a *f* sister-in-law. **~o** *m* brother-in-law

cuño *m* stamp. **de nuevo ~** new

cuota *f* quota; (*de sociedad etc*) membership, fee; (*LAm, plazo*) instalment; (*Mex, peaje*) toll

cupe *vb véase* CABER

cupo *m* cuota; (*LAm, capacidad*) room; (*Mex, plaza*) place

cupón *m* coupon

cúpula *f* dome

cura *f* cure; (*tratamiento*) treatment. ● *m* priest. **~ción** *f* healing. **~ndero** *m* faith-healer. **~r** *vt* (*incl Culin*) cure; dress (herida); (*tratar*) treat; (*fig*) remedy; tan (pieles). **~rse** *vpr* get better

curios|ear *vi* pry; (*mirar*) browse. **~idad** *f* curiosity. **~o** *adj* curious; (*raro*) odd, unusual ● *m* onlooker; (*fisgón*) busybody

curita *f* (*LAm*) (sticking) plaster

curriculum (vitae) *m* curriculum vitae, CV

cursar *vt* issue; (*estudiar*) study

cursi *adj* pretentious, showy

cursillo *m* short course

cursiva *f* italics

curso *m* course; (*Univ etc*) year. **en ~** under way; (año etc) current

cursor *m* cursor

curtir *vt* tan; (*fig*) harden. **~se** *vpr* become tanned; (*fig*) become hardened

curv|a *f* curve; (*de carretera*) bend. **~ar** *vt* bend; bow (estante). **~arse** *vpr* bend; (estante) bow; (madera) warp. **~ilíneo** *adj* curvilinear; (mujer) curvaceous. **~o** *adj* curved

cúspide *f* top; (*fig*) pinnacle

custodi|a *f* safe-keeping; (*Jurid*) custody. **~ar** *vt* guard; (*guardar*) look after. **~o** *m* guardian

cutáneo *adj* skin

cutis *m* skin, complexion

cuyo *pron* (*de persona*) whose, of whom; (*de cosa*) whose, of which. **en ~ caso** in which case

Dd

dactilógrafo *m* typist

dado *m* dice. ● *adj* given. **~ que** since, given that

daltónico *adj* colour-blind

dama *f* lady. **~ de honor** bridesmaid. **~s** *fpl* draughts (*Brit*), checkers (*Amer*)

damasco *m* damask; (*LAm, fruta*) apricot

danés *adj* Danish. ● *m* Dane; (*idioma*) Danish

danza *f* dance; (*acción*) dancing. **~r** 10 *vt/i* dance

dañ|ar *vt* damage. **~se** *vpr* get

damaged. **~ino** *adj* harmful. **~o** *m* damage; (*a una persona*) harm. **~os y perjuicios** damages. **hacer ~o a** harm, hurt. **hacerse ~o** hurt o.s.

dar 26 *vt* give; bear (frutos); give out (calor); strike (la hora). ● *vi* give. **da igual** it doesn't matter. **¡dale!** go on! **da lo mismo** it doesn't matter. **~ a** (ventana) look on to; (edificio) face. **~ a luz** give birth. **~ con** meet (persona); find (cosa). **¿qué más da?** it doesn't matter! **~se** *vpr* have (baño). **dárselas de** make o.s. out to be. **~se por** consider o.s.

dardo *m* dart

datar *vi.* **~ de** date from

dátil *m* date

dato *m* piece of information. **~s** *mpl* data, information. **~s personales** personal details

de *preposición*

Note that **de** before **el** becomes **del**, e.g. **es del norte**

····➤ (*contenido, material*) of. **un vaso de agua** a glass of water. **es de madera** it's made of wood (*pertenencia*) **el coche de Juan** Juan's car. **es de ella** it's hers. **es de María** It's María's. **las llaves del coche** the car keys (*procedencia, origen, época*) from. **soy de Madrid** I'm from Madrid. **una llamada de Lima** a call from Lima. **es del siglo V** it's from the 5th century (*causa, modo*) **se murió de cáncer** he died of cancer. **temblar de miedo** to tremble with fear. **de dos en dos** two by two

····➤ (*parte del día, hora*) **de noche** at night. **de madrugada** early in the morning. **las diez de la mañana** ten (o'clock) in the morning. **de 9 a 12** from 9 to 12

····➤ (*en oraciones pasivas*) by. **rodeado de agua** surrounded by water. **va seguido de coma** it's followed by a comma. **es de Mozart** it's by Mozart

····➤ (*al especificar*) **el cajón de arriba** the top drawer. **la clase de inglés** the English lesson. **la chica de verde** the girl in green. **el de debajo** the one underneath

····➤ (*en calidad de*) as. **trabaja de oficinista** he works as a clerk. **vino de chaperón** he came as a chaperon

····➤ (*en comparaciones*) than. **pesa más de un kilo** it weighs more than a kilo

····➤ (*con superlativo*) **el más alto del mundo** the tallest in the world. **el mejor de todos** the best of all

····➤ (*sentido condicional*) if. **de haberlo sabido** if I had known. **de continuar así** if this goes on

➡ Cuando la preposición **de** se emplea como parte de expresiones como **de prisa, de acuerdo** etc., y de nombres compuestos como **hombre de negocios, saco de dormir** etc., ver bajo el respectivo nombre

deambular *vi* roam (**por** about)

debajo *adv* underneath. **~ de** under(neath). **el de ~** the one underneath. **por ~** underneath. **por ~ de** below

debat|e *m* debate. **~ir** *vt* debate

deber *vt* owe. ● *verbo auxiliar* have to, must; (*en condicional*) should. **debo marcharme** I must go, I have to go. ● *m* duty. **~es** *mpl* homework. **~se** *vpr.* **~se a** be due to

debido *adj* due; (*correcto*) proper. **~ a** due to. **como es ~** as is proper

débil *adj* weak; (sonido) faint; (luz) dim

debili|dad *f* weakness. **~tar** *vt* weaken. **~tarse** *vpr* weaken, get weak

débito *m* debit. **~ bancario** (*LAm*) direct debit

debut *m* debut

debutar *vi* make one's debut

década *f* decade

deca|dencia *f* decline. **~dente** *adj* decadent. **~er** 29 *vi* decline; (*debilitarse*) weaken. **~ído** *adj* in low spirits. **~imiento** *m* decline, weakening

decano *m* dean; (*miembro más antiguo*) senior member

decapitar *vt* behead

decena *f* ten. **una ~ de** about ten

decencia *f* decency

decenio *m* decade

decente *adj* decent; (*decoroso*) respectable; (*limpio*) clean, tidy

decepci|ón *f* disappointment. **~onar** *vt* disappoint

decidi|do *adj* decided; (persona) determined, resolute. **~r** *vt* decide; settle (cuestión etc). ● *vi* decide. **~rse** *vpr* make up one's mind

decimal *adj & m* decimal

décimo *adj & m* tenth. ● *m* (*de lotería*) tenth part of a lottery ticket

decir 46 *vt* say; (*contar*) tell. ● *m* saying. **~ que no** say no. **~ que sí** say yes. **dicho de otro modo** in other words. **dicho y hecho** no sooner said than done. **¿dígame?** can I help you? **¡dígame!** (*al teléfono*) hello! **digamos** let's say. **es ~** that is to say. **mejor dicho** rather. **¡no me digas!** you don't say!, really! **por así ~, por ~lo así** so to speak, as it were. **querer ~** mean. **se dice que** it is said that, they say that

decisi|ón *f* decision. **~vo** *adj* decisive

declara|ción *f* declaration; (*a autoridad, prensa*) statement. **~ción de renta** income tax return. **~r** *vt/i* declare. **~rse** *vpr* declare o.s.; (epidemia etc) break out

declinar *vt* turn down; (*Gram*) decline

declive *m* slope; (*fig*) decline. **en ~** sloping

decola|je *m* (*LAm*) take-off. **~r** *vi* (*LAm*) take off

decolorarse *vpr* become discoloured, fade

decora|ción *f* decoration. **~do** *m* (*en el teatro*) set. **~r** *vt* decorate. **~tivo** *adj* decorative

decoro *m* decorum. **~so** *adj* decent, respectable

decrépito *adj* decrepit

decret|ar *vt* decree. **~o** *m* decree

dedal *m* thimble

dedica|ción *f* dedication. **~r** 7 *vt* dedicate; devote (tiempo). **~rse** *vpr.* **~rse a** devote o.s. to. **¿a qué se dedica?** what does he do? **~toria** *f* dedication

dedo *m* finger; (*del pie*) toe. **~**

anular ring finger. **~ corazón** middle finger. **~ gordo** thumb; (*del pie*) big toe. **~ índice** index finger. **~ meñique** little finger. **~ pulgar** thumb

deduc|ción *f* deduction. **~ir** 47 *vt* deduce; (*descontar*) deduct

defect|o *m* fault, defect. **~uoso** *adj* defective

defen|der 1 *vt* defend. **~sa** *f* defence. **~derse** *vpr* defend o.s. **~sivo** *adj* defensive. **~sor** *m* defender. **abogado** *m* **~sor** defence counsel

defeño *m* (*Mex*) person from the Federal District

deficien|cia *f* deficiency. **~cia mental** mental handicap. **~te** *adj* poor, deficient. ● *m & f* **~te mental** mentally handicapped person

déficit *m invar* deficit

defini|ción *f* definition. **~do** *adj* defined. **~r** *vt* define. **~tivo** *adj* definitive. **en ~tiva** all in all

deform|ación *f* deformation; (*de imagen etc*) distortion. **~ar** *vt* deform; distort (imagen, metal). **~arse** *vpr* go out of shape. **~e** *adj* deformed

defraudar *vt* defraud; (*decepcionar*) disappoint

defunción *f* death

degenera|ción *f* degeneration; (*cualidad*) degeneracy. **~do** *adj* degenerate. **~r** *vi* degenerate

degollar 16 *vt* cut s.o.'s throat

degradar *vt* degrade; (*Mil*) demote. **~se** *vpr* demean o.s..

degusta|ción *f* tasting. **~r** *vt* taste

dehesa *f* pasture

deja|dez *f* slovenliness; (*pereza*) laziness. **~do** *adj* slovenly; (*descuidado*) slack, negligent. **~r** *vt* leave; (*abandonar*) abandon; give up (estudios); (*prestar*) lend; (*permitir*) let. **~r a un lado** leave aside. **~r de** stop

dejo *m* aftertaste; (*tonillo*) slight accent; (*toque*) touch

del = **de + el**

delantal *m* apron

delante *adv* in front. **~ de** in front of. **de ~** front. **~ra** *f* front; (*de teatro etc*) front row; (*ventaja*) lead; (*de equipo*) forward line. **llevar la ~ra** be in the lead. **~ro** *adj* front. ● *m* forward

delat|ar *vt* denounce. **~or** *m* informer

delega|ción *f* delegation; (*oficina*) regional office; (*Mex, comisaría*) police station. **~do** *m* delegate; (*Com*) agent, representative. **~r** 12 *vt* delegate

deleit|ar *vt* delight. **~e** *m* delight

deletrear *vt* spell (out)

delfín *m* dolphin

delgad|ez *f* thinness. **~o** *adj* thin; (*esbelto*) slim. **~ucho** *adj* skinny

delibera|ción *f* deliberation. **~do** *adj* deliberate. **~r** *vi* deliberate (**sobre** on)

delicad|eza *f* gentleness; (*fragilidad*) frailty; (*tacto*) tact. **falta de ~eza** tactlessness. **tener la ~ de** have the courtesy to. **~o** *adj* delicate; (*refinado*) refined; (*sensible*) sensitive

delici|a *f* delight. **~oso** *adj* delightful; (sabor etc) delicious

delimitar *vt* delimit

delincuen|cia *f* delinquency. **~te** *m & f* criminal, delinquent

delinquir 8 *vi* commit a criminal offence

delir|ante *adj* delirious. **~ar** *vi* be delirious; (*fig*) talk nonsense. **~io**

m delirium; (*fig*) frenzy
delito *m* crime, offence
demacrado *adj* haggard
demagogo *m* demagogue
demanda *f* demand; (*Jurid*) lawsuit. **~do** *m* defendant. **~nte** *m & f* (*Jurid*) plaintiff. **~r** *vt* (*Jurid*) sue; (*LAm, requerir*) require
demarcación *f* demarcation
demás *adj* rest of the, other. • *pron* rest, others. **lo ~** the rest. **por ~** extremely. **por lo ~** otherwise
demas|ía *f.* **en ~ía** in excess. **~iado** *adj* too much; (*en plural*) too many. • *adv* too much; (*con adjetivo*) too
demen|cia *f* madness. **~te** *adj* demented, mad
dem|ocracia *f* democracy. **~ócrata** *m & f* democrat. **~ocrático** *adj* democratic
demol|er 2 *vt* demolish. **~ición** *f* demolition
demonio *m* devil, demon. **¡~s!** hell! **¿cómo ~s?** how the hell? **¡qué ~s!** what the hell!
demora *f* delay. **~r** *vt* delay. • *vi* stay on. **~rse** *vpr* be too long; (*LAm, cierto tiempo*). **se ~ una hora en llegar** it takes him an hour to get there
demostra|ción *f* demonstration, show. **~r** 2 *vt* demonstrate; (*mostrar*) show; (*probar*) prove. **~tivo** *adj* demonstrative
dengue *m* dengue fever
denigrar *vt* denigrate
denominado *adj* named; (*supuesto*) so-called
dens|idad *f* density. **~o** *adj* dense, thick
denta|dura *f* teeth. **~dura postiza** dentures, false teeth. **~l** *adj* dental
dent|era *f.* **darle ~era a uno** set s.o.'s teeth on edge. **~ífrico** *m* toothpaste. **~ista** *m & f* dentist
dentro *adv* inside; (*de un edificio*) indoors. **~ de** in. **~ de poco** soon. **por ~** inside
denuncia *f* report; (*acusación*) accusation. **~r** *vt* report; (periódico etc) denounce
departamento *m* department; (*LAm, apartamento*) flat (*Brit*), apartment (*Amer*)
depend|encia *f* dependence; (*sección*) section; (*oficina*) office. **~encias** *fpl* buildings. **~er** *vi* depend (**de** on). **~ienta** *f* shop assistant. **~iente** *adj* dependent (**de** on). • *m* shop assistant
depila|r *vt* depilate. **~torio** *adj* depilatory
deplora|ble *adj* deplorable. **~r** *vt* deplore, regret
deponer 34 *vt* remove from office; depose (rey); lay down (armas). • *vi* give evidence
deporta|ción *f* deportation. **~r** *vt* deport
deport|e *m* sport. **hacer ~e** take part in sports. **~ista** *m* sportsman. • *f* sportswoman. **~ivo** *adj* sports. • *m* sports car
dep|ositante *m & f* depositor. **~ositar** *vt* deposit; (*poner*) put, place. **~ósito** *m* deposit; (*almacén*) warehouse; (*Mil*) depot; (*de líquidos*) tank
depravado *adj* depraved
deprecia|ción *f* depreciation. **~r** *vt* depreciate. **~rse** *vpr* depreciate
depr|esión *f* depression. **~imido** *adj* depressed. **~imir** *vt* depress. **~imirse** *vpr* get

depressed

depura|ción *f* purification. **~do** *adj* refined. **~r** *vt* purify; (*Pol*) purge; refine (estilo)

derech|a *f* (*mano*) right hand; (*lado*) right. **a la ~a** on the right; (*hacia el lado derecho*) to the right. **~ista** *adj* right-wing. • *m & f* right-winger. **~o** *adj* right; (*vertical*) upright; (*recto*) straight. • *adv* straight. **todo ~o** straight on. • *m* right; (*Jurid*) law; (*lado*) right side. **~os** *mpl* dues. **~os de autor** royalties

deriva *f* drift. **a la ~** drifting, adrift

deriva|do *adj* derived. • *m* derivative, by-product. **~r** *vt* divert. • *vi*. **~r de** derive from, be derived from. **~rse** *vpr*. **~rse de** be derived from

derram|amiento *m* spilling. **~amiento de sangre** bloodshed. **~ar** *vt* spill; shed (lágrimas). **~arse** *vpr* spill. **~e** *m* spilling; (*pérdida*) leakage; (*Med*) discharge; (*Med, de sangre*) haemorrhage

derretir **5** *vt* melt

derribar *vt* knock down; bring down, overthrow (gobierno etc)

derrocar **7** *vt* bring down, overthrow (gobierno etc)

derroch|ar *vt* squander. **~e** *m* waste

derrot|a *f* defeat. **~ar** *vt* defeat. **~ado** *adj* defeated. **~ero** *m* course

derrumba|r *vt* knock down **~rse** *vpr* collapse; (persona) go to pieces

desabotonar *vt* unbutton, undo. **~se** *vpr* come undone; (persona) undo

desabrido *adj* tasteless; (persona) surly; (*LAm*) dull

desabrochar *vt* undo. **~se** *vpr* come undone; (persona) undo

desacato *m* defiance; (*Jurid*) contempt of court

desac|ertado *adj* ill-advised; (*erróneo*) wrong. **~ierto** *m* mistake

desacreditar *vt* discredit

desactivar *vt* defuse

desacuerdo *m* disagreement

desafiar **20** *vt* challenge; (*afrontar*) defy

desafina|do *adj* out of tune. **~r** *vi* be out of tune. **~rse** *vpr* go out of tune

desafío *m* challenge; (*a la muerte*) defiance; (*combate*) duel

desafortunad|amente *adv* unfortunately. **~o** *adj* unfortunate

desagrada|ble *adj* unpleasant. **~r** *vt* displease. • *vi* be unpleasant. **me ~ el sabor** I don't like the taste

desagradecido *adj* ungrateful

desagrado *m* displeasure. **con ~** unwillingly

desagüe *m* drain; (*acción*) drainage. **tubo** *m* **de ~** drain-pipe

desahog|ado *adj* roomy; (*acomodado*) comfortable. **~ar** **12** *vt* vent. **~arse** *vpr* let off steam. **~o** *m* comfort; (*alivio*) relief

desahuci|ar *vt* declare terminally ill (enfermo); evict (inquilino). **~o** *m* eviction

desair|ar *vt* snub. **~e** *m* snub

desajuste *m* maladjustment; (*desequilibrio*) imbalance

desala|dora *f* desalination plant. **~r** *vt* to desalinate

desal|entador *adj* disheartening. **~entar** **1** *vt* discourage. **~iento** *m* discouragement

d

desaliñado *adj* slovenly
desalmado *adj* heartless
desalojar *vt* (ocupantes) evacuate; (policía) to clear; (*LAm*) evict (inquilino)
desampar|ado *adj* helpless; (lugar) unprotected. **~ar** *vt* abandon. **~o** *m* helplessness; (*abandono*) lack of protection
desangrar *vt* bleed. **~se** *vpr* bleed
desanima|do *adj* down-hearted. **~r** *vt* discourage. **~rse** *vpr* lose heart
desapar|ecer **11** *vi* disappear; (efecto) wear off. **~ecido** *adj* missing. ● *m* missing person. **~ición** *f* disappearance
desapego *m* indifference
desapercibido *adj*. **pasar ~** go unnoticed
desaprobar **2** *vt* disapprove of
desarm|able *adj* collapsible; (estante) easy to dismantle. **~ar** *vt* disarm; (*desmontar*) dismantle; take apart; (*LAm*) take down (carpa). **~e** *m* disarmament
desarraig|ado *adj* rootless. **~ar** **12** *vt* uproot. **~o** *m* uprooting
desarregl|ar *vt* mess up; (*alterar*) disrupt. **~o** *m* disorder
desarroll|ar *vt* develop. **~arse** *vpr* (*incl Foto*) develop; (suceso) take place. **~o** *m* development
desaseado *adj* dirty; (*desordenado*) untidy
desasosiego *m* anxiety; (*intranquilidad*) restlessness
desastr|ado *adj* scruffy. **~e** *m* disaster. **~oso** *adj* disastrous
desatar *vt* untie; (*fig, soltar*) unleash. **~se** *vpr* come undone; to undo (zapatos)
desatascar **7** *vt* unblock
desaten|der **1** *vt* not pay attention to; neglect (deber etc). **~to** *adj* inattentive; (*descortés*) discourteous
desatin|ado *adj* silly. **~o** *m* silliness; (*error*) mistake
desatornillar *vt* unscrew
desautorizar **10** *vt* declare unauthorized; discredit (persona); (*desmentir*) deny
desavenencia *f* disagreement
desayun|ar *vt* have for breakfast. ● *vi* have breakfast. **~o** *m* breakfast
desazón *m* (*fig*) unease
desbandarse *vpr* (*Mil*) disband; (*dispersarse*) disperse
desbarajust|ar *vt* mess up. **~e** *m* mess
desbaratar *vt* spoil; (*Mex*) mess up (papeles)
desbloquear *vt* clear; release (mecanismo); unfreeze (cuenta)
desbocado *adj* (caballo) runaway; (escote) wide
desbordarse *vpr* overflow; (río) burst its banks
descabellado *adj* crazy
descafeinado *adj* decaffeinated. ● *m* decaffeinated coffee
descalabro *m* disaster
descalificar **7** *vt* disqualify; (*desacreditar*) discredit
descalz|ar **10** *vt* take off (zapatos). **~o** *adj* barefoot
descampado *m* open ground. **al ~** (*LAm*) in the open air
descans|ado *adj* rested; (trabajo) easy. **~ar** *vt/i* rest. **~illo** *m* landing. **~o** *m* rest; (*del trabajo*) break; (*LAm, rellano*) landing; (*en deportes*) half-time; (*en el teatro etc*) interval
descapotable *adj* convertible

descarado *adj* cheeky; (*sin vergüenza*) shameless

descarg|a *f* unloading; (*Mil, Elec*) discharge. **~ar** 12 *vt* unload; (*Mil, Elec*) discharge; (*Informática*) download. **~o** *m* (*recibo*) receipt; (*Jurid*) evidence

descaro *m* cheek, nerve

descarriarse 20 *vpr* go the wrong way; (res) stray; (*fig*) go astray

descarrila|miento *m* derailment. **~r** *vi* be derailed. **~rse** *vpr* (*LAm*) be derailed

descartar *vt* rule out

descascararse *vpr* (pintura) peel; (taza) chip

descen|dencia *f* descent; (*personas*) descendants. **~der** 1 *vt* go down (escalera etc). • *vi* go down; (temperatura) fall, drop; (*provenir*) be descended (**de** from). **~diente** *m & f* descendent. **~so** *m* descent; (*de temperatura, fiebre etc*) fall, drop

descifrar *vt* decipher; decode (clave)

descolgar 2 & 12 *vt* take down; pick up (el teléfono). **~se** *vpr* lower o.s.

descolor|ar *vt* discolour, fade. **~ido** *adj* discoloured, faded; (persona) pale

descomp|oner 34 *vt* break down; decompose (materia); upset (estómago); (*esp LAm, estropear*) break; (*esp LAm, desarreglar*) mess up. **~onerse** *vpr* decompose; (*esp LAm, estropearse*) break down; (persona) feel sick. **~ostura** *f* (*esp LAm, de máquina*) breakdown; (*esp LAm, náuseas*) sickness; (*esp LAm, diarrea*) diarrhoea; (*LAm, falla*) fault. **~uesto** *adj* decomposed; (*encolerizado*) angry; (*esp LAm, estropeado*) broken. **estar ~uesto** (*del estómago*) have diarrhoea

descomunal *adj* enormous

desconc|ertante *adj* disconcerting. **~ertar** 1 *vt* disconcert; (*dejar perplejo*) puzzle. **~ertarse** *vpr* be put out, be disconcerted

desconectar *vt* disconnect

desconfia|do *adj* distrustful. **~nza** *f* distrust, suspicion. **~r** 20 *vi*. **~r de** mistrust; (*no creer*) doubt

descongelar *vt* defrost; (*Com*) unfreeze

desconoc|er 11 *vt* not know, not recognize. **~ido** *adj* unknown; (*cambiado*) unrecognizable. • *m* stranger. **~imiento** *m* ignorance

desconsidera|ción *f* lack of consideration. **~do** *adj* inconsiderate

descons|olado *adj* distressed. **~uelo** *m* distress; (*tristeza*) sadness

desconta|do *adj*. **dar por ~do (que)** take for granted (that). **~r** 2 *vt* discount; deduct (impuestos etc)

descontento *adj* unhappy (**con** with), dissatisfied (**con** with). • *m* discontent

descorazonar *vt* discourage. **~se** *vpr* lose heart

descorchar *vt* uncork

descorrer *vt* draw (cortina). **~ el cerrojo** unbolt the door

descort|és *adj* rude, discourteous. **~esía** *f* rudeness

descos|er *vt* unpick. **~erse** *vpr* come undone. **~ido** *adj* unstitched

descrédito *m* disrepute. **ir en ~ de** damage the reputation of

descremado *adj* skimmed

descri|bir (*pp* **descrito**) *vt* describe. **~pción** *f* description

d

descuartizar [10] *vt* cut up
descubierto *adj* discovered; (*no cubierto*) uncovered; (vehículo) open-top; (piscina) open-air; (cielo) clear; (cabeza) bare. • *m* overdraft. **poner al ~** expose
descubri|miento *m* discovery. **~r** (*pp* **descubierto**) *vt* discover; (*destapar*) uncover; (*revelar*) reveal; unveil (estatua). **~rse** *vpr* (*quitarse el sombrero*) take off one's hat
descuento *m* discount; (*del sueldo*) deduction; (*en deportes*) injury time
descuid|ado *adj* careless; (aspecto etc) untidy; (*desprevenido*) unprepared. **~ar** *vt* neglect. • *vi* not worry. **¡~a!** don't worry!. **~arse** *vpr* be careless **~o** *m* carelessness; (*negligencia*) negligence
desde *prep* (*lugar etc*) from; (*tiempo*) since, from. **~ ahora** from now on. **~ hace un mes** for a month. **~ luego** of course. **~ Madrid hasta Barcelona** from Madrid to Barcelona. **~ niño** since childhood
desdecirse [46] *vpr.* **~ de** take back (palabras etc); go back on (promesa)
desd|én *m* scorn. **~eñable** *adj* insignificant. **nada ~eñable** significant. **~eñar** *vt* scorn
desdicha *f* misfortune. **por ~** unfortunately. **~do** *adj* unfortunate
desdoblar *vt* (*desplegar*) unfold
desear *vt* want; wish (suerte etc). **le deseo un buen viaje** I hope you have a good journey. **¿qué desea Vd?** can I help you?
desech|able *adj* disposable. **~ar** *vt* throw out; (*rechazar*) reject. **~o** *m* waste
desembalar *vt* unpack
desembarcar [7] *vt* unload. • *vi* disembark
desemboca|dura *f* (*de río*) mouth; (*de calle*) opening. **~r** [7] *vi*. **~r en** (río) flow into; (calle) lead to
desembolso *m* payment
desembragar [12] *vi* declutch
desempaquetar *vt* unwrap
desempat|ar *vi* break a tie. **~e** *m* tie-breaker
desempeñ|ar *vt* redeem; play (papel); hold (cargo); perform, carry out (deber etc). **~arse** *vpr* (*LAm*) perform. **~arse bien** manage well. **~o** *m* redemption; (*de un deber, una función*) discharge; (*LAm, actuación*) performance
desemple|ado *adj* unemployed. • *m* unemployed person. **los ~ados** the unemployed. **~o** *m* unemployment
desencadenar *vt* unchain (preso); unleash (perro); (*causar*) trigger. **~se** *vpr* be triggered off; (guerra etc) break out
desencajar *vt* dislocate; (*desconectar*) disconnect. **~se** *vpr* become dislocated
desenchufar *vt* unplug
desenfad|ado *adj* uninhibited; (*desenvuelto*) self-assured. **~o** *m* lack of inhibition; (*desenvoltura*) self-assurance
desenfocado *adj* out of focus
desenfren|ado *adj* unrestrained. **~o** *m* licentiousness
desenganchar *vt* unhook; uncouple (vagón)
desengañ|ar *vt* disillusion. **~arse** *vpr* become disillusioned; (*darse cuenta*) realize. **~o** *m* disillusionment, disappointment
desenlace *m* outcome

desenmascarar *vt* unmask
desenredar *vt* untangle. **~se** *vpr* untangle
desenro|llar *vt* unroll, unwind. **~scar** 7 *vt* unscrew
desentend|erse 1 *vpr* want nothing to do with. **~ido** *m*. **hacerse el ~ido** (*fingir no oír*) pretend not to hear; (*fingir ignorancia*) pretend not to know
desenterrar 1 *vt* exhume; (*fig*) unearth
desentonar *vi* be out of tune; (colores) clash
desenvoltura *f* ease; (*falta de timidez*) confidence
desenvolver 2 (*pp* **desenvuelto**) *vt* unwrap; expound (idea etc). **~se** *vpr* perform; (*manejarse*) manage
deseo *m* wish, desire. **~so** *adj* eager. **estar ~so de** be eager to
desequilibr|ado *adj* unbalanced. **~io** *m* imbalance
des|ertar *vt* desert; (*Pol*) defect. **~értico** *adj* desert-like. **~ertor** *m* deserter; (*Pol*) defector
desespera|ción *f* despair. **~do** *adj* desperate. **~nte** *adj* infuriating. **~r** *vt* drive to despair. **~rse** *vpr* despair
desestimar *vt* (*rechazar*) reject
desfachat|ado *adj* brazen, shameless. **~ez** *f* nerve, cheek
desfallec|er 11 *vt* weaken. • *vi* become weak; (*desmayarse*) faint. **~imiento** *m* weakness; (*desmayo*) faint
desfasado *adj* out of phase; (idea) outdated; (persona) out of touch
desfavorable *adj* unfavourable
desfil|adero *m* narrow mountain pass; (*cañón*) narrow gorge. **~ar** *vi* march (past). **~e** *m* procession, parade. **~e de modelos** fashion show
desgana *f*, (*LAm*) **desgano** *m* (*falta de apetito*) lack of appetite; (*Med*) weakness, faintness; (*fig*) unwillingness
desgarr|ador *adj* heart-rending. **~ar** *vt* tear; (*fig*) break (corazón). **~o** *m* tear, rip
desgast|ar *vt* wear away; wear out (ropa). **~arse** *vpr* wear away; (ropa) be worn out; (persona) wear o.s. out. **~e** *m* wear
desgracia *f* misfortune; (*accidente*) accident; **por ~** unfortunately. **¡qué ~!** what a shame!. **~do** *adj* unlucky; (*pobre*) poor. • *m* unfortunate person, poor devil [!]
desgranar *vt* shell (habas etc)
desgreñado *adj* ruffled, dishevelled
deshabitado *adj* uninhabited; (edificio) unoccupied
deshacer 31 *vt* undo; strip (cama); unpack (maleta); (*desmontar*) take to pieces; break (trato); (*derretir*) melt; (*disolver*) dissolve. **~se** *vpr* come undone; (*disolverse*) dissolve; (*derretirse*) melt. **~se de algo** get rid of sth. **~se en lágrimas** dissolve into tears. **~se por hacer algo** go out of one's way to do sth
desheredar *vt* disinherit
deshidratarse *vpr* become dehydrated
deshielo *m* thaw
deshilachado *adj* frayed
deshincha|do *adj* (neumático) flat. **~r** *vt* deflate; (*Med*) reduce the swelling in. **~rse** *vpr* go down
deshollinador *m* chimney sweep

deshon|esto *adj* dishonest; (*obsceno*) indecent. **~ra** *f* disgrace. **~rar** *vt* dishonour

deshora *f*. **a ~** out of hours. **comer a ~s** eat between meals

d

deshuesar *vt* bone (carne); stone (fruta)

desidia *f* slackness; (pereza) laziness

desierto *adj* deserted. ● *m* desert

designar *vt* designate; (*fijar*) fix

desigual *adj* unequal; (terreno) uneven; (*distinto*) different. **~dad** *f* inequality

desilusi|ón *f* disappointment; (*pérdida de ilusiones*) disillusionment. **~onar** *vt* disappoint; (*quitar las ilusiones*) disillusion. **~onarse** *vpr* be disappointed; (*perder las ilusiones*) become disillusioned

desinfecta|nte *m* disinfectant. **~r** *vt* disinfect

desinflar *vt* deflate. **~se** *vpr* go down

desinhibido *adj* uninhibited

desintegrar *vt* disintegrate. **~se** *vpr* disintegrate

desinter|és *m* lack of interest; (*generosidad*) unselfishness. **~esado** *adj* uninterested; (*liberal*) unselfish

desistir *vi*. **~ de** give up

desleal *adj* disloyal. **~tad** *f* disloyalty

desligar 12 *vt* untie; (*separar*) separate; (*fig, librar*) free. **~se** *vpr* break away; (*de un compromiso*) free o.s. (**de** from)

desliza|dor *m* (*Mex*) hang glider. **~r** 10 *vt* slide, slip. **~se** *vpr* slide, slip; (patinador) glide; (tiempo) slip by, pass; (*fluir*) flow

deslucido *adj* tarnished; (*gastado*) worn out; (*fig*) undistinguished

deslumbrar *vt* dazzle

desmadr|arse *vpr* get out of control. **~e** *m* excess

desmán *m* outrage

desmanchar *vt* (*LAm*) remove the stains from

desmantelar *vt* dismantle; (*despojar*) strip

desmaquillador *m* make-up remover

desmay|ado *adj* unconscious. **~arse** *vpr* faint. **~o** *m* faint

desmedido *adj* excessive

desmemoriado *adj* forgetful

desmenti|do *m* denial. **~r** 4 *vt* deny; (*contradecir*) contradict

desmenuzar 10 *vt* crumble; shred (carne etc)

desmerecer 11 *vi*. **no ~ de** compare favourably with

desmesurado *adj* excessive; (*enorme*) enormous

desmonta|ble *adj* collapsible; (armario) easy to dismantle; (*separable*) removable. **~r** *vt* (*quitar*) remove; (*desarmar*) dismantle, take apart. ● *vi* dismount

desmoralizar 10 *vt* demoralize

desmoronarse *vpr* crumble; (edificio) collapse

desnatado *adj* skimmed

desnivel *m* unevenness; (*fig*) difference, inequality

desnud|ar *vt* strip; undress, strip (persona). **~arse** *vpr* undress. **~ez** *f* nudity. **~o** *adj* naked; (*fig*) bare. ● *m* nude

desnutri|ción *f* malnutrition. **~do** *adj* undernourished

desobed|ecer 11 *vt* disobey. **~iencia** *f* disobedience

desocupa|do *adj* (asiento etc) vacant, free; (*sin trabajo*) unemployed; (*ocioso*) idle. **~r** *vt* vacate; (*vaciar*) empty; (*desalojar*) clear

desodorante *m* deodorant

desolado *adj* desolate; (persona) sorry, sad

desorbitante *adj* excessive

desorden *m* disorder, untidiness; (*confusión*) confusion. **~ado** *adj* untidy. **~ar** *vt* disarrange, make a mess of

desorganizar **10** *vt* disorganize; (*trastornar*) disturb

desorienta|do *adj* confused. **~r** *vt* disorientate. **~rse** *vpr* lose one's bearings

despabila|do *adj* wide awake; (*listo*) quick. **~r** *vt* (*despertar*) wake up; (*avivar*) wise up. **~rse** *vpr* wake up; (*avivarse*) wise up

despach|ar *vt* finish; (*tratar con*) deal with; (*atender*) serve; (*vender*) sell; (*enviar*) send; (*despedir*) fire. **~o** *m* dispatch; (*oficina*) office; (*venta*) sale; (*de localidades*) box office

despacio *adv* slowly

despampanante *adj* stunning

desparpajo *m* confidence; (*descaro*) impudence

desparramar *vt* scatter; spill (líquidos)

despavorido *adj* terrified

despecho *m* spite. **a ~ de** in spite of. **por ~** out of spite

despectivo *adj* contemptuous; (sentido etc) pejorative

despedazar **10** *vt* tear to pieces

despedi|da *f* goodbye, farewell. **~da de soltero** stag-party. **~r** **5** *vt* say goodbye to, see off; dismiss (empleado); evict (inquilino); (*arrojar*) throw; give off (olor etc). **~rse** *vpr* say goodbye (**de** to)

despeg|ar **12** *vt* unstick. • *vi* (avión) take off. **~ue** *m* take-off

despeinar *vt* ruffle the hair of

despeja|do *adj* clear; (persona) wide awake. **~r** *vt* clear; (*aclarar*) clarify. • *vi* clear. **~rse** *vpr* (*aclararse*) become clear; (tiempo) clear up

despellejar *vt* skin

despenalizar *vt* decriminalize

despensa *f* pantry, larder

despeñadero *m* cliff

desperdici|ar *vt* waste. **~o** *m* waste. **~os** *mpl* rubbish

desperta|dor *m* alarm clock. **~r** **1** *vt* wake (up); (*fig*) awaken. **~rse** *vpr* wake up

despiadado *adj* merciless

despido *m* dismissal

despierto *adj* awake; (*listo*) bright

despilfarr|ar *vt* waste. **~o** *m* squandering

despintarse *vpr* (*Mex*) run

despista|do *adj* (*con estar*) confused; (*con ser*) absent-minded. **~r** *vt* throw off the scent; (*fig*) mislead. **~rse** *vpr* (*fig*) get confused

despiste *m* mistake; (*confusión*) muddle

desplaza|miento *m* displacement; (*de opinión etc*) swing, shift. **~r** **10** *vt* displace. **~rse** *vpr* travel

desplegar **1** & **12** *vt* open out; spread (alas); (*fig*) show

desplomarse *vpr* collapse

despoblado *m* deserted area

despoj|ar *vt* deprive (persona); strip (cosa). **~os** *mpl* remains; (*de res*) offal; (*de ave*) giblets

despreci|able *adj* despicable; (cantidad) negligible. **~ar** *vt* despise; (*rechazar*) scorn. **~o** *m* contempt; (*desaire*) snub

desprender *vt* remove; give off

(olor). **~se** *vpr* fall off; (*fig*) part with; (*deducirse*) follow

despreocupa|do *adj* unconcerned; (*descuidado*) careless. **~rse** *vpr* not worry

desprestigiar *vt* discredit

desprevenido *adj* unprepared. **pillar a uno ~** catch s.o. unawares

desproporcionado *adj* disproportionate

desprovisto *adj.* **~ de** lacking in, without

después *adv* after, afterwards; (*más tarde*) later; (*a continuación*) then. **~ de** after. **~ de comer** after eating. **~ de todo** after all. **~ (de) que** after. **poco ~** soon after

desquit|arse *vpr* get even (**de** with). **~e** *m* revenge

destaca|do *adj* outstanding. **~r** **7** *vt* emphasize. • *vi* stand out. **~rse** *vpr* stand out. **~rse en** excel at

destajo *m.* **trabajar a ~** do piece-work

destap|ar *vt* uncover; open (botella). **~arse** *vpr* reveal one's true self. **~e** *m* (*fig*) permissiveness

destartalado *adj* (coche) clapped-out; (casa) ramshackle

destello *m* sparkle; (*de estrella*) twinkle; (*fig*) glimmer

destemplado *adj* discordant; (nervios) frayed

desteñir **5** & **22** *vt* fade. • *vi* fade; (color) run. **~se** *vpr* fade; (color) run

desterra|do *m* exile. **~r** **1** *vt* banish

destetar *vt* wean

destiempo *m.* **a ~** at the wrong moment; (*Mus*) out of time

destierro *m* exile

destil|ar *vt* distil. **~ería** *f* distillery

destin|ar *vt* destine; (*nombrar*) post. **~atario** *m* addressee. **~o** *m* (*uso*) use, function; (*lugar*) destination; (*suerte*) destiny. **con ~o a** (going) to

destituir **17** *vt* dismiss

destornilla|dor *m* screwdriver. **~r** *vt* unscrew

destreza *f* skill

destroz|ar **10** *vt* destroy; (*fig*) shatter. **~os** *mpl* destruction, damage

destru|cción *f* destruction. **~ir** **17** *vt* destroy

desus|ado *adj* old-fashioned; (*insólito*) unusual. **~o** *m* disuse. **caer en ~o** fall into disuse

desvalido *adj* needy, destitute

desvalijar *vt* rob; ransack (casa)

desvalorizar **10** *vt* devalue

desván *m* loft

desvanec|er **11** *vt* make disappear; (*borrar*) blur; (*fig*) dispel. **~erse** *vpr* disappear; (*desmayarse*) faint. **~imiento** *m* (*Med*) faint

desvariar **20** *vi* be delirious; (*fig*) talk nonsense

desvel|ar *vt* keep awake. **~arse** *vpr* stay awake, have a sleepless night. **~o** *m* sleeplessness

desvencijado *adj* (mueble) rickety

desventaja *f* disadvantage

desventura *f* misfortune. **~do** *adj* unfortunate

desverg|onzado *adj* impudent, cheeky. **~üenza** *f* impudence, cheek

desvestirse **5** *vpr* undress

desv|iación *f* deviation; (*Auto*) diversion. **~iar** **20** *vt* divert; deflect (pelota). **~iarse** *vpr* (carretera) branch off; (*del camino*) make a detour; (*del tema*) stray. **~ío** *m* diversion

desvivirse *vpr.* **~se por** be completely devoted to; (*esforzarse*) go out of one's way to

detall|ar *vt* relate in detail. **~e** *m* detail; (*fig*) gesture. **al ~e** retail. **entrar en ~es** go into detail. **¡qué ~e!** how thoughtful! **~ista** *m & f* retailer

detect|ar *vt* detect. **~ive** *m* detective

deten|ción *f* stopping; (*Jurid*) arrest; (*en la cárcel*) detention. **~er** 40 *vt* stop; (*Jurid*) arrest; (*encarcelar*) detain; (*retrasar*) delay. **~erse** *vpr* stop; (*entretenerse*) spend a lot of time. **~idamente** *adv* at length. **~ido** *adj* (*Jurid*) under arrest. ● *m* prisoner

detergente *adj & m* detergent

deterior|ar *vt* damage, spoil. **~arse** *vpr* deteriorate. **~o** *m* deterioration

determina|ción *f* determination; (*decisión*) decison. **~nte** *adj* decisive. **~r** *vt* determine; (*decidir*) decide

detestar *vt* detest

detrás *adv* behind; (*en la parte posterior*) on the back. **~ de** behind. **por ~** at the back; (*por la espalda*) from behind

detrimento *m* detriment. **en ~ de** to the detriment of

deud|a *f* debt. **~or** *m* debtor

devalua|ción *f* devaluation. **~r** 21 *vt* devalue. **~se** *vpr* depreciate

devastador *adj* devastating

devoción *f* devotion

devol|ución *f* return; (*Com*) repayment, refund. **~ver** 5 (*pp* **devuelto**) *vt* return; (*Com*) repay, refund. ● *vi* be sick

devorar *vt* devour

devoto *adj* devout; (amigo etc) devoted. ● *m* admirer

di *vb véase* DAR, DECIR

día *m* day. **~ de fiesta** (public) holiday. **~ del santo** saint's day. **~ feriado** (*LAm*), **~ festivo** (public) holiday. **al ~** up to date. **al ~ siguiente** (on) the following day. **¡buenos ~s!** good morning! **de ~** by day. **el ~ de hoy** today. **el ~ de mañana** tomorrow. **un ~ sí y otro no** every other day. **vivir al ~** live from hand to mouth

> **Día de la raza** In Latin America, the anniversary of Columbus's discovery of America, October 12. In Spain it is known as *Día de la Hispanidad*. It is a celebration of the cultural ties shared by Spanish-speaking countries.

diab|etes *f* diabetes. **~ético** *adj* diabetic

diab|lo *m* devil. **~lura** *f* mischief. **~ólico** *adj* diabolical

diadema *f* diadem

diáfano *adj* diaphanous; (cielo) clear

diafragma *m* diaphragm

diagn|osis *f* diagnosis. **~osticar** 7 *vt* diagnose. **~óstico** *m* diagnosis

diagonal *adj & f* diagonal

diagrama *m* diagram

dialecto *m* dialect

di|alogar 12 *vi* talk. **~álogo** *m* dialogue; (*Pol*) talks

diamante *m* diamond

diámetro *m* diameter

diana *f* reveille; (*blanco*) bull's-eye

diapositiva *f* slide, transparency

diario *adj* daily. ● *m* newspaper; (*libro*) diary. **a ~o** daily. **de ~o** everyday, ordinary

diarrea *f* diarrhoea

d **dibuj|ante** *m* draughtsman. ● *f* draughtswoman. **~ar** *vt* draw. **~o** *m* drawing. **~os animados** cartoons

diccionario *m* dictionary

dich|a *f* happiness. **por ~a** fortunately. **~o** *adj* said; (*tal*) such. ● *m* saying. **~o y hecho** no sooner said than done. **mejor ~o** rather. **propiamente ~o** strictly speaking. **~oso** *adj* happy; (*afortunado*) fortunate

diciembre *m* December

dicta|do *m* dictation. **~dor** *m* dictator. **~dura** *f* dictatorship. **~men** *m* opinion; (*informe*) report. **~r** *vt* dictate; pronounce (sentencia etc); (*LAm*) give (clase)

didáctico *adj* didactic

dieci|nueve *adj & m* nineteen. **~ocho** *adj & m* eighteen. **~séis** *adj & m* sixteen. **~siete** *adj & m* seventeen

diente *m* tooth; (*de tenedor*) prong; (*de ajo*) clove. **~ de león** dandelion. **hablar entre ~s** mumble

diestro *adj* right-handed; (*hábil*) skillful

dieta *f* diet

diez *adj & m* ten

diezmar *vt* decimate

difamación *f* (*con palabras*) slander; (*por escrito*) libel

diferen|cia *f* difference; (*desacuerdo*) disagreement. **~ciar** *vt* differentiate between. **~ciarse** *vpr* differ. **~te** *adj* different; (*diversos*) various

diferido *adj* (*TV etc*) **en ~** recorded

dif|ícil *adj* difficult; (*poco probable*) unlikely. **~icultad** *f* difficulty. **~icultar** *vt* make difficult

difteria *f* diphtheria

difundir *vt* spread; (*TV etc*) broadcast

difunto *adj* late, deceased. ● *m* deceased

difusión *f* spreading

dige|rir **4** *vt* digest. **~stión** *f* digestion. **~stivo** *adj* digestive

digital *adj* digital; (*de los dedos*) finger

dign|arse *vpr* deign to. **~atario** *m* dignitary. **~idad** *f* dignity. **~o** *adj* honourable; (*decoroso*) decent; (*merecedor*) worthy (**de** of). **~ de elogio** praiseworthy

digo *vb véase* **DECIR**

dije *vb véase* **DECIR**

dilatar *vt* expand; (*Med*) dilate; (*prolongar*) prolong. **~se** *vpr* expand; (*Med*) dilate; (*extenderse*) extend; (*Mex, demorarse*) be late

dilema *m* dilemma

diligen|cia *f* diligence; (*gestión*) job; (*carruaje*) stagecoach. **~te** *adj* diligent

dilucidar *vt* clarify; solve (misterio)

diluir **17** *vt* dilute

diluvio *m* flood

dimensión *f* dimension; (*tamaño*) size

diminut|ivo *adj & m* diminutive. **~o** *adj* minute

dimitir *vt/i* resign

Dinamarca *f* Denmark

dinamarqués *adj* Danish. ● *m* Dane

dinámic|a *f* dynamics. **~o** *adj*

dynamic

dinamita *f* dynamite

dínamo *m* dynamo

dinastía *f* dynasty

diner|al *m* fortune. **~o** *m* money. **~o efectivo** cash. **~o suelto** change

dinosaurio *m* dinosaur

dios *m* god. **~a** *f* goddess. **¡D~ mío!** good heavens! **¡gracias a D~!** thank God!

diplom|a *m* diploma. **~acia** *f* diplomacy. **~ado** *adj* qualified. **~arse** *vpr* (*LAm*) graduate. **~ático** *adj* diplomatic. • *m* diplomat

diptongo *m* diphthong

diputa|ción *f* delegation. **~ción provincial** county council. **~do** *m* deputy; (*Pol, en España*) member of the Cortes; (*Pol, en Inglaterra*) Member of Parliament; (*Pol, en Estados Unidos*) congressman

dique *m* dike

direc|ción *f* direction; (*señas*) address; (*los que dirigen*) management; (*Pol*) leadership; (*Auto*) steering. **~ción prohibida** no entry. **~ción única** one-way. **~ta** *f* (*Auto*) top gear. **~tiva** *f* board; (*Pol*) executive committee. **~tivas** *fpl* guidelines. **~to** *adj* direct; (línea) straight; (tren) through. **en ~to** (*TV etc*) live. **~tor** *m* director; (*Mus*) conductor; (*de escuela*) headmaster; (*de periódico*) editor; (*gerente*) manager. **~tora** *f* (*de escuela etc*) headmistress. **~torio** *m* board of directors; (*LAm, de teléfonos*) telephone directory

dirig|ente *adj* ruling. • *m & f* leader; (*de empresa*) manager. **~ir** **14** *vt* direct; (*Mus*) conduct; run (empresa etc); address (carta etc). **~irse** *vpr* make one's way; (*hablar*) address

disciplina *f* discipline. **~r** *vt* discipline. **~rio** *adj* disciplinary

discípulo *m* disciple; (*alumno*) pupil

disco *m* disc; (*Mus*) record; (*deportes*) discus; (*de teléfono*) dial; (*de tráfico*) sign; (*Rail*) signal. **~ duro** hard disk. **~ flexible** floppy disk

disconforme *adj* not in agreement

discord|e *adj* discordant. **~ia** *f* discord

discoteca *f* discothèque, disco **!**; (*colección de discos*) record collection

discreción *f* discretion

discrepa|ncia *f* discrepancy; (*desacuerdo*) disagreement. **~r** *vi* differ

discreto *adj* discreet; (*moderado*) moderate

discrimina|ción *f* discrimination. **~r** *vt* (*distinguir*) discriminate between; (*tratar injustamente*) discriminate against

disculpa *f* apology; (*excusa*) excuse. **pedir ~s** apologize. **~r** *vt* excuse, forgive. **~rse** *vpr* apologize

discurs|ar *vi* speak (**sobre** about). **~o** *m* speech

discusión *f* discussion; (*riña*) argument

discuti|ble *adj* debatable. **~r** *vt* discuss; (*contradecir*) contradict. • *vi* argue (**por** about)

disecar **7** *vt* stuff; (*cortar*) dissect

diseminar *vt* disseminate, spread

disentir **4** *vi* disagree (**de** with, **en** on)

diseñ|ador *m* designer. **~ar** *vt* design. **~o** *m* design; (*fig*) sketch

disertación *f* dissertation

disfraz *m* fancy dress; (*para engañar*) disguise. **~ar** 10 *vt* dress up; (*para engañar*) disguise. **~arse** *vpr.* **~arse de** dress up as; (*para engañar*) disguise o.s. as.

d

disfrutar *vt* enjoy. ● *vi* enjoy o.s. **~ de** enjoy

disgust|ar *vt* displease; (*molestar*) annoy. **~arse** *vpr* get annoyed, get upset; (dos personas) fall out. **~o** *m* annoyance; (*problema*) trouble; (*riña*) quarrel; (*dolor*) sorrow, grief

disidente *adj & m & f* dissident

disimular *vt* conceal. ● *vi* pretend

disipar *vt* dissipate; (*derrochar*) squander

dislocarse 7 *vpr* dislocate

disminu|ción *f* decrease. **~ir** 17 *vi* diminish

disolver 2 (*pp* **disuelto**) *vt* dissolve. **~se** *vpr* dissolve

dispar *adj* different

disparar *vt* fire; (*Mex, pagar*) buy. ● *vi* shoot (**contra** at)

disparate *m* silly thing; (*error*) mistake. **decir ~s** talk nonsense. **¡qué ~!** how ridiculous!

disparidad *f* disparity

disparo *m* (*acción*) firing; (*tiro*) shot

dispensar *vt* give; (*eximir*) exempt. ● *vi.* **¡Vd dispense!** forgive me

dispers|ar *vt* scatter, disperse. **~arse** *vpr* scatter, disperse. **~ión** *f* dispersion. **~o** *adj* scattered

dispon|er 34 *vt* arrange; (*Jurid*) order. ● *vi.* **~er de** have; (*vender etc*) dispose of. **~erse** *vpr* prepare (**a** to). **~ibilidad** *f* availability. **~ible** *adj* available

disposición *f* arrangement; (*aptitud*) talent; (*disponibilidad*) disposal; (*Jurid*) order, decree. **~ de ánimo** frame of mind. **a la ~ de** at the disposal of. **a su ~** at your service

dispositivo *m* device

dispuesto *adj* ready; (persona) disposed (**a** to); (*servicial*) helpful

disputa *f* dispute; (*pelea*) argument

disquete *m* diskette, floppy disk

dista|ncia *f* distance. **a ~ncia** from a distance. **guardar las ~ncias** keep one's distance. **~nciar** *vt* space out; distance (amigos). **~nciarse** *vpr* (dos personas) fall out. **~nte** *adj* distant. **~r** *vi* be away; (*fig*) be far. **~ 5 kilómetros** it's 5 kilometres away

distin|ción *f* distinction; (*honor*) award. **~guido** *adj* distinguished. **~guir** 13 *vt/i* distinguish. **~guirse** *vpr* distinguish o.s.; (*diferenciarse*) differ. **~tivo** *adj* distinctive. ● *m* badge. **~to** *adj* different, distinct

distra|cción *f* amusement; (*descuido*) absent-mindedness, inattention. **~er** 41 *vt* distract; (*divertir*) amuse. **~erse** *vpr* amuse o.s.; (*descuidarse*) not pay attention. **~ído** *adj* (*desatento*) absent-minded

distribu|ción *f* distribution. **~idor** *m* distributor. **~ir** 17 *vt* distribute

distrito *m* district

disturbio *m* disturbance

disuadir *vt* deter, dissuade

diurno *adj* daytime

divagar 12 *vi* digress; (*hablar sin sentido*) ramble

diván *m* settee, sofa

diversi|dad *f* diversity. **~ficar** 7 *vt* diversify

diversión *f* amusement, entertainment; (*pasatiempo*) pastime

diverso *adj* different
diverti|do *adj* amusing; (*que tiene gracia*) funny. **~r** 4 *vt* amuse, entertain. **~rse** *vpr* enjoy o.s.
dividir *vt* divide; (*repartir*) share out
divino *adj* divine
divisa *f* emblem. **~s** *fpl* currency
divisar *vt* make out
división *f* division
divorci|ado *adj* divorced. • *m* divorcee. **~ar** *vt* divorce. **~arse** *vpr* get divorced. **~o** *m* divorce
divulgar 12 *vt* spread; divulge (secreto)
dizque *adv* (*LAm*) apparently; (*supuestamente*) supposedly
do *m* C; (*solfa*) doh

> **DNI - Documento Nacional de Identidad** See
> ▷**DOCUMENTO DE IDENTIDAD**

dobl|adillo *m* hem; (*de pantalón*) turn-up (*Brit*), cuff (*Amer*). **~ar** *vt* double; (*plegar*) fold; (*torcer*) bend; turn (esquina); dub (película). • *vi* turn; (campana) toll. **~arse** *vpr* double; (*curvarse*) bend. **~e** *adj* double. • *m* double. **el ~e** twice as much (**de**, **que** as). **~egar** 12 *vt* (*fig*) force to give in. **~egarse** *vpr* give in
doce *adj & m* twelve. **~na** *f* dozen
docente *adj* teaching. • *m & f* teacher
dócil *adj* obedient
doctor *m* doctor. **~ado** *m* doctorate
doctrina *f* doctrine
document|ación *f* documentation, papers. **~al** *adj & m* documentary. **~o** *m* document. **D~o Nacional de Identidad** identity card

> **documento de identidad** An identity card that all residents over a certain age in Spain and Latin America must carry at all times. Holders must quote their identity card number on most official forms. The card is also known as *carné de identidad*, and in Spain as the *DNI* (*Documento Nacional de Identidad*).

dólar *m* dollar
dolarizar *vt* dollarize
dol|er 2 *vi* hurt, ache; (*fig*) grieve. **me duele la cabeza** I have a headache. **le duele el estómago** he has (a) stomach-ache. **~or** *m* pain; (*sordo*) ache; (*fig*) sorrow. **~or de cabeza** headache. **~or de muelas** toothache. **~oroso** *adj* painful
domar *vt* tame; break in (caballo)
dom|esticar 7 *vt* domesticate. **~éstico** *adj* domestic
domicili|ar *vt*. **~ar los pagos** pay by direct debit. **~o** *m* address. **~o particular** home address. **reparto a ~** home delivery service
domina|nte *adj* dominant; (persona) domineering. **~r** *vt* dominate; (*contener*) control; (*conocer*) have a good command of. • *vi* dominate. **~rse** *vpr* control o.s.
domingo *m* Sunday
dominio *m* authority; (*territorio*) domain; (*fig*) command
dominó *m* (*pl* **~s**) dominoes; (*ficha*) domino
don *m* talent, gift; (*en un sobre*) Mr. **~ Pedro** Pedro
donación *f* donation
donaire *m* grace, charm

dona|nte *m& f* (*de sangre*) donor. **~r** *vt* donate

doncella *f* maiden; (*criada*) maid

donde *adv* where

dónde *adv* where?; (*LAm, cómo*) how; **¿hasta ~?** how far? **¿por ~?** whereabouts?; (*por qué camino?*) which way? **¿a ~ vas?** where are you going? **¿de ~ eres?** where are you from?

dondequiera *adv.* **~ que** wherever. **por ~** everywhere

doña *f* (*en un sobre*) Mrs. **~ María** María

dora|do *adj* golden; (*cubierto de oro*) gilt. **~r** *vt* gilt; (*Culin*) brown

dormi|do *adj* asleep. **quedarse ~do** fall asleep; (*no despertar*) oversleep. **~r** **6** *vt* send to sleep. • *vi* sleep. **~rse** *vpr* fall asleep. **~r la siesta** have an afternoon nap, have a siesta. **~tar** *vi* doze. **~torio** *m* bedroom

dors|al *adj* back. • *m* (*en deportes*) number. **~o** *m* back. **nadar de ~** (*Mex*) do (the) backstroke

dos *adj & m* two. **de ~ en ~** in twos, in pairs. **los ~, las ~** both (of them). **~cientos** *adj & m* two hundred

dosi|ficar **7** *vt* dose; (*fig*) measure out. **~s** *f invar* dose

dot|ado *adj* gifted. **~ar** *vt* give a dowry; (*proveer*) provide (**de** with). **~e** *m* dowry

doy *vb véase* **DAR**

dragar **12** *vt* dredge

drama *m* drama; (*obra de teatro*) play. **~turgo** *m* playwright

drástico *adj* drastic

droga *f* drug. **~dicto** *m* drug addict. **~do** *m* drug addict. **~r** **12** *vt* drug. **~rse** *vpr* take drugs

droguería *f* hardware store

ducha *f* shower. **~rse** *vpr* have a shower

dud|a *f* doubt. **poner en ~a** question. **sin ~a (alguna)** without a doubt. **~ar** *vt/i* doubt. **~oso** *adj* doubtful; (*sospechoso*) dubious

duelo *m* duel; (*luto*) mourning

duende *m* imp

dueñ|a *f* owner, proprietress; (*de una pensión*) landlady. **~o** *m* owner, proprietor; (*de una pensión*) landlord

duermo *vb véase* **DORMIR**

dul|ce *adj* sweet; (agua) fresh; (*suave*) soft, gentle. • *m* (*LAm*) sweet. **~zura** *f* sweetness; (*fig*) gentleness

duna *f* dune

dúo *m* duet, duo

duplica|do *adj* duplicated. **por ~** in duplicate. • *m* duplicate. **~r** **7** *vt* duplicate. **~rse** *vpr* double

duque *m* duke. **~sa** *f* duchess

dura|ción *f* duration, length. **~dero** *adj* lasting. **~nte** *prep* during; (*medida de tiempo*) for. **~ todo el año** all year round. **~r** *vi* last

durazno *m* (*LAm, fruta*) peach

dureza *f* hardness; (*Culin*) toughness; (*fig*) harshness

duro *adj* hard; (*Culin*) tough; (*fig*) harsh. • *adv* (*esp LAm*) hard

DVD *m* (**Disco Versátil Digital**) DVD. **~teca** *f* DVD library

Ee

e *conj* and
Ébola *m* ebola
ebrio *adj* drunk
ebullición *f* boiling
eccema *m* eczema
echar *vt* throw; post (carta); give off (olor); pour (líquido); (*expulsar*) expel; (*de recinto*) throw out; fire (empleado); (*poner*) put on; get (gasolina); put out (raíces); show (película). **~ a** start. **~ a perder** spoil. **~ de menos** miss. **~se atrás** (*fig*) back down. **echárselas de** feign. **~se** *vpr* throw o.s.; (*tumbarse*) lie down
eclesiástico *adj* ecclesiastical
eclipse *m* eclipse
eco *m* echo. **hacerse ~ de** echo
ecolog|ía *f* ecology. **~ista** *m & f* ecologist
economato *m* cooperative store
econ|omía *f* economy; (*ciencia*) economics. **~ómico** *adj* economic; (*no caro*) inexpensive. **~omista** *m & f* economist. **~omizar** **10** *vt/i* economize
ecoturismo *m* ecotourism
ecuación *f* equation
ecuador *m* equator. **el E~** the Equator. **E~** (*país*) Ecuador
ecuánime *adj* level-headed; (*imparcial*) impartial
ecuatoriano *adj & m* Ecuadorian
ecuestre *adj* equestrian
edad *f* age. **~ avanzada** old age. **E~ de Piedra** Stone Age. **E~ Media** Middle Ages. **¿qué ~ tiene?** how old is he?
edición *f* edition; (*publicación*) publication
edicto *m* edict
edific|ación *f* building. **~ante** *adj* edifying. **~ar** **7** *vt* build; (*fig*) edify. **~io** *m* building; (*fig*) structure
edit|ar *vt* edit; (*publicar*) publish. **~or** *adj* publishing. • *m* editor; (*que publica*) publisher. **~orial** *adj* editorial. • *m* leading article. • *f* publishing house
edredón *m* duvet
educa|ción *f* upbringing; (*modales*) (good) manners; (*enseñanza*) education. **falta de ~ción** rudeness, bad manners. **~do** *adj* polite. **bien ~do** polite. **mal ~do** rude. **~r** **7** *vt* bring up; (*enseñar*) educate. **~tivo** *adj* educational
edulcorante *m* sweetener
EE.UU. *abrev* (**Estados Unidos**) USA
efect|ivamente *adv* really; (*por supuesto*) indeed. **~ivo** *adj* effective; (*auténtico*) real. • *m* cash. **~o** *m* effect; (*impresión*) impression. **en ~o** really; (*como respuesta*) indeed. **~os** *mpl* belongings; (*Com*) goods. **~uar** **21** *vt* carry out; make (viaje, compras etc)
efervescente *adj* effervescent; (bebidas) fizzy
efica|cia *f* effectiveness; (*de persona*) efficiency. **~z** *adj* effective; (persona) efficient
eficien|cia *f* efficiency. **~te** *adj* efficient
efímero *adj* ephemeral
efusi|vidad *f* effusiveness. **~vo** *adj* effusive; (persona) demonstrative
egipcio *adj & m* Egyptian
Egipto *m* Egypt

ego|ísmo *m* selfishness, egotism. **~ísta** *adj* selfish

egresar *vi* (*LAm*) graduate; (*de colegio*) leave school, graduate (*Amer*)

eje *m* axis; (*Tec*) axle

ejecu|ción *f* execution; (*Mus*) performance. **~tar** *vt* carry out; (*Mus*) perform; (*matar*) execute. **~tivo** *m* executive

e

ejempl|ar *adj* exemplary; (*ideal*) model. ● *m* specimen; (*libro*) copy; (*revista*) issue, number. **~ificar** **7** *vt* exemplify. **~o** *m* example. **dar (el) ~o** set an example. **por ~o** for example

ejerc|er **9** *vt* exercise; practise (profesión); exert (influencia). ● *vi* practise. **~icio** *m* exercise; (*de profesión*) practice. **hacer ~icios** take exercise. **~itar** *vt* exercise

ejército *m* army

ejido *m* (*Mex*) cooperative

ejote *m* (*Mex*) green bean

el *artículo definido masculino* (*pl* **los**)

The masculine article **el** is also used before feminine nouns which begin with stressed **a** or **ha**, e.g. **el ala derecha, el hada madrina.** Also, **de** followed by **el** becomes **del** and **el** preceded by **a** becomes **al**

....➤ the. **el tren de las seis** the six o'clock train. **el vecino de al lado** the next-door neighbour. **cerca del hospital** near the hospital

....➤ *No se traduce en los siguientes casos:* (*con nombre abstracto, genérico*) **el tiempo vuela** time flies. **odio el queso** I hate cheese. **el hilo es muy durable** linen is very durable

....➤ (*con colores, días de la semana*) **el rojo está de moda** red is in fashion. **el lunes es fiesta** Monday is a holiday

....➤ (*con algunas instituciones*) **termino el colegio mañana** I finish school tomorrow. **lo ingresaron en el hospital** he was admitted to hospital

....➤ (*con nombres propios*) **el Sr. Díaz** Mr Díaz. **el doctor Lara** Doctor Lara

....➤ (*antes de infinitivo*) **es muy cuidadosa en el vestir** she takes great care in the way she dresses. **me di cuenta al verlo** I realized when I saw him

....➤ (*con partes del cuerpo, artículos personales*) *se traduce por un posesivo.* **apretó el puño** he clenched his fist. **tienes el zapato desatado** your shoe is undone

....➤ **el + de. es el de Pedro** it's Pedro's. **el del sombrero** the one with the hat

....➤ **el + que** (*persona*) **el que me atendió** the one who served me. (*cosa*) **el que se rompió** the one that broke.

....➤ **el + que** + *subjuntivo* (*quienquiera*) whoever. **el que gane la lotería** whoever wins the lottery. (*cualquiera*) whichever. **compra el que sea más barato** buy whichever is cheaper

él *pron* (*persona*) he; (*persona con prep*) him; (*cosa*) it. **es de ~** it's his

elabora|ción *f* elaboration; (*fabricación*) manufacture. **~r** *vt* elaborate; manufacture (producto);

(*producir*) produce

el|asticidad *f* elasticity. **~ástico** *adj & m* elastic

elec|ción *f* choice; (*de político etc*) election. **~ciones** *fpl* (*Pol*) election. **~tor** *m* voter. **~torado** *m* electorate. **~toral** *adj* electoral; (*campaña*) election

electrici|dad *f* electricity. **~sta** *m & f* electrician

eléctrico *adj* electric; (*aparato*) electrical

electri|ficar **7** *vt* electrify. **~zar** **10** *vt* electrify

electrocutar *vt* electrocute. **~se** *vpr* be electrocuted

electrodoméstico *adj* electrical appliance

electrónic|a *f* electronics. **~o** *adj* electronic

elefante *m* elephant

elegan|cia *f* elegance. **~te** *adj* elegant

elegía *f* elegy

elegi|ble *adj* eligible. **~do** *adj* chosen. **~r** **5** & **14** *vt* choose; (*por votación*) elect

element|al *adj* elementary; (*esencial*) fundamental. **~o** *m* element; (*persona*) person, bloke (*Brit, fam*). **~os** *mpl* (*nociones*) basic principles

elenco *m* (*en el teatro*) cast

eleva|ción *f* elevation; (*de precios*) rise, increase; (*acción*) raising. **~dor** *m* (*Mex*) lift (*Brit*), elevator (*Amer*). **~r** *vt* raise; (*promover*) promote

elimina|ción *f* elimination. **~r** *vt* eliminate; (*Informática*) delete. **~toria** *f* preliminary heat

élite /e'lit, e'lite/ *f* elite

ella *pron* (*persona*) she; (*persona con prep*) her; (*cosa*) it. **es de ~s** it's theirs. **~s** *pron* pl they; (*con prep*) them. **es de ~** it's hers

ello *pron* it

ellos *pron pl* they; (*con prep*) them. **es de ~** it's theirs

elocuen|cia *f* eloquence. **~te** *adj* eloquent

elogi|ar *vt* praise. **~o** *m* praise

elote *m* (*Mex*) corncob; (*Culin*) corn on the cob

eludir *vt* avoid, elude

emanar *vi* emanate (**de** from); (*originarse*) originate (**de** from, in)

emancipa|ción *f* emancipation. **~r** *vt* emancipate. **~rse** *vpr* become emancipated

embadurnar *vt* smear

embajad|a *f* embassy. **~or** *m* ambassador

embalar *vt* pack

embaldosar *vt* tile

embalsamar *vt* embalm

embalse *m* reservoir

embaraz|ada *adj* pregnant. • *f* pregnant woman. **~ar** **10** *vt* get pregnant. **~o** *m* pregnancy; (*apuro*) embarrassment; (*estorbo*) hindrance. **~oso** *adj* awkward, embarrassing

embar|cación *f* vessel. **~cadero** *m* jetty, pier. **~car** **7** *vt* load (mercancías etc). **~carse** *vpr* board. **~carse en** (*fig*) embark upon

embargo *m* embargo; (*Jurid*) seizure. **sin ~** however

embarque *m* loading; (*de pasajeros*) boarding

embaucar **7** *vt* trick

embelesar *vt* captivate

embellecer **11** *vt* make beautiful

embesti|da *f* charge. **~r** **5** *vt/i* charge

emblema *m* emblem

embolsarse *vpr* pocket

embonar *vt* (*Mex*) fit

emborrachar *vt* get drunk. **~se** *vpr* get drunk

emboscada *f* ambush

embotar *vt* dull

embotella|miento *m* (*de vehículos*) traffic jam. **~r** *vt* bottle

embrague *m* clutch

embriag|arse 12 *vpr* get drunk. **~uez** *f* drunkenness

embrión *m* embryo

embroll|ar *vt* mix up; involve (persona). **~arse** *vpr* get into a muddle; (*en un asunto*) get involved. **~o** *m* tangle; (*fig*) muddle

embruj|ado *adj* bewitched; (casa) haunted. **~ar** *vt* bewitch. **~o** *m* spell

embrutecer 11 *vt* brutalize

embudo *m* funnel

embuste *m* lie. **~ro** *adj* deceitful. • *m* liar

embuti|do *m* (*Culin*) sausage. **~r** *vt* stuff

emergencia *f* emergency

emerger 14 *vi* appear, emerge

emigra|ción *f* emigration. **~nte** *adj & m & f* emigrant. **~r** *vi* emigrate

eminen|cia *f* eminence. **~te** *adj* eminent

emisario *m* emissary

emi|sión *f* emission; (*de dinero*) issue; (*TV etc*) broadcast. **~sor** *adj* issuing; (*TV etc*) broadcasting. **~sora** *f* radio station. **~tir** *vt* emit, give out; (*TV etc*) broadcast; cast (voto); (*poner en circulación*) issue

emoci|ón *f* emotion; (*excitación*) excitement. **¡qué ~ón!** how exciting!. **~onado** *adj* moved. **~onante** *adj* exciting; (*conmovedor*) moving. **~onar** *vt* move. **~onarse** *vpr* get excited; (*conmoverse*) be moved

emotivo *adj* emotional; (*conmovedor*) moving

empacar 7 *vt* (*LAm*) pack

empacho *m* indigestion

empadronar *vt* register. **~se** *vpr* register

empalagoso *adj* sickly; (persona) cloying

empalizada *f* fence

empalm|ar *vt* connect, join. • *vi* meet. **~e** *m* junction; (*de trenes*) connection

empan|ada *f* (savoury) pie; (*LAm, individual*) pasty. **~adilla** *f* pasty

empantanarse *vpr* become swamped; (coche) get bogged down

empañar *vt* steam up; (*fig*) tarnish. **~se** *vpr* steam up

empapar *vt* soak. **~se** *vpr* get soaked

empapela|do *m* wallpaper. **~r** *vt* wallpaper

empaquetar *vt* package

emparedado *m* sandwich

emparentado *adj* related

empast|ar *vt* fill (muela). **~e** *m* filling

empat|ar *vi* draw. **~e** *m* draw

empedernido *adj* confirmed; (bebedor) inveterate

empedrar 1 *vt* pave

empeine *m* instep

empeñ|ado *adj* in debt; (*decidido*) determined (**en** to). **~ar** *vt* pawn; pledge (palabra). **~arse** *vpr* get into debt; (*estar decidido a*) be determined (**en** to). **~o** *m* pledge; (*resolución*) determination. **casa** *f*

de ~s pawnshop. **~oso** *adj* (*LAm*) hardworking

empeorar *vt* make worse. ● *vi* get worse. **~se** *vpr* get worse

empequeñecer [11] *vt* become smaller; (*fig*) belittle

empera|dor *m* emperor. **~triz** *f* empress

empezar [1] & [10] *vt/i* start, begin. **para ~** to begin with

empina|do *adj* (cuesta) steep. **~r** *vt* raise. **~rse** *vpr* (persona) stand on tiptoe

empírico *adj* empirical

emplasto *m* plaster

emplaza|miento *m* (*Jurid*) summons; (*lugar*) site. **~r** [10] *vt* summon; (*situar*) site

emple|ada *f* employee; (*doméstica*) maid. **~ado** *m* employee. **~ar** *vt* use; employ (persona); spend (tiempo). **~arse** *vpr* get a job. **~o** *m* use; (*trabajo*) employment; (*puesto*) job

empobrecer [11] *vt* impoverish. **~se** *vpr* become poor

empoll|ar *vt* incubate (huevos); (*arg, estudiar*) cram [!]. ● *vi* (ave) sit; (estudiante) [✱] cram. **~ón** *m* [✱] swot (*Brit, fam*), grind (*Amer, fam*)

empolvarse *vpr* powder

empotra|do *adj* built-in, fitted. **~r** *vt* fit

emprende|dor *adj* enterprising. **~r** *vt* undertake; set out on (viaje). **~rla con uno** pick a fight with s.o.

empresa *f* undertaking; (*Com*) company, firm. **~ puntocom** dotcom company. **~rio** *m* businessman; (*patrón*) employer; (*de teatro etc*) impresario

empuj|ar *vt* push. **~e** *m* (*fig*) drive. **~ón** *m* push, shove

empuña|dura *f* handle

emular *vt* emulate

en *prep* in; (*sobre*) on; (*dentro*) inside, in; (*medio de transporte*) by. **~ casa** at home. **~ coche** by car. **~ 10 días** in 10 days. **de pueblo ~ pueblo** from town to town

enagua *f* petticoat

enajena|ción *f* alienation. **~ción mental** insanity. **~r** *vt* alienate; (*volver loco*) derange

enamora|do *adj* in love. ● *m* lover. **~r** *vt* win the love of. **~rse** *vpr* fall in love (**de** with)

enano *adj* & *m* dwarf

enardecer [11] *vt* inflame. **~se** *vpr* get excited (**por** about)

encabeza|do *m* (*Mex*) headline. **~miento** *m* heading; (*de periódico*) headline. **~r** [10] *vt* head; lead (revolución etc)

encabritarse *vpr* rear up

encadenar *vt* chain; (*fig*) tie down

encaj|ar *vt* fit; fit together (varias piezas). ● *vi* fit; (*cuadrar*) tally. **~arse** *vpr* put on. **~e** *m* lace; (*Com*) reserve

encaminar *vt* direct. **~se** *vpr* make one's way

encandilar *vt* dazzle; (*estimular*) stimulate

encant|ado *adj* enchanted; (persona) delighted. **¡~ado!** pleased to meet you! **~ador** *adj* charming. **~amiento** *m* spell. **~ar** *vt* bewitch; (*fig*) charm, delight. **me ~a la leche** I love milk. **~o** *m* spell; (*fig*) delight

encapricharse *vpr.* **~ con** take a fancy to

encarar *vt* face; (*LAm*) stand up to (persona). **~se** *vpr.* **~se con** stand up to

e

encarcelar *vt* imprison
encarecer 11 *vt* put up the price of. **~se** *vpr* become more expensive
encarg|ado *adj* in charge. • *m* manager, person in charge. **~ar** 12 *vt* entrust; (*pedir*) order. **~arse** *vpr* take charge (**de** of). **~o** *m* job; (*Com*) order; (*recado*) errand. **hecho de ~o** made to measure
encariñarse *vpr.* **~ con** take to, become fond of
encarna|ción *f* incarnation. **~do** *adj* incarnate; (*rojo*) red; (uña) ingrowing. • *m* red
encarnizado *adj* bitter
encarpetar *vt* file; (*LAm, dar carpetazo*) shelve
encarrilar *vt* put back on the rails; (*fig*) direct, put on the right track
encasillar *vt* classify; (*fig*) pigeonhole
encauzar 10 *vt* channel
enceguecer *vt* 11 (*LAm*) blind
encend|edor *m* lighter. **~er** 1 *vt* light; switch on, turn on (aparato eléctrico); start (motor); (*fig*) arouse. **~erse** *vpr* light; (aparato eléctrico) come on; (*excitarse*) get excited; (*ruborizarse*) blush. **~ido** *adj* lit; (aparato eléctrico) on; (*rojo*) bright red. • *m* (*Auto*) ignition
encera|do *adj* waxed. • *m* (*pizarra*) blackboard. **~r** *vt* wax
encerr|ar 1 *vt* shut in; (*con llave*) lock up; (*fig, contener*) contain. **~ona** *f* trap
enchilar *vt* (*Mex*) add chili to
enchinar *vt* (*Mex*) perm
enchuf|ado *adj* switched on. **~ar** *vt* plug in; fit together (tubos etc). **~e** *m* socket; (*clavija*) plug; (*de tubos etc*) joint; (*fam, influencia*) contact. **tener ~e** have friends in the right places
encía *f* gum
enciclopedia *f* encyclopaedia
encierro *m* confinement; (*cárcel*) prison
encim|a *adv* on top; (*arriba*) above. **~ de** on, on top of; (*sobre*) over; (*además de*) besides, as well as. **por ~** on top; (*adj* la ligera) superficially. **por ~ de todo** above all. **~ar** *vt* (*Mex*) stack up. **~era** *f* worktop
encina *f* holm oak
encinta *adj* pregnant
enclenque *adj* weak; (*enfermizo*) sickly
encoger 14 *vt* shrink; (*contraer*) contract. **~se** *vpr* shrink. **~erse de hombros** shrug one's shoulders
encolar *vt* glue; (*pegar*) stick
encolerizar 10 *vt* make angry. **~se** *vpr* get furious
encomendar 1 *vt* entrust
encomi|ar *vt* praise. **~o** *m* praise. **~oso** *adj* (*LAm*) complimentary
encono *m* bitterness, ill will
encontra|do *adj* contrary, conflicting. **~r** 2 *vt* find; (*tropezar con*) meet. **~rse** *vpr* meet; (*hallarse*) be. **no ~rse** feel uncomfortable
encorvar *vt* hunch. **~se** *vpr* stoop
encrespa|do *adj* (pelo) curly; (mar) rough. **~r** *vt* curl (pelo); make rough (mar)
encrucijada *f* crossroads
encuaderna|ción *f* binding. **~dor** *m* bookbinder. **~r** *vt* bind
encub|ierto *adj* hidden. **~rir** (*pp* **encubierto**) *vt* hide, conceal; cover up (delito); shelter (delincuente)
encuentro *m* meeting; (*en depor-*

tes) match; (*Mil*) encounter
encuesta *f* survey; (*investigación*) inquiry
encumbrado *adj* eminent; (*alto*) high
encurtidos *mpl* pickles
endeble *adj* weak
endemoniado *adj* possessed; (*muy malo*) wretched
enderezar 10 *vt* straighten out; (*poner vertical*) put upright; (*fig, arreglar*) put right, sort out; (*dirigir*) direct. **~se** *vpr* straighten out
endeudarse *vpr* get into debt
endiablado *adj* possessed; (*malo*) terrible; (*difícil*) difficult
endosar *vt* endorse (cheque)
endulzar 10 *vt* sweeten; (*fig*) soften
endurecer 11 *vt* harden. **~se** *vpr* harden
enemi|go *adj* enemy. • *m* enemy. **~stad** *f* enmity. **~star** *vt* make an enemy of. **~starse** *vpr* fall out (**con** with)
en|ergía *f* energy. **~érgico** *adj* (persona) lively; (decisión) forceful
energúmeno *m* madman
enero *m* January
enésimo *adj* nth, umpteenth I
enfad|ado *adj* angry; (*molesto*) annoyed. **~ar** *vt* make cross, anger; (*molestar*) annoy. **~arse** *vpr* get angry; (*molestarse*) get annoyed. **~o** *m* anger; (*molestia*) annoyance
énfasis *m invar* emphasis, stress. **poner ~** stress, emphasize
enfático *adj* emphatic
enferm|ar *vi* fall ill. **~arse** *vpr* (*LAm*) fall ill. **~edad** *f* illness. **~era** *f* nurse. **~ería** *f* sick bay; (*carrera*) nursing. **~ero** *m* (male) nurse
~izo *adj* sickly. **~o** *adj* ill. • *m* patient
enflaquecer 11 *vt* make thin. • *vi* lose weight
enfo|car 7 *vt* shine on; focus (lente); (*fig*) approach. **~que** *m* focus; (*fig*) approach
enfrentar *vt* face, confront; (*poner frente a frente*) bring face to face. **~se** *vpr.* **~se con** confront; (*en deportes*) meet
enfrente *adv* opposite. **~ de** opposite. **de ~** opposite
enfria|miento *m* cooling; (*catarro*) cold. **~r** 20 *vt* cool (down); (*fig*) cool down. **~rse** *vpr* go cold; (*fig*) cool off
enfurecer 11 *vt* infuriate. **~se** *vpr* get furious
engalanar *vt* adorn. **~se** *vpr* dress up
enganchar *vt* hook; hang up (ropa). **~se** *vpr* get caught; (*Mil*) enlist
engañ|ar *vt* deceive, trick; (*ser infiel*) be unfaithful. **~arse** *vpr* be wrong, be mistaken; (*no admitir la verdad*) deceive o.s. **~o** *m* deceit, trickery; (*error*) mistake. **~oso** *adj* deceptive; (persona) deceitful
engarzar 10 *vt* string (cuentas); set (joyas)
engatusar *vt* I coax
engendr|ar *vt* father; (*fig*) breed. **~o** *m* (*monstruo*) monster; (*fig*) brainchild
englobar *vt* include
engomar *vt* glue
engordar *vt* fatten, gain (kilo). • *vi* get fatter, put on weight
engorro *m* nuisance
engranaje *m* (*Auto*) gear
engrandecer 11 *vt* (*enaltecer*) exalt, raise

engrasar *vt* grease; (*con aceite*) oil; (*ensuciar*) get grease on
engreído *adj* arrogant
engullir 22 *vt* gulp down
enhebrar *vt* thread
enhorabuena *f* congratulations. dar la ~ congratulate
enigm|a *m* enigma. **~ático** *adj* enigmatic
enjabonar *vt* soap. **~se** *vpr* to soap o.s.
enjambre *m* swarm
enjaular *vt* put in a cage
enjuag|ar 12 *vt* rinse. **~ue** *m* rinsing; (*para la boca*) mouthwash
enjugar 12 *vt* wipe (away)
enjuiciar *vt* pass judgement on
enjuto *adj* (persona) skinny
enlace *m* connection; (*matrimonial*) wedding
enlatar *vt* tin, can
enlazar 10 *vt* link; tie together (cintas); (*Mex, casar*) marry
enlodar *vt*, **enlodazar** 10 *vt* cover in mud
enloquecer 11 *vt* drive mad. • *vi* go mad. **~se** *vpr* go mad
enlosar *vt* (*con losas*) pave; (*con baldosas*) tile
enmarañar *vt* tangle (up), entangle; (*confundir*) confuse. **~se** *vpr* get into a tangle; (*confundirse*) get confused
enmarcar 7 *vt* frame
enm|endar *vt* correct. **~endarse** *vpr* mend one's way. **~ienda** *f* correction; (*de ley etc*) amendment
enmohecerse 11 *vpr* (*con óxido*) go rusty; (*con hongos*) go mouldy
enmudecer 11 *vi* be dumbstruck; (*callar*) fall silent
ennegrecer 11 *vt* blacken
ennoblecer 11 *vt* ennoble; (*fig*) add style to
enoj|adizo *adj* irritable. **~ado** *adj* angry; (*molesto*) annoyed. **~ar** *vt* anger; (*molestar*) annoy. **~arse** *vpr* get angry; (*molestarse*) get annoyed. **~o** *m* anger; (*molestia*) annoyance. **~oso** *adj* annoying
enorgullecerse 11 *vpr* be proud
enorm|e *adj* huge, enormous. **~emente** *adv* enormously. **~idad** *f* immensity; (*de crimer*) enormity
enraizado *adj* deeply rooted
enrarecido *adj* rarefied
enred|adera *f* creeper. **~ar** *vt* tangle (up), entangle; (*confundir*) confuse; (*involucrar*) involve. **~arse** *vpr* get tangled; (*confundirse*) get confused; (persona) get involved (**con** with). **~o** *m* tangle; (*fig*) muddle, mess
enrejado *m* bars
enriquecer 11 *vt* make rich; (*fig*) enrich. **~se** *vpr* get rich
enrojecerse 11 *vpr* (persona) go red, blush
enrolar *vt* enlist
enrollar *vt* roll (up), wind (hilo etc)
enroscar 7 *vt* coil; (*atornillar*) screw in
ensalad|a *f* salad. **armar una ~a** make a mess. **~era** *f* salad bowl. **~illa** *f* Russian salad
ensalzar 10 *vt* praise; (*enaltecer*) exalt
ensambla|dura *f*, **ensamblaje** *m* (*acción*) assembling; (*efecto*) joint. **~r** *vt* join
ensanch|ar *vt* widen; (*agrandar*) enlarge. **~arse** *vpr* get wider. **~e** *m* widening
ensangrentar 1 *vt* stain with blood

ensañarse *vpr.* **~ con** treat cruelly

ensartar *vt* string (cuentas etc)

ensay|ar *vt* test; rehearse (obra de teatro etc). **~o** *m* test, trial; (*composición literaria*) essay

enseguida *adv* at once, immediately

ensenada *f* inlet, cove

enseña|nza *f* education; (*acción de enseñar*) teaching. **~nza media** secondary education. **~r** *vt* teach; (*mostrar*) show

enseres *mpl* equipment

ensillar *vt* saddle

ensimismarse *vpr* be lost in thought

ensombrecer **11** *vt* darken

ensordecer **11** *vt* deafen. ● *vi* go deaf

ensuciar *vt* dirty. **~se** *vpr* get dirty

ensueño *m* dream

entablar *vt* (*empezar*) start

entablillar *vt* put in a splint

entallar *vt* tailor (un vestido). ● *vi* fit

entarimado *m* parquet; (*plataforma*) platform

ente *m* entity, being; (*fam, persona rara*) weirdo; (*Com*) firm, company

entend|er **1** *vt* understand; (*opinar*) believe, think. ● *vi* understand. **~er de** know about. **a mi ~er** in my opinion. **dar a ~er** hint. **darse a ~er** (*LAm*) make o.s. understood **~erse** *vpr* make o.s. understood; (*comprenderse*) be understood. **~erse con** get on with. **~ido** *adj* understood; (*enterado*) well-informed. **no darse por ~ido** pretend not to understand. ● *interj* agreed!, OK! **!**. **~imiento** *m* understanding

entera|do *adj* well-informed; (*que sabe*) aware. **darse por ~do** take the hint. **~r** *vt* inform (**de** of). **~rse** *vpr.* **~rse de** find out about, hear of. **¡entérate!** listen! **¿te ~s?** do you understand?

entereza *f* (*carácter*) strength of character

enternecer **11** *vt* (*fig*) move, touch. **~se** *vpr* be moved, be touched

entero *adj* entire, whole. **por ~** entirely, completely

enterra|dor *m* gravedigger. **~r** **1** *vt* bury

entibiar *vt* (*enfriar*) cool; (*calentar*) warm (up). **~se** *vpr* (*enfriarse*) cool down; (*fig*) cool; (*calentarse*) get warm

entidad *f* entity; (*organización*) organization; (*Com*) company; (*importancia*) significance

entierro *m* burial; (*ceremonia*) funeral

entona|ción *f* intonation. **~r** *vt* intone; sing (nota). ● *vi* (*Mus*) be in tune; (colores) match. **~rse** *vpr* (*emborracharse*) get tipsy

entonces *adv* then. **en aquel ~** at that time, then

entorn|ado *adj* (puerta) ajar; (ventana) slightly open. **~o** *m* environment; (*en literatura*) setting

entorpecer **11** *vt* dull; slow down (tráfico); (*dificultar*) hinder

entra|da *f* entrance; (*incorporación*) admission, entry; (*para cine etc*) ticket; (*de datos, Tec*) input; (*de una comida*) starter. **de ~da** right away. **~do** *adj.* **~do en años** elderly. **ya ~da la noche** late at night. **~nte** *adj* next, coming

entraña *f* (*fig*) heart. **~s** *fpl* entrails; (*fig*) heart. **~ble** *adj* (cariño) deep; (amigo) close. **~r** *vt* involve

entrar *vt* (*traer*) bring in; (*llevar*) take in. • *vi* go in, enter; (*venir*) come in, enter; (*empezar*) start, begin; (*incorporarse*) join. **~ en,** (*LAm*) **~ a** go into

e

entre *prep* (*dos personas o cosas*) between; (*más de dos*) among(st)

entre|abierto *adj* half-open. **~abrir** (*pp* **entreabierto**) *vt* half open. **~acto** *m* interval. **~cejo** *m* forehead. **fruncir el ~cejo** frown. **~cerrar** 1 *vt* (*LAm*) half close. **~cortado** *adj* (voz) faltering; (respiración) laboured. **~cruzar** 10 *vt* intertwine

entrega *f* handing over; (*de mercancías etc*) delivery; (*de novela etc*) instalment; (*dedicación*) commitment. **~r** 12 *vt* deliver; (*dar*) give; hand in (deberes); hand over (poder). **~rse** *vpr* surrender, give o.s. up; (*dedicarse*) devote o.s. (**a** to)

entre|lazar 10 *vt* intertwine. **~més** *m* hors-d'oeuvre; (*en el teatro*) short comedy. **~mezclar** *vt* intermingle

entrena|dor *m* trainer. **~miento** *m* training. **~r** *vt* train. **~rse** *vpr* train

entre|pierna *f* crotch; *medida* inside leg measurement. **~piso** *m* (*LAm*) mezzanine. **~sacar** 7 *vt* pick out; (*peluquería*) thin out **~suelo** *m* mezzanine; (*de cine*) dress circle **~tanto** *adv* meanwhile, in the meantime **~tejer** *vt* weave; (*entrelazar*) interweave

entreten|ción *f* (*LAm*) entertainment. **~er** 40 *vt* entertain, amuse; (*detener*) delay, keep. **~erse** *vpr* amuse o.s.; (*tardar*) delay, linger. **~ido** *adj* (*con ser*) entertaining; (*con estar*) busy. **~imiento** *m* entertainment

entrever 43 *vt* make out, glimpse

entrevista *f* interview; (*reunión*) meeting. **~rse** *vpr* have an interview

entristecer 11 *vt* sadden, make sad. **~se** *vpr* grow sad

entromet|erse *vpr* interfere. **~ido** *adj* interfering

entumec|erse 11 *vpr* go numb. **~ido** *adj* numb

enturbiar *vt* cloud

entusi|asmar *vt* fill with enthusiasm; (*gustar mucho*) delight. **~asmarse** *vpr*. **~asmarse con** get enthusiastic about. **~asmo** *m* enthusiasm. **~asta** *adj* enthusiastic. • *m & f* enthusiast

enumerar *vt* enumerate

envalentonar *vt* encourage. **~se** *vpr* become bolder

envas|ado *m* packaging; (*en latas*) canning; (*en botellas*) bottling. **~ar** *vt* package; (*en latas*) tin, can; (*en botellas*) bottle. **~e** *m* packing; (*lata*) tin, can; (*botella*) bottle

envejec|er 11 *vt* make (look) older. • *vi* age, grow old. **~erse** *vpr* age, grow old

envenenar *vt* poison

envergadura *f* importance

envia|do *m* envoy; (*de la prensa*) correspondent. **~r** 20 *vt* send

enviciarse *vpr* become addicted (**con** to)

envidi|a *f* envy; (*celos*) jealousy. **~ar** *vt* envy, be envious of. **~oso** *adj* envious; (*celoso*) jealous. **tener ~a a** envy

envío *m* sending, dispatch; (*de*

mercancías) consignment; (*de dinero*) remittance. **~ contra reembolso** cash on delivery. **gastos** *mpl* **de ~** postage and packing (costs)
enviudar *vi* be widowed
env|oltura *f* wrapping. **~olver** **2** (*pp* **envuelto**) *vt* wrap; (*cubrir*) cover; (*rodear*) surround; (*fig, enredar*) involve. **~uelto** *adj* wrapped (up)
enyesar *vt* plaster; (*Med*) put in plaster
épica *f* epic
épico *adj* epic
epid|emia *f* epidemic. **~émico** *adj* epidemic
epil|epsia *f* epilepsy. **~éptico** *adj* epileptic
epílogo *m* epilogue
episodio *m* episode
epístola *f* epistle
epitafio *m* epitaph
época *f* age; (*período*) period. **hacer ~** make history, be epoch-making
equidad *f* equity
equilibr|ado *adj* (well-)balanced. **~ar** *vt* balance. **~io** *m* balance; (*de balanza*) equilibrium. **~ista** *m & f* tightrope walker
equinoccio *m* equinox
equipaje *m* luggage (*esp Brit*), baggage (*esp Amer*)
equipar *vt* equip; (*de ropa*) fit out
equiparar *vt* make equal; (*comparar*) compare
equipo *m* equipment; (*de personas*) team
equitación *f* riding
equivale|nte *adj* equivalent. **~r** **42** *vi* be equivalent; (*significar*) mean
equivoca|ción *f* mistake, error. **~do** *adj* wrong. **~rse** *vpr* make a mistake; (*estar en error*) be wrong, be mistaken. **~rse de** be wrong about. **~rse de número** dial the wrong number. **si no me equivoco** if I'm not mistaken
equívoco *adj* equivocal; (*sospechoso*) suspicious • *m* misunderstanding; (*error*) mistake
era *f* era. • *vb véase* **SER**
erario *m* treasury
erección *f* erection
eres *vb véase* **SER**
erguir **48** *vt* raise. **~se** *vpr* raise
erigir **14** *vt* erect. **~se** *vpr*. **~se en** set o.s. up as; (*llegar a ser*) become
eriza|do *adj* prickly. **~rse** **10** *vpr* stand on end; (*LAm*) (persona) get goose pimples
erizo *m* hedgehog; (*de mar*) sea urchin. **~ de mar** sea urchin
ermita *f* hermitage. **~ño** *m* hermit
erosi|ón *f* erosion. **~onar** *vt* erode
er|ótico *adj* erotic. **~otismo** *m* eroticism
err|ar **1** (*la* **i** *inicial pasa a ser* **y**) *vt* miss. • *vi* wander; (*equivocarse*) make a mistake, be wrong. **~ata** *f* misprint. **~óneo** *adj* erroneous, wrong. **~or** *m* error, mistake. **estar en un ~or** be wrong, be mistaken
eruct|ar *vi* belch. **~o** *m* belch
erudi|ción *f* learning, erudition. **~to** *adj* learned; (palabra) erudite
erupción *f* eruption; (*Med*) rash
es *vb véase* **SER**
esa *adj véase* **ESE**
ésa *pron véase* **ÉSE**
esbelto *adj* slender, slim
esboz|ar **10** *vt* sketch, outline. **~o**

e

m sketch, outline

escabeche *m* brine. **en ~** pickled

escabroso *adj* (terreno) rough; (asunto) difficult; (*atrevido*) crude

escabullirse 22 *vpr* slip away

escafandra *f* diving-suit

e

escala *f* scale; (*escalera de mano*) ladder; (*Aviac*) stopover. **hacer ~ en** stop at. **vuelo sin ~s** non-stop flight. **~da** *f* climbing; (*Pol*) escalation. **~r** *vt* climb; break into (una casa). ● *vi* climb, go climbing

escaldar *vt* scald

escalera *f* staircase, stairs; (*de mano*) ladder. **~ de caracol** spiral staircase. **~ de incendios** fire escape. **~ de tijera** step-ladder. **~ mecánica** escalator

escalfa|do *adj* poached. **~r** *vt* poach

escalinata *f* flight of steps

escalofrío *m* shiver. **tener ~s** be shivering

escalón *m* step, stair; (*de escala*) rung

escalope *m* escalope

escam|a *f* scale; (*de jabón, de la piel*) flake. **~oso** *adj* scaly; (piel) flaky

escamotear *vt* make disappear; (*robar*) steal, pinch

escampar *vi* stop raining

esc|andalizar 10 *vt* scandalize, shock. **~andalizarse** *vpr* be shocked. **~ándalo** *m* scandal; (*alboroto*) commotion, racket. **armar un ~** make a scene. **~andaloso** *adj* scandalous; (*alborotador*) noisy

escandinavo *adj* & *m* Scandinavian

escaño *m* bench; (*Pol*) seat

escapa|da *f* escape; (*visita*) flying visit. **~r** *vi* escape. **dejar ~r** let out **~rse** *vpr* escape; (líquido, gas) leak

escaparate *m* (shop) window

escap|atoria *f* (*fig*) way out. **~e** *m* (*de gas, de líquido*) leak; (*fuga*) escape; (*Auto*) exhaust

escarabajo *m* beetle

escaramuza *f* skirmish

escarbar *vt* scratch; pick (dientes, herida); (*fig, escudriñar*) pry (**en** into). **~se** *vpr* pick

escarcha *f* frost. **~do** *adj* (fruta) crystallized

escarlat|a *adj invar* scarlet. **~ina** *f* scarlet fever

escarm|entar 1 *vt* teach a lesson to. ● *vi* learn one's lesson. **~iento** *m* punishment; (*lección*) lesson

escarola *f* endive

escarpado *adj* steep

escas|ear *vi* be scarce. **~ez** *f* scarcity, shortage; (*pobreza*) poverty. **~o** *adj* scarce; (*poco*) little; (*muy justo*) barely. **~o de** short of

escatimar *vt* be sparing with

escayola *f* plaster

esc|ena *f* scene; (*escenario*) stage. **~enario** *m* stage; (*fig*) scene. **~énico** *adj* stage. **~enografía** *f* set design

esc|epticismo *m* scepticism. **~éptico** *adj* sceptical. ● *m* sceptic

esclarecer 11 *vt* (*fig*) throw light on, clarify

esclav|itud *f* slavery. **~izar** 10 *vt* enslave. **~o** *m* slave

esclusa *f* lock; (*de presa*) floodgate

escoba *f* broom

escocer 2 & 9 *vi* sting

escocés *adj* Scottish. ● *m* Scot

Escocia *f* Scotland

escog|er [14] *vt* choose. **~ido** *adj* chosen; (mercancía) choice; (clientela) select

escolar *adj* school. ● *m* schoolboy. ● *f* schoolgirl

escolta *f* escort

escombros *mpl* rubble

escond|er *vt* hide. **~erse** *vpr* hide. **~idas** *fpl* (*LAm*, *juego*) hide-and-seek. **a ~idas** secretly. **~ite** *m* hiding place; (*juego*) hide-and-seek. **~rijo** *m* hiding place

escopeta *f* shotgun

escoria *f* slag; (*fig*) dregs

escorpión *m* scorpion

Escorpión *m* Scorpio

escot|ado *adj* low-cut. **~e** *m* low neckline. **pagar a ~e** share the expenses

escozor *m* stinging

escri|bano *m* clerk. **~bir** (*pp* **escrito**) *vt/i* write. **~bir a máquina** type. **¿cómo se escribe...?** how do you spell...? **~birse** *vpr* write to each other. **~to** *adj* written. **por ~to** in writing. ● *m* document. **~tor** *m* writer. **~torio** *m* desk; (*oficina*) office; (*LAm*, *en una casa*) study. **~tura** *f* (hand)writing; (*Jurid*) deed

escr|úpulo *m* scruple. **~upuloso** *adj* scrupulous

escrut|ar *vt* scrutinize; count (votos). **~inio** *m* count

escuadr|a *f* (*instrumento*) square; (*Mil*) squad; (*Naut*) fleet. **~ón** *m* squadron

escuálido *adj* skinny

escuchar *vt* listen to; (*esp LAm*, *oír*) hear. ● *vi* listen

escudo *m* shield. **~ de armas** coat of arms

escudriñar *vt* examine

escuela *f* school. **~ normal** teachers' training college

escueto *adj* simple

escuincle *m* (*Mex fam*) kid [!]

escul|pir *vt* sculpture. **~tor** *m* sculptor. **~tora** *f* sculptress. **~tura** *f* sculpture

escupir *vt/i* spit

escurr|eplatos *m invar* plate rack. **~idizo** *adj* slippery. **~ir** *vt* drain; wring out (ropa). ● *vi* drain; (ropa) drip. **~irse** *vpr* slip

ese *adj* (*f* **esa**) that; (*mpl* **esos**, *fpl* **esas**) those

ése *pron* (*f* **ésa**) that one: (*mpl* **ésos**, *fpl* **ésas**) those; (*primero de dos*) the former

esencia *f* essence. **~l** *adj* essential. **lo ~l** the main thing

esf|era *f* sphere; (*de reloj*) face. **~érico** *adj* spherical

esf|orzarse [2] & [10] *vpr* make an effort. **~uerzo** *m* effort

esfumarse *vpr* fade away; (persona) vanish

esgrim|a *f* fencing. **~ir** *vt* brandish; (*fig*) use

esguince *m* sprain

eslabón *m* link

eslavo *adj* Slavic, Slavonic

eslogan *m* slogan

esmalt|ar *vt* enamel. **~e** *m* enamel. **~e de uñas** nail polish

esmerado *adj* careful; (persona) painstaking

esmeralda *f* emerald

esmer|arse *vpr* take care (**en** over).

esmero *m* care

esmoquin (*pl* **esmóquines**) *m* dinner jacket, tuxedo (*Amer*)

esnob *adj invar* snobbish. ● *m & f* (*pl* **~s**) snob. **~ismo** *m* snobbery

esnórkel *m* snorkel

eso *pron* that. **¡~ es!** that's it! **~ mismo** exactly. **a ~ de** about. **en ~** at that moment. **¿no es ~?** isn't that right? **por ~** that's why. **y ~ que** even though

esos *adj pl véase* **ESE**

e

ésos *pron pl véase* **ÉSE**

espabila|do *adj* bright; (*despierto*) awake. **~r** *vt* (*avivar*) brighten up; (*despertar*) wake up. **~rse** *vpr* wake up; (*avivarse*) wise up; (*apresurarse*) hurry up

espaci|al *adj* space. **~ar** *vt* space out. **~o** *m* space. **~oso** *adj* spacious

espada *f* sword. **~s** *fpl* (*en naipes*) spades

espaguetis *mpl* spaghetti

espald|a *f* back. **a ~as de uno** behind s.o.'s back. **volver la(s) ~a(s) a uno** give s.o. the cold shoulder. **~ mojada** wetback. **~illa** *f* shoulder-blade

espant|ajo *m*, **~apájaros** *m invar* scarecrow. **~ar** *vt* frighten; (*ahuyentar*) frighten away. **~arse** *vpr* be frightened; (*ahuyentarse*) be frightened away. **~o** *m* terror; (*horror*) horror. **¡qué ~o!** how awful! **~oso** *adj* horrific; (*terrible*) terrible

España *f* Spain

español *adj* Spanish. ● *m* (*persona*) Spaniard; (*lengua*) Spanish. **los ~es** the Spanish

esparadrapo *m* (sticking) plaster

esparcir **9** *vt* scatter; (*difundir*) spread. **~rse** *vpr* be scattered; (*difundirse*) spread; (*divertirse*) enjoy o.s.

espárrago *m* asparagus

espasm|o *m* spasm. **~ódico** *adj* spasmodic

espátula *f* spatula; (*en pintura*) palette knife

especia *f* spice

especial *adj* special. **en ~** especially. **~idad** *f* speciality (*Brit*), specialty (*Amer*). **~ista** *adj & m & f* specialist. **~ización** *f* specialization. **~izarse** **10** *vpr* specialize. **~mente** *adv* especially

especie *f* kind, sort; (*en biología*) species. **en ~** in kind

especifica|ción *f* specification. **~r** **7** *vt* specify

específico *adj* specific

espect|áculo *m* sight; (*de circo etc*) show. **~acular** *adj* spectacular. **~ador** *m & f* spectator

espectro *m* spectre; (*en física*) spectrum

especula|dor *m* speculator. **~r** *vi* speculate

espej|ismo *m* mirage. **~o** *m* mirror. **~o retrovisor** (*Auto*) rear-view mirror

espeluznante *adj* horrifying

espera *f* wait. **a la ~** waiting (**de** for). **~nza** *f* hope. **~r** *vt* hope; (*aguardar*) wait for; expect (vista, carta, bebé). **espero que no** I hope not. **espero que sí** I hope so. ● *vi* (*aguardar*) wait. **~rse** *vpr* hang on; (*prever*) expect

esperma *f* sperm

esperpento *m* fright

espes|ar *vt/i* thicken. **~arse** *vpr* thicken. **~o** *adj* thick. **~or** *m* thickness

espetón *m* spit

esp|ía *f* spy. **~iar** **20** *vt* spy on. ● *vi* spy

espiga *f* (*de trigo etc*) ear

espina *f* thorn; (*de pez*) bone; (*en anatomía*) spine. **~ dorsal** spine

espinaca *f* spinach

espinazo *m* spine
espinilla *f* shin; (*Med*) blackhead; (*LAm, grano*) spot
espino *m* hawthorn. **~so** *adj* thorny; (*fig*) difficult
espionaje *m* espionage
espiral *adj* & *f* spiral
esp|iritista *m* & *f* spiritualist. **~íritu** *m* spirit; (*mente*) mind. **~iritual** *adj* spiritual
espl|éndido *adj* splendid; (persona) generous. **~endor** *m* splendour
espolear *vt* spur (on)
espolvorear *vt* sprinkle
esponj|a *f* sponge. **~oso** *adj* spongy
espont|aneidad *f* spontaneity. **~áneo** *adj* spontaneous
esporádico *adj* sporadic
espos|a *f* wife. **~as** *fpl* handcuffs. **~ar** *vt* handcuff. **~o** *m* husband
espuela *f* spur; (*fig*) incentive
espum|a *f* foam; (*en bebidas*) froth; (*de jabón*) lather; (*de las olas*) surf. **echar ~a** foam, froth. **~oso** *adj* (vino) sparkling
esqueleto *m* skeleton; (*estructura*) framework
esquema *m* outline
esqu|í *m* (*pl* **~ís**, **~íes**) ski; (*deporte*) skiing. **~iar** 20 *vi* ski
esquilar *vt* shear
esquimal *adj* & *m* Eskimo
esquina *f* corner
esquiv|ar *vt* avoid; dodge (golpe). **~o** *adj* elusive
esquizofrénico *adj* & *m* schizophrenic
esta *adj* véase ESTE
ésta *pron* véase ÉSTE
estab|ilidad *f* stability. **~le** *adj* stable
establec|er 11 *vt* establish. **~erse** *vpr* settle; (*Com*) set up. **~imiento** *m* establishment
establo *m* cattleshed
estaca *f* stake
estación *f* station; (*del año*) season. **~ de invierno** winter (sports) resort. **~ de servicio** service station
estaciona|miento *m* parking; (*LAm, lugar*) car park (*Brit*), parking lot (*Amer*). **~r** *vt* station; (*Auto*) park. **~rio** *adj* stationary
estadía *f* (*LAm*) stay
estadio *m* stadium; (*fase*) stage
estadista *m* statesman. • *f* stateswoman
estadístic|a *f* statistics; (*cifra*) statistic. **~o** *adj* statistical
estado *m* state; (*Med*) condition. **~ civil** marital status. **~ de ánimo** frame of mind. **~ de cuenta** bank statement. **~ mayor** (*Mil*) staff. **en buen ~** in good condition
Estados Unidos *mpl* United States
estadounidense *adj* American, United States. • *m* & *f* American
estafa *f* swindle. **~r** *vt* swindle
estafeta *f* (*oficina de correos*) (sub-)post office
estala|ctita *f* stalactite. **~gmita** *f* stalagmite
estall|ar *vi* explode; (olas) break; (guerra etc) break out; (*fig*) burst. **~ar en llanto** burst into tears. **~ar de risa** burst out laughing. **~ido** *m* explosion; (*de guerra etc*) outbreak
estamp|a *f* print; (*aspecto*) appearance. **~ado** *adj* printed. • *m* printing; (*motivo*) pattern; (*tela*) cotton print. **~ar** *vt* stamp;

(*imprimir*) print
estampido *m* bang
estampilla *f* (*LAm*, *de correos*) (postage) stamp
estanca|do *adj* stagnant. **~r** 7 *vt* stem. **~rse** *vpr* stagnate
estancia *f* stay; (*cuarto*) large room
estanco *adj* watertight. ● *m* tobacconist's (shop)

> **estanco** In Spain, an establishment selling tobacco, stamps, bus and metro passes and other products whose sale is restricted. Cigarettes etc are sold in bars and cafés but at higher prices. *Estancos* also sell stationery and sometimes papers.

estandarte *m* standard, banner
estanque *m* pond; (*depósito de agua*) (water) tank
estanquero *m* tobacconist
estante *m* shelf. **~ría** *f* shelves; (*para libros*) bookcase
estaño *m* tin

estar 27
● *verbo intransitivo*
····➤ to be **¿cómo estás?** how are you?. **estoy enfermo** I'm ill. **está muy cerca** it's very near. **¿está Pedro?** is Pedro in? **¿cómo está el tiempo?** what's the weather like? **ya estamos en invierno** it's winter already
····➤ (*quedarse*) to stay. **sólo ~é una semana** I'll only be staying for a week. **estoy en un hotel** I'm staying in a hotel
····➤ (*con fecha*) **¿a cuánto estamos?** what's the date today? **estamos a 8 de mayo** it's the 8th of May.
····➤ (*en locuciones*) **¿estamos?** all right? **¡ahí está!** that's it! **~ por** (*apoyar a*) to support; (*LAm*, *encontrarse a punto de*) to be about to; (*quedar por*) **eso está por verse** that remains to be seen. **son cuentas que están por pagar** they're bills still to be paid
● *verbo auxiliar*
····➤ (*con gerundio*) **estaba estudiando** I was studying
····➤ (*con participio*) **está condenado a muerte** he's been sentenced to death. **está mal traducido** it's wrongly translated.
estarse *verbo pronominal* to stay. **no se está quieto** he won't stay still

➡ Cuando el verbo **estar** forma parte de expresiones como **estar de acuerdo**, **estar a la vista**, **estar constipado**, etc., ver bajo el respectivo nombre o adjetivo

estatal *adj* state
estático *adj* static
estatua *f* statue
estatura *f* height
estatuto *m* statute; (*norma*) rule
este *adj* (región) eastern; (viento, lado) east. ● *m* east. ● *adj* (*f* **esta**) this; (*mpl* **estos**, *fpl* **estas**) these. ● *int* (*LAm*) well, er
éste *pron* (*f* **ésta**) this one; (*mpl* **éstos**, *fpl* **éstas**) these; (*segundo de dos*) the latter
estela *f* wake; (*de avión*) trail; (*lápida*) carved stone
estera *f* mat; (*tejido*) matting

est|éreo *adj* stereo. **~ereofónico** *adj* stereo, stereophonic
estereotipo *m* stereotype
estéril *adj* sterile; (terreno) barren
esterilla *f* mat
esterlina *adj*. **libra** *f* **~** pound sterling
estético *adj* aesthetic
estiércol *m* dung; (*abono*) manure
estigma *m* stigma. **~s** *mpl* (*Relig*) stigmata
estil|arse *vpr* be used. **~o** *m* style; (*en natación*) stroke. **~ mariposa** butterfly. **~ pecho** (*LAm*) breaststroke. **por el ~o** of that sort
estilográfica *f* fountain pen
estima *f* esteem. **~do** *adj* (amigo, colega) valued. **~do señor** (*en cartas*) Dear Sir. **~r** *vt* esteem; have great respect for (persona); (*valorar*) value; (*juzgar*) consider
est|imulante *adj* stimulating. • *m* stimulant. **~imular** *vt* stimulate; (*incitar*) incite. **~ímulo** *m* stimulus
estir|ado *adj* stretched; (persona) haughty. **~ar** *vt* stretch; (*fig*) stretch out. **~ón** *m* pull, tug; (*crecimiento*) sudden growth
estirpe *m* stock
esto *pron neutro* this; (*este asunto*) this business. **en ~** at this point. **en ~ de** in this business of. **por ~** therefore
estofa|do *adj* stewed. • *m* stew. **~r** *vt* stew
estómago *m* stomach. **dolor** *m* **de ~** stomach ache
estorb|ar *vt* obstruct; (*molestar*) bother. • *vi* be in the way. **~o** *m* hindrance; (*molestia*) nuisance
estornud|ar *vi* sneeze. **~o** *m* sneeze
estos *adj mpl véase* ESTE
éstos *pron mpl véase* ÉSTE
estoy *vb véase* ESTAR
estrabismo *m* squint
estrado *m* stage; (*Mus*) bandstand
estrafalario *adj* eccentric; (ropa) outlandish
estrago *m* devastation. **hacer ~os** devastate
estragón *m* tarragon
estrambótico *adj* eccentric; (ropa) outlandish
estrangula|dor *m* strangler; (*Auto*) choke. **~r** *vt* strangle
estratagema *f* stratagem
estrat|ega *m & f* strategist. **~egia** *f* strategy. **~égico** *adj* strategic
estrato *m* stratum
estrech|ar *vt* make narrower; take in (vestido); embrace (persona). **~ar la mano a uno** shake hands with s.o. **~arse** *vpr* become narrower; (*abrazarse*) embrace. **~ez** *f* narrowness. **~eces** *fpl* financial difficulties. **~o** *adj* narrow; (vestido etc) tight; (*fig, íntimo*) close. **~o de miras** narrow-minded. • *m* strait(s)
estrella *f* star. **~ de mar** starfish. **~ado** *adj* starry
estrellar *vt* smash; crash (coche). **~se** *vpr* crash (**contra** into)
estremec|er [11] *vt* shake. **~erse** *vpr* shake; (*de emoción etc*) tremble (**de** with). **~imiento** *m* shaking
estren|ar *vt* wear for the first time (vestido etc); show for the first time (película). **~arse** *vpr* make one's début. **~o** *m* (*de película*) première; (*de obra de teatro*) first night; (*de persona*) debut
estreñi|do *adj* constipated. **~miento** *m* constipation

estrés *m* stress
estría *f* groove; (*de la piel*) stretch mark
estribillo *m* (*incl Mus*) refrain
estribo *m* stirrup; (*de coche*) step. **perder los ~s** lose one's temper
estribor *m* starboard
estricto *adj* strict
estridente *adj* strident, raucous
estrofa *f* stanza, verse
estropajo *m* scourer
estropear *vt* damage; (*plan*) spoil; ruin (ropa). **~se** *vpr* be damaged; (*averiarse*) break down; (ropa) get ruined; (fruta etc) go bad; (*fracasar*) fail
estructura *f* structure. **~l** *adj* structural
estruendo *m* roar; (*de mucha gente*) uproar
estrujar *vt* squeeze; wring (out) (ropa); (*fig*) drain
estuario *m* estuary
estuche *m* case
estudi|ante *m & f* student. **~antil** *adj* student. **~ar** *vt* study. **~o** *m* study; (*de artista*) studio. **~oso** *adj* studious
estufa *f* heater; (*Mex, cocina*) cooker
estupefac|iente *m* narcotic. **~to** *adj* astonished
estupendo *adj* marvellous; (persona) fantastic; **¡~!** that's great!
est|upidez *f* stupidity; (*acto*) stupid thing. **~úpido** *adj* stupid
estupor *m* amazement
estuve *vb véase* ESTAR
etapa *f* stage. **por ~s** in stages
etéreo *adj* ethereal
etern|idad *f* eternity. **~o** *adj* eternal
étic|a *f* ethics. **~o** *adj* ethical
etimología *f* etymology
etiqueta *f* ticket, tag; (*ceremonial*) etiquette. **de ~** formal
étnico *adj* ethnic
eucalipto *m* eucalyptus
eufemismo *m* euphemism
euforia *f* euphoria
euro *m* euro. **~escéptico** *adj & m* Eurosceptic
Europa *f* Europe
euro|peo *adj & m* European. **~zona** *f* eurozone
eutanasia *f* euthanasia
evacua|ción *f* evacuation. **~r** **21** *vt* evacuate
evadir *vt* avoid; evade (impuestos).. **~se** *vpr* escape
evalua|ción *f* evaluation. **~r** **21** *vt* assess; evaluate (datos)
evangeli|o *m* gospel. **~sta** *m & f* evangelist; (*Mex, escribiente*) scribe
evapora|ción *f* evaporation. **~rse** *vpr* evaporate; (*fig*) disappear
evasi|ón *f* evasion; (*fuga*) escape. **~vo** *adj* evasive
evento *m* event; (*caso*) case
eventual *adj* possible. **~idad** *f* eventuality
eviden|cia *f* evidence. **poner en ~cia a uno** show s.o. up. **~ciar** *vt* show. **~ciarse** *vpr* be obvious. **~te** *adj* obvious. **~temente** *adv* obviously
evitar *vt* avoid; (*ahorrar*) spare; (*prevenir*) prevent
evocar **7** *vt* evoke
evoluci|ón *f* evolution. **~onar** *vi* evolve; (*Mil*) manoeuvre
ex *prefijo* ex-, former
exacerbar *vt* exacerbate
exact|amente *adv* exactly. **~itud** *f* exactness. **~o** *adj* exact; (*preciso*) accurate; (*puntual*) punc-

tual. ¡~! exactly!

exagera|ción *f* exaggeration. **~do** *adj* exaggerated. **~r** *vt/i* exaggerate

exalta|do *adj* exalted; (*excitado*) (over)excited; (*fanático*) hot-headed. **~r** *vt* exalt. **~rse** *vpr* get excited

exam|en *m* exam, examination. **~inar** *vt* examine. **~inarse** *vpr* take an exam

exasperar *vt* exasperate. **~se** *vpr* get exasperated

excarcela|ción *f* release (from prison). **~r** *vt* release

excava|ción *f* excavation. **~dora** *f* digger. **~r** *vt* excavate

excede|ncia *f* leave of absence. **~nte** *adj & m* surplus. **~r** *vi* exceed. **~rse** *vpr* go too far

excelen|cia *f* excellence; (*tratamiento*) Excellency. **~te** *adj* excellent

exc|entricidad *f* eccentricity. **~éntrico** *adj & m* eccentric

excepci|ón *f* exception. **~onal** *adj* exceptional. **a ~ón de, con ~ón de** except (for)

except|o *prep* except (for). **~uar** **21** *vt* except

exces|ivo *adj* excessive. **~o** *m* excess. **~o de equipaje** excess luggage (*esp Brit*), excess baggage (*esp Amer*)

excita|ción *f* excitement. **~r** *vt* excite; (*incitar*) incite. **~rse** *vpr* get excited

exclama|ción *f* exclamation. **~r** *vi* exclaim

exclu|ir **17** *vt* exclude. **~sión** *f* exclusion. **~siva** *f* sole right; (*reportaje*) exclusive (story). **~sivo** *adj* exclusive

excomu|lgar **12** *vt* excommunicate. **~nión** *f* excommunication

excremento *m* excrement

excursi|ón *f* excursion, outing. **~onista** *m & f* day-tripper

excusa *f* excuse; (*disculpa*) apology. **presentar sus ~s** apologize. **~r** *vt* excuse

exento *adj* exempt; (*libre*) free

exhalar *vt* exhale, breath out; give off (olor etc)

exhaust|ivo *adj* exhaustive. **~o** *adj* exhausted

exhibi|ción *f* exhibition; (*demostración*) display. **~cionista** *m & f* exhibitionist. **~r** *vt* exhibit **~rse** *vpr* show o.s.; (*hacerse notar*) draw attention to o.s.

exhumar *vt* exhume; (*fig*) dig up

exig|encia *f* demand. **~ente** *adj* demanding. **~ir** **14** *vt* demand

exiguo *adj* meagre

exil|(i)ado *adj* exiled. ● *m* exile. **~(i)arse** *vpr* go into exile. **~io** *m* exile

exim|ente *m* reason for exemption; (*Jurid*) grounds for acquittal. **~ir** *vt* exempt

existencia *f* existence. **~s** *fpl* stock. **~lismo** *m* existentialism

exist|ente *adj* existing. **~ir** *vi* exist

éxito *m* success. **no tener ~** fail. **tener ~** be successful

exitoso *adj* successful

éxodo *m* exodus

exonerar *vt* exonerate

exorbitante *adj* exorbitant

exorci|smo *m* exorcism. **~zar** **10** *vt* exorcise

exótico *adj* exotic

expan|dir *vt* expand; (*fig*) spread. **~dirse** *vpr* expand. **~sión** *f* ex-

e

pansion. **~sivo** *adj* expansive

expatria|do *adj & m* expatriate. **~rse** *vpr* emigrate; (*exiliarse*) go into exile

expectativa *f* prospect; (*esperanza*) expectation. **estar a la ~** be waiting

expedi|ción *f* expedition; (*de documento*) issue; (*de mercancías*) dispatch. **~ente** *m* record, file; (*Jurid*) proceedings. **~r** 5 *vt* issue; (*enviar*) dispatch, send. **~to** *adj* clear; (*LAm, fácil*) easy

expeler *vt* expel

expend|edor *m* dealer. **~edor automático** vending machine. **~io** *m* (*LAm*) shop; (*venta*) sale

expensas *fpl* (*Jurid*) costs. **a ~ de** at the expense of. **a mis ~** at my expense

experiencia *f* experience

experiment|al *adj* experimental. **~ar** *vt* test, experiment with; (*sentir*) experience. **~o** *m* experiment

experto *adj & m* expert

expiar 20 *vt* atone for

expirar *vi* expire

explanada *f* levelled area; (*paseo*) esplanade

explayarse *vpr* speak at length; (*desahogarse*) unburden o.s. (**con** to)

explica|ción *f* explanation. **~r** 7 *vt* explain. **~rse** *vpr* understand; (*hacerse comprender*) explain o.s. **no me lo explico** I can't understand it

explícito *adj* explicit

explora|ción *f* exploration. **~dor** *m* explorer; (*muchacho*) boy scout. **~r** *vt* explore

explosi|ón *f* explosion; (*fig*) outburst. **~onar** *vt* blow up. **~vo** *adj & m* explosive

explota|ción *f* working; (*abuso*) exploitation. **~r** *vt* work (mina); farm (tierra); (*abusar*) exploit. • *vi* explode

expone|nte *m* exponent. **~r** 34 *vt* expose; display (mercancías); present (tema); set out (hechos); exhibit (cuadros etc); (*arriesgar*) risk. • *vi* exhibit. **~rse** *vpr.* **~se a que** run the risk of

exporta|ción *f* export. **~dor** *m* exporter. **~r** *vt* export

exposición *f* exposure; (*de cuadros etc*) exhibition; (*de hechos*) exposition

expres|ar *vt* express. **~arse** *vpr* express o.s. **~ión** *f* expression. **~ivo** *adj* expressive; (*cariñoso*) affectionate

expreso *adj* express. • *m* express; (*café*) expresso

exprimi|dor *m* squeezer. **~r** *vt* squeeze

expropiar *vt* expropriate

expuesto *adj* on display; (lugar etc) exposed; (*peligroso*) dangerous. **estar ~ a** be exposed to

expuls|ar *vt* expel; throw out (persona); send off (jugador). **~ión** *f* expulsion

exquisito *adj* exquisite; (*de sabor*) delicious

éxtasis *m invar* ecstasy

extend|er 1 *vt* spread (out); (*ampliar*) extend; issue (documento). **~erse** *vpr* spread; (paisaje etc) extend, stretch. **~ido** *adj* spread out; (*generalizado*) widespread; (brazos) outstretched

extens|amente *adv* widely; (*detalladamente*) in full. **~ión** *f* extension; (*área*) expanse; (*largo*) length.

~o *adj* extensive
extenuar 21 *vt* exhaust
exterior *adj* external, exterior; (*del extranjero*) foreign; (aspecto etc) outward. ● *m* outside, exterior; (*países extranjeros*) abroad
extermin|ación *f* extermination. **~ar** *vt* exterminate. **~io** *m* extermination
externo *adj* external; (signo etc) outward. ● *m* day pupil
extin|ción *f* extinction. **~guidor** *m* (*LAm*) fire extinguisher. **~guir** 13 *vt* extinguish. **~guirse** *vpr* die out; (fuego) go out. **~to** *adj* (raza etc) extinct. **~tor** *m* fire extinguisher
extirpar *vt* eradicate; remove (tumor)
extorsión *f* extortion
extra *adj invar* extra; (*de buena calidad*) good-quality; (huevos) large. **paga** *f* **~** bonus
extracto *m* extract
extradición *f* extradition
extraer 41 *vt* extract
extranjer|ía *f* (*Esp*) **la ley de ~** immigration law. **~o** *adj* foreign. ● *m* foreigner; (*países*) foreign countries. **del ~** from abroad. **en el ~**, **por el ~** abroad
extrañ|ar *vt* surprise; (*encontrar extraño*) find strange; (*LAm, echar de menos*) miss. **~arse** *vpr* be surprised (**de** at). **~eza** *f* strangeness; (*asombro*) surprise. **~o** *adj* strange. ● *m* stranger
extraoficial *adj* unofficial
extraordinario *adj* extraordinary
extrarradio *m* outlying districts
extraterrestre *adj* extraterrestrial. ● *m* alien
extravagan|cia *f* oddness, eccentricity. **~te** *adj* odd, eccentric
extrav|iado *adj* lost. **~iar** 20 *vt* lose. **~iarse** *vpr* get lost; (objetos) go missing. **~ío** *m* loss
extremar *vt* take extra (precauciones); tighten up (vigilancia). **~se** *vpr* make every effort
extremeño *adj* from Extremadura
extrem|idad *f* end. **~idades** *fpl* extremities. **~ista** *adj* & *m* & *f* extremist. **~o** *adj* extreme. ● *m* end; (*colmo*) extreme. **en ~o** extremely. **en último ~o** as a last resort
extrovertido *adj* & *m* extrovert
exuberan|cia *f* exuberance. **~te** *adj* exuberant
eyacular *vt/i* ejaculate

Ff

fa *m* F; (*solfa*) fah
fabada *f* bean and pork stew
fábrica *f* factory. **marca** *f* **de ~** trade mark
fabrica|ción *f* manufacture. **~ción en serie** mass production. **~nte** *m* & *f* manufacturer. **~r** 7 *vt* manufacture
fábula *f* fable; (*mentira*) fabrication
fabuloso *adj* fabulous
facci|ón *f* faction. **~ones** *fpl* (*de la cara*) features
faceta *f* facet
facha *f* (*fam, aspecto*) look. **~da** *f* façade
fácil *adj* easy; (*probable*) likely

facili|dad *f* ease; (*disposición*) aptitude. **~dades** *fpl* facilities. **~tar** *vt* facilitate; (*proporcionar*) provide
factible *adj* feasible
factor *m* factor
factura *f* bill, invoice. **~r** *vt* (*hacer la factura*) invoice; (*al embarcar*) check in
faculta|d *f* faculty; (*capacidad*) ability; (*poder*) power. **~tivo** *adj* optional
faena *f* job. **~s domésticas** housework
faisán *m* pheasant
faja *f* (*de tierra*) strip; (*corsé*) corset; (*Mil etc*) sash
fajo *m* bundle; (*de billetes*) wad
falda *f* skirt; (*de montaña*) side
falla *f* fault; (*defecto*) flaw. **~ humana** (*LAm*) human error. **~r** *vi* fail. **me falló** he let me down. **sin ~r** without fail. ● *vt* (*errar*) miss
fallec|er 11 *vi* die. **~ido** *m* deceased
fallido *adj* vain; (*fracasado*) unsuccessful
fallo *m* (*defecto*) fault; (*error*) mistake. **~ humano** human error; (*en certamen*) decision; (*Jurid*) ruling
falluca *f* (*Mex*) smuggled goods
fals|ear *vt* falsify, distort. **~ificación** *f* forgery. **~ificador** *m* forger. **~ificar** 7 *vt* forge. **~o** *adj* false; (*falsificado*) forged; (joya) fake
falt|a *f* lack; (*ausencia*) absence; (*escasez*) shortage; (*defecto*) fault, defect; (*culpa*) fault; (*error*) mistake; (*en fútbol etc*) foul; (*en tenis*) fault. **a ~a de** for lack of. **echar en ~a** miss. **hacer ~a** be necessary. **me hace ~a** I need. **sacar ~as** find fault. **~o** *adj* lacking (**de** in)

faltar *verbo intransitivo*

! cuando el verbo **faltar** va precedido del complemento indirecto **le** (o **les, nos** etc) el sujeto en español pasa a ser el objeto en inglés p.ej: **les falta experiencia** *they lack experience*

····▸ (*no estar*) to be missing **¿quién falta?** who's missing? **falta una de las chicas** one of the girls is missing. **al abrigo le faltan 3 botones** the coat has three buttons missing. **~ a algo** (*no asistir*) to be absent from sth; (*no acudir*) to miss sth
····▸ (*no haber suficiente*) **va a ~ leche** there won't be enough milk. **nos faltó tiempo** we didn't have enough time
····▸ (*no tener*) **le falta cariño** he lacks affection
····▸ (*hacer falta*) **le falta sal** it needs more salt. **¡es lo que nos faltaba!** that's all we needed!
····▸ (*quedar*) **¿te falta mucho?** are you going to be much longer? **falta poco para Navidad** it's not long until Christmas. **aún falta mucho** (*distancia*) there's a long way to go yet **¡no faltaba más!** of course!

fama *f* fame; (*reputación*) reputation
famélico *adj* starving
familia *f* family; (*hijos*) children. **~ numerosa** large family. **~r** *adj* familiar; (*de la familia*) family; (*sin ceremonia*) informal; (lenguaje) colloquial. ● *m & f* relative. **~ridad** *f* familiarity. **~rizarse** 10 *vpr* be-

come familiar (**con** with)
famoso *adj* famous
fanático *adj* fanatical. ● *m* fanatic
fanfarr|ón *adj* boastful. ● *m* braggart. **~onear** *vi* show off
fango *m* mud. **~so** *adj* muddy
fantasía *f* fantasy. **de ~** fancy; (joya) imitation
fantasma *m* ghost
fantástico *adj* fantastic
fardo *m* bundle
faringe *f* pharynx
farmac|eútico *m* chemist (*Brit*), pharmacist, druggist (*Amer*). **~ia** *f* (*ciencia*) pharmacy; (*tienda*) chemist's (shop) (*Brit*), pharmacy
faro *m* lighthouse; (*Aviac*) beacon; (*Auto*) headlight
farol *m* lantern; (*de la calle*) street lamp. **~a** *f* street lamp
farr|a *f* partying. **~ear** *vi* (*LAm*) go out partying
farsa *f* farce. **~nte** *m & f* fraud
fascículo *m* instalment
fascinar *vt* fascinate
fascis|mo *m* fascism
fase *f* phase
fastidi|ar *vt* annoy; (*estropear*) spoil. **~arse** *vpr* (máquina) break down; hurt (pierna); (*LAm, molestarse*) get annoyed. **¡para que te ~es!** so there!. **~o** *m* nuisance; (*aburrimiento*) boredom. **~oso** *adj* annoying
fatal *adj* fateful; (*mortal*) fatal; (*fam, pésimo*) terrible. **~idad** *f* fate; (*desgracia*) misfortune
fatig|a *f* fatigue. **~ar** **12** *vt* tire. **~arse** *vpr* get tired. **~oso** *adj* tiring
fauna *f* fauna
favor *m* favour. **a ~ de, en ~ de** in favour of. **haga el ~ de** would you be so kind as to, please. **por ~** please
favorec|er **11** *vt* favour; (vestido, peinado etc) suit. **~ido** *adj* favoured
favorito *adj & m* favourite
fax *m* fax
faxear *vt* fax
faz *f* face
fe *f* faith. **dar ~ de** certify. **de buena ~** in good faith
febrero *m* February
febril *adj* feverish
fecha *f* date. **a estas ~s** now; (*todavía*) still. **hasta la ~** so far. **poner la ~** date. **~r** *vt* date
fecund|ación *f* fertilization. **~ación artificial** artificial insemination. **~ar** *vt* fertilize. **~o** *adj* fertile; (*fig*) prolific
federa|ción *f* federation. **~l** *adj* federal
felici|dad *f* happiness. **~dades** *fpl* best wishes; (*congratulaciones*) congratulations. **~tación** *f* letter of congratulation. **¡~taciones!** (*LAm*) congratulations! **~tar** *vt* congratulate
feligrés *m* parishioner
feliz *adj* happy; (*afortunado*) lucky. **¡Felices Pascuas!** Happy Christmas! **¡F~ Año Nuevo!** Happy New Year!
felpudo *m* doormat
fem|enil *adj* (*Mex*) women's. **~enino** *adj* feminine; (equipo) women's; (*en biología*) female. ● *m* feminine. **~inista** *adj & m & f* feminist.
fen|omenal *adj* phenomenal. **~ómeno** *m* phenomenon; (*monstruo*) freak
feo *adj* ugly; (*desagradable*) nasty. ● *adv* (*LAm*) (*mal*) bad

feria *f* fair; (*verbena*) carnival; (*Mex, cambio*) small change. **~do** *m* (*LAm*) public holiday

ferment|ar *vt/i* ferment. **~o** *m* ferment

fero|cidad *f* ferocity. **~z** *adj* fierce

férreo *adj* iron; (disciplina) strict

f

ferreter|ía *f* hardware store, ironmonger's (*Brit*). **~o** *m* hardware dealer, ironmonger (*Brit*)

ferro|carril *m* railway (*Brit*), railroad (*Amer*). **~viario** *adj* rail. ● *m* railwayman (*Brit*), railroader (*Amer*)

fértil *adj* fertile

fertili|dad *f* fertility. **~zante** *m* fertilizer. **~zar** 10 *vt* fertilize

ferv|iente *adj* fervent. **~or** *m* fervour

festej|ar *vt* celebrate; entertain (persona). **~o** *m* celebration

festiv|al *m* festival. **~idad** *f* festivity. **~o** *adj* festive. ● *m* public holiday

fétido *adj* stinking

feto *m* foetus

fiable *adj* reliable

fiado *m*. **al ~** on credit. **~r** *m* (*Jurid*) guarantor

fiambre *m* cold meat. **~ría** *f* (*LAm*) delicatessen

fianza *f* (*dinero*) deposit; (*objeto*) surety. **bajo ~** on bail

fiar 20 *vt* (*vender*) sell on credit; (*confiar*) confide. ● *vi* give credit. **~se** *vpr*. **~se de** trust

fibra *f* fibre. **~ de vidrio** fibreglass

ficción *f* fiction

fich|a *f* token; (*tarjeta*) index card; (*en juegos*) counter. **~ar** *vt* open a file on. **estar ~ado** have a (police) record. **~ero** *m* card index; (*en informática*) file

fidedigno *adj* reliable

fidelidad *f* faithfulness

fideos *mpl* noodles

fiebre *f* fever. **~ aftosa** foot-and-mouth disease. **~ del heno** hay fever. **~ porcina** swine fever. **tener ~** have a temperature

fiel *adj* faithful; (memoria, relato etc) reliable. ● *m* believer

fieltro *m* felt

fier|a *f* wild animal. **~o** *adj* fierce

fierro *m* (*LAm*) metal bar; (*hierro*) iron

fiesta *f* party; (*día festivo*) holiday. **~s** *fpl* celebrations

> i
>
> **fiestas** A *fiesta* in Spain can be a day of local celebrations, a larger event for a town or city, or a national holiday to commemorate a saint's day or a historical event. Famous Spanish *fiestas* include The *Fallas* in Valencia, the *Sanfermines* in Pamplona, and the *Feria de Sevilla*. In Latin America *fiestas patrias* are a period of one or more days when each country celebrates its independence. There are usually military parades, firework displays, and cultural events typical of the country.

figura *f* figure; (*forma*) shape. **~r** *vi* appear; (*destacar*) show off. **~rse** *vpr* imagine. **¡figúrate!** just imagine!

fij|ación *f* fixing; (*obsesión*) fixation. **~ar** *vt* fix; establish (residencia). **~arse** *vpr* (*poner atención*) pay attention; (*percatarse*) notice. **¡fíjate!** just imagine! **~o** *adj* fixed; (*firme*) stable; (*permanente*) permanent. ● *adv*. **mirar ~o** stare

fila *f* line; (*de soldados etc*) file; (*en el teatro, cine etc*) row; (*cola*) queue. **ponerse en ~** line up

filántropo *m* philanthropist

filat|elia *f* stamp collecting, philately. **~élico** *adj* philatelic. • *m* stamp collector, philatelist

filete *m* fillet

filial *adj* filial. • *f* subsidiary

Filipinas *fpl.* **las (islas) ~** the Philippines

filipino *adj* Philippine, Filipino

filmar *vt* film; shoot (película)

filo *m* edge; (*de hoja*) cutting edge. **al ~ de las doce** at exactly twelve o'clock. **sacar ~ a** sharpen

filología *f* philology

filón *m* vein; (*fig*) gold-mine

fil|osofía *f* philosophy. **~ósofo** *m* philosopher

filtr|ar *vt* filter. **~arse** *vpr* filter; (dinero) disappear; (noticia) leak. **~o** *m* filter; (*bebida*) philtre. **~ solar** sunscreen

fin *m* end; (*objetivo*) aim. **~ de semana** weekend. **a ~ de** in order to. **a ~ de cuentas** at the end of the day. **a ~ de que** in order that. **a ~es de** at the end of. **al ~** finally. **al ~ y al cabo** after all. **dar ~ a** end. **en ~** in short. **por ~** finally. **sin ~** endless

final *adj* final. • *m* end. • *f* final. **~idad** *f* aim. **~ista** *m & f* finalist. **~izar** 10 *vt* finish. • *vi* end

financi|ación *f* financing; (*fondos*) funds; (*facilidades*) credit facilities. **~ar** *vt* finance. **~ero** *adj* financial. • *m* financier

finca *f* property; (*tierras*) estate; (*rural*) farm; (*de recreo*) country house

fingir 14 *vt* feign; (*simular*) simulate. • *vi* pretend. **~se** *vpr* pretend to be

finlandés *adj* Finnish. • *m* (*persona*) Finn; (*lengua*) Finnish

Finlandia *f* Finland

fino *adj* fine; (*delgado*) thin; (oído) acute; (*de modales*) refined; (*sutil*) subtle

firma *f* signature; (*acto*) signing; (*empresa*) firm

firmar *vt/i* sign

firme *adj* firm; (*estable*) stable, steady; (color) fast. • *m* (*pavimento*) (road) surface. • *adv* hard. **~za** *f* firmness

fisc|al *adj* fiscal, tax. • *m & f* public prosecutor. **~o** *m* treasury

fisg|ar 12 *vi* snoop (around). **~ón** *adj* nosy. • *m* snooper

físic|a *f* physics. **~o** *adj* physical. • *m* physique; (*persona*) physicist

fisonomista *m & f.* **ser buen ~** be good at remembering faces

fistol *m* (*Mex*) tiepin

flaco *adj* thin, skinny; (*débil*) weak

flagelo *m* scourge

flagrante *adj* flagrant. **en ~** red-handed

flama *f* (*Mex*) flame

flamante *adj* splendid; (*nuevo*) brand-new

flamear *vi* flame; (bandera etc) flap

flamenco *adj* flamenco; (*de Flandes*) Flemish. • *m* (*ave*) flamingo; (*música etc*) flamenco; (*idioma*) Flemish

i

flamenco Flamenco is performed in three forms: guitar, singing and dancing. Originally a gypsy art form, it also has Arabic and North African influences. Modern flamenco blends traditional forms with rock, jazz and salsa. In its pure form the music and lyrics are improvised, but tourists are more likely to see rehearsed performances.

flan *m* crème caramel
flaqueza *f* thinness; (*debilidad*) weakness
f
flauta *f* flute
flecha *f* arrow. **~zo** *m* love at first sight
fleco *m* fringe; (*Mex, en el pelo*) fringe (*Brit*), bangs (*Amer*)
flem|a *f* phlegm. **~ático** *adj* phlegmatic
flequillo *m* fringe (*Brit*), bangs (*Amer*)
fletar *vt* charter; (*LAm, transportar*) transport
flexible *adj* flexible
flirte|ar *vi* flirt. **~o** *m* flirting
floj|ear *vi* flag; (*holgazanear*) laze around. **~o** *adj* loose; (*poco fuerte*) weak; (*perezoso*) lazy
flor *f* flower. **la ~ y nata** the cream. **~a** *f* flora. **~ecer** 11 *vi* flower, bloom; (*fig*) flourish. **~eciente** *adj* (*fig*) flourishing. **~ero** *m* flower vase. **~ista** *m & f* florist
flot|a *f* fleet. **~ador** *m* float; (*de niño*) rubber band. **~ar** *vi* float. **~e. a ~e** afloat
fluctua|ción *f* fluctuation. **~r** 21 *vi* fluctuate
flu|idez *f* fluidity; (*fig*) fluency. **~ido** *adj* fluid; (*fig*) fluent. • *m* fluid. **~ir** 17 *vi* flow
fluoruro *m* fluoride
fluvial *adj* river
fobia *f* phobia
foca *f* seal
foco *m* focus; (*lámpara*) floodlight; (*LAm, de coche*) (head)light; (*Mex, bombilla*) light bulb
fogón *m* cooker; (*LAm, fogata*) bonfire
folio *m* sheet
folklórico *adj* folk
follaje *m* foliage
follet|ín *m* newspaper serial. **~o** *m* pamphlet
follón *m* I mess; (*alboroto*) row; (*problema*) trouble
fomentar *vt* promote; boost (ahorro); stir up (odio)
fonda *f* (*pensión*) boarding-house; (*LAm, restaurant*) cheap restaurant
fondo *m* bottom; (*de calle, pasillo*) end; (*de sala etc*) back; (*de escenario, pintura etc*) background. **~ de reptiles** slush fund. **~s** *mpl* funds, money. **a ~** thoroughly
fonétic|a *f* phonetics. **~o** *adj* phonetic
fontanero *m* plumber
footing /'futin/ *m* jogging
forastero *m* stranger
forcejear *vi* struggle
forense *adj* forensic. • *m & f* forensic scientist
forjar *vt* forge. **~se** *vpr* forge; build up (ilusiones)
forma *f* form; (*contorno*) shape; (*modo*) way; (*Mex, formulario*) form. **~s** *fpl* conventions. **de todas ~s** anyway. **estar en ~** be in good form. **~ción** *f* formation; (*educación*) training. **~l** *adj* formal; (*de fiar*) reliable; (*serio*) serious. **~lidad** *f* formality; (*fiabilidad*) reliability; (*seriedad*) seriousness. **~r** *vt* form; (*componer*) make up; (*enseñar*) train. **~rse** *vpr* form; (*desarrollarse*) develop; (*educarse*) to be educated. **~to** *m* format
formidable *adj* formidable; (*muy*

grande) enormous

fórmula *f* formula; (*sistema*) way. **~ de cortesía** polite expression

formular *vt* formulate; make (queja etc). **~io** *m* form

fornido *adj* well-built

forr|ar *vt* (*en el interior*) line; (*en el exterior*) cover. **~o** *m* lining; (*cubierta*) cover

fortale|cer **11** *vt* strengthen. **~za** *f* strength; (*Mil*) fortress; (*fuerza moral*) fortitude

fortuito *adj* fortuitous; (encuentro) chance

fortuna *f* fortune; (*suerte*) luck

forz|ar **2** & **10** *vt* force; strain (vista). **~osamente** *adv* necessarily. **~oso** *adj* necessary

fosa *f* ditch; (*tumba*) grave. **~s** *fpl* **nasales** nostrils

fósforo *m* phosphorus; (*cerilla*) match

fósil *adj* & *m* fossil

foso *m* ditch; (*en castillo*) moat; (*de teatro*) pit

foto *f* photo. **sacar ~s** take photos

fotocopia *f* photocopy. **~dora** *f* photocopier. **~r** *vt* photocopy

fotogénico *adj* photogenic

fot|ografía *f* photography; (*Foto*) photograph. **~ografiar** **20** *vt* photograph. **~ógrafo** *m* photographer

foul /faul/ *m* (*pl* **~s**) (*LAm*) foul

frac *m* (*pl* **~s** *o* **fraques**) tails

fracas|ar *vi* fail. **~o** *m* failure

fracción *f* fraction; (*Pol*) faction

fractura *f* fracture. **~r** *vt* fracture. **~rse** *vpr* fracture

fragan|cia *f* fragrance. **~te** *adj* fragrant

frágil *adj* fragile

fragmento *m* fragment; (*de canción etc*) extract

fragua *f* forge. **~r** **15** *vt* forge; (*fig*) concoct. ● *vi* set

fraile *m* friar; (*monje*) monk

frambuesa *f* raspberry

franc|és *adj* French. ● *m* (*persona*) Frenchman; (*lengua*) French. **~esa** *f* Frenchwoman

Francia *f* France

franco *adj* frank; (*evidente*) marked; (*Com*) free. ● *m* (*moneda*) franc

francotirador *m* sniper

franela *f* flannel

franja *f* border; (*banda*) stripe; (*de terreno*) strip

franque|ar *vt* clear; (*atravesar*) cross; pay the postage on (carta). **~o** *m* postage

franqueza *f* frankness

frasco *m* bottle; (*de mermelada etc*) jar

frase *f* phrase; (*oración*) sentence. **~ hecha** set phrase

fratern|al *adj* fraternal. **~idad** *f* fraternity

fraud|e *m* fraud. **~ulento** *adj* fraudulent

fray *m* brother, friar

frecuen|cia *f* frequency. **con ~cia** frequently. **~tar** *vt* frequent. **~te** *adj* frequent

frega|dero *m* sink. **~r** **1** & **12** *vt* scrub; wash (los platos); mop (el suelo); (*LAm, fam, molestar*) annoy

freír **51** (*pp* **frito**) *vt* fry. **~se** *vpr* fry; (persona) roast

frenar *vt* brake; (*fig*) check

frenético *adj* frenzied; (*furioso*) furious

freno *m* (*de caballería*) bit; (*Auto*)

brake; (*fig*) check

frente *m* front. **~ a** opposite. **~ a ~** face to face. **al ~** at the head; (*hacia delante*) forward. **chocar de ~** crash head on. **de ~ a** (*LAm*) facing. **hacer ~ a** face (cosa); stand up to (persona). ● *f* forehead. **arrugar la ~** frown

f

fresa *f* strawberry

fresc|o *adj* (*frío*) cool; (*reciente*) fresh; (*descarado*) cheeky. ● *m* fresh air; (*frescor*) coolness; (*mural*) fresco; (*persona*) impudent person. **al ~o** in the open air. **hacer ~o** be cool. **tomar el ~o** get some fresh air. **~or** *m* coolness. **~ura** *f* freshness; (*frío*) coolness; (*descaro*) cheek

frialdad *f* coldness; (*fig*) indifference

fricci|ón *f* rubbing; (*fig, Tec*) friction; (*masaje*) massage. **~onar** *vt* rub

frigidez *f* frigidity

frígido *adj* frigid

frigorífico *m* fridge, refrigerator

frijol *m* (*LAm*) bean. **~es refritos** (*Mex*) fried purée of beans

frío *adj & m* cold. **tomar ~** catch cold. **hacer ~** be cold. **tener ~** be cold

frito *adj* fried; (I, *harto*) fed up. **me tiene ~** I'm sick of him

fr|ivolidad *f* frivolity. **~ívolo** *adj* frivolous

fronter|a *f* border, frontier. **~izo** *adj* border; (país) bordering

frontón *m* pelota court; (*pared*) fronton

frotar *vt* rub; strike (cerilla)

fructífero *adj* fruitful

fruncir 9 *vt* gather (tela). **~ el ceño** frown

frustra|ción *f* frustration. **~r** *vt* frustrate. **~rse** *vpr* (*fracasar*) fail. **quedar ~do** be disappointed

frut|a *f* fruit. **~al** *adj* fruit. **~ería** *f* fruit shop. **~ero** *m* fruit seller; (*recipiente*) fruit bowl. **~icultura** *f* fruit-growing. **~o** *m* fruit

fucsia *f* fuchsia. ● *m* fuchsia

fuego *m* fire. **~s artificiales** fireworks. **a ~ lento** on a low heat. **tener ~** have a light

fuente *f* fountain; (*manantial*) spring; (*plato*) serving dish; (*fig*) source

fuera *adv* out; (*al exterior*) outside; (*en otra parte*) away; (*en el extranjero*) abroad. **~ de** outside; (*excepto*) except for, besides. **por ~** on the outside. ● *vb véase* **IR** *y* **SER**

fuerte *adj* strong; (color) bright; (sonido) loud; (dolor) severe; (*duro*) hard; (*grande*) large; (lluvia, nevada) heavy. ● *m* fort; (*fig*) strong point. ● *adv* hard; (*con hablar etc*) loudly; (llover) heavily; (*mucho*) a lot

fuerza *f* strength; (*poder*) power; (*en física*) force; (*Mil*) forces. **~ de voluntad** will-power. **a ~ de** by (dint of). **a la ~** by necessity. **por ~** by force; (*por necesidad*) by necessity. **tener ~s para** have the strength to

fuese *vb véase* **IR** *y* **SER**

fug|a *f* flight, escape; (*de gas etc*) leak; (*Mus*) fugue. **~arse** 12 *vpr* flee, escape. **~az** *adj* fleeting. **~itivo** *adj & m* fugitive

fui *vb véase* **IR**, **SER**

fulano *m* so-and-so. **~, mengano y zutano** every Tom, Dick and Harry

fulminar *vt* (*fig, con mirada*) look daggers at

fuma|dor *adj* smoking. • *m* smoker. **~r** *vt/i* smoke. **~r en pipa** smoke a pipe. **~rse** *vpr* smoke. **~rada** *f* puff of smoke

funci|ón *f* function; (*de un cargo etc*) duty; (*de teatro*) show, performance. **~onal** *adj* functional. **~onar** *vi* work, function. **no ~ona** out of order. **~onario** *m* civil servant

funda *f* cover. **~ de almohada** pillowcase

funda|ción *f* foundation. **~mental** *adj* fundamental. **~mentar** *vt* base (**en** on). **~mento** *m* foundation. **~r** *vt* found; (*fig*) base. **~rse** *vpr* be based

fundi|ción *f* melting; (*de metales*) smelting; (*taller*) foundry. **~r** *vt* melt; smelt (metales); cast (objeto); blend (colores); (*fusionar*) merge; (*Elec*) blow; (*LAm*) seize up (motor). **~rse** *vpr* melt; (*unirse*) merge

fúnebre *adj* funeral; (*sombrío*) gloomy

funeral *adj* funeral. • *m* funeral. **~es** *mpl* funeral

funicular *adj & m* funicular

furg|ón *m* van. **~oneta** *f* van

fur|ia *f* fury; (*violencia*) violence. **~ibundo** *adj* furious. **~ioso** *adj* furious. **~or** *m* fury

furtivo *adj* furtive. **cazador ~** poacher

furúnculo *m* boil

fusible *m* fuse

fusil *m* rifle. **~ar** *vt* shoot

fusión *f* melting; (*unión*) fusion; (*Com*) merger

fútbol *m*, (*Mex*) **futbol** *m* football

futbolista *m & f* footballer

futur|ista *adj* futuristic. • *m & f* futurist. **~o** *adj & m* future

Gg

gabardina *f* raincoat

gabinete *m* (*Pol*) cabinet; (*en museo etc*) room; (*de dentista, médico etc*) consulting room

gaceta *f* gazette

gafa *f* hook. **~s** *fpl* glasses, spectacles. **~s de sol** sunglasses

gaf|ar *vt* [I] bring bad luck to. **~e** *m* jinx

gaita *f* bagpipes

gajo *m* segment

gala *f* gala. **~s** *fpl* finery, best clothes. **estar de ~** be dressed up. **hacer ~ de** show off

galán *m* (*en el teatro*) (romantic) hero; (*enamorado*) lover

galante *adj* gallant. **~ar** *vt* court. **~ría** *f* gallantry

galápago *m* turtle

galardón *m* award

galaxia *f* galaxy

galera *f* galley

galer|ía *f* gallery. **~ía comercial** (shopping) arcade. **~ón** *m* (*Mex*) hall

Gales *m* Wales. **país de ~** Wales

gal|és *adj* Welsh. • *m* Welshman; (*lengua*) Welsh. **~esa** *f* Welshwoman

galgo *m* greyhound

Galicia *f* Galicia

galimatías *m invar* gibberish

gallard|ía *f* elegance. **~o** *adj* elegant

gallego *adj & m* Galician
galleta *f* biscuit (*Brit*), cookie (*Amer*)
gall|ina *f* hen, chicken; (*fig, fam*) coward. **~o** *m* cock
galón *m* gallon; (*cinta*) braid; (*Mil*) stripe
galop|ar *vi* gallop. **~e** *m* gallop
gama *f* scale; (*fig*) range

g

gamba *f* prawn (*Brit*), shrimp (*Amer*)
gamberro *m* hooligan
gamuza *f* (*piel*) chamois leather; (*de otro animal*) suede
gana *f* wish, desire; (*apetito*) appetite. **de buena ~** willingly. **de mala ~** reluctantly. **no me da la ~** I don't feel like it. **tener ~s de** (+ *infinitivo*) feel like (+ *gerundio*)
ganad|ería *f* cattle raising; (*ganado*) livestock. **~o** *m* livestock. **~o lanar** sheep. **~o porcino** pigs. **~o vacuno** cattle
gana|dor *adj* winning. • *m* winner. **~ncia** *f* gain; (*Com*) profit. **~r** *vt* earn; (*en concurso, juego etc*) win; (*alcanzar*) reach. • *vi* (*vencer*) win; (*mejorar*) improve. **~rle a uno** beat s.o. **~rse la vida** earn a living. **salir ~ndo** come out better off
ganch|illo *m* crochet. **hacer ~illo** crochet. **~o** *m* hook; (*LAm, colgador*) hanger. **tener ~o** be very attractive
ganga *f* bargain
ganso *m* goose
garabat|ear *vt/i* scribble. **~o** *m* scribble
garaje *m* garage
garant|e *m & f* guarantor. **~ía** *f* guarantee. **~izar** 10 *vt* guarantee
garapiña *f* (*Mex*) pineapple squash. **~do** *adj*. **almendras** *fpl* **~das** sugared almonds
garbanzo *m* chick-pea
garbo *m* poise; (*de escrito*) style. **~so** *adj* elegant
garganta *f* throat; (*valle*) gorge
gárgaras *fpl*. **hacer ~** gargle
garita *f* hut; (*de centinela*) sentry box
garra *f* (*de animal*) claw; (*de ave*) talon
garrafa *f* carafe
garrafal *adj* huge
garrapata *f* tick
garrapat|ear *vi* scribble. **~o** *m* scribble
garrote *m* club, cudgel; (*tormento*) garrotte
gar|úa *f* (*LAm*) drizzle. **~uar** *vi* 21 (*LAm*) drizzle
garza *f* heron
gas *m* gas. **con ~** fizzy. **sin ~** still
gasa *f* gauze
gaseosa *f* fizzy drink
gas|óleo *m* diesel. **~olina** *f* petrol (*Brit*), gasoline (*Amer*), gas (*Amer*). **~olinera** *f* petrol station (*Brit*), gas station (*Amer*)
gast|ado *adj* spent; (vestido etc) worn out. **~ador** *m* spendthrift. **~ar** *vt* spend; (*consumir*) use; (*malgastar*) waste; (*desgastar*) wear out; wear (vestido etc); crack (broma). **~arse** *vpr* wear out. **~o** *m* expense; (*acción de gastar*) spending
gastronomía *f* gastronomy
gat|a *f* cat. **a ~as** on all fours. **~ear** *vi* crawl
gatillo *m* trigger
gat|ito *m* kitten. **~o** *m* cat. **dar ~o por liebre** take s.o. in
gaucho *m* Gaucho

> **gaucho** A peasant of the pampas of Argentina, Uruguay and Brazil. Modern gauchos work as foremen on farms and ranches and take part in rodeos.Traditionally, a gaucho's outfit was characterized by its baggy trousers, leather chaps, and *chiripá*, a waist-high garment. They also used *boleadoras* for catching cattle.

gaveta *f* drawer
gaviota *f* seagull
gazpacho *m* gazpacho
gelatina *f* gelatine; (*jalea*) jelly
gema *f* gem
gemelo *m* twin. **~s** *mpl* (*anteojos*) binoculars; (*de camisa*) cuff-links
gemido *m* groan
Géminis *m* Gemini
gemir 5 *vi* moan; (animal) whine, howl
gen *m*, **gene** *m* gene
geneal|ogía *f* genealogy. **~ógico** *adj* genealogical. **árbol** *m* **~ógico** family tree
generaci|ón *f* generation. **~onal** *adj* generation
general *adj* general. **en ~** in general. **por lo ~** generally. ● *m* general. **~izar** 10 *vt/i* generalize. **~mente** *adv* generally
generar *vt* generate
género *m* type, sort; (*en biología*) genus; (*Gram*) gender; (*en literatura etc*) genre; (*producto*) product; (*tela*) material. **~s de punto** knitwear. **~ humano** mankind
generos|idad *f* generosity. **~o** *adj* generous
genétic|a *f* genetics. **~o** *adj* genetic
geni|al *adj* brilliant; (*divertido*) funny. **~o** *m* temper; (*carácter*) nature; (*talento, persona*) genius
genital *adj* genital. **~es** *mpl* genitals
genoma *m* genome
gente *f* people; (*nación*) nation; (*fam, familia*) family, folks; (*Mex, persona*) person. ● *adj* (*LAm*) respectable; (*amable*) kind
gentil *adj* charming. **~eza** *f* kindness. **tener la ~eza de** be kind enough to
gentío *m* crowd
genuflexión *f* genuflection
genuino *adj* genuine
ge|ografía *f* geography. **~ográfico** *adj* geographical.
ge|ología *f* geology. **~ólogo** *m* geologist
geom|etría *f* geometry. **~étrico** *adj* geometrical
geranio *m* geranium
geren|cia *f* management. **~ciar** *vt* (*LAm*) manage. **~te** *m & f* manager
germen *m* germ
germinar *vi* germinate
gestación *f* gestation
gesticula|ción *f* gesticulation. **~r** *vi* gesticulate
gesti|ón *f* step; (*administración*) management. **~onar** *vt* take steps to arrange; (*dirigir*) manage
gesto *m* expression; (*ademán*) gesture; (*mueca*) grimace
gibraltareño *adj & m* Gibraltarian
gigante *adj* gigantic. ● *m* giant. **~sco** *adj* gigantic
gimn|asia *f* gymnastics. **~asio** *m* gymnasium, gym I. **~asta** *m & f* gymnast. **~ástic** *adj* gymnastic
gimotear *vi* whine

g

ginebra *f* gin
ginec|ólogo *m* gynaecologist
gira *f* tour. **~r** *vt* spin; draw (cheque); transfer (dinero). ● *vi* rotate, go round; (en camino) turn
girasol *m* sunflower
gir|atorio *adj* revolving. **~o** *m* turn; (*Com*) draft; (*locución*) expression. **~o postal** money order
gitano *adj & m* gypsy

g

glacia|l *adj* icy. **~r** *m* glacier
glándula *f* gland
glasear *vt* glaze; (*Culin*) ice
glob|al *adj* global; (*fig*) overall. **~o** *m* globe; (*aerostato, juguete*) balloon
glóbulo *m* globule
gloria *f* glory; (*placer*) delight. **~rse** *vpr* boast (**de** about)
glorieta *f* square; (*Auto*) roundabout (*Brit*), (traffic) circle (*Amer*)
glorificar **7** *vt* glorify
glorioso *adj* glorious
glotón *adj* gluttonous. ● *m* glutton
gnomo /ˈnomo/ *m* gnome
gob|ernación *f* government. **Ministerio** *m* **de la G~ernación** Home Office (*Brit*), Department of the Interior (*Amer*). **~ernador** *adj* governing. ● *m* governor. **~ernante** *adj* governing. ● *m & f* leader. **~ernar** **1** *vt* govern. **~ierno** *m* government
goce *m* enjoyment
gol *m* goal
golf *m* golf
golfo *m* gulf; (*niño*) urchin; (*holgazán*) layabout
golondrina *f* swallow
golos|ina *f* titbit; (*dulce*) sweet. **~o** *adj* fond of sweets
golpe *m* blow; (*puñetazo*) punch; (*choque*) bump; (*de emoción*) shock; (*arg, atraco*) job **I**; (*en golf, en tenis, de remo*) stroke. **~ de estado** coup d'etat. **~ de fortuna** stroke of luck. **~ de vista** glance. **~ militar** military coup. **de ~** suddenly. **de un ~** in one go. **~ar** *vt* hit; (*dar varios golpes*) beat; (*con mucho ruido*) bang; (*con el puño*) punch. ● *vi* knock
goma *f* rubber; (*para pegar*) glue; (*banda*) rubber band; (*de borrar*) eraser. **~ de mascar** chewing gum. **~ espuma** foam rubber
googlear ® *vt/i* **I** to google
gord|a *f* (*Mex*) small thick tortilla. **~o** *adj* (persona) (*con ser*) fat; (*con estar*) have put on weight; (carne) fatty; (*grueso*) thick; (*grande*) large, big. ● *m* first prize. **~ura** *f* fatness; (*grasa*) fat
gorila *f* gorilla
gorje|ar *vi* chirp. **~o** *m* chirping
gorra *f* cap. **~ de baño** (*LAm*) bathing cap
gorrión *m* sparrow
gorro *m* cap; (*de niño*) bonnet. **~ de baño** bathing cap
got|a *f* drop; (*Med*) gout. **ni ~a** nothing. **~ear** *vi* drip. **~era** *f* leak
gozar **10** *vt* enjoy. ● *vi*. **~ de** enjoy
gozne *m* hinge
gozo *m* pleasure; (*alegría*) joy. **~so** *adj* delighted
graba|ción *f* recording. **~do** *m* engraving, print; (*en libro*) illustration. **~dora** *f* tape-recorder. **~r** *vt* engrave; record (discos etc)
graci|a *f* grace; (*favor*) favour; (*humor*) wit. **~as** *fpl* thanks. **¡~as!** thank you!, thanks! **dar las ~as** thank. **hacer ~a** amuse; (*gustar*) please. **¡muchas ~as!** thank you

very much! **tener ~a** be funny. **~oso** *adj* funny. • *m* fool, comic character

grad|a *f* step. **~as** *fpl* stand(s). **~ación** *f* gradation. **~o** *m* degree; (*en enseñanza*) year (*Brit*), grade (*Amer*). **de buen ~o** willingly

gradua|ción *f* graduation; (*de alcohol*) proof. **~do** *m* graduate. **~l** *adj* gradual. **~r** 21 *vt* graduate; (*regular*) adjust. **~rse** *vpr* graduate

gráfic|a *f* graph. **~o** *adj* graphic. • *m* graph

gram|ática *f* grammar. **~atical** *adj* grammatical

gramo *m* gram, gramme (*Brit*)

gran *adj véase* GRANDE

grana *f* (*color*) deep red

granada *f* pomegranate; (*Mil*) grenade

granate *m* (*color*) maroon

Gran Bretaña *f* Great Britain

grande *adj* (*delante de nombre en singular* **gran**) big, large; (*alto*) tall; (*fig*) great; (*LAm, de edad*) grown up. **~za** *f* greatness

grandioso *adj* magnificent

granel *m*. **a ~** in bulk; (*suelto*) loose; (*fig*) in abundance

granero *m* barn

granito *m* granite; (*grano*) small grain

graniz|ado *m* iced drink. **~ar** 10 *vi* hail. **~o** *m* hail

granj|a *f* farm. **~ero** *m* farmer

grano *m* grain; (*semilla*) seed; (*de café*) bean; (*Med*) spot. **~s** *mpl* cereals

granuja *m & f* rogue

grapa *f* staple. **~r** *vt* staple

gras|a *f* grease; (*Culin*) fat. **~iento** *adj* greasy

gratifica|ción *f* (*de sueldo*) bonus (*recompensa*) reward. **~r** 7 *vt* reward

grat|is *adv* free. **~itud** *f* gratitude. **~o** *adj* pleasant **~uito** *adj* free; (*fig*) uncalled for

grava|men *m* tax; (*carga*) burden; (*sobre inmueble*) encumbrance. **~r** *vt* tax; (*cargar*) burden

grave *adj* serious; (voz) deep; (sonido) low; (acento) grave. **~dad** *f* gravity

gravilla *f* gravel

gravitar *vi* gravitate; (*apoyarse*) rest (**sobre** on); (peligro) hang (**sobre** over)

gravoso *adj* costly

graznar *vi* (cuervo) caw; (pato) quack; honk (ganso)

Grecia *f* Greece

gremio *m* union

greña *f* mop of hair

gresca *f* rumpus; (*riña*) quarrel

griego *adj & m* Greek

grieta *f* crack

grifo *m* tap, faucet (*Amer*)

grilletes *mpl* shackles

grillo *m* cricket. **~s** *mpl* shackles

gringo *m* (*LAm*) foreigner; (*norteamericano*) Yankee [!]

gripe *f* flu

gris *adj* grey. • *m* grey; (*fam, policía*) policeman

grit|ar *vi* shout. **~ería** *f*, **~erío** *m* uproar. **~o** *m* shout; (*de dolor, sorpresa*) cry; (*chillido*) scream. **dar ~s** shout

grosella *f* redcurrant. **~ negra** blackcurrant

groser|ía *f* rudeness; (*ordinariez*) coarseness; (*comentario etc*) coarse remark; (*palabra*) swearword. **~o** *adj* coarse; (*descortés*) rude

grosor *m* thickness

g

grotesco *adj* grotesque
grúa *f* crane
grueso *adj* thick; (persona) fat, stout. ● *m* thickness; (*fig*) main body
grumo *m* lump
gruñi|do *m* grunt; (*de perro*) growl. **~r** 22 *vi* grunt; (perro) growl
grupa *f* hindquarters
g
grupo *m* group
gruta *f* grotto
guacamole *m* guacamole
guadaña *f* scythe
guaje *m* (*Mex*) gourd
guajolote *m* (*Mex*) turkey
guante *m* glove
guapo *adj* good-looking; (chica) pretty; (*elegante*) smart
guarda *m & f* guard; (*de parque etc*) keeper. **~barros** *m invar* mudguard. **~bosque** *m* gamekeeper. **~costas** *m invar* coastguard vessel. **~espaldas** *m invar* bodyguard. **~meta** *m* goalkeeper. **~r** *vt* keep; (*proteger*) protect; (*en un lugar*) put away; (*reservar*) save, keep. **~rse** *vpr*. **~rse de** (+ *infinitivo*) avoid (+ *gerundio*). **~rropa** *m* wardrobe; (*en local público*) cloakroom. **~vallas** *m invar* (*LAm*) goalkeeper
guardería *f* nursery
guardia *f* guard; (*policía*) policewoman; (*de médico*) shift. **G~ Civil** Civil Guard. **~ municipal** police. **estar de ~** be on duty. **estar en ~** be on one's guard. **montar la ~** mount guard. ● *m* policeman. **~ jurado** *m & f* security guard. **~ de tráfico** *m* traffic policeman. ● *f* traffic policewoman
guardián *m* guardian; (*de parque etc*) keeper; (*de edificio*) security guard
guar|ecer 11 *vt* (*albergar*) give shelter to. **~ecerse** *vpr* take shelter. **~ida** *f* den, lair; (*de personas*) hideout
guarn|ecer 11 *vt* (*adornar*) adorn; (*Culin*) garnish. **~ición** *m* adornment; (*de caballo*) harness; (*Culin*) garnish; (*Mil*) garrison; (*de piedra preciosa*) setting
guas|a *f* joke. **~ón** *adj* humorous. ● *m* joker
Guatemala *f* Guatemala
guatemalteco *adj & m* Guatemalan
guateque *m* party, bash
guayab|a *f* guava; (*dulce*) guava jelly. **~era** *f* lightweight jacket
gubernatura *f* (*Mex*) government
güero *adj* (*Mex*) fair
guerr|a *f* war; (*método*) warfare. **dar ~a** annoy. **~ero** *adj* warlike; (*belicoso*) fighting. ● *m* warrior. **~illa** *f* band of guerrillas. **~illero** *m* guerrilla
guía *m & f* guide. ● *f* guidebook; (*de teléfonos*) directory
guiar 20 *vt* guide; (*llevar*) lead; (*Auto*) drive. **~se** *vpr* be guided (**por** by)
guijarro *m* pebble
guillotina *f* guillotine
guind|a *f* morello cherry. **~illa** *f* chilli
guiñapo *m* rag; (*fig, persona*) wreck
guiñ|ar *vt/i* wink. **~o** *m* wink. **hacer ~os** wink
gui|ón *m* hyphen, dash; (*de película etc*) script. **~onista** *m & f* scriptwriter
guirnalda *f* garland
guisado *m* stew

guisante *m* pea. ~ **de olor** sweet pea

guis|ar *vt/i* cook. ~**o** *m* stew

guitarr|a *f* guitar. ~**ista** *m & f* guitarist

gula *f* gluttony

gusano *m* worm; (*larva de mosca*) maggot

gustar

● *verbo intransitivo*

! Cuando el verbo **gustar** va precedido del complemento indirecto **le** (o **les, nos** etc), el sujeto en español pasa a ser el objeto en inglés. **me gusta mucho la música** *I like music very much*. **le gustan los helados** *he likes ice cream*. **a Juan no le gusta** *Juan doesn't like it* (or *her* etc)

····➤ **gustar** + *infinitivo*. **les gusta ver televisión** they like watching television

····➤ **gustar que** + *subjuntivo*. **me** ~**ía que vinieras** I'd like you to come. **no le gusta que lo corrijan** he doesn't like being corrected. **¿te** ~**ía que te lo comprara?** would you like me to buy it for you?

····➤ **gustar de algo** to like sth. **gustan de las fiestas** they like parties

····➤ (*tener acogida*) to go down well. **ese tipo de cosas que siempre gusta** those sort of things always go down well. **el libro no gustó** the book didn't go down well

····➤ (*en frases de cortesía*) to wish. **como guste** as you wish. **cuando gustes** whenever you wish

● *verbo transitivo*

····➤ (*LAm, querer*) **¿gusta un café?** would you like a coffee? **¿gustan pasar?** would you like to come in? **gustarse** *verbo pronominal* to like each other

gusto *m* taste; (*placer*) pleasure. **a** ~ comfortable. **a mi** ~ to my liking. **buen** ~ good taste. **con mucho** ~ with pleasure. **dar** ~ please. **mucho** ~ pleased to meet you. ~**so** *adj* tasty; (*de buen grado*) willingly

gutural *adj* guttural

Hh

ha *vb véase* HABER

haba *f* broad bean

Habana *f* **La** ~ Havana

habano *m* (*puro*) Havana

haber *verbo auxiliar* 30 have. ● *v impersonal* (*presente s & pl* **hay**, *imperfecto s & pl* **había**, *pretérito s & pl* **hubo**). **hay una carta para ti** there's a letter for you. **hay 5 bancos en la plaza** there are 5 banks in the square. **hay que hacerlo** it must be done, you have to do it. **he aquí** here is, here are. **no hay de qué** don't mention it, not at all. **¿qué hay?** (*¿qué pasa?*) what's the matter?; (*¿qué tal?*) how are you?

habichuela *f* bean

hábil *adj* skilful; (*listo*) clever; (día) working; (*Jurid*) competent

habili|dad *f* skill; (*astucia*) cleverness; (*Jurid*) competence. **~tar** *vt* qualify

habita|ción *f* room; (*dormitorio*) bedroom; (*en biología*) habitat. **~ción de matrimonio**, **~ción doble** double room. **~ción individual**, **~ción sencilla** single room. **~do** *adj* inhabited. **~nte** *m* inhabitant. **~r** *vt* live in. ● *vi* live

hábito *m* habit

habitua|l *adj* usual, habitual; (cliente) regular. **~r** [21] *vt* accustom. **~rse** *vpr.* **~rse a** get used to

h

habla *f* speech; (*idioma*) language; (*dialecto*) dialect. **al ~** (*al teléfono*) speaking. **ponerse al ~ con** get in touch with. **~dor** *adj* talkative. ● *m* chatterbox. **~duría** *f* rumour. **~durías** *fpl* gossip. **~nte** *adj* speaking. ● *m & f* speaker. **~r** *vt* speak. ● *vi* speak, talk (**con** to); (*Mex, por teléfono*) call. **¡ni ~r!** out of the question! **se ~ español** Spanish spoken

hacend|ado *m* landowner; (*LAm*) farmer. **~oso** *adj* hard-working

hacer [31]

● *verbo transitivo*

····➤ to do. **¿qué haces?** what are you doing? **~ los deberes** to do one's homework. **no sé qué ~** I don't know what to do. **hazme un favor** can you do me a favour?

····➤ (*fabricar, preparar, producir*) to make. **me hizo un vestido** she made me a dress. **~ un café** to make a (cup of) coffee. **no hagas tanto ruido** don't make so much noise

····➤ (*construir*) to build (casa, puente)

····➤ **hacer que uno haga algo** to make s.o. do sth. **haz que se vaya** make him leave. **hizo que se equivocara** he made her go wrong

····➤ **hacer hacer algo** to have sth done. **hizo arreglar el techo** he had the roof repaired

➡ Cuando el verbo **hacer** se emplea en expresiones como **hacer una pregunta, hacer trampa** etc., ver bajo el respectivo nombre

● *verbo intransitivo*

····➤ (*actuar, obrar*) to do. **hiciste bien en llamar** you did the right thing to call **¿cómo haces para parecer tan joven?** what do you do to look so young?

····➤ (*fingir, simular*) **hacer como que** to pretend. **hizo como que no me conocía** he pretended not to know me. **haz como que estás dormido** pretend you're asleep

····➤ **hacer de** (*en teatro*) to play the part of; (*ejercer la función de*) to act as

····➤ (*LAm, sentar*) **tanta sal hace mal** so much salt is not good for you. **dormir le hizo bien** the sleep did him good. **el pepino me hace mal** cucumber doesn't agree with me

verbo impersonal

····➤ (*hablando del tiempo atmosférico*) to be. **hace sol** it's sunny. **hace 3 grados** it's 3 degrees

····➤ (*con expresiones temporales*) **hace una hora que espero** I've been waiting for an hour.

llegó hace 3 días he arrived 3 days ago. **hace mucho tiempo** a long time ago. **hasta hace poco** until recently

● **hacerse** *verbo pronominal*

····➤ (*para sí*) to make o.s. (falda, café)

····➤ (*hacer que otro haga*) **se hizo la permanente** she had her hair permed. **me hice una piscina** I had a pool built

····➤ (*convertirse en*) to become. **se hicieron amigos** they became friends

····➤ (*acostumbrarse*) **~se a algo** to get used to sth

····➤ (*fingirse*) to pretend. **~se el enfermo** to pretend to be ill

····➤ (*moverse*) to move. **hazte para atrás** move back

····➤ **hacerse de** (*LAm*) to make (amigo, dinero)

hacha *f* axe; (*antorcha*) torch

hacia *prep* towards; (*cerca de*) near; (*con tiempo*) at about. **~ abajo** downwards. **~ arriba** upwards. **~ atrás** backwards. **~ las dos** (at) about two o'clock

hacienda *f* country estate; (*en LAm*) ranch; **la ~ pública** the Treasury. **Ministerio** *m* **de H~** Ministry of Finance; (*en Gran Bretaña*) Exchequer; (*en Estados Unidos*) Treasury

hada *f* fairy. **el ~ madrina** the fairy godmother

hago *vb véase* HACER

Haití *m* Haiti

halag|ar 12 *vt* flatter. **~üeño** *adj* flattering; (*esperanzador*) promising

halcón *m* falcon

halla|r *vt* find; (*descubrir*) discover. **~rse** *vpr* be. **~zgo** *m* discovery

hamaca *f* hammock; (*asiento*) deck-chair

hambr|e *f* hunger; (*de muchos*) famine. **tener ~e** be hungry. **~iento** *adj* starving

hamburguesa *f* hamburger

harag|án *adj* lazy, idle. ● *m* layabout. **~anear** *vi* laze around

harap|iento *adj* in rags. **~o** *m* rag

harina *f* flour

hart|ar *vt* (*fastidiar*) annoy. **me estás ~ando** you're annoying me. **~arse** *vpr* (*llenarse*) gorge o.s. (**de** on); (*cansarse*) get fed up (**de** with). **~o** *adj* full; (*cansado*) tired; (*fastidiado*) fed up (**de** with). ● *adv* (*LAm*) (*muy*) very; (*mucho*) a lot

hasta *prep* as far as; (*en el tiempo*) until, till; (*Mex*) not until. ● *adv* even. **¡~ la vista!** goodbye!, see you! ! **¡~ luego!** see you later! **¡~ mañana!** see you tomorrow! **¡~ pronto!** see you soon!

hast|iar 20 *vt* (*cansar*) weary, tire; (*aburrir*) bore. **~iarse** *vpr* get fed up (**de** with). **~ío** *m* weariness; (*aburrimiento*) boredom

haya *f* beech (tree). ● *vb véase* HABER

hazaña *f* exploit

hazmerreír *m* laughing stock

he *vb véase* HABER

hebilla *f* buckle

hebra *f* thread; (*fibra*) fibre

hebreo *adj & m* Hebrew

hechi|cera *f* witch. **~cería** *f* witchcraft. **~cero** *m* wizard. **~zar** 10 *vt* cast a spell on; (*fig*) captivate. **~zo** *m* spell; (*fig*) charm

hech|o *pp de* **hacer**. ● *adj* (*manufacturado*) made; (*terminado*) done; (vestidos etc) ready-made; (*Culin*)

h

done. • *m* fact; (*acto*) deed; (*cuestión*) matter; (*suceso*) event. **de ~o** in fact. **~ura** *f* making; (*forma*) form; (*del cuerpo*) build; (*calidad de fabricación*) workmanship

hed|er 1 *vi* stink. **~iondez** *f* stench. **~iondo** *adj* stinking, smelly. **~or** *m* stench

hela|da *f* frost. **~dera** *f* (*LAm*) fridge, refrigerator. **~dería** *f* ice-cream shop. **~do** *adj* freezing; (*congelado*) frozen; (*LAm, bebida*) chilled. • *m* ice-cream. **~r** 1 *vt/i* freeze. **anoche heló** there was a frost last night. **~rse** *vpr* freeze

helecho *m* fern

hélice *f* propeller

helicóptero *m* helicopter

hembra *f* female; (*mujer*) woman

hemorr|agia *f* haemorrhage. **~oides** *fpl* haemorrhoids

hendidura *f* crack, split; (*en geología*) fissure

heno *m* hay

heráldica *f* heraldry

hered|ar *vt/i* inherit. **~era** *f* heiress. **~ero** *m* heir. **~itario** *adj* hereditary

herej|e *m* heretic. **~ía** *f* heresy

herencia *f* inheritance; (*fig*) heritage

heri|da *f* injury; (*con arma*) wound. **~do** *adj* injured; (*con arma*) wounded; (*fig*) hurt. • *m* injured person. **~r** 4 *vt* injure; (*con arma*) wound; (*fig*) hurt. **~rse** *vpr* hurt o.s.

herman|a *f* sister. **~a política** sister-in-law. **~astra** *f* stepsister. **~astro** *m* stepbrother. **~o** *m* brother. **~o político** brother-in-law. **~os** *mpl* brothers; (*chicos y chicas*) brothers and sisters. **~os gemelos** twins

hermético *adj* hermetic; (*fig*) watertight

hermos|o *adj* beautiful; (*espléndido*) splendid. **~ura** *f* beauty

héroe *m* hero

hero|ico *adj* heroic. **~ína** *f* heroine; (*droga*) heroin. **~ísmo** *m* heroism

herr|adura *f* horseshoe. **~amienta** *f* tool. **~ero** *m* blacksmith

herv|idero *m* (*fig*) hotbed; (*multitud*) throng. **~ir** 4 *vt/i* boil. **~or** *m* (*fig*) ardour. **romper el ~** come to the boil

hiberna|ción *f* hibernation. **~r** *vi* hibernate

híbrido *adj & m* hybrid

hice *vb véase* HACER

hidalgo *m* nobleman

hidrata|nte *adj* moisturizing. **~r** *vt* hydrate; (crema etc) moisturize

hidráulico *adj* hydraulic

hidr|oavión *m* seaplane. **~oeléctrico** *adj* hydroelectric. **~ofobia** *f* rabies. **~ófobo** *adj* rabid. **~ógeno** *m* hydrogen

hiedra *f* ivy

hielo *m* ice

hiena *f* hyena

hierba *f* grass; (*Culin, Med*) herb **mala ~** weed. **~buena** *f* mint.

hierro *m* iron

hígado *m* liver

higi|ene *f* hygiene. **~énico** *adj* hygienic

hig|o *m* fig. **~uera** *f* fig tree

hij|a *f* daughter. **~astra** *f* stepdaughter. **~astro** *m* stepson. **~o** *m* son. **~os** *mpl* sons; (*chicos y chicas*) children

hilar *vt* spin. **~ delgado** split hairs

hilera *f* row; (*Mil*) file

hilo *m* thread; (*Elec*) wire; (*de líquido*) trickle; (*lino*) linen

hilv|án *m* tacking. **~anar** *vt* tack; (*fig*) put together

himno *m* hymn. **~ nacional** anthem

hincapié *m*. **hacer ~ en** stress, insist on

hincar 7 *vt* drive (estaca) (**en** into). **~se** *vpr*. **~se de rodillas** kneel down

hincha *f* 1 grudge. ● *m* & *f* (*fam, aficionado*) fan

hincha|do *adj* inflated; (*Med*) swollen. **~r** *vt* inflate, blow up. **~rse** *vpr* swell up; (*fig, fam, comer mucho*) gorge o.s. **~zón** *f* swelling

hinojo *m* fennel

hiper|mercado *m* hypermarket. **~sensible** *adj* hypersensitive. **~tensión** *f* high blood pressure

hípic|a *f* horse racing. **~o** *adj* horse

hipn|osis *f* hypnosis. **~otismo** *m* hypnotism. **~otizar** 10 *vt* hypnotize

hipo *m* hiccup. **tener ~** have hiccups

hipo|alérgeno *adj* hypoallergenic. **~condríaco** *adj* & *m* hypochondriac

hip|ocresía *f* hypocrisy. **~ócrita** *adj* hypocritical. ● *m* & *f* hypocrite

hipódromo *m* racecourse

hipopótamo *m* hippopotamus

hipoteca *f* mortgage. **~r** 7 *vt* mortgage

hip|ótesis *f invar* hypothesis. **~otético** *adj* hypothetical

hiriente *adj* offensive, wounding

hirsuto *adj* (barba) bristly; (pelo) wiry

hispánico *adj* Hispanic

> **Hispanidad - Día de la**
> See ▷**Día de la Raza**

Hispanoamérica *f* Spanish America

hispano|americano *adj* Spanish American. **~hablante** *adj* Spanish-speaking

hist|eria *f* hysteria. **~érico** *adj* hysterical

hist|oria *f* history; (*relato*) story; (*excusa*) tale, excuse. **pasar a la ~oria** go down in history. **~oriador** *m* historian. **~órico** *adj* historical. **~orieta** *f* tale; (*con dibujos*) strip cartoon

hito *m* milestone

hizo *vb véase* **hacer**

hocico *m* snout

hockey /'(x)oki/ *m* hockey. **~ sobre hielo** ice hockey

hogar *m* home; (*chimenea*) hearth. **~eño** *adj* domestic; (persona) home-loving

hoguera *f* bonfire

hoja *f* leaf; (*de papel, metal etc*) sheet; (*de cuchillo, espada etc*) blade. **~ de afeitar** razor blade. **~lata** *f* tin

hojaldre *m* puff pastry

hojear *vt* leaf through

hola *int* hello!

Holanda *f* Holland

holand|és *adj* Dutch. ● *m* Dutchman; (*lengua*) Dutch. **~esa** *f* Dutchwoman. **los ~eses** the Dutch

holg|ado *adj* loose; (*fig*) comfortable. **~ar** 2 & 12 *vi*. **huelga decir que** needless to say. **~azán** *adj* lazy. ● *m* idler. **~ura** *f* looseness; (*fig*) comfort

hollín *m* soot

h

hombre *m* man; (*especie humana*) man(kind). ● *int* Good Heavens!; (*de duda*) well. **~ de negocios** businessman. **~ rana** frogman

hombr|era *f* shoulder pad. **~o** *m* shoulder

homenaje *m* homage, tribute. **rendir ~ a** pay tribute to

home|ópata *m* homoeopath. **~opatía** *f* homoeopathy. **~opático** *adj* homoeopathic

h

homicid|a *adj* murderous. ● *m & f* murderer. **~io** *m* murder

homosexual *adj & m & f* homosexual. **~idad** *f* homosexuality

hond|o *adj* deep. **~onada** *f* hollow

Honduras *f* Honduras

hondureño *adj & m* Honduran

honest|idad *f* honesty. **~o** *adj* honest

hongo *m* fungus; (*LAm, Culin*) mushroom; (*venenoso*) toadstool

hon|or *m* honour. **~orable** *adj* honourable. **~orario** *adj* honorary. **~orarios** *mpl* fees. **~ra** *f* honour; (*buena fama*) good name. **~radez** *f* honesty. **~rado** *adj* honest. **~rar** *vt* honour

hora *f* hour; (*momento puntual*) time; (*cita*) appointment. **~ pico**, **~ punta** rush hour. **~s** *fpl* **de trabajo** working hours. **~s** *fpl* **extraordinarias** overtime. **~s** *fpl* **libres** free time. **a estas ~s** now. **¿a qué ~?** (at) what time? **a última ~** at the last moment. **de última ~** last-minute. **en buena ~** at the right time. **media ~** half an hour. **pedir ~** to make an appointment. **¿qué ~ es?** what time is it?

horario *adj* hourly. ● *m* timetable. **~ de trabajo** working hours

horca *f* gallows

horcajadas *fpl*. **a ~** astride

horchata *f* tiger-nut milk

horizont|al *adj & f* horizontal. **~e** *m* horizon

horma *f* mould; (*para fabricar calzado*) last; (*para conservar su forma*) shoe-tree. **de ~ ancha** broad-fitting

hormiga *f* ant

hormigón *m* concrete

hormigue|ar *vi* tingle; (*bullir*) swarm. **me ~a la mano** I've got pins and needles in my hand. **~o** *m* tingling; (*fig*) anxiety

hormiguero *m* anthill; (*de gente*) swarm

hormona *f* hormone

horn|ada *f* batch. **~illa** *f* (*LAm*) burner. **~illo** *m* burner; (*cocina portátil*) portable electric cooker. **~o** *m* oven; (*para cerámica etc*) kiln; (*Tec*) furnace

horóscopo *m* horoscope

horquilla *f* pitchfork; (*para el pelo*) hairpin

horr|endo *adj* awful. **~ible** *adj* horrible. **~ipilante** *adj* terrifying. **~or** *m* horror; (*atrocidad*) atrocity. **¡qué ~or!** how awful!. **~orizar** **10** *vt* horrify. **~orizarse** *vpr* be horrified. **~oroso** *adj* horrifying

hort|aliza *f* vegetable. **~elano** *m* market gardener

hosco *adj* surly

hospeda|je *m* accommodation. **~r** *vt* put up. **~rse** *vpr* stay

hospital *m* hospital. **~ario** *adj* hospitable. **~idad** *f* hospitality

hostal *m* boarding-house

hostería *f* inn

hostia *f* (*Relig*) host

hostigar **12** *vt* whip; (*fig, molestar*) pester

hostil *adj* hostile. **~idad** *f* hostility
hotel *m* hotel. **~ero** *adj* hotel. • *m* hotelier
hoy *adv* today. **~ (en) día** nowadays. **~ por ~** at the present time. **de ~ en adelante** from now on
hoy|o *m* hole. **~uelo** *m* dimple
hoz *f* sickle
hube *vb véase* **HABER**
hucha *f* money box
hueco *adj* hollow; (palabras) empty; (voz) resonant; (persona) superficial. • *m* hollow; (*espacio*) space; (*vacío*) gap
huelg|a *f* strike. **~a de brazos caídos** sit-down strike. **~a de hambre** hunger strike. **declararse en ~a** come out on strike. **~uista** *m & f* striker
huella *f* footprint; (*de animal, vehículo etc*) track. **~ digital** fingerprint
huelo *vb véase* **OLER**
huérfano *adj* orphaned. • *m* orphan. **~ de** without
huert|a *f* market garden (*Brit*), truck farm (*Amer*); (*terreno de regadío*) irrigated plain. **~o** *m* vegetable garden; (*de árboles frutales*) orchard
hueso *m* bone; (*de fruta*) stone
huésped *m* guest; (*que paga*) lodger
huesudo *adj* bony
huev|a *f* roe. **~o** *m* egg. **~o duro** hard-boiled egg. **~o escalfado** poached egg. **~o estrellado, ~o frito** fried egg. **~o pasado por agua** boiled egg. **~os revueltos** scrambled eggs. **~o tibio** (*Mex*) boiled egg
hui|da *f* flight, escape. **~dizo** *adj* (*tímido*) shy; (*esquivo*) elusive
huipil *m* (*Mex*) traditional embroidered smock

> *i* **huipil** A traditional garment worn by Indian and mestizo women in Mexico and Central America. *Huipiles* are generally made of richly embroidered cotton. They are very wide and low-cut, and are either waist- or thigh-length.

huir *vi* 17 flee, run away; (*evitar*). **~ de** avoid. **me huye** he avoids me
huitlacoche *m* (*Mex*) edible black fungus
hule *m* oilcloth; (*Mex, goma*) rubber
human|idad *f* mankind; (*fig*) humanity. **~itario** *adj* humanitarian. **~o** *adj* human; (*benévolo*) humane
humareda *f* cloud of smoke
humed|ad *f* dampness; (*en meteorología*) humidity; (*gotitas de agua*) moisture. **~ecer** 11 *vt* moisten. **~ecerse** *vpr* become moist
húmedo *adj* damp; (clima) humid; (labios) moist; (*mojado*) wet
humi|ldad *f* humility. **~lde** *adj* humble. **~llación** *f* humiliation. **~llar** *vt* humiliate. **~llarse** *vpr* lower o.s.
humo *m* smoke; (*vapor*) steam; (*gas nocivo*) fumes. **~s** *mpl* airs
humor *m* mood, temper; (*gracia*) humour. **estar de mal ~** be in a bad mood. **~ista** *m & f* humorist. **~ístico** *adj* humorous
hundi|miento *m* sinking. **~r** *vt* sink; destroy (persona). **~rse** *vpr* sink; (edificio) collapse
húngaro *adj & m* Hungarian
Hungría *f* Hungary
huracán *m* hurricane

huraño *adj* unsociable
hurgar [12] *vi* rummage (**en** through). **~se** *vpr.* **~se la nariz** pick one's nose
hurra *int* hurray!
hurtadillas *fpl.* **a ~** stealthily
hurt|ar *vt* steal. **~o** *m* theft; (*cosa robada*) stolen object
husmear *vt* sniff out; (*fig*) pry into
huyo *vb véase* HUIR

Ii

iba *véase* IR
ibérico *adj* Iberian
iberoamericano *adj & m* Latin American
iceberg /iθ'ber/ *m* (*pl* **~s**) iceberg
ictericia *f* jaundice
ida *f* outward journey; (*partida*) departure. **de ~ y vuelta** (billete) return (*Brit*), round-trip (*Amer*); (viaje) round
idea *f* idea; (*opinión*) opinion. **cambiar de ~** change one's mind. **no tener la más remota ~, no tener la menor ~** not have the slightest idea, not have a clue [I]
ideal *adj & m* ideal. **~ista** *m & f* idealist. **~izar** [10] *vt* idealize
idear *vt* think up, conceive; (*inventar*) invent
ídem *pron & adv* the same
idéntico *adj* identical
identi|dad *f* identity. **~ficación** *f* identification. **~ficar** [7] *vt* identify. **~ficarse** *vpr* identify o.s. **~ficarse con** identify with
ideol|ogía *f* ideology. **~ógico** *adj* ideological
idílico *adj* idyllic
idilio *m* idyll
idiom|a *m* language. **~ático** *adj* idiomatic
idiosincrasia *f* idiosyncrasy
idiot|a *adj* idiotic. ● *m & f* idiot. **~ez** *f* stupidity
idolatrar *vt* worship; (*fig*) idolize
ídolo *m* idol
idóneo *adj* suitable (**para** for)
iglesia *f* church
iglú *m* igloo
ignora|ncia *f* ignorance. **~nte** *adj* ignorant. ● *m* ignoramus. **~r** *vt* not know, be unaware of; (*no hacer caso de*) ignore
igual *adj* equal; (*mismo*) the same; (*similar*) like; (*llano*) even; (*liso*) smooth. ● *adv* the same. ● *m* equal. **~ que** (the same) as. **al ~ que** the same as. **da ~, es ~** it doesn't matter. **sin ~** unequalled
igual|ar *vt* make equal; equal (éxito, récord); (*allanar*) level. **~arse** *vpr* be equal. **~dad** *f* equality. **~mente** *adv* equally; (*también*) also, likewise; (*respuesta de cortesía*) the same to you
ilegal *adj* illegal
ilegible *adj* illegible
ilegítimo *adj* illegitimate
ileso *adj* unhurt
ilícito *adj* illicit
ilimitado *adj* unlimited
ilógico *adj* illogical
ilumina|ción *f* illumination; (*alumbrado*) lighting. **~r** *vt* light (up). **~rse** *vpr* light up
ilusi|ón *f* illusion; (*sueño*) dream; (*alegría*) joy. **hacerse ~ones** build up one's hopes. **me hace ~ón** I'm

thrilled; I'm looking forward to (algo en el futuro). **~onado** *adj* excited. **~onar** *vt* give false hope. **~onarse** *vpr* have false hopes

ilusionis|mo *m* conjuring. **~ta** *m & f* conjurer

iluso *adj* naive. ● *m* dreamer. **~rio** *adj* illusory

ilustra|ción *f* learning; (*dibujo*) illustration. **~do** *adj* learned; (*con dibujos*) illustrated. **~r** *vt* explain; (*instruir*) instruct; (*añadir dibujos etc*) illustrate. **~rse** *vpr* acquire knowledge. **~tivo** *adj* illustrative

ilustre *adj* illustrious

imagen *f* image; (*TV etc*) picture

imagina|ble *adj* imaginable. **~ción** *f* imagination. **~r** *vt* imagine. **~rse** *vpr* imagine. **~rio** *m* imaginary. **~tivo** *adj* imaginative

imán *m* magnet

imbécil *adj* stupid. ● *m & f* idiot

imborrable *adj* indelible; (recuerdo etc) unforgettable

imita|ción *f* imitation. **~r** *vt* imitate

impacien|cia *f* impatience. **~tarse** *vpr* lose one's patience. **~te** *adj* impatient

impacto *m* impact; (*huella*) mark. **~ de bala** bullet hole

impar *adj* odd

imparcial *adj* impartial. **~idad** *f* impartiality

impartir *vt* impart, give

impasible *adj* impassive

impávido *adj* fearless; (*impasible*) impassive

impecable *adj* impeccable

impedi|do *adj* disabled. **~mento** *m* impediment. **~r** **5** *vt* prevent; (*obstruir*) hinder

impenetrable *adj* impenetrable

impensa|ble *adj* unthinkable. **~do** *adj* unexpected

impera|r *vi* prevail. **~tivo** *adj* imperative; (necesidad) urgent

imperceptible *adj* imperceptible

imperdible *m* safety pin

imperdonable *adj* unforgivable

imperfec|ción *f* imperfection. **~to** *adj* imperfect

imperi|al *adj* imperial. **~alismo** *m* imperialism. **~o** *m* empire; (*poder*) rule. **~oso** *adj* imperious

impermeable *adj* waterproof. ● *m* raincoat

impersonal *adj* impersonal

impertinen|cia *f* impertinence. **~te** *adj* impertinent

imperturbable *adj* imperturbable

ímpetu *m* impetus; (*impulso*) impulse; (*violencia*) force

impetuos|idad *f* impetuosity. **~o** *adj* impetuous

implacable *adj* implacable

implantar *vt* introduce

implementación *f* implementation

implica|ción *f* implication. **~r** **7** *vt* implicate; (*significar*) imply

implícito *adj* implicit

implorar *vt* implore

impon|ente *adj* imposing; **!** terrific. **~er** **34** *vt* impose; (*requerir*) demand; deposit (dinero). **~erse** *vpr* (*hacerse obedecer*) assert o.s.; (*hacerse respetar*) command respect; (*prevalecer*) prevail. **~ible** *adj* taxable

importa|ción *f* importation; (*artículo*) import. **~ciones** *fpl* imports. **~dor** *adj* importing. ● *m* importer

importa|ncia *f* importance.

~**nte** *adj* important; (*en cantidad*) considerable. ~**r** *vt* import; (*ascender a*) amount to. ● *vi* be important, matter. **¿le ~ría...?** would you mind...? **no ~** it doesn't matter

importe *m* price; (*total*) amount

importun|ar *vt* bother. ~**o** *adj* troublesome; (*inoportuno*) inopportune

imposib|ilidad *f* impossibility. ~**le** *adj* impossible. **hacer lo ~le para** do all one can to

imposición *f* imposition; (*impuesto*) tax

impostor *m* impostor

impoten|cia *f* impotence. ~**te** *adj* impotent

impracticable *adj* impracticable; (*intransitable*) unpassable

imprecis|ión *f* vagueness; (*error*) inaccuracy. ~**o** *adj* imprecise

impregnar *vt* impregnate; (*empapar*) soak

imprenta *f* printing; (*taller*) printing house, printer's

imprescindible *adj* indispensable, essential

impresi|ón *f* impression; (*acción de imprimir*) printing; (*tirada*) edition; (*huella*) imprint. ~**onable** *adj* impressionable. ~**onante** *adj* impressive; (*espantoso*) frightening. ~**onar** *vt* impress; (*negativamente*) shock; (*conmover*) move; (*Foto*) expose. ~**onarse** *vpr* be impressed; (*negativamente*) be shocked; (*conmover*) be moved

impresionis|mo *m* impressionism. ~**ta** *adj & m & f* impressionist

impreso *adj* printed. ● *m* form. ~**s** *mpl* printed matter. ~**ra** *f* printer

imprevis|ible *adj* unforeseeable. ~**to** *adj* unforeseen

imprimir (*pp* **impreso**) *vt* print (libro etc)

improbab|ilidad *f* improbability. ~**le** *adj* unlikely, improbable

improcedente *adj* inadmissible; (conducta) improper; (despido) unfair

improductivo *adj* unproductive

improperio *m* insult. ~**s** *mpl* abuse

impropio *adj* improper

improvis|ación *f* improvisation. ~**ado** *adj* improvised. ~**ar** *vt* improvise. ~**o** *adj*. **de ~o** unexpectedly

impruden|cia *f* imprudence. ~**te** *adj* imprudent

imp|udicia *f* indecency; (*desvergüenza*) shamelessness. ~**údico** *adj* indecent; (*desvergonzado*) shameless. ~**udor** *m* indecency; (*desvergüenza*) shamelessness

impuesto *adj* imposed. ● *m* tax. **~ a la renta** income tax. **~ sobre el valor agregado** (*LAm*), **~ sobre el valor añadido** VAT, value added tax

impuls|ar *vt* propel; drive (persona); boost (producción etc). ~**ividad** *f* impulsiveness. ~**ivo** *adj* impulsive. ~**o** *m* impulse

impun|e *adj* unpunished. ~**idad** *f* impunity

impur|eza *f* impurity. ~**o** *adj* impure

imputa|ción *f* charge. ~**r** *vt* attribute; (*acusar*) charge

inaccesible *adj* inaccessible

inaceptable *adj* unacceptable

inactiv|idad *f* inactivity. ~**o** *adj* inactive

inadaptado *adj* maladjusted

inadecuado *adj* inadequate; (*inapropiado*) unsuitable
inadmisible *adj* inadmissible; (*inaceptable*) unacceptable
inadvertido *adj* distracted. **pasar ~** go unnoticed
inagotable *adj* inexhaustible
inaguantable *adj* unbearable
inaltera|ble *adj* impassive; (color) fast; (convicción) unalterable. **~do** *adj* unchanged
inapreciable *adj* invaluable; (*imperceptible*) imperceptible
inapropiado *adj* inappropriate
inasequible *adj* out of reach
inaudito *adj* unprecedented
inaugura|ción *f* inauguration. **~l** *adj* inaugural. **~r** *vt* inaugurate
inca *adj & m & f* Inca. **~ico** *adj* Inca

Incas Founded in the twelfth century, the Andean empire of the Quechua-speaking Incas grew and extended from southern Colombia to Argentina and central Chile. Its capital was Cuzco. The Incas built an extensive road network and impressive buildings, including Machu Picchu. The empire collapsed in 1533 after defeat by the Spaniards led by Francisco Pizarro.

incalculable *adj* incalculable
incandescente *adj* incandescent
incansable *adj* tireless
incapa|cidad *f* incapacity; (*física*) disability. **~citado** *adj* disabled. **~citar** *vt* incapacitate. **~z** *adj* incapable
incauto *adj* unwary; (*fácil de engañar*) gullible
incendi|ar *vt* set fire to. **~arse** *vpr* catch fire. **~ario** *adj* incendiary. • *m* arsonist. **~o** *m* fire
incentivo *m* incentive
incertidumbre *f* uncertainty
incesante *adj* incessant
incest|o *m* incest. **~uoso** *adj* incestuous
inciden|cia *f* incidence; (*efecto*) impact; (*incidente*) incident. **~tal** *adj* incidental. **~te** *m* incident
incidir *vi* fall (**en** into); (*influir*) influence
incienso *m* incense
incierto *adj* uncertain
incinera|dor *m* incinerator. **~r** *vt* incinerate; cremate (cadáver)
incipiente *adj* incipient
incisi|ón *f* incision. **~vo** *adj* incisive. • *m* incisor
incitar *vt* incite
inclemen|cia *f* harshness. **~te** *adj* harsh
inclina|ción *f* slope; (*de la cabeza*) nod; (*fig*) inclination. **~r** *vt* tilt; (*inducir*) incline. **~rse** *vpr* lean; (*en saludo*) bow; (*tender*) be inclined (**a** to)
inclu|ido *adj* included; (precio) inclusive. **~ir** 17 *vt* include; (*en cartas*) enclose. **~sión** *f* inclusion. **~sive** *adv* inclusive. **hasta el lunes ~sive** up to and including Monday. **~so** *adv* even
incógnito *adj* unknown. **de ~** incognito
incoheren|cia *f* incoherence. **~te** *adj* incoherent
incoloro *adj* colourless
incomestible *adj*, **incomible** *adj* uneatable, inedible
incomodar *vt* inconvenience; (*causar vergüenza*) make feel uncomfortable. **~se** *vpr* feel uncom-

fortable; (*enojarse*) get angry
incómodo *adj* uncomfortable; (*inconveniente*) inconvenient
incomparable *adj* incomparable
incompatib|ilidad *f* incompatibility. **~le** *adj* incompatible
incompeten|cia *f* incompetence. **~te** *adj & m & f* incompetent
incompleto *adj* incomplete
incompren|dido *adj* misunderstood. **~sible** *adj* incomprehensible. **~sión** *f* incomprehension
incomunicado *adj* cut off; (preso) in solitary confinement
inconcebible *adj* inconceivable
inconcluso *adj* unfinished
incondicional *adj* unconditional
inconfundible *adj* unmistakable
incongruente *adj* incoherent; (*contradictorio*) inconsistent
inconmensurable *adj* immeasurable
inconscien|cia *f* unconsciousness; (*irreflexión*) recklessness. **~te** *adj* unconscious; (*irreflexivo*) reckless
inconsecuente *adj* inconsistent
inconsistente *adj* flimsy
inconsolable *adj* unconsolable
inconstan|cia *f* lack of perseverance. **~te** *adj* changeable; (persona) lacking in perseverance; (*voluble*) fickle
incontable *adj* countless
incontenible *adj* irrepressible
incontinen|cia *f* incontinence. **~te** *adj* incontinent
inconvenien|cia *f* inconvenience. **~te** *adj* inconvenient; (*inapropiado*) inappropriate; (*incorrecto*) improper. • *m* problem; (*desventaja*) drawback
incorpora|ción *f* incorporation. **~r** *vt* incorporate; (*Culin*) add. **~rse** *vpr* sit up; join (sociedad, regimiento etc)
incorrecto *adj* incorrect; (*descortés*) discourteous
incorregible *adj* incorrigible
incorruptible *adj* incorruptible
incrédulo *adj* sceptical; (mirada, gesto) incredulous
increíble *adj* incredible
increment|ar *vt* increase. **~o** *m* increase
incriminar *vt* incriminate
incrustar *vt* encrust
incuba|ción *f* incubation. **~dora** *f* incubator. **~r** *vt* incubate; (*fig*) hatch
incuestionable *adj* unquestionable
inculcar **7** *vt* inculcate
inculpar *vt* accuse
inculto *adj* uneducated
incumplimiento *m* nonfulfilment; (*de un contrato*) breach
incurable *adj* incurable
incurrir *vi.* **~ en** incur (gasto); fall into (error); commit (crimen)
incursión *f* raid
indagar **12** *vt* investigate
indebido *adj* unjust; (uso) improper
indecen|cia *f* indecency. **~te** *adj* indecent
indecible *adj* indescribable
indecis|ión *f* indecision. **~o** *adj* (*con ser*) indecisive; (*con estar*) undecided
indefenso *adj* defenceless
indefini|ble *adj* indefinable. **~do** *adj* indefinite; (*impreciso*) undefined
indemnizar **10** *vt* compensate
independ|encia *f* independ-

ence. **~iente** *adj* independent. **~izarse** 10 *vpr* become independent

indes|cifrable *adj* indecipherable. **~criptible** *adj* indescribable

indeseable *adj* undesirable

indestructible *adj* indestructible

indetermina|ble *adj* indeterminable. **~do** *adj* indeterminate; (tiempo) indefinite

India *f*. la ~ India

indica|ción *f* indication; (*señal*) signal. **~ciones** *fpl* directions. **~dor** *m* indicator; (*Tec*) gauge. **~r** 7 *vt* show, indicate; (*apuntar*) point at; (*hacer saber*) point out; (*aconsejar*) advise. **~tivo** *adj* indicative. • *m* indicative; (*al teléfono*) dialling code

índice *m* index; (*dedo*) index finger; (*catálogo*) catalogue; (*indicación*) indication; (*aguja*) pointer

indicio *m* indication, sign; (*vestigio*) trace

indiferen|cia *f* indifference. **~te** *adj* indifferent. **me es ~te** it's all the same to me

indígena *adj* indigenous. • *m & f* native

indigen|cia *f* poverty. **~te** *adj* needy

indigest|ión *f* indigestion. **~o** *adj* indigestible

indign|ación *f* indignation. **~ado** *adj* indignant. **~ar** *vt* make indignant. **~arse** *vpr* become indignant. **~o** *adj* unworthy; (*despreciable*) contemptible

indio *adj & m* Indian

indirect|a *f* hint. **~o** *adj* indirect

indisciplinado *adj* undisciplined

indiscre|ción *f* indiscretion. **~to** *adj* indiscreet

indiscutible *adj* unquestionable

indisoluble *adj* indissoluble

indispensable *adj* indispensable

indisp|oner 34 *vt* (*enemistar*) set against. **~onerse** *vpr* fall out; (*ponerse enfermo*) fall ill. **~osición** *f* indisposition. **~uesto** *adj* indisposed

individu|al *adj* individual; (cama) single. • *m* (*en tenis etc*) singles. **~alidad** *f* individuality. **~alista** *m & f* individualist. **~alizar** 10 *vt* individualize. **~o** *m* individual

indocumentado *m person without identity papers*; (*inmigrante*) illegal immigrant

índole *f* nature; (*clase*) type

indolen|cia *f* indolence. **~te** *adj* indolent

indoloro *adj* painless

indomable *adj* untameable

inducir 47 *vt* induce. **~ a error** be misleading

indudable *adj* undoubted

indulgen|cia *f* indulgence. **~te** *adj* indulgent

indult|ar *vt* pardon. **~o** *m* pardon

industria *f* industry. **~l** *adj* industrial. • *m & f* industrialist. **~lización** *f* industrialization. **~lizar** 10 *vt* industrialize

inédito *adj* unpublished; (*fig*) unknown

inefable *adj* indescribable

ineficaz *adj* ineffective; (*sistema etc*) inefficient

ineficiente *adj* inefficient

ineludible *adj* inescapable, unavoidable

inept|itud *f* ineptitude. **~o** *adj* inept

inequívoco *adj* unequivocal

inercia *f* inertia

inerte *adj* inert; (*sin vida*) lifeless

inesperado *adj* unexpected
inestable *adj* unstable
inestimable *adj* inestimable
inevitable *adj* inevitable
inexistente *adj* non-existent
inexorable *adj* inexorable
inexper|iencia *f* inexperience. **~to** *adj* inexperienced
inexplicable *adj* inexplicable
infalible *adj* infallible
infam|ar *vt* defame. **~atorio** *adj* defamatory. **~e** *adj* infamous; (*fig, fam, muy malo*) awful. **~ia** *f* infamy
infancia *f* infancy
infant|a *f* infanta, princess. **~e** *m* infante, prince. **~ería** *f* infantry. **~il** *adj* children's; (población) child; (actitud etc) childish, infantile
infarto *m* heart attack
infec|ción *f* infection. **~cioso** *adj* infectious. **~tar** *vt* infect. **~tarse** *vpr* become infected. **~to** *adj* infected; I disgusting
infeli|cidad *f* unhappiness. **~z** *adj* unhappy
inferior *adj* inferior. ● *m & f* inferior. **~idad** *f* inferiority
infernal *adj* infernal, hellish
infestar *vt* infest; (*fig*) inundate
infi|delidad *f* unfaithfulness. **~el** *adj* unfaithful
infierno *m* hell
infiltra|ción *f* infiltration. **~rse** *vpr* infiltrate
ínfimo *adj* lowest; (calidad) very poor
infini|dad *f* infinity. **~tivo** *m* infinitive. **~to** *adj* infinite. ● *m*. **el ~to** the infinite; (*en matemáticas*) infinity. **~dad de** countless
inflación *f* inflation
inflama|ble *adj* (in)flammable. **~ción** *f* inflammation. **~r** *vt* set on fire; (*fig, Med*) inflame. **~rse** *vpr* catch fire; (*Med*) become inflamed
inflar *vt* inflate; blow up (globo); (*fig, exagerar*) exaggerate
inflexi|ble *adj* inflexible. **~ón** *f* inflexion
influ|encia *f* influence (**en** on). **~ir** 17 *vt* influence. ● *vi*. **~ en** influence. **~jo** *m* influence. **~yente** *adj* influential
informa|ción *f* information; (*noticias*) news; (*en aeropuerto etc*) information desk; (*de teléfonos*) directory enquiries. **~dor** *m* informant
informal *adj* informal; (persona) unreliable
inform|ante *m & f* informant. **~ar** *vt/i* inform. **~arse** *vpr* find out. **~ática** *f* information technology, computing. **~ativo** *adj* informative; (programa) news. **~atizar** 10 *vt* computerize
informe *adj* shapeless. ● *m* report. **~s** *fpl* references, information
infracción *f* infringement. **~ de tráfico** traffic offence
infraestructura *f* infrastructure
infranqueable *adj* impassable; (*fig*) insuperable
infrarrojo *adj* infrared
infringir 14 *vt* infringe
infructuoso *adj* fruitless
ínfulas *fpl*. **darse ~** give o.s. airs. **tener ~ de** fancy o.s. as
infundado *adj* unfounded
infu|ndir *vt* instil. **~sión** *f* infusion
ingeni|ar *vt* invent. **~ársela**s **para** find a way to
ingenier|ía *f* engineering. **~o** *m* engineer

ingenio *m* ingenuity; (*agudeza*) wit; (*LAm, de azúcar*) refinery. **~so** *adj* ingenious

ingenu|idad *f* naivety. **~o** *adj* naive

Inglaterra *f* England

ingl|és *adj* English. ● *m* Englishman; (*lengua*) English. **~esa** *f* Englishwoman. **los ~eses** the English

ingrat|itud *f* ingratitude. **~o** *adj* ungrateful; (*desagradable*) thankless

ingrediente *m* ingredient

ingres|ar *vt* deposit. ● *vi*. **~ar en** come in, enter; join (sociedad). **~o** *m* entrance; (*de dinero*) deposit; (*en sociedad, hospital*) admission. **~os** *mpl* income

inh|ábil *adj* unskilful; (*no apto*) unfit. **~abilidad** *f* unskilfulness; (*para cargo*) ineligibility

inhabitable *adj* uninhabitable

inhala|dor *m* inhaler. **~r** *vt* inhale

inherente *adj* inherent

inhibi|ción *f* inhibition. **~r** *vt* inhibit

inhóspito *adj* inhospitable

inhumano *adj* inhuman

inici|ación *f* beginning. **~al** *adj* & *f* initial. **~ar** *vt* initiate; (*comenzar*) begin, start. **~ativa** *f* initiative. **~o** *m* beginning

inigualado *adj* unequalled

ininterrumpido *adj* uninterrupted

injert|ar *vt* graft. **~to** *m* graft

injuri|a *f* insult. **~ar** *vt* insult. **~oso** *adj* insulting

injust|icia *f* injustice. **~o** *adj* unjust, unfair

inmaculado *adj* immaculate

inmaduro *adj* unripe; (persona) immature

inmediaciones *fpl*. **las ~** the vicinity, the surrounding area

inmediat|amente *adv* immediately. **~o** *adj* immediate; (*contiguo*) next. **de ~o** immediately

inmejorable *adj* excellent

inmemorable *adj* immemorial

inmens|idad *f* immensity. **~o** *adj* immense

inmersión *f* immersion

inmigra|ción *f* immigration. **~nte** *adj* & *m* & *f* immigrant. **~r** *vt* immigrate

inminen|cia *f* imminence. **~te** *adj* imminent

inmiscuirse **17** *vpr* interfere

inmobiliario *adj* property

inmolar *vt* sacrifice

inmoral *adj* immoral. **~idad** *f* immorality

inmortal *adj* immortal. **~izar** **10** *vt* immortalize

inmóvil *adj* immobile

inmovilizador *m* immobilizer

inmueble *adj*. **bienes ~s** property

inmund|icia *f* filth. **~o** *adj* filthy

inmun|e *adj* immune. **~idad** *f* immunity. **~ización** *f* immunization. **~izar** **10** *vt* immunize

inmuta|ble *adj* unchangeable. **~rse** *vpr* be perturbed. **sin ~rse** unperturbed

innato *adj* innate

innecesario *adj* unnecessary

innegable *adj* undeniable

innova|ción *f* innovation. **~r** *vi* innovate. ● *vt* make innovations in

innumerable *adj* innumerable

inocen|cia *f* innocence. **~tada** *f* practical joke. **~te** *adj* innocent. **~tón** *adj* naïve

inocuo *adj* innocuous

i

inodoro *adj* odourless. • *m* toilet
inofensivo *adj* inoffensive
inolvidable *adj* unforgettable
inoperable *adj* inoperable
inoportuno *adj* untimely; (comentario) ill-timed
inoxidable *adj* stainless
inquiet|ar *vt* worry. **~arse** *vpr* get worried. **~o** *adj* worried; (*agitado*) restless. **~ud** *f* anxiety
inquilino *m* tenant
inquirir **4** *vt* enquire into, investigate

i

insaciable *adj* insatiable
insalubre *adj* unhealthy
insatisfecho *adj* unsatisfied; (*descontento*) dissatisfied
inscri|bir (*pp* **inscrito**) *vt* (*en registro*) register; (*en curso*) enrol; (*grabar*) inscribe. **~birse** *vpr* register. **~pción** *f* inscription; (*registro*) registration
insect|icida *m* insecticide. **~o** *m* insect
insegur|idad *f* insecurity. **~o** *adj* insecure; (ciudad) unsafe, dangerous
insemina|ción *f* insemination. **~r** *vt* inseminate
insensato *adj* foolish
insensible *adj* insensitive
inseparable *adj* inseparable
insertar *vt* insert
insidi|a *f* malice. **~oso** *adj* insidious
insigne *adj* famous
insignia *f* badge; (*bandera*) flag
insignificante *adj* insignificant
insinu|ación *f* insinuation. **~ante** *adj* insinuating. **~ar** **21** *vt* imply; insinuate (algo ofensivo). **~arse** *vpr*. **~ársele a** make a pass at
insípido *adj* insipid
insist|encia *f* insistence. **~ente** *adj* insistent. **~ir** *vi* insist; (*hacer hincapié*) stress
insolación *f* sunstroke
insolen|cia *f* rudeness, insolence. **~te** *adj* rude, insolent
insólito *adj* unusual
insolven|cia *f* insolvency. **~te** *adj & m & f* insolvent
insomn|e *adj* sleepless. • *m & f* insomniac. **~io** *m* insomnia
insondable *adj* unfathomable
insoportable *adj* unbearable
insospechado *adj* unexpected
insostenible *adj* untenable
inspec|ción *f* inspection. **~cionar** *vt* inspect. **~tor** *m* inspector
inspira|ción *f* inspiration. **~r** *vt* inspire. **~rse** *vpr* be inspired
instala|ción *f* installation. **~r** *vt* install. **~rse** *vpr* settle
instancia *f* request. **en última ~** as a last resort
instant|ánea *f* snapshot. **~áneo** *adj* instantaneous; (café etc) instant. **~e** *m* instant. **a cada ~e** constantly. **al ~e** immediately
instaura|ción *f* establishment. **~r** *vt* establish
instiga|ción *f* instigation. **~dor** *m* instigator. **~r** **12** *vt* instigate; (*incitar*) incite
instint|ivo *adj* instinctive. **~o** *m* instinct
institu|ción *f* institution. **~cional** *adj* institutional. **~ir** **17** *vt* establish. **~to** *m* institute; (*en enseñanza*) (secondary) school. **~triz** *f* governess
instru|cción *f* education; (*Mil*) training. **~cciones** *fpl* instruction. **~ctivo** *adj* instructive; (película

etc) educational. **~ctor** *m* instructor. **~ir** 17 *vt* instruct, teach; (*Mil*) train

instrument|ación *f* instrumentation. **~al** *adj* instrumental. **~o** *m* instrument; (*herramienta*) tool

insubordina|ción *f* insubordination. **~r** *vt* stir up. **~rse** *vpr* rebel

insuficien|cia *f* insufficiency; (*inadecuación*) inadequacy. **~te** *adj* insufficient

insufrible *adj* insufferable

insular *adj* insular

insulina *f* insulin

insulso *adj* tasteless; (*fig*) insipid

insult|ar *vt* insult. **~o** *m* insult

insuperable *adj* insuperable; (*inmejorable*) unbeatable

insurgente *adj* insurgent

insurrec|ción *f* insurrection. **~to** *adj* insurgent

intachable *adj* irreproachable

intacto *adj* intact

intangible *adj* intangible

integra|ción *f* integration. **~l** *adj* integral; (*completo*) complete; (*incorporado*) built-in; (pan) wholemeal (*Brit*), wholewheat (*Amer*). **~r** *vt* make up

integridad *f* integrity; (*entereza*) wholeness

íntegro *adj* complete; (*fig*) upright

intelect|o *m* intellect. **~ual** *adj & m* & f intellectual

inteligen|cia *f* intelligence. **~te** *adj* intelligent

inteligible *adj* intelligible

intemperie *f.* **a la ~** in the open

intempestivo *adj* untimely

intenci|ón *f* intention. **con doble ~ón** implying sth else. **~onado** *adj* deliberate. **bien ~onado** well-meaning. **mal ~onado** malicious. **~onal** *adj* intentional

intens|idad *f* intensity. **~ificar** 7 *vt* intensify. **~ivo** *adj* intensive. **~o** *adj* intense

intent|ar *vt* try. **~o** *m* attempt; (*Mex, propósito*) intention

inter|calar *vt* insert. **~cambio** *m* exchange. **~ceder** *vt* intercede

interceptar *vt* intercept

interdicto *m* ban

inter|és *m* interest; (*egoísmo*) self-interest. **~esado** *adj* interested; (*parcial*) biassed; (*egoísta*) selfish. **~esante** *adj* interesting. **~esar** *vt* interest; (*afectar*) concern. ● *vi* be of interest. **~esarse** *vpr* take an interest (**por** in)

interfaz *m & f* interface

interfer|encia *f* interference. **~ir** 4 *vi* interfere

interfono *m* intercom

interino *adj* temporary; (persona) acting. ● *m* stand-in

interior *adj* interior; (comercio etc) domestic. ● *m* inside. **Ministerio del I~** Interior Ministry

interjección *f* interjection

inter|locutor *m* speaker. **~mediario** *adj & m* intermediary. **~medio** *adj* intermediate. ● *m* interval

interminable *adj* interminable

intermitente *adj* intermittent. ● *m* indicator

internacional *adj* international

intern|ado *m* (*Escol*) boarding-school. **~ar** *vt* (*en manicomio*) commit; (*en hospital*) admit. **~arse** *vpr* penetrate

internauta *m & f* netsurfer

Internet *m* Internet

interno *adj* internal; (*en enseñanza*) boarding. ● *m* boarder

interponer 34 *vt* interpose. **~se** *vpr* intervene

int|erpretación *f* interpretation. **~erpretar** *vt* interpret; (*Mús etc*) play. **~érprete** *m* interpreter; (*Mus*) performer

interroga|ción *f* interrogation; (*signo*) question mark. **~r** 12 *vt* question. **~tivo** *adj* interrogative

interru|mpir *vt* interrupt; cut off (suministro); cut short (viaje etc); block (tráfico). **~pción** *f* interruption. **~ptor** *m* switch

inter|sección *f* intersection. **~urbano** *adj* inter-city; (llamada) long-distance

intervalo *m* interval; (*espacio*) space. **a ~s** at intervals

interven|ir 53 *vt* control; (*Med*) operate on. ● *vi* intervene; (*participar*) take part. **~tor** *m* inspector; (*Com*) auditor

intestino *m* intestine

intim|ar *vi* become friendly. **~idad** *f* intimacy

intimidar *vt* intimidate

íntimo *adj* intimate; (amigo) close. ● *m* close friend

intolera|ble *adj* intolerable. **~nte** *adj* intolerant

intoxicar 7 *vt* poison

intranquilo *adj* worried

intransigente *adj* intransigent

intransitable *adj* impassable

intransitivo *adj* intransitive

intratable *adj* impossible

intrépido *adj* intrepid

intriga *f* intrigue. **~nte** *adj* intriguing. **~r** 12 *vt* intrigue

intrincado *adj* intricate

intrínseco *adj* intrinsic

introduc|ción *f* introduction. **~ir** 47 *vt* introduce; (*meter*) insert. **~irse** *vpr* get into

intromisión *f* interference

introvertido *adj* introverted. ● *m* introvert

intruso *m* intruder

intui|ción *f* intuition. **~r** 17 *vt* sense. **~tivo** *adj* intuitive

inunda|ción *f* flooding. **~r** *vt* flood

inusitado *adj* unusual

in|útil *adj* useless; (*vano*) futile. **~utilidad** *f* uselessness

invadir *vt* invade

inv|alidez *f* invalidity; (*Med*) disability. **~álido** *adj & m* invalid

invariable *adj* invariable

invas|ión *f* invasion. **~or** *adj* invading. ● *m* invader

invencible *adj* invincible

inven|ción *f* invention. **~tar** *vt* invent

inventario *m* inventory

invent|iva *f* inventiveness. **~ivo** *adj* inventive. **~or** *m* inventor

invernadero *m* greenhouse

invernal *adj* winter

inverosímil *adj* implausible

inver|sión *f* inversion; (*Com*) investment. **~sionista** *m & f* investor

inverso *adj* inverse; (*contrario*) opposite. **a la inversa** the other way round. **a la inversa de** contrary to

inversor *m* investor

invertir 4 *vt* reverse; (*Com*) invest; put in (tiempo)

investidura *f* investiture

investiga|ción *f* investigation; (*Univ*) research. **~dor** *m* investigator; (*Univ*) researcher. **~r** 12 *vt* investigate; (*Univ*) research

investir 5 *vt* invest

invicto *adj* unbeaten

invierno *m* winter
inviolable *adj* inviolate
invisible *adj* invisible
invita|ción *f* invitation. **~do** *m* guest. **~r** *vt* invite. **te invito a una copa** I'll buy you a drink
invocar 7 *vt* invoke
involuntario *adj* involuntary
invulnerable *adj* invulnerable
inyec|ción *f* injection. **~tar** *vt* inject

ir 49

● *verbo intransitivo*

····➤ to go. **fui a verla** I went to see her. **ir a pie** to go on foot. **ir en coche** to go by car. **vamos a casa** let's go home. **fue (a) por el pan** he went to get some bread

! Cuando la acción del verbo **ir** significa trasladarse hacia o con el interlocutor la traducción es *to come*, p.ej: **¡ya voy!** *I'm coming!* **yo voy contigo** *I'll come with you*

····➤ (*estar*) to be. **iba con su novio** she was with her boyfriend. **¿cómo te va?** how are you?

····➤ (*sentar*) to suit. **ese color no le va** that colour doesn't suit her. **no me va ni me viene** I don't mind at all

····➤ (*Méx, apoyar*) **irle a** to support. **le va al equipo local** he supports the local team

····➤ (*en exclamaciones*) **¡vamos!** come on! **¡vaya!** what a surprise!; (*contrariedad*) oh, dear! **¡vaya noche!** what a night! **¡qué va!** nonsense!

➡ Cuando el verbo intransitivo se emplea con expresiones como **ir de paseo, ir de compras, ir tirando** etc., ver bajo el respectivo nombre, verbo etc.

● *verbo auxiliar*

····➤ **ir a** + *infinitivo* (*para expresar futuro, propósito*) to be going to + *infinitive;* (*al prevenir*) **no te vayas a caer** be careful you don't fall. **no vaya a ser que llueva** in case it rains; (*en sugerencias*) **vamos a dormir** let's go to sleep. **vamos a ver** let's see

····➤ **ir** + *gerundio.* **ve arreglándote** start getting ready. **el tiempo va mejorando** the weather is gradually getting better.

● **irse** *verbo pronominal*

····➤ to go. **se ha ido a casa** he's gone home

····➤ (*marcharse*) to leave. **se fue sin despedirse** he left without saying goodbye. **se fue de casa** she left home

ira *f* anger. **~cundo** *adj* irascible
Irak *m* Iraq
Irán *m* Iran
iraní *adj & m & f* Iranian
iraquí *adj & m & f* Iraqi
iris *m* (*del ojo*) iris
Irlanda *f* Ireland
irland|és *adj* Irish. ● *m* Irishman; (*lengua*) Irish. **~esa** *f* Irishwoman. **los ~eses** the Irish
ir|onía *f* irony. **~ónico** *adj* ironic
irracional *adj* irrational

i

irradiar *vt* radiate
irreal *adj* unreal. **~idad** *f* unreality
irrealizable *adj* unattainable
irreconciliable *adj* irreconcilable
irreconocible *adj* unrecognizable
irrecuperable *adj* irretrievable
irreflexión *f* impetuosity
irregular *adj* irregular. **~idad** *f* irregularity
irreparable *adj* irreparable
irreprimible *adj* irrepressible
irreprochable *adj* irreproachable
irresistible *adj* irresistible
irrespetuoso *adj* disrespectful
irresponsable *adj* irresponsible
irriga|ción *f* irrigation. **~r** 12 *vt* irrigate
irrisorio *adj* derisory
irrita|ble *adj* irritable. **~ción** *f* irritation. **~r** *vt* irritate. **~rse** *vpr* get annoyed
irrumpir *vi* burst (**en** in)
isla *f* island. **las I~s Británicas** the British Isles
islámico *adj* Islamic
islandés *adj* Icelandic. • *m* Icelander; (*lengua*) Icelandic
Islandia *f* Iceland
isleño *adj* island. • *m* islander
Israel *m* Israel
israelí *adj & m* Israeli
Italia *f* Italy
italiano *adj & m* Italian
itinerario *adj* itinerary
IVA *abrev* (**impuesto sobre el valor agregado** (*LAm*), **impuesto sobre el valor añadido**) VAT
izar 10 *vt* hoist
izquierd|a *f*. **la ~a** the left hand; (*Pol*) left. **a la ~a** on the left; (*con movimiento*) to the left. **de ~a** left-wing. **~ista** *m & f* leftist. **~o** *adj* left

Jj

ja *int* ha!
jabalí *m* (*pl* **~es**) wild boar
jabalina *f* javelin
jab|ón *m* soap. **~onar** *vt* soap. **~onoso** *adj* soapy
jaca *f* pony
jacinto *m* hyacinth
jactarse *vpr* boast
jadea|nte *adj* panting. **~r** *vi* pant
jaguar *m* jaguar
jaiba *f* (*LAm*) crab
jalar *vt* (*LAm*) pull
jalea *f* jelly
jaleo *m* row, uproar. **armar un ~** kick up a fuss
jalón *m* (*LAm, tirón*) pull; (*Mex fam, trago*) drink; (*Mex, tramo*) stretch
jamás *adv* never. **nunca ~** never ever
jamelgo *m* nag
jamón *m* ham. **~ de York** boiled ham. **~ serrano** cured ham
Japón *m*. **el ~** Japan
japonés *adj & m* Japanese
jaque *m* check. **~ mate** checkmate
jaqueca *f* migraine
jarabe *m* syrup
jardín *m* garden. **~ de la infancia**, (*Mex*) **~ de niños** kindergarten, nursery school
jardiner|ía *f* gardening. **~o** *m* gardener

jarr|a *f* jug. **en ~as** with hands on hips. **~o** *m* jug. **caer como un ~o de agua fría** come as a shock. **~ón** *m* vase

jaula *f* cage

jauría *f* pack of hounds

jazmín *m* jasmine

jef|a *f* boss. **~atura** *f* leadership; (*sede*) headquarters. **~e** *m* boss; (*Pol etc*) leader. **~e de camareros** head waiter. **~e de estación** station-master. **~e de ventas** sales manager

jengibre *m* ginger

jer|arquía *f* hierarchy. **~árquico** *adj* hierarchical

jerez *m* sherry. **al ~** with sherry

> **jerez** Sherry is produced in an area around Jerez de la Frontera near Cádiz. Sherries are drunk worldwide as an aperitif, and in Spain as an accompaniment to tapas. The main types are: the pale *fino* and *manzanilla* and the darker *oloroso* and *amontillado*. It is from *Jerez* that sherry takes its English name.

jerga *f* coarse cloth; (*argot*) jargon

jerigonza *f* jargon; (*galimatías*) gibberish

jeringa *f* syringe; (*LAm fam, molestia*) nuisance. **~r** [12] *vt* (*fig, fam, molestar*) annoy

jeroglífico *m* hieroglyph(ic)

jersey *m* (*pl* **~s**) jersey

Jesucristo *m* Jesus Christ. **antes de ~** BC, before Christ

jesuita *adj* & *m* Jesuit

Jesús *m* Jesus. • *int* good heavens!; (*al estornudar*) bless you!

jícara *f* (*Mex*) gourd

jilguero *m* goldfinch

jinete *m* & *f* rider

jipijapa *m* panama hat

jirafa *f* giraffe

jirón *m* shred, tatter

jitomate *m* (*Mex*) tomato

jorna|da *f* working day; (*viaje*) journey; (*etapa*) stage. **~l** *m* day's wage. **~lero** *m* day labourer

joroba *f* hump. **~do** *adj* hunchbacked. • *m* hunchback. **~r** *vt* [!] annoy

jota *f* letter J; (*danza*) jota, popular dance. **ni ~** nothing

joven (*pl* **jóvenes**) *adj* young. • *m* young man. • *f* young woman

jovial *adj* jovial

joy|a *f* jewel. **~as** *fpl* jewellery. **~ería** *f* jeweller's (shop). **~ero** *m* jeweller; (*estuche*) jewellery box

juanete *m* bunion

jubil|ación *f* retirement. **~ado** *adj* retired. **~ar** *vt* pension off. **~arse** *vpr* retire. **~eo** *m* jubilee

júbilo *m* joy

judaísmo *m* Judaism

judía *f* Jewish woman; (*alubia*) bean. **~ blanca** haricot bean. **~ escarlata** runner bean. **~ verde** French bean

judicial *adj* judicial

judío *adj* Jewish. • *m* Jewish man

judo *m* judo

juego *m* play; (*de mesa, niños*) game; (*de azar*) gambling; (*conjunto*) set. **estar en ~** be at stake. **estar fuera de ~** be offside. **hacer ~** match. **~s** *mpl* **malabares** juggling. **J~s** *mpl* **Olímpicos** Olympic Games. • *vb véase* **JUGAR**

juerga *f* spree

jueves *m invar* Thursday

juez *m* judge. **~ de instrucción** examining magistrate. **~ de línea**

J

linesman

juga|dor *m* player; (*habitual, por dinero*) gambler. **~r** 3 *vt* play. • *vi* play; (*apostar fuerte*) gamble. **~rse** *vpr* risk. **~r al fútbol**, (*LAm*) **~r fútbol** play football

juglar *m* minstrel

jugo *m* juice; (*de carne*) gravy; (*fig*) substance. **~so** *adj* juicy; (*fig*) substantial

juguet|e *m* toy. **~ear** *vi* play. **~ón** *adj* playful

juicio *m* judgement; (*opinión*) opinion; (*razón*) reason. **a mi ~** in my opinion. **~so** *adj* wise

juliana *f* vegetable soup

julio *m* July

junco *m* rush, reed

jungla *f* jungle

junio *m* June

junt|a *f* meeting; (*consejo*) board, committee; (*Pol*) junta; (*Tec*) joint. **~ar** *vt* join; (*reunir*) collect. **~arse** *vpr* join; (gente) meet. **~o** *adj* joined; (*en plural*) together. **~o a** next to. **~ura** *f* joint

jura|do *adj* sworn. • *m* jury; (*miembro de jurado*) juror. **~mento** *m* oath. **prestar ~mento** take an oath. **~r** *vt/i* swear. **~r en falso** commit perjury. **jurárselas a uno** have it in for s.o.

jurel *m* (type of) mackerel

jurídico *adj* legal

juris|dicción *f* jurisdiction. **~prudencia** *f* jurisprudence

justamente *adj* exactly; (*con justicia*) fairly

justicia *f* justice

justifica|ción *f* justification. **~r** 7 *vt* justify

justo *adj* fair, just; (*exacto*) exact; (*ropa*) tight. • *adv* just. **~ a tiempo** just in time

juven|il *adj* youthful. **~tud** *f* youth; (*gente joven*) young people

juzga|do *m* (*tribunal*) court. **~r** 12 *vt* judge. **a ~r por** judging by

Kk

kilo *m*, **kilogramo** *m* kilo, kilogram

kil|ometraje *m* distance in kilometres, mileage. **~ométrico** *adj* I endless. **~ómetro** *m* kilometre. **~ómetro cuadrado** square kilometre

kilovatio *m* kilowatt

kiosco *m* kiosk

Ll

la *artículo definido femenino* (*pl* **las**)

- the. **la flor azul** the blue flower. **la casa de al lado** the house next door. **cerca de la iglesia** near the church *No se traduce en los siguientes casos:*
- (*con nombre abstracto, genérico*) **la paciencia es una virtud** patience is a virtue. **odio la leche** I hate milk. **la madera es muy versátil** wood is very versatile
- (*con algunas instituciones*)

termino la universidad mañana I finish university tomorrow. **no va nunca a la iglesia** he never goes to church. **está en la cárcel** he's in jail

····➤ (*con nombres propios*) **la Sra. Díaz** Mrs Díaz. **la doctora Lara** doctor Lara

····➤ (*con partes del cuerpo, artículos personales*) *se traduce por un posesivo.* **apretó la mano** he clenched his fist. **tienes la camisa desabrochada** your shirt is undone

····➤ **la + de. es la de Ana** it's Ana's. **la del sombrero** the one with the hat

····➤ **la + que** (*persona*) **la que me atendió** the one who served me. (*cosa*) **la que se rompió** the one that broke

····➤ **la + que** + *subjuntivo* (*quienquiera*) whoever. **la que gane pasará a la final** whoever wins will go to the final. (*cualquiera*) whichever. **compra la que sea más barata** buy whichever is cheaper

laberinto *m* labyrinth, maze

labia *f* gift of the gab

labio *m* lip

labor *f* work. **~es de aguja** needlework. **~es de ganchillo** crochet. **~es de punto** knitting. **~es domésticas** housework. **~able** *adj* working. **~ar** *vi* work

laboratorio *m* laboratory

laborioso *adj* laborious

laborista *adj* Labour. • *m & f* member of the Labour Party

labra|do *adj* worked; (madera) carved; (metal) wrought; (tierra) ploughed. **~dor** *m* farmer; (*obrero*) farm labourer. **~nza** *f* farming. **~r** *vt* work; carve (madera); cut (piedra); till (la tierra). **~rse** *vpr.* **~rse un porvenir** carve out a future for o.s.

labriego *m* peasant

laca *f* lacquer

lacayo *m* lackey

lacio *adj* straight; (*flojo*) limp

lacón *m* shoulder of pork

lacónico *adj* laconic

lacr|ar *vt* seal. **~e** *m* sealing wax

lactante *adj* (niño) still on milk

lácteo *adj* milky. **productos** *mpl* **~s** dairy products

ladear *vt* tilt. **~se** *vpr* lean

ladera *f* slope

ladino *adj* astute

lado *m* side. **al ~** near. **al ~ de** next to, beside. **de ~** sideways. **en todos ~s** everywhere. **los de al ~** the next door neighbours. **por otro ~** on the other hand. **por todos ~s** everywhere. **por un ~** on the one hand

ladr|ar *vi* bark. **~ido** *m* bark

ladrillo *m* brick

ladrón *m* thief, robber; (*de casas*) burglar

lagart|ija *f* (small) lizard. **~o** *m* lizard

lago *m* lake

lágrima *f* tear

lagrimoso *adj* tearful

laguna *f* small lake; (*fig, omisión*) gap

laico *adj* lay

lament|able *adj* deplorable; (*que da pena*) pitiful; (pérdida) sad. **~ar** *vt* be sorry about. **~arse** *vpr* lament; (*quejarse*) complain. **~o** *m* moan

lamer *vt* lick

lámina *f* sheet; (*ilustración*) plate; (*estampa*) picture card

lamina|do *adj* laminated. **~r** *vt* laminate

lámpara *f* lamp. **~ de pie** standard lamp

lamparón *m* stain

lampiño *adj* beardless; (cuerpo) hairless

lana *f* wool. **de ~** wool(len)

lanceta *f* lancet

lancha *f* boat. **~ motora** motor boat. **~ salvavidas** lifeboat

langost|a *f* (*de mar*) lobster; (*insecto*) locust. **~ino** *m* king prawn

languide|cer [11] *vi* languish. **~z** *f* languor

lánguido *adj* languid; (*decaído*) listless

lanilla *f* nap; (*tela fina*) flannel

lanudo *adj* woolly; (perro) shaggy

lanza *f* lance, spear

lanza|llamas *m invar* flame-thrower. **~miento** *m* throw; (*acción de lanzar*) throwing; (*de proyectil, de producto*) launch. **~miento de peso**, (*LAm*) **~miento de bala** shot put. **~r** [10] *vt* throw; (*de un avión*) drop; launch (proyectil, producto). **~rse** *vpr* throw o.s.

lapicero *m* (propelling) pencil

lápida *f* tombstone; (*placa conmemorativa*) memorial tablet

lapidar *vt* stone

lápiz *m* pencil. **~ de labios** lipstick. **a ~** in pencil

lapso *m* lapse

laptop *m* laptop

larg|a *f*. **a la ~a** in the long run. **dar ~as** put off. **~ar** [12] *vt* (*Naut*) let out; (*fam, dar*) give; [I] deal (bofetada etc). **~arse** *vpr* [I] beat it [I]. **~o** *adj* long. ● *m* length. **¡~o!** go away! **a lo ~o** lengthwise. **a lo ~o de** along. **tener 100 metros de ~o** be 100 metres long

laring|e *f* larynx. **~itis** *f* laryngitis

larva *f* larva

las *artículo definido fpl* the. *véase tb* **LA**. ● *pron* them. **~ de** those, the ones. **~ de Vd** your ones, yours. **~ que** whoever, the ones

láser *m* laser

lástima *f* pity; (*queja*) complaint. **da ~ verlo así** it's sad to see him like that. **ella me da ~** I feel sorry for her. **¡qué ~!** what a pity!

lastim|ado *adj* hurt. **~ar** *vt* hurt. **~arse** *vpr* hurt o.s. **~ero** *adj* doleful. **~oso** *adj* pitiful

lastre *m* ballast; (*fig*) burden

lata *f* tinplate; (*envase*) tin (*esp Brit*), can; (*fam, molestia*) nuisance. **dar la ~** be a nuisance. **¡qué ~!** what a nuisance!

latente *adj* latent

lateral *adj* side, lateral

latido *m* beating; (*cada golpe*) beat

latifundio *m* large estate

latigazo *m* (*golpe*) lash; (*chasquido*) crack

látigo *m* whip

latín *m* Latin. **saber ~** [I] know what's what [I]

latino *adj* Latin. **L~américa** *f* Latin America. **~americano** *adj* & *m* Latin American

latir *vi* beat; (herida) throb

latitud *f* latitude

latón *m* brass

latoso *adj* annoying; (*pesado*) boring

laúd *m* lute
laureado *adj* honoured; (*premiado*) prize-winning
laurel *m* laurel; (*Culin*) bay
lava *f* lava
lava|ble *adj* washable. **~bo** *m* wash-basin; (*retrete*) toilet. **~dero** *m* sink. **~do** *m* washing. **~do de cerebro** brainwashing. **~do en seco** dry-cleaning. **~dora** *f* washing machine. **~ndería** *f* laundry. **~ndería automática** launderette, laundromat (*esp Amer*). **~platos** *m & f invar* dishwasher. ● *m* (*Mex, fregadero*) sink. **~r** *vt* wash. **~r en seco** dry-clean. **~rse** *vpr* have a wash. **~rse las manos** (*incl fig*) wash one's hands. **~tiva** *f* enema. **~vajillas** *m invar* dishwasher; (*detergente*) washing-up liquid (*Brit*), dishwashing liquid (*Amer*)
laxante *adj & m* laxative
lazada *f* bow
lazarillo *m* guide for a blind person
lazo *m* knot; (*lazada*) bow; (*fig, vínculo*) tie; (*con nudo corredizo*) lasso; (*Mex, cuerda*) rope
le *pron* (*acusativo, él*) him; (*acusativo, Vd*) you; (*dativo, él*) (to) him; (*dativo, ella*) (to) her; (*dativo, cosa*) (to) it; (*dativo, Vd*) (to) you
leal *adj* loyal; (*fiel*) faithful. **~tad** *f* loyalty; (*fidelidad*) faithfulness
lección *f* lesson
leche *f* milk; (*golpe*) bash. **~ condensada** condensed milk. **~ desnatada** skimmed milk. **~ en polvo** powdered milk. **~ sin desnatar** whole milk. **tener mala ~** be spiteful. **~ra** *f* (*vasija*) milk jug. **~ría** *f* dairy. **~ro** *adj* milk, dairy. ● *m* milkman
lecho *m* (*en literatura*) bed. **~ de río** river bed
lechoso *adj* milky
lechuga *f* lettuce
lechuza *f* owl
lect|or *m* reader; (*Univ*) language assistant. **~ura** *f* reading
leer 18 *vt/i* read
legación *f* legation
legado *m* legacy; (*enviado*) legate
legajo *m* bundle, file
legal *adj* legal. **~idad** *f* legality. **~izar** 10 *vt* legalize; (*certificar*) authenticate. **~mente** *adv* legally
legar 12 *vt* bequeath
legible *adj* legible
legi|ón *f* legion. **~onario** *m* legionary. **~onella** *f* legionnaire's disease
legisla|ción *f* legislation. **~dor** *m* legislator. **~r** *vi* legislate. **~tura** *f* term (of office); (*año parlamentario*) session; (*LAm, cuerpo*) legislature
leg|itimidad *f* legitimacy. **~ítimo** *adj* legitimate; (*verdadero*) real
lego *adj* lay; (*ignorante*) ignorant. ● *m* layman
legua *f* league
legumbre *f* vegetable
lejan|ía *f* distance. **~o** *adj* distant
lejía *f* bleach
lejos *adv* far. **~ de** far from. **a lo ~** in the distance. **desde ~** from a distance, from afar
lema *m* motto
lencería *f* linen; (*de mujer*) lingerie
lengua *f* tongue; (*idioma*) language. **irse de la ~** talk too much. **morderse la ~** hold one's tongue

lenguas cooficiales The regional languages of Spain, *catalán*, *euskera* and *gallego*, which now have equal status with Castilian in the regions where they are spoken. Banned under Franco, they continued to be spoken privately. They are now widely used in public life, education, the media, cinema and literature.

lenguado *m* sole
lenguaje *m* language
lengüeta *f* (*de zapato*) tongue. **~da** *f*, **~zo** *m* lick
lente *f* lens. **~s** *mpl* glasses. **~s de contacto** contact lenses
lentej|a *f* lentil. **~uela** *f* sequin
lentilla *f* contact lens
lent|itud *f* slowness. **~o** *adj* slow
leñ|a *f* firewood. **~ador** *m* woodcutter. **~o** *m* log
Leo *m* Leo
le|ón *m* lion. **~ona** *f* lioness
leopardo *m* leopard
leotardo *m* thick tights
lepr|a *f* leprosy. **~oso** *m* leper
lerdo *adj* dim; (*torpe*) clumsy
les *pron* (*acusativo*) them; (*acusativo, Vds*) you; (*dativo*) (to) them; (*dativo, Vds*) (to) you
lesbiana *f* lesbian
lesi|ón *f* wound. **~onado** *adj* injured. **~onar** *vt* injure; (*dañar*) damage
letal *adj* lethal
let|árgico *adj* lethargic. **~argo** *m* lethargy
letr|a *f* letter; (*escritura*) handwriting; (*de una canción*) words, lyrics. **~a de cambio** bill of exchange. **~a de imprenta** print. **~ado** *adj* learned. **~ero** *m* notice; (*cartel*) poster
letrina *f* latrine
leucemia *f* leukaemia
levadura *f* yeast. **~ en polvo** baking powder
levanta|miento *m* lifting; (*sublevación*) uprising. **~r** *vt* raise, lift; (*construir*) build; (*recoger*) pick up. **~rse** *vpr* get up; (*ponerse de pie*) stand up; (*erguirse, sublevarse*) rise up
levante *m* east; (*viento*) east wind
levar *vt*. **~ anclas** weigh anchor
leve *adj* light; (sospecha etc) slight; (enfermedad) mild; (*de poca importancia*) trivial. **~dad** *f* lightness; (*fig*) slightness
léxico *m* vocabulary
lexicografía *f* lexicography
ley *f* law; (*parlamentaria*) act
leyenda *f* legend
liar **20** *vt* tie; (*envolver*) wrap up; roll (cigarrillo); (*fig, confundir*) confuse; (*fig, enredar*) involve. **~se** *vpr* get involved
libanés *adj & m* Lebanese
libelo *m* (*escrito*) libellous article; (*Jurid*) petition
libélula *f* dragonfly
libera|ción *f* liberation. **~dor** *adj* liberating. ● *m* liberator
liberal *adj & m & f* liberal. **~idad** *f* liberality
liber|ar *vt* free. **~tad** *f* freedom. **~tad de cultos** freedom of worship. **~tad de imprenta** freedom of the press. **~tad provisional** bail. **en ~tad** free. **~tador** *m* liberator. **~tar** *vt* free
libertino *m* libertine
libido *f* libido
libio *adj & m* Libyan

libra *f* pound. ~ **esterlina** pound sterling

Libra *m* Libra

libra|dor *m* (*Com*) drawer. **~r** *vt* free; (*de un peligro*) save. **~rse** *vpr* free o.s. **~rse de** get rid of

libre *adj* free. **estilo ~** (*en natación*) freestyle. **~ de impuestos** tax-free

librea *f* livery

libr|ería *f* bookshop (*Brit*), bookstore (*Amer*); (*mueble*) bookcase. **~ero** *m* bookseller; (*Mex, mueble*) bookcase. **~eta** *f* notebook. **~o** *m* book. **~o de bolsillo** paperback. **~o de ejercicios** exercise book. **~o de reclamaciones** complaints book

licencia *f* permission; (*documento*) licence. **~do** *m* graduate; (*Mex, abogado*) lawyer. **~ para manejar** (*Mex*) driving licence. **~r** *vt* (*Mil*) discharge; (*echar*) dismiss. **~tura** *f* degree

licencioso *adj* licentious

licitar *vt* bid for

lícito *adj* legal; (*permisible*) permissible

licor *m* liquor; (*dulce*) liqueur

licua|dora *f* blender. **~r** **21** liquefy; (*Culin*) blend

lid *f* fight. **en buena ~** by fair means. **~es** *fpl* matters

líder *m* leader

liderato *m*, **liderazgo** *m* leadership

lidia *f* bullfighting; (*lucha*) fight. **~r** *vt/i* fight

liebre *f* hare

lienzo *m* linen; (*del pintor*) canvas; (*muro, pared*) wall

liga *f* garter; (*alianza*) league; (*LAm, gomita*) rubber band. **~dura** *f* bond; (*Mus*) slur; (*Med*) ligature. **~mento** *m* ligament. **~r** **12** *vt* bind; (*atar*) tie; (*Mus*) slur. ● *vi* mix. **~r con** (*fig*) pick up. **~rse** *vpr* (*fig*) commit o.s.

liger|eza *f* lightness; (*agilidad*) agility; (*rapidez*) swiftness; (*de carácter*) fickleness. **~o** *adj* light; (*rápido*) quick; (*ágil*) agile; (*superficial*) superficial; (*de poca importancia*) slight. ● *adv* quickly. **a la ~a** lightly, superficially

liguero *m* suspender belt

lija *f* dogfish; (*papel de lija*) sandpaper. **~r** *vt* sand

lila *f* lilac. ● *m* (*color*) lilac

lima *f* file; (*fruta*) lime. **~duras** *fpl* filings. **~r** *vt* file (down)

limita|ción *f* limitation. **~do** *adj* limited. **~r** *vt* limit. **~r con** border on. **~tivo** *adj* limiting

límite *m* limit. **~ de velocidad** speed limit

limítrofe *adj* bordering

lim|ón *m* lemon; (*Mex*) lime. **~onada** *f* lemonade

limosn|a *f* alms. **pedir ~a** beg. **~ear** *vi* beg

limpia|botas *m invar* bootblack. **~parabrisas** *m invar* windscreen wiper (*Brit*), windshield wiper (*Amer*). **~pipas** *m invar* pipe-cleaner. **~r** *vt* clean; (*enjugar*) wipe. **~vidrios** *m invar* (*LAm*) window cleaner

limpi|eza *f* cleanliness; (*acción de limpiar*) cleaning. **~eza en seco** dry-cleaning. **~o** *adj* clean; (cielo) clear; (*fig, honrado*) honest; (*neto*) net. **pasar a ~o**, (*LAm*) **pasar en ~o** make a fair copy. ● *adv* fairly. **jugar ~o** play fair

linaje *m* lineage; (*fig, clase*) kind

lince *m* lynx

linchar *vt* lynch

lind|ar *vi* border (**con** on). **~e** *f*

boundary. **~ero** *m* border

lindo *adj* pretty, lovely. **de lo ~** ⊞ a lot

línea *f* line. **en ~s generales** broadly speaking. **guardar la ~** watch one's figure

lingote *m* ingot

lingü|ista *m & f* linguist. **~ística** *f* linguistics. **~ístico** *adj* linguistic

lino *m* flax; (*tela*) linen

linterna *f* lantern; (*de bolsillo*) torch, flashlight (*Amer*)

lío *m* bundle; (*jaleo*) fuss; (*embrollo*) muddle; (*amorío*) affair

liquida|ción *f* liquidation; (*venta especial*) sale. **~r** *vt* liquify; (*Com*) liquidate; settle (cuenta)

líquido *adj* liquid; (*Com*) net. ● *m* liquid; (*Com*) cash

lira *f* lyre; (*moneda italiana*) lira

líric|a *f* lyric poetry. **~o** *adj* lyric(al)

lirio *m* iris

lirón *m* dormouse; (*fig*) sleepy-head. **dormir como un ~** sleep like a log

lisiado *adj* crippled

liso *adj* smooth; (pelo) straight; (tierra) flat; (*sencillo*) plain

lisonj|a *f* flattery. **~eador** *adj* flattering. ● *m* flatterer. **~ear** *vt* flatter. **~ero** *adj* flattering

lista *f* stripe; (*enumeración*) list. **~ de correos** poste restante. **a ~s** striped. **pasar ~** take the register. **~do** *adj* striped

listo *adj* clever; (*preparado*) ready

listón *m* strip; (*en saltos*) bar; (*Mex, cinta*) ribbon

litera *f* (*en barco, tren*) berth; (*en habitación*) bunk bed

literal *adj* literal

litera|rio *adj* literary. **~tura** *f* literature

litig|ar 12 *vi* dispute; (*Jurid*) litigate. **~io** *m* dispute; (*Jurid*) litigation

litografía *f* (*arte*) lithography; (*cuadro*) lithograph

litoral *adj* coastal. ● *m* coast

litro *m* litre

lituano *adj & m* Lithuanian

liturgia *f* liturgy

liviano *adj* fickle; (*LAm, de poco peso*) light

lívido *adj* livid

llaga *f* wound; (*úlcera*) ulcer

llama *f* flame; (*animal*) llama

llamada *f* call

llama|do *adj* called. ● *m* (*LAm*) call. **~miento** *m* call. **~r** *vt* call; (*por teléfono*) phone. ● *vi* call; (*golpear en la puerta*) knock; (*tocar el timbre*) ring. **~r por teléfono** phone, telephone. **~rse** *vpr* be called. **¿cómo te ~s?** what's your name?

llamarada *f* sudden blaze; (*fig, de pasión etc*) outburst

llamativo *adj* flashy; (color) loud; (persona) striking

llamear *vi* blaze

llano *adj* flat, level; (persona) natural; (*sencillo*) plain. ● *m* plain

llanta *f* (*Auto*) (wheel) rim; (*LAm, neumático*) tyre

llanto *m* crying

llanura *f* plain

llave *f* key; (*para tuercas*) spanner; (*LAm, del baño etc*) tap (*Brit*), faucet (*Amer*); (*Elec*) switch. **~ inglesa** monkey wrench. **cerrar con ~** lock. **echar la ~** lock up. **~ro** *m* key-ring

llega|da *f* arrival. **~r** 12 *vi* arrive, come; (*alcanzar*) reach; (*bastar*) be enough. **~r a** (*conseguir*) manage to. **~r a saber** find out. **~r a ser** become. **~r hasta** go as far as

llen|ar *vt* fill (up); (*rellenar*) fill in; (*cubrir*) cover (**de** with). **~o** *adj* full. ● *m* (*en el teatro etc*) full house. **de ~** entirely

lleva|dero *adj* tolerable. **~r** *vt* carry; (*inducir, conducir*) lead; (*acompañar*) take; wear (ropa). **¿cuánto tiempo ~s aquí?** how long have you been here? **llevo 3 años estudiando inglés** I've been studying English for 3 years. **~rse** *vpr* take away; win (premio etc); (*comprar*) take. **~rse bien** get on well together

llor|ar *vi* cry; (ojos) water. **~iquear** *vi* whine. **~iqueo** *m* whining. **~o** *m* crying. **~ón** *adj* whining. ● *m* cry-baby. **~oso** *adj* tearful

llov|er **2** *vi* rain. **~izna** *f* drizzle. **~iznar** *vi* drizzle

llueve *vb véase* **LLOVER**

lluvi|a *f* rain; (*fig*) shower. **~oso** *adj* rainy; (clima) wet

lo *artículo definido neutro*. **~ importante** what is important, the important thing. ● *pron* (*él*) him; (*cosa*) it. **~ que** what, that which

loa *f* praise. **~ble** *adj* praiseworthy. **~r** *vt* praise

lobo *m* wolf

lóbrego *adj* gloomy

lóbulo *m* lobe

local *adj* local. ● *m* premises. **~idad** *f* locality; (*de un espectáculo*) seat; (*entrada*) ticket. **~izador** *m* pager; (*de reserva*) booking reference. **~izar** **10** *vt* find, locate

loción *f* lotion

loco *adj* mad, crazy. ● *m* lunatic. **~ de alegría** mad with joy. **estar ~ por** be crazy about. **volverse ~** go mad

locomo|ción *f* locomotion. **~tora** *f* locomotive

locuaz *adj* talkative

locución *f* expression

locura *f* madness; (*acto*) crazy thing. **con ~** madly

locutor *m* broadcaster

lod|azal *m* quagmire. **~o** *m* mud

lógic|a *f* logic. **~o** *adj* logical

logr|ar *vt* get; win (premio). **~ hacer** manage to do. **~o** *m* achievement; (*de premio*) winning; (*éxito*) success

loma *f* small hill

lombriz *f* worm

lomo *m* back; (*de libro*) spine. **~ de cerdo** loin of pork

lona *f* canvas

loncha *f* slice; (*de tocino*) rasher

londinense *adj* from London. ● *m* Londoner

Londres *m* London

loneta *f* thin canvas

longaniza *f* sausage

longev|idad *f* longevity. **~o** *adj* long-lived

longitud *f* length; (*en geografía*) longitude

lonja *f* slice; (*de tocino*) rasher; (*Com*) market

loro *m* parrot

los *artículo definido mpl* the. *véase tb* **EL**. ● *pron* them. **~ de Antonio** Antonio's. **~ que** whoever, the ones

losa *f* (*baldosa*) flagstone. **~ sepulcral** tombstone

lote *m* share; (*de productos*) batch; (*terreno*) plot (*Brit*), lot (*Amer*)

lotería *f* lottery

loto *m* lotus

loza *f* crockery; (*fina*) china
lozano *adj* fresh; (vegetación) lush; (persona) healthy-looking
lubina *f* sea bass
lubrica|nte *adj* lubricating. ● *m* lubricant. **~r** 7 *vt* lubricate
lucero *m* bright star. **~ del alba** morning star
lucha *f* fight; (*fig*) struggle. **~dor** *m* fighter. **~r** *vi* fight; (*fig*) struggle
lucid|ez *f* lucidity. **~o** *adj* splendid
lúcido *adj* lucid
luciérnaga *f* glow-worm
lucimiento *m* brilliance
lucio *m* pike
lucir 11 *vt* (*fig*) show off. ● *vi* shine; (joya) sparkle; (*LAm*, *mostrarse*) look. **~se** *vpr* (*fig*) shine, excel; (*presumir*) show off
lucr|ativo *adj* lucrative. **~o** *m* gain
luego *adv* then; (*más tarde*) later (on); (*Mex*, *pronto*) soon. ● *conj* therefore. **~ que** as soon as. **desde ~** of course
lugar *m* place; (*espacio libre*) room. **~ común** cliché. **dar ~ a** give rise to. **en ~ de** instead of. **en primer ~** first. **hacer ~** make room. **tener ~** take place. **~eño** *adj* local, village
lugarteniente *m* deputy
lúgubre *adj* gloomy
lujo *m* luxury. **~so** *adj* luxurious. **de ~** luxury
lumbago *m* lumbago
lumbre *f* fire; (*luz*) light
luminoso *adj* luminous; (*fig*) bright; (letrero) illuminated
luna *f* moon; (*espejo*) mirror. **~ de miel** honeymoon. **claro de ~** moonlight. **estar en la ~** be miles away. **~r** *adj* lunar. ● *m* mole; (*en tela*) spot
lunes *m invar* Monday
lupa *f* magnifying glass
lustr|abotas *m invar* (*LAm*) bootblack. **~ar** *vt* shine, polish. **~e** *m* shine; (*fig*, *esplendor*) splendour. **dar ~e a**, **sacar ~e a** polish. **~oso** *adj* shining
luto *m* mourning. **estar de ~** be in mourning
luz *f* light; (*electricidad*) electricity. **luces altas** (*LAm*) headlights on full beam. **luces bajas** (*LAm*), **luces cortas** dipped headlights. **luces antiniebla** fog light. **luces largas** headlights on full beam. **a la ~ de** in the light of. **a todas luces** obviously. **dar a ~** give birth. **hacer la ~ sobre** shed light on. **sacar a la ~** bring to light

Mm

macabro *adj* macabre
macaco *m* macaque (monkey)
macanudo *adj* Ⓘ great Ⓘ
macarrones *mpl* macaroni
macerar *vt* macerate (fruta); marinade (carne etc)
maceta *f* mallet; (*tiesto*) flowerpot
machacar 7 *vt* crush. ● *vi* go on (**sobre** about)
machamartillo. **a ~** *adj* ardent; (*como adv*) firmly
machet|azo *m* blow with a machete; (*herida*) wound from a machete. **~e** *m* machete
mach|ista *m* male chauvinist. **~o** *adj* male; (*varonil*) macho

machu|car 7 *vt* bruise; (*aplastar*) crush. **~cón** *m* (*LAm*) bruise
macizo *adj* solid. ● *m* mass; (*de plantas*) bed
madeja *f* skein
madera *m* (*vino*) Madeira. ● *f* wood; (*naturaleza*) nature. **~ble** *adj* yielding timber. **~men** *m* woodwork
madero *m* log; (*de construcción*) timber
madona *f* Madonna
madr|astra *f* stepmother. **~e** *f* mother. **~eperla** *f* mother-of-pearl. **~eselva** *f* honeysuckle
madrigal *m* madrigal
madriguera *f* den; (*de conejo*) burrow
madrileño *adj* of Madrid. ● *m* person from Madrid
madrina *f* godmother; (*en una boda*) matron of honour
madrug|ada *f* dawn. **de ~ada** at dawn. **~ador** *adj* who gets up early. ● *m* early riser. **~ar** 12 *vi* get up early
madur|ación *f* maturing; (*de fruta*) ripening. **~ar** *vt/i* mature; (fruta) ripen. **~ez** *f* maturity; (*de fruta*) ripeness. **~o** *adj* mature; (fruta) ripe
maestr|ía *f* skill; (*Univ*) master's degree. **~o** *m* master; (*de escuela*) schoolteacher
mafia *f* mafia
magdalena *f* fairy cake (*Brit*), cup cake (*Amer*)
magia *f* magic
mágico *adj* magic; (*maravilloso*) magical
magist|erio *m* teaching (profession); (*conjunto de maestros*) teachers. **~rado** *m* magistrate; (*juez*) judge. **~ral** *adj* teaching; (*bien hecho*) masterly. **~ratura** *f* magistracy
magn|animidad *f* magnanimity. **~ánimo** *adj* magnanimous. **~ate** *m* magnate, tycoon
magnavoz *m* (*Mex*) megaphone
magnético *adj* magnetic
magneti|smo *m* magnetism. **~zar** 10 *vt* magnetize
magn|ificar *vt* extol; (*LAm*) magnify (objeto). **~ificencia** *f* magnificence. **~ífico** *adj* magnificent. **~itud** *f* magnitude
magnolia *f* magnolia
mago *m* magician; (*en cuentos*) wizard
magro *adj* lean; (tierra) poor
magulla|dura *f* bruise. **~r** *vt* bruise. **~rse** *vpr* bruise
mahometano *adj* Islamic
maíz *m* maize, corn (*Amer*)
majada *f* sheepfold; (*estiércol*) manure; (*LAm*) flock of sheep
majader|ía *f* silly thing. **~o** *m* idiot. ● *adj* stupid
majest|ad *f* majesty. **~uoso** *adj* majestic
majo *adj* nice
mal *adv* badly; (*poco*) poorly; (*difícilmente*) hardly; (*equivocadamente*) wrongly; (*desagradablemente*) bad. ● *adj*. **estar ~** be ill; (*anímicamente*) be in a bad way; (*incorrecto*) be wrong. **estar ~ de** (*escaso de*) be short of. *véase tb* **MALO**. ● *m* evil; (*daño*) harm; (*enfermedad*) illness. **~ que bien** somehow (or other). **de ~ en peor** from bad to worse. **hacer ~ en** be wrong to. **¡menos ~!** thank goodness!
malabaris|mo *m* juggling. **~ta** *m & f* juggler
mala|consejado *adj* ill-advised.

~costumbrado *adj* spoilt. **~crianza** (*LAm*) rudeness. **~gradecido** *adj* ungrateful

malagueño *adj* of Málaga. • *m* person from Málaga

malaria *f* malaria

Malasia *f* Malaysia

malavenido *adj* incompatible

malaventura *adj* unfortunate

malayo *adj* Malay(an)

malbaratar *vt* sell off cheap; (*malgastar*) squander

malcarado *adj* nasty looking

malcriado *adj* (niño) spoilt

maldad *f* evil; (*acción*) wicked thing

maldecir 46 (*pero imperativo* **maldice**, *futuro y condicional regulares*, *pp* **maldecido** *o* **maldito**) *vt* curse. • *vi* curse; speak ill (**de** of)

m

maldi|ciente *adj* backbiting; (*que blasfema*) foul-mouthed. **~ción** *f* curse. **~to** *adj* damned. **¡~to sea!** damn (it)!

maleab|ilidad *f* malleability. **~le** *adj* malleable

malea|nte *m* criminal. **~r** *vt* damage; (*pervertir*) corrupt. **~rse** *vpr* be spoilt; (*pervertirse*) be corrupted

malecón *m* breakwater; (*embarcadero*) jetty; (*Rail*) embankment; (*LAm, paseo marítimo*) seafront

maledicencia *f* slander

mal|eficio *m* curse. **~éfico** *adj* evil

malestar *m* discomfort; (*fig*) uneasiness

malet|a *f* (suit)case. **hacer la ~a** pack (one's case). **~ero** *m* porter; (*Auto*) boot, trunk (*Amer*). **~ín** *m* small case; (*para documentos*) briefcase

mal|evolencia *f* malevolence. **~évolo** *adj* malevolent

maleza *f* weeds; (*matorral*) undergrowth

mal|gastar *vt* waste. **~hablado** *adj* foul-mouthed. **~hechor** *m* criminal. **~humorado** *adj* bad-tempered

malici|a *f* malice; (*picardía*) mischief. **~arse** *vpr* suspect. **~oso** *adj* malicious; (*pícaro*) mischievous

maligno *adj* malignant; (persona) evil

malintencionado *adj* malicious

malla *f* mesh; (*de armadura*) mail; (*de gimnasia*) leotard

Mallorca *f* Majorca

mallorquín *adj* & *m* Majorcan

malmirado *adj* (*con estar*) frowned upon

malo *adj* (*delante de nombre masculino en singular* **mal**) bad; (*enfermo*) ill. **~ de** difficult to. **estar de malas** (*malhumorado*) be in a bad mood; (*LAm, con mala suerte*) be out of luck. **lo ~ es que** the trouble is that. **por las malas** by force

malogr|ar *vt* waste; (*estropear*) spoil. **~arse** *vpr* fall through

maloliente *adj* smelly

malpensado *adj* nasty, malicious

malsano *adj* unhealthy

malsonante *adj* ill-sounding; (*grosero*) offensive

malt|a *f* malt. **~eada** *f* (*LAm*) milk shake. **~ear** *vt* malt

maltr|atar *vt* ill-treat; (*pegar*) batter; mistreat (juguete etc). **~echo** *adj* battered

malucho *adj* [!] under the weather

malva *f* mallow. **(color de) ~** *adj invar* mauve

malvado *adj* wicked
malvavisco *m* marshmallow
malversa|ción *f* embezzlement. **~dor** *adj* embezzling. ● *m* embezzler. **~r** *vt* embezzle
Malvinas *fpl*. **las (islas) ~** the Falklands, the Falkland Islands
mama *f* mammary gland; (*de mujer*) breast
mamá *f* mum; (*usado por niños*) mummy
mama|da *f* sucking. **~r** *vt* suck; (*fig*) grow up with. ● *vi* (bebé) feed; (animal) suckle. **dar de ~** breastfeed
mamario *adj* mammary
mamarracho *m* clown; (*cosa ridícula*) (ridiculous) sight; (*cosa mal hecha*) botch; (*cosa fea*) mess. **ir hecho un ~** look a sight
mameluco *m* (*LAm*) overalls; (*de niño*) rompers
mamífero *adj* mammalian. ● *m* mammal
mamila *f* (*Mex*) feeding bottle
mamotreto *m* (*libro*) hefty volume; (*armatoste*) huge thing
mampara *f* screen
mampostería *f* masonry
mamut *m* mammoth
manada *f* herd; (*de lobos*) pack; (*de leones*) pride. **en ~** in crowds
mana|ntial *m* spring; (*fig*) source. **~r** *vi* flow; (*fig*) abound. ● *vt* drip with
manaza *f* big hand
mancha *f* stain; (*en la piel*) blotch. **~do** *adj* stained; (*sucio*) dirty; (animal) spotted. **~r** *vt* stain; (*ensuciar*) dirty. **~rse** *vpr* get stained; (*ensuciarse*) get dirty
manchego *adj* of la Mancha. ● *m* person from la Mancha
manchón *m* large stain
mancilla *f* blemish. **~r** *vt* stain
manco *adj* (*de una mano*) one-handed; (*de las dos manos*) handless; (*de un brazo*) one-armed; (*de los dos brazos*) armless
mancomun|adamente *adv* jointly. **~ar** *vt* unite; (*Jurid*) make jointly liable. **~arse** *vpr* unite. **~idad** *f* union
manda *f* (*Mex*) religious offering
manda|dero *m* messenger. **~do** *m* (*LAm*) shopping; (*diligencia*) errand. **hacer los ~dos** (*LAm*) do the shopping. **~miento** *m* order; (*Relig*) commandment. **~r** *vt* order; (*enviar*) send; (*gobernar*) rule. ● *vi* be in command. **¿mande?** (*Mex*) pardon?
mandarin|a *f* (*naranja*) mandarin (orange). **~o** *m* mandarin tree
mandat|ario *m* attorney; (*Pol*) head of state. **~o** *m* mandate; (*Pol*) term of office
mandíbula *f* jaw
mando *m* command. **~ a distancia** remote control. **al ~ de** in charge of. **altos ~s** *mpl* high-ranking officers
mandolina *f* mandolin
mandón *adj* bossy
manducar **7** *vt* **!** stuff oneself with
manecilla *f* hand
manej|able *adj* manageable. **~ar** *vt* use; handle (asunto etc); (*fig*) manage; (*LAm, conducir*) drive. **~arse** *vpr* get by. **~o** *m* handling. **~os** *mpl* scheming
manera *f* way. **~s** *fpl* manners. **de alguna ~** somehow. **de ~ que** so (that). **de ninguna ~** by no means. **de otra ~** otherwise. **de todas ~s** anyway

m

manga *f* sleeve; (*tubo de goma*) hose; (*red*) net; (*para colar*) filter; (*LAm, de langostas*) swarm
mango *m* handle; (*fruta*) mango. **~near** *vt* boss about. ● *vi* (*entrometerse*) interfere
manguera *f* hose(pipe)
manguito *m* muff
maní *m* (*pl* **~es**) (*LAm*) peanut
manía *f* mania; (*antipatía*) dislike. **tener la ~ de** have an obsession with
maniaco *adj*, **maníaco** *adj* maniac(al). ● *m* maniac
maniatar *vt* tie s.o.'s hands
maniático *adj* maniac(al); (*obsesivo*) obsessive; (*loco*) crazy; (*delicado*) finicky
manicomio *m* lunatic asylum
m **manicura** *f* manicure; (*mujer*) manicurist
manido *adj* stale
manifesta|ción *f* manifestation, sign; (*Pol*) demonstration. **~nte** *m* demonstrator. **~r** 1 *vt* show; (*Pol*) state. **~rse** *vpr* show; (*Pol*) demonstrate
manifiesto *adj* clear; (error) obvious; (verdad) manifest. ● *m* manifesto
manilargo *adj* light-fingered
manilla *f* (*de cajón etc*) handle; (*de reloj*) hand. **~r** *m* handlebar(s)
maniobra *f* manoeuvre. **~r** *vt* operate; (*Rail*) shunt. ● *vt/i* manoeuvre. **~s** *fpl* (*Mil*) manoeuvres
manipula|ción *f* manipulation. **~r** *vt* manipulate
maniquí *m* dummy. ● *m & f* model
mani|rroto *adj & m* spendthrift. **~ta** *f*, (*LAm*) **~to** *m* little hand
manivela *f* crank
manjar *m* delicacy
mano *f* hand; (*de animales*) front foot; (*de perros, gatos*) front paw. **~ de obra** work force. **¡~s arriba!** hands up! **a ~** by hand; (*próximo*) handy. **a ~ derecha** on the right. **de segunda ~** second hand. **echar una ~** lend a hand. **tener buena ~ para** be good at. ● *m* (*LAm, fam*) mate (*Brit*), buddy (*Amer*)
manojo *m* bunch
manose|ar *vt* handle. **~o** *m* handling
manotada *f*, **manotazo** *m* slap
manote|ar *vi* gesticulate. **~o** *m* gesticulation
mansalva: **a ~** *adv* without risk
mansarda *f* attic
mansión *f* mansion. **~ señorial** stately home
manso *adj* gentle; (animal) tame
manta *f* blanket
mantec|a *f* fat. **~oso** *adj* greasy
mantel *m* tablecloth; (*del altar*) altar cloth. **~ería** *f* table linen
manten|er 40 *vt* support; (*conservar*) keep; (*sostener*) maintain. **~erse** *vpr* support o.s.; (*permanecer*) remain. **~se de/con** live off. **~imiento** *m* maintenance
mantequ|era *f* butter churn. **~illa** *f* butter
mant|illa *f* mantilla. **~o** *m* cloak. **~ón** *m* shawl
manual *adj & m* manual
manubrio *m* crank; (*LAm, de bicicleta*) handlebars
manufactura *f* manufacture. **~r** *vt* manufacture, make
manuscrito *adj* handwritten. ● *m* manuscript
manutención *f* maintenance
manzana *f* apple; (*de edificios*)

block. **~r** *m* (*apple*) orchard. **~ de Adán** (*LAm*) Adam's apple

manzan|illa *f* camomile tea. ● *m* manzanilla, pale dry sherry. **~o** *m* apple tree

maña *f* skill. **~s** *fpl* cunning

mañan|a *f* morning. **~a por la ~a** tomorrow morning. **pasado ~a** the day after tomorrow. **en la ~a** (*LAm*), **por la ~a** in the morning. ● *m* future. ● *adv* tomorrow. **~ero** *adj* who gets up early. ● *m* early riser

mañoso *adj* clever; (*astuto*) crafty; (*LAm, caprichoso*) difficult

mapa *m* map

mapache *m* racoon

maqueta *f* scale model

maquiladora *f* (*Mex*) cross-border assembly plant

maquilla|je *m* make-up. **~r** *vt* make up. **~rse** *vpr* make up

máquina *f* machine; (*Rail*) engine. **~ de afeitar** shaver. **~ de escribir** typewriter. **~ fotográfica** camera

maquin|ación *f* machination. **~al** *adj* mechanical. **~aria** *f* machinery. **~ista** *m & f* operator; (*Rail*) engine driver

mar *m & f* sea. **alta ~** high seas. **la ~ de** [!] lots of

maraña *f* thicket; (*enredo*) tangle; (*embrollo*) muddle

maratón *m & f* marathon

maravill|a *f* wonder. **a las mil ~as, de ~as** marvellously. **contar/decir ~as de** speak wonderfully of. **hacer ~as** work wonders. **~ar** *vt* astonish. **~arse** *vpr* be astonished (**de** at). **~oso** *adj* marvellous, wonderful

marca *f* mark; (*de coches etc*) make; (*de alimentos, cosméticos*) brand; (*Deportes*) record. **~ de fábrica** trade mark. **de ~** brand name; (*fig*) excellent. **de ~ mayor** [!] absolute. **~do** *adj* marked. **~dor** *m* marker; (*Deportes*) scoreboard. **~r** [7] *vt* mark; (*señalar*) show; score (un gol); dial (número de teléfono). ● *vi* score

marcha *f* (*incl Mus*) march; (*Auto*) gear; (*desarrollo*) course; (*partida*) departure. **a toda ~** at full speed. **dar/hacer ~ atrás** put into reverse. **poner en ~** start; (*fig*) set in motion

marchante *m* (*f* **marchanta**) art dealer; (*Mex, en mercado*) stall holder

marchar *vi* go; (*funcionar*) work, go; (*Mil*) march. **~se** *vpr* leave

marchit|ar *vt* wither. **~arse** *vpr* wither. **~o** *adj* withered

marcial *adj* martial

marciano *adj & m* Martian

marco *m* frame; (*moneda alemana*) mark; (*deportes*) goal-posts

marea *f* tide. **~do** *adj* sick; (*en el mar*) seasick; (*aturdido*) dizzy; (*borracho*) drunk. **~r** *vt* make feel sick; (*aturdir*) make feel dizzy; (*confundir*) confuse. **~rse** *vpr* feel sick; (*en un barco*) get seasick; (*estar aturdido*) feel dizzy; (*irse la cabeza*) feel faint; (*emborracharse*) get slightly drunk; (*confundirse*) get confused

marejada *f* swell; (*fig*) wave

mareo *m* sickness; (*en el mar*) seasickness; (*aturdimiento*) dizziness; (*confusión*) muddle

marfil *m* ivory

margarina *f* margarine

margarita *f* daisy; (*cóctel*) margarita

marg|en *m* margin; (*de un ca-*

mino) side. • *f* (*de un río*) bank. **~inado** *adj* excluded. • *m* outcast. **al ~en** (*fig*) outside. **~inal** *adj* marginal. **~inar** *vt* (*excluir*) exclude; (*fijar márgenes*) set margins

mariachi *m* (*Mex*) (*música popular de Jalisco*) Mariachi music; (*conjunto*) Mariachi band; (*músico*) Mariachi musician

> **mariachi** The word can mean the traditional Mexican musical ensemble, the musicians and the lively mestizo music they play. *Mariachis* wearing costumes based on those worn by *charros* can be seen in the Plaza Garibaldi, in Mexico City, where they are hired for parties, or to sing *mañanitas* or serenades.

maric|a *m* [!] sissy [!]. **~ón** *m* [!] homosexual, queer [!]; (*LAm, cobarde*) wimp

marido *m* husband

mariguana *f*, **marihuana** *f* marijuana

marimacho *f* mannish woman

marimba *f* (type of) drum (*LAm, especie de xilofón*) marimba

marin|a *f* navy; (*barcos*) fleet; (*cuadro*) seascape. **~a de guerra** navy. **~a mercante** merchant navy. **~ería** *f* seamanship; (*marineros*) sailors. **~ero** *adj* marine; (barco) seaworthy. • *m* sailor. **a la ~era** in tomato and garlic sauce. **~o** *adj* marine

marioneta *f* puppet. **~s** *fpl* puppet show

maripos|a *f* butterfly. **~a nocturna** moth. **~ear** *vi* be fickle; (*galantear*) flirt. **~ón** *m* flirt

mariquita *f* ladybird (*Brit*), ladybug (*Amer*). • *m* [!] sissy [!]

mariscador *m* shell-fisher

mariscal *m* marshal

maris|car *vt* fish for shellfish. **~co** *m* seafood, shellfish. **~quero** *m* (*pescador de mariscos*) seafood fisherman; (*vendedor de mariscos*) seafood seller

marital *adj* marital; (vida) married

marítimo *adj* maritime; (ciudad etc) coastal, seaside

marmita *f* cooking pot

mármol *m* marble

marmota *f* marmot

maroma *f* rope; (*Mex, voltereta*) somersault

marqu|és *m* marquess. **~esa** *f* marchioness. **~esina** *f* glass canopy; (*en estadio*) roof

marran|a *f* sow. **~ada** *f* filthy thing; (*cochinada*) dirty trick. **~o** *adj* filthy. • *m* hog

marrón *adj* & *m* brown

marroqu|í *adj* & *m* & *f* Moroccan. • *m* (*leather*) morocco. **~inería** *f* leather goods

Marruecos *m* Morocco

marsopa *f* porpoise

marsupial *adj* & *m* marsupial

marta *f* marten

martajar *vt* (*Mex*) crush (maíz)

Marte *m* Mars

martes *m invar* Tuesday. **~ de carnaval** Shrove Tuesday

martill|ar *vt* hammer. **~azo** *m* blow with a hammer. **~ear** *vt* hammer. **~eo** *m* hammering. **~o** *m* hammer

martín *m* **pescador** kingfisher

martinete *m* (*del piano*) hammer; (*ave*) heron

martingala *f* (*ardid*) trick

mártir *m* & *f* martyr

martir|io *m* martyrdom; (*fig*) torment. ~izar [10] *vt* martyr; (*fig*) torment, torture

marxis|mo *m* Marxism. **~ta** *adj & m & f* Marxist

marzo *m* March

más *adv & adj* (*comparativo*) more; (*superlativo*) most. **~ caro** dearer. **~ doloroso** more painful. **el ~ caro** the dearest; (*de dos*) the dearer. **el ~ curioso** the most curious; (*de dos*) the more curious. • *prep* plus. • *m* plus (sign). **~ bien** rather. **~ de** (*cantidad indeterminada*) more than. **~ o menos** more or less. **~ que** more than. **~ y ~** more and more. **a lo ~** at (the) most. **dos ~ dos** two plus two. **de ~** too many. **es ~** moreover. **nadie ~** nobody else. **no ~** no more

masa *f* mass; (*Culin*) dough. **en ~** en masse

masacre *f* massacre

masaj|e *m* massage. **~ear** *vt* massage. **~ista** *m* masseur. • *f* masseuse

mascada *f* (*Mex*) scarf

mascar [7] *vt* chew

máscara *f* mask

mascar|ada *f* masquerade. **~illa** *f* mask. **~ón** *m* (*Naut*) figurehead

mascota *f* mascot

masculin|idad *f* masculinity. **~o** *adj* masculine; (sexo) male. • *m* masculine

mascullar [3] *vt* mumble

masilla *f* putty

masivo *adj* massive, large-scale

mas|ón *m* Freemason. **~onería** *f* Freemasonry. **~ónico** *adj* Masonic

masoquis|mo *m* masochism. **~ta** *adj* masochistic. • *m & f* masochist

mastica|ción *f* chewing. **~r** [7] *vt* chew

mástil *m* (*Naut*) mast; (*de bandera*) flagpole; (*de guitarra, violín*) neck

mastín *m* mastiff

mastodonte *m* mastodon; (*fig*) giant

masturba|ción *f* masturbation. **~rse** *vpr* masturbate

mata *f* (*arbusto*) bush; (*LAm, planta*) plant

matad|ero *m* slaughterhouse. **~or** *adj* killing. • *m* (*torero*) matador

matamoscas *m invar* fly swatter

mata|nza *f* killing. **~r** *vt* kill (personas); slaughter (reses). **~rife** *m* butcher. **~rse** *vpr* kill o.s.; (*en un accidente*) be killed; (*Mex, para un examen*) cram. **~rse trabajando** work like mad

mata|polillas *m invar* moth killer. **~rratas** *m invar* rat poison

matasanos *m invar* quack

matasellos *m invar* postmark

mate *adj* matt. • *m* (*ajedrez*) (check)mate (*LAm, bebida*) maté

matemátic|as *fpl* mathematics, maths (*Brit*), math (*Amer*). **~o** *adj* mathematical. • *m* mathematician

materia *f* matter; (*material*) material; (*LAm, asignatura*) subject. **~ prima** raw material. **en ~ de** on the question of

material *adj & m* material. **~idad** *f* material nature. **~ismo** *m* materialism. **~ista** *adj* materialistic. • *m & f* materialist; (*Mex, constructor*) building contractor. **~izar** [10] *vt* materialize. **~izarse** *vpr* materialize. **~mente** *adv* materially; (*absolutamente*) absolutely

matern|al *adj* maternal; (amor) motherly. **~idad** *f* motherhood; (*hospital*) maternity hospital; (*sala*) maternity ward. **~o** *adj* motherly; (lengua) mother

matin|al *adj* morning. **~ée** *m* matinée

matiz *m* shade; (*fig*) nuance. **~ación** *f* combination of colours. **~ar** 10 *vt* blend (colores); (*introducir variedad*) vary; (*teñir*) tinge (**de** with)

mat|ón *m* bully; (*de barrio*) thug. **~onismo** *m* bullying; (*de barrio*) thuggery

matorral *m* scrub; (*conjunto de matas*) thicket

matraca *f* rattle. **dar ~** pester

matraz *m* flask

matriarca *f* matriarch. **~do** *m* matriarchy. **~l** *adj* matriarchal

matr|ícula *f* (*lista*) register, list; (*inscripción*) registration; (*Auto*) registration number; (*placa*) licence plate. **~icular** *vt* register. **~icularse** *vpr* enrol, register

matrimoni|al *adj* matrimonial. **~o** *m* marriage; (*pareja*) married couple

matriz *f* matrix; (*molde*) mould; (*útero*) womb, uterus

matrona *f* matron; (*partera*) midwife

matutino *adj* morning

maull|ar *vi* miaow. **~ido** *m* miaow

mausoleo *m* mausoleum

maxilar *adj* maxillary. • *m* jaw(bone)

máxim|a *f* maxim. **~e** *adv* especially. **~o** *adj* maximum; (punto) highest. • *m* maximum

maya *f* daisy. • *adj* Mayan. • *m & f* (*persona*) Maya

mayo *m* May

mayonesa *f* mayonnaise

mayor *adj* (*más grande, comparativo*) bigger; (*más grande, superlativo*) biggest; (*de edad, comparativo*) older; (*de edad, superlativo*) oldest; (*adulto*) grown-up; (*principal*) main, major; (*Mus*) major. • *m & f* (*adulto*) adult. **al por ~** wholesale. **~al** *m* foreman. **~azgo** *m* entailed estate

mayordomo *m* butler

mayor|ía *f* majority. **~ista** *m & f* wholesaler. **~itario** *adj* majority; (socio) principal. **~mente** *adv* especially

mayúscul|a *f* capital (letter). **~o** *adj* capital; (*fig, grande*) big

mazacote *m* hard mass

mazapán *m* marzipan

mazmorra *f* dungeon

mazo *m* mallet; (*manojo*) bunch; (*LAm, de naipes*) pack (*Brit*), deck (*Amer*)

mazorca *f* cob. **~ de maíz** corncob

me *pron* (*acusativo*) me; (*dativo*) (to) me; (*reflexivo*) (to) myself

mecánic|a *f* mechanics. **~o** *adj* mechanical. • *m* mechanic

mecani|smo *m* mechanism. **~zación** *f* mechanization. **~zar** 10 *vt* mechanize

mecanograf|ía *f* typing. **~iado** *adj* typed, typewritten. **~iar** 20 *vt* type

mecanógrafo *m* typist

mecate *m* (*Mex*) string; (*más grueso*) rope

mecedora *f* rocking chair

mecenas *m & f invar* patron

mecer 9 *vt* rock; swing (columpio). **~se** *vpr* rock; (*en un columpio*) swing

mecha *f* (*de vela*) wick; (*de explosivo*) fuse. **~s** *fpl* highlights

mechar *vt* stuff, lard
mechero *m* (cigarette) lighter
mechón *m* (*de pelo*) lock
medall|a *f* medal. **~ón** *m* medallion; (*relicario*) locket
media *f* stocking; (*promedio*) average. **a ~s** half each
mediación *f* mediation
mediado *adj* half full; (*a mitad de*) halfway through. **~s** *mpl*. **a ~s de marzo** in mid-March
mediador *m* mediator
medialuna *f* (*pl* **mediaslunas**) croissant
median|amente *adv* fairly. **~a** *f* (*Auto*) central reservation (*Brit*), median strip (*Amer*). **~era** *f* party wall. **~ero** *adj* (muro) party. **~o** *adj* medium; (*mediocre*) average, mediocre
medianoche *f* (*pl* **mediasnoches**) midnight; (*Culin*) type of roll
mediante *prep* through, by means of
mediar *vi* mediate; (*llegar a la mitad*) be halfway through; (*interceder*) intercede (**por** for)
medic|ación *f* medication. **~amento** *m* medicine. **~ina** *f* medicine. **~inal** *adj* medicinal
medición *f* measurement
médico *adj* medical. • *m* doctor. **~ de cabecera** GP, general practitioner
medid|a *f* measurement; (*unidad*) measure; (*disposición*) measure, step; (*prudencia*) moderation. **a la ~a** made to measure. **a ~a que** as. **en cierta ~a** to a certain extent. **~or** *m* (*LAm*) meter
medieval *adj* medieval. **~ista** *m & f* medievalist
medio *adj* half (a); (*mediano*) average. **dos horas y media** two and a half hours. **~ litro** half a litre. **las dos y media** half past two. • *m* middle; (*Math*) half; (*manera*) means; (*en deportes*) half(-back). **en ~** in the middle (**de** of). **por ~ de** through. **~ ambiente** *m* environment
medioambiental *adj* environmental
mediocr|e *adj* mediocre. **~idad** *f* mediocrity
mediodía *m* midday, noon; (*sur*) south
medioevo *m* Middle Ages
Medio Oriente *m* Middle East
medir **5** *vt* measure; weigh up (palabras etc). • *vi* measure, be. **¿cuánto mide de alto?** how tall is it? **~se** *vpr* (*moderarse*) measure o.s.; (*Mex*, *probarse*) try on
medita|bundo *adj* thoughtful. **~ción** *f* meditation. **~r** *vt* think about. • *vi* meditate
mediterráneo *adj* Mediterranean
Mediterráneo *m* Mediterranean
médium *m & f* medium
médula *f* marrow
medusa *f* jellyfish
megáfono *m* megaphone
megalómano *m* megalomaniac
mejicano *adj & m* Mexican
Méjico *m* Mexico
mejilla *f* cheek
mejillón *m* mussel
mejor *adj & adv* (*comparativo*) better; (*superlativo*) best. **~ dicho** rather. **a lo ~** perhaps. **tanto ~** so much the better. **~a** *f* improvement. **~able** *adj* improvable. **~amiento** *m* improvement
mejorana *f* marjoram
mejorar *vt* improve, better. • *vi*

m

get better. **~se** *vpr* get better

mejunje *m* mixture

melanc|olía *f* melancholy. **~ólico** *adj* melancholic

melaza *f* molasses

melen|a *f* long hair; (*de león*) mane. **~udo** *adj* long-haired

melindr|es *mpl* affectation. **hacer ~es con la comida** be picky about food. **~oso** *adj* affected

mellizo *adj* & *m* twin

melocot|ón *m* peach. **~onero** *m* peach tree

mel|odía *f* melody. **~ódico** *adj* melodic. **~odioso** *adj* melodious

melodram|a *m* melodrama. **~ático** *adj* melodramatic

melómano *m* music lover

melón *m* melon

m

meloso *adj* sickly-sweet; (canción) slushy

membran|a *f* membrane. **~oso** *adj* membranous

membrete *m* letterhead

membrill|ero *m* quince tree. **~o** *m* quince

memo *adj* stupid. • *m* idiot

memorable *adj* memorable

memorando *m*, **memorándum** *m* notebook; (*nota*) memorandum, memo

memori|a *f* memory; (*informe*) report; (*tesis*) thesis. **~as** *fpl* (*autobiografía*) memoirs. **de ~a** by heart; (citar) from memory. **~al** *m* memorial. **~ón** *m* good memory. **~zación** *f* memorizing. **~zar** 10 *vt* memorize

menaje *m* household goods. **~ de cocina** kitchenware

menci|ón *f* mention. **~onado** *adj* aforementioned. **~onar** *vt* mention

mendi|cidad *f* begging. **~gar** 12 *vt* beg for. • *vi* beg. **~go** *m* beggar

mendrugo *m* piece of stale bread

mene|ar *vt* wag (rabo); shake (cabeza); wiggle (caderas). **~arse** *vpr* move; (*con inquietud*) fidget; (*balancearse*) swing. **~o** *m* movement; (sacudida) shake

menester *m* occupation. **ser ~** be necessary. **~oso** *adj* needy

menestra *f* vegetable stew

mengano *m* so-and-so

mengua *f* decrease; (*falta*) lack. **~do** *adj* diminished. **~nte** *adj* (luna) waning; (marea) ebb. **~r** 15 *vt/i* decrease, diminish

meningitis *f* meningitis

menjurje *m* mixture

menopausia *f* menopause

menor *adj* (*más pequeño, comparativo*) smaller; (*más pequeño, superlativo*) smallest; (*más joven, comparativo*) younger; (*más joven, superlativo*) youngest; (*Mus*) minor. • *m* & *f* (*menor de edad*) minor. **al por ~** retail

menos *adj* (*comparativo*) less; (*comparativo, con plural*) fewer; (*superlativo*) least; (*superlativo, con plural*) fewest. • *adv* (*comparativo*) less; (*superlativo*) least. • *prep* except. **al ~** at least. **a ~ que** unless. **las dos ~ diez** ten to two. **ni mucho ~** far from it. **por lo ~** at least. **~cabar** *vt* lessen; (*fig, estropear*) damage. **~cabo** *m* lessening. **~preciable** *adj* contemptible. **~preciar** *vt* despise. **~precio** *m* contempt

mensaje *m* message. **~ro** *m* messenger

menso *adj* (*LAm, fam*) stupid

menstru|ación *f* menstruation. **~al** *adj* menstrual. **~ar** 21 *vi* menstruate

mensual *adj* monthly. **~idad** *f* monthly pay; (*cuota*) monthly payment

mensurable *adj* measurable

menta *f* mint

mental *adj* mental. **~idad** *f* mentality. **~mente** *adv* mentally

mentar 1 *vt* mention, name

mente *f* mind

mentecato *adj* stupid. • *m* idiot

mentir 4 *vi* lie. **~a** *f* lie. **~ijillas** *fpl*. **de ~ijillas** for a joke. **~oso** *adj* lying. • *m* liar

mentís *m invar* denial

mentor *m* mentor

menú *m* menu

menud|ear *vi* happen frequently; (*Mex, Com*) sell retail. **~encia** *f* trifle. **~encias** *fpl* (*LAm*) giblets. **~eo** *m* (*Mex*) retail trade. **~illos** *mpl* giblets. **~o** *adj* small; (lluvia) fine. **a ~o** often. **~os** *mpl* giblets

meñique *adj* (dedo) little. • *m* little finger

meollo *m* (*médula*) marrow; (*de tema etc*) heart

merca|chifle *m* hawker; (*fig*) profiteer. **~der** *m* merchant. **~dería** *f* (*LAm*) merchandise. **~do** *m* market. **M~do Común** Common Market. **~do negro** black market

mercan|cía(s) *f(pl)* goods, merchandise. **~te** *adj* merchant. • *m* merchant ship. **~til** *adj* mercantile, commercial. **~tilismo** *m* mercantilism

merced *f* favour. **su/vuestra ~** your honour

mercenario *adj & m* mercenary

mercer|ía *f* haberdashery (*Brit*), notions (*Amer*).

mercurial *adj* mercurial

mercurio *m* mercury

merec|edor *adj* worthy (**de** of). **~er** 11 *vt* deserve. **~erse** *vpr* deserve. **~idamente** *adv* deservedly. **~ido** *adj* well deserved. **~imiento** *m* (*mérito*) merit

merend|ar 1 *vt* have as an afternoon snack. • *vi* have an afternoon snack. **~ero** *m* snack bar; (*lugar*) picnic area

merengue *m* meringue

meridi|ano *adj* midday; (*fig*) dazzling. • *m* meridian. **~onal** *adj* southern. • *m* southerner

merienda *f* afternoon snack

merino *adj* merino

mérito *m* merit; (*valor*) worth

meritorio *adj* praiseworthy. • *m* unpaid trainee

merluza *f* hake

merma *f* decrease. **~r** *vt/i* decrease, reduce

mermelada *f* jam

mero *adj* mere; (*Mex, verdadero*) real. • *adv* (*Mex, precisamente*) exactly; (*Mex, casi*) nearly. • *m* grouper

merode|ador *m* prowler. **~ar** *vi* prowl

mes *m* month

mesa *f* table; (*para escribir o estudiar*) desk. **poner la ~** lay the table

mesarse *vpr* tear at one's hair

meser|a *f* (*LAm*) waitress. **~o** *m* (*LAm*) waiter

meseta *f* plateau; (*descansillo*) landing

Mesías *m* Messiah

mesilla *f*, **mesita** *f* small table. **~**

de noche bedside table
mesón *m* inn
mesoner|a *f* landlady. **~o** *m* landlord
mestiz|aje *m* crossbreeding. **~o** *adj* (persona) half-caste; (animal) cross-bred. ● *m* (*persona*) half-caste; (*animal*) cross-breed
mesura *f* moderation. **~do** *adj* moderate
meta *f* goal; (*de una carrera*) finish
metabolismo *m* metabolism
metafísic|a *f* metaphysics. **~o** *adj* metaphysical
met|áfora *f* metaphor. **~afórico** *adj* metaphorical
met|al *m* metal; (*de la voz*) timbre. **~ales** *mpl* (*instrumentos de latón*) brass. **~álico** *adj* (objeto) metal; (sonido) metallic
metal|urgia *f* metallurgy. **~úrgico** *adj* metallurgical
metamorfosis *f invar* metamorphosis
metedura de pata *f* blunder
mete|órico *adj* meteoric. **~orito** *m* meteorite. **~oro** *m* meteor. **~orología** *f* meteorology. **~orológico** *adj* meteorological. **~orólogo** *m* meteorologist
meter *vt* put; score (un gol); (*enredar*) involve; (*causar*) make. **~se** *vpr* get involved (**en** in); (*entrometerse*) meddle. **~se con uno** pick a quarrel with s.o.
meticulos|idad *f* meticulousness. **~o** *adj* meticulous
metida de pata *f* (*LAm*) blunder
metido *m* reprimand. ● *adj*. **~ en años** getting on. **estar ~ en algo** be involved in sth. **estar muy ~ con uno** be well in with s.o.
metódico *adj* methodical
metodis|mo *m* Methodism. **~ta** *adj & m & f* Methodist
método *m* method
metodología *f* methodology
metraje *m* length. **de largo ~** (película) feature
metrall|a *f* shrapnel. **~eta** *f* submachine gun
métric|a *f* metrics. **~o** *adj* metric; (verso) metrical
metro *m* metre; (*tren*) underground (*Brit*), subway (*Amer*). **~ cuadrado** square metre
metrónomo *m* metronome
metr|ópoli *f* metropolis. **~opolitano** *adj* metropolitan. ● *m* metropolitan; (*tren*) underground (*Brit*), subway (*Amer*)
mexicano *adj & m* Mexican
México *m* Mexico. **~ D. F.** Mexico City
mezcal *m* (*Mex*) mescal
mezc|la *f* (*acción*) mixing; (*substancia*) mixture; (*argamasa*) mortar. **~lador** *m* mixer. **~lar** *vt* mix; shuffle (los naipes). **~larse** *vpr* mix; (*intervenir*) interfere. **~olanza** *f* mixture
mezquin|dad *f* meanness. **~o** *adj* mean; (*escaso*) meagre. ● *m* mean person
mezquita *f* mosque
mi *adj* my. ● *m* (*Mus*) E; (*solfa*) mi
mí *pron* me
miau *m* miaow
mica *f* (*silicato*) mica
mico *m* (long-tailed) monkey
micro|bio *m* microbe. **~biología** *f* microbiology. **~cosmos** *m invar* microcosm. **~film(e)** *m* microfilm
micrófono *m* microphone
microonda *f* microwave. **~s** *m invar* microwave oven

microordenador *m* microcomputer

micros|cópico *adj* microscopic. **~copio** *m* microscope. **~urco** *m* long-playing record

miedo *m* fear (**a** for). **dar ~** frighten. **morirse de ~** be scared to death. **tener ~** be frightened. **~so** *adj* fearful

miel *f* honey

miembro *m* limb; (*persona*) member

mientras *conj* while. • *adv* meanwhile. **~ que** whereas. **~ tanto** in the meantime

miércoles *m invar* Wednesday. **~ de ceniza** Ash Wednesday

mierda *f* (✱) shit

mies *f* ripe, grain

miga *f* crumb; (*fig, meollo*) essence. **~jas** *fpl* crumbs; (*sobras*) scraps. **~r** 12 *vt* crumble

migra|ción *f* migration. **~torio** *adj* migratory

mijo *m* millet

mil *adj & m* a/one thousand. **~es de** thousands of. **~ novecientos noventa y nueve** nineteen ninety-nine. **~ euros** a thousand euros

milagro *m* miracle. **~so** *adj* miraculous

milen|ario *adj* millenial. **~io** *m* millennium

milésimo *adj & m* thousandth

mili *f* ! military service. **~cia** *f* soldiering; (*gente armada*) militia

mili|gramo *m* milligram. **~litro** *m* millilitre

milímetro *m* millimetre

militante *adj & m & f* activist

militar *adj* military. • *m* soldier. **~ismo** *m* militarism. **~ista** *adj* militaristic. • *m & f* militarist. **~izar** 10 *vt* militarize

milla *f* mile

millar *m* thousand. **a ~es** by the thousand

mill|ón *m* million. **un ~ón de libros** a million books. **~onada** *f* fortune. **~onario** *m* millionaire. **~onésimo** *adj & m* millionth

milonga *f* popular dance and music from the River Plate region

milpa *f* (*Mex*) maize field, cornfield (*Amer*)

milpies *m invar* woodlouse

mimar *vt* spoil

mimbre *m & f* wicker. **~arse** *vpr* sway. **~ra** *f* osier. **~ral** *m* osier-bed

mimetismo *m* mimicry

mímic|a *f* mime. **~o** *adj* mimic

mimo *m* mime; (*adj un niño*) spoiling; (*caricia*) cuddle

mimosa *f* mimosa

mina *f* mine. **~r** *vt* mine; (*fig*) undermine

minarete *m* minaret

mineral *m* mineral; (*mena*) ore. **~ogía** *f* mineralogy. **~ogista** *m & f* mineralogist

miner|ía *f* mining. **~o** *adj* mining. • *m* miner

miniatura *f* miniature

minifundio *m* smallholding

minimizar 10 *vt* minimize

mínim|o *adj & m* minimum. **como ~** at least. **~um** *m* minimum

minino *m* ! cat, puss !

minist|erial *adj* ministerial; (reunión) cabinet. **~erio** *m* ministry. **~ro** *m* minister

minor|ía *f* minority. **~idad** *f* minority. **~ista** *m & f* retailer

minuci|a *f* trifle. **~osidad** *f* thoroughness. **~oso** *adj* thorough; (*de-*

m

tallado) detailed
minúscul|a *f* lower case letter. **~o** *adj* tiny
minuta *f* draft copy; (*de abogado*) bill
minut|ero *m* minute hand. **~o** *m* minute
mío *adj & pron* mine. **un amigo ~** a friend of mine
miop|e *adj* short-sighted. • *m & f* short-sighted person. **~ía** *f* short-sightedness
mira *f* sight; (*fig, intención*) aim. **a la ~** on the lookout. **con ~s a** with a view to. **~da** *f* look. **echar una ~da a** glance at. **~do** *adj* careful with money; (*comedido*) considerate. **bien ~do** highly regarded. **no estar bien ~do** be frowned upon. **~dor** *m* viewpoint. **~miento** *m* consideration. **~r** *vt* look at; (*observar*) watch; (*considerar*) consider. **~r fijamente a** stare at. • *vi* look (edificio etc). **~ hacia** face. **~rse** *vpr* (personas) look at each other
mirilla *f* peephole
miriñaque *m* crinoline
mirlo *m* blackbird
mirón *adj* nosey. • *m* nosey-parker; (*espectador*) onlooker
mirto *m* myrtle
misa *f* mass. **~l** *m* missal
misántropo *m* misanthropist
miscelánea *f* miscellany; (*Mex, tienda*) corner shop (*Brit*), small general store (*Amer*)
miser|able *adj* very poor; (*lastimoso*) miserable; (*tacaño*) mean. **~ia** *f* extreme poverty; (*suciedad*) squalor
misericordi|a *f* pity; (*piedad*) mercy. **~oso** *adj* merciful
mísero *adj* miserable; (*tacaño*) mean; (*malvado*) wicked
misil *m* missile
misi|ón *f* mission. **~onero** *m* missionary
misiva *f* missive
mism|ísimo *adj* very same. **~o** *adj* same; (*después de pronombre personal*) myself, yourself, himself, herself, itself, ourselves, yourselves, themselves; (enfático) very. • *adv.* **ahora ~** right now. **aquí ~** right here. **lo ~** the same
misterio *m* mystery. **~so** *adj* mysterious
místic|a *f* mysticism. **~o** *adj* mystical. • *m* mystic
mistifica|ción *f* mystification. **~r** **7** *vt* mystify
mitad *f* half; (*centro*) middle. **cortar algo por la ~** cut sth in half
mitigar **12** *vt* mitigate; quench (sed); relieve (dolor etc)
mitin *m*, **mitín** *m* meeting
mito *m* myth. **~logía** *f* mythology. **~lógico** *adj* mythological
mitón *m* mitten
mitote *m* (*Mex*) Aztec dance
mixt|o *adj* mixed. **educación mixta** coeducation
mobbing *m* harassment
mobiliario *m* furniture
moce|dad *f* youth. **~río** *m* young people. **~tón** *m* strapping lad. **~tona** *f* strapping girl
mochales *adj invar.* **estar ~** be round the bend
mochila *f* rucksack
mocho *adj* blunt. • *m* butt end
mochuelo *m* little owl
moción *f* motion
moco *m* mucus. **limpiarse los ~s** blow one's nose
moda *f* fashion. **estar de ~** be in

fashion. **~l** *adj* modal. **~les** *mpl* manners. **~lidad** *f* kind

model|ado *m* modelling. **~ador** *m* modeller. **~ar** *vt* model; (*fig, configurar*) form. **~o** *m & f* model

módem *m* modem

modera|ción *f* moderation. **~do** *adj* moderate. **~r** *vt* moderate; reduce (velocidad). **~rse** *vpr* control oneself

modern|idad *f* modernity. **~ismo** *m* modernism. **~ista** *m & f* modernist. **~izar** 10 *vt* modernize. **~o** *adj* modern; (*a la moda*) fashionable

modest|ia *f* modesty. **~o** *adj* modest

módico *adj* moderate

modifica|ción *f* modification. **~r** 7 *vt* modify

modismo *m* idiom

modist|a *f* dressmaker. **~o** *m* designer

modo *m* manner, way; (*Gram*) mood; (*Mus*) mode. **~ de ser** character. **de ~ que** so that. **de ningún ~** certainly not. **de todos ~s** anyhow. **ni ~** (*LAm*) no way

modorra *f* drowsiness

modula|ción *f* modulation. **~dor** *m* modulator. **~r** *vt* modulate

módulo *m* module

mofa *f* mockery. **~rse** *vpr*. **~rse de** make fun of

mofeta *f* skunk

moflet|e *m* chubby cheek. **~udo** *adj* with chubby cheeks

mohín *m* grimace. **hacer un ~** pull a face

moho *m* mould; (*óxido*) rust. **~so** *adj* mouldy; (metales) rusty

moisés *m* Moses basket

mojado *adj* wet

mojar *vt* wet; (*empapar*) soak; (*humedecer*) moisten, dampen

mojigat|ería *f* prudishness. **~o** *m* prude. • *adj* prudish

mojón *m* boundary post; (*señal*) signpost

molar *m* molar

mold|e *m* mould; (*aguja*) knitting needle. **~ear** *vt* mould, shape; (*fig*) form. **~ura** *f* moulding

mole *f* mass, bulk. • *m* (*Mex, salsa*) chili sauce with chocolate and sesame

mol|écula *f* molecule. **~ecular** *adj* molecular

mole|dor *adj* grinding. • *m* grinder. **~r** 2 grind

molest|ar *vt* annoy; (*incomodar*) bother. **¿le ~a que fume?** do you mind if I smoke? • *vi* be a nuisance. **no ~ar** do not disturb. **~arse** *vpr* bother; (*ofenderse*) take offence. **~ia** *f* bother, nuisance; (*inconveniente*) inconvenience; (*incomodidad*) discomfort. **~o** *adj* annoying; (*inconveniente*) inconvenient; (*ofendido*) offended

molicie *f* softness; (*excesiva comodidad*) easy life

molido *adj* ground; (*fig, muy cansado*) worn out

molienda *f* grinding

molin|ero *m* miller. **~ete** *m* toy windmill. **~illo** *m* mill; (*juguete*) toy windmill. **~o** *m* mill. **~ de agua** watermill. **~o de viento** windmill

molleja *f* gizzard

mollera *f* (*de la cabeza*) crown; (*fig, sesera*) brains

molusco *m* mollusc

moment|áneamente *adv* momentarily. **~áneo** *adj* (*breve*) momentary; (*pasajero*) temporary. **~o** *m* moment; (*ocasión*) time. **al ~o** at once. **de ~o** for the moment

momi|a *f* mummy. **~ficar** 7 *vt* mummify. **~ficarse** *vpr* become mummified

monacal *adj* monastic

monada *f* beautiful thing; (*niño bonito*) cute kid; (*acción tonta*) silliness

monaguillo *m* altar boy

mon|arca *m & f* monarch. **~arquía** *f* monarchy. **~árquico** *adj* monarchical

monasterio *m* monastery

mond|a *f* peeling; (*piel*) peel. **~adientes** *m invar* toothpick. **~adura** *f* peeling; (*piel*) peel. **~ar** *vt* peel (fruta etc). **~o** *adj* (*sin pelo*) bald

m

mondongo *m* innards

moned|a *f* coin; (*de un país*) currency. **~ero** *m* purse (*Brit*), change purse (*Amer*)

monetario *adj* monetary

mongolismo *m* Down's syndrome

monigote *m* weak character; (*muñeco*) rag doll; (*dibujo*) doodle

monitor *m* monitor

monj|a *f* nun. **~e** *m* monk. **~il** *adj* nun's; (*como de monja*) like a nun

mono *m* monkey; (*sobretodo*) overalls. • *adj* pretty

monocromo *adj & m* monochrome

monóculo *m* monocle

mon|ogamia *f* monogamy. **~ógamo** *adj* monogamous

monogra|fía *f* monograph. **~ma** *m* monogram

mon|ologar 12 *vi* soliloquize. **~ólogo** *m* monologue

monoplano *m* monoplane

monopoli|o *m* monopoly. **~zar** 10 *vt* monopolize

monos|ilábico *adj* monosyllabic. **~ílabo** *m* monosyllable

monoteís|mo *m* monotheism. **~ta** *adj* monotheistic. • *m & f* monotheist

mon|otonía *f* monotony. **~ótono** *adj* monotonous

monseñor *m* monsignor

monstruo *m* monster. **~sidad** *f* monstrosity; (*atrocidad*) atrocity. **~so** *adj* monstrous

monta *f* mounting; (*valor*) total value

montacargas *m invar* service lift (*Brit*), service elevator (*Amer*)

monta|dor *m* fitter. **~je** *m* assembly; (*Cine*) montage; (*teatro*) staging, production

montañ|a *f* mountain. **~a rusa** roller coaster. **~ero** *adj* mountaineer. **~és** *adj* mountain. • *m* highlander. **~ismo** *m* mountaineering. **~oso** *adj* mountainous

montaplatos *m invar* dumb waiter

montar *vt* ride; (*subirse a*) get on; (*ensamblar*) assemble; cock (arma); set up (una casa, un negocio). • *vi* ride; (*subirse*) mount. **~ a caballo** ride a horse

monte *m* (*montaña*) mountain; (*terreno inculto*) scrub; (*bosque*) woodland. **~ de piedad** pawnshop

montepío *m* charitable fund for dependents

montés *adj* wild

montevideano *adj & m* Montevidean

montículo *m* hillock

montón *m* heap, pile. **a montones** in abundance. **un ~ de**

loads of

montura *f* mount; (*silla*) saddle

monument|al *adj* monumental; (*fig, muy grande*) enormous. **~o** *m* monument

monzón *m & f* monsoon

moñ|a *f* ribbon. **~o** *m* bun; (*LAm, lazo*) bow

moque|o *m* runny nose. **~ro** *m* ① handkerchief

moqueta *f* fitted carpet

moquillo *m* distemper

mora *f* mulberry; (*de zarzamora*) blackberry; (*Jurid*) default

morada *f* dwelling

morado *adj* purple

morador *m* inhabitant

moral *m* mulberry tree. ● *f* morals. ● *adj* moral. **~eja** *f* moral. **~idad** *f* morality. **~ista** *m & f* moralist. **~izador** *adj* moralizing. ● *m* moralist. **~izar** ⑩ *vt* moralize

morar *vi* live

moratoria *f* moratorium

mórbido *adj* soft; (*malsano*) morbid

morbo *m* illness. **~sidad** *f* morbidity. **~so** *adj* unhealthy

morcilla *f* black pudding

morda|cidad *f* sharpness. **~z** *adj* scathing

mordaza *f* gag

morde|dura *f* bite. **~r** ② *vt* bite; (*Mex, exigir soborno a*) extract a bribe from. ● *vi* bite. **~rse** *vpr* bite o.s. **~rse las uñas** bite one's nails

mordi|da *f* (*Mex*) bribe. **~sco** *m* bite. **~squear** *vt* nibble (at)

moreno *adj* (*con ser*) dark; (*de pelo obscuro*) dark-haired; (*de raza negra*) dark-skinned; (*con estar*) brown, tanned

morera *f* white mulberry tree

moretón *m* bruise

morfema *m* morpheme

morfin|a *f* morphine. **~ómano** *m* morphine addict

morfol|ogía *f* morphology. **~ógico** *adj* morphological

moribundo *adj* dying

morir ⑥ (*pp* **muerto**) *vi* die; (*fig, extinguirse*) die away; (*fig, terminar*) end. **~ ahogado** drown. **~se** *vpr* die. **~se de hambre** starve to death; (*fig*) be starving. **se muere por una flauta** she's dying to have a flute

morisco *adj* Moorish. ● *m* Moor

morm|ón *m* Mormon. **~ónico** *adj* Mormon. **~onismo** *m* Mormonism

moro *adj* Moorish. ● *m* Moor

morral *m* (*mochila*) rucksack; (*de cazador*) gamebag; (*para caballos*) nosebag

morrillo *m* nape of the neck

morriña *f* homesickness

morro *m* snout

morrocotudo *adj* (①, *tremendo*) terrible; (*estupendo*) terrific ①

morsa *f* walrus

mortaja *f* shroud

mortal *adj & m & f* mortal. **~idad** *f* mortality. **~mente** *adv* mortally

mortandad *f* loss of life; (*Mil*) carnage

mortecino *adj* failing; (color) pale

mortero *m* mortar

mortífero *adj* deadly

mortifica|ción *f* mortification. **~r** ⑦ *vt* (*atormentar*) torment. **~rse** *vpr* distress o.s.

mortuorio *adj* death

mosaico *m* mosaic; (*Mex, baldosa*) floor tile

mosca *f* fly. **~rda** *f* blowfly. **~rdón** *m* botfly; (*de cuerpo azul*)

m

bluebottle
moscatel *adj* muscatel
moscón *m* botfly; (*mosca de cuerpo azul*) bluebottle
moscovita *adj & m & f* Muscovite
mosque|arse *vpr* get cross. **~o** *m* resentment
mosquete *m* musket. **~ro** *m* musketeer
mosquit|ero *m* mosquito net. **~o** *m* mosquito
mostacho *m* moustache
mostaza *f* mustard
mosto *m* must, grape juice
mostrador *m* counter
mostrar 2 *vt* show. **~se** *vpr* (show oneself to) be. **se mostró muy amable** he was very kind
mota *f* spot, speck
mote *m* nickname
motea|do *adj* speckled. **~r** *vt* speckle
motejar *vt* call
motel *m* motel
motete *m* motet
motín *m* riot; (*de tropas, tripulación*) mutiny
motiv|ación *f* motivation. **~ar** *vt* motivate. **~o** *m* reason. **con ~o de** because of
motocicl|eta *f* motor cycle, motor bike 🅃. **~ista** *m & f* motorcyclist
motoneta *f* (*LAm*) (motor) scooter
motor *adj* motor. • *m* motor, engine. **~ de arranque** starter motor. **~a** *f* motor boat. **~ismo** *m* motorcycling. **~ista** *m & f* motorist; (*de una moto*) motorcyclist. **~izar** 10 *vt* motorize
motriz *adj* motor
move|dizo *adj* movable; (*poco firme*) unstable; (persona) fickle. **~r** 2 *vt* move; shake (la cabeza); (*provocar*) cause. **~rse** *vpr* move; (*darse prisa*) hurry up
movi|ble *adj* movable. **~do** *adj* moved; (*Foto*) blurred
móvil *adj* mobile; (*Esp, teléfono*) mobile phone, cellphone. • *m* motive
movili|dad *f* mobility. **~zación** *f* mobilization. **~zar** 10 *vt* mobilize
movimiento *m* movement, motion; (*agitación*) bustle
moza *f* young girl. **~lbete** *m* lad
mozárabe *adj* Mozarabic. • *m & f* Mozarab
moz|o *m* young boy. **~uela** *f* young girl. **~uelo** *m* young boy/lad
mucam|a *f* (*LAm*) servant. **~o** *m* (*LAm*) servant
muchach|a *f* girl; (*sirvienta*) servant, maid. **~o** *m* boy, lad
muchedumbre *f* crowd
mucho *adj* a lot of; (*en negativas, preguntas*) much, a lot of. **~s** a lot of; (*en negativas, preguntas*) many, a lot of. • *pron* a lot; (*personas*) many (people). **como ~** at the most. **ni ~ menos** by no means. **por ~ que** however much. • *adv* a lot, very much; (*tiempo*) long, a long time
mucos|idad *f* mucus. **~o** *adj* mucous
muda *f* change of clothing; (*de animales*) shedding. **~ble** *adj* changeable; (personas) fickle. **~nza** *f* move, removal (*Brit*). **~r** *vt* change; shed (piel). **~rse** *vpr* (*de ropa*) change one's clothes; (*de casa*) move (house)
mudéjar *adj & m & f* Mudejar
mud|ez *f* dumbness. **~o** *adj*

m

dumb; (*callado*) silent
mueble *adj* movable. ● *m* piece of furniture. **~s** *mpl* furniture
mueca *f* grimace, face. **hacer una ~** pull a face
muela *f* back tooth, molar; (*piedra de afilar*) grindstone; (*piedra de molino*) millstone. **~ del juicio** wisdom tooth
muelle *adj* soft. ● *m* spring; (*Naut*) wharf; (*malecón*) jetty
muérdago *m* mistletoe
muero *vb véase* **MORIR**
muert|e *f* death; (*homicidio*) murder. **~o** *adj* dead. ● *m* dead person
muesca *f* nick; (*ranura*) slot
muestra *f* sample; (*prueba*) proof; (*modelo*) model; (*señal*) sign. **~rio** *m* collection of samples
muestro *vb véase* **MOSTRAR**
muevo *vb véase* **MOVER**
mugi|do *m* moo. **~r** **14** *vi* moo
mugr|e *m* dirt. **~iento** *adj* dirty, filthy
mugrón *m* sucker
mujer *f* woman; (*esposa*) wife. ● *int* my dear! **~iego** *adj* fond of the women. ● *m* womanizer. **~zuela** *f* prostitute
mula *f* mule. **~da** *f* drove of mules
mulato *adj* of mixed race (*black and white*). ● *m* person of mixed race
mulero *m* muleteer
muleta *f* crutch; (*toreo*) stick with a red flag
mulli|do *adj* soft. **~r** **22** *vt* soften
mulo *m* mule
multa *f* fine. **~r** *vt* fine
multi|color *adj* multicoloured. **~copista** *m* duplicator. **~cultural** *adj* multicultural. **~forme** *adj* multiform. **~lateral** *adj* multilateral. **~lingüe** *adj* multilingual. **~millonario** *m* multimillionaire
múltiple *adj* multiple
multiplic|ación *f* multiplication. **~ar** **7** *vt* multiply. **~arse** *vpr* multiply. **~idad** *f* multiplicity
múltiplo *m* multiple
multitud *f* multitude, crowd. **~inario** *adj* mass; (concierto) with mass audience
mund|ano *adj* wordly; (*de la sociedad elegante*) society. **~ial** *adj* world-wide. **la segunda guerra ~ial** the Second World War. **~illo** *m* world, circles. **~o** *m* world. **todo el ~o** everybody
munición *f* ammunition; (*provisiones*) supplies
municip|al *adj* municipal. **~alidad** *f* municipality. **~io** *m* municipality; (*ayuntamiento*) town council
muñe|ca *f* (*en anatomía*) wrist; (*juguete*) doll; (*maniquí*) dummy. **~co** *m* doll. **~quera** *f* wristband
muñón *m* stump
mura|l *adj* mural, wall. ● *m* mural. **~lla** *f* (city) wall. **~r** *vt* wall
murciélago *m* bat
murga *f* street band
murmullo *m* (*incl fig*) murmur
murmura|ción *f* gossip. **~dor** *adj* gossiping. ● *m* gossip. **~r** *vi* murmur; (*criticar*) gossip
muro *m* wall
murria *f* depression
mus *m* card game
musa *f* muse
musaraña *f* shrew
muscula|r *adj* muscular. **~tura** *f* muscles
músculo *m* muscle
musculoso *adj* muscular

muselina *f* muslin
museo *m* museum. ~ **de arte** art gallery
musgo *m* moss. ~**so** *adj* mossy
música *f* music
musical *adj & m* musical
músico *adj* musical. • *m* musician
music|ología *f* musicology. ~**ólogo** *m* musicologist
muslo *m* thigh
mustio *adj* (plantas) withered; (cosas) faded; (personas) gloomy; (*Mex, hipócrita*) two-faced
musulmán *adj & m* Muslim
muta|bilidad *f* mutability. ~**ción** *f* mutation
mutila|ción *f* mutilation. ~**do** *adj* crippled. • *m* cripple. ~**r** *vt* mutilate; maim (persona)
mutis *m* (*en el teatro*) exit. ~**mo** *m* silence
mutu|alidad *f* mutuality; (*asociación*) friendly society. ~**amente** *adv* mutually. ~**o** *adj* mutual
muy *adv* very; (*demasiado*) too

Nn

nabo *m* turnip
nácar *m* mother-of-pearl
nac|er 11 *vi* be born; (pollito) hatch out; (planta) sprout. ~**ido** *adj* born. **recien** ~**ido** newborn. ~**iente** *adj* (sol) rising. ~**imiento** *m* birth; (*de río*) source; (*belén*) crib. **lugar** *m* **de** ~**imiento** place of birth
naci|ón *f* nation. ~**onal** *adj* national. ~**onalidad** *f* nationality. ~**onalismo** *m* nationalism. ~**onalista** *m & f* nationalist. ~**onalizar** 10 *vt* nationalize. ~**onalizarse** *vpr* become naturalized
nada *pron* nothing, not anything. • *adv* not at all. ¡~ **de eso!** nothing of the sort! **antes que** ~ first of all. **¡de** ~**!** (*después de 'gracias'*) don't mention it! **para** ~ (not) at all. **por** ~ **del mundo** not for anything in the world
nada|dor *m* swimmer. ~**r** *vi* swim. ~**r de espalda(s)** do (the) backstroke
nadería *f* trifle
nadie *pron* no one, nobody
nado *m* (*Mex*) swimming. • *adv* **a** ~ swimming
naipe *m* (playing) card. **juegos** *mpl* **de** ~**s** card games
nalga *f* buttock. ~**s** *fpl* bottom. ~**da** *f* (*Mex*) smack on the bottom
nana *f* lullaby
naranj|a *f* orange. ~**ada** *f* orangeade. ~**al** *m* orange grove. ~**ero** *m* orange tree
narcótico *adj & m* narcotic
nariz *f* nose. **¡narices!** rubbish!
narra|ción *f* narration. ~**dor** *m* narrator. ~**r** *vt* tell. ~**tivo** *adj* narrative
nasal *adj* nasal
nata *f* cream
natación *f* swimming
natal *adj* native; (pueblo etc) home. ~**idad** *f* birth rate
natillas *fpl* custard
nativo *adj & m* native
nato *adj* born
natural *adj* natural. • *m* native. ~**eza** *f* nature. ~**eza muerta** still life. ~**idad** *f* naturalness. ~**ista** *m & f* naturalist. ~**izar** 10 *vt* natural-

ize. **~izarse** *vpr* become naturalized. **~mente** *adv* naturally. ● *int* of course!

naufrag|ar 12 *vi* (barco) sink; (persona) be shipwrecked; (*fig*) fail. **~io** *m* shipwreck

náufrago *adj* shipwrecked. ● *m* shipwrecked person

náuseas *fpl* nausea. **dar ~s a uno** make s.o. feel sick. **sentir ~s** feel sick

náutico *adj* nautical

navaja *f* penknife; (*de afeitar*) razor. **~zo** *m* slash

naval *adj* naval

nave *f* ship; (*de iglesia*) nave. **~ espacial** spaceship. **quemar las ~s** burn one's boats

navega|ble *adj* navigable; (barco) seaworthy. **~ción** *f* navigation; (*tráfico*) shipping. **~dor** *m* (*Informática*) browser. **~nte** *m & f* navigator. **~r** 12 *vi* sail; (*Informática*) browse

Navid|ad *f* Christmas. **~eño** *adj* Christmas. **en ~ades** at Christmas. **¡feliz ~ad!** Happy Christmas! **por ~ad** at Christmas

nazi *adj & m & f* Nazi. **~smo** *m* Nazism

neblina *f* mist

nebuloso *adj* misty; (*fig*) vague

necedad *f* foolishness. **decir ~es** talk nonsense. **hacer una ~** do sth stupid

necesari|amente *adv* necessarily. **~o** *adj* necessary

necesi|dad *f* need; (*cosa esencial*) necessity; (*pobreza*) poverty. **~dades** *fpl* hardships. **no hay ~dad** there's no need. **por ~dad** (out) of necessity. **~tado** *adj* in need (**de** of). **~tar** *vt* need. ● *vi*. **~tar de** need

necio *adj* silly. ● *m* idiot

néctar *m* nectar

nectarina *f* nectarine

nefasto *adj* unfortunate; (consecuencia) disastrous; (influencia) harmful

nega|ción *f* denial; (*Gram*) negative. **~do** *adj* useless. **~r** 1 & 12 *vt* deny; (*rehusar*) refuse. **~rse** *vpr* refuse (**a** to). **~tiva** *f* (*acción*) denial; (*acción de rehusar*) refusal. **~tivo** *adj & m* negative

negligen|cia *f* negligence. **~te** *adj* negligent

negoci|able *adj* negotiable. **~ación** *f* negotiation. **~ante** *m & f* dealer. **~ar** *vt/i* negotiate. **~ar en** trade in. **~o** *m* business; (*Com, trato*) deal. **~os** *mpl* business. **hombre** *m* **de ~os** businessman

negr|a *f* black woman; (*Mus*) crotchet. **~o** *adj* black; (ojos) dark. ● *m* (*color*) black; (*persona*) black man. **~ura** *f* blackness. **~uzco** *adj* blackish

nen|a *f* little girl. **~o** *m* little boy

nenúfar *m* water lily

neocelandés *adj* from New Zealand. ● *m* New Zealander

neón *m* neon

nepotismo *m* nepotism

nervio *m* nerve; (*tendón*) sinew; (*en botánica*) vein. **~sidad** *f*, **~sismo** *m* nervousness; (*impaciencia*) impatience. **~so** *adj* nervous; (*de temperamento*) highly-strung. **ponerse ~so** get nervous

neto *adj* clear; (verdad) simple; (*Com*) net

neumático *adj* pneumatic. ● *m* tyre

neumonía *f* pneumonia

neur|algia *f* neuralgia. **~ología** *f* neurology. **~ólogo** *m* neurologist. **~osis** *f* neurosis. **~ótico** *adj* neurotic

neutr|al *adj* neutral. **~alidad** *f* neutrality. **~alizar** 10 *vt* neutralize. **~o** *adj* neutral; (*Gram*) neuter

neva|da *f* snowfall. **~r** 1 *vi* snow. **~sca** *f* blizzard

nevera *f* refrigerator, fridge (*Brit*)

nevisca *f* light snowfall

nexo *m* link

ni *conj*. **~... ~** neither... nor. **~ aunque** not even if. **~ siquiera** not even. **sin...~ ...** without ... or...

Nicaragua *f* Nicaragua

nicaragüense *adj & m & f* Nicaraguan

nicho *m* niche

nicotina *f* nicotine

nido *m* nest; (*de ladrones*) den

niebla *f* fog. **hay ~** it's foggy. **un día de ~** a foggy day

n

niet|a *f* granddaughter. **~o** *m* grandson. **~os** *mpl* grandchildren

nieve *f* snow; (*Mex, helado*) sorbet

niki *m* polo shirt

nimi|edad *f* triviality. **~o** *adj* insignificant

ninfa *f* nymph

ningún *véase* **NINGUNO**

ninguno *adj* (*delante de nombre masculino en singular* **ningún**) no; (*con otro negativo*) any. **de ninguna manera, de ningún modo** by no means. **en ninguna parte** nowhere. **sin ningún amigo** without any friends. • *pron* (*de dos*) neither; (*de más de dos*) none; (*nadie*) no-one, nobody

niñ|a *f* (little) girl. **~era** *f* nanny. **~ería** *f* childish thing. **~ez** *f* childhood. **~o** *adj* childish. • *m* (little) boy **de ~o** as a child. **desde ~o** from childhood

níquel *m* nickel

níspero *m* medlar

nitidez *f* clarity; (*de foto, imagen*) sharpness

nítido *adj* clear; (*foto, imagen*) sharp

nitrógeno *m* nitrogen

nivel *m* level; (*fig*) standard. **~ de vida** standard of living. **~ar** *vt* level. **~arse** *vpr* become level

no *adv* not; (*como respuesta*) no. **¿~?** isn't it? **¡a que ~!** I bet you don't! **¡cómo ~!** of course! **Felipe ~ tiene hijos** Felipe has no children. **¡que ~!** certainly not!

nob|iliario *adj* noble. **~le** *adj & m & f* noble. **~leza** *f* nobility

noche *f* night. **~ vieja** New Year's Eve. **de ~** at night. **hacerse de ~** get dark. **hacer ~** spend the night. **media ~** midnight. **en la ~** (*LAm*), **por la ~** at night

> i
>
> **Nochevieja** In Spain and other Spanish-speaking countries, where it is known as Año Nuevo, it is customary to see the New Year in by eating twelve grapes for good luck, one on each chime of the clock at midnight.

Nochebuena *f* Christmas Eve

noción *f* notion. **nociones** *fpl* rudiments

nocivo *adj* harmful

nocturno *adj* nocturnal; (*clase*) evening; (*tren etc*) night. • *m* nocturne

nodriza *f* wet nurse

nogal *m* walnut tree; (*madera*) walnut

nómada *adj* nomadic. • *m & f* nomad

nombr|ado *adj* famous; (*susodicho*) aforementioned. **~amiento** *m* appointment. **~ar** *vt* appoint; (*citar*) mention. **~e** *m* name; (*Gram*) noun; (*fama*) renown. **~e de pila** Christian name. **en ~e de** in the name of. **no tener ~e** be unspeakable. **poner de ~e** call

nomeolvides *m invar* forget-me-not

nómina *f* payroll

nomina|l *adj* nominal. **~tivo** *adj & m* nominative. **~tivo a** (cheque etc) made out to

non *adj* odd. • *m* odd number. **pares y ~es** odds and evens

nono *adj* ninth

nordeste *adj* (región) north-eastern; (viento) north-easterly. • *m* northeast

nórdico *adj* Nordic. • *m* Northern European

noria *f* water-wheel; (*en una feria*) big wheel (*Brit*), Ferris wheel (*Amer*)

norma *f* rule

normal *adj* normal. • *f* teachers' training college. **~idad** *f* normality (*Brit*), normalcy (*Amer*). **~izar** 10 *vt* normalize. **~mente** *adv* normally, usually

noroeste *adj* (región) north-western; (viento) north-westerly. • *m* northwest

norte *adj* (región) northern; (viento, lado) north. • *m* north; (*fig, meta*) aim

Norteamérica *f* (North) America

norteamericano *adj & m* (North) American

norteño *adj* northern. • *m* northerner

Noruega *f* Norway

noruego *adj & m* Norwegian

nos *pron* (*acusativo*) us; (*dativo*) (to) us; (*reflexivo*) (to) ourselves; (*recíproco*) (to) each other

nosotros *pron* we; (*con prep*) us

nost|algia *f* nostalgia; (*de casa, de patria*) homesickness. **~álgico** *adj* nostalgic

nota *f* note; (*de examen etc*) mark. **de ~** famous. **de mala ~** notorious. **digno de ~** notable. **~ble** *adj* notable. **~ción** *f* notation. **~r** *vt* notice. **es de ~r** it should be noted. **hacerse ~r** stand out

notario *m* notary

notici|a *f* (piece of) news. **~as** *fpl* news. **atrasado de ~as** behind with the news. **tener ~as de** hear from. **~ario**, (*LAm*) **~ero** *m* news

notifica|ción *f* notification. **~r** 7 *vt* notify

notori|edad *f* notoriety. **~o** *adj* well-known; (*evidente*) obvious; (*notable*) marked

novato *adj* inexperienced. • *m* novice

novecientos *adj & m* nine hundred

noved|ad *f* newness; (*cosa nueva*) innovation; (*cambio*) change; (*moda*) latest fashion. **llegar sin ~ad** arrive safely. **~oso** *adj* novel

novel|a *f* novel. **~ista** *m & f* novelist

noveno *adj* ninth

noventa *adj & m* ninety; (*nonagésimo*) ninetieth

novia *f* girlfriend; (*prometida*) fiancée; (*en boda*) bride. **~r** *vi* (*LAm*) go out together. **~zgo** *m* engagement

novicio *m* novice

noviembre *m* November

novill|a *f* heifer. **~o** *m* bullock. **hacer ~os** play truant

novio *m* boyfriend; (*prometido*) fiancé; (*en boda*) bridegroom. **los ~s** the bride and groom

nub|arrón *m* large dark cloud. **~e** *f* cloud; (*de insectos etc*) swarm. **~lado** *adj* cloudy, overcast. • *m* cloud. **~lar** *vt* cloud. **~larse** *vpr* become cloudy; (vista) cloud over. **~oso** *adj* cloudy

nuca *f* back of the neck

nuclear *adj* nuclear

núcleo *m* nucleus

nudillo *m* knuckle

nudis|mo *m* nudism. **~ta** *m & f* nudist

nudo *m* knot; (*de asunto etc*) crux. **tener un ~ en la garganta** have a lump in one's throat. **~so** *adj* knotty

nuera *f* daughter-in-law

nuestro *adj* our. • *pron* ours. **~ amigo** our friend. **un coche ~** a car of ours

n

ñ

o

nueva *f* (piece of) news. **~s** *fpl* news. **~mente** *adv* again

Nueva Zelanda *f*, (*LAm*) **Nueva Zelandia** *f* New Zealand

nueve *adj & m* nine

nuevo *adj* new. **de ~** again. **estar ~** be as good as new

nuez *f* walnut. **~ de Adán** Adam's apple. **~ moscada** nutmeg

nul|idad *f* nullity; (*fam, persona*) dead loss 🅸. **~o** *adj* useless; (*Jurid*) null and void

num|eración *f* numbering. **~eral** *adj & m* numeral. **~erar** *vt* number. **~érico** *adj* numerical

número *m* number; (*arábigo, romano*) numeral; (*de zapatos etc*) size; (*billete de lotería*) lottery ticket; (*de publicación*) issue. **sin ~** countless

numeroso *adj* numerous

nunca *adv* never. **~ (ja)más** never again. **casi ~** hardly ever. **como ~** like never before. **más que ~** more than ever

nupcial *adj* nuptial. **banquete ~** wedding breakfast

nutria *f* otter

nutri|ción *f* nutrition. **~do** *adj* nourished, fed; (*fig*) large; (aplausos) loud; (fuego) heavy. **~r** *vt* nourish, feed; (*fig*) feed. **~tivo** *adj* nutritious. **valor** *m* **~tivo** nutritional value

nylon *m* nylon

Ññ

ñapa *f* (*LAm*) extra goods given free

ñato *adj* (*LAm*) snub-nosed

ñoñ|ería *f*, **~ez** *f* insipidity. **~o** *adj* insipid; (*tímido*) bashful; (*quisquilloso*) prudish

Oo

o *conj* or. **~ bien** rather. **~... ~** either ... or

oasis *m invar* oasis

obed|ecer 🅸🅸 *vt/i* obey. **~iencia** *f* obedience. **~iente** *adj* obedient

obes|idad *f* obesity. **~o** *adj* obese

obispo *m* bishop

obje|ción *f* objection. **~tar** *vt/i* object
objetivo *adj* objective. • *m* objective; (*foto etc*) lens
objeto *m* object. **~r** *m* objector. **~ de conciencia** conscientious objector
oblicuo *adj* oblique
obliga|ción *f* obligation; (*Com*) bond. **~do** *adj* obliged; (*forzoso*) obligatory; **~r** 12 *vt* force, oblige. **~rse** *vpr*. **~rse a** undertake to. **~torio** *adj* obligatory
oboe *m* oboe. • *m & f* (*músico*) oboist
obra *f* work; (*acción*) deed; (*de teatro*) play; (*construcción*) building work. **~ maestra** masterpiece. **en ~s** under construction. **por ~ de** thanks to. **~r** *vt* do
obrero *adj* labour; (clase) working. • *m* workman; (*de fábrica, construcción*) worker
obscen|idad *f* obscenity. **~o** *adj* obscene
obscu... *véase* **oscu...**
obsequi|ar *vt* lavish attention on. **~ar con** give, present with. **~o** *m* gift, present; (*agasajo*) attention. **~oso** *adj* obliging
observa|ción *f* observation. **hacer una ~ción** make a remark. **~dor** *m* observer. **~ncia** *f* observance. **~r** *vt* observe; (*notar*) notice. **~torio** *m* observatory
obses|ión *f* obsession. **~ionar** *vt* obsess. **~ivo** *adj* obsessive. **~o** *adj* obsessed
obst|aculizar 10 *vt* hinder; hold up (tráfico). **~áculo** *m* obstacle
obstante: **no ~** *adv* however, nevertheless; (*como prep*) in spite of
obstar *vi*. **eso no obsta para que vaya** that should not prevent him from going
obstina|do *adj* obstinate. **~rse** *vpr*. **~rse en** (+ *infinitivo*) insist on (+ *gerundio*)
obstru|cción *f* obstruction. **~ir** 17 *vt* obstruct
obtener 40 *vt* get, obtain
obtura|dor *m* (*Foto*) shutter. **~r** *vt* plug; fill (muela etc)
obvio *adj* obvious
oca *f* goose
ocasi|ón *f* occasion; (*oportunidad*) opportunity. **aprovechar la ~ón** take the opportunity. **con ~ón de** on the occasion of. **de ~ón** bargain; (*usado*) second-hand. **en ~ones** sometimes. **perder una ~ón** miss a chance. **~onal** *adj* chance. **~onar** *vt* cause
ocaso *m* sunset; (*fig*) decline
occident|al *adj* western. • *m & f* westerner. **~e** *m* west
océano *m* ocean
ochenta *adj & m* eighty
ocho *adj & m* eight. **~cientos** *adj & m* eight hundred
ocio *m* idleness; (*tiempo libre*) leisure time. **~sidad** *f* idleness. **~so** *adj* idle; (*inútil*) pointless
oct|agonal *adj* octagonal. **~ágono** *m* octagon
octano *m* octane
octav|a *f* octave. **~o** *adj & m* eighth
octogenario *adj & m* octogenarian
octubre *m* October
ocular *adj* eye
oculista *m & f* ophthalmologist, ophthalmic optician
ocult|ar *vt* hide. **~arse** *vpr* hide. **~o** *adj* hidden; (*secreto*) secret
ocupa|ción *f* occupation. **~do**

adj occupied; (persona) busy. **estar ~do** (asiento) be taken; (línea telefónica) be engaged (*Brit*), be busy (*Amer*). **~nte** *m & f* occupant. **~r** *vt* occupy, take up (espacio). **~rse** *vpr* look after

ocurr|encia *f* occurrence, event; (*idea*) idea; (*que tiene gracia*) witty remark. **~ir** *vi* happen. **¿qué ~e?** what's the matter? **~irse** *vpr* occur. **se me ~e que** it occurs to me that

oda *f* ode

odi|ar *vt* hate. **~o** *m* hatred. **~oso** *adj* hateful; (persona) horrible

oeste *adj* (región) western; (viento, lado) west. • *m* west

ofen|der *vt* offend; (*insultar*) insult. **~derse** *vpr* take offence. **~sa** *f* offence. **~siva** *f* offensive. **~sivo** *adj* offensive

oferta *f* offer; (*en subasta*) bid. **~s de empleo** situations vacant. **en ~** on (special) offer

O

oficial *adj* official. • *m* skilled worker; (*Mil*) officer

oficin|a *f* office. **~a de colocación** employment office. **~a de turismo** tourist office. **horas** *fpl* **de ~a** business hours. **~ista** *m & f* office worker

oficio *m* trade. **~so** *adj* (*no oficial*) unofficial

ofrec|er 11 *vt* offer; give (fiesta, banquete etc); (*prometer*) promise. **~erse** *vpr* (persona) volunteer. **~imiento** *m* offer

ofrenda *f* offering. **~r** *vt* offer

ofuscar 7 *vt* blind; (*confundir*) confuse. **~se** *vpr* get worked up

oí|ble *adj* audible. **~do** *m* ear; (*sentido*) hearing. **al ~do** in one's ear. **de ~das** by hearsay. **conocer de ~das** have heard of. **de ~do** by ear. **duro de ~do** hard of hearing

oigo *vb véase* **OÍR**

oír 50 *vt* hear. **¡oiga!** listen!; (*al teléfono*) hello!

ojal *m* buttonhole

ojalá *int* I hope so! • *conj* if only

ojea|da *f* glance. **dar una ~da a, echar una ~da a** have a quick glance at. **~r** *vt* have a look at

ojeras *fpl* rings under one's eyes

ojeriza *f* ill will. **tener ~ a** have a grudge against

ojo *m* eye; (*de cerradura*) keyhole; (*de un puente*) span. **¡~!** careful!

ola *f* wave

olé *int* bravo!

olea|da *f* wave. **~je** *m* swell

óleo *m* oil; (*cuadro*) oil painting

oleoducto *m* oil pipeline

oler 2 (*las formas que empiecen por* **ue** *se escriben* **hue**) *vt* smell. • *vi* smell (**a** of). **me huele mal** (*fig*) it sounds fishy to me

olfat|ear *vt* sniff; scent (rastro). **~o** *m* (sense of) smell; (*fig*) intuition

olimpiada *f*, **olimpíada** *f* Olympic games, Olympics

olímpico *adj* Olympic; (*fig, fam*) total

oliv|a *f* olive. **~ar** *m* olive grove. **~o** *m* olive tree

olla *f* pot, casserole. **~ a/de presión, ~ exprés** pressure cooker

olmo *m* elm (tree)

olor *m* smell. **~oso** *adj* sweet-smelling

olvid|adizo *adj* forgetful. **~ar** *vt* forget. **~arse** *vpr* forget. **~arse de** forget. **se me ~ó** I forgot. **~o** *m* oblivion; (*acto*) omission

ombligo *m* navel
omi|sión *f* omission. **~tir** *vt* omit
ómnibus *adj* omnibus
omnipotente *adj* omnipotent
omóplato *m* shoulder blade
once *adj & m* eleven
ond|a *f* wave. **~a corta** short wave. **~a larga** long wave. **longitud** *f* **de ~a** wavelength. **~ear** *vi* wave; (agua) ripple. **~ulación** *f* undulation; (*del pelo*) wave. **~ular** *vi* wave
onomásti|co *adj* (índice) of names. • *m* (*LAm*) saint's day

onomástica See ▷**SANTO**

ONU *abrev* (**Organización de las Naciones Unidas**) UN
OPA *f* take-over bid
opac|ar **7** (*LAm*) make opaque; (*deslucir*) mar; (*anular*) overshadow. **~o** *adj* opaque; (*fig*) dull
opci|ón *f* option. **~onal** *adj* optional
open-jaw *m* open jaws ticket
ópera *f* opera
opera|ción *f* operation; (*Com*) transaction; **~ retorno** (*Esp*) *return to work* (*after the holidays*). **~dor** *m* operator; (*TV*) cameraman; (*Mex, obrero*) machinist. **~r** *vt* operate on; work (milagro etc); (*Mex*) operate (máquina). • *vi* operate; (*Com*) deal. **~rio** *m* machinist. **~rse** *vpr* take place; (*Med*) have an operation. **~torio** *adj* operative
opereta *f* operetta
opin|ar *vi* express one's opinion. • *vt* think. **~ que** think that. **¿qué opinas?** what do you think? **~ión** *f* opinion. **la ~ión pública** public opinion
opio *m* opium
opone|nte *adj* opposing. • *m & f* opponent. **~r** *vt* oppose; offer (resistencia); raise (objeción). **~rse** *vpr* be opposed; (dos personas) oppose each other
oporto *m* port (wine)
oportun|idad *f* opportunity; (*cualidad de oportuno*) timeliness; (*LAm, ocasión*) occasion. **~ista** *m & f* opportunist. **~o** *adj* opportune; (*apropiado*) suitable
oposi|ción *f* opposition. **~ciones** *fpl* public examination. **~tor** *m* candidate; (*Pol*) opponent
opres|ión *f* oppression; (*ahogo*) difficulty in breathing. **~ivo** *adj* oppressive. **~or** *m* oppressor
oprimir *vt* squeeze; press (botón etc); (ropa) be too tight for; (*fig*) oppress
optar *vi* choose. **~ por** opt for
óptic|a *f* optics; (*tienda*) optician's (shop). **~o** *adj* optic(al). • *m* optician
optimis|mo *m* optimism. **~ta** *adj* optimistic. • *m & f* optimist
óptimo *adj* ideal; (condiciones) perfect
opuesto *adj* opposite; (opiniones) conflicting
opulen|cia *f* opulence. **~to** *adj* opulent
oración *f* prayer; (*Gram*) sentence
ora|dor *m* speaker. **~l** *adj* oral
órale *int* (*Mex*) come on!; (*de acuerdo*) OK!
orar *vi* pray (**por** for)
órbita *f* orbit
orden *f* order. **~ del día** agenda. **órdenes** *fpl* **sagradas** Holy Orders. **a sus órdenes** (*esp Mex*) can I help you? **~ de arresto** arrest warrant. **en ~** in order. **por ~** in turn.

~**ado** *adj* tidy

ordenador *m* computer

ordena|nza *f* ordinance. ● *m* (*Mil*) orderly. ~**r** *vt* put in order; (*mandar*) order; (*Relig*) ordain; (*LAm, en restaurante*) order

ordeñar *vt* milk

ordinario *adj* ordinary; (*grosero*) common; (*de mala calidad*) poor-quality

orear *vt* air

orégano *m* oregano

oreja *f* ear

orfanato *m* orphanage

orfebre *m* goldsmith, silversmith

orfeón *m* choral society

orgánico *adj* organic

organillo *m* barrel-organ

organismo *m* organism

organista *m & f* organist

organiza|ción *f* organization. ~**dor** *m* organizer. ~**r** 10 *vt* organize. ~**rse** *vpr* get organized

O

órgano *m* organ

orgasmo *m* orgasm

orgía *f* orgy

orgullo *m* pride. ~**so** *adj* proud

orientación *f* orientation; (*guía*) guidance; (*Archit*) aspect

oriental *adj & m & f* oriental

orientar *vt* position; advise (persona). ~**se** *vpr* point; (persona) find one's bearings

oriente *m* east

orificio *m* hole

orig|en *m* origin. **dar** ~**en a** give rise to. ~**inal** *adj* original; (*excéntrico*) odd. ~**inalidad** *f* originality. ~**inar** *vt* give rise to. ~**inario** *adj* original; (*nativo*) native. **ser** ~**inario de** come from. ~**inarse** *vpr* originate; (incendio) start

orilla *f* (*del mar*) shore; (*de río*) bank; (*borde*) edge. **a** ~**s del mar** by the sea

orina *f* urine. ~**l** *m* chamber-pot. ~**r** *vi* urinate

oriundo *adj* native. **ser** ~ **de** (persona) come from; (especie etc) native to

ornamental *adj* ornamental

ornitología *f* ornithology

oro *m* gold. ~**s** *mpl* Spanish card suit. ~ **de ley** 9 carat gold. **hacerse de** ~ make a fortune. **prometer el** ~ **y el moro** promise the moon

orquesta *f* orchestra. ~**l** *adj* orchestral. ~**r** *vt* orchestrate

orquídea *f* orchid

ortiga *f* nettle

ortodoxo *adj* orthodox

ortografía *f* spelling

ortopédico *adj* orthopaedic

oruga *f* caterpillar

orzuelo *m* sty

os *pron* (*acusativo*) you; (*dativo*) (to) you; (*reflexivo*) (to) yourselves; (*recíproco*) (to) each other

osad|ía *f* boldness. ~**o** *adj* bold

oscila|ción *f* swinging; (*de precios*) fluctuation; (*Tec*) oscillation. ~**r** *vi* swing; (precio) fluctuate; (*Tec*) oscillate

oscur|ecer 11 *vi* get dark. ● *vt* darken; (*fig*) obscure. ~**ecerse** *vpr* grow dark; (*nublarse*) cloud over. ~**idad** *f* darkness; (*fig*) obscurity. ~**o** *adj* dark; (*fig*) obscure. **a** ~**as** in the dark

óseo *adj* bone

oso *m* bear. ~ **de felpa**, ~ **de peluche** teddy bear

ostensible *adj* obvious

ostent|ación *f* ostentation. ~**ar**

vt show off; (*mostrar*) show. **~oso** *adj* ostentatious

osteópata *m & f* osteopath

ostión *m* (*esp Mex*) oyster

ostra *f* oyster

ostracismo *m* ostracism

Otan *abrev* (**Organización del Tratado del Atlántico Norte**) NATO, North Atlantic Treaty Organization

otitis *f* inflammation of the ear

otoño *m* autumn (*Brit*), fall (*Amer*)

otorga|miento *m* granting. **~r** 12 *vt* give; grant (préstamo); (*Jurid*) draw up (testamento)

otorrinolaringólogo *m* ear, nose and throat specialist

otro, otra

● *adjetivo*

····➤ another; (*con artículo, posesivo*) other. **come ~ pedazo** have another piece. **el ~ día** the other day. **mi ~ coche** my other car. **otra cosa** something else. **otra persona** somebody else. **otra vez** again

····➤ (*en plural*) other; (*con numeral*) another. **en otras ocasiones** on other occasions. **~s 3 vasos** another 3 glasses

····➤ (*siguiente*) next. **al ~ día** the next day. **me bajo en la otra estación** I get off at the next station

● *pronombre*

····➤ (*cosa*) another one. **lo cambié por ~** I changed it for another one

····➤ (*persona*) someone else. **invitó a ~** she invited someone else

····➤ (*en plural*) (some) others. **tengo ~s en casa** I have (some) others at home. **~s piensan lo contrario** others think the opposite

····➤ (*con artículo*) **el ~** the other one. **los ~s** the others. **uno detrás del ~** one after the other. **los ~s no vinieron** the others didn't come. **esta semana no, la otra** not this week, next week. **de un día para el ~** from one day to the next

➡ Para usos complementarios ver **uno, tanto**

ovación *f* ovation

oval *adj*, **ovalado** *adj* oval

óvalo *m* oval

ovario *m* ovary

oveja *f* sheep; (*hembra*) ewe

overol *m* (*LAm*) overalls

ovillo *m* ball. **hacerse un ~** curl up

OVNI *abrev* (**objeto volante no identificado**) UFO

ovulación *f* ovulation

oxida|ción *f* rusting. **~r** *vi* rust. **~rse** *vpr* go rusty

óxido *m* rust; (*en química*) oxide

oxígeno *m* oxygen

oye *vb véase* **OÍR**

oyente *adj* listening. ● *m & f* listener; (*Univ*) occasional student

ozono *m* ozone

Pp

pabellón *m* pavilion; (*en jardín*) summerhouse; (*en hospital*) block; (*de instrumento*) bell; (*bandera*) flag
pacer 11 *vi* graze
pachucho *adj* (fruta) overripe; (persona) poorly
pacien|cia *f* patience. **perder la ~cia** lose patience. **~te** *adj & m & f* patient
pacificar 7 *vt* pacify. **~se** *vpr* calm down
pacífico *adj* peaceful. **el (Océano) P~** the Pacific (Ocean)
pacifis|mo *m* pacifism. **~ta** *adj & m & f* pacifist
pact|ar *vi* agree, make a pact. **~o** *m* pact, agreement
padec|er 11 *vt/i* suffer (**de** from); (*soportar*) bear. **~er del corazón** have heart trouble. **~imiento** *m* suffering
P
padrastro *m* stepfather
padre *adj* I terrible; (*Mex, estupendo*) great. • *m* father. **~s** *mpl* parents
padrino *m* godfather; (*en boda*) man who gives away the bride
padrón *m* register. **~ electoral** (*LAm*) electoral roll
paella *f* paella
paga *f* payment; (*sueldo*) pay. **~dero** *adj* payable
pagano *adj & m* pagan
pagar 12 *vt* pay; pay for (compras). • *vi* pay. **~é** *m* IOU
página *f* page
pago *m* payment
país *m* country; (*ciudadanos*) nation. **~ natal** native land. **el P~ Vasco** the Basque Country. **los P~es Bajos** the Low Countries
paisaje *m* landscape, scenery
paisano *m* compatriot
paja *f* straw; (*en texto*) padding
pájaro *m* bird. **~ carpintero** woodpecker
paje *m* page
pala *f* shovel; (*para cavar*) spade; (*para basura*) dustpan; (*de pimpón*) bat
palabr|a *f* word; (*habla*) speech. **pedir la ~a** ask to speak. **tomar la ~a** take the floor. **~ota** *f* swear-word. **decir ~otas** swear
palacio *m* palace
paladar *m* palate
palanca *f* lever; (*fig*) influence. **~ de cambio (de velocidades)** gear lever (*Brit*), gear shift (*Amer*)
palangana *f* washbasin (*Brit*), washbowl (*Amer*)
palco *m* (*en el teatro*) box
palestino *adj & m* Palestinian
paleta *f* (*de pintor*) palette; (*de albañil*) trowel
paleto *m* yokel
paliativo *adj & m* palliative
palide|cer 11 *vi* turn pale. **~z** *f* paleness
pálido *adj* pale. **ponerse ~** turn pale
palillo *m* (*de dientes*) toothpick; (*para comer*) chopstick
paliza *f* beating
palma *f* (*de la mano*) palm; (*árbol*) palm (tree); (*de dátiles*) date palm. **dar ~s** clap. **~da** *f* pat; (*LAm*) slap. **~das** *fpl* applause
palmera *f* palm tree
palmo *m* span; (*fig*) few inches. **~ a ~** inch by inch

palmote|ar *vi* clap. **~o** *m* clapping, applause

palo *m* stick; (*de valla*) post; (*de golf*) club; (*golpe*) blow; (*de naipes*) suit; (*mástil*) mast

paloma *f* pigeon; (*blanca, símbolo*) dove

palomitas *fpl* popcorn

palpar *vt* feel

palpita|ción *f* palpitation. **~nte** *adj* throbbing. **~r** *vi* beat; (*latir con fuerza*) pound; (vena, sien) throb

palta *f* (*LAm*) avocado (pear)

paludismo *m* malaria

pamela *f* (*woman's*) *broad-brimmed dress hat*

pamp|a *f* pampas. **~ero** *adj* of the pampas

pan *m* bread; (*barra*) loaf. **~ integral** wholewheat bread, wholemeal bread (*Brit*). **~ tostado** toast. **~ rallado** breadcrumbs. **ganarse el ~** earn one's living

pana *f* corduroy

panader|ía *f* bakery; (*tienda*) baker's (shop). **~o** *m* baker

panal *m* honeycomb

panameño *adj & m* Panamanian

pancarta *f* banner, placard

panda *m* panda

pander|eta *f* (small) tambourine **~o** *m* tambourine

pandilla *f* gang

panecillo *m* (bread) roll

panel *m* panel

panfleto *m* pamphlet

pánico *m* panic. **tener ~** be terrified (**a** of)

panor|ama *m* panorama. **~ámico** *adj* panoramic

panque *m* (*Mex*) sponge cake

pantaletas *fpl* (*Mex*) panties, knickers (*Brit*)

pantalla *f* screen; (*de lámpara*) (lamp)shade

pantalón *m*, **pantalones** *mpl* trousers. **~ a la cadera** bumsters

pantano *m* marsh; (*embalse*) reservoir. **~so** *adj* marshy

pantera *f* panther

panti *m*, (*Mex*) **pantimedias** *fpl* tights (*Brit*), pantyhose (*Amer*)

pantomima *f* pantomime

pantorrilla *f* calf

pantufla *f* slipper

panz|a *f* belly. **~udo** *adj* potbellied

pañal *m* nappy (*Brit*), diaper (*Amer*)

paño *m* material; (*de lana*) woollen cloth; (*trapo*) cloth. **~ de cocina** dishcloth; (*para secar*) tea towel. **~ higiénico** sanitary towel. **en ~s menores** in one's underclothes

pañuelo *m* handkerchief; (*de cabeza*) scarf

papa *m* pope. ●*f* (*LAm*) potato. **~s fritas** (*LAm*) chips (*Brit*), French fries (*Amer*); (*de paquete*) crisps (*Brit*), chips (*Amer*)

papá *m* dad(dy). **~s** *mpl* parents. **P~ Noel** Father Christmas

papada *f* (*de persona*) double chin

papagayo *m* parrot

papalote *m* (*Mex*) kite

papanatas *m invar* simpleton

paparrucha *f* (*tontería*) silly thing

papaya *f* papaya, pawpaw

papel *m* paper; (*en el teatro etc*) role. **~ carbón** carbon paper. **~ de calcar** tracing paper. **~ de envolver** wrapping paper. **~ de plata** silver paper. **~ higiénico** toilet paper. ~ **pintado** wallpaper. ~ **secante** blotting paper. **~eo** *m* paperwork. **~era** *f* waste-paper basket. **~ería** *f* stationer's (shop). **~eta** *f* (*para votar*) (ballot) paper

paperas *fpl* mumps

paquete *m* packet; (*bulto*) parcel; (*LAm, de papas fritas*) bag; (*Mex, problema*) headache. ~ **postal** parcel

Paquistán *m* Pakistan

paquistaní *adj & m* Pakistani

par *adj* (número) even. ● *m* couple; (*dos cosas iguales*) pair. **a ~es** two by two. **de ~ en ~** wide open. **~es y nones** odds and evens. **sin ~** without equal. ● *f* par. **a la ~** (*Com*) at par. **a la ~ que** at the same time

para *preposición*

····➤ for. **es ~ ti** it's for you. ~ **siempre** for ever. **¿~ qué?** what for? ~ **mi cumpleaños** for my birthday

····➤ (*con infinitivo*) to. **es muy tarde ~ llamar** it's too late to call. **salió ~ divertirse** he went out to have fun. **lo hago ~ ahorrar** I do it (in order) to save money

····➤ (*dirección*) **iba ~ la oficina** he was going to the office. **empújalo ~ atrás** push it back. **¿vas ~ casa?** are you going home?

····➤ (*tiempo*) by. **debe estar listo ~ el 5** it must be ready by the 5th. ~ **entonces** by then

····➤ (*LAm, hora*) to. **son 5 ~ la una** it's 5 to one

····➤ ~ **que** so (that). **grité ~ que me oyera** I shouted so (that) he could hear me.

Note that **para que** is always followed by a verb in the subjunctive

parabienes *mpl* congratulations

parábola *f* (*narración*) parable

parabólica *f* satellite dish

para|brisas *m invar* windscreen (*Brit*), windshield (*Amer*). **~caídas** *m invar* parachute. **~caidista** *m & f* parachutist; (*Mil*) paratrooper. **~choques** *m invar* bumper (*Brit*), fender (*Amer*) (*Rail*) buffer

parad|a *f* (*acción*) stop; (*lugar*) bus stop; (*de taxis*) rank; (*Mil*) parade. **~ero** *m* whereabouts; (*LAm, lugar*) bus stop. **~o** *adj* stationary; (desempleado) unemployed. **estar ~** (*LAm, de pie*) be standing

paradoja *f* paradox

parador *m* state-owned hotel

i

parador (nacional de turismo) A national chain of hotels in Spain. They are often converted castles, palaces and monasteries. They provide a high standard of accommodation but are relatively inexpensive and often act as showcases for local craftsmanship and cooking.

parafina *f* paraffin

paraguas *m invar* umbrella

Paraguay *m* Paraguay

paraguayo *adj & m* Paraguayan

paraíso *m* paradise; (*en el teatro*) gallery

paralel|a *f* parallel (line). **~as** *fpl* parallel bars. **~o** *adj & m* parallel

par|álisis *f invar* paralysis. **~alítico** *adj* paralytic. **~alizar** 10 *vt* paralyse

parámetro *m* parameter

paramilitar *adj* paramilitary

páramo *m* bleak upland

parangón *m* comparison.

paraninfo *m* main hall

paranoi|a *f* paranoia. **~co** *adj* paranoiac

parar *vt/i* stop. **sin ~** continuously. **~se** *vpr* stop; (*LAm, ponerse de pie*) stand

pararrayos *m invar* lightning conductor

parásito *adj* parasitic. ● *m* parasite

parcela *f* plot. **~r** *vt* divide into plots

parche *m* patch

parcial *adj* partial. **a tiempo ~** part-time. **~idad** *f* prejudice

parco *adj* laconic; (*sobrio*) sparing, frugal

parear *vt* put into pairs

parec|er *m* opinion. **al ~er** apparently. **a mi ~er** in my opinion. ● *vi* 11 seem; (*asemejarse*) look like; (*tener aspecto de*) look. **me ~e** I think. **~e fácil** it looks easy. **¿qué te ~e?** what do you think? **según ~e** apparently. **~erse** *vpr* resemble, look like. **~ido** *adj* similar. **bien ~ido** good-looking. ● *m* similarity

pared *f* wall. **~ por medio** next door. **~ón** *m* (*de fusilamiento*) wall. **llevar al ~ón** shoot

parej|a *f* pair; (*hombre y mujer*) couple; (*compañero*) partner. **~o** *adj* the same; (*LAm, sin desniveles*) even; (*LAm, liso*) smooth; (*Mex, equitativo*) equal. ● *adv* (*LAm*) evenly

parente|la *f* relations. **~sco** *m* relationship

paréntesis *m invar* parenthesis, bracket (*Brit*); (*intervalo*) break. **entre ~** in brackets (*Brit*), in parenthesis; (*fig*) by the way

paria *m & f* outcast

paridad *f* equality; (*Com*) parity

pariente *m & f* relation, relative

parir *vt* give birth to. ● *vi* give birth

parisiense *adj & m & f*, **parisino** *adj & m* Parisian

parking /ˈparkin/ *m* car park (*Brit*), parking lot (*Amer*)

parlament|ar *vi* talk. **~ario** *adj* parliamentary. ● *m* member of parliament (*Brit*), congressman (*Amer*). **~o** *m* parliament

parlanchín *adj* talkative. ● *m* chatterbox

parlante *m* (*LAm*) loudspeaker

paro *m* stoppage; (*desempleo*) unemployment; (*subsidio*) unemployment benefit; (*LAm, huelga*) strike. **~ cardíaco** cardiac arrest

parodia *f* parody

parpadear *vi* blink; (luz) flicker

párpado *m* eyelid

parque *m* park. **~ de atracciones** funfair. **~ eólico** wind farm. **~ infantil** playground. **~ zoológico** zoo, zoological gardens

parquímetro *m* parking meter

parra *f* grapevine

párrafo *m* paragraph

parrilla *f* grill; (*LAm, Auto*) luggage rack. **a la ~** grilled. **~da** *f* grill

párroco *m* parish priest

parroquia *f* parish; (*iglesia*) parish church. **~no** *m* parishioner

parte *m* (*informe*) report. **dar ~** report. **de mi ~** for me ● *f* part; (*porción*) share; (*Jurid*) party; (*Mex,* *repuesto*) spare (part). **de ~ de** from. **¿de ~ de quién?** (*al teléfono*) who's speaking? **en cualquier ~** anywhere. **en gran ~** largely. **en ~** partly. **en todas ~s** everywhere. **la mayor ~** the majority. **la ~ superior** the top. **ninguna ~** nowhere. **por otra ~** on the other hand. **por todas ~s** everywhere

partera *f* midwife

partición *f* division; (*Pol*) partition

participa|ción *f* participation; (*noticia*) announcement; (*de lotería*) share. **~nte** *adj* participating. ● *m & f* participant. **~r** *vt* announce. ● *vi* take part

participio *m* participle

particular *adj* particular; (clase) private. **nada de ~** nothing special. ● *m* private individual.

partida *f* departure; (*en registro*) entry; (*documento*) certificate; (*de mercancías*) consignment; (*juego*) game; (*de gente*) group

P

partidario *adj & m* partisan. **~ de** in favour of

parti|do *m* (*Pol*) party; (*encuentro*) match, game; (*LAm, de ajedrez*) game. **~r** *vt* cut; (*romper*) break; crack (nueces). ● *vi* leave. **a ~r de** from. **~ de** start from. **~rse** *vpr* (*romperse*) break; (*dividirse*) split

partitura *f* (*Mus*) score

parto *m* labour. **estar de ~** be in labour

parvulario *m* kindergarten, nursery school (*Brit*)

pasa *f* raisin. **~ de Corinto** currant

pasa|da *f* passing; (*de puntos*) row. **de ~da** in passing. **~dero** *adj* passable. **~dizo** *m* passage. **~do** *adj* past; (día, mes etc) last; (*anticuado*) old-fashioned; (comida) bad, off. **~do mañana** the day after tomorrow. **~dos tres días** after three days. **~dor** *m* bolt; (*de pelo*) hair-slide

pasaje *m* passage; (*pasajeros*) passengers; (*LAm, de avión etc*) ticket. **~ro** *adj* passing. ● *m* passenger

pasamano(s) *m* handrail; (*barandilla de escalera*) banister(s)

pasamontañas *m invar* balaclava

pasaporte *m* passport

pasar *vt* pass; (*atravesar*) go through; (*filtrar*) strain; spend (tiempo); show (película); (*tolerar*) tolerate; give (mensaje, enfermedad). ● *vi* pass; (*suceder*) happen; (*ir*) go; (*venir*) come; (tiempo) go by. **~ de** have no interest in. **~lo bien** have a good time. **~ frío** be cold. **~ la aspiradora** vacuum. **~ por alto** leave out. **lo que pasa es que** the fact is that. **pase lo que pase** whatever happens. **¡pase Vd!** come in!, go in! **¡que lo pases bien!** have a good time! **¿qué pasa?** what's the matter?, what's happening? **~se** *vpr* pass; (dolor) go away; (flores) wither; (comida) go bad; spend (tiempo); (*excederse*) go too far

pasarela *f* footbridge; (*Naut*) gangway

pasatiempo *m* hobby, pastime

Pascua *f* (*fiesta de los hebreos*) Passover; (*de Resurrección*) Easter; (*Navidad*) Christmas. **~s** *fpl* Christmas

pase *m* pass

pase|ante *m & f* passer-by. **~ar** *vt* walk (perro); (*exhibir*) show off. ● *vi* walk. **ir a ~ar, salir a ~ar** walk. **~arse** *vpr* walk. **~o** *m* walk; (*en coche etc*) ride; (*calle*) avenue. **~o**

marítimo promenade. **dar un ~o, ir de ~** go for a walk. **¡vete a ~o!** [!] get lost! [!]

pasillo *m* corridor; (*de cine, avión*) aisle

pasión *f* passion

pasivo *adj* passive

pasm|ar *vt* astonish. **~arse** *vpr* be astonished

paso *m* step; (*acción de pasar*) passing; (*camino*) way; (*entre montañas*) pass; (*estrecho*) strait(s). **~ a nivel** level crossing (*Brit*), grade crossing (*Amer*). **~ de cebra** zebra crossing. **~ de peatones** pedestrian crossing. **~ elevado** flyover (*Brit*), overpass (*Amer*). **a cada ~** at every turn. **a dos ~s** very near. **de ~** in passing. **de ~ por** just passing through. **oír ~s** hear footsteps. **prohibido el ~** no entry

pasota *m & f* drop-out

pasta *f* paste; (*masa*) dough; (*sl, dinero*) dough [x]. **~s** *fpl* pasta; (*pasteles*) pastries. **~ de dientes, ~ dentífrica** toothpaste

pastel *m* cake; (*empanada*) pie; (*lápiz*) pastel. **~ería** *f* cake shop

pasteurizado *adj* pasteurized

pastilla *f* pastille; (*de jabón*) bar; (*de chocolate*) piece

pasto *m* pasture; (*hierba*) grass; (*LAm, césped*) lawn. **~r** *m* shepherd; (*Relig*) minister. **~ra** *f* shepherdess

pata *f* leg; (*pie de perro, gato*) paw; (*de ave*) foot. **~s arriba** upside down. **a cuatro ~s** on all fours. **meter la ~** put one's foot in it. **tener mala ~** have bad luck. **~da** *f* kick. **~lear** *vi* stamp one's feet; (niño) kick

patata *f* potato. **~s fritas** chips (*Brit*), French fries (*Amer*); (*de bolsa*) (potato) crisps (*Brit*), (potato) chips (*Amer*)

patente *adj* obvious. • *f* licence

patern|al *adj* paternal; (cariño etc) fatherly. **~idad** *f* paternity. **~o** *adj* paternal; (cariño etc) fatherly

patético *adj* moving

patillas *fpl* sideburns

patín *m* skate; (*con ruedas*) roller skate. **patines en línea** Rollerblades (P)

patina|dor *m* skater. **~je** *m* skating. **~r** *vi* skate; (*resbalar*) slide; (coche) skid

patio *m* patio. **~ de butacas** stalls (*Brit*), orchestra (*Amer*)

pato *m* duck

patológico *adj* pathological

patoso *adj* clumsy

patraña *f* hoax

patria *f* homeland

patriarca *m* patriarch

patrimonio *m* patrimony; (*fig*) heritage

patri|ota *adj* patriotic. • *m & f* patriot. **~otismo** *m* patriotism

patrocin|ar *vt* sponsor. **~io** *m* sponsorship

patrón *m* (*jefe*) boss; (*de pensión etc*) landlord; (*en costura*) pattern

patrulla *f* patrol; (*fig, cuadrilla*) group. **~r** *vt/i* patrol

pausa *f* pause. **~do** *adj* slow

pauta *f* guideline

paviment|ar *vt* pave. **~o** *m* pavement

pavo *m* turkey. **~ real** peacock

pavor *m* terror

payas|ada *f* buffoonery. **~o** *m* clown

paz *f* peace

P

peaje *m* toll
peatón *m* pedestrian
peca *f* freckle
peca|do *m* sin; (*defecto*) fault. **~dor** *m* sinner. **~minoso** *adj* sinful. **~r** **7** *vi* sin
pech|o *m* chest; (*de mujer*) breast; (*fig, corazón*) heart. **dar el ~o a un niño** breast-feed a child. **tomar a ~o** take to heart. **~uga** *f* breast
pecoso *adj* freckled
peculiar *adj* peculiar, particular. **~idad** *f* peculiarity
pedal *m* pedal. **~ear** *vi* pedal
pedante *adj* pedantic
pedazo *m* piece, bit. **a ~s** in pieces. **hacer(se) ~s** smash
pediatra *m & f* paediatrician
pedicuro *m* chiropodist
pedi|do *m* order; (*LAm, solicitud*) request. **~r** **5** *vt* ask for; (*Com, en restaurante*) order. ● *vi* ask. **~r prestado** borrow
pega|dizo *adj* catchy. **~joso** *adj* sticky
P **pega|mento** *m* glue. **~r** **12** *vt* stick (on); (*coser*) sew on; give (enfermedad etc); (*juntar*) join; (*golpear*) hit; (*dar*) give. **~r fuego a** set fire to ● *vi* stick. **~rse** *vpr* stick; (*pelearse*) hit each other. **~tina** *f* sticker
pein|ado *m* hairstyle. **~ar** *vt* comb. **~arse** *vpr* comb one's hair. **~e** *m* comb. **~eta** *f* ornamental comb
p.ej. *abrev* (**por ejemplo**) e.g.
pelado *adj* (fruta) peeled; (cabeza) bald; (terreno) bare
pela|je *m* (*de animal*) fur; (*fig, aspecto*) appearance. **~mbre** *m* (*de animal*) fur; (*de persona*) thick hair
pelar *vt* peel; shell (habas); skin (tomates); pluck (ave)
peldaño *m* step; (*de escalera de mano*) rung
pelea *f* fight; (*discusión*) quarrel. **~r** *vi* fight; (*discutir*) quarrel. **~rse** *vpr* fight; (*discutir*) quarrel
peletería *f* fur shop
peliagudo *adj* difficult, tricky
pelícano *m* pelican
película *f* film (*esp Brit*), movie (*esp Amer*). **~ de dibujos animados** cartoon (film)
peligro *m* danger; (*riesgo*) hazard, risk. **poner en ~** endanger. **~so** *adj* dangerous
pelirrojo *adj* red-haired
pellejo *m* skin
pellizc|ar **7** *vt* pinch. **~o** *m* pinch
pelma *m & f*, **pelmazo** *m* bore, nuisance
pelo *m* hair. **no tener ~s en la lengua** be outspoken. **tomar el ~ a uno** pull s.o.'s leg
pelota *f* ball. **~ vasca** pelota. **hacer la ~ a uno** suck up to s.o.
pelotera *f* squabble
peluca *f* wig
peludo *adj* hairy
peluquer|ía *f* hairdresser's. **~o** *m* hairdresser
pelusa *f* down
pena *f* sadness; (lástima) pity; (*LAm, vergüenza*) embarrassment; (*Jurid*) sentence. **~ de muerte** death penalty. **a duras ~s** with difficulty. **da ~ que** it's a pity that. **me da ~** it makes me sad. **merecer la ~** be worthwhile. **pasar ~s** suffer hardship. **¡qué ~!** what a pity! **valer la ~** be worthwhile
penal *adj* penal; (derecho) criminal. ● *m* prison; (*LAm, penalty*)

penalty. **~idad** *f* suffering; (*Jurid*) penalty. **~ty** *m* penalty

pendiente *adj* hanging; (cuenta) outstanding; (asunto etc) pending. • *m* earring. • *f* slope

péndulo *m* pendulum

pene *m* penis

penetra|nte *adj* penetrating; (sonido) piercing; (viento) bitter. **~r** *vt* penetrate; (*fig*) pierce. • *vi*. **~r en** penetrate; (*entrar*) go into

penicilina *f* penicillin

pen|ínsula *f* peninsula. **~insular** *adj* peninsular

penique *m* penny

penitencia *f* penitence; (*castigo*) penance

penoso *adj* painful; (*difícil*) difficult; (*LAm, tímido*) shy; (*LAm, embarazoso*) embarrassing

pensa|do *adj*. **bien ~do** all things considered. **menos ~do** least expected. **~dor** *m* thinker. **~miento** *m* thought. **~r** **1** *vt* think; (*considerar*) consider. **cuando menos se piensa** when least expected. **¡ni ~rlo!** no way! **pienso que sí** I think so. • *vi* think. **~r en** think about. **~tivo** *adj* thoughtful

pensi|ón *f* pension; (*casa de huéspedes*) guest-house. **~ón completa** full board. **~onista** *m & f* pensioner; (*huésped*) lodger

penúltimo *adj & m* penultimate, last but one

penumbra *f* half-light

penuria *f* shortage. **pasar ~s** suffer hardship

peñ|a *f* rock; (*de amigos*) group; (*LAm, club*) folk club. **~ón** *m* rock. **el P~ón de Gibraltar** The Rock (of Gibraltar)

peón *m* labourer; (*en ajedrez*) pawn; (*en damas*) piece

peonza *f* (spinning) top

peor *adj* (*comparativo*) worse; (*superlativo*) worst. • *adv* worse. **de mal en ~** from bad to worse. **lo ~** the worst thing. **tanto ~** so much the worse

pepin|illo *m* gherkin. **~o** *m* cucumber. **(no) me importa un ~o** I couldn't care less

pepita *f* pip; (*de oro*) nugget

pequeñ|ez *f* smallness; (*minucia*) trifle. **~o** *adj* small, little; (*de edad*) young; (*menor*) younger. • *m* little one. **es el ~o** he's the youngest

pera *f* (*fruta*) pear. **~l** *m* pear (tree)

percance *m* mishap

percatarse *vpr*. **~ de** notice

perc|epción *f* perception. **~ibir** *vt* perceive; earn (dinero)

percha *f* hanger; (*de aves*) perch

percusión *f* percussion

perde|dor *adj* losing. • *m* loser. **~r** **1** *vt* lose; (*malgastar*) waste; miss (tren etc). • *vi* lose. **~rse** *vpr* get lost; (*desaparecer*) disappear; (*desperdiciarse*) be wasted; (*estropearse*) be spoilt. **echar(se) a ~r** spoil

pérdida *f* loss; (*de líquido*) leak; (*de tiempo*) waste

perdido *adj* lost

perdiz *f* partridge

perd|ón *m* pardon, forgiveness. **pedir ~ón** apologize. • *int* sorry! **~onar** *vt* excuse, forgive; (*Jurid*) pardon. **¡~one (Vd)!** sorry!

perdura|ble *adj* lasting. **~r** *vi* last

perece|dero *adj* perishable. **~r** **11** *vi* perish

peregrin|ación *f* pilgrimage.

P

~o *adj* strange. ● *m* pilgrim
perejil *m* parsley
perengano *m* so-and-so
perenne *adj* everlasting; (*planta*) perennial
perez|a *f* laziness. **~oso** *adj* lazy
perfec|ción *f* perfection. **a la ~ción** perfectly, to perfection. **~cionar** *vt* perfect; (*mejorar*) improve. **~cionista** *m & f* perfectionist. **~to** *adj* perfect; (*completo*) complete
perfil *m* profile; (*contorno*) outline. **~ado** *adj* well-shaped
perfora|ción *f* perforation. **~dora** *f* punch. **~r** *vt* pierce, perforate; punch (papel, tarjeta etc)
perfum|ar *vt* perfume. **~arse** *vpr* put perfume on. **~e** *m* perfume, scent. **~ería** *f* perfumery
pericia *f* skill
perif|eria *f* (*de ciudad*) outskirts. **~érico** *adj* (barrio) outlying. ● *m* (*Mex, carretera*) ring road
perilla *f* (*barba*) goatee
perímetro *m* perimeter
P
periódico *adj* periodic(al). ● *m* newspaper
periodis|mo *m* journalism. **~ta** *m & f* journalist
período *m*, **periodo** *m* period
periquito *m* budgerigar
periscopio *m* periscope
perito *adj & m* expert
perju|dicar 7 *vt* damage; (*desfavorecer*) not suit. **~dicial** *adj* damaging. **~icio** *m* damage. **en ~icio de** to the detriment of
perla *f* pearl. **de ~s** *adv* very well
permane|cer 11 *vi* remain. **~ncia** *f* permanence; (*estancia*) stay. **~nte** *adj* permanent. ● *f* perm. ● *m* (*Mex*) perm
permi|sivo *adj* permissive. **~so** *m* permission; (*documento*) licence; (*Mil etc*) leave. **~so de conducir** driving licence (*Brit*), driver's license (*Amer*). **con ~so** excuse me. **~tir** *vt* allow, permit. **¿me ~te?** may I? **~tirse** *vpr* allow s.o.
pernicioso *adj* pernicious; (persona) wicked
perno *m* bolt
pero *conj* but. ● *m* fault; (*objeción*) objection
perogrullada *f* platitude
perpendicular *adj & f* perpendicular
perpetrar *vt* perpetrate
perpetu|ar 21 *vt* perpetuate. **~o** *adj* perpetual
perplejo *adj* perplexed
perr|a *f* (*animal*) bitch; (*moneda*) coin, penny (*Brit*), cent (*Amer*); (*rabieta*) tantrum. **estar sin una ~a** be broke. **~era** *f* dog pound; (*vehículo*) dog catcher's van. **~o** *adj* awful. ● *m* dog. **~o galgo** greyhound. **de ~os** awful
persa *adj & m & f* Persian
perse|cución *f* pursuit; (*política etc*) persecution. **~guir** 5 & 13 *vt* pursue; (*por ideología etc*) persecute
persevera|nte *adj* persevering. **~r** *vi* persevere
persiana *f* blind; (*LAm, contraventana*) shutter
persignarse *vpr* cross o.s.
persist|ente *adj* persistent. **~ir** *vi* persist
person|a *f* person. **~as** *fpl* people. **~aje** *m* (*persona importante*) important figure; (*de obra literaria*) character. **~al** *adj* personal. ● *m* staff. **~alidad** *f* personality. **~arse** *vpr* appear in person. **~ifi-**

car **7** *vt* personify
perspectiva *f* perspective
perspica|cia *f* shrewdness; (*de vista*) keen eyesight. **~z** *adj* shrewd; (vista) keen
persua|dir *vt* persuade. **~sión** *f* persuasion. **~sivo** *adj* persuasive
pertenecer **11** *vi* belong
pértiga *f* pole. **salto** *m* **con ~** pole vault
pertinente *adj* relevant
perturba|ción *f* disturbance. **~ción del orden público** breach of the peace. **~r** *vt* disturb; disrupt (orden)
Perú *m*. **el ~** Peru
peruano *adj & m* Peruvian
perver|so *adj* evil. ● *m* evil person. **~tir** **4** *vt* pervert
pesa *f* weight. **~dez** *f* weight; (*de cabeza etc*) heaviness; (*lentitud*) sluggishness; (*cualidad de fastidioso*) tediousness; (*cosa fastidiosa*) bore, nuisance
pesadilla *f* nightmare
pesado *adj* heavy; (sueño) deep; (viaje) tiring; (*duro*) hard; (*aburrido*) boring, tedious
pésame *m* sympathy, condolences
pesar *vt* weigh. ● *vi* be heavy. ● *m* sorrow; (*remordimiento*) regret. **a ~ de (que)** in spite of. **pese a (que)** in spite of
pesca *f* fishing; (*peces*) fish; (*pescado*) catch. **ir de ~** go fishing. **~da** *f* hake. **~dería** *f* fish shop. **~dilla** *f* whiting. **~do** *m* fish. **~dor** *adj* fishing. ● *m* fisherman. **~r** **7** *vt* catch. ● *vi* fish
pescuezo *m* neck
pesebre *m* manger
pesero *m* (*Mex*) minibus
peseta *f* peseta
pesimista *adj* pessimistic. ● *m & f* pessimist
pésimo *adj* very bad, awful
peso *m* weight; (*moneda*) peso. **~ bruto** gross weight. **~ neto** net weight. **al ~** by weight. **de ~** influential
pesquero *adj* fishing
pestañ|a *f* eyelash. **~ear** *vi* blink
pest|e *f* plague; (*hedor*) stench. **~icida** *m* pesticide
pestillo *m* bolt; (*de cerradura*) latch
petaca *f* cigarette case; (*Mex, maleta*) suitcase
pétalo *m* petal
petardo *m* firecracker
petición *f* request; (*escrito*) petition
petirrojo *m* robin
petrificar **7** *vt* petrify
petr|óleo *m* oil. **~olero** *adj* oil. ● *m* oil tanker
petulante *adj* smug
peyorativo *adj* pejorative
pez *f* fish; (*substancia negruzca*) pitch. **~ espada** swordfish
pezón *m* nipple
pezuña *f* hoof
piadoso *adj* compassionate; (*devoto*) devout
pian|ista *m & f* pianist. **~o** *m* piano. **~o de cola** grand piano
piar **20** *vi* chirp
picad|a *f*. **caer en ~a** (*LAm*) nosedive. **~o** *adj* perforated; (carne) minced (*Brit*), ground (*Amer*); (*ofendido*) offended; (mar) choppy; (diente) bad. ● *m*. **caer en ~o** nosedive. **~ura** *f* bite, sting; (*de polilla*) moth hole
picaflor *m* (*LAm*) hummingbird

P

picante *adj* hot; (chiste etc) risqué

picaporte *m* door-handle; (*aldaba*) knocker

picar 7 *vt* (ave) peck; (insecto, pez) bite; (abeja, avispa) sting; (*comer poco*) pick at; mince (*Brit*), grind (*Amer*) (carne); chop (up) (cebolla etc); (*Mex, pinchar*) prick. • *vi* itch; (ave) peck; (insecto, pez) bite; (sol) scorch; (comida) be hot

picardía *f* craftiness; (*travesura*) naughty thing

pícaro *adj* crafty; (niño) mischievous. • *m* rogue

picazón *f* itch

pichón *m* pigeon; (*Mex, novato*) beginner

pico *m* beak; (*punta*) corner; (*herramienta*) pickaxe; (*cima*) peak. **y ~** (*con tiempo*) a little after; (*con cantidad*) a little more than. **~tear** *vt* peck; (*fam, comer*) pick at

picudo *adj* pointed

pido *vb véase* PEDIR

pie *m* foot; (*Bot, de vaso*) stem. **~ cuadrado** square foot. **a cuatro ~s** on all fours. **al ~ de la letra** literally. **a ~** on foot. **a ~(s) juntillas** (*fig*) firmly. **buscarle tres ~s al gato** split hairs. **de ~** standing (up). **de ~s a cabeza** from head to toe. **en ~** standing (up). **ponerse de ~** stand up

piedad *f* pity; (*Relig*) piety

piedra *f* stone; (*de mechero*) flint

piel *f* skin; (*cuero*) leather

pienso *vb véase* PENSAR

pierdo *vb véase* PERDER

pierna *f* leg

pieza *f* piece; (*parte*) part; (*obra teatral*) play; (*moneda*) coin; (*habitación*) room. **~ de recambio** spare part

pijama *m* pyjamas

pila *f* (*montón*) pile; (*recipiente*) basin; (*eléctrica*) battery. **~ bautismal** font. **~r** *m* pillar

píldora *f* pill

pilla|je *m* pillage. **~r** *vt* catch

pillo *adj* wicked. • *m* rogue

pilot|ar *vt* pilot. **~o** *m* pilot

pim|entero *m* (*vasija*) pepperpot. **~entón** *m* paprika; (*LAm, fruto*) pepper. **~ienta** *f* pepper. **grano** *m* **de ~ienta** peppercorn. **~iento** *m* pepper

pináculo *m* pinnacle

pinar *m* pine forest

pincel *m* paintbrush. **~ada** *f* brush-stroke. **la última ~ada** (*fig*) the finishing touch

pinch|ar *vt* pierce, prick; puncture (neumático); (*fig, incitar*) push; (*Med, fam*) give an injection to. **~azo** *m* prick; (*en neumático*) puncture. **~itos** *mpl* kebab(s); (*tapas*) savoury snacks. **~o** *m* point

ping-pong *m* table tennis, ping-pong

pingüino *m* penguin

pino *m* pine (tree)

pint|a *f* spot; (*fig, aspecto*) appearance. **tener ~a de** look like. **~ada** *f* graffiti. **~ar** *vt* paint. **no ~a nada** (*fig*) it doesn't count. **~arse** *vpr* put on make-up. **~or** *m* painter. **~oresco** *adj* picturesque. **~ura** *f* painting; (*material*) paint

pinza *f* (clothes-)peg (*Brit*), clothes-pin (*Amer*); (*de cangrejo etc*) claw. **~s** *fpl* tweezers

piñ|a *f* pine cone; (*fruta*) pineapple. **~ón** *m* (*semilla*) pine nut

pío *adj* pious. • *m* chirp. **no decir ni ~** not say a word

piojo *m* louse

pionero *m* pioneer

pipa *f* pipe; (*semilla*) seed; (*de girasol*) sunflower seed

pique *m* resentment; (*rivalidad*) rivalry. **irse a ~** sink

piquete *m* picket; (*Mex, herida*) prick; (*Mex, de insecto*) sting

piragua *f* canoe

pirámide *f* pyramid

pirata *adj invar* pirate. ● *m & f* pirate

Pirineos *mpl.* **los ~**the Pyrenees

piropo *m* flattering comment

pirueta *f* pirouette

pirulí *m* lollipop

pisa|da *f* footstep; (*huella*) footprint. **~papeles** *m invar* paperweight. **~r** *vt* tread on. ● *vi* tread

piscina *f* swimming pool

Piscis *m* Pisces

piso *m* floor; (*vivienda*) flat (*Brit*), apartment (*Amer*); (*de autobús*) deck

pisotear *vt* trample (on)

pista *f* track; (*fig, indicio*) clue. **~ de aterrizaje** runway. **~ de baile** dance floor. **~ de carreras** racing track. **~ de hielo** ice-rink. **~ de tenis** tennis court

pistol|a *f* pistol. **~era** *f* holster. **~ero** *m* gunman

pistón *m* piston

pit|ar, (*LAm*) **~ear** *vt* whistle at; (conductor) hoot at; award (falta). ● *vi* blow a whistle; (*Auto*) sound one's horn. **~ido** *m* whistle

pitill|era *f* cigarette case. **~o** *m* cigarette

pito *m* whistle; (*Auto*) horn

pitón *m* python

pitorre|arse *vpr.* **~arse de** make fun of. **~o** *m* teasing

pitorro *m* spout

piyama *m* (*LAm*) pyjamas

pizarr|a *f* slate; (*en aula*) blackboard. **~ón** *m* (*LAm*) blackboard

pizca *f* **I** tiny piece; (*de sal*) pinch. **ni ~** not at all

placa *f* plate; (*con inscripción*) plaque; (*distintivo*) badge. **~ de matrícula** number plate

place|ntero *adj* pleasant. **~r** **32** *vi.* **haz lo que te plazca** do as you please. **me ~ hacerlo** I'm pleased to do it. ● *m* pleasure

plácido *adj* placid

plaga *f* (*also fig*) plague. **~do** *adj.* **~do de** filled with

plagio *m* plagiarism

plan *m* plan. **en ~ de** as

plana *f* page. **en primera ~** on the front page

plancha *f* iron; (*lámina*) sheet. **a la ~** grilled. **tirarse una ~** put one's foot in it. **~do** *m* ironing. **~r** *vt* iron. ● *vi* do the ironing

planeador *m* glider

planear *vt* plan. ● *vi* glide

planeta *m* planet

planicie *f* plain

planifica|ción *f* planning. **~r** **7** *vt* plan

planilla *f* (*LAm*) payroll; (*personal*) staff

plano *adj* flat. ● *m* plane; (*de edificio*) plan; (*de ciudad*) street plan. **primer ~** foreground; (*Foto*) close-up

planta *f* (*del pie*) sole; (*en botánica, fábrica*) plant; (*plano*) ground plan; (*piso*) floor. **~ baja** ground floor (*Brit*), first floor (*Amer*)

planta|ción *f* plantation. **~r** *vt* plant; deal (golpe). **~r en la calle** throw out. **~rse** *vpr* stand; (*fig*) stand firm

P

plantear *vt* (*exponer*) expound; (*causar*) create; raise (cuestión)
plantilla *f* insole; (*nómina*) payroll; (*personal*) personnel
plaqué *m* plating. **de ~** plated
plástico *adj & m* plastic
plata *f* silver; (*fig, fam, dinero*) money. **~ de ley** hallmarked silver
plataforma *f* platform
plátano *m* plane (tree); (*fruta*) banana. **platanero** *m* banana tree
platea *f* stalls (*Brit*), orchestra (*Amer*)
plateado *adj* silver-plated; (*color de plata*) silver
pl|ática *f* talk. **~aticar** **7** *vi* (*Mex*) talk. ● *vt* (*Mex*) tell
platija *f* plaice
platillo *m* saucer; (*Mus*) cymbal. **~ volador** (*LAm*), **~ volante** flying saucer
platino *m* platinum. **~s** *mpl* (*Auto*) points
plato *m* plate; (*comida*) dish; (*parte de una comida*) course
P **platónico** *adj* platonic
playa *f* beach; (*fig*) seaside
plaza *f* square; (*mercado*) market (place); (*sitio*) place; (*empleo*) job. **~ de toros** bullring
plazco *vb véase* **PLACER**
plazo *m* period; (*pago*) instalment; (*fecha*) date. **comprar a ~s** buy on hire purchase (*Brit*), buy on the installment plan (*Amer*)
plazuela *f* little square
pleamar *f* high tide
pleb|e *f* common people. **~eyo** *adj & m* plebeian. **~iscito** *m* plebiscite
plega|ble *adj* pliable; (silla) folding. **~r** **1** & **12** *vt* fold. **~rse** *vpr* bend; (*fig*) yield
pleito *m* (court) case; (*fig*) dispute
plenilunio *m* full moon
plen|itud *f* fullness; (*fig*) height. **~o** *adj* full. **en ~o día** in broad daylight. **en ~o verano** at the height of the summer
plieg|o *m* sheet. **~ue** *m* fold; (*en ropa*) pleat
plisar *vt* pleat
plom|ero *m* (*LAm*) plumber. **~o** *m* lead; (*Elec*) fuse. **con ~o** leaded. **sin ~o** unleaded
pluma *f* feather; (*para escribir*) pen. **~ atómica** (*Mex*) ballpoint pen. **~ estilográfica** fountain pen. **~je** *m* plumage
plum|ero *m* feather duster; (*para plumas, lápices etc*) pencil-case. **~ón** *m* down; (*edredón*) down-filled quilt
plural *adj & m* plural. **en ~** in the plural
pluri|empleo *m* having more than one job. **~partidismo** *m* multi-party system. **~étnico** *adj* multiethnic
plus *m* bonus
pluscuamperfecto *m* pluperfect
plusvalía *f* capital gain
pluvial *adj* rain
pobla|ción *f* population; (*ciudad*) city, town; (*pueblo*) village. **~do** *adj* populated. ● *m* village. **~r** **2** *vt* populate; (*habitar*) inhabit. **~rse** *vpr* get crowded
pobre *adj* poor. ● *m & f* poor person; (*fig*) poor thing. **¡~cito!** poor (little) thing! **¡~ de mí!** poor (old) me! **~za** *f* poverty
pocilga *f* pigsty
poción *f* potion

poco

● *adjetivo/pronombre*

····➤ **poco, poca** little, not much. **tiene poca paciencia** he has little patience. **¿cuánta leche queda? - poca** how much milk is there left? - not much

····➤ **pocos, pocas** few. **muy ~s días** very few days. **unos ~s dólares** a few dollars. **compré unos ~s** I bought a few. **aceptaron a muy ~s** very few (people) were accepted

····➤ **a ~ de llegar** soon after he arrived. **¡a ~ !** (*Mex*) really? **dentro de ~** soon. **~ a ~**, (*LAm*) **de a ~** gradually, little by little. **hace ~** recently, not long ago. **por ~** nearly. **un ~** (*cantidad*) a little; (*tiempo*) a while. **un ~ de** a (little) bit of, a little, some

● *adverbio*

····➤ (*con verbo*) not much. **lee muy ~** he doesn't read very much

····➤ (*con adjetivo*) **un lugar ~ conocido** a little known place. **es ~ inteligente** he's not very intelligent

! Cuando **poco** modifica a un adjetivo, muchas veces el inglés prefiere el uso del prefijo *un-*, p. ej. **poco amistoso** *unfriendly*. **poco agradecido** *ungrateful*

podar *vt* prune

poder 33 *verbo auxiliar* be able to. **no voy a ~ terminar** I won't be able to finish. **no pudo venir** he couldn't come. **¿puedo hacer algo?** can I do anything? **¿puedo pasar?** may I come in? **no ~ con** not be able to cope with; (*no aguantar*) not be able to stand. **no ~ más** be exhausted; (*estar harto de algo*) not be able to manage any more. **no ~ menos que** have no alternative but. **puede que** it is possible that. **puede ser** it is possible. **¿se puede ...?** may I...? ● *m* power. **en el ~** in power. **~es públicos** authorities. **~oso** *adj* powerful

podrido *adj* rotten

po|ema *m* poem. **~esía** *f* poetry; (*poema*) poem. **~eta** *m & f* poet. **~ético** *adj* poetic

polaco *adj* Polish. ● *m* Pole; (*lengua*) Polish

polar *adj* polar. **estrella ~** polestar

polea *f* pulley

pol|émica *f* controversy. **~emizar** 10 *vi* argue

polen *m* pollen

policía *f* police (force); (*persona*) policewoman. ● *m* policeman. **~co** *adj* police; (novela etc) detective

policromo *adj*, **polícromo** *adj* polychrome

polideportivo *m* sports centre

polietileno *m* polythene

poligamia *f* polygamy

polígono *m* polygon

polilla *f* moth

polio(mielitis) *f* polio(myelitis)

polític|a *f* politics; (*postura*) policy; (*mujer*) politician. **~ interior** domestic policy. **~o** *adj* political. **familia ~a** in-laws. ● *m* politician

póliza *f* (*de seguros*) policy

poll|o *m* chicken; (*gallo joven*) chick. **~uelo** *m* chick

polo *m* pole; (*helado*) ice lolly (*Brit*),

P

Popsicle (P) (*Amer*); (*juego*) polo. **P~ norte** North Pole

Polonia *f* Poland

poltrona *f* armchair

polución *f* pollution

polv|areda *f* dust cloud; (*fig, escándalo*) uproar. **~era** *f* compact. **~o** *m* powder; (*suciedad*) dust. **~os** *mpl* powder. **en ~o** powdered. **estar hecho ~o** be exhausted. **quitar el ~o** dust

pólvora *f* gunpowder; (*fuegos artificiales*) fireworks

polvoriento *adj* dusty

pomada *f* ointment

pomelo *m* grapefruit

pómez *adj*. **piedra** *f* **~** pumice stone

pomp|a *f* bubble; (*esplendor*) pomp. **~as fúnebres** funeral. **~oso** *adj* pompous; (*espléndido*) splendid

pómulo *m* cheekbone

ponchar *vt* (*Mex*) puncture

ponche *m* punch

poncho *m* poncho

P

ponderar *vt* (*alabar*) speak highly of

poner 34 *vt* put; put on (ropa, obra de teatro, TV etc); lay (la mesa, un huevo); set (examen, deberes); (*contribuir*) contribute; give (nombre); make (nervioso); pay (atención); show (película, interés); open (una tienda); equip (una casa). **~ con** (*al teléfono*) put through to. **~ por escrito** put into writing. **~ una multa** fine. **pongamos** let's suppose. • *vi* lay. **~se** *vpr* put o.s.; (*volverse*) get; put on (ropa); (sol) set. **~se a** start to. **~se a mal con uno** fall out with s.o.

pongo *vb véase* **PONER**

poniente *m* west; (*viento*) west wind

pont|ificar 7 *vi* pontificate. **~ífice** *m* pontiff

popa *f* stern

popote *m* (*Mex*) (drinking) straw

popul|acho *m* masses. **~ar** *adj* popular; (costumbre) traditional; (lenguaje) colloquial. **~aridad** *f* popularity. **~arizar** 10 *vt* popularize.

póquer *m* poker

poquito *m*. **un ~** a little bit. • *adv* a little

por *preposición*

- for. **es ~ tu bien** it's for your own good. **lo compró por 5 dólares** he bought it for 5 dollars. **si no fuera por ti** if it weren't for you. **vino por una semana** he came for a week

> Para expresiones como **por la mañana, por la noche** etc., ver bajo el respectivo nombre

- (*causa*) because of. **se retrasó ~ la lluvia** he was late because of the rain. **no hay trenes ~ la huelga** there aren't any trains because of the strike
- (*medio, agente*) by. **lo envié ~ correo** I sent it by post. **fue destruida ~ las bombas** it was destroyed by the bombs
- (*a través de*) through. **entró ~ la ventana** he got in through the window. **me enteré ~ un amigo** I found out through a friend. **~ todo el**

país throughout the country

····➤ (*a lo largo de*) along. **caminar ~ la playa** to walk along the beach. **cortar ~ la línea de puntos** cut along the dotted line

····➤ (*proporción*) per. **cobra 30 dólares ~ hora** he charges 30 dollars per hour. **uno ~ persona** one per person. **10 ~ ciento** 10 per cent

····➤ (*Mat*) times. **dos ~ dos (son) cuatro** two times two is four

····➤ (*modo*) in. **~ escrito** in writing. **pagar ~ adelantado** to pay in advance

➡ Para expresiones como **por dentro, por fuera** etc., ver bajo el respectivo adverbio

····➤ (*en locuciones*) **~ más que** no matter how much. **¿~ qué?** why? **~ si** in case. **~ supuesto** of course

porcelana *f* china

porcentaje *m* percentage

porcino *adj* pig

porción *f* portion; (*de chocolate*) piece

pordiosero *m* beggar

porfia|do *adj* stubborn. **~r** 20 *vi* insist

pormenor *m* detail

pornogr|afía *f* pornography. **~áfico** *adj* pornographic

poro *m* pore; (*Mex, puerro*) leek. **~so** *adj* porous

porque *conj* because; (*para que*) so that

porqué *m* reason

porquería *f* filth; (*basura*) rubbish; (*grosería*) dirty trick

porra *f* club

porrón *m* wine jug (with a long spout)

portaaviones *m invar* aircraft carrier

portada *f* (*de libro*) title page; (*de revista*) cover

portadocumentos *m invar* (*LAm*) briefcase

portador *m* bearer

portaequipaje(s) *m invar* boot (*Brit*), trunk (*Amer*); (*encima del coche*) roof-rack

portal *m* hall; (*puerta principal*) main entrance. **~es** *mpl* arcade

porta|ligas *m invar* suspender belt. **~monedas** *m invar* purse

portarse *vpr* behave

portátil *adj* portable. ● *m* portable computer, laptop

portavoz *m* spokesman. ● *f* spokeswoman

portazo *m* bang. **dar un ~** slam the door

porte *m* transport; (*precio*) carriage; (*LAm, tamaño*) size. **~ador** *m* carrier

portento *m* marvel

porteño *adj* from Buenos Aires

porter|ía *f* porter's lodge; (*en deportes*) goal. **~o** *m* caretaker, porter; (*en deportes*) goalkeeper. **~o automático** entryphone

pórtico *m* portico

portorriqueño *adj & m* Puerto Rican

Portugal *m* Portugal

portugués *adj & m* Portuguese

porvenir *m* future

posada *f* inn. **dar ~** give shelter

posar *vt* put. ● *vi* pose. **~se** *vpr*

P

(pájaro) perch; (avión) land
posdata *f* postscript
pose|edor *m* owner; (*de récord, billete, etc*) holder. **~er** 18 *vt* own; hold (récord); have (conocimientos). **~sión** *f* possession. **~sionarse** *vpr.* **~sionarse de** take possession of. **~sivo** *adj* possessive
posgraduado *adj & m* postgraduate
posguerra *f* post-war years
posib|ilidad *f* possibility. **~le** *adj* possible. **de ser ~le** if possible. **en lo ~le** as far as possible. **si es ~le** if possible
posición *f* position; (*en sociedad*) social standing
positivo *adj* positive
poso *m* sediment
posponer 34 *vt* put after; (*diferir*) postpone
posta *f.* **a ~** on purpose
postal *adj* postal. ● *f* postcard
poste *m* pole; (*de valla*) post
póster *m* (*pl* **~s**) poster
postergar 12 *vt* pass over; (*diferir*) postpone
posteri|dad *f* posterity. **~or** *adj* back; (años) later; (capítulos) subsequent. **~ormente** *adv* later
postigo *m* door; (*contraventana*) shutter
postizo *adj* false, artificial. ● *m* hairpiece
postrarse *vpr* prostrate o.s.
postre *m* dessert, pudding (*Brit*)
postular *vt* postulate; (*LAm*) nominate (candidato)
póstumo *adj* posthumous
postura *f* position, stance
potable *adj* drinkable; (agua) drinking
potaje *m* vegetable stew
potasio *m* potassium
pote *m* pot
poten|cia *f* power. **~cial** *adj & m* potential. **~te** *adj* powerful
potro *m* colt; (*en gimnasia*) horse
pozo *m* well; (*hoyo seco*) pit; (*de mina*) shaft; (*fondo común*) pool
práctica *f* practice. **en la ~** in practice
practica|nte *m & f* nurse. **~r** 7 *vt* practise; play (deportes); (*ejecutar*) carry out
práctico *adj* practical; (*conveniente, útil*) handy. ● *m* practitioner
prad|era *f* meadow; (*terreno grande*) prairie. **~o** *m* meadow
pragmático *adj* pragmatic
preámbulo *m* preamble
precario *adj* precarious; (medios) scarce
precaución *f* precaution; (*cautela*) caution. **con ~** cautiously
precaverse *vpr* take precautions
precede|ncia *f* precedence; (*prioridad*) priority. **~nte** *adj* preceding. ● *m* precedent **~r** *vt/i* precede
precepto *m* precept. **~r** *m* tutor
precia|do *adj* valued; (don) valuable. **~rse** *vpr.* **~rse de** pride o.s. on
precio *m* price. **~ de venta al público** retail price. **al ~ de** at the cost of. **no tener ~** be priceless. **¿qué ~ tiene?** how much is it?
precios|idad *f* (*cosa preciosa*) beautiful thing. **¡es una ~idad!** it's beautiful! **~o** *adj* precious; (*bonito*) beautiful
precipicio *m* precipice
precipita|ción *f* precipitation; (*prisa*) rush. **~damente** *adv* hastily. **~do** *adj* hasty. **~r** *vt* (*apre-*

P

surar) hasten; (*arrojar*) hurl. **~rse** *vpr* throw o.s.; (*correr*) rush; (*actuar sin reflexionar*) act rashly

precis|amente *adj* exactly. **~ar** *vt* require; (*determinar*) determine. **~ión** *f* precision. **~o** *adj* precise; (*necesario*) necessary. **si es ~o** if necessary

preconcebido *adj* preconceived

precoz *adj* early; (niño) precocious

precursor *m* forerunner

predecesor *m* predecessor

predecir 46, (*pero imperativo* **predice**, *futuro y condicional regulares*) *vt* foretell

predestinado *adj* predestined

prédica *f* sermon

predicar 7 *vt/i* preach

predicción *f* prediction; (*del tiempo*) forecast

predilec|ción *f* predilection. **~to** *adj* favourite

predisponer 34 *vt* predispose

predomin|ante *adj* predominant. **~ar** *vi* predominate. **~io** *m* predominance

preeminente *adj* pre-eminent

prefabricado *adj* prefabricated

prefacio *m* preface

prefer|encia *f* preference; (*Auto*) right of way. **de ~encia** preferably. **~ente** *adj* preferential. **~ible** *adj* preferable. **~ido** *adj* favourite. **~ir** 4 *vt* prefer

prefijo *m* prefix; (*telefónico*) dialling code

pregonar *vt* announce

pregunta *f* question. **hacer una ~** ask a question. **~r** *vt/i* ask (**por** about). **~rse** *vpr* wonder

prehistórico *adj* prehistoric

preju|icio *m* prejudice. **~zgar** 12 *vt* prejudge

preliminar *adj & m* preliminary

preludio *m* prelude

premarital *adj*, **prematrimonial** *adj* premarital

prematuro *adj* premature

premedita|ción *f* premeditation. **~r** *vt* premeditate

premi|ar *vt* give a prize to; (*recompensar*) reward. **~o** *m* prize; (*recompensa*) reward. **~o gordo** jackpot

premonición *f* premonition

prenatal *adj* antenatal

prenda *f* garment; (*garantía*) surety; (*en juegos*) forfeit. **en ~ de** as a token of. **~r** *vt* captivate. **~rse** *vpr* fall in love (**de** with)

prende|dor *m* brooch. **~r** *vt* capture; (*sujetar*) fasten; light (cigarrillo); (*LAm*) turn on (gas, radio, etc). • *vi* catch; (*arraigar*) take root. **~rse** *vpr* (*encenderse*) catch fire

prensa *f* press. **~r** *vt* press

preñado *adj* pregnant; (*fig*) full

preocupa|ción *f* worry. **~do** *adj* worried. **~r** *vt* worry. **~rse** *vpr* worry. **~rse de** look after

prepara|ción *f* preparation. **~do** *adj* prepared. • *m* preparation. **~r** *vt* prepare. **~rse** *vpr* get ready. **~tivos** *mpl* preparations. **~torio** *adj* preparatory

preposición *f* preposition

prepotente *adj* arrogant; (actitud) high-handed

prerrogativa *f* prerogative

presa *f* (*cosa*) prey; (*embalse*) dam

presagi|ar *vt* presage. **~o** *m* omen

presb|iteriano *adj & m* Presbyterian. **~ítero** *m* priest

prescindir *vi*. **~ de** do without;

(*deshacerse de*) dispense with

prescri|bir (*pp* **prescrito**) *vt* prescribe. **~pción** *f* prescription

presencia *f* presence; (*aspecto*) appearance. **en ~ de** in the presence of. **~r** *vt* be present at; (*ver*) witness

presenta|ble *adj* presentable. **~ción** *f* presentation; (*de una persona a otra*) introduction. **~dor** *m* presenter. **~r** *vt* present; (*ofrecer*) offer; (*entregar*) hand in; (*hacer conocer*) introduce; show (película). **~rse** *vpr* present o.s.; (*hacerse conocer*) introduce o.s.; (*aparecer*) turn up

presente *adj* present; (*actual*) this. • *m* present. **los ~s** those present. **tener ~** remember

presenti|miento *m* premonition. **~r** **4** *vt* have a feeling (**que** that)

preserva|r *vt* preserve. **~tivo** *m* condom

presiden|cia *f* presidency; (*de asamblea*) chairmanship. **~cial** *adj* presidential. **~ta** *f* (woman) president. **~te** *m* president; (*de asamblea*) chairman. **~te del gobierno** prime minister

P

presidi|ario *m* convict. **~o** *m* prison

presidir *vt* be president of; preside over (tribunal); chair (reunión, comité)

presi|ón *f* pressure. **a ~ón** under pressure. **hacer ~ón** press. **~onar** *vt* press; (*fig*) put pressure on

preso *adj*. **estar ~** be in prison. **llevarse ~ a uno** take s.o. away under arrest. • *m* prisoner

presta|do *adj* (*de uno*) lent; (*a uno*) borrowed. **pedir ~do** borrow. **~mista** *m & f* moneylender

préstamo *m* loan; (*acción de pedir prestado*) borrowing; (*acción de prestar*) lending

prestar *vt* lend; give (ayuda etc); pay (atención). **~se** *vpr*. **~se a** be open to; (*ser apto*) be suitable (**para** for)

prestidigita|ción *f* conjuring. **~dor** *m* conjurer

prestigio *m* prestige. **~so** *adj* prestigious

presu|mido *adj* conceited. **~mir** *vi* show off; boast (**de** about). **~nción** *f* conceit; (*suposición*) presumption. **~nto** *adj* alleged. **~ntuoso** *adj* conceited

presup|oner **34** *vt* presuppose. **~uesto** *m* budget; (*precio estimado*) estimate

preten|cioso *adj* pretentious. **~der** *vt* try to; (*afirmar*) claim; (*solicitar*) apply for; (*cortejar*) court. **~diente** *m* pretender; (*a una mujer*) suitor. **~sión** *f* pretension; (*aspiración*) aspiration

pretérito *m* preterite, past

pretexto *m* pretext. **con el ~ de** on the pretext of

prevalecer **11** *vi* prevail (**sobre** over)

preven|ción *f* prevention; (*prejuicio*) prejudice. **~ido** *adj* ready; (*precavido*) cautious. **~ir** **53** *vt* prevent; (*advertir*) warn. **~tiva** *f* (*Mex*) amber light. **~tivo** *adj* preventive

prever **43** *vt* foresee; (*planear*) plan

previo *adj* previous

previs|ible *adj* predictable. **~ión** *f* forecast; (*prudencia*) precaution

prima *f* (*pariente*) cousin; (*cantidad*) bonus

primario *adj* primary

primavera *f* spring. **~l** *adj* spring

primer *adj véase* PRIMERO. **~a** *f* (*Auto*) first (gear); (*en tren etc*) first class. **~o** *adj* (*delante de nombre masculino en singular* **primer**) first; (*mejor*) best; (*principal*) leading. **la ~a fila** the front row. **lo ~o es** the most important thing is. **~a enseñanza** primary education. **a ~os de** at the beginning of. **de ~a** first-class. • *n* (the) first. • *adv* first

primitivo *adj* primitive

primo *m* cousin; [!] fool. **hacer el ~** be taken for a ride

primogénito *adj & m* first-born, eldest

primor *m* delicacy; (*cosa*) beautiful thing

primordial *adj* fundamental; (interés) paramount

princesa *f* princess

principal *adj* main. **lo ~ es que** the main thing is that

príncipe *m* prince

principi|ante *m & f* beginner. **~o** *m* beginning; (*moral, idea*) principle; (*origen*) origin. **al ~o** at first. **a ~o(s) de** at the beginning of. **desde el ~o** from the start. **en ~o** in principle. **~os** *mpl* (*nociones*) rudiments

prión *m* prion

prioridad *f* priority

prisa *f* hurry, haste. **darse ~** hurry (up). **de ~** quickly. **tener ~** be in a hurry

prisi|ón *f* prison; (*encarcelamiento*) imprisonment. **~onero** *m* prisoner

prismáticos *mpl* binoculars

priva|ción *f* deprivation. **~da** *f* (*Mex*) private road. **~do** *adj* (*particular*) private. **~r** *vt* deprive (**de** of). **~tivo** *adj* exclusive (**de** to)

privilegi|ado *adj* privileged; (*muy bueno*) exceptional. **~o** *m* privilege

pro *prep.* **en ~ de** for, in favour of. • *m* advantage. **los ~s y los contras** the pros and cons

proa *f* bow

probab|ilidad *f* probability. **~le** *adj* probable, likely. **~lemente** *adv* probably

proba|dor *m* fitting-room. **~r** [2] *vt* try; try on (ropa); (*demostrar*) prove. • *vi* try. **~rse** *vpr* try on

probeta *f* test-tube

problema *m* problem. **hacerse ~as** (*LAm*) worry

procaz *adj* indecent

proced|encia *f* origin. **~ente** *adj* (*razonable*) reasonable. **~ente de** (coming) from. **~er** *m* conduct. • *vi* proceed. **~er contra** start legal proceedings against. **~er de** come from. **~imiento** *m* procedure; (*sistema*) process; (*Jurid*) proceedings

proces|ador *m.* **~ de textos** word processor. **~al** *adj* procedural. **costas ~ales** legal costs. **~amiento** *m* processing; (*Jurid*) prosecution. **~amiento de textos** word-processing.. **~ar** *vt* process; (*Jurid*) prosecute

procesión *f* procession

proceso *m* process; (*Jurid*) trial; (*transcurso*) course

proclamar *vt* proclaim

procrea|ción *f* procreation. **~r** *vt* procreate

procura|dor *m* attorney, solicitor; (*asistente*) clerk (*Brit*), paralegal (*Amer*). **~r** *vt* try; (*obtener*) obtain

prodigar [12] *vt* lavish

prodigio *m* prodigy; (*maravilla*) wonder; (*milagro*) miracle. **~so** *adj* prodigious

pródigo *adj* prodigal

produc|ción *f* production. **~ir** [47] *vt* produce; (*causar*) cause. **~irse** *vpr* (*suceder*) happen. **~tivo** *adj* productive. **~to** *m* product. **~tos agrícolas** farm produce. **~tos alimenticios** foodstuffs. **~tos de belleza** cosmetics. **~tos de consumo** consumer goods. **~tor** *m* producer.

proeza *f* exploit

profan|ación *f* desecration. **~ar** *vt* desecrate. **~o** *adj* profane

profecía *f* prophecy

proferir [4] *vt* utter; hurl (insultos etc)

profes|ión *f* profession. **~ional** *adj* professional. **~or** *m* teacher; (*en universidad*) lecturer. **~orado** *m* teaching profession; (*conjunto de profesores*) staff

prof|eta *m* prophet. **~etizar** [10] *vt/i* prophesize

prófugo *adj & m* fugitive

profund|idad *f* depth. **~o** *adj* deep; (*fig*) profound. **poco ~o** shallow

progenitor *m* ancestor

programa *m* programme; (*de estudios*) syllabus. **~ concurso** quiz show. **~ de entrevistas** chat show. **~ción** *f* programming; (*TV etc*) programmes; (*en periódico*) TV guide. **~r** *vt* programme. **~dor** *m* computer programmer

progres|ar *vi* (make) progress. **~ión** *f* progression. **~ista** *adj* progressive. **~ivo** *adj* progressive. **~o** *m* progress. **hacer ~os** make progress

prohibi|ción *f* prohibition. **~do** *adj* forbidden. **prohibido fumar** no smoking. **~r** *vt* forbid. **~tivo** *adj* prohibitive

prójimo *m* fellow man

prole *f* offspring

proletari|ado *m* proletariat. **~o** *adj & m* proletarian

prol|iferación *f* proliferation. **~iferar** *vi* proliferate. **~ífico** *adj* prolific

prolijo *adj* long-winded

prólogo *m* prologue

prolongar [12] *vt* prolong; (*alargar*) lengthen. **~se** *vpr* go on

promedio *m* average. **como ~** on average

prome|sa *f* promise. **~ter** *vt* promise. ● *vi* show promise. **~terse** *vpr* (novios) get engaged. **~tida** *f* fiancée. **~tido** *adj* promised; (novios) engaged. ● *m* fiancé

prominente *f* prominence

promiscu|idad *f* promiscuity. **~o** *adj* promiscuous

promo|ción *f* promotion. **~tor** *m* promoter. **~ver** [2] *vt* promote; (*causar*) cause

promulgar [12] *vt* promulgate

pronombre *m* pronoun

pron|osticar [7] *vt* predict; forecast (tiempo). **~óstico** *m* prediction; (*del tiempo*) forecast; (*Med*) prognosis

pront|itud *f* promptness. **~o** *adj* quick. ● *adv* quickly; (*dentro de poco*) soon; (*temprano*) early. **de ~o** suddenly. **por lo ~o** for the time being. **tan ~o como** as soon as

pronuncia|ción *f* pronunciation. **~miento** *m* revolt. **~r** *vt* pronounce; deliver (discurso). **~rse** *vpr* (*declararse*) declare o.s.; (*sublevarse*) rise up

propagación *f* propagation

propaganda *f* propaganda;

(*anuncios*) advertising
propagar 12 *vt/i* propagate. **~se** *vpr* spread
propasarse *vpr* go too far
propens|ión *f* inclination. **~o** *adj* inclined
propici|ar *vt* favour; (*provocar*) bring about. **~o** *adj* favourable
propie|dad *f* property. **~tario** *m* owner
propina *f* tip
propio *adj* own; (*característico*) typical; (*natural*) natural; (*apropiado*) proper. **el ~ médico** the doctor himself
proponer 34 *vt* propose; put forward (persona). **~se** *vpr*. **~se hacer** intend to do
proporci|ón *f* proportion. **~onado** *adj* proportioned. **~onal** *adj* proportional. **~onar** *vt* provide
proposición *f* proposition
propósito *m* intention. **a ~** (*adrede*) on purpose; (*de paso*) by the way. **a ~ de** with regard to
propuesta *f* proposal
propuls|ar *vt* propel; (*fig*) promote. **~ión** *f* propulsion. **~ión a chorro** jet propulsion
prórroga *f* extension
prorrogar 12 *vt* extend
prosa *f* prose. **~ico** *adj* prosaic
proscri|bir (*pp* **proscrito**) *vt* exile; (*prohibir*) ban. **~to** *adj* banned. ● *m* exile; (*bandido*) outlaw
proseguir 5 & 13 *vt/i* continue
prospecto *m* prospectus; (*de fármaco*) directions for use
prosper|ar *vi* prosper; (persona) do well. **~idad** *f* prosperity
próspero *adj* prosperous. **¡P~ Año Nuevo!** Happy New Year!
prostit|ución *f* prostitution. **~uta** *f* prostitute
protagonista *m & f* protagonist
prote|cción *f* protection. **~ctor** *adj* protective. ● *m* protector; (*benefactor*) patron. **~ger** 14 *vt* protect. **~gida** *f* protegée. **~gido** *adj* protected. ● *m* protegé
proteína *f* protein
protesta *f* protest; (*manifestación*) demonstration; (*Mex, promesa*) promise; (*Mex, juramento*) oath
protestante *adj & m & f* Protestant
protestar *vt/i* protest
protocolo *m* protocol
provecho *m* benefit. **¡buen ~!** enjoy your meal! **de ~** useful. **en ~ de** to the benefit of. **sacar ~ de** benefit from
proveer 18 (*pp* **proveído** *y* **provisto**) *vt* supply, provide
provenir 53 *vi* come (**de** from)
proverbi|al *adj* proverbial. **~o** *m* proverb
provincia *f* province. **~l** *adj*, **~no** *adj* provincial
provisional *adj* provisional
provisto *adj* provided (**de** with)
provoca|ción *f* provocation. **~r** 7 *vt* provoke; (*causar*) cause. **~tivo** *adj* provocative
proximidad *f* proximity
próximo *adj* next; (*cerca*) near
proyec|ción *f* projection. **~tar** *vt* hurl; cast (luz); show (película). **~til** *m* missile. **~to** *m* plan. **~to de ley** bill. **en ~to** planned. **~tor** *m* projector
pruden|cia *f* prudence; (*cuidado*) caution. **~te** *adj* prudent, sensible

P

prueba *f* proof; (*examen*) test; (*de ropa*) fitting. **a ~** on trial. **a ~ de** proof against. **a ~ de agua** waterproof. **poner a ~** test

pruebo *vb véase* PROBAR

psicoan|álisis *f* psychoanalysis. **~alista** *m & f* psychoanalyst. **~alizar** 10 *vt* psychoanalyse

psic|ología *f* psychology. **~ológico** *adj* psychological. **~ólogo** *m* psychologist. **~ópata** *m & f* psychopath. **~osis** *f invar* psychosis

psiqu|e *f* psyche. **~iatra** *m & f* psychiatrist. **~iátrico** *adj* psychiatric

psíquico *adj* psychic

ptas, pts *abrev* (**pesetas**) pesetas

púa *f* sharp point; (*espina*) thorn; (*de erizo*) quill; (*de peine*) tooth; (*Mus*) plectrum

pubertad *f* puberty

publica|ción *f* publication. **~r** 7 *vt* publish

publici|dad *f* publicity; (*Com*) advertising. **~tario** *adj* advertising

P

público *adj* public. ● *m* public; (*de espectáculo etc*) audience

puchero *m* cooking pot; (*guisado*) stew. **hacer ~s** (*fig, fam*) pout

pude *vb véase* PODER

pudor *m* modesty. **~oso** *adj* modest

pudrir (*pp* **podrido**) *vt* rot; (*fig, molestar*) annoy. **~se** *vpr* rot

puebl|ecito *m* small village. **~erino** *m* country bumpkin. **~o** *m* town; (*aldea*) village; (*nación*) nation, people

puedo *vb véase* PODER

puente *m* bridge; (*fig, fam*) long weekend. **~ colgante** suspension bridge. **~ levadizo** drawbridge. **hacer ~** I have a long weekend

> **i** **puente** *Puentes* are very important in Spain and Latin America. *Hacer Puente* means that when a working day falls between two public holidays, it too is taken as a holiday.

puerco *adj* filthy; (*grosero*) coarse. ● *m* pig. **~ espín** porcupine

puerro *m* leek

puerta *f* door; (*en deportes*) goal; (*de ciudad, en jardín*) gate. **~ principal** main entrance. **a ~ cerrada** behind closed doors

puerto *m* port; (*fig, refugio*) refuge; (*entre montañas*) pass. **~ franco** free port

puertorriqueño *adj & m* Puerto Rican

pues *adv* (*entonces*) then; (*bueno*) well. ● *conj* since

puest|a *f* setting; (*en juegos*) bet. **~a de sol** sunset. **~a en escena** staging. **~a en marcha** starting. **~o** *adj* put; (*vestido*) dressed. ● *m* place; (*empleo*) position, job; (*en mercado etc*) stall. ● *conj.* **~o que** since

pugna *f* struggle. **~r** *vi*. **~r por** strive to

puja *f* struggle (**por** to); (*en subasta*) bid. **~r** *vt* struggle; (*en subasta*) bid

pulcro *adj* neat

pulga *f* flea. **tener malas ~s** be bad-tempered

pulga|da *f* inch. **~r** *m* thumb; (*del pie*) big toe

puli|do *adj* polished; (modales) refined. **~r** *vt* polish; (*suavizar*) smooth

pulla *f* gibe

pulm|ón *m* lung. **~onar** *adj* pulmonary. **~onía** *f* pneumonia

pulpa *f* pulp
pulpería *f* (*LAm*) grocer's shop (*Brit*), grocery store (*Amer*)
púlpito *m* pulpit
pulpo *m* octopus
pulque *m* (*Mex*) pulque, alcoholic Mexican drink. **~ría** *f* bar
pulsa|ción *f* pulsation. **~dor** *m* button. **~r** *vt* press; (*Mus*) pluck
pulsera *f* bracelet
pulso *m* pulse; (*firmeza*) steady hand. **echar un ~** arm wrestle. **tomar el ~ a uno** take s.o.'s pulse
pulular *vi* teem with
puma *m* puma
puna *f* puna, high plateau
punitivo *adj* punitive
punta *f* point; (*extremo*) tip. **estar de ~** be in a bad mood. **ponerse de ~ con uno** fall out with s.o. **sacar ~ a** sharpen
puntada *f* stitch
puntaje *m* (*LAm*) score
puntal *m* prop, support
puntapié *m* kick
puntear *vt* mark; (*Mus*) pluck; (*LAm, en deportes*) lead
puntería *f* aim; (*destreza*) markmanship
puntiagudo *adj* pointed; (*afilado*) sharp
puntilla *f* (*encaje*) lace. **en ~s** (*LAm*), **de ~s** on tiptoe
punto *m* point; (*señal, trazo*) dot; (*de examen*) mark; (*lugar*) spot, place; (*de taxis*) stand; (*momento*) moment; (*punto final*) full stop (*Brit*), period (*Amer*); (*puntada*) stitch. **~ de vista** point of view. **~ com** dot-com. **~ final** full stop (*Brit*), period (*Amer*). **~ muerto** (*Auto*) neutral (gear). **~ y aparte** full stop, new paragraph (*Brit*), period, new paragraph (*Amer*). **~ y coma** semicolon. **a ~** on time; (*listo*) ready. **a ~ de** on the point of. **de ~** knitted. **dos ~s** colon. **en ~** exactly. **hacer ~** knit. **hasta cierto ~** to a certain extent
puntuación *f* punctuation; (*en deportes, acción*) scoring; (*en deportes, número de puntos*) score
puntual *adj* punctual; (*exacto*) accurate. **~idad** *f* punctuality; (*exactitud*) accuracy
puntuar 21 *vt* punctuate; mark (*Brit*), grade (*Amer*) (examen). ● *vi* score (points)
punza|da *f* sharp pain; (*fig*) pang. **~nte** *adj* sharp. **~r** 10 *vt* prick
puñado *m* handful. **a ~s** by the handful
puñal *m* dagger. **~ada** *f* stab
puñ|etazo *m* punch. **~o** *m* fist; (*de ropa*) cuff; (*mango*) handle. **de su ~o (y letra)** in his own handwriting
pupa *f* (*fam, en los labios*) cold sore
pupila *f* pupil
pupitre *m* desk
puré *m* purée; (*sopa*) thick soup. **~ de papas** (*LAm*), **~ de patatas** mashed potatoes
pureza *f* purity
purga *f* purge. **~torio** *m* purgatory
puri|ficación *f* purification. **~ificar** 7 *vt* purify. **~sta** *m & f* purist. **~tano** *adj* puritanical. ● *m* puritan
puro *adj* pure; (cielo) clear. **de pura casualidad** by sheer chance. **de ~ tonto** out of sheer stupidity. ● *m* cigar
púrpura *f* purple
pus *m* pus
puse *vb véase* **PONER**

P

pusilánime *adj* fainthearted
puta *f* (*vulg*) whore

Qq

que *pron rel* (*personas, sujeto*) who; (*personas, complemento*) whom; (*cosas*) which, that. ● *conj* that. **¡~ tengan Vds buen viaje!** have a good journey! **¡~ venga!** let him come! **~ venga o no venga** whether he comes or not. **creo ~ tiene razón** I think (that) he is right. **más ~** more than. **lo ~** what. **yo ~ tú** if I were you
qué *adj* (*con sustantivo*) what; (*con a o adv*) how. ● *pron* what. **¡~ bonito!** how nice!. **¿en ~ piensas?** what are you thinking about?
quebra|da *f* gorge; (*paso*) pass. **~dizo** *adj* fragile. **~do** *adj* broken; (*Com*) bankrupt. ● *m* (*Math*) fraction. **~ntar** *vt* break; disturb (paz). **~nto** *m* (*pérdida*) loss; (*daño*) damage. **~r** **1** *vt* break. ● *vi* break; (*Com*) go bankrupt. **~rse** *vpr* break
quechua *adj* Quechua. ● *m & f* Quechuan. ● *m* (*lengua*) Quechua
quedar *vi* stay, remain; (*estar*) be; (*haber todavía*) be left. **~ bien** come off well. **~se** *vpr* stay. **~ con** arrange to meet. **~ en** agree to. **~ en nada** come to nothing. **~ por** (+ *infinitivo*) remain to be (+ *pp*)
quehacer *m* work. **~es domésticos** household chores
quej|a *f* complaint; (*de dolor*) moan. **~arse** *vpr* complain (**de** about); (*gemir*) moan. **~ido** *m* moan
quema|do *adj* burnt; (*LAm, bronceado*) tanned; (*fig*) annoyed. **~dor** *m* burner. **~dura** *f* burn. **~r** *vt/i* burn. **~rse** *vpr* burn o.s.; (*consumirse*) burn up; (*con el sol*) get sunburnt. **~rropa** *adv.* **a ~rropa** point-blank
quena *f* Indian flute
quepo *vb véase* **CABER**
querella *f* (*riña*) quarrel, dispute; (*Jurid*) criminal action
quer|er **35** *vt* want; (*amar*) love; (*necesitar*) need. **~er decir** mean. ● *m* love; (*amante*) lover. **como quiera que** however. **cuando quiera que** whenever. **donde quiera** wherever. **¿quieres darme ese libro?** would you pass me that book? **¿quieres un helado?** would you like an ice-cream? **quisiera ir a la playa** I'd like to go to the beach. **sin ~er** without meaning to. **~ido** *adj* dear; (*amado*) loved
querosén *m*, **queroseno** *m* kerosene
querubín *m* cherub
ques|adilla *f* (*Mex*) tortilla filled with cheese. **~o** *m* cheese
quetzal *m* (*unidad monetaria ecuatoriana*) quetzal
quicio *m* frame. **sacar de ~ a uno** infuriate s.o.
quiebra *f* (*Com*) bankruptcy
quien *pron rel* (*sujeto*) who; (*complemento*) whom
quién *pron interrogativo* (*sujeto*) who; (*tras preposición*) **¿con ~?** who with?, to whom?. **¿de ~ son estos libros?** whose are these books?
quienquiera *pron* whoever
quiero *vb véase* **QUERER**

p q

quiet|o *adj* still; (*inmóvil*) motionless; (carácter etc) calm. **~ud** *f* stillness

quijada *f* jaw

quilate *m* carat

quilla *f* keel

quimera *f* (*fig*) illusion

químic|a *f* chemistry. **~o** *adj* chemical. ● *m* chemist

quince *adj & m* fifteen. **~ días** a fortnight. **~na** *f* fortnight. **~nal** *adj* fortnightly

quincuagésimo *adj* fiftieth

quiniela *f* pools coupon. **~s** *fpl* (football) pools

quinientos *adj & m* five hundred

quinquenio *m* (period of) five years

quinta *f* (*casa*) villa

quintal *m* a hundred kilograms

quinteto *m* quintet

quinto *adj & m* fifth

quiosco *m* kiosk; (*en jardín*) summerhouse; (*en parque etc*) bandstand

quirúrgico *adj* surgical

quise *vb véase* QUERER

quisquill|a *f* trifle; (*camarón*) shrimp. **~oso** *adj* irritable; (*exigente*) fussy

quita|esmalte *m* nail polish remover. **~manchas** *m invar* stain remover. **~nieves** *m invar* snow plough. **~r** *vt* remove, take away; take off (ropa); (*robar*) steal. **~ndo** (*fam, a excepción de*) apart from. **~rse** *vpr* get rid of (dolor); take off (ropa). **~rse de** (*no hacerlo más*) stop. **~rse de en medio** get out of the way. **~sol** *m* sunshade

quizá(s) *adv* perhaps

quórum *m* quorum

Rr

rábano *m* radish. **~ picante** horseradish. **me importa un ~** I couldn't care less

rabi|a *f* rabies; (*fig*) rage. **~ar** *vi* (*de dolor*) be in great pain; (*estar enfadado*) be furious. **dar ~a** infuriate. **~eta** *f* tantrum

rabino *m* rabbi

rabioso *adj* rabid; (*furioso*) furious

rabo *m* tail

racha *f* gust of wind; (*fig*) spate. **pasar por una mala ~** go through a bad patch

racial *adj* racial

racimo *m* bunch

ración *f* share, ration; (*de comida*) portion

raciona|l *adj* rational. **~lizar** **10** *vt* rationalize. **~r** *vt* (*limitar*) ration; (*repartir*) ration out

racis|mo *m* racism. **~ta** *adj* racist

radar *m* radar

radiación *f* radiation

radiactiv|idad *f* radioactivity. **~o** *adj* radioactive

radiador *m* radiator

radiante *adj* radiant; (*brillante*) brilliant

radical *adj & m & f* radical

radicar **7** *vi* lie (**en** in). **~se** *vpr* settle

radio *m* radius; (*de rueda*) spoke; (*LAm*) radio. ● *f* radio. **~actividad** *f* radioactivity. **~activo** *adj* radioactive. **~difusión** *f* broadcasting. **~emisora** *f* radio station. **~escucha** *m & f* listener. **~grafía** *f* radiography

radi|ólogo *m* radiologist. **~oterapia** *f* radiotherapy
radioyente *m & f* listener
raer 36 *vt* scrape; (*quitar*) scrape off
ráfaga *f* (*de viento*) gust; (*de ametralladora*) burst
rafia *f* raffia
raído *adj* threadbare
raíz *f* root. **a ~ de** as a result of. **echar raíces** (*fig*) settle
raja *f* split; (*Culin*) slice. **~r** *vt* split. **~rse** *vpr* split; (*fig*) back out
rajatabla. **a ~** rigorously
ralea *f* sort
ralla|dor *m* grater. **~r** *vt* grate
ralo *adj* (pelo) thin
rama *f* branch. **~je** *m* branches. **~l** *m* branch
rambla *f* watercourse; (*avenida*) avenue
ramera *f* prostitute
ramifica|ción *f* ramification. **~rse** 7 *vpr* branch out
ram|illete *m* bunch. **~o** *m* branch; (*de flores*) bunch, bouquet
rampa *f* ramp, slope
rana *f* frog
ranch|era *f* (*Mex*) folk song. **~ero** *m* cook; (*Mex, hacendado*) rancher. **~o** *m* (*LAm, choza*) hut; (*LAm, casucha*) shanty; (*Mex, hacienda*) ranch
rancio *adj* rancid; (vino) old; (*fig*) ancient
rango *m* rank
ranúnculo *m* buttercup
ranura *f* groove; (*para moneda*) slot
rapar *vt* shave; crop (pelo)
rapaz *adj* rapacious; (ave) of prey
rape *m* monkfish
rapidez *f* speed
rápido *adj* fast, quick. • *adv* quickly. • *m* (*tren*) express. **~s** *mpl* rapids
rapiña *f* robbery. **ave** *f* **de ~** bird of prey
rapsodia *f* rhapsody
rapt|ar *vt* kidnap. **~o** *m* kidnapping; (*de ira etc*) fit
raqueta *f* racquet
rar|eza *f* rarity; (*cosa rara*) oddity. **~o** *adj* rare; (*extraño*) odd. **es ~o que** it is strange that. **¡qué ~o!** how strange!
ras. **a ~ de** level with
rasca|cielos *m invar* skyscraper. **~r** 7 *vt* scratch; (*raspar*) scrape
rasgar 12 *vt* tear
rasgo *m* characteristic; (*gesto*) gesture; (*de pincel*) stroke. **~s** *mpl* (*facciones*) features
rasguear *vt* strum
rasguñ|ar *vt* scratch. **~o** *m* scratch
raso *adj* (cucharada etc) level; (vuelo etc) low. **al ~** in the open air. • *m* satin
raspa|dura *f* scratch; (*acción*) scratching. **~r** *vt* scratch; (*rozar*) scrape
rastr|a. **a ~as** dragging. **~ear** *vt* track. **~ero** *adj* creeping. **~illar** *vt* rake. **~illo** *m* rake. **~o** *m* track; (*señal*) sign. **ni ~o** not a trace
rata *f* rat
ratero *m* petty thief
ratifica|ción *f* ratification. **~r** 7 *vt* ratify
rato *m* moment, short time. **~s libres** spare time. **a ~s** at times. **a cada ~** (*LAm*) always. **hace un ~** a moment ago. **pasar un mal ~** have a rough time
rat|ón *m* mouse. **~onera** *f*

mousetrap; (*madriguera*) mouse hole

raudal *m* torrent. **a ~les** in abundance

raya *f* line; (*lista*) stripe; (*de pelo*) parting. **a ~s** striped. **pasarse de la ~** go too far. **~r** *vt* scratch. **~r en** border on

rayo *m* ray; (*descarga eléctrica*) lightning. **~ de luna** moonbeam. **~ láser** laser beam. **~s X** X-rays

raza *f* race; (*de animal*) breed. **de ~** (caballo) thoroughbred; (perro) pedigree

raz|ón *f* reason. **a ~ón de** at the rate of. **tener ~ón** be right. **~onable** *adj* reasonable. **~onar** *vt* reason out. ● *vi* reason

RDSI *abrev* (**Red Digital de Servicios Integrados**) ISDN

re *m* D; (*solfa*) re

reac|ción *f* reaction; (*LAm, Pol*) right wing. **~ción en cadena** chain reaction. **~cionario** *adj & m* reactionary. **~tor** *m* reactor; (*avión*) jet

real *adj* real; (*de rey etc*) royal; (hecho) true. ● *m* real, old Spanish coin

realidad *f* reality; (*verdad*) truth. **en ~** in fact. **hacerse ~** come true

realis|mo *m* realism. **~ta** *adj* realistic. ● *m & f* realist

realiza|ción *f* fulfilment. **~r** 10 *vt* carry out; make (viaje); fulfil (ilusión); (*vender*) sell. **~rse** *vpr* (sueño, predicción etc) come true; (persona) fulfil o.s.

realzar 10 *vt* (*fig*) enhance

reanimar *vt* revive. **~se** *vpr* revive

reanudar *vt* resume; renew (amistad)

reavivar *vt* revive

rebaja *f* reduction. **en ~s** in the sale. **~do** *adj* (precio) reduced. **~r** *vt* lower; lose (peso)

rebanada *f* slice

rebaño *m* herd; (*de ovejas*) flock

rebasar *vt* exceed; (*dejar atrás*) leave behind; (*Mex, Auto*) overtake

rebatir *vt* refute

rebel|arse *vpr* rebel. **~de** *adj* rebellious; (grupo) rebel. ● *m* rebel. **~día** *f* rebelliousness. **~ión** *f* rebellion

rebosa|nte *adj* brimming (**de** with). **~r** *vi* overflow; (*abundar*) abound

rebot|ar *vt* bounce; (*rechazar*) repel. ● *vi* bounce; (bala) ricochet. **~e** *m* bounce, rebound. **de ~e** on the rebound

reboz|ar 10 *vt* wrap up; (*Culin*) coat in batter. **~o** *m* (*LAm*) shawl

rebusca|do *adj* affected; (*complicado*) over-elaborate. **~r** 7 *vt* search through

rebuznar *vi* bray

recado *m* errand; (*mensaje*) message

reca|er 29 *vi* fall back; (*Med*) relapse; (*fig*) fall. **~ída** *f* relapse

recalcar 7 *vt* stress

recalcitrante *adj* recalcitrant

recalentar 1 *vt* reheat; (*demasiado*) overheat

recámara *f* small room; (*de arma de fuego*) chamber; (*Mex, dormitorio*) bedroom

recambio *m* (*Mec*) spare (part); (*de pluma etc*) refill. **de ~** spare

recapitular *vt* sum up

recarg|ar 12 *vt* overload; (*aumentar*) increase; recharge (batería). **~o** *m* increase

r

recat|ado *adj* modest. **~o** *m* prudence; (*modestia*) modesty. **sin ~o** openly

recauda|ción *f* (*cantidad*) takings. **~dor** *m* tax collector. **~r** *vt* collect

recel|ar *vt* suspect. • *vi* be suspicious (**de** of). **~o** *m* distrust; (*temor*) fear. **~oso** *adj* suspicious

recepci|ón *f* reception. **~onista** *m & f* receptionist

receptáculo *m* receptacle

receptor *m* receiver

recesión *f* recession

receta *f* recipe; (*Med*) prescription

rechaz|ar 10 *vt* reject; defeat (moción); repel (ataque); (*no aceptar*) turn down. **~o** *m* rejection

rechifla *f* booing

rechinar *vi* squeak. **le rechinan los dientes** he grinds his teeth

rechoncho *adj* stout

recib|imiento *m* (*acogida*) welcome. **~ir** *vt* receive; (*acoger*) welcome • *vi* entertain. **~irse** *vpr* graduate. **~o** *m* receipt. **acusar ~o** acknowledge receipt

reci|én *adv* recently; (*LAm, hace poco*) just. **~ casado** newly married. **~ nacido** newborn. **~ente** *adj* recent; (*Culin*) fresh

recinto *m* enclosure; (*local*) premises

recio *adj* strong; (voz) loud. • *adv* hard; (*en voz alta*) loudly

recipiente *m* receptacle. • *m & f* recipient

recíproco *adj* reciprocal; (sentimiento) mutual

recita|l *m* recital; (*de poesías*) reading. **~r** *vt* recite

reclama|ción *f* claim; (*queja*) complaint. **~r** *vt* claim. • *vi* appeal

réclame *m* (*LAm*) advertisement

reclamo *m* (*LAm*) complaint

reclinar *vi* lean. **~se** *vpr* lean

reclus|ión *f* imprisonment. **~o** *m* prisoner

recluta *m & f* recruit. **~miento** *m* recruitment. **~r** *vt* recruit

recobrar *vt* recover. **~se** *vpr* recover

recodo *m* bend

recog|er 14 *vt* collect; pick up (cosa caída); (*cosechar*) harvest. **~erse** *vpr* withdraw; (*ir a casa*) go home; (*acostarse*) go to bed. **~ida** *f* collection; (*cosecha*) harvest

recomenda|ción *f* recommendation. **~r** 1 *vt* recommend; (*encomendar*) entrust

recomenzar 1 & 10 *vt/i* start again

recompensa *f* reward. **~r** *vt* reward

reconcilia|ción *f* reconciliation. **~r** *vt* reconcile. **~rse** *vpr* be reconciled

reconoc|er 11 *vt* recognize; (*admitir*) acknowledge; (*examinar*) examine. **~imiento** *m* recognition; (*admisión*) acknowledgement; (*agradecimiento*) gratitude; (*examen*) examination

reconozco *vb véase* **RECONOCER**

reconquista *f* reconquest. **~r** *vt* reconquer; (*fig*) win back

> **i** **Reconquista** The period in Spain's history during which the Christian kingdoms slowly recovered the territories occupied by the Moslem Moors of North Africa. The Moorish invasion began in 711 AD and was halted in 718. The expulsion of

the last Moorish ruler of Granada in 1492 completed the *Reconquista*.

reconsiderar *vt* reconsider
reconstruir **17** *vt* reconstruct
récord /'rekor/ *m* (*pl* **~s**) record
recordar **2** *vt* remember; (*hacer acordar*) remind. ● *vi* remember. **que yo recuerde** as far as I remember. **si mal no recuerdo** if I remember rightly
recorr|er *vt* tour (país); go round (zona, museo); cover (distancia). **~ mundo** travel all around the world. **~ido** *m* journey; (*trayecto*) route
recort|ar *vt* cut (out). **~e** *m* cutting (out); (*de periódico etc*) cutting
recostar **2** *vt* lean. **~se** *vpr* lie down
recoveco *m* bend; (*rincón*) nook
recre|ación *f* recreation. **~ar** *vt* recreate; (*divertir*) entertain. **~arse** *vpr* amuse o.s. **~ativo** *adj* recreational. **~o** *m* recreation; (*en escuela*) break
recrudecer **11** *vi* intensify
recta *f* straight line. **~ final** home stretch
rect|angular *adj* rectangular. **~ángulo** *adj* rectangular; (triángulo) right-angled. ● *m* rectangle
rectifica|ción *f* rectification. **~r** **7** *vt* rectify
rect|itud *f* straightness; (*fig*) honesty. **~o** *adj* straight; (*fig, justo*) fair; (*fig, honrado*) honest. **todo ~o** straight on. ● *m* rectum
rector *adj* governing. ● *m* rector
recubrir (*pp* **recubierto**) *vt* cover (**con, de** with)
recuerdo *m* memory; (*regalo*) souvenir. **~s** *mpl* (*saludos*) regards. ● *vb véase* **RECORDAR**
recupera|ción *f* recovery. **~r** *vt* recover. **~r el tiempo perdido** make up for lost time. **~rse** *vpr* recover
recur|rir *vi*. **~rir a** resort to (cosa); turn to (persona). **~so** *m* resort; (*medio*) resource; (*Jurid*) appeal. **~sos** *mpl* resources
red *f* network; (*malla*) net; (*para equipaje*) luggage rack; (*Com*) chain; (*Elec, gas*) mains. **la R~** the Net
redac|ción *f* writing; (*lenguaje*) wording; (*conjunto de redactores*) editorial staff; (*oficina*) editorial office; (*Escol, Univ*) essay. **~tar** *vt* write. **~tor** *m* writer; (*de periódico*) editor
redada *f* catch; (*de policía*) raid
redecilla *f* small net; (*para el pelo*) hairnet
redentor *adj* redeeming
redimir *vt* redeem
redoblar *vt* redouble; step up (vigilancia)
redomado *adj* utter
redond|a *f* (*de imprenta*) roman (type); (*Mus*) semibreve (*Brit*), whole note (*Amer*). **a la ~a** around. **~ear** *vt* round off. **~el** *m* circle; (*de plaza de toros*) arena. **~o** *adj* round; (*completo*) complete; (*Mex, boleto*) return, round-trip (*Amer*). **en ~o** round; (*categóricamente*) flatly
reduc|ción *f* reduction. **~ido** *adj* reduced; (*limitado*) limited; (*pequeño*) small; (precio) low. **~ir** **47** *vt* reduce. **~irse** *vpr* be reduced; (*fig*) amount
reduje *vb véase* **REDUCIR**
redundan|cia *f* redundancy. **~te** *adj* redundant
reduzco *vb véase* **REDUCIR**

reembols|ar *vt* reimburse. **~o** *m* repayment. **contra ~o** cash on delivery

reemplaz|ar [10] *vt* replace. **~o** *m* replacement

refacci|ón *f* (*LAm*) refurbishment; (*Mex, Mec*) spare part. **~onar** *vt* (*LAm*) refurbish. **~onaria** *f* (*Mex*) repair shop

referencia *f* reference; (*información*) report. **con ~ a** with reference to. **hacer ~ a** refer to

referéndum *m* (*pl* **~s**) referendum

referir [4] *vt* tell; (*remitir*) refer. **~se** *vpr* refer. **por lo que se refiere a** as regards

refiero *vb véase* REFERIR

refilón. **de ~** obliquely

refin|amiento *m* refinement. **~ar** *vt* refine. **~ería** *f* refinery

reflector *m* reflector; (*proyector*) searchlight

reflej|ar *vt* reflect. **~o** *adj* reflex. ● *m* reflection; (*Med*) reflex; (*en el pelo*) highlights

reflexi|ón *f* reflection. **sin ~ón** without thinking. **~onar** *vi* reflect. **~vo** *adj* (persona) thoughtful; (*Gram*) reflexive

reforma *f* reform. **~s** *fpl* (*reparaciones*) repairs. **~r** *vt* reform. **~rse** *vpr* reform

reforzar [2] & [10] *vt* reinforce

refrac|ción *f* refraction. **~tario** *adj* heat-resistant

refrán *m* saying

refregar [1] & [12] *vt* scrub

refresc|ar [7] *vt* refresh; (*enfriar*) cool. ● *vi* get cooler. **~arse** *vpr* refresh o.s. **~o** *m* cold drink. **~os** *mpl* refreshments

refrigera|ción *f* refrigeration; (*aire acondicionado*) air-conditioning; (*de motor*) cooling. **~r** *vt* refrigerate; air-condition (lugar); cool (motor). **~dor** *m* refrigerator

refuerzo *m* reinforcement

refugi|ado *m* refugee. **~arse** *vpr* take refuge. **~o** *m* refuge, shelter

refunfuñar *vi* grumble

refutar *vt* refute

regadera *f* watering-can; (*Mex, ducha*) shower

regala|do *adj* as a present, free; (*cómodo*) comfortable. **~r** *vt* give

regalo *m* present, gift

regañ|adientes. **a ~adientes** reluctantly. **~ar** *vt* scold. ● *vi* moan; (*dos personas*) quarrel. **~o** *m* (*reprensión*) scolding

regar [1] & [12] *vt* water

regata *f* boat race; (*serie*) regatta

regate|ar *vt* haggle over; (*economizar*) economize on. ● *vi* haggle; (*en deportes*) dribble. **~o** *m* haggling; (*en deportes*) dribbling

regazo *m* lap

regenerar *vt* regenerate

régimen *m* (*pl* **regímenes**) regime; (*Med*) diet; (*de lluvias*) pattern

regimiento *m* regiment

regi|ón *f* region. **~onal** *adj* regional

regir [5] & [14] *vt* govern. ● *vi* apply, be in force

registr|ado *adj* registered. **~ar** *vt* register; (*Mex*) check in (equipaje); (*grabar*) record; (*examinar*) search. **~arse** *vpr* register; (*darse*) be reported. **~o** *m* (*acción de registrar*) registration; (*libro*) register; (*cosa anotada*) entry; (*inspección*) search. **~o civil** (*oficina*) registry office

regla *f* ruler; (*norma*) rule; (*mens-

truación) period. **en ~** in order. **por ~ general** as a rule. **~mentación** *f* regulation. **~mentar** *vt* regulate. **~mentario** *adj* regulation; (horario) set. **~mento** *m* regulations

regocij|arse *vpr* be delighted. **~o** *m* delight

regode|arse *vpr* (+ *gerundio*) delight in (+ *gerund*). **~o** *m* delight

regordete *adj* chubby

regres|ar *vi* return; (*LAm*) send back (persona). **~arse** *vpr* (*LAm*) return. **~ivo** *adj* backward. **~o** *m* return

regula|ble *adj* adjustable. **~dor** *m* control. **~r** *adj* regular; (*mediano*) average; (*no bueno*) so-so. ● *vt* regulate; adjust (volumen etc). **~ridad** *f* regularity. **con ~ridad** regularly

rehabilita|ción *f* rehabilitation; (*en empleo etc*) reinstatement. **~r** *vt* rehabilitate; (*en cargo*) reinstate

rehacer 31 *vt* redo; (*repetir*) repeat; rebuild (vida). **~se** *vpr* recover

rehén *m* hostage

rehogar 12 *vt* sauté

rehuir 17 *vt* avoid

rehusar *vt/i* refuse

reimpr|esión *f* reprinting. **~imir** (*pp* **reimpreso**) *vt* reprint

reina *f* queen. **~do** *m* reign. **~nte** *adj* ruling; (*fig*) prevailing. **~r** *vi* reign; (*fig*) prevail

reincidir *vi* (*Jurid*) reoffend

reino *m* kingdom. **R~ Unido** United Kingdom

reintegr|ar *vt* reinstate (persona); refund (cantidad). **~arse** *vpr* return. **~o** *m* refund

reír 51 *vi* laugh. **~se** *vpr* laugh. **~se de** laugh at. **echarse a ~** burst out laughing

reivindica|ción *f* claim. **~r** 7 *vt* claim; (*rehabilitar*) restore

rej|a *f* grille; (*verja*) railing. **entre ~as** behind bars. **~illa** *f* grille, grating; (*red*) luggage rack

rejuvenecer 11 *vt/i* rejuvenate. **~se** *vpr* be rejuvenated

relaci|ón *f* connection; (*trato*) relation(ship); (*relato*) account; (*lista*) list. **con ~ón a**, **en ~ón a** in relation to. **~onado** *adj* related. **bien ~onado** well-connected. **~onar** *vt* relate (**con** to). **~onarse** *vpr* be connected; (*tratar*) mix (**con** with)

relaja|ción *f* relaxation; (*aflojamiento*) slackening. **~do** *adj* relaxed. **~r** *vt* relax; (*aflojar*) slacken. **~rse** *vpr* relax

relamerse *vpr* lick one's lips

relámpago *m* (flash of) lightning

relatar *vt* tell, relate

relativ|idad *f* relativity. **~o** *adj* relative

relato *m* tale; (*relación*) account

relegar 12 *vt* relegate. **~ al olvido** consign to oblivion

relev|ante *adj* outstanding. **~ar** *vt* relieve; (*substituir*) replace. **~o** *m* relief. **carrera** *f* **de ~os** relay race

relieve *m* relief; (*fig*) importance. **de ~** important. **poner de ~** emphasize

religi|ón *f* religion. **~osa** *f* nun. **~oso** *adj* religious. ● *m* monk

relinch|ar *vi* neigh. **~o** *m* neigh

reliquia *f* relic

rellano *m* landing

rellen|ar *vt* refill; (*Culin*) stuff; fill in (formulario). **~o** *adj* full up; (*Culin*) stuffed. ● *m* filling; (*Culin*) stuffing

reloj *m* clock; (*de bolsillo o pulsera*)

r

watch. **~ de caja** grandfather clock. **~ de pulsera** wrist-watch. **~ de sol** sundial. **~ despertador** alarm clock. **~ería** *f* watchmaker's (shop). **~ero** *m* watchmaker

reluci|ente *adj* shining. **~r** 11 *vi* shine; (*destellar*) sparkle

relumbrar *vi* shine

remach|ar *vt* rivet. **~e** *m* rivet

remangar 12 *vt* roll up

remar *vi* row

remat|ado *adj* (*total*) complete. **~ar** *vt* finish off; (*agotar*) use up; (*Com*) sell off cheap; (*LAm, subasta*) auction; (*en tenis*) smash. **~e** *m* end; (*fig*) finishing touch; (*LAm, subastar*) auction; (*en tenis*) smash. **de ~e** completely

remedar *vt* imitate

remedi|ar *vt* remedy; repair (daño); (*fig, resolver*) solve. **no lo pude ~ar** I couldn't help it. **~o** *m* remedy; (*fig*) solution; (*LAm, medicamento*) medicine. **como último ~o** as a last resort. **no hay más ~o** there's no other way. **no tener más ~o** have no choice

remedo *m* poor imitation.

rem|endar 1 *vt* repair. **~iendo** *m* patch

remilg|ado *adj* fussy; (*afectado*) affected. **~o** *m* fussiness; (*afectación*) affectation. **~oso** *adj* (*Mex*) fussy

reminiscencia *f* reminiscence

remisión *f* remission; (*envío*) sending; (*referencia*) reference

remit|e *m* sender's name and address. **~ente** *m* sender. **~ir** *vt* send; (*referir*) refer • *vi* diminish

remo *m* oar

remoj|ar *vt* soak; (*fig, fam*) celebrate. **~o** *m* soaking. **poner a ~o** soak

remolacha *f* beetroot. **~ azucarera** sugar beet

remolcar 7 *vt* tow

remolino *m* swirl; (*de aire etc*) whirl

remolque *m* towing; (*cabo*) towrope; (*vehículo*) trailer. **a ~** on tow. **dar ~ a** tow

remontar *vt* overcome. **~ el vuelo** soar up; (avión) gain height. **~se** *vpr* soar up; (*en el tiempo*) go back to

remord|er 2 *vi*. **eso le remuerde** he feels guilty for it. **me remuerde la conciencia** I have a guilty conscience. **~imiento** *m* remorse. **tener ~imientos** feel remorse

remoto *adj* remote; (época) distant

remover 2 *vt* stir (líquido); turn over (tierra); (*quitar*) remove; (*fig, activar*) revive

remunera|ción *f* remuneration. **~r** *vt* remunerate

renac|er 11 *vi* be reborn; (*fig*) revive. **~imiento** *m* rebirth. **R~imiento** Renaissance

renacuajo *m* tadpole; (*fig*) tiddler

rencilla *f* quarrel

rencor *m* bitterness. **guardar ~ a** have a grudge against. **~oso** *adj* resentful

rendi|ción *f* surrender. **~do** *adj* submissive; (*agotado*) exhausted

rendija *f* crack

rendi|miento *m* performance; (*Com*) yield. **~r** 5 *vt* yield; (*agotar*) exhaust; pay (homenaje); present (informe). • *vi* pay; (*producir*) produce. **~rse** *vpr* surrender

renegar 1 & 12 *vt* deny. • *vi* grumble. **~ de** renounce (fe etc); disown (personas)

renglón *m* line; (*Com*) item. **a ~ seguido** straight away

reno *m* reindeer

renombr|ado *adj* renowned. **~e** *m* renown

renova|ción *f* renewal; (*de edificio*) renovation; (*de mobiliario*) complete change. **~r** *vt* renew; renovate (edificio); change (mobiliario)

rent|a *f* income; (*Mex, alquiler*) rent. **~a vitalicia** (life) annuity. **~able** *adj* profitable. **~ar** *vt* yield; (*Mex, alquilar*) rent, hire. **~ista** *m & f* person of independent means

renuncia *f* renunciation; (*dimisión*) resignation. **~r** *vi*. **~r a** renounce, give up; (*dimitir*) resign

reñi|do *adj* hard-fought. **estar ~do con** be incompatible with (cosa); be on bad terms with (persona). **~r** **5** & **22** *vt* scold. • *vi* quarrel

reo *m & f* (*Jurid*) accused; (*condenado*) convicted offender; (*pez*) sea trout

reojo. **mirar de ~** look out of the corner of one's eye at

reorganizar **10** *vt* reorganize

repar|ación *f* repair; (*acción*) repairing (*fig, compensación*) reparation. **~ar** *vt* repair; (*fig*) make amends for; (*notar*) notice. • *vi*. **~ar en** notice; (*hacer caso de*) pay attention to. **~o** *m* fault; (*objeción*) objection. **poner ~os** raise objections

repart|ición *f* distribution. **~idor** *m* delivery man. **~imiento** *m* distribution. **~ir** *vt* distribute, share out; deliver (cartas, leche etc); hand out (folleto, premio). **~o** *m* distribution; (*de cartas, leche etc*) delivery; (*actores*) cast

repas|ar *vt* go over; check (cuenta); revise (texto); (*leer a la ligera*) glance through; (*coser*) mend. • *vi* revise. **~o** *m* revision; (*de ropa*) mending. **dar un ~o** look through

repatria|ción *f* repatriation. **~r** *vt* repatriate

repele|nte *adj* repulsive. • *m* insect repellent. **~r** *vt* repel

repent|e. **de ~** suddenly. **~ino** *adj* sudden

repercu|sión *f* repercussion. **~tir** *vi* reverberate; (*fig*) have repercussions (**en** on)

repertorio *m* repertoire

repeti|ción *f* repetition; (*de programa*) repeat. **~damente** *adv* repeatedly. **~r** **5** *vt* repeat; have a second helping of (plato); (*imitar*) copy. • *vi* have a second helping of

repi|car **7** *vt* ring (campanas). **~que** *m* peal

repisa *f* shelf. **~ de chimenea** mantlepiece

repito *vb véase* REPETIR

replegarse **1** & **12** *vpr* withdraw

repleto *adj* full up. **~ de gente** packed with people

réplica *adj* reply; (*copia*) replica

replicar **7** *vi* reply

repollo *m* cabbage

reponer **34** *vt* replace; revive (obra de teatro); (*contestar*) reply. **~se** *vpr* recover

report|aje *m* report; (*LAm, entrevista*) interview. **~ar** *vt* yield; (*LAm, denunciar*) report. **~e** *m* (*Mex, informe*) report; (*Mex, queja*) complaint. **~ero** *m* reporter

repos|ado *adj* quiet; (*sin prisa*) unhurried. **~ar** *vi* rest; (líquido) settle. **~o** *m* rest

repost|ar *vt* replenish. • *vi* (avión)

refuel; (*Auto*) fill up. **~ería** *f* pastrymaking
reprender *vt* reprimand
represalia *f* reprisal. **tomar ~s** retaliate
representa|ción *f* representation; (*en el teatro*) performance. **en ~ción de** representing. **~nte** *m* representative. **~r** *vt* represent; perform (obra de teatro); play (papel); (*aparentar*) look. **~rse** *vpr* imagine. **~tivo** *adj* representative
represi|ón *f* repression. **~vo** *adj* repressive
reprimenda *f* reprimand
reprimir *vt* supress. **~se** *vpr* control o.s.
reprobar **2** *vt* condemn; (*LAm, Univ, etc*) fail
reproch|ar *vt* reproach. **~e** *m* reproach
reproduc|ción *f* reproduction. **~ir** **47** *vt* reproduce. **~tor** *adj* reproductive; (animal) breeding
reptil *m* reptile
rep|ública *f* republic. **~ublicano** *adj & m* republican
repudiar *vt* condemn; (*Jurid*) repudiate
r
repuesto *m* (*Mec*) spare (part). **de ~** spare
repugna|ncia *f* disgust. **~nte** *adj* repugnant; (olor) disgusting. **~r** *vt* disgust
repuls|a *f* rebuff. **~ión** *f* repulsion. **~ivo** *adj* repulsive
reputa|ción *f* reputation. **~do** *adj* reputable. **~r** *vt* consider
requeri|miento *m* request; (*necesidad*) requirement. **~r** **4** *vt* require; summons (persona)
requesón *m* curd cheese
requete... *prefijo* (*fam*) extremely
requis|a *f* requisition; (*confiscación*) seizure; (*inspección*) inspection; (*Mil*) requisition. **~ar** *vt* requisition; (*confiscar*) seize; (*inspeccionar*) inspect. **~ito** *m* requirement
res *f* animal. **~ lanar** sheep. **~ vacuna** (*vaca*) cow; (*toro*) bull; (*buey*) ox. **carne de ~** (*Mex*) beef
resabido *adj* well-known; (persona) pedantic
resaca *f* undercurrent; (*después de beber*) hangover
resaltar *vi* stand out. **hacer ~** emphasize
resarcir **9** *vt* repay; (*compensar*) compensate. **~se** *vpr* make up for
resbal|adilla *f* (*Mex*) slide. **~adizo** *adj* slippery. **~ar** *vi* slip; (*Auto*) skid; (líquido) trickle. **~arse** *vpr* slip; (*Auto*) skid; (líquido) trickle. **~ón** *m* slip; (*de vehículo*) skid. **~oso** *adj* (*LAm*) slippery
rescat|ar *vt* rescue; (*fig*) recover. **~e** *m* ransom; (*recuperación*) recovery; (*salvamento*) rescue
rescoldo *m* embers
resecar **7** *vt* dry up. **~se** *vpr* dry up
resenti|do *adj* resentful. **~miento** *m* resentment. **~rse** *vpr* feel the effects; (*debilitarse*) be weakened; (*ofenderse*) take offence (**de** at)
reseña *f* summary; (*de persona*) description; (*en periódico*) report, review. **~r** *vt* describe; (*en periódico*) report on, review
reserva *f* reservation; (*provisión*) reserve(s). **de ~** in reserve. **~ción** *f* (*LAm*) reservation. **~do** *adj* reserved. **~r** *vt* reserve; (*guardar*) keep, save. **~rse** *vpr* save o.s.
resfria|do *m* cold. **~rse** *vpr* catch

a cold

resguard|ar *vt* protect. **~arse** *vpr* protect o.s.; (*fig*) take care. **~o** *m* protection; (*garantía*) guarantee; (*recibo*) receipt

resid|encia *f* residence; (*Univ*) hall of residence (*Brit*), dormitory (*Amer*); (*de ancianos etc*) home. **~encial** *adj* residential. **~ente** *adj & m & f* resident. **~ir** *vi* reside; (*fig*) lie (**en** in)

residu|al *adj* residual. **~o** *m* residue. **~os** *mpl* waste

resigna|ción *f* resignation. **~rse** *vpr* resign o.s. (**a** to)

resist|encia *f* resistence. **~ente** *adj* resistent. **~ir** *vt* resist; (*soportar*) bear. ● *vi* resist. **ya no resisto más** I can't take it any more

resol|ución *f* resolution; (*solución*) solution; (*decisión*) decision. **~ver** **2** (*pp* **resuelto**) resolve; solve (problema etc). **~verse** *vpr* resolve itself; (*resultar bien*) work out; (*decidir*) decide

resona|ncia *f* resonance. **tener ~ncia** cause a stir. **~nte** *adj* resonant; (*fig*) resounding. **~r** **2** *vi* resound

resorte *m* spring; (*Mex, elástico*) elastic. **tocar (todos los) ~s** (*fig*) pull strings

respald|ar *vt* back; (*escribir*) endorse. **~arse** *vpr* lean back. **~o** *m* backing; (*de asiento*) back

respect|ar *vi.* **en lo que ~a a** with regard to. **en lo que a mí ~a** as far as I'm concerned. **~ivo** *adj* respective. **~o** *m* respect. **al ~o** on this matter. **(con) ~o a** with regard to

respet|able *adj* respectable. ● *m* audience. **~ar** *vt* respect. **~o** *m* respect. **faltar al ~o a** be disrespectful to. **~uoso** *adj* respectful

respir|ación *f* breathing; (*ventilación*) ventilation. **~ar** *vi* breathe; (*fig*) breathe a sigh of relief. **~o** *m* breathing; (*fig*) rest

respland|ecer **11** *vi* shine. **~eciente** *adj* shining. **~or** *m* brilliance; (*de llamas*) glow

responder *vi* answer; (*replicar*) answer back; (*reaccionar*) respond. **~ de** be responsible for. **~ por uno** vouch for s.o.

responsab|ilidad *f* responsibility. **~le** *adj* responsible

respuesta *f* reply, answer

resquebrajar *vt* crack. **~se** *vpr* crack

resquemor *m* (*fig*) uneasiness

resquicio *m* crack; (*fig*) possibility

resta *f* subtraction

restablecer **11** *vt* restore. **~se** *vpr* recover

rest|ante *adj* remaining. **lo ~nte** the rest. **~ar** *vt* take away; (*substraer*) subtract. ● *vi* be left

restaura|ción *f* restoration. **~nte** *m* restaurant. **~r** *vt* restore

restitu|ción *f* restitution. **~ir** **17** *vt* return; (*restaurar*) restore

resto *m* rest, remainder; (*en matemática*) remainder. **~s** *mpl* remains; (*de comida*) leftovers

restorán *m* restaurant

restregar **1** & **12** *vt* rub

restri|cción *f* restriction. **~ngir** **14** *vt* restrict, limit

resucitar *vt* resuscitate; (*fig*) revive. ● *vi* return to life

resuello *m* breath; (*respiración*) heavy breathing

resuelto *adj* resolute

resulta|do *m* result (**en** in). **~r** *vi* result; (*salir*) turn out; (*dar resul-*

r

tado) work; (*ser*) be; (*costar*) come to

resum|en *m* summary. **en ~en** in short. **~ir** *vt* summarize; (*recapitular*) sum up

resur|gir 14 *vi* reemerge; (*fig*) revive. **~gimiento** *m* resurgence. **~rección** *f* resurrection

retaguardia *f* (*Mil*) rearguard

retahíla *f* string

retar *vt* challenge

retardar *vt* slow down; (*demorar*) delay

retazo *m* remnant; (*fig*) piece, bit

reten|ción *f* retention. **~er** 40 *vt* keep; (*en la memoria*) retain; (*no dar*) withhold

reticencia *f* insinuation; (*reserva*) reluctance

retina *f* retina

retir|ada *f* withdrawal. **~ado** *adj* remote; (vida) secluded; (*jubilado*) retired. **~ar** *vt* move away; (*quitar*) remove; withdraw (dinero); (*jubilar*) pension off. **~arse** *vpr* draw back; (*Mil*) withdraw; (*jubilarse*) retire; (*acostarse*) go to bed. **~o** *m* retirement; (*pensión*) pension; (*lugar apartado*) retreat; (*LAm, de apoyo, fondos*) withdrawal

reto *m* challenge

retocar 7 *vt* retouch

retoño *m* shoot; (*fig*) kid

retoque *m* (*acción*) retouching; (*efecto*) finishing touch

retorc|er 2 & 9 *vt* twist; wring (ropa). **~erse** *vpr* get twisted up; (*de dolor*) writhe. **~ijón** *m* (*LAm*) stomach cramp

retóric|a *f* rhetoric; (*grandilocuencia*) grandiloquence. **~o** *m* rhetorical

retorn|ar *vt/i* return. **~o** *m* return

retortijón *m* twist; (*de tripas*) stomach cramp

retractarse *vpr* retract. **~ de lo dicho** withdraw what one said

retransmitir *vt* repeat; (*radio, TV*) broadcast. **~ en directo** broadcast live

retras|ado *adj* (*con ser*) mentally handicapped; (*con estar*) behind; (reloj) slow; (*poco desarrollado*) backward; (*anticuado*) old-fashioned. **~ar** *vt* delay; put back (reloj); (*retardar*) slow down; (*posponer*) postpone. ● *vi* (reloj) be slow. **~arse** *vpr* be late; (reloj) be slow. **~o** *m* delay; (*poco desarrollo*) backwardness; (*de reloj*) slowness. **traer ~o** be late. **~os** *mpl* arrears

retrato *m* portrait; (*fig, descripción*) description. **ser el vivo ~ de** be the living image of

retrete *m* toilet

retribu|ción *f* payment; (*recompensa*) reward. **~ir** 17 *vt* pay; (*recompensar*) reward; (*LAm*) return (favor)

retroce|der *vi* move back; (*fig*) back down. **~so** *m* backward movement; (*de arma de fuego*) recoil; (*Med*) relapse

retrógrado *adj* & *m* (*Pol*) reactionary

retrospectivo *adj* retrospective

retrovisor *m* rear-view mirror

retumbar *vt* echo; (trueno etc) boom

reum|a *m*, **reúma** *m* rheumatism. **~ático** *adj* rheumatic. **~atismo** *m* rheumatism

reuni|ón *f* meeting; (*entre amigos*) reunion. **~r** 23 *vt* join together; (*recoger*) gather (together); raise (fondos). **~rse** *vpr* meet; (amigos etc) get together

revalidar *vt* confirm; (*Mex, estudios*) validate

revalorizar 10 *vt*, (*LAm*) **revaluar** 21 *vt* revalue; increase (pensiones). **~se** *vpr* appreciate

revancha *f* revenge; (*en deportes*) return match. **tomar la ~** get one's own back

revela|ción *f* revelation. **~do** *m* developing. **~dor** *adj* revealing. **~r** *vt* reveal; (*Foto*) develop

revent|ar 1 *vi* burst; (*tener ganas*) be dying to. **~arse** *vpr* burst. **~ón** *m* burst; (*Auto*) blow out; (*Mex, fiesta*) party

reveren|cia *f* reverence; (*de hombre, niño*) bow; (*de mujer*) curtsy. **~ciar** *vt* revere. **~do** *adj* (*Relig*) reverend. **~te** *adj* reverent

revers|ible *adj* reversible. **~o** *m* reverse; (*de papel*) back

revertir 4 *vi* revert (**a** to)

revés *m* wrong side; (*de prenda*) inside; (*contratiempo*) setback; (*en deportes*) backhand. **al ~** the other way round; (*con lo de arriba abajo*) upside down; (*con lo de dentro fuera*) inside out

revesti|miento *m* coating. **~r** 5 *vt* cover

revis|ar *vt* check; overhaul (mecanismo); service (coche etc); (*LAm, equipaje*) search. **~ión** *f* check(ing)); (*Med*) checkup; (*de coche etc*) service; (*LAm, de equipaje*) inspection. **~or** *m* inspector

revista *f* magazine; (*inspección*) inspection; (*artículo*) review; (*espectáculo*) revue. **pasar ~ a** inspect

revivir *vi* revive

revolcar 2 & 7 *vt* knock over. **~se** *vpr* roll around

revolotear *vi* flutter

revoltijo *m*, **revoltillo** *m* mess

revoltoso *adj* rebellious; (niño) naughty

revoluci|ón *f* revolution. **~onar** *vt* revolutionize. **~onario** *adj & m* revolutionary

revolver 2 (*pp* **revuelto**) *vt* mix; stir (líquido); (*desordenar*) mess up

revólver *m* revolver

revuelo *m* fluttering; (*fig*) stir

revuelt|a *f* revolt; (*conmoción*) disturbance. **~o** *adj* mixed up; (líquido) cloudy; (mar) rough; (tiempo) unsettled; (huevos) scrambled

rey *m* king. **los ~es** the king and queen. **los R~es Magos** the Three Wise Men

reyerta *f* brawl

rezagarse 12 *vpr* fall behind

rez|ar 10 *vt* say. • *vi* pray; (*decir*) say. **~o** *m* praying; (*oración*) prayer

rezongar 12 *vi* grumble

ría *f* estuary

riachuelo *m* stream

riada *f* flood

ribera *f* bank

ribete *m* border; (*fig*) embellishment

rico *adj* rich; (*Culin, fam*) good, nice. • *m* rich person

rid|ículo *adj* ridiculous. **~iculizar** 10 *vt* ridicule

riego *m* watering; (*irrigación*) irrigation

riel *m* rail

rienda *f* rein

riesgo *m* risk. **correr (el) ~ de** run the risk of

rifa *f* raffle. **~r** *vt* raffle

rifle *m* rifle

rigidez *f* rigidity; (*fig*) inflexibility

rígido *adj* rigid; (*fig*) inflexible

rig|or *m* strictness; (*exactitud*) exactness; (*de clima*) severity. **de ~or** compulsory. **en ~or** strictly speaking. **~uroso** *adj* rigorous
rima *f* rhyme. **~r** *vt/i* rhyme
rimbombante *adj* resounding; (lenguaje) pompous; (*fig, ostentoso*) showy
rímel *m* mascara
rin *m* (*Mex*) rim
rincón *m* corner
rinoceronte *m* rhinoceros
riña *f* quarrel; (*pelea*) fight
riñón *m* kidney
río *m* river; (*fig*) stream. **~ abajo** downstream. **~ arriba** upstream. ● *vb véase* **REÍR**
riqueza *f* wealth; (*fig*) richness. **~s** *fpl* riches
ris|a *f* laugh. **desternillarse de ~a** split one's sides laughing. **la ~a** laughter. **~otada** *f* guffaw. **~ueño** *adj* smiling; (*fig*) cheerful
rítmico *adj* rhythmic(al)
ritmo *m* rhythm; (*fig*) rate
rit|o *m* rite; (*fig*) ritual. **~ual** *adj & m* ritual
rival *adj & m & f* rival. **~idad** *f* rivalry. **~izar** **10** *vi* rival
r
riz|ado *adj* curly. **~ar** **10** *vt* curl; ripple (agua). **~o** *m* curl; (*en agua*) ripple
róbalo *m* bass
robar *vt* steal (cosa); rob (banco); (*raptar*) kidnap
roble *m* oak (tree)
robo *m* theft; (*de banco, museo*) robbery; (*en vivienda*) burglary
robusto *adj* robust
roca *f* rock
roce *m* rubbing; (*señal*) mark; (*fig, entre personas*) regular contact; (*Pol*) friction. **tener un ~ con uno** have a brush with s.o.
rociar **20** *vt* spray
rocín *m* nag
rocío *m* dew
rodaballo *m* turbot
rodaja *f* slice. **en ~s** sliced
roda|je *m* (*de película*) shooting; (*de coche*) running in. **~r** **2** *vt* shoot (película); run in (coche). ● *vi* roll; (coche) run; (*hacer una película*) shoot
rode|ar *vt* surround; (*LAm*) round up (ganado). **~arse** *vpr* surround o.s. (**de** with). **~o** *m* detour; (*de ganado*) round-up. **andar con ~os** beat about the bush. **sin ~os** plainly
rodill|a *f* knee. **ponerse de ~as** kneel down. **~era** *f* knee-pad
rodillo *m* roller; (*Culin*) rolling-pin
roe|dor *m* rodent. **~r** **37** *vt* gnaw
rogar **2** & **12** *vt/i* beg; (*Relig*) pray; **se ruega a los Sres. pasajeros...** passengers are requested.... **se ruega no fumar** please do not smoke
roj|izo *adj* reddish. **~o** *adj & m* red. **ponerse ~o** blush
roll|izo *adj* plump; (bebé) chubby. **~o** *m* roll; (*de cuerda*) coil; (*Culin, rodillo*) rolling-pin; (*fig, fam, pesadez*) bore
romance *adj* Romance. ● *m* (*idilio*) romance; (*poema*) ballad
roman|o *adj & m* Roman. **a la ~a** (*Culin*) (deep-)fried in batter
rom|anticismo *m* romanticism. **~ántico** *adj* romantic
romería *f* pilgrimage; (*LAm, multitud*) mass
romero *m* rosemary
romo *adj* blunt; (nariz) snub
rompe|cabezas *m invar* puzzle;

(*de piezas*) jigsaw (puzzle). **~olas** *m invar* breakwater

romp|er (*pp* **roto**) *vt* break; tear (hoja, camisa etc); break off (relaciones etc). ● *vi* break; (novios) break up. **~er a** burst out. **~erse** *vpr* break

ron *m* rum

ronc|ar 7 *vi* snore. **~o** *adj* hoarse

roncha *f* lump; (*por alergia*) rash

ronda *f* round; (*patrulla*) patrol; (*serenata*) serenade. **~r** *vt* patrol. ● *vi* be on patrol; (*merodear*) hang around

ronqu|era *f* hoarseness. **~ido** *m* snore

ronronear *vi* purr

roñ|a *f* (*suciedad*) grime. **~oso** *adj* dirty; (*oxidado*) rusty; (*tacaño*) mean

rop|a *f* clothes, clothing. **~a blanca** linen, underwear. **~a de cama** bedclothes. **~a interior** underwear. **~aje** *m* robes; (*excesivo*) heavy clothing. **~ero** *m* wardrobe

ros|a *adj invar* pink. ● *f* rose. ● *m* pink. **~áceo** *adj* pinkish. **~ado** *adj* pink; (mejillas) rosy. ● *m* (*vino*) rosé. **~al** *m* rose-bush

rosario *m* rosary; (*fig*) series

ros|ca *f* (*de tornillo*) thread; (*de pan*) roll; (*bollo*) type of doughnut. **~co** *m* roll. **~quilla** *f* type of doughnut

rostro *m* face

rota|ción *f* rotation. **~r** *vt/i* rotate. **~rse** *vpr* take turns. **~tivo** *adj* rotary

roto *adj* broken

rótula *f* kneecap

rotulador *m* felt-tip pen

rótulo *m* sign; (*etiqueta*) label; (*logotipo*) logo

rotundo *adj* categorical

rotura *f* tear; (*grieta*) crack

rozadura *f* scratch

rozagante *adj* (*LAm*) healthy

rozar 10 *vt* rub against; (*ligeramente*) brush against; (*raspar*) graze. **~se** *vpr* rub; (*con otras personas*) mix

Rte. *abrev* (**Remite(nte)**) sender

rubéola *f* German measles

rubí *m* ruby

rubicundo *adj* ruddy

rubio *adj* (pelo) fair; (persona) fair-haired; (tabaco) Virginia

rubor *m* blush; (*Mex, cosmético*) blusher. **~izarse** 10 *vpr* blush

rúbrica *f* (*de firma*) flourish; (*firma*) signature; (*título*) heading

rudeza *f* roughness

rudiment|ario *adj* rudimentary. **~os** *mpl* rudiments

rueca *f* distaff

rueda *f* wheel; (*de mueble*) castor; (*de personas*) ring; (*Culin*) slice. **~ de prensa** press conference

ruedo *m* edge; (*redondel*) bullring

ruego *m* request; (*súplica*) entreaty. ● *vb véase* ROGAR

rufián *m* pimp; (*granuja*) rogue

rugby *m* rugby

rugi|do *m* roar. **~r** 14 *vi* roar

ruibarbo *m* rhubarb

ruido *m* noise. **~so** *adj* noisy; (*fig*) sensational

ruin *adj* despicable; (*tacaño*) mean

ruin|a *f* ruin; (*colapso*) collapse. **~oso** *adj* ruinous

ruiseñor *m* nightingale

ruleta *f* roulette

rulo *m* curler

rumano *adj* & *m* Romanian

rumbo *m* direction; (*fig*) course;

(*fig, esplendidez*) lavishness. **con ~ a** in the direction of. **~so** *adj* lavish

rumia|nte *adj & m* ruminant. **~r** *vt* chew; (*fig*) brood over. ● *vi* ruminate

rumor *m* rumour; (*ruido*) murmur. **~earse** *vpr* **se ~ea que** rumour has it that. **~oso** *adj* murmuring

runrún *m* (*de voces*) murmur; (*de motor*) whirr

ruptura *f* breakup; (*de relaciones etc*) breaking off; (*de contrato*) breach

rural *adj* rural

ruso *adj & m* Russian

rústico *adj* rural; (*de carácter*) coarse. **en rústica** paperback

ruta *f* route; (*fig*) course

rutina *f* routine. **~rio** *adj* routine; (trabajo) monotonous

Ss

S.A. *abrev* (**Sociedad Anónima**) Ltd, plc, Inc (*Amer*)

sábado *m* Saturday

sábana *f* sheet

sabañón *m* chilblain

sabático *adj* sabbatical

sab|elotodo *m & f invar* know-all 🅸. **~er** 38 *vt* know; (*ser capaz de*) be able to, know how to; (*enterarse de*) find out. ● *vi* know. **~er a** taste of. **hacer ~er** let know. **¡qué sé yo!** how should I know? **que yo sepa** as far as I know. **¿~es nadar?** can you swim? **un no sé qué** a certain sth. **¡yo qué sé!** how should I know? **¡vete a ~er!** who knows? **~er** *m* knowledge. **~ido** *adj* well-known. **~iduría** *f* wisdom; (*conocimientos*) knowledge

sabi|endas. a ~ knowingly; (*a propósito*) on purpose. **~hondo** *m* know-all. **~o** *adj* learned; (*prudente*) wise

sabor *m* taste, flavour; (*fig*) flavour. **~ear** *vt* taste; (*fig*) savour

sabot|aje *m* sabotage. **~eador** *m* saboteur. **~ear** *vt* sabotage

sabroso *adj* tasty; (chisme) juicy; (*LAm, agradable*) pleasant

sabueso *m* (*perro*) bloodhound; (*fig, detective*) detective

saca|corchos *m invar* corkscrew. **~puntas** *m invar* pencil-sharpener

sacar 7 *vt* take out; put out (parte del cuerpo); (*quitar*) remove; take (foto); win (premio); get (billete, entrada); withdraw (dinero); reach (solución); draw (conclusión); make (copia). **~ adelante** bring up (niño); carry on (negocio)

sacarina *f* saccharin

sacerdo|cio *m* priesthood. **~te** *m* priest

saciar *vt* satisfy; quench (sed)

saco *m* sack; (*LAm, chaqueta*) jacket. **~ de dormir** sleeping-bag

sacramento *m* sacrament

sacrific|ar 7 *vt* sacrifice; slaughter (res); put to sleep (perro, gato). **~arse** *vpr* sacrifice o.s. **~io** *m* sacrifice; (*de res*) slaughter

sacr|ilegio *m* sacrilege. **~ílego** *adj* sacrilegious

sacudi|da *f* shake; (*movimiento brusco*) jolt, jerk; (*fig*) shock. **~da eléctrica** electric shock. **~r** *vt* shake; (*golpear*) beat. **~rse** *vpr* shake off; (*fig*) get rid of

sádico *adj* sadistic. ● *m* sadist

sadismo *m* sadism
safari *m* safari
sagaz *adj* shrewd
Sagitario *m* Sagittarius
sagrado *adj* (lugar) holy, sacred; (altar, escrituras) holy; (*fig*) sacred
sal *f* salt. ● *vb véase* SALIR
sala *f* room; (*en casa*) living room; (*en hospital*) ward; (*para reuniones etc*) hall; (*en teatro*) house; (*Jurid*) courtroom. ~ **de embarque** departure lounge. ~ **de espera** waiting room. ~ **de estar** living room. ~ **de fiestas** nightclub
salado *adj* salty; (agua del mar) salt; (*no dulce*) savoury; (*fig*) witty
salario *m* wage
salchich|a *f* (pork) sausage. **~ón** *m* salami
sald|ar *vt* settle (cuenta); (*vender*) sell off. **~o** *m* balance. **~os** *mpl* sales. **venta de ~os** clearance sale
salero *m* salt-cellar
salgo *vb véase* SALIR
sali|da *f* departure; (*puerta*) exit, way out; (*de gas, de líquido*) leak; (*de astro*) rising; (*Com, venta*) sale; (*chiste*) witty remark; (*fig*) way out; **~da de emergencia** emergency exit. **~ente** *adj* (*Archit*) projecting; (pómulo etc) prominent. **~r** 52 *vi* leave; (*ir afuera*) go out; (*Informática*) exit; (revista etc) be published; (*resultar*) turn out; (astro) rise; (*aparecer*) appear. **~r adelante** get by. **~rse** *vpr* leave; (recipiente, líquido etc) leak. **~rse con la suya** get one's own way
saliva *f* saliva
salmo *m* psalm
salm|ón *m* salmon. **~onete** *m* red mullet
salón *m* living-room, lounge. ~ **de actos** assembly hall. ~ **de clases** classroom. ~ **de fiestas** dancehall
salpica|dera *f* (*Mex*) mudguard. **~dero** *m* (*Auto*) dashboard. **~dura** *f* splash; (*acción*) splashing. **~r** 7 *vt* splash; (*fig*) sprinkle
sals|a *f* sauce; (*para carne asada*) gravy; (*Mus*) salsa. **~a verde** parsley sauce. **~era** *f* sauce-boat
salt|amontes *m invar* grasshopper. **~ar** *vt* jump (over); (*fig*) miss out. ● *vi* jump; (*romperse*) break; (líquido) spurt out; (*desprenderse*) come off; (pelota) bounce; (*estallar*) explode. **~eador** *m* highwayman. **~ear** *vt* (*Culin*) sauté
salt|o *m* jump; (*al agua*) dive. **~o de agua** waterfall. ~ **mortal** somersault. **de un ~o** with one jump. **~ón** *adj* (ojos) bulging
salud *f* health. ● *int* cheers!; (*LAm, al estornudar*) bless you! **~able** *adj* healthy
salud|ar *vt* greet, say hello to; (*Mil*) salute. **lo ~a atentamente** (*en cartas*) yours faithfully. ~ **con la mano** wave. **~o** *m* greeting; (*Mil*) salute. **~os** *mpl* best wishes
salva *f* salvo. **una ~ de aplausos** a burst of applause
salvación *f* salvation
salvado *m* bran
salvaguardia *f* safeguard
salvaje *adj* (*planta, animal*) wild; (*primitivo*) savage. ● *m & f* savage
salva|mento *m* rescue. **~r** *vt* save, rescue; (*atravesar*); cross (*recorrer*); travel (*fig*) overcome. **~rse** *vpr* save o.s. **~vidas** *m & f invar* lifeguard. ● *m* lifebelt. **chaleco** *m* **~vidas** life-jacket
salvo *adj* safe. ● *adv & prep* except (for). **a ~** out of danger. **poner a ~** put in a safe place. ~ **que** un-

S

less. **~conducto** *m* safe-conduct.

San *adj* Saint, St. **~ Miguel** St Michael

sana|r *vt* cure. ● *vi* recover; heal (herida). **~torio** *m* sanatorium

sanci|ón *f* sanction. **~onar** *vt* sanction

sandalia *f* sandal

sandía *f* watermelon

sándwich /'saŋgwitʃ/ *m* (*pl* **~s, ~es**) sandwich

sangr|ante *adj* bleeding; (*fig*) flagrant. **~ar** *vt/i* bleed. **~e** *f* blood. **a ~e fría** in cold blood

sangría *f* (*bebida*) sangria

sangriento *adj* bloody

sangu|ijuela *f* leech. **~íneo** *adj* blood

san|idad *f* health. **~itario** *adj* sanitary. ● *m* (*Mex*) toilet. **~o** *adj* healthy; (mente) sound. **~o y salvo** safe and sound. **cortar por lo ~o** settle things once and for all

santiamén *m*. **en un ~** in an instant

sant|idad *f* sanctity. **~ificar** 7 *vt* sanctify. **~iguarse** 15 *vpr* cross o.s. **~o** *adj* holy; (*delante de nombre*) Saint, St. ● *m* saint; (*día*) saint's day, name day. **~uario** *m* sanctuary. **~urrón** *adj* sanctimonious

> *i*
> **santo** Most first names in Spanish-speaking countries are those of saints. A person's *santo* (also known as *onomástico* in Latin America and *onomástica* in Spain) is the saint's day of the saint they are named after. As well as celebrating their calendar birthday many people also celebrate their *santo*.

saña *f* viciousness. **con ~** viciously

sapo *m* toad

saque *m* (*en tenis*) service; (*inicial en fútbol*) kick-off. **~ de banda** throw-in; (*en rugby*) line-out. **~ de esquina** corner (kick)

saque|ar *vt* loot. **~o** *m* looting

sarampión *m* measles

sarape *m* (*Mex*) colourful blanket

sarc|asmo *m* sarcasm. **~ástico** *adj* sarcastic

sardina *f* sardine

sargento *m* sergeant

sarpullido *m* rash

sartén *f or m* frying-pan (*Brit*), frypan (*Amer*)

sastre *m* tailor. **~ría** *f* tailoring; (*tienda*) tailor's (shop)

Sat|anás *m* Satan. **~ánico** *adj* satanic

satélite *m* satellite

satinado *adj* shiny

sátira *f* satire

satírico *adj* satirical. ● *m* satirist

satisf|acción *f* satisfaction. **~acer** 31 *vt* satisfy; (*pagar*) pay; (*gustar*) please; meet (gastos, requisitos). **~acerse** *vpr* satisfy o.s.; (*vengarse*) take revenge. **~actorio** *adj* satisfactory. **~echo** *adj* satisfied. **~echo de sí mismo** smug

satura|ción *f* saturation. **~r** *vt* saturate

Saturno *m* Saturn

sauce *m* willow. **~ llorón** weeping willow

sauna *f*, (*LAm*) **sauna** *m* sauna

saxofón *m*, **saxófono** *m* saxophone

sazona|do *adj* ripe; (*Culin*) seasoned. **~r** *vt* ripen; (*Culin*) season

S

se *pronombre*

● (*en lugar de le, les*) **se lo di** (*a él*) I gave it to him; (*a ella*) I gave it to her; (*a usted, ustedes*) I gave it to you; (*a ellos, ellas*) I gave it to them. **se lo compré** I bought it for him (*or* her *etc*). **se lo quité** I took it away from him (*or* her *etc*). **se lo dije** I told him (*or* her *etc*)

....> (*reflexivo*) **se secó** (*él*) he dried himself; (*ella*) she dried herself; (*usted*) you dried yourself. (*sujeto no humano*) it dried itself. **se secaron** (*ellos, ellas*) they dried themselves. (*ustedes*) you dried yourselves. (*con partes del cuerpo*) **se lavó la cara** (*él*) he washed his face; (*con efectos personales*) **se limpian los zapatos** they clean their shoes

....> (*recíproco*) each other, one another. **se ayudan mucho** they help each other a lot. **no se hablan** they don't speak to each other

....> (*cuando otro hace la acción*) **va a operarse** she's going to have an operation. **se cortó el pelo** he had his hair cut

....> (*enfático*) **se bebió el café** he drank his coffee. **se subió al tren** he got on the train

➡ **se** also forms part of certain pronominal verbs such as **equivocarse, arrepentirse, caerse** etc., which are treated under the respective entries

....> (*voz pasiva*) **se construyeron muchas casas** many houses were built. **se vendió rápidamente** it was sold very quickly

....> (*impersonal*) **antes se escuchaba más radio** people used to listen to the radio more in the past. **no se puede entrar** you can't get in. **se está bien aquí** it's very nice here

....> (*en instrucciones*) **sírvase frío** serve cold

sé *vb véase* **SABER** *y* **SER**

sea *vb véase* **SER**

seca|dor *m* drier; (*de pelo*) hairdrier. **~nte** *adj* drying. ● *m* blotting-paper. **~r** **7** *vt* dry. **~rse** *vpr* dry; (río etc) dry up; (persona) dry o.s.

sección *f* section

seco *adj* dry; (frutos, flores) dried; (*flaco*) thin; (respuesta) curt. **a secas** just. **en ~** (*bruscamente*) suddenly. **lavar en ~** dry-clean

secretar|ía *f* secretariat; (*Mex, ministerio*) ministry. **~io** *m* secretary; (*Mex, Pol*) minister

secreto *adj* & *m* secret

secta *f* sect. **~rio** *adj* sectarian

sector *m* sector

secuela *f* consequence

secuencia *f* sequence

secuestr|ar *vt* confiscate; kidnap (persona); hijack (avión). **~o** *m* seizure; (*de persona*) kidnapping; (*de avión*) hijack(ing)

secundar *vt* second, help. **~io** *adj* secondary

sed *f* thirst. ● *vb véase* **SER**. **tener ~** be thirsty. **tener ~ de** (*fig*) be hungry for

seda *f* silk. **~ dental** dental floss

sedante *adj* & *m* sedative

sede *f* seat; (*Relig*) see; (*de organismo*) headquarters; (*de congreso,* *juegos etc*) venue

sedentario *adj* sedentary

sedici|ón *f* sedition. **~oso** *adj* seditious

sediento *adj* thirsty

seduc|ción *f* seduction. **~ir** [47] *vt* seduce; (*atraer*) attract. **~tor** *adj* seductive. • *m* seducer

seglar *adj* secular. • *m* layman

segrega|ción *f* segregation. **~r** [12] *vt* segregate

segui|da *f*. **en ~da** immediately. **~do** *adj* continuous; (*en plural*) consecutive. **~ de** followed by. • *adv* straight; (*LAm, a menudo*) often. **todo ~do** straight ahead. **~dor** *m* follower; (*en deportes*) supporter. **~r** [5] & [13] *vt* follow. • *vi* (*continuar*) continue; (*por un camino*) go on. **~r adelante** carry on

según *prep* according to. • *adv* it depends; (*a medida que*) as

segund|a *f* (*Auto*) second gear; (*en tren, avión etc*) second class. **~o** *adj* & *m* second

segur|amente *adv* certainly; (*muy probablemente*) surely. **~idad** *f* security; (*ausencia de peligro*) safety; (*certeza*) certainty; (*aplomo*) confidence. **~idad en sí mismo** self-confidence. **~idad social** social security. **~o** *adj* safe; (*cierto*) certain, sure; (*estable*) secure; (*de fiar*) reliable. • *adv* for certain. • *m* insurance; (*dispositivo de seguridad*) safety device. **~o de sí mismo** self-confident. **~o contra terceros** third-party insurance

seis *adj* & *m* six. **~cientos** *adj* & *m* six hundred

seísmo *m* earthquake

selec|ción *f* selection. **~cionar** *vt* select, choose. **~tivo** *adj* selective. **~to** *adj* selected; (*fig*) choice

sell|ar *vt* stamp; (*cerrar*) seal. **~o** *m* stamp; (*precinto*) seal; (*fig, distintivo*) hallmark; (*LAm, en moneda*) reverse

selva *f* forest; (*jungla*) jungle

semáforo *m* (*Auto*) traffic lights; (*Rail*) signal; (*Naut*) semaphore

semana *f* week. **S~ Santa** Holy Week. **~l** *adj* weekly. **~rio** *adj* & *m* weekly

> **Semana Santa** The most famous Holy Week celebrations in the Spanish-speaking world are held in Sevilla between Palm Sunday and Easter Sunday. Lay brotherhoods, *cofradías*, process through the city in huge parades. During the processions they sing *saetas*, flamenco verses mourning Christ's passion.

semántic|a *f* semantics. **~o** *adj* semantic

semblante *m* face; (*fig*) look

sembrar [1] *vt* sow; (*fig*) scatter

semeja|nte *adj* similar; (*tal*) such. • *m* fellow man. **~nza** *f* similarity. **a ~nza de** like. **~r** *vi*. **~r a** resemble

semen *m* semen. **~tal** *adj* stud. • *m* stud animal

semestr|al *adj* half-yearly. **~e** *m* six months

semi|circular *adj* semicircular. **~círculo** *m* semicircle. **~final** *f* semifinal

semill|a *f* seed. **~ero** *m* seedbed; (*fig*) hotbed

seminario *m* (*Univ*) seminar; (*Relig*) seminary

sémola *f* semolina

senado *m* senate. **~r** *m* senator

sencill|ez *f* simplicity. **~o** *adj* simple; (*para viajar*) single ticket; (*disco*) single; (*LAm, dinero suelto*) change

senda *f*, **sendero** *m* path

sendos *adj pl* each

seno *m* bosom. **~ materno** womb

sensaci|ón *f* sensation; (*percepción, impresión*) feeling. **~onal** *adj* sensational

sensat|ez *f* good sense. **~o** *adj* sensible

sensi|bilidad *f* sensibility. **~ble** *adj* sensitive; (*notable*) notable; (*lamentable*) lamentable. **~tivo** *adj* (órgano) sense

sensual *adj* sensual. **~idad** *f* sensuality

senta|do *adj* sitting (down); **dar algo por ~do** take something for granted. **~dor** *adj* (*LAm*) flattering. **~r** **1** *vt* sit; (*establecer*) establish. • *vi* suit; (*de medidas*) fit; (comida) agree with. **~rse** *vpr* sit (down)

sentencia *f* (*Jurid*) sentence. **~r** *vt* sentence (**a** to)

sentido *adj* heartfelt; (*sensible*) sensitive. • *m* sense; (*dirección*) direction; (*conocimiento*) consciousness. **~ común** common sense. **~ del humor** sense of humour. **~ único** one-way. **doble ~** double meaning. **no tener ~** not make sense. **perder el ~** faint. **sin ~** senseless

sentim|ental *adj* sentimental. **~iento** *m* feeling; (*sentido*) sense; (*pesar*) regret

sentir **4** *vt* feel; (*oír*) hear; (*lamentar*) be sorry for. **lo siento mucho** I'm really sorry. • *m* (*opinión*) opinion. **~se** *vpr* feel; (*Mex, ofenderse*) be offended

seña *f* sign. **~s** *fpl* (*dirección*) address; (*descripción*) description. **dar ~s de** show signs of

señal *f* signal; (*letrero, aviso*) sign; (*telefónica*) tone; (*Com*) deposit. **dar ~es de** show signs of. **en ~ de** as a token of. **~ado** *adj* (hora, día) appointed. **~ar** *vt* signal; (*poner señales en*) mark; (*apuntar*) point out; (manecilla, aguja) point to; (*determinar*) fix. **~arse** *vpr* stand out

señor *m* man, gentleman; (*delante de nombre propio*) Mr; (*tratamiento directo*) sir. **~a** *f* lady, woman; (*delante de nombre propio*) Mrs; (*esposa*) wife; (*tratamiento directo*) madam. **el ~** Mr. **muy ~ mío** Dear Sir. **¡no ~!** certainly not!. **~ial** *adj* (casa) stately. **~ita** *f* young lady; (*delante de nombre propio*) Miss; (*tratamiento directo*) miss. **~ito** *m* young gentleman

señuelo *m* lure

sepa *vb véase* **SABER**

separa|ción *f* separation. **~do** *adj* separate. **por ~do** separately. **~r** *vt* separate; (*de empleo*) dismiss. **~rse** *vpr* separate; (amigos) part. **~tista** *adj & m & f* separatist

septentrional *adj* north(ern)

septiembre *m* September

séptimo *adj* seventh

sepulcro *m* sepulchre

sepult|ar *vt* bury. **~ura** *f* burial; (*tumba*) grave. **~urero** *m* gravedigger

sequ|edad *f* dryness. **~ía** *f* drought

séquito *m* entourage; (*fig*) train

ser **39**

• verbo intransitivo

····➤ to be. **es bajo** he's short. **es abogado** he's a lawyer.

S

ábreme, soy yo open up, it's me. **¿cómo es?** (*como persona*) what's he like?; (*físicamente*) what does he look like? **era invierno** it was winter

····➤ **ser de** (*indicando composición*) to be made of. **es de hierro** it's made of iron. (*provenir de*) to be from. **es de México** he's from Mexico. (*pertenecer a*) to belong to. **el coche es de Juan** the car belongs to Juan, it's Juan's car

····➤ (*sumar*) **¿cuánto es todo?** how much is that altogether? **son 40 dólares** that's 40 dollars. **somos 10** there are 10 of us

····➤ (*con la hora*) **son las 3** it's 3 o'clock. **~ía la una** it must have been one o'clock

····➤ (*tener lugar*) to be held. **~á en la iglesia** it will be held in the church

····➤ (*ocurrir*) to happen **¿dónde fue el accidente?** where did the accident happen? **me contó cómo fue** he told me how it happened

····➤ (*en locuciones*) **a no ~ que** unless. **como sea** no matter what. **cuando sea** whenever. **donde sea** wherever. **¡eso es!** that's it! **es que** the thing is. **lo que sea** anything. **no sea que, no vaya a ~ que** in case. **o sea** in other words. **sea ... sea ...** either ... or ... **sea como sea** at all costs

● *nombre masculino* being; (*persona*) person. **el ~ humano** the human being. **un ~ amargado** a bitter person. **los ~es queridos** the loved ones

S

seren|ar *vt* calm down. **~arse** *vpr* calm down. **~ata** *f* serenade. **~idad** *f* serenity. **~o** *adj* serene; (cielo) clear; (mar) calm

seri|al *m* serial. **~e** *f* series. **fuera de ~e** (*fig*) out of this world. **producción** *f* **en ~e** mass production

seri|edad *f* seriousness. **~o** *adj* serious; (*confiable*) reliable; **en ~o** seriously. **poco ~o** frivolous

sermón *m* sermon; (*fig*) lecture

serp|enteante *adj* winding. **~entear** *vi* wind. **~iente** *f* snake. **~iente de cascabel** rattlesnake

serr|ar 1 *vt* saw. **~ín** *m* sawdust. **~uchar** *vt* (*LAm*) saw. **~ucho** *m* (hand)saw

servi|cial *adj* helpful. **~cio** *m* service; (*conjunto*) set; (*aseo*) toilet; **~cio a domicilio** delivery service. **~dor** *m* servant. **su (seguro) ~dor** (*en cartas*) yours faithfully. **~dumbre** *f* servitude; (*criados*) servants, staff. **~l** *adj* servile

servidor *m* server; (*criado*) servant

servilleta *f* napkin, serviette

servir 5 *vt* serve; (*en restaurante*) wait on. ● *vi* serve; (*ser útil*) be of use. **~se** *vpr* help o.s.. **~se de** use. **no ~ de nada** be useless. **para ~le** at your service. **sírvase sentarse** please sit down

sesent|a *adj & m* sixty. **~ón** *adj & m* sixty-year-old

seseo *m* pronunciation of the Spanish *c* as an *s*

sesión *f* session; (*en el cine, teatro*) performance

seso *m* brain

seta *f* mushroom

sete|cientos *adj & m* seven hundred. **~nta** *adj & m* seventy. **~ntón** *adj & m* seventy-year-old
setiembre *m* September
seto *m* fence; (*de plantas*) hedge. **~ vivo** hedge
seudónimo *m* pseudonym
sever|idad *f* severity; (*de profesor etc*) strictness. **~o** *adj* severe; (profesor etc) strict
sevillan|as *fpl* popular dance from Seville. **~o** *m* person from Seville
sexo *m* sex
sext|eto *m* sextet. **~o** *adj* sixth
sexual *adj* sexual. **~idad** *f* sexuality
si *m* (*Mus*) B; (*solfa*) te. • *conj* if; (*dubitativo*) whether; **~ no** otherwise. **por ~ (acaso)** in case
sí[1] *pron reflexivo* (*él*) himself; (*ella*) herself; (*de cosa*) itself; (*uno*) oneself; (*Vd*) yourself; (*ellos, ellas*) themselves; (*Vds*) yourselves; (*recíproco*) each other
sí[2] *adv* yes. • *m* consent
sida *m* Aids
sidra *f* cider
siembra *f* sowing; (*época*) sowing time
siempre *adv* always; (*LAm, todavía*) still; (*Mex, por fin*) after all. **~ que** if; (*cada vez*) whenever. **como ~** as usual. **de ~** (*acostumbrado*) usual. **lo de ~** the usual thing. **para ~** for ever
sien *f* temple
siento *vb véase* **SENTAR** *y* **SENTIR**
sierra *f* saw; (*cordillera*) mountain range
siesta *f* nap, siesta
siete *adj & m* seven
sífilis *f* syphilis
sifón *m* U-bend; (*de soda*) syphon
sigilo *m* stealth; (*fig*) secrecy
sigla *f* abbreviation
siglo *m* century; (*época*) age. **hace ~s que no escribe** he hasn't written for ages
significa|ción *f* significance. **~do** *adj* (*conocido*) well-known. • *m* meaning; (*importancia*) significance. **~r** **7** *vt* mean; (*expresar*) express. **~tivo** *adj* meaningful; (*importante*) significant
signo *m* sign. **~ de admiración** exclamation mark. **~ de interrogación** question mark
sigo *vb véase* **SEGUIR**
siguiente *adj* following, next. **lo ~** the following
sílaba *f* syllable
silb|ar *vt/i* whistle. **~ato** *m*, **~ido** *m* whistle
silenci|ador *m* silencer. **~ar** *vt* hush up. **~o** *m* silence. **~oso** *adj* silent
sill|a *f* chair; (*de montar*) saddle (*Relig*) see **~a de ruedas** wheelchair. **~ín** *m* saddle. **~ón** *m* armchair
silueta *f* silhouette; (*dibujo*) outline
silvestre *adj* wild
simb|ólico *adj* symbolic(al). **~olismo** *m* symbolism. **~olizar** **10** *vt* symbolize
símbolo *m* symbol
sim|etría *f* symmetry. **~étrico** *adj* symmetric(al)
similar *adj* similar (**a** to)
simp|atía *f* friendliness; (*cariño*) affection. **~ático** *adj* nice, likeable; (ambiente) pleasant. **~atizante** *m & f* sympathizer. **~atizar** **10** *vi* get on (well together)

S

simpl|e *adj* simple; (*mero*) mere. **~eza** *f* simplicity; (*tontería*) stupid thing; (*insignificancia*) trifle. **~icidad** *f* simplicity. **~ificar** 7 *vt* simplify. **~ista** *adj* simplistic. **~ón** *m* simpleton

simula|ción *f* simulation. **~r** *vt* simulate; (*fingir*) feign

simultáneo *adj* simultaneous

sin *prep* without. **~ saber** without knowing. **~ querer** accidentally

sinagoga *f* synagogue

sincer|idad *f* sincerity. **~o** *adj* sincere

sincronizar 10 *vt* synchronize

sindica|l *adj* (trade-)union. **~lista** *m & f* trade-unionist. **~to** *m* trade union

síndrome *m* syndrome

sinfín *m* endless number (**de** of)

sinfonía *f* symphony

singular *adj* singular; (*excepcional*) exceptional. **~izarse** *vpr* stand out

siniestro *adj* sinister. ● *m* disaster; (*accidente*) accident

sinnúmero *m* endless number (**de** of)

sino *m* fate. ● *conj* but

sinónimo *adj* synonymous. ● *m* synonym (**de** for)

sintaxis *f* syntax

síntesis *f invar* synthesis; (*resumen*) summary

sint|ético *adj* synthetic. **~etizar** 10 *vt* synthesize; (*resumir*) summarize

síntoma *f* symptom

sintomático *adj* symptomatic

sinton|ía *f* tuning; (*Mus*) signature tune. **~izar** 10 *vt* (*con la radio*) tune (in) to

sinvergüenza *m & f* crook

siquiera *conj* even if. ● *adv* at least. **ni ~** not even

sirena *f* siren; (*en cuentos*) mermaid

sirio *adj & m* Syrian

sirvient|a *f* maid. **~e** *m* servant

sirvo *vb véase* SERVIR

sísmico *adj* seismic

sismo *m* earthquake

sistem|a *m* system. **por ~a** as a rule. **~ático** *adj* systematic

sitiar *vt* besiege; (*fig*) surround

sitio *m* place; (*espacio*) space; (*Mil*) siege; (*Mex, parada de taxi*) taxi rank. **en cualquier ~** anywhere. **~ web** website

situa|ción *f* situation; (*estado, condición*) position. **~r** 21 *vt* place, put; locate (edificio). **~rse** *vpr* be successful, establish o.s.

slip /es'lip/ *m* (*pl* **~s**) underpants, briefs

smoking /es'mokin/ *m* (*pl* **~s**) dinner jacket (*Brit*), tuxedo (*Amer*)

sobaco *m* armpit

sobar *vt* handle; knead (masa)

soberan|ía *f* sovereignty. **~o** *adj* sovereign; (*fig*) supreme. ● *m* sovereign

soberbi|a *f* pride; (*altanería*) arrogance. **~o** *adj* proud; (*altivo*) arrogant

soborn|ar *vt* bribe. **~o** *m* bribe

sobra *f* surplus. **de ~** more than enough. **~s** *fpl* leftovers. **~do** *adj* more than enough. **~nte** *adj* surplus. **~r** *vi* be left over; (*estorbar*) be in the way

sobre *prep* on; (*encima de*) on top of; (*más o menos*) about; (*por encima de*) above; (*sin tocar*) over. **~ todo** above all, especially. ● *m* envelope. **~cargar** 12 *vt* overload. **~coger** 14 *vt* startle; (*conmover*) move. **~cubierta** *f* dustcover. **~dosis** *f invar* overdose. **~entender** **1** *vt* understand, infer. **~girar** *vt* (*LAm*) overdraw. **~giro** *m* (*LAm*) overdraft. **~humano** *adj* superhuman. **~llevar** *vt* bear. **~mesa** *f*. **de ~mesa** after-dinner. **~natural** *adj* supernatural. **~nombre** *m* nickname. **~pasar** *vt* exceed. **~peso** *m* (*LAm*) excess baggage. **~poner** **34** *vt* superimpose. **~ponerse** *vpr* overcome. **~saliente** *adj* (*fig*) outstanding. ● *m* excellent mark. **~salir** **52** *vi* stick out; (*fig*) stand out. **~saltar** *vt* startle. **~salto** *m* fright. **~sueldo** *m* bonus. **~todo** *m* overcoat. **~venir** **53** *vi* happen. **~viviente** *adj* surviving. ● *m* & *f* survivor. **~vivir** *vi* survive. **~volar** *vt* fly over

sobriedad *f* moderation; (*de estilo*) simplicity

sobrin|a *f* niece. **~o** *m* nephew. **~os** (*varones*) nephews; (*varones y mujeres*) nieces and nephews

sobrio *adj* moderate, sober

socavar *vt* undermine

soci|able *adj* sociable. **~al** *adj* social. **~aldemócrata** *m* & *f* social democrat. **~alismo** *m* socialism. **~alista** *adj* & *m* & *f* socialist. **~edad** *f* society; (*Com*) company. **~edad anónima** limited company. **~o** *m* member; (*Com*) partner. **~ología** *f* sociology. **~ólogo** *m* sociologist

socorr|er *vt* help. **~o** *m* help

soda *f* (*bebida*) soda (water)

sodio *m* sodium

sofá *m* sofa, settee

sofistica|ción *f* sophistication. **~do** *adj* sophisticated

sofo|cante *adj* suffocating; (*fig*) stifling. **~car** **7** *vt* smother (fuego); (*fig*) stifle. **~carse** *vpr* get upset

soga *f* rope

soja *f* soya (bean)

sojuzgar **12** *vt* subdue

sol *m* sun; (*luz*) sunlight; (*Mus*) G; (*solfa*) soh. **al ~** in the sun. **día** *m* **de ~** sunny day. **hace ~, hay ~** it is sunny. **tomar el ~** sunbathe

solamente *adv* only

solapa *f* lapel; (*de bolsillo etc*) flap. **~do** *adj* sly

solar *adj* solar. ● *m* plot

solariego *adj* (casa) ancestral

soldado *m* soldier. **~ raso** private

solda|dor *m* welder; (*utensilio*) soldering iron. **~r** **2** *vt* weld, solder

soleado *adj* sunny

soledad *f* solitude; (*aislamiento*) loneliness

solemn|e *adj* solemn. **~idad** *f* solemnity

soler **2** *vi* be in the habit of. **suele despertarse a las 6** he usually wakes up at 6 o'clock

sol|icitante *m* applicant. **~ de asilo** asylum seeker. **~icitar** *vt* request, ask for; apply for (empleo). **~ícito** *adj* solicitous. **~icitud** *f* request; (*para un puesto*) application; (*formulario*) application form; (*preocupación*) concern

solidaridad *f* solidarity

solid|ez *f* solidity; (*de argumento etc*) soundness. **~ificarse** **7** *vpr* solidify

sólido *adj* solid; (argumento etc) sound. ● *m* solid

soliloquio *m* soliloquy

solista *m* & *f* soloist

solitario *adj* solitary; (*aislado*) lonely. ● *m* loner; (*juego, diamante*) solitaire

sollоz|ar 10 *vi* sob. **~o** *m* sob

solo *adj* (*sin compañía*) alone; (*aislado*) lonely; (*sin ayuda*) by oneself; (*único*) only; (*Mus*) solo; (café) black. • *m* solo; (*juego*) solitaire. **a solas** alone

sólo *adv* only. **~ que** except that. **no ~... sino también** not only... but also.... **tan ~** only

solomillo *m* sirloin

soltar 2 *vt* let go of; (*dejar ir*) release; (*dejar caer*) drop; (*dejar salir, decir*) let out; give (golpe etc). **~se** *vpr* come undone; (*librarse*) break loose

solter|a *f* single woman. **~o** *adj* single. • *m* bachelor

soltura *f* looseness; (*fig*) ease, fluency

solu|ble *adj* soluble. **~ción** *f* solution. **~cionar** *vt* solve; settle (huelga, asunto)

solvente *adj & m* solvent

sombr|a *f* shadow; (*lugar sin sol*) shade. **a la ~a** in the shade. **~eado** *adj* shady

sombrero *m* hat. **~ hongo** bowler hat

sombrío *adj* sombre

somero *adj* superficial

someter *vt* subdue; subject (persona); (*presentar*) submit. **~se** *vpr* give in

somn|oliento *adj* sleepy. **~ífero** *m* sleeping-pill

somos *vb véase* **SER**

son *m* sound. • *vb véase* **SER**

sonámbulo *m* sleepwalker. **ser ~** walk in one's sleep

sonar 2 *vt* blow; ring (timbre). • *vi* sound; (timbre, teléfono etc) ring; (despertador) go off; (*Mus*) play; (*fig, ser conocido*) be familiar. **~ a** sound like. **~se** *vpr* blow one's nose

sonde|ar *vt* sound out; explore (espacio); (*Naut*) sound. **~o** *m* poll; (*Naut*) sounding

soneto *m* sonnet

sonido *m* sound

sonoro *adj* sonorous; (*ruidoso*) loud

sonr|eír 51 *vi* smile. **~eírse** *vpr* smile. **~isa** *f* smile

sonroj|arse *vpr* blush. **~o** *m* blush

sonrosado *adj* rosy, pink

sonsacar 7 *vt* wheedle out

soñ|ado *adj* dream. **~ador** *m* dreamer. **~ar** 2 *vi* dream (**con** of). **¡ni ~arlo!** not likely!

sopa *f* soup

sopesar *vt* (*fig*) weigh up

sopl|ar *vt* blow; blow out (vela); blow off (polvo); (*inflar*) blow up. • *vi* blow. **~ete** *m* blowlamp. **~o** *m* puff

soport|al *m* porch. **~ales** *mpl* arcade. **~ar** *vt* support; (*fig*) bear, put up with. **~e** *m* support

soprano *f* soprano

sor *f* sister

sorb|er *vt* sip; (*con ruido*) slurp; (*absorber*) absorb. **~ por la nariz** sniff. **~ete** *m* sorbet, water-ice. **~o** *m* (*pequeña cantidad*) sip; (*trago grande*) gulp

sordera *f* deafness

sórdido *adj* squalid; (asunto) sordid

sordo *adj* deaf; (ruido etc) dull. • *m* deaf person. **hacerse el ~** turn a deaf ear. **~mudo** *adj* deaf and dumb

soroche *m* (*LAm*) mountain sickness

sorpre|ndente *adj* surprising.

~nder *vt* surprise. **~nderse** *vpr* be surprised. **~sa** *f* surprise

sorte|ar *vt* draw lots for; (*fig*) avoid. **~o** *m* draw. **por ~o** by drawing lots

sortija *f* ring; (*de pelo*) ringlet

sortilegio *m* sorcery; (*embrujo*) spell

sos|egar 1 & 12 *vt* calm. **~iego** *m* calmness

soslayo. **de ~** sideways

soso *adj* tasteless; (*fig*) dull

sospech|a *f* suspicion. **~ar** *vt* suspect. ● *vi*. **~ de** suspect. **~oso** *adj* suspicious. ● *m* suspect

sost|én *m* support; (*prenda femenina*) bra [!], brassière. **~ener** 40 *vt* support; bear (peso); (*sujetar*) hold; (*sustentar*) maintain; (*alimentar*) sustain. **~enerse** *vpr* support o.s.; (*continuar*) remain. **~enido** *adj* sustained; (*Mus*) sharp. ● *m* (*Mus*) sharp

sota *f* (*de naipes*) jack

sótano *m* basement

soviético *adj* (*Historia*) Soviet

soy *vb véase* SER

Sr. *abrev* (**Señor**) Mr. **~a.** *abrev* (**Señora**) Mrs. **~ta.** *abrev* (**Señorita**) Miss

su *adj* (*de él*) his; (*de ella*) her; (*de animal, objeto*) its; (*de uno*) one's; (*de Vd*) your; (*de ellos, de ellas*) their; (*de Vds*) your

suav|e *adj* smooth; (*fig*) gentle; (color, sonido) soft; (tabaco, sedante) mild. **~idad** *f* smoothness, softness. **~izante** *m* conditioner; (*para ropa*) softener. **~izar** 10 *vt* smooth, soften

subalimentado *adj* underfed

subarrendar 1 *vt* sublet

subasta *f* auction. **~r** *vt* auction

sub|campeón *m* runner-up. **~consciencia** *f* subconscious. **~consciente** *adj & m* subconscious. **~continente** *m* subcontinent. **~desarrollado** *adj* underdeveloped. **~director** *m* assistant manager

súbdito *m* subject

sub|dividir *vt* subdivide. **~estimar** *vt* underestimate

subi|da *f* rise; (*a montaña*) ascent; (*pendiente*) slope. **~do** *adj* (color) intense. **~r** *vt* go up; climb (mountain); (*llevar*) take up; (*aumentar*) raise; turn up (radio, calefacción). ● *vi* go up. **~r a** get into (coche); get on (autobús, avión, barco, tren); (*aumentar*) rise. **~ a pie** walk up. **~rse** *vpr* climb up. **~rse a** get on (tren etc)

súbito *adj* sudden. **de ~** suddenly

subjetivo *adj* subjective

subjuntivo *adj & m* subjunctive

subleva|ción *f* uprising. **~rse** *vpr* rebel

sublim|ar *vt* sublimate. **~e** *adj* sublime

submarino *adj* underwater. ● *m* submarine

subordinado *adj & m* subordinate

subrayar *vt* underline

subsanar *vt* rectify; overcome (dificultad); make up for (carencia)

subscri|bir *vt* (*pp* **subscrito**) sign. **~birse** *vpr* subscribe (**a** to). **~pción** *f* subscription

subsidi|ario *adj* subsidiary. **~o** *m* subsidy. **~o de desempleo, ~ de paro** unemployment benefit

subsiguiente *adj* subsequent

subsist|encia *f* subsistence. **~ir** *vi* subsist; (*perdurar*) survive

substraer 41 *vt* take away

subterráneo *adj* underground
subtítulo *m* subtitle
suburb|ano *adj* suburban. **~io** *m* suburb; (*barrio pobre*) depressed area
subvenci|ón *f* subsidy. **~onar** *vt* subsidize
subver|sión *f* subversion. **~sivo** *adj* subversive. **~tir** 4 *vt* subvert
succi|ón *f* suction. **~onar** *vt* suck
suce|der *vi* happen; (*seguir*) **~ a** follow. ● *vt* (*substituir*) succeed. **lo que ~de es que** the trouble is that. **¿qué ~de?** what's the matter? **~sión** *f* succession. **~sivo** *adj* successive; (*consecutivo*) consecutive. **en lo ~sivo** in future. **~so** *m* event; (*incidente*) incident. **~sor** *m* successor
suciedad *f* dirt; (*estado*) dirtiness
sucinto *adj* concise; (prenda) scanty
sucio *adj* dirty; (conciencia) guilty. **en ~** in rough
sucre *m* (*unidad monetaria del Ecuador*) sucre
suculento *adj* succulent
sucumbir *vi* succumb (**a** to)
sucursal *f* branch (office)
Sudáfrica *f* South Africa
S
sudafricano *adj* & *m* South African
Sudamérica *f* South America
sudamericano *adj* & *m* South American
sudar *vi* sweat
sud|este *m* south-east. **~oeste** *m* south-west
sudor *m* sweat
Suecia *f* Sweden
sueco *adj* Swedish. ● *m* (*persona*) Swede; (*lengua*) Swedish. **hacerse el ~** pretend not to hear
suegr|a *f* mother-in-law. **~o** *m* father-in-law. **mis ~os** my in-laws
suela *f* sole
sueldo *m* salary
suelo *m* ground; (*dentro de edificio*) floor; (*territorio*) soil; (*en la calle etc*) road surface. ● *vb véase* SOLER
suelto *adj* loose; (cordones) undone; (*sin pareja*) odd; (lenguaje) fluent. **con el pelo ~** with one's hair down. ● *m* change
sueño *m* sleep; (*lo soñado, ilusión*) dream. **tener ~** be sleepy
suerte *f* luck; (*destino*) fate; (*azar*) chance. **de otra ~** otherwise. **de ~ que** so. **echar ~s** draw lots. **por ~** fortunately. **tener ~** be lucky
suéter *m* sweater, jersey
suficien|cia *f* (*aptitud*) aptitude; (*presunción*) smugness. **~te** *adj* enough, sufficient; (*presumido*) smug. **~temente** *adv* sufficiently
sufijo *m* suffix
sufragio *m* (*voto*) vote
sufri|miento *m* suffering. **~r** *vt* suffer; undergo (cambio); have (accident). ● *vi* suffer
suge|rencia *f* suggestion. **~rir** 4 *vt* suggest. **~stión** *f* (*en psicología*) suggestion. **es pura ~stión** it's all in one's mind. **~stionable** *adj* impressionable. **~stionar** *vt* influence. **~stivo** *adj* (*estimulante*) stimulating; (*atractivo*) sexy
suicid|a *adj* suicidal. ● *m* & *f* suicide victim; (*fig*) maniac. **~arse** *vpr* commit suicide. **~io** *m* suicide
Suiza *f* Switzerland
suizo *adj* & *m* Swiss
suje|ción *f* subjection. **con ~ a** in accordance with. **~tador** *m* bra 🅘, brassière. **~tapapeles** *m invar* paper-clip. **~tar** *vt* fasten; (*agarrar*)

hold. **~tarse** *vpr.* **~se a** hold on to; (*someterse*) abide by. **~to** *adj* fastened; (*susceptible*) subject (**a** to). ● *m* individual; (*Gram*) subject.

suma *f* sum; (*Math*) addition; (*combinación*) combination. **en ~** in short. **~mente** *adv* extremely. **~r** *vt* add (up); (*totalizar*) add up to. ● *vi* add up. **~rse** *vpr.* **~rse a** join in

sumario *adj* brief; (*Jurid*) summary. ● *m* table of contents; (*Jurid*) pre-trial proceedings

sumergi|ble *adj* submersible. **~r** 14 *vt* submerge

suministr|ar *vt* supply. **~o** *m* supply; (*acción*) supplying

sumir *vt* sink; (*fig*) plunge

sumis|ión *f* submission. **~o** *adj* submissive

sumo *adj* great; (*supremo*) supreme. **a lo ~** at the most

suntuoso *adj* sumptuous

supe *vb véase* SABER

superar *vt* surpass; (*vencer*) overcome; beat (marca); (*dejar atrás*) get over. **~se** *vpr* better o.s.

supercheria *f* swindle

superfici|al *adj* superficial. **~e** *f* surface; (*extensión*) area. **de ~e** surface

superfluo *adj* superfluous

superior *adj* superior; (*más alto*) higher; (*mejor*) better; (piso) upper. ● *m* superior. **~idad** *f* superiority

superlativo *adj* & *m* superlative

supermercado *m* supermarket

supersticí|ón *f* superstition. **~oso** *adj* superstitious

supervis|ar *vt* supervise. **~ión** *f* supervision. **~or** *m* supervisor

superviv|encia *f* survival. **~iente** *adj* surviving. ● *m* & *f* survivor

suplantar *vt* supplant

suplement|ario *adj* supplementary. **~o** *m* supplement

suplente *adj* & *m* & *f* substitute

súplica *f* entreaty; (*Jurid*) request

suplicar 7 *vt* beg

suplicio *m* torture

suplir *vt* make up for; (*reemplazar*) replace

supo|ner 34 *vt* suppose; (*significar*) mean; involve (gasto, trabajo). **~sición** *f* supposition

suprem|acía *f* supremacy. **~o** *adj* supreme

supr|esión *f* suppression; (*de impuesto*) abolition; (*de restricción*) lifting. **~imir** *vt* suppress; abolish (impuesto); lift (restricción); delete (párrafo)

supuesto *adj* supposed; (falso) false; (*denominado*) so-called. ● *m* assumption. **¡por ~!** of course!

sur *m* south; (*viento*) south wind

surc|ar 7 *vt* plough; cut through (agua). **~o** *m* furrow; (*de rueda*) rut

surfear *vi* (*Informática*) surf

surgir 14 *vi* spring up; (*elevarse*) loom up; (*aparecer*) appear; (dificultad, oportunidad) arise

surrealis|mo *m* surrealism. **~ta** *adj* & *m* & *f* surrealist

surti|do *adj* well-stocked; (*variado*) assorted. ● *m* assortment, selection. **~dor** *m* (*de gasolina*) petrol pump (*Brit*), gas pump (*Amer*). **~r** *vt* supply; have (efecto). **~rse** *vpr* provide o.s. (**de** with)

susceptib|ilidad *f* sensitivity. **~le** *adj* susceptible; (*sensible*) sensitive

suscitar *vt* provoke; arouse

(curiosidad, interés)

suscr... *véase* **SUBSCR...**

susodicho *adj* aforementioned

suspen|der *vt* suspend; stop (tratamiento); call off (viaje); (*en examen*) fail; (*colgar*) hang (**de** from). **~se** *m* suspense. **novela de ~se** thriller. **~sión** *f* suspension. **~so** *m* fail; (*LAm, en libro, película*) suspense. **en ~so** suspended

suspir|ar *vi* sigh. **~o** *m* sigh

sust... *véase* **SUBST...**

sustanci|a *f* substance. **~al** *adj* substantial. **~oso** *adj* substantial

sustantivo *m* noun

sustent|ación *f* support. **~ar** *vt* support; (*alimentar*) sustain; (*mantener*) maintain. **~o** *m* support; (*alimento*) sustenance

sustitu|ción *f* substitution; (*permanente*) replacement. **~ir** 17 *vt* substitute, replace. **~to** *m* substitute; (*permanente*) replacement

susto *m* fright

susurr|ar *vi* (persona) whisper; (agua) murmur; (hojas) rustle

sutil *adj* fine; (*fig*) subtle. **~eza** *f* subtlety

suyo *adj & pron* (*de él*) his; (*de ella*) hers; (*de animal*) its; (*de Vd*) yours; (*de ellos, de ellas*) theirs; (*de Vds*) yours. **un amigo ~** a friend of his, a friend of theirs, etc

Tt

tabac|alera *f* (state) tobacco monopoly. **~o** *m* tobacco; (*cigarrillos*) cigarettes

tabern|a *f* bar. **~ero** *m* barman; (*dueño*) landlord

tabique *m* partition wall; (*Mex, ladrillo*) brick

tabl|a *f* plank; (*del suelo*) floorboard; (*de vestido*) pleat; (*índice*) index; (*gráfico, en matemática etc*) table. **hacer ~as** (*en ajedrez*) draw. **~a de surf** surfboard. **~ado** *m* platform; (*en el teatro*) stage. **~ao** *m* place where flamenco shows are held. **~ero** *m* board. **~ero de mandos** dashboard

tableta *f* tablet; (*de chocolate*) bar

tabl|illa *f* splint; (*Mex, de chocolate*) bar. **~ón** *m* plank. **~ón de anuncios** notice board (*esp Brit*), bulletin board (*Amer*)

tabú *m* (*pl* **~es**, **~s**) taboo

tabular *vt* tabulate

taburete *m* stool

tacaño *adj* mean

tacha *f* stain, blemish. **sin ~** unblemished; (conducta) irreproachable. **~r** *vt* (*con raya*) cross out; (*Jurid*) impeach. **~ de** accuse of

tácito *adj* tacit

taciturno *adj* taciturn; (*triste*) glum

taco *m* plug; (*LAm, tacón*) heel; (*de billar*) cue; (*de billetes*) book; (*fig, fam, lío*) mess; (*palabrota*) swearword; (*Mex, Culin*) taco, filled tortilla

tacón *m* heel

táctic|a *f* tactics. **~o** *adj* tactical

s t

táctil *adj* tactile
tacto *m* touch; (*fig*) tact
tahúr *m* card-sharp
tailandés *adj & m* Thai
Tailandia *f* Thailand
taimado *adj* sly
taj|ada *f* slice. **sacar ~ada** profit. **~ante** *adj* categorical; (tono) sharp. **~ear** *vt* (*LAm*) slash. **~o** *m* cut; (*en mina*) face
tal *adj* such. **de ~ manera** in such a way. **un ~** someone called. ● *pron*. **como ~** as such. **y ~** and things like that. ● *adv*. **con ~ de que** as long as. **~ como** the way. **~ para cual** [!] two of a kind. **~ vez** maybe. **¿qué ~?** how are you? **¿qué ~ es ella?** what's she like?
taladr|ar *vt* drill. **~o** *m* drill
talante *m* mood. **de buen ~** (estar) in a good mood; (ayudar) willingly
talar *vt* fell
talco *m* talcum powder
talega *f*, **talego** *m* sack
talento *m* talent; (*fig*) talented person
talismán *m* talisman
talla *f* carving; (*de diamante etc*) cutting; (*estatura*) height; (*tamaño*) size. **~do** *m* carving; (*de diamante etc*) cutting. **~dor** *m* carver; (*cortador*) cutter; (*LAm, de naipes*) dealer. **~r** *vt* carve; sculpt (escultura); cut (diamante); (*Mex, restregar*) scrub. **~rse** *vpr* (*Mex*) rub o.s.
tallarín *m* noodle
talle *m* waist; (*figura*) figure
taller *m* workshop; (*de pintor etc*) studio; (*Auto*) garage
tallo *m* stem, stalk
tal|ón *m* heel; (*recibo*) counterfoil; (*cheque*) cheque. **~onario** *m* receipt book; (*de cheques*) cheque book
tamal *m* (*LAm*) tamale
tamaño *adj* such a. ● *m* size. **de ~ natural** life-size
tambalearse *vpr* (*persona*) stagger; (cosa) wobble
también *adv* also, too
tambor *m* drum. **~ del freno** brake drum. **~ilear** *vi* drum
tamiz *m* sieve. **~ar** [10] *vt* sieve
tampoco *adv* neither, nor, not either. **yo ~ fui** I didn't go either
tampón *m* tampon; (*para entintar*) ink-pad
tan *adv* so. **~... como** as... as. **¿qué ~...?** (*LAm*) how...?
tanda *f* group; (*de obreros*) shift
tang|ente *adj & f* tangent. **~ible** *adj* tangible
tango *m* tango
tanque *m* tank
tante|ar *vt* estimate; sound up (persona); (*ensayar*) test; (*fig*) weigh up; (*LAm, palpar*) feel. ● *vi* (*LAm*) feel one's way. **~o** *m* estimate; (*prueba*) test; (*en deportes*) score
tanto *adj* (*en singular*) so much; (*en plural*) so many; (*comparación en singular*) as much; (*comparación en plural*) as many. ● *pron* so much; (*en plural*) so many. ● *adv* so; (*con verbo*) so much. **hace ~ tiempo** it's been so long. **~... como** both ...and. **¿qué ~...?** (*LAm*) how much...? **~ como** as well as; (*cantidad*) as much as. **~ más... cuanto que** all the more ... because. **~ si... como si** whether ... or. **a ~s de** sometime in. **en ~**, **entre ~** meanwhile. **en ~ que** while. **entre ~** meanwhile. **hasta**

~ **que** until. **no es para** ~ it's not as bad as all that. **otro** ~ the same; (*el doble*) as much again. **por (lo)** ~ therefore. • *m* certain amount; (*punto*) point; (*gol*) goal. **estar al** ~ **de** be up to date with

tañer 22 *vi* peal

tapa *f* lid; (*de botella*) top; (*de libro*) cover. ~**s** *fpl* savoury snacks. ~**dera** *f* cover, lid; (*fig*) cover. ~**r** *vt* cover; (*abrigar*) wrap up; (*obturar*) plug. ~**rrabo(s)** *m invar* loincloth

> **i** **tapas** In Spain these are small portions of food served in bars and cafés with a drink. There is a wide variety, including Spanish omelette, seafood, different kinds of cooked potatoes, cheese, ham, chorizo etc. The practice of going out for a drink and *tapas* is known as *tapeo*.

tapete *m* (*de mesa*) table cover; (*Mex, alfombra*) rug

tapia *f* wall. ~**r** *vt* enclose

tapi|cería *f* tapestry; (*de muebles*) upholstery. ~**z** *m* tapestry. ~**zar** 10 *vt* upholster (muebles)

tapón *m* stopper; (*Tec*) plug

taqu|igrafía *f* shorthand. ~**ígrafo** *m* shorthand writer

t

taquill|a *f* ticket office; (*fig, dinero*) takings. ~**ero** *adj* box-office

tara *f* (*peso*) tare; (*defecto*) defect

tarántula *f* tarantula

tararear *vt/i* hum

tarda|nza *f* delay. ~**r** *vt* take. • *vi* (*retrasarse*) be late; (*emplear mucho tiempo*) take a long time. **a más** ~**r** at the latest. **sin** ~**r** without delay

tard|e *adv* late. • *f* (*antes del atardecer*) afternoon; (*después del atardecer*) evening. **en la** ~**e** (*LAm*), **por la** ~**e** in the afternoon. ~**ío** *adj* late

tarea *f* task, job

tarifa *f* rate; (*en transporte*) fare; (*lista de precios*) tariff

tarima *f* dais

tarjeta *f* card. ~ **de crédito** credit card. ~ **de fidelidad** loyalty card. ~ **postal** postcard. ~ **telefónica** telephone card

tarro *m* jar; (*Mex, taza*) mug

tarta *f* cake; (*con base de masa*) tart. ~ **helada** ice-cream gateau

tartamud|ear *vi* stammer. ~**o** *adj*. **es** ~**o** he stammers

tasa *f* valuation; (*impuesto*) tax; (*índice*) rate. ~**r** *vt* value; (*limitar*) ration

tasca *f* bar

tatarabuel|a *f* great-great-grandmother. ~**o** *m* great-great-grandfather. ~**os** *mpl* great-great-grandparents

tatua|je *m* (*acción*) tattooing; (*dibujo*) tattoo. ~**r** 21 *vt* tattoo

taurino *adj* bullfighting

Tauro *m* Taurus

tauromaquia *f* bullfighting

taxi *m* taxi. ~**ista** *m & f* taxi-driver

taz|a *f* cup. ~**ón** *m* bowl

te *pron* (*acusativo*) you; (*dativo*) (to) you; (*reflexivo*) (to) yourself

té *m* tea; (*LAm, reunión*) tea party

teatr|al *adj* theatre; (*exagerado*) theatrical. ~**o** *m* theatre; (*literatura*) drama

tebeo *m* comic

tech|ado *m* roof. ~**ar** *vt* roof. ~**o** *m* (*interior*) ceiling; (*LAm, tejado*) roof. ~**umbre** *f* roof

tecl|a *f* key. **~ado** *m* keyboard. **~ear** *vt* key in
técnica *f* technique
tecnicismo *m* technical nature; (*palabra*) technical term
técnico *adj* technical. ● *m* technician; (*en deportes*) trainer
tecnol|ogía *f* technology. **~ógico** *adj* technological
tecolote *m* (*Mex*) owl
teja *f* tile. **~s de pizarra** slates. **~do** *m* roof. **a toca ~** cash
teje|dor *m* weaver. **~r** *vt* weave; (*hacer punto*) knit
tejemaneje *m* 🅸 intrigue. **~s** *mpl* scheming
tejido *m* material; (*Anat, fig*) tissue. **~s** *mpl* textiles
tejón *m* badger
tela *f* material, fabric; (*de araña*) web; (*en líquido*) skin
telar *m* loom. **~es** *mpl* textile mill
telaraña *f* spider's web, cobweb
tele *f* 🅸 TV, telly
tele|banca *f* telephone banking. **~comunicación** *f* telecommunication. **~diario** *m* television news. **~dirigido** *adj* remote-controlled; (misil) guided. **~férico** *m* cable-car
tel|efonear *vt/i* telephone. **~efónico** *adj* telephone. **~efonista** *m & f* telephonist.
teléfono *m* telephone. **~ celular** (*LAm*) mobile phone, cellular phone. **~ móvil** (*Esp*) mobile phone, cellular phone. **~ satélite** satphone
tel|egrafía *f* telegraphy. **~égrafo** *m* telegraph. **~egrama** *m* telegram
telenovela *f* television soap opera
teleobjetivo *m* telephoto lens
telep|atía *f* telepathy. **~ático** *adj* telepathic
telesc|ópico *adj* telescopic. **~opio** *m* telescope
telesilla *m & f* chair-lift
telespectador *m* viewer
telesquí *m* ski-lift
televi|dente *m & f* viewer. **~sar** *vt* televise. **~sión** *f* television. **~sor** *m* television (set)
télex *m invar* telex
telón *m* curtain
tema *m* subject; (*Mus*) theme
tembl|ar 🅸 *vi* shake; (*de miedo*) tremble; (*de frío*) shiver. **~or** *m* shaking; (*de miedo*) trembling; (*de frío*) shivering; **~or de tierra** earth tremor. **~oroso** *adj* trembling
tem|er *vt* be afraid (of). ● *vi* be afraid. **~erse** *vpr* be afraid. **~erario** *adj* reckless. **~eroso** *adj* frightened. **~ible** *adj* fearsome. **~or** *m* fear
témpano *m* floe
temperamento *m* temperament
temperatura *f* temperature
tempest|ad *f* storm. **~uoso** *adj* stormy
templ|ado *adj* (*tibio*) warm; (clima, tiempo) mild; (*valiente*) courageous. **~anza** *f* mildness. **~ar** *vt* temper; (*calentar*) warm up. **~e** *m* tempering; (coraje) courage; (*humor*) mood
templo *m* temple
tempora|da *f* season. **~l** *adj* temporary. ● *m* storm
tempran|ero *adj* (frutos) early. ser **~ero** be an early riser. **~o** *adj & adv* early
tenacidad *f* tenacity
tenacillas *fpl* tongs

tenaz *adj* tenacious

tenaza *f*, **tenazas** *fpl* pliers; (*de chimenea, Culin*) tongs; (*de cangrejo*) pincer

tende|ncia *f* tendency. **~nte** *adj*. **~nte a** aimed at. **~r** **1** *vt* spread (out); hang out (ropa a secar); (*colocar*) lay. ● *vi* tend (**a** to). **~rse** *vpr* lie down

tender|ete *m* stall. **~o** *m* shopkeeper

tendido *adj* spread out; (ropa) hung out; (persona) lying down. ● *m* (*en plaza de toros*) front rows

tendón *m* tendon

tenebroso *adj* gloomy; (asunto) sinister

tenedor *m* fork; (*poseedor*) holder

tener 40

● *verbo transitivo*

! El presente del verbo **tener** admite dos traducciones: *to have* y *to have got*, este último de uso más extendido en el inglés británico

····➤ to have. **¿tienen hijos?** do you have any children?, have you got any children? **no tenemos coche** we don't have a car, we haven't got a car. **tiene gripe** he has (the) flu, he's got (the) flu

····➤ to be. (dimensiones, edad) **tiene 1 metro de largo** it's 1 meter long. **tengo 20 años** I'm 20 (years old)

····➤ (*sentir*) **tener** + *nombre* to be + *adjective*. **~ celos** to be jealous. **~ frío** to be cold

····➤ (*sujetar, sostener*) to hold. **tenme la escalera** hold the ladder for me

····➤ (*indicando estado*) **tiene las manos sucias** his hands are dirty. **me tiene preocupada** I'm worried about him. **me tuvo esperando** he kept me waiting

····➤ (*llevar puesto*) to be wearing, to have on. **¡qué zapatos más elegantes tienes!** those are very smart shoes you're wearing! **tienes el suéter al revés** you have your sweater on inside out

····➤ (*considerar*) **~ a uno por algo** to think s.o. is sth. **lo tenía por tímido** I thought he was shy

● *verbo auxiliar*

····➤ **~ que hacer algo** to have to do sth. **tengo que irme** I have to go

····➤ **tener** + *participio pasado*. **tengo pensado comprarlo** I'm thinking of buying it. **tenía entendido otra cosa** I understood something else

····➤ (*LAm, con expresiones temporales*) **tienen 2 años de estar aquí** they've been here for 2 months. **tiene mucho tiempo sin verlo** she hasn't seen him for a long time

····➤ (*en locuciones*) **aquí tiene** here you are. **¿qué tienes?** what's the matter with you? **¿y eso qué tiene?** (*LAm*) and what's wrong with that?

● **tenerse** *verbo pronominal*

····➤ (*sostenerse*) **no podía ~se en pie** (*de cansancio*) he was dead on his feet; (*de borracho*) he could hardly stand

···➤ (*considerarse*) to consider o.s. **se tiene por afortunado** he considers himself lucky

tengo *vb véase* **TENER**

teniente *m* lieutenant

tenis *m* tennis. ~ **de mesa** table tennis. ~**ta** *m & f* tennis player

tenor *m* sense; (*Mus*) tenor. **a** ~ **de** according to

tens|ión *f* tension; (*arterial*) blood pressure; (*Elec*) voltage; (*estrés*) strain. ~**o** *adj* tense

tentación *f* temptation

tentáculo *m* tentacle

tenta|dor *adj* tempting. ~**r** **1** *vt* tempt; (*palpar*) feel

tentativa *f* attempt

tenue *adj* thin; (luz, voz) faint; (color) subdued

teñi|r **5** & **22** *vt* dye; (*fig*) tinge (**de** with). ~**rse** *vpr* dye one's hair

teología *f* theology

te|oría *f* theory. ~**órico** *adj* theoretical

tequila *f* tequila

terap|euta *m & f* therapist. ~**éutico** *adj* therapeutic. ~**ia** *f* therapy

terc|er *adj véase* **TERCERO**. ~**era** *f* (*Auto*) third (gear). ~**ero** *adj* (*delante de nombre masculino en singular* **tercer**) third. ● *m* third party. ~**io** *m* third

terciopelo *m* velvet

terco *adj* obstinate

tergiversar *vt* distort

termal *adj* thermal

térmico *adj* thermal

termina|ción *f* ending; (*conclusión*) conclusion. ~**l** *adj & m* terminal. ~**nte** *adj* categorical. ~**r** *vt* finish, end. ~**r por** end up. ~**rse** *vpr* come to an end

término *m* end; (*palabra*) term; (*plazo*) period. ~ **medio** average. **dar** ~ **a** finish off. **en primer** ~ first of all. **en último** ~ as a last resort. **estar en buenos** ~**s con** be on good terms with. **llevar a** ~ carry out

terminología *f* terminology

termita *f* termite

termo *m* Thermos (P) flask, flask

termómetro *m* thermometer

termo|nuclear *adj* thermonuclear. ~**stato** *m* thermostat

terner|a *f* (*carne*) veal. ~**o** *m* calf

ternura *f* tenderness

terquedad *f* stubbornness

terrado *m* flat roof

terraplén *m* embankment

terrateniente *m & f* landowner

terraza *f* terrace; (*balcón*) balcony; (*terrado*) flat roof

terremoto *m* earthquake

terre|no *adj* earthly. ● *m* land; (*solar*) plot (*fig*) field. ~**stre** *adj* land; (*Mil*) ground

terrible *adj* terrible. ~**mente** *adv* awfully

territori|al *adj* territorial. ~**o** *m* territory

terrón *m* (*de tierra*) clod; (*Culin*) lump

terror *m* terror. ~**ífico** *adj* terrifying. ~**ismo** *m* terrorism. ~**ista** *m & f* terrorist

terso *adj* smooth

tertulia *f* gathering

tesina *f* dissertation

tesón *m* tenacity

tesor|ería *f* treasury. ~**ero** *m* treasurer. ~**o** *m* treasure; (*tesorería*) treasury; (*libro*) thesaurus

testaferro *m* figurehead

testa|mento *m* will. **T~mento** (*Relig*) Testament. ~**r** *vi* make a will

testarudo *adj* stubborn
testículo *m* testicle
testi|ficar [7] *vt/i* testify. **~go** *m* witness. **~go ocular**, **~go presencial** eyewitness. **ser ~go de** witness. **~monio** *m* testimony
teta *f* tit (*fam o vulg*); (*de biberón*) teat
tétanos *m* tetanus
tetera *f* (*para el té*) teapot
tetilla *f* nipple; (*de biberón*) teat
tétrico *adj* gloomy
textil *adj & m* textile
text|o *m* text. **~ual** *adj* textual; (traducción) literal; (palabras) exact
textura *f* texture
tez *f* complexion
ti *pron* you
tía *f* aunt; [!] woman
tiara *f* tiara
tibio *adj* lukewarm
tiburón *m* shark
tiempo *m* time; (*atmosférico*) weather; (*Mus*) tempo; (*Gram*) tense; (*en partido*) half. **a su ~** in due course. **a ~** in time. **¿cuánto ~?** how long? **hace buen ~** the weather is fine. **hace ~** some time ago. **mucho ~** a long time. **perder el ~** waste time
tienda *f* shop (*esp Brit*), store (*esp Amer*); (*de campaña*) tent. **~ de comestibles**, **~ de ultramarinos** grocer's (shop) (*Brit*), grocery store (*Amer*)
tiene *vb véase* TENER
tienta. **andar a ~s** feel one's way
tierno *adj* tender; (*joven*) young
tierra *f* land; (*planeta, Elec*) earth; (*suelo*) ground; (*en geología*) soil, earth; (*LAm, polvo*) dust. **por ~** overland, by land
tieso *adj* stiff; (*engreído*) conceited
tiesto *m* flowerpot
tifón *m* typhoon
tifus *m* typhus; (*fiebre tifoidea*) typhoid (fever)
tigre *m* tiger. **~sa** *f* tigress
tijera *f*, **tijeras** *fpl* scissors; (*de jardín*) shears
tijeretear *vt* snip
tila *f* (*infusión*) lime tea
tild|ar *vt*. **~ar de** (*fig*) brand as. **~e** *f* tilde
tilo *m* lime(-tree)
timar *vt* swindle
timbal *m* kettledrum; (*Culin*) timbale, meat pie. **~es** *mpl* (*Mus*) timpani
timbr|ar *vt* stamp. **~e** *m* (*sello*) fiscal stamp; (*Mex*) postage stamp; (*Elec*) bell; (*sonido*) timbre
timidez *f* shyness
tímido *adj* shy
timo *m* swindle
timón *m* rudder; (*rueda*) wheel; (*fig*) helm
tímpano *m* eardrum
tina *f* tub. **~co** *m* (*Mex*) water tank. **~ja** *f* large earthenware jar
tinglado *m* mess; (*asunto*) racket
tinieblas *fpl* darkness; (*fig*) confusion
tino *f* good sense; (*tacto*) tact
tint|a *f* ink. **de buena ~a** on good authority. **~e** *m* dyeing; (*color*) dye; (*fig*) tinge. **~ero** *m* ink-well
tintinear *vi* tinkle; (vasos) chink, clink
tinto *adj* (vino) red
tintorería *f* dry cleaner's
tintura *f* dyeing; (*color*) dye
tío *m* uncle; [!] man. **~s** *mpl* uncle and aunt
tiovivo *m* merry-go-round

típico *adj* typical
tipo *m* type; (*fam, persona*) person; (*figura de mujer*) figure; (*figura de hombre*) build; (*Com*) rate
tip|ografía *f* typography. **~ográfico** *adj* typographic(al)
tira *f* strip. **la ~ de** lots of
tirabuzón *m* corkscrew; (*de pelo*) ringlet
tirad|a *f* distance; (*serie*) series; (*de periódico etc*) print-run. **de una ~a** in one go. **~o** *adj* (*barato*) very cheap; (*fam, fácil*) very easy. **~or** *m* (*asa*) handle
tiran|ía *f* tyranny. **~izar** 10 *vt* tyrannize. **~o** *adj* tyrannical. ● *m* tyrant
tirante *adj* tight; (*fig*) tense; (relaciones) strained. ● *m* strap. **~s** *mpl* braces (*esp Brit*), suspenders (*Amer*)
tirar *vt* throw; (*desechar*) throw away; (*derribar*) knock over; drop (bomba); fire (cohete); (*imprimir*) print. ● *vi* (*disparar*) shoot. **~ a** tend to (be); (*parecerse a*) resemble. **~ abajo** knock down. **~ de** pull. **a todo ~** at the most. **ir tirando** get by. **~se** *vpr* throw o.s.; (*tumbarse*) lie down
tirita *f* (sticking) plaster
tiritar *vi* shiver (**de** with)
tiro *m* throw; (*disparo*) shot. **~ libre** free kick. **a ~** within range. **errar el ~** miss. **pegarse un ~** shoot o.s.
tiroides *m* thyroid (gland)
tirón *m* tug. **de un ~** in one go
tirote|ar *vt* shoot at. **~o** *m* shooting
tisana *f* herb tea
tisú *m* (*pl* **~s, ~es**) tissue
títere *m* puppet. **~s** *mpl* puppet show
titilar *vi* (estrella) twinkle
titiritero *m* puppeteer; (*acróbata*) acrobat
titube|ante *adj* faltering; (*fig*) hesitant. **~ar** *vi* falter. **~o** *m* hesitation
titula|do *adj* (libro) entitled; (persona) qualified. **~r** *m* headline; (*persona*) holder. ● *vt* call. **~rse** *vpr* be called; (persona) graduate
título *m* title; (*académico*) qualification; (*Univ*) degree. **a ~ de** as, by way of
tiza *f* chalk
tiz|nar *vt* dirty. **~ne** *m* soot
toall|a *f* towel. **~ero** *m* towel-rail
tobillo *m* ankle
tobogán *m* slide; (*para la nieve*) toboggan
tocadiscos *m invar* record-player
toca|do *adj* touched !. ● *m* headdress. **~dor** *m* dressing-table. **~nte** *adj*. **en lo ~nte a** with regard to. **~r** 7 *vt* touch; (*palpar*) feel; (*Mus*) play; ring (timbre); (*mencionar*) touch on; (barco) stop at. ● *vi* ring; (*corresponder a uno*). **te ~ a ti** it's your turn. **en lo que ~ a** as for. **~rse** *vpr* touch; (personas); touch each other
tocayo *m* namesake
tocino *m* bacon
tocólogo *m* obstetrician
todavía *adv* still; (*con negativos*) yet. **~ no** not yet

todo , **toda**
● *adjetivo*
····➤ (*la totalidad*) all. **~ el vino** all the wine. **~s los edificios** all the buildings. **~ ese dinero** all that money. **~ el mundo**

everyone. (*como adv*) **está toda sucia** it's all dirty

....▸ (*entero*) whole. ~ **el día** the whole day, all day. **toda su familia** his whole family. ~ **el tiempo** the whole time, all the time

....▸ (*cada, cualquiera*) every. ~ **tipo de coche** every type of car. ~**s los días** every day

....▸ (*enfático*) **a toda velocidad** at top speed. **es** ~ **un caballero** he's a real gentleman

....▸ (*en locuciones*) **ante** ~ above all. **a** ~ **esto** meanwhile. **con** ~ even so. **del** ~ totally. ~ **lo contrario** quite the opposite

➡ Para expresiones como **todo recto, todo seguido** etc., ver bajo el respectivo adjetivo

● *pronombre*

....▸ all; (*todas las cosas*) everything. **eso es** ~ that's all. **lo perdieron** ~ they lost everything. **quiere comprar** ~ he wants to buy everything

....▸ **todos, todas** all; (*todo el mundo*) everyone. **los compró** ~**s** he bought them all, he bought all of them. ~**s queríamos ir** we all wanted to go. **vinieron** ~**s** everyone came

● *nombre masculino* **el**/**un** ~ the/a whole

toldo *m* awning

tolera|ncia *f* tolerance. ~**nte** *adj* tolerant. ~**r** *vt* tolerate

toma *f* taking; (*de universidad etc*) occupation; (*Med*) dose; (*de agua*) intake; (*Elec*) socket; (*LAm, acequia*) irrigation channel. ● *int* well!, fancy that! ~ **de corriente** power point. ~**dura** *f.* ~**dura de pelo** hoax. ~**r** *vt* take; catch (autobús, tren); occupy (universidad etc); (*beber*) drink, have; (*comer*) eat, have. ● *vi* take; (*esp LAm, beber*) drink; (*LAm, dirigirse*) go. ~**r a bien** take well. ~**r a mal** take badly. ~**r en serio** take seriously. ~**rla con uno** pick on s.o. ~**r por** take for. ~ **y daca** give and take. **¿qué va a** ~**r?** what would you like? ~**rse** *vpr* take; (*beber*) drink, have; (*comer*) eat, have

tomate *m* tomato

tomillo *m* thyme

tomo *m* volume

ton: **sin** ~ **ni son** without rhyme or reason

tonad|a *f* tune; (*canción*) popular song; (*LAm, acento*) accent. ~**illa** *f* tune

tonel *m* barrel. ~**ada** *f* ton. ~**aje** *m* tonnage

tónic|a *f* trend; (*bebida*) tonic water. ~**o** *adj* tonic; (sílaba) stressed. ● *m* tonic

tonificar 7 *vt* invigorate

tono *m* tone; (*Mus, modo*) key; (*color*) shade

tont|ería *f* silliness; (*cosa*) silly thing; (*dicho*) silly remark. **dejarse de** ~**erías** stop fooling around. ~**o** *adj* silly. ● *m* fool, idiot; (*payaso*) clown. **hacer el** ~**o** act the fool. **hacerse el** ~**o** act dumb

topacio *m* topaz

topar *vi.* ~ **con** run into

tope *adj* maximum. ● *m* end; (*de tren*) buffer; (*Mex, Auto*) speed bump. **hasta los** ~**s** crammed full. **ir a** ~ go flat out

tópico *adj* trite. **de uso** ~ (*Med*) for external use only. ● *m* cliché

topo *m* mole

topogr|afía *f* topography. **~áfico** *adj* topographical

toque *m* touch; (*sonido*) sound; (*de campana*) peal; (*de reloj*) stroke. **~ de queda** curfew. **dar los últimos ~s** put the finishing touches. **~tear** *vt* fiddle with

toquilla *f* shawl

tórax *m invar* thorax

torcer 2 & 9 *vt* twist; (*doblar*) bend; wring out (ropa). ● *vi* turn. **~se** *vpr* twist

tordo *adj* dapple grey. ● *m* thrush

tore|ar *vt* fight; (*evitar*) dodge. ● *vi* fight (bulls). **~o** *m* bullfighting. **~ro** *m* bullfighter

torment|a *f* storm. **~o** *m* torture. **~oso** *adj* stormy

tornado *m* tornado

tornasolado *adj* irridescent

torneo *m* tournament

tornillo *m* screw

torniquete *m* (*Med*) tourniquet; (*entrada*) turnstile

torno *m* lathe; (*de alfarero*) wheel. **en ~ a** around

toro *m* bull. **~s** *mpl* bullfighting. **ir a los ~s** go to a bullfight

> **(la fiesta de) los toros** *i*
> Bullfighting is popular in Spain and some Latin American countries. The season runs from March to October in Spain, from November to March in Latin America. The bullfighters who take part in a corrida gather in *cuadrillas*. The principal bullfighter or *matador* is assisted by *peones*.

toronja *f* (*LAm*) grapefruit

torpe *adj* clumsy; (*estúpido*) stupid

torpedo *m* torpedo

torpeza *f* clumsiness; (*de inteligencia*) slowness. **una ~** a blunder

torre *f* tower; (*en ajedrez*) castle, rook; (*Elec*) pylon; (*edificio*) tower block (*Brit*), apartment block (*Amer*)

torren|cial *adj* torrential. **~te** *m* torrent; (*circulatorio*) bloodstream; (*fig*) flood

tórrido *adj* torrid

torsión *f* twisting

torso *m* torso

torta *f* tart; (*LAm*, *de verduras*) pie; (*golpe*) slap, punch; (*Mex*, *bocadillo*) filled roll. **no entender ni ~** not understand a thing. **~zo** *m* slap, punch. **pegarse un ~zo** have a bad accident

tortícolis *f* stiff neck

tortilla *f* omelette; (*Mex*, *de maíz*) tortilla. **~ española** potato omelette. **~ francesa** plain omelette

tórtola *f* turtle-dove

tortuoso *adj* winding; (*fig*) devious

tortura *f* torture. **~r** *vt* torture

tos *f* cough. **~ ferina** whooping cough

tosco *adj* crude; (persona) coarse

toser *vi* cough

tost|ada *f* piece of toast. **~adas** *fpl* toast; (*Mex*, *de tortilla*) fried tortillas. **~ado** *adj* (pan) toasted; (café) roasted; (persona, color) tanned. **~ar** *vt* toast (pan); roast (café); tan (piel)

total *adj* total. ● *adv* after all. **~ que** so, to cut a long story short. ● *m* total; (*totalidad*) whole. **~idad** *f* whole. **~itario** *adj* totalitarian. **~izar** 10 *vt* total

tóxico *adj* toxic

toxi|cómano *m* drug addict. **~na** *f* toxin

t

tozudo *adj* stubborn

traba *f* catch; (*fig, obstáculo*) obstacle. **poner ~s a** hinder

trabaj|ador *adj* hard-working. ● *m* worker. **~ar** *vt* work; knead (masa). ● *vi* work (**de** as); (actor) act. **¿en qué ~as?** what do you do? **~o** *m* work. **costar ~o** be difficult. **~oso** *adj* hard

trabalenguas *m invar* tongue-twister

traba|r *vt* (*sujetar*) fasten; (*unir*) join; (*entablar*) strike up. **~rse** *vpr* get stuck. **trabársele la lengua** get tongue-tied

trácala *m* (*Mex*) cheat. ● *f* (*Mex*) trick

tracción *f* traction

tractor *m* tractor

tradici|ón *f* tradition. **~onal** *adj* traditional

traduc|ción *f* translation. **~ir** 47 *vt* translate (**a** into). **~tor** *m* translator

traer 41 *vt* bring; (*llevar*) carry; (*causar*) cause. **traérselas** be difficult

trafica|nte *m & f* dealer. **~r** 7 *vi* deal

tráfico *m* traffic; (*Com*) trade

traga|luz *m* skylight. **~perras** *f invar* slot-machine. **~r** 12 *vt* swallow; (*comer mucho*) devour; (*soportar*) put up with. **no lo trago** I can't stand him. **~rse** *vpr* swallow; (*fig*) swallow up

tragedia *f* tragedy

trágico *adj* tragic. ● *m* tragedian

trag|o *m* swallow, gulp; (*pequeña porción*) sip; (*fig, disgusto*) blow; (*LAm, bebida alcohólica*) drink. **echar(se) un ~o** have a drink. **~ón** *adj* greedy. ● *m* glutton.

trai|ción *f* treachery; (*Pol*) treason. **~cionar** *vt* betray. **~cionero** *adj* treacherous. **~dor** *adj* treacherous. ● *m* traitor

traigo *vb véase* TRAER

traje *m* dress; (*de hombre*) suit. **~ de baño** swimming-costume. **~ de etiqueta**, **~ de noche** evening dress. ● *vb véase* TRAER.

traj|ín *m* coming and going; (*ajetreo*) hustle and bustle. **~inar** *vi* bustle about

trama *f* weft; (*fig, argumento*) plot. **~r** *vt* weave; (*fig*) plot

tramitar *vt* negotiate

trámite *m* step. **~s** *mpl* procedure

tramo *m* (*parte*) section; (*de escalera*) flight

tramp|a *f* trap; (*fig*) trick. **hacer ~a** cheat. **~illa** *f* trapdoor

trampolín *m* trampoline; (*de piscina*) springboard; (*rígido*) diving board

tramposo *adj* cheating. ● *m* cheat

tranca *f* bar. **~r** *vt* bar

trance *m* moment; (*hipnótico etc*) trance

tranco *m* stride

tranquil|idad *f* peace; (*de espíritu*) peace of mind. **con ~** calmly. **~izar** 10 *vt* calm down; (*reconfortar*) reassure. **~o** *adj* calm; (lugar) quiet; (conciencia) clear. **estáte ~o** don't worry

transa|cción *f* transaction; (*acuerdo*) settlement. **~r** *vi* (*LAm*) compromise

transatlántico *adj* transatlantic. ● *m* (ocean) liner

transbord|ador *m* ferry. **~ar** *vt* transfer. **~o** *m* transfer. **hacer ~o** change (**en** at)

transcri|bir (*pp* **transcrito**) *vt* transcribe. **~pción** *f* transcription

transcur|rir *vi* pass. **~so** *m* course

transeúnte *m & f* passer-by

transfer|encia *f* transfer. **~ir** 4 *vt* transfer

transforma|ción *f* transformation. **~dor** *m* transformer. **~r** *vt* transform

transfusión *f* transfusion

transgre|dir *vt* transgress. **~sión** *f* transgression

transición *f* transition

transigir 14 *vi* give in, compromise

transistor *m* transistor

transita|ble *adj* passable. **~r** *vi* go

transitivo *adj* transitive

tránsito *m* transit; (*tráfico*) traffic

transitorio *adj* transitory

transmi|sión *f* transmission; (*radio, TV*) broadcast **~sor** *m* transmitter. **~sora** *f* broadcasting station. **~tir** *vt* transmit; (*radio, TV*) broadcast; (*fig*) pass on

transparen|cia *f* transparency. **~tar** *vt* show. **~te** *adj* transparent

transpira|ción *f* perspiration. **~r** *vi* transpire; (*sudar*) sweat

transport|ar *vt* transport. **~e** *m* transport. **empresa** *f* **de ~es** removals company

transversal *adj* transverse. **una calle ~ a la Gran Vía** a street which crosses the Gran Vía

tranvía *m* tram

trapear *vt* (*LAm*) mop

trapecio *m* trapeze; (*Math*) trapezium

trapo *m* cloth. **~s** *mpl* rags; (!, *ropa*) clothes **a todo ~** out of control

tráquea *f* windpipe, trachea

traquete|ar *vt* bang, rattle; (*persona*) rush around. **~o** *m* banging, rattle

tras *prep* after; (*detrás*) behind

trascende|ncia *f* significance; (*alcance*) implication. **~ntal** *adj* transcendental; (*importante*) important. **~r** 1 *vi* (*saberse*) become known; (*extenderse*) spread

trasero *adj* back, rear. ● *m* (*de persona*) bottom

trasfondo *m* background

traslad|ar *vt* move; transfer (empleado etc); (*aplazar*) postpone. **~o** *m* transfer; (*copia*) copy. (*mudanza*) removal. **dar ~o** notify

trasl|úcido *adj* translucent. **~ucirse** 11 *vpr* be translucent; (*dejarse ver*) show through; (*fig, revelarse*) be revealed. **~uz** *m*. **al ~uz** against the light

trasmano. a ~ out of the way

trasnochar *vt* (*acostarse tarde*) go to bed late; (*no acostarse*) stay up all night; (*no dormir*) be unable to sleep

traspas|ar *vt* go through; (*transferir*) transfer; go beyond (límite). **se ~a** for sale. **~o** *m* transfer

traspié *m* trip; (*fig*) slip. **dar un ~** stumble; (*fig*) slip up

trasplant|ar *vt* transplant. **~e** *m* transplant

trastada *f* prank; (*jugada*) dirty trick

traste *m* fret. **dar al ~ con** ruin. **ir al ~** fall through. **~s** *mpl* (*Mex*) junk

trastero *m* storeroom

trasto *m* piece of junk. ● **~s** *mpl* junk

trastorn|ado *adj* mad. **~ar** *vt* upset; (*volver loco*) drive mad; (*fig, fam, gustar mucho*) delight. **~arse**

vpr get upset; (*volverse loco*) go mad. **~o** *m* (*incl Med*) upset; (*Pol*) disturbance; (*fig*) confusion

trat|able *adj* friendly; (*Med*) treatable. **~ado** *m* treatise; (*acuerdo*) treaty. **~amiento** *m* treatment; (*título*) title. **~ante** *m & f* dealer. **~ar** *vt* (*incl Med*) treat; deal with (asunto etc); (*manejar*) handle; (*de tú, de Vd*) address (**de** as). • *vi* deal (with). **~ar con** have to do with; (*Com*) deal in. **~ar de** be about; (*intentar*) try. **¿de qué se ~a?** what's it about? **~o** *m* treatment; (*acuerdo*) agreement; (*título*) title; (*relación*) relationship. **¡~o hecho!** agreed! **~os** *mpl* dealings

traum|a *m* trauma. **~ático** *adj* traumatic

través: **a ~ de** through; (*de lado a lado*) crossways

travesaño *m* crossbeam; (*de portería*) crossbar

travesía *f* crossing; (*calle*) side-street

trav|esura *f* prank. **~ieso** *adj* (niño) mischievous, naughty

trayecto *m* (*tramo*) stretch; (*ruta*) route; (*viaje*) journey. **~ria** *f* trajectory; (*fig*) course

traz|a *f* (*aspecto*) appearance. **~as** *fpl* signs. **~ado** *m* plan. **~ar** 10 *vt* draw; (*bosquejar*) sketch. **~o** *m* stroke; (*línea*) line

t

trébol *m* clover. **~es** *mpl* (*en naipes*) clubs

trece *adj & m* thirteen

trecho *m* stretch; (*distancia*) distance; (*tiempo*) while. **a ~s** here and there. **de ~ en ~** at intervals

tregua *f* truce; (*fig*) respite

treinta *adj & m* thirty

tremendo *adj* terrible; (*extraordinario*) terrific

tren *m* train. **~ de aterrizaje** landing gear. **~ de vida** lifestyle

tren|cilla *f* braid. **~za** *f* braid; (*de pelo*) plait. **~zar** 10 *vt* plait

trepa|dor *adj* climbing. **~dora** *f* climber. **~r** *vt/i* climb. **~rse** *vpr*. **~rse a** climb (árbol); climb onto (silla etc)

tres *adj & m* three. **~cientos** *adj & m* three hundred. **~illo** *m* three-piece suite; (*Mus*) triplet

treta *f* trick

tri|angular *adj* triangular. **~ángulo** *m* triangle

trib|al *adj* tribal. **~u** *f* tribe

tribuna *f* platform; (*de espectadores*) stand. **~l** *m* court; (*de examen etc*) board; (*fig*) tribunal

tribut|ar *vt* pay. **~o** *m* tribute; (*impuesto*) tax

triciclo *m* tricycle

tricolor *adj* three-coloured

tricotar *vt/i* knit

tridimensional *adj* three-dimensional

trig|al *m* wheat field. **~o** *m* wheat

trigésimo *adj* thirtieth

trigueño *adj* olive-skinned; (pelo) dark blonde

trilla|do *adj* (*fig, manoseado*) trite; (*fig, conocido*) well-known. **~r** *vt* thresh

trilogía *f* trilogy

trimestr|al *adj* quarterly. **~e** *m* quarter; (*en enseñanza*) term

trin|ar *vi* warble. **estar que trina** be furious

trinchar *vt* carve

trinchera *f* ditch; (*Mil*) trench; (*abrigo*) trench coat

trineo *m* sledge

trinidad *f* trinity

trino *m* warble

trío *m* trio

tripa *f* intestine; (*fig*, *vientre*) tummy, belly. **~s** *fpl* (*de máquina etc*) parts, workings. **revolver las ~s** turn one's stomach

tripl|e *adj* triple. • *m*. **el ~e (de)** three times as much (as). **~icado** *adj*. **por ~icado** in triplicate. **~icar** 7 *vt* treble

tripula|ción *f* crew. **~nte** *m & f* member of the crew. **~r** *vt* man

tris *m*. **estar en un ~** be on the point of

triste *adj* sad; (paisaje, tiempo etc) gloomy; (*fig*, *insignificante*) miserable. **~za** *f* sadness

triturar *vt* crush

triunf|al *adj* triumphal. **~ante** *adj* triumphant. **~ar** *vi* triumph (**de, sobre** over). **~o** *m* triumph

trivial *adj* trivial. **~idad** *f* triviality

trizas. **hacer algo ~** smash sth to pieces. **hacerse ~** smash

trocear *vt* cut up, chop

trocha *f* narrow path; (*LAm*, *rail*) gauge

trofeo *m* trophy

tromba *f* whirlwind; (*marina*) waterspout. **~ de agua** heavy downpour

trombón *m* trombone

trombosis *f invar* thrombosis

trompa *f* horn; (*de orquesta*) French horn; (*de elefante*) trunk; (*hocico*) snout; (*en anatomía*) tube. **coger una ~** ! get drunk. **~zo** *m* bump

trompet|a *f* trumpet; (*músico*) trumpet player; (*Mil*) trumpeter. **~illa** *f* ear-trumpet

trompo *m* (*juguete*) (spinning) top

tronar *vt* (*Mex*) shoot. • *vi* thunder

tronchar *vt* bring down; (*fig*) cut short. **~se de risa** laugh a lot

tronco *m* trunk. **dormir como un ~** sleep like a log

trono *m* throne

trop|a *f* troops. **~el** *m* mob

tropez|ar 1 & 10 *vi* trip; (*fig*) slip up. **~ar con** run into. **~ón** *m* stumble; (*fig*) slip

tropical *adj* tropical

trópico *adj* tropical. • *m* tropic

tropiezo *m* slip; (*desgracia*) hitch

trot|ar *vi* trot. **~e** *m* trot; (*fig*) toing and froing. **al ~e** at a trot; (*de prisa*) in a rush. **de mucho ~e** hard-wearing

trozo *m* piece, bit. **a ~s** in bits

trucha *f* trout

truco *m* trick. **coger el ~** get the knack

trueno *m* thunder; (*estampido*) bang

trueque *m* exchange; (*Com*) barter

trufa *f* truffle

truhán *m* rogue

truncar 7 *vt* truncate; (*fig*) cut short

tu *adj* your

tú *pron* you

tuba *f* tuba

tubérculo *m* tuber

tuberculosis *f* tuberculosis

tub|ería *f* pipes; (*oleoducto etc*) pipeline. **~o** *m* tube. **~o de ensayo** test tube. **~o de escape** (*Auto*) exhaust (pipe). **~ular** *adj* tubular

tuerca *f* nut

tuerto *adj* one-eyed, blind in one eye. • *m* one-eyed person

tuétano *m* marrow; (*fig*) heart. **hasta los ~s** completely

t

tufo *m* stench
tugurio *m* hovel
tul *m* tulle
tulipán *m* tulip
tulli|do *adj* paralysed. **~r** 22 *vt* cripple
tumba *f* grave, tomb
tumb|ar *vt* knock over, knock down (estructura); (*fig, fam, en examen*) fail. **~arse** *vpr* lie down. **~o** *m* jolt. **dar un ~o** tumble. **~ona** *f* sun lounger
tumor *m* tumour
tumulto *m* turmoil; (*Pol*) riot
tuna *f* prickly pear; (*de estudiantes*) student band
tunante *m & f* rogue
túnel *m* tunnel
túnica *f* tunic
tupé *m* toupee; (*fig*) nerve
tupido *adj* thick
turba *f* peat; (*muchedumbre*) mob
turbado *adj* upset
turbante *m* turban
turbar *vt* upset; (*molestar*) disturb. **~se** *vpr* be upset
turbina *f* turbine
turbi|o *adj* cloudy; (vista) blurred; (asunto etc) shady. **~ón** *m* squall
turbulen|cia *f* turbulence; (*disturbio*) disturbance. **~te** *adj* turbulent
turco *adj* Turkish. ● *m* Turk; (*lengua*) Turkish
tur|ismo *m* tourism; (*coche*) car. **hacer ~** travel around. **~ cultural** heritage tourism. **~ patrimonial** (*LAm*) heritage tourism. **~ista** *m & f* tourist. **~ístico** *adj* tourist
turn|arse *vpr* take turns (**para** to). **~o** *m* turn; (*de trabajo*) shift. **de ~** on duty
turquesa *f* turquoise
Turquía *f* Turkey
turrón *m* nougat
tutear *vt* address as *tú*. **~se** *vpr* be on familiar terms
tutela *f* (*Jurid*) guardianship; (*fig*) protection
tutor *m* guardian; (*en enseñanza*) form master
tuve *vb véase* **TENER**
tuyo *adj & pron* yours. **un amigo ~** a friend of yours

Uu

u *conj* or
ubic|ar *vt* (*LAm*) place; (*localizar*) find. **~arse** *vpr* (*LAm*) be situated; (*orientarse*) find one's way around
ubre *f* udder
Ud. *abrev* (**Usted**) you
UE *abrev* (**Unión Europea**) EU
uf *int* phew!; (*de repugnancia*) ugh!
ufan|arse *vpr* be proud (**con, de** of); (*jactarse*) boast (**con, de** about). **~o** *adj* proud
úlcera *f* ulcer
últimamente *adv* (*recientemente*) recently; (*finalmente*) finally
ultim|ar *vt* complete; (*LAm, matar*) kill. **~átum** *m* ultimatum
último *adj* last; (*más reciente*) latest; (*más lejano*) furthest; (*más alto*) top; (*más bajo*) bottom; (*definitivo*) final. ● *m* last one. **estar en las últimas** be on one's last legs; (*sin dinero*) be down to one's last penny. **por ~** finally. **vestido a la última** dressed in the latest fashion

ultra *adj* ultra, extreme
ultraj|ante *adj* offensive. **~e** *m* insult, outrage
ultramar *m*. **de ~** overseas; (productos) foreign. **~inos** *mpl* groceries. **tienda de ~s** grocer's (shop) (*Brit*), grocery store (*Amer*)
ultranza. **a ~** (*con decisión*) decisively; (*extremo*) out-and-out
ultravioleta *adj invar* ultraviolet
umbilical *adj* umbilical
umbral *m* threshold

un, **una** *artículo indefinido*

! The masculine article **un** is also used before feminine nouns which begin with stressed **a** or **ha**, e.g. **un alma piadosa, un hada madrina**

····► (*en sing*) a; (*antes de sonido vocálico*) an. **un perro** a dog. **una hora** an hour
····► **unos, unas** (*cantidad incierta*) some. **compré ~os libros** I bought some books. (*cantidad cierta*) **tiene ~os ojos preciosos** she has beautiful eyes. **tiene ~os hijos muy buenos** her children are very good. (*en aproximaciones*) about. **en ~as 3 horas** in about 3 hours

➡ For further information see **uno**

un|ánime *adj* unanimous. **~animidad** *f* unanimity
undécimo *adj* eleventh
ungüento *m* ointment
únic|amente *adv* only. **~o** *adj* only; (*fig, incomparable*) unique
unicornio *m* unicorn
unid|ad *f* unit; (*cualidad*) unity. **~ad de disco** disk drive. **~o** *adj* united
unifica|ción *f* unification. **~r** **7** *vt* unite, unify
uniform|ar *vt* standardize. **~e** *adj* & *m* uniform. **~idad** *f* uniformity
unilateral *adj* unilateral
uni|ón *f* union; (*cualidad*) unity; (*Tec*) joint. **~r** *vt* join; mix (líquidos). **~rse** *vpr* join together; (caminos) converge; (compañías) merge
unísono *m* unison. **al ~** in unison
univers|al *adj* universal. **~idad** *f* university. **~itario** *adj* university. **~o** *m* universe

uno, **una**

● *adjetivo*

Note that **uno** becomes **un** before masculine nouns

one. **una peseta** one peseta. **un dólar** one dollar. **ni una persona** not one person, not a single person. **treinta y un años** thirty one years

● *pronombre*

····► one. **~ es mío** one (of them) is mine. **es la una** it's one o'clock. **se ayudan el ~ al otro** they help one another, they help each other. **lo que sienten el ~ por el otro** what they feel for each other
····► (*fam, alguien*) someone. **le pregunté a ~** I asked someone
····► **unos, unas** some. **no tenía vasos así es que le presté ~s** she didn't have any glasses so I lent her some. **a ~s les**

u

gusta, a otros no** some like it, others don't. **los ~s a los otros** one another, each other ····➤ (*impersonal*) you. **~ no sabe qué decir** you don't know what to say

untar *vt* grease; (*cubrir*) spread; (*fig, fam, sobornar*) bribe
uña *f* nail; (*de animal*) claw; (*casco*) hoof
uranio *m* uranium
Urano *m* Uranus
urban|idad *f* politeness. **~ismo** *m* town planning. **~ización** *f* development. **~izar** 10 *vt* develop. **~o** *adj* urban
urbe *f* big city
urdir *vt* (*fig*) plot
urg|encia *f* urgency; (*emergencia*) emergency. **~encias** A & E, (*Amer*) emergency room. **~ente** *adj* urgent; (carta) express. **~ir** 14 *vi* be urgent.
urinario *m* urinal
urna *f* urn; (*Pol*) ballot box
urraca *f* magpie
URSS *abrev* (*Historia*) USSR
Uruguay *m.* **el ~** Uruguay
uruguayo *adj & m* Uruguayan
us|ado *adj* (*con estar*) used; (ropa etc) worn; (*con ser*) secondhand. **~ar** *vt* use; (*llevar*) wear. **~arse** *vpr* (*LAm*) be in fashion. **~o** *m* use; (*costumbre*) custom. **al ~o de** in the style of
usted *pron* you. **~es** you
usual *adj* usual
usuario *adj* user
usur|a *f* usury. **~ero** *m* usurer
usurpar *vt* usurp
utensilio *m* utensil; (*herramienta*) tool
útero *m* womb, uterus
útil *adj* useful. **~es** *mpl* implements; (*equipo*) equipment
utili|dad *f* usefulness. **~dades** *fpl* (*LAm*) profits. **~zación** *f* use, utilization. **~zar** 10 *vt* use, utilize
utopía *f* Utopia
uva *f* grape. **~ pasa** raisin. **mala ~** bad mood

Vv

vaca *f* cow. **carne de ~** beef
vacaciones *fpl* holiday(s), vacation(s) (*Amer*). **de ~** on holiday, on vacation (*Amer*)
vacante *adj* vacant. ● *f* vacancy
vaciar 20 *vt* empty; (*ahuecar*) hollow out; (*en molde*) cast
vacila|ción *f* hesitation. **~nte** *adj* unsteady; (*fig*) hesitant. **~r** *vi* hesitate (🅸, *bromear*) tease; (*LAm, divertirse*) have fun
vacío *adj* empty; (*frívolo*) frivolous. ● *m* empty space; (*estado*) emptiness; (*en física*) vacuum; (*fig*) void
vacuna *f* vaccine. **~ción** *f* vaccination. **~r** *vt* vaccinate
vacuno *adj* bovine
vad|ear *vt* ford. **~o** *m* ford
vaga|bundear *vi* wander. **~bundo** *adj* vagrant; (perro) stray. **niño ~** street urchin. ● *m* tramp, vagrant. **~ncia** *f* vagrancy; (*fig*) laziness. **~r** 12 *vi* wander (about)
vagina *f* vagina
vago *adj* vague; (*holgazán*) lazy. ● *m* layabout
vag|ón *m* coach, carriage; (*de mer-*

u v

cancías) wagon. **~ón restaurante** dining-car. **~oneta** *f* small freight wagon; (*Mex, para pasajeros*) van

vaho *m* breath; (*vapor*) steam. **~s** *mpl* inhalation

vain|a *f* sheath; (*de semillas*) pod. **~illa** *f* vanilla

vaiv|én *m* swinging; (*de tren etc*) rocking. **~enes** *mpl* (*fig, de suerte*) swings

vajilla *f* dishes, crockery

vale *m* voucher; (*pagaré*) IOU. **~dero** *adj* valid

valenciano *adj* from Valencia

valentía *f* bravery, courage

valer 42 *vt* be worth; (*costar*) cost; (*fig, significar*) mean. • *vi* be worth; (*costar*) cost; (*servir*) be of use; (*ser valedero*) be valid; (*estar permitido*) be allowed. **~ la pena** be worthwhile, be worth it. **¿cuánto vale?** how much is it? **no ~ para nada** be useless. **eso no me vale** (*Mex, fam*) I don't give a damn about that. **¡vale!** all right!, OK! !

valeroso *adj* courageous

valgo *vb véase* **VALER**

valía *f* worth

validez *f* validity. **dar ~ a** validate

válido *adj* valid

valiente *adj* brave; (*en sentido irónico*) fine. • *m* brave person

valija *f* suitcase. **~ diplomática** diplomatic bag

valioso *adj* valuable

valla *f* fence; (*en atletismo*) hurdle

valle *m* valley

val|or *m* value, worth; (*coraje*) courage. **objetos** *mpl* **de ~or** valuables. **sin ~or** worthless. **~ores** *mpl* securities. **~oración** *f* valuation. **~orar** *vt* value

vals *m invar* waltz

válvula *f* valve

vampiro *m* vampire

vanagloriarse *vpr* boast

vandalismo *m* vandalism

vándalo *m & f* vandal

vanguardia *f* vanguard. **de ~** (*en arte, música etc*) avant-garde

van|idad *f* vanity. **~idoso** *adj* vain. **~o** *adj* vain; (*inútil*) futile; (palabras) empty. **en ~** in vain

vapor *m* steam, vapour; (*Naut*) steamer. **al ~** (*Culin*) steamed. **~izador** *m* vaporizer. **~izar** 10 vaporize

vaquer|o *m* cowherd, cowboy. **~os** *mpl* jeans

vara *f* stick; (*de autoridad*) staff (*medida*) yard

varar *vi* run aground

varia|ble *adj & f* variable. **~ción** *f* variation. **~do** *adj* varied. **~nte** *f* variant; (*Auto*) by-pass. **~ntes** *fpl* hors d'oeuvres. **~r** 20 *vt* change; (*dar variedad a*) vary. • *vi* vary; (*cambiar*) change

varicela *f* chickenpox

variedad *f* variety

varilla *f* stick; (*de metal*) rod

varios *adj* several

varita *f* wand

variz *f* (*pl* **varices**, (*LAm*) **várices**) varicose vein

var|ón *adj* male. • *m* man; (*niño*) boy. **~onil** *adj* manly

vasco *adj & m* Basque

vaselina *f* Vaseline (P), petroleum jelly

vasija *f* vessel, pot

vaso *m* glass; (*en anatomía*) vessel

vástago *m* shoot; (*descendiente*) descendant

vasto *adj* vast
vaticin|ar *vt* forecast. **~io** *m* prediction, forecast
vatio *m* watt
vaya *vb véase* **IR**
Vd. *abrev* (**Usted**) you
vecin|al *adj* local. **~dad** *f* neighbourhood; (*vecinos*) residents; (*Mex, edificio*) tenement house. **~dario** *m* neighbourhood; (*vecinos*) residents. **~o** *adj* neighbouring. ● *m* neighbour; (*de barrio, edificio*) resident
ve|da *f* close season. **~do** *m* reserve. **~do de caza** game reserve. **~r** *vt* prohibit
vega *f* fertile plain
vegeta|ción *f* vegetation. **~l** *adj & m* plant, vegetable. **~r** *vi* grow; (persona) vegetate. **~riano** *adj & m* vegetarian
vehemente *adj* vehement
vehículo *m* vehicle
veinte *adj & m* twenty
veinti|cinco *adj & m* twenty-five. **~cuatro** *adj & m* twenty-four. **~dós** *adj & m* twenty-two. **~nueve** *adj & m* twenty-nine; **~ocho** *adj & m* twenty-eight. **~séis** *adj & m* twenty-six. **~siete** *adj & m* twenty-seven. **~trés** *adj & m* twenty-three. **~uno** *adj & m* (*delante de nombre masculino* **veintiún**) twenty-one
vejación *f* humiliation
vejar *vt* ill-treat
veje|storio *m* old crock; (*LAm, cosa*) old relic. **~z** *f* old age
vejiga *f* bladder
vela *f* (*Naut*) sail; (*de cera*) candle; (*vigilia*) vigil. **pasar la noche en ~** have a sleepless night
velada *f* evening
vela|do *adj* veiled; (*Foto*) exposed. **~r** *vt* watch over; hold a wake over (difunto); (*encubrir*) veil; (*Foto*) expose. ● *vi* stay awake. **~r por** look after. **~rse** *vpr* (*Foto*) get exposed
velero *m* sailing-ship
veleta *f* weather vane
vell|o *m* hair; (*pelusa*) down. **~ón** *m* fleece
velo *m* veil
veloc|idad *f* speed; (*Auto, Mec*) gear. **a toda ~idad** at full speed. **~ímetro** *m* speedometer. **~ista** *m & f* sprinter
velódromo *m* cycle-track
veloz *adj* fast, quick
vena *f* vein; (*en madera*) grain. **estar de/en ~** be in the mood
venado *m* deer; (*Culin*) venison
vencedor *adj* winning. ● *m* winner
venc|er **9** *vt* defeat; (*superar*) overcome. ● *vi* win; (pasaporte) expire. **~erse** *vpr* collapse; (*LAm, pasaporte*) expire. **~ido** *adj* beaten; (pasaporte) expired; (*Com, atrasado*) in arrears. **darse por ~ido** give up. **~imiento** *m* due date; (*de pasaporte*) expiry date
venda *f* bandage. **~je** *m* dressing. **~r** *vt* bandage
vendaval *m* gale
vende|dor *adj* selling. ● *m* seller; (*en tienda*) salesperson. **~dor ambulante** pedlar. **~r** *vt* sell. **se ~** for sale. **~rse** *vpr* (persona) sell out
vendimia *f* grape harvest
veneciano *adj* Venetian
veneno *m* poison; (*malevolencia*) venom. **~so** *adj* poisonous
venera|ble *adj* venerable. **~ción** *f* reverence. **~r** *vt* revere
venéreo *adj* venereal

venezolano *adj & m* Venezuelan
Venezuela *f* Venezuela
venga|nza *f* revenge. **~r** 12 *vt* avenge. **~rse** *vpr* take revenge (**de, por** for) (**en** on). **~tivo** *adj* vindictive
vengo *vb véase* **VENIR**
venia *f* (*permiso*) permission. **~l** *adj* venial
veni|da *f* arrival; (*vuelta*) return. **~dero** *adj* coming. **~r** 53 *vi* come. **~r bien** suit. **la semana que viene** next week. **¡venga!** come on!
venta *f* sale; (*posada*) inn. **en ~** for sale
ventaj|a *f* advantage. **~oso** *adj* advantageous
ventan|a *f* (*inc informática*) window; (*de la nariz*) nostril. **~illa** *f* window
ventarrón *m* [I] strong wind
ventila|ción *f* ventilation. **~dor** *m* fan. **~r** *vt* air
vent|isca *f* blizzard. **~olera** *f* gust of wind. **~osa** *f* sucker. **~osidad** *f* wind, flatulence. **~oso** *adj* windy
ventrílocuo *m* ventriloquist
ventur|a *f* happiness; (*suerte*) luck. **a la ~a** with no fixed plan. **echar la buena ~a a uno** tell s.o.'s fortune. **por ~a** fortunately; (*acaso*) perhaps. **~oso** *adj* happy, lucky
Venus *m* Venus
ver 43 *vt* see; watch (televisión). • *vi* see. **a mi modo de ~** in my view. **a ~** let's see. **dejarse ~** show. **no lo puedo ~** I can't stand him. **no tener nada que ~ con** have nothing to do with. **vamos a ~** let's see. **ya lo veo** that's obvious. **ya ~emos** we'll see. **~se** *vpr* see o.s.; (*encontrarse*) find o.s.; (dos personas) meet; (*LAm, parecer*) look
veran|eante *m & f* holidaymaker, vacationer (*Amer*). **~ear** *vi* spend one's summer holiday. **~eo** *m*. **ir de ~eo** spend one's summer holiday. **lugar** *m* **de ~eo** summer resort. **~iego** *adj* summer. **~o** *m* summer
vera|s. de ~ really; (*verdadero*) real. **~z** *adj* truthful
verbal *adj* verbal
verbena *f* (*fiesta*) fair; (*baile*) dance
verbo *m* verb. **~so** *adj* verbose
verdad *f* truth. **¿~?** isn't it?, aren't they?, won't it? etc. **a decir ~** to tell the truth. **de ~** really. **~eramente** *adv* really. **~ero** *adj* true; (*fig*) real
verd|e *adj* green; (fruta) unripe; (chiste) dirty. • *m* green; (*hierba*) grass. **~or** *m* greenness
verdugo *m* executioner; (*fig*) tyrant
verdu|lería *f* greengrocer's (shop). **~lero** *m* greengrocer
vereda *f* path; (*LAm, acera*) pavement (*Brit*), sidewalk (*Amer*)
veredicto *m* verdict
verg|onzoso *adj* shameful; (*tímido*) shy. **~üenza** *f* shame; (*bochorno*) embarrassment. **¡es una ~üenza!** it's a disgrace! **me da ~üenza** I'm ashamed/embarrassed. **tener ~üenza** be ashamed/embarrassed
verídico *adj* true
verifica|ción *f* verification. **~r** 7 *vt* check. **~rse** *vpr* take place; (*resultar verdad*) come true
verja *f* (*cerca*) railings; (*puerta*) iron gate

vermú *m*, **vermut** *m* vermouth
verosímil *adj* likely; (relato) credible
verruga *f* wart
versa|do *adj* versed. **~r** *vi*. **~ sobre** deal with
versátil *adj* versatile; (*fig*) fickle
versión *f* version; (*traducción*) translation
verso *m* verse; (*poema*) poem
vértebra *f* vertebra
verte|dero *m* dump; (*desagüe*) drain **~r** **1** *vt* pour; (*derramar*) spill ● *vi* flow
vertical *adj* & *f* vertical
vértice *f* vertex
vertiente *f* slope
vertiginoso *adj* dizzy
vértigo *m* (*Med*) vertigo. **dar ~** make dizzy
vesícula *f* vesicle. **~ biliar** gall bladder
vespertino *adj* evening
vestíbulo *m* hall; (*de hotel, teatro*) foyer
vestido *m* dress
vestigio *m* trace. **~s** *mpl* remains
vest|imenta *f* clothes. **~ir** **5** *vt* (*llevar*) wear; dress (niño etc). ● *vi* dress. **~ir de** wear. **~irse** *vpr* get dressed. **~irse de** wear; (*disfrazarse*) dress up as. **~uario** *m* wardrobe; (*en gimnasio etc*) changing room (*Brit*), locker room (*Amer*)
vetar *vt* veto
veterano *adj* veteran
veterinari|a *f* veterinary science. **~o** *adj* veterinary. ● *m* vet **!**, veterinary surgeon (*Brit*), veterinarian (*Amer*)
veto *m* veto
vez *f* time; (*turno*) turn. **a la ~** at the same time. **alguna ~** sometimes; (*en preguntas*) ever. **algunas veces** sometimes. **a su ~** in turn. **a veces** sometimes. **cada ~** each time. **cada ~ más** more and more. **de una ~** in one go. **de una ~ para siempre** once and for all. **de ~ en cuando** from time to time. **dos veces** twice. **en ~ de** instead of. **érase una ~, había una ~** once upon a time there was. **otra ~** again. **pocas veces, rara ~** seldom. **una ~ (que)** once
vía *f* road; (*Rail*) line; (*en anatomía*) tract; (*fig*) way. **~ férrea** railway (*Brit*), railroad (*Amer*). **~ rápida** fast lane. **estar en ~s de** be in the process of. ● *prep* via. **~ aérea** by air. **~ de comunicación** means of communication.
viab|ilidad *f* viability. **~le** *adj* viable
viaducto *m* viaduct
viaj|ante *m* & *f* commercial traveller. **~ar** *vi* travel. **~e** *m* journey; (*corto*) trip. **~e de novios** honeymoon. **¡buen ~e!** have a good journey!. **estar de ~** be away. **salir de ~** go on a trip. **~ero** *m* traveller; (*pasajero*) passenger
víbora *f* viper
vibra|ción *f* vibration. **~nte** *adj* vibrant. **~r** *vt/i* vibrate
vicario *m* vicar
viceversa *adv* vice versa
vici|ado *adj* (texto) corrupt; (aire) stale. **~ar** *vt* corrupt; (*estropear*) spoil. **~o** *m* vice; (*mala costumbre*) bad habit. **~oso** *adj* dissolute; (círculo) vicious
víctima *f* victim; (*de un accidente*) casualty
victori|a *f* victory. **~oso** *adj* victorious
vid *f* vine

V

vida *f* life; (*duración*) lifetime. **¡~ mía!** my darling! **de por ~** for life. **en mi ~** never (in my life). **estar con ~** be still alive

vídeo *m*, (*LAm*) **video** *m* video; (*cinta*) videotape; (*aparato*) video recorder

videojuego *m* video game

vidri|era *f* stained glass window; (*puerta*) glass door; (*LAm, escaparate*) shop window. **~ería** *f* glass works. **~ero** *m* glazier. **~o** *m* glass; (*LAm, en ventana*) window pane. **limpiar los ~os** clean the windows. **~oso** *adj* glassy

vieira *f* scallop

viejo *adj* old. • *m* old person

viene *vb véase* **VENIR**

viento *m* wind. **hacer ~** be windy

vientre *m* stomach; (*cavidad*) abdomen; (*matriz*) womb; (*intestino*) bowels; (*de vasija etc*) belly

viernes *m invar* Friday. **V~ Santo** Good Friday

viga *f* beam; (*de metal*) girder

vigen|cia *f* validity. **~te** *adj* valid; (ley) in force. **entrar en ~cia** come into force

vigésimo *adj* twentieth

vigía *f* watch-tower. • *m & f* (*persona*) lookout

vigil|ancia *f* vigilance. **~ante** *adj* vigilant. • *m & f* security guard; (*nocturno*) watchman. **~ar** *vt* keep an eye on. • *vi* be vigilant; (vigía) keep watch. **~ia** *f* vigil; (*Relig*) fasting

vigor *m* vigour; (*vigencia*) force. **entrar en ~** come into force. **~oso** *adj* vigorous

vil *adj* vile. **~eza** *f* vileness; (*acción*) vile deed

villa *f* (*casa*) villa; (*Historia*) town. **la V~** Madrid

villancico *m* (Christmas) carol

villano *adj* villanous; (*Historia*) peasant

vilo. **en ~** in the air

vinagre *m* vinegar. **~ra** *f* vinegar bottle. **~ras** *fpl* cruet. **~ta** *f* vinaigrette

vincular *vt* bind

vínculo *m* tie, bond

vindicar **7** *vt* (*rehabilitar*) vindicate

vine *vb véase* **VENIR**

vinicult|or *m* wine-grower. **~ura** *f* wine growing

vino *m* wine. **~ de la casa** house wine. **~ de mesa** table wine. **~ tinto** red wine

viñ|a *f* vineyard. **~atero** *m* (*LAm*) wine-grower. **~edo** *m* vineyard

viola *f* viola

viola|ción *f* violation; (*de una mujer*) rape. **~r** *vt* violate; break (ley); rape (mujer)

violen|cia *f* violence; (*fuerza*) force. **~tarse** *vpr* get embarrassed. **~to** *adj* violent; (*fig*) awkward

violeta *adj invar & f* violet

viol|ín *m* violin. • *m & f* (*músico*) violinist. **~inista** *m & f* violinist. **~ón** *m* double bass. **~onc(h)elista** *m & f* cellist. **~onc(h)elo** *m* cello

vira|je *m* turn. **~r** *vt* turn. • *vi* turn; (*fig*) change direction. **~r bruscamente** swerve

virg|en *adj*. **ser ~en** be a virgin. • *f* virgin. **~inal** *adj* virginal. **~inidad** *f* virginity

Virgo *m* Virgo

viril *adj* virile. **~idad** *f* virility

virtu|al *adj* virtual. **~d** *f* virtue; (*capacidad*) power. **en ~ de** by virtue of. **~oso** *adj* virtuous. • *m* virtuoso

viruela *f* smallpox

virulento *adj* virulent

virus *m invar* virus

visa *f* (*LAm*) visa. **~ado** *m* visa. **~r** *vt* endorse

vísceras *fpl* entrails

viscoso *adj* viscous

visera *f* visor; (*de gorra*) peak

visib|ilidad *f* visibility. **~le** *adj* visible

visillo *m* (*cortina*) net curtain

visi|ón *f* vision; (*vista*) sight. **~onario** *adj & m* visionary

visita *f* visit; (*visitante*) visitor; (*invitado*) guest; (*Internet*) hit. **~nte** *m & f* visitor. **~r** *vt* visit

vislumbrar *vt* glimpse

viso *m* sheen; (*aspecto*) appearance

visón *m* mink

visor *m* viewfinder

víspera *f* day before, eve

vista *f* sight, vision; (*aspecto, mirada*) look; (*panorama*) view. **apartar la ~** look away. **a primera ~**, **a simple ~** at first sight. **con ~s a** with a view to. **en ~ de** in view of. **estar a la ~** be obvious. **hacer la ~ gorda** turn a blind eye. **perder la ~** lose one's sight. **tener a la ~** have in front of one. **volver la ~ atrás** look back. **~zo** *m* glance. **dar/echar un ~zo a** glance at

V

visto *adj* seen; (*poco original*) common (*considerado*) considered. **~ que** since. **bien ~** acceptable. **está ~ que** it's obvious that. **mal ~** unacceptable. **por lo ~** apparently. ● *vb véase* VESTIR. **~ bueno** *m* approval. **~so** *adj* colourful, bright

visual *adj* visual. **campo ~** field of vision

vital *adj* vital. **~icio** *adj* life; (cargo) held for life. **~idad** *f* vitality

vitamina *f* vitamin

viticult|or *m* wine-grower. **~ura** *f* wine growing

vitorear *vt* cheer

vítreo *adj* vitreous

vitrina *f* showcase; (*en casa*) glass cabinet; (*LAm, escaparate*) shop window

viud|a *f* widow. **~ez** *f* widowhood. **~o** *adj* widowed. ● *m* widower

viva *m* cheer. **~cidad** *f* liveliness. **~mente** *adv* vividly. **~z** *adj* lively

víveres *mpl* supplies

vivero *m* nursery; (*de peces*) hatchery; (*de moluscos*) bed

viveza *f* vividness; (*de inteligencia*) sharpness; (*de carácter*) liveliness

vívido *adj* vivid

vividor *m* pleasure seeker

vivienda *f* housing; (*casa*) house; (*piso*) flat (*Brit*), apartment (*esp Amer*). **sin ~** homeless

viviente *adj* living

vivificar **7** *vt* (*animar*) enliven

vivir *vt* live through. ● *vi* live; (*estar vivo*) be alive. **¡viva!** hurray! **¡viva el rey!** long live the king! ● *m* life. **~ de** live on. **de mal ~** dissolute

vivisección *f* vivisection

vivo *adj* alive; (*viviente*) living; (color) bright; (*listo*) clever; (*fig*) lively. ● *m* sharp operator

vocab|lo *m* word. **~ulario** *m* vocabulary

vocación *f* vocation

vocal *adj* vocal. ● *f* vowel. ● *m & f* member. **~ista** *m & f* vocalist

voce|ar *vt* call (mercancías); (*fig*)

proclaim; (*Mex*) page (persona). ● *vi* shout. **~río** *m* shouting. **~ro** (*LAm*) spokeperson

vociferar *vi* shout

vola|dor *adj* flying. ● *m* rocket. **~ndas**. **en ~ndas** in the air. **~nte** *adj* flying. ● *m* (*Auto*) steering-wheel; (*nota*) note; (*rehilete*) shuttlecock. **~r** **2** *vt* blow up. ● *vi* fly; (*fam*, *desaparecer*) disappear

volátil *adj* volatile

volcán *m* volcano. **~ico** *adj* volcanic

volcar **2** & **7** *vt* knock over; (*vaciar*) empty out; turn over (molde). ● *vi* overturn. **~se** *vpr* fall over; (vehículo) overturn; (*fig*) do one's utmost. **~se en** throw o.s. into

vóleibol *m*, (*Mex*) **volibol** *m* volleyball

voltaje *m* voltage

volte|ar *vt* turn over; (*en el aire*) toss; ring (campanas); (*LAm*) turn over (colchón etc). **~arse** *vpr* (*LAm*) turn around; (carro) overturn. **~reta** *f* somersault

voltio *m* volt

voluble *adj* (*fig*) fickle

volum|en *m* volume. **~inoso** *adj* voluminous

voluntad *f* will; (*fuerza de voluntad*) willpower; (*deseo*) wish; (*intención*) intention. **buena ~** goodwill. **mala ~** ill will

voluntario *adj* voluntary. ● *m* volunteer

voluptuoso *adj* voluptuous

volver **2** (*pp* **vuelto**) *vt* turn; (*de arriba a abajo*) turn over; (*devolver*) restore. ● *vi* return; (*fig*) revert. **~ a hacer algo** do sth again. **~ en sí** come round. **~se** *vpr* turn round; (*hacerse*) become

vomit|ar *vt* bring up. ● *vi* be sick, vomit. **~ivo** *adj* disgusting

vómito *m* vomit; (*acción*) vomiting

voraz *adj* voracious

vos *pron* (*LAm*) you. **~otros** *pron* you; (*reflexivo*) yourselves

vot|ación *f* voting; (*voto*) vote. **~ante** *m* & *f* voter. **~ar** *vt* vote for. ● *vi* vote (**por** for). **~o** *m* vote; (*Relig*) vow

voy *vb véase* **IR**

voz *f* voice; (*rumor*) rumour; (*palabra*) word. **~ pública** public opinion. **a media ~** softly. **a una ~** unanimously. **dar voces** shout. **en ~ alta** loudly

vuelco *m* upset. **el corazón me dio un ~** my heart missed a beat

vuelo *m* flight; (*acción*) flying; (*de ropa*) flare. **al ~** in flight; (*fig*) in passing

vuelta *f* turn; (*curva*) bend; (*paseo*) walk; (*revolución*) revolution; (*regreso*) return; (*dinero*) change. **a la ~** on one's return. **a la ~ de la esquina** round the corner. **dar la ~ al mundo** go round the world. **dar una ~** go for a walk. **estar de ~** be back

vuelvo *vb véase* **VOLVER**

vuestro *adj* your. ● *pron* yours. **un amigo ~** a friend of yours

vulg|ar *adj* vulgar; (persona) common. **~aridad** *f* vulgarity. **~arizar** **10** *vt* popularize. **~o** *m* common people

vulnerable *adj* vulnerable

Ww

wáter /'(g)water/ *m* toilet
Web *m* /'(g)web/. **el ~** the Web
whisky /'(g)wiski/ *m* whisky

Xx

xenofobia *f* xenophobia
xilófono *m* xylophone

Yy

y *conj* and
ya *adv* already; (*ahora*) now; (*con negativos*) any more; (*para afirmar*) yes, sure; (*en seguida*) immediately; (*pronto*) soon. **~ mismo** (*LAm*) right away. • *int* of course! **~ no** no longer. **~ que** since. **¡~, ~!** oh sure!
yacaré *m* (*LAm*) alligator
yac|er 44 *vi* lie. **~imiento** *m* deposit; (*de petróleo*) oilfield
yanqui *m & f* American, Yank(ee)
yate *m* yacht
yegua *f* mare
yelmo *m* helmet
yema *f* (*en botánica*) bud; (*de huevo*) yolk; (*golosina*) sweet. **~ del dedo** fingertip
yerba *f* (*LAm*) grass; (*Med*) herb
yergo *vb véase* **ERGUIR**
yermo *adj* uninhabited; (*no cultivable*) barren. • *m* wasteland
yerno *m* son-in-law
yerro *m* mistake. • *vb véase* **ERRAR**
yeso *m* plaster; (*mineral*) gypsum
yo *pron* I. **~ mismo** myself. **¿quién, ~?** who, me? **soy ~** it's me
yodo *m* iodine
yoga *m* yoga
yogur *m* yog(h)urt
yuca *f* yucca
yugo *m* yoke
Yugoslavia *f* Yugoslavia
yugoslavo *adj & m* Yugoslav
yunque *m* anvil
yunta *f* yoke

Zz

zafarrancho *m* (*confusión*) mess; (*riña*) quarrel
zafarse *vpr* escape; get out of (obligación etc); (*Mex, dislocarse*) dislocate
zafiro *m* sapphire
zaga *f* rear; (*en deportes*) defence. **a la ~** behind
zaguán *m* hall
zaherir 4 *vt* hurt
zahorí *m* dowser
zaino *adj* (caballo) chestnut; (vaca) black
zalamer|ía *f* flattery. **~o** *adj* flattering. • *m* flatterer
zamarra *f* (*piel*) sheepskin; (*prenda*) sheepskin jacket

w x y z

zamarrear *vt* shake

zamba *f* South American dance

zambulli|da *f* dive; (*baño*) dip. **~rse** *vpr* dive

zamparse *vpr* gobble up

zanahoria *f* carrot

zancad|a *f* stride. **~illa** *f* trip. **hacer una ~illa a uno** trip s.o. up

zanc|o *m* stilt. **~udo** *adj* long-legged; (ave) wading. • *m* (*LAm*) mosquito

zanganear *vi* idle

zángano *m* drone. • *m & f* (*persona*) idler

zangolotear *vt* shake. • *vi* rattle; (persona) fidget

zanja *f* ditch; (*para tuberías etc*) trench. **~r** *vt* (*fig*) settle

zapat|ear *vi* tap with one's feet. **~ería** *f* shoe shop; (*arte*) shoemaking. **~ero** *m* shoemaker; (*el que remienda zapatos*) cobbler. **~illa** *f* slipper; (*de deportes*) trainer. **~illa de ballet** ballet shoe. **~o** *m* shoe

zarand|a *f* sieve. **~ear** *vt* (*sacudir*) shake

zarcillo *m* earring

zarpa *f* paw

zarpar *vi* set sail, weigh anchor

zarza *f* bramble. **~mora** *f* blackberry

zarzuela *f* Spanish operetta

> **i**
> **zarzuela** A musical drama consisting of alternating passages of dialogue, songs, choruses, and dancing that originated in Spain in the seventeenth century. Also popular in Latin America, its name derives from the Palacio de la Zarzuela, the Madrid palace where the Royal family now lives.

zigzag *m* zigzag. **~uear** *vi* zigzag

zinc *m* zinc

zócalo *m* skirting-board; (*pedestal*) plinth; (*Mex, plaza*) main square

zodiaco *m*, **zodíaco** *m* zodiac

zona *f* zone; (*área*) area

zoo *m* zoo. **~logía** *f* zoology. **~lógico** *adj* zoological

zoólogo *m* zoologist

zopenco *adj* stupid. • *m* idiot

zoquete *m* blockhead

zorr|a *f* vixen **~illo** *m* (*LAm*) skunk.. **~o** *m* fox

zorzal *m* thrush

zozobra *f* (*fig*) anxiety. **~r** *vi* founder

zueco *m* clog

zumb|ar *vt* **I** give (golpe etc). • *vi* buzz. **~ido** *m* buzzing

zumo *m* juice

zurci|do *m* darning. **~r** **9** *vt* darn

zurdo *adj* left-handed; (mano) left

zurrar *vt* (*fig, fam, dar golpes*) beat (up)

zutano *m* so-and-so

Phrasefinder

Useful phrases	Expresiones útiles
yes, please/no, thank you	sí, por favor/no, gracias
sorry	perdone
excuse me	disculpe
I'm sorry, I don't understand	perdone, pero no le entiendo
Meeting people	**Saludos**
hello/goodbye	hola/adiós
how are you?	¿cómo está usted?
nice to meet you	mucho gusto
Asking questions	**Preguntas**
do you speak English/Spanish?	¿habla usted inglés/español?
what's your name?	¿cómo se llama?
where are you from?	¿de dónde es?
how much is it?	¿cuánto es?
where is...?	¿dónde está…?
can I have...?	¿me da…?
would you like...?	¿quiere usted…?
Statements about yourself	**Información personal**
my name is...	me llamo…
I'm American/I'm Mexican	soy americano/-a/mexicano/-a
I don't speak Spanish/English	no hablo español/inglés
I live near Seville/Chester	vivo cerca de Sevilla/Chester
I'm a student	soy estudiante
I work in an office	trabajo en una oficina
Emergencies	**Emergencias**
can you help me, please?	¿me ayuda, por favor?
I'm lost	me he perdido
I'm ill	no me encuentro bien
call an ambulance	llamen a una ambulancia
Reading signs	**Carteles y señales**
no entry	prohibido el paso
no smoking	prohibido fumar
fire exit	salida de emergencia
for sale	en venta

❶ Going Places

On the road	Por carretera
where's the nearest garage/ petrol station, (*Amer*) gas station	¿dónde está el taller más cercano/ la gasolinera más cercana?
what's the best way to get there?	¿cuál es la mejor forma de llegar allí?
I've got a puncture	he pinchado, (*Mex*) se nos ponchó una llanta
I'd like to hire a bike/car	quisiera alquilar, (*Mex*) rentar una bicicleta/un coche
there's been an accident	ha habido un accidente
my car's broken down	se me ha estropeado el coche, (*LAm*) se me descompuso el carro
the car won't start	el coche no arranca

By rail	En tren
where can I buy a ticket?	¿dónde se sacan los billetes, (*LAm*) boletos?
what time is the next train to Barcelona/York?	¿a qué hora sale el próximo tren para Barcelona/York?
do I have to change?	¿tengo que hacer algún transbordo?
can I take my bike on the train?	¿puedo llevar la bicicleta en el tren?
which platform for the train to San Sebastian/Bath?	¿de qué andén sale el tren para San Sebastián/Bath?
there's a train to London at 10 o'clock	hay un tren que sale para Londres a las 10
a single/return to Leeds/Valencia, please	un billete, (*LAm*) boleto de ida/ida y vuelta para Leeds/Valencia, por favor
I'd like an all-day ticket	quiero un billete, (*LAm*) boleto que valga para todo el día
I'd like to reserve a seat	quisiera reservar una plaza

At the airport	**En el aeropuerto**
when's the next flight to Paris/Rome?	¿cuándo sale el próximo vuelo para París/Roma?
where do I check in?	¿dónde puedo facturar, (*LAm*) chequear, (*Mex*) registrar el equipaje?
I'd like to confirm my flight	quisiera confirmar mi vuelo
I'd like a window seat/an aisle seat	quisiera un asiento de ventanilla/pasillo
I want to change/cancel my reservation	quiero cambiar/cancelar mi reserva

Getting there	**Cómo llegar a los sitios**
could you tell me the way to the castle?	¿me podría decir cómo se llega al castillo?
how long will it take to get there?	¿cuánto tiempo se tarda en llegar?
how far is it from here?	¿a qué distancia está?
which bus do I take for the cathedral?	¿qué autobús debo tomar para ir a la catedral?
can you tell me where to get off?	¿podría decirme dónde me tengo que bajar?
what time is the last bus?	¿a qué hora sale el último autobús?
how do I get to the airport?	¿cómo se llega al aeropuerto?
where's the nearest underground station, (*Amer*) subway station?	¿dónde está la estación de metro más cercana?
can you call me a taxi?	¿me puede pedir un taxi?
take the first turning on the right	gire por la primera (calle) a la derecha
turn left at the traffic lights/just past the church	al llegar al semáforo/después de pasar la iglesia, gire a la izquierda
I'll take a taxi	tomaré un taxi

❷ Keeping in touch

On the phone	Por teléfono
where can I buy a phone card?	¿dónde puedo comprar una tarjeta para el teléfono?
may I use your phone?	¿puedo llamar por teléfono?
do you have a mobile, (*Amer*) cell phone?	¿tiene usted un móvil, (*LAm*) un celular?
what is the code for Alava/Cardiff?	¿cuál es el prefijo de Álava/Cardiff?
I want to make a phone call	quiero hacer una llamada
I'd like to reverse the charges, (*Amer*) call collect	quisiera hacer una llamada a cobro revertido, (*LAm*) una llamada por cobrar
the line's engaged/busy	está comunicando, (esp *LAm*) está ocupado
there's no answer	no contestan
hello, this is Natalia	hola, soy, (esp *LAm*) habla Natalia
is Juan there, please?	¿está Juan, por favor?
who's calling?	¿de parte de quién?
sorry, wrong number	perdone, se ha confundido
just a moment, please	un momento, por favor
would you like to hold?	¿quiere esperar?
please tell him/her I called	dígale que lo/la he llamado, por favor
I'd like to leave a message for him/her	quisiera dejarle un mensaje
...I'll try again later	lo/la volveré a llamar más tarde
please tell him/her that Maria called	dígale que lo/la ha llamado María, por favor
can he/she ring me back?	¿le puede decir que me llame?
my home number is...	mi número (de teléfono) es el...
my business number is...	el número del trabajo es el...
my fax number is...	mi número de fax es el...
we were cut off	se ha cortado

Cómo mantenerse en contacto ❷

Writing	Por carta
what's your address?	¿cuál es su dirección?
where is the nearest post office?	¿dónde está la oficina de correos más cercana?, (*LAm*) ¿dónde está el correo más cercano?
could I have a stamp for Argentina/Italy, please?	¿me da un sello, (*LAm*) una estampilla, (*Mex*) un timbre para Argentina/Italia, por favor?
I'd like to send a parcel/a telegram	quisiera mandar un paquete/telegrama

On line	En línea
are you on the Internet?	¿está conectado/-a a Internet?
what's your e-mail address?	¿cuál es su dirección de correo electrónico?
we could send it by e-mail	lo podríamos mandar por correo electrónico
I'll e-mail it to you on Tuesday	se lo mandaré por correo electrónico el martes
I looked it up on the Internet	lo he mirado en Internet
the information is on their website	la información está en su página web

Meeting up	Citas, encuentros
what shall we do this evening?	¿qué hacemos esta tarde?
where shall we meet?	¿dónde podemos encontrarnos?
I'll see you outside the café at 6 o'clock	nos vemos a las 6 en la puerta de la cafetería
see you later	hasta luego
I can't today, I'm busy	hoy no puedo, estoy ocupado/-a

❸ Food and Drink

Booking a restaurant	Reservar mesa en un restaurante
can you recommend a good restaurant?	¿me puede recomendar un buen restaurante?
I'd like to reserve a table for four	quisiera reservar una mesa para cuatro
a reservation for tomorrow evening at eight o'clock	una reserva para mañana a las ocho de la tarde

Ordering	Pedir la comida
could we see the menu/wine list, please?	¿nos enseña el menú/la carta de vinos, por favor?
do you have a vegetarian/children's menu?	¿tienen un menú especial para vegeterianos/niños?
as a starter... and to follow	de primero.. y de segundo…
could we have some more bread/rice?	¿nos puede traer más pan/arroz?
what would you recommend?	¿qué recomienda?
I'd like a ...white coffee ...black coffee ...a decaffeinated coffee ...a liqueur	Quisiera …un café con leche …café solo, (*LAm*) café negro …un café descafeinado …un licor
could I have the bill, (*Amer*) check	¿me trae la cuenta, por favor?

You will hear	Oirás
¿Ya han decidido lo que van a pedir?	Are you ready to order?
¿Quieren un aperitivo?	Would you like an aperitif?
¿Quieren entrada?	Would you like a starter?
¿Qué van a pedir de segundo plato?	What will you have for the main course?
¿Quieren postre?	Would you like a dessert?
¿Quieren café?/licores?	Would you like coffee?/liqueurs?
¿Algo más?	Anything else?
¡Buen provecho!	Enjoy your meal!
El servicio (no) está incluido.	Service is (not) included.

The menu

starters/entradas, (*Esp*) entrantes	
hors d'oeuvres	entremeses, (*Mex*) botanas
omelette	omelette, tortilla
soup	sopa
fish/pescado	
bass	lubina
cod	bacalao
eel	anguila
hake	merluza
herring	arenque
monk fish	rapé
mullet	mújol, (*LAm*) lisa
mussels	mejillones
oyster	ostra
prawns	gambas
salmon	salmón
sardines	sardinas
shrimps	gambas
sole	lenguado
squid	calamares
trout	trucha
tuna	atún
turbot	rodaballo
meat/carne	
beef	carne de vaca
chicken	pollo
duck	pato
goose	ganso
hare	liebre
ham	jamón
kidneys	riñones
lamb	cordero
liver	hígado
pork	cerdo
rabbit	conejo
steak	bistec, filete

La carta/El menú

entradas, (*Esp*) entrantes/starters	
entremeses, botanas (*Mex*)	hors d'oeuvres
omelette, tortilla	omelette
sopa	soup
pescado/fish	
anguila	eel
arenque	herring
atún	tuna
bacalao	cod
calamares	squid
camarones (*LAm*)	prawns, shrimps
gambas	prawns,
lenguado	sole
lisa (*LAm*)	mullet
lubina	bass
mejillones	mussels
merluza	hake
mújol	mullet
ostra, (*Mex*) ostión	oyster
rapé	monk fish
róbalo	bass
rodaballo	turbot
trucha	trout
carne/meat	
bistec, filete	steak
carne de vaca, de res (*Mex*)	beef
cerdo	pork
conejo	rabbit
cordero	lamb
ganso	goose
hígado	liver
jamón	ham
liebre	hare
pato	duck
pollo	chicken

❸ Food and Drink

tenderloin	lomo
turkey	pavo
veal	ternera
venison	venado
white meat	carne blanca

puerco (*Mex*)	pork
riñones	kidneys
solomillo (*Esp*)	sirloin steak
ternera	veal
venado	venison

vegetables/verduras

artichoke	alcachofa
asparagus	espárragos
aubergine	berenjena
beans	frijoles
carrots	zanahorias
cabbage	col, repollo
celery	apio
endive	endivia
lettuce	lechuga
mushrooms	champiñones
peas	guisantes, (*LAm*) arvejas
pepper	pimiento
potatoes	patatas, (*LAm*) papas
runner bean	habichuela
tomato	tomate, (*Mex*) jitomate
sweet potato	batata, camote (*LAm*)
zucchini	calabacines

verduras/vegetables

alcachofa	artichoke
arvejas (*LAm*)	peas
apio	celery
batata	sweet potato
berenjena	aubergine
camote (*LAm*)	sweet potato
cebollas	onions
champiñones	mushrooms
chícharos (*Mex*)	peas
col, repollo	cabbage
coliflor	cauliflower
espárragos	asparagus
frijoles	beans
guisantes	peas
haba	broad bean
jitomate (*Mex*)	tomato
papas	potatoes
patatas	potatoes
pimiento	pepper
zanahorias	carrots

the way it's cooked/cómo se prepara

boiled	cocido -da
roast	asado -da
fried	frito -ta
pureed	puré de
grilled	a la parilla
griddled	a la plancha
stewed	estofado -da, guisado -da
rare	poco hecho
well done	bien hecho

cómo se prepara/the way it's cooked

a la parilla	grilled
a la plancha	griddled
asado -da	roast
bien cocido	well done
bien hecho	well done
cocido -da	boiled
estofado -da	stewed
guisado -da	stewed
frito -ta	fried
poco hecho	rare

desserts/postres

ice cream	helados
fruits	fruta
pie	tarta, (*LAm*) pay
tart	tarta

other

bread	pan
butter	mantequilla
cheese	queso
cheeseboard	tabla de quesos
garlic	ajo
mayonnaise	mayonesa
mustard	mostaza
olive oil	aceite de oliva
pepper	pimienta
rice	arroz
salt	sal
sauce	salsa
seasoning	condimento
vinegar	vinagre

drinks/bebidas

beer	cerveza
bottle	botella
carbonated	con gas
half-bottle	media botella
liqueur	licor
mineral water	agua mineral
red wine	vino tinto
rosé	vino rosado
soft drink	bebida no alcohólica
still	sin gas
house wine	vino de la casa
table wine	vino de mesa
white wine	vino blanco
wine	vino

postres/desserts

fruta	fruit
helados	ice cream
pastel, (*LAm*) pay	pie
tarta	tart

otros

aceite de oliva	olive oil
ajo	garlic
arroz	rice
condimento	seasoning
mantequilla	butter
mayonesa	mayonnaise
mostaza	mustard
pan	bread
pimienta	pepper
queso	cheese
sal	salt
salsa	sauce
tabla de quesos	cheeseboard
vinagre	vinegar

bebidas/drinks

agua mineral	mineral water
bebida no alcohólica	soft drink
botella	botella
cerveza	beer
con gas	carbonated
licor	liqueur
media botella	half-bottle
sin gas	still
vino	wine
vino blanco	white wine
vino de la casa	house wine
vino de mesa	table wine
vino rosado	rosé
vino tinto	red wine

4 Places to stay

Camping	Campings
can we pitch our tent here?	¿podemos montar la tienda (de campaña) aquí?
can we park our caravan here?	¿podemos aparcar la caravana aquí?, (LAm) ¿podemos estacionar el tráiler aquí?
what are the facilities like?	¿cómo son las instalaciones?
how much is it per night?	¿cuánto cobran por (pasar la) noche?
where do we park the car?	¿dónde podemos aparcar, (esp *LAm*) estacionar?
we're looking for a campsite	estamos buscando un camping
this is a list of local campsites	ésta es una lista de los campings de la zona
we go on a camping holiday every year	todos los años pasamos las vacaciones en un camping

At the hotel	Hoteles
I'd like a double/single room with bath	quisiera una habitación individual/doble con baño
we have a reservation in the name of Morris	tenemos una reserva a nombre de Morris
we'll be staying three nights, from Friday to Sunday	nos quedaremos tres noches, de viernes a domingo
how much does the room cost?	¿cuánto cuesta la habitación?
I'd like to see the room	quisiera ver la habitación
what time is breakfast?	¿a qué hora se sirve el desayuno?
can I leave this in your safe?	¿puedo dejar esto en la caja fuerte?
bed and breakfast	(lugar donde dan) alojamiento y desayuno
we'd like to stay another night	nos gustaría quedarnos una noche más
please call me at 7:30	¿me podría despertar a las 7:30, por favor?
are there any messages for me?	¿hay algún mensaje para mí?

Hostels	Albergues
could you tell me where the youth hostel is?	¿me podría indicar dónde está el albergue?
what time does the hostel close?	¿a qué hora cierra el albergue?
I'll be staying in a hostel	me alojaré en un albergue
the hostel we're staying in is great value	el albergue donde nos alojamos ofrece una buena relación calidad-precio
I know a really good hostel in Dublin	conozco un albergue estupendo en Dublín
I'd like to go backpacking in Australia	me gustaría irme a Australia con la mochila al hombro

Rooms to rent	Alquiler de habitaciones
I'm looking for a room with a reasonable rent	quiero alquilar, (*Mex*) rentar una habitación que tenga un precio razonable
I'd like to rent an apartment for a few weeks	me gustaría alquilar, (*Mex*) rentar un apartamento para unas cuantas semanas
where do I find out about rooms to rent?	¿dónde me puedo informar sobre alquileres, (*Mex*) rentas de habitaciones?
what's the weekly rent?	¿cuánto cuesta el alquiler, (*Mex*) la renta semanal?
I'm staying with friends at the moment	en este momento estoy alojado en casa de unos amigos
I rent an apartment on the outskirts of town	vivo en un apartamento alquilado, (*Mex*) rentado en las afueras
the room's fine — I'll take it	la habitación está muy bien, me la quedo
the deposit is one month's rent in advance	como depósito, se paga un mes de alquiler, (*Mex*) renta por adelantado

❺ Shopping and money

At the bank	En el banco
I'd like to change some money	quisiera cambiar dinero
I want to change some dollars into euros	quisiera cambiar dólares a euros
do you take Eurocheques?	¿aceptan Eurocheques?
what's the exchange rate today?	¿a cuánto está hoy el cambio?
I prefer traveller's cheques, (*Amer*) traveler's checks to cash	prefiero cheques de viaje que dinero en metálico, (esp *LAm*) en efectivo
I'd like to transfer some money from my account	quisiera hacer una transferencia desde mi cuenta corriente
I'll get some money from the cash machine	sacaré dinero del cajero (automático)
I usually pay by direct debit, (*Amer*) direct billing	suelo domiciliar los pagos en mi cuenta, (*LAm*) acostumbro a pagar por débito bancario
I'm with another bank	no soy cliente/-a de este banco

Finding the right shop	Dar con la tienda adecuada
where's the main shopping district?	¿dónde está la zona de tiendas?
where can I buy batteries/postcards?	¿dónde puedo comprar unas pilas/postales?
where's the nearest pharmacy/bookshop?	¿dónde está la farmacia/librería más cercana?
is there a good food shop around here?	¿hay una buena tienda de comestibles por aquí?
what time do the shops open/close?	¿a qué hora abren/cierran las tiendas?
where did you get those?	¿dónde los/las ha comprado?
I'm looking for presents for my family	estoy buscando regalos para mi familia
we'll do our shopping on Saturday	(nosotros) haremos las compras el sábado
I love shopping	me encanta ir de compras

Las compras y el dinero 5

Are you being served?	¿Lo/La atienden?
how much does that cost?	¿cuánto cuesta?
can I try it on?	¿me lo puedo probar?
could you wrap it for me, please?	¿me lo envuelve, por favor?
can I pay by credit card/cheque, (*Amer*) check?	¿puedo pagar con tarjeta/cheque?
do you have this in another colour, (*Amer*) color?	¿tiene éste/-a en otro color?
could I have a bag, please?	¿me da una bolsa, por favor?
I'm just looking	sólo estoy mirando
I'll think about it	me lo voy a pensar
I'd like a receipt, please	¿me da el recibo, por favor?
I need a bigger/smaller size	necesito una talla más grande/más pequeña
I take a size 10/a medium	uso la talla 38/mediana
it doesn't suit me	no me queda bien
I'm sorry, I don't have any change/ anything smaller	perdone, pero no tengo cambio/ billetes más pequeños
that's all, thank you	nada más, gracias

Changing things	Devoluciones
can I have a refund?	¿me podría devolver el dinero?
can you mend it for me?	¿me lo/la podrían arreglar?
can I speak to the manager?	quisiera hablar con el encargado/la encargada
it doesn't work	no funciona
I'd like to change it, please	quisiera cambiarlo/-a, por favor
I bought this here yesterday	compré esto ayer

❻ Sport and leisure

Keeping fit	Mantenerse en forma
where can we play football/squash?	¿dónde se puede jugar al fútbol/ squash, (*LAm*) jugar fútbol/squash?
where is the local sports centre, (*Amer*) center?	¿dónde está el polideportivo?
what's the charge per day?	¿cuánto cobran (al día)?
is there a reduction for children/ a student discount?	¿hacen descuentos a niños/ estudiantes?
I'm looking for a swimming pool/ tennis court	estoy buscando una piscina, (*Mex*) alberca/un club de tenis
you have to be a member	(para entrar) hace falta ser socio
I play tennis on Mondays	los lunes juego al tenis, (*LAm*) juego tenis
I would like to go fishing/riding	me gustaría ir a pescar/montar a caballo
I want to do aerobics	quiero hacer aerobic
I love swimming/rollerblading	me encanta nadar/patinar con patines en línea
we want to hire skis/snowboards	queremos alquilar unos esquís/ unas tablas de nieve

Watching sport	Ver espectáculos deportivos
is there a football match on Saturday?	¿hay algún partido de fútbol el sábado?
which teams are playing?	¿qué equipos juegan?
where can I get tickets?	¿dónde se compran las entradas?
I'd like to see a rugby/football match	me gustaría ver un partido de rugby/fútbol
my favourite, (*Amer*) favorite team is...	mi equipo favorito es el…
let's watch the match on TV	veamos el partido en la tele

Going to the cinema/theatre/club	Cine/Teatro/Discotecas
what's on?	¿qué ponen, (esp *LAm*) dan (en el cine/teatro)?
when does the box office open/close?	¿a qué hora abren/cierran la taquilla, (*LAm*) boletería?
what time does the concert/ performance start?	¿a qué hora empieza el concierto/ la representación?
when does it finish?	¿a qué hora termina?
are there any seats left for tonight?	¿quedan entradas para esta noche?
how much are the tickets?	¿cuánto cuestan las entradas?
where can I get a programme, (*Amer*) program?	¿dónde puedo conseguir un programa?
I want to book tickets for tonight's performance	quiero reservar entradas para esta noche
I'll book seats in the circle	reservaré entradas de platea
I'd rather have seats in the stalls	prefiero el patio de butacas
somewhere in the middle, but not too far back	que sean centrales, pero no demasiado atrás
four, please	cuatro, por favor
for Saturday	para el sábado
we'd like to go to a club	nos gustaría ir a una discoteca
I go clubbing every weekend	voy a la discoteca todos los fines de semana

Hobbies	Aficiones y hobbies
what do you do at the weekend?	¿qué hace los fines de semana?
I like yoga/listening to music	me gusta el yoga/escuchar música
I spend a lot of time surfing the Net	me paso mucho tiempo navegando por la Red
I read a lot	leo mucho
I collect musical instruments	colecciono instrumentos musicales

7 Good timing

Telling the time	La hora
what time is it?	¿qué hora es?
it's 2 o'clock	son las 2
at about 8 o'clock	hacia las 8
from 10 o'clock onwards	a partir de las 10
at 5 o'clock in the morning/afternoon	a las cinco de la mañana/tarde
it's five past/quarter past/half past one	es la una y cinco/y cuarto/y media
it's twenty-five to/quarter to one	es la una menos veinticinco/menos cuarto/(*LAm*) son veinticinco/un cuarto para la una
a quarter/three quarters of an hour	un cuarto/tres cuartos de hora

Days and dates	Días y fechas
Sunday*, Monday, Tuesday, Wednesday, Thursday, Friday, Saturday	domingo, lunes, martes, miércoles, jueves, viernes, sábado
January, February, March, April, May, June, July, August, September, October, November, December	enero, febrero, marzo, abril, mayo, junio, julio, agosto, septiembre, octubre, noviembre, diciembre
what's the date?	¿qué fecha es hoy?
it's the second of June	(es el) dos de junio
we meet up every Monday	nos vemos todos los lunes
we're going away in August	nos vamos fuera en agosto
on November 8th	el 8 de noviembre

* Para los anglosajones la semana empieza un domingo y acaba el sábado siguiente, meintras que los latinos solemos empezar la semana el lunes.

Public holidays and special days	Fiestas y celebraciones especiales
Bank holiday	día festivo en el Reino Unido
Bank holiday Monday	lunes de puente
New Year's Day (Jan 1)	Año Nuevo (1 de enero)
Epiphany (Jan 6)	Reyes (6 de enero)
St Valentine's Day (Feb 14)	San Valentín (14 de febrero)
Shrove Tuesday/Pancake Day	Martes de Carnaval (este día es tradicional merendar crêpes con azúcar y zumo de limón)
Ash Wednesday	Miércoles de Ceniza
Independence Day	4 de julio, fiesta de la independencia de los EEUU
Maundy Thursday	Jueves Santo
Good Friday	Viernes Santo
May Day (May 1)	1 de mayo, día del trabajador
Thanksgiving	día de Acción de Gracias, fiesta típica de EEUU y Canadá
Halloween (Oct 31)	Halloween (fiesta de fantasmas y brujas que se celebra la víspera de Todos los Santos)
All Saints' Day	Todos los Santos
Guy Fawkes Day/Bonfire Night (Nov 5)	fiesta de Guy Fawkes (5 de noviembre: se celebra que el católico Guy Fawkes fracasó en su intento de incendiar el parlamento)
Remembrance Sunday	fiesta en recuerdo a los caídos en las dos guerras mundiales
St Nicholas' Day (Dec 6)	San Nicolás (6 de diciembre)
Christmas Eve (Dec 24)	Nochebuena (24 de diciembre)
Christmas Day (Dec 25)	Navidad (25 de diciembre)
Boxing Day (Dec 26)	día de fiesta que sigue al día de Navidad
New Year's Eve (Dec 31)	Nochevieja (31 de diciembre)

❽ Weights & measures/Pesos y medidas

Length/Longitud

inches/pulgadas	0.39	3.9	7.8	11.7	15.6	19.7	39
cm/centímetros	1	10	20	30	40	50	100

Distance/Distancia

miles/millas	0.62	6.2	12.4	18.6	24.9	31	62
km/km	1	10	20	30	40	50	100

Weight/Peso

pounds/libras	2.2	22	44	66	88	110	220
kg/kilos	1	10	20	30	40	50	100

Capacity/Capacidad

gallons/galones	0.22	2.2	4.4	6.6	8.8	11	22
litres/litros	1	10	20	30	40	50	100

Temperature/Temperatura

°C	0	5	10	15	20	25	30	37	38	40
°F	32	41	50	59	68	77	86	98.4	100	104

Clothing and shoe sizes/Tallas de ropa y calzado

Women's clothing sizes/Ropa de señora

UK	8	10	12	14	16	18
US	6	8	10	12	14	16
Continent	36	38	40	42	44	46

Men's clothing sizes/Ropa de caballero

UK/US	36	38	40	42	44	46
Continent	46	48	50	52	54	56

Men's and women's shoes/Calzado de señora y caballero

UK women	4	5	6	7	7.5	8			
UK men				6	7	8	9	10	11
US	6.5	7.5	8.5	9.5	10.5	11.5	12.5	13.5	14.5
Continent	37	38	39	40	41	42	43	44	45

Aa

a /ə/, *stressed form* /eɪ/

before vowel sound or silent 'h' **an**

indefinite article

····➤ un (*m*), una (*f*). **a problem** un problema. **an apple** una manzana. **have you got a pencil?** ¿tienes un lápiz?

! Feminine singular nouns beginning with stressed or accented *a* or *ha* take the article *un* instead of *una*, e.g. *un águila, un hada*

····➤ (*when talking about prices and quantities*) por. **30 miles an hour** 30 millas por hora. **twice a week** dos veces por semana, dos veces a la semana

! There are many cases in which **a** is not translated, such as when talking about people's professions, in exclamations, etc: **she's a lawyer** *es abogada.* **what a beautiful day!** *¡qué día más precioso!.* **have you got a car?** *¿tienes coche?* **half a cup** *media taza*

A & E /eɪənd'iː/ *n* urgencias *fpl*

aback /ə'bæk/ *adv.* **be taken ~** quedar desconcertado

abandon /ə'bændən/ *vt* abandonar. ● *n* abandono *m*, desenfado *m*. **~ed** *a* abandonado

abashed /ə'bæʃt/ *adj* confuso

abate /ə'beɪt/ *vi* disminuir; (storm etc) calmarse

abattoir /'æbətwɑː(r)/ *n* matadero *m*

abbess /'æbɪs/ *n* abadesa *f*

abbey /'æbɪ/ *n* abadía *f*

abbot /'æbət/ *n* abad *m*

abbreviat|e /ə'briːvɪeɪt/ *vt* abreviar. **~ion** /-'eɪʃn/ *n* abreviatura *f*; (*act*) abreviación *f*

abdicat|e /'æbdɪkeɪt/ *vt/i* abdicar. **~ion** /-'eɪʃn/ *n* abdicación *f*

abdom|en /'æbdəmən/ *n* abdomen *m*. **~inal** /-'dɒmɪnl/ *adj* abdominal

abduct /æb'dʌkt/ *vt* secuestrar. **~ion** /-ʃn/ *n* secuestro *m*

abhor /əb'hɔː(r)/ *vt* (*pt* **abhorred**) aborrecer. **~rence** /-'hɒrəns/ *n* aborrecimiento *m*. **~rent** /-'hɒrənt/ *adj* aborrecible

abide /ə'baɪd/ *vt* (*pt* **abided**) soportar. ● *vi* (*old use*, *pt* **abode**) morar. □ **~ by** *vt* atenerse a; cumplir (promise)

ability /ə'bɪlətɪ/ *n* capacidad *f*; (*cleverness*) habilidad *f*

abject /'æbdʒekt/ *adj* (*wretched*) miserable

ablaze /ə'bleɪz/ *adj* en llamas

able /'eɪbl/ *adj* (**-er**, **-est**) capaz. **be ~** poder; (*know how to*) saber. **~-bodied** /-'bɒdɪd/ *adj* sano, no discapacitado

ably /'eɪblɪ/ *adv* hábilmente

abnormal /æb'nɔːml/ *adj* anormal. **~ity** /-'mælətɪ/ *n* anormali-

a

dad *f*

aboard /ə'bɔ:d/ *adv* a bordo. ● *prep* a bordo de

abode /ə'bəʊd/ *see* ABIDE. ● *n* (*old use*) domicilio *m*

aboli|sh /ə'bɒlɪʃ/ *vt* abolir. **~tion** /æbə'lɪʃn/ *n* abolición *f*

abominable /ə'bɒmɪnəbl/ *adj* abominable

aborigin|al /æbə'rɪdʒənl/ *adj & n* aborigen (*m & f*), indígena (*m & f*). **~es** /-i:z/ *npl* aborígenes *mpl*

abort /ə'bɔ:t/ *vt* hacer abortar. **~ion** /-ʃn/ *n* aborto *m* provocado; (*fig*) aborto *m*. **have an ~ion** hacerse un aborto. **~ive** *adj* fracasado

abound /ə'baʊnd/ *vi* abundar (**in** en)

about /ə'baʊt/ *adv* (*approximately*) alrededor de; (*here and there*) por todas partes; (*in existence*) por aquí. **~ here** por aquí. **be ~ to** estar a punto de. ● *prep* sobre; (*around*) alrededor de; (*somewhere in*) en. **talk ~** hablar de. **~-face**, **~-turn** *n* (*fig*) cambio *m* rotundo

above /ə'bʌv/ *adv* arriba. ● *prep* encima de; (*more than*) más de. **~ all** sobre todo. **~ board** *adj* legítimo. ● *adv* abiertamente. **~-mentioned** *adj* susodicho

abrasi|on /ə'breɪʒn/ *n* abrasión *f*. **~ve** /-sɪv/ *adj* abrasivo

abreast /ə'brest/ *adv*. **march four ~** marchar en columna de cuatro en fondo. **keep ~ of** mantenerse al corriente de

abroad /ə'brɔ:d/ *adv* (*be*) en el extranjero; (*go*) al extranjero; (*far and wide*) por todas partes

abrupt /ə'brʌpt/ *adj* brusco. **~ly** *adv* (*suddenly*) repentinamente; (*curtly*) bruscamente

abscess /'æbsɪs/ *n* absceso *m*

abscond /əb'skɒnd/ *vi* fugarse

absen|ce /'æbsəns/ *n* ausencia *f*; (*lack*) falta *f*. **~t** /'æbsənt/ *adj* ausente. **~t-minded** /-'maɪndɪd/ *adj* distraído. **~t-mindedness** *n* distracción *f*, despiste *m*. **~tee** /-'ti:/ *n* ausente *m & f*. **~teeism** *n* absentismo *m*, ausentismo *m* (*LAm*)

absolute /'æbsəlu:t/ *adj* absoluto. **~ly** *adv* absolutamente

absolve /əb'zɒlv/ *vt* (*from sin*) absolver; (*from obligation*) liberar

absor|b /əb'zɔ:b/ *vt* absorber. **~bent** /-bent/ *adj* absorbente. **~bent cotton** *n* (*Amer*) algodón *m* hidrófilo. **~ption** /əb'zɔ:pʃən/ *n* absorción *f*

abstain /əb'steɪn/ *vi* abstenerse (**from** de)

abstemious /əb'sti:mɪəs/ *adj* abstemio

abstention /əb'stenʃn/ *n* abstención *f*

abstract /'æbstrækt/ *adj* abstracto. ● *n* (*summary*) resumen *m*; (*painting*) cuadro *m* abstracto. ● /əb'strækt/ *vt* extraer; (*summarize*) resumir. **~ion** /-ʃn/ *n* abstracción *f*

absurd /əb'sɜ:d/ *adj* absurdo. **~ity** *n* absurdo *m*, disparate *m*

abundan|ce /ə'bʌndəns/ *n* abundancia *f*. **~t** *adj* abundante

abus|e /ə'bju:z/ *vt* (*misuse*) abusar de; (*ill-treat*) maltratar; (*insult*) insultar. ● /ə'bju:s/ *n* abuso *m*; (*insults*) insultos *mpl*. **~ive** /ə'bju:sɪv/ *adj* injurioso

abysmal /ə'bɪzməl/ *adj* [!] pésimo

abyss /ə'bɪs/ *n* abismo *m*

academic /ækə'demɪk/ *adj* académico; (*pej*) teórico. ● *n* universitario *m*, catedrático *m*

academy /ə'kædəmɪ/ *n* academia *f*.

accelerat|e /ək'seləreɪt/ *vt* acelerar. ● *vi* acelerar; (*Auto*) apretar el acelerador. **~ion** /-'reɪʃn/ *n* aceleración *f*. **~or** *n* acelerador *m*

accent /'æksənt/ *n* acento *m*

accept /ək'sept/ *vt* aceptar. **~able** *adj* aceptable. **~ance** *n* aceptación *f*; (*approval*) aprobación *f*

access /'ækses/ *n* acceso *m*. **~ible** /ək'sesəbl/ *adj* accesible; (person) tratable

accession /æk'seʃn/ *n* (*to power, throne etc*) ascenso *m*; (*thing added*) adquisición *f*

accessory /ək'sesərɪ/ *adj* accesorio. ● *n* accesorio *m*, complemento *m*; (*Jurid*) cómplice *m & f*

accident /'æksɪdənt/ *n* accidente *m*; (*chance*) casualidad *f*. **by ~** sin querer; (*by chance*) por casualidad. **~al** /-'dentl/ *adj* accidental, fortuito. **~ally** /-'dentəlɪ/ *adv* sin querer; (*by chance*) por casualidad. **~-prone** *adj* propenso a los accidentes

acclaim /ə'kleɪm/ *vt* aclamar. ● *n* aclamación *f*

accolade /'ækəleɪd/ *n* (*praise*) encomio *m*

accommodat|e /ə'kɒmədeɪt/ *vt* (*give hospitality to*) alojar; (*adapt*) acomodar; (*oblige*) complacer. **~ing** *adj* complaciente. **~ion** /-'deɪʃn/ *n*, **~ions** *npl* (*Amer*) alojamiento *m*

accompan|iment /ə'kʌmpənɪmənt/ *n* acompañamiento *m*. **~ist** *n* acompañante *m & f*. **~y** /ə'kʌmpənɪ/ *vt* acompañar

accomplice /ə'kʌmplɪs/ *n* cómplice *m & f*

accomplish /ə'kʌmplɪʃ/ *vt* (*complete*) acabar; (*achieve*) realizar; (*carry out*) llevar a cabo. **~ed** *adj* consumado. **~ment** *n* realización *f*; (*ability*) talento *m*; (*thing achieved*) triunfo *m*, logro *m*

accord /ə'kɔːd/ *vi* concordar. ● *vt* conceder. ● *n* acuerdo *m*; (*harmony*) armonía *f*. **of one's own ~** espontáneamente. **~ance** *n*. **in ~ance with** de acuerdo con. **~ing** *adv*. **~ing to** según. **~ingly** *adv* en conformidad; (*therefore*) por consiguiente

accordion /ə'kɔːdɪən/ *n* acordeón *m*

accost /ə'kɒst/ *vt* abordar

account /ə'kaʊnt/ *n* cuenta *f*; (*description*) relato *m*. **~s** *npl* (*in business*) contabilidad *f*. **on ~ of** a causa de. **on no ~** de ninguna manera. **on this ~** por eso. **take into ~** tener en cuenta. ● *vt* considerar. □ **~ for** *vt* dar cuenta de, explicar

accountan|cy /ə'kaʊntənsɪ/ *n* contabilidad *f*. **~t** *n* contable *m & f*, contador *m* (*LAm*)

accumulat|e /ə'kjuːmjʊleɪt/ *vt* acumular. ● *vi* acumularse. **~ion** /-'leɪʃn/ *n* acumulación *f*

accura|cy /'ækjərəsɪ/ *n* exactitud *f*, precisión *f*. **~te** /-ət/ *adj* exacto, preciso

accus|ation /ækjuː'zeɪʃn/ *n* acusación *f*. **~e** /ə'kjuːz/ *vt* acusar

accustom /ə'kʌstəm/ *vt* acostumbrar. **~ed** *adj*. **be ~ed (to)** estar acostumbrado (a). **get ~ed (to)** acostumbrarse (a)

ace /eɪs/ *n* as *m*

ache /eɪk/ *n* dolor *m*. ● *vi* doler. **my leg ~s** me duele la pierna

achieve /ə'tʃiːv/ *vt* realizar; lograr

(success). **~ment** *n* realización *f*; (*feat*) proeza *f*; (*thing achieved*) logro *m*

acid /'æsɪd/ *adj & n* ácido (*m*). **~ic** *adj* /ə'sɪdɪk/ *adj* ácido. **~ rain** *n* lluvia *f* ácida

acknowledge /ək'nɒlɪdʒ/ *vt* reconocer. **~ receipt of** acusar recibo de. **~ment** *n* reconocimiento *m*; (*Com*) acuse *m* de recibo

acne /'æknɪ/ *n* acné *m*

acorn /'eɪkɔ:n/ *n* bellota *f*

acoustic /ə'ku:stɪk/ *adj* acústico. **~s** *npl* acústica *f*

acquaint /ə'kweɪnt/ *vt*. **~ s.o. with** poner a uno al corriente de. **be ~ed with** conocer (person); saber (fact). **~ance** *n* conocimiento *m*; (*person*) conocido *m*

acquiesce /ækwɪ'es/ *vi* consentir (**in** en). **~nce** *n* aquiescencia *f*, consentimiento *m*

acqui|re /ə'kwaɪə(r)/ *vt* adquirir; aprender (language). **~re a taste for** tomar gusto a. **~sition** /ækwɪ'zɪʃn/ *n* adquisición *f*. **~sitive** /ə'kwɪzətɪv/ *adj* codicioso

acquit /ə'kwɪt/ *vt* (*pt* **acquitted**) absolver. **~tal** *n* absolución *f*

acre /'eɪkə(r)/ *n* acre *m*

acrid /'ækrɪd/ *adj* acre

acrimonious /ækrɪ'məʊnɪəs/ *adj* cáustico, mordaz

acrobat /'ækrəbæt/ *n* acróbata *m & f*. **~ic** /-'bætɪk/ *adj* acrobático. **~ics** *npl* acrobacia *f*

acronym /'ækrənɪm/ *n* acrónimo *m*, siglas *fpl*

across /ə'krɒs/ *adv & prep* (*side to side*) de un lado al otro; (*on other side*) al otro lado de; (*crosswise*) a través. **it is 20 metres ~** tiene 20 metros de ancho. **go** *or* **walk ~** atravesar, cruzar

act /ækt/ *n* acto *m*; (*action*) acción *f*; (*in variety show*) número *m*; (*decree*) decreto *m*. ● *vt* hacer (part, role). ● *vi* actuar; (*pretend*) fingir. **~ as** actuar de; (object) servir de. **~ for** representar. **~ing** *adj* interino. ● *n* (*of play*) representación *f*; (*by actor*) interpretación *f*; (*profession*) profesión *f* de actor

action /'ækʃn/ *n* acción *f*; (*Jurid*) demanda *f*; (*plot*) argumento *m*. **out of ~** (*on sign*) no funciona. **put out of ~** inutilizar. **take ~** tomar medidas **~ replay** *n* repetición *f* de la jugada

activate /'æktɪveɪt/ *vt* activar

activ|e /'æktɪv/ *adj* activo; (*energetic*) lleno de energía; (volcano) en actividad. **~ist** *n* activista *m & f*. **~ity** /-'tɪvətɪ/ *n* actividad *f*

act|or /'æktə(r)/ *n* actor *m*. **~ress** /-trɪs/ *n* actriz *f*

actual /'æktʃʊəl/ *adj* verdadero. **~ly** *adv* en realidad, efectivamente; (*even*) incluso

acute /ə'kju:t/ *adj* agudo. **~ly** *adv* agudamente

ad /æd/ *n* [!] anuncio *m*, aviso *m* (*LAm*)

AD /eɪ'di:/ *abbr* (= **Anno Domini**) d. de J.C.

Adam's apple /ædəmz'æpl/ *n* nuez *f* (de Adán)

adapt /ə'dæpt/ *vt* adaptar. ● *vi* adaptarse. **~ability** /-ə'bɪlətɪ/ *n* adaptabilidad *f*. **~able** /-əbl/ *adj* adaptable. **~ation** /ædæp'teɪʃn/ *n* adaptación *f*; (*of book etc*) versión *f*. **~or** /ə'dæptə(r)/ *n* (*Elec, with several sockets*) enchufe *m* múltiple; (*Elec, for different sockets*) adaptador *m*

add /æd/ *vt* añadir. ● *vi* sumar. □ **~ up** *vt* sumar; (*fig*) tener sentido. **~**

up to equivaler a

adder /'ædə(r)/ *n* víbora *f*

addict /'ædɪkt/ *n* adicto *m*; (*fig*) entusiasta *m & f*. **~ed** /ə'dɪktɪd/ *adj*. **~ed to** adicto a; (*fig*) fanático de. **~ion** /ə'dɪkʃn/ *n* (*Med*) dependencia *f*; (*fig*) afición *f*. **~ive** /ə'dɪktɪv/ *adj* que crea adicción; (*fig*) que crea hábito

addition /ə'dɪʃn/ *n* suma *f*. **in ~** además. **~al** *adj* suplementario

address /ə'dres/ *n* dirección *f*; (*on form*) domicilio *m*; (*speech*) discurso *m*. • *vt* poner la dirección en; (*speak to*) dirigirse a. **~ book** *n* libreta *f* de direcciones. **~ee** /ædre'si:/ *n* destinatario *m*

adept /'ædept/ *adj & n* experto (*m*)

adequa|cy /'ædɪkwəsɪ/ *n* suficiencia *f*. **~te** /-ət/ *adj* suficiente, adecuado. **~tely** *adv* suficientemente, adecuadamente

adhere /əd'hɪə(r)/ *vi* adherirse (**to** a); observar (rule). **~nce** /-rəns/ *n* adhesión *f*; (*to rules*) observancia *f*

adhesi|on /əd'hi:ʒn/ *n* adherencia *f*. **~ve** /-sɪv/ *adj & n* adhesivo (*m*)

adjacent /ə'dʒeɪsnt/ *adj* contiguo

adjective /'ædʒɪktɪv/ *n* adjetivo *m*

adjourn /ə'dʒɜ:n/ *vt* aplazar; suspender (meeting etc). • *vi* suspenderse

adjust /ə'dʒʌst/ *vt* ajustar (machine); (*arrange*) arreglar. • *vi*. **~ (to)** adaptarse (a). **~able** *adj* ajustable. **~ment** *n* adaptación *f*; (*Tec*) ajuste *m*

administer /əd'mɪnɪstə(r)/ *vt* administrar

administrat|ion /ədmɪnɪ'streɪʃn/ *n* administración *f*. **~ive** /əd'mɪnɪstrətɪv/ *adj* administrativo. **~or** /əd'mɪnɪstreɪtə(r)/ *n* administrador *m*

admirable /'ædmərəbl/ *adj* admirable

admiral /'ædmərəl/ *n* almirante *m*

admir|ation /ædmə'reɪʃn/ *n* admiración *f*. **~e** /əd'maɪə(r)/ *vt* admirar. **~er** /əd'maɪərə(r)/ *n* admirador *m*

admission /əd'mɪʃn/ *n* admisión *f*; (*entry*) entrada *f*

admit /əd'mɪt/ *vt* (*pt* **admitted**) dejar entrar; (*acknowledge*) admitir, reconocer. **~ to** confesar. **be ~ted** (*to hospital etc*) ingresar. **~tance** *n* entrada *f*. **~tedly** *adv* es verdad que

admonish /əd'mɒnɪʃ/ *vt* reprender; (*advise*) aconsejar

ado /ə'du:/ *n* alboroto m; (*trouble*) dificultad *f*. **without more** *or* **further ~** en seguida, sin más

adolescen|ce /ædə'lesns/ *n* adolescencia *f*. **~t** *adj & n* adolescente (*m & f*)

adopt /ə'dɒpt/ *vt* adoptar. **~ed** *adj* (child) adoptivo. **~ion** /-ʃn/ *n* adopción *f*

ador|able /ə'dɔ:rəbl/ *adj* adorable. **~ation** /ædə'reɪʃn/ *n* adoración *f*. **~e** /ə'dɔ:(r)/ *vt* adorar

adorn /ə'dɔ:n/ *vt* adornar. **~ment** *n* adorno *m*

adrift /ə'drɪft/ *adj & adv* a la deriva

adult /'ædʌlt/ *adj & n* adulto (*m*)

adulter|er /ə'dʌltərə(r)/ *n* adúltero *m*. **~ess** /-ɪs/ *n* adúltera *f*. **~y** *n* adulterio *m*

advance /əd'vɑ:ns/ *vt* adelantar. • *vi* adelantarse. • *n* adelanto *m*. **in ~** con anticipación, por adelantado. **~d** *adj* avanzado; (studies) superior

advantage /əd'vɑ:ntɪdʒ/ *n* ventaja *f*. **take ~ of** aprovecharse de; abusar de (person). **~ous** /ædvən

ˈteɪdʒəs/ *adj* ventajoso

advent /ˈædvənt/ *n* venida *f*. **A~** *n* adviento *m*

adventur|e /ədˈventʃə(r)/ *n* aventura *f*. **~er** *n* aventurero *m*. **~ous** *adj* (person) aventurero; (thing) arriesgado; (*fig, bold*) audaz

adverb /ˈædvɜːb/ *n* adverbio *m*

adversary /ˈædvəsərɪ/ *n* adversario *m*

advers|e /ˈædvɜːs/ *adj* adverso, contrario, desfavorable. **~ity** /ədˈvɜːsətɪ/ *n* infortunio *m*

advert /ˈædvɜːt/ *n* ⊞ anuncio *m*, aviso *m* (*LAm*). **~ise** /ˈædvətaɪz/ *vt* anunciar. ● *vi* hacer publicidad; (*seek, sell*) poner un anuncio. **~isement** /ədˈvɜːtɪsmənt/ *n* anuncio *m*, aviso *m* (*LAm*). **~iser** /ˈædvətaɪzə(r)/ *n* anunciante *m & f*

advice /ədˈvaɪs/ *n* consejo *m*; (*report*) informe *m*

advis|able /ədˈvaɪzəbl/ *adj* aconsejable. **~e** /ədˈvaɪz/ *vt* aconsejar; (*inform*) avisar. **~e against** aconsejar en contra de. **~er** *n* consejero *m*; (*consultant*) asesor *m*. **~ory** *adj* consultivo

advocate /ˈædvəkət/ *n* defensor *m*; (*Jurid*) abogado *m*. ● /ˈædvəkeɪt/ *vt* recomendar

aerial /ˈeərɪəl/ *adj* aéreo. ● *n* antena *f*

aerobics /eəˈrəʊbɪks/ *npl* aeróbica *f*

aerodrome /ˈeərədrəʊm/ *n* aeródromo *m*

aerodynamic /eərəʊdaɪˈnæmɪk/ *adj* aerodinámico

aeroplane /ˈeərəpleɪn/ *n* avión *m*

aerosol /ˈeərəsɒl/ *n* aerosol *m*

aesthetic /iːsˈθetɪk/ *adj* estético

afar /əˈfɑː(r)/ *adv* lejos

affable /ˈæfəbl/ *adj* afable

affair /əˈfeə(r)/ *n* asunto *m*. **(love) ~** aventura *f*, amorío *m*. **~s** *npl* (*business*) negocios *mpl*

affect /əˈfekt/ *vt* afectar; (*pretend*) fingir. **~ation** /æfekˈteɪʃn/ *n* afectación *f*. **~ed** *adj* afectado, amanerado

affection /əˈfekʃn/ *n* cariño *m*. **~ate** /-ət/ *adj* cariñoso

affiliate /əˈfɪlɪeɪt/ *vt* afiliar

affirm /əˈfɜːm/ *vt* afirmar. **~ative** /-ətɪv/ *adj* afirmativo. ● *n* respuesta *f* afirmativa

afflict /əˈflɪkt/ *vt* afligir. **~ion** /-ʃn/ *n* aflicción *f*, pena *f*

affluen|ce /ˈæflʊəns/ *n* riqueza *f*. **~t** *adj* rico.

afford /əˈfɔːd/ *vt* permitirse; (*provide*) dar. **he can't ~ a car** no le alcanza el dinero para comprar un coche

affront /əˈfrʌnt/ *n* afrenta *f*, ofensa *f*. ● *vt* afrentar, ofender

afield /əˈfiːld/ *adv*. **far ~** muy lejos

afloat /əˈfləʊt/ *adv* a flote

afraid /əˈfreɪd/ *adj*. **be ~** tener miedo (**of** a); (*be sorry*) sentir, lamentar

afresh /əˈfreʃ/ *adv* de nuevo

Africa /ˈæfrɪkə/ *n* África *f*. **~n** *adj & n* africano (*m*). **~n-American** *adj & n* norteamericano (*m*) de origen africano

after /ˈɑːftə(r)/ *adv* después; (*behind*) detrás. ● *prep* después de; (*behind*) detrás de. **it's twenty ~ four** (*Amer*) son las cuatro y veinte. **be ~** (*seek*) andar en busca de. ● *conj* después de que. ● *adj* posterior. **~-effect** *n* consecuencia *f*, efecto *m* secundario. **~math** /ˈɑːftəmæθ/ *n* secuelas *fpl*. **~noon** /-ˈnuːn/ *n* tarde *f*. **~shave** *n* loción *f* para después de afeitarse. **~thought** *n* ocurrencia *f* tardía. **~wards** /-wədz/ *adv* después

again /ə'gen/ *adv* otra vez; (*besides*) además. **do ~** volver a hacer, hacer otra vez. **~ and ~** una y otra vez

against /ə'genst/ *prep* contra; (*in opposition to*) en contra de, contra

age /eɪdʒ/ *n* edad *f*. **at four years of ~** a los cuatro años. **under ~** menor de edad. **~s** *npl* 🅸 siglos *mpl*. ● *vt/i* (*pres p* **ageing**) envejecer. **~d** /'eɪdʒd/ *adj* de ... años. **~d 10** de 10 años. **~d** /'eɪdʒɪd/ *adj* viejo, anciano

agency /'eɪdʒənsɪ/ *n* agencia *f*; (*department*) organismo *m*

agenda /ə'dʒendə/ *n* orden *m* del día

agent /'eɪdʒənt/ *n* agente *m & f*; (*representative*) representante *m & f*

aggravat|e /'ægrəveɪt/ *vt* agravar; (*fam, irritate*) irritar. **~ion** /-'veɪʃn/ *n* agravación *f*; (*fam, irritation*) irritación *f*

aggress|ion /ə'greʃn/ *n* agresión *f*. **~ive** *adj* agresivo. **~iveness** *n* agresividad *f*. **~or** *n* agresor *m*

aggrieved /ə'gri:vd/ *adj* apenado, ofendido

aghast /ə'gɑ:st/ *adj* horrorizado

agil|e /'ædʒaɪl/ *adj* ágil. **~ity** /ə'dʒɪlətɪ/ *n* agilidad *f*

aging /'eɪdʒɪŋ/ *adj* envejecido. ● *n* envejecimiento *m*

agitat|e /'ædʒɪteɪt/ *vt* agitar. **~ed** *adj* nervioso. **~ion** /-'teɪʃn/ *n* agitación *f*, excitación *f*. **~or** *n* agitador *m*

ago /ə'gəʊ/ *adv*. **a long time ~** hace mucho tiempo. **3 days ~** hace 3 días

agon|ize /'ægənaɪz/ *vi* atormentarse. **~izing** *adj* (pain) atroz; (experience) angustioso. **~y** *n* dolor *m* (agudo); (*mental*) angustia *f*

agree /ə'gri:/ *vt* acordar. ● *vi* estar de acuerdo; (*of figures*) concordar; (*get on*) entenderse. □ **~ on** *vt* acordar (date, details). □ **~ with** *vt* (*of food etc*) sentarle bien a. **~able** /ə'gri:əbl/ *adj* agradable. **be ~able** (*willing*) estar de acuerdo. **~d** *adj* (time, place) convenido. **~ment** /-mənt/ *n* acuerdo *m*. **in ~ment** de acuerdo

agricultur|al /ægrɪ'kʌltʃərəl/ *adj* agrícola. **~e** /'ægrɪkʌltʃə(r)/ *n* agricultura *f*

aground /ə'graʊnd/ *adv*. **run ~** (*of ship*) varar, encallar

ahead /ə'hed/ *adv* delante; (*in time*) antes de. **be ~** ir delante

aid /eɪd/ *vt* ayudar. ● *n* ayuda *f*. **in ~ of** a beneficio de

AIDS /eɪdz/ *n* sida *m*

ailment /'eɪlmənt/ *n* enfermedad *f*

aim /eɪm/ *vt* apuntar; (*fig*) dirigir. ● *vi* apuntar; (*fig*) pretender. ● *n* puntería *f*; (*fig*) objetivo *m*. **~less** *adj*, **~lessly** *adv* sin objeto, sin rumbo

air /eə(r)/ *n* aire *m*. **be on the ~** (*Radio, TV*) estar en el aire. **put on ~s** darse aires. ● *vt* airear. **~ bag** *n* (*Auto*) bolsa *f* de aire. **~ base** *n* base *f* aérea. **~borne** *adj* en el aire; (*Mil*) aerotransportado. **~-conditioned** *adj* climatizado, con aire acondicionado. **~ conditioning** *n* aire *m* acondicionado. **~craft** *n* (*pl invar*) avión *m*. **~craft carrier** *n* portaaviones *m*. **~field** *n* aeródromo *m*. **A~ Force** *n* fuerzas *fpl* aéreas. **~ freshener** *n* ambientador *m*. **~gun** *n* escopeta *f* de aire comprimido. **~ hostess** *n* azafata *f*, aeromoza *f* (*LAm*). **~line** *n* línea *f* aérea. **~ mail** *n* correo *m* aéreo. **~plane** *n* (*Amer*) avión *m*. **~port** *n* aeropuerto *m*. **~sick** *adj* mareado (en un avión). **~tight** *adj* hermético. **~ traffic controller** *n* controlador *m* aéreo. **~y** *adj* (**-ier, -iest**) aireado; (manner) desenfadado

aisle /aɪl/ *n* nave *f* lateral; (*gangway*) pasillo *m*

ajar /ə'dʒɑː(r)/ *adj* entreabierto

alarm /ə'lɑːm/ *n* alarma *f*. ● *vt* asustar. **~ clock** *n* despertador *m*. **~ist** *n* alarmista *m & f*

Albania /æl'beɪnɪə/ *n* Albania *f*. **~n** *adj & n* albanés (*m*)

albatross /'ælbətrɒs/ *n* albatros *m*

album /'ælbəm/ *n* álbum *m*

alcohol /'ælkəhɒl/ *n* alcohol *m*. **~ic** /-'hɒlɪk/ *adj & n* alcohólico (*m*)

alcove /'ælkəʊv/ *n* nicho *m*

ale /eɪl/ *n* cerveza *f*

alert /ə'lɜːt/ *adj* vivo; (*watchful*) vigilante. ● *n* alerta *f*. **on the ~** alerta. ● *vt* avisar

algebra /'ældʒɪbrə/ *n* álgebra *f*

Algeria /æl'dʒɪərɪə/ *n* Argelia *f*. **~n** *adj & n* argelino (*m*)

alias /'eɪlɪəs/ *n* (*pl* **-ases**) alias *m*. ● *adv* alias

alibi /'ælɪbaɪ/ *n* (*pl* **-is**) coartada *f*

alien /'eɪlɪən/ *n* extranjero *m*. ● *adj* ajeno. **~ate** /-eɪt/ *vt* enajenar. **~ation** /-'neɪʃn/ *n* enajenación *f*

alienat|e /'eɪlɪəneɪt/ *vt* enajenar. **~ion** /-'neɪʃn/ *n* enajenación *f*

alight /ə'laɪt/ *adj* ardiendo; (light) encendido

align /ə'laɪn/ *vt* alinear. **~ment** *n* alineación *f*

alike /ə'laɪk/ *adj* parecido, semejante. **look** *or* **be ~** parecerse. ● *adv* de la misma manera

alive /ə'laɪv/ *adj* vivo. **~ with** lleno de

alkali /'ælkəlaɪ/ *n* (*pl* **-is**) álcali *m*. **~ne** *adj* alcalino

all /ɔːl/

● *adjective* todo, -da; (*pl*) todos, -das. **~ day** todo el día. **~ the windows** todas las ventanas. **~ four of us went** fuimos los cuatro

● *pronoun*

····➤ (*everything*) todo. **that's ~** eso es todo. **I did ~ I could to persuade her** hice todo lo que pude para convencerla

····➤ (*after pronoun*) todo, -da; (*pl*) todos, -das. **he helped us ~** nos ayudó a todos

····➤ **all of** todo, -da, (*pl*) todos, -das. **~ of the paintings** todos los cuadros. **~ of the milk** toda la leche

····➤ (*in phrases*) **all in all** en general. **not at all** (*in no way*) de ninguna manera; (*after thanks*) de nada, no hay de qué. **it's not at ~ bad** no está nada mal. **I don't like it at ~** no me gusta nada

● *adverb*

····➤ (*completely*) completamente. **she was ~ alone** estaba completamente sola. **I got ~ dirty** me ensucié todo/toda. **I don't know him ~ that well** no lo conozco tan bien

····➤ (*in scores*) **the score was one ~** iban empatados uno a uno

····➤ (*in phrases*) **to be all for sth**

estar completamente a favor de algo. **to be all in** ⊡ estar rendido

all-around /ɔ:lə'raʊnd/ *adj* (*Amer*) completo

allay /ə'leɪ/ *vt* aliviar (pain); aquietar (fears etc)

all-clear /ɔ:l'klɪə(r)/ *n* fin *m* de (la) alarma; (*permission*) visto *m* bueno

alleg|ation /ælɪ'geɪʃn/ *n* alegato *m*. **~e** /ə'ledʒ/ *vt* alegar. **~ed** *adj* presunto. **~edly** /-ɪdlɪ/ *adv* según se dice, supuestamente

allegiance /ə'li:dʒəns/ *n* lealtad *f*

allegory /'ælɪgərɪ/ *n* alegoría *f*

allerg|ic /ə'lɜ:dʒɪk/ *adj* alérgico (**to** a). **~y** /'ælədʒɪ/ *n* alergia *f*

alleviate /ə'li:vɪeɪt/ *vt* aliviar

alley /'ælɪ/ (*pl* **-eys**) *n* callejuela *f*

alliance /ə'laɪəns/ *n* alianza *f*

alligator /'ælɪgeɪtə(r)/ *n* caimán *m*

allocat|e /'æləkeɪt/ *vt* asignar; (*share out*) repartir. **~ion** /-'keɪʃn/ *n* asignación *f*; (*distribution*) reparto *m*

allot /ə'lɒt/ *vt* (*pt* **allotted**) asignar. **~ment** *n* asignación *f*; (*land*) parcela *f*

allow /ə'laʊ/ *vt* permitir; (*grant*) conceder; (*reckon on*) prever; (*agree*) admitir. □ **~ for** *vt* tener en cuenta. **~ance** /ə'laʊəns/ *n* concesión *f*; (*pension*) pensión *f*; (*Com*) rebaja *f*. **make ~ances for** ser indulgente con (person); (*take into account*) tener en cuenta

alloy /'ælɔɪ/ *n* aleación *f*

all: ~ right *adj & adv* bien. ● *int* ¡vale!, ¡okey! (*esp LAm*), ¡órale! (*Mex*). **~-round** *adj* completo

allusion /ə'lu:ʒn/ *n* alusión *f*

ally /'ælaɪ/ *n* aliado *m*. ● /ə'laɪ/ *vt*. **~ o.s.** aliarse (**with** con)

almighty /ɔ:l'maɪtɪ/ *adj* todopoderoso

almond /'ɑ:mənd/ *n* almendra *f*

almost /'ɔ:lməʊst/ *adv* casi

alone /ə'ləʊn/ *adj* solo. ● *adv* sólo, solamente

along /ə'lɒŋ/ *prep* por, a lo largo de. ● *adv*. **~ with** junto con. **all ~** todo el tiempo. **come ~** venga. **~side** /-'saɪd/ *adv* (*Naut*) al costado. ● *prep* al lado de

aloof /ə'lu:f/ *adv* apartado. ● *adj* reservado

aloud /ə'laʊd/ *adv* en voz alta

alphabet /'ælfəbet/ *n* alfabeto *m*. **~ical** /-'betɪkl/ *adj* alfabético

Alps /ælps/ *npl*. **the ~** los Alpes

already /ɔ:l'redɪ/ *adv* ya

Alsatian /æl'seɪʃn/ *n* pastor *m* alemán

also /'ɔ:lsəʊ/ *adv* también; (*moreover*) además

altar /'ɔ:ltə(r)/ *n* altar *m*

alter /'ɔ:ltə(r)/ *vt* cambiar. ● *vi* cambiarse. **~ation** /-'reɪʃn/ *n* modificación *f*; (*to garment*) arreglo *m*

alternate /ɔ:l'tɜ:nət/ *adj* alterno; (*Amer*) *see* **ALTERNATIVE**. ● /'ɔ:ltəneɪt/ *vt/i* alternar. **~ly** /ɔ:l'tɜ:nətlɪ/ *adv* alternativamente

alternative /ɔ:l'tɜ:nətɪv/ *adj* alternativo. ● *n* alternativa *f*. **~ly** *adv* en cambio, por otra parte

although /ɔ:l'ðəʊ/ *conj* aunque

altitude /'æltɪtju:d/ *n* altitud *f*

altogether /ɔ:ltə'geðə(r)/ *adv* completamente; (*on the whole*) en total

aluminium /æljʊ'mɪnɪəm/, **aluminum** /ə'lu:mɪnəm/ (*Amer*) *n* aluminio *m*

a

always /'ɔ:lweɪz/ *adv* siempre

am /æm/ *see* **BE**

a.m. *abbr* (= **ante meridiem**) de la mañana

amalgamate /ə'mælgəmeɪt/ *vt* amalgamar. ● *vi* amalgamarse

amass /ə'mæs/ *vt* acumular

amateur /'æmətə(r)/ *adj & n* amateur (*m & f*). **~ish** *adj* (*pej*) torpe, chapucero

amaz|e /ə'meɪz/ *vt* asombrar. **~ed** *adj* asombrado, estupefacto. **be ~ed at** quedarse asombrado de, asombrarse de. **~ement** *n* asombro *m*. **~ing** *adj* increíble

ambassador /æm'bæsədə(r)/ *n* embajador *m*

ambigu|ity /æmbɪ'gju:ətɪ/ *n* ambigüedad *f*. **~ous** /æm'bɪgjʊəs/ *adj* ambiguo

ambiti|on /æm'bɪʃn/ *n* ambición *f*. **~ous** /-ʃəs/ *adj* ambicioso

ambivalent /æm'bɪvələnt/ *adj* ambivalente

amble /'æmbl/ *vi* andar despacio, andar sin prisa

ambulance /'æmbjʊləns/ *n* ambulancia *f*

ambush /'æmbʊʃ/ *n* emboscada *f*. ● *vt* tender una emboscada a

amen /ɑ:'men/ *int* amén

amend /ə'mend/ *vt* enmendar. **~ment** *n* enmienda *f*. **~s** *npl*. **make ~s** reparar

amenities /ə'mi:nətɪz/ *npl* servicios *mpl*; (*of hotel, club*) instalaciones *fpl*

America /ə'merɪkə/ *n* (*continent*) América; (*North America*) Estados *mpl* Unidos, Norteamérica *f*. **~n** *adj & n* americano (*m*); (*North American*) estadounidense (*m & f*), norteamericano (*m*). **~nism** *n* americanismo *m*

> **i** **American dream** El sueño americano se basa en la idea de que cualquier persona en los Estados Unidos puede prosperar mediante el trabajo duro. Para los inmigrantes y las minorías, el concepto abarca la libertad y la igualdad de derechos.

amiable /'eɪmɪəbl/ *adj* simpático

amicable /'æmɪkəbl/ *adj* amistoso

amid(st) /ə'mɪd(st)/ *prep* entre, en medio de

ammonia /ə'məʊnɪə/ *n* amoníaco *m*, amoniaco *m*

ammunition /æmjʊ'nɪʃn/ *n* municiones *fpl*

amnesty /'æmnəstɪ/ *n* amnistía *f*

amok /ə'mɒk/ *adv*. **run ~** volverse loco

among(st) /ə'mʌŋ(st)/ *prep* entre

amount /ə'maʊnt/ *n* cantidad *f*; (*total*) total *m*, suma *f*. ▫ **~ to** *vt* sumar; (*fig*) equivaler a, significar

amp(ere) /'amp(eə(r))/ *n* amperio *m*

amphibi|an /æm'fɪbɪən/ *n* anfibio *m*. **~ous** /-əs/ *adj* anfibio

amphitheatre /'æmfɪθɪətə(r)/ *n* anfiteatro *m*

ampl|e /'æmpl/ *adj* (**-er**, **-est**) amplio; (*enough*) suficiente; (*plentiful*) abundante. **~y** *adv* ampliamente, bastante

amplif|ier /'æmplɪfaɪə(r)/ *n* amplificador *m*. **~y** /'æmplɪfaɪ/ *vt* amplificar

amputat|e /'æmpjʊteɪt/ *vt* amputar. **~ion** /-'teɪʃn/ *n* amputación *f*

amus|e /ə'mju:z/ *vt* divertir. **~ed** *adj* (expression) divertido. **keep s.o. ~ed** entretener a uno. **~ement** *n* diversión *f*. **~ing** *adj* divertido

an /ən, æn/ *see* **A**

anaemi|a /əˈniːmɪə/ *n* anemia *f*. **~c** *adj* anémico

anaesthe|tic /ænɪsˈθetɪk/ *n* anestésico *m*. **~tist** /əˈniːsθɪtɪst/ *n* anestesista *m & f*

anagram /ˈænəgræm/ *n* anagrama *m*

analogy /əˈnælədʒɪ/ *n* analogía *f*

analy|se /ˈænəlaɪz/ *vt* analizar. **~sis** /əˈnæləsɪs/ *n* (*pl* **-ses** /-siːz/) *n* análisis *m*. **~st** /ˈænəlɪst/ *n* analista *m & f*. **~tic(al)** /ænəˈlɪtɪk(əl)/ *adj* analítico

anarch|ist /ˈænəkɪst/ *n* anarquista *m & f*. **~y** *n* anarquía *f*

anatom|ical /ænəˈtɒmɪkl/ *adj* anatómico. **~y** /əˈnætəmɪ/ *n* anatomía *f*

ancest|or /ˈænsestə(r)/ *n* antepasado *m*. **~ral** /-ˈsestrəl/ *adj* ancestral. **~ry** /ˈænsestrɪ/ *n* ascendencia *f*

anchor /ˈæŋkə(r)/ *n* ancla *f*. ● *vt* anclar; (*fig*) sujetar. ● *vi* anclar. **~man** *n* (*on TV*) presentador *m*. **~woman** *n* (*on TV*) presentadora *f*.

ancient /ˈeɪnʃənt/ *adj* antiguo, viejo

ancillary /ænˈsɪlərɪ/ *adj* auxiliar

and /ənd, ænd/ *conj* y; (*before* **i-** *and* **hi-**) e. **bread ~ butter** pan *m* con mantequilla. **go ~ see him** ve a verlo. **more ~ more** cada vez más. **try ~ come** trata de venir

anecdot|al /ænɪkˈdəʊtl/ *adj* anecdótico. **~e** /ˈænɪkdəʊt/ *n* anécdota *f*

anew /əˈnjuː/ *adv* de nuevo

angel /ˈeɪndʒl/ *n* ángel *m*. **~ic** /ænˈdʒelɪk/ *adj* angélico

anger /ˈæŋgə(r)/ *n* ira *f*. ● *vt* enfadar, (*esp LAm*) enojar

angle /ˈæŋgl/ *n* ángulo *m*; (*fig*) punto *m* de vista. **~r** /ˈæŋglə(r)/ *n* pescador *m*

Anglican /ˈæŋglɪkən/ *adj & n* anglicano (*m*)

angr|ily /ˈæŋgrɪlɪ/ *adv* con enfado, (*esp LAm*) con enojo. **~y** /ˈæŋgrɪ/ *adj* (**-ier**, **-iest**) enfadado, (*esp LAm*) enojado. **get ~y** enfadarse, enojarse (*esp LAm*)

anguish /ˈæŋgwɪʃ/ *n* angustia *f*

animal /ˈænɪməl/ *adj & n* animal (*m*)

animat|e /ˈænɪmeɪt/ *vt* animar. **~ion** /-ˈmeɪʃn/ *n* animación *f*

animosity /ænɪˈmɒsətɪ/ *n* animosidad *f*

ankle /ˈæŋkl/ *n* tobillo *m*. **~ boot** botín *m*. **~ sock** calcetín *m* corto

annexe /ˈæneks/ *n* anexo *m*

annihilat|e /əˈnaɪəleɪt/ *vt* aniquilar. **~ion** /-ˈleɪʃn/ *n* aniquilación *f*

anniversary /ænɪˈvɜːsərɪ/ *n* aniversario *m*

announce /əˈnaʊns/ *vt* anunciar, comunicar. **~ment** *n* anuncio *m*; (*official*) comunicado *m*. **~r** *n* (*Radio, TV*) locutor *m*

annoy /əˈnɔɪ/ *vt* molestar. **~ance** *n* molestia *m*. **~ed** *adj* enfadado, enojado (*LAm*). **~ing** *adj* molesto

annual /ˈænjʊəl/ *adj* anual. ● *n* anuario *m*. **~ly** *adv* cada año

annul /əˈnʌl/ *vt* (*pt* **annulled**) anular. **~ment** *n* anulación *f*

anonymous /əˈnɒnɪməs/ *adj* anónimo

anorak /ˈænəræk/ *n* anorac *m*

another /əˈnʌðə(r)/ *adj & pron* otro. **~ 10 minutes** 10 minutos más. **in ~ way** de otra manera. **one ~** el uno al otro; (*pl*) unos a otros

a

answer /'ɑ:nsə(r)/ *n* respuesta *f*; (*solution*) solución *f*. ● *vt* contestar; escuchar, oír (prayer). ~ **the door** abrir la puerta. ● *vi* contestar. □ ~ **back** *vi* contestar. □ ~ **for** *vt* ser responsable de. ~**able** *adj* responsable. ~**ing machine** *n* contestador *m* automático

ant /ænt/ *n* hormiga *f*

antagoni|sm /æn'tægənızəm/ *n* antagonismo *m*. ~**stic** /-'nıstık/ *adj* antagónico, opuesto. ~**ze** /æn 'tægənaız/ *vt* provocar la enemistad de

Antarctic /æn'tɑ:ktık/ *adj* antártico. ● *n* **the** ~ la región antártica

antelope /'æntıləʊp/ *n* antílope *m*

antenatal /'æntıneıtl/ *adj* prenatal

antenna /æn'tenə/ (*pl* **-nae** /-ni:/) (*of insect etc*) *n* antena *f*; (*pl* **-nas**) (*of radio, TV*) antena *f*

anthem /'ænθəm/ *n* himno *m*

anthology /æn'θɒlədʒı/ *n* antología *f*

anthrax /'ænθræks/ *n* ántrax *m*

anthropolog|ist /ænθrə 'pɒlədʒıst/ *n* antropológo *m*. ~**y** *n* antropología *f*

anti-... /æntı/ *pref* anti... ~**aircraft** /-'eəkrɑ:ft/ *adj* antiaéreo

antibiotic /æntıbaı'ɒtık/ *adj* & *n* antibiótico (*m*)

anticipat|e /æn'tısıpeıt/ *vt* anticiparse a; (*foresee*) prever; (*forestall*) prevenir. ~**ion** /-'peıʃn/ *n* (*foresight*) previsión *f*; (*expectation*) expectativa *f*

anti: ~**climax** /-'klaımæks/ *n* decepción *f*. ~**clockwise** /-'klɒkwaız/ *adv* & *adj* en sentido contrario al de las agujas del reloj

antidote /'æntıdəʊt/ *m* antídoto *m*

antifreeze /'æntıfri:z/ *n* anticongelante *m*

antiperspirant /æntı 'pɜ:spırənt/ *n* antitranspirante *m*

antiquated /'æntıkweıtıd/ *adj* anticuado

antique /æn'ti:k/ *adj* antiguo. ● *n* antigüedad *f*. ~ **dealer** anticuario *m*. ~ **shop** tienda *f* de antigüedades

antiquity /æn'tıkwətı/ *n* antigüedad *f*

anti: ~**septic** /-'septık/ *adj* & *n* antiséptico (*m*). ~**social** /-'səʊʃl/ *adj* antisocial

antlers /'æntləz/ *npl* cornamenta *f*

anus /'eınəs/ *n* ano *m*

anvil /'ænvıl/ *n* yunque *m*

anxi|ety /æŋ'zaıətı/ *n* ansiedad *f*; (*worry*) inquietud *f*; (*eagerness*) anhelo *m*. ~**ous** /'æŋkʃəs/ *adj* inquieto; (*eager*) deseoso. ~**ously** *adv* con inquietud; (*eagerly*) con impaciencia

any /'enı/ *adj* algún; (*negative*) ningún *m*; (*whatever*) cualquier; (*every*) todo. **at** ~ **moment** en cualquier momento. **have you** ~ **wine?** ¿tienes vino? ● *pron* alguno; (*negative*) ninguno. **have we** ~**?** ¿tenemos algunos? **not** ~ ninguno. ● *adv* (*a little*) un poco, algo. **is it** ~ **better?** ¿está algo mejor?

anybody /'enıbɒdı/ *pron* alguien; (*after negative*) nadie. ~ **can do it** cualquiera puede hacerlo

anyhow /'enıhaʊ/ *adv* de todas formas; (*in spite of all*) a pesar de todo; (*badly*) de cualquier manera

anyone /'enıwʌn/ *pron see* ANYBODY

anything /'enıθıŋ/ *pron* algo; (*whatever*) cualquier cosa; (*after negative*) nada. ~ **but** todo menos

anyway /'enɪweɪ/ *adv* de todas formas

anywhere /'enɪweə(r)/ *adv* en cualquier parte; (*after negative*) en ningún sitio. **~ else** en cualquier otro lugar. **~ you go** dondequiera que vayas

apart /ə'pɑ:t/ *adv* aparte; (*separated*) separado. **~ from** aparte de. **come ~** romperse. **take ~** desmontar

apartheid /ə'pɑ:theɪt/ *n* apartheid *m*

apartment /ə'pɑ:tmənt/ *n* (*Amer*) apartamento *m*, piso *m*. **~ building** *n* (*Amer*) edificio *m* de apartamentos, casa *f* de pisos

apath|etic /æpə'θetɪk/ *adj* apático. **~y** /'æpəθɪ/ *n* apatía *f*

ape /eɪp/ *n* mono *m*. ● *vt* imitar

aperitif /ə'perətɪf/ *n* aperitivo *m*

aperture /'æpətʃʊə(r)/ *n* abertura *f*

apex /'eɪpeks/ *n* ápice *m*

aphrodisiac /æfrə'dɪzɪæk/ *adj* & *n* afrodisíaco (*m*), afrodisiaco (*m*)

apolog|etic /əpɒlə'dʒetɪk/ *adj* lleno de disculpas. **be ~etic** disculparse. **~ize** /ə'pɒlədʒaɪz/ *vi* disculparse (**for** de). **~y** /ə'pɒlədʒɪ/ *n* disculpa *f*

apostle /ə'pɒsl/ *n* apóstol *m*

apostrophe /ə'pɒstrəfɪ/ *n* apóstrofo *m*

appal /ə'pɔ:l/ *vt* (*pt* **appalled**) horrorizar. **~ling** *adj* espantoso

apparatus /æpə'reɪtəs/ *n* aparato *m*

apparel /ə'pærəl/ *n* (*Amer*) ropa *f*

apparent /ə'pærənt/ *adj* aparente; (*clear*) evidente. **~ly** *adv* por lo visto

apparition /æpə'rɪʃn/ *n* aparición *f*

appeal /ə'pi:l/ *vi* apelar; (*attract*) atraer. ● *n* llamamiento *m*; (*attraction*) atractivo *m*; (*Jurid*) apelación *f*. **~ing** *adj* atrayente

appear /ə'pɪə(r)/ *vi* aparecer; (*seem*) parecer; (*in court*) comparecer. **~ance** *n* aparición *f*; (*aspect*) aspecto *m*; (*in court*) comparecencia *f*

appease /ə'pi:z/ *vt* aplacar; (*pacify*) apaciguar

append /ə'pend/ *vt* adjuntar

appendicitis /əpendɪ'saɪtɪs/ *n* apendicitis *f*

appendix /ə'pendɪks/ *n* (*pl* **-ices** /-ɪsi:z/) (*of book*) apéndice *m*. (*pl* **-ixes**) (*organ*) apéndice *m*

appetite /'æpɪtaɪt/ *n* apetito *m*

applau|d /ə'plɔ:d/ *vt/i* aplaudir. **~se** /ə'plɔ:z/ *n* aplausos *mpl*. **round of ~se** aplauso *m*

apple /'æpl/ *n* manzana *f*. **~ tree** *n* manzano *m*

appliance /ə'plaɪəns/ *n* aparato *m*. **electrical ~** electrodoméstico *m*

applic|able /'æplɪkəbl/ *adj* aplicable; (*relevant*) pertinente. **~ant** /'æplɪkənt/ *n* candidato *m*, solicitante *m* & *f*. **~ation** /æplɪ'keɪʃn/ *n* aplicación *f*; (*request*) solicitud *f*. **~ation form** formulario *m* (de solicitud)

appl|ied /ə'plaɪd/ *adj* aplicado. **~y** /ə'plaɪ/ *vt* aplicar. ● *vi* aplicarse; (*ask*) presentar una solicitud. **~y for** solicitar (job etc)

appoint /ə'pɔɪnt/ *vt* nombrar; (*fix*) señalar. **~ment** *n* cita *f*

apprais|al /ə'preɪzl/ *n* evaluación *f*. **~e** /ə'preɪz/ *vt* evaluar

appreciable /ə'pri:ʃəbl/ *adj* (*considerable*) considerable

appreciat|e /ə'pri:ʃɪeɪt/ *vt* (*value*)

a

apreciar; (*understand*) comprender; (*be grateful for*) agradecer. **~ion** /-'eɪʃn/ *n* aprecio *m*; (*gratitude*) agradecimiento *m*. **~ive** /ə 'pri:ʃɪətɪv/ *adj* agradecido

apprehen|sion /æprɪ'henʃn/ *n* (*fear*) recelo *f*. **~sive** *adj* aprensivo

apprentice /ə'prentɪs/ *n* aprendiz *m*. ● *vt*. **be ~d to s.o.** estar de aprendiz con uno. **~ship** *n* aprendizaje *m*

approach /ə'prəʊtʃ/ *vt* acercarse a. ● *vi* acercarse. ● *n* acercamiento *m*; (*to problem*) enfoque *m*; (*access*) acceso *m*

appropriate /ə'prəʊprɪət/ *adj* apropiado. ● /ə'prəʊprɪeɪt/ *vt* apropiarse de. **~ly** /-ətli/ *adv* apropiadamente

approv|al /ə'pru:vl/ *n* aprobación *f*. **on ~al** a prueba. **~e** /ə'pru:v/ *vt/i* aprobar. **~ingly** *adv* con aprobación

approximat|e /ə'prɒksɪmət/ *adj* aproximado. ● /ə'prɒksɪmeɪt/ *vt* aproximarse a. **~ely** /-ətlɪ/ *adv* aproximadamente. **~ion** /-'meɪʃn/ *n* aproximación *f*

apricot /'eɪprɪkɒt/ *n* albaricoque *m*, chabacano *m* (*Mex*)

April /'eɪprəl/ *n* abril *m*. **~ fool!** ¡inocentón!

apron /'eɪprən/ *n* delantal *m*

apt /æpt/ *adj* apropiado. **be ~ to** tener tendencia a. **~itude** /'æptɪtju:d/ *n* aptitud *f*. **~ly** *adv* acertadamente

aquarium /ə'kweərɪəm/ *n* (*pl* **-ums**) acuario *m*

Aquarius /ə'kweərɪəs/ *n* Acuario *m*

aquatic /ə'kwætɪk/ *adj* acuático

aqueduct /'ækwɪdʌkt/ *n* acueducto *m*

Arab /'ærəb/ *adj & n* árabe (*m & f*). **~ian** /ə'reɪbɪən/ *adj* árabe. **~ic** /'ærəbɪk/ *adj & n* árabe (*m*). **~ic numerals** números *mpl* arábigos

arable /'ærəbl/ *adj* cultivable

arbitrary /'ɑ:bɪtrərɪ/ *adj* arbitrario

arbitrat|e /'ɑ:bɪtreɪt/ *vi* arbitrar. **~ion** /-'treɪʃn/ *n* arbitraje *m*. **~or** *n* árbitro *m*

arc /ɑ:k/ *n* arco *m*

arcade /ɑ:'keɪd/ *n* arcada *f*; (*around square*) soportales *mpl*; (*shops*) galería *f*

arch /ɑ:tʃ/ *n* arco *m*. ● *vt* arquear. ● *vi* arquearse

archaeolog|ical /ɑ:kɪə'lɒdʒɪkl/ *adj* arqueológico. **~ist** /ɑ:kɪ 'ɒlədʒɪst/ *n* arqueólogo *m*. **~y** /ɑ:kɪ'ɒlədʒɪ/ *n* arqueología *f*

archaic /ɑ:'keɪɪk/ *adj* arcaico

archbishop /ɑ:tʃ'bɪʃəp/ *n* arzobispo *m*

archer /'ɑ:tʃə(r)/ *n* arquero *m*. **~y** *n* tiro *m* con arco

architect /'ɑ:kɪtekt/ *n* arquitecto *m*. **~ure** /-tʃə(r)/ *n* arquitectura *f*. **~ural** /-'tektʃərəl/ *adj* arquitectónico

archives /'ɑ:kaɪvz/ *npl* archivo *m*

archway /'ɑ:tʃweɪ/ *n* arco *m*

Arctic /'ɑ:ktɪk/ *adj* ártico. ● *n*. **the ~** el Ártico

ard|ent /'ɑ:dənt/ *adj* fervoroso; (supporter, lover) apasionado. **~our** /'ɑ:də(r)/ *n* fervor *m*; (*love*) pasión *f*

arduous /'ɑ:djʊəs/ *adj* arduo

are /ɑ:(r)/ *see* BE

area /'eərɪə/ *n* (*Math*) superficie *f*; (*of country*) zona *f*; (*of city*) barrio *m*

arena /ə'ri:nə/ *n* arena *f*; (*scene of activity*) ruedo *m*

aren't /ɑ:nt/ = **are not**

Argentin|a /ɑːdʒən'tiːnə/ *n* Argentina *f*. **~ian** /-'tɪnɪən/ *adj & n* argentino (*m*)

argu|able /'ɑːgjʊəbl/ *adj* discutible. **~e** /'ɑːgjuː/ *vi* discutir; (*reason*) razonar. **~ment** /'ɑːgjʊmənt/ *n* disputa *f*; (*reasoning*) argumento *m*. **~mentative** /ɑːgjʊ'mentətɪv/ *adj* discutidor

arid /'ærɪd/ *adj* árido

Aries /'eəriːz/ *n* Aries *m*

arise /ə'raɪz/ *vi* (*pt* **arose**, *pp* **arisen**) surgir (**from** de)

aristocra|cy /ærɪ'stɒkrəsɪ/ *n* aristocracia *f*. **~t** /'ærɪstəkræt/ *n* aristócrata *m & f*. **~tic** /-'krætɪk/ *adj* aristocrático

arithmetic /ə'rɪθmətɪk/ *n* aritmética *f*

ark /ɑːk/ *n* (*Relig*) arca *f*

arm /ɑːm/ *n* brazo *m*; (*of garment*) manga *f*. **~s** *npl* armas *fpl*. ● *vt* armar

armament /'ɑːməmənt/ *n* armamento *m*

arm: ~band *n* brazalete *m*. **~chair** *n* sillón *m*

armed /ɑːmd/ *adj* armado. **~ robbery** *n* robo *m* a mano armada

armful /'ɑːmfʊl/ *n* brazada *f*

armour /'ɑːmə(r)/ *n* armadura *f*. **~ed** /'ɑːməd/ *adj* blindado. **~y** /'ɑːmərɪ/ *n* arsenal *m*

armpit /'ɑːmpɪt/ *n* sobaco *m*, axila *f*

army /'ɑːmɪ/ *n* ejército *m*

aroma /ə'rəʊmə/ *n* aroma *m*

arose /ə'rəʊz/ *see* ARISE

around /ə'raʊnd/ *adv* alrededor; (*near*) cerca. **all ~** por todas partes. ● *prep* alrededor de; (*with time*) a eso de

arouse /ə'raʊz/ *vt* despertar

arrange /ə'reɪndʒ/ *vt* arreglar; (*fix*) fijar. **~ment** *n* arreglo *m*; (*agreement*) acuerdo *m*. **~ments** *npl* (*plans*) preparativos *mpl*

arrears /ə'rɪəz/ *npl* atrasos *mpl*. **in ~** atrasado en el pago (**with** de)

arrest /ə'rest/ *vt* detener. ● *n* detención *f*. **under ~** detenido

arriv|al /ə'raɪvl/ *n* llegada *f*. **new ~al** recién llegado *m*. **~e** /ə'raɪv/ *vi* llegar

arrogan|ce /'ærəgəns/ *n* arrogancia *f*. **~t** *adj* arrogante. **~tly** *adv* con arrogancia

arrow /'ærəʊ/ *n* flecha *f*

arse /ɑːs/ *n* (*vulgar*) culo *m*

arsenal /'ɑːsənl/ *n* arsenal *m*

arsenic /'ɑːsnɪk/ *n* arsénico *m*

arson /'ɑːsn/ *n* incendio *m* provocado. **~ist** *n* incendiario *m*

art¹ /ɑːt/ *n* arte *m*. **A~s** *npl* (*Univ*) Filosofía y Letras *fpl*. **fine ~s** bellas artes *fpl*

art² /ɑːt/ (*old use, with* **thou**) *see* ARE

artery /'ɑːtərɪ/ *n* arteria *f*

art gallery *n* museo *m* de arte, pinacoteca *f*; (commercial) galería *f* de arte

arthritis /ɑː'θraɪtɪs/ *n* artritis *f*

article /'ɑːtɪkl/ *n* artículo *m*. **~ of clothing** prenda *f* de vestir

articulat|e /ɑː'tɪkjʊlət/ *adj* (utterance) articulado; (person) que sabe expresarse. ● /ɑː'tɪkjʊleɪt/ *vt/i* articular. **~ed lorry** *n* camión *m* articulado. **~ion** /-'leɪʃn/ *n* articulación *f*

artificial /ɑːtɪ'fɪʃl/ *adj* artificial. **~ respiration** respiración *f* artificial

artillery /ɑː'tɪlərɪ/ *n* artillería *f*

artist /'ɑːtɪst/ *n* artista *m & f*. **~tic** /ɑː'tɪstɪk/ *adj* artístico. **~ry** /'ɑːtɪstrɪ/ *n* arte *m*, habilidad *f*

as /æz, əz/ *adv & conj* como; (*since*) ya que; (*while*) mientras. **~ big ~**

a

tan grande como. ~ **far** ~ (*distance*) hasta; (*qualitative*) en cuanto a. ~ **far** ~ **I know** que yo sepa. ~ **if** como si. ~ **long** ~ mientras. ~ **much** ~ tanto como. ~ **soon** ~ tan pronto como. ~ **well** también

asbestos /æz'bestɒs/ *n* amianto *m*, asbesto *m*

ascen|d /ə'send/ *vt/i* subir. **A~sion** /ə'senʃn/ *n*. **the A~sion** la Ascensión. **~t** /ə'sent/ *n* subida *f*

ascertain /æsə'teɪn/ *vt* averiguar

ash /æʃ/ *n* ceniza *f*. ● *n*. ~ **(tree)** fresno *m*

ashamed /ə'ʃeɪmd/ *adj* avergonzado (**of** de). **be** ~ **of s.o.** avergonzarse de uno

ashore /ə'ʃɔ:(r)/ *adv* a tierra. **go** ~ desembarcar

ash: ~tray *n* cenicero *m*. **A~ Wednesday** *n* Miércoles *m* de Ceniza

Asia /'eɪʃə/ *n* Asia *f*. **~n** *adj & n* asiático (*m*). **~tic** /-ɪ'ætɪk/ *adj* asiático

aside /ə'saɪd/ *adv* a un lado. ● *n* (*in theatre*) aparte *m*

ask /ɑ:sk/ *vt* pedir; hacer (question); (*invite*) invitar. ~ **about** enterarse de. ~ **s.o. to do something** pedirle a uno que haga algo. □ ~ **after** *vt* preguntar por. □ ~ **for** *vt*. ~ **for help** pedir ayuda. ~ **for trouble** buscarse problemas. □ ~ **in** *vt*. ~ **s.o. in** invitar a uno a pasar

askew /ə'skju:/ *adv & adj* torcido

asleep /ə'sli:p/ *adv & adj* dormido. **fall** ~ dormirse

asparagus /ə'spærəgəs/ *n* espárrago *m*

aspect /'æspekt/ *n* aspecto *m*

asphalt /'æsfælt/ *n* asfalto *m*. ● *vt* asfaltar

aspir|ation /æspə'reɪʃn/ *n* aspiración *f*. **~e** /əs'paɪə(r)/ *vi* aspirar

aspirin /'æsprɪn/ *n* aspirina *f*

ass /æs/ *n* asno *m*; (*fig, fam*) imbécil *m*; (*Amer vulgar*) culo *m*

assassin /ə'sæsɪn/ *n* asesino *m*. **~ate** /-eɪt/ *vt* asesinar. **~ation** /-'eɪʃn/ *n* asesinato *m*

assault /ə'sɔ:lt/ *n* (*Mil*) ataque *m*; (*Jurid*) atentado *m*. ● *vt* asaltar

assembl|e /ə'sembl/ *vt* reunir; (*Mec*) montar. ● *vi* reunirse. **~y** *n* reunión *f*; (*Pol etc*) asamblea *f*. **~y line** *n* línea *f* de montaje

assent /ə'sent/ *n* asentimiento *m*. ● *vi* asentir

assert /ə'sɜ:t/ *vt* afirmar; hacer valer (one's rights). **~ion** /-ʃn/ *n* afirmación *f*. **~ive** *adj* positivo, firme

assess /ə'ses/ *vt* evaluar; (*determine*) determinar; fijar (tax etc). **~ment** *n* evaluación *f*

asset /'æset/ *n* (*advantage*) ventaja *f*. **~s** *npl* (*Com*) bienes *mpl*

assign /ə'saɪn/ *vt* asignar; (*appoint*) nombrar. **~ment** *n* asignación *f*; (*mission*) misión *f*; (*task*) función *f*; (*for school*) trabajo *m*

assimilate /ə'sɪmɪleɪt/ *vt* asimilar. ● *vi* asimilarse

assist /ə'sɪst/ *vt/i* ayudar. **~ance** *n* ayuda *f*. **~ant** *n* ayudante *m & f*; (*shop*) dependienta *f*, dependiente *m*. ● *adj* auxiliar, adjunto

associat|e /ə'səʊʃɪeɪt/ *vt* asociar. ● *vi* asociarse. ● /ə'səʊʃɪət/ *adj* asociado. ● *n* colega *m & f*; (*Com*) socio *m*. **~ion** /-'eɪʃn/ *n* asociación *f*.

assort|ed /ə'sɔ:tɪd/ *adj* surtido. **~ment** *n* surtido *m*

assum|e /ə'sju:m/ *vt* suponer; tomar (power, attitude); asumir (role, burden). **~ption** /ə'sʌmpʃn/ *n* suposición *f*

assur|ance /ə'ʃʊərəns/ *n* seguridad *f*; (*insurance*) seguro *m*. **~e** /ə'ʃʊə(r)/ *vt* asegurar. **~ed** *adj* seguro

asterisk /'æstərɪsk/ *n* asterisco *m*

asthma /'æsmə/ *n* asma *f*. **~tic** /-'mætɪk/ *adj & n* asmático (*m*)

astonish /ə'stɒnɪʃ/ *vt* asombrar. **~ed** *adj* asombrado. **~ing** *adj* asombroso. **~ment** *n* asombro *m*

astound /ə'staʊnd/ *vt* asombrar. **~ed** *adj* atónito. **~ing** *adj* increíble

astray /ə'streɪ/ *adv*. **go ~** extraviarse. **lead ~** llevar por mal camino

astrology /ə'strɒlədʒɪ/ *n* astrología *f*

astronaut /'æstrənɔ:t/ *n* astronauta *m & f*

astronom|er /ə'strɒnəmə(r)/ *n* astrónomo *m*. **~ical** /æstrə'nɒmɪkl/ *adj* astronómico. **~y** /ə'strɒnəmɪ/ *n* astronomía *f*

astute /ə'stju:t/ *adj* astuto

asylum /ə'saɪləm/ *n* asilo *m*. **lunatic ~** manicomio *m*. **~ seeker** *n* solicitante *m & f* de asilo

at /æt/ *preposition*

····➤ (*location*) en. **she's at the office** está en la oficina. **at home** en casa. **call me at the office** llámame a la oficina

➡ For translations of phrases such as **at the top, at the front of, at the back of** see entries **top, front** etc

····➤ (*at the house of*) en casa de. **I'll be at Rachel's** estaré en casa de Rachel

····➤ (*Comput*: @) arroba *f*

····➤ (*talking about time*) **at 7 o'clock** a las siete. **at night** por la noche, de noche, en la noche (*LAm*). **at Christmas** en Navidad

····➤ (*talking about age*) a. **at six (years of age)** a los seis años

····➤ (*with measurements, numbers etc*) a. **at 60 miles an hour** a 60 millas por hora. **at a depth of** a una profundidad de. **three at a time** de tres en tres

➡ For translations of phrasal verbs with **at**, such as **look at**, see entries for those verbs

ate /et/ *see* EAT

atheis|m /'eɪθɪɪzəm/ *n* ateísmo *m*. **~t** *n* ateo *m*

athlet|e /'æθli:t/ *n* atleta *m & f*. **~ic** /-'letɪk/ *adj* atlético. **~ics** *npl* atletismo *m*; (*Amer, Sport*) deportes *mpl*

Atlantic /ət'læntɪk/ *adj* atlántico. ● *n*. **the ~ (Ocean)** el (Océano) Atlántico

atlas /'ætləs/ *n* atlas *m*

ATM *abbr* (= **automated teller machine**) cajero *m* automático

atmospher|e /'ætməsfɪə(r)/ *n* atmósfera *f*; (*fig*) ambiente *m*. **~ic** /-'ferɪk/ *adj* atmosférico

atom /'ætəm/ *n* átomo *m*. **~ic** /ə'tɒmɪk/ *adj* atómico

atroci|ous /ə'trəʊʃəs/ *adj* atroz. **~ty** /ə'trɒsətɪ/ *n* atrocidad *f*

attach /ə'tætʃ/ *vt* sujetar; adjuntar (document etc). **be ~ed to** (*be fond of*) tener cariño a. **~ment** *n* (*affection*) cariño *m*; (*tool*) accesorio *m*

attack /ə'tæk/ *n* ataque *m*. ● *vt/i* atacar. **~er** *n* agresor *m*

attain /ə'teɪn/ *vt* conseguir. **~able** *adj* alcanzable

attempt /ə'tempt/ *vt* intentar. ● *n* tentativa *f*; (*attack*) atentado *m*

attend /ə'tend/ *vt* asistir a; (*escort*) acompañar. ● *vi* prestar atención. □ **~ to** *vt* (*look after*) ocuparse de. **~ance** *n* asistencia *f*; (*people present*) concurrencia *f*.

atten|tion /ə'tenʃn/ *n* atención *f*. **~tion!** (*Mil*) ¡firmes! **pay ~tion** prestar atención. **~tive** *adj* atento

attic /'ætɪk/ *n* desván *m*

attire /ə'taɪə(r)/ *n* atavío *m*. ● *vt* ataviar

attitude /'ætɪtju:d/ *n* postura *f*

attorney /ə'tɜ:nɪ/ *n* (*pl* **-eys**) (*Amer*) abogado *m*

attract /ə'trækt/ *vt* atraer. **~ion** /-ʃn/ *n* atracción *f*; (*charm*) atractivo *m*. **~ive** *adj* atractivo; (*interesting*) atrayente

attribute /ə'trɪbju:t/ *vt* atribuir. ● /'ætrɪbju:t/ *n* atributo *m*

aubergine /'əʊbəʒi:n/ *n* berenjena *f*

auction /'ɔ:kʃn/ *n* subasta *f*. ● *vt* subastar. **~eer** /-ə'nɪə(r)/ *n* subastador *m*

audaci|ous /ɔ:'deɪʃəs/ *adj* audaz. **~ty** /ɔ:'dæsətɪ/ *n* audacia *f*

audible /'ɔ:dəbl/ *adj* audible

audience /'ɔ:dɪəns/ *n* (*at play, film*) público *m*; (*TV*) audiencia *f*; (*interview*) audiencia *f*

audiovisual /ɔ:dɪəʊ'vɪʒʊəl/ *adj* audiovisual

audit /'ɔ:dɪt/ *n* revisión *f* de cuentas. ● *vt* revisar

audition /ɔ:'dɪʃn/ *n* audición *f*. ● *vt* hacerle una audición a. ● *vi* dar una audición (**for** para)

auditor /'ɔ:dɪtə(r)/ *n* interventor *m* de cuentas

auditorium /ɔ:dɪ'tɔ:rɪəm/ (*pl* **-riums** *or* **-ria** /-rɪə/) *n* sala *f*, auditorio *m*

augment /ɔ:g'ment/ *vt* aumentar

augur /'ɔ:gə(r)/ *vt* augurar. **it ~s well** es de buen agüero

August /'ɔ:gəst/ *n* agosto *m*

aunt /ɑ:nt/ *n* tía *f*

au pair /əʊ'peə(r)/ *n* chica *f* au pair

aura /'ɔ:rə/ *n* aura *f*, halo *m*

auster|e /ɔ:'stɪə(r)/ *adj* austero. **~ity** /ɔ:'sterətɪ/ *n* austeridad *f*

Australia /ɒ'streɪlɪə/ *n* Australia *f*. **~n** *adj & n* australiano (*m*)

Austria /'ɒstrɪə/ *n* Austria *f*. **~n** *adj & n* austríaco (*m*)

authentic /ɔ:'θentɪk/ *adj* auténtico. **~ate** /-keɪt/ *vt* autenticar. **~ity** /-ən'tɪsətɪ/ *n* autenticidad *f*

author /'ɔ:θə(r)/ *n* autor *m*. **~ess** /-ɪs/ *n* autora *f*

authoritative /ɔ:'θɒrɪtətɪv/ *adj* autorizado; (*manner*) autoritario

authority /ɔ:'θɒrətɪ/ *n* autoridad *f*; (*permission*) autorización *f*

authoriz|ation /ɔ:θəraɪ'zeɪʃn/ *n* autorización *f*. **~e** /'ɔ:θəraɪz/ *vt* autorizar

autobiography /ɔ:təʊbaɪ'ɒgrəfɪ/ *n* autobiografía *f*

autograph /'ɔ:təgrɑ:f/ *n* autógrafo *m*. ● *vt* firmar, autografiar

automat|e /'ɔ:təmeɪt/ *vt* automatizar. **~ic** /-'mætɪk/ *adj* automático. **~ion** /-'meɪʃn/ *n* automatización *f*. **~on** /ɔ:'tɒmətən/ *n* (*pl* **-tons** *or* **-ta** /-tə/) autómata *m*

automobile /'ɔ:təməbi:l/ *n*

(*Amer*) coche *m*, carro *m* (*LAm*), automóvil *m*

autonom|ous /ɔ:'tɒnəməs/ *adj* autónomo. **~y** *n* autonomía *f*

autopsy /'ɔ:tɒpsɪ/ *n* autopsia *f*

autumn /'ɔ:təm/ *n* otoño *m*. **~al** /ɔ:'tʌmnəl/ *adj* otoñal

auxiliary /ɔ:g'zɪlɪərɪ/ *adj & n* auxiliar (*m & f*)

avail /ə'veɪl/ *n*. **to no ~** inútil

availab|ility /əveɪlə'bɪlətɪ/ *n* disponibilidad *f*. **~le** /ə'veɪləbl/ *adj* disponible

avalanche /'ævəlɑ:nʃ/ *n* avalancha *f*

avaric|e /'ævərɪs/ *n* avaricia *f*. **~ious** /-'rɪʃəs/ *adj* avaro

avenue /'ævənju:/ *n* avenida *f*; (*fig*) vía *f*

average /'ævərɪdʒ/ *n* promedio *m*. **on ~** por término medio. ● *adj* medio

avers|e /ə'vɜ:s/ *adj*. **be ~e to** ser reacio a. **~ion** /-ʃn/ *n* repugnancia *f*

avert /ə'vɜ:t/ *vt* (*turn away*) apartar; (*ward off*) desviar

aviation /eɪvɪ'eɪʃn/ *n* aviación *f*

avid /'ævɪd/ *adj* ávido

avocado /ævə'kɑ:dəʊ/ *n* (*pl* **-os**) aguacate *m*

avoid /ə'vɔɪd/ *vt* evitar. **~able** *adj* evitable. **~ance** *n* el evitar

await /ə'weɪt/ *vt* esperar

awake /ə'weɪk/ *vt/i* (*pt* **awoke**, *pp* **awoken**) despertar. ● *adj* despierto. **wide ~** completamente despierto; (*fig*) despabilado. **~n** /ə'weɪkən/ *vt/i* despertar. **~ning** *n* el despertar

award /ə'wɔ:d/ *vt* otorgar; (*Jurid*) adjudicar. ● *n* premio *m*; (*Jurid*) adjudicación *f*; (*scholarship*) beca *f*

aware /ə'weə(r)/ *adj*. **be ~ of sth** ser consciente de algo, darse cuenta de algo. **~ness** *n* conciencia *f*

awash /ə'wɒʃ/ *adj* inundado

away /ə'weɪ/ *adv* (*absent*) fuera. **far ~** muy lejos. ● *adj* **~ match** partido *m* fuera de casa

awe /ɔ:/ *n* temor *m*. **~-inspiring** *adj* impresionante. **~some** /-səm/ *adj* imponente

awful /'ɔ:fʊl/ *adj* terrible, malísimo. **feel ~** sentirse muy mal

awkward /'ɔ:kwəd/ *adj* difícil; (*inconvenient*) inoportuno; (*clumsy*) desmañado; (*embarrassed*) incómodo. **~ness** *n* dificultad *f*; (*discomfort*) molestia *f*; (*clumsiness*) torpeza *f*

awning /'ɔ:nɪŋ/ *n* toldo *m*

awoke/ə'wəʊk/, **awoken** /ə'wəʊkən/ *see* **AWAKE**

axe /æks/ *n* hacha *f*. ● *vt* (*pres p* **axing**) cortar con hacha; (*fig*) recortar

axis /'æksɪs/ *n* (*pl* **axes**/-i:z/) eje *m*

axle /'æksl/ *n* eje *m*

Bb

BA /bi:'eɪ/ *abbr see* **BACHELOR**

babble /'bæbl/ *vi* balbucir; (*chatter*) parlotear; (stream) murmullar.

baboon /bə'bu:n/ *n* mandril *m*

baby /'beɪbɪ/ *n* niño *m*, bebé *m*. **~ buggy**, **~ carriage** *n* (*Amer*) cochecito *m*. **~ish** *adj* /'beɪbɪɪʃ/ infantil. **~-sit** *vi* cuidar a los niños, hacer de canguro. **~-sitter** *n* baby sitter *m & f*, canguro *m & f*

bachelor /ˈbætʃələ(r)/ *n* soltero *m*. **B~ of Arts (BA)** licenciado *m* en filosofía y letras. **B~ of Science (BSc)** licenciado *m* en ciencias

back /bæk/ *n* espalda *f*; (*of car*) parte *f* trasera; (*of chair*) respaldo *m*; (*of cloth*) revés *m*; (*of house*) parte *f* de atrás; (*of animal, book*) lomo *m*; (*of hand, document*) dorso *m*; (*football*) defensa *m & f*. **in the ~ of beyond** en el quinto infierno. ● *adj* trasero. **the ~ door** la puerta trasera. ● *adv* atrás; (*returned*) de vuelta. ● *vt* apoyar; (*betting*) apostar a; dar marcha atrás a (car). ● *vi* retroceder; (car) dar marcha atrás. □ **~ down** *vi* volverse atrás. □ **~ out** *vi* retirarse. □ **~ up** *vt* apoyar; (*Comp*) hacer una copia de seguridad de. **~ache** *n* dolor *m* de espalda. **~bone** *n* columna *f* vertebral; (*fig*) pilar *m*. **~date** /-ˈdeɪt/ *vt* antedatar. **~er** *n* partidario *m*; (*Com*) financiador *m*. **~fire** /-ˈfaɪə(r)/ *vi* (*Auto*) petardear; (*fig*) fallar. **his plan ~fired on him** le salió el tiro por la culata. **~ground** *n* fondo *m*; (*environment*) antecedentes *mpl*. **~hand** *n* (*Sport*) revés *m*. **~ing** *n* apoyo *m*. **~lash** *n* reacción *f*. **~log** *n* atrasos *mpl*. **~side** /-ˈsaɪd/ *n* [I] trasero *m*. **~stage** /-ˈsteɪdʒ/ *adj* de bastidores. ● *adv* entre bastidores. **~stroke** *n* (*tennis etc*) revés *m*; (*swimming*) estilo *m* espalda, estilo *m* dorso (*Mex*). **~-up** *n* apoyo *m*; (*Comp*) copia *f* de seguridad. **~ward** /-wəd/ *adj* (step etc) hacia atrás; (*retarded*) retrasado; (*undeveloped*) atrasado. ● *adv* (*Amer*) *see* **BACKWARDS**. **~wards** *adv* hacia atrás; (*fall*) de espaldas; (*back to front*) al revés. **go ~wards and forwards** ir de acá para allá. **~water** *n* agua *f* estancada; (*fig*) lugar *m* apartado

bacon /ˈbeɪkən/ *n* tocino *m*

bacteria /bækˈtɪərɪə/ *npl* bacterias *fpl*

bad /bæd/ *adj* (**worse**, **worst**) malo, (*before masculine singular noun*) mal; (*serious*) grave; (*harmful*) nocivo; (language) indecente. **feel ~** sentirse mal

bade /beɪd/ *see* **BID**

badge /bædʒ/ *n* distintivo *m*, chapa *f*

badger /ˈbædʒə(r)/ *n* tejón *m*. ● *vt* acosar

bad: ~ly *adv* mal. **want ~ly** desear muchísimo. **~ly injured** gravemente herido. **~ly off** mal de dinero. **~-mannered** /-ˈmænəd/ *adj* mal educado

badminton /ˈbædmɪntən/ *n* bádminton *m*

bad-tempered /bædˈtempəd/ *adj* (*always*) de mal carácter; (*temporarily*) de mal humor

baffle /ˈbæfl/ *vt* desconcertar. **~d** *adj* perplejo

bag /bæg/ *n* bolsa *f*; (*handbag*) bolso *m*. ● *vt* (*pt* **bagged**) ensacar; (*take*) coger (*esp Spain*), agarrar (*LAm*). **~s** *npl* (*luggage*) equipaje *m*

baggage /ˈbægɪdʒ/ *n* equipaje *m*. **~ room** *n* (*Amer*) consigna *f*

baggy /ˈbægɪ/ *adj* (clothes) holgado

bagpipes /ˈbægpaɪps/ *npl* gaita *f*

baguette /bæˈget/ *n* baguette *f*

bail¹ /beɪl/ *n* fianza *f*. ● *vt* poner en libertad bajo fianza. **~ s.o. out** pagar la fianza a uno

bail² *vt*. **~ out** (*Naut*) achicar

bait /beɪt/ *n* cebo *m*

bak|e /beɪk/ *vt* cocer al horno. ● *vi* cocerse. **~er** *n* panadero *m*. **~ery**

n panadería *f*

balance /'bæləns/ *n* equilibrio *m*; (*Com*) balance *m*; (*sum*) saldo *m*; (*scales*) balanza *f*; (*remainder*) resto *m*. ● *vt* equilibrar (load); mantener en equilibrio (object); nivelar (budget). ● *vi* equilibrarse; (*Com*) cuadrar. **~d** *adj* equilibrado

balcony /'bælkənɪ/ *n* balcón *m*

bald /bɔ:ld/ *adj* (**-er**, **-est**) calvo, pelón (*Mex*)

bale /beɪl/ *n* bala *f*, fardo *m*. ● *vi*. **~ out** lanzarse en paracaídas

Balearic /bælɪ'ærɪk/ *adj*. **the ~ Islands** las Islas *fpl* Baleares

ball /bɔ:l/ *n* bola *f*; (*tennis etc*) pelota *f*; (*football etc*) balón *m*, pelota *f* (*esp LAm*); (*of yarn*) ovillo *m*; (*dance*) baile *m*

ballad /'bæləd/ *n* balada *f*

ballast /'bæləst/ *n* lastre *m*

ball bearing *n* cojinete *m* de bolas

ballerina /bælə'ri:nə/ *f* bailarina *f*

ballet /'bæleɪ/ *n* ballet *m*. **~ dancer** *n* bailarín *m* de ballet, bailarina *f* de ballet

balloon /bə'lu:n/ *n* globo *m*

ballot /'bælət/ *n* votación *f*. **~ box** *n* urna *f*. **~ paper** *n* papeleta *f*.

ball: ~point *n*. **~point (pen)** bolígrafo *m*, pluma *f* atómica (*Mex*). **~room** *n* salón *m* de baile

bamboo /bæm'bu:/ *n* bambú *m*

ban /bæn/ *vt* (*pt* **banned**) prohibir. **~ s.o. from sth** prohibir algo a uno. ● *n* prohibición *f*

banal /bə'nɑ:l/ *adj* banal. **~ity** /bə'næləti/ *n* banalidad *f*

banana /bə'nɑ:nə/ *n* plátano *m*

band /bænd/ *n* (*strip*) banda *f*. ● *n* (*Mus*) orquesta *f*; (*military, brass*) banda *f*. □ **~ together** *vi* juntarse

bandage /'bændɪdʒ/ *n* venda *f*. ● *vt* vendar

Band-Aid /'bændeɪd/ *n* (*Amer*, ®) tirita *f*, curita *f* (*LAm*)

B & B /'bi:ənbi:/ *abbr* (= **bed and breakfast**) cama *f* y desayuno; (*place*) pensión *f*

bandit /'bændɪt/ *n* bandido *m*

band: ~stand *n* quiosco *m* de música. **~wagon** *n*. **jump on the ~wagon** (*fig*) subirse al carro

bandy /'bændɪ/ *adj* (**-ier**, **-iest**) patizambo

bang /bæŋ/ *n* (*noise*) ruido *m*; (*blow*) golpe *m*; (*of gun*) estampido *m*; (*of door*) golpe *m*. ● *vt* (*strike*) golpear. **~ the door** dar un portazo. ● *adv* exactamente. ● *int* ¡pum! **~s** *npl* (*Amer*) flequillo *m*, cerquillo *m* (*LAm*), fleco *m* (*Mex*)

banger /'bæŋə(r)/ *n* petardo *m*; (Ⓘ, *Culin*) salchicha *f*

bangle /'bæŋgl/ *n* brazalete *m*

banish /'bænɪʃ/ *vt* desterrar

banisters /'bænɪstəz/ *npl* pasamanos *m*

banjo /'bændʒəʊ/ *n* (*pl* **-os**) banjo *m*

bank /bæŋk/ *n* (*Com*) banco *m*; (*of river*) orilla *f*. ● *vt* depositar. ● *vi* (*in flying*) ladearse. □ **~ on** *vt* contar con. □ **~ with** *vi* tener una cuenta con. **~ card** *n* tarjeta *f* bancaria; (*Amer*) tarjeta *f* de crédito (*expedida por un banco*). **~er** *n* banquero *m*. **~ holiday** *n* día *m* festivo, día *m* feriado (*LAm*). **~ing** *n* (*Com*) banca *f*. **~note** *n* billete *m* de banco

bankrupt /'bæŋkrʌpt/ *adj* & *n* quebrado (*m*). **go ~** quebrar. ● *vt* hacer quebrar. **~cy** /-rʌpsɪ/ *n* bancarrota *f*, quiebra *f*

bank statement *n* estado *m*

b

de cuenta

banner /'bænə(r)/ *n* bandera *f*; (*in demonstration*) pancarta *f*

banquet /'bæŋkwɪt/ *n* banquete *m*

banter /'bæntə(r)/ *n* chanza *f*

bap /bæp/ *n* panecillo *m* blando

baptism /'bæptɪzəm/ *n* bautismo *m*; (*act*) bautizo *m*

Baptist /'bæptɪst/ *n* bautista *m & f*

baptize /bæp'taɪz/ *vt* bautizar

bar /bɑ:(r)/ *n* barra *f*; (*on window*) reja *f*; (*of chocolate*) tableta *f*; (*of soap*) pastilla *f*; (*pub*) bar *m*; (*Mus*) compás *m*; (*Jurid*) abogacía *f*; (*fig*) obstáculo *m*. ● *vt* (*pt* **barred**) atrancar (door); (*exclude*) excluir; (*prohibit*) prohibir. ● *prep* excepto

barbar|ian /bɑ:'beərɪən/ *adj & n* bárbaro (*m*). **~ic** /bɑ:'bærɪk/ *adj* bárbaro

barbecue /'bɑ:bɪkju:/ *n* barbacoa *f*. ● *vt* asar a la parilla

barbed wire /bɑ:bd 'waɪə(r)/ *n* alambre *m* de púas

barber /'bɑ:bə(r)/ *n* peluquero *m*, barbero *m*

barbwire /'bɑ:b'waɪə(r)/ *n* (*Amer*) *see* **BARBED WIRE**

bare /beə(r)/ *adj* (**-er**, **-est**) desnudo; (*room*) con pocos muebles; (*mere*) simple; (*empty*) vacío. ● *vt* desnudar; (*uncover*) descubrir. **~ one's teeth** mostrar los dientes. **~back** *adv* a pelo. **~faced** *adj* descarado. **~foot** *adj* descalzo. **~headed** /-'hedɪd/ *adj* descubierto. **~ly** *adv* apenas.

bargain /'bɑ:gɪn/ *n* (*agreement*) pacto *m*; (*good buy*) ganga *f*. ● *vi* negociar; (*haggle*) regatear. □ **~ for** *vt* esperar, contar con

barge /bɑ:dʒ/ *n* barcaza *f*. ● *vi*. **~ in** irrumpir

baritone /'bærɪtəʊn/ *n* barítono *m*

bark /bɑ:k/ *n* (*of dog*) ladrido *m*; (*of tree*) corteza *f*. ● *vi* ladrar

barley /'bɑ:lɪ/ *n* cebada *f*

bar: ~maid *n* camarera *f*. **~man** /-mən/ *n* camarero *m*, barman *m*

barmy /'bɑ:mɪ/ *adj* ⊠ chiflado

barn /bɑ:n/ *n* granero *m*

barometer /bə'rɒmɪtə(r)/ *n* barómetro *m*

baron /'bærən/ *n* barón *m*. **~ess** /-ɪs/ *n* baronesa *f*

barracks /'bærəks/ *npl* cuartel *m*

barrage /'bærɑ:ʒ/ *n* (*Mil*) barrera *f*; (*dam*) presa *f*. **a ~ of questions** un aluvión de preguntas

barrel /'bærəl/ *n* barril *m*; (*of gun*) cañón *m*

barren /'bærən/ *adj* estéril

barrette /bə'ret/ *n* (*Amer*) pasador *m*

barricade /bærɪ'keɪd/ *n* barricada *f*. ● *vt* cerrar con barricadas

barrier /'bærɪə(r)/ *n* barrera *f*

barrister /'bærɪstə(r)/ *n* abogado *m*

bartender /'bɑ:tendə(r)/ *n* (*Amer*) (*male*) camarero *m*, barman *m*; (*female*) camarera *f*

barter /'bɑ:tə(r)/ *n* trueque *m*. ● *vt* trocar

base /beɪs/ *n* base *f*. ● *vt* basar. **~ball** *n* béisbol *m*, beisbol *m* (*Mex*)

basement /'beɪsmənt/ *n* sótano *m*

bash /bæʃ/ *vt* golpear. ● *n* golpe *m*. **have a ~** 🅸 probar

bashful /'bæʃfl/ *adj* tímido

basic /'beɪsɪk/ *adj* básico, fundamental. **~ally** *adv* fundamentalmente

basin /ˈbeɪsn/ *n* (*for washing*) palangana *f*; (*for food*) cuenco *m*; (*of river*) cuenca *f*

basis /ˈbeɪsɪs/ *n* (*pl* **bases**/-siːz/) base *f*

bask /bɑːsk/ *vi* asolearse; (*fig*) gozar (**in** de)

basket /ˈbɑːskɪt/ *n* cesta *f*; (*big*) cesto *m*. **~ball** *n* baloncesto *m*, básquetbol *m* (*LAm*)

bass[1] /beɪs/ *adj* bajo. ● *n* (*Mus*) bajo *m*

bass[2] /bæs/ *n* (*fish*) lubina *f*

bassoon /bəˈsuːn/ *n* fagot *m*

bastard /ˈbɑːstəd/ *n* bastardo *m*. **you ~!** (*vulgar*) ¡cabrón! (*vulgar*)

bat /bæt/ *n* (*for baseball, cricket*) bate *m*; (*for table tennis*) raqueta *f*; (*mammal*) murciélago *m*. **off one's own ~** por sí solo. ● *vt* (*pt* **batted**) golpear. **without ~ting an eyelid** sin pestañear. ● *vi* batear

batch /bætʃ/ *n* (*of people*) grupo *m*; (*of papers*) pila *f*; (*of goods*) remesa *f*; (*of bread*) hornada *f*; (*Comp*) lote *m*

bated /ˈbeɪtɪd/ *adj*. **with ~ breath** con aliento entrecortado

bath /bɑːθ/ *n* (*pl* **-s** /bɑːðz/) baño *m*; (*tub*) bañera *f*, tina *f* (*LAm*). **~s** *npl* (*swimming pool*) piscina *f*, alberca *f* (*Mex*). **have a ~, take a ~** (*Amer*) bañarse. ● *vt* bañar. ● *vi* bañarse

bathe /beɪð/ *vt* bañar. ● *vi* bañarse. ● *n* baño *m*. **~r** *n* bañista *m & f*

bathing /ˈbeɪðɪŋ/ *n* baños *mpl*. **~ costume**, **~ suit** *n* traje *m* de baño

bathroom /ˈbɑːθrʊm/ *n* cuarto *m* de baño; (*Amer, toilet*) servicio *m*, baño *m* (*LAm*)

batsman /ˈbætsmən/ *n* (*pl* **-men**) bateador *m*

battalion /bəˈtælɪən/ *n* batallón *m*

batter /ˈbætə(r)/ *vt* (*beat*) apalear; (*cover with batter*) rebozar. ● *n* batido *m* para rebozar; (*Amer, for cake*) masa *f*. **~ed** /ˈbætəd/ *adj* (car etc) estropeado; (wife etc) maltratado

battery /ˈbætərɪ/ *n* (*Mil, Auto*) batería *f*; (*of torch, radio*) pila *f*

battle /ˈbætl/ *n* batalla *f*; (*fig*) lucha *f*. ● *vi* luchar. **~field** *n* campo *m* de batalla. **~ship** *n* acorazado *m*

bawl /bɔːl/ *vt/i* gritar

bay /beɪ/ *n* (*on coast*) bahía *f*. **keep at ~** mantener a raya

bayonet /ˈbeɪənet/ *n* bayoneta *f*

bay window /beɪ ˈwɪndəʊ/ *n* ventana *f* salediza

bazaar /bəˈzɑː(r)/ *n* bazar *m*

BC *abbr* (= **before Christ**) a. de C., antes de Cristo

be /biː/

present **am, are, is;** past **was, were;** past participle **been**

● *intransitive verb*

! Spanish has two verbs meaning **be**, *ser* and *estar*. See those entries for further information about the differences between them.

····➤ (*position, changed condition or state*) estar. **where is the library?** ¿dónde está la biblioteca? **she's tired** está cansada. **how are you?** ¿cómo estás?

····➤ (*identity, nature or permanent characteristics*) ser. **she's tall** es alta. **he's Scottish** es escocés. **I'm a journalist** soy periodista. **he's very kind** es muy bondadoso

····➤ (*feel*) **to be** + *adjective* tener + *sustantivo*. **to be cold/hot** tener frío/calor. **he's hungry/thirsty** tiene hambre/sed

····➤ (*age*) **he's thirty** tiene treinta años

····➤ (*weather*) **it's cold/hot** hace frío/calor. **it was 40 degrees** hacía 40 grados

● *auxiliary verb*

····➤ (*in tenses*) estar. **I'm working** estoy trabajando. **they were singing** estaban cantando, cantaban

····➤ (*in tag questions*) **it's a beautiful house, isn't it?** es una casa preciosa, ¿verdad? *or* ¿no? *or* ¿no es cierto?

····➤ (*in short answers*) **are you disappointed? - yes, I am** ¿estás desilusionado? - sí (,lo estoy). **I'm surprised, aren't you?** estoy sorprendido, ¿tú no?

····➤ (*in passive sentences*) **it was built in 1834** fue construido en 1834, se construyó en 1834. **she was told that ...** le dijeron que..., se le dijo que ...

! Note that passive sentences in English are often translated using the pronoun *se* or using the third person plural.

beach /bi:tʃ/ *n* playa *f*

beacon /'bi:kən/ *n* faro *m*

bead /bi:d/ *n* cuenta *f*; (*of glass*) abalorio *m*

beak /bi:k/ *n* pico *m*

beaker /'bi:kə(r)/ *n* taza *f* (*alta y sin asa*)

beam /bi:m/ *n* (*of wood*) viga *f*; (*of light*) rayo *m*; (*Naut*) bao *m*. ● *vt* emitir. ● *vi* irradiar; (*smile*) sonreír

bean /bi:n/ *n* alubia *f*, frijol *m* (*LAm*); (*broad bean*) haba *f*; (*of coffee*) grano *m*

bear /beə(r)/ *vt* (*pt* **bore**, *pp* **borne**) llevar; parir (niño); (*endure*) soportar. ~ **right** torcer a la derecha. ~ **in mind** tener en cuenta. □ ~ **with** *vt* tener paciencia con. ● *n* oso *m*. ~**able** *adj* soportable

beard /bɪəd/ *n* barba *f*. ~**ed** *adj* barbudo

bearer /'beərə(r)/ *n* portador *m*; (*of passport*) titular *m & f*

bearing /'beərɪŋ/ *n* comportamiento *m*; (*relevance*) relación *f*; (*Mec*) cojinete *m*. **get one's** ~**s** orientarse. **lose one's** ~**s** desorientarse

beast /bi:st/ *n* bestia *f*; (*person*) bruto *m*. ~**ly** *adj* (**-ier**, **-iest**) bestial; ▣ horrible

beat /bi:t/ *vt* (*pt* **beat**, *pp* **beaten**) (*hit*) pegar; (*Culin*) batir; (*defeat*) derrotar; (*better*) sobrepasar; batir (record); (*baffle*) dejar perplejo. ~ **it** ▣ largarse. ● *vi* (heart) latir. ● *n* latido *m*; (*Mus*) ritmo *m*; (*of policeman*) ronda *f*. □ ~ **up** *vt* darle una paliza a; (*Culin*) batir. ~ **up on** (*Amer, fam*) darle una paliza a. ~**er** *n* batidor *m*. ~**ing** *n* paliza *f*

beautician /bju:'tɪʃn/ *n* esteticista *m & f*

beautiful /'bju:tɪfl/ *adj* hermoso. ~**ly** *adv* maravillosamente

beauty /'bju:tɪ/ *n* belleza *f*. ~ **salon**, ~ **shop** (*Amer*) *n* salón *m* de belleza. ~ **spot** *n* (*on face*) lunar *m*; (*site*) lugar *m* pintoresco

beaver /'bi:və(r)/ *n* castor *m*

became /bɪ'keɪm/ *see* **BECOME**

because /bɪ'kɒz/ *conj* porque. ● *adv.* ~ **of** por, a causa de

beckon /'bekən/ *vt/i.* ~ **(to)** hacer señas (a)

become /bɪ'kʌm/ *vi* (*pt* **became**, *pp* **become**) hacerse, llegar a ser, volverse, convertirse en. **what has ~ of her?** ¿qué es de ella?

bed /bed/ *n* cama *f*; (*layer*) estrato *m*; (*of sea, river*) fondo *m*; (*of flowers*) macizo *m*. **go to ~** acostarse. ● *vi* (*pt* **bedded**). ~ **and breakfast (B & B)** cama y desayuno; (*place*) pensión *f*. **~bug** *n* chinche *f*. **~clothes** *npl*, **~ding** *n* ropa *f* de cama, cobijas *fpl* (*LAm*)

> **Bed and breakfast** Los bed & breakfast o B&B son casas privadas o pequeños hoteles que ofrecen alojamiento y desayuno a precios generalmente módicos.

bed: ~room *n* dormitorio *m*, cuarto *m*, habitación *f*, recámara *f* (*Mex*). **~-sitter** /-'sɪtə(r)/ *n* habitación *f* con cama y uso de cocina y baño compartidos, estudio *m*. **~spread** *n* colcha *f*. **~time** *n* hora *f* de acostarse

bee /bi:/ *n* abeja *f*; (*Amer, social gathering*) círculo *m*

beech /bi:tʃ/ *n* haya *f*

beef /bi:f/ *n* carne *f* de vaca, carne *f* de res (*Mex*). ● *vi* ⊠ quejarse. **~burger** *n* hamburguesa *f*. **~y** *adj* (**-ier, -iest**) musculoso

bee: ~hive *n* colmena *f*. **~line** *n*. **make a ~line for** ir en línea recta hacia

been /bi:n/ *see* **BE**

beer /bɪə(r)/ *n* cerveza *f*

beet /bi:t/ *n* (*Amer*) remolacha *f*, betabel *f* (*Mex*)

beetle /'bi:tl/ *n* escarabajo *m*

beetroot /'bi:tru:t/ *n invar* remolacha *f*, betabel *f* (*Mex*)

befall /bɪ'fɔ:l/ *vt* (*pt* **befell**, *pp* **befallen**) ocurrirle a. ● *vi* ocurrir

before /bɪ'fɔ:(r)/ *prep* (*time*) antes de; (*place*) delante de. **~ leaving** antes de marcharse. ● *adv* (*place*) delante; (*time*) antes. **a week ~** una semana antes. **the week ~** la semana anterior. ● *conj* (*time*) antes de que. **~ he leaves** antes de que se vaya. **~hand** *adv* de antemano

befriend /bɪ'frend/ *vt* hacerse amigo de

beg /beg/ *vt/i* (*pt* **begged**) mendigar; (*entreat*) suplicar; (*ask*) pedir. **~ s.o.'s pardon** pedir perdón a uno. **I ~ your pardon!** ¡perdone Vd! **I ~ your pardon?** ¿cómo?

began /bɪ'gæn/ *see* **BEGIN**

beggar /'begə(r)/ *n* mendigo *m*

begin /bɪ'gɪn/ *vt/i* (*pt* **began**, *pp* **begun**, *pres p* **beginning**) comenzar, empezar. **~ner** *n* principiante *m & f*. **~ning** *n* principio *m*

begrudge /bɪ'grʌdʒ/ *vt* envidiar; (*give*) dar de mala gana

begun /bɪ'gʌn/ *see* **BEGIN**

behalf /bɪ'hɑ:f/ *n*. **on ~ of, in ~ of** (*Amer*) de parte de, en nombre de

behav|e /bɪ'heɪv/ *vi* comportarse, portarse. **~e (o.s.)** portarse bien. **~iour** /bɪ'heɪvjə(r)/ *n* comportamiento *m*

behead /bɪ'hed/ *vt* decapitar

behind /bɪ'haɪnd/ *prep* detrás de, atrás de (*LAm*). ● *adv* detrás; (*late*) atrasado. ● *n* ⊡ trasero *m*

beige /beɪʒ/ *adj & n* beige (*m*)

being /'bi:ɪŋ/ *n* ser *m*. **come into ~** nacer

b

belated /bɪ'leɪtɪd/ *adj* tardío

belch /beltʃ/ *vi* eructar. ▫ ~ **out** *vt* arrojar (smoke)

belfry /'belfrɪ/ *n* campanario *m*

Belgi|an /'beldʒən/ *adj & n* belga (*m & f*). **~um** /'beldʒəm/ *n* Bélgica *f*

belie|f /bɪ'li:f/ *n* (*trust*) fe *f*; (*opinion*) creencia *f*. **~ve** /bɪ'li:v/ *vt/i* creer. **~ve in** creer en. **make ~ve** fingir

belittle /bɪ'lɪtl/ *vt* menospreciar (achievements); denigrar (person)

bell /bel/ *n* campana *f*; (*on door, bicycle*) timbre *m*

belligerent /bɪ'lɪdʒərənt/ *adj* beligerante

bellow /'beləʊ/ *vt* gritar. ● *vi* bramar. **~s** *npl* fuelle *m*

bell pepper *n* (*Amer*) pimiento *m*

belly /'belɪ/ *n* barriga *f*

belong /bɪ'lɒŋ/ *vi* pertenecer (**to** a); (*club*) ser socio (**to** de); (*have as usual place*) ir. **~ings** /bɪ'lɒŋɪŋz/ *npl* pertenencias *fpl*. **personal ~ings** efectos *mpl* personales

beloved /bɪ'lʌvɪd/ *adj* querido

below /bɪ'ləʊ/ *prep* debajo de, abajo de (*LAm*); (*fig*) inferior a. ● *adv* abajo

belt /belt/ *n* cinturón *m*; (*area*) zona *f*. ● *vt* (*fig*) rodear; ⊠ darle una paliza a. **~way** *n* (*Amer*) carretera *f* de circunvalación

bench /bentʃ/ *n* banco *m*

bend /bend/ *n* curva *f*. ● *vt* (*pt & pp* **bent**) doblar; torcer (arm, leg). ● *vi* doblarse; (road) torcerse. ▫ ~ **down** *vi* inclinarse ▫ ~ **over** *vi* agacharse

beneath /bɪ'ni:θ/ *prep* debajo de; (*fig*) inferior a. ● *adv* abajo

beneficial /benɪ'fɪʃl/ *adj* provechoso

beneficiary /benɪ'fɪʃərɪ/ *n* beneficiario *m*

benefit /'benɪfɪt/ *n* provecho *m*, ventaja *f*; (*allowance*) prestación *f*; (*for unemployed*) subsidio *m*; (*perk*) beneficio *m*. ● *vt* (*pt* **benefited**, *pres p* **benefiting**) beneficiar. ● *vi* beneficiarse

benevolent /bə'nevələnt/ *adj* benévolo

benign /bɪ'naɪn/ *adj* benigno

bent /bent/ *see* BEND. ● *n* inclinación *f*. ● *adj* torcido; (⊠, *corrupt*) corrompido

bereave|d /bɪ'ri:vd/ *n*. **the ~d** la familia del difunto. **~ment** *n* pérdida *f*; (*mourning*) luto *m*

beret /'bereɪ/ *n* boina *f*

berry /'berɪ/ *n* baya *f*

berserk /bə'sɜ:k/ *adj*. **go ~** volverse loco

berth /bɜ:θ/ *n* litera *f*; (*anchorage*) amarradero *m*. **give a wide ~ to** evitar. ● *vt/i* atracar

beside /bɪ'saɪd/ *prep* al lado de. **be ~ o.s.** estar fuera de sí

besides /bɪ'saɪdz/ *prep* además de; (*except*) excepto. ● *adv* además

besiege /bɪ'si:dʒ/ *vt* sitiar, asediar; (*fig*) acosar

best /best/ *adj* (el) mejor. **the ~ thing is to...** lo mejor es... ● *adv* mejor. **like ~** preferir. ● *n* lo mejor. **at ~** a lo más. **do one's ~** hacer todo lo posible. **make the ~ of** contentarse con. **~ man** *n* padrino *m* (de boda)

bestow /bɪ'stəʊ/ *vt* conceder

bestseller /best'selə(r)/ *n* éxito *m* de librería, bestseller *m*

bet /bet/ *n* apuesta *f*. ● *vt/i* (*pt* **bet** *or* **betted**) apostar

betray /bɪ'treɪ/ *vt* traicionar. **~al** *n* traición *f*

better /'betə(r)/ *adj & adv* mejor. ~ **off** en mejores condiciones; (*richer*) más rico. **get** ~ mejorar. **all the** ~ tanto mejor. **I'd** ~ **be off** me tengo que ir. **the** ~ **part of** la mayor parte de. ● *vt* mejorar; (*beat*) sobrepasar. ~ **o.s.** superarse. ● *n* superior *m*. **get the** ~ **of** vencer a. **my** ~**s** mis superiores *mpl*

between /bɪ'twi:n/ *prep* entre. ● *adv* en medio

beverage /'bevərɪdʒ/ *n* bebida *f*

beware /bɪ'weə(r)/ *vi* tener cuidado. ● *int* ¡cuidado!

bewilder /bɪ'wɪldə(r)/ *vt* desconcertar. ~**ment** *n* aturdimiento *m*

bewitch /bɪ'wɪtʃ/ *vt* hechizar; (*delight*) cautivar

beyond /bɪ'jɒnd/ *prep* más allá de; (*fig*) fuera de. ~ **doubt** sin lugar a duda. ● *adv* más allá

bias /'baɪəs/ *n* tendencia *f*; (*prejudice*) prejuicio *m*. ● *vt* (*pt* **biased**) influir en. ~**ed** *adj* parcial

bib /bɪb/ *n* babero *m*

Bible /'baɪbl/ *n* Biblia *f*

biblical /'bɪblɪkl/ *adj* bíblico

bibliography /bɪblɪ'ɒgrəfɪ/ *n* bibliografía *f*

biceps /'baɪseps/ *n invar* bíceps *m*

bicker /'bɪkə(r)/ *vi* altercar

bicycle /'baɪsɪkl/ *n* bicicleta *f*

bid /bɪd/ *n* (*offer*) oferta *f*; (*attempt*) tentativa *f*. ● *vi* hacer una oferta. ● *vt* (*pt & pp* **bid**, *pres p* **bidding**) ofrecer; (*pt* **bid**, *pp* **bidden**, *pres p* **bidding**) mandar; dar (welcome, good day etc). ~**der** *n* postor *m*. ~**ding** *n* (*at auction*) ofertas *fpl*; (*order*) mandato *m*

bide /baɪd/ *vt*. ~ **one's time** esperar el momento oportuno

bifocals /baɪ'fəʊklz/ *npl* gafas *fpl* bifocales, anteojos *mpl* bifocales (*LAm*)

big /bɪg/ *adj* (**bigger**, **biggest**) grande, (*before singular noun*) gran. ● *adv*. **talk** ~ fanfarronear

bigam|ist /'bɪgəmɪst/ *n* bígamo *m*. ~**ous** /'bɪgəməs/ *adj* bígamo. ~**y** *n* bigamia *f*

big-headed /-'hedɪd/ *adj* engreído

bigot /'bɪgət/ *n* fanático *m*. ~**ed** *adj* fanático

bike /baɪk/ *n* ⓘ bici *f* ⓘ

bikini /bɪ'ki:nɪ/ *n* (*pl* **-is**) bikini *m*

bile /baɪl/ *n* bilis *f*

bilingual /baɪ'lɪŋgwəl/ *adj* bilingüe

bill /bɪl/ *n* cuenta *f*; (*invoice*) factura *f*; (*notice*) cartel *m*; (*Amer, banknote*) billete *m*; (*Pol*) proyecto *m* de ley; (*of bird*) pico *m*

billet /'bɪlɪt/ *n* (*Mil*) alojamiento *m*. ● *vt* alojar

billfold /'bɪlfəʊld/ *n* (*Amer*) cartera *f*, billetera *f*

billiards /'bɪlɪədz/ *n* billar *m*

billion /'bɪlɪən/ *n* billón *m*; (*Amer*) mil millones *mpl*

bin /bɪn/ *n* recipiente *m*; (*for rubbish*) cubo *m* de basura, bote *m* de basura (*Mex*); (*for waste paper*) papelera *f*

bind /baɪnd/ *vt* (*pt* **bound**) atar; encuadernar (book); (*Jurid*) obligar. ● *n* ⓘ lata *f*. ~**ing** *n* (*of books*) encuadernación *f*; (*braid*) ribete *m*

binge /bɪndʒ/ *n* ⊠, (*of food*) comilona *f*; (*of drink*) borrachera *f*. **go on a** ~ ir de juerga

bingo /'bɪŋgəʊ/ *n* bingo *m*

binoculars /bɪ'nɒkjʊləz/ *npl* gemelos *mpl*

biograph|er /baɪ'ɒgrəfə(r)/ *n*

b

biógrafo *m*. **~y** *n* biografía *f*

biolog|ical /baɪəˈlɒdʒɪkl/ *adj* biológico. **~ist** /baɪˈɒlədʒɪst/ *n* biólogo *m*. **~y** /baɪˈɒlədʒɪ/ *n* biología *f*

bioterrorism /baɪəʊˈterərɪzm/ *n* bioterrorismo *m*

birch /bɜːtʃ/ *n* (*tree*) abedul *m*

bird /bɜːd/ *n* ave *f*; (*small*) pájaro *m*; (*sl, girl*) chica *f*

Biro /ˈbaɪərəʊ/ *n* (*pl* **-os**) (®) bolígrafo *m*

birth /bɜːθ/ *n* nacimiento *m*. **give ~** dar a luz. **~ certificate** *n* partida *f* de nacimiento. **~ control** *n* control *m* de la natalidad. **~day** *n* cumpleaños *m*. **~mark** *n* marca *f* de nacimiento. **~place** *n* lugar *m* de nacimiento. **~ rate** *n* natalidad *f*

biscuit /ˈbɪskɪt/ *n* galleta *f*

bisect /baɪˈsekt/ *vt* bisecar

bishop /ˈbɪʃəp/ *n* obispo *m*; (*Chess*) alfil *m*

bit /bɪt/ *see* BITE. ● *n* trozo *m*; (*quantity*) poco *m*; (*of horse*) bocado *m*; (*Mec*) broca *f*; (*Comp*) bit *m*

bitch /bɪtʃ/ *n* perra *f*; (*fam, woman*) bruja *f* [!]

bit|e /baɪt/ *vt/i* (*pt* **bit**, *pp* **bitten**) morder; (*insect*) picar. **~e one's nails** morderse las uñas. ● *n* mordisco *m*; (*mouthful*) bocado *m*; (*of insect etc*) picadura *f*. **~ing** /ˈbaɪtɪŋ/ *adj* mordaz

bitter /ˈbɪtə(r)/ *adj* amargo; (*of weather*) glacial. ● *n* cerveza *f* amarga. **~ly** *adv* amargamente. **it's ~ly cold** hace un frío glacial. **~ness** *n* amargor *m*; (*resentment*) amargura *f*

bizarre /bɪˈzɑː(r)/ *adj* extraño

black /blæk/ *adj* (**-er**, **-est**) negro. **~ and blue** amoratado. ● *n* negro *m*; (*coffee*) solo, negro (*LAm*). ● *vt* ennegrecer; limpiar (shoes). **~ out** *vi* desmayarse. **~ and white** *n* blanco y negro *m*. **~-and-white** *adj* en blanco y negro. **~berry** /-bərɪ/ *n* zarzamora *f*. **~bird** *n* mirlo *m*. **~board** *n* pizarra *f*. **~currant** /-ˈkʌrənt/ *n* grosella *f* negra. **~en** *vt* ennegrecer. **~ eye** *n* ojo *m* morado. **~list** *vt* poner en la lista negra. **~mail** *n* chantaje *m*. ● *vt* chantajear. **~mailer** *n* chantajista *m & f*. **~out** *n* apagón *m*; (*Med*) desmayo *m*; (*of news*) censura *f*. **~smith** *n* herrero *m*

bladder /ˈblædə(r)/ *n* vejiga *f*

blade /bleɪd/ *n* (*of knife, sword*) hoja *f*. **~ of grass** brizna *f* de hierba

blame /bleɪm/ *vt* echar la culpa a. **be to ~** tener la culpa. ● *n* culpa *f*. **~less** *adj* inocente

bland /blænd/ *adj* (**-er**, **-est**) suave

blank /blæŋk/ *adj* (page, space) en blanco; (cassette) virgen; (cartridge) sin bala; (*fig*) vacío. ● *n* blanco *m*

blanket /ˈblæŋkɪt/ *n* manta *f*, cobija *f* (*LAm*), frazada (*LAm*); (*fig*) capa *f*. ● *vt* (*pt* **blanketed**) (*fig*) cubrir (**in**, **with** de)

blare /bleə(r)/ *vi* sonar muy fuerte. ● *n* estrépito *m*

blasphem|e /blæsˈfiːm/ *vt/i* blasfemar. **~ous** /ˈblæsfəməs/ *adj* blasfemo. **~y** /ˈblæsfəmɪ/ *n* blasfemia *f*

blast /blɑːst/ *n* explosión *f*; (*gust*) ráfaga *f*; (*sound*) toque *m*. ● *vt* volar. **~ed** *adj* maldito. **~-off** *n* (*of missile*) despegue *m*

blatant /ˈbleɪtnt/ *adj* patente; (*shameless*) descarado

blaze /ˈbleɪz/ *n* llamarada *f*; (*of light*) resplandor *m*; (*fig*) arranque *m*. ● *vi* arder en llamas; (*fig*) brillar

blazer /ˈbleɪzə(r)/ *n* chaqueta *f*

bleach /bliːtʃ/ *n* lejía *f*, cloro *m* (*LAm*), blanqueador *m* (*LAm*). • *vt* blanquear; decolorar (hair).

bleak /bliːk/ *adj* (**-er**, **-est**) desolado; (*fig*) sombrío

bleat /bliːt/ *n* balido *m*. • *vi* balar

bleed /bliːd/ *vt/i* (*pt* **bled** /bled/) sangrar

bleep /bliːp/ *n* pitido *m*

blemish /ˈblemɪʃ/ *n* mancha *f*

blend /blend/ *n* mezcla *f*. • *vt* mezclar. • *vi* combinarse. **~er** *n* licuadora *f*

bless /bles/ *vt* bendecir. **~ you!** (*on sneezing*) ¡Jesús!, ¡salud! (*Mex*). **~ed** /ˈblesɪd/ *adj* bendito. **~ing** *n* bendición *f*; (*advantage*) ventaja *f*

blew /bluː/ *see* BLOW

blight /blaɪt/ *n* añublo *m*, tizón *m*; (*fig*) plaga *f*. • *vt* añublar, atizonar; (*fig*) destrozar

blind /blaɪnd/ *adj* ciego. **~ alley** callejón *m* sin salida. • *n* persiana *f*; (*fig*) pretexto *m*. • *vt* dejar ciego; (*dazzle*) deslumbrar. **~fold** *adj* & *adv* con los ojos vendados. • *n* venda *f*. • *vt* vendar los ojos a. **~ly** *adv* a ciegas. **~ness** *n* ceguera *f*

blink /blɪŋk/ *vi* parpadear; (light) centellear. **~ers** *npl* (*on horse*) anteojeras *fpl*

bliss /blɪs/ *n* felicidad *f*. **~ful** *adj* feliz

blister /ˈblɪstə(r)/ *n* ampolla *f*

blizzard /ˈblɪzəd/ *n* ventisca *f*

bloated /ˈbləʊtɪd/ *adj* hinchado (with de)

blob /blɒb/ *n* (*drip*) gota *f*; (*stain*) mancha *f*

bloc /blɒk/ *n* (*Pol*) bloque *m*

block /blɒk/ *n* bloque *m*; (*of wood*) zoquete *m*; (*of buildings*) manzana *f*, cuadra *f* (*LAm*). **in ~ letters** en letra de imprenta. **~ of flats** edificio *m* de apartamentos, casa *f* de pisos. • *vt* bloquear. **~ade** /blɒˈkeɪd/ *n* bloqueo *m*. • *vt* bloquear. **~age** /-ɪdʒ/ *n* obstrucción *f*. **~head** *n* [!] zopenco *m*

bloke /bləʊk/ *n* [!] tipo *m*, tío *m* [!]

blond /blɒnd/ *adj* & *n* rubio (*m*), güero (*m*) (*Mex fam*). **~e** *adj* & *n* rubia (*f*), güera (*f*) (*Mex fam*)

blood /blʌd/ *n* sangre *f*. **~bath** *n* masacre *m*. **~-curdling** /-kɜːdlɪŋ/*adj* horripilante. **~hound** *n* sabueso *m*. **~ pressure** *n* tensión *f* arterial. **high ~ pressure** hipertensión *f*. **~shed** *n* derramamiento *m* de sangre. **~shot** *adj* sanguinolento; (eye) inyectado de sangre. **~stream** *n* torrente *m* sanguíneo. **~thirsty** *adj* sanguinario. **~y** *adj* (**-ier**, **-iest**) sangriento; (*stained*) ensangrentado; [✖] maldito

bloom /bluːm/ *n* flor *f*. • *vi* florecer

blossom /ˈblɒsəm/ *n* flor *f*. • *vi* florecer. **~ (out) into** (*fig*) llegar a ser

blot /blɒt/ *n* borrón *m*. • *vt* (*pt* **blotted**) manchar; (*dry*) secar. □ **~ out** *vt* oscurecer

blotch /blɒtʃ/ *n* mancha *f*. **~y** *adj* lleno de manchas

blotting-paper /ˈblɒtɪŋ/ *n* papel *m* secante

blouse /blaʊz/ *n* blusa *f*

blow /bləʊ/ *vt* (*pt* **blew**, *pp* **blown**) soplar; fundir (fuse); tocar (trumpet). • *vi* soplar; (fuse) fundirse; (*sound*) sonar. • *n* golpe *m*. □ **~ down** *vt* derribar. □ **~ out** *vi* apagar (candle). □ **~ over** *vi* pasar. □ **~ up** *vt* inflar; (*explode*) volar;

(*Photo*) ampliar. *vi* (*explode*) estallar; (*burst*) reventar. **~-dry** *vt* secar con secador. **~lamp** *n* soplete *m*. **~out** *n* (*of tyre*) reventón *m*. **~ torch** *n* soplete *m*

blue /blu:/ *adj* (**-er**, **-est**) azul; (joke) verde. ● *n* azul *m*. **out of the ~** totalmente inesperado. **~s** *npl*. **have the ~s** tener tristeza. **~bell** *n* campanilla *f*. **~berry** *n* arándano *m*. **~bottle** *n* moscarda *f*. **~print** *n* plano *m*; (*fig, plan*) programa *m*

bluff /blʌf/ *n* (*poker*) farol *m*, bluff *m* (*LAm*), blof *m* (*Mex*). ● *vt* engañar. ● *vi* tirarse un farol, hacer un bluf (*LAm*), blofear (*Mex*)

blunder /ˈblʌndə(r)/ *vi* cometer un error. ● *n* metedura *f* de pata

blunt /blʌnt/ *adj* desafilado; (person) directo, abrupto. ● *vt* desafilar. **~ly** *adv* francamente

blur /blɜ:(r)/ *n* impresión *f* indistinta. ● *vt* (*pt* **blurred**) hacer borroso

blurb /blɜ:b/ *n* resumen *m* publicitario

blurt /blɜ:t/ *vt*. **~ out** dejar escapar

blush /blʌʃ/ *vi* ruborizarse. ● *n* rubor *m*

boar /bɔ:(r)/ *n* verraco *m*. **wild ~** jabalí *m*

board /bɔ:d/ *n* tabla *f*, tablero *m*; (*for notices*) tablón *m* de anuncios, tablero *m* de anuncios (*LAm*); (*blackboard*) pizarra *f*; (*food*) pensión *f*; (*of company*) junta *f*. **~ and lodging** casa y comida. **full ~** pensión *f* completa. **go by the ~** ser abandonado. ● *vt* alojar; **~ a ship** embarcarse. ● *vi* alojarse (**with** en casa de); (*at school*) ser interno. **~er** *n* huésped *m & f*; (*school*) interno *m*. **~ing card** *n* tarjeta *f* de embarque. **~ing house** *n* casa *f* de huéspedes, pensión *f*. **~ing pass** *n* see **~ING CARD**. **~ing school** *n* internado *m*

boast /bəʊst/ *vt* enorgullecerse de. ● *vi* jactarse. ● *n* jactancia *f*. **~ful** *adj* jactancioso

boat /bəʊt/ *n* barco *m*; (*small*) bote *m*, barca *f*

bob /bɒb/ *vi* (*pt* **bobbed**) menearse, subir y bajar. □ **~ up** *vi* presentarse súbitamente

bobbin /ˈbɒbɪn/ *n* carrete *m*; (*in sewing machine*) canilla *f*, bobina *f*

bobby pin /ˈbɒbɪ/ *n* (*Amer*) horquilla *f*, pasador *m* (*Mex*). **~ sox** /sɒks/ *npl* (*Amer*) calcetines *mpl* cortos

bobsleigh /ˈbɒbsleɪ/ *n* bob (sleigh) *m*

bode /bəʊd/ *vi*. **~ well/ill** ser de buen/mal agüero

bodice /ˈbɒdɪs/ *n* corpiño *m*

bodily /ˈbɒdɪlɪ/ *adj* físico, corporal. ● *adv* físicamente

body /ˈbɒdɪ/ *n* cuerpo *m*; (*dead*) cadáver *m*. **~guard** *n* guardaespaldas *m*. **~ part** *n* pedazo *m* de cuerpo. **~work** *n* carrocería *f*

bog /bɒg/ *n* ciénaga *f*. □ **~ down** *vt* (*pt* **bogged**). **get ~ged down** empantanarse

boggle /ˈbɒgl/ *vi* sobresaltarse. **the mind ~s** uno se queda atónito

bogus /ˈbəʊgəs/ *adj* falso

boil /bɔɪl/ *vt/i* hervir. **be ~ing hot** estar ardiendo; (weather) hacer mucho calor. ● *n* furúnculo *m*. □ **~ away** *vi* evaporarse. □ **~ down to** *vt* reducirse a. □ **~ over** *vi* rebosar. **~ed** *adj* hervido; (egg) pasado por agua. **~er** *n* caldera *f*. **~er suit** *n* mono *m*, overol *m* (*LAm*)

boisterous /ˈbɔɪstərəs/ *adj* ruidoso, bullicioso

bold /bəʊld/ *adj* (**-er**, **-est**) audaz. **~ly** *adv* con audacia, audazmente

Bolivia /bəˈlɪvɪə/ *n* Bolivia *f*. **~n** *adj & n* boliviano (*m*)

bolster /ˈbəʊlstə(r)/ ▫ **~ up** *vt* sostener

bolt /bəʊlt/ *n* (*on door*) cerrojo *m*; (*for nut*) perno *m*; (*lightning*) rayo *m*; (*leap*) fuga *f*. • *vt* echar el cerrojo a (door); engullir (food). • *vi* fugarse. • *adv*. **~ upright** rígido

bomb /bɒm/ *n* bomba *f*. • *vt* bombardear. **~ard** /bɒmˈbɑːd/ *vt* bombardear **~er** /ˈbɒmə(r)/ *n* (*plane*) bombardero *m*; (*terrorist*) terrorista *m & f*. **~ing** /ˈbɒmɪŋ/ *n* bombardeo *m*. **~shell** *n* bomba *f*

bond /bɒnd/ *n* (*agreement*) obligación *f*; (*link*) lazo *m*; (*Com*) bono *m*. • *vi* (*stick*) adherirse. **~age** /-ɪdʒ/ *n* esclavitud *f*

bone /bəʊn/ *n* hueso *m*; (*of fish*) espina *f*. • *vt* deshuesar; quitar las espinas a (fish). **~-dry** *adj* completamente seco. **~ idle** *adj* holgazán

bonfire /ˈbɒnfaɪə(r)/ *n* hoguera *f*, fogata *f*

bonnet /ˈbɒnɪt/ *n* gorra *f*; (*Auto*) capó *m*, capote *m* (*Mex*)

bonus /ˈbəʊnəs/ *n* (*payment*) bonificación *f*; (*fig*) ventaja *f*

bony /ˈbəʊnɪ/ *adj* (**-ier**, **-iest**) huesudo; (fish) lleno de espinas

boo /buː/ *int* ¡bu! • *vt/i* abuchear

boob /buːb/ *n* (*fam*, *mistake*) metedura *f* de pata. • *vi* 🅸 meter la pata

book /bʊk/ *n* libro *m*; (*of cheques etc*) talonario *m*, chequera *f*; (*notebook*) libreta *f*; (*exercise book*) cuaderno *m*. **~s** (*mpl*) (*Com*) cuentas *fpl*. • *vt* (*enter*) registrar; (*reserve*) reservar. • *vi* reservar. **~case** *n* biblioteca *f*, librería *f*, librero *m* (*Mex*). **~ing** *n* reserva *f*, reservación *f* (*LAm*). **~ing office** *n* (*in theatre*) taquilla *f*, boletría *f* (*LAm*). **~keeping** *n* contabilidad *f*. **~let** /ˈbʊklɪt/ *n* folleto *m*. **~maker** *n* corredor *m* de apuestas. **~mark** *n* señal *f*. **~seller** *n* librero *m*. **~shop**, (*Amer*) **~store** *n* librería *f*. **~worm** *n* (*fig*) ratón *m* de biblioteca

boom /buːm/ *vi* retumbar; (*fig*) prosperar. • *n* estampido *m*; (*Com*) boom *m*

boost /buːst/ *vt* estimular; reforzar (morale). • *n* empuje *m*. **~er** *n* (*Med*) revacunación *f*. **~er cable** *n* (*Amer*) cable *m* de arranque

boot /buːt/ *n* bota *f*; (*Auto*) maletero *m*, cajuela *f* (*Mex*). ▫ **~ up** *vt* (*Comp*) cargar

booth /buːð/ *n* cabina *f*; (*at fair*) puesto *m*

booze /buːz/ *vi* 🅸 beber mucho. • *n* 🅸 alcohol *m*

border /ˈbɔːdə(r)/ *n* borde *m*; (*frontier*) frontera *f*; (*in garden*) arriate *m*. ▫ **~ on** *vt* lindar con. **~line** *n* línea *f* divisoria. **~line case** *n* caso *m* dudoso

bor|e /bɔː(r)/ *see* BEAR. • *vt* (*annoy*) aburrir; (*Tec*) taladrar. • *vi* taladrar. • *n* (*person*) pelmazo *m*; (*thing*) lata *f*. **~ed** *adj* aburrido. **be ~ed** estar aburrido. **get ~ed** aburrirse. **~edom** /ˈbɔːdəm/ *n* aburrimiento *m*. **~ing** *adj* aburrido, pesado

born /bɔːn/ *adj* nato. **be ~** nacer

borne /bɔːn/ *see* BEAR

borough /ˈbʌrə/ *n* municipio *m*

borrow /ˈbɒrəʊ/ *vt* pedir prestado

boss /bɒs/ *n* 🅸 jefe *m*. • *vt*. **~ (about)** 🅸 dar órdenes a. **~y** *adj* mandón

b

botan|ical /bəˈtænɪkl/ *adj* botánico. **~ist** /ˈbɒtənɪst/ *n* botánico *m*. **~y** /ˈbɒtənɪ/ *n* botánica *f*

both /bəʊθ/ *adj & pron* ambos (*mpl*), los dos (*mpl*). ● *adv* al mismo tiempo, a la vez. **~ Ann and Brian came** tanto Ann como Bob vinieron.

bother /ˈbɒðə(r)/ *vt* (*inconvenience*) molestar; (*worry*) preocupar. **~ it!** ¡caramba! ● *vi* molestarse. **~ about** preocuparse de. **~ doing** tomarse la molestia de hacer. ● *n* molestia *f*

bottle /ˈbɒtl/ *n* botella, mamila *f* (*Mex*); (*for baby*) biberón *m*. ● *vt* embotellar. □ **~ up** *vt* (*fig*) reprimir. **~neck** *n* (*traffic jam*) embotellamiento *m*. **~ opener** *n* abrebotellas *m*, destapador *m* (*LAm*)

bottom /ˈbɒtəm/ *n* fondo *m*; (*of hill*) pie *m*; (*buttocks*) trasero *m*. ● *adj* de más abajo; (price) más bajo; (lip, edge) inferior. **~less** *adj* sin fondo

bough /baʊ/ *n* rama *f*

bought /bɔːt/ *see* BUY

boulder /ˈbəʊldə(r)/ *n* canto *m*

bounce /baʊns/ *vt* hacer rebotar. ● *vi* rebotar; (person) saltar; [!] (cheque) ser rechazado. ● *n* rebote *m*

bound /baʊnd/ *see* BIND. ● *vi* saltar. ● *n* (*jump*) salto *m*. **~s** *npl* (*limits*) límites *mpl*. **out of ~s** zona *f* prohibida. ● *adj*. **be ~ for** dirigirse a. **~ to** obligado a; (*certain*) seguro de

boundary /ˈbaʊndərɪ/ *n* límite *m*

bouquet /bʊˈkeɪ/ *n* ramo *m*; (*of wine*) buqué *m*, aroma *m*

bout /baʊt/ *n* período *m*; (*Med*) ataque *m*; (*Sport*) encuentro *m*

bow¹ /bəʊ/ *n* (*weapon, Mus*) arco *m*; (*knot*) lazo *m*, moño *m* (*LAm*)

bow² /baʊ/ *n* reverencia *f*; (*Naut*) proa *f*; ● *vi* inclinarse. ● *vt* inclinar

bowels /ˈbaʊəlz/ *npl* intestinos *mpl*; (*fig*) entrañas *fpl*

bowl /bəʊl/ *n* (*container*) cuenco *m*; (*for washing*) palangana *f*; (*ball*) bola *f*. ● *vt* (*cricket*) arrojar. ● *vi* (*cricket*) arrojar la pelota. □ **~ over** *vt* derribar

bowl: ~er *n* (*cricket*) lanzador *m*. **~er (hat)** sombrero *m* de hongo, bombín *m*. **~ing** *n* bolos *mpl*. **~ing alley** *n* bolera *f*

bow tie /bəʊ ˈtaɪ/ *n* corbata *f* de lazo, pajarita *f*

box /bɒks/ *n* caja *f*; (*for jewels etc*) estuche *m*; (*in theatre*) palco *m*. ● *vt* boxear contra. **~ s.o.'s ears** dar una manotada a uno. ● *vi* boxear. **~er** *n* boxeador *m*. **~ing** *n* boxeo *m*. **B~ing Day** *n* el 26 de diciembre. **~ office** *n* taquilla *f*, boletería *f* (*LAm*). **~ room** *n* trastero *m*

boy /bɔɪ/ *n* chico *m*, muchacho *m*; (*young*) niño *m*

boy: ~ band *n* grupo *m* pop de chicos. **~friend** *n* novio *m*. **~hood** *n* niñez *f*. **~ish** *adj* de muchacho; (*childish*) infantil

boycott /ˈbɔɪkɒt/ *vt* boicotear. ● *n* boicoteo *m*

bra /brɑː/ *n* sostén *m*, sujetador *m*, brasier *m* (*Mex*)

brace /breɪs/ *n* abrazadera *f*. ● *vt* asegurar. **~ o.s.** prepararse. **~s** *npl* tirantes *mpl*; (*Amer, dental*) aparato(s) *m*(*pl*)

bracelet /ˈbreɪslɪt/ *n* pulsera *f*

bracken /ˈbrækən/ *n* helecho *m*

bracket /ˈbrækɪt/ *n* soporte *m*; (*group*) categoría *f*; (*parenthesis*) paréntesis *m*. **square ~s** corchetes *mpl*. ● *vt* poner entre paréntesis;

(*join together*) agrupar

brag /bræg/ *vi* (*pt* **bragged**) jactarse (**about** de)

braid /breɪd/ *n* galón *m*; (*Amer, in hair*) trenza *f*

brain /breɪn/ *n* cerebro *m*. ● *vt* romper la cabeza a. **~child** *n* invento *m*. **~ drain** *n* 🄸 fuga *f* de cerebros. **~storm** *n* ataque *m* de locura; (*Amer, brainwave*) idea *f* genial. **~wash** *vt* lavar el cerebro. **~wave** *n* idea *f* genial. **~y** *adj* (**-ier**, **-iest**) inteligente

brake /breɪk/ *n* freno *m*. ● *vt/i* frenar. **~ fluid** *n* líquido *m* de freno. **~ lights** *npl* luces *fpl* de freno

bramble /'bræmbl/ *n* zarza *f*

bran /bræn/ *n* salvado *m*

branch /brɑːntʃ/ *n* rama *f*; (*of road*) bifurcación *f*; (*Com*) sucursal *m*; (*fig*) ramo *m*. □ **~ off** *vi* bifurcarse. □ **~ out** *vi* ramificarse

brand /brænd/ *n* marca *f*. ● *vt* marcar; (*label*) tildar de

brandish /'brændɪʃ/ *vt* blandir

brand: ~ name: *n* marca *f*. **~-new** /-'njuː/ *adj* flamante

brandy /'brændɪ/ *n* coñac *m*

brash /bræʃ/ *adj* descarado

brass /brɑːs/ *n* latón *m*. **get down to ~ tacks** (*fig*) ir al grano. **~ band** *n* banda *f* de música

brassière /'bræsjeə(r)/ *n see* **BRA**

brat /bræt/ *n* (*pej*) mocoso *m*

bravado /brə'vɑːdəʊ/ *n* bravata *f*

brave /breɪv/ *adj* (**-er**, **-est**) valiente. ● *n* (*North American Indian*) guerrero *m* indio. **the ~** *npl* los valientes. ● *vt* afrontar. **~ry** /-ərɪ/ *n* valentía *f*, valor *m*

brawl /brɔːl/ *n* alboroto *m*. ● *vi* pelearse

brazen /'breɪzn/ *adj* descarado

Brazil /brə'zɪl/ *n* Brasil *m*. **~ian** /-jən/ *adj & n* brasileño (*m*)

breach /briːtʃ/ *n* infracción *f*, violación *f*; (*of contract*) incumplimiento *m*; (*gap*) brecha *f*. **~ of the peace** alteración *f* del orden público. ● *vt* abrir una brecha en

bread /bred/ *n* pan *m*. **a loaf of ~** un pan. **~crumbs** *npl* migajas *fpl*; (*Culin*) pan *m* rallado, pan *m* molido (*Mex*)

breadth /bredθ/ *n* anchura *f*

breadwinner /'bredwɪnə(r)/ *n* sostén *m* de la familia

break /breɪk/ *vt* (*pt* **broke**, *pp* **broken**) romper; infringir, violar (law); batir (record); comunicar (news); interrumpir (journey). ● *vi* romperse; (news) divulgarse. ● *n* ruptura *f*; (*interval*) intervalo *m*; (*fam, chance*) oportunidad *f*; (*in weather*) cambio *m*. □ **~ away** *vi* escapar. □ **~ down** *vt* derribar; analizar (figures). *vi* estropearse, descomponerse (*LAm*); (*Auto*) averiarse; (*cry*) deshacerse en lágrimas. □ **~ in** *vi* (intruder) entrar (*para robar*). □ **~ into** *vt* entrar en (*para robar*) (house etc); (*start doing*) ponerse a. □ **~ off** *vi* interrumpirse. □ **~ out** *vi* (war, disease) estallar; (*run away*) escaparse. □ **~ up** *vi* romperse; (band, lovers) separarse; (schools) terminar. **~able** *adj* frágil. **~age** /-ɪdʒ/ *n* rotura *f*. **~down** *n* (*Tec*) falla *f*; (*Med*) colapso *m*, crisis *f* nerviosa; (*of figures*) análisis *f*. **~er** *n* (*wave*) ola *f* grande

breakfast /'brekfəst/ *n* desayuno *m*. **have ~** desayunar

break: ~through *n* adelanto *m*. **~water** *n* rompeolas *m*

breast /brest/ *n* pecho *m*; (*of chicken etc*) pechuga *f*. (estilo *m*)

b

~stroke *n* braza *f*, (estilo *m*) pecho *m* (*LAm*)

breath /breθ/ *n* aliento *m*, respiración *f*. **be out of ~** estar sin aliento. **hold one's ~** aguantar la respiración. **under one's ~** a media voz

breath|e /bri:ð/ *vt/i* respirar. **~er** *n* descanso *m*, pausa *f*. **~ing** *n* respiración *f*

breathtaking /'breθteɪkɪŋ/ *adj* impresionante

bred /bred/ *see* BREED

breed /bri:d/ *vt* (*pt* **bred**) criar; (*fig*) engendrar. ● *vi* reproducirse. ● *n* raza *f*

breez|e /bri:z/ *n* brisa *f*. **~y** *adj* de mucho viento

brew /bru:/ *vt* hacer (beer); preparar (tea). ● *vi* hacer cerveza; (tea) reposar; (*fig*) prepararse. ● *n* infusión *f*. **~er** *n* cervecero *m*. **~ery** *n* cervecería *f*, fábrica *f* de cerveza

bribe /braɪb/ *n* soborno *m*. ● *vt* sobornar. **~ry** /braɪbərɪ/ *n* soborno *m*

brick /brɪk/ *n* ladrillo *m*. **~layer** *n* albañil *m*

bridal /'braɪdl/ *adj* nupcial

bride /braɪd/ *m* novia *f*. **~groom** *n* novio *m*. **~smaid** /'braɪdzmeɪd/ *n* dama *f* de honor

bridge /brɪdʒ/ *n* puente *m*; (*of nose*) caballete *m*; (*Cards*) bridge *m*. ● *vt* tender un puente sobre. **~ a gap** llenar un vacío

bridle /'braɪdl/ *n* brida *f*. **~ path** *n* camino *m* de herradura

brief /bri:f/ *adj* (**-er**, **-est**) breve. ● *n* (*Jurid*) escrito *m*. ● *vt* dar instrucciones a. **~case** *n* maletín *m*, portafolio(s) *m* (*LAm*). **~ly** *adv* brevemente. **~s** *npl* (*man's*) calzoncillos *mpl*; (*woman's*) bragas *fpl*, calzones *mpl* (*LAm*), pantaletas *fpl* (*Mex*)

brigade /brɪ'geɪd/ *n* brigada *f*

bright /braɪt/ *adj* (**-er**, **-est**) brillante, claro; (*clever*) listo; (*cheerful*) alegre. **~en** *vt* aclarar; hacer más alegre (house etc). ● *vi* (*weather*) aclararse; (face) illuminarse

brillian|ce /'brɪljəns/ *n* brillantez *f*, brillo *m*. **~t** *adj* brillante

brim /brɪm/ *n* borde *m*; (*of hat*) ala *f*. □ **~ over** *vi* (*pt* **brimmed**) desbordarse

brine /braɪn/ *n* salmuera *f*

bring /brɪŋ/ *vt* (*pt* **brought**) traer; (*lead*) llevar. □ **~ about** *vt* causar. □ **~ back** *vt* devolver. □ **~ down** *vt* derribar. □ **~ off** *vt* lograr. □ **~ on** *vt* causar. □ **~ out** *vt* sacar; lanzar (product); publicar (book). □ **~ round/to** *vt* hacer volver en sí. □ **~ up** *vt* (*Med*) vomitar; educar (children); plantear (question)

brink /brɪŋk/ *n* borde *m*

brisk /brɪsk/ *adj* (**-er**, **-est**) enérgico, vivo

bristle /'brɪsl/ *n* cerda *f*. ● *vi* erizarse

Brit|ain /'brɪtən/ *n* Gran Bretaña *f*. **~ish** /'brɪtɪʃ/ *adj* británico. ● *npl* **the ~ish** los británicos. **~on** /'brɪtən/ *n* británico *m*

Brittany /'brɪtənɪ/ *n* Bretaña *f*

brittle /'brɪtl/ *adj* frágil, quebradizo

broach /brəʊtʃ/ *vt* abordar

broad /brɔ:d/ *adj* (**-er**, **-est**) ancho. **in ~ daylight** a plena luz del día. **~ bean** *n* haba *f* **~cast** *n* emisión *f*. ● *vt* (*pt* **broadcast**) emitir. ● *vi* hablar por la radio. **~caster** *n* locutor *m*. **~casting** *n* radio-difusión *f*. **~en** *vt* ensanchar. ● *vi* ensancharse. **~ly** *adv* en general. **~-minded** /-'maɪndɪd/ *adj* de miras amplias, tolerante

broccoli /ˈbrɒkəlɪ/ *n invar* brécol *m*

brochure /ˈbrəʊʃə(r)/ *n* folleto *m*

broil /brɔɪl/ *vt* (*Amer*) asar a la parrilla. **~er** *n* (*Amer*) parrilla *f*

broke /brəʊk/ *see* **BREAK**. ● *adj* 🅸 sin blanca, en la ruina

broken /ˈbrəʊkən/ *see* **BREAK**. ● *adj* roto

broker /ˈbrəʊkə(r)/ *n* corredor *m*

brolly /ˈbrɒlɪ/ *n* 🅸 paraguas *m*

bronchitis /brɒŋˈkaɪtɪs/ *n* bronquitis *f*

bronze /brɒnz/ *n* bronce *m*. ● *adj* de bronce

brooch /brəʊtʃ/ *n* broche *m*

brood /bru:d/ *n* cría *f*; (*humorous*) prole *m*. ● *vi* empollar; (*fig*) meditar

brook /brʊk/ *n* arroyo *m*. ● *vt* soportar

broom /bru:m/ *n* escoba *f*. **~stick** *n* palo *m* de escoba

broth /brɒθ/ *n* caldo *m*

brothel /ˈbrɒθl/ *n* burdel *m*

brother /ˈbrʌðə(r)/ *n* hermano *m*. **~hood** *n* fraternidad *f*. **~-in-law** (*pl* **~s-in-law**) *n* cuñado *m*. **~ly** *adj* fraternal

brought /brɔ:t/ *see* **BRING**

brow /braʊ/ *n* frente *f*; (*of hill*) cima *f*. **~beat** *vt* (*pt* **-beaten**, *pp* **-beat**) intimidar

brown /braʊn/ *adj* (**-er**, **-est**) marrón, café (*Mex*); (hair) castaño; (skin) moreno; (*tanned*) bronceado. ● *n* marrón *m*, café *m* (*Mex*). ● *vt* poner moreno; (*Culin*) dorar. **~ bread** *n* pan *m* integral. **~ sugar** /braʊn ˈʃʊgə(r)/ *n* azúcar *m* moreno, azúcar *f* morena

browse /braʊz/ *vi* (*in a shop*) curiosear; (animal) pacer; (*Comp*) navegar. **~r** (*Comp*) browser *m*, navegador *m*

bruise /bru:z/ *n* magulladura *f*. ● *vt* magullar; machucar (fruit)

brunch /brʌntʃ/ *n* 🅸 desayuno *m* tardío

brunette /bru:ˈnet/ *n* morena *f*

brunt /brʌnt/ *n*. **bear** *o* **take the ~ of sth** sufrir algo

brush /brʌʃ/ *n* cepillo *m*; (*large*) escoba; (*for decorating*) brocha *f*; (*artist's*) pincel; (*skirmish*) escaramuza *f*. ● *vt* cepillar. ▫ **~ against** *vt* rozar. ▫ **~ aside** *vt* rechazar. ▫ **~ off** *vt* (*rebuff*) desairar. ▫ **~ up (on)** *vt* refrescar

brusque /bru:sk/ *adj* brusco. **~ly** *adv* bruscamente

Brussels /ˈbrʌslz/ *n* Bruselas *f*. **~ sprout** *n* col *f* de Bruselas

brutal /ˈbru:tl/ *adj* brutal. **~ity** /-ˈtælətɪ/ *n* brutalidad *f*. **~ly** *adv* brutalmente

brute /bru:t/ *n* bestia *f*. **~ force** fuerza *f* bruta

BSc *abbr see* **BACHELOR**

BSE *abbr* (**bovine spongiform encephalopathy**) EBE *f*

bubbl|e /ˈbʌbl/ *n* burbuja *f*. ● *vi* burbujear. ▫ **~ over** *vi* desbordarse. **~ly** *adj* burbujeante

buck /bʌk/ *adj* macho. ● *n* (*deer*) ciervo *m*; (*Amer fam*) dólar *m*. **pass the ~** pasar la pelota

bucket /ˈbʌkɪt/ *n* balde *m*, cubo *m*, cubeta *f* (*Mex*)

buckle /ˈbʌkl/ *n* hebilla *f*. ● *vt* abrochar. ● *vi* torcerse

bud /bʌd/ *n* brote *m*. ● *vi* (*pt* **budded**) brotar.

Buddhis|m /ˈbʊdɪzəm/ *n* budismo *m*. **~t** *adj* & *n* budista (*m & f*)

budding /ˈbʌdɪŋ/ *adj* (*fig*) en ciernes

b

b

buddy /'bʌdɪ/ *n* 🅸 amigo *m*, cuate *m* (*Mex*)

budge /bʌdʒ/ *vt* mover. ● *vi* moverse

budgerigar /'bʌdʒərɪgɑ:(r)/ *n* periquito *m*

budget /'bʌdʒɪt/ *n* presupuesto *m*

buffalo /'bʌfələʊ/ *n* (*pl* **-oes** *or* **-o**) búfalo *m*

buffer /'bʌfə(r)/ *n* parachoques *m*

buffet¹ /'bʊfeɪ/ *n* (*meal*) buffet *m*; (*in train*) bar *m*

buffet² /'bʌfɪt/ *n* golpe *m*

bug /bʌg/ *n* bicho *m*; 🅸 (*germ*) microbio *m*; (*fam, device*) micrófono *m* oculto. ● *vt* (*pt* **bugged**) 🅸 ocultar un micrófono en; (*bother*) molestar

buggy /'bʌgɪ/ *n*. **baby ~** sillita *f* de paseo (*plegable*); (*Amer*) cochecito *m*

bugle /'bju:gl/ *n* corneta *f*

build /bɪld/ *vt/i* (*pt* **built**) construir. ● *n* (*of person*) figura *f*, tipo *m*. □ **~ up** *vt/i* fortalecer; (*increase*) aumentar. **~er** *n* (*contractor*) contratista *m & f*; (*labourer*) albañil *m*. **~ing** *n* edificio *m*; (*construction*) construcción *f*. **~up** *n* aumento *m*; (*of gas etc*) acumulación *f*

built /bɪlt/ *see* BUILD. **~-in** *adj* empotrado. **~-up area** *n* zona *f* urbanizada

bulb /bʌlb/ *n* bulbo *m*; (*Elec*) bombilla *f*, foco *m* (*Mex*)

Bulgaria /bʌl'geərɪə/ *n* Bulgaria *f*. **~n** *adj & n* búlgaro (*m*)

bulg|e /bʌldʒ/ *n* protuberancia *f*. ● *vi* pandearse. **~ing** *adj* abultado; (eyes) saltón

bulk /bʌlk/ *n* bulto *m*, volumen *m*. **in ~** a granel; (*loose*) suelto. **the ~ of** la mayor parte de. **~y** *adj* voluminoso

bull /bʊl/ *n* toro *m*. **~dog** *n* buldog *m*. **~dozer** /-dəʊzə(r)/ *n* bulldozer *m*

bullet /'bʊlɪt/ *n* bala *f*

bulletin /'bʊlətɪn/ *n* anuncio *m*; (*journal*) boletín *m*. **~ board** *n* (*Amer*) tablón *m* de anuncios, tablero *m* de anuncios (*LAm*)

bulletproof /'bʊlɪtpru:f/ *adj* a prueba de balas

bullfight /'bʊlfaɪt/ *n* corrida *f* (de toros). **~er** *n* torero *m*. **~ing** *n* (deporte *m* de) los toros

bull: ~ring *n* plaza *f* de toros. **~'s-eye** *n* diana *f*. **~shit** *n* (*vulgar*) sandeces *fpl* 🅸, gillipolleces *fpl* 🆇

bully /'bʊlɪ/ *n* matón *m*. ● *vt* intimidar. **~ing** *n* intimidación *f*

bum /bʌm/ *n* (*fam, backside*) trasero *m*; (*Amer fam, tramp*) holgazán *m*

bumblebee /'bʌmblbi:/ *n* abejorro *m*

bump /bʌmp/ *vt* chocar contra. ● *vi* dar sacudidas. ● *n* (*blow*) golpe *m*; (*jolt*) sacudida *f*. □ **~ into** *vt* chocar contra; (*meet*) encontrar.

bumper /'bʌmpə(r)/ *n* parachoques *m*. ● *adj* récord. **~ edition** *n* edición *f* especial

bun /bʌn/ *n* bollo *m*; (*bread roll*) panecillo *m*, bolillo *m* (*Mex*); (*hair*) moño *m*, chongo *m* (*Mex*)

bunch /bʌntʃ/ *n* (*of people*) grupo *m*; (*of bananas, grapes*) racimo *m*; (*of flowers*) ramo *m*

bundle /'bʌndl/ *n* bulto *m*; (*of papers*) legajo *m*. □ **~ up** *vt* atar

bungalow /'bʌŋgələʊ/ *n* casa *f* de un solo piso

bungle /'bʌŋgl/ *vt* echar a perder

bunk /bʌŋk/ *n* litera *f*

bunker /'bʌŋkə(r)/ *n* carbonera *f*;

(*Golf, Mil*) búnker *m*

bunny /ˈbʌnɪ/ *n* conejito *m*

buoy /bɔɪ/ *n* boya *f*. □ ~ **up** *vt* hacer flotar; (*fig*) animar

buoyant /ˈbɔɪənt/ *adj* flotante; (*fig*) optimista

burden /ˈbɜ:dn/ *n* carga *f*. ● *vt* cargar (**with** de)

bureau /ˈbjʊərəʊ/ *n* (*pl* **-eaux** /-əʊz/) agencia *f*; (*desk*) escritorio *m*; (*Amer, chest of drawers*) cómoda *f*

bureaucra|cy /bjʊəˈrɒkrəsɪ/ *n* burocracia *f*. ~**t** /ˈbjʊərəkræt/ *n* burócrata *m & f*. ~**tic** /-ˈkrætɪk/ *adj* burocrático

burger /ˈbɜ:gə(r)/ *n* [!] hamburguesa *f*

burgl|ar /ˈbɜ:glə(r)/ *n* ladrón *m*. ~**ar alarm** *n* alarma *f* antirrobo. ~**ary** *n* robo *m* (*en casa o edificio*). ~**e** /ˈbɜ:gl/ *vt* entrar a robar en. **we were** ~**ed** nos entraron a robar

burial /ˈberɪəl/ *n* entierro *m*

burly /ˈbɜ:lɪ/ *adj* (**-ier**, **-iest**) corpulento

burn /bɜ:n/ *vt* (*pt* **burned** *or* **burnt**) quemar. ● *vi* quemarse. ● *n* quemadura *f*. ~**er** *n* quemador *m*. □ ~ **down** *vt* incendiar. *vi* incendiarse

burnt /bɜ:nt/ *see* BURN

burp /bɜ:p/ *n* [!] eructo *m*. ● *vi* [!] eructar

burrow /ˈbʌrəʊ/ *n* madriguera *f*. ● *vt* excavar

burst /bɜ:st/ *vt* (*pt* **burst**) reventar. ● *vi* reventarse. ~ **into tears** echarse a llorar. ~ **out laughing** echarse a reír. ● *n* (*Mil*) ráfaga *f*; (*of activity*) arrebato; (*of applause*) salva *f*

bury /ˈberɪ/ *vt* enterrar; (*hide*) ocultar

bus /bʌs/ *n* (*pl* **buses**) autobús *m*, camión *m* (*Mex*)

bush /bʊʃ/ *n* arbusto *m*; (*land*) monte *m*. ~**y** *adj* espeso

business /ˈbɪznɪs/ *n* negocio *m*; (*Com*) negocios *mpl*; (*profession*) ocupación *f*; (*fig*) asunto *m*. **mind one's own** ~ ocuparse de sus propios asuntos. ~**like** *adj* práctico, serio. ~**man** /-mən/ *n* hombre *m* de negocios. ~**woman** *n* mujer *f* de negocios

busker /ˈbʌskə(r)/ *n* músico *m* ambulante

bus stop *n* parada *f* de autobús, paradero *m* de autobús (*LAm*)

bust /bʌst/ *n* busto *m*; (*chest*) pecho *m*. ● *vt* (*pt* **busted** *or* **bust**) [!] romper. ● *vi* romperse. ● *adj* roto. **go** ~ [!] quebrar

bust-up /ˈbʌstʌp/ *n* [!] riña *f*

busy /ˈbɪzɪ/ *adj* (**-ier**, **-iest**) ocupado; (street) concurrido. **be** ~ (*Amer*) (phone) estar comunicando, estar ocupado (*LAm*). ● *vt*. ~ **o.s.** with ocuparse de. ~**body** *n* entrometido *m*

but /bʌt/ *conj* pero; (*after negative*) sino. ● *prep* menos. ~ **for** si no fuera por. **last** ~ **one** penúltimo

butcher /ˈbʊtʃə(r)/ *n* carnicero *m*. ● *vt* matar; (*fig*) hacer una carnicería con

butler /ˈbʌtlə(r)/ *n* mayordomo *m*

butt /bʌt/ *n* (*of gun*) culata *f*; (*of cigarette*) colilla *f*; (*target*) blanco *m*; (*Amer fam, backside*) trasero *m*. ● *vi* topar. □ ~ **in** *vi* interrumpir

butter /ˈbʌtə(r)/ *n* mantequilla *f*. ● *vt* untar con mantequilla. ~**cup** *n* ranúnculo *m*. ~**fingers** *n* manazas *m*, torpe *m*. ~**fly** *n* mariposa *f*; (*swimming*) estilo *m* mariposa

buttock /ˈbʌtək/ *n* nalga *f*

button /ˈbʌtn/ *n* botón *m*. • *vt* abotonar. • *vi* abotonarse. **~hole** *n* ojal *m*. • *vt* (*fig*) detener

buy /baɪ/ *vt/i* (*pt* **bought**) comprar. • *n* compra *f*. **~er** *n* comprador *m*

buzz /bʌz/ *n* zumbido *m*. • *vi* zumbar. ▫ **~ off** *vi* ☒ largarse. **~er** *n* timbre *m*

by /baɪ/ *prep* por; (*near*) cerca de; (*before*) antes de; (*according to*) según. **~ and large** en conjunto, en general. **~ car** en coche. **~ oneself** por sí solo

bye/baɪ/, **bye-bye** /ˈbaɪbaɪ/ *int* [!] ¡adiós!

by: ~-election *n* elección *f* parcial. **~-law** *n* reglamento *m* (local). **~pass** *n* carretera *f* de circunvalación. • *vt* eludir; (road) circunvalar. **~-product** *n* subproducto *m*. **~stander** /-stændə(r)/ *n* espectador *m*

byte /baɪt/ *n* (*Comp*) byte *m*, octeto *m*

Cc

cab /kæb/ *n* taxi *m*; (*of lorry, train*) cabina *f*

cabaret /ˈkæbəreɪ/ *n* cabaret *m*

cabbage /ˈkæbɪdʒ/ *n* col *f*, repollo *m*

cabin /ˈkæbɪn/ *n* (*house*) cabaña *f*; (*in ship*) camarote *m*; (*in plane*) cabina *f*

cabinet /ˈkæbɪnɪt/ *n* (*cupboard*) armario *m*; (*for display*) vitrina *f*. **C~** (*Pol*) gabinete *m*

cable /ˈkeɪbl/ *n* cable *m*. **~ car** *n* teleférico *m*. **~ TV** *n* televisión *f* por cable, cablevisión *f* (*LAm*)

cackle /ˈkækl/ *n* (*of hen*) cacareo *m*; (*laugh*) risotada *f*. • *vi* cacarear; (*laugh*) reírse a carcajadas

cactus /ˈkæktəs/ *n* (*pl* **-ti** /-taɪ/ *or* **-tuses**) cacto *m*

caddie, **caddy** /ˈkædɪ/ *n* (*golf*) portador *m* de palos

cadet /kəˈdet/ *n* cadete *m*

cadge /kædʒ/ *vt/i* gorronear

café /ˈkæfeɪ/ *n* cafetería *f*

cafeteria /kæfɪˈtɪərɪə/ *n* restaurante *m* autoservicio

caffeine /ˈkæfiːn/ *n* cafeína *f*

cage /keɪdʒ/ *n* jaula *f*. • *vt* enjaular

cake /keɪk/ *n* pastel *m*, tarta *f*; (*sponge*) bizcocho *m*. **~ of soap** pastilla *f* de jabón

calamity /kəˈlæmətɪ/ *n* calamidad *f*

calcium /ˈkælsɪəm/ *n* calcio *m*

calculat|e /ˈkælkjʊleɪt/ *vt/i* calcular. **~ion** /-ˈleɪʃn/ *n* cálculo *m*. **~or** *n* calculadora *f*

calculus /ˈkælkjʊləs/ *n* (*Math*) cálculo *m*

calendar /ˈkælɪndə(r)/ *n* calendario *m*

calf /kɑːf/ *n* (*pl* **calves**) (*animal*) ternero *m*; (*of leg*) pantorrilla *f*

calibre /ˈkælɪbə(r)/ *n* calibre *m*

call /kɔːl/ *vt/i* llamar. • *n* llamada *f*; (*shout*) grito *m*; (*visit*) visita *f*. **be on ~** estar de guardia. **long-distance ~** llamada *f* de larga distancia, conferencia *f*. ▫ **~ back** *vt* hacer volver; (*on phone*) volver a llamar. *vi* volver; (*on phone*) volver a llamar. ▫ **~ for** *vt* pedir; (*fetch*) ir a buscar. ▫ **~ off** *vt* suspender. ▫ **~ on** *vt* pasar a visitar. ▫ **~ out** *vi* dar voces. ▫ **~ together** *vt* convocar. ▫ **~ up** *vt* (*Mil*) llamar al servicio militar; (*phone*) llamar. **~**

box *n* cabina *f* telefónica. ~ **centre** *n* centro *m* de llamadas. ~**er** *n* visita *f*; (*phone*) persona que llama *m*. ~**ing** *n* vocación *f*

callous /ˈkæləs/ *adj* insensible, cruel

calm /kɑːm/ *adj* (**-er**, **-est**) tranquilo; (sea) en calma. ● *n* tranquilidad *f*, calma *f*. ● *vt* calmar. ● *vi* calmarse. ~ **down** *vi* tranquilizarse. *vt* calmar. ~**ly** *adv* con calma

calorie /ˈkælərɪ/ *n* caloría *f*

calves /kɑːvz/ *npl* see **CALF**

camcorder /ˈkæmkɔːdə(r)/ *n* videocámara *f*, camcórder *m*

came /keɪm/ see **COME**

camel /ˈkæml/ *n* camello *m*

camera /ˈkæmərə/ *n* cámara *f*, máquina *f* fotográfica ~**man** /-mən/ *n* camarógrafo *m*, cámara *m*

camouflage /ˈkæməflɑːʒ/ *n* camuflaje *m*. ● *vt* camuflar

camp /kæmp/ *n* campamento *m*. ● *vi* acampar. **go** ~**ing** hacer camping

campaign /kæmˈpeɪn/ *n* campaña *f*. ● *vi* hacer campaña

camp: ~**bed** *n* catre *m* de tijera. ~**er** *n* campista *m* & *f*; (*vehicle*) cámper *m*. ~**ground** *n* (*Amer*) see ~**SITE**. ~**ing** *n* camping *m*. ~**site** *n* camping *m*

campus /ˈkæmpəs/ *n* (*pl* **-puses**) campus *m*, ciudad *f* universitaria

can¹ /kæn//kən/

negative **can't, cannot** (formal); past **could**

auxiliary verb

····➤ (*be able to*) poder. **I** ~**'t lift it** no lo puedo levantar. **she says she** ~ **come** dice que puede venir

····➤ (*be allowed to*) poder. ~ **I smoke?** ¿puedo fumar?

····➤ (*know how to*) saber. ~ **you swim?** ¿sabes nadar?

····➤ (*with verbs of perception*) *not translated*. **I** ~**'t see you** no te veo. **I** ~ **hear you better now** ahora te oigo mejor

····➤ (*in requests*) ~ **I have a glass of water, please?** ¿me trae un vaso de agua, por favor?. ~ **I have a kilo of cheese, please?** ¿me da un kilo de queso, por favor?

····➤ (*in offers*) ~ **I help you?** ¿te ayudo?; (*in shop*) ¿lo/la atienden?

can² /kæn/ *n* lata *f*, bote *m*. ● *vt* (*pt* **canned**) enlatar. ~**ned music** música *f* grabada

Canad|a /ˈkænədə/ *n* (el) Canadá *m*. ~**ian** /kəˈneɪdɪən/ *adj* & *n* canadiense (*m* & *f*)

canal /kəˈnæl/ *n* canal *m*

Canaries /kəˈneərɪz/ *npl* = **CANARY ISLANDS**

canary /kəˈneərɪ/ *n* canario *m*. **C**~ **Islands** *npl*. **the C**~ **Islands** las Islas Canarias

cancel /ˈkænsl/ *vt* (*pt* **cancelled**) cancelar; anular (command, cheque); (*delete*) tachar. ~**lation** /-ˈleɪʃn/ *n* cancelación *f*

cancer /ˈkænsə(r)/ *n* cáncer *m*. **C**~ *n* (*in astrology*) Cáncer *m*. ~**ous** *adj* canceroso

candid /ˈkændɪd/ *adj* franco

candidate /ˈkændɪdeɪt/ *n* candidato *m*

candle /ˈkændl/ *n* vela *f*. ~**stick** *n* candelero *m*

candour /ˈkændə(r)/ *n* franqueza *f*

candy /ˈkændɪ/ *n* (*Amer*) caramelo *m*, dulce *f* (*LAm*). **~floss** /-flɒs/ *n* algodón *m* de azúcar

cane /keɪn/ *n* caña *f*; (*for baskets*) mimbre *m*; (*stick*) bastón *m*; (*for punishment*) palmeta *f*. ● *vt* castigar con palmeta

canister /ˈkænɪstə(r)/ *n* bote *m*

cannabis /ˈkænəbɪs/ *n* cáñamo *m* índico, hachís *m*, cannabis *m*

cannibal /ˈkænɪbl/ *n* caníbal *m*. **~ism** *n* canibalismo *m*

cannon /ˈkænən/ *n invar* cañón *m*. **~ ball** *n* bala *f* de cañón

cannot /ˈkænət/ *see* CAN[1]

canoe /kəˈnuː/ *n* canoa *f*, piragua *f*. ● *vi* ir en canoa

canon /ˈkænən/ *n* canon *m*; (*person*) canónigo *m*. **~ize** *vt* canonizar

can opener *n* abrelatas *m*

canopy /ˈkænəpɪ/ *n* dosel *m*

can't /kɑːnt/ *see* CAN[1]

cantankerous /kænˈtæŋkərəs/ *adj* mal humorado

canteen /kænˈtiːn/ *n* cantina *f*; (*of cutlery*) juego *m* de cubiertos

canter /ˈkæntə(r)/ *n* medio galope *m*. ● *vi* ir a medio galope

canvas /ˈkænvəs/ *n* lona *f*; (*artist's*) lienzo *m*

canvass /ˈkænvəs/ *vi* hacer campaña, solicitar votos. **~ing** *n* solicitación *f* (de votos)

canyon /ˈkænjən/ *n* cañón *m*

cap /kæp/ *n* gorra *f*; (*lid*) tapa *f*; (*of cartridge*) cápsula *f*; (*of pen*) capuchón *m*. ● *vt* (*pt* **capped**) tapar, poner cápsula a; (*outdo*) superar

capab|ility /keɪpəˈbɪlətɪ/ *n* capacidad *f*. **~le** /ˈkeɪpəbl/ *adj* capaz

capacity /kəˈpæsətɪ/ *n* capacidad *f*; (*function*) calidad *f*

cape /keɪp/ *n* (*cloak*) capa *f*; (*headland*) cabo *m*

capital /ˈkæpɪtl/ *adj* capital. **~ letter** mayúscula *f*. ● *n* (*town*) capital *f*; (*money*) capital *m*. **~ism** *n* capitalismo *m*. **~ist** *adj* & *n* capitalista (*m* & *f*.) **~ize** *vt* capitalizar; escribir con mayúsculas (word). ● *vi*. **~ize on** aprovechar

capitulat|e /kəˈpɪtʃʊleɪt/ *vi* capitular. **~ion** /-ˈleɪʃn/ *n* capitulación *f*

> *i* **Capitol** El Capitolio o sede del Congreso (*Congress*) de EE.UU., en Washington DC. Situado en *Capitol Hill*, a menudo la prensa emplea este nombre para hacer referencia al Congreso de EE.UU.

Capricorn /ˈkæprɪkɔːn/ *n* Capricornio *m*

capsize /kæpˈsaɪz/ *vt* hacer volcar. ● *vi* volcarse

capsule /ˈkæpsjuːl/ *n* cápsula *f*

captain /ˈkæptɪn/ *n* capitán *m*; (*of plane*) comandante *m* & *f*. ● *vt* capitanear

caption /ˈkæpʃn/ *n* (*heading*) título *m*; (*of cartoon etc*) leyenda *f*

captivate /ˈkæptɪveɪt/ *vt* encantar

captiv|e /ˈkæptɪv/ *adj* & *n* cautivo (*m*). **~ity** /-ˈtɪvətɪ/ *n* cautiverio *m*, cautividad *f*

capture /ˈkæptʃə(r)/ *vt* capturar; atraer (attention); (*Mil*) tomar. ● *n* apresamiento *m*; (*Mil*) toma *f*

car /kɑː(r)/ *n* coche *m*, carro *m* (*LAm*); (*Amer, of train*) vagón *m*

caramel /ˈkærəmel/ *n* azúcar *m* quemado; (*sweet*) caramelo *m*, dulce *m* (*LAm*)

caravan /'kærəvæn/ *n* caravana *f*

carbohydrate /kɑːbəʊ'haɪdreɪt/ *n* hidrato *m* de carbono

carbon /'kɑːbən/ *n* carbono *m*; (*paper*) carbón *m*. ~ **copy** *n* copia *f* al carbón. ~ **dioxide** /daɪ'ɒksaɪd/ *n* anhídrido *m* carbónico. ~ **monoxide** /mə'nɒksaɪd/ *n* monóxido de carbono

carburettor /kɑːbjʊ'retə(r)/ *n* carburador *m*

carcass /'kɑːkəs/ *n* cuerpo *m* de animal muerto; (*for meat*) res *f* muerta

card /kɑːd/ *n* tarjeta *f*; (*for games*) carta *f*; (*membership*) carnet *m*; (*records*) ficha *f*. ~**board** *n* cartón *m*

cardigan /'kɑːdɪgən/ *n* chaqueta *f* de punto, rebeca *f*

cardinal /'kɑːdɪnəl/ *adj* cardinal. ● *n* cardenal *m*

care /keə(r)/ *n* cuidado *m*; (*worry*) preocupación *f*; (*protection*) cargo *m*. ~ **of** a cuidado de, en casa de. **take** ~ tener cuidado. **take** ~ **of** cuidar de (person); ocuparse de (matter). ● *vi* interesarse. **I don't** ~ me da igual. □ ~ **about** *vt* preocuparse por. □ ~ **for** *vt* cuidar de; (*like*) querer

career /kə'rɪə(r)/ *n* carrera *f*. ● *vi* correr a toda velocidad

care: ~**free** *adj* despreocupado. ~**ful** *adj* cuidadoso; (*cautious*) prudente. **be** ~**ful** tener cuidado. ~**fully** *adv* con cuidado. ~**less** *adj* negligente; (*not worried*) indiferente. ~**lessly** *adv* descuidadamente. ~**lessness** *n* descuido *m* ~**r** *n persona que cuida de un discapacitado*

caress /kə'res/ *n* caricia *f*. ● *vt* acariciar

caretaker /'keəteɪkə(r)/ *n* vigilante *m*; (*of flats etc*) portero *m*

car ferry *n* transbordador *m* de coches

cargo /'kɑːgəʊ/ *n* (*pl* **-oes**) carga *f*

Caribbean /kærɪ'biːən/ *adj* caribeño. **the** ~ **(Sea)** *n* el mar Caribe

caricature /'kærɪkətʃʊə(r)/ *n* caricatura *f*. ● *vt* caricaturizar

carnage /'kɑːnɪdʒ/ *n* carnicería *f*, matanza *f*

carnation /kɑː'neɪʃn/ *n* clavel *m*

carnival /'kɑːnɪvl/ *n* carnaval *m*

carol /'kærəl/ *n* villancico *m*

carousel /kærə'sel/ *n* tiovivo *m*, carrusel *m* (*LAm*); (*for baggage*) cinta *f* transportadora

carp /kɑːp/ *n invar* carpa *f*. □ ~ **at** *vi* quejarse de

car park *n* aparcamiento *m*, estacionamiento *m*

carpent|er /'kɑːpɪntə(r)/ *n* carpintero *m*. ~**ry** /-trɪ/ *n* carpintería *f*

carpet /'kɑːpɪt/ *n* alfombra *f*. ~ **sweeper** *n* cepillo *m* mecánico

carriage /'kærɪdʒ/ *n* coche *m*; (*Mec*) carro *m*; (*transport*) transporte *m*; (*cost, bearing*) porte *m*; (*of train*) vagón *m*. ~**way** *n* calzada *f*, carretera *f*

carrier /'kærɪə(r)/ *n* transportista *m & f*; (*company*) empresa *f* de transportes; (*Med*) portador *m*. ~ **bag** *n* bolsa *f*

carrot /'kærət/ *n* zanahoria *f*

carry /'kærɪ/ *vt* llevar; transportar (goods); (*involve*) llevar consigo, implicar. ● *vi* (sounds) llegar, oírse. □ ~ **off** *vt* llevarse. □ ~ **on** *vi* seguir, continuar. □ ~ **out** *vt* realizar; cumplir (promise, threat). ~ **cot** *n* cuna *f* portátil

carsick /'kɑːsɪk/ *adj* mareado (*por viajar en coche*)

C

cart /kɑ:t/ *n* carro *m*; (*Amer, in supermarket, airport*) carrito *m*. • *vt* acarrear; (*fam, carry*) llevar

carton /'kɑ:tən/ *n* caja *f* de cartón

cartoon /kɑ:'tu:n/ *n* caricatura *f*, chiste *m*; (*strip*) historieta *f*; (*film*) dibujos *mpl* animados

cartridge /'kɑ:trɪdʒ/ *n* cartucho *m*

carve /kɑ:v/ *vt* tallar; trinchar (meat)

cascade /kæs'keɪd/ *n* cascada *f*. • *vi* caer en cascadas

case /keɪs/ *n* caso *m*; (*Jurid*) proceso *m*; (*crate*) cajón *m*; (*box*) caja *f*; (*suitcase*) maleta *f*, petaca *f* (*Mex*). **in any ~** en todo caso. **in ~ he comes** por si viene. **in ~ of** en caso de

cash /kæʃ/ *n* dinero *m* efectivo. **pay (in) ~** pagar al contado. • *vt* cobrar. **~ in (on)** aprovecharse de. **~ desk** *n* caja *f*. **~ dispenser** *n* cajero *m* automático

cashier /kæ'ʃɪə(r)/ *n* cajero *m*

cashpoint /'kæʃpɔɪnt/ *n* cajero *m* automático

casino /kə'si:nəʊ/ *n* (*pl* **-os**) casino *m*

cask /kɑ:sk/ *n* barril *m*

casket /'kɑ:skɪt/ *n* cajita *f*; (*Amer*) ataúd *m*, cajón *m* (*LAm*)

casserole /'kæsərəʊl/ *n* cacerola *f*; (*stew*) guiso *m*, guisado *m* (*Mex*)

cassette /kə'set/ *n* cassette *m & f*

cast /kɑ:st/ *vt* (*pt* **cast**) arrojar; fundir (metal); emitir (vote). • *n* lanzamiento *m*; (*in play*) reparto *m*; (*mould*) molde *m*

castanets /kæstə'nets/ *npl* castañuelas *fpl*

castaway /'kɑ:stəweɪ/ *n* náufrago *m*

caster /'kɑ:stə(r)/ *n* ruedecita *f*. **~ sugar** *n* azúcar *m* extrafino

Castil|e /kæ'sti:l/ *n* Castilla *f*. **~ian** /kæ'stɪlɪən/ *adj & n* castellano (*m*)

cast: ~ iron *n* hierro *m* fundido. **~-iron** *adj* (*fig*) sólido

castle /'kɑ:sl/ *n* castillo *m*; (*Chess*) torre *f*

cast-offs /'kɑ:stɒfs/ *npl* desechos *mpl*

castrat|e /kæ'streɪt/ *vt* castrar. **~ion** /-ʃn/ *n* castración *f*

casual /'kæʒʊəl/ *adj* casual; (meeting) fortuito; (work) ocasional; (attitude) despreocupado; (clothes) informal, de sport. **~ly** *adv* de paso

casualt|y /'kæʒʊəltɪ/ *n* (*injured*) herido *m*; (*dead*) víctima *f*; (*in hospital*) urgencias *fpl*. **~ies** *npl* (*Mil*) bajas *fpl*

cat /kæt/ *n* gato *m*

Catalan /'kætəlæn/ *adj & n* catalán (*m*)

catalogue /'kætəlɒg/ *n* catálogo *m*. • *vt* catalogar

Catalonia /kætə'ləʊnɪə/ *n* Cataluña *f*

catalyst /'kætəlɪst/ *n* catalizador *m*

catamaran /kætəmə'ræn/ *n* catamarán *m*

catapult /'kætəpʌlt/ *n* catapulta *f*; (*child's*) tirachinas *f*, resortera *f* (*Mex*)

catarrh /kə'tɑ:(r)/ *n* catarro *m*

catastroph|e /kə'tæstrəfɪ/ *n* catástrofe *m*. **~ic** /kætə'strɒfɪk/ *adj* catastrófico

catch /kætʃ/ *vt* (*pt* **caught**) coger (*esp Spain*), agarrar; tomar (train, bus); (*unawares*) sorprender, pillar; (*understand*) entender; contagiarse de (disease). **~ a cold** resfriarse.

~ sight of avistar. ● *vi* (*get stuck*) engancharse; (fire) prenderse. ● *n* (*by goalkeeper*) parada *f*; (*of fish*) pesca *f*; (*on door*) pestillo *m*; (*on window*) cerradura *f*. □ **~ on** *vi* 🅸 hacerse popular. □ **~ up** *vi* poner al día. **~ up with** alcanzar; ponerse al corriente de (news etc). **~ing** *adj* contagioso. **~phrase** *n* eslogan *m*. **~y** *adj* pegadizo

categor|ical /kætɪ'gɒrɪkl/ *adj* categórico. **~y** /'kætɪgərɪ/ *n* categoría *f*

cater /'keɪtə(r)/ *vi* encargarse del servicio de comida. **~ for** proveer a (needs). **~er** *n* proveedor *m*

caterpillar /'kætəpɪlə(r)/ *n* oruga *f*, azotador *m* (*Mex*)

cathedral /kə'θi:drəl/ *n* catedral *f*

catholic /'kæθəlɪk/ *adj* universal. **C~** *adj* & *n* católico (*m*). **C~ism** /kə'θɒlɪsɪzəm/ *n* catolicismo *m*

cat: ~nap *n* sueñecito *m*. **C~seyes** *npl* (®) catafaros *mpl*

cattle /'kætl/ *npl* ganado *m*

catwalk *n* pasarela *f*

Caucasian /kɔ:'keɪʒən/ *n*. **a male ~** (*Amer*) un hombre de raza blanca

caught /kɔ:t/ *see* CATCH

cauliflower /'kɒlɪflaʊə(r)/ *n* coliflor *f*

cause /kɔ:z/ *n* causa *f*, motivo *m*. ● *vt* causar

cautio|n /'kɔ:ʃn/ *n* cautela *f*; (*warning*) advertencia *f*. ● *vt* advertir; (*Jurid*) amonestar. **~us** /-ʃəs/ *adj* cauteloso, prudente

cavalry /'kævəlrɪ/ *n* caballería *f*

cave /keɪv/ *n* cueva *f*. □ **~ in** *vi* hundirse. **~man** *n* troglodita *m*

cavern /'kævən/ *n* caverna *f*

caviare /'kævɪɑ:(r)/ *n* caviar *m*

cavity /'kævətɪ/ *n* cavidad *f*; (*in tooth*) caries *f*

CCTV *abbr* (**closed circuit television**) CCTV *m*

CD *abbr* (= **compact disc**) CD *m*. **~ player** (reproductor *m* de) compact-disc *m*. **~-ROM** *n* CD-ROM *m*

cease /si:s/ *vt/i* cesar. **~fire** *n* alto *m* el fuego

cedar /'si:də(r)/ *n* cedro *m*

ceiling /'si:lɪŋ/ *n* techo *m*

celebrat|e /'selɪbreɪt/ *vt* celebrar. ● *vi* divertirse. **~ed** *adj* célebre. **~ion** /-'breɪʃn/ *n* celebración *f*; (*party*) fiesta *f*

celebrity /sɪ'lebrətɪ/ *n* celebridad *f*

celery /'selərɪ/ *n* apio *m*

cell /sel/ *n* celda *f*; (*in plants, electricity*) célula *f*

cellar /'selə(r)/ *n* sótano *m*; (*for wine*) bodega *f*

cello /'tʃeləʊ/ *n* (*pl* **-os**) violonc(h)elo *m*, chelo *m*

Cellophane /'seləfeɪn/ *n* (®) celofán *m* (®)

cellphone /'selfəʊn/ *n* celular *m* (*LAm*), móvil *m* (*Esp*)

cellul|ar /'seljʊlə(r)/ *adj* celular. **~ phone** *n* teléfono celular *m* (*LAm*), teléfono móvil *m* (*Esp*). **~oid** *n* celuloide *m*

Celsius /'selsɪəs/ *adj*. **20 degrees ~** 20 grados centígrados *or* Celsio(s)

cement /sɪ'ment/ *n* cemento *m*. ● *vt* cementar

cemetery /'semətrɪ/ *n* cementerio *m*

cens|or /'sensə(r)/ *n* censor *m*. ● *vt* censurar. **~ship** *n* censura *f*. **~ure** /'senʃə(r)/ *vt* censurar

census /'sensəs/ *n* censo *m*

C

cent /sent/ *n* ($) centavo *m*; (€) céntimo *m*

centenary /sen'ti:nərɪ/ *n* centenario *m*

centi|grade /'sentɪgreɪd/ *adj* centígrado. **~litre** *n* centilitro *m*. **~metre** *n* centímetro *m*. **~pede** /-pi:d/ *n* ciempiés *m*

central /'sentrəl/ *adj* central; (*of town*) céntrico. ~ **heating** *n* calefacción *f* central. **~ize** *vt* centralizar

centre /'sentə(r)/ *n* centro *m*. ● *vt* (*pt* **centred**) centrar. ● *vi* centrarse (**on** en)

century /'sentʃərɪ/ *n* siglo *m*

cereal /'sɪərɪəl/ *n* cereal *m*

ceremon|ial /serɪ'məʊnɪəl/ *adj* & *n* ceremonial (*m*). **~y** /'serɪmənɪ/ *n* ceremonia *f*

certain /'sɜ:tn/ *adj* cierto. **for ~** seguro. **make ~ of** asegurarse de. **~ly** *adv* desde luego

certificate /sə'tɪfɪkət/ *n* certificado *m*; (*of birth, death etc*) partida *f*

certify /'sɜ:tɪfaɪ/ *vt* certificar

chafe /tʃeɪf/ *vt* rozar. ● *vi* rozarse

chaffinch /'tʃæfɪntʃ/ *n* pinzón *m*

chagrin /'ʃægrɪn/ *n* disgusto *m*

chain /tʃeɪn/ *n* cadena *f*. ● *vt* encadenar. ~ **reaction** *n* reacción *f* en cadena. **~-smoker** *n* fumador *m* que siempre tiene un cigarrillo encendido. ~ **store** *n* tienda *f* de una cadena

chair /tʃeə(r)/ *n* silla *f*; (*Univ*) cátedra *f*. ● *vt* presidir. **~lift** *n* telesquí *m*, telesilla *m* (*LAm*). **~man** /-mən/ *n* presidente *m*

chalet /'ʃæleɪ/ *n* chalé *m*

chalk /tʃɔ:k/ *n* (*in geology*) creta *f*; (*stick*) tiza *f*, gis *m* (*Mex*)

challeng|e /'tʃælɪndʒ/ *n* desafío *m*; (*fig*) reto *m*. ● *vt* desafiar; (*question*) poner en duda. **~ing** *adj* estimulante

chamber /'tʃeɪmbə(r)/ *n* (*old use*) cámara *f*. **~maid** *n* camarera *f*. **~ pot** *n* orinal *m*

champagne /ʃæm'peɪn/ *n* champaña *m*, champán *m*

champion /'tʃæmpɪən/ *n* campeón *m*. ● *vt* defender. **~ship** *n* campeonato *m*

chance /tʃɑ:ns/ *n* casualidad *f*; (*likelihood*) posibilidad *f*; (*opportunity*) oportunidad *f*; (*risk*) riesgo *m*. **by ~** por casualidad. ● *adj* fortuito

chancellor /'tʃɑ:nsələ(r)/ *n* canciller *m*; (*Univ*) rector *m*. **C~ of the Exchequer** Ministro *m* de Hacienda

chandelier /ʃændə'lɪə(r)/ *n* araña *f* (de luces)

chang|e /tʃeɪndʒ/ *vt* cambiar; (*substitute*) reemplazar. ~ **one's mind** cambiar de idea. ● *vi* cambiarse. ● *n* cambio *m*; (*coins*) cambio *m*, sencillo *m* (*LAm*), feria *f* (*Mex*); (*money returned*) cambio *m*, vuelta *f*, vuelto *m* (*LAm*). **~eable** *adj* cambiable; (weather) variable. **~ing room** *n* (*Sport*) vestuario *m*, vestidor *m* (*Mex*); (*in shop*) probador *m*

channel /'tʃænl/ *n* canal *m*; (*fig*) medio *m*. ● *vt* (*pt* **channelled**) acanalar; (*fig*) encauzar. **the (English) C~** el Canal de la Mancha. **C~ Islands** *npl*. **the C~ Islands** las islas Anglonormandas. **C~ Tunnel** *n*. **the C~ Tunnel** el Eurotúnel

chant /tʃɑ:nt/ *n* canto *m*. ● *vt/i* cantar

chao|s /'keɪɒs/ *n* caos *m*. **~tic** /-'ɒtɪk/ *adj* caótico

chap /tʃæp/ *n* [I] tipo *m*, tío *m* [I]. ● *vt* (*pt* **chapped**) agrietar. ● *vi* agrietarse

chapel /'tʃæpl/ *n* capilla *f*
chaperon /'ʃæpərəʊn/ *n* acompañante *f*
chapter /'tʃæptə(r)/ *n* capítulo *m*
char /tʃɑ:(r)/ *vt* (*pt* **charred**) carbonizar
character /'kærəktə(r)/ *n* carácter *m*; (*in book, play*) personaje *m*. **in ~** característico. **~istic** /-'rɪstɪk/ *adj* típico. ● *n* característica *f*. **~ize** *vt* caracterizar
charade /ʃə'rɑ:d/ *n* farsa *f*. **~s** *npl* (*game*) charada *f*
charcoal /'tʃɑ:kəʊl/ *n* carbón *m* vegetal; (*for drawing*) carboncillo *m*
charge /tʃɑ:dʒ/ *n* precio *m*; (*Elec, Mil*) carga *f*; (*Jurid*) acusación *f*; (*task, custody*) encargo *m*; (*responsibility*) responsabilidad *f*. **in ~ of** responsable de, encargado de. **the person in ~** la persona responsable. **take ~ of** encargarse de. ● *vt* pedir; (*Elec, Mil*) cargar; (*Jurid*) acusar. ● *vi* cargar; (animal) embestir (**at** contra)
charit|able /'tʃærɪtəbl/ *adj* caritativo. **~y** /'tʃærɪtɪ/ *n* caridad *f*; (*society*) institución *f* benéfica
charm /tʃɑ:m/ *n* encanto *m*; (*spell*) hechizo *m*; (*on bracelet*) dije *m*, amuleto *m*. ● *vt* encantar. **~ing** *adj* encantador
chart /tʃɑ:t/ *n* (*for navigation*) carta *f* de navegación; (*table*) tabla *f*
charter /'tʃɑ:tə(r)/ *n* carta *f*. ● *vt* alquilar (bus, train); fletar (plane, ship). **~ flight** *n* vuelo *m* chárter
chase /tʃeɪs/ *vt* perseguir. ● *vi* correr (**after** tras). ● *n* persecución *f*. □ **~ away**, **~ off** *vt* ahuyentar
chassis /'ʃæsɪ/ *n* chasis *m*
chastise /tʃæs'taɪz/ *vt* castigar
chastity /'tʃæstətɪ/ *n* castidad *f*
chat /tʃæt/ *n* charla *f*, conversación *f* (*LAm*), plática *f* (*Mex*). ● *vi* (*pt* **chatted**) charlar, conversar (*LAm*), platicar (*Mex*)
chatter /'tʃætə(r)/ *n* charla *f*. ● *vi* charlar. **his teeth are ~ing** le castañetean los dientes. **~box** *n* parlanchín *m*
chauffeur /'ʃəʊfə(r)/ *n* chófer *m*
chauvinis|m /'ʃəʊvɪnɪzəm/ *n* patriotería *f*; (*male*) machismo *m*. **~t** *n* patriotero *m*; (*male*) machista *m*
cheap /tʃi:p/ *adj* (**-er**, **-est**) barato; (*poor quality*) de baja calidad; (rate) económico. **~(ly)** *adv* barato, a bajo precio
cheat /'tʃi:t/ *vt* defraudar; (*deceive*) engañar. ● *vi* (*at cards*) hacer trampas. ● *n* trampa *f*; (*person*) tramposo *m*
check /tʃek/ *vt* comprobar; (*examine*) inspeccionar; (*curb*) frenar. ● *vi* comprobar. ● *n* comprobación *f*; (*of tickets*) control *m*; (*curb*) freno *m*; (*Chess*) jaque *m*; (*pattern*) cuadro *m*; (*Amer, bill*) cuenta *f*; (*Amer, cheque*) cheque *m*. □ **~ in** *vi* registrarse; (*at airport*) facturar el equipaje, chequear el equipaje (*LAm*), registrar el equipaje (*Mex*). □ **~ out** *vi* pagar la cuenta y marcharse. □ **~ up** *vi* confirmar. □ **~ up on** *vt* investigar. **~book** *n* (*Amer*) *see* CHEQUEBOOK. **~ered** /'tʃekəd/ *adj* (*Amer*) *see* CHEQUERED
checkers /'tʃekəz/ *n* (*Amer*) damas *fpl*
check: ~mate *n* jaque *m* mate. ● *vt* dar mate a. **~out** *n* caja *f*. **~point** control *m*. **~up** *n* chequeo *m*, revisión
cheek /tʃi:k/ *n* mejilla *f*; (*fig*) descaro *m*. **~bone** *n* pómulo *m*. **~y** *adj* descarado
cheep /tʃi:p/ *vi* piar

c

cheer /tʃɪə(r)/ *n* alegría *f*; (*applause*) viva *m*. **~s!** ¡salud!. ● *vt* alegrar; (*applaud*) aplaudir. ● *vi* alegrarse; (*applaud*) aplaudir. **~ up!** ¡anímate! **~ful** *adj* alegre

cheerio /tʃɪərɪ'əʊ/ *int* [!] ¡adiós!, ¡hasta luego!

cheerless /'tʃɪəlɪs/ *adj* triste

cheese /tʃi:z/ *n* queso *m*

cheetah /'tʃi:tə/ *n* guepardo *m*

chef /ʃef/ *n* jefe *m* de cocina

chemical /'kemɪkl/ *adj* químico. ● *n* producto *m* químico

chemist /'kemɪst/ *n* farmacéutico *m*; (*scientist*) químico *m*. **~ry** *n* química *f*. **~'s (shop)** *n* farmacia *f*

cheque /tʃek/ *n* cheque *m*, talón *m*. **~book** *n* chequera *f*, talonario *m*

cherish /'tʃerɪʃ/ *vt* cuidar; (*love*) querer; abrigar (hope)

cherry /'tʃerɪ/ *n* cereza *f*. **~ tree** *n* cerezo *m*

chess /tʃes/ *n* ajedrez *m*. **~board** *n* tablero *m* de ajedrez

chest /tʃest/ *n* pecho *m*; (*box*) cofre *m*, cajón *m*

chestnut /'tʃesnʌt/ *n* castaña *f*. ● *adj* castaño. **~ tree** *n* castaño *m*

chest of drawers *n* cómoda *f*

chew /tʃu:/ *vt* masticar. **~ing gum** *n* chicle *m*

chic /ʃi:k/ *adj* elegante

chick /tʃɪk/ *n* polluelo *m*. **~en** /'tʃɪkɪn/ *n* pollo *m*. ● *adj* [!] cobarde. ▫ **~en out** *vi* [!] acobardarse. **~enpox** /'tʃɪkɪnpɒks/ *n* varicela *f*. **~pea** *n* garbanzo *m*

chicory /'tʃɪkərɪ/ *n* (*in coffee*) achicoria *f*; (*in salad*) escarola *f*

chief /tʃi:f/ *n* jefe *m*. ● *adj* principal. **~ly** *adv* principalmente

chilblain /'tʃɪlbleɪn/ *n* sabañón *m*

child /tʃaɪld/ *n* (*pl* **children** /'tʃɪldrən/) niño *m*; (*offspring*) hijo *m*. **~birth** *n* parto *m*. **~hood** *n* niñez *f*. **~ish** *adj* infantil. **~less** *adj* sin hijos. **~like** *adj* ingenuo, de niño

Chile /'tʃɪlɪ/ *n* Chile *m*. **~an** *adj & n* chileno (*m*)

chill /tʃɪl/ *n* frío *m*; (*illness*) resfriado *m*. ● *adj* frío. ● *vt* enfriar; refrigerar (food)

chilli /'tʃɪlɪ/ *n* (*pl* **-ies**) chile *m*

chilly /'tʃɪlɪ/ *adj* frío

chime /tʃaɪm/ *n* carillón *m*. ● *vt* tocar (bells); dar (hours). ● *vi* repicar

chimney /'tʃɪmnɪ/ *n* (*pl* **-eys**) chimenea *f*. **~ sweep** *n* deshollinador *m*

chimpanzee /tʃɪmpæn'zi:/ *n* chimpancé *m*

chin /tʃɪn/ *n* barbilla *f*

china /'tʃaɪnə/ *n* porcelana *f*

Chin|a /'tʃaɪnə/ *n* China *f*. **~ese** /-'ni:z/ *adj & n* chino (*m*)

chink /tʃɪŋk/ *n* (*crack*) grieta *f*; (*sound*) tintín *m*. ● *vi* tintinear

chip /tʃɪp/ *n* pedacito *m*; (*splinter*) astilla *f*; (*Culin*) patata *f* frita, papa *f* frita (*LAm*); (*in gambling*) ficha *f*; (*Comp*) chip *m*. **have a ~ on one's shoulder** guardar rencor. ● *vt* (*pt* **chipped**) desportillar. ▫ **~ in** *vi* [!] interrumpir; (*with money*) contribuir

chiropodist /kɪ'rɒpədɪst/ *n* callista *m & f*, pedicuro *m*

chirp /tʃɜ:p/ *n* pío *m*. ● *vi* piar. **~y** *adj* alegre

chisel /'tʃɪzl/ *n* formón *m*. ● *vt* (*pt* **chiselled**) cincelar

chivalr|ous /'ʃɪvəlrəs/ *adj* caballeroso. **~y** /-rɪ/ *n* caballerosidad *f*

chlorine /'klɔ:ri:n/ *n* cloro *m*

chock /tʃɒk/ *n* cuña *f*. **~-a-block** *adj*, **~-full** *adj* atestado
chocolate /ˈtʃɒklət/ *n* chocolate *m*; (*individual sweet*) bombón *m*, chocolate *m* (*LAm*)
choice /tʃɔɪs/ *n* elección *f*; (*preference*) preferencia *f*. ● *adj* escogido
choir /ˈkwaɪə(r)/ *n* coro *m*
choke /tʃəʊk/ *vt* sofocar. ● *vi* sofocarse. ● *n* (*Auto*) choke *m*, estárter *m*, ahogador *m* (*Mex*)
cholera /ˈkɒlərə/ *n* cólera *m*
cholesterol /kəˈlestərɒl/ *n* colesterol *m*
choose /tʃuːz/ *vt/i* (*pt* **chose**, *pp* **chosen**) elegir, escoger. **~y** *adj* [!] exigente
chop /tʃɒp/ *vt* (*pt* **chopped**) cortar. ● *n* (*Culin*) chuleta *f*. □ **~ down** *vt* talar. □ **~ off** *vt* cortar. **~per** *n* hacha *f*; (*butcher's*) cuchilla *f*. **~py** *adj* picado
chord /kɔːd/ *n* (*Mus*) acorde *m*
chore /tʃɔː(r)/ *n* tarea *f*, faena *f*. **household ~s** *npl* quehaceres *mpl* domésticos
chorus /ˈkɔːrəs/ *n* coro *m*; (*of song*) estribillo *m*
chose/tʃəʊz/, **chosen** /ˈtʃəʊzn/ *see* CHOOSE
Christ /kraɪst/ *n* Cristo *m*
christen /ˈkrɪsn/ *vt* bautizar. **~ing** *n* bautizo *m*
Christian /ˈkrɪstjən/ *adj* & *n* cristiano (*m*). **~ity** /krɪstɪˈænətɪ/ *n* cristianismo *m*. **~ name** *n* nombre *m* de pila
Christmas /ˈkrɪsməs/ *n* Navidad *f*. **Merry ~!** ¡Feliz Navidad!, ¡Felices Pascuas! **Father ~** Papá *m* Noel. ● *adj* de Navidad, navideño. **~ card** *n* tarjeta *f* de Navidad *f*. **~ day** *n* día *m* de Navidad. **~ Eve** *n* Nochebuena *f*. **~ tree** *n* árbol *m* de Navidad
chrom|e /krəʊm/ *n* cromo *m*. **~ium** /ˈkrəʊmɪəm/ *n* cromo *m*
chromosome /ˈkrəʊməsəʊm/ *n* cromosoma *m*
chronic /ˈkrɒnɪk/ *adj* crónico; (*fam, bad*) terrible
chronicle /ˈkrɒnɪkl/ *n* crónica *f*. ● *vt* historiar
chronological /krɒnəˈlɒdʒɪkl/ *adj* cronológico
chubby /ˈtʃʌbɪ/ *adj* (**-ier**, **-iest**) regordete; (person) gordinflón [!]
chuck /tʃʌk/ *vt* [!] tirar. □ **~ out** *vt* tirar
chuckle /ˈtʃʌkl/ *n* risa *f* ahogada. ● *vi* reírse entre dientes
chug /tʃʌg/ *vi* (*pt* **chugged**) (*of motor*) traquetear
chum /tʃʌm/ *n* amigo *m*, compinche *m*, cuate *m* (*Mex*)
chunk /tʃʌŋk/ *n* trozo *m* grueso. **~y** *adj* macizo
church /ˈtʃɜːtʃ/ *n* iglesia *f*. **~yard** *n* cementerio *m*
churn /ˈtʃɜːn/ *n* (*for milk*) lechera *f*, cántara *f*; (*for making butter*) mantequera *f*. ● *vt* agitar. □ **~ out** *vt* producir en profusión
chute /ʃuːt/ *n* tobogán *m*
cider /ˈsaɪdə(r)/ *n* sidra *f*
cigar /sɪˈgɑː(r)/ *n* puro *m*
cigarette /sɪgəˈret/ *n* cigarrillo *m*. **~ end** *n* colilla *f*. **~ holder** *n* boquilla *f*. **~ lighter** *n* mechero *m*, encendedor *m*
cinecamera /ˈsɪnɪkæmərə/ *n* tomavistas *m*, filmadora *f* (*LAm*)
cinema /ˈsɪnəmə/ *n* cine *m*
cipher /ˈsaɪfə(r)/ *n* (*Math, fig*) cero *m*; (*code*) clave *f*
circle /ˈsɜːkl/ *n* círculo *m*; (*in theatre*) anfiteatro *m*. ● *vt* girar alrede-

dor de. ● *vi* dar vueltas

circuit /'sɜ:kɪt/ *n* circuito *m*

circular /'sɜ:kjʊlə(r)/ *adj & n* circular (*f*)

circulat|e /'sɜ:kjʊleɪt/ *vt* hacer circular. ● *vi* circular. **~ion** /-'leɪʃn/ *n* circulación *f*; (*number of copies*) tirada *f*

circumcise /'sɜ:kəmsaɪz/ *vt* circuncidar

circumference /sə'kʌmfərəns/ *n* circunferencia *f*

circumstance /'sɜ:kəmstəns/ *n* circunstancia *f*. **~s** (*means*) *npl* situación *f* económica

circus /'sɜ:kəs/ *n* circo *m*

cistern /'sɪstən/ *n* cisterna *f*

cite /saɪt/ *vt* citar

citizen /'sɪtɪzn/ *n* ciudadano *m*; (*inhabitant*) habitante *m & f*

citrus /'sɪtrəs/ *n*. **~ fruits** cítricos *mpl*

city /'sɪtɪ/ *n* ciudad *f*; **the C~** el centro *m* financiero de Londres

> **City - the** Área ubicada dentro de los límites de la antigua ciudad de Londres. Actualmente es el centro financiero de la capital donde tienen sus sedes centrales muchas instituciones financieras. A menudo, cuando se habla de *The City*, se está refiriendo a ésas y no a la zona propiamente dicha.

civic /'sɪvɪk/ *adj* cívico

civil /'sɪvl/ *adj* civil; (*polite*) cortés

civilian /sɪ'vɪlɪən/ *adj & n* civil (*m & f*)

civiliz|ation /sɪvɪlaɪ'zeɪʃn/ *n* civilización *f*. **~ed** /'sɪvəlaɪzd/ *adj* civilizado.

civil: ~ servant *n* funcionario *m* (del Estado), burócrata *m & f* (*Mex*). **~ service** *n* administración *f* pública. **~ war** *n* guerra *f* civil

clad /klæd/ *see* CLOTHE

claim /kleɪm/ *vt* reclamar; (*assert*) pretender. ● *n* reclamación *f*; (*right*) derecho *m*; (*Jurid*) demanda *f*

clairvoyant /kleə'vɔɪənt/ *n* clarividente *m & f*

clam /klæm/ *n* almeja *f*. ● *vi* (*pt* **clammed**). **~ up** [!] ponerse muy poco comunicativo

clamber /'klæmbə(r)/ *vi* trepar a gatas

clammy /'klæmɪ/ *adj* (**-ier**, **-iest**) húmedo

clamour /'klæmə(r)/ *n* clamor *m*. ● *vi*. **~ for** pedir a gritos

clamp /klæmp/ *n* abrazadera *f*; (*Auto*) cepo *m*. ● *vt* sujetar con abrazadera; poner cepo a (car). □ **~ down on** *vt* reprimir

clan /klæn/ *n* clan *m*

clang /klæŋ/ *n* sonido *m* metálico

clap /klæp/ *vt* (*pt* **clapped**) aplaudir; batir (hands). ● *vi* aplaudir. ● *n* palmada *f*; (*of thunder*) trueno *m*

clarif|ication /klærɪfɪ'keɪʃn/ *n* aclaración *f*. **~y** /'klærɪfaɪ/ *vt* aclarar. ● *vi* aclararse

clarinet /klærɪ'net/ *n* clarinete *m*

clarity /'klærətɪ/ *n* claridad *f*

clash /klæʃ/ *n* choque *m*; (*noise*) estruendo *m*; (*contrast*) contraste *m*; (*fig*) conflicto *m*. ● *vt* golpear. ● *vi* encontrarse; (colours) desentonar

clasp /klɑ:sp/ *n* cierre *m*. ● *vt* agarrar; apretar (hand)

class /klɑ:s/ *n* clase *f*. **evening ~** *n* clase nocturna. ● *vt* clasificar

classic /'klæsɪk/ *adj & n* clásico (*m*). **~al** *adj* clásico. **~s** *npl* estudios *mpl* clásicos

classif|ication /klæsɪfɪ'keɪʃn/ *n* clasificación *f*. **~y** /'klæsɪfaɪ/ *vt* clasificar

class: ~room *n* aula *f*, clase *f*. **~y** *adj* 🄸 elegante

clatter /'klætə(r)/ *n* ruido *m*; (*of train*) traqueteo *m*. ● *vi* hacer ruido

clause /klɔ:z/ *n* cláusula *f*; (*Gram*) oración *f*

claustrophobia /klɔ:strə'fəʊbɪə/ *n* claustrofobia *f*

claw /klɔ:/ *n* garra *f*; (*of cat*) uña *f*; (*of crab*) pinza *f*. ● *vt* arañar

clay /kleɪ/ *n* arcilla *f*

clean /kli:n/ *adj* (**-er**, **-est**) limpio; (stroke) bien definido. ● *adv* completamente. ● *vt* limpiar. ● *vi* limpiar. □ **~ up** *vt* hacer la limpieza. **~er** *n* persona *f* que hace la limpieza. **~liness** /'klenlɪnɪs/ *n* limpieza *f*

cleans|e /klenz/ *vt* limpiar. **~er** *n* producto *m* de limpieza; (*for skin*) crema *f* de limpieza. **~ing cream** *n* crema *f* de limpieza

clear /klɪə(r)/ *adj* (**-er**, **-est**) claro; (*transparent*) transparente; (*without obstacles*) libre; (profit) neto; (sky) despejado. **keep ~ of** evitar. ● *adv* claramente. ● *vt* despejar; liquidar (goods); (*Jurid*) absolver; (*jump over*) saltar por encima de; quitar, levantar (*LAm*) (table). □ **~ off** *vi* 🅇, **~ out** *vi* (🄸, *go away*) largarse. □ **~ up** *vt* (*tidy*) ordenar; aclarar (mystery). *vi* (weather) despejarse. **~ance** *n* (*removal of obstructions*) despeje *m*; (*authorization*) permiso *m*; (*by security*) acreditación *f*. **~ing** *n* claro *m*. **~ly** *adv* evidentemente. **~way** *n* carretera *f* en la que no se permite parar

cleavage /'kli:vɪdʒ/ *n* escote *m*

clef /klef/ *n* (*Mus*) clave *f*

clench /klentʃ/ *vt* apretar

clergy /'klɜ:dʒɪ/ *n* clero *m*. **~man** /-mən/ *n* clérigo *m*

cleric /'klerɪk/ *n* clérigo *m*. **~al** *adj* clerical; (*of clerks*) de oficina

clerk /klɑ:k/ *n* empleado *m*; (*Amer, salesclerk*) vendedor *m*

clever /'klevə(r)/ *adj* (**-er**, **-est**) inteligente; (*skilful*) hábil. **~ly** *adv* inteligentemente; (*with skill*) hábilmente. **~ness** *n* inteligencia *f*

cliché /'kli:ʃeɪ/ *n* lugar *m* común *m*, cliché *m*

click /klɪk/ *n* golpecito *m*. ● *vi* chascar; 🄸 llevarse bien. **~ on sth** hacer clic en algo. ● *vt* chasquear

client /'klaɪənt/ *n* cliente *m*

cliff /klɪf/ *n* acantilado *m*

climat|e /'klaɪmət/ *n* clima *m*. **~ic** /-'mætɪk/ *adj* climático

climax /'klaɪmæks/ *n* clímax *m*; (*orgasm*) orgasmo *m*

climb /klaɪm/ *vt* subir (stairs); trepar (tree); escalar (mountain). ● *vi* subir. ● *n* subida *f*. □ **~ down** *vi* bajar; (*fig*) ceder. **~er** *n* (*Sport*) alpinista *m & f*, andinista *m & f* (*LAm*); (*plant*) trepadora *f*

clinch /klɪntʃ/ *vt* cerrar (deal)

cling /klɪŋ/ *vi* (*pt* **clung**) agarrarse; (*stick*) pegarse

clinic /'klɪnɪk/ *n* centro *m* médico; (*private hospital*) clínica *f*. **~al** *adj* clínico

clink /klɪŋk/ *n* tintineo *m*. ● *vt* hacer tintinear. ● *vi* tintinear

clip /klɪp/ *n* (fastener) clip *m*; (*for paper*) sujetapapeles *m*; (*for hair*) horquilla *f*. ● *vt* (*pt* **clipped**) (*cut*) cortar; (*join*) sujetar. **~pers** /'klɪpəz/ *npl* (*for hair*) maquinilla *f* para cortar el pelo; (*for nails*) cor-

tauñas *m.* **~ping** *n* recorte *m*
cloak /kləʊk/ *n* capa *f.* **~room** *n* guardarropa *m*; (*toilet*) lavabo *m*, baño *m* (*LAm*)
clock /klɒk/ *n* reloj *m.* **~wise** *a/adv* en el sentido de las agujas del reloj. **~work** *n* mecanismo *m* de relojería. **like ~work** con precisión
clog /klɒg/ *n* zueco *m.* ● *vt* (*pt* **clogged**) atascar
cloister /ˈklɔɪstə(r)/ *n* claustro *m*
clone /kləʊn/ *n* clon *m*
close¹ /kləʊs/ *adj* (**-er**, **-est**) cercano; (*together*) apretado; (friend) íntimo; (weather) bochornoso; (link etc) estrecho; (game, battle) reñido. **have a ~ shave** (*fig*) escaparse de milagro. ● *adv* cerca
close² /kləʊz/ *vt* cerrar. ● *vi* cerrarse; (*end*) terminar. **~ down** *vt/i* cerrar. ● *n* fin *m.* **~d** *adj* cerrado
closely /ˈkləʊslɪ/ *adv* estrechamente; (*at a short distance*) de cerca; (*with attention*) detenidamente; (*precisely*) rigurosamente
closet /ˈklɒzɪt/ *n* (*Amer*) armario *m*; (*for clothes*) armario *m*, closet *m* (*LAm*)
close-up /ˈkləʊsʌp/ *n* (*Cinema etc*) primer plano *m*
closure /ˈkləʊʒə(r)/ *n* cierre *m*
clot /klɒt/ *n* (*Med*) coágulo *m*; **!** tonto *m.* ● *vi* (*pt* **clotted**) cuajarse; (blood) coagularse
cloth /klɒθ/ *n* tela *f*; (*duster*) trapo *m*; (*tablecloth*) mantel *m*
cloth|e /kləʊð/ *vt* (*pt* **clothed** *or* **clad**) vestir. **~es** /kləʊðz/ *npl* ropa. **~espin**, **~espeg** (*Amer*) *n* pinza *f* (para tender la ropa). **~ing** *n* ropa *f*
cloud /klaʊd/ *n* nube *f.* ● **~ over** *vi* nublarse. **~y** *adj* (**-ier**, **-iest**) nublado; (liquid) turbio
clout /klaʊt/ *n* bofetada *f.* ● *vt* abofetear
clove /kləʊv/ *n* clavo *m.* **~ of garlic** *n* diente *m* de ajo
clover /ˈkləʊvə(r)/ *n* trébol *m*
clown /klaʊn/ *n* payaso *m.* ● *vi* hacer el payaso
club /klʌb/ *n* club *m*; (*weapon*) porra *f*; (*golf club*) palo *m* de golf; (*at cards*) trébol *m.* ● *vt* (*pt* **clubbed**) aporrear. □ **~ together** *vi* contribuir con dinero (**to** para)
cluck /klʌk/ *vi* cloquear
clue /kluː/ *n* pista *f*; (*in crosswords*) indicación *f.* **not to have a ~** no tener la menor idea
clump /klʌmp/ *n* grupo *m.* ● *vt* agrupar
clums|iness /ˈklʌmzɪnɪs/ *n* torpeza *f.* **~y** /ˈklʌmzɪ/ *adj* (**-ier**, **-iest**) torpe
clung /klʌŋ/ *see* CLING
cluster /ˈklʌstə(r)/ *n* grupo *m.* ● *vi* agruparse
clutch /klʌtʃ/ *vt* agarrar. ● *n* (*Auto*) embrague *m*
clutter /ˈklʌtə(r)/ *n* desorden *m.* ● *vt.* **~ (up)** abarrotar. **~ed** /ˈklʌtəd/ *adj* abarratado de cosas
coach /kəʊtʃ/ *n* autocar *m*, autobús *m*; (*of train*) vagón *m*; (*horse-drawn*) coche *m*; (*Sport*) entrenador *m.* ● *vt* (*Sport*) entrenar
coal /kəʊl/ *n* carbón *m*
coalition /kəʊəˈlɪʃn/ *n* coalición *f*
coarse /kɔːs/ *adj* (**-er**, **-est**) grueso; (material) basto; (*person, language*) ordinario
coast /kəʊst/ *n* costa *f.* ● *vi* (*with cycle*) deslizarse sin pedalear; (*with car*) ir en punto muerto. **~al** *adj* costero. **~guard** *n* guardacostas *m.* **~line** *n* litoral *m*

coat /kəʊt/ *n* abrigo *m*; (*jacket*) chaqueta *f*; (*of animal*) pelo *m*; (*of paint*) mano *f*. ● *vt* cubrir, revestir. **~hanger** *n* percha *f*, gancho *m* (*LAm*). **~ing** *n* capa *f*. **~ of arms** *n* escudo *m* de armas

coax /kəʊks/ *vt* engatusar

cobbler /ˈkɒblə(r)/ *n* zapatero *m* (remendón)

cobblestone /ˈkɒbəlstəʊn/ *n* adoquín *m*

cobweb /ˈkɒbweb/ *n* telaraña *f*

cocaine /kəˈkeɪn/ *n* cocaína *f*

cock /kɒk/ *n* (*cockerel*) gallo *m*; (*male bird*) macho *m*. ● *vt* amartillar (gun); aguzar (ears). **~erel** /ˈkɒkərəl/ *n* gallo *m*. **~-eyed** /-aɪd/ *adj* 🅸 torcido

cockney /ˈkɒknɪ/ *adj & n* (*pl* **-eys**) londinense (*m & f*) (del este de Londres)

cockpit /ˈkɒkpɪt/ *n* (*in aircraft*) cabina *f* del piloto

cockroach /ˈkɒkrəʊtʃ/ *n* cucaracha *f*

cocktail /ˈkɒkteɪl/ *n* cóctel *m*

cock-up /ˈkɒkʌp/ *n* 🅧 lío *m*

cocky /ˈkɒkɪ/ *adj* (**-ier**, **-iest**) engreído

cocoa /ˈkəʊkəʊ/ *n* cacao *m*; (*drink*) chocolate *m*, cocoa *f* (*LAm*)

coconut /ˈkəʊkənʌt/ *n* coco *m*

cocoon /kəˈku:n/ *n* capullo *m*

cod /kɒd/ *n invar* bacalao *m*

code /kəʊd/ *n* código *m*; (*secret*) clave *f*; **in ~** en clave

coeducational /kəʊedʒʊˈkeɪʃənl/ *adj* mixto

coerc|e /kəʊˈɜ:s/ *vt* coaccionar. **~ion** /-ʃn/ *n* coacción *f*

coffee /ˈkɒfɪ/ *n* café *m*. **~ bean** *n* grano *m* de café. **~ maker** *n* cafetera *f*. **~pot** *n* cafetera *f*

coffin /ˈkɒfɪn/ *n* ataúd *m*, cajón *m* (*LAm*)

cog /kɒg/ *n* diente *m*; (*fig*) pieza *f*

coherent /kəʊˈhɪərənt/ *adj* coherente

coil /kɔɪl/ *vt* enrollar. ● *n* rollo *m*; (*one ring*) vuelta *f*

coin /kɔɪn/ *n* moneda *f*. ● *vt* acuñar

coincide /kəʊɪnˈsaɪd/ *vi* coincidir. **~nce** /kəʊˈɪnsɪdəns/ *n* casualidad *f*. **~ntal** /kəʊɪnsɪˈdentl/ *adj* casual

coke /kəʊk/ *n* (*coal*) coque *m*. **C~** (®) Coca-Cola *f* (®)

colander /ˈkʌləndə(r)/ *n* colador *m*

cold /kəʊld/ *adj* (**-er**, **-est**) frío. **be ~** (person) tener frío. **it is ~** (*weather*) hace frío. ● *n* frío *m*; (*Med*) resfriado *m*. **have a ~** estar resfriado. **~-blooded** /-ˈblʌdɪd/ *adj* (animal) de sangre fría; (murder) a sangre fría. **~-shoulder** /-ˈʃəʊldə(r)/ *vt* tratar con frialdad. **~ sore** *n* herpes *m* labial. **~ storage** *n* conservación *f* en frigorífico

coleslaw /ˈkəʊlslɔ:/ *n* ensalada *f* de col

collaborat|e /kəˈlæbəreɪt/ *vi* colaborar. **~ion** /-ˈreɪʃn/ *n* colaboración *f*. **~or** *n* colaborador *m*

collaps|e /kəˈlæps/ *vi* derrumbarse; (*Med*) sufrir un colapso. ● *n* derrumbamiento *m*; (*Med*) colapso *m*. **~ible** /-əbl/ *adj* plegable

collar /ˈkɒlə(r)/ *n* cuello *m*; (*for animals*) collar *m*. ● *vt* 🅸 hurtar. **~bone** *n* clavícula *f*

colleague /ˈkɒli:g/ *n* colega *m & f*

collect /kəˈlekt/ *vt* reunir; (*hobby*) coleccionar, juntar (*LAm*); (*pick up*) recoger; cobrar (rent). ● *vi* (people) reunirse; (things) acumularse. **~ion** /-ʃn/ *n* colección *f*; (*in church*) colecta *f*; (*of post*) recogida *f.* ~**or** *n* coleccionista *m & f*

college /ˈkɒlɪdʒ/ *n* colegio *m*; (*of art, music etc*) escuela *f*; (*Amer*) universidad *f*

colli|de /kəˈlaɪd/ *vi* chocar. ~**sion** /-ˈlɪʒn/ *n* choque *m*

colloquial /kəˈləʊkwɪəl/ *adj* coloquial

Colombia /kəˈlʌmbɪə/ *n* Colombia *f*. ~**n** *adj & n* colombiano (*m*)

colon /ˈkəʊlən/ *n* (*Gram*) dos puntos *mpl*; (*Med*) colon *m*

colonel /ˈkɜːnl/ *n* coronel *m*

colon|ial /kəˈləʊnɪəl/ *adj* colonial. ~**ize** /ˈkɒlənaɪz/ *vt* colonizar. ~**y** /ˈkɒlənɪ/ *n* colonia *f*

colossal /kəˈlɒsl/ *adj* colosal

colour /ˈkʌlə(r)/ *n* color *m*. **off** ~ (*fig*) indispuesto. ● *adj* de color(es), en color(es) ● *vt* colorear; (*dye*) teñir. ~**-blind** *adj* daltónico. ~**ed** /ˈkʌləd/ *adj* de color. ~**ful** *adj* lleno de color; (*fig*) pintoresco. ~**ing** *n* color; (*food colouring*) colorante *m*. ~**less** *adj* incoloro

column /ˈkɒləm/ *n* columna *f*. ~**ist** *n* columnista *m & f*

coma /ˈkəʊmə/ *n* coma *m*

comb /kəʊm/ *n* peine *m*. ● *vt* (*search*) registrar. ~ **one's hair** peinarse

combat /ˈkɒmbæt/ *n* combate *m*. ● *vt* (*pt* **combated**) combatir

combination /kɒmbɪˈneɪʃn/ *n* combinación *f*

combine /kəmˈbaɪn/ *vt* combinar. ● *vi* combinarse. ● /ˈkɒmbaɪn/ *n* asociación *f*. ~ **harvester** *n* cosechadora *f*

combustion /kəmˈbʌstʃən/ *n* combustión *f*

come /kʌm/ *vi* (*pt* **came**, *pp* **come**) venir; (*occur*) pasar. □ ~ **across** *vt* encontrarse con (person); encontrar (object). □ ~ **apart** *vi* deshacerse. □ ~ **away** *vi* (*leave*) salir; (*become detached*) salirse. □ ~ **back** *vi* volver. □ ~ **by** *vt* obtener. □ ~ **down** *vi* bajar. □ ~ **in** *vi* entrar; (*arrive*) llegar. □ ~ **into** *vt* entrar en; heredar (money). □ ~ **off** *vi* desprenderse; (*succeed*) tener éxito. *vt*. ~ **off it!** 🅸 ¡no me vengas con eso! □ ~ **on** *vi* (*start to work*) encenderse. ~ **on, hurry up!** ¡vamos, date prisa! □ ~ **out** *vi* salir. □ ~ **round** *vi* (*after fainting*) volver en sí; (*be converted*) cambiar de idea; (*visit*) venir. □ ~ **to** *vt* llegar a (decision etc). □ ~ **up** *vi* subir; (*fig*) surgir. □ ~ **up with** *vt* proponer (idea). ~**back** *n* retorno *m*; (*retort*) réplica *f*

comedian /kəˈmiːdɪən/ *n* cómico *m*

comedy /ˈkɒmədɪ/ *n* comedia *f*

comet /ˈkɒmɪt/ *n* cometa *m*

comfort /ˈkʌmfət/ *n* comodidad *f*; (*consolation*) consuelo *m*. ● *vt* consolar. ~**able** *adj* cómodo. ~**er** *n* (*for baby*) chupete *m*, chupón *m* (*LAm*); (*Amer, for bed*) edredón *m*

comic /ˈkɒmɪk/ *adj* cómico. ● *n* cómico *m*; (*periodical*) revista *f* de historietas, tebeo *m*. ~**al** *adj* cómico. ~ **strip** *n* tira *f* cómica

coming /ˈkʌmɪŋ/ *n* llegada *f*. ~**s and goings** idas *fpl* y venidas. ● *adj* próximo; (week, month etc) que viene

comma /ˈkɒmə/ *n* coma *f*

command /kəˈmɑːnd/ *n* orden *f*; (*mastery*) dominio *m*. ● *vt* ordenar; imponer (respect)

commandeer /kɒmənˈdɪə(r)/ *vt* requisar

command: ~er *n* comandante *m*. ~**ing** *adj* imponente. ~**ment** *n* mandamiento *m*

commando /kəˈmɑːndəʊ/ *n* (*pl* **-os**) comando *m*

commemorat|e /kəˈmeməreɪt/ *vt* conmemorar. **~ion** /-ˈreɪʃn/ *n* conmemoración *f*. **~ive** /-ətɪv/ *adj* conmemorativo

commence /kəˈmens/ *vt* dar comienzo a. ● *vi* iniciarse

commend /kəˈmend/ *vt* alabar. **~able** *adj* loable. **~ation** /kɒmenˈdeɪʃn/ *n* elogio *m*

comment /ˈkɒment/ *n* observación *f*. ● *vi* hacer observaciones (**on** sobre)

commentary /ˈkɒməntrɪ/ *n* comentario *m*; (*Radio, TV*) reportaje *m*

commentat|e /ˈkɒmənteɪt/ *vi* narrar. **~or** *n* (*Radio, TV*) locutor *m*

commerc|e /ˈkɒmɜːs/ *n* comercio *m*. **~ial** /kəˈmɜːʃl/ *adj* comercial. ● *n* anuncio *m*; aviso *m* (*LAm*). **~ialize** *vt* comercializar

commiserat|e /kəˈmɪzəreɪt/ *vi* compadecerse (**with** de). **~ion** /-ˈreɪʃn/ *n* conmiseración *f*

commission /kəˈmɪʃn/ *n* comisión *f*. **out of ~** fuera de servicio. ● *vt* encargar; (*Mil*) nombrar oficial

commissionaire /kəmɪʃəˈneə(r)/ *n* portero *m*

commit /kəˈmɪt/ *vt* (*pt* **committed**) cometer; (*entrust*) confiar. **~ o.s.** comprometerse. **~ment** *n* compromiso *m*

committee /kəˈmɪtɪ/ *n* comité *m*

commodity /kəˈmɒdətɪ/ *n* producto *m*, artículo *m*

common /ˈkɒmən/ *adj* (**-er**, **-est**) común; (*usual*) corriente; (*vulgar*) ordinario. ● *n*. **in ~** en común. **~er** *n* plebeyo *m*. **~ law** *n* derecho *m* consuetudinario. **~ly** *adv* comúnmente. **C~ Market** *n* Mercado *m* Común. **~place** *adj* banal. ● *n* banalidad *f*. **~ room** *n* sala *f* común, salón *m* común. **C~s** *n*. **the (House of) C~s** la Cámara de los Comunes. **~ sense** *n* sentido *m* común. **C~wealth** *n*. **the C~wealth** la Mancomunidad *f* Británica

commotion /kəˈməʊʃn/ *n* confusión *f*

> i
>
> **Commonwealth** *La Commonwealth* es una asociación de las antiguas colonias y territorios que conformaban el Imperio Británico. Cada dos años se celebra una reunión de sus jefes de gobierno. Entre los países miembros existen muchos vínculos culturales, educativos y deportivos. En EE.UU., es el término oficial para referirse a cuatro estados: Kentucky, Massachussets, Pensilvania y Virginia.

commune /ˈkɒmjuːn/ *n* comuna *f*

communicat|e /kəˈmjuːnɪkeɪt/ *vt* comunicar. ● *vi* comunicarse. **~ion** /-ˈkeɪʃn/ *n* comunicación *f*. **~ive** /-ətɪv/ *adj* comunicativo

communion /kəˈmjuːnɪən/ *n* comunión *f*

communis|m /ˈkɒmjʊnɪsəm/ *n* comunismo *m*. **~t** *n* comunista *m* & *f*

community /kəˈmjuːnətɪ/ *n* comunidad *f*. **~ centre** *n* centro *m* social

commute /kəˈmjuːt/ *vi* viajar diariamente (*entre el lugar de residencia y el trabajo*). ● *vt* (*Jurid*) conmutar. **~r** *n* viajero *m* diario

compact /kəmˈpækt/ *adj* compacto. ● /ˈkɒmpækt/ *n* (*for powder*) polvera *f*. **~ disc**, **~ disk** /ˈkɒmpækt/ *n* disco *m* compacto, compact-disc *m.* ~ **disc player** *n* (reproductor *m* de) compact-disc

companion /kəm'pænɪən/ *n* compañero *m.* ~**ship** *n* compañía *f*

company /'kʌmpənɪ/ *n* compañía *f*; (*guests*) visita *f*; (*Com*) sociedad *f*

compar|able /'kɒmpərəbl/ *adj* comparable. ~**ative** /kəm'pærətɪv/ *adj* comparativo; (*fig*) relativo. ● *n* (*Gram*) comparativo *m.* ~**e** /kəm'peə(r)/ *vt* comparar. ~**ison** /kəm'pærɪsn/ *n* comparación *f*

compartment /kəm'pɑ:tmənt/ *n* compartim(i)ento *m*

compass /'kʌmpəs/ *n* brújula *f.* ~**es** *npl* compás *m*

compassion /kəm'pæʃn/ *n* compasión *f.* ~**ate** /-ət/ *adj* compasivo

compatible /kəm'pætəbl/ *adj* compatible

compel /kəm'pel/ *vt* (*pt* **compelled**) obligar. ~**ling** *adj* irresistible

compensat|e /'kɒmpənseɪt/ *vt* compensar; (*for loss*) indemnizar. ● *vi.* ~**e for sth** compensar algo. ~**ion** /-'seɪʃn/ *n* compensación *f*; (*financial*) indemnización *f*

compère /'kɒmpeə(r)/ *n* presentador *m.* ● *vt* presentar

compete /kəm'pi:t/ *vi* competir

competen|ce /'kɒmpətəns/ *n* competencia *f.* ~**t** *adj* competente

competit|ion /kɒmpə'tɪʃn/ *n* (*contest*) concurso *m*; (*Sport*) competición *f*, competencia *f* (*LAm*); (*Com*) competencia *f.* ~**ive** /kəm'petətɪv/ *adj* competidor; (price) competitivo. ~**or** /kəm'petɪtə(r)/ *n* competidor *m*; (*in contest*) concursante *m & f*

compile /kəm'paɪl/ *vt* compilar

complacen|cy /kəm'pleɪsənsɪ/ *n* autosuficiencia *f.* ~**t** *adj* satisfecho de sí mismo

complain /kəm'pleɪn/ *vi.* ~ **(about)** quejarse (de). ● *vt.* ~ **that** quejarse de que. ~**t** *n* queja *f*; (*Med*) enfermedad *f*

complement /'kɒmplɪmənt/ *n* complemento *m.* ● *vt* complementar. ~**ary** /-'mentrɪ/ *adj* complementario

complet|e /kəm'pli:t/ *adj* completo; (*finished*) acabado; (*downright*) total. ● *vt* acabar; llenar (a form). ~**ely** *adv* completamente. ~**ion** /-ʃn/ *n* finalización *f*

complex /'kɒmpleks/ *adj* complejo. ● *n* complejo *m*

complexion /kəm'plekʃn/ *n* tez *f*; (*fig*) aspecto *m*

complexity /kəm'pleksətɪ/ *n* complejidad *f*

complicat|e /'kɒmplɪkeɪt/ *vt* complicar. ~**ed** *adj* complicado. ~**ion** /-'keɪʃn/ *n* complicación *f*

compliment /'kɒmplɪmənt/ *n* cumplido *m*; (*amorous*) piropo *m.* ● *vt* felicitar. ~**ary** /-'mentrɪ/ *adj* halagador; (*given free*) de regalo. ~**s** *npl* saludos *mpl*

comply /kəm'plaɪ/ *vi.* ~ **with** conformarse con

component /kəm'pəʊnənt/ *adj & n* componente (*m*)

compos|e /kəm'pəʊz/ *vt* componer. **be** ~**ed of** estar compuesto de. ~**er** *n* compositor *m.* ~**ition** /kɒmpə'zɪʃn/ *n* composición *f*

compost /'kɒmpɒst/ *n* abono *m*

composure /kəm'pəʊʒə(r)/ *n* serenidad *f*

compound /'kɒmpaʊnd/ *n* compuesto *m*; (*enclosure*) recinto *m.* ● *adj* compuesto; (fracture)

complicado
comprehen|d /kɒmprɪˈhend/ *vt* comprender. **~sion** /kɒmprɪˈhenʃn/ *n* comprensión *f.* **~sive** /kɒmprɪˈhensɪv/ *adj* extenso; (insurance) contra todo riesgo. **~sive (school)** *n* instituto *m* de enseñanza secundaria
compress /ˈkɒmpres/ *n* (*Med*) compresa *f.* ● /kəmˈpres/ *vt* comprimir. **~ion** /-ˈpreʃn/ *n* compresión *f*
comprise /kəmˈpraɪz/ *vt* comprender
compromis|e /ˈkɒmprəmaɪz/ *n* acuerdo *m*, compromiso *m*, arreglo *m.* ● *vt* comprometer. ● *vi* llegar a un acuerdo. **~ing** *adj* (situation) comprometido
compuls|ion /kəmˈpʌlʃn/ *n* (*force*) coacción *f*; (*obsession*) compulsión *f.* **~ive** /kəmˈpʌlsɪv/ *adj* compulsivo. **~ory** /kəmˈpʌlsərɪ/ *adj* obligatorio
comput|e /kəmˈpjuːt/ *vb* calcular. **comput|er** *n* ordenador *m*, computadora *f* (*LAm*). **~erize** *vt* computarizar, computerizar. **~er studies** *n*, **~ing** *n* informática *f*, computación *f*
comrade /ˈkɒmreɪd/ *n* camarada *m & f*
con /kɒn/ *vt* (*pt* **conned**) ⓘ estafar. ● *n* (*fraud*) estafa *f*; (*objection*) *see* **PRO**
concave /ˈkɒŋkeɪv/ *adj* cóncavo
conceal /kənˈsiːl/ *vt* ocultar
concede /kənˈsiːd/ *vt* conceder
conceit /kənˈsiːt/ *n* vanidad *f.* **~ed** *adj* engreído
conceiv|able /kənˈsiːvəbl/ *adj* concebible. **~e** /kənˈsiːv/ *vt/i* concebir
concentrat|e /ˈkɒnsəntreɪt/ *vt* concentrar. ● *vi* concentrarse (**on** en). **~ion** /-ˈtreɪʃn/ *n* concentración *f*
concept /ˈkɒnsept/ *n* concepto *m*
conception /kənˈsepʃn/ *n* concepción *f*
concern /kənˈsɜːn/ *n* asunto *m*; (*worry*) preocupación *f*; (*Com*) empresa *f.* ● *vt* tener que ver con; (*deal with*) tratar de. **as far as I'm ~ed** en cuanto a mí. **be ~ed about** preocuparse por. **~ing** *prep* acerca de
concert /ˈkɒnsət/ *n* concierto *m.* **~ed** /kənˈsɜːtɪd/ *adj* concertado
concertina /kɒnsəˈtiːnə/ *n* concertina *f*
concerto /kənˈtʃɜːtəʊ/ *n* (*pl* **-os** *or* **-ti** /-tɪ/) concierto *m*
concession /kənˈseʃn/ *n* concesión *f*
concise /kənˈsaɪs/ *adj* conciso
conclu|de /kənˈkluːd/ *vt/i* concluir. **~ding** *adj* final. **~sion** /-ʃn/ *n* conclusión *f.*. **~sive** /-sɪv/ *adj* decisivo. **~sively** *adv* concluyentemente
concoct /kənˈkɒkt/ *vt* confeccionar; (*fig*) inventar. **~ion** /-ʃn/ *n* mezcla *f*; (*drink*) brebaje *m*
concrete /ˈkɒŋkriːt/ *n* hormigón *m*, concreto *m* (*LAm*). ● *adj* concreto
concussion /kənˈkʌʃn/ *n* conmoción *f* cerebral
condemn /kənˈdem/ *vt* condenar. **~ation** /kɒndemˈneɪʃn/ *n* condena *f*
condens|ation /kɒndenˈseɪʃn/ *n* condensación *f.* **~e** /kənˈdens/ *vt* condensar. ● *vi* condensarse
condescend /kɒndɪˈsend/ *vi* dignarse (**to** a). **~ing** *adj* superior
condition /kənˈdɪʃn/ *n* condición

f. **on ~ that** a condición de que. ● *vt* condicionar. **~al** *adj* condicional. **~er** *n* (*for hair*) suavizante *m*, enjuague *m* (*LAm*)

C

condo /ˈkɒndəʊ/ *n* (*pl* **-os**) (*Amer fam*) *see* **CONDOMINIUM**

condolences /kənˈdəʊlənsɪz/ *npl* pésame *m*

condom /ˈkɒndɒm/ *n* condón *m*

condominium /kɒndəˈmɪnɪəm/ *n* (*Amer*) apartamento *m*, piso *m* (en régimen de propiedad horizontal)

condone /kənˈdəʊn/ *vt* condonar

conduct /kənˈdʌkt/ *vt* llevar a cabo (business, experiment); conducir (electricity); dirigir (orchestra). ● /ˈkɒndʌkt/ *n* conducta *f*. **~or** /kənˈdʌktə(r)/ *n* director *m*; (*of bus*) cobrador *m*. **~ress** /kənˈdʌktrɪs/ *n* cobradora *f*

cone /kəʊn/ *n* cono *m*; (*for ice cream*) cucurucho *m*, barquillo *m* (*Mex*)

confectionery /kənˈfekʃənrɪ/ *n* productos *mpl* de confitería

confederation /kənfedəˈreɪʃn/ *n* confederación *f*

conference /ˈkɒnfərəns/ *n* congreso *m*; **an international ~ on ...** un congreso internacional sobre ...

confess /kənˈfes/ *vt* confesar. ● *vi* confesarse. **~ion** /-ʃn/ *n* confesión *f*

confetti /kənˈfetɪ/ *n* confeti *m*

confide /kənˈfaɪd/ *vt/i* confiar

confiden|ce /ˈkɒnfɪdəns/ *n* confianza *f*; (*self-confidence*) confianza *f* en sí mismo; (*secret*) confidencia *f*. **~ce trick** *n* estafa *f*, timo *m*. **~t** /ˈkɒnfɪdənt/ *adj* seguro de sí mismo. **be ~t of** confiar en

confidential /kɒnfɪˈdenʃl/ *adj* confidencial. **~ity** /-denʃɪˈælətɪ/ *n* confidencialidad *f*

configur|ation /kənfɪgəˈreɪʃn/ *n* configuración *f*. **~e** /kənˈfɪgə(r)/ *vt* configurar

confine /kənˈfaɪn/ *vt* confinar; (*limit*) limitar. **~ment** *n* (*imprisonment*) prisión *f*

confirm /kənˈfɜːm/ *vt* confirmar. **~ation** /kɒnfəˈmeɪʃn/ *n* confirmación *f*. **~ed** *adj* inveterado

confiscat|e /ˈkɒnfɪskeɪt/ *vt* confiscar. **~ion** /-ˈkeɪʃn/ *n* confiscación *f*

conflict /ˈkɒnflɪkt/ *n* conflicto *m*. ● /kənˈflɪkt/ *vi* chocar. **~ing** /kənˈflɪktɪŋ/ *adj* contradictorio

conform /kənˈfɔːm/ *vi* conformarse. **~ist** *n* conformista *m & f*

confound /kənˈfaʊnd/ *vt* confundir. **~ed** *adj* ⓘ maldito

confront /kənˈfrʌnt/ *vt* hacer frente a; (*face*) enfrentarse con. **~ation** /kɒnfrʌnˈteɪʃn/ *n* confrontación *f*

confus|e /kənˈfjuːz/ *vt* confundir. **~ed** *adj* confundido. **get ~ed** confundirse. **~ing** *adj* confuso. **~ion** /-ʒn/ *n* confusión *f*

congeal /kənˈdʒiːl/ *vi* coagularse

congest|ed /kənˈdʒestɪd/ *adj* congestionado. **~ion** /-tʃən/ *n* congestión *f*

congratulat|e /kənˈgrætjʊleɪt/ *vt* felicitar. **~ions** /-ˈleɪʃnz/ *npl* enhorabuena *f*, felicitaciones *fpl* (*LAm*)

congregat|e /ˈkɒŋgrɪgeɪt/ *vi* congregarse. **~ion** /-ˈgeɪʃn/ *n* asamblea *f*; (*Relig*) fieles *mpl*, feligreses *mpl*

congress /ˈkɒŋgres/ *n* congreso *m*. **C~** (*Amer*) el Congreso. **~man** /-mən/ *n* (*Amer*) miembro *m* del Congreso. **~woman** *n* (*Amer*) miembro *f* del Congreso.

Congress El Congreso es el organismo legislativo de EE.UU. Se reúne en el Capitolio (*Capitol*) y está compuesto por dos cámaras: El Senado y la Cámara de Representantes. Se renueva cada dos años y su función es elaborar leyes que deben ser aprobadas, primero, por las dos cámaras y posteriormente por el Presidente.

conifer /'kɒnɪfə(r)/ *n* conífera *f*

conjugat|e /'kɒndʒʊgeɪt/ *vt* conjugar. **~ion** /-'geɪʃn/ *n* conjugación *f*

conjunction /kən'dʒʌŋkʃn/ *n* conjunción *f*

conjur|e /'kʌndʒə(r)/ *vi* hacer juegos de manos. ● *vt*. □ **~e up** *vt* evocar. **~er, ~or** *n* prestidigitador *m*

conk /kɒŋk/ *vi*. **~ out** [!] fallar; (person) desmayarse

conker /'kɒŋkə(r)/ *n* [!] castaña *f* de Indias

conman /'kɒnmæn/ *n* (*pl* **-men**) [!] estafador *m*, timador *m*

connect /kə'nekt/ *vt* conectar; (*associate*) relacionar. ● *vi* (*be fitted*) estar conectado (**to** a). □ **~ with** *vt* (train) enlazar con. **~ed** *adj* unido; (*related*) relacionado. **be ~ed with** tener que ver con, estar emparentado con. **~ion** /-ʃn/ *n* conexión *f*; (*Rail*) enlace *m*; (*fig*) relación *f*. **in ~ion with** a propósito de, con respecto a

connive /kə'naɪv/ *vi*. **~e at** ser cómplice en

connoisseur /kɒnə'sɜː(r)/ *n* experto *m*

connotation /kɒnə'teɪʃn/ *n* connotación *f*

conquer /'kɒŋkə(r)/ *vt* conquistar; (*fig*) vencer. **~or** *n* conquistador *m*

conquest /'kɒŋkwest/ *n* conquista *f*

conscience /'kɒnʃəns/ *n* conciencia *f*

conscientious /kɒnʃɪ'enʃəs/ *adj* concienzudo

conscious /'kɒnʃəs/ *adj* consciente; (*deliberate*) intencional. **~ly** *adv* a sabiendas. **~ness** *n* consciencia *f*; (*Med*) conocimiento *m*

conscript /'kɒnskrɪpt/ *n* recluta *m & f*, conscripto *m* (*LAm*). ● /kən'skrɪpt/ *vt* reclutar. **~ion** /kən'skrɪpʃn/ *n* reclutamiento *m*, conscripción *f* (*LAm*)

consecrate /'kɒnsɪkreɪt/ *vt* consagrar

consecutive /kən'sekjʊtɪv/ *adj* sucesivo

consensus /kən'sensəs/ *n* consenso *m*

consent /kən'sent/ *vi* consentir. ● *n* consentimiento *m*

consequen|ce /'kɒnsɪkwəns/ *n* consecuencia *f*. **~t** *adj* consiguiente. **~tly** *adv* por consiguiente

conservation /kɒnsə'veɪʃn/ *n* conservación *f*, preservación *f*. **~ist** *n* conservacionista *m & f*

conservative /kən'sɜːvətɪv/ *adj* conservador; (*modest*) prudente, moderado. **C~** *adj & n* conservador (*m*)

conservatory /kən'sɜːvətrɪ/ *n* invernadero *m*

conserve /kən'sɜːv/ *vt* conservar

consider /kən'sɪdə(r)/ *vt* considerar; (*take into account*) tomar en cuenta. **~able** *adj* considerable. **~ably** *adv* considerablemente

considerat|e /kən'sɪdərət/ *adj*

considerado. **~ion** /-ˈreɪʃn/ *n* consideración *f*. **take sth into ~ion** tomar algo en cuenta

considering /kənˈsɪdərɪŋ/ *prep* teniendo en cuenta. ● *conj*. **~ (that)** teniendo en cuenta que

consign /kənˈsaɪn/ *vt* consignar; (*send*) enviar. **~ment** *n* envío *m*

consist /kənˈsɪst/ *vi*. **~ of** consistir en. **~ency** *n* consistencia *f*; (*fig*) coherencia *f*. **~ent** *adj* coherente; (*unchanging*) constante. **~ent with** compatible con. **~ently** *adv* constantemente

consolation /kɒnsəˈleɪʃn/ *n* consuelo *m*

console /kənˈsəʊl/ *vt* consolar. ● /ˈkɒnsəʊl/ *n* consola *f*

consolidate /kənˈsɒlɪdeɪt/ *vt* consolidar

consonant /ˈkɒnsənənt/ *n* consonante *f*

conspicuous /kənˈspɪkjʊəs/ *adj* (*easily seen*) visible; (*showy*) llamativo; (*noteworthy*) notable

conspir|acy /kənˈspɪrəsɪ/ *n* conspiración *f*. **~ator** /kənˈspɪrətə(r)/ *n* conspirador *m*. **~e** /kənˈspaɪə(r)/ *vi* conspirar

constable /ˈkʌnstəbl/ *n* agente *m* & *f* de policía

constant /ˈkɒnstənt/ *adj* constante. **~ly** *adv* constantemente

constellation /kɒnstəˈleɪʃn/ *n* constelación *f*

consternation /kɒnstəˈneɪʃn/ *n* consternación *f*

constipat|ed /ˈkɒnstɪpeɪtɪd/ *adj* estreñido. **~ion** /-ˈpeɪʃn/ *n* estreñimiento *m*

constituen|cy /kənˈstɪtjʊənsɪ/ *n* distrito *m* electoral. **~t** *n* (*Pol*) elector *m*. ● *adj* constituyente, constitutivo

constitut|e /ˈkɒnstɪtjuːt/ *vt* constituir. **~ion** /-ˈtjuːʃn/ *n* constitución *f*. **~ional** /-ˈtjuːʃənl/ *adj* constitucional. ● *n* paseo *m*

constrict /kənˈstrɪkt/ *vt* apretar. **~ion** /-ʃn/ *n* constricción *f*

construct /kənˈstrʌkt/ *vt* construir. **~ion** /-ʃn/ *n* construcción *f*. **~ive** *adj* constructivo

consul /ˈkɒnsl/ *n* cónsul *m* & *f*. **~ate** /ˈkɒnsjʊlət/ *n* consulado *m*

consult /kənˈsʌlt/ *vt/i* consultar. **~ancy** *n* asesoría. **~ant** *n* asesor *m*; (*Med*) especialista *m* & *f*; (*Tec*) consejero *m* técnico. **~ation** /kɒnsəlˈteɪʃn/ *n* consulta *f*

consume /kənˈsjuːm/ *vt* consumir. **~r** *n* consumidor *m*. ● *adj* de consumo

consummate /ˈkɒnsəmət/ *adj* consumado. ● /ˈkɒnsəmeɪt/ *vt* consumar

consumption /kənˈsʌmpʃn/ *n* consumo *m*

contact /ˈkɒntækt/ *n* contacto *m*. ● *vt* ponerse en contacto con. **~ lens** *n* lentilla *f*, lente *f* de contacto (*LAm*)

contagious /kənˈteɪdʒəs/ *adj* contagioso

contain /kənˈteɪn/ *vt* contener. **~ o.s.** contenerse. **~er** *n* recipiente *m*; (*Com*) contenedor *m*

contaminat|e /kənˈtæmɪneɪt/ *vt* contaminar. **~ion** /-ˈneɪʃn/ *n* contaminación *f*

contemplate /ˈkɒntəmpleɪt/ *vt* contemplar; (*consider*) considerar

contemporary /kənˈtempərərɪ/ *adj* & *n* contemporáneo (*m*)

contempt /kənˈtempt/ *n* desprecio *m*. **~ible** *adj* despreciable. **~uous** /-tjʊəs/ *adj* desdeñoso

contend /kənˈtend/ *vt* competir.

~er *n* aspirante *m & f* (**for** a)

content /kən'tent/ *adj* satisfecho. ● /'kɒntent/ *n* contenido *m*. ● /kən 'tent/ *vt* contentar. **~ed** /kən 'tentɪd/ *adj* satisfecho. **~ment** /kən'tentmənt/ *n* satisfacción *f*. **~s** /'kɒntents/ *n* contenido *m*; (*of book*) índice *m* de materias

contest /'kɒntest/ *n* (*competition*) concurso *m*; (*Sport*) competición *f*, competencia *f* (*LAm*). ● /kən'test/ *vt* disputar. **~ant** /kən'testənt/ *n* concursante *m & f*

context /'kɒntekst/ *n* contexto *m*

continent /'kɒntɪnənt/ *n* continente *m*. **the C~** Europa *f*. **~al** /-'nentl/ *adj* continental. **~al quilt** *n* edredón *m*

contingen|cy /kən'tɪndʒənsɪ/ *n* contingencia *f*. **~t** *adj & n* contingente (*m*)

continu|al /kən'tɪnjʊəl/ *adj* continuo. **~ally** *adv* continuamente. **~ation** /-'eɪʃn/ *n* continuación *f*. **~e** /kən'tɪnju:/ *vt/i* continuar, seguir. **~ed** *adj* continuo. **~ity** /kɒntɪ'nju:ətɪ/ *n* continuidad *f*. **~ous** /kən'tɪnjʊəs/ *adj* continuo. **~ously** *adv* continuamente

contort /kən'tɔ:t/ *vt* retorcer. **~ion** /-ʃn/ *n* contorsión *f*. **~ionist** /-ʃənɪst/ *n* contorsionista *m & f*

contour /'kɒntʊə(r)/ *n* contorno *m*

contraband /'kɒntrəbænd/ *n* contrabando *m*

contracepti|on /kɒntrə'sepʃn/ *n* anticoncepción *f*. **~ve** /-tɪv/ *adj & n* anticonceptivo (*m*)

contract /'kɒntrækt/ *n* contrato *m*. ● /kən'trækt/ *vt* contraer. ● *vi* contraerse. **~ion** /kən'trækʃn/ *n* contracción *f*. **~or** /kən'træktə(r)/ *n* contratista *m & f*

contradict /kɒntrə'dɪkt/ *vt* contradecir. **~ion** /-ʃn/ *n* contradicción *f*. **~ory** *adj* contradictorio

contraption /kən'træpʃn/ *n* [I] artilugio *m*

contrary /'kɒntrərɪ/ *adj* contrario. **the ~** lo contrario. **on the ~** al contrario. ● *adv*. **~ to** contrariamente a. ● /kən'treərɪ/ *adj* (*obstinate*) terco

contrast /'kɒntrɑ:st/ *n* contraste *m*. ● /kən'trɑ:st/ *vt/i* contrastar. **~ing** *adj* contrastante

contravene /kɒntrə'vi:n/ *vt* contravenir

contribut|e /kən'trɪbju:t/ *vt* contribuir con. ● *vi* contribuir. **~e to** escribir para (newspaper). **~ion** /kɒntrɪ'bju:ʃn/ *n* contribución *f*. **~or** *n* contribuyente *m & f*; (*to newspaper*) colaborador *m*

contrite /'kɒntraɪt/ *adj* arrepentido, pesaroso

contriv|e /kən'traɪv/ *vt* idear. **~e to** conseguir. **~ed** *adj* artificioso

control /kən'trəʊl/ *vt* (*pt* **controlled**) controlar. ● *n* control *m*. **~ler** *n* director *m*. **~s** *npl* (*Mec*) mandos *mpl*

controvers|ial /kɒntrə'vɜ:ʃl/ controvertido. **~y** /'kɒntrəvɜ:sɪ/ *n* controversia *f*

conundrum /kə'nʌndrəm/ *n* adivinanza *f*

convalesce /kɒnvə'les/ *vi* convalecer. **~nce** *n* convalecencia *f*

convector /kən'vektə(r)/ *n* estufa *f* de convección

convene /kən'vi:n/ *vt* convocar. ● *vi* reunirse

convenien|ce /kən'vi:nɪəns/ *n* conveniencia *f*, comodidad *f*. **all modern ~ces** todas las comodidades. **at your ~ce** según le convenga. **~ces** *npl* servicios *mpl*, baños *mpl* (*LAm*). **~t** *adj* conveniente; (place) bien situado; (time) oportuno. **be ~t** convenir. **~tly** *adv* convenientemente

convent /'kɒnvənt/ *n* convento *m*

convention /kən'venʃn/ *n* convención *f*. **~al** *adj* convencional

converge /kən'vɜːdʒ/ *vi* converger

conversation /kɒnvə'seɪʃn/ *n* conversación *f*. **~al** *adj* familiar, coloquial.

converse /kən'vɜːs/ *vi* conversar. ● /'kɒnvɜːs/ *adj* inverso. ● *n* lo contrario. **~ly** *adv* a la inversa

conver|sion /kən'vɜːʃn/ *n* conversión *f*. **~t** /kən'vɜːt/ *vt* convertir. ● /'kɒnvɜːt/ *n* converso *m*. **~tible** /kən'vɜːtɪbl/ *adj* convertible. ● *n* (*Auto*) descapotable *m*, convertible *m* (*LAm*)

convex /'kɒnveks/ *adj* convexo

convey /kən'veɪ/ *vt* transportar (goods, people); comunicar (idea, feeling). **~or belt** *n* cinta *f* transportadora, banda *f* transportadora (*LAm*)

convict /kən'vɪkt/ *vt* condenar. ● /'kɒnvɪkt/ *n* presidiario *m*. **~ion** /kən'vɪkʃn/ *n* condena *f*; (*belief*) creencia *f*

convinc|e /kən'vɪns/ *vt* convencer. **~ing** *adj* convincente

convoluted /'kɒnvəluːtɪd/ *adj* (argument) intrincado

convoy /'kɒnvɔɪ/ *n* convoy *m*

convuls|e /kən'vʌls/ *vt* convulsionar. **be ~ed with laughter** desternillarse de risa. **~ion** /-ʃn/ *n* convulsión *f*

coo /kuː/ *vi* arrullar

cook /kʊk/ *vt* hacer, preparar. ● *vi* cocinar; (food) hacerse. ● *n* cocinero *m*. □ **~ up** *vt* [!] inventar. **~book** *n* libro *m* de cocina. **~er** *n* cocina *f*, estufa *f* (*Mex*). **~ery** *n* cocina *f*

cookie /'kʊkɪ/ *n* (*Amer*) galleta *f*

cool /kuːl/ *adj* (**-er**, **-est**) fresco; (*calm*) tranquilo; (*unfriendly*) frío. ● *n* fresco *m*; [x] calma *f*. ● *vt* enfriar. ● *vi* enfriarse. □ **~ down** *vi* (person) calmarse. **~ly** *adv* tranquilamente

coop /kuːp/ *n* gallinero *m*. □ **~ up** *vt* encerrar

co-op /'kəʊɒp/ *n* cooperativa *f*

cooperat|e /kəʊ'ɒpəreɪt/ *vi* cooperar. **~ion** /-'reɪʃn/ *n* cooperación *f*. **~ive** /kəʊ'ɒpərətɪv/ *adj* cooperativo. ● *n* cooperativa *f*

co-opt /kəʊ'ɒpt/ *vt* cooptar

co-ordinat|e /kəʊ'ɔːdɪneɪt/ *vt* coordinar. ● /kəʊ'ɔːdɪnət/ *n* (*Math*) coordenada *f*. **~es** *npl* prendas *fpl* para combinar. **~ion** /kəʊɔːdɪ'neɪʃn/ *n* coordinación *f*

cop /kɒp/ *n* [!] poli *m* & *f* [!], tira *m* & *f* (*Mex, fam*)

cope /kəʊp/ *vi* arreglárselas. **~ with** hacer frente a

copious /'kəʊpɪəs/ *adj* abundante

copper /'kɒpə(r)/ *n* cobre *m*; (*coin*) perra *f*; [!] poli *m* & *f* [!], tira *m* & *f* (*Mex, fam*). ● *adj* de cobre

copy /'kɒpɪ/ *n* copia *f*; (*of book, newspaper*) ejemplar *m*. ● *vt* copiar. **~right** *n* derechos *mpl* de reproducción

coral /'kɒrəl/ *n* coral *m*

cord /kɔːd/ *n* cuerda *f*; (*fabric*) pana *f*; (*Amer, Elec*) cordón *m*, cable *m*

cordial /'kɔːdɪəl/ *adj* cordial. ● *n* refresco *m* (concentrado)

cordon /'kɔːdn/ *n* cordón *m*. □ **~ off** *vt* acordonar

core /kɔ:(r)/ *n* (*of apple*) corazón *m*; (*of Earth*) centro *m*; (*of problem*) meollo *m*

cork /kɔ:k/ *n* corcho *m*. **~screw** *n* sacacorchos *m*

corn /kɔ:n/ *n* (*wheat*) trigo *m*; (*Amer*) maíz *m*; (*hard skin*) callo *m*

corned beef /kɔ:nd 'bi:f/ *n* carne *f* de vaca en lata

corner /'kɔ:nə(r)/ *n* ángulo *m*; (*inside*) rincón *m*; (*outside*) esquina *f*; (*football*) córner *m*. ● *vt* arrinconar; (*Com*) acaparar

cornet /'kɔ:nɪt/ *n* (*Mus*) corneta *f*; (*for ice cream*) cucurucho *m*, barquillo *m* (*Mex*)

corn: ~flakes *npl* copos *mpl* de maíz. **~flour** *n* maizena *f* (®)

Cornish /'kɔ:nɪʃ/ *adj* de Cornualles

cornstarch /'kɔ:nstɑ:tʃ/ *n* (*Amer*) maizena *f* (®)

corny /'kɔ:nɪ/ *adj* (*fam, trite*) gastado

coronation /kɒrə'neɪʃn/ *n* coronación *f*

coroner /'kɒrənə(r)/ *n* juez *m* de primera instancia

corporal /'kɔ:pərəl/ *n* cabo *m*. ● *adj* corporal

corporate /'kɔ:pərət/ *adj* corporativo

corporation /kɔ:pə'reɪʃn/ *n* corporación *f*; (*Amer*) sociedad *f* anónima

corps /kɔ:(r)/ *n* (*pl* **corps**/kɔ:z/) cuerpo *m*

corpse /kɔ:ps/ *n* cadáver *m*

corpulent /'kɔ:pjʊlənt/ *adj* corpulento

corral /kə'rɑ:l/ *n* (*Amer*) corral *m*

correct /kə'rekt/ *adj* correcto; (time) exacto. ● *vt* corregir. **~ion** /-ʃn/ *n* corrección *f*

correspond /kɒrɪ'spɒnd/ *vi* corresponder; (*write*) escribirse. **~ence** *n* correspondencia *f*. **~ent** *n* corresponsal *m & f*

corridor /'kɒrɪdɔ:(r)/ *n* pasillo *m*

corro|de /kə'rəʊd/ *vt* corroer. ● *vi* corroerse. **~sion** /-ʒn/ *n* corrosión *f*. **~sive** /-sɪv/ *adj* corrosivo

corrugated /'kɒrəgeɪtɪd/ *adj* ondulado. **~ iron** *n* chapa *f* de zinc

corrupt /kə'rʌpt/ *adj* corrompido. ● *vt* corromper. **~ion** /-ʃn/ *n* corrupción *f*

corset /'kɔ:sɪt/ *n* corsé *m*

cosmetic /kɒz'metɪk/ *adj & n* cosmético (*m*)

cosmic /'kɒzmɪk/ *adj* cósmico

cosmopolitan /kɒzmə'pɒlɪtən/ *adj & n* cosmopolita (*m & f*)

cosmos /'kɒzmɒs/ *n* cosmos *m*

cosset /'kɒsɪt/ *vt* (*pt* **cosseted**) mimar

cost /kɒst/ *vt* (*pt* **cost**) costar; (*pt* **costed**) calcular el coste de, calcular el costo de (*LAm*).● *n* coste *m*, costo *m* (*LAm*). **at all ~s** cueste lo que cueste. **to one's ~** a sus expensas. **~s** *npl* (*Jurid*) costas *fpl*

Costa Rica /kɒstə'ri:kə/ *n* Costa *f* Rica. **~n** *adj & n* costarricense (*m & f*), costarriqueño (*m & f*)

cost: ~-effective *adj* rentable. **~ly** *adj* (**-ier, -iest**) costoso

costume /'kɒstju:m/ *n* traje *m*; (*for party, disguise*) disfraz *m*

cosy /'kəʊzɪ/ *adj* (**-ier, -iest**) acogedor. ● *n* cubreteras *m*

cot /kɒt/ *n* cuna *f*

cottage /'kɒtɪdʒ/ *n* casita *f*. **~ cheese** *n* requesón *m*. **~ pie** *n* pastel *m* de carne cubierta con puré

cotton /'kɒtn/ *n* algodón *m*; (*thread*) hilo *m*; (*Amer*) *see* **~**

WOOL. □ ~ **on** *vi* 🅸 comprender. ~ **bud** *n* bastoncillo *m*, cotonete *m* (*Mex*). ~ **candy** *n* (*Amer*) algodón *m* de azúcar. ~ **swab** *n* (*Amer*) *see* ~ **BUD**. ~ **wool** *n* algodón *m* hidrófilo

couch /kaʊtʃ/ *n* sofá *m*

cough /kɒf/ *vi* toser. ● *n* tos *f*. □ ~ **up** *vt* 🅸 pagar. ~ **mixture** *n* jarabe *m* para la tos

could /kʊd/ *pt of* **CAN**[1]

couldn't /'kʊdnt/ = **could not**

council /'kaʊnsl/ *n* consejo *m*; (*of town*) ayuntamiento *m*. ~ **house** *n* vivienda *f* subvencionada. ~**lor** *n* concejal *m*

counsel /'kaʊnsl/ *n* consejo *m*; (*pl invar*) (*Jurid*) abogado *m*. ● *vt* (*pt* **counselled**) aconsejar. ~**ling** *n* terapia *f* de apoyo. ~**lor** *n* consejero *m*

count /kaʊnt/ *n* recuento *m*; (*nobleman*) conde *m*. ● *vt/i* contar. □ ~ **on** *vt* contar. ~**down** *n* cuenta *f* atrás

counter /'kaʊntə(r)/ *n* (*in shop*) mostrador *m*; (*in bank, post office*) ventanilla *f*; (*token*) ficha *f*. ● *adv*. ~ **to** en contra de. ● *adj* opuesto. ● *vt* oponerse a; parar (blow)

counter... /'kaʊntə(r)/ *pref* contra.... ~**act** /-'ækt/ *vt* contrarrestar. ~**-attack** *n* contraataque *m*. ● *vt/i* contraatacar. ~**balance** *n* contrapeso *m*. ● *vt/i* contrapesar. ~**clockwise** /-'klɒkwaɪz/ *a/adv* (*Amer*) en sentido contrario al de las agujas del reloj

counterfeit /'kaʊntəfɪt/ *adj* falsificado. ● *n* falsificación *f*. ● *vt* falsificar

counterfoil /'kaʊntəfɔɪl/ *n* matriz *f*, talón *m* (*LAm*)

counter-productive /kaʊntəprə'dʌktɪv/ *adj* contraproducente

countess /'kaʊntɪs/ *n* condesa *f*

countless /'kaʊntlɪs/ *adj* innumerable

country /'kʌntrɪ/ *n* (*native land*) país *m*; (*countryside*) campo *m*; (*Mus*) (música *f*) country *m*. ~**-and-western** /-en'westən/ (música *f*) country *m*. ~**man** /-mən/ *n* (*of one's own country*) compatriota *m*. ~**side** *n* campo *m*; (*landscape*) paisaje *m*

county /'kaʊntɪ/ *n* condado *m*

coup /ku:/ *n* golpe *m*

couple /'kʌpl/ *n* (*of things*) par *m*; (*of people*) pareja *f*; (*married*) matrimonio *m*. **a** ~ **of** un par de

coupon /'ku:pɒn/ *n* cupón *m*

courage /'kʌrɪdʒ/ *n* valor *m*. ~**ous** /kə'reɪdʒəs/ *adj* valiente

courgette /kʊə'ʒet/ *n* calabacín *m*

courier /'kʊrɪə(r)/ *n* mensajero *m*; (*for tourists*) guía *m* & *f*

course /kɔ:s/ *n* curso *m*; (*behaviour*) conducta *f*; (*in navigation*) rumbo *m*; (*Culin*) plato *m*; (*for golf*) campo *m*. **in due** ~ a su debido tiempo. **in the** ~ **of** en el transcurso de, durante. **of** ~ claro, por supuesto. **of** ~ **not** claro que no, por supuesto que no

court /kɔ:t/ *n* corte *f*; (*tennis*) pista *f*; cancha *f* (*LAm*); (*Jurid*) tribunal *m*. ● *vt* cortejar; buscar (danger)

courteous /'kɜ:tɪəs/ *adj* cortés

courtesy /'kɜ:təsɪ/ *n* cortesía *f*

courtier /'kɔ:tɪə(r)/ *n* (*old use*) cortesano *m*

court: ~ **martial** *n* (*pl* ~**s martial**) consejo *m* de guerra. **-martial** *vt* (*pt* ~**-martialled**) juzgar en consejo de guerra. ~**ship** *n* cortejo *m*. ~**yard** *n* patio *m*

cousin /ˈkʌzn/ *n* primo *m*. **first ~** primo carnal. **second ~** primo segundo

cove /kəʊv/ *n* ensenada *f*, cala *f*

Coventry /ˈkɒvntrɪ/ *n*. **send s.o. to ~** hacer el vacío a uno

cover /ˈkʌvə(r)/ *vt* cubrir. ● *n* cubierta *f*; (*shelter*) abrigo *m*; (*lid*) tapa *f*; (*for furniture*) funda *f*; (*pretext*) pretexto *m*; (*of magazine*) portada *f*. □ **~ up** *vt* cubrir; (*fig*) ocultar. **~age** *n* cobertura *f*. **~ charge** *n* precio *m* del cubierto. **~ing** *n* cubierta *f*. **~ing letter** *n* carta *f* adjunta

covet /ˈkʌvɪt/ *vt* codiciar

cow /kaʊ/ *n* vaca *f*

coward /ˈkaʊəd/ *n* cobarde *m*. **~ice** /ˈkaʊədɪs/ *n* cobardía *f*. **~ly** *adj* cobarde.

cowboy /ˈkaʊbɔɪ/ *n* vaquero *m*

cower /ˈkaʊə(r)/ *vi* encogerse, acobardarse

coxswain /ˈkɒksn/ *n* timonel *m*

coy /kɔɪ/ *adj* (**-er**, **-est**) (*shy*) tímido; (*evasive*) evasivo

crab /kræb/ *n* cangrejo *m*, jaiba *f* (*LAm*)

crack /kræk/ *n* grieta *f*; (*noise*) crujido *m*; (*of whip*) chasquido *m*; (*drug*) crack *m*. ● *adj* [!] de primera. ● *vt* agrietar; chasquear (whip, fingers); cascar (nut); gastar (joke); resolver (problem). ● *vi* agrietarse. **get ~ing** [!] darse prisa. □ **~ down on** *vt* [!] tomar medidas enérgicas contra

cracker /ˈkrækə(r)/ *n* (*Culin*) cracker *f*, galleta *f* (*salada*); (*Christmas cracker*) sorpresa *f* (que estalla al abrirla)

crackle /ˈkrækl/ *vi* crepitar. ● *n* crepitación *f*, crujido *m*

crackpot /ˈkrækpɒt/ *n* [!] chiflado *m*

cradle /ˈkreɪdl/ *n* cuna *f*. ● *vt* acunar

craft /krɑːft/ *n* destreza *f*; (*technique*) arte *f*; (*cunning*) astucia *f*. ● *n invar* (*boat*) barco *m*

craftsman /ˈkrɑːftsmən/ *n* (*pl* **-men**) artesano *m*. **~ship** *n* artesanía *f*

crafty /ˈkrɑːftɪ/ *adj* (**-ier**, **-iest**) astuto

cram /kræm/ *vt* (*pt* **crammed**) rellenar. **~ with** llenar de. ● *vi* (*for exams*) memorizar, empollar [✕], zambutir (*Mex*)

cramp /kræmp/ *n* calambre *m*

cramped /kræmpt/ *adj* apretado

crane /kreɪn/ *n* grúa *f*. ● *vt* estirar (neck)

crank /kræŋk/ *n* manivela *f*; (*person*) excéntrico *m*. **~y** *adj* excéntrico

cranny /ˈkrænɪ/ *n* grieta *f*

crash /kræʃ/ *n* accidente *m*; (*noise*) estruendo *m*; (*collision*) choque *m*; (*Com*) quiebra *f*. ● *vt* estrellar. ● *vi* quebrar con estrépito; (*have accident*) tener un accidente; (car etc) estrellarse, chocar; (*fail*) fracasar. **~ course** *n* curso *m* intensivo. **~ helmet** *n* casco *m* protector. **~-land** *vi* hacer un aterrizaje forzoso

crass /kræs/ *adj* craso, burdo

crate /kreɪt/ *n* cajón *m*. ● *vt* embalar

crater /ˈkreɪtə(r)/ *n* cráter *m*

crav|e /kreɪv/ *vt* ansiar. **~ing** *n* ansia *f*

crawl /krɔːl/ *vi* (baby) gatear; (*move slowly*) avanzar lentamente; (*drag o.s.*) arrastrarse. **~ to** humillarse ante. **~ with** hervir de. ● *n* (*swimming*) crol *m*. **at a ~** a paso lento

crayon /ˈkreɪən/ *n* lápiz *m* de color; (*made of wax*) lápiz *m* de cera, crayola *f* (®), crayón *m* (*Mex*)

craz|e /kreɪz/ *n* manía *f*. **~y** /ˈkreɪzɪ/ *adj* (**-ier**, **-iest**) loco. **be ~y about** estar loco por

creak /kri:k/ *n* crujido *m*; (*of hinge*) chirrido *m*. ● *vi* crujir; (hinge) chirriar

cream /kri:m/ *n* crema *f*; (*fresh*) nata *f*, crema *f* (*LAm*). ● *adj* (*colour*) color crema. ● *vt* (*beat*) batir. **~ cheese** *n* queso *m* para untar, queso *m* crema (*LAm*). **~y** *adj* cremoso

crease /kri:s/ *n* raya *f*, pliegue *m* (*Mex*); (*crumple*) arruga *f*. ● *vt* plegar; (*wrinkle*) arrugar. ● *vi* arrugarse

creat|e /kri:ˈeɪt/ *vt* crear. **~ion** /-ʃn/ *n* creación *f*. **~ive** *adj* creativo. **~or** *n* creador *m*

creature /ˈkri:tʃə(r)/ *n* criatura *f*

crèche /kreʃ/ *n* guardería *f* (infantil)

credib|ility /kredəˈbɪlətɪ/ *n* credibilidad *f*. **~le** /ˈkredəbl/ *adj* creíble

credit /ˈkredɪt/ *n* crédito *m*; (*honour*) mérito *m*. **take the ~ for** atribuirse el mérito de. ● *vt* (*pt* **credited**) acreditar; (*believe*) creer. **~ s.o. with** atribuir a uno. **~ card** *n* tarjeta *f* de crédito. **~or** *n* acreedor *m*

creed /kri:d/ *n* credo *m*

creek /kri:k/ *n* ensenada *f*. **up the ~** ☒ en apuros

creep /kri:p/ *vi* (*pt* **crept**) arrastrarse; (*plant*) trepar. ● *n* ⓘ adulador. **~s** /kri:ps/ *npl*. **give s.o. the ~s** poner los pelos de punta a uno. **~er** *n* enredadera *f*

cremat|e /krɪˈmeɪt/ *vt* incinerar. **~ion** /-ʃn/ *n* cremación *f*. **~orium** /kreməˈtɔ:rɪəm/ *n* (*pl* **-ia** /-ɪə/) crematorio *m*

crept /krept/ *see* **CREEP**

crescendo /krɪˈʃendəʊ/ *n* (*pl* **-os**) crescendo *m*

crescent /ˈkresnt/ *n* media luna *f*; (*street*) calle *f* en forma de media luna

crest /krest/ *n* cresta *f*; (*on coat of arms*) emblema *m*

crevice /ˈkrevɪs/ *n* grieta *f*

crew /kru:/ *n* tripulación *f*; (*gang*) pandilla *f*. **~ cut** *n* corte *m* al rape

crib /krɪb/ *n* (*Amer*) cuna *f*; (*Relig*) belén *m*. ● *vt/i* (*pt* **cribbed**) copiar

crick /krɪk/ *n* calambre *m*; (*in neck*) tortícolis *f*

cricket /ˈkrɪkɪt/ *n* (*Sport*) críquet *m*; (*insect*) grillo *m*

crim|e /kraɪm/ *n* delito *m*; (*murder*) crimen *m*; (*acts*) delincuencia *f*. **~inal** /ˈkrɪmɪnl/ *adj & n* criminal (*m & f*)

crimson /ˈkrɪmzn/ *adj & n* carmesí (*m*)

cringe /krɪndʒ/ *vi* encogerse; (*fig*) humillarse

crinkle /ˈkrɪŋkl/ *vt* arrugar. ● *vi* arrugarse. ● *n* arruga *f*

cripple /ˈkrɪpl/ *n* lisiado *m*. ● *vt* lisiar; (*fig*) paralizar

crisis /ˈkraɪsɪs/ *n* (*pl* **crises** /-si:z/) crisis *f*

crisp /krɪsp/ *adj* (**-er**, **-est**) (*Culin*) crujiente; (air) vigorizador. **~s** *npl* patatas *fpl* fritas, papas *fpl* fritas (*LAm*) (*de bolsa*)

crisscross /ˈkrɪskrɒs/ *adj* entrecruzado. ● *vt* entrecruzar. ● *vi* entrecruzarse

criterion /kraɪˈtɪərɪən/ *n* (*pl* **-ia** /-ɪə/) criterio *m*

critic /ˈkrɪtɪk/ *n* crítico *m*. **~al** *adj* crítico. **~ally** *adv* críticamente; (*ill*) gravemente

critici|sm /ˈkrɪtɪsɪzəm/ *n* crítica *f*. **~ze** /ˈkrɪtɪsaɪz/ *vt/i* criticar

croak /krəʊk/ *n* (*of person*) gruñido *m*; (*of frog*) canto *m*. ● *vi* gruñir; (frog) croar

Croat /ˈkrəʊæt/ *n* croata *m & f*. **~ia** /krəʊˈeɪʃə/ *n* Croacia *f*. **~ian** *adj* croata

crochet /ˈkrəʊʃeɪ/ *n* crochet *m*, ganchillo *m*. ● *vt* tejer a crochet *or* a ganchillo

crockery /ˈkrɒkərɪ/ *n* loza *f*

crocodile /ˈkrɒkədaɪl/ *n* cocodrilo *m*. **~ tears** *npl* lágrimas *fpl* de cocodrilo

crocus /ˈkrəʊkəs/ *n* (*pl* **-es**) azafrán *m* de primavera

crook /krʊk/ *n* 🄸 sinvergüenza *m & f*. **~ed** /ˈkrʊkɪd/ *adj* torcido, chueco (*LAm*); (*winding*) tortuoso; (*dishonest*) deshonesto

crop /krɒp/ *n* cosecha *f*; (*haircut*) corte *m* de pelo muy corto. ● *vt* (*pt* **cropped**) cortar. □ **~ up** *vi* surgir

croquet /ˈkrəʊkeɪ/ *n* croquet *m*

cross /krɒs/ *n* cruz *f*; (*of animals*) cruce *m*. ● *vt* cruzar; (*oppose*) contrariar. **~ s.o.'s mind** ocurrírsele a uno. ● *vi* cruzar. **~ o.s.** santiguarse. ● *adj* enfadado, enojado (*esp LAm*). □ **~ out** *vt* tachar. **~bar** *n* travesaño *m*. **~-examine** /-ɪgˈzæmɪn/ *vt* interrogar. **~-eyed** *adj* bizco. **~fire** *n* fuego *m* cruzado. **~ing** *n* (*by boat*) travesía *f*; (*on road*) cruce *m* peatonal. **~ly** *adv* con enfado, con enojo (*esp LAm*). **~-purposes** /-ˈpɜːpəsɪz/ *npl*. **talk at ~-purposes** hablar sin entenderse. **~-reference** /-ˈrefrəns/ *n* remisión *f*. **~roads** *n invar* cruce *m*. **~-section** /-ˈsekʃn/ *n* sección *f* transversal; (*fig*) muestra *f* representativa. **~walk** *n* (*Amer*) paso de peatones. **~word** *n* **~word (puzzle)** crucigrama *m*

crotch /krɒtʃ/ *n* entrepiernas *fpl*

crouch /kraʊtʃ/ *vi* agacharse

crow /krəʊ/ *n* cuervo *m*. **as the ~ flies** en línea recta. ● *vi* cacarear. **~bar** *n* palanca *f*

crowd /kraʊd/ *n* muchedumbre *f*. ● *vt* amontonar; (*fill*) llenar. ● *vi* amontonarse; (*gather*) reunirse. **~ed** *adj* atestado

crown /kraʊn/ *n* corona *f*; (*of hill*) cumbre *f*; (*of head*) coronilla *f*. ● *vt* coronar

crucial /ˈkruːʃl/ *adj* crucial

crucifix /ˈkruːsɪfɪks/ *n* crucifijo *m*. **~ion** /-ˈfɪkʃn/ *n* crucifixión *f*

crucify /ˈkruːsɪfaɪ/ *vt* crucificar

crude /kruːd/ *adj* (**-er**, **-est**) (*raw*) crudo; (*rough*) tosco; (*vulgar*) ordinario

cruel /ˈkrʊəl/ *adj* (**crueller**, **cruellest**) cruel. **~ty** *n* crueldad *f*

cruet /ˈkruːɪt/ *n* vinagrera *f*

cruise /kruːz/ *n* crucero *m*. ● *vi* hacer un crucero; (*of car*) circular lentamente. **~r** *n* crucero *m*

crumb /krʌm/ *n* miga *f*

crumble /ˈkrʌmbl/ *vt* desmenuzar. ● *vi* desmenuzarse; (*collapse*) derrumbarse

crummy /ˈkrʌmɪ/ *adj* (**-ier**, **-iest**) 🗵 miserable

crumpet /ˈkrʌmpɪt/ *n* bollo *m* blando

crumple /ˈkrʌmpl/ *vt* arrugar. ● *vi* arrugarse

crunch /krʌntʃ/ *vt* hacer crujir; (*bite*) masticar. **~y** *adj* crujiente

crusade /kruːˈseɪd/ *n* cruzada *f*.

C

~r *n* cruzado *m*

crush /krʌʃ/ *vt* aplastar; arrugar (clothes). ● *n* (*crowd*) aglomeración *f*. **have a ~ on** ⊡ estar chiflado por

crust /krʌst/ *n* corteza *f*. **~y** *adj* (bread) de corteza dura

crutch /krʌtʃ/ *n* muleta *f*; (*between legs*) entrepiernas *fpl*

crux /krʌks/ *n* (*pl* **cruxes**). **the ~ (of the matter)** el quid (de la cuestión)

cry /kraɪ/ *n* grito *m*. **be a far ~ from** (*fig*) distar mucho de. ● *vi* llorar; (*call out*) gritar. □ **~ off** *vi* echarse atrás, rajarse. **~baby** *n* llorón *m*

crypt /krɪpt/ *n* cripta *f*

cryptic /ˈkrɪptɪk/ *adj* enigmático

crystal /ˈkrɪstl/ *n* cristal *m*. **~lize** *vi* cristalizarse

cub /kʌb/ *n* cachorro *m*. **C~ (Scout)** *n* lobato *m*

Cuba /ˈkju:bə/ *n* Cuba *f*. **~n** *adj* & *n* cubano (*m*)

cubbyhole /ˈkʌbɪhəʊl/ *n* cuchitril *m*

cub|e /kju:b/ *n* cubo *m*. **~ic** *adj* cúbico

cubicle /ˈkju:bɪkl/ *n* cubículo *m*; (*changing room*) probador *m*

cuckoo /ˈkʊku:/ *n* cuco *m*, cuclillo *m*

cucumber /ˈkju:kʌmbə(r)/ *n* pepino *m*

cuddl|e /ˈkʌdl/ *vt* abrazar. ● *vi* abrazarse. ● *n* abrazo *m*. **~y** *adj* adorable

cue /kju:/ *n* (*Mus*) entrada *f*; (*in theatre*) pie *m*; (*in snooker*) taco *m*

cuff /kʌf/ *n* puño *m*; (*Amer, of trousers*) vuelta *f*, dobladillo *m*; (*blow*) bofetada *f*. **speak off the ~** hablar de improviso. ● *vt* abofetear. **~link** *n* gemelo *m*, mancuerna *f* (*Mex*)

cul-de-sac /ˈkʌldəsæk/ *n* callejón *m* sin salida

culinary /ˈkʌlɪnərɪ/ *adj* culinario

cull /kʌl/ *vt* sacrificar en forma selectiva (animals)

culminat|e /ˈkʌlmɪneɪt/ *vi* culminar. **~ion** /-ˈneɪʃn/ *n* culminación *f*

culprit /ˈkʌlprɪt/ *n* culpable *m* & *f*

cult /kʌlt/ *n* culto *m*

cultivat|e /ˈkʌltɪveɪt/ *vt* cultivar. **~ion** /-ˈveɪʃn/ *n* cultivo *m*

cultur|al /ˈkʌltʃərəl/ *adj* cultural. **~e** /ˈkʌltʃə(r)/ *n* cultura *f*; (*Bot etc*) cultivo *m*. **~ed** *adj* cultivado; (person) culto

cumbersome /ˈkʌmbəsəm/ *adj* incómodo; (*heavy*) pesado

cunning /ˈkʌnɪŋ/ *adj* astuto. ● *n* astucia *f*

cup /kʌp/ *n* taza *f*; (*trophy*) copa *f*

cupboard /ˈkʌbəd/ *n* armario *m*

curator /kjʊəˈreɪtə(r)/ *n* (*of museum*) conservador *m*

curb /kɜ:b/ *n* freno *m*; (*Amer*) bordillo *m* (de la acera), borde *m* de la banqueta (*Mex*). ● *vt* refrenar

curdle /ˈkɜ:dl/ *vt* cuajar. ● *vi* cuajarse; (*go bad*) cortarse

cure /kjʊə(r)/ *vt* curar. ● *n* cura *f*

curfew /ˈkɜ:fju:/ *n* toque *m* de queda

curio|sity /kjʊərɪˈɒsətɪ/ *n* curiosidad *f*. **~us** /ˈkjʊərɪəs/ *adj* curioso

curl /kɜ:l/ *vt* rizar, enchinar (*Mex*). **~ o.s. up** acurrucarse. ● *vi* (hair) rizarse, enchinarse (*Mex*); (paper) ondularse. ● *n* rizo *m*, chino *m* (*Mex*). **~er** *n* rulo *m*, chino *m* (*Mex*). **~y** *adj* (**-ier, -iest**) rizado, chino (*Mex*)

currant /ˈkʌrənt/ *n* pasa *f* de Corinto

currency /ˈkʌrənsɪ/ *n* moneda *f*
current /ˈkʌrənt/ *adj & n* corriente (*f*); (*existing*) actual. **~ affairs** *npl* sucesos de actualidad. **~ly** *adv* actualmente
curriculum /kəˈrɪkjʊləm/ *n* (*pl* **-la**) programa *m* de estudios. **~ vitae** *n* currículum *m* vitae
curry /ˈkʌrɪ/ *n* curry *m*. ● *vt* preparar al curry
curse /kɜːs/ *n* maldición *f*; (*oath*) palabrota *f*. ● *vt* maldecir. ● *vi* decir palabrotas
cursory /ˈkɜːsərɪ/ *adj* superficial
curt /kɜːt/ *adj* brusco
curtain /ˈkɜːtn/ *n* cortina *f*; (*in theatre*) telón *m*
curtsey, **curtsy** /ˈkɜːtsɪ/ *n* reverencia *f*. ● *vi* hacer una reverencia
curve /kɜːv/ *n* curva *f*. ● *vi* estar curvado; (road) torcerse
cushion /ˈkʊʃn/ *n* cojín *m*, almohadón *m*
cushy /ˈkʊʃɪ/ *adj* (**-ier**, **-iest**) [!] fácil
custard /ˈkʌstəd/ *n* natillas *fpl*
custody /ˈkʌstədɪ/ *n* custodia *f*; **be in ~** *Jurid* estar detenido
custom /ˈkʌstəm/ *n* costumbre *f*; (*Com*) clientela *f*. **~ary** /-ərɪ/ *adj* acostumbrado. **~er** *n* cliente *m*. **~s** *npl* aduana *f*. **~s officer** *n* aduanero *m*
cut /kʌt/ *vt/i* (*pt* **cut**, *pres p* **cutting**) cortar; reducir (prices). ● *n* corte *m*; (*reduction*) reducción *f*. □ **~ across** *vt* cortar camino por. □ **~ back**, **~ down** *vt* reducir. □ **~ in** *vi* interrumpir. □ **~ off** *vt* cortar; (*phone*) desconectar; (*fig*) aislar. □ **~ out** *vt* recortar; (*omit*) suprimir. □ **~ through** *vt* cortar camino por. □ **~ up** *vt* cortar en pedazos
cute /kjuːt/ *adj* (**-er**, **-est**) [!] mono, amoroso (*LAm*); (*Amer, attractive*) guapo, buen mozo (*LAm*)
cutlery /ˈkʌtlərɪ/ *n* cubiertos *mpl*
cutlet /ˈkʌtlɪt/ *n* chuleta *f*
cut: ~-price, (*Amer*) **~-rate** *adj* a precio reducido. **~-throat** *adj* despiadado. **~ting** *adj* cortante; (remark) mordaz. ● *n* (*from newspaper*) recorte *m*; (*of plant*) esqueje *m*
CV *n* (= **curriculum vitae**) currículum *m* (vitae)
cyberspace /ˈsaɪbəspeɪs/ ciberespacio *m*
cycl|e /ˈsaɪkl/ *n* ciclo *m*; (*bicycle*) bicicleta *f*. ● *vi* ir en bicicleta. **~ing** *n* ciclismo *m*. **~ist** *n* ciclista *m & f*
cylind|er /ˈsɪlɪndə(r)/ *n* cilindro *m*. **~er head** (*Auto*) *n* culata *f*. **~rical** /-ˈlɪndrɪkl/ *adj* cilíndrico
cymbal /ˈsɪmbl/ *n* címbalo *m*
cynic /ˈsɪnɪk/ *n* cínico *m*. **~al** *adj* cínico. **~ism** /-sɪzəm/ *n* cinismo *m*
Czech /tʃek/ *adj & n* checo (*m*). **~oslovakia** /-əsləˈvækɪə/ *n* (*History*) Checoslovaquia *f*. **~ Republic** *n*. **the ~ Republic** *n* la República Checa

Dd

dab /dæb/ *vt* (*pt* **dabbed**) tocar ligeramente. ● *n* toque *m* suave. **a ~ of** un poquito de
dad /dæd/ *n* [!] papá *m*. **~dy** *n* papi *m*. **~dy-long-legs** *n invar* (*cranefly*) típula *f*; (*Amer, harvestman*) segador *m*, falangio *m*
daffodil /ˈdæfədɪl/ *n* narciso *m*

daft /dɑːft/ *adj* (**-er**, **-est**) 🅸 tonto
dagger /ˈdægə(r)/ *n* daga *f*, puñal *m*
daily /ˈdeɪlɪ/ *adj* diario. ● *adv* diariamente, cada día

d

Dáil Éireann Es el nombre de la cámara baja del Parlamento de la República de Irlanda. Se pronuncia /dɔɪl/ y consta de 166 representantes o diputados, comúnmente llamados *TDs*, que representan 41 circunscripciones. Se eligen por medio del sistema de representación proporcional. Según la Constitución debe haber un diputado por cada 20.000 a 30.000 personas.

dainty /ˈdeɪntɪ/ *adj* (**-ier**, **-iest**) delicado
dairy /ˈdeərɪ/ *n* vaquería *f*; (*shop*) lechería *f*
daisy /ˈdeɪzɪ/ *n* margarita *f*
dam /dæm/ *n* presa *f*, represa *f* (*LAm*)
damag|e /ˈdæmɪdʒ/ *n* daño *m*; **~s** (*npl*, *Jurid*) daños *mpl* y perjuicios *mpl*. ● *vt* (*fig*) dañar, estropear. **~ing** *adj* perjudicial
dame /deɪm/ *n* (*old use*) dama *f*; (*Amer*, *sl*) chica *f*
damn /dæm/ *vt* condenar; (*curse*) maldecir. ● *int* 🅸 ¡caray! 🅸. ● *adj* maldito. ● *n* **I don't give a ~** (no) me importa un comino
damp /dæmp/ *n* humedad *f*. ● *adj* (**-er**, **-est**) húmedo. ● *vt* mojar. **~ness** *n* humedad *f*
danc|e /dɑːns/ *vt/i* bailar. ● *n* baile *m*. **~e hall** *n* salón *m* de baile. **~er** *n* bailador *m*; (*professional*) bailarín *m*. **~ing** *n* baile *m*
dandelion /ˈdændɪlaɪən/ *n* diente *m* de león
dandruff /ˈdændrʌf/ *n* caspa *f*
dandy /ˈdændɪ/ *n* petimetre *m*
Dane /deɪn/ *n* danés *m*
danger /ˈdeɪndʒə(r)/ *n* peligro *m*; (*risk*) riesgo *m*. **~ous** *adj* peligroso
dangle /ˈdæŋgl/ *vt* balancear. ● *vi* suspender, colgar
Danish /ˈdeɪnɪʃ/ *adj* danés. ● *m* (*language*) danés *m*
dar|e /deə(r)/ *vt* desafiar. ● *vi* atreverse a. **I ~ say** probablemente. ● *n* desafío *m*. **~edevil** *n* atrevido *m*. **~ing** *adj* atrevido
dark /dɑːk/ *adj* (**-er**, **-est**) oscuro; (skin, hair) moreno. ● *n* oscuridad *f*; (*nightfall*) atardecer. **in the ~** a oscuras. **~en** *vt* oscurecer. ● *vi* oscurecerse. **~ness** *n* oscuridad *f*. **~room** *n* cámara *f* oscura
darling /ˈdɑːlɪŋ/ *adj* querido. ● *n* cariño *m*
darn /dɑːn/ *vt* zurcir
dart /dɑːt/ *n* dardo *m*. ● *vi* lanzarse; (*run*) precipitarse. **~board** *n* diana *f*. **~s** *npl* los dardos *mpl*
dash /dæʃ/ *vi* precipitarse. ● *vt* tirar; (*break*) romper; defraudar (hopes). ● *n* (*small amount*) poquito *m*; (*punctuation mark*) guión *m*. □ **~ off** *vi* marcharse apresuradamente. **~ out** *vi* salir corriendo. **~board** *n* tablero *m* de mandos
data /ˈdeɪtə/ *npl* datos *mpl*. **~base** *n* base *f* de datos. **~ processing** *n* proceso *m* de datos
date /deɪt/ *n* fecha *f*; (*appointment*) cita *f*; (*fruit*) dátil *m*. **to ~** hasta la fecha. ● *vt* fechar. ● *vi* datar; datar (remains); (*be old-fashioned*) quedar anticuado. **~d** *adj* pasado de moda
daub /dɔːb/ *vt* embadurnar

daughter /ˈdɔːtə(r)/ *n* hija *f*. **~-in-law** *n* nuera *f*

dawdle /ˈdɔːdl/ *vi* andar despacio; (*waste time*) perder el tiempo

dawn /dɔːn/ *n* amanecer *m*. ● *vi* amanecer; (*fig*) nacer. **it ~ed on me that** caí en la cuenta de que

day /deɪ/ *n* día *m*; (*whole day*) jornada *f*; (*period*) época *f*. **~break** *n* amanecer *m*. **~ care center** *n* (*Amer*) guardería *f* infantil. **~dream** *n* ensueño *m*. ● *vi* soñar despierto. **~light** *n* luz *f* del día. **~time** *n* día *m*

daze /deɪz/ *vt* aturdir. ● *n* aturdimiento *m*. **in a ~** aturdido. **~d** *adj* aturdido

dazzle /ˈdæzl/ *vt* deslumbrar

dead /ded/ *adj* muerto; (*numb*) dormido. ● *adv* justo; (**[!]**, *completely*) completamente. **~ beat** rendido. **~ slow** muy lento. **stop ~** parar en seco. **~en** *vt* amortiguar (sound, blow); calmar (pain). **~ end** *n* callejón *m* sin salida. **~line** *n* fecha *f* tope, plazo *m* de entrega. **~lock** *n* punto *m* muerto. **~ly** *adj* (**-ier**, **-iest**) mortal

deaf /def/ *adj* (**-er**, **-est**) sordo. **~en** *vt* ensordecer. **~ness** *n* sordera *f*

deal /diːl/ *n* (*agreement*) acuerdo *m*; (*treatment*) trato *m*. **a good ~** bastante. **a great ~ (of)** muchísimo. ● *vt* (*pt* **dealt**) dar (a blow, cards). ● *vi* (*cards*) dar, repartir. □ **~ in** *vt* comerciar en. □ **~ out** *vt* repartir, distribuir. □ **~ with** *vt* tratar con (person); tratar de (subject); ocuparse de (problem). **~er** *n* comerciante *m*. **drug ~er** traficante *m & f* de drogas

dean /diːn/ *n* deán *m*; (*Univ*) decano *m*

dear /dɪə(r)/ *adj* (**-er**, **-est**) querido; (*expensive*) caro. ● *n* querido *m*. ● *adv* caro. ● *int*. **oh ~!** ¡ay por Dios! **~ me!** ¡Dios mío! **~ly** *adv* (*pay*) caro; (*very much*) muchísimo

death /deθ/ *n* muerte *f*. **~ sentence** *n* pena *f* de muerte. **~ trap** *n* lugar *m* peligroso.

debat|able /dɪˈbeɪtəbl/ *adj* discutible. **~e** /dɪˈbeɪt/ *n* debate *m*. ● *vt* debatir, discutir

debauchery /dɪˈbɔːtʃərɪ/ *vt* libertinaje *m*

debit /ˈdebɪt/ *n* débito *m*. ● *vt* debitar, cargar. **~ card** *n* tarjeta *f* de cobro automático

debris /ˈdebriː/ *n* escombros *mpl*

debt /det/ *n* deuda *f*. **be in ~** tener deudas. **~or** *n* deudor *m*

debut /ˈdebjuː/ debut *m*

decade /ˈdekeɪd/ *n* década *f*

decaden|ce /ˈdekədəns/ *n* decadencia *f*. **~t** *adj* decadente

decay /dɪˈkeɪ/ *vi* descomponerse; (tooth) cariarse. ● *n* decomposición *f*; (*of tooth*) caries *f*

deceased /dɪˈsiːst/ *adj* difunto

deceit /dɪˈsiːt/ *n* engaño *m*. **~ful** *adj* falso. **~fully** *adv* falsamente

deceive /dɪˈsiːv/ *vt* engañar

December /dɪˈsembə(r)/ *n* diciembre *m*

decen|cy /ˈdiːsənsɪ/ *n* decencia *f*. **~t** *adj* decente; (*fam, good*) bueno; (*fam, kind*) amable. **~tly** *adv* decentemente

decepti|on /dɪˈsepʃn/ *n* engaño *m*. **~ve** /-tɪv/ *adj* engañoso

decibel /ˈdesɪbel/ *n* decibel(io) *m*

decide /dɪˈsaɪd/ *vt/i* decidir. **~d** *adj* resuelto; (*unquestionable*) indudable

decimal /ˈdesɪml/ *adj & n* decimal (*m*). **~ point** *n* coma *f* (decimal), punto *m* decimal

decipher /dɪ'saɪfə(r)/ *vt* descifrar

decis|ion /dɪ'sɪʒn/ *n* decisión *f*. **~ive** /dɪ'saɪsɪv/ *adj* decisivo; (manner) decidido

d

deck /dek/ *n* (*Naut*) cubierta *f*; (*Amer, of cards*) baraja *f*; (*of bus*) piso *m*. ● *vt* adornar. **~chair** *n* tumbona *f*, silla *f* de playa

declar|ation /deklə'reɪʃn/ *n* declaración *f*. **~e** /dɪ'kleə(r)/ *vt* declarar

decline /dɪ'klaɪn/ *vt* rehusar; (*Gram*) declinar. ● *vi* disminuir; (*deteriorate*) deteriorarse. ● *n* decadencia *f*; (*decrease*) disminución *f*

decode /di:'kəʊd/ *vt* descifrar

decompose /di:kəm'pəʊz/ *vi* descomponerse

décor /'deɪkɔ:(r)/ *n* decoración *f*

decorat|e /'dekəreɪt/ *vt* adornar, decorar (*LAm*); empapelar y pintar (room). **~ion** /-'reɪʃn/ *n* (*act*) decoración *f*; (*ornament*) adorno *m*. **~ive** /-ətɪv/ *adj* decorativo. **~or** *n* pintor *m* decorador

decoy /'di:kɔɪ/ *n* señuelo *m*. ● /dɪ'kɔɪ/ *vt* atraer con señuelo

decrease /dɪ'kri:s/ *vt/i* disminuir. ● /'di:kri:s/ *n* disminución *f*

decree /dɪ'kri:/ *n* decreto *m*. ● *vt* decretar

decrepit /dɪ'krepɪt/ *adj* decrépito

decriminalize /di:'krɪmɪnəlaɪz/ *vt* despenalizar

dedicat|e /'dedɪkeɪt/ *vt* dedicar. **~ion** /-'keɪʃn/ *n* dedicación *f*

deduce /dɪ'dju:s/ *vt* deducir

deduct /dɪ'dʌkt/ *vt* deducir. **~ion** /-ʃn/ *n* deducción *f*

deed /di:d/ *n* hecho *m*; (*Jurid*) escritura *f*

deem /di:m/ *vt* juzgar, considerar

deep /di:p/ *adj* (**-er**, **-est**) *adv* profundo. ● *adv* profundamente. **be ~ in thought** estar absorto en sus pensamientos. **~en** *vt* hacer más profundo. ● *vi* hacerse más profundo. **~freeze** *n* congelador *m*, freezer *m* (*LAm*). **~ly** *adv* profundamente

deer /dɪə(r)/ *n invar* ciervo *m*

deface /dɪ'feɪs/ *vt* desfigurar

default /dɪ'fɔ:lt/ *vi* faltar. ● *n* opción por defecto. **by ~** en rebeldía

defeat /dɪ'fi:t/ *vt* vencer; (*frustrate*) frustrar. ● *n* derrota *f*. **~ism** *n* derrotismo *m*. **~ist** *n* derrotista *a* & (*m* & *f*)

defect /'di:fekt/ *n* defecto *m*. ● /dɪ'fekt/ *vi* desertar. **~ to** pasar a. **~ion** /dɪ'fekʃn/ *n* (*Pol*) defección *f*. **~ive** /dɪ'fektɪv/ *adj* defectuoso

defence /dɪ'fens/ *n* defensa *f*. **~less** *adj* indefenso

defen|d /dɪ'fend/ *vt* defender. **~dant** *n* (*Jurid*) acusado *m*. **~sive** /-sɪv/ *adj* defensivo. ● *n* defensiva *f*

defer /dɪ'fɜ:(r)/ *vt* (*pt* **deferred**) aplazar. **~ence** /'defərəns/ *n* deferencia *f*. **~ential** /defə'renʃl/ *adj* deferente

defian|ce /dɪ'faɪəns/ *n* desafío *m*. **in ~ce of** a despecho de. **~t** *adj* desafiante. **~tly** *adv* con actitud desafiante

deficien|cy /dɪ'fɪʃənsɪ/ *n* falta *f*. **~t** *adj* deficiente. **be ~t in** carecer de

deficit /'defɪsɪt/ *n* déficit *m*

define /dɪ'faɪn/ *vt* definir

definite /'defɪnɪt/ *adj* (*final*) definitivo; (*certain*) seguro; (*clear*) claro; (*firm*) firme. **~ly** *adv* seguramente; (*definitively*) definitivamente

definition /defɪ'nɪʃn/ *n* definición *f*

definitive /dɪ'fɪnətɪv/ *adj* definitivo

deflate /dɪ'fleɪt/ *vt* desinflar. ● *vi* desinflarse

deflect /dɪ'flekt/ *vt* desviar

deform /dɪ'fɔ:m/ *vt* deformar. **~ed** *adj* deforme. **~ity** *n* deformidad *f*

defrost /di:'frɒst/ *vt* descongelar. ● *vi* descongelarse

deft /deft/ *adj* (**-er**, **-est**) hábil. **~ly** *adv* hábilmente *f*

defuse /di:'fju:z/ *vt* desactivar (bomb); (*fig*) calmar

defy /dɪ'faɪ/ *vt* desafiar

degenerate /dɪ'dʒenəreɪt/ *vi* degenerar. ● /dɪ'dʒenərət/ *adj & n* degenerado (*m*)

degrad|ation /degrə'deɪʃn/ *n* degradación *f*. **~e** /dɪ'greɪd/ *vt* degradar

degree /dɪ'gri:/ *n* grado *m*; (*Univ*) licenciatura *f*; (*rank*) rango *m*. **to a certain ~** hasta cierto punto

deign /deɪn/ *vi*. **~ to** dignarse

deity /'di:ɪtɪ/ *n* deidad *f*

deject|ed /dɪ'dʒektɪd/ *adj* desanimado. **~ion** /-ʃn/ *n* abatimiento *m*

delay /dɪ'leɪ/ *vt* retrasar, demorar (*LAm*). ● *vi* tardar, demorar (*LAm*). ● *n* retraso *m*, demora *f* (*LAm*)

delegat|e /'delɪgeɪt/ *vt/i* delegar. ● /'delɪgət/ *n* delegado *m*. **~ion** /-'geɪʃn/ *n* delegación *f*

delet|e /dɪ'li:t/ *vt* tachar. **~ion** /-ʃn/ *n* supresión *f*

deliberat|e /dɪ'lɪbəreɪt/ *vt/i* deliberar. ● /dɪ'lɪbərət/ *adj* intencionado; (steps etc) pausado. **~ely** *adv* a propósito. **~ion** /-'reɪʃn/ *n* deliberación *f*

delica|cy /'delɪkəsɪ/ *n* delicadeza *f*; (*food*) manjar *m*. **~te** /'delɪkət/ *adj* delicado

delicatessen /delɪkə'tesn/ *n* charcutería *f*, salchichonería *f* (*Mex*)

delicious /dɪ'lɪʃəs/ *adj* delicioso

delight /dɪ'laɪt/ *n* placer *m*. ● *vt* encantar. ● *vi* deleitarse. **~ed** *adj* encantado. **~ful** *adj* delicioso

deliri|ous /dɪ'lɪrɪəs/ *adj* delirante. **~um** /-əm/ *n* delirio *m*

deliver /dɪ'lɪvə(r)/ *vt* entregar; (*distribute*) repartir; (*aim*) lanzar; (*Med*) **he ~ed the baby** la asistió en el parto. **~ance** *n* liberación *f*. **~y** *n* entrega *f*; (*of post*) reparto *m*; (*Med*) parto *m*

delta /'deltə/ *n* (*of river*) delta *m*

delude /dɪ'lu:d/ *vt* engañar. **~ o.s.** engañarse

deluge /'delju:dʒ/ *n* diluvio *m*

delusion /dɪ'lu:ʒn/ *n* ilusión *f*

deluxe /dɪ'lʌks/ *adj* de lujo

delve /delv/ *vi* hurgar. **~ into** (*investigate*) ahondar en

demand /dɪ'mɑ:nd/ *vt* exigir. ● *n* petición *f*, pedido *m* (*LAm*); (*claim*) exigencia *f*; (*Com*) demanda *f*. **in ~** muy popular, muy solicitado. **on ~** a solicitud. **~ing** *adj* exigente. **~s** *npl* exigencias *fpl*

demented /dɪ'mentɪd/ *adj* demente

demo /'deməʊ/ *n* (*pl* **-os**) [!] manifestación *f*

democra|cy /dɪ'mɒkrəsɪ/ *n* democracia *f*. **~t** /'deməkræt/ *n* demócrata *m & f*. **D~t** *a & n* (*in US*) demócrata (*m & f*). **~tic** /demə'krætɪk/ *adj* democrático

demoli|sh /dɪ'mɒlɪʃ/ *vt* derribar. **~tion** /demə'lɪʃn/ *n* demolición *f*

demon /'di:mən/ *n* demonio *m*

demonstrat|e /'demənstreɪt/ *vt* demostrar. ● *vi* manifestarse, hacer una manifestación. **~ion** /-'streɪʃn/ *n* demostración *f*; (*Pol*) manifestación *f*. **~or** /ˈdemənstreɪtə(r)/*n* (*Pol*) manifestante *m* & *f*; (*marketing*) demostrador *m*

demoralize /dɪˈmɒrəlaɪz/ *vt* desmoralizar

demote /dɪˈməʊt/ *vt* bajar de categoría

demure /dɪˈmjʊə(r)/ *adj* recatado

den /den/ *n* (*of animal*) guarida *f*, madriguera *f*

denial /dɪˈnaɪəl/ *n* denegación *f*; (*statement*) desmentimiento *m*

denim /ˈdenɪm/ *n* tela *f* vaquera *or* de jeans, mezclilla (*Mex*) *f*. **~s** *npl* vaqueros *mpl*, jeans *mpl*, tejanos *mpl*, pantalones *mpl* de mezclilla (*Mex*)

Denmark /ˈdenmɑːk/ *n* Dinamarca *f*

denote /dɪˈnəʊt/ *vt* denotar

denounce /dɪˈnaʊns/ *vt* denunciar

dens|e /dens/ *adj* (**-er**, **-est**) espeso; (person) torpe. **~ely** *adv* densamente. **~ity** *n* densidad *f*

dent /dent/ *n* abolladura *f*. ● *vt* abollar

dental /ˈdentl/ *adj* dental. **~ floss** /flɒs/ *n* hilo *m or* seda *f* dental. **~ surgeon** *n* dentista *m* & *f*

dentist /ˈdentɪst/ *n* dentista *m* & *f*. **~ry** *n* odontología *f*

dentures /ˈdentʃəz/ *npl* dentadura *f* postiza

deny /dɪˈnaɪ/ *vt* negar; desmentir (rumour); denegar (request)

deodorant /dɪˈəʊdərənt/ *adj* & *n* desodorante (*m*)

depart /dɪˈpɑːt/ *vi* partir, salir. **~ from** (*deviate from*) apartarse de

department /dɪˈpɑːtment/ *n* departamento *m*; (*Pol*) ministerio *m*, secretaría *f* (*Mex*). **~ store** *n* grandes almacenes *mpl*, tienda *f* de departamentos (*Mex*)

departure /dɪˈpɑːtʃə(r)/ *n* partida *f*; (*of train etc*) salida *f*

depend /dɪˈpend/ *vi* depender. **~ on** depender de. **~able** *adj* digno de confianza. **~ant** /dɪˈpendənt/ *n* familiar *m* & *f* dependiente. **~ence** *n* dependencia *f*. **~ent** *adj* dependiente. **be ~ent on** depender de

depict /dɪˈpɪkt/ *vt* representar; (*in words*) describir

deplete /dɪˈpliːt/ *vt* agotar

deplor|able /dɪˈplɔːrəbl/ *adj* deplorable. **~e** /dɪˈplɔː(r)/ *vt* deplorar

deploy /dɪˈplɔɪ/ *vt* desplegar

deport /dɪˈpɔːt/ *vt* deportar. **~ation** /-ˈteɪʃn/ *n* deportación *f*

depose /dɪˈpəʊz/ *vt* deponer

deposit /dɪˈpɒzɪt/ *vt* (*pt* **deposited**) depositar. ● *n* depósito *m*

depot /ˈdepəʊ/ *n* depósito *m*; (*Amer*) estación *f* de autobuses

deprav|ed /dɪˈpreɪvd/ *adj* depravado. **~ity** /dɪˈprævətɪ/ *n* depravación *f*

depress /dɪˈpres/ *vt* deprimir; (*press down*) apretar. **~ed** *adj* deprimido. **~ing** *adj* deprimente. **~ion** /-ʃn/ *n* depresión *f*

depriv|ation /deprɪˈveɪʃn/ *n* privación *f*. **~e** /dɪˈpraɪv/ *vt*. **~e of** privar de. **~d** *adj* carenciado

depth /depθ/ *n* profundidad *f*. **be out of one's ~** perder pie; (*fig*) meterse en honduras. **in ~** a fondo

deput|ize /ˈdepjʊtaɪz/ *vi*. **~ize for** sustituir a. **~y** /ˈdepjʊtɪ/ *n* sustituto *m*. **~y chairman** *n* vicepresidente *m*

derail /dɪˈreɪl/ *vt* hacer descarrilar. **~ment** *n* descarrilamiento *m*

derelict /ˈderəlɪkt/ *adj* abandonado y en ruinas

deri|de /dɪˈraɪd/ *vt* mofarse de.

~sion /dɪ'rɪʒn/ *n* mofa *f.* **~sive** /dɪ'raɪsɪv/ *adj* burlón. **~sory** /dɪ'raɪsərɪ/ *adj* (offer etc) irrisorio

deriv|ation /derɪ'veɪʃn/ *n* derivación *f.* **~ative** /dɪ'rɪvətɪv/ *n* derivado *m.* **~e** /dɪ'raɪv/ *vt/i* derivar

derogatory /dɪ'rɒgətrɪ/ *adj* despectivo

descen|d /dɪ'send/ *vt/i* descender, bajar. **~dant** *n* descendiente *m & f.* **~t** *n* descenso *m*, bajada *f*; (*lineage*) ascendencia *f*

descri|be /dɪs'kraɪb/ *vt* describir. **~ption** /-'krɪpʃn/ *n* descripción *f.* **~ptive** /-'krɪptɪv/ *adj* descriptivo

desecrate /'desɪkreɪt/ *vt* profanar

desert[1] /dɪ'zɜ:t/ *vt* abandonar. ● *vi* (*Mil*) desertar. **~er** /dɪ'zɜ:tə(r)/ *n* desertor *m*

desert[2] /'dezət/ *adj & n* desierto (*m*)

deserts /dɪ'zɜ:ts/ *npl* lo merecido. **get one's just ~** llevarse su merecido

deserv|e /dɪ'zɜ:v/ *vt* merecer. **~ing** *adj* (cause) meritorio

design /dɪ'zaɪn/ *n* diseño *m*; (*plan*) plan *m.* **~s** (*intentions*) propósitos *mpl.* ● *vt* diseñar; (*plan*) planear

designate /'dezɪgneɪt/ *vt* designar

designer /dɪ'zaɪnə(r)/ *n* diseñador *m*; (*fashion* **~**) diseñador *m* de modas. ● *adj* (clothes) de diseño exclusivo

desirable /dɪ'zaɪərəbl/ *adj* deseable

desire /dɪ'zaɪə(r)/ *n* deseo *m.* ● *vt* desear

desk /desk/ *n* escritorio *m*; (*at school*) pupitre *m*; (*in hotel*) recepción *f*; (*Com*) caja *f.* **~top publishing** *n* autoedición *f*, edición *f* electrónica

desolat|e /'desələt/ *adj* desolado; (*uninhabited*) deshabitado. **~ion** /-'leɪʃn/ *n* desolación *f*

despair /dɪ'speə(r)/ *n* desesperación *f.* **be in ~** estar desesperado. ● *vi.* **~ of** desesperarse de

despatch /dɪ'spætʃ/ *vt, n* see **DISPATCH**

desperat|e /'despərət/ *adj* desesperado. **~ely** *adv* desesperadamente. **~ion** /-'reɪʃn/ *n* desesperación *f*

despicable /dɪ'spɪkəbl/ *adj* despreciable

despise /dɪ'spaɪz/ *vt* despreciar

despite /dɪ'spaɪt/ *prep* a pesar de

despondent /dɪ'spɒndənt/ *adj* abatido

despot /'despɒt/ *n* déspota *m*

dessert /dɪ'zɜ:t/ *n* postre *m.* **~spoon** *n* cuchara *f* de postre

destination /destɪ'neɪʃn/ *n* destino *m*

destiny /'destɪnɪ/ *n* destino *m*

destitute /'destɪtju:t/ *adj* indigente

destroy /dɪ'strɔɪ/ *vt* destruir. **~er** *n* destructor *m*

destructi|on /dɪ'strʌkʃn/ *n* destrucción *f.* **~ve** /-ɪv/ *adj* destructivo

desultory /'desəltrɪ/ *adj* desganado

detach /dɪ'tætʃ/ *vt* separar. **~able** *adj* separable. **~ed** *adj* (*aloof*) distante; (*house*) no adosado. **~ment** *n* desprendimiento *m*; (*Mil*) destacamento *m*; (*aloofness*) indiferencia *f*

detail /'di:teɪl/ *n* detalle *m.* **explain sth in ~** explicar algo detalladamente. ● *vt* detallar; (*Mil*) destacar. **~ed** *adj* detallado

detain /dɪ'teɪn/ *vt* detener; (*delay*) retener. **~ee** /di:teɪ'ni:/ *n* detenido *m*

d

d

detect /dɪ'tekt/ *vt* percibir; (*discover*) descubrir. **~ive** *n* (*private*) detective *m*; (*in police*) agente *m & f*. **~or** *n* detector *m*

detention /dɪ'tenʃn/ *n* detención *f*

deter /dɪ'tɜ:(r)/ *vt* (*pt* **deterred**) disuadir; (*prevent*) impedir

detergent /dɪ'tɜ:dʒənt/ *adj & n* detergente (*m*)

deteriorat|e /dɪ'tɪərɪəreɪt/ *vi* deteriorarse. **~ion** /-'reɪʃn/ *n* deterioro *m*

determin|ation /dɪtɜ:mɪ'neɪʃn/ *n* determinación *f*. **~e** /dɪ'tɜ:mɪn/ *vt* determinar; (*decide*) decidir. **~ed** *adj* determinado; (*resolute*) decidido

deterrent /dɪ'terənt/ *n* elemento *m* de disuasión

detest /dɪ'test/ *vt* aborrecer. **~able** *adj* odioso

detonat|e /'detəneɪt/ *vt* hacer detonar. ● *vi* detonar. **~ion** /-'neɪʃn/ *n* detonación *f*. **~or** *n* detonador *m*

detour /'di:tʊə(r)/ *n* rodeo *m*; (*Amer, of transport*) desvío *m*, desviación *f*. ● *vt* (*Amer*) desviar

detract /dɪ'trækt/ *vi*. **~ from** disminuir

detriment /'detrɪmənt/ *n*. **to the ~ of** en perjuicio de. **~al** /-'mentl/ *adj* perjudicial

devalue /di:'vælju:/ *vt* desvalorizar

devastat|e /'devəsteɪt/ *vt* devastar. **~ing** *adj* devastador; (*fig*) arrollador. **~ion** /-'steɪʃn/ *n* devastación *f*

develop /dɪ'veləp/ *vt* desarrollar; contraer (illness); urbanizar (land). ● *vi* desarrollarse; (*appear*) surgir. **~ing** *adj* (country) en vías de desarrollo. **~ment** *n* desarrollo *m*. **(new) ~ment** novedad *f*

deviant /'di:vɪənt/ *adj* desviado

deviat|e /'di:vɪeɪt/ *vi* desviarse. **~ion** /-'eɪʃn/ *n* desviación *f*

device /dɪ'vaɪs/ *n* dispositivo *m*; (*scheme*) estratagema *f*

devil /'devl/ *n* diablo *m*

devious /'di:vɪəs/ *adj* taimado

devise /dɪ'vaɪz/ *vt* idear

devoid /dɪ'vɔɪd/ *adj*. **be ~ of** carecer de

devolution /di:və'lu:ʃn/ *n* descentralización *f*; (*of power*) delegación *f*

devot|e /dɪ'vəʊt/ *vt* dedicar. **~ed** *adj* (couple) unido; (service) leal. **~ee** /devə'ti:/ *n* partidario *m*. **~ion** /-ʃn/ *n* devoción *f*

devour /dɪ'vaʊə(r)/ *vt* devorar

devout /dɪ'vaʊt/ *adj* devoto

dew /dju:/ *n* rocío *m*

dexterity /dek'sterətɪ/ *n* destreza *f*

diabet|es /daɪə'bi:ti:z/ *n* diabetes *f*. **~ic** /-'betɪk/ *adj & n* diabético (*m*)

diabolical /daɪə'bɒlɪkl/ *adj* diabólico

diagnos|e /'daɪəgnəʊz/ *vt* diagnosticar. **~is** /-'nəʊsɪs/ *n* (*pl* **-oses**/-si:z/) diagnóstico *m*

diagonal /daɪ'ægənl/ *adj & n* diagonal (*f*)

diagram /'daɪəgræm/ *n* diagrama *m*

dial /'daɪəl/ *n* cuadrante *m*; (*on clock, watch*) esfera *f*; (*on phone*) disco *m*. ● *vt* (*pt* **dialled**) marcar, discar (*LAm*)

dialect /'daɪəlekt/ *n* dialecto *m*

dialling: ~ **code** *n* prefijo *m*, código *m* de la zona (*LAm*). ~ **tone** *n* tono *m* de marcar, tono *m* de discado (*LAm*)

dialogue /'daɪəlɒg/ *n* diálogo *m*

dial tone *n* (*Amer*) *see* **DIALLING TONE**

diameter /daɪ'æmɪtə(r)/ *n* diámetro *m*

diamond /'daɪəmənd/ *n* diamante *m*; (*shape*) rombo *m*. **~s** *npl* (*Cards*) diamantes *mpl*

diaper /'daɪəpə(r)/ *n* (*Amer*) pañal *m*

diaphragm /'daɪəfræm/ *n* diafragma *m*

diarrhoea /daɪə'rɪə/ *n* diarrea *f*

diary /'daɪərɪ/ *n* diario *m*; (*book*) agenda *f*

dice /daɪs/ *n invar* dado *m*. ● *vt* (*Culin*) cortar en cubitos

dictat|e /dɪk'teɪt/ *vt/i* dictar. **~ion** /dɪk'teɪʃn/ *n* dictado *m*. **~or** *n* dictador *m*. **~orship** *n* dictadura *f*

dictionary /'dɪkʃənərɪ/ *n* diccionario *m*

did /dɪd/ *see* **DO**

didn't /'dɪdnt/ = **did not**

die /daɪ/ *vi* (*pres p* **dying**) morir. **be dying to** morirse por. □ **~ down** *vi* irse apagando. □ **~ out** *vi* extinguirse

diesel /'di:zl/ *n* (*fuel*) gasóleo *m*. **~ engine** *n* motor *m* diesel

diet /'daɪət/ *n* alimentación *f*; (*restricted*) régimen *m*. **be on a ~** estar a régimen. ● *vi* estar a régimen

differ /'dɪfə(r)/ *vi* ser distinto; (*disagree*) no estar de acuerdo. **~ence** /'dɪfrəns/ *n* diferencia *f*; (*disagreement*) desacuerdo *m*. **~ent** /'dɪfrənt/ *adj* distinto, diferente. **~ently** *adv* de otra manera

difficult /'dɪfɪkəlt/ *adj* difícil. **~y** *n* dificultad *f*

diffus|e /dɪ'fju:s/ *adj* difuso. ● /dɪ'fju:z/ *vt* difundir. ● *vi* difundirse. **~ion** /-ʒn/ *n* difusión *f*

dig /dɪg/ *n* (*poke*) empujón *m*; (*poke with elbow*) codazo *m*; (*remark*) indirecta *f*. **~s** *npl* 🄸 alojamiento *m* ● *vt* (*pt* **dug**, *pres p* **digging**) cavar; (*thrust*) empujar. ● *vi* cavar. □ **~ out** *vt* extraer. □ **~ up** *vt* desenterrar

digest /'daɪdʒest/ *n* resumen *m*. ● /daɪ'dʒest/ *vt* digerir. **~ion** /-'dʒestʃn/ *n* digestión *f*. **~ive** /-'dʒestɪv/ *adj* digestivo

digger /'dɪgə(r)/ *n* (*Mec*) excavadora *f*

digit /'dɪdʒɪt/ *n* dígito *m*; (*finger*) dedo *m*. **~al** /'dɪdʒɪtl/ *adj* digital

dignified /'dɪgnɪfaɪd/ *adj* solemne

dignitary /'dɪgnɪtərɪ/ *n* dignatario *m*

dignity /'dɪgnətɪ/ *n* dignidad *f*

digress /daɪ'gres/ *vi* divagar. **~ from** apartarse de. **~ion** /-ʃn/ *n* digresión *f*

dike /daɪk/ *n* dique *m*

dilapidated /dɪ'læpɪdeɪtɪd/ *adj* ruinoso

dilate /daɪ'leɪt/ *vt* dilatar. ● *vi* dilatarse

dilemma /daɪ'lemə/ *n* dilema *m*

diligent /'dɪlɪdʒənt/ *adj* diligente

dilute /daɪ'lju:t/ *vt* diluir

dim /dɪm/ *adj* (**dimmer**, **dimmest**) (light) débil; (room) oscuro; (*fam, stupid*) torpe. ● *vt* (*pt* **dimmed**) atenuar. **~ one's headlights** (*Amer*) poner las (luces) cortas *or* de cruce, poner las (luces) bajas (*LAm*). ● *vi* (light) irse atenuando

dime /daɪm/ *n* (*Amer*) *moneda de diez centavos*

dimension /daɪ'menʃn/ *n* dimensión *f*

diminish /dɪ'mɪnɪʃ/ *vt/i* disminuir

dimple /'dɪmpl/ *n* hoyuelo *m*

din /dɪn/ *n* jaleo *m*

dine /daɪn/ *vi* cenar. **~r** *n* comensal *m & f*; (*Amer, restaurant*) cafetería *f*

dinghy /ˈdɪŋgɪ/ *n* bote *m*; (*inflatable*) bote *m* neumático

dingy /ˈdɪndʒɪ/ *adj* (**-ier**, **-iest**) miserable, sucio

dinner /ˈdɪnə(r)/ *n* cena *f*, comida *f* (*LAm*). **have ~** cenar, comer (*LAm*). **~ party** *n* cena *f*, comida *f* (*LAm*)

dinosaur /ˈdaɪnəsɔ:(r)/ *n* dinosaurio *m*

dint /dɪnt/ *n*. **by ~ of** a fuerza de

dip /dɪp/ *vt* (*pt* **dipped**) meter; (*in liquid*) mojar. **~ one's headlights** poner las (luces) cortas *or* de cruce, poner las (luces) bajas (*LAm*). ● *vi* bajar. ● *n* (*slope*) inclinación *f*; (*in sea*) baño *m*. □ **~ into** *vt* hojear (book)

diphthong /ˈdɪfθɒŋ/ *n* diptongo *m*

diploma /dɪˈpləʊmə/ *n* diploma *m*

diploma|cy /dɪˈpləʊməsɪ/ *n* diplomacia *f*. **~t** /ˈdɪpləmæt/ *n* diplomático *m*. **~tic** /-ˈmætɪk/ *adj* diplomático

dipstick /ˈdɪpstɪk/ *n* (*Auto*) varilla *f* del nivel de aceite

dire /daɪə(r)/ *adj* (**-er**, **-est**) terrible; (need, poverty) extremo

direct /dɪˈrekt/ *adj* directo. ● *adv* directamente. ● *vt* dirigir; (*show the way*) indicar. **~ion** /-ʃn/ *n* dirección *f*. **~ions** *npl* instrucciones *fpl*. **~ly** *adv* directamente; (*at once*) en seguida. ● *conj* [!] en cuanto. **~or** *n* director *m*; (*of company*) directivo *m*

directory /dɪˈrektərɪ/ *n* guía *f*; (*Comp*) directorio *m*

dirt /dɜ:t/ *n* suciedad *f*. **~y** *adj* (**-ier**, **-iest**) sucio. ● *vt* ensuciar

disab|ility /dɪsəˈbɪlətɪ/ *n* invalidez *f*. **~le** /dɪsˈeɪbl/ *vt* incapacitar. **~led** *adj* minusválido

disadvantage /dɪsədˈvɑ:ntɪdʒ/ *n* desventaja *f*. **~d** *adj* desfavorecido

disagree /dɪsəˈgri:/ *vi* no estar de acuerdo (**with** con). **~ with** (food, climate) sentarle mal a. **~able** *adj* desagradable. **~ment** *n* desacuerdo *m*; (*quarrel*) riña *f*

disappear /dɪsəˈpɪə(r)/ *vi* desaparecer. **~ance** *n* desaparición *f*

disappoint /dɪsəˈpɔɪnt/ *vt* decepcionar. **~ing** *adj* decepcionante. **~ment** *n* decepción *f*

disapprov|al /dɪsəˈpru:vl/ *n* desaprobación *f*. **~e** /dɪsəˈpru:v/ *vi*. **~e of** desaprobar. **~ing** *adj* de reproche

disarm /dɪsˈɑ:m/ *vt* desarmar. ● *vi* desarmarse. **~ament** *n* desarme *m*

disarray /dɪsəˈreɪ/ *n* desorden *m*

disast|er /dɪˈzɑ:stə(r)/ *n* desastre *m*. **~rous** /-strəs/ *adj* catastrófico

disband /dɪsˈbænd/ *vt* disolver. ● *vi* disolverse

disbelief /dɪsbɪˈli:f/ *n* incredulidad *f*

disc /dɪsk/ *n* disco *m*

discard /dɪsˈkɑ:d/ *vt* descartar; abandonar (beliefs etc)

discern /dɪˈsɜ:n/ *vt* percibir. **~ing** *adj* exigente; (ear, eye) educado

discharge /dɪsˈtʃɑ:dʒ/ *vt* descargar; cumplir (duty); (*Mil*) licenciar. ● /ˈdɪstʃɑ:dʒ/ *n* descarga *f*; (*Med*) secreción *f*; (*Mil*) licenciamiento *m*

disciple /dɪˈsaɪpl/ *n* discípulo *m*

disciplin|ary /dɪsəˈplɪnərɪ/ *adj* disciplinario. **~e** /ˈdɪsɪplɪn/ *n* disciplina *f*. ● *vt* disciplinar; (*punish*) sancionar

disc jockey /ˈdɪskdʒɒkɪ/ *n* pin-

chadiscos *m & f*
disclaim /dɪs'kleɪm/ *vt* desconocer. **~er** *n* (*Jurid*) descargo *m* de responsabilidad
disclos|e /dɪs'kləʊz/ *vt* revelar. **~ure** /-ʒə(r)/ *n* revelación *f*
disco /'dɪskəʊ/ *n* (*pl* **-os**) [!] discoteca *f*
discolour /dɪs'kʌlə(r)/ *vt* decolorar. ● *vi* decolorarse
discomfort /dɪs'kʌmfət/ *n* malestar *m*; (*lack of comfort*) incomodidad *f*
disconcert /dɪskən'sɜ:t/ *vt* desconcertar
disconnect /dɪskə'nekt/ *vt* separar; (*Elec*) desconectar
disconsolate /dɪs'kɒnsələt/ *adj* desconsolado
discontent /dɪskən'tent/ *n* descontento *m*. **~ed** *adj* descontento
discontinue /dɪskən'tɪnju:/ *vt* interrumpir
discord /'dɪskɔ:d/ *n* discordia *f*; (*Mus*) disonancia *f*. **~ant** /-'skɔ:dənt/ *adj* discorde; (*Mus*) disonante
discotheque /'dɪskətek/ *n* discoteca *f*
discount /'dɪskaʊnt/ *n* descuento *m*. ● /dɪs'kaʊnt/ *vt* hacer caso omiso de; (*Com*) descontar
discourag|e /dɪs'kʌrɪdʒ/ *vt* desanimar; (*dissuade*) disuadir. **~ing** *adj* desalentador
discourteous /dɪs'kɜ:tɪəs/ *adj* descortés
discover /dɪs'kʌvə(r)/ *vt* descubrir. **~y** *n* descubrimiento *m*
discredit /dɪs'kredɪt/ *vt* (*pt* **discredited**) desacreditar. ● *n* descrédito *m*
discreet /dɪs'kri:t/ *adj* discreto. **~ly** *adv* discretamente
discrepancy /dɪ'skrepənsɪ/ *n* discrepancia *f*
discretion /dɪ'skreʃn/ *n* discreción *f*
discriminat|e /dɪs'krɪmɪneɪt/ *vt* discriminar. **~e between** distinguir entre. **~ing** *adj* perspicaz. **~ion** /-'neɪʃn/ *n* discernimiento *m*; (*bias*) discriminación *f*
discus /'dɪskəs/ *n* disco *m*
discuss /dɪ'skʌs/ *vt* discutir. **~ion** /-ʃn/ *n* discusión *f*
disdain /dɪs'deɪn/ *n* desdén *m*. **~ful** *adj* desdeñoso
disease /dɪ'zi:z/ *n* enfermedad *f*
disembark /dɪsɪm'bɑ:k/ *vi* desembarcar
disenchant|ed /dɪsɪn'tʃɑ:ntɪd/ *adj* desilusionado. **~ment** *n* desencanto *m*
disentangle /dɪsɪn'tæŋgl/ *vt* desenredar
disfigure /dɪs'fɪgə(r)/ *vt* desfigurar
disgrace /dɪs'greɪs/ *n* vergüenza *f*. ● *vt* deshonrar. **~ful** *adj* vergonzoso
disgruntled /dɪs'grʌntld/ *adj* descontento
disguise /dɪs'gaɪz/ *vt* disfrazar. ● *n* disfraz *m*. **in ~** disfrazado
disgust /dɪs'gʌst/ *n* repugnancia *f*, asco *m*. ● *vt* dar asco a. **~ed** *adj* indignado; (*stronger*) asqueado. **~ing** *adj* repugnante, asqueroso
dish /dɪʃ/ *n* plato *m*. **wash** *or* **do the ~es** fregar los platos, lavar los trastes (*Mex*). □ **~ up** *vt/i* servir. **~cloth** *n* bayeta *f*
disheartening /dɪs'hɑ:tnɪŋ/ *adj* desalentador
dishonest /dɪs'ɒnɪst/ *adj* deshonesto. **~y** *n* falta *f* de honradez
dishonour /dɪs'ɒnə(r)/ *n* deshonra *f*

d

dish: ~ **soap** *n* (*Amer*) lavavajillas *m*. ~ **towel** *n* paño *m* de cocina. ~**washer** *n* lavaplatos *m*, lavavajillas *m*. ~**washing liquid** *n* (*Amer*) *see* ~ SOAP

disillusion /dɪsɪ'luːʒn/ *vt* desilusionar. ~**ment** *n* desilusión *f*

disinfect /dɪsɪn'fekt/ *vt* desinfectar. ~**ant** *n* desinfectante *m*

disintegrate /dɪs'ɪntɪgreɪt/ *vt* desintegrar. ● *vi* desintegrarse

disinterested /dɪs'ɪntrəstɪd/ *adj* desinteresado

disjointed /dɪs'dʒɔɪntɪd/ *adj* inconexo

disk /dɪsk/ *n* disco *m*. ~ **drive** (*Comp*) unidad *f* de discos. ~**ette** /dɪs'ket/ *n* disquete *m*

dislike /dɪs'laɪk/ *n* aversión *f*. ● *vt*. I ~ **dogs** no me gustan los perros

dislocate /'dɪsləkeɪt/ *vt* dislocar(se) (limb)

dislodge /dɪs'lɒdʒ/ *vt* sacar

disloyal /dɪs'lɔɪəl/ *adj* desleal. ~**ty** *n* deslealtad *f*

dismal /'dɪzməl/ *adj* triste; (*bad*) fatal

dismantle /dɪs'mæntl/ *vt* desmontar

dismay /dɪs'meɪ/ *n* consternación *f*. ● *vt* consternar

dismiss /dɪs'mɪs/ *vt* despedir; (*reject*) rechazar. ~**al** *n* despido *m*; (*of idea*) rechazo *m*

dismount /dɪs'maʊnt/ *vi* desmontar

disobe|dience /dɪsə'biːdɪəns/ *n* desobediencia *f*. ~**dient** *adj* desobediente. ~**y** /dɪsə'beɪ/ *vt/i* desobedecer

disorder /dɪs'ɔːdə(r)/ *n* desorden *m*; (*ailment*) afección *f*. ~**ly** *adj* desordenado

disorganized /dɪs'ɔːgənaɪzd/ *adj* desorganizado

disorientate /dɪs'ɔːrɪənteɪt/ *vt* desorientar

disown /dɪs'əʊn/ *vt* repudiar

disparaging /dɪs'pærɪdʒɪŋ/ *adj* despreciativo

dispatch /dɪs'pætʃ/ *vt* despachar. ● *n* despacho *m*. ~ **rider** *n* mensajero *m*

dispel /dɪs'pel/ *vt* (*pt* **dispelled**) disipar

dispens|able /dɪs'pensəbl/ *adj* prescindible. ~**e** *vt* distribuir; (*Med*) preparar. □ ~ **with** *vt* prescindir de

dispers|al /dɪ'spɜːsl/ *n* dispersión *f*. ~**e** /dɪ'spɜːs/ *vt* dispersar. ● *vi* dispersarse

dispirited /dɪs'pɪrɪtɪd/ *adj* desanimado

display /dɪs'pleɪ/ *vt* exponer (goods); demostrar (feelings). ● *n* exposición *f*; (*of feelings*) demostración *f*

displeas|e /dɪs'pliːz/ *vt* desagradar. **be** ~**ed with** estar disgustado con. ~**ure** /-'pleʒə(r)/ *n* desagrado *m*

dispos|able /dɪs'pəʊzəbl/ *adj* desechable. ~**al** /dɪs'pəʊzl/ *n* (*of waste*) eliminación *f*. **at s.o.'s** ~**al** a la disposición de uno. ~**e of** /dɪs 'pəʊz/ *vt* deshacerse de

disproportionate /dɪsprə 'pɔːʃənət/ *adj* desproporcionado

disprove /dɪs'pruːv/ *vt* desmentir (claim); refutar (theory)

dispute /dɪs'pjuːt/ *vt* discutir. ● *n* disputa *f*. **in** ~ disputado

disqualif|ication /dɪskwɒlɪfɪ 'keɪʃn/ *n* descalificación *f*. ~**y** /dɪs 'kwɒlɪfaɪ/ *vt* incapacitar; (*Sport*) descalificar

disregard /dɪsrɪ'gɑːd/ *vt* no hacer caso de. ● *n* indiferencia *f* (**for** a)

disreputable /dɪsˈrepjʊtəbl/ *adj* de mala fama

disrespect /dɪsrɪˈspekt/ *n* falta *f* de respeto

disrupt /dɪsˈrʌpt/ *vt* interrumpir; trastornar (plans). **~ion** /-ʃn/ *n* trastorno *m*. **~ive** *adj* (influence) perjudicial, negativo

dissatis|faction /dɪsætɪsˈfækʃn/ *n* descontento *m*. **~fied** /dɪˈsætɪsfaɪd/ *adj* descontento

dissect /dɪˈsekt/ *vt* disecar

dissent /dɪˈsent/ *vi* disentir. ● *n* disentimiento *m*

dissertation /dɪsəˈteɪʃn/ *n* (*Univ*) tesis *f*

dissident /ˈdɪsɪdənt/ *adj & n* disidente (*m & f*)

dissimilar /dɪˈsɪmɪlə(r)/ *adj* distinto

dissolute /ˈdɪsəluːt/ *adj* disoluto

dissolve /dɪˈzɒlv/ *vt* disolver. ● *vi* disolverse

dissuade /dɪˈsweɪd/ *vt* disuadir

distan|ce /ˈdɪstəns/ *n* distancia *f*. **from a ~ce** desde lejos. **in the ~ce** a lo lejos. **~t** *adj* distante, lejano; (*aloof*) distante

distaste /dɪsˈteɪst/ *n* desagrado *m*. **~ful** *adj* desagradable

distil /dɪsˈtɪl/ *vt* (*pt* **distilled**) destilar. **~lery** /dɪsˈtɪlərɪ/ *n* destilería *f*

distinct /dɪsˈtɪŋkt/ *adj* distinto; (*clear*) claro; (*marked*) marcado. **~ion** /-ʃn/ *n* distinción *f*; (*in exam*) sobresaliente *m*. **~ive** *adj* distintivo

distinguish /dɪsˈtɪŋgwɪʃ/ *vt/i* distinguir. **~ed** *adj* distinguido

distort /dɪsˈtɔːt/ *vt* torcer. **~ion** /-ʃn/ *n* deformación *f*

distract /dɪsˈtrækt/ *vt* distraer. **~ed** *adj* distraído. **~ion** /-ʃn/ *n* distracción *f*; (*confusion*) aturdimiento *m*

distraught /dɪsˈtrɔːt/ *adj* consternado, angustiado

distress /dɪsˈtres/ *n* angustia *f*. ● *vt* afligir. **~ed** *adj* afligido. **~ing** *adj* penoso

distribut|e /dɪˈstrɪbjuːt/ *vt* repartir, distribuir. **~ion** /-ˈbjuːʃn/ *n* distribución *f*. **~or** *n* distribuidor *m*; (*Auto*) distribuidor *m* (del encendido)

district /ˈdɪstrɪkt/ *n* zona *f*, región *f*; (*of town*) barrio *m*

distrust /dɪsˈtrʌst/ *n* desconfianza *f*. ● *vt* desconfiar de

disturb /dɪsˈtɜːb/ *vt* molestar; (*perturb*) inquietar; (*move*) desordenar; (*interrupt*) interrumpir. **~ance** *n* disturbio *m*; (*tumult*) alboroto *m*. **~ed** *adj* trastornado. **~ing** *adj* inquietante

disused /dɪsˈjuːzd/ *adj* fuera de uso

ditch /dɪtʃ/ *n* zanja *f*; (*for irrigation*) acequia *f*. ● *vt* ▣ abandonar

dither /ˈdɪðə(r)/ *vi* vacilar

ditto /ˈdɪtəʊ/ *adv* ídem

divan /dɪˈvæn/ *n* diván *m*

dive /daɪv/ *vi* tirarse (al agua), zambullirse; (*rush*) meterse (precipitadamente). ● *n* (*into water*) zambullida *f*; (*Sport*) salto *m* (de trampolín); (*of plane*) descenso *m* en picado, descenso *m* en picada (*LAm*); (▣, *place*) antro *m*. **~r** *n* saltador *m*; (*underwater*) buzo *m*

diverge /daɪˈvɜːdʒ/ *vi* divergir. **~nt** *adj* divergente

divers|e /daɪˈvɜːs/ *adj* diverso. **~ify** *vt* diversificar. **~ity** *n* diversidad *f*

diver|sion /daɪˈvɜːʃn/ *n* desvío *m*; desviación *f*; (*distraction*) diversión *f*. **~t** /daɪˈvɜːt/ *vt* desviar; (*entertain*) divertir

d

divide /dɪ'vaɪd/ *vt* dividir. ● *vi* dividirse. **~d highway** *n* (*Amer*) autovía *f*, carretera *f* de doble pista

dividend /'dɪvɪdend/ *n* dividendo *m*

divine /dɪ'vaɪn/ *adj* divino

division /dɪ'vɪʒn/ *n* división *f*

divorce /dɪ'vɔ:s/ *n* divorcio *m*. ● *vt* divorciarse de. **get ~d** divorciarse. ● *vi* divorciarse. **~e** /dɪvɔ:'si:/ *n* divorciado *m*

divulge /daɪ'vʌldʒ/ *vt* divulgar

DIY *abbr see* DO-IT-YOURSELF

dizz|iness /'dɪzɪnɪs/ *n* vértigo *m*. **~y** *adj* (**-ier**, **-iest**) mareado. **be** *or* **feel ~y** marearse

DJ *abbr see* DISC JOCKEY

do /du://dʊ, də/

3rd person singular present **does;** past **did;** past participle **done**

● *transitive verb*

····▸ hacer. **he does what he wants** hace lo que quiere. **to do one's homework** hacer los deberes. **to do the cooking** preparar la comida, cocinar. **well done!** ¡muy bien!

····▸ (*clean*) lavar (dishes). limpiar (windows)

····▸ (*as job*) **what does he do?** ¿en qué trabaja?

····▸ (*swindle*) estafar. **I've been done!** ¡me han estafado!

····▸ (*achieve*) **she's done it!** ¡lo ha logrado!

● *intransitive verb*

····▸ hacer. **do as you're told!** ¡haz lo que se te dice!

····▸ (*fare*) **how are you doing?** (*with a task*) ¿qué tal te va? **how do you do?,** (*as greeting*) mucho gusto, encantado

····▸ (*perform*) **she did well/badly** le fue bien/mal

····▸ (*be suitable*) **will this do?** ¿esto sirve?

····▸ (*be enough*) ser suficiente, bastar. **one box will do** con una caja basta, con una caja es suficiente

● *auxiliary verb*

····▸ (*to form interrogative and negative*) **do you speak Spanish?** ¿hablas español?. **I don't want to** no quiero. **don't shut the door** no cierres la puerta

····▸ (*in tag questions*) **you eat meat, don't you?** ¿comes carne, ¿verdad? *or* ¿no? **he lives in London, doesn't he?** vive en Londres, ¿no? *or* ¿verdad? *or* ¿no es cierto?

····▸ (*in short answers*) **do you like it? - yes, I do** ¿te gusta? - sí. **who wrote it? - I did** ¿quién lo escribió? - yo

····▸ (*emphasizing*) **do come in!** ¡pase Ud!. **you do exaggerate!** ¡cómo exageras! ▫ **do away with** *vt* abolir. ▫ **do in** *vt* (*sl, kill*) eliminar. ▫ **do up** *vt* abrochar (coat etc); arreglar (house). ▫ **do with** *vt* (*need*) (*with can, could*) necesitar; (*expressing connection*) **it has nothing to do with that** no tiene nada que ver con eso. ▫ **do without** *vt* prescindir de

docile /'dəʊsaɪl/ *adj* dócil

dock /dɒk/ *n* (*Naut*) dársena *f*; (*wharf, quay*) muelle *m*; (*Jurid*) banquillo *m* de los acusados. **~s** *npl* (*port*) puerto *m*. ● *vt* cortar (tail);

atracar (ship). ● *vi* (ship) atracar. **~er** *n* estibador *m*. **~yard** *n* astillero *m*

doctor /'dɒktə(r)/ *n* médico *m*, doctor *m*

doctrine /'dɒktrɪn/ *n* doctrina *f*

document /'dɒkjʊmənt/ *n* documento *m*. **~ary** /-'mentrɪ/ *adj & n* documental (*m*)

dodg|e /dɒdʒ/ *vt* esquivar. ● *vi* esquivarse. ● *n* treta *f*. **~ems** /'dɒdʒəmz/ *npl* autos *mpl* de choque. **~y** *adj* (**-ier**, **-iest**) (*awkward*) difícil

doe /dəʊ/ *n* (*rabbit*) coneja *f*; (*hare*) liebre *f* hembra; (*deer*) cierva *f*

does /dʌz/ *see* **DO**

doesn't /'dʌznt/ = **does not**

dog /dɒg/ *n* perro *m*. ● *vt* (*pt* **dogged**) perseguir

dogged /'dɒgɪd/ *adj* obstinado

doghouse /'dɒghaʊs/ *n* (*Amer*) casa *f* del perro. **in the ~** 🄸 en desgracia

dogma /'dɒgmə/ *n* dogma *m*. **~tic** /-'mætɪk/ *adj* dogmático

do|ings *npl* actividades *fpl*. **~-it-yourself** /du:ɪtjɔ:'self/ *n* bricolaje *m*

dole /dəʊl/ *n* 🄸 subsidio *m* de paro, subsidio *m* de desempleo. **on the ~** 🄸 parado, desempleado. ▫ **~ out** *vt* distribuir

doleful /'dəʊlfl/ *adj* triste

doll /dɒl/ *n* muñeca *f*

dollar /'dɒlə(r)/ *n* dólar *m*

dollarization /dolərar'zeɪʃn/ *n* dolarización *f*

dollop /'dɒləp/ *n* 🄸 porción *f*

dolphin /'dɒlfɪn/ *n* delfín *m*

domain /dəʊ'meɪn/ *n* dominio *m*

dome /dəʊm/ *n* cúpula *f*

domestic /də'mestɪk/ *adj* doméstico; (trade, flights, etc) nacional. **~ated** /də'mestɪkeɪtɪd/ *adj* (animal) domesticado. **~ science** *n* economía *f* doméstica

domin|ance /'dɒmɪnəns/ *n* dominio *m*. **~ant** *adj* dominante. **~ate** /-eɪt/ *vt/i* dominar. **~ation** /-'neɪʃn/ *n* dominación *f*. **~eering** *adj* dominante

Dominican Republic /də 'mɪnɪkən/ *n* República *f* Dominicana

dominion /də'mɪnjən/ *n* dominio *m*

domino /'dɒmɪnəʊ/ *n* (*pl* **-oes**) ficha *f* de dominó. **~es** *npl* (*game*) dominó *m*

donat|e /dəʊ'neɪt/ *vt* donar. **~ion** /-ʃn/ *n* donativo *m*, donación *f*

done /dʌn/ *see* **DO**

donkey /'dɒŋkɪ/ *n* burro *m*, asno *m*. **~'s years** 🄸 siglos *mpl*

donor /'dəʊnə(r)/ *n* donante *m & f*

don't /dəʊnt/ = **do not**

doodle /'du:dl/ *vi/t* garrapatear

doom /du:m/ *n* destino *m*; (*death*) muerte *f*. ● *vt*. **be ~ed to** estar condenado a

door /dɔ:(r)/ *n* puerta *f*. **~bell** *n* timbre *m*. **~ knob** *n* pomo *m* (de la puerta). **~mat** *n* felpudo *m*. **~step** *n* peldaño *m*. **~way** *n* entrada *f*

dope /dəʊp/ *n* 🄸 droga *f*; (*sl, idiot*) imbécil *m*. ● *vt* 🄸 drogar

dormant /'dɔ:mənt/ *adj* aletargado, (volcano) inactivo

dormice /'dɔ:maɪs/ *see* **DORMOUSE**

dormitory /'dɔ:mɪtrɪ/ *n* dormitorio *m*

dormouse /'dɔ:maʊs/ *n* (*pl* **-mice**) lirón *m*

DOS /dɒs/ *abbr* (= **disc-operating system**) DOS *m*

d

dos|age /ˈdəʊsɪdʒ/ *n* dosis *f.* **~e** /dəʊs/ *n* dosis *f*

dot /dɒt/ *n* punto *m.* **on the ~** en punto. **~-com** *n* punto *m* com. **~-com company** empresa *f* puntocom

dote /dəʊt/ *vi.* **~ on** adorar

dotty /ˈdɒtɪ/ *adj* **(-ier, -iest)** ⓘ chiflado

double /ˈdʌbl/ *adj* doble. ● *adv* el doble. ● *n* doble *m*; (*person*) doble *m & f.* **at the ~** corriendo. ● *vt* doblar; redoblar (efforts etc). ● *vi* doblarse. **~ bass** /beɪs/ *n* contrabajo *m.* **~ bed** *n* cama *f* de matrimonio, cama *f* de doa plazas (*LAm*). **~ chin** *n* papada *f.* **~ click** *vt* hacer doble clic en. **~-cross** /-ˈkrɒs/ *vt* traicionar. **~-decker** /-ˈdekə(r)/ *n* autobús *m* de dos pisos. **~ Dutch** *n* ⓘ chino *m.* **~ glazing** /-ˈgleɪzɪŋ/ *n* doble ventana *f.* **~s** *npl* (*tennis*) dobles *mpl*

doubly /ˈdʌblɪ/ *adv* doblemente

doubt /daʊt/ *n* duda *f.* ● *vt* dudar; (*distrust*) dudar de. **~ful** *adj* dudoso. **~less** *adv* sin duda

dough /dəʊ/ *n* masa *f*; (*sl, money*) pasta *f* ⊠, lana *f* (*LAm fam*). **~nut** *n* donut *m*, dona *f* (*Mex*)

dove /dʌv/ *n* paloma *f*

down /daʊn/ *adv* abajo. **~ with** abajo. **come ~** bajar. **go ~** bajar; (sun) ponerse. ● *prep* abajo. ● *adj* ⓘ deprimido. ● *vt* derribar; (*fam, drink*) beber. ● *n* (*feathers*) plumón *m.* **~ and out** *adj* en la miseria. **~cast** *adj* abatido. **~fall** *n* perdición *f*; (*of king, dictator*) caída *f.* **~-hearted** /-ˈhɑ:tɪd/ *adj* abatido. **~hill** /-ˈhɪl/ *adv* cuesta abajo. **~load** /-ˈləʊd/ *vt* (*Comp*) bajar. **~market** /-ˈmɑ:kɪt/ *adj* (newspaper) popular; (store) barato. **~ payment** *n* depósito *m.* **~pour** *n* aguacero *m.* **~right** *adj* completo. ● *adv* completamente. **~s** *npl* colinas *fpl.* **~stairs** /-ˈsteəz/ *adv* abajo. ● /-steəz/ *adj* de abajo. **~stream** *adv* río abajo. **~-to-earth** /-tʊˈɜ:θ/ *adj* práctico. **~town** /-ˈtaʊn/ *n* centro *m* (de la ciudad). ● *adv.* **go ~town** ir al centro. **~ under** *adv* en las antípodas; (*in Australia*) en Australia. **~ward** /-wəd/ *adj & adv*, **~wards** *adv* hacia abajo

dowry /ˈdaʊərɪ/ *n* dote *f*

> **i**
>
> **Downing Street** Es una calle en el barrio londinense de Westminster. El número 10 es la residencia oficial del Primer Ministro y el 11, la del *Chancellor of the Exchequer* (Ministro de Economía y Hacienda). Los periodistas suelen utilizar las expresiones *Downing Street* o *Number 10* para referirse al Primer Ministro y al Gobierno.

doze /dəʊz/ *vi* dormitar

dozen /ˈdʌzn/ *n* docena *f.* **a ~ eggs** una docena de huevos. **~s of** ⓘ miles de, muchos

Dr /ˈdɒktə(r)/ *abbr* (**Doctor**)

drab /dræb/ *adj* monótono

draft /drɑ:ft/ *n* borrador *m*; (*Com*) letra *f* de cambio; (*Amer, Mil*) reclutamiento *m*; (*Amer, of air*) corriente *f* de aire. ● *vt* redactar el borrador de; (*Amer, conscript*) reclutar

drag /dræg/ *vt* (*pt* **dragged**) arrastrar. ● *n* ⓘ lata *f*

dragon /ˈdrægən/ *n* dragón *m.* **~fly** *n* libélula *f*

drain /dreɪn/ *vt* vaciar (tank, glass); drenar (land); (*fig*) agotar. ● *vi* escurrirse. ● *n* (*pipe*) sumidero *m*, resumidero *m* (*LAm*); (*plughole*) desagüe *m.* **~board** (*Amer*), **~ing**

board *n* escurridero *m*

drama /'drɑ:mə/ *n* drama *m*; (*art*) arte *m* teatral. **~tic** /drə'mætɪk/ *adj* dramático. **~tist** /'dræmətɪst/ *n* dramaturgo *m*. **~tize** /'dræmətaɪz/ *vt* adaptar al teatro; (*fig*) dramatizar

drank /dræŋk/ *see* **DRINK**

drape /dreɪp/ *vt* cubrir; (*hang*) colgar. **~s** *npl* (*Amer*) cortinas *fpl*

drastic /'dræstɪk/ *adj* drástico

draught /drɑ:ft/ *n* corriente *f* de aire. **~ beer** *n* cerveza *f* de barril. **~s** *npl* (*game*) juego *m* de damas *fpl*. **~y** *adj* lleno de corrientes de aire

draw /drɔ:/ *vt* (*pt* **drew**, *pp* **drawn**) tirar; (*attract*) atraer; dibujar (picture); trazar (line). **~ the line** trazar el límite. ● *vi* (*Art*) dibujar; (*Sport*) empatar; **~ near** acercarse. ● *n* (*Sport*) empate *m*; (*in lottery*) sorteo *m*. □ **~ in** *vi* (days) acortarse. □ **~ out** *vt* sacar (money). □ **~ up** *vi* pararse. *vt* redactar (document); acercar (chair). **~back** *n* desventaja *f*. **~bridge** *n* puente *m* levadizo

drawer /drɔ:(r)/ *n* cajón *m*, gaveta *f* (*Mex*). **~s** *npl* calzones *mpl*

drawing /'drɔ:ɪŋ/ *n* dibujo *m*. **~ pin** *n* tachuela *f*, chincheta *f*, chinche *f*. **~ room** *n* salón *m*

drawl /drɔ:l/ *n* habla *f* lenta

drawn /drɔ:n/ *see* **DRAW**

dread /dred/ *n* terror *m*. ● *vt* temer. **~ful** *adj* terrible. **~fully** *adv* terriblemente

dream /dri:m/ *n* sueño *m*. ● *vt/i* (*pt* **dreamed** *or* **dreamt** /dremt/) soñar. □ **~ up** *vt* idear. *adj* ideal. **~er** *n* soñador *m*

dreary /'drɪərɪ/ *adj* (**-ier**, **-iest**) triste; (*boring*) monótono

dredge /dredʒ/ *n* draga *f*. ● *vt* dragar. **~r** *n* draga *f*

dregs /dregz/ *npl* posos *mpl*, heces *fpl*; (*fig*) hez *f*

drench /drentʃ/ *vt* empapar

dress /dres/ *n* vestido *m*; (*clothing*) ropa *f*. ● *vt* vestir; (*decorate*) adornar; (*Med*) vendar. ● *vi* vestirse. □ **~ up** *vi* ponerse elegante. **~ up as** disfrazarse de. **~ circle** *n* primer palco *m*

dressing /'dresɪŋ/ *n* (*sauce*) aliño *m*; (*bandage*) vendaje *m*. **~-down** /-'daʊn/ *n* rapapolvo *m*, reprensión *f*. **~ gown** *n* bata *f*. **~ room** *n* vestidor *m*; (*in theatre*) camarín *m*. **~ table** *n* tocador *m*

dress: ~maker *n* modista *m & f*. **~making** *n* costura *f*. **~ rehearsal** *n* ensayo *m* general

drew /dru:/ *see* **DRAW**

dribble /'drɪbl/ *vi* (baby) babear; (*in football*) driblar, driblear

drie|d /draɪd/ *adj* (food) seco; (milk) en polvo. **~r** /'draɪə(r)/ *n* secador *m*

drift /drɪft/ *vi* ir a la deriva; (snow) amontonarse. ● *n* (*movement*) dirección *f*; (*of snow*) montón *m*

drill /drɪl/ *n* (*tool*) taladro *m*; (*of dentist*) torno *m*; (*training*) ejercicio *m*. ● *vt* taladrar, perforar; (*train*) entrenar. ● *vi* entrenarse

drink /drɪŋk/ *vt/i* (*pt* **drank**, *pp* **drunk**) beber, tomar (*LAm*). ● *n* bebida *f*. **~able** *adj* bebible; (water) potable. **~er** *n* bebedor *m*. **~ing water** *n* agua *f* potable

drip /drɪp/ *vi* (*pt* **dripped**) gotear. ● *n* gota *f*; (*Med*) goteo *m* intravenoso; (*fam, person*) soso *m*. **~-dry** /-'draɪ/ *adj* de lava y pon. **~ping** *adj*. **be ~ping wet** estar chorreando

drive /draɪv/ *vt* (*pt* **drove**, *pp*

driven) conducir, manejar (*LAm*) (car etc). ~ **s.o. mad** volver loco a uno. ~ **s.o. to do sth** llevar a uno a hacer algo. ● *vi* conducir, manejar (*LAm*). ~ **at** querer decir. ~ **in** (*in car*) entrar en coche. ● *n* paseo *m*; (*road*) calle *f*; (*private road*) camino *m* de entrada; (*fig*) empuje *m*. ~**r** *n* conductor *m*, chofer *m* (*LAm*). ~**r's license** *n* (*Amer*) *see* DRIVING LICENSE

d

drivel /'drɪvl/ *n* tonterías *fpl*

driving /'draɪvɪŋ/ *n* conducción *f*. ~ **licence** *n* permiso *m* de conducir, licencia *f* de conducción (*LAm*), licencia *f* (de manejar) (*Mex*). ~ **test** *n* examen *m* de conducir, examen *m* de manejar (*LAm*)

drizzle /'drɪzl/ *n* llovizna *f*. ● *vi* lloviznar

drone /drəʊn/ *n* zumbido *m*. ● *vi* zumbar

drool /dru:l/ *vi* babear

droop /dru:p/ *vi* inclinarse; (flowers) marchitarse

drop /drɒp/ *n* gota *f*; (*fall*) caída *f*; (*decrease*) descenso *m*. ● *vt* (*pt* **dropped**) dejar caer; (*lower*) bajar. ● *vi* caer. □ ~ **in on** *vt* pasar por casa de. □ ~ **off** *vi* (*sleep*) dormirse. □ ~ **out** *vi* retirarse; (student) abandonar los estudios. ~**out** *n* marginado *m*

drought /draʊt/ *n* sequía *f*

drove /drəʊv/ *see* DRIVE. ● *n* manada *f*

drown /draʊn/ *vt* ahogar. ● *vi* ahogarse

drowsy /'draʊzɪ/ *adj* soñoliento

drudgery /'drʌdʒərɪ/ *n* trabajo *m* pesado

drug /drʌg/ *n* droga *f*; (*Med*) medicamento *m*. ● *vt* (*pt* **drugged**) drogar. ~ **addict** *n* drogadicto *m*. ~**gist** *n* (*Amer*) farmacéutico *m*. ~**store** *n* (*Amer*) farmacia *f* (que vende otros artículos también)

drum /drʌm/ *n* tambor *m*; (*for oil*) bidón *m*. ● *vi* (*pt* **drummed**) tocar el tambor. ● *vt*. ~ **sth into s.o.** hacerle aprender algo a uno a fuerza de repetírselo. ~**mer** *n* tambor *m*; (*in group*) batería *f*. ~**s** *npl* batería *f*. ~**stick** *n* baqueta *f*; (*Culin*) muslo *m*

drunk /drʌŋk/ *see* DRINK. ● *adj* borracho. **get** ~ emborracharse. ● *n* borracho *m*. ~**ard** /-əd/ *n* borracho *m*. ~**en** *adj* borracho

dry /draɪ/ *adj* (**drier**, **driest**) seco. ● *vt* secar. ● *vi* secarse. □ ~ **up** *vi* (stream) secarse; (funds) agotarse. ~**-clean** *vt* limpiar en seco. ~**-cleaner's** tintorería *f*. ~**er** *n see* DRIER

DTD *abbrev* **Document Type Definition** DTD *m*

dual /'dju:əl/ *adj* doble. ~ **carriageway** *n* autovía *f*, carretera *f* de doble pista

dub /dʌb/ *vt* (*pt* **dubbed**) doblar (film)

dubious /'dju:bɪəs/ *adj* dudoso; (person) sospechoso

duchess /'dʌtʃɪs/ *n* duquesa *f*

duck /dʌk/ *n* pato *m*. ● *vt* sumergir; bajar (head). ● *vi* agacharse. ~**ling** /'dʌklɪŋ/ *n* patito *m*

duct /dʌkt/ *n* conducto *m*

dud /dʌd/ *adj* inútil; (cheque) sin fondos

due /dju:/ *adj* debido; (*expected*) esperado. ~ **to** debido a. ● *adv*. ~ **north** derecho hacia el norte. ~**s** *npl* derechos *mpl*

duel /'dju:əl/ *n* duelo *m*

duet /dju:'et/ *n* dúo *m*

duffel, **duffle** /'dʌfl/: ~ **bag** *n* bolsa *f* de lona. ~ **coat** *n* trenca *f*

dug /dʌg/ *see* DIG

duke /djuːk/ *n* duque *m*

dull /dʌl/ *adj* (**-er**, **-est**) (weather) gris; (colour) apagado; (person, play, etc) pesado; (sound) sordo

dumb /dʌm/ *adj* (**-er**, **-est**) mudo; [I] estúpido. □ **~ down** *vt* reducir el valor intelectual de. **~found** /dʌm'faʊnd/ *vt* pasmar

dummy /'dʌmɪ/ *n* muñeco *m*; (*of tailor*) maniquí *m*; (*for baby*) chupete *m*. ● *adj* falso. **~ run** prueba *f*

dump /dʌmp/ *vt* tirar, botar (*LAm*). ● *n* vertedero *m*; (*Mil*) depósito *m*; [I] lugar *m* desagradable. **be down in the ~s** estar deprimido

dumpling /'dʌmplɪŋ/ *n* bola *f* de masa hervida

Dumpster /'dʌmpstə(r)/ *n* (*Amer*, ®) contenedor *m* (para escombros)

dumpy /'dʌmpɪ/ *adj* (**-ier**, **-iest**) regordete

dunce /dʌns/ *n* burro *m*

dung /dʌŋ/ *n* (*manure*) estiércol *m*

dungarees /dʌŋgə'riːz/ *npl* mono *m*, peto *m*

dungeon /'dʌndʒən/ *n* calabozo *m*

dunk /dʌŋk/ *vt* remojar

dupe /djuːp/ *vt* engañar. ● *n* inocentón *m*

duplicat|e /'djuːplɪkət/ *adj & n* duplicado (*m*). ● /'djuːplɪkeɪt/ *vt* duplicar; (*on machine*) reproducir. **~ing machine**, **~or** *n* multicopista *f*

durable /'djʊərəbl/ *adj* durable

duration /djʊ'reɪʃn/ *n* duración *f*

duress /djʊ'res/ *n*. **under ~** bajo coacción

during /'djʊərɪŋ/ *prep* durante

dusk /dʌsk/ *n* anochecer *m*

dust /dʌst/ *n* polvo *m*. ● *vt* quitar el polvo a; (*sprinkle*) espolvorear (**with** con). **~bin** *n* cubo *m* de la basura, bote *m* de la basura (*Mex*). **~ cloth** (*Amer*), **~er** *n* trapo *m*. **~jacket** *n* sobrecubierta *f*. **~man** /-mən/ *n* basurero *m*. **~pan** *n* recogedor *m*. **~y** *adj* (**-ier**, **-iest**) polvoriento

d

Dutch /dʌtʃ/ *adj* holandés. ● *n* (*language*) holandés *m*. **the ~** (*people*) los holandeses. **~man** /-mən/ *m* holandés *m*. **~woman** *n* holandesa *f*

duty /'djuːtɪ/ *n* deber *m*; (*tax*) derechos *mpl* de aduana. **on ~** de servicio. **~-free** /-'friː/ *adj* libre de impuestos

duvet /'djuːveɪ/ *n* edredón *m*

dwarf /dwɔːf/ *n* (*pl* **-s** *or* **dwarves**) enano *m*

dwell /dwel/ *vi* (*pt* **dwelt** *or* **dwelled**) morar. □ **~ on** *vt* detenerse en. **~ing** *n* morada *f*

dwindle /'dwɪndl/ *vi* disminuir

dye /daɪ/ *vt* (*pres p* **dyeing**) teñir. ● *n* tinte *m*

dying /'daɪɪŋ/ *see* DIE

dynamic /daɪ'næmɪk/ *adj* dinámico. **~s** *npl* dinámica *f*

dynamite /'daɪnəmaɪt/ *n* dinamita *f*. ● *vt* dinamitar

dynamo /'daɪnəməʊ/ *n* (*pl* **-os**) dinamo *f*, dínamo *f*, dinamo *m* (*LAm*), dínamo *m* (*LAm*)

dynasty /'dɪnəstɪ/ *n* dinastía *f*

Ee

E *abbr* (= **East**) E

e

each /iːtʃ/ *adj* cada. ● *pron* cada uno. ~ **one** cada uno. ~ **other** uno a otro, el uno al otro. **they love** ~ **other** se aman

eager /ˈiːgə(r)/ *adj* impaciente; (*enthusiastic*) ávido. ~**ness** *n* impaciencia *f*; (*enthusiasm*) entusiasmo *m*

eagle /ˈiːgl/ *n* águila *f*

ear /ɪə(r)/ *n* oído *m*; (*outer*) oreja *f*; (*of corn*) espiga *f*. ~**ache** *n* dolor *m* de oído. ~**drum** *n* tímpano *m*

earl /ɜːl/ *n* conde *m*

early /ˈɜːlɪ/ *adj* (**-ier**, **-iest**) temprano; (*before expected time*) prematuro. ● *adv* temprano; (*ahead of time*) con anticipación

earn /ɜːn/ *vt* ganar; (*deserve*) merecer

earnest /ˈɜːnɪst/ *adj* serio. **in** ~ en serio

earnings /ˈɜːnɪŋz/ *npl* ingresos *mpl*; (*Com*) ganancias *fpl*

ear: ~**phone** *n* audífono *m*. ~**ring** *n* pendiente *m*, arete *m* (*LAm*). ~**shot** *n*. **within** ~**shot** al alcance del oído

earth /ɜːθ/ *n* tierra *f*. **the E**~ (*planet*) la Tierra. ● *vt* (*Elec*) conectar a tierra. ~**quake** *n* terremoto *m*

earwig /ˈɪəwɪg/ *n* tijereta *f*

ease /iːz/ *n* facilidad *f*; (*comfort*) tranquilidad *f*. **at** ~ a gusto; (*Mil*) en posición de descanso. **ill at** ~ molesto. **with** ~ fácilmente. ● *vt* calmar; aliviar (pain). ● *vi* calmarse; (*lessen*) disminuir

easel /ˈiːzl/ *n* caballete *m*

easily /ˈiːzɪlɪ/ *adv* fácilmente

east /iːst/ *n* este *m*. ● *adj* este, oriental; (wind) del este. ● *adv* hacia el este.

Easter /ˈiːstə(r)/ *n* Semana *f* Santa; (*Relig*) Pascua *f* de Resurrección. ~ **egg** *n* huevo *m* de Pascua

east: ~**erly** /-əli/ *adj* (wind) del este. ~**ern** /-ən/ *adj* este, oriental. ~**ward**/-wəd/, ~**wards** *adv* hacia el este

easy /ˈiːzɪ/ *adj* (**-ier**, **-iest**) fácil. ● *adv*. **go** ~ **on sth** Ⓘ no pasarse con algo. **take it** ~ tomarse las cosas con calma. ● *int* ¡despacio! ~ **chair** *n* sillón *m*. ~**going** /-ˈgəʊɪŋ/ *adj* acomodadizo

eat /iːt/ *vt/i* (*pt* **ate**, *pp* **eaten**) comer. □ ~ **into** *vt* corroer. ~**er** *n* comedor *m*

eaves /iːvz/ *npl* alero *m*. ~**drop** *vi* (*pt* **-dropped**). ~**drop (on)** escuchar a escondidas

ebb /eb/ *n* reflujo *m*. ● *vi* bajar; (*fig*) decaer

ebola /iːˈbəʊlə/ *n* Ébola *m*

ebony /ˈebənɪ/ *n* ébano *m*

EC /iːˈsiː/ *abbr* (= **European Community**) CE *f* (Comunidad *f* Europea)

eccentric /ɪkˈsentrɪk/ *adj* & *n* excéntrico (*m*). ~**ity** /eksenˈtrɪsətɪ/ *n* excentricidad *f*

echo /ˈekəʊ/ *n* (*pl* **-oes**) eco *m*. ● *vi* hacer eco

eclipse /ɪˈklɪps/ *n* eclipse *m*. ● *vt* eclipsar

ecolog|ical /iːkəˈlɒdʒɪkl/ *adj* ecológico. ~**y** *n* ecología *f*

e-commerce /iːˈkɒmɜːs/ *n* comercio *m* electrónico

econom|ic /iːkəˈnɒmɪk/ *adj* económico; ~ **refugee** refugiado *m* económico. **~ical** *adj* económico. **~ics** *n* economía *f*. **~ist** /ɪ'kɒnəmɪst/ *n* economista *m & f*. **~ize** /ɪ'kɒnəmaɪz/ *vi* economizar. **~ize on sth** economizar algo. **~y** /ɪ'kɒnəmɪ/ *n* economía *f*

ecsta|sy /'ekstəsɪ/ *n* éxtasis *f*. **~tic** /ɪk'stætɪk/ *adj* extático

Ecuador /'ekwədɔ:(r)/ *n* Ecuador *m*. **~ean** /ekwə'dɔ:rɪən/ *adj & n* ecuatoriano (*m*)

edg|e /edʒ/ *n* borde *m*; (*of knife*) filo *m*; (*of town*) afueras *fpl*. **have the ~e on** [I] llevar la ventaja a. **on ~e** nervioso. ● *vt* ribetear. ● *vi* avanzar cautelosamente. **~eways** *adv* de lado. **~y** *adj* nervioso

edible /'edɪbl/ *adj* comestible

edit /'edɪt/ *vt* dirigir (newspaper); preparar una edición de (text); editar (film). **~ion** /ɪ'dɪʃn/ *n* edición *f*. **~or** *n* (*of newspaper*) director *m*; (*of text*) redactor *m*. **~orial** /edɪ'tɔ:rɪəl/ *adj* editorial. ● *n* artículo *m* de fondo

Edinburgh Festival Es el principal acontecimiento cultural británico que, desde 1947, se celebra en agosto, en la capital de Escocia. El festival atrae a un gran número de visitantes y un aspecto muy importante del mismo son los espectáculos que no forman parte del programa oficial, que se conocen como *the Fringe*.

educat|e /'edʒʊkeɪt/ *vt* educar. **~ed** *adj* culto. **~ion** /-'keɪʃn/ *n* educación *f*; (*knowledge, culture*) cultura *f*. **~ional** /-'keɪʃənl/ *adj* instructivo

EC /i:i:'si:/ *abbr* (= **European Commission**) CE *f* (Comisión *f* Europea)

eel /i:l/ *n* anguila *f*

eerie /'ɪərɪ/ *adj* (**-ier**, **-iest**) misterioso

effect /ɪ'fekt/ *n* efecto *m*. **in ~** efectivamente. **take ~** entrar en vigor. **~ive** *adj* eficaz; (*striking*) impresionante; (*real*) efectivo. **~ively** *adv* eficazmente. **~iveness** *n* eficacia *f*

effeminate /ɪ'femɪnət/ *adj* afeminado

efficien|cy /ɪ'fɪʃənsɪ/ *n* eficiencia *f*; (*Mec*) rendimiento *m*. **~t** *adj* eficiente. **~tly** *adv* eficientemente

effort /'efət/ *n* esfuerzo *m*. **~less** *adj* fácil

e.g. /i:'dʒi:/ *abbr* (= **exempli gratia**) p.ej., por ejemplo

egg /eg/ *n* huevo *m*. □ **~ on** *vt* [I] incitar. **~cup** *n* huevera *f*. **~plant** *n* (*Amer*) berenjena *f*. **~shell** *n* cáscara *f* de huevo

ego /'i:gəʊ/ *n* (*pl* **-os**) yo *m*. **~ism** *n* egoísmo *m*. **~ist** *n* egoísta *m & f*. **~centric** /i:gəʊ'sentrɪk/ *adj* egocéntrico. **~tism** *n* egotismo *m*. **~tist** *n* egotista *m & f*

eh /eɪ/ *int* [I] ¡eh!

eiderdown /'aɪdədaʊn/ *n* edredón *m*

eight /eɪt/ *adj & n* ocho (*m*). **~een** /eɪ'ti:n/ *adj & n* dieciocho (*m*). **~eenth** *adj* decimoctavo. ● *n* dieciochavo *m*. **~h** /eɪtθ/ *adj & n* octavo (*m*) **~ieth** /'eɪtɪəθ/ *adj* octogésimo. ● *n* ochentavo *m*. **~y** /'eɪtɪ/ *adj & n* ochenta (*m*)

either /'aɪðə(r)/ *adj* cualquiera de los dos; (*negative*) ninguno de los dos; (*each*) cada. ● *pron* uno u otro; (*with negative*) ni uno ni otro. ● *adv* (*negative*) tampoco. ● *conj* o. ~

Tuesday or Wednesday o el martes o el miércoles; (*with negative*) ni el martes ni el miércoles

eject /ɪ'dʒekt/ *vt* expulsar

eke /i:k/ *vt*. ~ **out** hacer alcanzar (resources). ~ **out a living** ganarse la vida a duras penas

elaborate /ɪ'læbərət/ *adj* complicado. ● /ɪ'læbəreɪt/ *vt* elaborar. ● /ɪ'læbəreɪt/ *vi* explicarse

elapse /ɪ'læps/ *vi* transcurrir

elastic /ɪ'læstɪk/ *adj* & *n* elástico (*m*). ~ **band** *n* goma *f* (elástica), liga *f* (*Mex*)

elat|ed /ɪ'leɪtɪd/ *adj* regocijado. ~**ion** /-ʃn/ *n* regocijo *m*

elbow /'elbəʊ/ *n* codo *m*. ● *vt* dar un codazo a

elder /'eldə(r)/ *adj* mayor. ● *n* mayor *m* & *f*; (*tree*) saúco *m*. ~**ly** /'eldəlɪ/ *adj* mayor, anciano

eldest /'eldɪst/ *adj* & *n* mayor (*m* & *f*)

elect /ɪ'lekt/ *vt* elegir. ~ **to do** decidir hacer. ● *adj* electo. ~**ion** /-ʃn/ *n* elección *f*. ~**or** *n* elector *m*. ~**oral** *adj* electoral. ~**orate** /-ət/ *n* electorado *m*

electric /ɪ'lektrɪk/ *adj* eléctrico. ~**al** *adj* eléctrico. ~ **blanket** *n* manta *f* eléctrica. ~**ian** /ɪlek'trɪʃn/ *n* electricista *m* & *f*. ~**ity** /ɪlek'trɪsətɪ/ *n* electricidad *f*

electrify /ɪ'lektrɪfaɪ/ *vt* electrificar; (*fig*) electrizar

electrocute /ɪ'lektrəkju:t/ *vt* electrocutar

electrode /ɪ'lektrəʊd/ *n* electrodo *m*

electron /ɪ'lektrɒn/ *n* electrón *m*

electronic /ɪlek'trɒnɪk/ *adj* electrónico. ~ **mail** *n* correo *m* electrónico. ~**s** *n* electrónica *f*

elegan|ce /'elɪgəns/ *n* elegancia *f*. ~**t** *adj* elegante. ~**tly** *adv* elegantemente

element /'elɪmənt/ *n* elemento *m*. ~**ary** /-'mentrɪ/ *adj* elemental. ~**ary school** *n* (*Amer*) escuela *f* primaria

elephant /'elɪfənt/ *n* elefante *m*

elevat|e /'elɪveɪt/ *vt* elevar. ~**ion** /-'veɪʃn/ *n* elevación *f*. ~**or** *n* (*Amer*) ascensor *m*

eleven /ɪ'levn/ *adj* & *n* once (*m*). ~**th** *adj* undécimo. ● *n* onceavo *m*

elf /elf/ *n* (*pl* **elves**) duende *m*

eligible /'elɪdʒəbl/ *adj* elegible. **be** ~ **for** tener derecho a

eliminat|e /ɪ'lɪmɪneɪt/ *vt* eliminar. ~**ion** /-'neɪʃn/ *n* eliminación *f*

élite /eɪ'li:t/ *n* elite *f*, élite *f*

ellip|se /ɪ'lɪps/ *n* elipse *f*. ~**tical** *adj* elíptico

elm /elm/ *n* olmo *m*

elope /ɪ'ləʊp/ *vi* fugarse con el amante

eloquen|ce /'eləkwəns/ *n* elocuencia *f*. ~**t** *adj* elocuente

El Salvador /el'sælvədɔ:(r)/ *n* El Salvador

else /els/ *adv*. **somebody** ~ otra persona. **everybody** ~ todos los demás. **nobody** ~ ningún otro, nadie más. **nothing** ~ nada más. **or** ~ o bien. **somewhere** ~ en otra parte. ~**where** *adv* en otra parte

elu|de /ɪ'lu:d/ *vt* eludir. ~**sive** /-sɪv/ *adj* esquivo

elves /elvz/ *see* ELF

emaciated /ɪ'meɪʃɪeɪtɪd/ *adj* consumido

email, e-mail /'i:meɪl/ *n* correo *m* electrónico, correo-e *m*. ● *vt* mandar por correo electrónico, emailear. ~ **address** *n* casilla *f* electrónica, dirección *f* de correo electrónico

emancipat|e /ɪ'mænsɪpeɪt/ *vt* emancipar. **~ion** /-'peɪʃn/ *n* emancipación *f*

embankment /ɪm'bæŋkmənt/ *n* terraplén *m*; (*of river*) dique *m*

embargo /ɪm'bɑːgəʊ/ *n* (*pl* **-oes**) embargo *m*

embark /ɪm'bɑːk/ *vi* embarcarse. **~ on** (*fig*) emprender. **~ation** /embɑː'keɪʃn/ *n* embarque *m*

embarrass /ɪm'bærəs/ *vt* avergonzar. **~ed** *adj* avergonzado. **~ing** *adj* embarazoso. **~ment** *n* vergüenza *f*

embassy /'embəsɪ/ *n* embajada *f*

embellish /ɪm'belɪʃ/ *vt* adornar. **~ment** *n* adorno *m*

embers /'embəz/ *npl* ascuas *fpl*

embezzle /ɪm'bezl/ *vt* desfalcar. **~ment** *n* desfalco *m*

emblem /'embləm/ *n* emblema *m*

embrace /ɪm'breɪs/ *vt* abrazar; (*fig*) abarcar. ● *vi* abrazarse. ● *n* abrazo *m*

embroider /ɪm'brɔɪdə(r)/ *vt* bordar. **~y** *n* bordado *m*

embroil /ɪm'brɔɪl/ *vt* enredar

embryo /'embrɪəʊ/ *n* (*pl* **-os**) embrión *m*. **~nic** /-'ɒnɪk/ *adj* embrionario

emend /ɪ'mend/ *vt* enmendar

emerald /'emərəld/ *n* esmeralda *f*

emerge /ɪ'mɜːdʒ/ *vi* salir. **~nce** /-əns/ *n* aparición *f*

emergency /ɪ'mɜːdʒənsɪ/ *n* emergencia *f*; (*Med*) urgencia *f*. **in an ~** en caso de emergencia. **~ exit** *n* salida *f* de emergencia. **~ room** urgencias *fpl*

emigra|nt /'emɪgrənt/ *n* emigrante *m & f*. **~te** /'emɪgreɪt/ *vi* emigrar. **~tion** /-'greɪʃn/ *n* emigración *f*

eminen|ce /'emɪnəns/ *n* eminencia *f*. **~t** *adj* eminente.

emi|ssion /ɪ'mɪʃn/ *n* emisión *f*. **~t** *vt* (*pt* **emitted**) emitir

emoti|on /ɪ'məʊʃn/ *n* emoción *f*. **~onal** *adj* emocional; (person) emotivo; (*moving*) conmovedor. **~ve** /ɪ'məʊtɪv/ *adj* emotivo

empathy /'empəθɪ/ *n* empatía *f*

emperor /'empərə(r)/ *n* emperador *m*

empha|sis /'emfəsɪs/ *n* (*pl* **~ses** /-siːz/) énfasis *m*. **~size** /'emfəsaɪz/ *vt* enfatizar. **~tic** /ɪm'fætɪk/ *adj* (gesture) enfático; (assertion) categórico

empire /'empaɪə(r)/ *n* imperio *m*

empirical /ɪm'pɪrɪkl/ *adj* empírico

employ /ɪm'plɔɪ/ *vt* emplear. **~ee** /emplɔɪ'iː/ *n* empleado *m*. **~er** *n* patrón *m*. **~ment** *n* empleo *m*. **~ment agency** *n* agencia *f* de trabajo

empower /ɪm'paʊə(r)/ *vt* autorizar (**to do** a hacer)

empress /'emprɪs/ *n* emperatriz *f*

empty /'emptɪ/ *adj* vacío; (promise) vano. **on an ~y stomach** con el estómago vacío. ● *n* ! envase *m* (vacío). ● *vt* vaciar. ● *vi* vaciarse

emulate /'emjʊleɪt/ *vt* emular

emulsion /ɪ'mʌlʃn/ *n* emulsión *f*

enable /ɪ'neɪbl/ *vt*. **~ s.o. to do sth** permitir a uno hacer algo

enact /ɪ'nækt/ *vt* (*Jurid*) decretar; (*in theatre*) representar

enamel /ɪ'næml/ *n* esmalte *m*. ● *vt* (*pt* **enamelled**) esmaltar

enchant /ɪn'tʃɑːnt/ *vt* encantar. **~ing** *adj* encantador. **~ment** *n* encanto *m*

encircle /ɪn'sɜːkl/ *vt* rodear

enclave /ˈenkleɪv/ *n* enclave *m*
enclos|e /ɪnˈkləʊz/ *vt* cercar (land); (*Com*) adjuntar. **~ed** *adj* (space) cerrado; (*Com*) adjunto. **~ure** /ɪnˈkləʊʒə(r)/ *n* cercamiento *m*
encode /ɪnˈkəʊd/ *vt* codificar, cifrar
encore /ˈɒŋkɔː(r)/ *int* ¡otra! ● *n* bis *m*, repetición *f*
encounter /ɪnˈkaʊntə(r)/ *vt* encontrar. ● *n* encuentro *m*
encourag|e /ɪnˈkʌrɪdʒ/ *vt* animar; (*stimulate*) fomentar. **~ement** *n* ánimo *m*. **~ing** *adj* alentador
encroach /ɪnˈkrəʊtʃ/ *vi*. **~ on** invadir (land); quitar (time)
encyclopaedi|a /ɪnsaɪkləˈpiːdɪə/ *n* enciclopedia *f*. **~c** *adj* enciclopédico
end /end/ *n* fin *m*; (*furthest point*) extremo *m*. **in the ~** por fin. **make ~s meet** poder llegar a fin de mes. **put an ~ to** poner fin a. **no ~ of** muchísimos. **on ~** de pie; (*consecutive*) seguido. ● *vt/i* terminar, acabar
endanger /ɪnˈdeɪndʒə(r)/ *vt* poner en peligro. **~ed** *adj* (species) en peligro
endearing /ɪnˈdɪərɪŋ/ *adj* simpático
endeavour /ɪnˈdevə(r)/ *n* esfuerzo *m*, intento *m*. ● *vi*. **~ to** esforzarse por
ending /ˈendɪŋ/ *n* fin *m*
endless /ˈendlɪs/ *adj* interminable
endorse /ɪnˈdɔːs/ *vt* endosar; (*fig*) aprobar. **~ment** *n* endoso *m*; (*fig*) aprobación *f*; (*Auto*) nota *f* de inhabilitación
endur|ance /ɪnˈdjʊərəns/ *n* resistencia *f*. **~e** /ɪnˈdjʊə(r)/ *vt* aguantar. **~ing** *adj* perdurable
enemy /ˈenəmɪ/ *n* & *a* enemigo (*m*)
energ|etic /enəˈdʒetɪk/ *adj* enérgico. **~y** /ˈenədʒɪ/ *n* energía *f*
enforce /ɪnˈfɔːs/ *vt* hacer cumplir (law); hacer valer (claim). **~d** *adj* forzado
engag|e /ɪnˈgeɪdʒ/ *vt* emplear (staff); captar (attention); (*Mec*) hacer engranar. ● *vi* (*Mec*) engranar. **~e in** dedicarse a. **~ed** *adj* prometido, comprometido (*LAm*); (*busy*) ocupado. **be ~ed** (*of phone*) estar comunicando, estar ocupado (*LAm*). **get ~ed** prometerse, comprometerse (*LAm*). **~ement** *n* compromiso *m*
engine /ˈendʒɪn/ *n* motor *m*; (*of train*) locomotora *f*. **~ driver** *n* maquinista *m*
engineer /endʒɪˈnɪə(r)/ *n* ingeniero *m*; (*mechanic*) mecánico *m*; (*Amer, Rail*) maquinista *m*. ● *vt* (*contrive*) fraguar. **~ing** *n* ingeniería *f*
England /ˈɪŋglənd/ *n* Inglaterra *f*
English /ˈɪŋglɪʃ/ *adj* inglés. ● *n* (*language*) inglés *m*. ● *npl*. **the ~** los ingleses. **~man** /-mən/ *n* inglés *m*. **~woman** *n* inglesa *f*
engrav|e /ɪnˈgreɪv/ *vt* grabar. **~ing** *n* grabado *m*
engrossed /ɪnˈgrəʊst/ *adj* absorto
engulf /ɪnˈgʌlf/ *vt* envolver
enhance /ɪnˈhɑːns/ *vt* realzar; aumentar (value)
enigma /ɪˈnɪgmə/ *n* enigma *m*. **~tic** /enɪgˈmætɪk/ *adj* enigmático
enjoy /ɪnˈdʒɔɪ/ *vt*. **I ~ reading** me gusta la lectura. **~ o.s.** divertirse. **~able** *adj* agradable. **~ment** *n* placer *m*
enlarge /ɪnˈlɑːdʒ/ *vt* agrandar;

(*Photo*) ampliar. ● *vi* agrandarse. ~ **upon** extenderse sobre. ~**ment** *n* (*Photo*) ampliación *f*

enlighten /ɪn'laɪtn/ *vt* ilustrar. ~**ment** *n*. **the E~ment** el siglo de la luces

enlist /ɪn'lɪst/ *vt* alistar; conseguir (support). ● *vi* alistarse

enliven /ɪn'laɪvn/ *vt* animar

enorm|ity /ɪ'nɔ:mətɪ/ *n* enormidad *f*. ~**ous** /ɪ'nɔ:məs/ *adj* enorme. ~**ously** *adv* enormemente

enough /ɪ'nʌf/ *adj & adv* bastante. ● *n* bastante *m*, suficiente *m*. ● *int* ¡basta!

enquir|e /ɪn'kwaɪə(r)/ *vt/i* preguntar. ~**e about** informarse de. ~**y** *n* pregunta *f*; (*investigation*) investigación *f*

enrage /ɪn'reɪdʒ/ *vt* enfurecer

enrol /ɪn'rəʊl/ *vt* (*pt* **enrolled**) inscribir, matricular (student). ● *vi* inscribirse, matricularse

ensue /ɪn'sju:/ *vi* seguir

ensure /ɪn'ʃʊə(r)/ *vt* asegurar

entail /ɪn'teɪl/ *vt* suponer; acarrear (expense)

entangle /ɪn'tæŋgl/ *vt* enredar. ~**ment** *n* enredo *m*

enter /'entə(r)/ *vt* entrar en, entrar a (*esp LAm*); presentarse a (competition); inscribirse en (race); (*write*) escribir. ● *vi* entrar

enterpris|e /'entəpraɪz/ *n* empresa *f*; (*fig*) iniciativa *f*. ~**ing** *adj* emprendedor

entertain /entə'teɪn/ *vt* entretener; recibir (guests); abrigar (ideas, hopes); (*consider*) considerar. ~**ing** *adj* entretenido. ~**ment** *n* entretenimiento *m*; (*show*) espectáculo *m*

enthral /ɪn'θrɔ:l/ *vt* (*pt* **enthralled**) cautivar

enthuse /ɪn'θju:z/ *vi*. ~ **over** entusiasmarse por

enthusias|m /ɪn'θju:zɪæzəm/ *n* entusiasmo *m*. ~**t** *n* entusiasta *m & f*. ~**tic** /-'æstɪk/ *adj* entusiasta. ~**tically** *adv* con entusiasmo

entice /ɪn'taɪs/ *vt* atraer

entire /ɪn'taɪə(r)/ *adj* entero. ~**ly** *adv* completamente. ~**ty** /ɪn'taɪərətɪ/ *n*. **in its** ~**ty** en su totalidad

entitle /ɪn'taɪtl/ *vt* titular; (*give a right*) dar derecho a. **be** ~**d to** tener derecho a. ~**ment** *n* derecho *m*

entity /'entətɪ/ *n* entidad *f*

entrails /'entreɪlz/ *npl* entrañas *fpl*

entrance /'entrəns/ *n* entrada *f*. ● /ɪn'trɑ:ns/ *vt* encantar

entrant /'entrənt/ *n* participante *m & f*; (*in exam*) candidato *m*

entreat /ɪn'tri:t/ *vt* suplicar. ~**y** *n* súplica *f*

entrenched /ɪn'trentʃt/ *adj* (position) afianzado

entrust /ɪn'trʌst/ *vt* confiar

entry /'entrɪ/ *n* entrada *f*

entwine /ɪn'twaɪn/ *vt* entrelazar

enumerate /ɪ'nju:məreɪt/ *vt* enumerar

envelop /ɪn'veləp/ *vt* envolver

envelope /'envələʊp/ *n* sobre *m*

enviable /'envɪəbl/ *adj* envidiable

envious /'envɪəs/ *adj* envidioso

environment /ɪn'vaɪərənmənt/ *n* medio *m* ambiente. ~**al** /-'mentl/ *adj* ambiental

envisage /ɪn'vɪzɪdʒ/ *vt* prever; (*imagine*) imaginar

envision /ɪn'vɪʒn/ *vt* (*Amer*) prever

envoy /'envɔɪ/ *n* enviado *m*

envy /'envɪ/ *n* envidia *f*. ● *vt* envidiar

enzyme /'enzaɪm/ *n* enzima *f*

ephemeral /ɪ'femərəl/ *adj*

efímero
epic /'epɪk/ *n* épica *f*. ● *adj* épico
epidemic /epɪ'demɪk/ *n* epidemia *f*. ● *adj* epidémico
epilep|sy /'epɪlepsɪ/ *n* epilepsia *f*. **~tic** /-'leptɪk/ *adj & n* epiléptico (*m*)
epilogue /'epɪlɒg/ *n* epílogo *m*
episode /'epɪsəʊd/ *n* episodio *m*
epitaph /'epɪtɑ:f/ *n* epitafio *m*
epitom|e /ɪ'pɪtəmɪ/ *n* personificación *f*, epítome *m*. **~ize** *vt* ser la personificación de
epoch /'i:pɒk/ *n* época *f*
equal /'i:kwəl/ *adj & n* igual (*m & f*). **~ to** (*a task*) a la altura de. ● *vt* (*pt* **equalled**) ser igual a; (*Math*) ser. **~ity** /ɪ'kwɒlətɪ/ *n* igualdad *f*. **~ize** *vt* igualar. ● *vi* (*Sport*) emapatar. **~izer** *n* (*Sport*) gol *m* del empate. **~ly** *adv* igualmente; (share) por igual
equation /ɪ'kweɪʒn/ *n* ecuación *f*
equator /ɪ'kweɪtə(r)/ *n* ecuador *m*. **~ial** /ekwə'tɔ:rɪəl/ *adj* ecuatorial
equilibrium /i:kwɪ'lɪbrɪəm/ *n* equilibrio *m*
equinox /'i:kwɪnɒks/ *n* equinoccio *m*
equip /ɪ'kwɪp/ *vt* (*pt* **equipped**) equipar. **~ sth with** proveer algo de. **~ment** *n* equipo *m*
equivalen|ce /ɪ'kwɪvələns/ *n* equivalencia *f*. **~t** *adj & n* equivalente (*m*). **be ~t to** equivaler
equivocal /ɪ'kwɪvəkl/ *adj* equívoco
era /'ɪərə/ *n* era *f*
eradicate /ɪ'rædɪkeɪt/ *vt* erradicar, extirpar
erase /ɪ'reɪz/ *vt* borrar. **~r** *n* goma *f* (de borrar)
erect /ɪ'rekt/ *adj* erguido. ● *vt* levantar. **~ion** /-ʃn/ *n* construcción *f*; (*physiology*) erección *f*
ero|de /ɪ'rəʊd/ *vt* erosionar. **~sion** /-ʒn/ *n* erosión *f*
erotic /ɪ'rɒtɪk/ *adj* erótico
err /ɜ:(r)/ *vi* errar; (*sin*) pecar
errand /'erənd/ *n* recado *m*, mandado *m* (*LAm*)
erratic /ɪ'rætɪk/ *adj* desigual; (person) voluble
erroneous /ɪ'rəʊnɪəs/ *adj* erróneo
error /'erə(r)/ *n* error *m*
erudit|e /'eru:daɪt/ *adj* erudito. **~ion** /-'dɪʃn/ *n* erudición *f*
erupt /ɪ'rʌpt/ *vi* entrar en erupción; (*fig*) estallar. **~ion** /-ʃn/ *n* erupción *f*
escalat|e /'eskəleɪt/ *vt* intensificar. ● *vi* intensificarse. **~ion** /-'leɪʃn/ *n* intensificación *f*. **~or** *n* escalera *f* mecánica
escapade /eskə'peɪd/ *n* aventura *f*
escap|e /ɪ'skeɪp/ *vi* escaparse. ● *vt* evitar. ● *n* fuga *f*; (*of gas, water*) escape *m*. **have a narrow ~e** escapar por un pelo. **~ism** /-ɪzəm/ *n* escapismo *m*
escort /'eskɔ:t/ *n* acompañante *m*; (*Mil*) escolta *f*. ● /ɪ'skɔ:t/ *vt* acompañar; (*Mil*) escoltar
Eskimo /'eskɪməʊ/ *n* (*pl* **-os** *or invar*) esquimal *m & f*
especial /ɪ'speʃl/ *adj* especial. **~ly** *adv* especialmente
espionage /'espɪənɑ:ʒ/ *n* espionaje *m*
Esq. /ɪ'skwaɪə(r)/ *abbr* (= **Esquire**) (*in address*) **E. Ashton, ~** Sr. Don E. Ashton
essay /'eseɪ/ *n* ensayo *m*; (*at school*) composición *f*
essence /'esns/ *n* esencia *f*. **in ~** esencialmente

essential /ɪ'senʃl/ *adj* esencial. ● *n* elemento *m* esencial. **~ly** *adv* esencialmente

establish /ɪ'stæblɪʃ/ *vt* establecer. **~ment** *n* establecimiento *m*. **the E~ment** los que mandan, el sistema

estate /ɪ'steɪt/ *n* finca *f*; (*housing estate*) complejo *m* habitacional, urbanización *f*, fraccionamiento *m* (*Mex*); (*possessions*) bienes *mpl*. **~ agent** *n* agente *m* inmobiliario. **~ car** *n* ranchera *f*, (coche *m*) familiar *m*, camioneta *f* (*LAm*)

esteem /ɪ'sti:m/ *n* estima *f*

estimat|e /'estɪmət/ *n* cálculo *m*; (*Com*) presupuesto *m*. ● /'estɪmeɪt/ *vt* calcular. **~ion** /-'meɪʃn/ *n* estimación *f*; (*opinion*) opinión *f*

estranged /ɪs'treɪndʒd/ *adj* alejado

estuary /'estʃʊərɪ/ *n* estuario *m*

etc /et'setrə/ *abbr* (= **et cetera**) etc., etcétera

etching /'etʃɪŋ/ *n* aguafuerte *m*

etern|al /ɪ'tɜ:nl/ *adj* eterno. **~ity** /-ətɪ/ *n* eternidad *f*

ether /'i:θə(r)/ *n* éter *m*

ethic /'eθɪk/ *n* ética *f*. **~al** *adj* ético. **~s** *npl* ética *f*

ethnic /'eθnɪk/ *adj* étnico

etiquette /'etɪket/ *n* etiqueta *f*

etymology /etɪ'mɒlədʒɪ/ *n* etimología *f*

EU /i:'ju:/ *abbr* (**European Union**) UE (Unión Europea)

euphemism /'ju:fəmɪzəm/ *n* eufemismo *m*

euphoria /ju:'fɔ:rɪə/ *n* euforia *f*

euro /'jʊərəʊ/ *n* euro *m*

Europe /'jʊərəp/ *n* Europa *f*. **~an** /-'pɪən/ *adj* & *n* europeo (*m*). **~an Union** *n* Unión *f* Europea

euthanasia /ju:θə'neɪzɪə/ *n* eutanasia *f*

evacuat|e /ɪ'vækjʊeɪt/ *vt* evacuar; desocupar (building). **~ion** /-'eɪʃn/ *n* evacuación *f*

evade /ɪ'veɪd/ *vt* evadir

evalua|te /ɪ'væljʊeɪt/ *vt* evaluar. **~tion** /-'eɪʃn/ *vt* evaluación *f*

evangelical /i:væn'dʒelɪkl/ *adj* evangélico

evaporat|e /ɪ'væpəreɪt/ *vi* evaporarse. **~ion** /-'reɪʃn/ *n* evaporación *f*

evasi|on /ɪ'veɪʒn/ *n* evasión *f*. **~ve** /ɪ'veɪsɪv/ *adj* evasivo

eve /i:v/ *n* víspera *f*

even /'i:vn/ *adj* (*flat, smooth*) plano; (colour) uniforme; (distribution) equitativo; (number) par. **get ~ with** desquitarse con. ● *vt* nivelar. □ **~ up** *vt* equilibrar. ● *adv* aun, hasta, incluso. **~ if** aunque. **~ so** aun así. **not ~** ni siquiera

evening /'i:vnɪŋ/ *n* tarde *f*; (*after dark*) noche *f*. **~ class** *n* clase *f* nocturna

event /ɪ'vent/ *n* acontecimiento *m*; (*Sport*) prueba *f*. **in the ~ of** en caso de. **~ful** *adj* lleno de acontecimientos

eventual /ɪ'ventʃʊəl/ *adj* final, definitivo. **~ity** /-'ælətɪ/ *n* eventualidad *f*. **~ly** *adv* finalmente

ever /'evə(r)/ *adv* (*negative*) nunca, jamás; (*at all times*) siempre. **have you ~ been to Greece?** ¿has estado (alguna vez) en Grecia?, **~ after** desde entonces. **~ since** desde entonces. **~ so** [!] muy. **for ~** para siempre. **hardly ~** casi nunca. **~green** *adj* de hoja perenne. ● *n* árbol *m* de hoja perenne. **~lasting** *adj* eterno.

every /'evrɪ/ *adj* cada, todo. **~**

child todos los niños. **~ one** cada uno. **~ other day** un día sí y otro no. **~body** *pron* todos, todo el mundo. **~day** *adj* de todos los días. **~one** *pron* todos, todo el mundo. **~thing** *pron* todo. **~where** *adv* (*be*) en todas partes, (*go*) a todos lados

e

evict /ɪ'vɪkt/ *vt* desahuciar. **~ion** /-ʃn/ *n* desahucio *m*

eviden|ce /'evɪdəns/ *n* evidencia *f*; (*proof*) pruebas *fpl*; (*Jurid*) testimonio *m*; **give ~ce** prestar declaración. **~ce of** señales de. **in ~ce** visible. **~t** *adj* evidente. **~tly** *adv* evidentemente

evil /'i:vl/ *adj* malvado. ● *n* mal *m*

evo|cative /ɪ'vɒkətɪv/ *adj* evocador. **~ke** /ɪ'vəʊk/ *vt* evocar

evolution /i:və'lu:ʃn/ *n* evolución *f*

evolve /ɪ'vɒlv/ *vt* desarrollar. ● *vi* evolucionar

ewe /ju:/ *n* oveja *f*

exact /ɪg'zækt/ *adj* exacto. ● *vt* exigir (**from** a). **~ing** *adj* exigente. **~ly** *adv* exactamente

exaggerat|e /ɪg'zædʒəreɪt/ *vt* exagerar. **~ion** /-'reɪʃn/ *n* exageración *f*

exam /ɪg'zæm/ *n* examen *m*. **~ination** /ɪgzæmɪ'neɪʃn/ *n* examen *m*. **~ine** /ɪg'zæmɪn/ *vt* examinar; interrogar (witness). **~iner** *n* examinador *m*

example /ɪg'zɑ:mpl/ *n* ejemplo *m*. **for ~** por ejemplo. **make an ~ of s.o.** darle un castigo ejemplar a uno

exasperat|e /ɪg'zæspəreɪt/ *vt* exasperar. **~ing** *adj* exasperante. **~ion** /-'reɪʃn/ *n* exasperación *f*

excavat|e /'ekskəveɪt/ *vt* excavar. **~ion** /-'veɪʃn/ *n* excavación *f*

exceed /ɪk'si:d/ *vt* exceder. **~ingly** *adv* sumamente

excel /ɪk'sel/ *vi* (*pt* **excelled**) sobresalir. ● *vt*. **~ o.s.** lucirse. **~lence** /'eksələns/ *n* excelencia *f*. **~lent** *adj* excelente

except /ɪk'sept/ *prep* menos, excepto. **~ for** si no fuera por. ● *vt* exceptuar. **~ing** *prep* con excepción de

exception /ɪk'sepʃən/ *n* excepción *f*. **take ~ to** ofenderse por. **~al** *adj* excepcional. **~ally** *adv* excepcionalmente

excerpt /'eksɜ:pt/ *n* extracto *m*

excess /ɪk'ses/ *n* exceso *m*. ● /'ekses/ *adj* excedente. **~ fare** suplemento *m*. **~ luggage** exceso *m* de equipaje. **~ive** *adj* excesivo

exchange /ɪk'stʃeɪndʒ/ *vt* cambiar. ● *n* intercambio *m*; (*of money*) cambio *m*. **(telephone) ~** central *f* telefónica

excise /'eksaɪz/ *n* impuestos *mpl* interos. ● /ek'saɪz/ *vt* quitar

excit|able /ɪk'saɪtəbl/ *adj* excitable. **~e** /ɪk'saɪt/ *vt* emocionar; (*stimulate*) excitar. **~ed** *adj* entusiasmado. **get ~ed** entusiasmarse. **~ement** *n* emoción *f*; (*enthusiasm*) entusiasmo *m*. **~ing** *adj* emocionante

excla|im /ɪk'skleɪm/ *vi/t* exclamar. **~mation** /eksklə'meɪʃn/ *n* exclamación *f*. **~mation mark** *n* signo *m* de admiración *f*

exclu|de /ɪk'sklu:d/ *vt* excluir. **~sion** /-ʒən/ *n* exclusión *f*. **~sive** /ɪk'sklu:sɪv/ *adj* exclusivo; (club) selecto. **~sive of** excluyendo. **~sively** *adv* exclusivamente

excruciating /ɪk'skru:ʃɪeɪtɪŋ/ *adj* atroz, insoportable

excursion /ɪk'skɜ:ʃn/ *n* ex-

cursión *f*
excus|able /ɪk'skju:zəbl/ *adj* perdonable. **~e** /ɪk'skju:z/ *vt* perdonar. **~e from** dispensar de. **~e me!** ¡perdón! ● /ɪk'skju:s/ *n* excusa *f*
ex-directory /eksdɪ'rektərɪ/ *adj* que no figura en la guía telefónica, privado (*Mex*)
execut|e /'eksɪkju:t/ *vt* ejecutar. **~ion** /eksɪ'kju:ʃn/ *n* ejecución *f*. **~ioner** *n* verdugo *m*
executive /ɪg'zekjʊtɪv/ *adj & n* ejecutivo (*m*)
exempt /ɪg'zempt/ *adj* exento (**from** de). ● *vt* dispensar. **~ion** /-ʃn/ *n* exención *f*
exercise /'eksəsaɪz/ *n* ejercicio *m*. ● *vt* ejercer. ● *vi* hacer ejercicio. **~ book** *n* cuaderno *m*
exert /ɪg'zɜ:t/ *vt* ejercer. **~ o.s.** hacer un gran esfuerzo. **~ion** /-ʃn/ *n* esfuerzo *m*
exhale /eks'heɪl/ *vt/i* exhalar
exhaust /ɪg'zɔ:st/ *vt* agotar. ● *n* (*Auto*) tubo *m* de escape. **~ed** *adj* agotado. **~ion** /-stʃən/ *n* agotamiento *m*. **~ive** *adj* exhaustivo
exhibit /ɪg'zɪbɪt/ *vt* exponer; (*fig*) mostrar. ● *n* objeto *m* expuesto; (*Jurid*) documento *m*. **~ion** /eksɪ'bɪʃn/ *n* exposición. **~ionist** *n* exhibicionista *m & f*. **~or** /ɪg'zɪbɪtə(r)/ *n* expositor *m*
exhilarat|ing /ɪg'zɪləreɪtɪŋ/ *adj* excitante. **~ion** /-'reɪʃn/ *n* regocijo *m*
exhort /ɪg'zɔ:t/ *vt* exhortar
exile /'eksaɪl/ *n* exilio *m*; (*person*) exiliado *m*. ● *vt* desterrar
exist /ɪg'zɪst/ *vi* existir. **~ence** *n* existencia *f*. **in ~ence** existente
exit /'eksɪt/ *n* salida *f*
exorbitant /ɪg'zɔ:bɪtənt/ *adj* exorbitante
exorcis|e /'eksɔ:saɪz/ *vt* exorcizar. **~m** /-sɪzəm/ *n* exorcismo *m*. **~t** *n* exorcista *m & f*
exotic /ɪg'zɒtɪk/ *adj* exótico
expand /ɪk'spænd/ *vt* expandir; (*develop*) desarrollar. ● *vi* expandirse
expanse /ɪk'spæns/ *n* extensión *f*
expansion /ɪk'spænʃn/ *n* expansión *f*
expatriate /eks'pætrɪət/ *adj & n* expatriado (*m*)
expect /ɪk'spekt/ *vt* esperar; (*suppose*) suponer; (*demand*) contar con. **I ~ so** supongo que sí. **~ancy** *n* esperanza *f*. **life ~ancy** esperanza *f* de vida. **~ant** *adj* expectante. **~ant mother** *n* futura madre *f*
expectation /ekspek'teɪʃn/ *n* expectativa *f*
expedient /ɪk'spi:dɪənt/ *adj* conveniente. ● *n* expediente *m*
expedition /ekspɪ'dɪʃn/ *n* expedición *f*
expel /ɪk'spel/ *vt* (*pt* **expelled**) expulsar
expend /ɪk'spend/ *vt* gastar. **~able** *adj* prescindible. **~iture** /-ɪtʃə(r)/ *n* gastos *mpl*
expens|e /ɪk'spens/ *n* gasto *m*. **at s.o.'s ~e** a costa de uno. **~es** *npl* (*Com*) gastos *mpl*. **~ive** *adj* caro
experience /ɪk'spɪərɪəns/ *n* experiencia. ● *vt* experimentar. **~d** *adj* con experiencia; (driver) experimentado
experiment /ɪk'sperɪmənt/ *n* experimento *m*. ● *vi* experimentar. **~al** /-'mentl/ *adj* experimental
expert /'ekspɜ:t/ *adj & n* experto (*m*). **~ise** /ekspɜ:'ti:z/ *n* pericia *f*. **~ly** *adv* hábilmente

e

expir|e /ɪk'spaɪə(r)/ *vi* (passport, ticket) caducar; (contract) vencer. **~y** *n* vencimiento *m*, caducidad *f*

expla|in /ɪk'spleɪn/ *vt* explicar. **~nation** /eksplə'neɪʃn/ *n* explicación *f*. **~natory** /ɪks'plænətərɪ/ *adj* explicativo

e

explicit /ɪk'splɪsɪt/ *adj* explícito

explode /ɪk'spləʊd/ *vt* hacer explotar. ● *vi* estallar

exploit /'eksplɔɪt/ *n* hazaña *f*. ● /ɪk'splɔɪt/ *vt* explotar. **~ation** /eksplɔɪ'teɪʃn/ *n* explotación *f*

explor|ation /eksplə'reɪʃn/ *n* exploración *f*. **~atory** /ɪk'splɒrətrɪ/ *adj* exploratorio. **~e** /ɪk'splɔ:(r)/ *vt* explorar. **~er** *n* explorador *m*

explosi|on /ɪk'spləʊʒn/ *n* explosión *f*. **~ve** /-sɪv/ *adj & n* explosivo (*m*)

export /ɪk'spɔ:t/ *vt* exportar. ● /'ekspɔ:t/ *n* exportación *f*; (*item*) artículo *m* de exportación. **~er** /ɪks'pɔ:tə(r)/ exportador *m*

expos|e /ɪk'spəʊz/ *vt* exponer; (*reveal*) descubrir. **~ure** /-ʒə(r)/ *n* exposición *f*. **die of ~ure** morir de frío

express /ɪk'spres/ *vt* expresar. ● *adj* expreso; (letter) urgente. ● *adv* (*by express post*) por correo urgente. ● *n* (*train*) rápido *m*, expreso *m*. **~ion** *n* expresión *f*. **~ive** *adj* expresivo. **~ly** *adv* expresadamente. **~way** *n* (*Amer*) autopista *f*

expulsion /ɪk'spʌlʃn/ *n* expulsión *f*

exquisite /'ekskwɪzɪt/ *adj* exquisito

exten|d /ɪk'stend/ *vt* extender; (*prolong*) prolongar; ampliar (house). ● *vi* extenderse. **~sion** /-ʃn/ *n* extensión *f*; (*of road, time*) prolongación *f*; (*building*) anejo *m*. **~sive** /-sɪv/ *adj* extenso. **~sively** *adv* extensamente. **~t** *n* extensión *f*; (*fig*) alcance. **to a certain ~t** hasta cierto punto

exterior /ɪk'stɪərɪə(r)/ *adj & n* exterior (*m*)

exterminat|e /ɪk'stɜ:mɪneɪt/ *vt* exterminar. **~ion** /-'neɪʃn/ *n* exterminio *m*

external /ɪk'stɜ:nl/ *adj* externo

extinct /ɪk'stɪŋkt/ *adj* extinto. **~ion** /-ʃn/ *n* extinción *f*

extinguish /ɪk'stɪŋgwɪʃ/ *vt* extinguir. **~er** *n* extintor *m*, extinguidor *m* (*LAm*)

extol /ɪk'stəʊl/ *vt* (*pt* **extolled**) alabar

extort /ɪk'stɔ:t/ *vt* sacar por la fuerza. **~ion** /-ʃn/ *n* exacción *f*. **~ionate** /-ənət/ *adj* exorbitante

extra /'ekstrə/ *adj* de más. ● *adv* extraordinariamente. ● *n* suplemento *m*; (*Cinema*) extra *m & f*

extract /'ekstrækt/ *n* extracto *m*. ● /ɪk'strækt/ *vt* extraer. **~ion** /ɪk'strækʃn/ *n* extracción *f*

extradit|e /'ekstrədaɪt/ *vt* extraditar. **~ion** /-'dɪʃn/ *n* extradición *f*

extra: ~ordinary /ɪk'strɔ:dnrɪ/ *adj* extraordinario. **~-sensory** /ekstrə'sensərɪ/ *adj* extrasensorial

extravagan|ce /ɪk'strævəgəns/ *n* prodigalidad *f*; (*of gestures, dress*) extravagancia *f*. **~t** *adj* pródigo; (behaviour) extravagante. **~za** *n* gran espectáculo *m*

extrem|e /ɪk'stri:m/ *adj & n* extremo (*m*). **~ely** *adv* extremadamente. **~ist** *n* extremista *m & f*

extricate /'ekstrɪkeɪt/ *vt* desenredar, librar

extrovert /'ekstrəvɜ:t/ *n* extrovertido *m*

exuberan|ce /ɪg'zju:bərəns/ *n*

exuberancia *f.* ~**t** *adj* exuberante
exude /ɪg'zju:d/ *vt* rezumar
exult /ɪg'zʌlt/ *vi* exultar. ~**ation** /egzʌl'teɪʃn/ *n* exultación *f*
eye /aɪ/ *n* ojo m. **keep an ~ on** no perder de vista. **see ~ to ~ with s.o.** estar de acuerdo con uno. ● *vt* (*pt* **eyed**, *pres p* **eyeing**) mirar. ~**ball** *n* globo *m* ocular. ~**brow** *n* ceja *f.* ~**drops** *npl* colirio *m.* ~**lash** *n* pestaña *f.* ~**lid** *n* párpado *m.* ~**-opener** *n* [!] revelación *f.* ~**-shadow** *n* sombra *f* de ojos. ~**sight** *n* vista *f.* ~**sore** *n* (*fig, fam*) monstruosidad *f*, adefesio *m.* ~**witness** *n* testigo *m* ocular

Ff

fable /'feɪbl/ *n* fábula *f*
fabric /'fæbrɪk/ *n* tejido *m*, tela *f*
fabricate /'fæbrɪkeɪt/ *vt* inventar. ~**ation** /-'keɪʃn/ *n* invención *f*
fabulous /'fæbjʊləs/ *adj* fabuloso
facade /fə'sɑ:d/ *n* fachada *f*
face /feɪs/ *n* cara *f*, rostro *m*; (*of watch*) esfera *f*, carátula *f* (*Mex*); (*aspect*) aspecto *m.* ~ **down(wards)** boca abajo. ~ **up(wards)** boca arriba. **in the ~ of** frente a. **lose ~** quedar mal. **pull ~s** hacer muecas. ● *vt* mirar hacia; (house) dar a; (*confront*) enfrentarse con. ● *vi* volverse. □ ~ **up to** *vt* enfrentarse con. ~ **flannel** *n* paño *m* (para lavarse la cara). ~**less** *adj* anónimo. ~ **lift** *n* cirugía *f* estética en la cara
facetious /fə'si:ʃəs/ *adj* burlón
facial /'feɪʃl/ *adj* facial
facile /'fæsaɪl/ *adj* superficial, simplista
facilitate /fə'sɪlɪteɪt/ *vt* facilitar
facility /fə'sɪlɪtɪ/ *n* facilidad *f*
fact /fækt/ *n* hecho *m.* **as a matter of ~, in ~** en realidad, de hecho
faction /'fækʃn/ *n* facción *f*
factor /'fæktə(r)/ *n* factor *m*
factory /'fæktərɪ/ *n* fábrica *f*
factual /'fæktʃʊəl/ *adj* basado en hechos, factual
faculty /'fækəltɪ/ *n* facultad *f*
fad /fæd/ *n* manía *f*, capricho *m*
fade /feɪd/ *vi* (colour) desteñirse; (flowers) marchitarse; (light) apagarse; (memory, sound) desvanecerse
fag /fæg/ *n* (*fam, chore*) faena *f*; (*sl, cigarette*) cigarrillo *m*, pitillo *m*
Fahrenheit /'færənhaɪt/ *adj* Fahrenheit
fail /feɪl/ *vi* fracasar; (brakes) fallar; (*in an exam*) suspender, ser reprobado (*LAm*). **he ~ed to arrive** no llegó. ● *vt* suspender, ser reprobado en (*LAm*) (exam); suspender, reprobar (*LAm*) (candidate). ● *n.* **without ~** sin falta. ~**ing** *n* defecto *m.* ● *prep.* ~**ing that, ...** si eso no resulta.... ~**ure** /'feɪljə(r)/ *n* fracaso *m*
faint /feɪnt/ *adj* (**-er, -est**) (*weak*) débil; (*indistinct*) indistinto. **feel ~** estar mareado. **the ~est idea** la más remota idea. ● *vi* desmayarse. ● *n* desmayo *m.* ~**-hearted** /-'hɑ:tɪd/ *adj* pusilánime, cobarde. ~**ly** *adv* (*weakly*) débilmente; (*indistinctly*) indistintamente; (*slightly*) ligeramente
fair /feə(r)/ *adj* (**-er, -est**) (*just*) justo; (weather) bueno; (amount) razonable; (hair) rubio, güero (*Mex fam*); (skin) blanco. ● *adv* limpio. ● *n*

e f

feria *f.* ~**-haired** /-'heəd/ *adj* rubio, güero (*Mex fam*). ~**ly** *adv* (*justly*) justamente; (*rather*) bastante. ~**ness** *n* justicia *f.* **in all** ~**ness** sinceramente. ~ **play** *n* juego *m* limpio

fairy /'feəri/ *n* hada *f.* ~ **story**, ~ **tale** *n* cuento *m* de hadas

f

faith /feɪθ/ *n* (*trust*) confianza *f*; (*Relig*) fe *f.* ~**ful** *adj* fiel. ~**fully** *adv* fielmente. **yours** ~**fully** (*in letters*) (le saluda) atentamente

fake /feɪk/ *n* falsificación *f*; (*person*) farsante *m*. ● *adj* falso. ● *vt* falsificar

falcon /'fɔːlkən/ *n* halcón *m*

Falkland Islands /'fɔːlklənd/ *npl*. **the Falkland Islands, the Falklands** las (Islas) Malvinas

fall /fɔːl/ *vi* (*pt* **fell**, *pp* **fallen**) caer; (*decrease*) bajar. ● *n* caída *f*; (*Amer, autumn*) otoño *m*; (*in price*) bajada *f.* □ ~ **apart** *vi* deshacerse. □ ~ **back on** *vt* recurrir a. □ ~ **down** *vi* (*fall*) caerse. □ ~ **for** *vt* 🅸 enamorarse de (person); dejarse engañar por (trick). □ ~ **in** *vi* (*Mil*) formar filas. □ ~ **off** *vi* caerse; (*diminish*) disminuir. □ ~ **out** *vi* (*quarrel*) reñir (**with** con); (*drop out*) caerse; (*Mil*) romper filas. □ ~ **over** *vi* caerse. *vt* tropezar con. □ ~ **through** *vi* no salir adelante

fallacy /'fæləsi/ *n* falacia *f*

fallible /'fæləbl/ *adj* falible

fallout /'fɔːlaʊt/ *n* lluvia *f* radiactiva. ~ **shelter** *n* refugio *m* antinuclear

fallow /'fæləʊ/ *adj* en barbecho

false /fɔːls/ *adj* falso. ~ **alarm** *n* falsa alarma. ~**hood** *n* mentira *f.* ~**ly** *adv* falsamente. ~ **teeth** *npl* dentadura *f* postiza

falsify /'fɔːlsɪfaɪ/ *vt* falsificar

falter /'fɔːltə(r)/ *vi* vacilar

fame /feɪm/ *n* fama *f.* ~**d** *adj* famoso

familiar /fə'mɪlɪə(r)/ *adj* familiar. **the name sounds** ~ el nombre me suena. **be** ~ **with** conocer. ~**ity** /-'ærətɪ/ *n* familiaridad *f.* ~**ize** *vt* familiarizar

family /'fæməlɪ/ *n* familia *f.* ● *adj* de (la) familia, familiar. ~ **tree** *n* árbol *m* genealógico

famine /'fæmɪn/ *n* hambre *f*, hambruna *f*

famished /'fæmɪʃt/ *adj* hambriento

famous /'feɪməs/ *adj* famoso

fan /fæn/ *n* abanico *m*; (*Mec*) ventilador *m*; (*enthusiast*) aficionado *m*; (*of group, actor*) fan *m & f*; (*of sport, team*) hincha *m & f.* ● *vt* (*pt* **fanned**) abanicar; avivar (interest). □ ~ **out** *vi* desparramarse en forma de abanico

fanatic /fə'nætɪk/ *n* fanático *m*. ~**al** *adj* fanático. ~**ism** /-sɪzəm/ *n* fanatismo *m*

fan belt *n* correa *f* de ventilador, banda *f* del ventilador (*Mex*)

fanciful /'fænsɪfl/ *adj* (*imaginative*) imaginativo; (*impractical*) extravagante

fancy /'fænsɪ/ *n* imaginación *f*; (*liking*) gusto *m*. **take a** ~ **to** tomar cariño a (person); aficionarse a (thing). ● *adj* de lujo. ● *vt* (*imagine*) imaginar; (*believe*) creer; (*fam, want*) apetecer a. ~ **dress** *n* disfraz *m*

fanfare /'fænfeə(r)/ *n* fanfarria *f*

fang /fæŋ/ *n* (*of animal*) colmillo *m*; (*of snake*) diente *m*

fantasize /'fæntəsaɪz/ *vi* fantasear

fantastic /fæn'tæstɪk/ *adj* fantástico

fantasy /ˈfæntəsɪ/ *n* fantasía *f*

far /fɑː(r)/ *adv* lejos; (*much*) mucho. **as ~ as** hasta. **as ~ as I know** que yo sepa. **by ~** con mucho. ● *adj* (**further**, **furthest** *or* **farther**, **farthest**) lejano. **~ away** lejano

farc|e /fɑːs/ *n* farsa *f*. **~ical** *adj* ridículo

fare /feə(r)/ *n* (*on bus*) precio *m* del billete, precio *m* del boleto (*LAm*); (*on train, plane*) precio *m* del billete, precio *m* del pasaje (*LAm*); (*food*) comida *f*

Far East /fɑːrˈiːst/ *n* Extremo *or* Lejano Oriente *m*

farewell /feəˈwel/ *int & n* adiós (*m*)

far-fetched /fɑːˈfetʃt/ *adj* improbable

farm /fɑːm/ *n* granja *f*. ● *vt* cultivar. □ **~ out** *vt* encargar (a terceros). ● *vi* ser agricultor. **~er** *n* agricultor *m*, granjero *m*. **~house** *n* granja *f*. **~ing** *n* agricultura *f*. **~yard** *n* corral *m*

far: ~-off *adj* lejano. **~-reaching** /fɑːˈriːtʃɪŋ/ *adj* trascendental. **~-sighted** /fɑːˈsaɪtɪd/ *adj* con visión del futuro; (*Med, Amer*) hipermétrope

farther, **farthest** /ˈfɑːðə(r), ˈfɑːðəst/ *see* **FAR**

fascinat|e /ˈfæsɪneɪt/ *vt* fascinar. **~ed** *adj* fascinado. **~ing** *adj* fascinante. **~ion** /-ˈneɪʃn/ *n* fascinación *f*

fascis|m /ˈfæʃɪzəm/ *n* fascismo *m*. **~t** *adj & n* fascista (*m & f*)

fashion /ˈfæʃn/ *n* (*manner*) manera *f*; (*vogue*) moda *f*. **be in**/**out of ~** estar de moda/estar pasado de moda. **~able** *adj* de moda

fast /fɑːst/ *adj* (**-er**, **-est**) rápido; (clock) adelantado; (*secure*) fijo; (colours) sólido. ● *adv* rápidamente; (*securely*) firmemente. **~ asleep** profundamente dormido. ● *vi* ayunar. ● *n* ayuno *m*

fasten /ˈfɑːsn/ *vt* sujetar; cerrar (case); abrochar (belt etc). ● *vi* (case) cerrar; (belt etc) cerrarse. **~er**, **~ing** *n* (*on box, window*) cierre *m*; (*on door*) cerrojo *m*

fat /fæt/ *n* grasa *f*. ● *adj* (**fatter**, **fattest**) gordo; (meat) que tiene mucha grasa; (*thick*) grueso. **get ~** engordar

fatal /ˈfeɪtl/ *adj* mortal; (*fateful*) fatídico. **~ity** /fəˈtælətɪ/ muerto *m*. **~ly** *adv* mortalmente

fate /feɪt/ *n* destino *m*; (*one's lot*) suerte *f*. **~d** *adj* predestinado. **~ful** *adj* fatídico

father /ˈfɑːðə(r)/ *n* padre *m*. **~hood** *m* paternidad *f*. **~-in-law** *m* (*pl* **~s-in-law**) *m* suegro *m*. **~ly** *adj* paternal

fathom /ˈfæðəm/ *n* braza *f*. ● *vt*. **~ (out)** comprender

fatigue /fəˈtiːg/ *n* fatiga *f*. ● *vt* fatigar

fat|ten *vt*. **~ten (up)** cebar (animal). **~tening** *adj* que engorda. **~ty** *adj* graso, grasoso (*LAm*). ● *n* ⊡ gordinflón *m*

fatuous /ˈfætjʊəs/ *adj* fatuo

faucet /ˈfɔːsɪt/ *n* (*Amer*) grifo *m*, llave *f* (*LAm*)

fault /fɔːlt/ *n* defecto *m*; (*blame*) culpa *f*; (*tennis*) falta *f*; (*in geology*) falla *f*. **at ~** culpable. ● *vt* encontrarle defectos a. **~less** *adj* impecable. **~y** *adj* defectuoso

favour /ˈfeɪvə(r)/ *n* favor *m*. ● *vt* favorecer; (*support*) estar a favor de; (*prefer*) preferir. **~able** *adj* favorable. **~ably** *adv* favorablemente. **~ite** *adj & n* preferido (*m*). **~itism** *n* favoritismo *m*

f

fawn /fɔːn/ *n* cervato *m*. ● *adj* beige, beis. ● *vi*. ~ **on** adular

fax /fæks/ *n* fax *m*. ● *vt* faxear

fear /fɪə(r)/ *n* miedo *m*. ● *vt* temer. ~**ful** *adj* (*frightening*) espantoso; (*frightened*) temeroso. ~**less** *adj* intrépido. ~**some** /-səm/ *adj* espantoso

feasib|ility /fiːzə'bɪlətɪ/ *n* viabilidad *f*. ~**le** /'fiːzəbl/ *adj* factible; (*likely*) posible

f

feast /fiːst/ *n* (*Relig*) fiesta *f*; (*meal*) banquete *m*

feat /fiːt/ *n* hazaña *f*

feather /'feðə(r)/ *n* pluma *f*. ~**weight** *n* peso *m* pluma

feature /'fiːtʃə(r)/ *n* (*on face*) rasgo *m*; (*characteristic*) característica *f*; (*in newspaper*) artículo *m*; ~ **(film)** película *f* principal, largometraje *m*. ● *vt* presentar; (*give prominence to*) destacar

February /'februərɪ/ *n* febrero *m*

fed /fed/ *see* **FEED**

feder|al /'fedərəl/ *adj* federal. ~**ation** /fedə'reɪʃn/ *n* federación *f*

fed up *adj* ⓘ harto (**with** de)

fee /fiː/ *n* (*professional*) honorarios *mpl*; (*enrolment*) derechos *mpl*; (*club*) cuota *f*

feeble /'fiːbl/ *adj* (**-er**, **-est**) débil

feed /fiːd/ *vt* (*pt* **fed**) dar de comer a; (*supply*) alimentar. ● *vi* comer. ● *n* (*for animals*) pienso *m*; (*for babies*) comida *f*. ~**back** *n* reacción *f*

feel /fiːl/ *vt* (*pt* **felt**) sentir; (*touch*) tocar; (*think*) considerar. **do you ~ it's a good idea?** ¿te parece buena idea? ~ **as if** tener la impresión de que. ~ **hot**/**hungry** tener calor/hambre. ~ **like** (*fam*, *want*) tener ganas de. ● *n* sensación *f*. **get the ~ of sth** acostumbrarse a algo. ~**er** *n* (*of insect*) antena *f*. ~**ing** *n* sentimiento *m*; (*physical*) sensación *f*

feet /fiːt/ *see* **FOOT**

feign /feɪn/ *vt* fingir

feint /feɪnt/ *n* finta *f*

fell /fel/ *see* **FALL**. ● *vt* derribar; talar (tree)

fellow /'feləʊ/ *n* ⓘ tipo *m*; (*comrade*) compañero *m*; (*of society*) socio *m*. ~ **countryman** *n* compatriota *m*. ~ **passenger**/**traveller** *n* compañero *m* de viaje

felony /'felənɪ/ *n* delito *m* grave

felt /felt/ *n see* **FEEL**. ● *n* fieltro *m*

female /'fiːmeɪl/ *adj* hembra; (voice, sex etc) femenino. ● *n* mujer *f*; (*animal*) hembra *f*

femini|ne /'femənɪn/ *adj* & *n* femenino (*m*). ~**nity** /-'nɪnətɪ/ *n* feminidad *f*. ~**st** *adj* & *n* feminista *m* & *f*

fenc|e /fens/ *n* cerca *f*, cerco *m* (*LAm*). ● *vt*. ~**e (in)** encerrar, cercar. ● *vi* (*Sport*) practicar la esgrima. ~**er** *n* esgrimidor *m*. ~**ing** *n* (*Sport*) esgrima *f*

fend /fend/ *vi*. ~ **for o.s.** valerse por sí mismo. □ ~ **off** *vt* defenderse de

fender /'fendə(r)/ *n* rejilla *f*; (*Amer*, *Auto*) guardabarros *m*, salpicadera *f* (*Mex*)

ferment /fə'ment/ *vt/i* fermentar. ~**ation** /-'teɪʃn/ *n* fermentación *f*

fern /fɜːn/ *n* helecho *m*

feroci|ous /fə'rəʊʃəs/ *adj* feroz. ~**ty** /fə'rɒsətɪ/ *n* ferocidad *f*

ferret /'ferɪt/ *n* hurón *m*. ● *vi* (*pt* **ferreted**) ~ **about** husmear. ● *vt*. ~ **out** descubrir

ferry /'ferɪ/ *n* ferry *m*. ● *vt* transportar

fertil|e /'fɜːtaɪl/ *adj* fértil. ~**ity** /-'tɪlətɪ/ *n* fertilidad *f*. ~**ize**

/'fɜːtəlaɪz/ *vt* fecundar, abonar (soil). **~izer** *n* fertilizante *m*

ferv|ent /'fɜːvənt/ *adj* ferviente. **~our** /-və(r)/ *n* fervor *m*

fester /'festə(r)/ *vi* enconarse

festival /'festəvl/ *n* fiesta *f*; (*of arts*) festival *m*

festiv|e /'festɪv/ *adj* festivo. **the ~e season** *n* las Navidades. **~ity** /fe'stɪvətɪ/ *n* festividad *f*

fetch /fetʃ/ *vt* (*go for*) ir a buscar; (*bring*) traer; (*be sold for*) venderse en. **~ing** *adj* atractivo

fête /feɪt/ *n* fiesta *f.* ● *vt* festejar

fetish /'fetɪʃ/ *n* fetiche *m*

fetter /'fetə(r)/ *vt* encadenar

feud /fjuːd/ *n* contienda *f*

feudal /'fjuːdl/ *adj* feudal. **~ism** *n* feudalismo m

fever /'fiːvə(r)/ *n* fiebre *f.* **~ish** *adj* febril

few /fjuː/ *adj* pocos. **a ~ houses** algunas casas. ● *n* pocos *mpl*. **a ~** unos (pocos). **a good ~, quite a ~** ⊡ muchos. **~er** *adj & n* menos. **~est** *adj* el menor número de

fiancé /fɪ'ɒnseɪ/ *n* novio *m.* **~e** /fɪ'ɒnseɪ/ *n* novia *f*

fiasco /fɪ'æskəʊ/ *n* (*pl* **-os**) fiasco *m*

fib /fɪb/ *n* ⊡ mentirilla *f.* ● *vi* ⊡ mentir, decir mentirillas

fibre /'faɪbə(r)/ *n* fibra *f.* **~glass** *n* fibra *f* de vidrio

fickle /'fɪkl/ *adj* inconstante

ficti|on /'fɪkʃn/ *n* ficción *f.* **(works of) ~** novelas *fpl.* **~onal** *adj* novelesco. **~tious** /fɪk'tɪʃəs/ *adj* ficticio

fiddle /'fɪdl/ *n* ⊡ violín *m*; (*fam, swindle*) trampa *f.* ● *vt* ⊡ falsificar. **~ with** juguetear con

fidget /'fɪdʒɪt/ *vi* (*pt* **fidgeted**) moverse, ponerse nervioso. **~ with** juguetear con. ● *n* persona *f* inquieta. **~y** *adj* inquieto

field /fiːld/ *n* campo *m.* **~ day** *n.* **have a ~ day** hacer su agosto. **~ glasses** *npl* gemelos *mpl.* **F~ Marshal** *n* mariscal *m* de campo. **~ trip** *n* viaje *m* de estudio. **~work** *n* investigaciones *fpl* en el terreno

fiend /fiːnd/ *n* demonio *m.* **~ish** *adj* diabólico

fierce /fɪəs/ *adj* (**-er, -est**) feroz; (attack) violento. **~ly** *adv* (growl) con ferocidad; (fight) con fiereza

fiery /'faɪərɪ/ *adj* (**-ier, -iest**) ardiente; (temper) exaltado

fifteen /fɪf'tiːn/ *adj & n* quince (*m*). **~th** *adj* decimoquinto. ● *n* quinceavo *m*

fifth /fɪfθ/ *adj & n* quinto (*m*)

fift|ieth /'fɪftɪəθ/ *adj* quincuagésimo. ● *n* cincuentavo *m.* **~y** *adj & n* cincuenta (*m*). **~y-~y** *adv* mitad y mitad, a medias. ● *adj.* **a ~y-~y chance** una posibilidad de cada dos

fig /fɪg/ *n* higo *m*

fight /faɪt/ *vi* (*pt* **fought**) luchar; (*quarrel*) disputar. ● *vt* luchar contra. ● *n* pelea *m*; (*struggle*) lucha *f*; (*quarrel*) disputa *f*; (*Mil*) combate *m.* □ **~ back** *vi* defenderse. □ **~ off** *vt* rechazar (attack); luchar contra (illness). **~er** *n* luchador *m*; (*aircraft*) avión *m* de caza. **~ing** *n* luchas *fpl*

figment /'fɪgmənt/ *n.* **~ of the imagination** producto *m* de la imaginación

figurative /'fɪgjʊrətɪv/ *adj* figurado

figure /'fɪgə(r)/ *n* (*number*) cifra *f*; (*person*) figura *f*; (*shape*) forma *f*; (*of woman*) tipo *m.* ● *vt* imaginar;

f

(*Amer fam, reckon*) calcular. ● *vi* figurar. **that ~s** (*fam*) es lógico. □ **~ out** *vt* entender. **~head** *n* testaferro *m*, mascarón *m* de proa. **~ of speech** *n* figura *f* retórica

filch /fɪltʃ/ *vt* 🅸 hurtar

file /faɪl/ *n* (*tool, for nails*) lima *f*; (*folder*) carpeta *f*; (*set of papers*) expediente *m*; (*Comp*) archivo *m*; (*row*) fila *f*. **in single ~** en fila india. ● *vt* archivar (papers); limar (metal, nails). ● **~ in** *vi* entrar en fila. **~ past** *vt* desfilar ante

filing cabinet /ˈfaɪlɪŋ/ *n* archivador *m*

fill /fɪl/ *vt* llenar. ● *vi* llenarse. ● *n*. **eat one's ~** hartarse de comer. **have had one's ~ of** estar harto de □ **~ in** *vt* rellenar (form, hole). □ **~ out** *vt* rellenar (form). *vi* (*get fatter*) engordar. □ **~ up** *vt* llenar. *vi* llenarse

fillet /ˈfɪlɪt/ *n* filete *m*. ● *vt* (*pt* **filleted**) cortar en filetes (meat); quitar la espina a (fish)

filling /ˈfɪlɪŋ/ *n* (*in tooth*) empaste *m*, tapadura *f* (*Mex*). **~ station** *n* gasolinera *f*

film /fɪlm/ *n* película *f*. ● *vt* filmar. **~ star** *n* estrella *f* de cine

filter /ˈfɪltə(r)/ *n* filtro *m*. ● *vt* filtrar. ● *vi* filtrarse. **~-tipped** *adj* con filtro

filth /fɪlθ/ *n* mugre *f*. **~y** *adj* mugriento

fin /fɪn/ *n* aleta *f*

final /ˈfaɪnl/ *adj* último; (*conclusive*) decisivo. ● *n* (*Sport*) final *f*. **~s** *npl* (*Schol*) exámenes *mpl* de fin de curso

finale /fɪˈnɑːlɪ/ *n* final *m*

final|ist *n* finalista *m & f*. **~ize** *vt* ultimar. **~ly** *adv* (*lastly*) finalmente, por fin

financ|e /ˈfaɪnæns/ *n* finanzas *fpl*. ● *vt* financiar. **~ial** /faɪˈnænʃl/ *adj* financiero; (difficulties) económico

find /faɪnd/ *vt* (*pt* **found**) encontrar. **~ out** *vt* descubrir. ● *vi* (*learn*) enterarse. **~ings** *npl* conclusiones *fpl*

fine /faɪn/ *adj* (**-er**, **-est**) (*delicate*) fino; (*excellent*) excelente. ● *adv* muy bien. ● *n* multa *f*. ● *vt* multar. **~ arts** *npl* bellas artes *fpl*. **~ly** *adv* (*cut*) en trozos pequeños; (adjust) con precisión

finger /ˈfɪŋgə(r)/ *n* dedo *m*. ● *vt* tocar. **~nail** *n* uña *f*. **~print** *n* huella *f* digital. **~tip** *n* punta *f* del dedo

finish /ˈfɪnɪʃ/ *vt/i* terminar, acabar. **~ doing** terminar de hacer. ● *n* fin *m*; (*of race*) llegada *f*

finite /ˈfaɪnaɪt/ *adj* finito

Fin|land /ˈfɪnlənd/ *n* Finlandia *f*. **~n** *n* finlandés *m*. **~nish** *adj & n* finlandés (*m*)

fiord /fjɔːd/ *n* fiordo *m*

fir /fɜː(r)/ *n* abeto *m*

fire /faɪə(r)/ *n* fuego *m*; (*conflagration*) incendio *m*. ● *vt* disparar (gun); (*dismiss*) despedir; avivar (imagination). ● *vi* disparar. **~ alarm** *n* alarma *f* contra incendios. **~arm** *n* arma *f* de fuego. **~ brigade**, **~ department** (*Amer*) *n* cuerpo *m* de bomberos. **~ engine** *n* coche *m* de bomberos, carro *m* de bomberos (*Mex*). **~-escape** *n* escalera *f* de incendios. **~ extinguisher** *n* extintor *m*, extinguidor *m* (*LAm*). **~fighter** *n* bombero *m*. **~man** /-mən/ *n* bombero *m*. **~place** *n* chimenea *f*. **~side** *n* hogar *m*. **~ truck** *n* (*Amer*) see **~ ENGINE**. **~wood** *n* leña *f*. **~work** *n* fuego *m* artificial

firm /fɜːm/ *n* empresa *f*. ● *adj* (**-er**,

-**est**) firme. **~ly** *adv* firmemente

first /fɜ:st/ *adj* primero, (*before masculine singular noun*) primer. **at ~ hand** directamente. ● *n* primero *m*. ● *adv* primero; (*first time*) por primera vez. **~ of all** primero. **~ aid** *n* primeros auxilios *mpl*. **~ aid kit** *n* botiquín *m*. **~ class** /-'klɑ:s/ *adv* (travel) en primera clase. **~-class** *adj* de primera clase. **~ floor** *n* primer piso *m*; (*Amer*) planta *f* baja. **F~ Lady** *n* (*Amer*) Primera Dama *f*. **~ly** *adv* en primer lugar. **~ name** *n* nombre *m* de pila. **~-rate** /-'reɪt/ *adj* excelente

fish /fɪʃ/ *n* (*pl invar or* **-es**) pez *m*; (*as food*) pescado *m*. ● *vi* pescar. **go ~ing** ir de pesca. □ **~ out** *vt* sacar. **~erman** *n* pescador *m*. **~ing** *n* pesca *f*. **~ing pole** (*Amer*), **~ing rod** *n* caña *f* de pesca. **~monger** *n* pescadero *m*. **~ shop** *n* pescadería *f*. **~y** *adj* (smell) a pescado; (*fam, questionable*) sospechoso

fission /'fɪʃn/ *n* fisión *f*

fist /fɪst/ *n* puño *m*

fit /fɪt/ *adj* (**fitter**, **fittest**) (*healthy*) en forma; (*good enough*) adecuado; (*able*) capaz. ● *n* (*attack*) ataque; (*of clothes*) corte *m*. ● *vt* (*pt* **fitted**) (*adapt*) adaptar; (*be the right size for*) quedarle bien a; (*install*) colocar. ● *vi* encajar; (*in certain space*) caber; (clothes) quedarle bien a uno. □ **~ in** *vi* caber. **~ful** *adj* irregular. **~ness** *n* salud *f*; (*Sport*) (buena) forma *f* física. **~ting** *adj* apropiado. ● *n* (*of clothes*) prueba *f*. **~ting room** *n* probador *m*

five /faɪv/ *adj* & *n* cinco (*m*)

fix /fɪks/ *vt* fijar; (*mend, deal with*) arreglar. ● *n*. **in a ~** en un aprieto. **~ed** *adj* fijo. **~ture** /'fɪkstʃə(r)/ *n* (*Sport*) partido *m*

fizz /fɪz/ *vi* burbujear. ● *n* efervescencia *f*. **~le** /fɪzl/ *vi*. **~le out** fracasar. **~y** *adj* efervescente; (water) con gas

fjord /fjɔ:d/ *n* fiordo *m*

flabbergasted /'flæbəgɑ:stɪd/ *adj* estupefacto

flabby /'flæbɪ/ *adj* flojo

flag /flæg/ *n* bandera *f*. ● *vi* (*pt* **flagged**) (*weaken*) flaquear; (conversation) languidecer

flagon /'flægən/ *n* botella *f* grande, jarro *m*

flagpole /'flægpəʊl/ *n* asta *f* de bandera

flagrant /'fleɪgrənt/ *adj* flagrante

flair /fleə(r)/ *n* don *m* (**for** de)

flak|e /fleɪk/ *n* copo *m*; (*of paint, metal*) escama *f*. ● *vi* desconcharse. **~y** *adj* escamoso

flamboyant /flæm'bɔɪənt/ *adj* (clothes) vistoso; (manner) extravagante

flame /fleɪm/ *n* llama *f*. **go up in ~s** incendiarse

flamingo /flə'mɪŋgəʊ/ *n* (*pl* **-o(e)s** flamenco *m*

flammable /'flæməbl/ *adj* inflamable

flan /flæn/ *n* tartaleta *f*

flank /flænk/ *n* (*of animal*) ijada *f*; (*of person*) costado *m*; (*Mil, Sport*) flanco *m*

flannel /'flænl/ *n* franela *f*; (*for face*) paño *m* (para lavarse la cara).

flap /flæp/ *vi* (*pt* **flapped**) ondear; (wings) aletear. ● *vt* batir (wings); agitar (arms). ● *n* (*cover*) tapa *f*; (*of pocket*) cartera *f*; (*of table*) ala *f*. **get into a ~** [I] ponerse nervioso

flare /fleə(r)/ ● *n* llamarada *f*; (*Mil*)

f

bengala *f*; (*in skirt*) vuelo *m*. □ ~ **up** *vi* llamear; (fighting) estallar; (person) encolerizarse

flash /flæʃ/ ● *vi* destellar. ● *vt* (*aim torch*) dirigir; (*flaunt*) hacer ostentación de. ~ **past** pasar como un rayo. ● *n* destello *m*; (*Photo*) flash *m*. **~back** *n* escena *f* retrospectiva. **~light** *n* (*Amer, torch*) linterna *f*. **~y** *adj* ostentoso

f

flask /flɑ:sk/ *n* frasco *m*; (*vacuum flask*) termo *m*

flat /flæt/ *adj* (**flatter, flattest**) plano; (tyre) desinflado; (refusal) categórico; (fare, rate) fijo; (*Mus*) bemol. ● *adv* (*Mus*) demasiado bajo. ~ **out** (*at top speed*) a toda velocidad. ● *n* (*rooms*) apartamento *m*, piso *m*; [!] pinchazo *m*; (*Mus*) (*Auto, esp Amer*) bemol *m*. **~ly** *adv* categóricamente. **~ten** *vt* allanar, aplanar

flatter /flætə(r)/ *vt* adular. **~ing** *adj* (person) lisonjero; (clothes) favorecedor. **~y** *n* adulación *f*

flaunt /flɔ:nt/ *vt* hacer ostentación de

flavour /ˈfleɪvə(r)/ *n* sabor *m*. ● *vt* sazonar. **~ing** *n* condimento *m*

flaw /flɔ:/ *n* defecto *m*. **~less** *adj* perfecto

flea /fli:/ *n* pulga *f*

fleck /flek/ *n* mancha *f*, pinta *f*

fled /fled/ *see* FLEE

flee /fli:/ *vi* (*pt* **fled**) huir. ● *vt* huir de

fleece /fli:s/ *n* vellón *m*. ● *vt* [!] desplumar

fleet /fli:t/ *n* flota *f*; (*of cars*) parque *m* móvil

fleeting /ˈfli:tɪŋ/ *adj* fugaz

Flemish /ˈflemɪʃ/ *adj* & *n* flamenco (*m*)

flesh /fleʃ/ *n* carne *f*. **in the** ~ en persona

flew /flu:/ *see* FLY

flex /fleks/ *vt* doblar; flexionar (muscle). ● *n* (*Elec*) cable *m*

flexib|ility /fleksəˈbɪlətɪ/ *n* flexibilidad *f*. **~le** /ˈfleksəbl/ *adj* flexible

flexitime /ˈfleksɪtaɪm/, (*Amer*) **flextime** /ˈflekstaɪm/ *n* horario *m* flexible

flick /flɪk/ *n* golpecito *m*. ● *vt* dar un golpecito a. □ ~ **through** *vt* hojear

flicker /ˈflɪkə(r)/ *vi* parpadear. ● *n* parpadeo *m*; (*of hope*) resquicio *m*

flies /flaɪz/ *npl* (*on trousers*) bragueta *f*

flight /flaɪt/ *n* vuelo *m*; (*fleeing*) huida *f*, fuga *f*. ~ **of stairs** tramo *m* de escalera *f*. **take (to)** ~ darse a la fuga. ~ **attendant** *n* (*male*) sobrecargo *m*, aeromozo *m* (*LAm*); (*female*) azafata *f*, aeromoza *f* (*LAm*). **~-deck** *n* cubierta *f* de vuelo

flimsy /ˈflɪmzɪ/ *adj* (**-ier, -iest**) flojo, débil, poco sólido

flinch /flɪntʃ/ *vi* retroceder (**from** ante)

fling /flɪŋ/ *vt* (*pt* **flung**) arrojar. ● *n* (*love affair*) aventura *f*; (*wild time*) juerga *f*

flint /flɪnt/ *n* pedernal *m*; (*for lighter*) piedra *f*

flip /flɪp/ *vt* (*pt* **flipped**) dar un golpecito a. ● *n* golpecito *m*. □ ~ **through** *vt* hojear.

flippant /ˈflɪpənt/ *adj* poco serio

flipper /ˈflɪpə(r)/ *n* aleta *f*

flirt /flɜ:t/ *vi* coquetear. ● *n* (*woman*) coqueta *f*; (*man*) coqueto *m*

flit /flɪt/ *vi* (*pt* **flitted**) revolotear

float /fləʊt/ *vi* flotar. ● *vt* hacer flotar; introducir en Bolsa (company).

● *n* flotador *m*; (*cash*) caja *f* chica

flock /flɒk/ *n* (*of birds*) bandada *f*; (*of sheep*) rebaño *m*. ● *vi* congregarse

flog /flɒg/ *vt* (*pt* **flogged**) (*beat*) azotar; (*fam, sell*) vender

flood /flʌd/ *n* inundación *f*; (*fig*) avalancha *f*. ● *vt* inundar. ● *vi* (building etc) inundarse; (river) desbordar. **~light** *n* foco *m*. ● *vt* (*pt* **~lit**) iluminar (con focos)

floor /flɔ:(r)/ *n* suelo *m*; (*storey*) piso *m*; (*for dancing*) pista *f*. ● *vt* derribar; (*baffle*) confundir

flop /flɒp/ *vi* (*pt* **flopped**) dejarse caer pesadamente; (*fam, fail*) fracasar. ● *n* [!] fracaso *m*. **~py** *adj* flojo. ● *n* see **~PY DISK**. **~py disk** *n* disquete *m*, floppy (disk) *m*

floral /'flɔ:rəl/ *adj* floral

florid /'flɒrɪd/ *adj* florido

florist /'flɒrɪst/ *n* florista *m & f*

flounder /'flaʊndə(r)/ *vi* (*in water*) luchar para mantenerse a flote; (speaker) quedar sin saber qué decir

flour /flaʊə(r)/ *n* harina *f*

flourish /'flʌrɪʃ/ *vi* florecer; (business) prosperar. ● *vt* blandir. ● *n* ademán *m* elegante; (*in handwriting*) rasgo *m*. **~ing** *adj* próspero

flout /flaʊt/ *vt* burlarse de

flow /fləʊ/ *vi* fluir; (blood) correr; (*hang loosely*) caer. ● *n* flujo *m*; (*stream*) corriente *f*; (*of traffic, information*) circulación *f*. **~ chart** *n* organigrama *m*

flower /'flaʊə(r)/ *n* flor *f*. ● *vi* florecer, florear (*Mex*). **~ bed** *n* macizo *m* de flores. **~y** *adj* florido

flown /fləʊn/ *see* **FLY**

flu /flu:/ *n* gripe *f*

fluctuat|e /'flʌktjʊeɪt/ *vi* fluctuar. **~ion** /-'eɪʃn/ *n* fluctuación *f*

flue /flu:/ *n* tiro *m*

fluen|cy /'flu:ənsɪ/ *n* fluidez *f*. **~t** *adj* (style) fluido; (speaker) elocuente. **be ~t in a language** hablar un idioma con fluidez. **~tly** *adv* con fluidez

fluff /flʌf/ *n* pelusa *f*. **~y** *adj* (**-ier, -iest**) velloso

fluid /'flu:ɪd/ *adj & n* fluido (*m*)

flung /flʌŋ/ *see* **FLING**

fluorescent /flʊə'resnt/ *adj* fluorescente

flush /flʌʃ/ *vi* ruborizarse. ● *vt*. **~ the toilet** tirar de la cadena, jalarle a la cadena (*LAm*). ● *n* (*blush*) rubor *m*

fluster /'flʌstə(r)/ *vt* poner nervioso

flute /flu:t/ *n* flauta *f*

flutter /'flʌtə(r)/ *vi* ondear; (bird) revolotear. ● *n* (*of wings*) revoloteo *m*; (*fig*) agitación *f*

flux /flʌks/ *n* flujo *m*. **be in a state of ~** estar siempre cambiando

fly /flaɪ/ *vi* (*pt* **flew**, *pp* **flown**) volar; (passenger) ir en avión; (flag) flotar; (*rush*) correr. ● *vt* pilotar, pilotear (*LAm*) (aircraft); transportar en avión (passengers, goods); izar (flag). ● *n* mosca *f*; (*of trousers*) *see* **FLIES**. **~ing** *adj* volante. **~ing visit** visita *f* relámpago. ● *n* (*activity*) aviación *f*. **~leaf** *n* guarda *f*. **~over** *n* paso *m* elevado

foal /fəʊl/ *n* potro *m*

foam /fəʊm/ *n* espuma *f*. ● *vi* espumar. **~ rubber** *n* goma *f* espuma, hule *m* espuma (*Mex*)

fob /fɒb/ *vt* (*pt* **fobbed**). **~ sth off onto s.o.** (*palm off*) encajarle algo a uno

focal /'fəʊkl/ *adj* focal

focus /'fəʊkəs/ *n* (*pl* **-cuses** *or* **-ci** /-saɪ/) foco *m*; (*fig*) centro *m*. **in ~**

enfocado. **out of ~** desenfocado. ● *vt* (*pt* **focused**) enfocar (*fig*) concentrar. ● *vi* enfocar; (*fig*) concentrarse (**on** en)

fodder /ˈfɒdə(r)/ *n* forraje *m*

foe /fəʊ/ *n* enemigo *m*

foetus /ˈfiːtəs/ *n* (*pl* **-tuses**) feto *m*

fog /fɒg/ *n* niebla *f*

f

fog|gy *adj* (**-ier, -iest**) nebuloso. **it is ~gy** hay niebla. **~horn** *n* sirena *f* de niebla

foible /ˈfɔɪbl/ *n* punto *m* débil

foil /fɔɪl/ *vt* (*thwart*) frustrar. ● *n* papel *m* de plata

foist /fɔɪst/ *vt* encajar (**on** a)

fold /fəʊld/ *vt* doblar; cruzar (arms). ● *vi* doblarse; (*fail*) fracasar. ● *n* pliegue *m*. (*for sheep*) redil *m*. **~er** *n* carpeta *f*. **~ing** *adj* plegable

foliage /ˈfəʊlɪɪdʒ/ *n* follaje *m*

folk /fəʊk/ *n* gente *f*. ● *adj* popular. **~lore** /-lɔː(r)/ *n* folklore *m*. **~ music** *n* música *f* folklórica; (*modern*) música *f* folk. **~s** *npl* (*one's relatives*) familia *f*

follow /ˈfɒləʊ/ *vt/i* seguir. □ **~ up** *vt* seguir. **~er** *n* seguidor *m*. **~ing** *n* partidarios *mpl*. ● *adj* siguiente. ● *prep* después de

folly /ˈfɒlɪ/ *n* locura *f*

fond /fɒnd/ *adj* (**-er, -est**) (*loving*) cariñoso; (hope) vivo. **be ~ of s.o.** tener(le) cariño a uno. **be ~ of sth** ser aficionado a algo

fondle /ˈfɒndl/ *vt* acariciar

fondness /ˈfɒndnɪs/ *n* cariño *m*; (*for things*) afición *f*

font /fɒnt/ *n* pila *f* bautismal

food /fuːd/ *n* comida *f*. **~ processor** *n* robot *m* de cocina

fool /fuːl/ *n* idiota *m & f* ● *vt* engañar. □ **~ about** *vi* hacer payasadas. **~hardy** *adj* temerario. **~ish** *adj* tonto. **~ishly** *adv* tontamente. **~ishness** *n* tontería *f*. **~proof** *adj* infalible

foot /fʊt/ *n* (*pl* **feet**) pie *m*; (*measure*) pie *m* (= *30,48cm*); (*of animal, furniture*) pata *f*. **get under s.o.'s feet** estorbar a uno. **on ~** a pie. **on/to one's feet** de pie. **put one's ~ in it** meter la pata. ● *vt* pagar (bill). **~age** /-ɪdʒ/ *n* (*of film*) secuencia *f*. **~-and-mouth disease** *n* fiebre *f* aftosa. **~ball** *n* (*ball*) balón *m*; (*game*) fútbol *m*; (*American ~ball*) fútbol *m* americano. **~baller** *n* futbolista *m & f*. **~bridge** *n* puente *m* para peatones. **~hills** *npl* estribaciones *fpl*. **~hold** *n* punto *m* de apoyo. **~ing** *n* pie *m*. **on an equal ~ing** en igualdad de condiciones. **~lights** *npl* candilejas *fpl*. **~man** /-mən/ *n* lacayo *m*. **~note** *n* nota *f* (al pie de la página). **~path** *n* (*in country*) senda *f*; (*in town*) acera *f*, banqueta *f* (*Mex*). **~print** *n* huella *f*. **~step** *n* paso *m*. **~wear** *n* calzado *m*

for /fɔː(r)//fə(r)/

● *preposition*

···➤ (*intended for*) para. **it's ~ my mother** es para mi madre. **she works ~ a multinational** trabaja para una multinacional

···➤ (*on behalf of*) por. **I did it ~ you** lo hice por ti

➡ See entries **para** and **por** for further information

···➤ (*expressing purpose*) para. **I use it ~ washing the car** lo uso para limpiar el coche. **what ~?** ¿para qué?. **to go out ~ a meal** salir a comer fuera

····➤ (*in favour of*) a favor de. **are you ~ or against the idea?** ¿estás a favor o en contra de la idea?

····➤ (*indicating cost, in exchage for*) por. **I bought it ~ 30 pounds** lo compré por 30 libras. **she left him ~ another man** lo dejó por otro. **thanks ~ everything** gracias por todo. **what's the Spanish ~ toad'?** ¿cómo se dice toad' en español?

····➤ (*expressing duration*) **he read ~ two hours** leyó durante dos horas. **how long are you going ~?** ¿por cuánto tiempo vas? **I've been waiting ~ three hours** hace tres horas que estoy esperando, llevo tres horas esperando

····➤ (*in the direction of*) para. **the train ~ Santiago** el tren para Santiago

● *conjunction* (*because*) porque, pues (*literary usage*). **she left at once, ~ it was getting late** se fue en seguida, porque or pues se hacía tarde

forage /'fɒrɪdʒ/ *vi* forrajear. ● *n* forraje *m*

forbade /fə'bæd/ *see* FORBID

forbearance /fɔ:'beərəns/ *n* paciencia *f*

forbid /fə'bɪd/ *vt* (*pt* **forbade**, *pp* **forbidden**) prohibir (**s.o. to do** a uno hacer). **~ s.o. sth** prohibir algo a uno. **~ding** *adj* imponente

force /fɔ:s/ *n* fuerza *f*. **by ~** a la fuerza. **come into ~** entrar en vigor. **the ~s** las fuerzas *fpl* armadas. ● *vt* forzar; (*compel*) obligar (**s.o. to do sth** a uno a hacer algo). **~ on** imponer a. **~ open** forzar. **~d** *adj* forzado. **~-feed** *vt* alimentar a la fuerza. **~ful** *adj* enérgico

forceps /'fɔ:seps/ *n* fórceps *m*

forcibl|e /'fɔ:səbl/ *adj* a la fuerza. **~y** *adv* a la fuerza

ford /fɔ:d/ *n* vado *m* ● *vt* vadear

fore /fɔ:(r)/ *adj* anterior. ● *n*. **come to the ~** hacerse evidente

forearm /'fɔ:rɑ:m/ *n* antebrazo *m*

foreboding /fɔ:'bəʊdɪŋ/ *n* presentimiento *m*

forecast /'fɔ:kɑ:st/ *vt* (*pt* **forecast**) pronosticar (weather); prever (result). ● *n* pronóstico *m*. **weather ~** pronóstico *m* del tiempo

forecourt /'fɔ:kɔ:t/ *n* patio *m* delantero

forefinger /'fɔ:fɪŋgə(r)/ *n* (dedo *m*) índice *m*

forefront /'fɔ:frʌnt/ *n* vanguardia *f*. **in the ~** a la vanguardia

forego /fɔ:'gəʊ/ *vt* (*pt* **forewent**, *pp* **foregone**) *see* FORGO

foregone /'fɔ:gɒn/ *adj*. **~ conclusion** resultado *m* previsto

foreground /'fɔ:graʊnd/ *n*. **in the ~** en primer plano

forehead /'fɒrɪd/ *n* frente *f*

foreign /'fɒrən/ *adj* extranjero; (trade) exterior; (travel) al extranjero, en el extranjero. **~er** *n* extranjero *m*

foreman /'fɔ:mən/ (*pl* **-men** /-mən/) *n* capataz *m*

foremost /'fɔ:məʊst/ *adj* primero. ● *adv*. **first and ~** ante todo

forerunner /'fɔ:rʌnə(r)/ *n* precursor *m*

foresee /fɔ:'si:/ *vt* (*pt* **-saw**, *pp* **-seen**) prever. **~able** *adj* previsible

foresight /'fɔ:saɪt/ *n* previsión *f*

forest /'fɒrɪst/ *n* bosque *m*
forestall /fɔː'stɔːl/ *vt* (*prevent*) prevenir; (*preempt*) anticiparse a
forestry /'fɒrɪstrɪ/ *n* silvicultura *f*
foretaste /'fɔːteɪst/ *n* anticipo *m*
foretell /fɔː'tel/ *vt* (*pt* **foretold**) predecir
forever /fə'revə(r)/ *adv* para siempre; (*always*) siempre
forewarn /fɔː'wɔːn/ *vt* advertir
forewent /fɔː'went/ *see* **FOREGO**
foreword /'fɔːwɜːd/ *n* prefacio *m*
forfeit /'fɔːfɪt/ *n* (*penalty*) pena *f*; (*in game*) prenda *f*. ● *vt* perder; perder el derecho a (property)
forgave /fə'geɪv/ *see* **FORGIVE**
forge /fɔːdʒ/ *n* fragua *f*. ● *vt* fraguar; (*copy*) falsificar. □ ~ **ahead** *vi* adelantarse rápidamente. ~**r** *n* falsificador *m*. ~**ry** *n* falsificación *f*
forget /fə'get/ *vt* (*pt* **forgot**, *pp* **forgotten**) olvidar, olvidarse de. ● *vi* olvidarse (**about** de). **I forgot** se me olvidó. ~**ful** *adj* olvidadizo
forgive /fə'gɪv/ *vt* (*pt* **forgave**, *pp* **forgiven**) perdonar. ~ **s.o. for sth** perdonar algo a uno. ~**ness** *n* perdón *m*
forgo /fɔː'gəʊ/ *vt* (*pt* **forwent**, *pp* **forgone**) renunciar a
fork /fɔːk/ *n* tenedor *m*; (*for digging*) horca *f*; (*in road*) bifurcación *f*. ● *vi* (road) bifurcarse. □ ~ **out** *vt* [!] desembolsar, aflojar [!]. ~**lift truck** *n* carretilla *f* elevadora
forlorn /fə'lɔːn/ *adj* (hope, attempt) desesperado; (smile) triste
form /fɔːm/ *n* forma *f*; (*document*) formulario *m*; (*Schol*) clase *f*. ● *vt* formar. ● *vi* formarse
formal /'fɔːml/ *adj* formal; (person) formalista; (dress) de etiqueta. ~**ity** /-'mælətɪ/ *n* formalidad *f*. ~**ly** *adv* oficialmente
format /'fɔːmæt/ *n* formato *m*. ● *vt* (*pt* **formatted**) (*Comp*) formatear
formation /fɔː'meɪʃn/ *n* formación *f*
former /'fɔːmə(r)/ *adj* anterior; (*first of two*) primero. ● *n*. **the** ~ el primero *m*, la primera *f*, los primeros *mpl*, las primeras *fpl*. ~**ly** *adv* antes
formidable /'fɔːmɪdəbl/ *adj* formidable
formula /'fɔːmjʊlə/ *n* (*pl* **-ae** /-iː/ *or* **-as**) fórmula *f*. ~**te** /-leɪt/ *vt* formular
forsake /fə'seɪk/ *vt* (*pt* **forsook**, *pp* **forsaken**) abandonar
fort /fɔːt/ *n* fuerte *m*
forth /fɔːθ/ *adv*. **and so** ~ y así sucesivamente. ~**coming** /-'kʌmɪŋ/ *adj* próximo, venidero; (*sociable*) comunicativo. ~**right** *adj* directo. ~**with** /-'wɪθ/ *adv* inmediatamente
fortieth /'fɔːtɪɪθ/ *adj* cuadragésimo. ● *n* cuadragésima parte *f*
fortnight /'fɔːtnaɪt/ *n* quince días *mpl*, quincena *f*. ~**ly** *adj* bimensual. ● *adv* cada quince días
fortress /'fɔːtrɪs/ *n* fortaleza *f*
fortunate /'fɔːtʃənət/ *adj* afortunado. **be** ~ tener suerte. ~**ly** *adv* afortunadamente
fortune /'fɔːtʃuːn/ *n* fortuna *f*. ~**-teller** *n* adivino *m*
forty /'fɔːtɪ/ *adj* & *n* cuarenta (*m*). ~ **winks** un sueñecito
forum /'fɔːrəm/ *n* foro *m*
forward /'fɔːwəd/ *adj* (movement) hacia adelante; (*advanced*) precoz; (*pert*) impertinente. ● *n* (*Sport*) delantero *m*. ● *adv* adelante. **go** ~ avanzar. ● *vt* hacer seguir (letter); enviar (goods). ~**s** *adv* adelante
forwent /fɔː'went/ *see* **FORGO**
fossil /'fɒsl/ *adj* & *n* fósil (*m*)

foster /'fɒstə(r)/ *vt* (*promote*) fomentar; criar (child). ~ **child** *n* hijo *m* adoptivo

fought /fɔ:t/ *see* FIGHT

foul /faʊl/ *adj* (**-er**, **-est**) (smell) nauseabundo; (weather) pésimo; (person) asqueroso; (*dirty*) sucio; (language) obsceno. ● *n* (*Sport*) falta *f*. ● *vt* contaminar; (*entangle*) enredar. ~ **play** *n* (*Sport*) jugada *f* sucia; (*crime*) delito *m*

found /faʊnd/ *see* FIND. ● *vt* fundar.

foundation /faʊn'deɪʃn/ *n* fundación *f*; (*basis*) fundamento. (*cosmetic*) base *f* (de maquillaje). ~**s** *npl* (*of building*) cimientos *mpl*

founder /'faʊndə(r)/ *n* fundador *m*. ● *vi* (ship) hundirse

fountain /'faʊntɪn/ *n* fuente *f*. ~ **pen** *n* pluma *f* (estilográfica) *f*, estilográfica *f*

four /fɔ:(r)/ *adj* & *n* cuatro (*m*). ~**fold** *adj* cuádruple. ● *adv* cuatro veces. ~**some** /-səm/ *n* grupo *m* de cuatro personas ~**teen** /'fɔ:ti:n/ *adj* & *n* catorce (*m*). ~**teenth** *adj* & *n* decimocuarto (*m*). ~**th** /fɔ:θ/ *adj* & *n* cuarto (*m*). ~**-wheel drive** *n* tracción *f* integral

fowl /faʊl/ *n* ave *f*

fox /fɒks/ *n* zorro *m*, zorra *f*. ● *vt* [!] confundir

foyer /'fɔɪeɪ/ *n* (*of theatre*) foyer *m*; (*of hotel*) vestíbulo *m*

fraction /'frækʃn/ *n* fracción *f*

fracture /'fræktʃə(r)/ *n* fractura *f*. ● *vt* fracturar. ● *vi* fracturarse

fragile /'frædʒaɪl/ *adj* frágil

fragment /'frægmənt/ *n* fragmento *m*. ~**ary** /-ərɪ/ *adj* fragmentario

fragran|ce /'freɪgrəns/ *n* fragancia *f*. ~**t** *adj* fragante

frail /freɪl/ *adj* (**-er**, **-est**) frágil

frame /freɪm/ *n* (*of picture, door, window*) marco *m*; (*of spectacles*) montura *f*; (*fig, structure*) estructura *f*. ● *vt* enmarcar (picture); formular (plan, question); (*fam, incriminate unjustly*) incriminar falsamente. ~**work** *n* estructura *f*; (*context*) marco *m*

France /frɑ:ns/ *n* Francia *f*

frank /fræŋk/ *adj* franco. ● *vt* franquear. ~**ly** *adv* francamente

frantic /'fræntɪk/ *adj* frenético. ~ **with** loco de

fratern|al /frə'tɜ:nl/ *adj* fraternal. ~**ity** /frə'tɜ:nɪtɪ/ *n* fraternidad *f*; (*club*) asociación *f*. ~**ize** /'frætənaɪz/ *vi* fraternizar

fraud /frɔ:d/ *n* fraude *m*; (*person*) impostor *m*. ~**ulent** /-jʊlənt/ *adj* fraudulento

fraught /frɔ:t/ *adj* (*tense*) tenso. ~ **with** cargado de

fray /freɪ/ *n* riña *f*

freak /fri:k/ *n* fenómeno *m*; (*monster*) monstruo *m*. ● *adj* anormal. ~**ish** *adj* anormal

freckle /'frekl/ *n* peca *f*. ~**d** *adj* pecoso

free /fri:/ *adj* (**freer** /'fri:ə(r)/, **freest** /'fri:ɪst/) libre; (*gratis*) gratuito. ~ **of charge** gratis. ● *vt* (*pt* **freed**) (*set at liberty*) poner en libertad; (*relieve from*) liberar (**from/of** de); (*untangle*) desenredar. ~**dom** *n* libertad *f*. ~**hold** *n* propiedad *f* absoluta. ~ **kick** *n* tiro *m* libre. ~**lance** *adj* & *adv* por cuenta propia. ~**ly** *adv* libremente. ~**mason** *n* masón *m*. ~**-range** *adj* (eggs) de granja. ~ **speech** *n* libertad *f* de expresión. ~**style** *n* estilo *m* libre. ~**way** *n* (*Amer*) autopista *f*

f

freez|e /'fri:z/ *vt* (*pt* **froze**, *pp* **frozen**) helar; congelar (food, wages). ● *vi* helarse; (*become motionless*) quedarse inmóvil. ● *n* (*on wages, prices*) congelación *f*. **~er** *n* congelador *m*. **~ing** *adj* glacial. ● *n*. **~ing (point)** punto *m* de congelación *f*. **below ~ing** bajo cero

freight /freɪt/ *n* (*goods*) mercancías *fpl*. **~er** *n* buque *m* de carga

French /frentʃ/ *adj* francés. ● *n* (*language*) francés *m*. ● *npl*. **the ~** (*people*) los franceses. **~ fries** *npl* patatas *fpl* fritas, papas *fpl* fritas (*LAm*). **~man** /-mən/ *n* francés *m*. **~ window** *n* puerta *f* ventana. **~woman** *f* francesa *f*

frenz|ied /'frenzɪd/ *adj* frenético. **~y** *n* frenesí *m*

frequency /'fri:kwənsɪ/ *n* frecuencia *f*

frequent /frɪ'kwent/ *vt* frecuentar. ● /'fri:kwənt/ *adj* frecuente. **~ly** *adv* frecuentemente

fresh /freʃ/ *adj* (**-er**, **-est**) fresco; (*different, additional*) nuevo; (water) dulce. **~en** *vi* refrescar. □ **~en up** *vi* (person) refrescarse. **~er** *n* ⊞ see **~MAN**. **~ly** *adv* recientemente. **~man** *n* /-mən/ estudiante *m* de primer año. **~ness** *n* frescura *f*

fret /fret/ *vi* (*pt* **fretted**) preocuparse. **~ful** *adj* (*discontented*) quejoso; (*irritable*) irritable

friction /'frɪkʃn/ *n* fricción *f*

Friday /'fraɪdeɪ/ *n* viernes *m*

fridge /frɪdʒ/ *n* ⊞ frigorífico *m*, nevera *f*, refrigerador *m* (*LAm*)

fried /fraɪd/ see **FRY**. ● *adj* frito

friend /frend/ *n* amigo *m*. **~liness** *n* simpatía *f*. **~ly** *adj* (**-ier**, **-iest**) simpático. **~ship** *n* amistad *f*

fries /fraɪz/ *npl* see **FRENCH FRIES**

frieze /fri:z/ *n* friso *m*

frigate /'frɪgət/ *n* fragata *f*

fright /fraɪt/ *n* miedo *m*; (*shock*) susto *m*. **~en** *vt* asustar. □ **~ off** *vt* ahuyentar. **~ened** *adj* asustado. **be ~ened** tener miedo (**of** de.) **~ful** *adj* espantoso, horrible. **~fully** *adv* terriblemente

frigid /'frɪdʒɪd/ *adj* frígido

frill /frɪl/ *n* volante *m*, olán *m* (*Mex*). **~s** *npl* (*fig*) adornos *mpl*. **with no ~s** sencillo

fringe /frɪndʒ/ *n* (*sewing*) fleco *m*; (*ornamental border*) franja *f*; (*of hair*) flequillo *m*, cerquillo *m* (*LAm*), fleco *m* (*Mex*); (*of area*) periferia *f*; (*of society*) margen *m*

fritter /'frɪtə(r)/ *vt*. □ **~ away** *vt* desperdiciar (time); malgastar (money)

frivol|ity /frɪ'vɒlətɪ/ *n* frivolidad *f*. **~ous** /'frɪvələs/ *adj* frívolo

fro /frəʊ/ see **TO AND FRO**

frock /frɒk/ *n* vestido *m*

frog /frɒg/ *n* rana *f*. **have a ~ in one's throat** tener carraspera. **~man** /-mən/ *n* hombre *m* rana. **~spawn** *n* huevos *mpl* de rana

frolic /'frɒlɪk/ *vi* (*pt* **frolicked**) retozar

from /frɒm//frəm/ *prep* de; (*indicating starting point*) desde; (*habit, conviction*) por; **~ then on** a partir de ahí

front /frʌnt/ *n* parte *f* delantera; (*of building*) fachada *f*; (*of clothes*) delantera *f*; (*Mil, Pol*) frente *f*; (*of book*) principio *m*; (*fig, appearance*) apariencia *f*; (*seafront*) paseo *m* marítimo, malecón *m* (*LAm*). **in ~ of** delante de. ● *adj* delantero; (*first*) primero. **~al** *adj* frontal; (attack) de frente. **~ door** *n* puerta *f* principal

frontier /'frʌntɪə(r)/ *n* frontera *f*

front page *n* (*of newspaper*) primera plana *f*

frost /frɒst/ *n* (*freezing*) helada *f*; (*frozen dew*) escarcha *f*. **~bite** *n* congelación *f*. **~bitten** *adj* congelado. **~ed** *adj* (glass) esmerilado. **~ing** *n* (*Amer*) glaseado *m*. **~y** *adj* (weather) helado; (night) de helada; (*fig*) glacial

froth /frɒθ/ *n* espuma *f*. ● *vi* espumar. **~y** *adj* espumoso

frown /fraʊn/ *vi* fruncir el entrecejo ● *n* ceño *m*. □ **~ on** *vt* desaprobar.

froze /frəʊz/ *see* FREEZE. **~n** /ˈfrəʊzn/ *see* FREEZE. ● *adj* congelado; (region) helado

frugal /ˈfru:gl/ *adj* frugal

fruit /fru:t/ *n* (*in botany*) fruto *m*; (*as food*) fruta *f*. **~ful** /ˈfru:tfl/ *adj* fértil; (*fig*) fructífero. **~ion** /fru:ˈɪʃn/ *n*. **come to ~ion** realizarse. **~less** *adj* infructuoso. **~ salad** *n* macedonia *f* de frutas. **~y** *adj* que sabe a fruta

frustrat|e /frʌˈstreɪt/ *vt* frustrar. **~ion** /-ʃn/ *n* frustración *f*. **~ed** *adj* frustrado. **~ing** *adj* frustrante

fry /fraɪ/ *vt* (*pt* **fried**) freír. ● *vi* freírse. **~ing pan** *n* sárten *f*, sartén *m* (*LAm*)

fudge /fʌdʒ/ *n* dulce *m* de azúcar

fuel /ˈfju:əl/ *n* combustible *m*

fugitive /ˈfju:dʒɪtɪv/ *adj & n* fugitivo (*m*)

fulfil /fʊlˈfɪl/ *vt* (*pt* **fulfilled**) cumplir (con) (promise, obligation); satisfacer (condition); hacer realidad (ambition). **~ment** *n* (*of promise, obligation*) cumplimiento *m*; (*of conditions*) satisfacción *f*; (*of hopes, plans*) realización *f*

full /fʊl/ *adj* (**-er**, **-est**) lleno; (bus, hotel) completo; (account) detallado. **at ~ speed** a máxima velocidad. **be ~ (up)** (*with food*) no poder más. ● *n*. **in ~** sin quitar nada. **to the ~** completamente. **write in ~** escribir con todas las letras. **~back** *n* (*Sport*) defensa *m & f*. **~-blown** /fʊlˈbləʊn/ *adj* verdadero. **~-fledged** /-ˈfledʒd/ *adj* (*Amer*) *see* FULLY-FLEDGED. **~ moon** *n* luna *f* llena. **~-scale** /-ˈskeɪl/ *adj* (drawing) de tamaño natural; (*fig*) amplio. **~ stop** *n* punto *m*. **~-time** *adj* (employment) de jornada completa. ● /-ˈtaɪm/ *adv* a tiempo completo. **~y** *adv* completamente. **~-fledged** /-ˈfledʒd/ *adj* (chick) capaz de volar; (lawyer, nurse) hecho y derecho

fulsome /ˈfʊlsəm/ *adj* excesivo

fumble /ˈfʌmbl/ *vi* buscar (a tientas)

fume /fju:m/ *vi* despedir gases; (*fig, be furious*) estar furioso. **~s** *npl* gases *mpl*

fumigate /ˈfju:mɪgeɪt/ *vt* fumigar

fun /fʌn/ *n* (*amusement*) diversión *f*; (*merriment*) alegría *f*. **for ~** en broma. **have ~** divertirse. **make ~ of** burlarse de

function /ˈfʌŋkʃn/ *n* (*purpose, duty*) función *f*; (*reception*) recepción *f*. ● *vi* funcionar. **~al** *adj* funcional

fund /fʌnd/ *n* fondo *m*. ● *vt* financiar

fundamental /fʌndəˈmentl/ *adj* fundamental. **~ist** *adj & n* fundamentalista (*m & f*)

funeral /ˈfju:nərəl/ *n* entierro *m*, funerales *mpl*. **~ director** *n* director *m* de pompas fúnebres

funfair /ˈfʌnfeə(r)/ *n* feria *f*; (*permanent*) parque *m* de atracciones, parque *m* de diversiones (*LAm*)

fungus /ˈfʌŋgəs/ *n* (*pl* **-gi**/-gaɪ/) hongo *m*

funnel /ˈfʌnl/ *n* (*for pouring*) embudo *m*; (*of ship*) chimenea *f*

funn|ily /ˈfʌnɪlɪ/ *adv* (*oddly*) curiosamente. **~y** *adj* (**-ier**, **-iest**) divertido, gracioso; (*odd*) curioso, raro

fur /fɜ:(r)/ *n* pelo *m*; (*pelt*) piel *f*

furious /ˈfjʊərɪəs/ *adj* furioso. **~ly** *adv* furiosamente

g

furlough /ˈfɜ:ləʊ/ *n* (*Amer*) permiso *m*. **on ~** de permiso

furnace /ˈfɜ:nɪs/ *n* horno *m*

furnish /ˈfɜ:nɪʃ/ *vt* amueblar, amoblar (*LAm*); (*supply*) proveer. **~ings** *npl* muebles *mpl*, mobiliario *m*

furniture /ˈfɜ:nɪtʃə(r)/ *n* muebles *mpl*, mobiliario *m*. **a piece of ~** un mueble

furrow /ˈfʌrəʊ/ *n* surco *m*

furry /ˈfɜ:rɪ/ *adj* peludo

furthe|r /ˈfɜ:ðə(r)/ *adj* más lejano; (*additional*) nuevo. ● *adv* más lejos; (*more*) además. ● *vt* fomentar. **~rmore** *adv* además. **~st** *adj* más lejano. ● *adv* más lejos

furtive /ˈfɜ:tɪv/ *adj* furtivo

fury /ˈfjʊərɪ/ *n* furia *f*

fuse /fju:z/ *vt* (*melt*) fundir; (*fig, unite*) fusionar. **~ the lights** fundir los plomos. ● *vi* fundirse; (*fig*) fusionarse. ● *n* fusible *m*, plomo *m*; (*of bomb*) mecha *f*. **~box** *n* caja *f* de fusibles

fuselage /ˈfju:zəlɑ:ʒ/ *n* fuselaje *m*

fusion /ˈfju:ʒn/ *n* fusión *f*

fuss /fʌs/ *n* (*commotion*) jaleo *m*. **kick up a ~** armar un lío, armar una bronca. **make a ~ of** tratar con mucha atención. ● *vi* preocuparse. **~y** *adj* (**-ier**, **-iest**) (*finicky*) remilgado; (*demanding*) exigente

futil|e /ˈfju:taɪl/ *adj* inútil, vano. **~ity** /fju:ˈtɪlətɪ/ *n* inutilidad *f*

futur|e /ˈfju:tʃə(r)/ *adj* futuro. ● *n* futuro *m*. **in ~e** de ahora en adelante. **~istic** /fju:tʃəˈrɪstɪk/ *adj* futurista

fuzz /fʌz/ *n* pelusa *f*. **~y** *adj* (hair) crespo; (photograph) borroso

Gg

gab /gæb/ *n*. **have the gift of the ~** tener un pico de oro

gabardine /gæbəˈdi:n/ *n* gabardina *f*

gabble /ˈgæbl/ *vi* hablar atropelladamente

gable /ˈgeɪbl/ *n* aguilón *m*

gad /gæd/ *vi* (*pt* **gadded**). **~ about** callejear

gadget /ˈgædʒɪt/ *n* chisme *m*

Gaelic /ˈgeɪlɪk/ *adj & n* gaélico (*m*)

gaffe /gæf/ *n* plancha *f*, metedura *f* de pata, metida *f* de pata (*LAm*)

gag /gæg/ *n* mordaza *f*; (*joke*) chiste *m*. ● *vt* (*pt* **gagged**) amordazar. ● *vi* hacer arcadas

gaiety /ˈgeɪətɪ/ *n* alegría *f*

gaily /ˈgeɪlɪ/ *adv* alegremente

gain /geɪn/ *vt* ganar; (*acquire*) adquirir; (*obtain*) conseguir. ● *vi* (clock) adelantar. ● *n* ganancia *f*; (*increase*) aumento *m*

gait /geɪt/ *n* modo *m* de andar

gala /ˈgɑ:lə/ *n* fiesta *f*. **~ performance** (función *f* de) gala *f*

galaxy /ˈgæləksɪ/ *n* galaxia *f*

gale /geɪl/ *n* vendaval *m*

gall /gɔ:l/ *n* bilis *f*; (*fig*) hiel *f*; (*impudence*) descaro *m*

gallant /ˈgælənt/ *adj* (*brave*) valiente; (*chivalrous*) galante. **~ry** *n* valor *m*

gall bladder /ˈgɔːlblædə(r)/ *n* vesícula *f* biliar

gallery /ˈgælərɪ/ *n* galería *f*

galley /ˈgælɪ/ *n* (*ship*) galera *f*; (*ship's kitchen*) cocina *f*. **~ (proof)** *n* galerada *f*

gallivant /ˈgælɪvænt/ *vi* [!] callejear

gallon /ˈgælən/ *n* galón *m* (*imperial = 4,546l; Amer = 3,785l*)

gallop /ˈgæləp/ *n* galope *m*. ● *vi* (*pt* **galloped**) galopar

gallows /ˈgæləʊz/ *n* horca *f*

galore /gəˈlɔː(r)/ *adj* en abundancia

galvanize /ˈgælvənaɪz/ *vt* galvanizar

gambl|e /ˈgæmbl/ *vi* jugar. **~e on** contar con. ● *vt* jugarse. ● *n* (*venture*) empresa *f* arriesgada; (*bet*) apuesta *f*; (*risk*) riesgo *m*. **~er** *n* jugador *m*. **~ing** *n* juego *m*

game /geɪm/ *n* juego *m*; (*match*) partido *m*; (*animals, birds*) caza *f*. ● *adj* valiente. **~ for** listo para. **~keeper** *n* guardabosque *m*. **~s** *n* (*in school*) deportes *mpl*

gammon /ˈgæmən/ *n* jamón *m* fresco

gamut /ˈgæmət/ *n* gama *f*

gander /ˈgændə(r)/ *n* ganso *m*

gang /gæŋ/ *n* pandilla *f*; (*of workmen*) equipo *m*. **~master** *n contratista de mano de obra indocumentada*. □ **~ up** *vi* unirse (**on** contra)

gangling /ˈgæŋglɪŋ/ *adj* larguirucho

gangrene /ˈgæŋgriːn/ *n* gangrena *f*

gangster /ˈgæŋstə(r)/ *n* bandido *m*, gángster *m & f*

gangway /ˈgæŋweɪ/ *n* pasillo *m*; (*of ship*) pasarela *f*

gaol /dʒeɪl/ *n* cárcel *f*. **~er** *n* carcelero *m*

gap /gæp/ *n* espacio *m*; (*in fence, hedge*) hueco *m*; (*in time*) intervalo *m*; (*in knowledge*) laguna *f*; (*difference*) diferencia *f*

> *i*
>
> **gap year** En Gran Bretaña, es el periodo, entre el final de los estudios secundarios y el ingreso a la universidad, que muchos estudiantes destinan a obtener experiencia laboral relacionada con sus futuras carreras. Otros emprenden actividades no relacionadas con los estudios y para algunos es la oportunidad para ahorrar dinero o viajar.

gap|e /geɪp/ *vi* quedarse boquiabierto; (*be wide open*) estar muy abierto. **~ing** *adj* abierto; (*person*) boquiabierto

garage /ˈgærɑːʒ/ *n* garaje *m*, garage *m* (*LAm*), cochera *f* (*Mex*); (*petrol station*) gasolinera *f*; (*for repairs, sales*) taller *m*, garage *m* (*LAm*)

garbage /ˈgɑːbɪdʒ/ *n* basura *f*. **~ can** *n* (*Amer*) cubo *m* de la basura, bote *m* de la basura (*Mex*). **~ collector**, **~ man** *n* (*Amer*) basurero *m*

garble /ˈgɑːbl/ *vt* tergiversar, embrollar

garden /ˈgɑːdn/ *n* (*of flowers*) jardín *m*; (*of vegetables/fruit*) huerto *m*. ● *vi* trabajar en el jardín. **~er** /ˈgɑːdnə(r)/ *n* jardinero *m*. **~ing** *n* jardinería *f*; (*vegetable growing*) horticultura *f*

gargle /ˈgɑːgl/ *vi* hacer gárgaras

gargoyle /ˈgɑːgɔɪl/ *n* gárgola *f*

garish /ˈgeərɪʃ/ *adj* chillón

garland /ˈgɑːlənd/ *n* guirnalda *f*
garlic / ˈgɑːlɪk/ *n* ajo *m*
garment /ˈgɑːmənt/ *n* prenda *f* (de vestir)
garnish /ˈgɑːnɪʃ/ *vt* adornar, decorar. ● *n* adorno *m*
garret /ˈgærət/ *n* buhardilla *f*
garrison /ˈgærɪsn/ *n* guarnición *f*
garrulous /ˈgærələs/ *adj* hablador
garter /ˈgɑːtə(r)/ *n* liga *f*
gas /gæs/ *n* (*pl* **gases**) gas *m*; (*anaesthetic*) anestésico *m*; (*Amer, petrol*) gasolina *f*. ● *vt* (*pt* **gassed**) asfixiar con gas
gash /gæʃ/ *n* tajo *m*. ● *vt* hacer un tajo de
gasket /ˈgæskɪt/ *n* junta *f*
gas: ~ **mask** *n* careta *f* antigás. ~ **meter** *n* contador *m* de gas
gasoline /ˈgæsəliːn/ *n* (*Amer*) gasolina *f*
gasp /gɑːsp/ *vi* jadear; (*with surprise*) dar un grito ahogado. ● *n* exclamación *f*, grito *m*
gas: ~ **ring** *n* hornillo *m* de gas. ~ **station** *n* (*Amer*) gasolinera *f*
gastric /ˈgæstrɪk/ *adj* gástrico
gate /geɪt/ *n* puerta *f*; (*of metal*) verja *f*; (*barrier*) barrera *f*
gate: ~**crash** *vt* colarse en. ~**crasher** *n* intruso *m* (que ha entrado sin ser invitado). ~**way** *n* puerta *f*
gather /ˈgæðə(r)/ *vt* reunir (people, things); (*accumulate*) acumular; (*pick up*) recoger; recoger (flowers); (*fig, infer*) deducir; (*sewing*) fruncir. ~ **speed** acelerar. ● *vi* (people) reunirse; (things) acumularse. ~**ing** *n* reunión *f*
gaudy /ˈgɔːdɪ/ *adj* (**-ier, -iest**) chillón
gauge /geɪdʒ/ *n* (*measurement*) medida *f*; (*Rail*) entrevía *f*; (*instrument*) indicador *m*. ● *vt* medir; (*fig*) estimar
gaunt /gɔːnt/ *adj* descarnado; (*from illness*) demacrado
gauntlet /ˈgɔːntlɪt/ *n*. **run the ~ of** aguantar el acoso de
gauze /gɔːz/ *n* gasa *f*
gave /geɪv/ *see* **GIVE**
gawky /ˈgɔːkɪ/ *adj* (**-ier, -iest**) torpe
gawp /gɔːp/ *vi*. ~ **at** mirar como un tonto
gay /geɪ/ *adj* (**-er, -est**) (*fam, homosexual*) homosexual, gay [!]; (*dated, joyful*) alegre
gaze /geɪz/ *vi*. ~ **(at)** mirar (fijamente). ● *n* mirada *f* (fija)
gazelle /gəˈzel/ *n* (*pl invar or* **-s**) gacela *f*
GB *abbr see* **GREAT BRITAIN**
gear /gɪə(r)/ *n* equipo *m*; (*Tec*) engranaje *m*; (*Auto*) marcha *f*, cambio *m*. **in ~** engranado. **out of ~** desengranado. **change ~, shift ~** (*Amer*) cambiar de marcha. ● *vt* adaptar. ~**box** *n* (*Auto*) caja *f* de cambios
geese /giːs/ *see* **GOOSE**
gel /dʒel/ *n* gel *m*
gelatine /ˈdʒelətiːn/ *n* gelatina *f*
gelignite /ˈdʒelɪgnaɪt/ *n* gelignita *f*
gem /dʒem/ *n* piedra *f* preciosa
Gemini /ˈdʒemɪnaɪ/ *n* Géminis *mpl*
gender /ˈdʒendə(r)/ *n* género *m*
gene /dʒiːn/ *n* gen *m*, gene *m*
genealogy /dʒiːnɪˈælədʒɪ/ *n* genealogía *f*
general /ˈdʒenərəl/ *adj* general. ● *n* general *m*. **in ~** en general. ~ **election** *n* elecciones *fpl* generales. ~**ization** /-ˈzeɪʃn/ *n* generalización

f. **~ize** *vt/i* generalizar. **~ knowledge** *n* cultura *f* general. **~ly** *adv* generalmente. **~ practitioner** *n* médico *m* de cabecera

generat|e /ˈdʒenəreɪt/ *vt* generar. **~ion** /-ˈreɪʃn/ *n* generación *f*. **~ion gap** *n* brecha *f* generacional. **~or** *n* generador *m*

genero|sity /dʒenəˈrɒsətɪ/ *n* generosidad *f*. **~us** /ˈdʒenərəs/ *adj* generoso; (*plentiful*) abundante

genetic /dʒɪˈnetɪk/ *adj* genético. **~s** *n* genética *f*

Geneva /dʒɪˈni:və/ *n* Ginebra *f*

genial /ˈdʒi:nɪəl/ *adj* simpático, afable

genital /ˈdʒenɪtl/ *adj* genital. **~s** *npl* genitales *mpl*

genitive /ˈdʒenɪtɪv/ *adj* & *n* genitivo (*m*)

genius /ˈdʒi:nɪəs/ *n* (*pl* **-uses**) genio *m*

genocide /ˈdʒenəsaɪd/ *n* genocidio *m*

genome /ˈdʒi:nəʊm/ *n* genoma *m*

genre /ʒɑ:ŋr/ *n* género *m*

gent /dʒent/ *n* 🄸 señor *m*. **~s** *n* aseo *m* de caballeros

genteel /dʒenˈti:l/ *adj* distinguido

gentl|e /ˈdʒentl/ *adj* (**-er, -est**) (person) dulce; (murmur, breeze) suave; (hint) discreto. **~eman** *n* señor *m*; (*well-bred*) caballero *m*. **~eness** *n* amabilidad *f*

genuine /ˈdʒenjʊɪn/ *adj* verdadero; (person) sincero

geograph|er /dʒɪˈɒgrəfə(r)/ *n* geógrafo *m*. **~ical** /dʒɪəˈgræfɪkl/ *adj* geográfico. **~y** /dʒɪˈɒgrəfɪ/ *n* geografía *f*

geolog|ical /dʒɪəˈlɒdʒɪkl/ *adj* geológico. **~ist** /dʒɪˈɒlədʒɪst/ *n* geólogo *m*. **~y** /dʒɪˈɒlədʒɪ/ *n* geología *f*

geometr|ic(al) /dʒɪəˈmetrɪk(l)/ *adj* geométrico. **~y** /dʒɪˈɒmətrɪ/ *n* geometría *f*

geranium /dʒəˈreɪnɪəm/ *n* geranio *m*

geriatric /dʒerɪˈætrɪk/ *adj* (patient) anciano; (ward) de geriatría. **~s** *n* geriatría *f*

germ /dʒɜ:m/ *n* microbio *m*, germen *m*

German /ˈdʒɜ:mən/ *adj* & *n* alemán (*m*). **~ic** /dʒɜ:ˈmænɪk/ *adj* germánico. **~ measles** *n* rubéola *f*. **~y** *n* Alemania *f*

germinate /ˈdʒɜ:mɪneɪt/ *vi* germinar

gesticulate /dʒeˈstɪkjʊleɪt/ *vi* hacer ademanes, gesticular

gesture /ˈdʒestʃə(r)/ *n* gesto *m*, ademán *m*; (*fig*) gesto *m*. ● *vi* hacer gestos

get /get/

past **got;** past participle **got, gotten** (*Amer*); present participle **getting**

● *transitive verb*

····➤ (*obtain*) conseguir, obtener. **did you get the job?** ¿conseguiste el trabajo?

····➤ (*buy*) comprar. **I got it in the sales** lo compré en las rebajas

····➤ (*achieve, win*) sacar. **she got very good marks** sacó muy buenas notas

····➤ (*receive*) recibir. **I got a letter from Alex** recibí una carta de Alex

····➤ (*fetch*) ir a buscar. **~ your coat** vete a buscar tu abrigo

g

····➤ (*experience*) llevarse. **I got a terrible shock** me llevé un shock espantoso
····➤ (*fam, understand*) entender. **I don't ~ what you mean** no entiendo lo que quieres decir
····➤ (*ask or persuade*) **to ~ s.o. to do sth** hacer que uno haga algo

Note that *hacer que* is followed by the subjunctive form of the verb

····➤ (*cause to be done or happen*) **I must ~ this watch fixed** tengo que llevar a arreglar este reloj. **they got the roof mended** hicieron arreglar el techo

● *intransitive verb*

····➤ (*arrive, reach*) llegar. **I got there late** llegué tarde. **how do you ~ to Paddington?** ¿cómo se llega a Paddington?
····➤ (*become*) **to ~ tired** cansarse. **she got very angry** se puso furiosa. **it's ~ting late** se está haciendo tarde

➡ For translations of expressions such as **get better, get old** see entries **better, old** etc. See also **got**

····➤ **to get to do sth** (*manage to*) llegar a. **did you get to see him?** ¿llegaste a verlo? ▫ **get along** *vi* (*manage*) arreglárselas; (*progress*) hacer progresos. ▫ **get along with** *vt* llevarse bien con. ▫ **get at** *vt* (*reach*) llegar a; (*imply*) querer decir. ▫ **get away** *vi* salir; (*escape*) escaparse. ▫ **get back** *vi* volver. *vt* (*recover*) recobrar. ▫ **get by** *vi* (*manage*) arreglárselas; (*pass*) pasar. ▫ **get down** *vi* bajar. *vt* (*make depressed*) deprimir. ▫ **get in** *vi* entrar. ▫ **get into** *vt* entrar en; subir a (car) ▫ **get off** *vt* bajar(se) de (train etc). *vi* (*from train etc*) bajarse; (*Jurid*) salir absuelto. ▫ **get on** *vi* (*progress*) hacer progresos; (*succeed*) tener éxito. *vt* subirse a (train etc). ▫ **get on with** *vt* (*be on good terms with*) llevarse bien con; (*continue*) seguir con. ▫ **get out** *vi* salir. *vt* (*take out*) sacar. ▫ **get out of** *vt* (*fig*) librarse de. ▫ **get over** *vt* reponerse de (illness). ▫ **get round** *vt* soslayar (difficulty etc); engatusar (person). ▫ **get through** *vi* pasar; (*on phone*) comunicarse (**to** con). ▫ **get together** *vi* (*meet up*) reunirse. *vt* (*assemble*) reunir. ▫ **get up** *vi* levantarse; (*climb*) subir

geyser /ˈgiːzə(r)/ *n* géiser *m*

ghastly /ˈgɑːstlɪ/ *adj* (**-ier, -iest**) horrible

gherkin /ˈgɜːkɪn/ *n* pepinillo *m*

ghetto /ˈgetəʊ/ *n* (*pl* **-os**) gueto *m*

ghost /gəʊst/ *n* fantasma *m*. **~ly** *adj* espectral

giant /ˈdʒaɪənt/ *n* gigante *m*. ● *adj* gigantesco

gibberish /ˈdʒɪbərɪʃ/ *n* jerigonza *f*

gibe /dʒaɪb/ *n* pulla *f*

giblets /ˈdʒɪblɪts/ *npl* menudillos *mpl*

gidd|iness /ˈgɪdɪnɪs/ *n* vértigo *m*. **~y** *adj* (**-ier, -iest**) mareado. **be/feel ~y** estar/sentirse mareado

gift /gɪft/ *n* regalo *m*; (*ability*) don

m. **~ed** *adj* dotado de talento. **~-wrap** *vt* envolver para regalo

gigantic /dʒaɪˈgæntɪk/ *adj* gigantesco

giggle /ˈgɪgl/ *vi* reírse tontamente. ● *n* risita *f*

gild /gɪld/ *vt* dorar

gills /gɪlz/ *npl* agallas *fpl*

gilt /gɪlt/ *n* dorado *m.* ● *adj* dorado

gimmick /ˈgɪmɪk/ *n* truco *m*

gin / dʒɪn/ *n* ginebra *f*

ginger /ˈdʒɪndʒə(r)/ *n* jengibre *m.* ● *adj* rojizo. **he has ~ hair** es pelirrojo. **~bread** *n* pan *m* de jengibre

gipsy /ˈdʒɪpsɪ/ *n* gitano *m*

giraffe /dʒɪˈrɑːf/ *n* jirafa *f*

girder /ˈgɜːdə(r)/ *n* viga *f*

girdle /ˈgɜːdl/ *n* (*belt*) cinturón *m*; (*corset*) corsé *m*

girl /gɜːl/ *n* chica *f*, muchacha *f*; (*child*) niña *f.* **~ band** *n* grupo *m* pop de chicas. **~friend** *n* amiga *f*; (*of boy*) novia *f.* **~ish** *adj* de niña; (boy) afeminado. **~ scout** *n* (*Amer*) exploradora *f*, guía *f*

giro /ˈdʒaɪrəʊ/ *n* (*pl* **-os**) giro *m* (bancario)

girth /gɜːθ/ *n* circunferencia *f*

gist /dʒɪst/ *n* lo esencial

give /gɪv/ *vt* (*pt* **gave**, *pp* **given**) dar; (*deliver*) entregar; regalar (present); prestar (aid, attention). **~ o.s. to** darse a. ● *vi* dar; (*yield*) ceder; (*stretch*) dar de sí. ● *n* elasticidad *f.* □ **~ away** *vt* regalar; revelar (secret). □ **~ back** *vt* devolver. □ **~ in** *vi* ceder. □ **~ off** *vt* emitir. □ **~ out** *vt* distribuir. (*become used up*) agotarse. □ **~ up** *vt* renunciar a; (*yield*) ceder. **~ up doing sth** dejar de hacer algo. **~ o.s. up** entregarse (**to** a). *vi* rendirse. **~n** /ˈgɪvn/ *see* **GIVE**. ● *adj* dado. **~n name** *n* nombre *m* de pila

glacier /ˈglæsɪə(r)/ *n* glaciar *m*

glad /glæd/ *adj* contento. **be ~** alegrarse (**about** de). **~den** *vt* alegrar

gladly /ˈglædlɪ/ *adv* alegremente; (*willingly*) con mucho gusto

glamo|rous /ˈglæmərəs/ *adj* glamoroso. **~ur** /ˈglæmə(r)/ *n* glamour *m*

glance /glɑːns/ *n* ojeada *f.* ● *vi.* **~ at** dar un vistazo a

gland /glænd/ *n* glándula *f*

glar|e /gleə(r)/ *vi* (light) deslumbrar; (*stare angrily*) mirar airadamente. ● *n* resplandor *m*; (*stare*) mirada *f* airada. **~ing** *adj* deslumbrante; (*obvious*) manifiesto

glass /glɑːs/ *n* (*material*) cristal *m*, vidrio *m*; (*without stem or for wine*) vaso *m*; (*with stem*) copa *f*; (*for beer*) caña *f*; (*mirror*) espejo *m.* **~es** *npl* (*spectacles*) gafas *fpl*, lentes *fpl* (*LAm*), anteojos *mpl* (*LAm*). **~y** *adj* vítreo

glaze /gleɪz/ *vt* poner cristal(es) *or* vidrio(s) a (windows, doors); vidriar (pottery). ● *vi.* **~ (over)** (eyes) vidriarse. ● *n* barniz *m*; (*for pottery*) esmalte *m*

gleam /gliːm/ *n* destello *m.* ● *vi* destellar

glean /gliːn/ *vt* espigar; recoger (information)

glee /gliː/ *n* regocijo *m*

glib /glɪb/ *adj* de mucha labia; (reply) fácil

glid|e /glaɪd/ *vi* deslizarse; (*plane*) planear. **~er** *n* planeador *m.* **~ing** *n* planeo *m*

glimmer /ˈglɪmə(r)/ *n* destello *m.* ● *vi* destellar

glimpse /glɪmps/ *n.* **catch a ~ of** vislumbrar, ver brevemente. ● *vt* vislumbrar

glint /glɪnt/ *n* destello *m*. ● *vi* destellar
glisten /'glɪsn/ *vi* brillar
glitter /'glɪtə(r)/ *vi* brillar. ● *n* brillo *m*
gloat /gləʊt/ *vi*. ~ **on/over** regodearse sobre
glob|al /gləʊbl/ *adj* (*worldwide*) mundial; (*all-embracing*) global. **~al warming** *n* calentamiento *m* global. **~e** /gləʊb/ *n* globo *m*
g
gloom /glu:m/ *n* oscuridad *f*; (*sadness, fig*) tristeza *f*. **~y** *adj* (**-ier, -iest**) triste; (*pessimistic*) pesimista
glor|ify /'glɔ:rɪfaɪ/ *vt* glorificar. **~ious** /'glɔ:rɪəs/ *adj* espléndido; (deed, hero etc) glorioso. **~y** /'glɔ:rɪ/ *n* gloria *f*
gloss /glɒs/ *n* lustre *m*. ~ **(paint)** (pintura *f* al *or* de) esmalte *m*. □ ~ **over** *vt* (*make light of*) minimizar; (*cover up*) encubrir
glossary /'glɒsərɪ/ *n* glosario *m*
glossy /'glɒsɪ/ *adj* brillante
glove /glʌv/ *n* guante *m*. ~ **compartment** *n* (*Auto*) guantera *f*, gaveta *f*
glow /gləʊ/ *vi* brillar. ● *n* brillo *m*. **~ing** /'gləʊɪŋ/ *adj* incandescente; (account) entusiasta; (complexion) rojo
glucose /'glu:kəʊs/ *n* glucosa *f*
glue /glu:/ *n* cola *f*, goma *f* de pegar. ● *vt* (*pres p* **gluing**) pegar
glum /glʌm/ *adj* (**glummer, glummest**) triste
glutton /'glʌtn/ *n* glotón *m*
gnarled /nɑ:ld/ *adj* nudoso
gnash /næʃ/ *vt*. ~ **one's teeth** rechinar los dientes
gnat /næt/ *n* jején *m*, mosquito *m*
gnaw /nɔ:/ *vt* roer. ● *vi*. ~ **at** roer
gnome /nəʊm/ *n* gnomo *m*

go /gəʊ/

3rd pers sing present **goes**; past **went**; past participle **gone**

● *intransitive verb*
····➤ ir. **I'm going to France** voy a Francia. **to go shopping** ir de compras. **to go swimming** ir a nadar
····➤ (*leave*) irse. **we're going on Friday** nos vamos el viernes
····➤ (*work, function*) (engine, clock) funcionar
····➤ (*become*) **to go deaf** quedarse sordo. **to go mad** volverse loco. **his face went red** se puso colorado
····➤ (*stop*) (headache, pain) irse (+ *me/te/le*). **the pain's gone** se me ha ido el dolor
····➤ (*turn out, progress*) ir. **everything's going very well** todo va muy bien. **how did the exam go?** ¿qué tal te fue en el examen?
····➤ (*match, suit*) combinar. **the jacket and the trousers go well together** la chaqueta y los pantalones combinan bien.
····➤ (*cease to function*) (bulb, fuse) fundirse. **the brakes have gone** los frenos no funcionan
● *auxiliary verb* **to be going to** + *infinitive* ir a + *infinitivo*. **it's going to rain** va a llover. **she's going to win!** ¡va a ganar!
● *noun* (*pl* **goes**)
····➤ (*turn*) turno *m*. **you have three goes** tienes tres turnos. **it's your go** te toca a ti
····➤ (*attempt*) **to have a go at**

doing sth intentar hacer algo. **have another go** inténtalo de nuevo

····▸ (*energy, drive*) empuje *m*. **she has a lot of go** tiene mucho empuje

····▸ (*in phrases*) **I've been on the go all day** no he parado en todo el día. **to make a go of sth** sacar algo adelante □ **go across** *vt/vi* cruzar. □ **go after** *vi* perseguir. □ **go away** *vi* irse. □ **go back** *vi* volver. □ **go back on** *vt* faltar a (promise etc). □ **go by** *vi* pasar. □ **go down** *vi* bajar; (sun) ponerse. □ **go for** *vt* (*fam, attack*) atacar. □ **go in** *vi* entrar. □ **go in for** *vt* presentarse para (exam); participar en (competition). □ **go off** *vi* (*leave*) irse; (*go bad*) pasarse; (*explode*) estallar; (lights) apagarse. □ **go on** *vi* seguir; (*happen*) pasar; (*be switched on*) encenderse, prenderse (*LAm*). □ **go out** *vi* salir; (fire, light) apagarse. □ **go over** *vt* (*check*) revisar; (*revise*) repasar. □ **go through** *vt* pasar por; (*search*) registrar; (*check*) examinar. □ **go up** *vi/vt* subir. □ **go without** *vt* pasar sin

goad /gəʊd/ *vt* aguijonear

go-ahead /'gəʊəhed/ *n* luz *f* verde. ● *adj* dinámico

goal /gəʊl/ *n* (*Sport*) gol *m*; (*objective*) meta *f*. **~ie** /'gəʊlɪ/ *n* [!], **~keeper** *n* portero *m*, arquero *m* (*LAm*). **~post** *n* poste *m* de la portería, poste *m* del arco (*LAm*)

goat /gəʊt/ *n* cabra *f*

gobble /'gɒbl/ *vt* engullir

goblin /'gɒblɪn/ *n* duende *m*

god /gɒd/ *n* dios *m*. **G~** *n* Dios *m*. **~child** *n* ahijado *m*. **~-daughter** *n* ahijada *f*. **~dess** /'gɒdes/ *n* diosa *f*. **~father** *n* padrino *m*. **~forsaken** *adj* olvidado de Dios. **~mother** *n* madrina *f*. **~send** *n* beneficio *m* inesperado. **~son** *n* ahijado *m*

going /'gəʊɪŋ/ *n* camino *m*; (*racing*) (estado *m* del) terreno *m*. **it is slow/hard ~** es lento/difícil. ● *adj* (price) actual; (concern) en funcionamiento

gold /gəʊld/ *n* oro *m*. ● *adj* de oro. **~en** *adj* de oro; (*in colour*) dorado; (opportunity) único. **~en wedding** *n* bodas *fpl* de oro. **~fish** *n invar* pez *m* de colores. **~mine** *n* mina *f* de oro; (*fig*) fuente *f* de gran riqueza. **~-plated** /-'pleɪtɪd/ *adj* chapado en oro. **~smith** *n* orfebre *m*

golf /gɒlf/ *n* golf *m*. **~ ball** *n* pelota *f* de golf. **~ club** *n* palo *m* de golf; (*place*) club *m* de golf. **~course** *n* campo *m* de golf. **~er** *n* jugador *m* de golf

gondola /'gɒndələ/ *n* góndola *f*

gone /gɒn/ *see* **GO**. ● *adj* pasado. **~ six o'clock** después de las seis

gong /gɒŋ/ *n* gong(o) *m*

good /gʊd/ *adj* (**better, best**) bueno, (*before masculine singular noun*) buen. **~ afternoon** buenas tardes. **~ evening** (*before dark*) buenas tardes; (*after dark*) buenas noches. **~ morning** buenos días. **~ night** buenas noches. **as ~ as** (*almost*) casi. **feel ~** sentirse bien. **have a ~ time** divertirse. ● *n* bien *m*. **for ~** para siempre. **it is no ~ shouting** es inútil gritar *etc*. **~bye** /-'baɪ/ *int* ¡adiós! ● *n* adiós *m*. **say ~bye to** despedirse de. **~-for-nothing** /-fənʌθɪŋ/ *adj & n* inútil (*m*). **G~ Friday** *n* Viernes *m* Santo. **~-looking**

/-ˈlʊkɪŋ/ *adj* guapo, buen mozo *m* (*LAm*), buena moza *f* (*LAm*). **~ness** *n* bondad *f*. **~ness!**, **~ness gracious!**, **~ness me!**, **my ~ness!** ¡Dios mío! **~s** *npl* mercancías *fpl*. **~will** /-ˈwɪl/ *n* buena voluntad *f*. **~y** *n* (*Culin, fam*) golosina *f*; (*in film*) bueno *m*

gooey /ˈguːɪ/ *adj* (**gooier, gooiest**) [!] pegajoso; (*fig*) sentimental

g

goofy /ˈguːfɪ/ *adj* (*Amer*) necio

google (®) /ˈguːgl/ *vt, vi* [!] googlear [!]

goose /guːs/ *n* (*pl* **geese**) oca *f*, ganso *m*. **~berry** /ˈgʊzbərɪ/ *n* uva *f* espina, grosella *f* espinosa. **~-flesh** *n*, **~-pimples** *npl* carne *f* de gallina

gore /gɔː(r)/ *n* sangre *f*. ● *vt* cornear

gorge /gɔːdʒ/ *n* (*of river*) garganta *f*. ● *vt*. **~ o.s.** hartarse (**on** de)

gorgeous /ˈgɔːdʒəs/ *adj* precioso; (*splendid*) magnífico

gorilla /gəˈrɪlə/ *n* gorila *m*

gorse /gɔːs/ *n* aulaga *f*

gory /ˈgɔːrɪ/ *adj* (**-ier, -iest**) [!] sangriento

gosh /gɒʃ/ *int* ¡caramba!

go-slow /gəʊˈsləʊ/ *n* huelga *f* de celo, huelga *f* pasiva

gospel /ˈgɒspl/ *n* evangelio *m*

gossip /ˈgɒsɪp/ *n* (*chatter*) chismorreo *m*; (*person*) chismoso *m*. ● *vi* (*pt* **gossiped**) (*chatter*) chismorrear; (*repeat scandal*) contar chismes

got /gɒt/ *see* GET. **have ~** tener. **I've ~ to do it** tengo que hacerlo.

gotten /ˈgɒtn/ *see* GET

gouge /gaʊdʒ/ *vt* abrir (hole). □ **~ out** *vt* sacar

gourmet /ˈgʊəmeɪ/ *n* gastrónomo *m*

govern /ˈgʌvən/ *vt/i* gobernar. **~ess** *n* institutriz *f*. **~ment** *n* gobierno *m*. **~or** *n* gobernador *m*

gown /gaʊn/ *n* vestido *m*; (*of judge, teacher*) toga *f*

GP *abbr see* GENERAL PRACTITIONER

GPS *abbrev* **Global Positioning System** GPS *m*

grab /græb/ *vt* (*pt* **grabbed**) agarrar

grace /greɪs/ *n* gracia *f*. **~ful** *adj* elegante

gracious /ˈgreɪʃəs/ *adj* (*kind*) amable; (*elegant*) elegante

grade /greɪd/ *n* clase *f*, categoría *f*; (*of goods*) clase *f*, calidad *f*; (*on scale*) grado *m*; (*school mark*) nota *f*; (*Amer, class*) curso *m*, año *m*

gradient /ˈgreɪdɪənt/ *n* pendiente *f*, gradiente *f* (*LAm*)

gradual /ˈgrædʒʊəl/ *adj* gradual. **~ly** *adv* gradualmente, poco a poco

graduat|e /ˈgrædjʊət/ *n* (*Univ*) licenciado. ● /ˈgrædjʊeɪt/ *vi* licenciarse. **~ion** /-ˈeɪʃn/ *n* graduación *f*

graffiti /grəˈfiːtɪ/ *npl* graffiti *mpl*, pintadas *fpl*

graft /grɑːft/ *n* (*Med, Bot*) injerto *m*; (*Amer fam, bribery*) chanchullos *mpl*. ● *vt* injertar

grain /greɪn/ *n* grano *m*

gram /græm/ *n* gramo *m*

gramma|r /ˈgræmə(r)/ *n* gramática *f*. **~tical** /grəˈmætɪkl/ *adj* gramatical

gramme /græm/ *n* gramo *m*

grand /grænd/ *adj* (**-er, -est**) magnífico; (*fam, excellent*) estupendo. **~child** *n* nieto *m*. **~daughter** *n* nieta *f*. **~eur** /ˈgrændʒə(r)/ *n* grandiosidad *f*. **~father** *n* abuelo *m*. **~father clock** *n* reloj *m* de caja. **~iose** /ˈgrændɪəʊs/ *adj* grandioso.

~mother *n* abuela *f.* **~parents** *npl* abuelos *mpl.* **~ piano** *n* piano *m* de cola. **~son** *n* nieto *m.* **~stand** /'grænstænd/ *n* tribuna *f*

granite /'grænɪt/ *n* granito *m*

granny /'grænɪ/ *n* [I] abuela *f*

grant /grɑːnt/ *vt* conceder; (*give*) donar; (*admit*) admitir (**that** que). **take for ~ed** dar por sentado. ● *n* concesión *f*; (*Univ*) beca *f*

granule /'grænuːl/ *n* gránulo *m*

grape /greɪp/ *n* uva *f.* **~fruit** *n invar* pomelo *m*, toronja *f* (*LAm*)

graph /grɑːf/ *n* gráfica *f*

graphic /'græfɪk/ *adj* gráfico. **~s** *npl* diseño *m* gráfico; (*Comp*) gráficos *mpl*

grapple /'græpl/ *vi.* **~ with** forcejear con; (*mentally*) lidiar con

grasp /grɑːsp/ *vt* agarrar. ● *n* (*hold*) agarro *m*; (*fig*) comprensión *f.* **~ing** *adj* avaro

grass /grɑːs/ *n* hierba *f.* **~hopper** *n* saltamontes *m.* **~ roots** *npl* base *f* popular. ● *adj* de las bases. **~y** *adj* cubierto de hierba

grate /greɪt/ *n* rejilla *f*; (*fireplace*) chimenea *f.* ● *vt* rallar. ● *vi* rechinar; (*be irritating*) ser crispante

grateful /'greɪtfl/ *adj* agradecido. **~ly** *adv* con gratitud

grater /'greɪtə(r)/ *n* rallador *m*

gratif|ied /'grætɪfaɪd/ *adj* contento. **~y** /'grætɪfaɪ/ *vt* satisfacer; (*please*) agradar a. **~ying** *adj* agradable

grating /'greɪtɪŋ/ *n* reja *f*

gratitude /'grætɪtjuːd/ *n* gratitud *f*

gratuitous /grə'tjuːɪtəs/ *adj* gratuito

gratuity /grə'tjuːətɪ/ *n* (*tip*) propina *f*

grave /greɪv/ *n* sepultura *f.* ● *adj* (**-er, -est**) (*serious*) grave

gravel /'grævl/ *n* grava *f*

gravely /'greɪvlɪ/ *adv* (*seriously*) seriamente; (*solemnly*) con gravedad

grave: ~stone *n* lápida *f.* **~yard** *n* cementerio *m*

gravitate /'grævɪteɪt/ *vi* gravitar

gravity /'grævətɪ/ *n* gravedad *f*

gravy /'greɪvɪ/ *n* salsa *f*

gray /greɪ/ *adj & n* (*Amer*) see **GREY**

graze /greɪz/ *vi* (*eat*) pacer. ● *vt* (*touch*) rozar; (*scrape*) raspar. ● *n* rasguño *m*

greas|e /griːs/ *n* grasa *f.* ● *vt* engrasar. **~eproof paper** *n* papel *m* encerado *or* de cera. **~y** *adj* (hands) grasiento; (food) graso; (hair, skin) graso, grasoso (*LAm*)

great /greɪt/ *adj* (**-er, -est**) grande, (*before singular noun*) gran; (*fam, very good*) estupendo. **G~ Britain** *n* Gran Bretaña *f.* **~-grandfather** /-'grænfɑːðə(r)/ *n* bisabuelo *m.* **~-grandmother** /-'grænmʌðə(r)/ *n* bisabuela *f.* **~ly** *adv* (*very*) muy; (*much*) mucho

Greece /griːs/ *n* Grecia *f*

greed /griːd/ *n* avaricia *f*; (*for food*) glotonería *f.* **~y** *adj* avaro; (*for food*) glotón

Greek /griːk/ *adj & n* griego (*m*)

green /griːn/ *adj* (**-er, -est**) verde. ● *n* verde *m*; (*grass*) césped *m.* **~ belt** *n* zona *f* verde. **~ card** *n* (*Amer*) permiso *m* de residencia y trabajo. **~ery** *n* verdor *m.* **~gage** /-geɪdʒ/ *n* claudia *f.* **~grocer** *n* verdulero *m.* **~house** *n* invernadero *m.* **the ~house effect** el efecto invernadero. **~ light** *n* luz *f* verde. **~s** *npl* verduras *fpl*

Green Card En EE.UU., documento oficial que toda persona que no sea ciudadana norteamericana debe obtener para residir y trabajar en este país. En el Reino Unido, es el documento que se debe obtener de la compañía de seguros, cuando se lleva un automóvil al extranjero, a fin de que siga vigente la cobertura de la póliza.

g

greet /gri:t/ *vt* saludar; (*receive*) recibir. **~ing** *n* saludo *m*

gregarious /grɪˈgeərɪəs/ *adj* gregario; (person) sociable

grenade /grɪˈneɪd/ *n* granada *f*

grew /gru:/ *see* GROW

grey /greɪ/ *adj* (**-er**, **-est**) gris. **have ~ hair** ser canoso. ● *n* gris *m*. **~hound** *n* galgo *m*

grid /grɪd/ *n* reja *f*; (*Elec*, *network*) red *f*; (*on map*) cuadriculado *m*

grief /gri:f/ *n* dolor *m*. **come to ~** (person) acabar mal; (*fail*) fracasar

grievance /ˈgri:vns/ *n* queja *f* formal

grieve /gri:v/ *vt* apenar. ● *vi* afligirse. **~ for** llorar

grievous /ˈgri:vəs/ *adj* doloroso; (*serious*) grave. **~ bodily harm** (*Jurid*) lesiones *fpl* (corporales) graves

grill /grɪl/ *n* parrilla *f*. ● *vt* asar a la parrilla; (🅸, *interrogate*) interrogar

grille /grɪl/ *n* rejilla *f*

grim /grɪm/ *adj* (**grimmer**, **grimmest**) severo

grimace /ˈgrɪməs/ *n* mueca *f*. ● *vi* hacer muecas

grim|e /graɪm/ *n* mugre *f*. **~y** *adj* mugriento

grin /grɪn/ *vt* (*pt* **grinned**) sonreír. ● *n* sonrisa *f* (abierta)

grind /graɪnd/ *vt* (*pt* **ground**) moler (coffee, corn etc); (*pulverize*) pulverizar; (*sharpen*) afilar; (*Amer*) picar, moler (meat)

grip /grɪp/ *vt* (*pt* **gripped**) agarrar; (*interest*) captar. ● *n* (*hold*) agarro *m*; (*strength of hand*) apretón *m*; (*hairgrip*) horquilla *f*, pasador *m* (*Mex*). **come to ~s with** entender (subject)

grisly /ˈgrɪzlɪ/ *adj* (**-ier**, **-iest**) horrible

gristle /ˈgrɪsl/ *n* cartílago *m*

grit /grɪt/ *n* arenilla *f*; (*fig*) agallas *fpl*. ● *vt* (*pt* **gritted**) echar arena en (road). **~ one's teeth** (*fig*) acorazarse

groan /grəʊn/ *vi* gemir. ● *n* gemido *m*

grocer /ˈgrəʊsə(r)/ *n* tendero *m*, abarrotero *m* (*Mex*). **~ies** *npl* comestibles *mpl*. **~y** *n* tienda *f* de comestibles, tienda *f* de abarrotes (*Mex*)

groggy /ˈgrɒgɪ/ *adj* (*weak*) débil; (*unsteady*) inseguro; (*ill*) malucho

groin /grɔɪn/ *n* ingle *f*

groom /gru:m/ *n* mozo *m* de caballos; (*bridegroom*) novio *m*. ● *vt* almohazar (horses); (*fig*) preparar

groove /gru:v/ *n* ranura *f*; (*in record*) surco *m*

grope /grəʊp/ *vi* (*find one's way*) moverse a tientas. **~ for** buscar a tientas

gross /grəʊs/ *adj* (**-er**, **-est**) (*coarse*) grosero; (*Com*) bruto; (*fat*) grueso; (*flagrant*) flagrante. ● *n invar* gruesa *f*. **~ly** *adv* (*very*) enormemente

grotesque /grəʊˈtesk/ *adj* grotesco

ground /graʊnd/ *see* GRIND. ● *n* suelo *m*; (*area*) terreno *m*; (*reason*) razón *f*; (*Amer, Elec*) toma *f* de tierra. ● *vt* fundar (theory); retirar del servicio (aircraft). **~s** *npl* jardines *mpl*; (*sediment*) poso *m*. **~ beef** *n* (*Amer*) carne *f* picada, carne *f* molida. **~ cloth** *n* (*Amer*) *see* **~SHEET**. **~ floor** *n* planta *f* baja. **~ing** *n* base *f*, conocimientos *mpl* (**in** de). **~less** *adj* infundado. **~sheet** *n* suelo *m* impermeable (de una tienda de campaña). **~work** *n* trabajo *m* preparatorio

group /gru:p/ *n* grupo *m*. ● *vt* agrupar. ● *vi* agruparse

grouse /graʊs/ *n invar* (*bird*) urogallo *m*. ● *vi* ☐ rezongar

grovel /'grɒvl/ *vi* (*pt* **grovelled**) postrarse; (*fig*) arrastrarse

grow /grəʊ/ *vi* (*pt* **grew**, *pp* **grown**) crecer; (*become*) volverse, ponerse. ● *vt* cultivar. **~ a beard** dejarse (crecer) la barba. □ **~ up** *vi* hacerse mayor. **~ing** *adj* (quantity) cada vez mayor; (influence) creciente

growl /graʊl/ *vi* gruñir. ● *n* gruñido *m*

grown /grəʊn/ *see* **GROW**. ● *adj* adulto. **~-up** *adj & n* adulto (*m*)

growth /grəʊθ/ *n* crecimiento *m*; (*increase*) aumento *m*; (*development*) desarrollo *m*; (*Med*) bulto *m*, tumor *m*

grub /grʌb/ *n* (*larva*) larva *f*; (*fam, food*) comida *f*

grubby /'grʌbɪ/ *adj* (**-ier**, **-iest**) mugriento

grudg|e /grʌdʒ/ *vt see* **BEGRUDGE**. ● *n* rencilla *f*. **bear/have a ~e against s.o.** guardarle rencor a uno. **~ingly** *adv* de mala gana

gruelling /'gru:əlɪŋ/ *adj* agotador

gruesome /'gru:səm/ *adj* horrible

gruff /grʌf/ *adj* (**-er**, **-est**) (manners) brusco; (voice) ronco

grumble /'grʌmbl/ *vi* rezongar

grumpy /'grʌmpɪ/ *adj* (**-ier**, **-iest**) malhumorado

grunt /grʌnt/ *vi* gruñir. ● *n* gruñido *m*

guarant|ee /gærən'ti:/ *n* garantía *f*. ● *vt* garantizar. **~or** *n* garante *m & f*

guard /gɑ:d/ *vt* proteger; (*watch*) vigilar. ● *n* (*vigilance, Mil group*) guardia *f*; (*person*) guardia *m*; (*on train*) jefe *m* de tren. □ **~ against** *vt* evitar; protegerse contra (risk). **~ed** *adj* cauteloso. **~ian** /-ɪən/ *n* guardián *m*; (*of orphan*) tutor *m*

g

Guatemala /gwɑ:tə'mɑ:lə/ *n* Guatemala *f*. **~n** *adj & n* guatemalteco (*m*)

guer(r)illa /gə'rɪlə/ *n* guerrillero *m*. **~ warfare** *n* guerrilla *f*

guess /ges/ *vt* adivinar; (*Amer, suppose*) suponer. ● *n* conjetura *f*. **~work** *n* conjeturas *fpl*

guest /gest/ *n* invitado *m*; (*in hotel*) huésped *m*. **~house** *n* casa *f* de huéspedes

guffaw /gʌ'fɔ:/ *n* carcajada *f*. ● *vi* reírse a carcajadas

guidance /'gaɪdəns/ *n* (*advice*) consejos *mpl*; (*information*) información *f*

guide /gaɪd/ *n* (*person*) guía *m & f*; (*book*) guía *f*. **Girl G~** exploradora *f*, guía *f*. ● *vt* guiar. **~book** *n* guía *f*. **~ dog** *n* perro *m* guía, perro *m* lazarillo. **~d missile** *n* proyectil *m* teledirigido. **~lines** *npl* pauta *f*

guild /gɪld/ *n* gremio *m*

guile /gaɪl/ *n* astucia *f*

guillotine /'gɪləti:n/ *n* guillotina *f*

guilt /gɪlt/ *n* culpa *f*; (*Jurid*) culpabilidad *f*. **~y** *adj* culpable

guinea pig /'gɪnɪ/ *n* conejillo *m*

de Indias, cobaya *f*

guitar /gɪ'tɑ:(r)/ *n* guitarra *f*. **~ist** *n* guitarrista *m & f*

gulf /gʌlf/ *n* (*part of sea*) golfo *m*; (*gap*) abismo *m*

gull /gʌl/ *n* gaviota *f*

gullet /'gʌlɪt/ *n* garganta *f*, gaznate *m* 🄸

gullible /'gʌləbl/ *adj* crédulo

gully /'gʌlɪ/ *n* (*ravine*) barranco *m*

gulp /gʌlp/ *vt*. □ **~ (down)** tragarse de prisa. ● *vi* tragar saliva. ● *n* trago *m*

gum /gʌm/ *n* (*in mouth*) encía *f*; (*glue*) goma *f* de pegar; (*for chewing*) chicle *m*. ● *vt* (*pt* **gummed**) engomar

gun /gʌn/ *n* (*pistol*) pistola *f*; (*rifle*) fusil *m*, escopeta *f*; (*artillery piece*) cañón *m*. ● *vt* (*pt* **gunned**). □ **~ down** *vt* abatir a tiros. **~fire** *n* tiros *mpl*

gun: ~man /-mən/ *n* pistolero *m*, gatillero *m* (*Mex*). **~powder** *n* pólvora *f*. **~shot** *n* disparo *m*

gurgle /'gɜ:gl/ *vi* (liquid) gorgotear; (baby) gorjear

gush /gʌʃ/ *vi*. **~ (out)** salir a borbotones. ● *n* (*of liquid*) chorro *m*; (*fig*) torrente *m*

gusset /'gʌsɪt/ *n* entretela *f*

gust /gʌst/ *n* ráfaga *f*

gusto /'gʌstəʊ/ *n* entusiasmo *m*

gusty /'gʌstɪ/ *adj* borrascoso

gut /gʌt/ *n* intestino *m*. ● *vt* (*pt* **gutted**) destripar; (fire) destruir. **~s** *npl* tripas *fpl*; (*fam, courage*) agallas *fpl*

gutter /'gʌtə(r)/ *n* (*on roof*) canalón *m*, canaleta *f*; (*in street*) cuneta *f*; (*fig, slum*) arroyo *m*

guttural /'gʌtərəl/ *adj* gutural

guy /gaɪ/ *n* (*fam, man*) tipo *m* 🄸, tío *m* 🄸

guzzle /'gʌzl/ *vt* (*drink*) chupar 🄸; (*eat*) tragarse

gym /dʒɪm/ *n* 🄸 (*gymnasium*) gimnasio *m*; (*gymnastics*) gimnasia *f*

gymnasium /dʒɪm'neɪzɪəm/ *n* gimnasio *m*

gymnast /'dʒɪmnæst/ *n* gimnasta *m & f*. **~ics** /dʒɪm'næstɪks/ *npl* gimnasia *f*

gymslip /'dʒɪmslɪp/ *n* túnica *f* (de gimnasia)

gynaecolog|ist /gaɪnɪ'kɒlədʒɪst/ *n* ginecólogo *m*. **~y** *n* ginecología *f*

gypsy /'dʒɪpsɪ/ *n* gitano *m*

gyrate /dʒaɪə'reɪt/ *vi* girar

Hh

haberdashery /'hæbədæʃərɪ/ *n* mercería *f*; (*Amer, clothes*) ropa *f* y accesorios *mpl* para caballeros

habit /'hæbɪt/ *n* costumbre *f*; (*Relig, costume*) hábito *m*. **be in the ~ of** (+ *gerund*) tener la costumbre de (+ *infinitivo*), soler (+ *infinitivo*). **get into the ~ of** (+ *gerund*) acostumbrarse a (+ *infinitivo*)

habitable /'hæbɪtəbl/ *adj* habitable

habitat /'hæbɪtæt/ *n* hábitat *m*

habitation /hæbɪ'teɪʃn/ *n* habitación *f*

habitual /hə'bɪtjʊəl/ *adj* habitual; (liar) inveterado. **~ly** *adv* de costumbre

hack /hæk/ *n* (*old horse*) jamelgo

m; (*writer*) escritorzuelo *m*. ● *vt* cortar. **~er** *n* (*Comp*) pirata *m* informático

hackneyed /ˈhæknɪd/ *adj* manido

had /hæd/ *see* **HAVE**

haddock /ˈhædək/ *n invar* eglefino *m*

haemorrhage /ˈhemərɪdʒ/ *n* hemorragia *f*

haemorrhoids /ˈhemərɔɪdz/ *npl* hemorroides *fpl*

hag /hæg/ *n* bruja *f*

haggard /ˈhægəd/ *adj* demacrado

hail /heɪl/ *n* granizo *m*. ● *vi* granizar. ● *vt* (*greet*) saludar; llamar (taxi). □ **~ from** *vt* venir de. **~stone** *n* grano *m* de granizo

hair /heə(r)/ *n* pelo *m*. **~band** *n* cinta *f*, banda *f* (*Mex*). **~brush** *n* cepillo *m* (para el pelo). **~cut** *n* corte *m* de pelo. **have a ~cut** cortarse el pelo. **~do** *n* [!] peinado *m*. **~dresser** *n* peluquero *m*. **~dresser's (shop)** *n* peluquería *f*. **~-dryer** *n* secador *m*, secadora *f* (*Mex*). **~grip** *n* horquilla *f*, pasador *m* (*Mex*). **~pin** *n* horquilla *f*. **~pin bend** *n* curva *f* cerrada. **~-raising** *adj* espeluznante. **~spray** *n* laca *f*, fijador *m* (para el pelo). **~style** *n* peinado *m*. **~y** *adj* (**-ier**, **-iest**) peludo

half /hɑ:f/ *n* (*pl* **halves**) mitad *f*. ● *adj* medio. **~ a dozen** media docena *f*. **~ an hour** media hora *f*. ● *adv* medio, a medias. **~-hearted** /-ˈhɑ:tɪd/ *adj* poco entusiasta. **~-mast** /-ˈmɑ:st/ *n*. **at ~-mast** a media asta. **~ term** *n* vacaciones *fpl* de medio trimestre. **~-time** *n* (*Sport*) descanso *m*, medio tiempo *m* (*LAm*). **~way** *adj* medio. ● *adv* a medio camino

hall /hɔ:l/ *n* (*entrance*) vestíbulo *m*; (*for public events*) sala *f*, salón *m*. **~ of residence** residencia *f* universitaria, colegio *m* mayor. **~mark** /-mɑ:k/ *n* (*on gold, silver*) contraste *m*; (*fig*) sello *m* (distintivo)

hallo /həˈləʊ/ *int see* **HELLO**

Hallowe'en /ˈhæləʊˈi:n/ *n* víspera *f* de Todos los Santos

hallucination /həlu:sɪˈneɪʃn/ *n* alucinación *f*

halo /ˈheɪləʊ/ *n* (*pl* **-oes**) aureola *f*

halt /hɔ:lt/ *n*. **come to a ~** pararse. ● *vt* parar. ● *vi* pararse

halve /hɑ:v/ *vt* reducir a la mitad; (*divide into halves*) partir por la mitad

halves /hɑ:vz/ *see* **HALF**

ham /hæm/ *n* jamón *m*

hamburger /ˈhæmbɜ:gə(r)/ *n* hamburguesa *f*

hammer /ˈhæmə(r)/ *n* martillo *m*. ● *vt* martill(e)ar

hammock /ˈhæmək/ *n* hamaca *f*

hamper /ˈhæmpə(r)/ *n* cesta *f*. ● *vt* estorbar

hamster /ˈhæmstə(r)/ *n* hámster *m*

hand /hænd/ *n* mano *f*; (*of clock, watch*) manecilla *f*; (*worker*) obrero *m*. **by ~** a mano. **lend a ~** echar una mano. **on ~** a mano. **on the one ~... on the other ~** por un lado... por otro. **out of ~** fuera de control. **to ~** a mano. ● *vt* pasar. □ **~ down** *vt* pasar. □ **~ in** *vt* entregar. □ **~ over** *vt* entregar. □ **~ out** *vt* distribuir. **~bag** *n* bolso *m*, cartera *f* (*LAm*), bolsa *f* (*Mex*). **~brake** *n* (*in car*) freno *m* de mano. **~cuffs** *npl* esposas *fpl*. **~ful** *n* puñado *m*; (*fam, person*) persona *f* difícil

handicap /ˈhændɪkæp/ *n* desventaja *f*; (*Sport*) hándicap *m*. **~ped** *adj* minusválido

handicraft /ˈhændɪkrɑːft/ *n* artesanía *f*

handkerchief /ˈhæŋkətʃɪf/ *n* (*pl* **-fs** *or* **-chieves** /-tʃiːvz/) pañuelo *m*

handle /ˈhændl/ *n* (*of door*) picaporte *m*; (*of drawer*) tirador *m*; (*of implement*) mango *m*; (*of cup, bag, jug*) asa *f*. ● *vt* manejar; (*touch*) tocar. **~bars** *npl* manillar *m*, manubrio *m* (*LAm*).

hand: ~out *n* folleto *m*; (*of money, food*) dádiva *f*. **~shake** *n* apretón *m* de manos

h

handsome /ˈhænsəm/ *adj* (*good-looking*) guapo, buen mozo, buena moza (*LAm*); (*generous*) generoso

handwriting /ˈhændraɪtɪŋ/ *n* letra *f*

handy /ˈhændɪ/ *adj* (**-ier**, **-iest**) (*useful*) práctico; (person) diestro; (*near*) a mano. **come in ~** venir muy bien. **~man** *n* hombre *m* habilidoso

hang /hæŋ/ *vt* (*pt* **hung**) colgar; (*pt* **hanged**) (*capital punishment*) ahorcar. ● *vi* colgar; (clothing) caer. ● *n*. **get the ~ of sth** coger el truco de algo. □ **~ about, ~ around** *vi* holgazanear. □ **~ on** *vi* (*wait*) esperar. □ **~ out** *vt* tender (washing). □ **~ up** *vi* (*also telephone*) colgar

hangar /ˈhæŋə(r)/ *n* hangar *m*

hang: ~er *n* (*for clothes*) percha *f*. **~-glider** *n* alta *f* delta, deslizador *m* (*Mex*). **~over** (*after drinking*) resaca *f*. **~-up** *n* ! complejo *m*

hankie, **hanky** /ˈhæŋkɪ/ *n* ! pañuelo *m*

haphazard /hæpˈhæzəd/ *adj* fortuito. **~ly** *adv* al azar

happen /ˈhæpən/ *vi* pasar, suceder, ocurrir. **if he ~s to come** si acaso viene. **~ing** *n* acontecimiento *m*

happ|ily /ˈhæpɪlɪ/ *adv* alegremente; (*fortunately*) afortunadamente. **~iness** *n* felicidad *f*. **~y** *adj* (**-ier**, **-iest**) feliz; (*satisfied*) contento

harass /ˈhærəs/ *vt* acosar. **~ment** *n* acoso *m*

harbour /ˈhɑːbə(r)/ *n* puerto *m*

hard /hɑːd/ *adj* (**-er**, **-est**) duro; (*difficult*) difícil. ● *adv* (work) mucho; (*pull*) con fuerza. **~ done by** tratado injustamente. **~-boiled egg** /-ˈbɔɪld/ *n* huevo *m* duro. **~ disk** *n* disco *m* duro. **~en** *vt* endurecer. ● *vi* endurecerse. **~-headed** /-ˈhedɪd/ *adj* realista

hardly /ˈhɑːdlɪ/ *adv* apenas. **~ ever** casi nunca

hard: ~ness *n* dureza *f*. **~ship** *n* apuro *m*. **~ shoulder** *n* arcén *m*, acotamiento *m* (*Mex*). **~ware** *n* /-weə(r)/ ferretería *f*; (*Comp*) hardware *m*. **~ware store** *n* (*Amer*) ferretería *f*. **~-working** /-ˈwɜːkɪŋ/ *adj* trabajador

hardy /ˈhɑːdɪ/ *adj* (**-ier**, **-iest**) fuerte; (plants) resistente

hare /heə(r)/ *n* liebre *f*

hark /hɑːk/ *vi* escuchar. □ **~ back to** *vt* volver a

harm /hɑːm/ *n* daño *m*. **there is no ~ in asking** con preguntar no se pierde nada. ● *vt* hacer daño a (person); dañar (thing); perjudicar (interests). **~ful** *adj* perjudicial. **~less** *adj* inofensivo

harmonica /hɑːˈmɒnɪkə/ *n* armónica *f*

harmon|ious /hɑːˈməʊnɪəs/ *adj* armonioso. **~y** /ˈhɑːmənɪ/ *n* armonía *f*

harness /ˈhɑːnɪs/ *n* arnés *m*. ● *vt* poner el arnés a (horse); (*fig*) aprovechar

harp /hɑːp/ *n* arpa *f*. ● *vi*. ~ **on (about)** machacar (con)

harpoon /hɑːˈpuːn/ *n* arpón *m*

harpsichord /ˈhɑːpsɪkɔːd/ *n* clavicémbalo *m*, clave *m*

harrowing / ˈhærəʊɪŋ/ *adj* desgarrador

harsh /hɑːʃ/ *adj* (**-er**, **-est**) duro, severo; (light) fuerte; (climate) riguroso. **~ly** *adv* severamente. **~ness** *n* severidad *f*

harvest /ˈhɑːvɪst/ *n* cosecha *f*. ● *vt* cosechar

has /hæz/ *see* **HAVE**

hassle /ˈhæsl/ *n* [!] lío *m* [!], rollo *m* [!]. ● *vt* (*harass*) fastidiar

hast|e /heɪst/ *n* prisa *f*, apuro *m* (*LAm*). **make ~e** darse prisa. **~ily** /ˈheɪstɪlɪ/ *adv* de prisa. **~y** /ˈheɪstɪ/ *adj* (**-ier**, **-iest**) rápido; (*rash*) precipitado

hat /hæt/ *n* sombrero *m*

hatch /hætʃ/ *n* (*for food*) ventanilla *f*; (*Naut*) escotilla *f*. ● *vt* empollar (eggs); tramar (plot). ● *vi* salir del cascarón. **~back** *n* coche *m* con tres/cinco puertas; (*door*) puerta *f* trasera

hatchet /ˈhætʃɪt/ *n* hacha *f*

hat|e /heɪt/ *n* odio *m*. ● *vt* odiar. **~eful** *adj* odioso. **~red** /ˈheɪtrɪd/ *n* odio *m*

haughty /ˈhɔːtɪ/ *adj* (**-ier**, **-iest**) altivo

haul /hɔːl/ *vt* arrastrar; transportar (goods). ● *n* (*catch*) redada *f*; (*stolen goods*) botín *m*; (*journey*) recorrido *m*. **~age** /-ɪdʒ/ *n* transporte *m*. **~er** (*Amer*), **~ier** *n* transportista *m* & *f*

haunt /hɔːnt/ *vt* frecuentar; (ghost) rondar. ● *n* sitio *m* preferido. **~ed** *adj* (house) embrujado; (look) angustiado

have /hæv//həv, əv/

3rd person singular present **has**, past **had**

● *transitive verb*

····➤ tener. **I ~ three sisters** tengo tres hermanas. **do you ~ a credit card?** ¿tiene una tarjeta de crédito?

····➤ (*in requests*) **can I ~ a kilo of apples, please?** ¿me da un kilo de manzanas, por favor?

····➤ (*eat*) comer. **I had a pizza** comí una pizza

····➤ (*drink*) tomar. **come and ~ a drink** ven a tomar una copa

····➤ (*smoke*) fumar (cigarette)

····➤ (*hold, organize*) hacer (party, meeting)

····➤ (*get, receive*) **I had a letter from Tony yesterday** recibí una carta de Tony ayer. **we've had no news of her** no hemos tenido noticias suyas

····➤ (*illness*) tener (flu, headache). **to ~ a cold** estar resfriado, tener catarro

····➤ **to have sth done: we had it painted** lo hicimos pintar. **I had my hair cut** me corté el pelo

····➤ **to have it in for s.o.** tenerle manía a uno

● *auxiliary verb*

····➤ haber. **I've seen her already** ya la he visto, ya la vi (*LAm*)

····➤ **to have just done sth** acabar de hacer algo. **I've just**

seen her acabo de verla

····➤ **to have to do sth** tener que hacer algo. **I ~ to** *or* **I've got to go to the bank** tengo que ir al banco

····➤ (*in tag questions*) **you've met her, ~n't you?** ya la conoces, ¿no? *or* ¿verdad? *or* ¿no es cierto?

····➤ (*in short answers*) **you've forgotten something - have I?** has olvidado algo - ¿sí?

h

haven /'heɪvn/ *n* puerto *m*; (*refuge*) refugio *m*

haversack /'hævəsæk/ *n* mochila *f*

havoc /'hævək/ *n* estragos *mpl*

hawk /hɔ:k/ *n* halcón *m*

hawthorn /'hɔ:θɔ:n/ *n* espino *m*

hay /heɪ/ *n* heno *m*. **~ fever** *n* fiebre *f* del heno. **~stack** *n* almiar *m*. **~wire** *adj*. **go ~wire** (*plans*) desorganizarse; (machine) estropearse

hazard /'hæzəd/ *n* riesgo *m*. **~ous** *adj* arriesgado

haze /heɪz/ *n* neblina *f*

hazel /'heɪzl/ *n* avellano *m*. **~nut** *n* avellana *f*

hazy /'heɪzɪ/ *adj* (**-ier**, **-iest**) nebuloso

he /hi:/ *pron* él

head /hed/ *n* cabeza *f*; (*of family, government*) jefe *m*; (*of organization*) director *m*; (*of beer*) espuma *f*. **~s or tails** cara o cruz. ● *adj* principal. ● *vt* encabezar, cabecear (ball). □ **~ for** *vt* dirigirse a. **~ache** *n* dolor *m* de cabeza. **~er** *n* (*football*) cabezazo *m*. **~first** /-'fɜ:st/ *adv* de cabeza. **~ing** *n* título *m*, encabezamiento *m*. **~lamp** *n* faro *m*, foco *m* (*LAm*). **~land** /-lənd/ *n* promontorio *m*. **~line** *n* titular *m*. **the news ~lines** el resumen informativo. **~long** *adv* de cabeza; (*precipitately*) precipitadamente. **~master** *n* director *m*. **~mistress** *n* directora *f*. **~-on** /-'ɒn/ *adj & adv* de frente. **~phones** *npl* auriculares *mpl*, cascos *mpl*. **~quarters** /-'kwɔ:təz/ *n* (*of business*) oficina *f* central; (*Mil*) cuartel *m* general. **~strong** *adj* testarudo. **~teacher** /-'ti:tʃə(r)/ *n* director *m*. **~y** *adj* (**-ier**, **-iest**) (scent) embriagador

heal /hi:l/ *vt* curar. ● *vi* cicatrizarse

health /helθ/ *n* salud *f*. **~y** *adj* sano

heap /hi:p/ *n* montón *m*. ● *vt* amontonar.

hear /hɪə(r)/ *vt/i* (*pt* **heard** /hɜ:d/) oír. **~, ~!** ¡bravo! **~ about** oír hablar de. **~ from** recibir noticias de. **~ing** *n* oído *m*; (*Jurid*) vista *f*. **~ing-aid** *n* audífono *m*. **~say** *n* rumores *mpl*

hearse /hɜ:s/ *n* coche *m* fúnebre

heart /hɑ:t/ *n* corazón *m*. **at ~** en el fondo. **by ~** de memoria. **lose ~** descorazonarse. **~ache** *n* congoja *f*. **~ attack** *n* ataque *m* al corazón, infarto *m*. **~break** *n* congoja *f*. **~breaking** *adj* desgarrador. **~burn** *n* ardor *m* de estómago. **~felt** *adj* sincero

hearth /hɑ:θ/ *n* hogar *m*

heart: ~ily *adv* de buena gana. **~less** *adj* cruel. **~y** *adj* (*welcome*) caluroso; (meal) abundante

heat /hi:t/ *n* calor *m*; (*contest*) (prueba *f*) eliminatoria *f*. ● *vt* calentar. ● *vi* calentarse. **~ed** *adj* (*fig*) acalorado. **~er** *n* calentador *m*

heath /hi:θ/ *n* brezal *m*, monte *m*

heathen /'hi:ðn/ *n & a* pagano (*m*)

heather /'heðə(r)/ *n* brezo *m*

heat: ~ing *n* calefacción *f*. **~stroke** *n* insolación *f*. **~wave** *n* ola *f* de calor

heave /hi:v/ *vt* (*lift*) levantar; exhalar (sigh); (*fam, throw*) tirar. ● *vi* (*pull*) tirar, jalar (*LAm*); (▣, *retch*) dar arcadas

heaven /ˈhevn/ *n* cielo *m*. **~ly** *adj* celestial; (*astronomy*) celeste; (*fam, excellent*) divino

heav|ily /ˈhevɪlɪ/ *adv* pesadamente; (*smoke, drink*) mucho. **~y** *adj* (**-ier, -iest**) pesado; (rain) fuerte; (traffic) denso. **~yweight** *n* peso *m* pesado

heckle /ˈhekl/ *vt* interrumpir

hectic /ˈhektɪk/ *adj* febril

he'd /hi:d/ = **he had, he would**

hedge /hedʒ/ *n* seto *m* (vivo). ● *vi* escaparse por la tangente. **~hog** *n* erizo *m*

heed /hi:d/ *vt* hacer caso de. ● *n*. **take ~** tener cuidado

heel /hi:l/ *n* talón *m*; (*of shoe*) tacón *m*

hefty /ˈheftɪ/ *adj* (**-ier, -iest**) (*sturdy*) fuerte; (*heavy*) pesado

heifer /ˈhefə(r)/ *n* novilla *f*

height /haɪt/ *n* altura *f*; (*of person*) estatura *f*; (*of fame, glory*) cumbre *f*. **~en** *vt* elevar; (*fig*) aumentar

heir /eə(r)/ *n* heredero *m*. **~ess** *n* heredera *f*. **~loom** *n* reliquia *f* heredada

held /held/ *see* **HOLD**

helicopter /ˈhelɪkɒptə(r)/ *n* helicóptero *m*

hell /hel/ *n* infierno *m*

he'll /hi:l/ = **he will**

hello /həˈləʊ/ *int* ¡hola!; (*Telephone, caller*) ¡oiga!, ¡bueno! (*Mex*); (*Telephone, person answering*) ¡diga!, ¡bueno! (*Mex*). **say ~ to** saludar

helm /helm/ *n* (*Naut*) timón *m*

helmet /ˈhelmɪt/ *n* casco *m*

help /help/ *vt/i* ayudar. **he cannot ~ laughing** no puede menos de reír. **~ o.s. to** servirse. **it cannot be ~ed** no hay más remedio. ● *n* ayuda *f*. ● *int* ¡socorro! **~er** *n* ayudante *m*. **~ful** *adj* útil; (person) amable. **~ing** *n* porción *f*. **~less** *adj* (*unable to manage*) incapaz; (*defenceless*) indefenso

hem /hem/ *n* dobladillo *m*

hemisphere /ˈhemɪsfɪə(r)/ *n* hemisferio *m*

hen /hen/ *n* (*chicken*) gallina *f*; (*female bird*) hembra *f*

hence /hens/ *adv* de aquí. **~forth** *adv* de ahora en adelante

henpecked /ˈhenpekt/ *adj* dominado por su mujer

her /hɜ:(r)/ *pron* (*direct object*) la; (*indirect object*) le; (*after prep*) ella. **I know ~** la conozco. ● *adj* su, sus *pl*

herb /hɜ:b/ *n* hierba *f*. **~al** *adj* de hierbas

herd /hɜ:d/ *n* (*of cattle, pigs*) manada *f*; (*of goats*) rebaño *m*. ● *vt* arrear. **~ together** reunir

here /hɪə(r)/ *adv* aquí, acá (*esp LAm*). **~!** (*take this*) ¡tenga! **~abouts** /-əˈbaʊts/ *adv* por aquí. **~after** /-ˈɑ:ftə(r)/ *adv* en el futuro. **~by** /-ˈbaɪ/ *adv* por este medio

heredit|ary /hɪˈredɪtərɪ/ *adj* hereditario

here|sy /ˈherəsɪ/ *n* herejía *f*. **~tic** *n* hereje *m & f*

herewith /hɪəˈwɪð/ *adv* adjunto

heritage /ˈherɪtɪdʒ/ *n* herencia *f*; (*fig*) patrimonio *m*. **~ tourism** *n* turismo *m* cultural, turismo *m* patrimonial (*LAm*)

hermetically /hɜ:ˈmetɪklɪ/ *adv*. **~ sealed** herméticamente cerrado

h

hermit /ˈhɜːmɪt/ *n* ermitaño *m*, eremita *m*
hernia /ˈhɜːnɪə/ *n* hernia *f*
hero /ˈhɪərəʊ/ *n* (*pl* **-oes**) héroe *m*. **~ic** /hɪˈrəʊɪk/ *adj* heroico
heroin /ˈherəʊɪn/ *n* heroína *f*
hero: ~ine /ˈherəʊɪn/ *n* heroína *f*. **~ism** /ˈherəʊɪzm/ *n* heroísmo *m*
heron /ˈherən/ *n* garza *f* (real)
herring /ˈherɪŋ/ *n* arenque *m*
hers /hɜːz/ *poss pron* (el) suyo *m*, (la) suya *f*, (los) suyos *mpl*, (las) suyas *fpl*
herself /hɜːˈself/ *pron* ella misma; (*reflexive*) se; (*after prep*) sí misma
he's /hiːz/ = **he is**, **he has**
hesit|ant /ˈhezɪtənt/ *adj* vacilante. **~ate** /-teɪt/ *vi* vacilar. **~ation** /-ˈteɪʃn/ *n* vacilación *f*
heterosexual /hetərəʊˈseksjʊəl/ *adj & n* heterosexual (*m & f*)
het up /hetˈʌp/ *adj* 🅸 nervioso
hew /hjuː/ *vt* (*pp* **hewed** *or* **hewn**) cortar; (*cut into shape*) tallar
hexagon /ˈheksəgən/ *n* hexágono *m*. **~al** /-ˈægənl/ *adj* hexagonal
hey /heɪ/ *int* ¡eh!; (*expressing dismay, protest*) ¡oye!
heyday /heɪdeɪ/ *n* apogeo *m*
hi /haɪ/ *int* 🅸 ¡hola!
hibernat|e /ˈhaɪbəneɪt/ *vi* hibernar. **~ion** /-ˈneɪʃn/ *n* hibernación *f*
hiccough, **hiccup** /ˈhɪkʌp/ *n* hipo *m*. **have (the) ~s** tener hipo. ● *vi* hipar
hide /haɪd/ *vt* (*pt* **hid**, *pp* **hidden**) esconder. ● *vi* esconderse. ● *n* piel *f*; (*tanned*) cuero *m*. **~-and-seek** /ˈhaɪdnsiːk/ *n*. **play ~-and-seek** jugar al escondite, jugar a las escondidas (*LAm*)
hideous /ˈhɪdɪəs/ *adj* (*dreadful*) horrible; (*ugly*) feo
hideout /ˈhaɪdaʊt/ *n* escondrijo *m*
hiding /ˈhaɪdɪŋ/ *n* (🅸, *thrashing*) paliza *f*. **go into ~** esconderse. **~ place** *n* escondite *m*, escondrijo *m*
hierarchy /ˈhaɪərɑːkɪ/ *n* jerarquía *f*
hieroglyphics /haɪərəˈglɪfɪks/ *n* jeroglíficos *mpl*
hi-fi /ˈhaɪfaɪ/ *adj* de alta fidelidad. ● *n* equipo *m* de alta fidelidad, hi-fi *m*
high /haɪ/ *adj* (**-er**, **-est**) alto; (ideals) elevado; (wind) fuerte; (*fam, drugged*) drogado, colocado 🅸; (voice) agudo; (meat) pasado. ● *n* alto nivel *m*. **a (new) ~** un récord. ● *adv* alto. **~er education** *n* enseñanza *f* superior. **~-handed** /-ˈhændɪd/ *adj* prepotente. **~ heels** *npl* zapatos *mpl* de tacón alto. **~lands** /-ləndz/ *npl* tierras *fpl* altas. **~-level** *adj* de alto nivel. **~light** *n* punto *m* culminante. ● *vt* destacar; (*Art*) realzar. **~ly** *adv* muy; (paid) muy bien. **~ly strung** *adj* nervioso. **H~ness** *n* (*title*) alteza *f*. **~-rise** *adj* (building) alto. **~ school** *n* (*Amer*) instituto *m*, colegio *m* secundario. **~ street** *n* calle *f* principal. **~-strung** *adj* (*Amer*) nervioso. **~way** *n* carretera *f*

> **High School** En EE.UU., el último ciclo del colegio secundario, generalmente para alumnos de edades comprendidas entre los 14 y los 18 años. En Gran Bretaña, algunos colegios secundarios también reciben el nombre de *high schools*.

hijack /ˈhaɪdʒæk/ *vt* secuestrar. ● *n* secuestro *m*. **~er** *n* secuestrador
hike /haɪk/ *n* caminata *f*. ● *vi* ir de

caminata. **~r** *n* excursionista *m & f*

hilarious /hɪ'leərɪəs/ *adj* muy divertido

hill /hɪl/ *n* colina *f*; (*slope*) cuesta *f*. **~side** *n* ladera *f*. **~y** *adj* accidentado

hilt /hɪlt/ *n* (*of sword*) puño *m*. **to the ~** (*fig*) totalmente

him /hɪm/ *pron* (*direct object*) lo, le (*only Spain*); (*indirect object*) le; (*after prep*) él. **I know ~** lo/le conozco. **~self** *pron* él mismo; (*reflexive*) se; (*after prep*) sí mismo

hind|er /'hɪndə(r)/ *vt* estorbar. **~rance** /'hɪndrəns/ *n* obstáculo *m*

hindsight /'haɪnsaɪt/ *n*. **with ~** retrospectivamente

Hindu /'hɪndu:/ *n & a* hindú (*m & f*). **~ism** *n* hinduismo *m*

hinge /hɪndʒ/ *n* bisagra *f*

hint /hɪnt/ *n* indirecta *f*; (*advice*) consejo *m*. ● *vi* soltar una indirecta. **~ at** dar a entender

hip /hɪp/ *n* cadera *f*

hippie /'hɪpɪ/ *n* hippy *m & f*

hippopotamus /hɪpə'pɒtəməs/ *n* (*pl* **-muses** *or* **-mi** /-maɪ/) hipopótamo *m*

hire /haɪə(r)/ *vt* alquilar (thing); contratar (person). ● *n* alquiler *m*. **car ~** alquiler *m* de coches. **~ purchase** *n* compra *f* a plazos

his /hɪz/ *adj* su, sus *pl*. ● *poss pron* (el) suyo *m*, (la) suya *f*, (los) suyos *mpl*, (las) suyas *fpl*

Hispan|ic /hɪ'spænɪk/ *adj* hispánico. ● *n* (*Amer*) hispano *m*. **~ist** /'hɪspənɪst/ *n* hispanista *m & f*

hiss /hɪs/ *n* silbido. ● *vt/i* silbar

histor|ian /hɪ'stɔ:rɪən/ *n* historiador *m*. **~ic(al)** /hɪ'stɒrɪk(l)/ *adj* histórico. **~y** /'hɪstərɪ/ *n* historia *f*.

hit /hɪt/ *vt* (*pt* **hit**, *pres p* **hitting**) golpear (object); pegarle a (person); (*collide with*) chocar con; (*affect*) afectar. **~ it off with** hacer buenas migas con. □ **~ on** *vt* dar con. ● *n* (*blow*) golpe *m*; (*success*) éxito *m*. (*Internet*) visita *f*

hitch /hɪtʃ/ *vt* (*fasten*) enganchar. ● *n* (*snag*) problema *m*. **~ a lift**, **~ a ride** (*Amer*) *see* **~HIKE**. **~hike** *vi* hacer autostop, hacer dedo, ir de aventón (*Mex*). **~hiker** *n* autoestopista *m & f*

hither /'hɪðə(r)/ *adv* aquí, acá. **~ and thither** acá y allá. **~to** *adv* hasta ahora

hit-or-miss /hɪtɔ:'mɪs/ *adj* (approach) poco científico

hive /haɪv/ *n* colmena *f*

hoard /hɔ:d/ *vt* acumular. ● *n* provisión *f*; (*of money*) tesoro *m*

hoarding /'hɔ:dɪŋ/ *n* valla *f* publicitaria

hoarse /hɔ:s/ *adj* (**-er**, **-est**) ronco. **~ly** *adv* con voz ronca

hoax /həʊks/ *n* engaño *m*. ● *vt* engañar

hob /hɒb/ *n* (*of cooker*) hornillos *mpl*, hornillas *fpl* (*LAm*)

hobble /'hɒbl/ *vi* cojear, renguear (*LAm*)

hobby /'hɒbɪ/ *n* pasatiempo *m*. **~horse** *n* (*toy*) caballito *m* (de niño); (*fixation*) caballo *m* de batalla

hockey /'hɒkɪ/ *n* hockey *m*; (*Amer*) hockey *m* sobre hielo

hoe /həʊ/ *n* azada *f*. ● *vt* (*pres p* **hoeing**) azadonar

hog / hɒg/ *n* (*Amer*) cerdo *m*. ● *vt* (*pt* **hogged**) ! acaparar

hoist /hɔɪst/ *vt* levantar; izar (flag). ● *n* montacargas *m*

hold /həʊld/ *vt* (*pt* **held**) tener; (*grasp*) coger (*esp Spain*), agarrar; (*contain*) contener; mantener

h

(interest); (*believe*) creer. ● *vi* mantenerse. ● *n* (*influence*) influencia *f*; (*Naut, Aviat*) bodega *f*. **get ~ of** agarrar; (*fig, acquire*) adquirir. □ **~ back** *vt* (*contain*) contener. □ **~ on** *vi* (*stand firm*) resistir; (*wait*) esperar. □ **~ on to** *vt* (*keep*) guardar; (*cling to*) agarrarse a. □ **~ out** *vt* (*offer*) ofrecer. *vi* (*resist*) resistir. □ **~ up** *vt* (*raise*) levantar; (*support*) sostener; (*delay*) retrasar; (*rob*) atracar. **~all** *n* bolsa *f* (de viaje). **~er** *n* tenedor *m*; (*of post*) titular *m*; (*wallet*) funda *f*. **~up** atraco *m*

hole /həʊl/ *n* agujero *m*; (*in ground*) hoyo *m*; (*in road*) bache *m*. ● *vt* agujerear

holiday /ˈhɒlɪdeɪ/ *n* vacaciones *fpl*; (*public*) fiesta *f*. **go on ~** ir de vacaciones. **~maker** *n* veraneante *m & f*

holiness /ˈhəʊlɪnɪs/ *n* santidad *f*

Holland /ˈhɒlənd/ *n* Holanda *f*

hollow /ˈhɒləʊ/ *adj & n* hueco (*m*)

holly /ˈhɒlɪ/ *n* acebo *m*

holocaust /ˈhɒləkɔːst/ *n* holocausto *m*

holster /ˈhəʊlstə(r)/ *n* pistolera *f*

holy /ˈhəʊlɪ/ *adj* (**-ier**, **-iest**) santo, sagrado. **H~ Ghost** *n*, **H~ Spirit** *n* Espíritu *m* Santo. **~ water** *n* agua *f* bendita

homage /ˈhɒmɪdʒ/ *n* homenaje *m*. **pay ~ to** rendir homenaje a

home /həʊm/ *n* casa *f*; (*for old people*) residencia *f* de ancianos; (*native land*) patria *f*. ● *adj* (cooking) casero; (*address*) particular; (background) familiar; (*Pol*) interior; (match) de casa. ● *adv*. **(at) ~** en casa. **~land** *n* patria *f*. **~land security** seguridad *f* nacional. **~less** *adj* sin hogar. **~ly** *adj* (**-ier**, **-iest**) casero; (*Amer, ugly*) feo. **~-made** *adj* hecho en casa. **~ page** *n* (*Comp*) página *f* frontal. **~sick** *adj*. **be ~sick** echar de menos a su familia/su país, extrañar a su familia/su país (*LAm*). **~ town** *n* ciudad *f* natal. **~work** *n* deberes *mpl*

homicide /ˈhɒmɪsaɪd/ *n* homicidio *m*

homoeopathic /həʊmɪəʊˈpæθɪk/ *adj* homeopático

homogeneous /hɒməʊˈdʒiːnɪəs/ *adj* homogéneo

homosexual /həʊməʊˈseksjʊəl/ *adj & n* homosexual (*m*)

honest /ˈɒnɪst/ *adj* honrado; (*frank*) sincero. **~ly** *adv* honradamente. **~y** *n* honradez *f*

honey /ˈhʌnɪ/ *n* miel *f*. **~comb** *n* panal *m*. **~moon** *n* luna *f* de miel. **~suckle** *n* madreselva *f*

honorary /ˈɒnərərɪ/ *adj* honorario

honour /ˈɒnə(r)/ *n* honor *m*. ● *vt* honrar; cumplir (con) (promise). **~able** *adj* honorable

hood /hʊd/ *n* capucha *f*; (*car roof*) capota *f*; (*Amer, car bonnet*) capó *m*, capote *m* (*Mex*)

hoodwink /ˈhʊdwɪŋk/ *vt* engañar

hoof /huːf/ *n* (*pl* **hoofs** *or* **hooves**) (*of horse*) casco *m*, pezuna *f* (*Mex*); (*of cow*) pezuña *f*

hook /hʊk/ *n* gancho *m*; (*on garment*) corchete *m*; (*for fishing*) anzuelo *m*. **let s.o. off the ~** dejar salir a uno del atolladero. **off the ~** (telephone) descolgado. ● *vt*. **~ed on** [!] adicto a. □ **~ up** *vt* enganchar. **~ed** *adj* (tool) en forma de gancho; (nose) aguileño

hookey /ˈhʊkɪ/ *n*. **play ~** (*Amer fam*) faltar a clase, hacer novillos

hooligan /ˈhuːlɪgən/ *n* vándalo *m*, gamberro *m*

hoop /huːp/ *n* aro *m*
hooray /hʊˈreɪ/ *int & n* ¡viva! (*m*)
hoot /huːt/ *n* (*of horn*) bocinazo *m*; (*of owl*) ululato *m*. ● *vi* tocar la bocina; (owl) ulular
Hoover /ˈhuːvə(r)/ *n* (®) aspiradora *f*. ● *vt* pasar la aspiradora por, aspirar (*LAm*)
hooves /huːvz/ *see* **HOOF**
hop /hɒp/ *vi* (*pt* **hopped**) saltar a la pata coja; (frog, rabbit) brincar, saltar; (bird) dar saltitos. ● *n* salto *m*; (*flight*) etapa *f*. **~(s)** (*plant*) lúpulo *m*
hope /həʊp/ *n* esperanza *f*. ● *vt/i* esperar. **~ for** esperar. **~ful** *adj* (*optimistic*) esperanzado; (*promising*) esperanzador. **~fully** *adv* con optimismo; (*it is hoped*) se espera. **~less** *adj* desesperado
horde /hɔːd/ *n* horda *f*
horizon /həˈraɪzn/ *n* horizonte *m*
horizontal /hɒrɪˈzɒntl/ *adj* horizontal. **~ly** *adv* horizontalmente
hormone /ˈhɔːməʊn/ *n* hormona *f*
horn /hɔːn/ *n* cuerno *m*, asta *f*, cacho *m* (*LAm*); (*of car*) bocina *f*; (*Mus*) trompa *f*. **~ed** *adj* con cuernos
hornet /ˈhɔːnɪt/ *n* avispón *m*
horoscope /ˈhɒrəskəʊp/ *n* horóscopo *m*
horrible /ˈhɒrəbl/ *adj* horrible
horrid /ˈhɒrɪd/ *adj* horrible
horrific /həˈrɪfɪk/ *adj* horroroso
horrify /ˈhɒrɪfaɪ/ *vt* horrorizar
horror /ˈhɒrə(r)/ *n* horror *m*
hors-d'oeuvre /ɔːˈdɜːvr/ *n* (*pl* **-s** /-ˈdɜːvr/ entremés *m*, botana *f* (*Mex*)
horse /hɔːs/ *n* caballo *m*. **~back** *n*. **on ~back** a caballo. **~power** *n* (*unit*) caballo *m* (de fuerza). **~racing** *n* carreras *fpl* de caballos. **~shoe** *n* herradura *f*
horticultur|al /hɔːtɪˈkʌltʃərəl/ *adj* hortícola. **~e** /ˈhɔːtɪkʌltʃə(r)/ *n* horticultura *f*
hose /həʊz/ *n* manguera *f*, manga *f*. ● *vt*. **~ down** lavar (con manguera). **~pipe** *n* manga *f*
hosiery /ˈhəʊzɪərɪ/ *n* calcetería *f*
hospice /ˈhɒspɪs/ *n* residencia *f* para enfermos desahuciados
hospitable /hɒˈspɪtəbl/ *adj* hospitalario
hospital /ˈhɒspɪtl/ *n* hospital *m*
hospitality /hɒspɪˈtælətɪ/ *n* hospitalidad *f*
host /həʊst/ *n* (*master of house*) anfitrión *m*; (*Radio, TV*) presentador *m*; (*multitude*) gran cantidad *f*; (*Relig*) hostia *f*
hostage /ˈhɒstɪdʒ/ *n* rehén *m*
hostel /ˈhɒstl/ *n* (*for students*) residencia *f*; (*for homeless people*) hogar *m*
hostess /ˈhəʊstɪs/ *n* anfitriona *f*
hostil|e /ˈhɒstaɪl/ *adj* hostil. **~ity** /-ˈtɪlətɪ/ *n* hostilidad *f*
hot /hɒt/ *adj* (**hotter**, **hottest**) caliente; (weather, day) caluroso; (climate) cálido; (*Culin*) picante; (news) de última hora. **be/feel ~** tener calor. **get ~** calentarse. **it is ~** hace calor. **~bed** *n* (*fig*) semillero *m*
hotchpotch /ˈhɒtʃpɒtʃ/ *n* mezcolanza *f*
hot dog *n* perrito *m* caliente
hotel /həʊˈtel/ *n* hotel *m*. **~ier** /-ɪeɪ/*n* hotelero *m*
hot: ~house *n* invernadero *m*. **~plate** *n* placa *f*, hornilla *f* (*LAm*). **~-water bottle** /-ˈwɔːtə(r)/ *n* bolsa *f* de agua caliente
hound /haʊnd/ *n* perro *m* de caza.

● *vt* perseguir

hour /aʊə(r)/ *n* hora *f.* **~ly** *adj* (rate) por hora. ● *adv* (*every hour*) cada hora; (*by the hour*) por hora

house /haʊs/ *n* (*pl* **-s** /'haʊzɪz/) casa *f*; (*Pol*) cámara *f.* ● /haʊz/ *vt* alojar; (*keep*) guardar. **~hold** *n* casa *f.* **~holder** *n* dueño *m* de una casa. **~keeper** *n* ama *f* de llaves. **~maid** *n* criada *f*, mucama *f* (*LAm*). **~-proud** *adj* meticuloso. **~warming** (*party*) *n* fiesta de inauguración de una casa. **~wife** *n* ama *f* de casa. **~work** *n* tareas *fpl* domésticas

h

housing /'haʊzɪŋ/ *n* alojamiento *m.* **~ development** (*Amer*), **~ estate** *n* complejo *m* habitacional, urbanización *f*

hovel /'hɒvl/ *n* casucha *f*

hover /'hɒvə(r)/ *vi* (bird, threat etc) cernerse; (*loiter*) rondar. **~craft** *n* (*pl invar or* **-crafts**) aerodeslizador *m*

how /haʊ/ *adv* cómo. **~ about a walk?** ¿qué te parece si damos un paseo? **~ are you?** ¿cómo está Vd? **~ do you do?** (*in introduction*) mucho gusto. **~ long?** (*in time*) ¿cuánto tiempo? **~ long is the room?** ¿cuánto mide de largo el cuarto? **~ often?** ¿cuántas veces?

however /haʊ'evə(r)/ *adv* (*nevertheless*) no obstante, sin embargo; (*with verb*) de cualquier manera que (+ *subjunctive*); (*with adjective or adverb*) por... que (+ *subjunctive*). **~ much it rains** por mucho que llueva

howl /haʊl/ *n* aullido. ● *vi* aullar

hp *abbr see* **HORSEPOWER**

HP *abbr see* **HIRE-PURCHASE**

hub /hʌb/ *n* (*of wheel*) cubo *m*; (*fig*) centro *m*

hubcap /'hʌbkæp/ *n* tapacubos *m*

huddle /'hʌdl/ *vi* apiñarse

hue /hju:/ *n* (*colour*) color *m*

huff /hʌf/ *n.* **be in a ~** estar enfurruñado

hug /hʌg/ *vt* (*pt* **hugged**) abrazar. ● *n* abrazo *m*

huge /hju:dʒ/ *adj* enorme. **~ly** *adv* enormemente

hulk /hʌlk/ *n* (*of ship*) barco *m* viejo

hull /hʌl/ *n* (*of ship*) casco *m*

hullo /hə'ləʊ/ *int see* **HELLO**

hum /hʌm/ *vt/i* (*pt* **hummed**) (person) canturrear; (insect, engine) zumbar. ● *n* zumbido *m*

human /'hju:mən/ *adj & n* humano (*m*). **~ being** *n* ser *m* humano. **~e** /hju:'meɪn/ *adj* humano. **~itarian** /hju:mænɪ'teərɪən/ *adj* humanitario. **~ity** /hju:'mænətɪ/ *n* humanidad *f*

humbl|e /'hʌmbl/ *adj* (**-er**, **-est**) humilde. ● *vt* humillar. **~y** *adv* humildemente

humdrum /'hʌmdrʌm/ *adj* monótono

humid /'hju:mɪd/ *adj* húmedo. **~ity** /hju:'mɪdətɪ/ *n* humedad *f*

humiliat|e /hju:'mɪlɪeɪt/ *vt* humillar. **~ion** /-'eɪʃn/ *n* humillación *f*

humility /hju:'mɪlətɪ/ *n* humildad *f*

humongous /hju:'mʌŋgəs/ *adj* [!] de primera

humo|rist /'hju:mərɪst/ *n* humorista *m & f.* **~rous** /-rəs/ *adj* humorístico. **~rously** *adv* con gracia. **~ur** /'hju:mə(r)/ *n* humor *m.* **sense of ~ur** sentido *m* del humor

hump /hʌmp/ *n* (*of person, camel*) joroba *f*; (*in ground*) montículo *m*

hunch /hʌntʃ/ *vt* encorvar. ● *n* presentimiento *m*; (*lump*) joroba *f*. **~back** *n* jorobado *m*

hundred /ˈhʌndrəd/ *adj* ciento, (*before noun*) cien. **one ~ and ninety-eight** ciento noventa y ocho. **two ~** doscientos. **three ~ pages** trescientas páginas. **four ~** cuatrocientos. **five ~** quinientos. ● *n* ciento *m*. **~s of** centenares de. **~th** *adj & n* centésimo (*m*). **~weight** *n* 50,8kg; (*Amer*) 45,36kg

hung /hʌŋ/ *see* HANG

Hungar|ian /hʌŋˈgeərɪən/ *adj & n* húngaro (*m*). **~y** /ˈhʌŋgərɪ/ *n* Hungría *f*

hung|er /ˈhʌŋgə(r)/ *n* hambre *f*. ● *vi*. **~er for** tener hambre de. **~rily** /ˈhʌŋgrəlɪ/ *adv* ávidamente. **~ry** *adj* (**-ier**, **-iest**) hambriento. **be ~ry** tener hambre

hunk /hʌŋk/ *n* (buen) pedazo *m*

hunt /hʌnt/ *vt* cazar. ● *vi* cazar. **~ for** buscar. ● *n* caza *f*. **~er** *n* cazador *m*. **~ing** *n* caza *f*. **go ~ing** ir de caza

hurl /hɜːl/ *vt* lanzar

hurrah/hʊˈrɑː/, **hurray** /hʊˈreɪ/ *int & n* ¡viva! (*m*)

hurricane /ˈhʌrɪkən/ *n* huracán *m*

hurr|ied /ˈhʌrɪd/ *adj* apresurado. **~iedly** *adv* apresuradamente. **~y** *vi* darse prisa, apurarse (*LAm*). ● *vt* meter prisa a, apurar (*LAm*). ● *n* prisa *f*. **be in a ~y** tener prisa, estar apurado (*LAm*)

hurt /hɜːt/ *vt* (*pt* **hurt**) hacer daño a, lastimar (*LAm*). **~ s.o.'s feelings** ofender a uno. ● *vi* doler. **my head ~s** me duele la cabeza. **~ful** *adj* hiriente

hurtle /ˈhɜːtl/ *vt* ir volando. ● *vi*. **~ along** mover rápidamente

husband /ˈhʌzbənd/ *n* marido *m*, esposo *m*

hush /hʌʃ/ *vt* acallar. ● *n* silencio *m*. □ **~ up** *vt* acallar (affair). **~-hush** *adj* [!] super secreto

husk /hʌsk/ *n* cáscara *f*

husky /ˈhʌskɪ/ *adj* (**-ier**, **-iest**) (*hoarse*) ronco

hustle /ˈhʌsl/ *vt* (*jostle*) empujar. ● *vi* (*hurry*) darse prisa, apurarse (*LAm*). ● *n* empuje *m*

hut /hʌt/ *n* cabaña *f*

hutch /hʌtʃ/ *n* conejera *f*

hybrid /ˈhaɪbrɪd/ *adj & n* híbrido (*m*)

hydrangea /haɪˈdreɪndʒə/ *n* hortensia *f*

hydrant /ˈhaɪdrənt/ *n*. **(fire) ~** *n* boca *f* de riego, boca *f* de incendios (*LAm*)

hydraulic /haɪˈdrɔːlɪk/ *adj* hidráulico

hydroelectric /haɪdrəʊɪˈlektrɪk/ *adj* hidroeléctrico

hydrofoil /ˈhaɪdrəfɔɪl/ *n* hidrodeslizador *m*

hydrogen /ˈhaɪdrədʒən/ *n* hidrógeno *m*

hyena /haɪˈiːnə/ *n* hiena *f*

hygien|e /ˈhaɪdʒiːn/ *n* higiene *f*. **~ic** /haɪˈdʒiːnɪk/ *adj* higiénico

hymn /hɪm/ *n* himno *m*

hyper... /ˈhaɪpə(r)/ *pref* hiper...

hyphen /ˈhaɪfn/ *n* guión *m*. **~ate** /-eɪt/ *vt* escribir con guión

hypno|sis /hɪpˈnəʊsɪs/ *n* hipnosis *f*. **~tic** /-ˈnɒtɪk/ *adj* hipnótico. **~tism** /ˈhɪpnətɪzəm/ *n* hipnotismo *m*. **~tist** /ˈhɪpnətɪst/ *n* hipnotista *m & f*. **~tize** /ˈhɪpnətaɪz/ *vt* hipnotizar

hypochondriac /haɪpəˈkɒndrɪæk/ *n* hipocondríaco *m*

hypocri|sy /hɪˈpɒkrəsɪ/ *n* hipo-

h

cresía *f.* **~te** /'hɪpəkrɪt/ *n* hipócrita *m & f.* **~tical** /hɪpə'krɪtɪkl/ *adj* hipócrita

hypodermic /haɪpə'dɜːmɪk/ *adj* hipodérmico. ● *n* hipodérmica *f*

hypothe|sis /haɪ'pɒθəsɪs/ *n* (*pl* **-theses**/-siːz/) hipótesis *f.* **~tical** /-ə'θetɪkl/ *adj* hipotético

hysteri|a /hɪ'stɪərɪə/ *n* histerismo *m.* **~cal** /-'terɪkl/ *adj* histérico. **~cs** /hɪ'sterɪks/ *npl* histerismo *m.* **have ~cs** ponerse histérico; (*laugh*) morir de risa

h
i

Ii

I /aɪ/ *pron* yo

ice /aɪs/ *n* hielo *m.* ● *vt* helar; glasear (cake). ● *vi.* **~ (up)** helarse, congelarse. **~berg** /-bɜːg/ *n* iceberg *m.* **~ box** *n* (*compartment*) congelador; (*Amer fam, refrigerator*) frigorífico *m*, refrigerador *m* (*LAm*). **~cream** *n* helado *m.* **~ cube** *n* cubito *m* de hielo

Iceland /'aɪslənd/ *n* Islandia *f*

ice: ~ lolly polo *m*, paleta *f* helada (*LAm*). **~ rink** *n* pista *f* de hielo. **~ skating** *n* patinaje *m* sobre hielo

icicle /'aɪsɪkl/ *n* carámbano *m*

icing /'aɪsɪŋ/ *n* glaseado *m*

icon /'aɪkɒn/ *n* icono *m*

icy /'aɪsɪ/ *adj* (**-ier**, **-iest**) helado; (*fig*) glacial

I'd /aɪd/ = **I had, I would**

idea /aɪ'dɪə/ *n* idea *f*

ideal /aɪ'dɪəl/ *adj & n* ideal (*m*). **~ism** *n* idealismo *m.* **~ist** *n* idealista *m & f.* **~istic** /-'lɪstɪk/ *adj* idealista. **~ize** *vt* idealizar. **~ly** *adv* idealmente

identical /aɪ'dentɪkl/ *adj* idéntico. **~ twins** *npl* gemelos *mpl* idénticos, gemelos *mpl* (*LAm*)

identif|ication /aɪdentɪfɪ'keɪʃn/ *n* identificación *f.* **~y** /aɪ'dentɪfaɪ/ *vt* identificar. ● *vi.* **~y with** identificarse con

identity /aɪ'dentɪtɪ/ *n* identidad *f.* **~ card** *n* carné *m* de identidad. **~ theft** *n* robo *m* de identidad

ideolog|ical /aɪdɪə'lɒdʒɪkl/ *adj* ideológico. **~y** /aɪdɪ'ɒlədʒɪ/ *n* ideología *f*

idiocy /'ɪdɪəsɪ/ *n* idiotez *f*

idiom /'ɪdɪəm/ *n* locución *f.* **~atic** /-'mætɪk/ *adj* idiomático

idiot /'ɪdɪət/ *n* idiota *m & f.* **~ic** /-'ɒtɪk/ *adj* idiota

idle /'aɪdl/ *adj* (**-er**, **-est**) ocioso; (*lazy*) holgazán; (*out of work*) desocupado; (machine) parado. ● *vi* (engine) andar al ralentí. **~ness** *n* ociosidad *f*; (*laziness*) holgazanería *f*

idol /'aɪdl/ *n* ídolo *m.* **~ize** *vt* idolatrar

idyllic /ɪ'dɪlɪk/ *adj* idílico

i.e. *abbr* (= **id est**) es decir

if /ɪf/ *conj* si

igloo /'ɪgluː/ *n* iglú *m*

ignit|e /ɪg'naɪt/ *vt* encender. ● *vi* encenderse. **~ion** /-'nɪʃn/ *n* ignición *f*; (*Auto*) encendido *m.* **~ion key** *n* llave *f* de contacto

ignoramus /ɪgnə'reɪməs/ *n* (*pl*-**muses**) ignorante

ignoran|ce /'ɪgnərəns/ *n* ignorancia *f.* **~t** *adj* ignorante

ignore /ɪg'nɔː(r)/ *vt* no hacer caso de; hacer caso omiso de (warning)

ill /ɪl/ *adj* enfermo. ● *adv* mal. ● *n* mal *m*

I'll /aɪl/ = **I will**
ill: ~**-advised** /-əd'vaɪzd/ *adj* imprudente. ~ **at ease** /-ət'iːz/ *adj* incómodo. ~**-bred** /-'bred/ *adj* mal educado
illegal /ɪ'liːgl/ *adj* ilegal
illegible /ɪ'ledʒəbl/ *adj* ilegible
illegitima|cy /ɪlɪ'dʒɪtɪməsɪ/ *n* ilegitimidad *f*. ~**te** /-ət/ *adj* ilegítimo
illitera|cy /ɪ'lɪtərəsɪ/ *n* analfabetismo *m*. ~**te** /-ət/ *adj* analfabeto
illness /'ɪlnɪs/ *n* enfermedad *f*
illogical /ɪ'lɒdʒɪkl/ *adj* ilógico
illuminat|e /ɪ'luːmɪneɪt/ *vt* iluminar. ~**ion** /-'neɪʃn/ *n* iluminación *f*
illus|ion /ɪ'luːʒn/ *n* ilusión *f*. ~**sory** /-sərɪ/ *adj* ilusorio
illustrat|e /'ɪləstreɪt/ *vt* ilustrar. ~**ion** /-'streɪʃn/ *n* ilustración *f*; (*example*) ejemplo *m*
illustrious /ɪ'lʌstrɪəs/ *adj* ilustre
ill will /ɪl'wɪl/ *n* mala voluntad *f*
I'm /aɪm/ = **I am**
image /'ɪmɪdʒ/ *n* imagen *f*. ~**ry** *n* imágenes *fpl*
imagin|able /ɪ'mædʒɪnəbl/ *adj* imaginable. ~**ary** *adj* imaginario. ~**ation** /-'neɪʃn/ *n* imaginación *f*. ~**ative** *adj* imaginativo. ~**e** /ɪ'mædʒɪn/ *vt* imaginar(se)
imbalance /ɪm'bæləns/ *n* desequilibrio *m*
imbecile /'ɪmbəsiːl/ *n* imbécil *m & f*
imitat|e /'ɪmɪteɪt/ *vt* imitar. ~**ion** /-'teɪʃn/ *n* imitación *f*. ● *adj* de imitación. ~**or** *n* imitador *m*
immaculate /ɪ'mækjʊlət/ *adj* inmaculado
immatur|e /ɪmə'tjʊə(r)/ *adj* inmaduro. ~**ity** *n* inmadurez *f*
immediate /ɪ'miːdɪət/ *adj* inmediato. ~**ly** *adv* inmediatamente. ● *conj* en cuanto (+ *subjunctive*)
immens|e /ɪ'mens/ *adj* inmenso. ~**ely** *adv* inmensamente; (*fam, very much*) muchísimo
immers|e /ɪ'mɜːs/ *vt* sumergir. ~**ion** /-ʃn/ *n* inmersión *f*. ~**ion heater** *n* calentador *m* de inmersión
immigra|nt /'ɪmɪgrənt/ *adj & n* inmigrante (*m & f*). ~**tion** /-'greɪʃn/ *n* inmigración *f*
imminent /'ɪmɪnənt/ *adj* inminente
immobil|e /ɪ'məʊbaɪl/ *adj* inmóvil. ~**ize** /-bɪlaɪz/ *vt* inmovilizar. ~**izer** /-bɪlaɪzə(r)/ *n* inmovilizador *m*
immoderate /ɪ'mɒdərət/ *adj* inmoderado
immodest /ɪ'mɒdɪst/ *adj* inmodesto
immoral /ɪ'mɒrəl/ *adj* inmoral. ~**ity** /ɪmə'rælətɪ/ *n* inmoralidad *f*
immortal /ɪ'mɔːtl/ *adj* inmortal. ~**ity** /-'tælətɪ/ *n* inmortalidad *f*. ~**ize** *vt* inmortalizar
immun|e /ɪ'mjuːn/ *adj* inmune (**to** a). ~**ity** *n* inmunidad *f*. ~**ization** /ɪmjʊnaɪ'zeɪʃn/ *n* inmunización *f*. ~**ize** /'ɪmjʊnaɪz/ *vt* inmunizar
imp /ɪmp/ *n* diablillo *m*
impact /'ɪmpækt/ *n* impacto *m*
impair /ɪm'peə(r)/ *vt* perjudicar
impale /ɪm'peɪl/ *vt* atravesar (**on** con)
impart /ɪm'pɑːt/ *vt* comunicar (news); impartir (knowledge)
impartial /ɪm'pɑːʃl/ *adj* imparcial. ~**ity** /-ɪ'ælətɪ/ *n* imparcialidad *f*
impassable /ɪm'pɑːsəbl/ *adj* (road) intransitable
impassive /ɪm'pæsɪv/ *adj* impasible

i

impatien|ce /ɪm'peɪʃəns/ *n* impaciencia *f*. **~t** *adj* impaciente. **get ~t** impacientarse. **~tly** *adv* con impaciencia

impeccable /ɪm'pekəbl/ *adj* impecable

impede /ɪm'pi:d/ *vt* estorbar

impediment /ɪm'pedɪmənt/ obstáculo *m*. **(speech)** ~ *n* defecto *m* del habla

impending /ɪm'pendɪŋ/ *adj* inminente

impenetrable /ɪm'penɪtrəbl/ *adj* impenetrable

imperative /ɪm'perətɪv/ *adj* imprescindible. ● *n* (*Gram*) imperativo *m*

imperceptible /ɪmpə'septəbl/ *adj* imperceptible

imperfect /ɪm'pɜ:fɪkt/ *adj* imperfecto. **~ion** /ɪmpə'fekʃn/ *n* imperfección *f*

imperial /ɪm'pɪərɪəl/ *adj* imperial. **~ism** *n* imperialismo *m*

impersonal /ɪm'pɜ:sənl/ *adj* impersonal

impersonat|e /ɪm'pɜ:səneɪt/ *vt* hacerse pasar por; (*mimic*) imitar. **~ion** /-'neɪʃn/ *n* imitación *f*. **~or** *n* imitador *m*

impertinen|ce /ɪm'pɜ:tɪnəns/ *n* impertinencia *f*. **~t** *adj* impertinente

impervious /ɪm'pɜ:vɪəs/ *adj*. **~ to** impermeable a

impetuous /ɪm'petjʊəs/ *adj* impetuoso

impetus /'ɪmpɪtəs/ *n* ímpetu *m*

implacable /ɪm'plækəbl/ *adj* implacable

implant /ɪm'plɑ:nt/ *vt* implantar

implement /'ɪmplɪmənt/ *n* instrumento *m*, implemento *m* (*LAm*). ● /'ɪmplɪment/ *vt* implementar

implementation /ɪmplɪmen'teɪʃn/ *n* implementación *f*

implicat|e /'ɪmplɪkeɪt/ *vt* implicar. **~ion** /-'keɪʃn/ *n* implicación *f*

implicit /ɪm'plɪsɪt/ *adj* (*implied*) implícito; (*unquestioning*) absoluto

implore /ɪm'plɔ:(r)/ *vt* implorar

imply /ɪm'plaɪ/ *vt* (*involve*) implicar; (*insinuate*) dar a entender, insinuar

impolite /ɪmpə'laɪt/ *adj* mal educado

import /ɪm'pɔ:t/ *vt* importar. ● /'ɪmpɔ:t/ *n* importación *f*; (*item*) artículo *m* de importación; (*meaning*) significación *f*

importan|ce /ɪm'pɔ:təns/ *n* importancia *f*. **~t** *adj* importante

importer /ɪm'pɔ:tə(r)/ *n* importador *m*

impos|e /ɪm'pəʊz/ *vt* imponer. ● *vi*. **~e on** abusar de la amabilidad de. **~ing** *adj* imponente. **~ition** /ɪmpə'zɪʃn/ *n* imposición *f*; (*fig*) abuso *m*

impossib|ility /ɪmpɒsə'bɪlətɪ/ *n* imposibilidad *f*. **~le** /ɪm'pɒsəbl/ *adj* imposible

impostor /ɪm'pɒstə(r)/ *n* impostor *m*

impoten|ce /'ɪmpətəns/ *n* impotencia *f*. **~t** *adj* impotente

impound /ɪm'paʊnd/ *vt* confiscar

impoverished /ɪm'pɒvərɪʃt/ *adj* empobrecido

impractical /ɪm'præktɪkl/ *adj* poco práctico

impregnable /im'pregnəbl/ *adj* inexpugnable

impregnate /'ɪmpregneɪt/ *vt* impregnar (**with** con, de)

impress /ɪm'pres/ *vt* impresionar; (*make good impression*) causar una buena impresión a. ● *vi* impresionar

impression /ɪm'preʃn/ *n* impresión *f*. **~able** *adj* impresionable. **~ism** *n* impresionismo *m*

impressive /ɪm'presɪv/ *adj* impresionante

imprint /'ɪmprɪnt/ *n* impresión *f*. ● /ɪm'prɪnt/ *vt* imprimir

imprison /ɪm'prɪzn/ *vt* encarcelar. **~ment** *n* encarcelamiento *m*

improbab|ility /ɪmprɒbə'bɪlətɪ/ *n* improbabilidad *f*. **~le** /ɪm'prɒbəbl/ *adj* improbable

impromptu /ɪm'prɒmptju:/ *adj* improvisado. ● *adv* de improviso

improper /ɪm'prɒpə(r)/ *adj* impropio; (*incorrect*) incorrecto

improve /ɪm'pru:v/ *vt* mejorar. ● *vi* mejorar. **~ment** *n* mejora *f*

improvis|ation /ɪmprəvaɪ'zeɪʃn/ *n* improvisación *f*. **~e** /'ɪmprəvaɪz/ *vt/i* improvisar

impuden|ce /'ɪmpjʊdəns/ *n* insolencia *f*. **~t** *adj* insolente

impuls|e /'ɪmpʌls/ *n* impulso *m*. **on ~e** sin reflexionar. **~ive** *adj* irreflexivo

impur|e /ɪm'pjʊə(r)/ *adj* impuro. **~ity** *n* impureza *f*

in /ɪn/ *prep* en; (*within*) dentro de. **~ a firm manner** de una manera terminante. **~ an hour('s time)** dentro de una hora. **~ doing** al hacer. **~ so far as** en la medida en que. **~ the evening** por la tarde. **~ the rain** bajo la lluvia. **~ the sun** al sol. **one ~ ten** uno de cada diez. **the best ~ the world** el mejor del mundo. ● *adv* (*inside*) dentro; (*at home*) en casa. **come ~** entrar. ● *n*. **the ~s and outs of** los detalles de

inability /ɪnə'bɪlətɪ/ *n* incapacidad *f*

inaccessible /ɪnæk'sesəbl/ *adj* inaccesible

inaccura|cy /ɪn'ækjʊrəsɪ/ *n* inexactitud *f*. **~te** /-ət/ *adj* inexacto

inactiv|e /ɪn'æktɪv/ *adj* inactivo. **~ity** /-'tɪvətɪ/ *n* inactividad *f*

inadequa|cy /ɪn'ædɪkwəsɪ/ *adj* insuficiencia *f*. **~te** /-ət/ *adj* insuficiente

inadvertently /ɪnəd'vɜ:təntlɪ/ *adv* sin querer

inadvisable /ɪnəd'vaɪzəbl/ *adj* desaconsejable

inane /ɪ'neɪn/ *adj* estúpido

inanimate /ɪn'ænɪmət/ *adj* inanimado

inappropriate /ɪnə'prəʊprɪət/ *adj* inoportuno

inarticulate /ɪnɑ:'tɪkjʊlət/ *adj* incapaz de expresarse claramente

inattentive /ɪnə'tentɪv/ *adj* desatento

inaudible /ɪn'ɔ:dəbl/ *adj* inaudible

inaugurate /ɪ'nɔ:gjʊreɪt/ *vt* inaugurar

inborn /'ɪnbɔ:n/ *adj* innato

inbred /ɪn'bred/ *adj* (*inborn*) innato; (social group) endogámico

Inc /ɪŋk/ *abbr* (*Amer*) (= **Incorporated**) S.A., Sociedad Anónima

incalculable /ɪn'kælkjʊləbl/ *adj* incalculable

incapable /ɪn'keɪpəbl/ *adj* incapaz

incapacit|ate /ɪnkə'pæsɪteɪt/ *vt* incapacitar. **~y** *n* incapacidad *f*

incarcerate /ɪn'kɑ:səreɪt/ *vt* encarcelar

incarnat|e /ɪn'kɑ:nət/ *adj* encarnado. **~ion** /-'neɪʃn/ *n* encarnación *f*

incendiary /ɪn'sendɪərɪ/ *adj* incendiario. **~ bomb** bomba *f*

incendiaria
incense /ˈɪnsens/ *n* incienso *m*. ● /ɪnˈsens/ *vt* enfurecer
incentive /ɪnˈsentɪv/ *n* incentivo *m*
incessant /ɪnˈsesnt/ *adj* incesante. **~ly** *adv* sin cesar
incest /ˈɪnsest/ *n* incesto *m*. **~uous** /ɪnˈsestjʊəs/ *adj* incestuoso
inch /ɪntʃ/ *n* pulgada *f*; (= 2,54cm). ● *vi*. **~ forward** avanzar lentamente
incidence /ˈɪnsɪdəns/ *n* frecuencia *f*
i
incident /ˈɪnsɪdənt/ *n* incidente *m*
incidental /ɪnsɪˈdentl/ *adj* (*effect*) secundario; (*minor*) incidental. **~ly** *adv* a propósito
incinerat|e /ɪnˈsɪnəreɪt/ *vt* incinerar. **~or** *n* incinerador *m*
incision /ɪnˈsɪʒn/ *n* incisión *f*
incite /ɪnˈsaɪt/ *vt* incitar. **~ment** *n* incitación *f*
inclination /ɪnklɪˈneɪʃn/ *n* inclinación *f*. **have no ~ to** no tener deseos de
incline /ɪnˈklaɪn/ *vt* inclinar. **be ~d to** tener tendencia a. ● *vi* inclinarse. ● /ˈɪnklaɪn/ *n* pendiente *f*
inclu|de /ɪnˈkluːd/ *vt* incluir. **~ding** *prep* incluso. **~sion** /-ʒn/ *n* inclusión *f*. **~sive** /-sɪv/ *adj* inclusivo
incognito /ɪnkɒgˈniːtəʊ/ *adv* de incógnito
incoherent /ɪnkəʊˈhɪərənt/ *adj* incoherente
incom|e /ˈɪnkʌm/ *n* ingresos *mpl*. **~e tax** *n* impuesto *m* sobre la renta. **~ing** *adj* (tide) ascendente
incomparable /ɪnˈkɒmpərəbl/ *adj* incomparable
incompatible /ɪnkəmˈpætəbl/ *adj* incompatible
incompeten|ce /ɪnˈkɒmpɪtəns/ *n* incompetencia *f*. **~t** *adj* incompetente
incomplete /ɪnkəmˈpliːt/ *adj* incompleto
incomprehensible /ɪnkɒmprɪˈhensəbl/ *adj* incomprensible
inconceivable /ɪnkənˈsiːvəbl/ *adj* inconcebible
inconclusive /ɪnkənˈkluːsɪv/ *adj* no concluyente
incongruous /ɪnˈkɒŋgrʊəs/ *adj* incongruente
inconsiderate /ɪnkənˈsɪdərət/ *adj* desconsiderado
inconsisten|cy /ɪnkənˈsɪstənsɪ/ *n* inconsecuencia *f*. **~t** *adj* inconsecuente. **be ~t with** no concordar con
inconspicuous /ɪnkənˈspɪkjʊəs/ *adj* que no llama la atención. **~ly** *adv* sin llamar la atención
incontinent /ɪnˈkɒntɪnənt/ *adj* incontinente
inconvenien|ce /ɪnkənˈviːnɪəns/ *adj* inconveniencia *f*; (*drawback*) inconveniente *m*. **~t** *adj* inconveniente
incorporate /ɪnˈkɔːpəreɪt/ *vt* incorporar; (*include*) incluir; (*Com*) constituir (en sociedad)
incorrect /ɪnkəˈrekt/ *adj* incorrecto
increas|e /ˈɪnkriːs/ *n* aumento *m* (**in** de). ● /ɪnˈkriːs/ *vt/i* aumentar. **~ing** /ɪnˈkriːsɪŋ/ *adj* creciente. **~ingly** *adv* cada vez más
incredible /ɪnˈkredəbl/ *adj* increíble
incredulous /ɪnˈkredjʊləs/ *adj* incrédulo
incriminat|e /ɪnˈkrɪmɪneɪt/ *vt* incriminar. **~ing** *adj* comprometedor

incubat|e /ˈɪŋkjʊbeɪt/ *vt* incubar. **~ion** /-ˈbeɪʃn/ *n* incubación *f*. **~or** *n* incubadora *f*

incur /ɪnˈkɜː(r)/ *vt* (*pt* **incurred**) incurrir en; contraer (debts)

incurable /ɪnˈkjʊərəbl/ *adj* (disease) incurable; (romantic) empedernido

indebted /ɪnˈdetɪd/ *adj*. **be ~ to s.o.** estar en deuda con uno

indecen|cy /ɪnˈdiːsnsɪ/ *n* indecencia *f*. **~t** *adj* indecente

indecisi|on /ɪndɪˈsɪʒn/ *n* indecisión *f*. **~ve** /-ˈsaɪsɪv/ *adj* indeciso

indeed /ɪnˈdiːd/ *adv* en efecto; (*really?*) ¿de veras?

indefinable /ɪndɪˈfaɪnəbl/ *adj* indefinible

indefinite /ɪnˈdefɪnət/ *adj* indefinido. **~ly** *adv* indefinidamente

indelible /ɪnˈdelɪbl/ *adj* indeleble

indemni|fy /ɪnˈdemnɪfaɪ/ *vt* (*insure*) asegurar; (*compensate*) indemnizar. **~ty** /-ətɪ/ *n* (*insurance*) indemnidad *f*; (*payment*) indemnización *f*

indent /ɪnˈdent/ *vt* sangrar (text). **~ation** /-ˈteɪʃn/ *n* mella *f*

independen|ce /ɪndɪˈpendəns/ *n* independencia *f*. **~t** *adj* independiente. **~tly** *adv* independientemente

in-depth /ɪnˈdepθ/ *adj* a fondo

indescribable /ɪndɪˈskraɪbəbl/ *adj* indescriptible

indestructible /ɪndɪˈstrʌktəbl/ *adj* indestructible

indeterminate /ɪndɪˈtɜːmɪnət/ *adj* indeterminado

index /ˈɪndeks/ *n* (*pl* **indexes**) (*in book*) índice *m*; (*pl* **indexes** *or* **indices**) (*Com, Math*) índice *m*. ● *vt* poner índice a; (*enter in index*) poner en un índice. **~ finger** *n* (dedo *m*) índice *m*. **~-linked** /-ˈlɪŋkt/ *adj* indexado

India /ˈɪndɪə/ *n* la India. **~n** *adj & n* indio (*m*)

indicat|e /ˈɪndɪkeɪt/ *vt* indicar. **~ion** /-ˈkeɪʃn/ *n* indicación *f*. **~ive** /ɪnˈdɪkətɪv/ *adj & n* indicativo (*m*). **~or** /ˈɪndɪkeɪtə(r)/ *n* indicador *m*; (*Auto*) intermitente *m*

indices /ˈɪndɪsiːz/ *see* **INDEX**

indict /ɪnˈdaɪt/ *vt* acusar. **~ment** *n* acusación *f*

indifferen|ce /ɪnˈdɪfrəns/ *n* indiferencia *f*. **~t** *adj* indiferente; (*not good*) mediocre

indigesti|ble /ɪndɪˈdʒestəbl/ *adj* indigesto. **~on** /-tʃən/ *n* indigestión *f*

indigna|nt /ɪnˈdɪgnənt/ *adj* indignado. **~tion** /-ˈneɪʃn/ *n* indignación *f*

indirect /ɪndɪˈrekt/ *adj* indirecto. **~ly** *adv* indirectamente

indiscre|et /ɪndɪˈskriːt/ *adj* indiscreto. **~tion** /-ˈkreʃn/ *n* indiscreción *f*

indiscriminate /ɪndɪˈskrɪmɪnət/ *adj* indistinto. **~ly** *adv* indistintamente

indispensable /ɪndɪˈspensəbl/ *adj* indispensable, imprescindible

indisposed /ɪndɪˈspəʊzd/ *adj* indispuesto

indisputable /ɪndɪˈspjuːtəbl/ *adj* indiscutible

indistinguishable /ɪndɪˈstɪŋgwɪʃəbl/ *adj* indistinguible (**from** de)

individual /ɪndɪˈvɪdjʊəl/ *adj* individual. ● *n* individuo *m*. **~ly** *adv* individualmente

indoctrinat|e /ɪnˈdɒktrɪmeɪt/ *vt* adoctrinar. **~ion** /-ˈneɪʃn/ *n* adoctrinamiento *m*

indolen|ce /ˈɪndələns/ *n* indolencia *f.* **~t** *adj* indolente

indomitable /ɪn'dɒmɪtəbl/ *adj* indómito

indoor /'ɪndɔ:(r)/ *adj* interior; (clothes etc) de casa; (*covered*) cubierto. **~s** *adv* dentro, adentro (*LAm*)

induc|e /ɪn'dju:s/ *vt* inducir. **~ement** *n* incentivo *m*

indulge /ɪn'dʌldʒ/ *vt* satisfacer (desires); complacer (person). ● *vi.* **~ in** permitirse. **~nce** /-əns/ *n* (*of desires*) satisfacción *f*; (*extravagance*) lujo *m.* **~nt** *adj* indulgente

industrial /ɪn'dʌstrɪəl/ *adj* industrial; (unrest) laboral. **~ist** *n* industrial *m & f.* **~ized** *adj* industrializado

industrious /ɪn'dʌstrɪəs/ *adj* trabajador

industry /'ɪndəstrɪ/ *n* industria *f*; (*zeal*) aplicación *f*

inebriated /ɪ'ni:brɪeɪtɪd/ *adj* beodo, ebrio

inedible /ɪn'edɪbl/ *adj* incomible

ineffective /ɪnɪ'fektɪv/ *adj* ineficaz; (person) incompetente

ineffectual /ɪnɪ'fektjʊəl/ *adj* ineficaz

inefficien|cy /ɪnɪ'fɪʃnsɪ/ *n* ineficacia *f*; (*of person*) incompetencia *f.* **~t** *adj* ineficaz; (person) incompetente

ineligible /ɪn'elɪdʒəbl/ *adj* inelegible. **be ~ for** no tener derecho a

inept /ɪ'nept/ *adj* inepto

inequality /ɪnɪ'kwɒlətɪ/ *n* desigualdad *f*

inert /ɪ'nɜ:t/ *adj* inerte. **~ia** /ɪ'nɜ:ʃə/ *n* inercia *f*

inescapable /ɪnɪ'skeɪpəbl/ *adj* ineludible

inevitabl|e /ɪn'evɪtəbl/ *adj* inevitable. ● *n.* **the ~e** lo inevitable. **~y** *adv* inevitablemente

inexact /ɪnɪg'zækt/ *adj* inexacto

inexcusable /ɪnɪk'skju:səbl/ *adj* imperdonable

inexpensive /ɪnɪk'spensɪv/ *adj* económico, barato

inexperience /ɪnɪk'spɪərɪəns/ *n* falta *f* de experiencia. **~d** *adj* inexperto

inexplicable /ɪnɪk'splɪkəbl/ *adj* inexplicable

infallib|ility /ɪnfælə'bɪlətɪ/ *n* infalibilidad *f.* **~le** /ɪn'fæləbl/ *adj* infalible

infam|ous /'ɪnfəməs/ *adj* infame. **~y** *n* infamia *f*

infan|cy /'ɪnfənsɪ/ *n* infancia *f.* **~t** *n* niño *m.* **~tile** /'ɪnfəntaɪl/ *adj* infantil

infantry /'ɪnfəntrɪ/ *n* infantería *f*

infatuat|ed /ɪn'fætjʊeɪtɪd/ *adj.* **be ~ed with** estar encaprichado con. **~ion** /-'eɪʃn/ *n* encaprichamiento *m*

infect /ɪn'fekt/ *vt* infectar; (*fig*) contagiar. **~ s.o. with sth** contagiarle algo a uno. **~ion** /-ʃn/ *n* infección *f.* **~ious** /-ʃəs/ *adj* contagioso

infer /ɪn'fɜ:(r)/ *vt* (*pt* **inferred**) deducir

inferior /ɪn'fɪərɪə(r)/ *adj & n* inferior (*m & f*). **~ity** /-'ɒrətɪ/ *n* inferioridad *f*

inferno /ɪn'fɜ:nəʊ/ *n* (*pl* **-os**) infierno *m*

infertil|e /ɪn'fɜ:taɪl/ *adj* estéril. **~ity** /-'tɪlətɪ/ *n* esterilidad *f*

infest /ɪn'fest/ *vt* infestar

infidelity /ɪnfɪ'delətɪ/ *n* infidelidad *f*

infiltrat|e /'ɪnfɪltreɪt/ *vt* infiltrarse en. ● *vi* infiltrarse. **~or** *n* infiltrado *m*

infinite /'ɪnfɪnət/ *adj* infinito. **~ly**

adv infinitamente

infinitesimal /ɪnfɪnɪ'tesɪml/ *adj* infinitesimal

infinitive /ɪn'fɪnətɪv/ *n* infinitivo *m*

infinity /ɪn'fɪnətɪ/ *n* (*infinite distance*) infinito *m*; (*infinite quantity*) infinidad *f*

infirm /ɪn'fɜːm/ *adj* enfermizo. **~ity** *n* enfermedad *f*

inflam|e /ɪn'fleɪm/ *vt* inflamar. **~mable** /ɪn'flæməbl/ *adj* inflamable. **~mation** /-ə'meɪʃn/ *n* inflamación *f*

inflat|e /ɪn'fleɪt/ *vt* inflar. **~ion** /-ʃn/ *n* inflación *f*. **~ionary** *adj* inflacionario

inflection /ɪn'flekʃn/ *n* inflexión *f*

inflexible /ɪn'fleksəbl/ *adj* inflexible

inflict /ɪn'flɪkt/ *vt* infligir (**on** a)

influen|ce /'ɪnflʊəns/ *n* influencia *f*. **under the ~ce** (*fam, drunk*) borracho. • *vt* influir (en). **~tial** /-'enʃl/ *adj* influyente

influenza /ɪnflʊ'enzə/ *n* gripe *f*

influx /'ɪnflʌks/ *n* afluencia *f*

inform /ɪn'fɔːm/ *vt* informar. **keep ~ed** tener al corriente. • *vi*. **~ on s.o.** delatar a uno

informal /ɪn'fɔːml/ *adj* informal; (language) familiar. **~ity** /-'mælətɪ/ *n* falta *f* de ceremonia. **~ly** *adv* (*casually*) de manera informal; (*unofficially*) informalmente

inform|ation /ɪnfə'meɪʃn/ *n* información *f*. **~ation technology** *n* informática *f*. **~ative** *adj* /ɪn'fɔːmətɪv/ informativo. **~er** /ɪb'fɔːmə(r)/ *n* informante *m*

infrared /ɪnfrə'red/ *adj* infrarrojo

infrequent /ɪn'friːkwənt/ *adj* poco frecuente. **~ly** *adv* raramente

infringe /ɪn'frɪndʒ/ *vt* infringir. **~ on** violar. **~ment** *n* violación *f*

infuriat|e /ɪn'fjʊərɪeɪt/ *vt* enfurecer. **~ing** *adj* exasperante

ingen|ious /ɪn'dʒiːnɪəs/ *adj* ingenioso. **~uity** /ɪndʒɪ'njuːətɪ/ *n* ingeniosidad *f*

ingot /'ɪŋgət/ *n* lingote *m*

ingrained /ɪn'greɪnd/ *adj* (*belief*) arraigado

ingratiate /ɪn'greɪʃɪeɪt/ *vt*. **~ o.s. with** congraciarse con

ingratitude /ɪn'grætɪtjuːd/ *n* ingratitud *f*

ingredient /ɪn'griːdɪənt/ *n* ingrediente *m*

ingrowing/'ɪngrəʊɪŋ/, **ingrown** /'ɪngrəʊn/ *adj*. **~ nail** *n* uñero *m*, uña *f* encarnada

inhabit /ɪn'hæbɪt/ *vt* habitar. **~able** *adj* habitable. **~ant** *n* habitante *m*

inhale /ɪn'heɪl/ *vt* aspirar. • *vi* (*when smoking*) aspirar el humo. **~r** *n* inhalador *m*

inherent /ɪn'hɪərənt/ *adj* inherente. **~ly** *adv* intrínsecamente

inherit /ɪn'herɪt/ *vt* heredar. **~ance** /-əns/ *n* herencia *f*

inhibit /ɪn'hɪbɪt/ *vt* inhibir. **~ed** *adj* inhibido. **~ion** /-'bɪʃn/ *n* inhibición *f*

inhospitable /ɪnhə'spɪtəbl/ *adj* (place) inhóspito; (person) inhospitalario

inhuman /ɪn'hjuːmən/ *adj* inhumano. **~e** /ɪnhjuː'meɪn/ *adj* inhumano. **~ity** /ɪnhjuː'mænətɪ/ *n* inhumanidad *f*

initial /ɪ'nɪʃl/ *n* inicial *f*. • *vt* (*pt* **initialled**) firmar con iniciales. • *adj* inicial. **~ly** *adv* al principio

initiat|e /ɪ'nɪʃɪeɪt/ *vt* iniciar; promover (scheme etc). **~ion** /-'eɪʃn/ *n* iniciación *f*

initiative /ɪ'nɪʃətɪv/ *n* iniciativa *f*. **on one's own ~** por iniciativa propia. **take the ~** tomar la iniciativa

inject /ɪn'dʒekt/ *vt* inyectar. **~ion** /-ʃn/ *n* inyección *f*

injur|e /'ɪndʒə(r)/ *vt* herir. **~y** *n* herida *f*

injustice /ɪn'dʒʌstɪs/ *n* injusticia *f*

ink /ɪŋk/ *n* tinta *f*. **~well** *n* tintero *m*. **~y** *adj* manchado de tinta

inland /'ɪnlənd/ *adj* interior. ● /ɪn'lænd/ *adv* tierra adentro. **I~ Revenue** /'ɪnlənd/ *n* Hacienda *f*

in-laws /'ɪnlɔ:z/ *npl* parientes *mpl* políticos

inlay /ɪn'leɪ/ *vt* (*pt* **inlaid**) taracear, incrustar. ● /'ɪnleɪ/ *n* taracea *f*, incrustación *f*

inlet /'ɪnlet/ *n* (*in coastline*) ensenada *f*; (*of river, sea*) brazo *m*

inmate /'ɪnmeɪt/ *n* (*of asylum*) interno *m*; (*of prison*) preso *m*

inn /ɪn/ *n* posada *f*

innate /ɪ'neɪt/ *adj* innato

inner /'ɪnə(r)/ *adj* interior; (*fig*) íntimo. **~most** *adj* más íntimo. **~ tube** *n* cámara *f*

innocen|ce /'ɪnəsns/ *n* inocencia *f*. **~t** *adj & n* inocente (*m & f*)

innocuous /ɪ'nɒkjʊəs/ *adj* inocuo

innovat|e /'ɪnəveɪt/ *vi* innovar. **~ion** /-'veɪʃn/ *n* innovación *f*. **~ive** /'ɪnəvətɪv/ *adj* innovador. **~or** *n* innovador *m*

innuendo /ɪnju:'endəʊ/ *n* (*pl* **-oes**) insinuación *f*

innumerable /ɪ'nju:mərəbl/ *adj* innumerable

inoculat|e /ɪ'nɒkjʊleɪt/ *vt* inocular. **~ion** /-'leɪʃn/ *n* inoculación *f*

inoffensive /ɪnə'fensɪv/ *adj* inofensivo

inopportune /ɪn'ɒpətju:n/ *adj* inoportuno

input /'ɪnpʊt/ *n* aportación *f*, aporte *m* (*LAm*); (*Comp*) entrada *f*. ● *vt* (*pt* **input**, *pres p* **inputting**) entrar (data)

inquest /'ɪnkwest/ *n* investigación *f* judicial

inquir|e /ɪn'kwaɪə(r)/ *vt/i* preguntar. **~e about** informarse de. **~y** *n* pregunta *f*; (*investigation*) investigación *f*

inquisition /ɪnkwɪ'zɪʃn/ *n* inquisición *f*

inquisitive /ɪn'kwɪzətɪv/ *adj* inquisitivo

insan|e /ɪn'seɪn/ *adj* loco. **~ity** /ɪn'sænətɪ/ *n* locura *f*

insatiable /ɪn'seɪʃəbl/ *adj* insaciable

inscri|be /ɪn'skraɪb/ *vt* inscribir (letters); grabar (design). **~ption** /-ɪpʃn/ *n* inscripción *f*

inscrutable /ɪn'skru:təbl/ *adj* inescrutable

insect /'ɪnsekt/ *n* insecto *m*. **~icide** /ɪn'sektɪsaɪd/ *n* insecticida *f*

insecur|e /ɪnsɪ'kjʊə(r)/ *adj* inseguro. **~ity** *n* inseguridad *f*

insensitive /ɪn'sensətɪv/ *adj* insensible

inseparable /ɪn'sepərəbl/ *adj* inseparable

insert /'ɪnsɜ:t/ *n* materia *f* insertada. ● /ɪn'sɜ:t/ *vt* insertar. **~ion** /ɪn'sɜ:ʃn/ *n* inserción *f*

inside /ɪn'saɪd/ *n* interior *m*. **~ out** al revés; (*thoroughly*) a fondo. ● *adj* interior. ● *adv* dentro, adentro (*LAm*). ● *prep* dentro de. **~s** *npl* tripas *fpl*

insight /'ɪnsaɪt/ *n* perspicacia *f*. **gain an ~ into** llegar a comprender bien

insignificant /ɪnsɪɡ'nɪfɪkənt/ *adj* insignificante

insincer|e /ɪnsɪn'sɪə(r)/ *adj* poco sincero. **~ity** /-'serətɪ/ *n* falta *f* de sinceridad

insinuat|e /ɪn'sɪnjʊeɪt/ *vt* insinuar. **~ion** /-'eɪʃn/ *n* insinuación *f*

insipid /ɪn'sɪpɪd/ *adj* insípido

insist /ɪn'sɪst/ *vt* insistir (**that** en que). ● *vi* insistir. **~ on** insistir en. **~ence** /-əns/ *n* insistencia *f*. **~ent** *adj* insistente. **~ently** *adv* con insistencia

insolen|ce /'ɪnsələns/ *n* insolencia *f*. **~t** *adj* insolente

insoluble /ɪn'sɒljʊbl/ *adj* insoluble

insolvent /ɪn'sɒlvənt/ *adj* insolvente

insomnia /ɪn'sɒmnɪə/ *n* insomnio *m*. **~c** /-ɪæk/ *n* insomne *m* & *f*

inspect /ɪn'spekt/ *vt* (*officially*) inspeccionar; (*look at closely*) revisar, examinar . **~ion** /-ʃn/ *n* inspección *f*. **~or** *n* inspector *m*; (*on train, bus*) revisor *m*, inspector *m* (*LAm*)

inspir|ation /ɪnspə'reɪʃn/ *n* inspiración *f*. **~e** /ɪn'spaɪə(r)/ *vt* inspirar. **~ing** *adj* inspirador

instability /ɪnstə'bɪlətɪ/ *n* inestabilidad *f*

install /ɪn'stɔ:l/ *vt* instalar. **~ation** /-ə'leɪʃn/ *n* instalación *f*

instalment /ɪn'stɔ:lmənt/ *n* (*payment*) plazo *m*; (*of publication*) entrega *f*; (*of radio, TV serial*) episodio *m*

instance /'ɪnstəns/ *n* ejemplo *m*; (*case*) caso *m*. **for ~** por ejemplo. **in the first ~** en primer lugar

instant /'ɪnstənt/ *adj* instantáneo. ● *n* instante *m*. **~aneous** /ɪnstən'teɪmɪəs/ *adj* instantáneo

instead /ɪn'sted/ *adv* en cambio. **~ of** en vez de, en lugar de

instigat|e /'ɪnstɪgeɪt/ *vt* instigar. **~ion** /-'geɪʃn/ *n* instigación *f*

instinct /'ɪnstɪŋkt/ *n* instinto *m*. **~ive** *adj* instintivo

institut|e /'ɪnstɪtju:t/ *n* instituto *m*. ● *vt* instituir; iniciar (enquiry etc). **~ion** /-'tju:ʃn/ *n* institución *f*. **~ional** *adj* institucional

instruct /ɪn'strʌkt/ *vt* instruir; (*order*) mandar. **~ s.o. in sth** enseñar algo a uno. **~ion** /-ʃn/ *n* instrucción *f*. **~ions** *npl* (*for use*) modo *m* de empleo. **~ive** *adj* instructivo. **~or** *n* instructor *m*

instrument /'ɪnstrəmənt/ *n* instrumento *m*. **~al** /ɪnstrə'mentl/ *adj* instrumental. **be ~al in** jugar un papel decisivo en

insubordinat|e /ɪnsə'bɔ:dɪnət/ *adj* insubordinado. **~ion** /-'neɪʃn/ *n* insubordinación *f*

insufferable /ɪn'sʌfərəbl/ *adj* (person) insufrible; (heat) insoportable

insufficient /ɪnsə'fɪʃnt/ *adj* insuficiente

insular /'ɪnsjʊlə(r)/ *adj* insular; (*narrow-minded*) estrecho de miras

insulat|e /'ɪnsjʊleɪt/ *vt* aislar. **~ion** /-'leɪʃn/ *n* aislamiento *m*

insulin /'ɪnsjʊlɪn/ *n* insulina *f*

insult /ɪn'sʌlt/ *vt* insultar. ● /'ɪnsʌlt/ *n* insulto *m*. **~ing** /ɪn'sʌltɪŋ/ *adj* insultante

insur|ance /ɪn'ʃʊərəns/ *n* seguro *m*. **~e** /ɪn'ʃʊə(r)/ *vt* (*Com*) asegurar; (*Amer*) *see* **ENSURE**

insurmountable /ɪnsə'maʊntəbl/ *adj* insuperable

intact /ɪn'tækt/ *adj* intacto

integral /'ɪntɪgrəl/ *adj* integral

integrat|e /'ɪntɪgreɪt/ *vt* integrar. ● *vi* integrarse. **~ion** /-'greɪʃn/ *n*

i

integración *f*
integrity /ɪn'tegrətɪ/ *n* integridad *f*
intellect /'ɪntəlekt/ *n* intelecto *m*. **~ual** /ɪntə'lektʃʊəl/ *adj & n* intelectual (*m*)
intelligen|ce /ɪn'telɪdʒəns/ *n* inteligencia *f*. **~t** *adj* inteligente. **~tly** *adv* inteligentemente
intelligible /ɪn'telɪdʒəbl/ *adj* inteligible
intend /ɪn'tend/ *vt*. **~ to do** pensar hacer
intens|e /ɪn'tens/ *adj* intenso; (person) apasionado. **~ely** *adv* intensamente; (*very*) sumamente. **~ify** /-ɪfaɪ/ *vt* intensificar. ● *vi* intensificarse. **~ity** /-ɪtɪ/ *n* intensidad *f*
intensive /ɪn'tensɪv/ *adj* intensivo. **~ care** *n* cuidados *mpl* intensivos
intent /ɪn'tent/ *n* propósito *m*. ● *adj* atento. **~ on** absorto en. **~ on doing** resuelto a hacer
intention /ɪn'tenʃn/ *n* intención *f*. **~al** *adj* intencional
intently /ɪn'tentlɪ/ *adv* atentamente
interact /ɪntər'ækt/ *vi* relacionarse. **~ion** /-ʃn/ *n* interacción *f*
intercept /ɪntə'sept/ *vt* interceptar. **~ion** /-ʃn/ *n* interceptación *f*
interchange /ɪntə'tʃeɪndʒ/ *vt* intercambiar. ● /'ɪntətʃeɪndʒ/ *n* intercambio *m*; (*road junction*) cruce *m*. **~able** /-'tʃeɪndʒəbl/ *adj* intercambiable
intercity /ɪntə'sɪtɪ/ *adj* rápido interurbano *m*
intercourse /'ɪntəkɔ:s/ *n* trato *m*; (*sexual*) acto *m* sexual
interest /'ɪntrest/ *n* interés *m*. ● *vt* interesar. **~ed** *adj* interesado. **be ~ed in** interesarse por. **~ing** *adj* interesante
interface /'ɪntəfeɪs/ interfaz *m & f*; (*interaction*) interrelación *f*
interfere /ɪntə'fɪə(r)/ *vi* entrometerse. **~ in** entrometerse en. **~ with** afectar (a); interferir (radio). **~nce** /-rəns/ *n* intromisión *f*; (*Radio*) interferencia *f*
interior /ɪn'tɪərɪə(r)/ *adj & n* interior (*m*)
interjection /ɪntə'dʒekʃn/ *n* interjección *f*
interlude /'ɪntəlu:d/ *n* intervalo *m*; (*theatre, music*) interludio *m*
intermediary /ɪntə'mi:dɪərɪ/ *adj & n* intermediario (*m*)
interminable /ɪn'tɜ:mɪnəbl/ *adj* interminable
intermittent /ɪntə'mɪtnt/ *adj* intermitente. **~ly** *adv* con discontinuidad
intern /ɪn'tɜ:n/ *vt* internar. ● /'ɪntɜ:n/ *n* (*Amer, doctor*) interno *m*
internal /ɪn'tɜ:nl/ *adj* interno. **~ly** *adv* internamente. **I~ Revenue Service** *n* (*Amer*) Hacienda *f*
international /ɪntə'næʃənl/ *adj* internacional
Internet /'ɪntənet/ *n*. **the ~** el Internet
interpret /ɪn'tɜ:prɪt/ *vt/i* interpretar. **~ation** /-'teɪʃn/ *n* interpretación *f*. **~er** *n* intérprete *m & f*
interrogat|e /ɪn'terəgeɪt/ *vt* interrogar. **~ion** /-'geɪʃn/ *n* interrogatorio *m*. **~ive** /-'rɒgətɪv/ *adj* interrogativo
interrupt /ɪntə'rʌpt/ *vt/i* interrumpir. **~ion** /-ʃn/ *n* interrupción *f*
intersect /ɪntə'sekt/ *vt* cruzar. ● *vi* (roads) cruzarse; (*geometry*) inter-

secarse. **~ion** /-ʃn/ *n* (*roads*) cruce *m*; (*geometry*) intersección *f*

intersperse /ɪntə'spɜ:s/ *vt* intercalar

interstate (highway) /'ɪntəsteɪt/ *n* (*Amer*) carretera *f* interestal

intertwine /ɪntə'twaɪn/ *vt* entrelazar. ● *vi* entrelazarse

interval /'ɪntəvl/ *n* intervalo *m*; (*theatre*) descanso *m*. **at ~s** a intervalos

interven|e /ɪntə'vi:n/ *vi* intervenir. **~tion** /-'venʃn/ *n* intervención *f*

interview /'ɪntəvju:/ *n* entrevista *f*. ● *vt* entrevistar. **~ee** /-'i:/ *n* entrevistado *m*. **~er** *n* entrevistador *m*

intestine /ɪn'testɪn/ *n* intestino *m*

intimacy /'ɪntɪməsɪ/ *n* intimidad *f*

intimate /'ɪntɪmət/ *adj* íntimo. ● /'ɪntɪmeɪt/ *vt* (*state*) anunciar; (*imply*) dar a entender. **~ly** /'ɪntɪmətlɪ/ *adv* íntimamente

intimidat|e /ɪn'tɪmɪdeɪt/ *vt* intimidar. **~ion** /-'deɪʃn/ *n* intimidación *f*

into /'ɪntu://'ɪntə/ *prep* en; (translate) a

intolerable /ɪn'tɒlərəbl/ *adj* intolerable

intoleran|ce /ɪn'tɒlərəns/ *n* intolerancia *f*. **~t** *adj* intolerante

intoxicat|e /ɪn'tɒksɪkeɪt/ *vt* embriagar; (*Med*) intoxicar. **~ed** *adj* ebrio. **~ing** *adj* (substance) estupefaciente. **~ion** /-'keɪʃn/ *n* embriaguez *f*; (*Med*) intoxicación *f*

intransitive /ɪn'trænsɪtɪv/ *adj* intransitivo

intravenous /ɪntrə'vi:nəs/ *adj* intravenoso

intrepid /ɪn'trepɪd/ *adj* intrépido

intrica|cy /'ɪntrɪkəsɪ/ *n* complejidad *f*. **~te** /-ət/ *adj* complejo

intrigu|e /ɪn'tri:g/ *vt/i* intrigar. ● /'ɪntri:g/ *n* intriga *f*. **~ing** /ɪn'tri:gɪŋ/ *adj* intrigante

intrinsic /ɪn'trɪnsɪk/ *adj* intrínseco. **~ally** *adv* intrínsecamente

introduc|e /ɪntrə'dju:s/ *vt* introducir; presentar (person). **~tion** /ɪntrə'dʌkʃn/ *n* introducción *f*; (*to person*) presentación *f*. **~tory** /ɪntrə'dʌktərɪ/ *adj* preliminar; (course) de introducción

introvert /'ɪntrəvɜ:t/ *n* introvertido *m*

intru|de /ɪn'tru:d/ *vi* entrometerse; (*disturb*) importunar. **~der** *n* intruso *m*. **~sion** /-ʒn/ *n* intrusión *f*. **~sive** /-sɪv/ *adj* impertinente

intuiti|on /ɪntju:'ɪʃn/ *n* intuición *f*. **~ve** /ɪn'tju:ɪtɪv/ *adj* intuitivo

inundat|e /'ɪnʌndeɪt/ *vt* inundar. **~ion** /-'deɪʃn/ *n* inundación *f*

invade /ɪn'veɪd/ *vt* invadir. **~r** *n* invasor *m*

invalid /'ɪnvəlɪd/ *n* inválido *m*. ● /ɪn'vælɪd/ *adj* inválido. **~ate** /ɪn'vælɪdeɪt/ *vt* invalidar

invaluable /ɪn'væljʊəbl/ *adj* inestimable, invalorable (*LAm*)

invariabl|e /ɪn'veərɪəbl/ *adj* invariable. **~y** *adv* invariablemente

invasion /ɪn'veɪʒn/ *n* invasión *f*

invent /ɪn'vent/ *vt* inventar. **~ion** /-'venʃn/ *n* invención *f*. **~ive** *adj* inventivo. **~or** *n* inventor *m*

inventory /'ɪnvəntrɪ/ *n* inventario *m*

invertebrate /ɪn'vɜ:tɪbrət/ *n* invertebrado *m*

inverted commas /ɪnvɜ:tɪd 'kɒməz/*npl* comillas *fpl*

invest /ɪn'vest/ *vt* invertir. ● *vi*. **~ in** invertir en

i

investigat|e /ɪn'vestɪgeɪt/ *vt* investigar. **~ion** /-'geɪʃn/ *n* investigación *f*. **under ~ion** sometido a examen. **~or** *n* investigador *m*

investment /ɪn'vestmənt/ inversión *f*

investor /ɪn'vestə(r)/ inversionista *m & f*

inveterate /ɪn'vetərət/ *adj* inveterado

invidious /ɪn'vɪdɪəs/ *adj* (*hateful*) odioso; (*unfair*) injusto

invigorating /ɪn'vɪgəreɪtɪŋ/ *adj* vigorizante; (*stimulating*) estimulante

i

invincible /ɪn'vɪnsɪbl/ *adj* invencible

invisible /ɪn'vɪzəbl/ *adj* invisible

invit|ation /ɪnvɪ'teɪʃn/ *n* invitación *f*. **~e** /ɪn'vaɪt/ *vt* invitar; (*ask for*) pedir. ● /'ɪnvaɪt/ *n* 🄸 invitación *f*. **~ing** /ɪn'vaɪtɪŋ/ *adj* atrayente

invoice /'ɪnvɔɪs/ *n* factura *f*. ● *vt*. **~ s.o. (for sth)** pasarle a uno factura (por algo)

involuntary /ɪn'vɒləntərɪ/ *adj* involuntario

involve /ɪn'vɒlv/ *vt* (*entail*) suponer; (*implicate*) implicar. **~d in** envuelto en. **~d** *adj* (*complex*) complicado. **~ment** *n* participación *f*; (*relationship*) enredo *m*

inward /'ɪnwəd/ *adj* interior. ● *adv* hacia adentro. **~s** *adv* hacia dentro

iodine /'aɪədi:n/ *n* yodo *m*

ion /'aɪən/ *n* ion *m*

iota /aɪ'əʊtə/ *n* (*amount*) pizca *f*

IOU /aɪəʊ'ju:/ *abbr* (= **I owe you**) pagaré *m*

IQ *abbr* (= **intelligence quotient**) CI *m*, cociente *m* intelectual

Iran /ɪ'rɑ:n/ *n* Irán *m*. **~ian** /ɪ'reɪmɪən/ *adj & n* iraní (*m*)

Iraq /ɪ'rɑ:k/ *n* Irak *m*. **~i** *adj & n* iraquí (*m & f*)

irate /aɪ'reɪt/ *adj* colérico

Ireland /'aɪələnd/ *n* Irlanda *f*

iris /'aɪərɪs/ *n* (*of eye*) iris *m*; (*flower*) lirio *m*

Irish /'aɪərɪʃ/ *adj* irlandés. ● *n* (*language*) irlandés *m*. *npl*. **the ~** (*people*) los irlandeses. **~man** /-mən/ *n* irlandés *m*. **~woman** *n* irlandesa *f*

iron /'aɪən/ *n* hierro *m*; (*appliance*) plancha *f*. ● *adj* de hierro. ● *vt* planchar. □ **~ out** *vt* allanar

ironic /aɪ'rɒnɪk/ *adj* irónico. **~ally** *adv* irónicamente

ironing board /'aɪənɪŋ/ *n* tabla *f* de planchar, burro *m* de planchar (*Mex*)

iron: ~monger /-mʌŋgə(r)/ *n* ferretero *m*. **~monger's** *n* ferretería *f*

irony /'aɪərənɪ/ *n* ironía *f*

irrational /ɪ'ræʃənl/ *adj* irracional

irrefutable /ɪrɪ'fju:təbl/ *adj* irrefutable

irregular /ɪ'regjʊlə(r)/ *adj* irregular. **~ity** /-'lærətɪ/ *n* irregularidad *f*

irrelevan|ce /ɪ'reləvəns/ *n* irrelevancia *f*. **~t** *adj* irrelevante

irreparable /ɪ'repərəbl/ *adj* irreparable

irreplaceable /ɪrɪ'pleɪsəbl/ *adj* irreemplazable

irresistible /ɪrɪ'zɪstəbl/ *adj* irresistible

irrespective /ɪrɪ'spektɪv/ *adj*. **~ of** sin tomar en cuenta

irresponsible /ɪrɪ'spɒnsəbl/ *adj* irresponsable

irretrievable /ɪrɪ'tri:vəbl/ *adj* irrecuperable

irreverent /ɪ'revərənt/ *adj* irreverente

irrevocable /ɪ'revəkəbl/ *adj* irrevocable

irrigat|e /'ɪrɪgeɪt/ *vt* regar, irrigar. **~ion** /-'geɪʃn/ *n* riego *m*, irrigación *f*

irritable /'ɪrɪtəbl/ *adj* irritable

irritat|e /'ɪrɪteɪt/ *vt* irritar. **~ed** *adj* irritado. **~ing** *adj* irritante. **~ion** /-'teɪʃn/ *n* irritación *f*

IRS *abbr* (*Amer*) *see* **INTERNAL REVENUE SERVICE**

is /ɪz/ *see* **BE**

ISDN *abbr* (**Integrated Services Digital Network**) RDSI

Islam /'ɪzlɑːm/ *n* el Islam. **~ic** /ɪz'læmɪk/ *adj* islámico

island /'aɪlənd/ *n* isla *f*. **~er** *n* isleño *m*

isolat|e /'aɪsəleɪt/ *vt* aislar. **~ion** /-'leɪʃn/ *n* aislamiento *m*

Israel /'ɪzreɪl/ *n* Israel *m*. **~i** /ɪz'reɪlɪ/ *adj & n* israelí (*m*)

issue /'ɪʃuː/ *n* tema *m*, asunto *m*; (*of magazine etc*) número *m*; (*of stamps, bank notes*) emisión *f*; (*of documents*) expedición *f*. **take ~ with** discrepar de. ● *vt* hacer público (statement); expedir (documents); emitir (stamps etc); prestar (library book)

it /ɪt/ *pronoun*

····➤ (*as subject*) *generally not translated*. **it's huge** es enorme. **where is it?** ¿dónde está?. **it's all lies** son todas mentiras

····➤ (*as direct object*) lo (*m*), la (*f*). **he read it to me** me lo/la leyó. **give it to me** dámelo/dámela

····➤ (*as indirect object*) le. **I gave it another coat of paint** le di otra mano de pintura

····➤ (*after a preposition*) *generally not translated*. **there's nothing behind it** no hay nada detrás

! Note, however, that in some cases *él* or *ella* must be used e.g. **he picked up the spoon and hit me with it** *agarró la cuchara y me golpeó con ella*

····➤ (*at door*) **who is it?** ¿quién es?. **it's me** soy yo; (*on telephone*) **who is it, please?** ¿quién habla, por favor?; (*before passing on to sb else*) ¿de parte de quién, por favor? **it's Carol** soy Carol (*Spain*), habla Carol

····➤ (*in impersonal constructions*) **it is well known that ...** bien se sabe que ... **it's five o'clock** son las cinco. **so it seems** así parece

····➤ **that's it** (*that's right*) eso es; (*that's enough, that's finished*) ya está

Italian /ɪ'tæljən/ *adj & n* italiano (*m*)

italics /ɪ'tælɪks/ *npl* (letra *f*) cursiva *f*

Italy /'ɪtəlɪ/ *n* Italia *f*

itch /ɪtʃ/ *n* picazón *f*. ● *vi* picar. **I'm ~ing to** estoy que me muero por. **my arm ~es** me pica el brazo. **~y** *adj* que pica. **I've got an ~y nose** me pica la nariz

it'd /ɪtəd/ = **it had, it would**

item /'aɪtəm/ *n* artículo *m*; (*on agenda*) punto *m*. **news ~** *n* noticia *f*. **~ize** *vt* detallar

itinerary /aɪ'tɪnərərɪ/ *n* itinerario *m*

it'll /'ɪtl/ = **it will**

its /ɪts/ *adj* su, sus (*pl*). ● *pron* (el)

suyo *m*, (la) suya *f*, (los) suyos *mpl*, (las) suyas *fpl*

it's /ɪts/ = **it is, it has**

itself /ɪt'self/ *pron* él mismo, ella misma, ello mismo; (*reflexive*) se; (*after prep*) sí mismo, sí misma

I've /aɪv/ = **I have**

ivory /'aɪvərɪ/ *n* marfil *m*. **~ tower** *n* torre *f* de marfil

ivy /'aɪvɪ/ *n* hiedra *f*

Ivy League - the El grupo de universidades más antiguas y respetadas de EE.UU. Situadas al noreste del país, son: Harvard, Yale, Columbia, Cornell, Dartmouth College, Brown, Princeton y Pensylvania. El término proviene de la hiedra que crece en los antiguos edificios de estos establecimientos.

Jj

jab /dʒæb/ *vt* (*pt* **jabbed**) pinchar; (*thrust*) hurgonear. ● *n* pinchazo *m*

jack /dʒæk/ *n* (*Mec*) gato *m*; (*socket*) enchufe *m* hembra; (*Cards*) sota *f*. □ **~ up** *vt* alzar con gato

jackal /'dʒækl/ *n* chacal *m*

jackdaw /'dʒækdɔ:/ *n* grajilla *f*

jacket /'dʒækɪt/ *n* chaqueta *f*; (*casual*) americana *f*, saco *m* (*LAm*); (*Amer, of book*) sobrecubierta *f*; (*of record*) funda *f*, carátula *f*

jack: ~ knife *vi* (lorry) plegarse. **~pot** *n* premio *m* gordo. **hit the ~pot** sacar el premio gordo

jade /dʒeɪd/ *n* (*stone*) jade *m*

jagged /'dʒægɪd/ *adj* (edge, cut) irregular; (rock) recortado

jaguar /'dʒægjʊə(r)/ *n* jaguar *m*

jail /dʒeɪl/ *n* cárcel *m*, prisión *f*. ● *vt* encarcelar. **~er** *n* carcelero *m*. **~house** *n* (*Amer*) cárcel *f*

jam /dʒæm/ *vt* (*pt* **jammed**) interferir con (radio); atestar (road). **~ sth into sth** meter algo a la fuerza en algo. ● *vi* (brakes) bloquearse; (machine) trancarse. ● *n* mermelada *f*; (*fam, situation*) apuro *m*

jangle /'dʒæŋgl/ *n* sonido *m* metálico (y áspero). ● *vi* hacer ruido (metálico)

janitor /'dʒænɪtə(r)/ *n* portero *m*

January /'dʒænjʊərɪ/ *n* enero *m*

Japan /dʒə'pæn/ *n* (el) Japón *m*. **~ese** /dʒæpə'ni:z/ *adj & n invar* japonés (*m*)

jar /dʒɑ:(r)/ *n* tarro *m*, bote *m*. ● *vi* (*pt* **jarred**) (clash) desentonar. ● *vt* sacudir

jargon /'dʒɑ:gən/ *n* jerga *f*

jaundice /'dʒɔ:ndɪs/ *n* ictericia *f*

jaunt /dʒɔ:nt/ *n* excursión *f*

jaunty /'dʒɔ:ntɪ/ *adj* (**-ier, -iest**) garboso

jaw /dʒɔ:/ *n* mandíbula *f*. **~s** *npl* fauces *fpl*. **~bone** *n* mandíbula *f*, maxilar *m*; (*of animal*) quijada *f*

jay /dʒeɪ/ *n* arrendajo *m*. **~walk** *vi* cruzar la calle descuidadamente. **~walker** *n* peatón *m* imprudente

jazz /dʒæz/ *n* jazz *m*. □ **~ up** *vt* animar. **~y** *adj* chillón

jealous /dʒeləs/ *adj* celoso; (*envious*) envidioso. **~y** *n* celos *mpl*

jeans /dʒi:nz/ *npl* vaqueros *mpl*, jeans *mpl*, tejanos *mpl*, pantalones *mpl* de mezclilla (*Mex*)

Jeep (*P*), **jeep** /dʒi:p/ *n* Jeep *m* (*P*)

jeer /dʒɪə(r)/ *vi*. **~ at** mofarse de;

(*boo*) abuchear. ● *n* burla *f*; (*boo*) abucheo *m*

Jell-O /ˈdʒeləʊ/ *n* (*P*) (*Amer*) gelatina *f* (con sabor a frutas)

jelly /dʒelɪ/ *n* (*clear jam*) jalea *f*; (*pudding*) *see* **Jell-O**; (*substance*) gelatina *f*. **~fish** *n* (*pl invar or* **-es**) medusa *f*

jeopardize /ˈdʒepədaɪz/ *vt* arriesgar

jerk /dʒɜːk/ *n* sacudida *f*; (*sl, fool*) idiota *m & f*. ● *vt* sacudir

jersey /ˈdʒɜːzɪ/ *n* (*pl* **-eys**) jersey *m*, suéter *m*, pulóver *m*

jest /dʒest/ *n* broma *f*. ● *vi* bromear

Jesus /ˈdʒiːzəs/ *n* Jesús *m*

jet /dʒet/ *n* (*stream*) chorro *m*; (*plane*) avión *m* (con motor a reacción); (*mineral*) azabache *m*. **~-black** /-ˈblæk/ *adj* azabache negro *a invar*. **~ lag** *n* jet lag *m*, desfase *f* horario. **have ~ lag** estar desfasado. **~-propelled** /-prəˈpeld/ *adj* (de propulsión) a reacción

jettison /ˈdʒetɪsn/ *vt* echar al mar; (*fig, discard*) deshacerse de

jetty /ˈdʒetɪ/ *n* muelle *m*

Jew /dʒuː/ *n* judío *m*

jewel /ˈdʒuːəl/ *n* joya *f*. **~ler** *n* joyero *m*. **~lery** *n* joyas *fpl*

Jewish /ˈdʒuːɪʃ/ *adj* judío

jiffy /ˈdʒɪfɪ/ *n* momentito *m*. **do sth in a ~** hacer algo en un santiamén

jig /dʒɪg/ *n* (*dance*) giga *f*

jigsaw /ˈdʒɪgsɔː/ *n*. **~ (puzzle)** rompecabezas *m*

jilt /dʒɪlt/ *vt* dejar plantado

jingle /ˈdʒɪŋgl/ *vt* hacer sonar. ● *vi* tintinear. ● *n* tintineo *m*; (*advert*) jingle *m* (publicitario)

job /dʒɒb/ *n* empleo *m*, trabajo *m*; (*piece of work*) trabajo *m*. **it is a good ~ that** menos mal que. **~less** *adj* desempleado

jockey /ˈdʒɒkɪ/ *n* jockey *m*

jocular /ˈdʒɒkjʊlə(r)/ *adj* jocoso

jog /dʒɒg/ *vt* (*pt* **jogged**) empujar; refrescar (memory). ● *vi* hacer footing, hacer jogging. **~er** *n* persona *f* que hace footing. **~ging** *n* footing *m*, jogging *m*. **go ~ging** salir a hacer footing *or* jogging

join /dʒɔɪn/ *vt* (*link*) unir; hacerse socio de (club); hacerse miembro de (political group); alistarse en (army); reunirse con (another person). ● *n* juntura. ● *vi*. **~ together** (parts) unirse; (roads etc) empalmar; (rivers) confluir. □ **~ in** *vi* participar (en). □ **~ up** *vi* (*Mil*) alistarse. **~er** *n* carpintero *m*

joint /dʒɔɪnt/ *adj* conjunto. ● *n* (*join*) unión *f*, junta *f*; (*in limbs*) articulación *f*. (*Culin*) trozo *m* de carne (para asar). **out of ~** descoyuntado. **~ account** *n* cuenta *f* conjunta. **~ly** *adv* conjuntamente. **~ owner** *n* copropietario *m*.

joist /dʒɔɪst/ *n* viga *f*

jok|e /dʒəʊk/ *n* (*story*) chiste *m*; (*practical joke*) broma *f*. ● *vi* bromear. **~er** *n* bromista *m & f*; (*Cards*) comodín *m*. **~y** *adj* jocoso

jolly /ˈdʒɒlɪ/ *adj* (**-ier**, **-iest**) alegre. ● *adv* [!] muy

jolt /dʒɒlt/ *vt* sacudir. ● *vi* (vehicle) dar una sacudida. ● *n* sacudida *f*

jostle /ˈdʒɒsl/ *vt* empujar. ● *vi* empujarse

jot /dʒɒt/ *n* pizca *f*. ● *vt* (*pt* **jotted**). □ **~ down** *vt* apuntar (rápidamente). **~ter** *n* bloc *m*

journal /ˈdʒɜːnl/ *n* (*diary*) diario *m*; (*newspaper*) periódico *m*; (*magazine*) revista *f*. **~ism** *n* periodismo *m*. **~ist** *n* periodista *m & f*

journey /ˈdʒɜːnɪ/ *n* viaje *m*. **go on a ~** hacer un viaje. ● *vi* viajar

jovial /ˈdʒəʊvɪəl/ *adj* jovial

joy /dʒɔɪ/ *n* alegría *f*. **~ful** *adj* feliz. **~ous** *adj* feliz. **~rider** *n* joven *m* que roba un coche para dar una vuelta. **~stick** *n* (*in aircraft*) palanca *f* de mando; (*Comp*) mando *m*, joystick *m*

jubila|nt /ˈdʒuːbɪlənt/ *adj* jubiloso. **~tion** /-ˈleɪʃn/ *n* júbilo *m*

jubilee /ˈdʒuːbɪliː/ *n* aniversario *m* especial

Judaism /ˈdʒuːdeɪɪzəm/ *n* judaísmo *m*

J

judge /dʒʌdʒ/ *n* juez *m*. ● *vt* juzgar. **~ment** *n* juicio *m*

judicia|l /dʒuːˈdɪʃl/ *adj* judicial. **~ry** /-ərɪ/ *n* judicatura *f*

judo /ˈdʒuːdəʊ/ *n* judo *m*

jug /dʒʌg/ *n* jarra *f*

juggernaut /ˈdʒʌgənɔːt/ *n* camión *m* grande

juggle /ˈdʒʌgl/ *vi* hacer malabarismos. ● *vt* hacer malabarismos con. **~r** *n* malabarista *m & f*

juic|e /dʒuːs/ *n* jugo *m*, zumo *m*. **~y** *adj* jugoso, zumoso; (story etc) [!] picante

jukebox /ˈdʒuːkbɒks/ *n* máquina *f* de discos, rocola *f* (*LAm*)

July /dʒuːˈlaɪ/ *n* julio *m*

jumble /ˈdʒʌmbl/ *vt*. **~ (up)** mezclar. ● *n* (*muddle*) revoltijo *m*. **~ sale** *n* venta *f* de objetos usados *m*

jumbo /ˈdʒʌmbəʊ/ *adj* gigante. **~ jet** *n* jumbo *m*

jump /dʒʌmp/ *vt* saltar. **~ rope** (*Amer*) saltar a la comba, saltar a la cuerda. **~ the gun** obrar prematuramente. **~ the queue** colarse. ● *vi* saltar; (*start*) sobresaltarse; (prices) alzarse. **~ at an opportunity** apresurarse a aprovechar una oportunidad. ● *n* salto *m*; (*start*) susto *m*; (*increase*) aumento *m*. **~er** *n* jersey *m*, suéter *m*, pulóver *m*; (*Amer, dress*) pichi *m*, jumper *m & f* (*LAm*). **~er cables** (*Amer*), **~ leads** *npl* cables *mpl* de arranque. **~ rope** (*Amer*) comba *f*, cuerda *f*, reata *f* (*Mex*). **~suit** *n* mono *m*. **~y** *adj* nervioso

junction /ˈdʒʌŋkʃn/ *n* (*of roads, rails*) cruce *m*; (*Elec*) empalme *m*

June /dʒuːn/ *n* junio *m*

jungle /ˈdʒʌŋgl/ *n* selva *f*, jungla *f*

junior /ˈdʒuːnɪə(r)/ *adj* (*in age*) más joven (**to** que); (*in rank*) subalterno. ● *n* menor *m*

junk /dʒʌŋk/ *n* trastos *mpl* viejos; (*worthless stuff*) basura *f*. ● *vt* [!] tirar. **~ food** *n* comida *f* basura, alimento *m* chatarra (*Mex*). **~ie** /ˈdʒʌnkɪ/ *n* [!] drogadicto *m*, yonqui *m & f* [!]. **~ mail** *n* propaganda *f* que se recibe por correo. **~ shop** *n* tienda *f* de trastos viejos

junta /ˈdʒʌntə/ *n* junta *f* militar

Jupiter /ˈdʒuːpɪtə(r)/ *n* Júpiter *m*

jurisdiction /dʒʊərɪsˈdɪkʃn/ *n* jurisdicción *f*

jur|or /ˈdʒʊərə(r)/ *n* (miembro *m* de un) jurado *m*. **~y** *n* jurado *m*

just /dʒʌst/ *adj* (*fair*) justo. ● *adv* exactamente, justo; (*barely*) justo; (*only*) sólo, solamente. **~ as tall** tan alto (**as** como). **~ listen!** ¡escucha! **he has ~ arrived** acaba de llegar, recién llegó (*LAm*)

justice /ˈdʒʌstɪs/ *n* justicia *f*. **J~ of the Peace** juez *m* de paz

justif|iable /dʒʌstɪˈfaɪəbl/ *adj* justificable. **~iably** *adv* con razón. **~ication** /dʒʌstɪfɪˈkeɪʃn/ *n* justificación *f*. **~y** /ˈdʒʌstɪfaɪ/ *vt* justificar

jut /dʒʌt/ *vi* (*pt* **jutted**). **~ (out)** ▫

sobresalir

juvenile /'dʒu:vənaɪl/ *adj* juvenil; (*childish*) infantil. ● *n* (*Jurid*) menor *m & f*

Kk

kaleidoscope /kə'laɪdəskəʊp/ *n* caleidoscopio *m*

kangaroo /kæŋgə'ru:/ *n* canguro *m*

karate /kə'rɑ:tɪ/ *n* kárate *m*, karate *m* (*LAm*)

keel /ki:l/ *n* (*of ship*) quilla *f*. □ ~ **over** *vi* volcar(se)

keen /ki:n/ *adj* (**-er**, **-est**) (interest, feeling) vivo; (wind, mind, analysis) penetrante; (eyesight) agudo; (*eager*) entusiasta. **I'm ~ on golf** me encanta el golf. **he's ~ on Shostakovich** le gusta Shostakovich. **~ly** *adv* vivamente; (*enthusiastically*) con entusiasmo. **~ness** *n* intensidad *f*; (*enthusiasm*) entusiasmo *m*.

keep /ki:p/ *vt* (*pt* **kept**) guardar; cumplir (promise); tener (shop, animals); mantener (family); observar (rule); (*celebrate*) celebrar; (*delay*) detener; (*prevent*) impedir. ● *vi* (food) conservarse; (*remain*) quedarse; (*continue*) seguir. **~ doing** seguir haciendo. ● *n* subsistencia *f*; (*of castle*) torreón *m*. **for ~s** 🄸 para siempre. □ ~ **back** *vt* retener. ● *vi* no acercarse. □ ~ **in** *vt* no dejar salir. □ ~ **off** *vt* mantenerse alejado de (land). **'~ off the grass'** 'prohibido pisar el césped'. □ ~ **on** *vi* seguir. **~ on doing sth** seguir haciendo. □ ~ **out** *vt* no dejar entrar. □ ~ **up** *vt* mantener. □ ~ **up with** *vt* estar al día en

kennel /'kenl/ *n* casa *f* del perro; (*Amer, for boarding*) residencia *f* canina. **~s** *n invar* residencia *f* canina

kept /kept/ *see* **KEEP**

kerb /kɜ:b/ *n* bordillo *m* (de la acera), borde *m* de la banqueta (*Mex*)

kerosene /'kerəsi:n/ *n* queroseno *m*

ketchup /'ketʃʌp/ *n* salsa *f* de tomate

kettle /'ketl/ *n* pava *f*, tetera *f* (para calentar agua)

key /ki:/ *n* llave *f*; (*of computer, piano*) tecla *f*; (*Mus*) tono *m*. **be off ~** no estar en el tono. ● *adj* clave. □ ~ **in** *vt* teclear. **~board** *n* teclado *m*. **~hole** *n* ojo *m* de la cerradura. **~ring** *n* llavero *m*

khaki /'kɑ:kɪ/ *adj* caqui

kick /kɪk/ *vt* dar una patada a (person); patear (ball). ● *vi* dar patadas; (horse) cocear. ● *n* patada *f*; (*of horse*) coz *f*; (*fam, thrill*) placer *m*. □ ~ **out** *vt* 🄸 echar. □ ~ **up** *vt* armar (fuss etc). **~off** *n* (*Sport*) saque *m* inicial. **~ start** *vt* arrancar (con el pedal de arranque) (engine)

kid /kɪd/ *n* (*young goat*) cabrito *m*; (*fam, child*) niño *m*, chaval *m*, escuincle *m* (*Mex*). ● *vt* (*pt* **kidded**) tomar el pelo a. ● *vi* bromear

kidnap /'kɪdnæp/ *vt* (*pt* **kidnapped**) secuestrar. **~per** *n* secuestrador *m*. **~ping** *n* secuestro *m*

kidney /'kɪdnɪ/ *n* riñón *m*

kill /kɪl/ *vt* matar; (*fig*) acabar con. ● *n* matanza *f*. □ ~ **off** *vt* matar. **~er** *n* asesino *m*. **~ing** *n* matanza *f*; (*murder*) asesinato *m*. **make a**

j k

~**ing** (*fig*) hacer un gran negocio

kiln /kɪln/ *n* horno *m*

kilo /'ki:ləʊ/ *n* (*pl* **-os**) kilo *m*. ~**gram(me)** /'kɪləgræm/ *n* kilogramo *m*. ~**metre**/'kɪləmi:tə(r)/, /kɪ'lɒmɪtə(r)/ *n* kilómetro *m*. ~**watt** /'kɪləwɒt/ *n* kilovatio *m*

kilt /kɪlt/ *n* falda *f* escocesa

kin /kɪn/ *n* familiares *mpl*

kind /kaɪnd/ *n* tipo *m*, clase *f*. ~ **of** (*fam, somewhat*) un poco. **in** ~ en especie. **be two of a** ~ ser tal para cual. ● *adj* amable

kindergarten /'kɪndəgɑ:tn/ *n* jardín *m* de infancia

kind-hearted /kaɪnd'hɑ:tɪd/ *adj* bondadoso

k

kindle /'kɪndl/ *vt* encender

kind|ly *adj* (**-ier**, **-iest**) bondadoso. ● *adv* amablemente; (*please*) haga el favor de. ~**ness** *n* bondad *f*; (*act*) favor *m*

king /kɪŋ/ *n* rey *m*. ~**dom** *n* reino *m*. ~**fisher** *n* martín *m* pescador. ~**-size(d)** *adj* extragrande

kink /kɪŋk/ *n* (*in rope*) vuelta *f*, curva *f*; (*in hair*) onda *f*. ~**y** *adj* [!] pervertido

kiosk /'ki:ɒsk/ *n* quiosco *m*

kipper /'kɪpə(r)/ *n* arenque *m* ahumado

kiss /kɪs/ *n* beso *m*. ● *vt* besar. ● *vi* besarse

kit /kɪt/ *n* avíos *mpl*. **tool** ~ caja *f* de herramientas. ▫ ~ **out** *vt* (*pt* **kitted**) equipar

kitchen /'kɪtʃɪn/ *n* cocina *f*

kite /kaɪt/ *n* cometa *f*, papalote *m* (*Mex*)

kitten /'kɪtn/ *n* gatito *m*

knack /næk/ *n* truco *m*

knapsack /'næpsæk/ *n* mochila *f*

knead /ni:d/ *vt* amasar

knee /ni:/ *n* rodilla *f*. ~**cap** *n* rótula *f*

kneel /ni:l/ *vi* (*pt* **kneeled** *or* **knelt**). ~ **(down)** arrodillarse; (*be on one's knees*) estar arrodillado

knelt /nelt/ *see* KNEEL

knew /nju:/ *see* KNOW

knickers /'nɪkəz/ *npl* bragas *fpl*, calzones *mpl* (*LAm*), pantaletas *fpl* (*Mex*)

knife /naɪf/ *n* (*pl* **knives**) cuchillo *m*. ● *vt* acuchillar

knight /naɪt/ *n* caballero *m*; (*Chess*) caballo *m*. ● *vt* conceder el título de Sir a. ~**hood** *n* título *m* de Sir

knit /nɪt/ *vt* (*pt* **knitted** *or* **knit**) hacer, tejer (*LAm*). ● *vi* tejer, hacer punto. ~ **one's brow** fruncir el ceño. ~**ting** *n* tejido *m*, punto *m*. ~**ting needle** *n* aguja *f* de hacer punto, aguja *f* de tejer

knives /naɪvz/ *see* KNIFE

knob /nɒb/ *n* botón *m*; (*of door, drawer etc*) tirador *m*. ~**bly** *adj* nudoso

knock /nɒk/ *vt* golpear; (*criticize*) criticar. ● *vi* golpear; (*at door*) llamar, golpear (*LAm*). ● *n* golpe *m*. ▫ ~ **about** *vt* maltratar. ▫ ~ **down** *vt* derribar; atropellar (person). ▫ ~ **off** *vt* hacer caer. ● *vi* (*fam, finish work*) terminar, salir del trabajo. ▫ ~ **out** *vt* (*by blow*) dejar sin sentido; (*eliminate*) eliminar. ▫ ~ **over** *vt* tirar; atropellar (person). ~**er** *n* aldaba *f*. ~**-kneed** /-'ni:d/ *adj* patizambo. ~**out** *n* (*Boxing*) nocaut *m*

knot /nɒt/ *n* nudo *m*. ● *vt* (*pt* **knotted**) anudar

know /nəʊ/ *vt* (*pt* **knew**) saber; (*be acquainted with*) conocer. **let s.o.** ~ **sth** decirle algo a uno;

(*warn*) avisarle algo a uno. ● *vi* saber. ~ **how to do sth** saber hacer algo. ~ **about** entender de (cars etc). ~ **of** saber de. ● *n*. **be in the** ~ estar enterado. **~-all** *n n* sabelotodo *m & f*. **~-how** *n* know-how *m*, conocimientos *mpl* y experiencia. **~ingly** *adv* a sabiendas. **~-it-all** *n* (*Amer*) *see* **~-ALL**

knowledge /'nɒlɪdʒ/ *n* saber *m*; (*awareness*) conocimiento *m*; (*learning*) conocimientos *mpl*. **~able** *adj* informado

known /nəʊn/ *see* **KNOW**. ● *adj* conocido

knuckle /'nʌkl/ *n* nudillo *m*. □ ~ **under** *vi* someterse

Korea /kə'rɪə/ *n* Corea *f*. **~n** *adj & n* coreano (*m*)

kudos /'kju:dɒs/ *n* prestigio *m*

Ll

lab /læb/ *n* [I] laboratorio *m*

label /'leɪbl/ *n* etiqueta *f*. ● *vt* (*pt* **labelled**) poner etiqueta a; (*fig, describe as*) tachar de

laboratory /lə'bɒrətərɪ/ *n* laboratorio *m*

laborious /lə'bɔ:rɪəs/ *adj* penoso

labour /'leɪbə(r)/ *n* trabajo *m*; (*workers*) mano *f* de obra; (*Med*) parto *m*. **in** ~ de parto. ● *vi* trabajar. ● *vt* insistir en. **L~** *n* el partido *m* laborista. ● *adj* laborista. **~er** *n* peón *m*

lace /leɪs/ *n* encaje *m*; (*of shoe*) cordón *m*, agujeta *f* (*Mex*). ● *vt* (*fasten*) atar

lacerate /'læsəreɪt/ *vt* lacerar

lack /læk/ *n* falta *f*. **for** ~ **of** por falta de. ● *vt* faltarle a uno. **he ~s confidence** le falta confianza en sí mismo. **~ing** *adj*. **be ~ing** faltar. **be ~ing in** no tener

lad /læd/ *n* muchacho *m*

ladder /'lædə(r)/ *n* escalera *f* (de mano); (*in stocking*) carrera *f*. ● *vt* hacerse una carrera en. ● *vi* hacérsele una carrera a

laden /'leɪdn/ *adj* cargado (**with** de)

ladle /'leɪdl/ *n* cucharón *m*

lady /'leɪdɪ/ *n* señora *f*. **young** ~ señorita *f*. **~bird** *n*, **~bug** *n* (*Amer*) mariquita *f*, catarina *f* (*Mex*). **~-in-waiting** *n* dama *f* de honor. **~like** *adj* fino

lag /læg/ *vi* (*pt* **lagged**). ~ **(behind)** retrasarse. ● *vt* revestir (*pipes*). ● *n* (*interval*) intervalo *m*

lager /'lɑ:gə(r)/ *n* cerveza *f* (rubia)

lagging /'lægɪŋ/ *n* revestimiento *m*

lagoon /lə'gu:n/ *n* laguna *f*

laid /leɪd/ *see* **LAY**

lain /leɪn/ *see* **LIE**[1]

lair /leə(r)/ *n* guarida *f*

lake /leɪk/ *n* lago *m*

lamb /læm/ *n* cordero *m*

lame /leɪm/ *adj* (**-er**, **-est**) cojo, rengo (*LAm*); (excuse) pobre, malo

lament /lə'ment/ *n* lamento *m*. ● *vt* lamentar. **~able** /'læməntəbl/ *adj* lamentable

lamp /læmp/ *n* lámpara *f*

lamp: ~post *n* farol *m*. **~shade** *n* pantalla *f*

lance /lɑ:ns/ *n* lanza *f*

land /lænd/ *n* tierra *f*; (*country*) país *m*; (*plot*) terreno *m*. ● *vt* desembarcar; (*obtain*) conseguir; dar (blow). ● *vi* (*from ship*) desembar-

k

l

car; (*aircraft*) aterrizar. □ ~ **up** *vi* ir a parar. ~**ing** *n* desembarque *m*; (*by aircraft*) aterrizaje *m*; (*top of stairs*) descanso *m*. ~**lady** *n* casera *f*; (*of inn*) dueña *f*. ~**lord** *n* casero *m*, dueño *m*; (*of inn*) dueño *m*. ~**mark** *n* punto *m* destacado. ~**scape** /-skeɪp/ *n* paisaje *m*. ~**slide** *n* desprendimiento *m* de tierras; (*Pol*) victoria *f* arrolladora

lane /leɪn/ *n* (*path, road*) camino *m*, sendero *m*; (*strip of road*) carril *m*

language /ˈlæŋgwɪdʒ/ *n* idioma *m*; (*speech, style*) lenguaje *m*

lank /læŋk/ *adj* (hair) lacio. ~**y** *adj* (**-ier**, **-iest**) larguirucho

lantern /ˈlæntən/ *n* linterna *f*

lap /læp/ *n* (*of body*) rodillas *fpl*; (*Sport*) vuelta *f*. □ ~ **up** *vt* (*pt* **lapped**) beber a lengüetazos; (*fig*) aceptar con entusiasmo. ● *vi* (waves) chapotear

lapel /ləˈpel/ *n* solapa *f*

lapse /læps/ *vi* (*decline*) degradarse; (*expire*) caducar; (time) transcurrir. ~ **into silence** callarse. ● *n* error *m*; (*of time*) intervalo *m*

laptop /ˈlæptɒp/ *n*. ~ **(computer)** laptop *m*, portátil *m*

lard /lɑːd/ *n* manteca *f* de cerdo

larder /ˈlɑːdə(r)/ *n* despensa *f*

large /lɑːdʒ/ *adj* (**-er**, **-est**) grande, (*before singular noun*) gran. ● *n*. **at** ~ en libertad. ~**ly** *adv* en gran parte

lark /lɑːk/ *n* (*bird*) alondra *f*; (*joke*) broma *f*; (*bit of fun*) travesura *f*. □ ~ **about** *vt* hacer el tonto 🅘

larva /ˈlɑːvə/ *n* (*pl* **-vae**/-viː/) larva *f*

laser /ˈleɪzə(r)/ *n* láser *m*. ~ **beam** *n* rayo *m* láser. ~ **printer** *n* impresora *f* láser

lash /læʃ/ *vt* azotar. □ ~ **out** *vi* atacar. ~ **out against** *vt* atacar. ● *n* latigazo *m*; (*eyelash*) pestaña *f*; (*whip*) látigo *m*

lashings /ˈlæʃɪŋz/ *npl*. ~ **of** (*fam, cream etc*) montones de

lass /læs/ *n* muchacha *f*

lasso /læˈsuː/ *n* (*pl* **-os**) lazo *m*

last /lɑːst/ *adj* último; (week etc) pasado. ~ **Monday** el lunes pasado. ~ **night** anoche. ● *adv* por último; (*most recently*) la última vez. **he came** ~ llegó el último. ● *n* último *m*; (*remainder*) lo que queda. ~ **but one** penúltimo. **at (long)** ~ por fin. ● *vi/t* durar. □ ~ **out** *vi* sobrevivir. ~**ing** *adj* duradero. ~**ly** *adv* por último

latch /lætʃ/ *n* pestillo *m*

late /leɪt/ *adj* (**-er**, **-est**) (*not on time*) tarde; (*recent*) reciente; (*former*) antiguo, ex. **be** ~ llegar tarde. **in** ~ **July** a fines de julio. **the** ~ **Dr Phillips** el difunto Dr. Phillips. ● *adv* tarde. ~**ly** *adv* últimamente

latent /ˈleɪtnt/ *adj* latente

later /ˈleɪtə(r)/ *adv* más tarde

lateral /ˈlætərəl/ *adj* lateral

latest /ˈleɪtɪst/ *adj* último. ● *n*. **at the** ~ a más tardar

lathe /leɪð/ *n* torno *m*

lather /ˈlɑːðə(r)/ *n* espuma *f*

Latin /ˈlætɪn/ *n* (*language*) latín *m*. ● *adj* latino. ~ **America** *n* América *f* Latina, Latinoamérica *f*. ~ **American** *adj* & *n* latinoamericano *f*

latitude /ˈlætɪtjuːd/ *n* latitud *m*

latter /ˈlætə(r)/ *adj* último; (*of two*) segundo. ● *n*. **the** ~ éste *m*, ésta *f*, éstos *mpl*, éstas *fpl*

laugh /lɑːf/ *vi* reír(se). ~ **at** reírse de. ● *n* risa *f*. ~**able** *adj* ridículo. ~**ing stock** *n* hazmerreír *m*. ~**ter**

n risas *fpl*

launch /lɔ:ntʃ/ *vt* lanzar; botar (new vessel). ● *n* lanzamiento *m*; (*of new vessel*) botadura; (*boat*) lancha *f* (a motor). **~ing pad**, **~ pad** *n* plataforma *f* de lanzamiento

laund|er /'lɔ:ndə(r)/ *vt* lavar (y planchar). **~erette** /-et/, **L~romat** /'lɔ:ndrəmæt/ (*Amer*) (*P*) *n* lavandería *f* automática. **~ry** *n* (*place*) lavandería *f*; (*dirty clothes*) ropa *f* sucia; (*clean clothes*) ropa *f* limpia

lava /'lɑ:və/ *n* lava *f*

lavatory /'lævətərɪ/ *n* (cuarto *m* de) baño *m*. **public ~** servicios *mpl*, baños *mpl* (*LAm*)

lavish /'lævɪʃ/ *adj* (lifestyle) de derroche; (*meal*) espléndido; (*production*) fastuoso. ● *vt* prodigar (**on** a)

law /lɔ:/ *n* ley *f*; (*profession, subject of study*) derecho *m*. **~ and order** *n* orden *m* público. **~ court** *n* tribunal *m*

lawn /lɔ:n/ *n* césped *m*, pasto *m* (*LAm*). **~mower** *n* cortacésped *f*, cortadora *f* de pasto (*LAm*)

lawsuit /'lɔ:su:t/ *n* juicio *m*

lawyer /'lɔjə(r)/ *n* abogado *m*

lax /læks/ *adj* descuidado; (morals etc) laxo

laxative /'læksətɪv/ *n* laxante *m*

lay /leɪ/ *see* LIE. ● *vt* (*pt* **laid**) poner (also table, eggs); tender (trap); formar (plan). **~ hands on** echar mano a. **~ hold of** agarrar. ● *adj* (*non-clerical*) laico; (opinion etc) profano. □ **~ down** *vt* dejar a un lado; imponer (condition). □ **~ into** *vt* ☒ dar una paliza a. □ **~ off** *vt* despedir (worker). *vi* ☒ terminar. □ **~ on** *vt* (*provide*) proveer. □ **~ out** *vt* (*design*) disponer; (*display*) exponer; gastar (money). **~about** *n* holgazán. **~-by** *n* área *f* de reposo

layer /'leɪə(r)/ *n* capa *f*

layette /leɪ'et/ *n* canastilla *f*

layman /'leɪmən/ *n* (*pl* **-men**) lego *m*

layout /'leɪaʊt/ *n* disposición *f*

laz|e /leɪz/ *vi* holgazanear; (*relax*) descansar. **~iness** *n* pereza *f*. **~y** *adj* perezoso. **~ybones** *n* holgazán *m*

lead[1] /li:d/ *vt* (*pt* **led**) conducir; dirigir (team); llevar (life); encabezar (parade, attack). **I was led to believe that ...** me dieron a entender que .... ● *vi* (*go first*) ir delante; (*in race*) aventajar. ● *n* mando *m*; (*clue*) pista *f*; (*leash*) correa *f*; (*wire*) cable *m*. **be in the ~** llevar la delantera

lead[2] /led/ *n* plomo *m*; (*of pencil*) mina *f*. **~ed** *adj* (fuel) con plomo

lead: /li:d/ **~er** *n* jefe *m*; (*Pol*) líder *m* & *f*; (*of gang*) cabecilla *m*. **~ership** *n* dirección *f*. **~ing** *adj* principal; (*in front*) delantero

leaf /li:f/ *n* (*pl* **leaves**) hoja *f*. □ **~ through** *vi* hojear **~let** /'li:flɪt/ *n* folleto *m*. **~y** *adj* frondoso

league /li:g/ *n* liga *f*. **be in ~ with** estar aliado con

leak /li:k/ *n* (*hole*) agujero *m*; (*of gas, liquid*) escape *m*; (*of information*) filtración *f*; (*in roof*) gotera *f*; (*in boat*) vía *f* de agua. ● *vi* gotear; (liquid) salirse; (boat) hacer agua. ● *vt* perder; filtrar (information). **~y** *adj* (receptacle) agujereado; (roof) que tiene goteras

lean /li:n/ (*pt* **leaned** *or* **leant** /lent/) *vt* apoyar. ● *vi* inclinarse. □ **~ against** *vt* apoyarse en. □ **~ on** *vt* apoyarse en. □ **~ out** *vt* asomarse (**of** a). □ **~ over** *vi* inclinarse ● *adj* (**-er, -est**) (person) delgado;

(animal) flaco; (meat) magro. **~ing** *adj* inclinado. **~-to** *n* colgadizo *m*

leap /li:p/ *vi* (*pt* **leaped** *or* **leapt** /lept/) saltar. ● *n* salto *m*. **~frog** *n*. **play ~frog** saltar al potro, jugar a la pídola, brincar al burro (*Mex*). ● *vi* (*pt* **-frogged**) saltar. **~ year** *n* año *m* bisiesto

learn /lɜ:n/ *vt/i* (*pt* **learned** *or* **learnt**) aprender (**to do** a hacer). **~ed** /-ɪd/ *adj* culto. **~er** *n* principiante *m & f*; (*apprentice*) aprendiz *m*. **~ing** *n* saber *m*. **~ing curve** *n* curva *f* del aprendizaje

lease /li:s/ *n* arriendo *m*. ● *vt* arrendar

leash /li:ʃ/ *n* correa *f*

least /li:st/ *adj* (*smallest amount of*) mínimo; (*slightest*) menor; (*smallest*) más pequeño. ● *n*. **the ~** lo menos. **at ~** por lo menos. **not in the ~** en absoluto. ● *adv* menos

leather /'leðə(r)/ *n* piel *f*, cuero *m*

leave /li:v/ *vt* (*pt* **left**) dejar; (*depart from*) salir de. **~ alone** dejar de tocar (thing); dejar en paz (person). ● *vi* marcharse; (train) salir. ● *n* permiso *m*. □ **~ behind** *vt* dejar. □ **~ out** *vt* omitir. □ **~ over** *vt*. **be left over** quedar. **on ~** (*Mil*) de permiso

leaves /li:vz/ *see* **LEAF**

lecture /'lektʃə(r)/ *n* conferencia *f*; (*Univ*) clase *f*; (*rebuke*) sermón *m*. ● *vi* dar clase. ● *vt* (*scold*) sermonear. **~r** *n* conferenciante *m & f*, conferencista *m & f* (*LAm*); (*Univ*) profesor *m* universitario

led /led/ *see* **LEAD**[1]

ledge /ledʒ/ *n* cornisa *f*; (*of window*) alféizar *m*

leek /li:k/ *n* puerro *m*

leer /'lɪə(r)/ *vi*. **~ at** mirar impúdicamente. ● *n* mirada impúdica *f*

left /left/ *see* **LEAVE**. *adj* izquierdo. ● *adv* a la izquierda. ● *n* izquierda *f*. **~-handed** /-'hændɪd/ *adj* zurdo. **~ luggage** *n* consigna *f*. **~overs** *npl* restos *mpl*. **~-wing** /-'wɪŋ/ *adj* izquierdista

leg /leg/ *n* pierna *f*; (*of animal, furniture*) pata *f*; (*of pork*) pernil *m*; (*of lamb*) pierna *f*; (*of journey*) etapa *f*. **on its last ~s** en las últimas. **pull s.o.'s ~** ▣ tomarle el pelo a uno

legacy /'legəsɪ/ *n* herencia *f*

legal /'li:gl/ *adj* (*permitted by law*) lícito; (*recognized by law*) legítimo; (system etc) jurídico. **~ity** /li:'gælətɪ/ *n* legalidad *f*. **~ize** *vt* legalizar. **~ly** *adv* legalmente

legend /'ledʒənd/ *n* leyenda *f*. **~ary** *adj* legendario

legible /'ledʒəbl/ *adj* legible

legislat|e /'ledʒɪsleɪt/ *vi* legislar. **~ion** /-'leɪʃn/ *n* legislación *f*

legitimate /lɪ'dʒɪtɪmət/ *adj* legítimo

leisure /'leʒə(r)/ *n* ocio *m*. **at your ~** cuando le venga bien. **~ly** *adj* lento, pausado

lemon /'lemən/ *n* limón *m*. **~ade** /-'neɪd/ *n* (*fizzy*) gaseosa *f* (de limón); (*still*) limonada *f*

lend /lend/ *vt* (*pt* **lent**) prestar. **~ing** *n* préstamo *m*

length /leŋθ/ *n* largo *m*; (*of time*) duración *f*; (*of cloth*) largo *m*. **at ~** (*at last*) por fin. **at (great) ~** detalladamente. **~en** /'leŋθən/ *vt* alargar. ● *vi* alargarse. **~ways** *adv* a lo largo. **~y** *adj* largo

lenient /'li:nɪənt/ *adj* indulgente

lens /lens/ *n* lente *f*; (*of camera*) objetivo *m*. **(contact) ~es** *npl* (*optics*) lentillas *fpl*, lentes *mpl* de

contacto (*LAm*)
lent /lent/ *see* **LEND**
Lent /lent/ *n* cuaresma *f*
Leo /ˈliːəʊ/ *n* Leo *m*
leopard /ˈlepəd/ *n* leopardo *m*
leotard /ˈliːətɑːd/ *n* malla *f*
lesbian /ˈlezbɪən/ *n* lesbiana *f*. ● *adj* lesbiano
less /les/ *adj & n & adv & prep* menos. ~ **than** menos que; (*with numbers*) menos de. ~ **and** ~ cada vez menos. **none the** ~ sin embargo. ~**en** *vt/i* disminuir
lesson /ˈlesn/ *n* clase *f*
lest /lest/ *conj* no sea que (+ *subjunctive*)
let /let/ *vt* (*pt* **let**, *pres p* **letting**) dejar; (*lease*) alquilar. ~ **me do it** déjame hacerlo. ● *modal verb*. ~**'s go!** ¡vamos!, ¡vámonos! ~**'s see** (vamos) a ver. ~**'s talk**/**drink** hablemos/bebamos. □ ~ **down** *vt* bajar; (*deflate*) desinflar; (*fig*) defraudar. □ ~ **go** *vt* soltar. □ ~ **in** *vt* dejar entrar. □ ~ **off** *vt* disparar (gun); (*cause to explode*) hacer explotar; hacer estallar (firework); (*excuse*) perdonar. □ ~ **out** *vt* dejar salir. □ ~ **through** *vt* dejar pasar. □ ~ **up** *vi* disminuir. ~**down** *n* desilusión *f*
lethal /ˈliːθl/ *adj* (dose, wound) mortal; (weapon) mortífero
letharg|ic /lɪˈθɑːdʒɪk/ *adj* letárgico. ~**y** /ˈleθədʒɪ/ *n* letargo *m*
letter /ˈletə(r)/ *n* (*of alphabet*) letra *f*; (*written message*) carta *f*. ~ **bomb** *n* carta *f* bomba. ~**box** *n* buzón *m*. ~**ing** *n* letras *fpl*
lettuce /ˈletɪs/ *n* lechuga *f*
let-up /ˈletʌp/ *n* interrupción *f*
leukaemia /luːˈkiːmɪə/ *n* leucemia *f*
level /ˈlevl/ *adj* (*flat, even*) plano, parejo (*LAm*); (spoonful) raso. ~ **with** (*at same height*) al nivel de. ● *n* nivel *m*. ● *vt* (*pt* **levelled**) nivelar; (*aim*) apuntar. ~ **crossing** *n* paso *m* a nivel, crucero *m* (*Mex*)
lever /ˈliːvə(r)/ *n* palanca *f*. ● *vt* apalancar. ~ **open** abrir haciendo palanca. ~**age** /-ɪdʒ/ *n* apalancamiento *m*
levy /ˈlevɪ/ *vt* imponer (tax). ● *n* impuesto *m*
lewd /luːd/ *adj* (**-er**, **-est**) lascivo
liab|ility /laɪəˈbɪlətɪ/ *n* responsabilidad *f*; (*fam, disadvantage*) lastre *m*. ~**ilities** *npl* (*debts*) deudas *fpl*. ~**le** /ˈlaɪəbl/ *adj*. **be** ~**le to do** tener tendencia a hacer. ~**le for** responsable de. ~**le to** susceptible de; expuesto a (fine)
liais|e /lɪˈeɪz/ *vi* actuar de enlace (**with** con). ~**on** /-ɒn/ *n* enlace *m*
liar /ˈlaɪə(r)/ *n* mentiroso *m*
libel /ˈlaɪbl/ *n* difamación *f*. ● *vt* (*pt* **libelled**) difamar (por escrito)
liberal /ˈlɪbərəl/ *adj* liberal; (*generous*) generoso. **L**~ (*Pol*) del Partido Liberal. ● *n* liberal *m & f*. ~**ly** *adv* liberalmente; (*generously*) generosamente
liberat|e /ˈlɪbəreɪt/ *vt* liberar. ~**ion** /-ˈreɪʃn/ *n* liberación *f*
liberty /ˈlɪbətɪ/ *n* libertad *f*. **take liberties** tomarse libertades. **take the** ~ **of** tomarse la libertad de
Libra /ˈliːbrə/ *n* Libra *f*
librar|ian /laɪˈbreərɪən/ *n* bibliotecario *m*. ~**y** /ˈlaɪbrərɪ/ *n* biblioteca *f*

i

Library of Congress La biblioteca nacional de EEUU, situada en Washington DC. Fundada por el Congreso *Congress*, alberga más de ochenta millones de libros en 470 idiomas, y otros objetos.

lice /laɪs/ *see* **LOUSE**

licence /ˈlaɪsns/ *n* licencia *f*, permiso *m*

license /ˈlaɪsns/ *vt* autorizar. ● *n* (*Amer*) *see* **LICENCE**. ~ **number** *n* (*Amer*) (número *m* de) matrícula *f*. ~ **plate** *n* (*Amer*) matrícula *f*, placa *f* (*LAm*)

lick /lɪk/ *vt* lamer; (*sl, defeat*) dar una paliza a. ● *n* lametón *m*

licorice /ˈlɪkərɪs/ *n* (*Amer*) regaliz *m*

lid /lɪd/ *n* tapa *f*; (*eyelid*) párpado *m*

lie[1] /laɪ/ *vi* (*pt* **lay**, *pp* **lain**, *pres p* **lying**) echarse, tenderse; (*be in lying position*) estar tendido; (*be*) estar, encontrarse. ~ **low** quedarse escondido. □ ~ **down** *vi* echarse, tenderse

lie[2] /laɪ/ *n* mentira *f*. ● *vi* (*pt* **lied**, *pres p* **lying**) mentir

lie-in /laɪˈɪn/ *n*. **have a** ~ quedarse en la cama

lieutenant /lefˈtenənt/ *n* (*Mil*) teniente *m*

life /laɪf/ *n* (*pl* **lives**) vida *f*. ~ **belt** *n* salvavidas *m*. ~**boat** *n* lancha *f* de salvamento; (*on ship*) bote *m* salvavidas. ~**buoy** *n* boya *f* salvavidas. ~ **coach** *n* coach *m* & *f* personal. ~**guard** *n* salvavidas *m* & *f*, socorrista *m* & *f*. ~ **jacket** *n* chaleco *m* salvavidas. ~**less** *adj* sin vida. ~**like** *adj* verosímil. ~**line** *n* cuerda *f* de salvamento; (*fig*) tabla *f* de salvación. ~**long** *adj* de toda la vida. ~ **preserver** *n* (*Amer, buoy*) *see* ~**BUOY**; (*jacket*) *see* ~ **JACKET**. ~ **ring** *n* (*Amer*) *see* ~ **BELT**. ~**saver** *n* (*person*) salvavidas *m* & *f*; (*fig*) salvación *f*. ~**-size(d)** *adj* (de) tamaño natural. ~**time** *n* vida *f*. ~ **vest** *n* (*Amer*) *see* ~ **JACKET**

lift /lɪft/ *vt* levantar. ● *vi* (*fog*) disiparse. ● *n* ascensor *m*. **give a** ~ **to s.o.** llevar a uno en su coche, dar aventón a uno (*Mex*). □ ~ **up** *vt* levantar. ~**-off** *n* despegue *m*

light /laɪt/ *n* luz *f*; (*lamp*) lámpara *f*, luz *f*; (*flame*) fuego *m*. **come to** ~ salir a la luz. **have you got a** ~**?** ¿tienes fuego? **the** ~**s** *npl* (*traffic signals*) el semáforo; (*on vehicle*) las luces. ● *adj* (**-er**, **-est**) (*in colour*) claro; (*not heavy*) ligero. ● *vt* (*pt* **lit** *or* **lighted**) encender, prender (*LAm*); (*illuminate*) iluminar. ● *vi* encenderse, prenderse (*LAm*). ~ **up** *vt* iluminar. ● *vi* iluminarse. ~ **bulb** *n* bombilla *f*, foco *m* (*Mex*). ~**en** *vt* (*make less heavy*) aligerar, alivianar (*LAm*); (*give light to*) iluminar; (*make brighter*) aclarar. ~**er** *n* (*for cigarettes*) mechero *m*, encendedor *m*. ~**-hearted** /-ˈhɑːtɪd/ *adj* alegre. ~**house** *n* faro *m*. ~**ly** *adv* ligeramente

lightning /ˈlaɪtnɪŋ/ *n*. **flash of** ~ relámpago *m*. ● *adj* relámpago

lightweight *adj* ligero, liviano (*LAm*)

like /laɪk/ *adj* parecido. ● *prep* como. ● *conj* [!] como. ● *vt*. **I** ~ **chocolate** me gusta el chocolate. **they** ~ **swimming** (a ellos) les gusta nadar. **would you** ~ **a coffee?** ¿quieres un café?. ~**able** *adj* simpático.

like|lihood /ˈlaɪklɪhʊd/ *n* probabilidad *f*. ~**ly** *adj* (**-ier**, **-iest**) probable. **he is** ~**ly to come** es probable que venga. ● *adv* probablemente. **not** ~**ly!** ¡ni hablar! ~**n** *vt* comparar (**to** con, a). ~**ness** *n* parecido *m*. **be a good** ~**ness** parecerse mucho. ~**wise**

adv (*also*) también; (*the same way*) lo mismo

liking /ˈlaɪkɪŋ/ *n* (*for thing*) afición *f*; (*for person*) simpatía *f*

lilac /ˈlaɪlək/ *adj* lila. ● *n* lila *f*; (*color*) lila *m*

lily /ˈlɪlɪ/ *n* lirio *m*; (*white*) azucena *f*

limb /lɪm/ *n* miembro *m*. **out on a ~** aislado

lime /laɪm/ *n* (*white substance*) cal *f*; (*fruit*) lima *f*. **~light** *n*. **be in the ~light** ser el centro de atención

limerick /ˈlɪmərɪk/ *n* quintilla *f* humorística

limit /ˈlɪmɪt/ *n* límite *m*. ● *vt* limitar. **~ation** /-ˈteɪʃn/ *n* limitación *f*. **~ed** *adj* limitado. **~ed company** *n* sociedad *f* anónima

limousine /ˈlɪməziːn/ *n* limusina *f*

limp /lɪmp/ *vi* cojear, renguear (*LAm*). ● *n* cojera *f*, renguera *f* (*LAm*). **have a ~** cojear. ● *adj* (**-er**, **-est**) flojo

linden /ˈlɪndn/ *n* (*Amer*) tilo *m*

line /laɪn/ *n* línea *f*; (*track*) vía *f*; (*wrinkle*) arruga *f*; (*row*) fila *f*; (*of poem*) verso *m*; (*rope*) cuerda *f*; (*of goods*) surtido *m*; (*Amer, queue*) cola *f*. **stand in ~** (*Amer*) hacer cola. **get in ~** (*Amer*) ponerse en la cola.. **cut in ~** (*Amer*) colarse. **in ~ with** de acuerdo con. ● *vt* forrar (skirt, box); bordear (streets etc). □ **~ up** *vi* alinearse; (*in queue*) hacer cola. *vt* (*form into line*) poner en fila; (*align*) alinear. **~d** /laɪnd/ *adj* (paper) con renglones; (*with fabric*) forrado

linen /ˈlɪnɪn/ *n* (*sheets etc*) ropa *f* blanca; (*material*) lino *m*

liner /ˈlaɪnə(r)/ *n* (*ship*) transatlántico *m*

linger /ˈlɪŋgə(r)/ *vi* tardar en marcharse. **~ (on)** (smells etc) persistir. □ **~ over** *vt* dilatarse en

lingerie /ˈlænʒərɪ/ *n* lencería *f*

linguist /ˈlɪŋgwɪst/ *n* políglota *m* & *f*; lingüista *m* & *f*. **~ic** /lɪŋˈgwɪstɪk/ *adj* lingüístico. **~ics** *n* lingüística *f*

lining /ˈlaɪnɪŋ/ *n* forro *m*

link /lɪŋk/ *n* (*of chain*) eslabón *m*; (*connection*) conexión *f*; (*bond*) vínculo *m*; (*transport, telecommunications*) conexión *f*, enlace *m*. ● *vt* conectar; relacionar (facts, events). □ **~ up** *vt*/*i* conectar

lino /ˈlaɪnəʊ/ *n* (*pl* **-os**) linóleo *m*

lint /lɪnt/ *n* (*Med*) hilas *fpl*

lion /ˈlaɪən/ *n* león *m*. **~ess** /-nɪs/ *n* leona *f*

lip /lɪp/ *n* labio *m*; (*edge*) borde *m*. **~read** *vi* leer los labios. **~salve** *n* crema *f* para los labios. **~ service** *n*. **pay ~ service to** aprobar de boquilla, aprobar de los dientes para afuera (*Mex*). **~stick** *n* lápiz *m* de labios

liqueur /lɪˈkjʊə(r)/ *n* licor *m*

liquid /ˈlɪkwɪd/ *adj* & *n* líquido (*m*)

liquidate /ˈlɪkwɪdeɪt/ *vt* liquidar

liquidize /ˈlɪkwɪdaɪz/ *vt* licuar. **~r** *n* licuadora *f*

liquor /ˈlɪkə(r)/ *n* bebidas *fpl* alcohólicas

liquorice /ˈlɪkərɪs/ *n* regaliz *m*

liquor store *n* (*Amer*) tienda *f* de bebidas alcohólicas

lisp /lɪsp/ *n* ceceo *m*. **speak with a ~** cecear. ● *vi* cecear

list /lɪst/ *n* lista *f*. ● *vt* hacer una lista de; (*enter in a list*) inscribir. ● *vi* (*ship*) escorar

listen /ˈlɪsn/ *vi* escuchar. **~ in (to)** escuchar. **~ to** escuchar. **~er** *n* oyente *m* & *f*

listless /ˈlɪstlɪs/ *adj* apático

lit /lɪt/ *see* LIGHT

literacy /ˈlɪtərəsɪ/ *n* alfabetismo *m*

literal /ˈlɪtərəl/ *adj* literal. **~ly** *adv* literalmente

literary /ˈlɪtərərɪ/ *adj* literario

literate /ˈlɪtərət/ *adj* alfabetizado

literature /ˈlɪtərətʃə(r)/ *n* literatura *f*; (*fig*) folletos *mpl*

lithe /laɪð/ *adj* ágil

litre /ˈliːtə(r)/ *n* litro *m*

litter /ˈlɪtə(r)/ *n* basura *f*; (*of animals*) camada *f*. ● *vt* ensuciar; (*scatter*) esparcir. **~ed with** lleno de. **~ bin** *n* papelera *f*. **~bug**, **~ lout** *n* persona *f* que tira basura en lugares públicos

little /ˈlɪtl/ *adj* pequeño; (*not much*) poco. **a ~ water** un poco de agua. ● *pron* poco, poca. **a ~** un poco. ● *adv* poco. **~ by ~** poco a poco. **~ finger** *n* (dedo *m*) meñique *m*

live /lɪv/ *vt/i* vivir. □ **~ down** *vt* lograr borrar. □ **~ off** *vt* vivir a costa de (family, friends); (*feed on*) alimentarse de. □ **~ on** *vt* (*feed o.s. on*) vivir de. *vi* (memory) seguir presente; (tradition) seguir existiendo. □ **~ up** *vt*. **~ it up** [!] darse la gran vida. □ **~ up to** *vt* vivir de acuerdo con; cumplir (promise). ● /laɪv/ *adj* vivo; (wire) con corriente; (broadcast) en directo

livelihood /ˈlaɪvlɪhʊd/ *n* sustento *m*

lively /ˈlaɪvlɪ/ *adj* (**-ier**, **-iest**) vivo

liven up /ˈlaɪvn/ *vt* animar. ● *vi* animar(se)

liver /ˈlɪvə(r)/ *n* hígado *m*

lives /laɪvz/ *see* LIFE

livestock /ˈlaɪvstɒk/ *n* animales *mpl* (de cría); (*cattle*) ganado *m*

livid /ˈlɪvɪd/ *adj* lívido; (*fam, angry*) furioso

living /ˈlɪvɪŋ/ *adj* vivo. ● *n* vida *f*. **make a ~** ganarse la vida. **~ room** *n* salón *m*, sala *f* (de estar), living *m* (*LAm*)

lizard /ˈlɪzəd/ *n* lagartija *f*; (*big*) lagarto *m*

load /ləʊd/ *n* (*also Elec*) carga *f*; (*quantity*) cantidad *f*; (*weight, strain*) peso *m*. **~s of** [!] montones de. ● *vt* cargar. **~ed** *adj* cargado

loaf /ləʊf/ *n* (*pl* **loaves**) pan *m*; (*stick of bread*) barra *f* de pan. ● *vi*. **~ (about)** holgazanear

loan /ləʊn/ *n* préstamo *m*. **on ~** prestado. ● *vt* prestar

loath|e /ləʊð/ *vt* odiar. **~ing** *n* odio *m* (**of** a). **~esome** /-səm/ *adj* repugnante

lobby /ˈlɒbɪ/ *n* vestíbulo *m*; (*Pol*) grupo *m* de presión. ● *vt* ejercer presión sobre. ● *vi*. **~ for sth** ejercer presión para obtener algo

lobe /ləʊb/ *n* lóbulo *m*

lobster /ˈlɒbstə(r)/ *n* langosta *f*, bogavante m

local /ˈləʊkl/ *adj* local. **~ (phone) call** llamada *f* urbana. ● *n* (*fam, pub*) bar *m*. **the ~s** los vecinos *mpl*. **~ government** *n* administración *f* municipal. **~ity** /-ˈkælətɪ/ *n* localidad *f*. **~ization** *n* localización *f*. **~ly** *adv* (live, work) en la zona

locat|e /ləʊˈkeɪt/ *vt* (*situate*) situar, ubicar (*LAm*); (*find*) localizar, ubicar (*LAm*). **~ion** /-ʃn/ *n* situación *f*, ubicación *f* (*LAm*). **on ~ion** fuera del estudio. **to film on ~ion in Andalusia** rodar en Andalucía

lock /lɒk/ *n* (*of door etc*) cerradura *f*; (*on canal*) esclusa *f*; (*of hair*) mechón *m*. ● *vt* cerrar con llave. ● *vi* cerrarse con llave. □ ~ **in** *vt* encerrar. □ ~ **out** *vt* cerrar la puerta a. □ ~ **up** *vt* encerrar (person); cerrar con llave (building)

locker /'lɒkə(r)/ *n* armario *m*, locker *m* (*LAm*). ~ **room** *n* (*Amer*) vestuario *m*, vestidor *m* (*Mex*)

locket /'lɒkɪt/ *n* medallón *m*

lock: ~out /'lɒkaʊt/ *n* cierre *m* patronal, paro *m* patronal (*LAm*). **~smith** *n* cerrajero *m*

locomotive /ləʊkə'məʊtɪv/ *n* locomotora *f*

lodg|e /lɒdʒ/ *n* (*of porter*) portería *f*. ● *vt* alojar; presentar (complaint). **~er** *n* huésped *m*. **~ings** *n* alojamiento *m*; (*room*) habitación *f* alquilada

loft /lɒft/ *n* desván *m*, altillo *m* (*LAm*)

lofty /'lɒftɪ/ *adj* (**-ier**, **-iest**) elevado; (*haughty*) altanero

log /lɒg/ *n* (*of wood*) tronco *m*; (*as fuel*) leño *m*; (*record*) diario *m*. **sleep like a ~** dormir como un tronco. ● *vt* (*pt* **logged**) registrar. □ ~ **in**, ~ **on** *vi* (*Comp*) entrar (al sistema). □ ~ **off**, ~ **out** *vi* (*Comp*) salir (del sistema)

logarithm /'lɒgərɪðəm/ *n* logaritmo *m*

loggerheads /'lɒgəhedz/ *npl*. **be at ~ with** estar a matar con

logic /'lɒdʒɪk/ *adj* lógica *f*. **~al** *adj* lógico. **~ally** *adv* lógicamente

logistics /lə'dʒɪstɪks/ *n* logística *f*. ● *npl* (*practicalities*) problemas *mpl* logísticos

logo /'ləʊgəʊ/ *n* (*pl* **-os**) logo *m*

loin /lɔɪn/ *n* (*Culin*) lomo *m*. **~s** *npl* entrañas *fpl*

loiter /'lɔɪtə(r)/ *vi* perder el tiempo

loll /lɒl/ *vi* repantigarse

loll|ipop /'lɒlɪpɒp/ *n* pirulí *m*. **~y** *n* polo *m*, paleta *f* (helada) (*LAm*)

London /'lʌndən/ *n* Londres *m*. ● *adj* londinense. **~er** *n* londinense *m & f*

lone /ləʊn/ *adj* solitario. **~ly** *adj* (**-ier**, **-iest**) solitario. **feel ~ly** sentirse muy solo. **~r** *n* solitario *m*. **~some** /-səm/ *adj* solitario

long /lɒŋ/ *adj* (**-er**, **-est**) largo. **a ~ time** mucho tiempo. **how ~ is it?** ¿cuánto tiene de largo? ● *adv* largo/mucho tiempo. **as ~ as** (*while*) mientras; (*provided that*) con tal que (+ *subjunctive*). **before ~** dentro de poco. **so ~!** ¡hasta luego! **so ~ as** (*provided that*) con tal que (+ *subjunctive*). □ ~ **for** *vi* anhelar. ~ **to do** estar deseando hacer. **~-distance** /-'dɪstəns/ *adj* de larga distancia. **~-distance phone call** llamada *f* de larga distancia, conferencia *f*. **~er** *adv*. **no ~er** ya no. **~-haul** /-'hɔːl/ *adj* de larga distancia. **~ing** *n* anhelo *m*, ansia *f*

longitude /'lɒŋgɪtjuːd/ *n* longitud *f*

long: ~ jump *n* salto *m* de longitud. **~-playing record** *n* elepé *m*. **~-range** *adj* de largo alcance. **~-sighted** /-'saɪtɪd/ *adj* hipermétrope. **~-term** *adj* a largo plazo. **~-winded** /-'wɪndɪd/ *adj* prolijo

loo /luː/ *n* ⓘ váter *m*, baño *m* (*LAm*)

look /lʊk/ *vt* mirar; representar (age). ● *vi* mirar; (*seem*) parecer; (*search*) buscar. ● *n* mirada *f*; (*appearance*) aspecto *m*. **good ~s** belleza *f*. □ ~ **after** *vt* cuidar (person); (*be responsible for*) encargarse de. □ ~ **at** *vt* mirar; (*consider*) considerar. □ ~ **down on** *vt* despre-

l

ciar. □~ **for** *vt* buscar. □~ **forward to** *vt* esperar con ansia. □~ **into** *vt* investigar. □~ **like** *vt* parecerse a. □~ **on** *vi* mirar. □~ **out** *vi* tener cuidado. □~ **out for** *vt* buscar; (*watch*) tener cuidado con. □~ **round** *vi* volver la cabeza. □~ **through** *vt* hojear. □~ **up** *vt* buscar (word); (*visit*) ir a ver. □~ **up to** *vt* admirar. ~**-alike** *n* [I] doble *m & f*. ~**out** *n* (*Mil, person*) vigía *m*. **be on the ~out for** andar a la caza de. ~**s** *npl* belleza *f*

loom /lu:m/ *n* telar *m*. ● *vi* aparecerse

looney, **loony** /'lu:nɪ/ *adj & n* [X] chiflado (*m*) [I], loco (*m*)

loop /lu:p/ *n* (*shape*) curva *f*; (*in string*) lazada *f*. ● *vt* hacer una lazada con. ~**hole** *n* (*in rule*) escapatoria *f*

loose /lu:s/ *adj* (**-er**, **-est**) suelto; (garment, thread, hair) flojo; (*inexact*) vago; (*not packed*) suelto. **be at a ~ end** no tener nada que hacer. ~**ly** *adv* sueltamente; (*roughly*) aproximadamente. ~**n** *vt* aflojar

loot /lu:t/ *n* botín *m*. ● *vt/i* saquear. ~**er** *n* saqueador *m*

lop /lɒp/ *vt* (*pt* **lopped**). ~ **off** cortar

lop-sided /-'saɪdɪd/ *adj* ladeado

lord /lɔ:d/ *n* señor *m*; (*British title*) lord *m*. **(good) L~!** ¡Dios mío! **the L~** el Señor. **the (House of) L~s** la Cámara de los Lores

lorry /'lɒrɪ/ *n* camión *m*. ~ **driver** *n* camionero *m*

lose /lu:z/ *vt/i* (*pt* **lost**) perder. ~**r** *n* perdedor *m*

loss /lɒs/ *n* pérdida *f*. **be at a ~** estar perplejo. **be at a ~ for words** no encontrar palabras

lost /lɒst/ *see* LOSE. ● *adj* perdido. **get ~** perderse. ~ **property** *n*, ~ **and found** (*Amer*) oficina *f* de objetos perdidos

lot /lɒt/ *n* (*fate*) suerte *f*; (*at auction*) lote *m*; (*land*) solar *m*. **a ~ (of)** muchos. **quite a ~ of** [I] bastante. ~**s (of)** [I] muchos. **they ate the ~** se lo comieron todo

lotion /'ləʊʃn/ *n* loción *f*

lottery /'lɒtərɪ/ *n* lotería *f*

loud /laʊd/ *adj* (**-er**, **-est**) fuerte; (*noisy*) ruidoso; (*gaudy*) chillón. **out ~** en voz alta. ~**hailer** /-'heɪlə(r)/ *n* megáfono *m*. ~**ly** *adv* (speak) en voz alta; (shout) fuerte; (complain) a voz en grito. ~**speaker** /-'spi:kə(r)/ *n* altavoz *m*, altoparlante *m* (*LAm*)

lounge /laʊndʒ/ *vi* repantigarse. ● *n* salón *m*, sala *f* (de estar), living *m* (*LAm*)

lous|e /laʊs/ *n* (*pl* **lice**) piojo *m*. ~**y** /'laʊzɪ/ *adj* (**-ier**, **-iest**) (*sl, bad*) malísimo

lout /laʊt/ *n* patán *m*

lov|able /'lʌvəbl/ *adj* adorable. ~**e** /lʌv/ *n* amor *m*; (*tennis*) cero *m*. **be in ~e (with)** estar enamorado (de). **fall in ~e (with)** enamorarse (de). ● *vt* querer, amar (person). **I ~e milk** me encanta la leche. ~**e affair** *n* aventura *f*, amorío *m*

lovely /'lʌvlɪ/ *adj* (**-ier**, **-iest**) (appearance) precioso, lindo (*LAm*); (person) encantador, amoroso (*LAm*)

lover /'lʌvə(r)/ *n* amante *m & f*

loving /'lʌvɪŋ/ *adj* cariñoso

low /ləʊ/ *adj & adv* (**-er**, **-est**) bajo. ● *vi* (cattle) mugir. ~**er** *vt* bajar. ~**er o.s.** envilecerse. ~**-level** *adj* a bajo nivel. ~**ly** *adj* (**-ier**, **-iest**) humilde

loyal /ˈlɔɪəl/ *adj* leal, fiel. **~ty** *n* lealtad *f*. **~ty card** tarjeta *f* de fidelidad

lozenge /ˈlɒzɪndʒ/ *n* (*shape*) rombo *m*; (*tablet*) pastilla *f*

LP *abbr* (= **long-playing record**) elepé *m*

Ltd /ˈlɪmɪtɪd/ *abbr* (= **Limited**) S.A., Sociedad Anónima

lubricate /ˈlu:brɪkeɪt/ *vt* lubricar

lucid /ˈlu:sɪd/ *adj* lúcido

luck /lʌk/ *n* suerte *f*. **good ~!** ¡(buena) suerte! **~ily** *adv* por suerte. **~y** *adj* (**-ier**, **-iest**) (person) con suerte. **be ~y** tener suerte. **~y number** número *m* de la suerte

lucrative /ˈlu:krətɪv/ *adj* lucrativo

ludicrous /ˈlu:dɪkrəs/ *adj* ridículo

lug /lʌg/ *vt* (*pt* **lugged**) 🅸 arrastrar

luggage /ˈlʌgɪdʒ/ *n* equipaje *m*. **~ rack** *n* rejilla *f*

lukewarm /ˈlu:kwɔ:m/ *adj* tibio; (*fig*) poco entusiasta

lull /lʌl/ *vt* (*soothe, send to sleep*) adormecer; (*calm*) calmar. ● *n* periodo *m* de calma

lullaby /ˈlʌləbaɪ/ *n* canción *f* de cuna

lumber /ˈlʌmbə(r)/ *n* trastos *mpl* viejos; (*wood*) maderos *mpl*. ● *vt*. **~ s.o. with sth** 🅸 endilgar algo a uno. **~jack** *n* leñador *m*

luminous /ˈlu:mɪnəs/ *adj* luminoso

lump /ˈlʌmp/ *n* (*swelling*) bulto *m*; (*as result of knock*) chichón *m*; (*in liquid*) grumo *m*; (*of sugar*) terrón *m*. ● *vt*. **~ together** agrupar. **~ it** 🅸 aguantarse. **~ sum** *n* suma *f* global. **~y** *adj* (sauce) grumoso; (mattress, cushions) lleno de protuberancias

lunacy /ˈlu:nəsɪ/ *n* locura *f*

lunar /ˈlu:nə(r)/ *adj* lunar

lunatic /ˈlu:nətɪk/ *n* loco *m*

lunch /lʌntʃ/ *n* comida *f*, almuerzo *m*. **have ~** comer, almorzar

luncheon /ˈlʌntʃən/ *n* comida *f*, almuerzo *m*. **~ voucher** *n* vale *m* de comida

lung /lʌŋ/ *n* pulmón *m*

lunge /lʌndʒ/ *n* arremetida *f*. ● *vi*. **~ at** arremeter contra

lurch /lɜ:tʃ/ *vi* tambalearse. ● *n*. **leave in the ~** dejar plantado

lure /ljʊə(r)/ *vt* atraer

lurid /ˈljʊərɪd/ *adj* (colour) chillón; (*shocking*) morboso

lurk /lɜ:k/ *vi* merodear; (*in ambush*) estar al acecho

luscious /ˈlʌʃəs/ *adj* delicioso

lush /lʌʃ/ *adj* exuberante

lust /lʌst/ *n* lujuria *f*; (*craving*) deseo *m*. ● *vi*. **~ after** codiciar

lute /lu:t/ *n* laúd *m*

Luxembourg, **Luxemburg** /ˈlʌksəmbɜ:g/ *n* Luxemburgo *m*

luxuriant /lʌgˈzjʊərɪənt/ *adj* exuberante

luxur|ious /lʌgˈzjʊərɪəs/ *adj* lujoso. **~y** /ˈlʌkʃərɪ/ *n* lujo *m*. ● *adj* de lujo

lying /ˈlaɪɪŋ/ *see* LIE[1], LIE[2]. ● *n* mentiras *fpl*. ● *adj* mentiroso

lynch /lɪntʃ/ *vt* linchar

lyric /ˈlɪrɪk/ *adj* lírico. **~al** *adj* lírico. **~s** *npl* letra *f*

Mm

MA /em'eɪ/ *abbr see* **Master**
mac /mæk/ *n* [!] impermeable *m*
macabre /mə'kɑ:brə/ *adj* macabro
macaroni /mækə'rəʊnɪ/ *n* macarrones *mpl*
mace /meɪs/ *n* (*staff*) maza *f*; (*spice*) macis *f*. **M~** (*P*) (*Amer*) gas *m* para defensa personal
machine /mə'ʃi:n/ *n* máquina *f*. **~ gun** *n* ametralladora *f*. **~ry** *n* maquinaria *f*; (*working parts, fig*) mecanismo *m*
mackintosh /'mækɪntɒʃ/ *n* impermeable *m*
macro /'mækrəʊ/ *n* (*pl* **-os**) (*Comp*) macro *m*
macrobiotic /mækrəʊbaɪ'ɒtɪk/ *adj* macrobiótico
mad /mæd/ *adj* (**madder, maddest**) loco; (*fam, angry*) furioso. **be ~ about** estar loco por
madam /'mædəm/ *n* señora *f*
mad: ~cap *adj* atolondrado. **~ cow disease** *f* enfermedad *f* de las vacas locas. **~den** *vt* (*make mad*) enloquecer; (*make angry*) enfurecer
made /meɪd/ *see* **make**. **~-to-measure** hecho a (la) medida
mad: ~house *n* manicomio *m*. **~ly** *adv* (*interested, in love etc*) locamente; (*frantically*) como un loco. **~man** /-mən/ *n* loco *m*. **~ness** *n* locura *f*
Madonna /mə'dɒnə/ *n*. **the ~** (*Relig*) la Virgen
maestro /'maɪstrəʊ/ *n* (*pl* **maestri** /-stri:/ *or* **-os**) maestro *m*
Mafia /'mæfɪə/ *n* mafia *f*
magazine /mægə'zi:n/ *n* revista *f*; (*of gun*) recámara *f*
magenta /mə'dʒentə/ *adj* magenta, morado
maggot /'mægət/ *n* gusano *m*
magic /'mædʒɪk/ *n* magia *f*. • *adj* mágico. **~al** *adj* mágico. **~ian** /mə'dʒɪʃn/ *n* mago *m*
magistrate /'mædʒɪstreɪt/ *n* juez *m* que conoce de faltas y asuntos civiles de menor importancia
magnet /'mægnɪt/ *n* imán *m*. **~ic** /-'netɪk/ *adj* magnético; (*fig*) lleno de magnetismo. **~ism** *n* magnetismo *m*. **~ize** *vt* imantar, magnetizar
magnif|ication /mægnɪfɪ'keɪʃn/ *n* aumento *m*. **~y** /'mægnɪfaɪ/ *vt* aumentar. **~ying glass** *n* lupa *f*
magnificen|ce /mæg'nɪfɪsns/ *adj* magnificencia *f*. **~t** *adj* magnífico
magnitude /'mægnɪtju:d/ *n* magnitud *f*
magpie /'mægpaɪ/ *n* urraca *f*
mahogany /mə'hɒgənɪ/ *n* caoba *f*
maid /meɪd/ *n* (*servant*) criada *f*, sirvienta *f*; (*girl, old use*) doncella *f*. **old ~** solterona *f*
maiden /'meɪdn/ *n* doncella *f*. • *adj* (voyage) inaugural. **~ name** *n* apellido *m* de soltera
mail /meɪl/ *n* correo *m*; (*armour*) (cota *f* de) malla *f*. • *adj* correo. • *vt* echar al correo (letter); (*send*) enviar por correo. **~box** *n* (*Amer*) buzón m. **~ing list** *n* lista *f* de direcciones. **~man** /-mən/ *n* (*Amer*) cartero *m*. **~ order** *n* venta *f* por correo
maim /meɪm/ *vt* mutilar
main /meɪn/ *n*. **(water/gas) ~** ca-

ñería *f* principal. **in the ~** en su mayor parte. **the ~s** *npl* (*Elec*) la red *f* de suministro. ● *adj* principal. **~ course** *n* plato *m* principal, plato *m* fuerte. **~ frame** *n* (*Comp*) unidad *f* central. **~land** *n*. **the ~land** la masa territorial de un país excluyendo sus islas. ● *adj*. **~land China** (la) China continental. **~ly** *adv* principalmente. **~ road** *n* carretera *f* principal. **~stream** *adj* (culture) establecido. **~ street** *n* calle *f* principal

maint|ain /meɪn'teɪn/ *vt* mantener. **~enance** /'meɪntənəns/ *n* mantenimiento *m*

maisonette /meɪzə'net/ *n* (*small house*) casita *f*; (*part of house*) dúplex *m*

maize /meɪz/ *n* maíz *m*

majestic /mə'dʒestɪk/ *adj* majestuoso

majesty /'mædʒəstɪ/ *n* majestad *f*

major /'meɪdʒə(r)/ *adj* (*important*) muy importante; (*Mus*) mayor. **a ~ road** una calle prioritaria. ● *n* comandante *m & f*, mayor *m & f* (*LAm*). ● *vi*. **~ in** (*Amer, Univ*) especializarse en

Majorca /mə'jɔ:kə/ *n* Mallorca *f*

majority /mə'dʒɒrətɪ/ *n* mayoría *f*. ● *adj* mayoritario

make /meɪk/ *vt* (*pt* **made**) hacer; (*manufacture*) fabricar; ganar (money); tomar (decision); llegar a (destination). **~ s.o. do sth** obligar a uno a hacer algo. **be made of** estar hecho de. **I ~ it two o'clock** yo tengo las dos. **~ believe** fingir. **~ do** (*manage*) arreglarse. **~ do with** (*content o.s.*) contentarse con. **~ it** llegar; (*succeed*) tener éxito. ● *n* marca *f*. **~ for** *vt* dirigirse a. **~ good** *vt* compensar; (*repair*) reparar. □ **~ off** *vi* escaparse (**with** con). □ **~ out** *vt* distinguir; (*understand*) entender; (*write out*) hacer; (*assert*) dar a entender. *vi* (*cope*) arreglárselas. □ **~ up** *vt* (*constitute*) formar; (*prepare*) preparar; inventar (story); **~ it up** (*become reconciled*) hacer las paces. **~ up (one's face)** maquillarse. □ **~ up for** *vt* compensar. **~-believe** *adj* fingido, simulado. *n* ficción *f*. **~over** *n* (*Amer*) maquillaje *m*. **~r** *n* fabricante *m & f*. **~shift** *adj* (*temporary*) provisional, provisorio (*LAm*); (*improvised*) improvisado. **~up** *n* maquillaje *m*. **put on ~up** maquillarse.

making /'meɪkɪŋ/ *n*. **he has the ~s of** tiene madera de. **in the ~** en vías de formación

maladjusted /mælə'dʒʌstɪd/ *adj* inadaptado

malaria /mə'leərɪə/ *n* malaria *f*, paludismo *m*

Malaysia /mə'leɪzɪə/ *n* Malasia *f*. **~n** *adj & n* malaisio (*m*)

male /meɪl/ *adj* macho; (voice, attitude) masculino. ● *n* macho *m*; (*man*) varón *m*

malevolent /mə'levələnt/ *adj* malévolo

malfunction /mæl'fʌŋkʃn/ *vi* fallar, funcionar mal

malic|e /'mælɪs/ *n* mala intención *f*, maldad *f*. **bear s.o. ~e** guardar rencor a uno. **~ious** /mə'lɪʃəs/ *adj* malintencionado. **~iously** *adv* con malevolencia

malignant /mə'lɪgnənt/ *adj* maligno

mallet /'mælɪt/ *n* mazo *m*

malnutrition /mælnju:'trɪʃn/ *n* desnutrición *f*

malpractice /mæl'præktɪs/ *n* mala práctica *f* (en el ejercicio de

una profesión)
malt /mɔːlt/ *n* malta *f*
Malt|a /'mɔːltə/ *n* Malta *f*. **~ese** /-'tiːz/ *adj & n* maltés (*m*)
mammal /'mæml/ *n* mamífero *m*
mammoth /'mæməθ/ *n* mamut *m*. ● *adj* gigantesco
man /mæn/ *n* (*pl* **men** /men/) hombre *m*; (*Chess*) pieza *f*. **~ in the street** hombre *m* de la calle. ● *vt* (*pt* **manned**) encargarse de (switchboard); tripular (ship); servir (guns)
manacles /'mænəklz/ *n* (*for wrists*) esposas *fpl*; (*for legs*) grillos *mpl*
manag|e /'mænɪdʒ/ *vt* dirigir; administrar (land, finances); (*handle*) manejar. ● *vi* (*Com*) dirigir; (*cope*) arreglárselas. **~e to do** lograr hacer. **~eable** *adj* (task) posible de alcanzar; (size) razonable. **~ement** *n* dirección *f*. **~er** *n* director *m*; (*of shop*) encargado *m*; (*of soccer team*) entrenador *m*, director *m* técnico (*LAm*). **~eress** /-'res/ *n* encargada *f*. **~erial** /-'dʒɪərɪəl/ *adj* directivo, gerencial (*LAm*). **~ing director** *n* director *m* ejecutivo
mandate /'mændeɪt/ *n* mandato *m*
mandatory /'mændətərɪ/ *adj* obligatorio
mane /meɪn/ *n* (*of horse*) crin(es) *f*(*pl*); (*of lion*) melena *f*
mangle /'mæŋgl/ *n* rodillo *m* (escurridor). ● *vt* destrozar
man: ~handle *vt* mover a pulso; (*treat roughly*) maltratar. **~hole** *n* registro *m*. **~hood** *n* madurez *f*; (*quality*) virilidad *f*. **~-hour** *n* hora *f* hombre. **~-hunt** *n* persecución *f*
mania /'meɪnɪə/ *n* manía *f*. **~c** /-ɪæk/ *n* maníaco *m*
manicure /'mænɪkjʊə(r)/ *n* manicura *f*, manicure *f* (*LAm*)
manifest /'mænɪfest/ *adj* manifiesto. ● *vt* manifestar. **~ation** /-'steɪʃn/ *n* manifestación *f*
manifesto /mænɪ'festəʊ/ *n* (*pl* **-os**) manifiesto *m*
manipulat|e /mə'nɪpjʊleɪt/ *vt* manipular. **~ion** /-'leɪʃn/ *n* manipulación *f*. **~ive** /-lətɪv/ *adj* manipulador
man: ~kind *n* humanidad *f*. **~ly** *adj* viril. **~-made** *adj* artificial
manner /'mænə(r)/ *n* manera *f*; (*demeanour*) actitud *f*; (*kind*) clase *f*. **~ed** *adj* amanerado. **~s** *npl* modales *mpl*, educación *f*. **bad ~s** mala educación
manoeuvre /mə'nuːvə(r)/ *n* maniobra *f*. ● *vt/i* maniobrar
manor /'mænə(r)/ *n*. **~ house** casa *f* solariega
manpower *n* mano *f* de obra
mansion /'mænʃn/ *n* mansión *f*
man: ~-size(d) *adj* grande. **~slaughter** *n* homicidio *m* sin premeditación
mantelpiece /'mæntlpiːs/ *n* repisa *f* de la chimenea
manual /'mænjʊəl/ *adj* manual. ● *n* (*handbook*) manual *m*
manufacture /mænjʊ'fæktʃə(r)/ *vt* fabricar. ● *n* fabricación *f*. **~r** *n* fabricante *m & f*
manure /mə'njʊə(r)/ *n* estiércol *m*
manuscript /'mænjʊskrɪpt/ *n* manuscrito *m*
many /'menɪ/ *adj & pron* muchos, muchas. **~ people** mucha gente. **a great/good ~** muchísimos. **how ~?** ¿cuántos? **so ~** tantos. **too ~** demasiados

map /mæp/ *n* mapa *m*; (*of streets etc*) plano *m*

mar /mɑː(r)/ *vt* (*pt* **marred**) estropear

marathon /ˈmærəθən/ *n* maratón *m & f*

marble /ˈmɑːbl/ *n* mármol *m*; (*for game*) canica *f*

march /mɑːtʃ/ *vi* (*Mil*) marchar. **~ off** *vi* irse. ● *n* marcha *f*

March /mɑːtʃ/ *n* marzo *m*

march-past /ˈmɑːtʃpɑːst/ *n* desfile *m*

mare /meə(r)/ *n* yegua *f*

margarine /mɑːdʒəˈriːn/ *n* margarina *f*

margin /ˈmɑːdʒɪn/ *n* margen *f*. **~al** *adj* marginal

marijuana /mærɪˈhwɑːnə/ *n* marihuana *f*

marina /məˈriːnə/ *n* puerto *m* deportivo

marine /məˈriːn/ *adj* marino. ● *n* (*sailor*) infante *m* de marina

marionette /mærɪəˈnet/ *n* marioneta *f*

marital status /mærɪtl ˈsteɪtəs/ *n* estado *m* civil

mark /mɑːk/ *n* marca *f*; (*stain*) mancha *f*; (*Schol*) nota *f*; (*target*) blanco *m*. ● *vt* (*indicate*) señalar, marcar; (*stain*) manchar; corregir (exam). **~ time** marcar el paso. □ **~ out** *vt* (*select*) señalar; (*distinguish*) distinguir. **~ed** *adj* marcado. **~edly** /-kɪdlɪ/ *adv* marcadamente. **~er** *n* marcador *m*. **~er (pen)** *n* rotulador *m*, marcador *m* (*LAm*)

market /ˈmɑːkɪt/ *n* mercado *m*. **on the ~** en venta. ● *vt* comercializar. **~ garden** *n* huerta *f*. **~ing** *n* marketing *m*

marking /ˈmɑːkɪŋ/ *n* marcas *fpl*; (*on animal, plant*) mancha *f*

marksman /ˈmɑːksmən/ *n* (*pl* **-men**) tirador *m*. **~ship** *n* puntería *f*

marmalade /ˈmɑːməleɪd/ *n* mermelada *f* (de cítricos)

maroon /məˈruːn/ *adj & n* granate (*m*). ● *vt* abandonar (en una isla desierta)

marquee /mɑːˈkiː/ *n* toldo *m*, entoldado *m*; (*Amer, awning*) marquesina *f*

marriage /ˈmærɪdʒ/ *n* matrimonio *m*; (*ceremony*) casamiento *m*

married /ˈmærɪd/ *adj* casado; (life) conyugal

marrow /ˈmærəʊ/ *n* (*of bone*) tuétano *m*; (*vegetable*) calabaza *f* verde alargada. **~ squash** *n* (*Amer*) calabaza *f* verde alargada

marry /ˈmærɪ/ *vt* casarse con; (*give or unite in marriage*) casar. ● *vi* casarse. **get married** casarse (**to** con)

Mars /mɑːz/ *n* Marte *m*

marsh /mɑːʃ/ *n* pantano *m*

marshal /ˈmɑːʃl/ *n* (*Mil*) mariscal *m*; (*Amer, police chief*) jefe *m* de policía. ● *vt* (*pt* **marshalled**) reunir; poner en orden (thoughts)

marsh: ~mallow /-ˈmæləʊ/ *n* malvavisco *m*, bombón *m* (*LAm*). **~y** *adj* pantanoso

martial /ˈmɑːʃl/ *adj* marcial. **~ arts** *npl* artes *fpl* marciales. **~ law** *n* ley *f* marcial

martyr /ˈmɑːtə(r)/ *n* mártir *m & f*

marvel /ˈmɑːvl/ *n* maravilla *f*. ● *vi* (*pt* **marvelled**) maravillarse (**at** de). **~lous** *adj* maravilloso

Marxis|m /ˈmɑːksɪzəm/ *n* marxismo *m*. **~t** *adj & n* marxista (*m & f*)

marzipan /ˈmɑːzɪpæn/ *n* mazapán *m*

mascara /mæˈskɑːrə/ *n* rímel® *m*

mascot /'mæskɒt/ *n* mascota *f*

masculin|e /'mæskjʊlɪn/ *adj & n* masculino (*m*). **~ity** /-'lɪnətɪ/ *n* masculinidad *f*

mash /mæʃ/ *n* (*Brit* ☐, *potatoes*) puré *m* de patatas, puré *m* de papas (*LAm*). ● *vt* hacer puré de, moler (*Mex*). **~ed potatoes** *n* puré *m* de patatas, puré *m* de papas (*LAm*)

mask /mɑ:sk/ *n* máscara *f*; (*Sport*) careta *f*. ● *vt* ocultar

masochis|m /'mæsəkɪzəm/ *n* masoquismo *m*. **~t** *n* masoquista *m & f*. **~tic** /-'kɪstɪk/ *adj* masoquista

mason /'meɪsn/ *n* (*stone* **~**) mampostero *m*. **M~** (*freemason*) masón *m*. **~ry** /'meɪsnrɪ/ *n* albañilería *f*

masquerade /mɑ:skə'reɪd/ *n* mascarada *f*. ● *vi*. **~ as** hacerse pasar por

mass /mæs/ *n* masa *f*; (*Relig*) misa *f*; (*large quantity*) montón *m*. **the ~es** las masas. ● *vi* concentrarse

massacre /'mæsəkə(r)/ *n* masacre *f*, matanza *f*. ● *vt* masacrar

mass|age /'mæsɑ:ʒ/ *n* masaje *m*. ● *vt* masajear. **~eur** /mæ'sɜ:(r)/ *n* masajista *m*. **~euse** /mæ'sɜ:z/ *n* masajista *f*

massive /'mæsɪv/ *adj* masivo; (*heavy*) macizo; (*huge*) enorme

mass: ~ media *n* medios *mpl* de comunicación. **~-produce** /-prə 'dju:s/ *vt* fabricar en serie

mast /mɑ:st/ *n* mástil *m*; (*for radio, TV*) antena *f* repetidora

master /'mɑ:stə(r)/ *n* amo *m*; (*expert*) maestro *m*; (*in secondary school*) profesor *m*; (*of ship*) capitán *m*; (*master copy*) original *m*. **~'s degree** master *m*, maestría *f*. **M~ of Arts (MA)** poseedor *m* de una maestría en folosofía y letras. **M~ of Science (MSc)** poseedor *m* de una maestría en ciencias. ● *vt* llegar a dominar. **~ key** *n* llave *f* maestra. **~mind** *n* cerebro *m*. ● *vt* dirigir. **~piece** *n* obra *f* maestra. **~stroke** *n* golpe *m* de maestro. **~y** *n* dominio *m*; (*skill*) maestría *f*

masturbat|e /'mæstəbeɪt/ *vi* masturbarse. **~ion** /-'beɪʃn/ *n* masturbación *f*

mat /mæt/ *n* estera *f*; (*at door*) felpudo *m*. ● *adj* (*Amer*) see **MATT**

match /mætʃ/ *n* (*Sport*) partido *m*; (*for fire*) cerilla *f*, fósforo *m* (*LAm*), cerillo *m* (*Mex*); (*equal*) igual *m*. ● *vt* emparejar; (*equal*) igualar; (clothes, colours) hacer juego con. ● *vi* hacer juego. **~box** *n* caja *f* de cerillas, caja *f* de fósforos (*LAm*), caja *f* de cerillos (*Mex*). **~ing** *adj* que hace juego. **~stick** *n* cerilla *f*, fósforo *m* (*LAm*), cerillo *m* (*Mex*)

mate /meɪt/ *n* (*of person*) pareja *f*; (*of animals, male*) macho *m*; (*of animals, female*) hembra *f*; (*assistant*) ayudante *m*; (☐, *friend*) amigo *m*, cuate *m* (*Mex*); (*Chess*) (jaque *m*) mate *m*. ● *vi* aparearse

material /mə'tɪərɪəl/ *n* material *m*; (*cloth*) tela *f*. ● *adj* material. **~istic** /-'lɪstɪk/ *adj* materialista. **~ize** *vi* materializarse. **~s** *npl* materiales *mpl*

matern|al /mə'tɜ:nl/ *adj* maternal. **~ity** /-ətɪ/ *n* maternidad *f*. ● *adj* (ward) de obstetricia; (clothes) premamá, de embarazada

math /mæθ/ *n* (*Amer*) see **MATHS**

mathematic|ian /mæθəmə'tɪʃn/ *n* matemático *m*. **~al** /-'mætɪkl/ *adj* matemático. **~s** /-'mætɪks/ *n* matemática(s) *f(pl)*

maths /mæθs/ *n* matemática(s) *f(pl)*

matinée, **matinee** /ˈmætɪneɪ/ *n* (*Theatre*) función *f* de tarde; (*Cinema*) primera sesión *f* (de la tarde)

matrices /ˈmeɪtrɪsiːz/ *see* **MATRIX**

matriculat|e /məˈtrɪkjʊleɪt/ *vi* matricularse. **~ion** /-ˈleɪʃn/ *n* matrícula *f*

matrimon|ial /mætrɪˈməʊnɪəl/ *adj* matrimonial. **~y** /ˈmætrɪmənɪ/ *n* matrimonio *m*

matrix /ˈmeɪtrɪks/ *n* (*pl* **matrices**) matriz *f*

matron /ˈmeɪtrən/ *n* (*married, elderly*) matrona *f*; (*in school*) ama *f* de llaves; (*former use, in hospital*) enfermera *f* jefe

matt, **matte** (*Amer*) /mæt/ *adj* mate

matted /ˈmætɪd/ *adj* enmarañado y apelmazado

matter /ˈmætə(r)/ *n* (*substance*) materia *f*; (*affair*) asunto *m*; (*pus*) pus *m*. **as a ~ of fact** en realidad. **no ~** no importa. **what is the ~?** ¿qué pasa? **to make ~s worse** para colmo (de males). ● *vi* importar. **it doesn't ~** no importa. **~-of-fact** /-əvˈfækt/ *adj* (person) práctico

mattress /ˈmætrɪs/ *n* colchón *m*

matur|e /məˈtjʊə(r)/ *adj* maduro. ● *vi* madurar. **~ity** *n* madurez *f*

maudlin /ˈmɔːdlɪn/ *adj* llorón

maul /mɔːl/ *vt* atacar (y herir)

mauve /məʊv/ *adj & n* malva (*m*)

maverick /ˈmævərɪk/ *n* inconformista *m & f*

maxim /ˈmæksɪm/ *n* máxima *f*

maxim|ize /ˈmæksɪmaɪz/ *vt* maximizar. **~um** /-əm/ *adj & n* máximo (*m*)

may /meɪ/,

past **might**

auxiliary verb

····➤ (*expressing possibility*) **he ~ come** puede que venga, es posible que venga. **it ~ be true** puede ser verdad. **she ~ not have seen him** es posible que *or* puede que no lo haya visto

····➤ (*asking for or giving permission*) **~ I smoke?** ¿puedo fumar?, ¿se puede fumar? **~ I have your name and address, please?** ¿quiere darme su nombre y dirección, por favor?

····➤ (*expressing a wish*) **~ he be happy** que sea feliz

····➤ (*conceding*) **he ~ not have much experience, but he's very hardworking** no tendrá mucha experiencia, pero es muy trabajador. **that's as ~ be** puede ser

····➤ **I ~ as well stay** más vale quedarme

May /meɪ/ *n* mayo *m*

maybe /ˈmeɪbɪ/ *adv* quizá(s), tal vez, a lo mejor

May Day *n* el primero de mayo

mayhem /ˈmeɪhem/ *n* caos *m*

mayonnaise /meɪəˈneɪz/ *n* mayonesa *f*, mahonesa *f*

mayor /meə(r)/ *n* alcalde *m*, alcaldesa *f*. **~ess** /-ɪs/ *n* alcaldesa *f*

maze /meɪz/ *n* laberinto *m*

me /miː/ *pron* me; (*after prep*) mí. **he knows ~** me conoce. **it's ~** soy yo

meadow /ˈmedəʊ/ *n* prado *m*, pradera *f*

meagre /ˈmiːgə(r)/ *adj* escaso

meal /miːl/ *n* comida *f*. **~time** *n* hora *f* de comer

mean /miːn/ *vt* (*pt* **meant**) (*intend*) tener la intención de, querer; (*signify*) querer decir, significar. **~ to do** tener la intención de hacer. **~ well** tener buenas intenciones. **be meant for** estar destinado a. ● *adj* (**-er**, **-est**) (*miserly*) tacaño; (*unkind*) malo; (*Math*) medio. ● *n* media *f*; (*average*) promedio *m*

meander /mɪˈændə(r)/ *vi* (river) serpentear

meaning /ˈmiːnɪŋ/ *n* sentido *m*. **~ful** *adj* significativo. **~less** *adj* sin sentido

meanness /ˈmiːnnɪs/ *n* (*miserliness*) tacañería *f*; (*unkindness*) maldad *f*

means /miːnz/ *n* medio *m*. **by ~ of** por medio de, mediante. **by all ~** por supuesto. **by no ~** de ninguna manera. ● *npl* (*wealth*) medios *mpl*, recursos *mpl*. **~ test** *n* investigación *f* de ingresos

meant /ment/ *see* MEAN

meantime /ˈmiːntaɪm/ *adv* mientras tanto, entretanto. ● *n*. **in the ~** mientras tanto, entretanto

meanwhile /ˈmiːnwaɪl/ *adv* mientras tanto, entretanto

measl|es /ˈmiːzlz/ *n* sarampión *m*. **~y** /ˈmiːzlɪ/ *adj* [!] miserable

measure /ˈmeʒə(r)/ *n* medida *f*; (*ruler*) regla *f*. ● *vt/i* medir. □ **~ up to** *vt* estar a la altura de. **~ment** *n* medida *f*

meat /miːt/ *n* carne *f*. **~ball** *n* albóndiga *f*. **~y** *adj* (taste, smell) a carne; (soup, stew) con mucha carne

mechan|ic /mɪˈkænɪk/ *n* mecánico *m*. **~ical** *adj* mecánico. **~ics** *n* mecánica *f*. **~ism** /ˈmekənɪzəm/ *n* mecanismo *m*. **~ize** /ˈmekənaɪz/ *vt* mecanizar

medal /ˈmedl/ *n* medalla *f*. **~list** /ˈmedəlɪst/ *n* medallista *m* & *f*. **be a gold ~list** ganar una medalla de oro

meddle /ˈmedl/ *vi* meterse, entrometerse (**in** en). **~ with** (*tinker*) toquetear

media /ˈmiːdɪə/ *see* MEDIUM. ● *npl*. **the ~** los medios de comunicación

mediat|e /ˈmiːdɪeɪt/ *vi* mediar. **~ion** /-ˈeɪʃn/ *n* mediación *f*. **~or** *n* mediador *m*

medical /ˈmedɪkl/ *adj* médico; (student) de medicina. ● *n* revisión *m* médica

medicat|ed /ˈmedɪkeɪtɪd/ *adj* medicinal. **~ion** /-ˈkeɪʃn/ *n* medicación *f*

medicin|al /mɪˈdɪsɪnl/ *adj* medicinal. **~e** /ˈmedsɪn/ *n* medicina *f*

medieval /medɪˈiːvl/ *adj* medieval

mediocre /miːdɪˈəʊkə(r)/ *adj* mediocre

meditat|e /ˈmedɪteɪt/ *vi* meditar. **~ion** /-ˈteɪʃn/ *n* meditación *f*

Mediterranean /medɪtəˈreɪnɪən/ *adj* mediterráneo. ● *n*. **the ~** el Mediterráneo

medium /ˈmiːdɪəm/ *n* (*pl* **media**) medio *m*. **happy ~** término *m* medio. ● *adj* mediano. **~-size(d)** /-saɪz(d)/ *adj* de tamaño mediano

medley /ˈmedlɪ/ *n* (*Mus*) popurrí *m*; (*mixture*) mezcla *f*

meek /miːk/ *adj* (**-er**, **-est**) dócil

meet /miːt/ *vt* (*pt* **met**) encontrar; (*bump into s.o.*) encontrarse con; (*fetch*) ir a buscar; (*get to know, be introduced to*) conocer. ● *vi* encontrarse; (*get to know*) conocerse; (*have meeting*) reunirse. **~ up** *vi* encontrarse (**with** con). □~ **with** *vt* ser recibido con; (*Amer, meet*) encontrarse con. ~**ing** *n* reunión *f*; (*accidental between two people*) encuentro *m*

megabyte /ˈmegəbaɪt/ *n* (*Comp*) megabyte *m*, megaocteto *m*

megaphone /ˈmegəfəʊn/ *n* megáfono *m*

melanchol|ic /melənˈkɒlɪk/ *adj* melancólico. ~**y** /ˈmelənkɒlɪ/ *n* melancolía *f*. ● *adj* melancólico

mellow /ˈmeləʊ/ *adj* (**-er, -est**) (fruit) maduro; (sound) dulce; (colour) tenue; (person) apacible

melodrama /ˈmelədrɑːmə/ *n* melodrama *m*. ~**tic** /melədrəˈmætɪk/ *adj* melodramático

melody /ˈmelədɪ/ *n* melodía *f*

melon /ˈmelən/ *n* melón *m*

melt /melt/ *vt* (*make liquid*) derretir; fundir (metals). ● *vi* (*become liquid*) derretirse; (metals) fundirse. □~ **down** *vt* fundir

member /ˈmembə(r)/ *n* miembro *m* & *f*; (*of club*) socio *m*. ~ **of staff** empleado *m*. **M~ of Congress** *n* (*Amer*) miembro *m* & *f* del Congreso. **M~ of Parliament** *n* diputado *m*. ~**ship** *n* calidad *f* de socio; (*members*) socios *mpl*, membresía *f* (*LAm*)

membrane /ˈmembreɪn/ *n* membrana *f*

memento /mɪˈmentəʊ/ *n* (*pl* **-os** *or* **-oes**) recuerdo *m*

memo /ˈmeməʊ/ *n* (*pl* **-os**) memorándum *m*, memo *m*

memoir /ˈmemwɑː(r)/ *n* memoria *f*

memorable /ˈmemərəbl/ *adj* memorable

memorandum /meməˈrændəm/ *n* (*pl* **-ums** *or* **-da** /-də/) memorándum *m*

memorial /mɪˈmɔːrɪəl/ *n* monumento *m*. ● *adj* conmemorativo

memor|ize /ˈmeməraɪz/ *vt* aprender de memoria. ~**y** /ˈmemərɪ/ *n* (*faculty*) memoria *f*; (*thing remembered*) recuerdo *m*. **from** ~**y** de memoria. **in** ~**y of** a la memoria de

men /men/ *see* **MAN**

menac|e /ˈmenəs/ *n* amenaza *f*; (*fam, nuisance*) peligro *m* público. ● *vt* amenazar. ~**ing** *adj* amenazador

mend /mend/ *vt* reparar; arreglar (garment). ~ **one's ways** enmendarse. ● *n* remiendo *m*. **be on the** ~ ir mejorando

menfolk /ˈmenfəʊk/ *n* hombres *mpl*

menial /ˈmiːnɪəl/ *adj* servil

meningitis /menɪnˈdʒaɪtɪs/ *n* meningitis *f*

menopause /ˈmenəpɔːz/ *n* menopausia *f*

menstruat|e /ˈmenstrʊeɪt/ *vi* menstruar. ~**ion** /-ˈeɪʃn/ *n* menstruación *f*

mental /ˈmentl/ *adj* mental; (hospital) psiquiátrico. ~**ity** /-ˈtælətɪ/ *n* mentalidad *f*. ~**ly** *adv* mentalmente. **be** ~**ly ill** ser un enfermo mental

mention /ˈmenʃn/ *vt* mencionar. **don't** ~ **it!** ¡no hay de qué! ● *n* mención *f*

mentor /ˈmentɔː(r)/ *n* mentor *m*

menu /ˈmenjuː/ *n* menú *m*

meow /mɪˈaʊ/ *n* & *vi see* **MEW**

mercenary /ˈmɜːsɪnərɪ/ *adj* & *n* mercenario (*m*)

merchandise /ˈmɜːtʃəndaɪz/ *n* mercancías *fpl*, mercadería *f* (*LAm*)

merchant /ˈmɜːtʃənt/ *n* comerciante *m*. ● *adj* (ship, navy) mercante. ~ **bank** *n* banco *m* mercantil

merci|ful /'mɜ:sɪfl/ *adj* misericordioso. ~**less** *adj* despiadado

mercury /'mɜ:kjʊrɪ/ *n* mercurio *m*. **M~** (*planet*) Mercurio *m*

mercy /'mɜ:sɪ/ *n* compasión *f*. **at the ~ of** a merced de

mere /mɪə(r)/ *adj* simple. ~**ly** *adv* simplemente

merge /mɜ:dʒ/ *vt* unir; fusionar (companies). ● *vi* unirse; (companies) fusionarse. ~**r** *n* fusión *f*

meridian /mə'rɪdɪən/ *n* meridiano *m*

meringue /mə'ræŋ/ *n* merengue *m*

merit /'merɪt/ *n* mérito *m*. ● *vt* (*pt* merited) merecer

mermaid /'mɜ:meɪd/ *n* sirena *f*

m

merr|ily /'merəlɪ/ *adv* alegremente. ~**iment** /'merɪmənt/ *n* alegría *f*. ~**y** /'merɪ/ *adj* (**-ier, -iest**) alegre. **make ~** divertirse. ~**y-go-round** *n* tiovivo *m*, carrusel *m* (*LAm*). ~**y-making** *n* jolgorio *m*

mesh /meʃ/ *n* malla *f*

mesmerize /'mezməraɪz/ *vt* hipnotizar; (*fascinate*) cautivar

mess /mes/ *n* desorden *m*; (*dirt*) suciedad *f*; (*Mil*) rancho *m*. **make a ~ of** estropear. □ ~ **up** *vt* desordenar; (*dirty*) ensuciar; estropear (plans). □ ~ **about** *vi* tontear. □ ~ **with** *vt* (*tinker with*) manosear

mess|age /'mesɪdʒ/ *n* mensaje *m*; (*when phoning*) recado *m*. ~**enger** /'mesɪndʒə(r)/ *n* mensajero *m*

Messiah /mɪ'saɪə/ *n* Mesías *m*

Messrs /'mesəz/ *npl*. ~ **Smith** los señores Smith, los Sres. Smith

messy /'mesɪ/ *adj* (**-ier, -iest**) en desorden; (*dirty*) sucio

met /met/ *see* **MEET**

metabolism /mɪ'tæbəlɪzəm/ *n* metabolismo *m*

metal /'metl/ *n* metal. ● *adj* de metal. ~**lic** /mə'tælɪk/ *adj* metálico

metaphor /'metəfə(r)/ *n* metáfora *f*. ~**ical** /-'fɒrɪkl/ *adj* metafórico

mete /mi:t/ *vt*. ~ **out** repartir; dar (punishment)

meteor /'mi:tɪə(r)/ *n* meteoro *m*. ~**ic** /-'ɒrɪk/ *adj* meteórico. ~**ite** /'mi:tɪəraɪt/ *n* meteorito *m*

meteorolog|ical /mi:tɪərə'lɒdʒɪkl/ *adj* meteorológico. ~**ist** /-'rɒlədʒɪst/ *n* meteorólogo *m*. ~**y** /-'rɒlədʒɪ/ *n* meteorología *f*

meter /'mi:tə(r)/ *n* contador *m*, medidor *m* (*LAm*); (*Amer*) *see* **METRE**

method /'meθəd/ *n* método *m*. ~**ical** /mɪ'θɒdɪkl/ *adj* metódico. **M~ist** /'meθədɪst/ *adj* & *n* metodista (*m* & *f*)

methylated /'meθɪleɪtɪd/ *adj*. ~ **spirit(s)** *n* alcohol *m* desnaturalizado

meticulous /mɪ'tɪkjʊləs/ *adj* meticuloso

metre /'mi:tə(r)/ *n* metro *m*

metric /'metrɪk/ *adj* métrico

metropoli|s /mɪ'trɒpəlɪs/ *n* metrópoli(s) *f*

mettle /'metl/ *n*. **be on one's ~** (*fig*) estar dispuesto a dar lo mejor de sí

mew /mju:/ *n* maullido *m*. ● *vi* maullar

Mexic|an /'meksɪkən/ *adj* & *n* mejicano (*m*), mexicano (*m*). ~**o** /-kəʊ/ *n* Méjico *m*, México *m*

miaow /mi:'aʊ/ *n* & *vi see* **MEW**

mice /maɪs/ *see* **MOUSE**

mickey /'mɪkɪ/ *n*. **take the ~ out of** Ⅰ tomar el pelo a

micro... /'maɪkrəʊ/ *pref* micro...

microbe /'maɪkrəʊb/ *n* microbio *m*

micro: ~chip *n* pastilla *f*. **~film** *n* microfilme *m*. **~light** *n* aeroligero *m*. **~phone** *n* micrófono *m*. **~processor** /-'prəʊsesə(r)/ *n* microprocesador *m*. **~scope** *n* microscopio *m*. **~scopic** /-'skɒpɪk/ *adj* microscópico. **~wave** *n* microonda *f*. **~wave oven** *n* horno *m* de microondas

mid- /mɪd/ *pref*. **in ~ air** en pleno aire. **in ~ March** a mediados de marzo

midday /mɪd'deɪ/ *n* mediodía *m*

middl|e /'mɪdl/ *adj* de en medio. ● *n* medio *m*. **in the ~e of** en medio de. **~e-aged** /-'eɪdʒd/ *adj* de mediana edad. **M~e Ages** *npl* Edad *f* Media. **~e class** *n* clase *f* media. **~e-class** *adj* de la clase media. **M~e East** *n* Oriente *m* Medio. **~eman** *n* intermediario *m*. **~e name** *n* segundo nombre *m*. **~ing** *adj* regular

midge /mɪdʒ/ *n* mosquito *m*

midget /'mɪdʒɪt/ *n* enano *m*. ● *adj* minúsculo

Midlands /'mɪdləndz/ *npl* región *f* central de Inglaterra

midnight /'mɪdnaɪt/ *n* medianoche *f*

midriff /'mɪdrɪf/ *n* diafragma *m*

midst /mɪdst/ *n*. **in our ~** entre nosotros. **in the ~ of** en medio de

midsummer /mɪd'sʌmə(r)/ *n* pleno verano *m*; (*solstice*) solsticio *m* de verano

midway /mɪd'weɪ/ *adv* a mitad de camino

Midwest /'mɪd'west/ región *f* central de los EE.UU.

midwife /'mɪdwaɪf/ *n* comadrona *f*, partera *f*

midwinter /mɪd'wɪntə(r)/ *n* pleno invierno *m*

might /maɪt/ *see* MAY. ● *n* (*strength*) fuerza *f*; (*power*) poder *m*. **~y** *adj* (*strong*) fuerte; (*powerful*) poderoso. ● *adv* 🄸 muy

migraine /'mi:greɪn/ *n* jaqueca *f*

migra|nt /'maɪgrənt/ *adj* migratorio. ● *n* (*person*) emigrante *m* & *f*. **~te** /maɪ'greɪt/ *vi* emigrar. **~tion** /-'greɪʃn/ *n* migración *f*

mild /maɪld/ *adj* (**-er**, **-est**) (person) afable; (climate) templado; (*slight*) ligero; (taste, manner) suave

mildew /'mɪldju:/ *n* moho *m*; (*on plants*) mildeu *m*, mildiu *m*

mildly /'maɪldlɪ/ *adv* (*gently*) suavemente; (*slightly*) ligeramente

mile /maɪl/ *n* milla *f*. **~s better** 🄸 mucho mejor. **~s too big** 🄸 demasiado grande. **~age** /-ɪdʒ/ *n* (*loosely*) kilometraje *m*. **~ometer** /maɪ'lɒmɪtə(r)/ *n* (*loosely*) cuentakilómetros *m*. **~stone** *n* mojón *m*; (*event, stage, fig*) hito *m*

militant /'mɪlɪtənt/ *adj* & *n* militante (*m* & *f*)

military /'mɪlɪtərɪ/ *adj* militar

militia /mɪ'lɪʃə/ *n* milicia *f*

milk /mɪlk/ *n* leche *f*. ● *adj* (product) lácteo; (chocolate) con leche. ● *vt* ordeñar (cow). **~man** /-mən/ *n* lechero *m*. **~ shake** *n* batido *m*, (leche *f*) malteada *f* (*LAm*), licuado *m* con leche (*LAm*). **~y** *adj* lechoso. **M~y Way** *n* Vía *f* Láctea

mill /mɪl/ *n* molino *m*; (*for coffee, pepper*) molinillo *m*; (*factory*) fábrica *f* de tejidos de algodón. ● *vt* moler. ▫ **~ about, mill around** *vi* dar vueltas

m

millennium /mɪ'lenɪəm/ *n* (*pl* **-ia** /-ɪə/ *or* **-iums**) milenio *m*

miller /'mɪlə(r)/ *n* molinero *m*

milli... /'mɪlɪ/ *pref* mili... **~gram(me)** *n* miligramo *m*. **~metre** *n* milímetro *m*

milliner /'mɪlɪnə(r)/ *n* sombrerero *m*

million /'mɪlɪən/ *n* millón *m*. **a ~ pounds** un millón de libras. **~aire** /-'eə(r)/ *n* millonario *m*

millstone /'mɪlstəʊn/ *n* muela *f* (de molino); (*fig, burden*) carga *f*

mime /maɪm/ *n* mímica *f*. ● *vt* imitar, hacer la mímica de. ● *vi* hacer la mímica

mimic /'mɪmɪk/ *vt* (*pt* **mimicked**) imitar. ● *n* imitador *m*. **~ry** *n* imitación *f*

mince /mɪns/ *vt* picar, moler (*LAm*) (meat). **not to ~ matters/words** no andar(se) con rodeos. ● *n* carne *f* picada, carne *f* molida (*LAm*). **~ pie** *n* pastelito *m* de Navidad (pastelito relleno de picadillo de frutos secos). **~r** *n* máquina *f* de picar carne, máquina *f* de moler carne (*LAm*)

m

mind /maɪnd/ *n* mente *f*; (*sanity*) juicio *m*. **to my ~** a mi parecer. **be on one's mind** preocuparle a uno. **make up one's ~** decidirse. ● *vt* (*look after*) cuidar (de); atender (shop). **~ the steps!** ¡cuidado con las escaleras! **never ~ him** no le hagas caso. **I don't ~ the noise** no me molesta el ruido. **would you ~ closing the door?** ¿le importaría cerrar la puerta? ● *vi*. **never ~** no importa, no te preocupes. **I don't ~** (*don't object*) me da igual. **do you ~ if I smoke?** ¿le importa si fumo? **~ful** *adj* atento (**of** a). **~less** *adj* (activity) mecánico; (violence) ciego

mine¹ /maɪn/ *poss pron* (*sing*) mío, mía; (*pl*) míos, mías. **it is ~** es mío. **~ are blue** los míos/las mías son azules. **a friend of ~** un amigo mío/una amiga mía

mine² /maɪn/ *n* mina *f*; (*Mil*) mina *f*. ● *vt* extraer. **~field** *n* campo *m* de minas. **~r** *n* minero *m*

mineral /'mɪnərəl/ *adj & n* mineral (*m*). **~ water** *n* agua *f* mineral

mingle /'mɪŋgl/ *vi* mezclarse

mini... /'mɪnɪ/ *pref* mini...

miniature /'mɪnɪtʃə(r)/ *n* miniatura *f*. ● *adj* en miniatura

mini: ~bus *n* microbús *m*. **~cab** *n* taxi *m* (que se pide por teléfono)

minim|al /'mɪnɪml/ *adj* mínimo. **~ize** *vt* reducir al mínimo. **~um** /-məm/ *adj & n* (*pl* **-ima** /-mə/) mínimo (*m*)

mining /'maɪnɪŋ/ *n* minería *f*. ● *adj* minero

miniskirt /'mɪnɪskɜːt/ *n* minifalda *f*

minist|er /'mɪnɪstə(r)/ *n* ministro *m*, secretario *m* (*Mex*); (*Relig*) pastor *m*. **~erial** /-'stɪərɪəl/ *adj* ministerial. **~ry** *n* ministerio *m*, secretaría *f* (*Mex*)

mink /mɪŋk/ *n* visón *m*

minor /'maɪnə(r)/ *adj* (*also Mus*) menor; (injury) leve; (change) pequeño; (operation) de poca importancia. ● *n* menor *m & f* de edad. **~ity** /maɪ'nɒrətɪ/ *n* minoría *f*. ● *adj* minoritario

minstrel /'mɪnstrəl/ *n* juglar *m*

mint /mɪnt/ *n* (*plant*) menta *f*; (*sweet*) pastilla *f* de menta; (*Finance*) casa *f* de la moneda. **in ~ condition** como nuevo. ● *vt* acuñar

minus /'maɪnəs/ *prep* menos; (*fam, without*) sin. ● *n* (*sign*) menos *m*. **five ~ three is two** cinco menos tres is igual a dos. **~ sign** *n* (signo *m* de) menos *m*

minute[1] /ˈmɪnɪt/ *n* minuto *m*. **the ~s** *npl* (*of meeting*) el acta *f*

minute[2] /maɪˈnjuːt/ *adj* diminuto; (*detailed*) minucioso

mirac|le /ˈmɪrəkl/ *n* milagro *m*. **~ulous** /mɪˈrækjʊləs/ *adj* milagroso

mirage /ˈmɪrɑːʒ/ *n* espejismo *m*

mirror /ˈmɪrə(r)/ *n* espejo *m*; (*driving ~*) (espejo *m*) retrovisor *m*. ● *vt* reflejar

mirth /mɜːθ/ *n* regocijo *m*; (*laughter*) risas *fpl*

misapprehension /mɪsæprɪˈhenʃn/ *n* malentendido *m*

misbehav|e /mɪsbɪˈheɪv/ *vi* portarse mal. **~iour** *n* mala conducta

miscalculat|e /mɪsˈkælkjʊleɪt/ *vt/i* calcular mal. **~ion** /-ˈleɪʃn/ *n* error *m* de cálculo

miscarr|iage /ˈmɪskærɪdʒ/ *n* aborto *m* espontáneo. **~iage of justice** *n* injusticia *f*. **~y** *vi* abortar

miscellaneous /mɪsəˈleɪnɪəs/ *adj* heterogéneo

mischie|f /ˈmɪstʃɪf/ *n* (*foolish conduct*) travesura *f*; (*harm*) daño *m*. **get into ~f** hacer travesuras. **make ~f** causar daños. **~vous** /ˈmɪstʃɪvəs/ *adj* travieso; (grin) pícaro

misconception /mɪskənˈsepʃn/ *n* equivocación *f*

misconduct /mɪsˈkɒndʌkt/ *n* mala conducta *f*

misdeed /mɪsˈdiːd/ *n* fechoría *f*

misdemeanour /mɪsdɪˈmiːnə(r)/ *n* delito *m* menor, falta *f*

miser /ˈmaɪzə(r)/ *n* avaro *m*

miserable /ˈmɪzərəbl/ *adj* (*sad*) triste; (*in low spirits*) abatido; (*wretched, poor*) mísero; (weather) pésimo

miserly /ˈmaɪzəlɪ/ *adj* avariento

misery /ˈmɪzərɪ/ *n* (*unhappiness*) tristeza *f*; (*pain*) sufrimiento *m*

misfire /mɪsˈfaɪə(r)/ *vi* fallar

misfit /ˈmɪsfɪt/ *n* inadaptado *m*

misfortune /mɪsˈfɔːtʃuːn/ *n* desgracia *f*

misgiving /mɪsˈgɪvɪŋ/ *n* recelo *m*

misguided /mɪsˈgaɪdɪd/ *adj* equivocado

mishap /ˈmɪshæp/ *n* percance *m*

misinform /mɪsɪnˈfɔːm/ *vt* informar mal

misinterpret /mɪsɪnˈtɜːprɪt/ *vt* interpretar mal

misjudge /mɪsˈdʒʌdʒ/ *vt* juzgar mal; (*miscalculate*) calcular mal

mislay /mɪsˈleɪ/ *vt* (*pt* **mislaid**) extraviar, perder

m

mislead /mɪsˈliːd/ *vt* (*pt* **misled** /mɪsˈled/) engañar. **~ing** *adj* engañoso

mismanage /mɪsˈmænɪdʒ/ *vt* administrar mal. **~ment** *n* mala administración *f*

misplace /mɪsˈpleɪs/ *vt* (*lose*) extraviar, perder

misprint /ˈmɪsprɪnt/ *n* errata *f*

miss /mɪs/ *vt* (*fail to hit*) no dar en; (*regret absence of*) echar de menos, extrañar (*LAm*); perder (train, party); perder (chance). **~ the point** no comprender. ● *vi* errar el tiro, fallar; (bullet) no dar en el blanco. ● *n* fallo *m*, falla *f* (*LAm*); (*title*) señorita *f*. □ **~ out** *vt* saltarse (line). **~out on sth** perderse algo

misshapen /mɪsˈʃeɪpən/ *adj* deforme

missile /ˈmɪsaɪl/ *n* (*Mil*) misil *m*

missing /'mɪsɪŋ/ *adj* (*lost*) perdido. **be ~** faltar. **go ~** desaparecer. **~ person** desaparecido *m*

mission /'mɪʃn/ *n* misión *f*. **~ary** /'mɪʃənərɪ/ *n* misionero *m*

mist /mɪst/ *n* neblina *f*; (*at sea*) bruma *f*. □ **~ up** *vi* empañarse

mistake /mɪ'steɪk/ *n* error *m*. **make a ~** cometer un error. **by ~** por error. ● *vt* (*pt* **mistook**, *pp* **mistaken**) confundir. **~ for** confundir con. **~n** /-ən/ *adj* equivocado. **be ~n** equivocarse

mistletoe /'mɪsltəʊ/ *n* muérdago *m*

mistreat /mɪs'triːt/ *vt* maltratar

mistress /'mɪstrɪs/ *n* (*of house*) señora *f*; (*lover*) amante *f*

mistrust /mɪs'trʌst/ *vt* desconfiar de. ● *n* desconfianza *f*. **~ful** *adj* desconfiado

misty /'mɪstɪ/ *adj* (**-ier**, **-iest**) neblinoso; (day) de neblina. **it's ~** hay neblina

misunderstand /mɪsʌndə'stænd/ *vt* (*pt* **-stood**) entender mal. **~ing** *n* malentendido *m*

misuse /mɪs'juːz/ *vt* emplear mal; malversar (funds). ● /mɪs'juːs/ *n* mal uso *m*; (*unfair use*) abuso *m*; (*of funds*) malversación *f*

mite /maɪt/ *n* (*insect*) ácaro *m*

mitten /'mɪtn/ *n* mitón *m*

mix /mɪks/ *vt* mezclar. ● *vi* mezclarse; (*go together*) combinar. **~ with** tratarse con (people). ● *n* mezcla *f*. □ **~ up** *vt* mezclar; (*confuse*) confundir. **~ed** *adj* (school etc) mixto; (*assorted*) mezclado. **be ~ed up** estar confuso. **~er** *n* (*Culin*) batidora *f*; (*TV, machine*) mezcladora *f*. **~ture** /'mɪkstʃə(r)/ *n* mezcla *f*. **~-up** *n* lío *m*

moan /məʊn/ *n* gemido *m*. ● *vi* gemir; (*complain*) quejarse (**about** de)

moat /məʊt/ *n* foso *m*

mob /mɒb/ *n* turba *f*. ● *vt* (*pt* **mobbed**) acosar

mobil|e /'məʊbaɪl/ *adj* móvil. **~e home** *n* caravana *f* fija, trailer *m* (*LAm*). **~e (phone)** *n* (teléfono *m*) móvil *m*, (teléfono *m*) celular *m* (*LAm*). ● *n* móvil *m*. **~ize** /'məʊbɪlaɪz/ *vt* movilizar. ● *vi* movilizarse

mock /mɒk/ *vt* burlarse de. ● *adj* (anger) fingido; (exam) de práctica. **~ery** /'mɒkərɪ/ *n* burla *f*. **make a ~ery of sth** ridiculizar algo

model /'mɒdl/ *n* (*example*) modelo *m*; (*mock-up*) maqueta *f*; (*person*) modelo *m*. ● *adj* (*exemplary*) modelo; (car etc) en miniatura. ● *vt* (*pt* **modelled**) modelar. **~ s.o. on s.o.** tomar a uno como modelo

modem /'məʊdem/ *n* (*Comp*) módem *m*

moderat|e /'mɒdərət/ *adj & n* moderado (*m*). ● /'mɒdəreɪt/ *vt* moderar. **~ely** /'mɒdərətlɪ/ *adv* (*fairly*) medianamente. **~ion** /-'reɪʃn/ *n* moderación *f*. **in ~ion** con moderación

modern /'mɒdn/ *adj* moderno. **~ize** *vt* modernizar

modest /'mɒdɪst/ *adj* modesto. **~y** *n* modestia *f*

modif|ication /mɒdɪfɪ'keɪʃn/ *n* modificación *f*. **~y** /-faɪ/ *vt* modificar

module /'mɒdjuːl/ *n* módulo *m*

moist /mɔɪst/ *adj* (**-er**, **-est**) húmedo. **~en** /'mɔɪsn/ *vt* humedecer

moistur|e /'mɔɪstʃə(r)/ *n* humedad *f*. **~ize** *vt* hidratar. **~izer**, **~izing cream** *n* crema *f* hidratante

mole /məʊl/ *n* (*animal*) topo *m*; (*on skin*) lunar *m*
molecule /ˈmɒlɪkjuːl/ *n* molécula *f*
molest /məˈlest/ *vt* abusar (sexualmente) de
mollify /ˈmɒlɪfaɪ/ *vt* aplacar
mollusc /ˈmɒləsk/ *n* molusco *m*
mollycoddle /ˈmɒlɪkɒdl/ *vt* mimar
molten /ˈməʊltən/ *adj* fundido; (lava) líquido
mom /mɒm/ *n* (*Amer*, [!]) mamá *f* [!]
moment /ˈməʊmənt/ *n* momento *m*. **at the ~** en este momento. **for the ~** de momento. **~ary** /ˈməʊməntərɪ/ *adj* momentáneo
momentous /məˈmentəs/ *adj* trascendental
momentum /məˈmentəm/ *n* momento *m*; (*speed*) velocidad *f*
mommy /ˈmɒmɪ/ *n* (*Amer, fam*) mamá *m* [!]
monarch /ˈmɒnək/ *n* monarca *m*. **~y** *n* monarquía *f*
monastery /ˈmɒnəstərɪ/ *n* monasterio *m*
Monday /ˈmʌndeɪ/ *n* lunes *m*
money /ˈmʌnɪ/ *n* dinero *m*, plata *f* (*LAm*). **~box** *n* hucha *f*, alcancía *f* (*LAm*). **~ order** *n* giro *m* postal
mongrel /ˈmʌŋgrəl/ *n* perro *m* mestizo, chucho *m* [!]
monitor /ˈmɒnɪtə(r)/ *n* (*Tec*) monitor *m*. ● *vt* observar (elections); seguir (progress); (*electronically*) monitorizar, escuchar
monk /mʌŋk/ *n* monje *m*. **~fish** *n* rape *m*
monkey /ˈmʌŋkɪ/ *n* mono *m*. **~-nut** *n* cacahuete *m*, cacahuate *m* (*Mex*), maní *m* (*LAm*). **~wrench** *n* llave *f* inglesa
mono /ˈmɒnəʊ/ *n* monofonía *f*
monologue /ˈmɒnəlɒg/ *n* monólogo *m*
monopol|ize /məˈnɒpəlaɪz/ *vt* monopolizar; acaparar (conversation). **~y** *n* monopolio *m*
monoton|e /ˈmɒnətəʊn/ *n* tono *m* monocorde. **~ous** /məˈnɒtənəs/ *adj* monótono. **~y** *n* monotonía *f*
monsoon /mɒnˈsuːn/ *n* monzón *m*
monst|er /ˈmɒnstə(r)/ *n* monstruo *m*. **~rous** /-strəs/ *adj* monstruoso
month /mʌnθ/ *n* mes *m*. **£200 a ~** 200 libras mensuales *or* al mes. **~ly** *adj* mensual. **~ly payment** mensualidad *f*, cuota *f* mensual (*LAm*). ● *adv* mensualmente
monument /ˈmɒnjʊmənt/ *n* monumento *m*. **~al** /-ˈmentl/ *adj* monumental
moo /muː/ *n* mugido *m*. ● *vi* mugir
mood /muːd/ *n* humor *m*. **be in a good/bad ~** estar de buen/mal humor. **~y** *adj* (**-ier**, **-iest**) temperamental; (*bad-tempered*) malhumorado
moon /muːn/ *n* luna *f*. **~light** *n* luz *f* de la luna. **~lighting** *n* pluriempleo *m*. **~lit** *adj* iluminado por la luna; (night) de luna
moor /mʊə(r)/ *n* páramo *m*; (*of heather*) brezal *m*. ● *vt* amarrar. **~ing** *n* (*place*) amarradero *m*. **~ings** *npl* (*ropes*) amarras *fpl*
moose /muːs/ *n invar* alce *m* americano
mop /mɒp/ *n* fregona *f*, trapeador *m* (*LAm*). **~ of hair** pelambrera *f*. ● *vt* (*pt* **mopped**). **~ (up)** limpiar
mope /məʊp/ *vi* estar abatido
moped /ˈməʊped/ *n* ciclomotor *m*

moral /'mɒrəl/ *adj* moral. ● *n* (*of tale*) moraleja *f*
morale /mə'rɑːl/ *n* moral *f*
moral|ity /mə'rælətɪ/ *n* moralidad *f*. **~ly** *adv* moralmente. **~s** *npl* moralidad *f*
morbid /'mɔːbɪd/ *adj* morboso
more /mɔː(r)/ *adj* más. **two ~ bottles** dos botellas más. ● *pron* más. **you ate ~ than me** comiste más que yo. **some ~** más. **~ than six** más de seis. **the ~ he has, the ~ he wants** cuánto más tiene, más quiere. ● *adv* más. **~ and ~** cada vez más. **~ or less** más o menos. **once ~** una vez más. **she doesn't live here any ~** ya no vive aquí. **~over** /mɔː'rəʊvə(r)/ *adv* además
morgue /mɔːg/ *n* depósito *m* de cadáveres, morgue *f* (*LAm*)
morning /'mɔːnɪŋ/ *n* mañana *f*; (*early hours*) madrugada *f*. **at 11 o'clock in the ~** a las once de la mañana. **in the ~** por la mañana, en la mañana (*LAm*). **tomorrow/yesterday ~** mañana/ayer por la mañana *or* (*LAm*) en la mañana. **(good) ~!** ¡buenos días!
Morocc|an /mə'rɒkən/ *adj & n* marroquí (*m & f*). **~o** /-kəʊ/ *n* Marruecos *m*
moron /'mɔːrɒn/ *n* imbécil *m & f*
morose /mə'rəʊs/ *adj* taciturno
Morse /mɔːs/ *n* Morse *m*. **in ~ (code)** *n* en (código) morse
morsel /'mɔːsl/ *n* bocado *m*
mortal /'mɔːtl/ *adj & n* mortal (*m*). **~ity** /-'tælətɪ/ *n* mortalidad *f*
mortar /'mɔːtə(r)/ *n* (*all senses*) mortero *m*
mortgage /'mɔːgɪdʒ/ *n* hipoteca *f*. ● *vt* hipotecar
mortify /'mɔːtɪfaɪ/ *vt* darle mucha vergüenza a
mortuary /'mɔːtjʊərɪ/ *n* depósito *m* de cadáveres, morgue *f* (*LAm*)
mosaic /məʊ'zeɪk/ *n* mosaico *m*
mosque /mɒsk/ *n* mezquita *f*
mosquito /mɒs'kiːtəʊ/ *n* (*pl* **-oes**) mosquito *m*, zancudo *m* (*LAm*)
moss /mɒs/ *n* musgo *m*
most /məʊst/ *adj* la mayoría de, la mayor parte de. **~ days** casi todos los días. ● *pron* la mayoría, la mayor parte. **at ~** como máximo. **make the ~ of** aprovechar al máximo. ● *adv* más; (*very*) muy; (*Amer, almost*) casi. **~ly** *adv* principalmente
MOT *n*. **~ (test)** ITV *f*, inspección *f* técnica de vehículos
motel /məʊ'tel/ *n* motel *m*
moth /mɒθ/ *n* mariposa *f* de la luz, palomilla *f*; (*in clothes*) polilla *f*
mother /'mʌðə(r)/ *n* madre *f*. ● *vt* mimar. **~-in-law** *n* (*pl* **~s-in-law**) suegra *f*. **~land** *n* patria *f*. **~ly** *adj* maternal. **~-of-pearl** *n* nácar *m*, madreperla *f*. **M~'s Day** *n* el día *m* de la Madre. **~-to-be** *n* futura madre *f*. **~ tongue** *n* lengua *f* materna
motif /məʊ'tiːf/ *n* motivo *m*
motion /'məʊʃn/ *n* movimiento *m*; (*proposal*) moción *f*. **put** *or* **set in ~** poner algo en marcha. ● *vt/i*. **~ (to) s.o. to** hacerle señas a uno para que. **~less** *adj* inmóvil
motiv|ate /'məʊtɪveɪt/ *vt* motivar. **~ation** /-'veɪʃn/ *n* motivación *f*. **~e** /'məʊtɪv/ *n* motivo *m*
motley /'mɒtlɪ/ *adj* variopinto
motor /'məʊtə(r)/ *n* motor *m*. ● *adj* motor; (*fem*) motora, motriz. **~ bike** *n* [!] motocicleta *f*, moto *f* [!]. **~ boat** *n* lancha *f* a motor. **~ car** *n* automóvil *m*. **~ cycle** *n* motocicleta *f*. **~cyclist** *n* motoci-

clista *m & f.* **~ing** *n* automovilismo *m.* **~ist** *n* automovilista *m & f.* **~way** *n* autopista *f*

motto /ˈmɒtəʊ/ *n* (*pl* **-oes**) lema *m*

mould /məʊld/ *n* molde *m*; (*fungus*) moho *m.* ● *vt* moldear; formar (character). **~ing** *n* (*on wall etc*) moldura *f.* **~y** *adj* mohoso

moult /məʊlt/ *vi* mudar de pelo/piel/plumas

mound /maʊnd/ *n* montículo *m*; (*pile, fig*) montón *m*

mount /maʊnt/ *vt* montar (horse); engarzar (gem); preparar (attack). ● *vi* subir, crecer. ● *n.* montura *f*; (*mountain*) monte *m.* □ **~ up** *vi* irse acumulando

mountain /ˈmaʊntɪn/ *n* montaña *f.* **~eer** /maʊntɪˈnɪə(r)/ *n* alpinista *m & f.* **~eering** *n* alpinismo *m.* **~ous** *adj* montañoso

mourn /mɔːn/ *vt* llorar. ● *vi* lamentarse. **~ for s.o.** llorar a uno. **~er** *n* doliente *m & f.* **~ful** *adj* triste. **~ing** *n* duelo *m*, luto *m.* **be in ~ing** estar de duelo

mouse /maʊs/ *n* (*pl* **mice**) ratón *m.* **~trap** *n* ratonera *f*

mousse /muːs/ *n* (*Culin*) mousse *f or m*; (*for hair*) mousse *f*

moustache /məˈstɑːʃ/ *n* bigote *m*

mouth /maʊθ/ *n* boca *f*; (*of cave*) entrada *f*; (*of river*) desembocadura *f.* **~ful** *n* bocado *m.* **~-organ** *n* armónica *f.* **~wash** *n* enjuague *m* bucal

move /muːv/ *vt* mover; (*relocate*) trasladar; (*with emotion*) conmover; (*propose*) proponer. **~ the television** cambiar de lugar la televisión. **~ house** mudarse de casa. ● *vi* moverse; (*be in motion*) estar en movimiento; (*take action*) tomar medidas. ● *n* movimiento *m*; (*in game*) jugada *f*; (*player's turn*) turno *m*; (*removal*) mudanza *f.* □ **~ away** *vi* alejarse. □ **~ in** *vi* instalarse. **~ in with s.o.** irse a vivir con uno. □ **~ over** *vi* correrse. **~ment** *n* movimiento *m*

movie /ˈmuːvɪ/ *n* (*Amer*) película *f.* **the ~s** *npl* el cine. **~ camera** *n* (*Amer*) tomavistas *m*, filmadora *f* (*LAm*)

moving /ˈmuːvɪŋ/ *adj* en movimiento; (*touching*) conmovedor

mow /məʊ/ *vt* (*pt* **mowed** *or* **mown** /məʊn/) cortar (lawn); segar (hay). □ **~ down** *vt* acribillar. **~er** *n* (*for lawn*) cortacésped *m*

MP *abbr see* **MEMBER OF PARLIAMENT**

Mr /ˈmɪstə(r)/ *abbr* (*pl* **Messrs**) (= **Mister**) Sr. **~ Coldbeck** Sr. Coldbeck

Mrs /ˈmɪsɪz/ *abbr* (*pl* **Mrs**) (= **Missis**) Sra. **~ Andrews** Sra. Andrews

Ms /mɪz/ *abbr* (title of married or unmarried woman)

MSc *abbr see* **MASTER**

much /mʌtʃ/ *adj & pron* mucho, mucha. ● *adv* mucho; (*before pp*) muy. **~ as** por mucho que. **~ the same** más o menos lo mismo. **how ~?** ¿cuánto?. **so ~** tanto. **too ~** demasiado

muck /mʌk/ *n* estiércol *m*; (*fam, dirt*) mugre *f.* □ **~ about** *vi* [!] tontear

mud /mʌd/ *n* barro *m*, lodo *m*

muddle /ˈmʌdl/ *vt* embrollar. ● *n* desorden *m*; (*mix-up*) lío *m.* □ **~ through** *vi* salir del paso

muddy *adj* lodoso; (hands etc) cubierto de lodo. **~guard** *n* guardabarros *m*, salpicadera *f* (*Mex*)

muffle /ˈmʌfl/ *vt* amortiguar (sound). **~r** *n* (*scarf*) bufanda *f*;

(*Amer, Auto*) silenciador *m*

mug /mʌg/ *n* taza *f* (*alta y sin platillo*), tarro *m* (*Mex*); (*for beer*) jarra *f*; (*fam, face*) cara *f*, jeta *f* ☒; (*fam, fool*) idiota *m & f*. ● *vt* (*pt* **mugged**) asaltar. **~ger** *n* asaltante *m & f*. **~ging** *n* asalto *m*

muggy /'mʌgɪ/ *adj* bochornoso

mule /mju:l/ *n* mula *f*

mull /mʌl/ (*Amer*), **~ over** *vt* reflexionar sobre

multi|coloured /mʌltɪ'kʌləd/ *adj* multicolor. **~national** /-'næʃənl/ *adj & n* multinacional (*f*)

multipl|e /'mʌltɪpl/ *adj* múltiple. ● *n* múltiplo *m*. **~ication** /mʌltɪplɪ'keɪʃn/ *n* multiplicación *f*. **~y** /'mʌltɪplaɪ/ *vt* multiplicar. ● *vi* (*Math*) multiplicar; (*increase*) multiplicarse

multitude /'mʌltɪtju:d/ *n*. **a ~ of problems** múltiples problemas

mum /mʌm/ *n* [!] mamá *f* [!]

mumble /'mʌmbl/ *vt* mascullar. ● *vi* hablar entre dientes

mummy /'mʌmɪ/ *n* (*fam, mother*) mamá *f* [!]; (*archaeology*) momia *f*

mumps /mʌmps/ *n* paperas *fpl*

munch /mʌntʃ/ *vt/i* mascar

mundane /mʌn'deɪn/ *adj* mundano

municipal /mju:'nɪsɪpl/ *adj* municipal

mural /'mjʊərəl/ *adj & n* mural (*f*)

murder /'mɜ:də(r)/ *n* asesinato *m*. ● *vt* asesinar. **~er** *n* asesino *m*

murky /'mɜ:kɪ/ *adj* (**-ier**, **-iest**) turbio

murmur /'mɜ:mə(r)/ *n* murmullo *m*. ● *vt/i* murmurar

musc|le /'mʌsl/ *n* músculo *m*. **~ular** /'mʌskjʊlə(r)/ *adj* muscular; (arm, body) musculoso

muse /mju:z/ *vi* meditar (**on** sobre)

museum /mju:'zɪəm/ *n* museo *m*

mush /mʌʃ/ *n* papilla *f*

mushroom /'mʌʃrʊm/ *n* champiñón *m*; (*in botany*) seta *f*. ● *vi* aparecer como hongos

mushy /'mʌʃɪ/ *adj* blando

music /'mju:zɪk/ *n* música *f*. **~al** *adj* musical. **be ~** tener sentido musical. ● *n* musical *m*. **~ian** /mju:'zɪʃn/ *n* músico *m*

Muslim /'mʊzlɪm/ *adj & n* musulmán (*m*)

mussel /'mʌsl/ *n* mejillón *m*

must /mʌst/ *modal verb* deber, tener que; (*expressing supposition*) deber (de). **he ~ be old** debe (de) ser viejo. **I ~ have done it** debo (de) haberlo hecho. ● *n*. **be a ~** ser imprescindible

mustache /'mʌstæʃ/ *n* (*Amer*) bigote *m*

mustard /'mʌstəd/ *n* mostaza *f*

muster /'mʌstə(r)/ *vt* reunir

musty /'mʌstɪ/ *adj* (**-ier**, **-iest**) que huele a humedad

mutation /mju:'teɪʃn/ *n* mutación *f*

mute /mju:t/ *adj* mudo

mutilate /'mju:tɪleɪt/ *vt* mutilar

mutiny /'mju:tɪnɪ/ *n* motín *m*. ● *vi* amotinarse

mutter /'mʌtə(r)/ *vt/i* murmurar

mutton /'mʌtn/ *n* carne *f* de ovino

mutual /'mju:tʃʊəl/ *adj* mutuo; (*fam, common*) común

muzzle /'mʌzl/ *n* (*snout*) hocico *m*; (*device*) bozal *m*

my /maɪ/ *adj* (*sing*) mi; (*pl*) mis

myself /maɪ'self/ *pron* (*reflexive*) me; (*used for emphasis*) yo mismo *m*, yo misma *f*. **I cut ~** me corté. **I made it ~** lo hice yo mismo/ misma. **I was by ~** estaba solo/ sola

myster|ious /mɪˈstɪərɪəs/ *adj* misterioso. **~y** /ˈmɪstərɪ/ *n* misterio *m*

mystical /ˈmɪstɪkl/ *adj* místico

mystify /ˈmɪstɪfaɪ/ *vt* dejar perplejo

mystique /mɪˈstiːk/ *n* mística *f*

myth /mɪθ/ *n* mito *m*. **~ical** *adj* mítico. **~ology** /mɪˈθɒlədʒɪ/ *n* mitología *f*

Nn

N *abbr* (= **north**) N

nab /næb/ *vt* (*pt* **nabbed**) (*sl, arrest*) pescar; (*snatch*) agarrar

nag /næg/ *vt* (*pt* **nagged**) fastidiar; (*scold*) estarle encima a. ● *vi* criticar

nail /neɪl/ *n* clavo *m*; (*of finger, toe*) uña *f*. **~ polish** esmalte *m* para las uñas. ● *vt*. **~ (down)** clavar

naive /naɪˈiːv/ *adj* ingenuo

naked /ˈneɪkɪd/ *adj* desnudo. **to the ~ eye** a simple vista

name /neɪm/ *n* nombre *m*; (*of book, film*) título *m*; (*fig*) fama *f*. **my ~ is Chris** me llamo Chris. **good ~** buena reputación. ● *vt* ponerle nombre a; (*appoint*) nombrar. **a man ~d Jones** un hombre llamado Jones. **she was ~d after** *or* (*Amer*) **for her grandmother** le pusieron el nombre de su abuela. **~less** *adj* anónimo. **~ly** *adv* a saber. **~sake** *n* (*person*) tocayo *m*

nanny /ˈnænɪ/ *n* niñera *f*

nap /næp/ *n* (*sleep*) sueñecito *m*; (*after lunch*) siesta *f*. **have a ~** echarse un sueño

napkin /ˈnæpkɪn/ *n* servilleta *f*

nappy /ˈnæpɪ/ *n* pañal *m*

narcotic /nɑːˈkɒtɪk/ *adj & n* narcótico (*m*)

narrat|e /nəˈreɪt/ *vt* narrar. **~ive** /ˈnærətɪv/ *n* narración *f*. **~or** /nəˈreɪtə(r)/ *n* narrador *m*

narrow /ˈnærəʊ/ *adj* (**-er, -est**) estrecho, angosto (*LAm*). **have a ~ escape** salvarse de milagro. ● *vt* estrechar; (*limit*) limitar. ● *vi* estrecharse. **~ly** *adv* (*just*) por poco. **~-minded** /-ˈmaɪndɪd/ *adj* de miras estrechas

nasal /ˈneɪzl/ *adj* nasal; (voice) gangoso

nasty /ˈnɑːstɪ/ *adj* (**-ier, -iest**) desagradable; (*spiteful*) malo (**to** con); (taste, smell) asqueroso; (cut) feo

nation /ˈneɪʃn/ *n* nación *f*

national /ˈnæʃənl/ *adj* nacional. ● *n* ciudadano *m*. **~ anthem** *n* himno *m* nacional. **~ism** *n* nacionalismo *m*. **~ity** /næʃəˈnælətɪ/ *n* nacionalidad *f*. **~ize** *vt* nacionalizar. **~ly** *adv* a escala nacional

> **National Trust** Fundación británica cuyo objetivo es la conservación de lugares de interés histórico o de belleza natural. Se financia mediante legados y subvenciones privadas. Es la mayor propietaria de tierras de Gran Bretaña. En Escocia, es independiente y recibe el nombre de *National Trust for Scotland*.

nationwide /ˈneɪʃnwaɪd/ *adj & adv* a escala nacional

native /ˈneɪtɪv/ *n* natural *m & f*. **be**

a ~ **of** ser natural de. ● *adj* nativo; (country, town) natal; (language) materno; (plant, animal) autóctono. **N~ American** indio *m* americano

nativity /nə'tɪvətɪ/ *n.* **the N~** la Natividad *f*

NATO /'neɪtəʊ/ *abbr* (= **North Atlantic Treaty Organization**) OTAN *f*

natter /'nætə(r)/ 🅸 *vi* charlar. ● *n* charla *f*

natural /'nætʃərəl/ *adj* natural. ~ **history** *n* historia *f* natural. **~ist** *n* naturalista *m & f*. **~ized** *adj* (citizen) naturalizado. **~ly** *adv* (*of course*) naturalmente; (*by nature*) por naturaleza

nature /'neɪtʃə(r)/ *n* naturaleza *f*; (*of person*) carácter *m*; (*of things*) naturaleza *f*

naught /nɔ:t/ *n* cero *m*

naughty /'nɔ:tɪ/ *adj* (**-ier**, **-iest**) malo, travieso

n

nause|a /'nɔ:zɪə/ *n* náuseas *fpl*. **~ous** /-ɪəs/ *adj* nauseabundo

nautical /'nɔ:tɪkl/ *adj* náutico. ~ **mile** *n* milla *f* marina

naval /'neɪvl/ *adj* naval; (officer) de marina

nave /neɪv/ *n* nave *f*

navel /'neɪvl/ *n* ombligo *m*

naviga|ble /'nævɪgəbl/ *adj* navegable. **~te** /'nævɪgeɪt/ *vt* navegar por (sea etc); gobernar (ship). ● *vi* navegar. **~tion** /-'geɪʃn/ *n* navegación *f*. **~tor** *n* oficial *m & f* de derrota

navy /'neɪvɪ/ *n* marina *f* de guerra. ~ **(blue)** *a & n* azul (*m*) marino

NE *abbr* (= **north-east**) NE

near /'nɪə(r)/ *adv* cerca. **draw ~** acercarse. ● *prep.* ~ **(to)** cerca de. **go ~ (to) sth** acercarse a algo. ● *adj* cercano. ● *vt* acercarse a. **~by** *adj* cercano. **~ly** *adv* casi. **he ~ly died** por poco se muere, casi se muere. **not ~ly** ni con mucho. **~sighted** /-'saɪtɪd/ *adj* miope, corto de vista

neat /ni:t/ *adj* (**-er**, **-est**) (person) pulcro; (room etc) bien arreglado; (*ingenious*) hábil; (whisky, gin) solo; ; (*Amer fam, great*) fantástico 🅸. **~ly** *adv* pulcramente; (organized) cuidadosamente

necessar|ily /nesə'serɪlɪ/ *adv* necesariamente. **~y** /'nesəserɪ/ *adj* necesario

necessit|ate /nə'sesɪteɪt/ *vt* exigir. **~y** /nɪ'sesətɪ/ *n* necesidad *f*. **the bare ~ies** lo indispensable

neck /nek/ *n* (*of person, bottle, dress*) cuello *m*; (*of animal*) pescuezo *m*. ~ **and** ~ a la par, parejos (*LAm*). **~lace** /'nekləs/ *n* collar *m*. **~line** *n* escote *m*

nectar /'nektə(r)/ *n* néctar *m*

nectarine /'nektərɪn/ *n* nectarina *f*

née /neɪ/ *adj* de soltera

need /ni:d/ *n* necesidad *f* (**for** de). ● *vt* necesitar; (*demand*) exigir. **you ~ not speak** no tienes que hablar

needle /'ni:dl/ *n* aguja *f*. ● *vt* (*fam, annoy*) pinchar

needless /'ni:dlɪs/ *adj* innecesario

needlework /'ni:dlwɜ:k/ *n* labores *fpl* de aguja; (*embroidery*) bordado *m*

needy /'ni:dɪ/ *adj* (**-ier**, **-iest**) necesitado

negative /'negətɪv/ *adj* negativo. ● *n* (*of photograph*) negativo *m*; (*no*) negativa *f*

neglect /nɪ'glekt/ *vt* descuidar (house); desatender (children); no cumplir con (duty). ● *n* negligencia *f.* **(state of) ~** abandono *m.* **~ful** *adj* negligente

neglig|ence /'neglɪdʒəns/ *n* negligencia *f*, descuido *m.* **~ent** *adj* negligente. **~ible** /'neglɪdʒəbl/ *adj* insignificante

negotia|ble /nɪ'gəʊʃəbl/ *adj* negociable. **~te** /nɪ'gəʊʃɪeɪt/ *vt/i* negociar. **~tion** /-'eɪʃn/ *n* negociación *f.* **~tor** *n* negociador *m*

neigh /neɪ/ *vi* relinchar

neighbour /'neɪbə(r)/ *n* vecino *m.* **~hood** *n* vecindad *f*, barrio *m.* **in the ~hood of** alrededor de. **~ing** *adj* vecino

neither /'naɪðə(r)/ *adj.* **~ book** ninguno de los libros. ● *pron* ninguno, -na. ● *conj.* **neither...nor** ni...ni. **~ do I** yo tampoco

neon /'ni:ɒn/ *n* neón *m.* ● *adj* (lamp etc) de neón

nephew /'nevju:/ *n* sobrino *m*

Neptune /'neptju:n/ *n* Neptuno *m*

nerv|e /nɜ:v/ *n* nervio *m*; (*courage*) valor *m*; (*calm*) sangre *f* fría; (*fam, impudence*) descaro *m.* **~es** *npl* (*before exams etc*) nervios *mpl.* **get on s.o.'s ~es** ponerle los nervios de punta a uno. **~e-racking** *adj* exasperante. **~ous** /'nɜ:vəs/ *adj* nervioso. **be/feel ~ous** estar nervioso. **~ousness** *n* nerviosismo *m.* **~y** /'nɜ:vɪ/ *adj* nervioso; (*Amer fam*) descarado

nest /nest/ *n* nido *m.* ● *vi* anidar

nestle /'nesl/ *vi* acurrucarse

net /net/ *n* red *f.* **the N~** (*Comp*) la Red. ● *vt* (*pt* **netted**) pescar (*con red*) (fish). ● *adj* neto. **~ball** *n* *especie de baloncesto*

Netherlands /'neðələndz/ *npl.* **the ~** los Países Bajos

netting /'netɪŋ/ *n* redes *fpl.* **wire ~** tela *f* metálica

nettle /'netl/ *n* ortiga *f*

network /'netwɜ:k/ *n* red *f*; (*TV*) cadena *f*

neuro|sis /njʊə'rəʊsɪs/ *n* (*pl* **-oses** /-si:z/) neurosis *f.* **~tic** /-'rɒtɪk/ *adj & n* neurótico (*m*)

neuter /'nju:tə(r)/ *adj & n* neutro (*m*). ● *vt* castrar (animals)

neutral /'nju:trəl/ *adj* neutral; (colour) neutro; (*Elec*) neutro. **~ (gear)** (*Auto*) punto *m* muerto. **~ize** *vt* neutralizar

neutron /'nju:trɒn/ *n* neutrón *m*

never /nevə(r)/ *adv* nunca; (*more emphatic*) jamás; (*fam, not*) no. **~ again** nunca más. **he ~ smiles** no sonríe nunca, nunca sonríe. **I ~ saw him** [!] no lo vi. **~-ending** *adj* interminable. **~theless** /-ðə'les/ *adv* sin embargo, no obstante

new /nju:/ *adj* (**-er, -est**) nuevo. **~born** *adj* recién nacido. **~comer** *n* recién llegado *m.* **~fangled** /-'fæŋgld/ *adj* (*pej*) moderno. **~ly** *adv* recién. **~ly-weds** *npl* recién casados *mpl*

news /nju:z/ *n.* **a piece of ~** una noticia. **good/bad ~** buenas/malas noticias. **the ~** (*TV, Radio*) las noticias. **~agent** *n* vendedor *m* de periódicos. **~caster** *n* locutor *m.* **~dealer** *n* (*Amer*) *see* **~AGENT**. **~flash** *n* información *f* de última hora. **~letter** *n* boletín *m*, informativo *m.* **~paper** *n* periódico *m*, diario *m.* **~reader** *n* locutor *m*

newt /nju:t/ *n* tritón *m*

New Year /nju:'jɪə(r)/ *n* Año *m* Nuevo. **N~'s Day** *n* día *m* de Año Nuevo. **N~'s Eve** *n* noche *f* vieja, noche *f* de fin de Año

New Zealand /nju:'zi:lənd/ *n* Nueva Zeland(i)a *f*

next /nekst/ *adj* próximo; (week,

month etc) que viene, próximo; (*adjoining*) vecino; (*following*) siguiente. ● *adv* luego, después. ~ **to** al lado de. **when you see me ~** la próxima vez que me veas. ~ **to nothing** casi nada. ~ **door** al lado (**to** de). **~-door** *adj* de al lado. ~ **of kin** *n* familiar(es) *m(pl)* más cercano(s)

nib /nɪb/ *n* plumilla *f*

nibble /'nɪbl/ *vt/i* mordisquear. ● *n* mordisco *m*

Nicaragua /nɪkə'rægjʊə/ *n* Nicaragua *f*. **~n** *adj & n* nicaragüense (*m & f*)

nice /naɪs/ *adj* (**-er**, **-est**) agradable; (*likeable*) simpático; (*kind*) amable; (weather, food) bueno. **we had a ~ time** lo pasamos bien. **~ly** *adv* (*kindly*) amablemente; (*politely*) con buenos modales

niche /nɪtʃ, niːʃ/ *n* nicho *m*

n **nick** /nɪk/ *n* corte *m* pequeño. **in the ~ of time** justo a tiempo. ● *vt* (*sl, steal*) afanar ☒

nickel /'nɪkl/ *n* (*metal*) níquel *m*; (*Amer*) moneda *f* de cinco centavos

nickname /'nɪkneɪm/ *n* apodo *m*. ● *vt* apodar

nicotine /'nɪkətiːn/ *n* nicotina *f*

niece /niːs/ *n* sobrina *f*

niggling /'nɪglɪŋ/ *adj* (doubt) constante

night /naɪt/ *n* noche *f*; (*evening*) tarde *f*. **at ~** por la noche, de noche. **good ~** ¡buenas noches! ● *adj* nocturno, de noche. **~cap** *n* (*drink*) bebida *f* (tomada antes de acostarse). **~club** *n* club *m* nocturno. **~dress** *n* camisón *m*. **~fall** *n* anochecer *m*. **~gown**, **~ie** /'naɪtɪ/ ☐ *n* camisón *m*. **~life** *n* vida *f* nocturna. **~ly** *adj* de todas las noches. **~mare** *n* pesadilla *f*. **~ school** *n* escuela *f* nocturna. **~-time** *n* noche *f*. **~watchman** *n* sereno *m*

nil /nɪl/ *n* nada *f*; (*Sport*) cero *m*

nimble /'nɪmbl/ *adj* (**-er**, **-est**) ágil

nine /naɪn/ *adj & n* nueve (*m*). **~teen** /naɪn'tiːn/ *adj & n* diecinueve (*m*). **~teenth** *adj* decimonoveno. ● *n* diecinueveavo *m*. **~tieth** /'naɪntɪəθ/ *adj* nonagésimo. ● *n* noventavo *m*. **~ty** *adj & n* noventa (*m*)

ninth /'naɪnθ/ *adj & n* noveno (*m*)

nip /nɪp/ *vt* (*pt* **nipped**) (*pinch*) pellizcar; (*bite*) mordisquear. ● *vi* (*fam, rush*) correr

nipple /'nɪpl/ *n* (*of woman*) pezón *m*; (*of man*) tetilla *f*; (*of baby's bottle*) tetina *f*, chupón *m* (*Mex*)

nippy /'nɪpɪ/ *adj* (**-ier**, **-iest**) (*fam, chilly*) fresquito

nitrogen /'naɪtrədʒən/ *n* nitrógeno *m*

no /nəʊ/ *adj* ninguno, (*before masculine singular noun*) ningún. **I have ~ money** no tengo dinero. **there's ~ food left** no queda nada de comida. **it has ~ windows** no tiene ventanas. **I'm ~ expert** no soy ningún experto. **~ smoking** prohibido fumar. **~ way!** ☐ ¡ni hablar! ● *adv & int* no. ● *n* (*pl* **noes**) no *m*

noble /'nəʊbl/ *adj* (**-er**, **-est**) noble. **~man** /-mən/ *n* noble *m*

nobody /'nəʊbədɪ/ *pron* nadie. **there's ~ there** no hay nadie

nocturnal /nɒk'tɜːnl/ *adj* nocturno

nod /nɒd/ *vt* (*pt* **nodded**). **~ one's head** asentir con la cabeza. ● *vi* (*in agreement*) asentir con la cabeza; (*in greeting*) saludar con la cabeza.

□ ~ **off** *vi* dormirse

nois|e /nɔɪz/ *n* ruido *m.* **~ily** *adv* ruidosamente. **~y** *adj* (**-ier**, **-iest**) ruidoso. **it's too ~y here** hay demasiado ruido aquí

nomad /'nəʊmæd/ *n* nómada *m & f.* **~ic** /-'mædɪk/ *adj* nómada

no man's land *n* tierra *f* de nadie

nominat|e /'nɒmɪneɪt/ *vt* (*put forward*) proponer; postular (*LAm*); (*appoint*) nombrar. **~ion** /-'neɪʃn/ *n* nombramiento *m*; (*Amer, Pol*) proclamación *f*

non-... /nɒn/ *pref* no ...

nonchalant /'nɒnʃələnt/ *adj* despreocupado

non-committal /nɒnkə'mɪtl/ *adj* evasivo

nondescript /'nɒndɪskrɪpt/ *adj* anodino

none /nʌn/ *pron* ninguno, ninguna. **there were ~ left** no quedaba ninguno/ninguna. **~ of us** ninguno de nosotros. ● *adv* no, de ninguna manera. **he is ~ the happier** no está más contento

nonentity /nɒ'nentətɪ/ *n* persona *f* insignificante

non-existent /nɒnɪg'zɪstənt/ *adj* inexistente

nonplussed /nɒn'plʌst/ *adj* perplejo

nonsens|e /'nɒnsns/ *n* tonterías *fpl*, disparates *mpl.* **~ical** /-'sensɪkl/ *adj* disparatado

non-smoker /nɒn'sməʊkə(r)/ *n* no fumador *m.* **I'm a ~** no fumo

non-stop /nɒn'stɒp/ *adj* (train) directo; (flight) sin escalas. ● *adv* sin parar; (*by train*) directamente; (*by air*) sin escalas

noodles /'nu:dlz/ *npl* fideos *mpl*

nook /nʊk/ *n* rincón *m*

noon /nu:n/ *n* mediodía *m*

no-one /'nəʊwʌn/ *pron* nadie

noose /nu:s/ *n* soga *f*

nor /nɔ:(r)/ *conj* ni, tampoco. **neither blue ~ red** ni azul ni rojo. **he doesn't play the piano, ~ do I** no sabe tocar el piano, ni yo tampoco

norm /nɔ:m/ *n* norma *f*

normal /'nɔ:ml/ *adj* normal. **~cy** *n* (*Amer*) normalidad *f.* **~ity** /-'mælətɪ/ *n* normalidad *f.* **~ly** *adv* normalmente

north /nɔ:θ/ *n* norte *m.* ● *adj* norte. ● *adv* hacia el norte. **N~ America** *n* América *f* del Norte, Norteamérica *f.* **N~ American** *adj & n* norteamericano (*m*). **~east** *n* nor(d)este *m.* ● *adj* nor(d)este. ● *adv* (go) hacia el nor(d)este. **it's ~east of Leeds** está al nor(d)este de Leeds. **~erly** /'nɔ:ðəlɪ/ *adj* (wind) del norte. **~ern** /'nɔ:ðən/ *adj* del norte. **~erner** *n* norteño *m.* **N~ern Ireland** *n* Irlanda *f* del Norte. **N~ Sea** *n* mar *m* del Norte. **~ward**/'nɔ:θwəd/, **~wards** *adv* hacia el norte. **~west** *n* noroeste *m.* ● *adj* noroeste. ● *adv* hacia el noroeste

Norw|ay /'nɔ:weɪ/ *n* Noruega *f.* **~egian** /-'wi:dʒən/ *adj & n* noruego (*m*)

nose /nəʊz/ *n* nariz *f.* **~bleed** *n* hemorragia *f* nasal. **~dive** *vi* descender en picado, descender en picada (*LAm*)

nostalgi|a /nɒ'stældʒə/ *n* nostalgia *f.* **~c** *adj* nostálgico

nostril /'nɒstrɪl/ *n* ventana *f* de la nariz *f*

nosy /'nəʊzɪ/ *adj* (**-ier**, **-iest**) 🅸 entrometido, metiche (*LAm*)

not /nɒt/

> Cuando **not** va precedido del verbo auxiliar **do** or **have** o de un verbo modal como **should** etc, se suele emplear la forma contraída **don't, haven't, shouldn't** etc

adverb

- ····➤ no. **I don't know** no sé. **~ yet** todavía no. **~ me** yo no
- ····➤ (*replacing a clause*) **I suppose ~** supongo que no. **of course ~** por supuesto que no. **are you going to help me or ~?** ¿me vas a ayudar o no?
- ····➤ (*emphatic*) ni. **~ a penny more!** ¡ni un penique más!
- ····➤ (*in phrases*) **certainly ~** de ninguna manera . **~ you again!** ¡tú otra vez!

n

notabl|e /ˈnəʊtəbl/ *adj* notable; (author) distinguido. **~y** /ˈnəʊtəblɪ/ *adv* notablemente; (*in particular*) particularmente

notch /nɒtʃ/ *n* muesca *f*. □ **~ up** *vt* apuntarse

note /nəʊt/ *n* (*incl Mus*) nota *f*; (*banknote*) billete *m*. **take ~s** tomar apuntes. ● *vt* (*notice*) observar; (*record*) anotar. □ **~ down** *vt* apuntar. **~book** *n* cuaderno *m*. **~d** *adj* célebre. **~paper** *n* papel *m* de carta(s)

nothing /ˈnʌθɪŋ/ *pron* nada. **he eats ~** no come nada. **for ~** (*free*) gratis; (*in vain*) en vano. **~ else** nada más. **~ much happened** no pasó gran cosa. **he does ~ but complain** no hace más que quejarse

notice /ˈnəʊtɪs/ *n* (*sign*) letrero *m*; (*item of information*) anuncio *m*; (*notification*) aviso *m*; (*of termination of employment*) preaviso *m*; **~ (of dismissal)** despido *m*. **take ~ of** hacer caso a (person). ● *vt* notar. ● *vi* darse cuenta. **~able** *adj* perceptible. **~ably** *adv* perceptiblemente. **~board** *n* tablón *m* de anuncios, tablero *m* de anuncios (*LAm*)

notif|ication /nəʊtɪfɪˈkeɪʃn/ *n* notificación *f*. **~y** /ˈnəʊtɪfaɪ/ *vt* informar; (*in writing*) notificar. **~y s.o. of sth** comunicarle algo a uno

notion /ˈnəʊʃn/ *n* (*concept*) concepto *m*; (*idea*) idea *f*

notorious /nəʊˈtɔːrɪəs/ *adj* notorio

notwithstanding /nɒtwɪθˈstændɪŋ/ *prep* a pesar de. ● *adv* no obstante

nougat /ˈnuːgɑː/ *n* turrón *m*

nought /nɔːt/ *n* cero *m*

noun /naʊn/ *n* sustantivo *m*, nombre *m*

nourish /ˈnʌrɪʃ/ *vt* alimentar. **~ment** *n* alimento *m*

novel /ˈnɒvl/ *n* novela *f*. ● *adj* original, novedoso. **~ist** *n* novelista *m & f*. **~ty** *n* novedad *f*

November /nəʊˈvembə(r)/ *n* noviembre *m*

novice /ˈnɒvɪs/ *n* principiante *m & f*

now /naʊ/ *adv* ahora. **~ and again, ~ and then** de vez en cuando. **right ~** ahora mismo. **from ~ on** a partir de ahora. ● *conj*. **~ (that)** ahora que. **~adays** /ˈnaʊədeɪz/ *adv* hoy (en) día

nowhere /ˈnəʊweə(r)/ *adv* por ninguna parte, por ningún lado; (*after motion towards*) a ninguna parte, a ningún lado

nozzle /ˈnɒzl/ *n* (*on hose*) boca *f*; (*on fire extinguisher*) boquilla *f*

nuance /ˈnjʊɑːns/ *n* matiz *m*

nuclear /ˈnjuːklɪə(r)/ *adj* nuclear

nucleus /ˈnjuːklɪəs/ *n* (*pl* **-lei** /-lɪaɪ/) núcleo *m*

nude /njuːd/ *adj & n* desnudo (*m*). **in the ~** desnudo

nudge /nʌdʒ/ *vt* codear (ligeramente). ● *n* golpe *m* (suave) con el codo

nudi|st /ˈnjuːdɪst/ *n* nudista *m & f*. **~ty** /ˈnjuːdətɪ/ *n* desnudez *f*

nuisance /ˈnjuːsns/ *n* (*thing, event*) molestia *f*, fastidio *m*; (*person*) pesado *m*

null /nʌl/ *adj* nulo

numb /nʌm/ *adj* entumecido. **go ~** entumecerse ● *vt* entumecer

number /ˈnʌmbə(r)/ *n* número *m*; (*telephone number*) número *m* de teléfono. **a ~ of people** varias personas. ● *vt* numerar; (*count, include*) contar. **~plate** *n* matrícula *f*, placa *f* (*LAm*)

numer|al /ˈnjuːmərəl/ *n* número *m*. **~ical** /njuːˈmerɪkl/ *adj* numérico. **~ous** /ˈnjuːmərəs/ *adj* numeroso

nun /nʌn/ *n* monja *f*

nurse /nɜːs/ *n* enfermero *m*, enfermera *f*; (*nanny*) niñera *f*. ● *vt* cuidar; abrigar (hope etc)

nursery /ˈnɜːsərɪ/ *n* (*for plants*) vivero *m*; (*day ~*) guardería *f*. **~ rhyme** *n* canción *f* infantil. **~ school** *n* jardín *m* de infancia, jardín *m* infantil (*LAm*)

nursing home /ˈnɜːsɪŋ/ *n* (*for older people*) residencia *f* de ancianos (con mayor nivel de asistencia médica)

nut /nʌt/ *n* fruto *m* seco (*nuez, almendra, avellana etc*); (*Tec*) tuerca *f*. **~case** *n* ⓘ chiflado *m*. **~crackers** *npl* cascanueces *m*. **~meg** /-meg/ *n* nuez *f* moscada

nutri|ent /ˈnjuːtrɪənt/ *n* nutriente *m*. **~tion** /njuːˈtrɪʃn/ *n* nutrición *f*. **~tious** /njuːˈtrɪʃəs/ *adj* nutritivo

nuts /nʌts/ *adj* (*fam, crazy*) chiflado

nutshell /ˈnʌtʃel/ *n* cáscara *f* de nuez. **in a ~** en pocas palabras

NW *abbr* (= **north-west**) NO

nylon /ˈnaɪlɒn/ *n* nylon *m*

Oo

oaf /əʊf/ *n* zoquete *m*

oak /əʊk/ *n* roble *m*

OAP /əʊeɪˈpiː/ *abbr* (= **old-age pensioner**) *n* pensionista *m & f*, pensionado *m*

oar /ɔː(r)/ *n* remo *m*

oasis /əʊˈeɪsɪs/ *n* (*pl* **oases** /-siːz/) oasis *m*

oath /əʊθ/ *n* juramento *m*

oat|meal /ˈəʊtmiːl/ *n* harina *f* de avena; (*Amer, flakes*) avena *f* (*en copos*). **~s** /əʊts/ *npl* avena *f*

obedien|ce /əʊˈbiːdɪəns/ *n* obediencia *f*. **~t** *adj* obediente. **~tly** *adv* obedientemente

obes|e /əʊˈbiːs/ *adj* obeso. **~ity** *n* obesidad *f*

obey /əʊˈbeɪ/ *vt/i* obedecer

obituary /əˈbɪtʃʊərɪ/ *n* nota *f* necrológica, obituario *m*

object /ˈɒbdʒɪkt/ *n* objeto *m*; (*aim*) objetivo *m*. ● /əbˈdʒekt/ *vi* oponerse (**to** a). **~ion** /əbˈdʒekʃn/ *n* objeción *f.* **~ionable** *adj* censurable; (*unpleasant*) desagradable. **~ive** /əb'dʒektɪv/ *adj & n* objetivo (*m*)

oblig|ation /ɒblɪ'geɪʃn/ *n* obligación *f.* **be under an ~ation to** estar obligado a. **~atory** /ə 'blɪgətrɪ/ *adj* obligatorio. **~e** /ə 'blaɪdʒ/ *vt* obligar. **I'd be much ~ed if you could help me** le quedaría muy agradecido si pudiera ayudarme. ● *vi* hacer un favor. **~ing** *adj* atento

oblique /ə'bli:k/ *adj* oblicuo

obliterate /ə'blɪtəreɪt/ *vt* arrasar; (*erase*) borrar

oblivio|n /ə'blɪvɪən/ *n* olvido *m.* **~us** /-vɪəs/ *adj* (*unaware*) inconsciente (**to, of** de)

oblong /'ɒblɒŋ/ *adj* oblongo. ● *n* rectángulo *m*

obnoxious /əb'nɒkʃəs/ *adj* odioso

oboe /'əʊbəʊ/ *n* oboe *m*

obscen|e /əb'si:n/ *adj* obsceno. **~ity** /əb'senətɪ/ *n* obscenidad *f*

obscur|e /əb'skjʊə(r)/ *adj* oscuro. ● *vt* ocultar; impedir ver claramente (issue). **~ity** *n* oscuridad *f*

obsequious /əb'si:kwɪəs/ *adj* servil

observ|ant /əb'zɜ:vənt/ *adj* observador. **~ation** /ɒbzə'veɪʃn/ *n* observación *f.* **~atory** /əb'zɜ:vətrɪ/ *n* observatorio *m.* **~e** /əb'zɜ:v/ *vt* observar. **~er** *n* observador *m*

obsess /əb'ses/ *vt* obsesionar. **~ed** /əb'sest/ *adj* obsesionado. **~ion** /-ʃn/ *n* obsesión *f.* **~ive** *adj* obsesivo

obsolete /'ɒbsəli:t/ *adj* obsoleto

obstacle /'ɒbstəkl/ *n* obstáculo *m*

obstina|cy /'ɒbstɪnəsɪ/ *n* obstinación *f.* **~te** /-ət/ *adj* obstinado. **~tely** *adv* obstinadamente

O

obstruct /əb'strʌkt/ *vt* obstruir; bloquear (traffic). **~ion** /-ʃn/ *n* obstrucción *f*

obtain /əb'teɪn/ *vt* conseguir, obtener. **~able** *adj* asequible

obtrusive /əb'tru:sɪv/ *adj* (presence) demasiado prominente; (noise) molesto

obtuse /əb'tju:s/ *adj* obtuso

obvious /'ɒbvɪəs/ *adj* obvio. **~ly** *adv* obviamente

occasion /ə'keɪʒn/ *n* ocasión *f.* **~al** *adj* esporádico. **~ally** *adv* de vez en cuando

occult /ɒ'kʌlt/ *adj* oculto

occup|ant /'ɒkjʊpənt/ *n* ocupante *m & f.* **~ation** /ɒkjʊ'peɪʃn/ *n* ocupación *f.* **~ier** /'ɒkjʊpaɪə(r)/ *n* ocupante *m & f.* **~y** /'ɒkjʊpaɪ/ *vt* ocupar. **keep o.s. ~ied** entretenerse

occur /ə'kɜ:(r)/ *vi* (*pt* **occurred**) tener lugar, ocurrir; (change) producirse; (*exist*) encontrarse. **it ~red to me that** se me ocurrió que. **~rence** /ə'kʌrəns/ *n* (*incidence*) incidencia *f.* **it is a rare ~rence** no es algo frecuente

ocean /'əʊʃn/ *n* océano *m*

o'clock /ə'klɒk/ *adv.* **it is 7 ~** son las siete. **it's one ~** es la una

octagon /'ɒktəgən/ *n* octágono *m*

octave /'ɒktɪv/ *n* octava *f*

October /ɒk'təʊbə(r)/ *n* octubre *m*

octopus /'ɒktəpəs/ *n* (*pl* **-puses**) pulpo *m*

odd /ɒd/ *adj* (**-er, -est**) extraño, raro; (number) impar; (*one of pair*) desparejado. **smoke the ~ cigarette** fumarse algún que otro cigarillo. **fifty-~** unos cincuenta, cincuenta y pico. **the ~ one out** la excepción. **~ity** *n* (*thing*) rareza *f*;

(*person*) bicho *m* raro. **~ly** *adv* de una manera extraña. **~ly enough** por extraño que parezca. **~ment** *n* retazo *m*. **~s** *npl* probabilidades *fpl*; (*in betting*) apuesta *f*. **be at ~s** estar en desacuerdo. **~s and ends** *mpl* ⓘ cosas *fpl* sueltas

odious /ˈəʊdɪəs/ *adj* odioso

odometer /ɒˈdɒmətə(r)/ *n* (*Amer*) cuentakilómetros *m*

odour /ˈəʊdə(r)/ *n* olor *m*

of /ɒv//əv/ *preposition*

- ····➤ de. **a pound of cheese** una libra de queso. **it's made of wood** es de madera. **a girl of ten** una niña de diez años
- ····➤ (*in dates*) de. **the fifth of November** el cinco de noviembre
- ····➤ (*Amer, when telling the time*) **it's ten (minutes) of five** son las cinco menos diez, son diez para las cinco (*LAm*)

! **of** is not translated in cases such as the following: **a colleague of mine** *un colega mío;* **there were six of us** *éramos seis;* **that's very kind of you** *es Ud muy amable*

off /ɒf/ *prep* (*from*) de. **he picked it up ~ the floor** lo recogió del suelo; (*distant from*) **just ~ the coast of Texas** a poca distancia de la costa de Tejas. **2 ft ~ the ground** a dos pies del suelo; (*absent from*) **I've been ~ work for a week** hace una semana que no voy a trabajar. ● *adv* (*removed*) **the lid was ~** la tapa no estaba puesta; (*distant*) **some way ~** a cierta distancia; (*leaving*) **I'm ~** me voy; (*switched off*) (light, TV) apagado; (water) cortado; (*cancelled*) (match) cancelado; (*not on duty*) (day) libre. ● *adj*. **be ~** (meat) estar malo, estar pasado; (milk) estar cortado. **~-beat** *adj* poco convencional. **~ chance** *n*. **on the ~ chance** por si acaso

off-licence En el Reino Unido, es una tienda que tiene licencia para vender bebidas alcohólicas que se deben consumir fuera del local. Abren cuando los bares y *pubs* están cerrados y también suelen vender bebidas no alcohólicas, tabaco, golosinas etc. A menudo alquilan vasos y copas para fiestas, etc.

offen|ce /əˈfens/ *n* (*breach of law*) infracción *f*; (*criminal* **~ce**) delito *m*; (*cause of outrage*) atentado *m*; (*Amer, attack*) ataque *m*. **take ~ce** ofenderse. **~d** *vt* ofender. **~der** *n* delincuente *m & f*. **~sive** /-sɪv/ *adj* ofensivo; (*disgusting*) desagradable

offer /ˈɒfə(r)/ *vt* ofrecer. **~ to do sth** ofrecerse a hacer algo. ● *n* oferta *f*. **on ~** de oferta

offhand /ɒfˈhænd/ *adj* (*brusque*) brusco. **say sth in an ~ way** decir algo a la ligera. ● *adv* de improviso

office /ˈɒfɪs/ *n* oficina *f*; (*post*) cargo *m*. **doctor's ~** (*Amer*) consultorio *m*, consulta *m*. **~ block** *n* edificio *m* de oficinas **~r** *n* oficial *m & f*; (*police* **~r**) policía *m & f*; (*as form of address*) agente

offici|al /əˈfɪʃl/ *adj* oficial. ● *n* funcionario *m* del Estado; (*of party, union*) dirigente *m & f*. **~ally** *adv* oficialmente. **~ous** /əˈfɪʃəs/ *adj* oficioso

offing /ˈɒfɪŋ/ *n*. **in the ~** en perspectiva

off: ~-licence *n* tienda *f* de vinos y licores. **~-putting** *adj* (*disconcerting*) desconcertante; (*disagreeable*) desagradable. **~set** *vt* (*pt* **-set**, *pres p* **-setting**) compensar. **~shore** *adj* (breeze) que sopla desde la tierra; (drilling) offshore; (well) submarino. ● *adv* a un lugar de mano de obra barata. **~side** /ɒfˈsaɪd/ *adj* (*Sport*) fuera de juego. **~spring** *n invar* prole *f*. **~-stage** /-ˈsteɪdʒ/ *adv* fuera del escenario. **~-white** *adj* color hueso

often /ˈɒfn/ *adv* a menudo, con frecuencia. **how ~?** ¿con qué frecuencia? **more ~** con más frecuencia

ogle /ˈəʊgl/ *vt* comerse con los ojos

ogre /ˈəʊgə(r)/ *n* ogro *m*

oh /əʊ/ *int* ¡ah!; (*expressing dismay*) ¡ay!

oil /ɔɪl/ *n* aceite *m*; (*petroleum*) petróleo *m*. ● *vt* lubricar. **~field** *n* yacimiento *m* petrolífero. **~ painting** *n* pintura *f* al óleo; (*picture*) óleo *m*. **~ rig** *n* plataforma *f* petrolífera. **~y** *adj* (substance) oleaginoso; (food) aceitoso

ointment /ˈɔɪntmənt/ *n* ungüento *m*

OK /əʊˈkeɪ/ *int* ¡vale!, ¡de acuerdo!, ¡bueno! (*LAm*). ● *adj* **~, thanks** bien, gracias. **the job's ~** el trabajo no está mal

old /əʊld/ *adj* (**-er**, **-est**) viejo; (*not modern*) antiguo; (*former*) antiguo; **an ~ friend** un viejo amigo. **how ~ is she?** ¿cuántos años tiene? **she is ten years ~** tiene diez años. **his ~er sister** su hermana mayor. **~ age** *n* vejez *f*. **~-fashioned** /-ˈfæʃənd/ *adj* anticuado

olive /ˈɒlɪv/ *n* aceituna *f*.

Olympic /əˈlɪmpɪk/ *adj* olímpico. **the ~s** *npl*, **the ~ Games** *npl* los Juegos Olímpicos

omelette /ˈɒmlɪt/ *n* tortilla *f* francesa, omelette *m* (*LAm*)

omen /ˈəʊmen/ *n* agüero *m*

omi|ssion /əˈmɪʃn/ *n* omisión *f*. **~t** /əʊˈmɪt/ *vt* (*pt* **omitted**) omitir

on /ɒn/ *prep* en, sobre; (*about*) sobre. **~ foot** a pie. **~ Monday** el lunes. **~ seeing** al ver. **I heard it ~ the radio** lo oí por la radio. ● *adv* (*light etc*) encendido, prendido (*LAm*); (*machine*) en marcha; (*tap*) abierto. **~ and ~** sin cesar. **and so ~** y así sucesivamente. **have a hat ~** llevar (puesto) un sombrero. **further ~** un poco más allá. **what's ~ at the Odeon?** ¿qué dan en el Odeon? **go ~** continuar. **later ~** más tarde

once /wʌns/ *adv* una vez; (*formerly*) antes. **at ~** inmediatamente. **~ upon a time there was...** érase una vez.... **~ and for all** de una vez por todas. ● *conj* una vez que

one /wʌn/ *adj* uno, (*before masculine singular noun*) un. **the ~ person I trusted** la única persona en la que confiaba.● *n* uno *m*. **~ by ~** uno a uno.. ● *pron* uno (*m*), una (*f*). **the blue ~** el/la azul. **this ~** éste/ésta. **~ another** el uno al otro

onerous /ˈɒnərəs/ *adj* (task) pesado

one: ~self /-ˈself/ *pron* (*reflexive*) se; (*after prep*) sí (mismo); (*emphatic use*) uno mismo, una misma. **by ~self** solo. **~-way** *adj* (street) de sentido único; (ticket) de ida, sencillo

onion /ˈʌnɪən/ *n* cebolla *f*

O

onlooker /ˈɒnlʊkə(r)/ *n* espectador *m*

only /ˈəʊnlɪ/ *adj* único. **she's an ~ child** es hija única. ● *adv* sólo, solamente. **~ just** (*barely*) apenas. **I've ~ just arrived** acabo de llegar. ● *conj* pero, sólo que

onset /ˈɒnset/ *n* comienzo *m*; (*of disease*) aparición *f*

onshore /ˈɒnʃɔ:(r)/ *adj* (breeze) que sopla desde el mar; (oil field) en tierra

onslaught /ˈɒnslɔ:t/ *n* ataque *m*

onus /ˈəʊnəs/ *n* responsabilidad *f*

onward(s) /ˈɒnwəd(z)/ *adj & adv* hacia adelante

ooze /u:z/ *vt/i* rezumar

opaque /əʊˈpeɪk/ *adj* opaco

open /ˈəʊpən/ *adj* abierto; (question) discutible. ● *n*. **in the ~** al aire libre. ● *vt/i* abrir. **~ing** *n* abertura *f*; (*beginning*) principio *m*. **~ly** *adv* abiertamente. **~-minded** /-ˈmaɪndɪd/ *adj* de actitud abierta

> **Open University** La universidad a distancia británica, fundada en 1969. La enseñanza se imparte fundamentalmente por correspondencia, mediante materiales impresos, material enviado por internet y programas de televisión emitidos por la BBC. También hay cursos de verano a los que los alumnos deben asistir. No se exigen calificaciones académicas para su ingreso.

opera /ˈɒprə/ *n* ópera *f*

operate /ˈɒpəreɪt/ *vt* manejar, operar (*Mex*) (machine). ● *vi* funcionar; (company) operar. **~ (on)** (*Med*) operar (a)

operatic /ɒpəˈrætɪk/ *adj* operístico

operation /ɒpəˈreɪʃn/ *n* operación *f*; (*Mec*) funcionamiento *m*; (*using of machine*) manejo *m*. **he had an ~** lo operaron. **in ~** en vigor. **~al** *adj* operacional

operative /ˈɒpərətɪv/ *adj*. **be ~** estar en vigor

operator *n* operador *m*

opinion /əˈpɪnɪən/ *n* opinión *f*. **in my ~** en mi opinión, a mi parecer

opponent /əˈpəʊnənt/ *n* adversario *m*; (*in sport*) contrincante *m & f*

opportun|e /ˈɒpətju:n/ *adj* oportuno. **~ist** /ɒpəˈtju:nɪst/ *n* oportunista *m & f*. **~ity** /ɒpəˈtju:nətɪ/ *n* oportunidad *f*

oppos|e /əˈpəʊz/ *vt* oponerse a. **be ~ed to** oponerse a, estar en contra de. **~ing** *adj* opuesto. **~ite** /ˈɒpəzɪt/ *adj* (*contrary*) opuesto; (*facing*) de enfrente. ● *n*. **the ~ite** lo contrario. **quite the ~ite** al contrario. ● *adv* enfrente. ● *prep* enfrente de. **~ite number** *n* homólogo *m*. **~ition** /ɒpəˈzɪʃn/ *n* oposición *f*; (*resistance*) resistencia *f*

oppress /əˈpres/ *vt* oprimir. **~ion** /-ʃn/ *n* opresión *f*. **~ive** *adj* (*cruel*) opresivo; (heat) sofocante

opt /ɒpt/ *vi*. **~ to** optar por. □ **~ out** *vi* decidir no tomar parte

optic|al /ˈɒptɪkl/ *adj* óptico. **~ian** /ɒpˈtɪʃn/ *n* óptico *m*

optimis|m /ˈɒptɪmɪzəm/ *n* optimismo *m*. **~t** *n* optimista *m & f*. **~tic** /-ˈmɪstɪk/ *adj* optimista

option /ˈɒpʃn/ *n* opción *f*. **~al** *adj* facultativo

or /ɔ:(r)/ *conj* o; (*before* **o-** *and* **ho-**) u; (*after negative*) ni. **~ else** si no, o bien

oral /ˈɔ:rəl/ *adj* oral. ● *n* [!] examen *m* oral

orange /ˈɒrɪndʒ/ *n* naranja *f*; (*colour*) naranja *m*. ● *adj* naranja. **~ade** /-ˈeɪd/ *n* naranjada *f*

orbit /ˈɔːbɪt/ *n* órbita *f*. ● *vt* orbitar

orchard /ˈɔːtʃəd/ *n* huerto *m*

orchestra /ˈɔːkɪstrə/ *n* orquesta *f*; (*Amer, in theatre*) platea *f*. **~l** /-ˈkestrəl/ *adj* orquestal. **~te** /-eɪt/ *vt* orquestar

orchid /ˈɔːkɪd/ *n* orquídea *f*

ordain /ɔːˈdeɪn/ *vt* (*Relig*) ordenar; (*decree*) decretar

ordeal /ɔːˈdiːl/ *n* dura prueba *f*

order /ˈɔːdə(r)/ *n* orden *m*; (*Com*) pedido *m*; (*command*) orden *f*. **in ~ that** para que. **in ~ to** para. ● *vt* (*command*) ordenar, mandar; (*Com*) pedir; (*in restaurant*) pedir, ordenar (*LAm*); encargar (book); llamar, ordenar (*LAm*) (taxi). **~ly** *adj* ordenado. ● *n* camillero *m*

ordinary /ˈɔːdɪnrɪ/ *adj* corriente; (*average*) medio; (*mediocre*) ordinario

O

ore /ɔː(r)/ *n* mena *f*

organ /ˈɔːgən/ *n* órgano *m*

organ|ic /ɔːˈgænɪk/ *adj* orgánico. **~ism** /ˈɔːgənɪzəm/ *n* organismo *m*. **~ist** /ˈɔːgənɪst/ *n* organista *m & f*. **~ization** /ɔːgənaɪˈzeɪʃn/ *n* organización *f*. **~ize** /ˈɔːgənaɪz/ *vt* organizar. **~izer** *n* organizador *m*

orgasm /ˈɔːgæzəm/ *n* orgasmo *m*

orgy /ˈɔːdʒɪ/ *n* orgía *f*

Orient /ˈɔːrɪənt/ *n* Oriente *m*. **~al** /-ˈentl/ *adj* oriental

orientat|e /ˈɔːrɪənteɪt/ *vt* orientar. **~ion** /-ˈteɪʃn/ *n* orientación *f*

origin /ˈɒrɪdʒɪn/ *n* origen *m*. **~al** /əˈrɪdʒənl/ *adj* original. **~ally** *adv* originariamente. **~ate** /əˈrɪdʒɪneɪt/ *vi*. **~ate from** provenir de

ornament /ˈɔːnəmənt/ *n* adorno *m*. **~al** /-ˈmentl/ *adj* de adorno

ornate /ɔːˈneɪt/ *adj* ornamentado; (style) recargado

ornithology /ɔːnɪˈθɒlədʒɪ/ *n* ornitología *f*

orphan /ˈɔːfn/ *n* huérfano *m*. ● *vt*. **be ~ed** quedar huérfano. **~age** /-ɪdʒ/ *n* orfanato *m*

orthodox /ˈɔːθədɒks/ *adj* ortodoxo

oscillate /ˈɒsɪleɪt/ *vi* oscilar

ostentatious /ɒstenˈteɪʃəs/ *adj* ostentoso

osteopath /ˈɒstɪəpæθ/ *n* osteópata *m & f*

ostracize /ˈɒstrəsaɪz/ *vt* hacerle vacío a

ostrich /ˈɒstrɪtʃ/ *n* avestruz *m*

other /ˈʌðə(r)/ *adj & pron* otro. **~ than** aparte de. **the ~ one** el otro. **~wise** *adv* de lo contrario, si no

otter /ˈɒtə(r)/ *n* nutria *f*

ouch /aʊtʃ/ *int* ¡ay!

ought /ɔːt/ *modal verb*. **I ~ to see it** debería verlo. **he ~ to have done it** debería haberlo hecho

ounce /aʊns/ *n* onza *f* (= *28.35 gr.*)

our /ˈaʊə(r)/ *adj* (*sing*) nuestro, nuestra, (*pl*) nuestros, nuestras. **~s** /ˈaʊəz/ *poss pron* (*sing*) nuestro, nuestra; (*pl*) nuestros, nuestras. **~s is red** el nuestro es rojo. **a friend of ~s** un amigo nuestro. **~selves** /-ˈselvz/ *pron* (*reflexive*) nos; (*used for emphasis and after prepositions*) nosotros mismos, nosotras mismas. **we behaved ~selves** nos portamos bien. **we did it ~selves** lo hicimos nosotros mismos/nosotras mismas

oust /aʊst/ *vt* desbancar; derrocar (government)

out /aʊt/ *adv* (*outside*) fuera, afuera

(*LAm*). (*not lighted, not on*) apagado; (*in blossom*) en flor; (*in error*) equivocado. **he's ~** (*not at home*) no está; **be ~ to** estar resuelto a. **~ of** *prep* (*from inside*) de; (*outside*) fuera, afuera (*LAm*). **five ~ of six** cinco de cada seis. **made ~ of** hecho de. **we're ~ of bread** nos hemos quedado sin pan. **~break** *n* (*of war*) estallido *m*; (*of disease*) brote *m*. **~burst** *n* arrebato *m*. **~cast** *n* paria *m & f*. **~come** *n* resultado *m*. **~cry** *n* protesta *f*. **~dated** /-ˈdeɪtɪd/ *adj* anticuado. **~do** /-ˈduː/ *vt* (*pt* **-did**, *pp* **-done**) superar. **~door** *adj* (clothes) de calle; (pool) descubierto. **~doors** /-ˈdɔːz/ *adv* al aire libre

outer /ˈaʊtə(r)/ *adj* exterior

out: ~fit *n* equipo *m*; (*clothes*) conjunto *m*. **~going** *adj* (minister etc) saliente; (*sociable*) abierto. **~goings** *npl* gastos *mpl*. **~grow** /-ˈgrəʊ/ *vt* (*pt* **-grew**, *pp* **-grown**) crecer más que (person). **he's ~grown his new shoes** le han quedado pequeños los zapatos nuevos. **~ing** *n* excursión *f*

outlandish /aʊtˈlændɪʃ/ *adj* extravagante

out: ~law *n* forajido *m*. ● *vt* proscribir. **~lay** *n* gastos *mpl*. **~let** *n* salida *f*; (*Com*) punto *m* de venta; (*Amer, Elec*) toma *f* de corriente. **~line** *n* contorno *m*; (*summary*) resumen *m*; (*plan of project*) esquema *m*. ● *vt* trazar; (*summarize*) esbozar. **~live** /-ˈlɪv/ *vt* sobrevivir a. **~look** *n* perspectivas *fpl*; (*attitude*) punto *m* de vista. **~lying** *adj* alejado. **~number** /-ˈnʌmbə(r)/ *vt* superar en número. **~-of-date** *adj* (ideas) desfasado; (clothes) pasado de moda. **~patient** *n* paciente *m* externo. **~post** *n* avanzada *f*. **~put** *n* producción *f*; (*of machine, worker*) rendimiento *m*. **~right** *adv* completamente; (*frankly*) abiertamente; (kill) en el acto. ● *adj* completo; (refusal) rotundo. **~set** *n* principio *m*. **~side** *adj & n* exterior (*m*). **at the ~** como máximo. ● /-ˈsaɪd/ *adv* fuera, afuera (*LAm*). ● *prep* fuera de. **~size** *adj* de talla gigante. **~skirts** *npl* afueras *fpl*. **~spoken** /-ˈspəʊkn/ *adj* directo, franco. **~standing** /-ˈstændɪŋ/ *adj* excepcional; (debt) pendiente. **~stretched** /aʊtˈstretʃt/ *adj* extendido. **~strip** /-ˈstrɪp/ *vt* (*pt* **-stripped**) (*run faster than*) tomarle la delantera a; (*exceed*) sobrepasar. **~ward** /-wəd/ *adj* (appearance) exterior; (sign) externo; (journey) de ida. **~wardly** *adv* por fuera, exteriormente. **~(s)** *adv* hacia afuera. **~weigh** /-ˈweɪ/ *vt* ser mayor que. **~wit** /-ˈwɪt/ *vt* (*pt* **-witted**) burlar

oval /ˈəʊvl/ *adj* ovalado, oval. ● *n* óvalo *m*

> **Oval Office** El Despacho Oval es el despacho oficial del Presidente de los Estados Unidos, ubicado en el ala oeste de la Casa Blanca. La forma oval fue determinada por George Washington, lo que le permitiría tener contacto visual con todos durante las reuniones. Originariamente, quería que todas las habitaciones de la Casa Blanca fueran ovales, pero pronto comprendió que este diseño era poco práctico.

ovary /ˈəʊvərɪ/ *n* ovario *m*

ovation /əʊˈveɪʃn/ *n* ovación *f*

oven /ˈʌvn/ *n* horno *m*

over /ˈəʊvə(r)/ *prep* por encima de; (*across*) al otro lado de; (*during*) durante; (*more than*) más de. **~ and above** por encima de. ● *adv* por encima; (*ended*) terminado; (*more*) más; (*in excess*) de sobra. **~ again** otra vez. **~ and ~** una y otra vez. **~ here** por aquí. **~ there** por allí. **all ~** (*finished*) acabado; (*everywhere*) por todas partes

over... /ˈəʊvə(r)/ *pref* excesivamente, demasiado

over: ~all /-ˈɔːl/ *adj* global; (length, cost) total. ● *adv* en conjunto. ● /ˈəʊvərɔːl/ *n*, **~alls** *npl* mono *m*, overol *m* (*LAm*); (*Amer, dungarees*) peto *m*, overol *m*. **~awe** /-ˈɔː/ *vt* intimidar. **~balance** /-ˈbæləns/ *vi* perder el equilibrio. **~bearing** /-ˈbeərɪŋ/ *adj* dominante. **~board** *adv* (throw) por la borda. **~cast** /-ˈkɑːst/ *adj* (day) nublado; (sky) cubierto. **~charge** /-ˈtʃɑːdʒ/ *vt* cobrarle de más a. **~coat** *n* abrigo *m*. **~come** /-ˈkʌm/ *vt* (*pt* **-came**, *pp* **-come**) superar, vencer. **~crowded** /-ˈkraʊdɪd/ *adj* abarrotado (de gente). **~do** /-ˈduː/ *vt* (*pt* **-did**, *pp* **-done**) exagerar; (*Culin*) recocer. **~dose** *n* sobredosis *f*. **~draft** *n* descubierto *m*. **~draw** /-ˈdrɔː/ *vt* (*pt* **-drew**, *pp* **-drawn**) girar en descubierto. **be ~drawn** tener un descubierto. **~due** /-ˈdjuː/ *adj*. **the book is a month ~due** el plazo de devolución del libro venció hace un mes. **~estimate** /-ˈestɪmeɪt/ *vt* sobreestimar. **~flow** /-ˈfləʊ/ *vi* desbordarse. ● *n* /-fləʊ/ (*excess*) exceso *m*; (*outlet*) rebosadero *m*. **~flow car park** *n* estacionamento *m* extra (*LAm*), aparcamiento *m* extra (*Esp*). **~grown** /-ˈgrəʊn/ *adj* demasiado grande; (garden) lleno de maleza. **~haul** /-ˈhɔːl/ *vt* revisar. ● /-hɔːl/ *n* revisión *f*. **~head** /-ˈhed/ *adv* por encima. ● /-hed/ *adj* de arriba. **~heads** /-hedz/ *npl*, **~head** *n* (*Amer*) gastos *mpl* indirectos. **~hear** /-ˈhɪə(r)/ *vt* (*pt* **-heard**) oír por casualidad. **~joyed** /-ˈdʒɔɪd/ *adj* encantado. **~land** *a/adv* por tierra. **~lap** /-ˈlæp/ *vi* (*pt* **-lapped**) traslaparse. **~leaf** /-ˈliːf/ *adv* al dorso. **~load** /-ˈləʊd/ *vt* sobrecargar. **~look** /-ˈlʊk/ *vt* (room) dar a; (*not notice*) pasar por alto; (*disregard*) disculpar. **~night** /-ˈnaɪt/ *adv* durante la noche. **stay ~night** quedarse a pasar la noche. ● *adj* (journey) de noche; (stay) de una noche. **~pass** *n* paso *m* elevado, paso *m* a desnivel (*Mex*). **~pay** /-ˈpeɪ/ *vt* (*pt* **-paid**) pagar demasiado. **~power** /-ˈpaʊə(r)/ *vt* dominar (opponent); (emotion) abrumar. **~powering** /-ˈpaʊərɪŋ/ *adj* (smell) muy fuerte; (desire) irrestible. **~priced** /-ˈpraɪst/ *adj* demasiado caro. **~rated** /-ˈreɪtɪd/ *adj* sobrevalorado. **~react** /-rɪˈækt/ *vi* reaccionar en forma exagerada. **~ride** /-ˈraɪd/ *vt* (*pt* **-rode**, *pp* **-ridden**) invalidar. **~riding** /-ˈraɪdɪŋ/ *adj* dominante. **~rule** /-ˈruːl/ *vt* anular; rechazar (objection). **~run** /-ˈrʌn/ *vt* (*pt* **-ran**, *pp* **-run**, *pres p* **-running**) invadir; exceder (limit). **~seas** /-ˈsiːz/ *adj* (trade) exterior; (investments) en el exterior; (visitor) extranjero. ● *adv* al extranjero. **~see** /-ˈsiː/ *vt* (*pt* **-saw**, *pp* **-seen**) supervisar. **~seer** /-sɪə(r)/ *n* capataz *m & f*, supervisor *m*. **~shadow** /-ˈʃædəʊ/ *vt* eclipsar. **~shoot** /-ˈʃuːt/ *vt* (*pt* **-shot**) excederse. **~sight** *n* descuido *m*. **~sleep** /-ˈsliːp/ *vi* (*pt*

-slept) quedarse dormido. **~step** /-'step/ *vt* (*pt* **-stepped**) sobrepasar. **~step the mark** pasarse de la raya

overt /'əʊvɜ:t/ *adj* manifiesto

over:: ~take /-'teɪk/ *vt/i* (*pt* **-took**, *pp* **-taken**) sobrepasar; (*Auto*) adelantar, rebasar (*Mex*). **~throw** /-'θrəʊ/ *vt* (*pt* **-threw**, *pp* **-thrown**) derrocar. **~time** *n* horas *fpl* extra

overture /'əʊvətjʊə(r)/ *n* obertura *f*

over:: ~turn /-'tɜ:n/ *vt* darle la vuelta a. ● *vi* volcar. **~weight** /-'weɪt/ *adj* demasiado gordo. **be ~weight** pesar demasiado. **~whelm** /-'welm/ *vt* aplastar; (*with emotion*) abrumar. **~whelming** *adj* aplastante; (*fig*) abrumador. **~work** /-'wɜ:k/ *vt* hacer trabajar demasiado. ● *vi* trabajar demasiado. ● *n* agotamiento *m*

ow|e /əʊ/ *vt* deber. **~ing to** debido a

owl /aʊl/ *n* búho *m*

own /əʊn/ *adj* propio. **my ~ house** mi propia casa. ● *pron.* **it's my ~** es mío (propio)/mía (propia). **on one's ~** solo. **get one's ~ back** 🄸 desquitarse. ● *vt* tener. □ **~ up** *vi.* 🄸 confesarse culpable. **~er** *n* propietario *m*, dueño *m*. **~ership** *n* propiedad *f*

oxygen /'ɒksɪdʒən/ *n* oxígeno *m*

> **Oxbridge** Término usado para referirse conjuntamente a las universidades más antiguas y de más prestigio en el Reino Unido; Oxford y Cambridge, especialmente cuando se quiere destacar el ambiente de privilegio con el que se las relaciona. Últimamente se han hecho grandes esfuerzos para atraer a estudiantes de todos los medios sociales.

oyster /'ɔɪstə(r)/ *n* ostra *f*

Pp

p *abbr* (= **pence, penny**) penique(s) (*m*(*pl*))

p. (*pl* **pp.**) (= **page**) pág., p.

pace /peɪs/ *n* paso *m*. **keep ~ with s.o.** seguirle el ritmo a uno. ● *vi*. **~ up and down** andar de un lado para otro. **~maker** *n* (*runner*) liebre *f*; (*Med*) marcapasos *m*

Pacific /pə'sɪfɪk/ *n*. **the ~ (Ocean)** el (Océano) Pacífico *m*

pacif|ist /'pæsɪfɪst/ *n* pacifista *m & f*. **~y** /'pæsɪfaɪ/ *vt* apaciguar

pack /pæk/ *n* fardo *m*; (*of cigarettes*) paquete *m*, cajetilla *f*; (*of cards*) baraja *f*; (*of hounds*) jauría *f*; (*of wolves*) manada *f*. **a ~ of lies** una sarta de mentiras. ● *vt* empaquetar; hacer (suitcase); (*press down*) apisonar. ● *vi* hacer la maleta, empacar (*LAm*). **~age** /-ɪdʒ/ *n* paquete *m*. **~age holiday** *n* vacaciones *fpl* organizadas. **~ed** /pækt/ *adj* lleno (de gente). **~et** /'pækɪt/ *n* paquete *m*

pact /pækt/ *n* pacto *m*, acuerdo *m*

pad /pæd/ *n* (*for writing*) bloc *m*. **shoulder ~s** hombreras *fpl*. ● *vt* (*pt* **padded**) rellenar

paddle /'pædl/ *n* pala *f*. ● *vi* mojarse los pies; (*in canoe*) remar (con pala)

paddock /'pædək/ *n* prado *m*

o p

padlock /'pædlɒk/ *n* candado *m*. ● *vt* cerrar con candado

paed|iatrician /pi:dɪə'trɪʃn/ *n* pediatra *m & f*. **~ophile** /'pi:dəfaɪl/ *n* pedófilo *m*

pagan /'peɪgən/ *adj & n* pagano (*m*)

page /peɪdʒ/ *n* página *f*; (*attendant*) paje *m*; (*in hotel*) botones *m*. ● *vt* llamar por megafonía/por buscapersonas, vocear (*LAm*)

paid /peɪd/ *see* PAY. ● *adj*. **put ~ to** [I] acabar con

pail /peɪl/ *n* balde *m*, cubo *m*

pain /peɪn/ *n* dolor *m*. **I have a ~ in my back** me duele la espalda. *m*. **be in ~** tener dolores. **be a ~ in the neck** [I] ser un pesado; (*thing*) ser una lata. ● *vt* doler. **~ful** *adj* doloroso. **it's very ~ful** duele mucho. **~-killer** *n* analgésico *m*. **~less** *adj* indoloro. **~staking** /'peɪnzteɪkɪŋ/ *adj* concienzudo

paint /peɪnt/ *n* pintura *f*. ● *vt/i* pintar. **~er** *n* pintor *m*. **~ing** *n* (*medium*) pintura *f*; (*picture*) cuadro *m*

P

pair /peə(r)/ *n* par *m*; (*of people*) pareja *f*. **a ~ of trousers** unos pantalones. □ **~off, ~ up** *vi* formar parejas

pajamas /pə'dʒɑ:məz/ *npl* (*Amer*) pijama *m*

Pakistan /pɑ:kɪ'stɑ:n/ *n* Pakistán *m*. **~i** *adj & n* paquistaní (*m & f*)

pal /pæl/ *n* [I] amigo *m*

palace /'pælɪs/ *n* palacio *m*

palat|able /'pælətəbl/ *adj* agradable. **~e** /'pælət/ *n* paladar *m*

pale /peɪl/ *adj* (**-er, -est**) pálido. **go ~, turn ~** palidecer. **~ness** *n* palidez *f*

Palestin|e /'pælɪstaɪn/ *n* Palestina *f*. **~ian** /-'stɪnɪən/ *adj & n* palestino (*m*)

palette /'pælɪt/ *n* paleta *f*

palm /pɑ:m/ *n* palma *f*. □ **~ off** *vt* encajar (**on** a). **P~ Sunday** *n* Domingo *m* de Ramos

palpable /'pælpəbl/ *adj* palpable

palpitat|e /'pælpɪteɪt/ *vi* palpitar. **~ion** /-'teɪʃn/ *n* palpitación *f*

pamper /'pæmpə(r)/ *vt* mimar

pamphlet /'pæmflɪt/ *n* folleto *m*

pan /pæn/ *n* cacerola *f*; (*for frying*) sartén *f*

panacea /pænə'sɪə/ *n* panacea *f*

Panama /'pænəmɑ:/ *n* Panamá *m*. **~nian** /-'meɪnɪən/ *adj & n* panameño (*m*)

pancake /'pænkeɪk/ *n* crep(e) *m*, panqueque *m* (*LAm*)

panda /'pændə/ *n* panda *m*

pandemonium /pændɪ'məʊnɪəm/ *n* pandemonio *m*

pander /'pændə(r)/ *vi*. **~ to s.o.** consentirle los caprichos a uno

pane /peɪn/ *n* vidrio *m*, cristal *m*

panel /'pænl/ *n* panel *m*; (*group of people*) jurado *m*. **~ling** *n* paneles *mpl*

pang /pæŋ/ *n* punzada *f*

panic /'pænɪk/ *n* pánico *m*. ● *vi* (*pt* **panicked**) dejarse llevar por el pánico. **~-stricken** *adj* aterrorizado

panoram|a /pænə'rɑ:mə/ *n* panorama *m*. **~ic** /-'ræmɪk/ *adj* panorámico

pansy /'pænzɪ/ *n* (*flower*) pensamiento *m*

pant /pænt/ *vi* jadear

panther /'pænθə(r)/ *n* pantera *f*

panties /'pæntɪz/ *npl* bragas *fpl*, calzones *mpl* (*LAm*), pantaletas *fpl* (*Mex*)

pantihose /'pæntɪhəuz/ *npl see* PANTYHOSE

pantomime /'pæntəmaɪm/ *n* pantomima *f*

pantry /ˈpæntrɪ/ *n* despensa *f*

pants /pænts/ *npl* (*man's*) calzoncillos *mpl*; (*woman's*) bragas *fpl*, calzones *mpl* (*LAm*), pantaletas *fpl* (*Mex*); (*Amer, trousers*) pantalones *mpl*

pantyhose /ˈpæntɪhəʊz/ *npl* (*Amer*) panty *m*, medias *fpl*, pantimedias *fpl* (*Mex*)

paper /ˈpeɪpə(r)/ *n* papel *m*; (*newspaper*) diario *m*, periódico *m*; (*exam*) examen *m*; (*document*) documento *m*. ● *vt* empapelar, tapizar (*Mex*). **~back** *n* libro *m* en rústica. **~ clip** *n* sujetapapeles *m*, clip *m*. **~weight** *n* pisapapeles *m*. **~work** *n* papeleo *m*, trabajo *m* administrativo

parable /ˈpærəbl/ *n* parábola *f*

parachut|e /ˈpærəʃuːt/ *n* paracaídas *m*. ● *vi* saltar en paracaídas. **~ist** *n* paracaidista *m & f*

parade /pəˈreɪd/ *n* desfile *m*; (*Mil*) formación *f*. ● *vi* desfilar. ● *vt* hacer alarde de

paradise /ˈpærədaɪs/ *n* paraíso *m*

paraffin /ˈpærəfɪn/ *n* queroseno *m*

paragraph /ˈpærəgrɑːf/ *n* párrafo *m*

Paraguay /ˈpærəgwaɪ/ *n* Paraguay *m*. **~an** *adj & n* paraguayo (*m*)

parallel /ˈpærəlel/ *adj* paralelo. ● *n* paralelo *m*; (*line*) paralela *f*

paraly|se /ˈpærəlaɪz/ *vt* paralizar. **~sis** /pəˈræləsɪs/ *n* (*pl* **-ses** /-siːz/) parálisis *f*

parameter /pəˈræmɪtə(r)/ *n* parámetro *m*

paranoia /pærəˈnɔɪə/ *n* paranoia *f*

parapet /ˈpærəpɪt/ *n* parapeto *m*

paraphernalia /pærəfəˈneɪlɪə/ *n* trastos *mpl*

parasite /ˈpærəsaɪt/ *n* parásito *m*

paratrooper /ˈpærətruːpə(r)/ *n* paracaidista *m* (del ejército)

parcel /ˈpɑːsl/ *n* paquete *m*

parch /pɑːtʃ/ *vt* resecar. **be ~ed** [I] estar muerto de sed

parchment /ˈpɑːtʃmənt/ *n* pergamino *m*

pardon /ˈpɑːdn/ *n* perdón *m*; (*Jurid*) indulto *m*. **I beg your ~** perdón. **(I beg your) ~?** ¿cómo?, ¿mande? (*Mex*). ● *vt* perdonar; (*Jurid*) indultar. **~ me?** (*Amer*) ¿cómo?

parent /ˈpeərənt/ *n* (*father*) padre *m*; (*mother*) madre *f*. **my ~s** mis padres. **~al** /pəˈrentl/ *adj* de los padres

parenthesis /pəˈrenθəsɪs/ *n* (*pl* **-theses** /-siːz/) paréntesis *m*

parenthood /ˈpeərənthʊd/ *n* el ser padre/madre

Paris /ˈpærɪs/ *n* París *m*

parish /ˈpærɪʃ/ *n* parroquia *f*; (*municipal*) distrito *m*. **~ioner** /pəˈrɪʃənə(r)/ *n* feligrés *m*

park /pɑːk/ *n* parque *m*. **~-and-ride** estacionamiento *m* disuasorio (*LAm*), aparcamiento *m* disuasorio (*Esp*). ● *vt/i* aparcar, estacionar (*LAm*)

parking: /ˈpɑːkɪŋ/ *n*: **~ lot** *n* (*Amer*) aparcamiento *m*, estacionamiento *m* (*LAm*). **~ meter** *n* parquímetro *m*

parkway /ˈpɑːkweɪ/ *n* (*Amer*) carretera *f* ajardinada

parliament /ˈpɑːləmənt/ *n* parlamento *m*. **~ary** /-ˈmentrɪ/ *adj* parlamentario

Parliament El Parlamento británico, el más alto organismo legislativo. Está formado por la Cámara de los Lores y la Cámara de los Comunes. La primera, consta de 703 miembros, en la mayoría nombrados, con un número de cargos hereditarios, lo que es objeto de reforma en la actualidad. La Cámara de los Comunes consta de 659 miembros elegidos por el pueblo. Ver ▷**Dáil Éireann**, ▷**Scottish Parliament**, ▷**Welsh Assembly**.

parlour /'pɑːlə(r)/ *n* salón *m*

parochial /pə'rəʊkɪəl/ *adj* (*fig*) provinciano

parody /'pærədɪ/ *n* parodia *f*. ● *vt* parodiar

parole /pə'rəʊl/ *n* libertad *f* condicional

parrot /'pærət/ *n* loro *m*, papagayo *m*

parsley /'pɑːslɪ/ *n* perejil *m*

parsnip /'pɑːsnɪp/ *n* pastinaca *f*

part /pɑːt/ *n* parte *f*; (*of machine*) pieza *f*; (*of serial*) episodio *m*; (*in play*) papel *m*; (*Amer, in hair*) raya *f*. **take ~ in** tomar parte en, participar en. **for the most ~** en su mayor parte. ● *adv* en parte. ● *vt* separar. ● *vi* separarse. □ **~ with** *vt* desprenderse de

P

partial /'pɑːʃl/ *adj* parcial. **be ~ to** tener debilidad por. **~ly** *adv* parcialmente

participa|nt /pɑː'tɪsɪpənt/ *n* participante *m & f*. **~te** /-peɪt/ *vi* participar. **~tion** /-'peɪʃn/ *n* participación *f*

particle /'pɑːtɪkl/ *n* partícula *f*

particular /pə'tɪkjʊlə(r)/ *adj* particular; (*precise*) meticuloso; (*fastidious*) quisquilloso. **in ~** en particular. ● *n* detalle *m*. **~ly** *adv* particularmente; (*specifically*) específicamente

parting /'pɑːtɪŋ/ *n* despedida *f*; (*in hair*) raya *f*. ● *adj* de despedida

partition /pɑː'tɪʃn/ *n* partición *f*; (*wall*) tabique *m*. ● *vt* dividir

partly /'pɑːtlɪ/ *adv* en parte

partner /'pɑːtnə(r)/ *n* socio *m*; (*Sport*) pareja *f*. **~ship** *n* asociación *f*; (*Com*) sociedad *f*

partridge /'pɑːtrɪdʒ/ *n* perdiz *f*

part-time /pɑːt'taɪm/ *adj & adv* a tiempo parcial, de medio tiempo (*LAm*)

party /'pɑːtɪ/ *n* reunión *f*, fiesta *f*; (*group*) grupo *m*; (*Pol*) partido *m*; (*Jurid*) parte *f*

pass /pɑːs/ *vt* (*hand, convey*) pasar; (*go past*) pasar por delante de; (*overtake*) adelantar, rebasar (*Mex*); (*approve*) aprobar (exam, bill, law); pronunciar (judgement). ● *vi* pasar; (pain) pasarse; (*Sport*) pasar la pelota. □ **~ away** *vi* fallecer. □ **~ down** *vt* transmitir. □ **~ out** *vi* desmayarse. □ **~ round** *vt* distribuir. □ **~ up** *vt* ⊡ dejar pasar. ● *n* (*permit*) pase *m*; (*ticket*) abono *m*; (*in mountains*) puerto *m*, desfiladero *m*; (*Sport*) pase *m*; (*in exam*) aprobado *m*. **make a ~ at** ⊡ intentar besar. **~able** *adj* pasable; (road) transitable

passage /'pæsɪdʒ/ *n* (*voyage*) travesía *f*; (*corridor*) pasillo *m*; (*alleyway*) pasaje *m*; (*in book*) pasaje *m*

passenger /'pæsɪndʒə(r)/ *n* pasajero *m*

passer-by /pɑːsə'baɪ/ *n* (*pl* **passers-by**) transeúnte *m & f*

passion /'pæʃn/ *n* pasión *f*. **~ate** /-ət/ *adj* apasionado. **~ately** *adv* apasionadamente

passive /'pæsɪv/ *adj* pasivo

Passover /'pɑːsəʊvə(r)/ *n* Pascua *f* de los hebreos

pass: ~port *n* pasaporte *m*. **~word** *n* contraseña *f*

past /pɑ:st/ *adj* anterior; (life) pasado; (week, year) último. **in times ~** en tiempos pasados. ● *n* pasado *m*. **in the ~** (*formerly*) antes, antiguamente. ● *prep* por delante de; (*beyond*) más allá de. **it's twenty four** son las cuatro y veinte. ● *adv*. **drive ~** pasar en coche. **go ~** pasar

paste /peɪst/ *n* pasta *f*; (*glue*) engrudo *m*; (*wallpaper ~*) pegamento *m*; (*jewellery*) estrás *m*

pastel /'pæstl/ *adj & n* pastel (*m*)

pasteurize /'pɑ:stʃəraɪz/ *vt* pasteurizar

pastime /'pɑ:staɪm/ *n* pasatiempo *m*

pastry /'peɪstrɪ/ *n* masa *f*; (*cake*) pastelito *m*

pasture /'pɑ:stʃə(r)/ *n* pasto(s) *mpl*

pasty /'pæstɪ/ *n* empanadilla *f*, empanada *f* (*LAm*)

pat /pæt/ *vt* (*pt* **patted**) darle palmaditas. ● *n* palmadita *f*; (*of butter*) porción *f*

patch /pætʃ/ *n* (*on clothes*) remiendo *m*, parche *m*; (*over eye*) parche *m*. **a bad ~** una mala racha. ● *vt* remendar. □ **~ up** *vt* hacerle un arreglo a

patent /'peɪtnt/ *adj* patente. ● *n* patente *f*. ● *vt* patentar. **~ leather** *n* charol *m*. **~ly** *adv*. **it's ~ly obvious that...** está clarísimo que...

patern|al /pə'tɜ:nl/ *adj* paterno. **~ity** /-ətɪ/ *n* paternidad *f*

path /pɑ:θ/ *n* (*pl* **-s**/pɑ:ðz/) sendero *m*; (*Sport*) pista *f*; (*of rocket*) trayectoria *f*; (*fig*) camino *m*

pathetic /pə'θetɪk/ *adj* (*pitiful*) patético; (excuse) pobre. **don't be so ~** no seas tan pusilánime

patien|ce /'peɪʃns/ *n* paciencia *f*. **~t** *adj & n* paciente (*m & f*). **be ~t with s.o.** tener paciencia con uno. **~tly** *adv* pacientemente

patio /'pætɪəʊ/ *n* (*pl* **-os**) patio *m*

patriot /'pætrɪət/ *n* patriota *m & f*. **~ic** /-'ɒtɪk/ *adj* patriótico. **~ism** *n* patriotismo *m*

patrol /pə'trəʊl/ *n* patrulla *f*. ● *vt/i* patrullar

patron /'peɪtrən/ *n* (*of the arts*) mecenas *m & f*; (*of charity*) patrocinador *m*; (*customer*) cliente *m & f*. **~age** /'pætrənɪdʒ/ *n* (*sponsorship*) patrocinio *m*; (*of the arts*) mecenazgo *m*. **~ize** /'pætrənaɪz/ *vt* ser cliente de; (*fig*) tratar con condescendencia. **~izing** *adj* condescendiente

pattern /'pætn/ *n* diseño *m*; (*sample*) muestra *f*; (*in dressmaking*) patrón *m*

paunch /pɔ:ntʃ/ *n* panza *f*

pause /pɔ:z/ *n* pausa *f*. ● *vi* hacer una pausa

pave /peɪv/ *vt* pavimentar; (*with flagstones*) enlosar. **~ment** *n* pavimento *m*; (*at side of road*) acera *f*, banqueta *f* (*Mex*)

paving stone /'peɪvɪŋstəʊn/ *n* losa *f*

paw /pɔ:/ *n* pata *f*

pawn /pɔ:n/ *n* (*Chess*) peón *m*; (*fig*) títere *m*. ● *vt* empeñar. **~broker** *n* prestamista *m & f*

pay /peɪ/ *vt* (*pt* **paid**) pagar; prestar (attention); hacer (compliment, visit). **~ cash** pagar al contado. ● *vi* pagar; (*be profitable*) rendir. ● *n* paga *f*. **in the ~ of** al servicio de. □ **~ back** *vt* devolver; pagar (loan). □ **~ in** *vt* ingresar, depositar (*LAm*). □ **~ off** *vt* cancelar, saldar (debt). *vi*

P

valer la pena. □ ~ **up** *vi* pagar. **~able** *adj* pagadero. **~ment** *n* pago *m*. **~roll** *n* nómina *f*

pea /piː/ *n* guisante *m*, arveja *f* (*LAm*), chícharo *m* (*Mex*)

peace /piːs/ *n* paz *f*. ~ **of mind** tranquilidad *f*. **~ful** *adj* tranquilo. **~maker** *n* conciliador *m*

peach /piːtʃ/ *n* melocotón *m*, durazno *m* (*LAm*)

peacock /ˈpiːkɒk/ *n* pavo *m* real

peak /piːk/ *n* cumbre *f*; (*of career*) apogeo *m*; (*maximum*) máximo *m*. ~ **hours** *npl* horas *fpl* de mayor demanda (o consumo etc)

peal /piːl/ *n* repique *m*. **~s of laughter** risotadas *fpl*

peanut /ˈpiːnʌt/ *n* cacahuete *m*, maní *m* (*LAm*), cacahuate *m* (*Mex*)

pear /peə(r)/ *n* pera *f*. ~ **(tree)** peral *m*

pearl /pɜːl/ *n* perla *f*

peasant /ˈpeznt/ *n* campesino *m*

peat /piːt/ *n* turba *f*

pebble /ˈpebl/ *n* guijarro *m*

P

peck /pek/ *vt* picotear. ● *n* picotazo *m*; (*kiss*) besito *m*

peculiar /pɪˈkjuːlɪə(r)/ *adj* raro; (*special*) especial. **~ity** /-ˈærətɪ/ *n* rareza *f*; (*feature*) particularidad *f*

pedal /ˈpedl/ *n* pedal *m*. ● *vi* pedalear

pedantic /pɪˈdæntɪk/ *adj* pedante

peddle /ˈpedl/ *vt* vender por las calles

pedestal /ˈpedɪstl/ *n* pedestal *m*

pedestrian /pɪˈdestrɪən/ *n* peatón *m*. ~ **crossing** paso *m* de peatones. ● *adj* pedestre; (*dull*) prosaico

pedigree /ˈpedɪgriː/ linaje *m*; (*of animal*) pedigrí *m*. ● *adj* (animal) de raza

peek /piːk/ *vi* mirar a hurtadillas

peel /piːl/ *n* piel *f*, cáscara *f*. ● *vt* pelar (fruit, vegetables). ● *vi* pelarse

peep /piːp/ *vi*. ~ **at** echarle un vistazo a. ● *n* (*look*) vistazo *m*; (*bird sound*) pío *m*

peer /pɪə(r)/ *vi* mirar. ~ **at** escudriñar. ● *n* (*equal*) par *m* & *f*; (*contemporary*) coetáneo *m*; (*lord*) par *m*. **~age** /-ɪdʒ/ *n* nobleza *f*

peg /peg/ *n* (*in ground*) estaca *f*; (*on violin*) clavija *f*; (*for washing*) pinza *f*; (*hook*) gancho *m*; (*for tent*) estaquilla *f*. **off the** ~ de confección. ● *vt* (*pt* **pegged**) sujetar (*con estacas, etc*); fijar (precios)

pejorative /pɪˈdʒɒrətɪv/ *adj* peyorativo, despectivo

pelican /ˈpelɪkən/ *n* pelícano *m*

pellet /ˈpelɪt/ *n* bolita *f*; (*for gun*) perdigón *m*

pelt /pelt/ *n* pellejo *m*. ● *vt*. ~ **s.o. with sth** lanzarle algo a uno. ● *vi*. ~ **with rain,** ~ **down** llover a cántaros

pelvis /ˈpelvɪs/ *n* pelvis *f*

pen /pen/ (*for writing*) pluma *f*; (*ballpoint*) bolígrafo *m*; (*sheep* ~) redil *m*; (*cattle* ~) corral *m*

penal /ˈpiːnl/ *adj* penal. **~ize** *vt* sancionar. **~ty** /ˈpenltɪ/ *n* pena *f*; (*fine*) multa *f*; (*in soccer*) penalty *m*; (*in US football*) castigo *m*. **~ty kick** *n* (*in soccer*) penalty *m*

penance /ˈpenəns/ *n* penitencia *f*

pence /pens/ *see* **PENNY**

pencil /ˈpensl/ *n* lápiz *m*. ● *vt* (*pt* **pencilled**) escribir con lápiz. **~-sharpener** *n* sacapuntas *m*

pendulum /ˈpendjʊləm/ *n* péndulo *m*

penetrat|e /ˈpenɪtreɪt/ *vt/i* penetrar. **~ing** *adj* penetrante. **~ion**

/-ˈtreɪʃn/ *n* penetración *f*

penguin /ˈpeŋgwɪn/ *n* pingüino *m*

penicillin /penɪˈsɪlɪn/ *n* penicilina *f*

peninsula /pəˈnɪnsjʊlə/ *n* península *f*

penis /ˈpiːnɪs/ *n* pene *m*

pen: ~knife /ˈpennaɪf/ *n* (*pl* **pen-knives**) navaja *f*. **~-name** *n* seudónimo *m*

penn|iless /ˈpenɪlɪs/ *adj* sin un céntimo. **~y** /ˈpenɪ/ *n* (*pl* **pennies** *or* **pence**) penique *m*

pension /ˈpenʃn/ *n* pensión *f*; (*for retirement*) pensión *f* de jubilación. **~er** *n* jubilado *m*

pensive /ˈpensɪv/ *adj* pensativo

Pentecost /ˈpentɪkɒst/ *n* Pentecostés *m*

penthouse /ˈpenthaʊs/ *n* penthouse *m*

pent-up /pentˈʌp/ *adj* reprimido; (*confined*) encerrado

penultimate /penˈʌltɪmət/ *adj* penúltimo

people /ˈpiːpl/ *npl* gente *f*; (*citizens*) pueblo *m*. **~ say (that)** se dice que, dicen que. **English ~** los ingleses. **young ~** los jóvenes. **the ~** (*nation*) el pueblo. ● *vt* poblar

pepper /ˈpepə(r)/ *n* pimienta *f*; (*vegetable*) pimiento *m*. ● *vt* (*intersperse*) salpicar (**with** de). **~box** *n* (*Amer*) pimentero *m*. **~corn** *n* grano *m* de pimienta. **~mint** *n* menta *f*; (*sweet*) caramelo *m* de menta. **~pot** *n* pimentero *m*

per /pɜː(r)/ *prep* por. **~ annum** al año. **~ cent** *see* PERCENT. **~ head** por cabeza, por persona. **ten miles ~ hour** diez millas por hora

perceive /pəˈsiːv/ *vt* percibir; (*notice*) darse cuenta de

percent, per cent /pəˈsent/ *n* (*no pl*) porcentaje *m*. ● *adv* por ciento. **~age** /-ɪdʒ/ *n* porcentaje *m*

percepti|ble /pəˈseptəbl/ *adj* perceptible. **~on** /-ʃn/ *n* percepción *f*. **~ve** /-tɪv/ *adj* perspicaz

perch /pɜːtʃ/ *n* (*of bird*) percha *f*; (*fish*) perca *f*. ● *vi* (bird) posarse. **~ on** (person) sentarse en el borde de

percolat|e /ˈpɜːkəleɪt/ *vi* filtrarse. **~or** *n* cafetera *f* eléctrica

percussion /pəˈkʌʃn/ *n* percusión *f*

perfect /ˈpɜːfɪkt/ *adj* perfecto; (place, day) ideal. ● /pəˈfekt/ *vt* perfeccionar. **~ion** /pəˈfekʃn/ *n* perfección *f*. **to ~ion** a la perfección. **~ly** /ˈpɜːfɪktlɪ/ *adv* perfectamente

perform /pəˈfɔːm/ *vt* desempeñar (function, role); ejecutar (task); realizar (experiment); representar (*play*); (*Mus*) interpretar. **~ an operation** (*Med*) operar. ● *vi* (actor) actuar; (musician) tocar; (*produce results*) (vehicle) responder; (company) rendir. **~ance** /-əns/ *n* ejecución *f*; (*of play*) representación *f*; (*of actor, musician*) interpretación *f*; (*of team*) actuación *f*; (*of car*) rendimiento *m*. **~er** *n* (*actor*) actor *m*; (*entertainer*) artista *m & f*

perfume /ˈpɜːfjuːm/ *n* perfume *m*

perhaps /pəˈhæps/ *adv* quizá(s), tal vez, a lo mejor

peril /ˈperəl/ *n* peligro *m*. **~ous** *adj* arriesgado, peligroso

perimeter /pəˈrɪmɪtə(r)/ *n* perímetro *m*

period /ˈpɪərɪəd/ *n* período *m*; (*in history*) época *f*; (*lesson*) clase *f*; (*Amer, Gram*) punto *m*; (*menstruation*) período *m*, regla *f*. ● *adj* de (la) época. **~ic** /-ˈɒdɪk/ *adj* periódico. **~ical** /pɪərɪˈɒdɪkl/ *n* revista *f*.

P

~ically *adv* periódico
peripher|al /pəˈrɪfərəl/ *adj* secundario; (*Comp*) periférico. **~y** /pəˈrɪfərɪ/ *n* periferia *f*
perish /ˈperɪʃ/ *vi* perecer; (*rot*) deteriorarse. **~able** *adj* perecedero. **~ing** *adj* 🄸 glacial
perjur|e /ˈpɜːdʒə(r)/ *vr.* **~e o.s.** perjurarse. **~y** *n* perjurio *m*
perk /pɜːk/ *n* gaje *m*. □ **~ up** *vt* reanimar. *vi* reanimarse
perm /pɜːm/ *n* permanente *f*. ● *vt*. **have one's hair ~ed** hacerse la permanente
permanen|ce /ˈpɜːmənəns/ *n* permanencia *f*. **~t** *adj* permanente. **~tly** *adv* permanentemente
permissible /pəˈmɪsəbl/ *adj* permisible
permission /pəˈmɪʃn/ *n* permiso *m*
permit /pəˈmɪt/ *vt* (*pt* **permitted**) permitir. ● /ˈpɜːmɪt/ *n* permiso *m*
peroxide /pəˈrɒksaɪd/ *n* peróxido *m*
P
perpendicular /pɜːpənˈdɪkjʊlə(r)/ *adj* & *n* perpendicular (*f*)
perpetrat|e /ˈpɜːpɪtreɪt/ *vt* cometer. **~or** *n* autor *m*
perpetua|l /pəˈpetʃʊəl/ *adj* perpetuo. **~te** /pəˈpetʃʊeɪt/ *vt* perpetuar
perplex /pəˈpleks/ *vt* dejar perplejo. **~ed** *adj* perplejo
persecut|e /ˈpɜːsɪkjuːt/ *vt* perseguir. **~ion** /-ˈkjuːʃn/ *n* persecución *f*
persever|ance /pɜːsɪˈvɪərəns/ *n* perseverancia *f*. **~e** /pɜːsɪˈvɪə(r)/ *vi* perseverar, persistir
Persian /ˈpɜːʃn/ *adj* persa. **the ~ Gulf** *n* el golfo Pérsico
persist /pəˈsɪst/ *vi* persistir. **~ence** /-əns/ *n* persistencia *f*. **~ent** *adj* persistente; (*continual*) continuo
person /ˈpɜːsn/ *n* persona *f*. **in ~** en persona. **~al** *adj* personal; (call) particular; (property) privado. **~al assistant** *n* secretario *m* personal. **~ality** /-ˈnælətɪ/ *n* personalidad *f*. **~ally** *adv* personalmente. **~nel** /pɜːsəˈnel/ *n* personal *m*. **P~** (*department*) sección *f* de personal
perspective /pəˈspektɪv/ *n* perspectiva *f*
perspir|ation /pɜːspəˈreɪʃn/ *n* transpiración *f*. **~e** /pəsˈpaɪə(r)/ *vi* transpirar
persua|de /pəˈsweɪd/ *vt* convencer, persuadir. **~e s.o. to do sth** convencer a uno para que haga algo. **~sion** *n* /-ʃn/ persuasión *f*. **~sive** /-sɪv/ *adj* persuasivo
pertinent /ˈpɜːtɪnənt/ *adj* pertinente. **~ly** *adv* pertinentemente
perturb /pəˈtɜːb/ *vt* perturbar
Peru /pəˈruː/ *n* el Perú *m*
peruse /pəˈruːz/ *vt* leer cuidadosamente
Peruvian /pəˈruːvɪən/ *adj* & *n* peruano (*m*)
perver|se /pəˈvɜːs/ *adj* retorcido; (*stubborn*) obstinado. **~sion** *n* perversión *f*. **~t** /pəˈvɜːt/ *vt* pervertir. ● /ˈpɜːvɜːt/ *n* pervertido *m*
pessimis|m /ˈpesɪmɪzəm/ *n* pesimismo *m*. **~t** *n* pesimista *m* & *f*. **~tic** /-ˈmɪstɪk/ *adj* pesimista
pest /pest/ *n* plaga *f*; (🄸, *person, thing*) peste *f*
pester /ˈpestə(r)/ *vt* importunar
pesticide /ˈpestɪsaɪd/ *n* pesticida *f*
pet /pet/ *n* animal *m* doméstico; (*favourite*) favorito *m*. ● *adj* preferido. **my ~ hate** lo que más odio. ● *vt* (*pt* **petted**) acariciar
petal /ˈpetl/ *n* pétalo *m*

petition /pɪ'tɪʃn/ *n* petición *f*
pet name *n* apodo *m*
petrified /'petrɪfaɪd/ *adj* (*terrified*) muerto de miedo; (rock) petrificado
petrol /'petrəl/ *n* gasolina *f*. ~ **pump** *n* surtidor *m*. ~ **station** *n* gasolinera *f*. ~ **tank** *n* depósito *m* de gasolina ~**eum** /pɪ'trəʊlɪəm/ *n* petróleo *m*.
petticoat /'petɪkəʊt/ *n* enagua *f*; (*slip*) combinación *f*
petty /'petɪ/ *adj* (**-ier**, **-iest**) insignificante; (*mean*) mezquino. ~**y cash** *n* dinero *m* para gastos menores
petulant /'petjʊlənt/ *adj* irritable
pew /pju:/ *n* banco *m* (de iglesia)
phantom /'fæntəm/ *n* fantasma *m*
pharma|ceutical /fɑ:mə'sju:tɪkl/ *adj* farmacéutico. ~**cist** /'fɑ:məsɪst/ *n* farmacéutico *m*. ~**cy** /'fɑ:məsɪ/ *n* farmacia *f*
phase /feɪz/ *n* etapa *f*. □ ~ **out** *vt* retirar progresivamente
PhD *abbr* (= **Doctor of Philosophy**) *n* doctorado *m*; (*person*) Dr., Dra.
pheasant /'feznt/ *n* faisán *m*
phenomen|al /fɪ'nɒmɪnl/ *adj* fenomenal. ~**on** /-ɪnən/ *n* (*pl* **-ena** /-ɪnə/) fenómeno *m*
philistine /'fɪlɪstaɪn/ *adj & n* filisteo (*m*)
philosoph|er /fɪ'lɒsəfə(r)/ *n* filósofo *m*. ~**ical** /-ə'sɒfɪkl/ *adj* filosófico. ~**y** /fɪ'lɒsəfɪ/ *n* filosofía *f*
phlegm /flem/ *n* flema *f*. ~**atic** /fleg'mætɪk/ *adj* flemático
phobia /'fəʊbɪə/ *n* fobia *f*
phone /fəʊn/ *n* 🄸 teléfono *m*. ● *vt/i* llamar (por teléfono). ~ **back** (*call again*) volver a llamar; (*return call*) llamar (más tarde). ~ **book** *n* guía *f* telefónica, directorio *m* (*LAm*). ~ **booth**, ~ **box** *n* cabina *f* telefónica. ~ **call** *n* llamada *f* (telefónica). ~ **card** *n* tarjeta *f* telefónica. ~ **number** *n* número *m* de teléfono
phonetic /fə'netɪk/ *adj* fonético. ~**s** *n* fonética *f*
phoney /'fəʊnɪ/ *adj* (**-ier**, **-iest**) 🄸 falso
phosph|ate /'fɒsfeɪt/ *n* fosfato *m*. ~**orus** /'fɒsfərəs/ *n* fósforo *m*
photo /'fəʊtəʊ/ *n* (*pl* **-os**) 🄸 foto *f*. **take a** ~ sacar una foto. ~**copier** /-kɒpɪə(r)/ *n* fotocopiadora *f*. ~**copy** *n* fotocopia *f*. ● *vt* fotocopiar. ~**genic** /-'dʒenɪk/ *adj* fotogénico. ~**graph** /-grɑ:f/ *n* fotografía *f*. ● *vt* fotografiar, sacarle una fotografía a. ~**grapher** /fə'tɒgrəfə(r)/ *n* fotógrafo *m*. ~**graphic** /-'græfɪk/ *adj* fotográfico. ~**graphy** /fə'tɒgrəfɪ/ *n* fotografía *f*
phrase /freɪz/ *n* frase *f*. ● *vt* expresar. ~ **book** *n* manual *m* de conversación
physi|cal /'fɪzɪkl/ *adj* físico. ~**cian** /fɪ'zɪʃn/ *n* médico *m*. ~**cist** /'fɪzɪsɪst/ *n* físico *m*. ~**cs** /'fɪzɪks/ *n* física *f*. ~**ology** /fɪzɪ'ɒlədʒɪ/ *n* fisiología *f*. ~**otherapist** /fɪzɪəʊ'θerəpɪst/ *n* fisioterapeuta *m & f*. ~**otherapy** /fɪzɪəʊ'θerəpɪ/ *n* fisioterapia *f*. ~**que** /fɪ'zi:k/ *n* físico *m*
pian|ist /'pɪənɪst/ *n* pianista *m & f*. ~**o** /pɪ'ænəʊ/ *n* (*pl* **-os**) piano *m*
pick /pɪk/ (*tool*) pico *m*. ● *vt* escoger; cortar (flowers); recoger (fruit, cotton); abrir con una ganzúa (lock). ~ **a quarrel** buscar camorra. ~ **holes in** criticar. □ ~ **on** *vt* meterse con. □ ~ **out** *vt* escoger; (*identify*) reconocer. □ ~ **up** *vt* re-

coger; (*lift*) levantar; (*learn*) aprender; adquirir (habit, etc); contagiarse de (illness). ● *vi* mejorar; (sales) subir. **~axe** *n* pico *m*

picket /ˈpɪkɪt/ *n* (*group*) piquete *m*. **~ line** *n* piquete *m*. ● *vt* formar un piquete frente a

pickle /ˈpɪkl/ *n* (*in vinegar*) encurtido *m*; (*Amer, gherkin*) pepinillo *m*; (*relish*) salsa *f* (*a base de encurtidos*). ● *vt* encurtir

pick: ~pocket *n* carterista *m & f*. **~-up** *n* (*truck*) camioneta *f*

picnic /ˈpɪknɪk/ *n* picnic *m*

picture /ˈpɪktʃə(r)/ *n* (*painting*) cuadro *m*; (*photo*) foto *f*; (*drawing*) dibujo *m*; (*illustration*) ilustración *f*; (*film*) película *f*; (*fig*) descripción *f*. ● *vt* imaginarse. **~sque** /-ˈresk/ *adj* pintoresco

pie /paɪ/ *n* empanada *f*; (*sweet*) pastel *m*, tarta *f*

piece /piːs/ *n* pedazo *m*, trozo *m*; (*part of machine*) pieza *f*; (*coin*) moneda *f*; (*in chess*) figura *f*. **a ~ of advice** un consejo. **a ~ of furniture** un mueble. **a ~ of news** una noticia. **take to ~s** desmontar. ▫ **~ together** *vt* juntar. **~meal** *adj* gradual; (*unsystematic*) poco sistemático. ● *adv* poco a poco

P

pier /pɪə(r)/ *n* muelle *m*; (*with amusements*) paseo con atracciones sobre un muelle

pierc|e /pɪəs/ *vt* perforar. **~ing** *adj* penetrante

piety /ˈpaɪətɪ/ *n* piedad *f*

pig /pɪg/ *n* cerdo *m*, chancho *m* (*LAm*)

pigeon /ˈpɪdʒɪn/ *n* paloma *f*; (*Culin*) pichón *m*. **~-hole** *n* casillero *m*; (*fig*) casilla *f*

piggy /ˈpɪgɪ/ *n* cerdito *m*. **~back** *n*. **give s.o. a ~back** llevar a uno a cuestas. **~ bank** *n* hucha *f*

pig-headed /-ˈhedɪd/ *adj* terco

pigment /ˈpɪgmənt/ *n* pigmento *m*

pig|sty /ˈpɪgstaɪ/ *n* pocilga *f*. **~tail** *n* (*plait*) trenza *f*; (*bunch*) coleta *f*

pike /paɪk/ *n invar* (*fish*) lucio *m*

pilchard /ˈpɪltʃəd/ *n* sardina *f*

pile /paɪl/ *n* (*heap*) montón *m*; (*of fabric*) pelo *m*. ● *vt* amontonar. **~ it on** exagerar. ● *vi* amontonarse. ▫ **~ up** *vt* amontonar. ● *vi* amontonarse. **~s** /paɪlz/ *npl* (*Med*) almorranas *fpl*. **~-up** *n* choque *m* múltiple

pilgrim /ˈpɪlgrɪm/ *n* peregrino. **~age** /-ɪdʒ/ *n* peregrinación *f*

pill /pɪl/ *n* pastilla *f*

pillar /ˈpɪlə(r)/ *n* columna *f*. **~ box** *n* buzón *m*

pillow /ˈpɪləʊ/ *n* almohada *f*. **~case** *n* funda *f* de almohada

pilot /ˈpaɪlət/ *n* piloto *m*. ● *vt* pilotar. **~ light** *n* fuego *m* piloto

pimple /ˈpɪmpl/ *n* grano *m*, espinilla *f* (*LAm*)

pin /pɪn/ *n* alfiler *m*; (*Mec*) perno *m*. **~s and needles** hormigueo *m*. ● *vt* (*pt* **pinned**) prender con alfileres; (*fix*) sujetar

PIN /pɪn/ *n* (= **personal identification number**) NIP *m*

pinafore /ˈpɪnəfɔː(r)/ *n* delantal *m*. **~ dress** *n* pichi *m*, jumper *m & f* (*LAm*)

pincers /ˈpɪnsəz/ *npl* tenazas *fpl*

pinch /pɪntʃ/ *vt* pellizcar; (*fam, steal*) hurtar. ● *vi* (shoe) apretar. ● *n* pellizco *m*; (*small amount*) pizca *f*. **at a ~** si fuera necesario

pine /paɪn/ *n* pino *m*. ● *vi*. **~ for sth** suspirar por algo. ▫ **~ away** *vi* languidecer de añoranza. **~apple** /'paɪnæpl/ *n* piña *f*

ping-pong /'pɪŋpɒŋ/ *n* ping-pong *m*

pink /pɪŋk/ *adj & n* rosa (*m*), rosado (*m*)

pinnacle /'pɪnəkl/ *n* pináculo *m*

pin: ~point *vt* determinar con precisión *f.* **~stripe** *n* raya *f* fina

pint /paɪnt/ *n* pinta *f* (= *0.57 litros*)

pioneer /paɪə'nɪə(r)/ *n* pionero *m*

pious /'paɪəs/ *adj* piadoso

pip /pɪp/ *n* (*seed*) pepita *f*; (*time signal*) señal *f*

pipe /paɪp/ *n* tubo *m*; (*Mus*) caramillo *m*; (*for smoking*) pipa *f.* ● *vt* llevar por tuberías. **~-dream** *n* ilusión *f.* **~line** *n* conducto *m*; (*for oil*) oleoducto *m.* **in the ~line** en preparación *f*

piping /'paɪpɪŋ/ *n* tubería *f.* ● *adv.* **~ hot** muy caliente, hirviendo

pira|cy /'paɪərəsɪ/ *n* piratería *f.* **~te** /'paɪərət/ *n* pirata *m*

Pisces /'paɪsi:z/ *n* Piscis *m*

piss /pɪs/ *vi* ☒ mear. □ **~ off** *vi* ☒. **~ off!** ¡vete a la mierda! **~ed** /pɪst/ *adj* (☒, *drunk*) como una cuba; (*Amer, fed up*) cabreado

pistol /'pɪstl/ *n* pistola *f*

piston /'pɪstən/ *n* pistón *m*

pit /pɪt/ *n* hoyo *m*; (*mine*) mina *f*; (*Amer, in fruit*) hueso *m*

pitch /pɪtʃ/ *n* (*substance*) brea *f*; (*degree*) grado *m*; (*Mus*) tono *m*; (*Sport*) campo *m.* ● *vt* (*throw*) lanzar; armar (tent). ● *vi* (ship) cabecear. **~-black** /-'blæk/ *adj* oscuro como boca de lobo. **~er** *n* jarra *f*

pitfall /'pɪtfɔ:l/ *n* trampa *f*

pith /pɪθ/ *n* (*of orange, lemon*) médula *f*; (*fig*) meollo *m*

pitiful /'pɪtɪfl/ *adj* lastimoso

pittance /'pɪtns/ *n* miseria *f*

pity /'pɪtɪ/ *n* lástima *f*, pena *f*; (*compassion*) piedad *f.* **it's a ~ you can't come** es una lástima que no puedas venir. ● *vt* tenerle lástima a

pivot /'pɪvət/ *n* pivote *m.* ● *vi* pivotar; (*fig*) depender (**on** de)

placard /'plækɑ:d/ *n* pancarta *f*; (*sign*) letrero *m*

placate /plə'keɪt/ *vt* apaciguar

place /pleɪs/ *n* lugar *m*; (*seat*) asiento *m*; (*in firm, team*) puesto *m*; (*fam, house*) casa *f.* **feel out of ~** sentirse fuera de lugar. **take ~** tener lugar. ● *vt* poner, colocar; (*identify*) identificar. **be ~d** (*in race*) colocarse. **~-mat** *n* mantel *m* individual

placid /'plæsɪd/ *adj* plácido

plague /pleɪg/ *n* peste *f*; (*fig*) plaga *f.* ● *vt* atormentar

plaice /pleɪs/ *n invar* platija *f*

plain /pleɪn/ *adj* (**-er**, **-est**) (*clear*) claro; (*simple*) sencillo; (*candid*) franco; (*ugly*) feo. **in ~ clothes** de civil. ● *adv* totalmente. ● *n* llanura *f.* **~ly** *adv* claramente; (*frankly*) francamente; (*simply*) con sencillez

plaintiff /'pleɪntɪf/ *n* demandante *m & f*

plait /plæt/ *vt* trenzar. ● *n* trenza *f*

plan /plæn/ *n* plan *m*; (*map*) plano *m*; (*of book, essay*) esquema *f.* ● *vt* (*pt* **planned**) planear; planificar (strategies). **I'm ~ning to go to Greece** pienso ir a Grecia

plane /pleɪn/ *n* (*tree*) plátano *m*; (*level*) nivel *m*; (*aircraft*) avión *m*; (*tool*) cepillo *m.* ● *vt* cepillar

planet /'plænɪt/ *n* planeta *m.* **~ary** *adj* planetario

plank /plæŋk/ *n* tabla *f*

planning /'plænɪŋ/ *n* planificación *f.* **family ~** planificación familiar. **town ~** urbanismo *m*

plant /plɑ:nt/ *n* planta *f*; (*Mec*) maquinaria *f*; (*factory*) fábrica *f*. ● *vt* plantar; (*place in position*) colocar. **~ation** /plæn'teɪʃn/ *n* plantación *f*

plaque /plæk/ *n* placa *f*

plasma /'plæzmə/ *n* plasma *m*

plaster /'plɑ:stə(r)/ *n* yeso *m*; (*on walls*) revoque *m*; (*sticking plaster*) tirita *f* (®), curita *f* (®) (*LAm*); (*for setting bones*) yeso *m*, escayola *f*. ● *vt* revocar; rellenar con yeso (cracks)

plastic /'plæstɪk/ *adj & n* plástico (*m*)

Plasticine /'plæstɪsi:n/ *n* (®) plastilina *f* (®)

plastic surgery /plæstɪk 'sɜ:dʒərɪ/ *n* cirugía *f* estética

plate /pleɪt/ *n* plato *m*; (*of metal*) chapa *f*; (*silverware*) vajilla *f* de plata; (*in book*) lámina *f*. ● *vt* recubrir (**with** de)

platform /'plætfɔ:m/ *n* plataforma *f*; (*Rail*) andén *m*

P

platinum /'plætɪnəm/ *n* platino *m*

platitude /'plætɪtju:d/ *n* lugar *m* común

platonic /plə'tɒnɪk/ *adj* platónico

plausible /'plɔ:zəbl/ *adj* verosímil; (person) convincente

play /pleɪ/ *vt* jugar a (game, cards); jugar a, jugar (*LAm*) (football, chess); tocar (instrument); (*act role*) representar el papel de. ● *vi* jugar. ● *n* juego *m*; (*drama*) obra *f* de teatro. ▫ **~ down** *vt* minimizar. ▫ **~ up** *vi* 🄸 (child) dar guerra; (car, TV) no funcionar bien. **~er** *n* jugador *m*; (*Mus*) músico *m*. **~ful** *adj* juguetón. **~ground** *n* parque *m* de juegos infantiles; (*in school*) patio *m* de recreo. **~group** *n* jardín *m* de la infancia. **~ing card** *n* naipe *m*. **~ing field** *n* campo *m* de deportes. **~pen** *n* corralito *m*. **~wright** /-raɪt/ *n* dramaturgo *m*

plc *abbr* (= **public limited company**) S.A.

plea /pli:/ *n* súplica *f*; (*excuse*) excusa *f*; (*Jurid*) defensa *f*

plead /pli:d/ *vt* (*Jurid*) alegar; (*as excuse*) pretextar. ● *vi* suplicar. **~ with** suplicarle a. **~ guilty** declararse culpable

pleasant /'pleznt/ *adj* agradable

pleas|e /pli:z/ *int* por favor. ● *vt* complacer; (*satisfy*) contentar. ● *vi* agradar; (*wish*) querer. **~ed** *adj* (*satisfied*) satisfecho; (*happy*) contento. **~ed with** satisfecho de. **~ing** *adj* agradable; (*news*) grato. **~ure** /'pleʒə(r)/ *n* placer *m*

pleat /pli:t/ *n* pliegue *m*

pledge /pledʒ/ *n* cantidad *f* prometida

plent|iful /'plentɪfl/ *adj* abundante. **~y** /'plentɪ/ *n* abundancia *f*. ● *pron*. **~y of** muchos, -chas; (*of sth uncountable*) mucho, -cha

pliable /'plaɪəbl/ *adj* flexible

pliers /'plaɪəz/ *npl* alicates *mpl*

plight /plaɪt/ *n* situación *f* difícil

plimsolls /'plɪmsəlz/ *npl* zapatillas *fpl* de lona

plod /plɒd/ *vi* (*pt* **plodded**) caminar con paso pesado

plot /plɒt/ *n* complot *m*; (*of novel etc*) argumento *m*; (*piece of land*) parcela *f*. ● *vt* (*pt* **plotted**) tramar; (*mark out*) trazar. ● *vi* conspirar

plough /plaʊ/ *n* arado *m*. ● *vt/i* arar. ▫ **~ into** *vt* estrellarse contra. ▫ **~ through** *vt* avanzar laboriosamente por

ploy /plɔɪ/ *n* treta *f*

pluck /plʌk/ *vt* arrancar; depilarse

(eyebrows); desplumar (bird). ~ **up courage to** armarse de valor para. ● *n* valor *m*. **~y** *adj* (**-ier**, **-iest**) valiente

plug /plʌg/ *n* (*in bath*) tapón *m*; (*Elec*) enchufe *m*; (*spark* ~) bujía *f*. ● *vt* (*pt* **plugged**) tapar; (*fam, advertise*) hacerle propaganda a. □ ~ **in** *vt* (*Elec*) enchufar. **~hole** *n* desagüe *m*

plum /plʌm/ *n* ciruela *f*

plumage /'plu:mɪdʒ/ *n* plumaje *m*

plumb|er /'plʌmə(r)/ *n* fontanero *m*, plomero *m* (*LAm*). **~ing** *n* instalación *f* sanitaria, instalación *f* de cañerías

plume /plu:m/ *n* pluma *f*

plump /plʌmp/ *adj* (**-er**, **-est**) rechoncho

plunge /plʌndʒ/ *vt* hundir (knife); (*in water*) sumergir; (*into state, condition*) sumir. ● *vi* zambullirse; (*fall*) caer. ● *n* zambullida *f*

plural /'plʊərəl/ *n* plural *m*. ● *adj* en plural

plus /plʌs/ *prep* más. ● *adj* positivo. ● *n* signo *m* de más; (*fig*) ventaja *f*

plush /plʌʃ/ *adj* lujoso

Pluto /'plu:təʊ/ *n* Plutón *m*

plutonium /plu:'təʊnɪəm/ *n* plutonio *m*

ply /plaɪ/ *vt* manejar (tool); ejercer (trade). ~ **s.o. with drink** dar continuamente de beber a uno. **~wood** *n* contrachapado *m*

p.m. *abbr* (= **post meridiem**) de la tarde

pneumatic drill /nju:'mætɪk/ *adj* martillo *m* neumático

pneumonia /nju:'məʊnjə/ *n* pulmonía *f*

poach /pəʊtʃ/ *vt* escalfar (egg); cocer (fish etc); (*steal*) cazar furtivamente. **~er** *n* cazador *m* furtivo

PO box /pi:'əʊ/ *n* Apdo. postal

pocket /'pɒkɪt/ *n* bolsillo *m*; (*of air, resistance*) bolsa *f*. ● *vt* poner en el bolsillo. **~book** *n* (*notebook*) libro *m* de bolsillo; (*Amer, wallet*) cartera *f*; (*Amer, handbag*) bolso *m*, cartera *f* (*LAm*), bolsa *f* (*Mex*). ~ **money** *n* dinero *m* de bolsillo, mesada *f* (*LAm*)

pod /pɒd/ *n* vaina *f*

poem /'pəʊɪm/ *n* poema *f*

poet /'pəʊɪt/ *n* poeta *m*. **~ic** /-'etɪk/ *adj* poético. **~ry** /'pəʊɪtrɪ/ *n* poesía *f*

poignant /'pɔɪnjənt/ *adj* conmovedor

point /pɔɪnt/ *n* (*dot, on scale*) punto *m*; (*sharp end*) punta *f*; (*in time*) momento *m*; (*statement*) observación; (*on agenda, in discussion*) punto *m*; (*Elec*) toma *f* de corriente. **to the ~** pertinente. **up to a ~** hasta cierto punto. **be on the ~ of** estar a punto de. **get to the ~** ir al grano. **there's no ~ (in) arguing** no sirve de nada discutir. ● *vt* (*aim*) apuntar; (*show*) indicar. ● *vi* señalar. ~ **at/to sth** señalar algo. □ ~ **out** *vt* señalar. **~-blank** *adj & adv* a quemarropa. **~ed** *adj* (*chin, nose*) puntiagudo; (*fig*) mordaz. **~less** *adj* inútil

poise /pɔɪz/ *n* porte *m*; (*composure*) desenvoltura *f*

poison /'pɔɪzn/ *n* veneno *m*. ● *vt* envenenar. **~ous** *adj* venenoso; (chemical etc) tóxico

poke /pəʊk/ *vt* empujar; atizar (fire). ● *vi* hurgar; (*pry*) meterse. ● *n* golpe *m*. □ ~ **about** *vi* fisgonear. **~r** /'pəʊkə(r)/ *n* atizador *m*; (*Cards*) póquer *m*

poky /'pəʊkɪ/ *adj* (**-ier**, **-iest**) diminuto

Poland /ˈpəʊlənd/ *n* Polonia *f*

polar /ˈpəʊlə(r)/ *adj* polar. **~ bear** *n* oso *m* blanco

pole /pəʊl/ *n* palo *m*; (*fixed*) poste *m*; (*for flag*) mástil *m*; (*in geography*) polo *m*

police /pəˈliːs/ *n* policía *f*. **~man** /-mən/ *n* policía *m*, agente *m*. **~ station** *n* comisaría *f*. **~woman** *n* policía *f*, agente *f*

policy /ˈpɒlɪsɪ/ *n* política *f*; (*insurance*) póliza *f* (de seguros)

polish /ˈpɒlɪʃ/ *n* (*for shoes*) betún *m*; (*furniture* **~**) cera *f* para muebles; (*floor* **~**) abrillantador *m* de suelos; (*shine*) brillo *m*; (*fig*) finura *f*. ● *vt* darle brillo a; limpiar (shoes); (*refine*) pulir. □ **~ off** *vt* despachar. **~ed** *adj* pulido

Polish /ˈpəʊlɪʃ/ *adj* & *n* polaco (*m*)

polite /pəˈlaɪt/ *adj* cortés. **~ly** *adv* cortésmente. **~ness** *n* cortesía *f*

politic|al /pəˈlɪtɪkl/ *adj* político. **~ian** /pɒlɪˈtɪʃn/ *n* político *m*. **~s** /ˈpɒlətɪks/ *n* política *f*

poll /pəʊl/ *n* elección *f*; (*survey*) encuesta *f*. ● *vt* obtener (votes)

pollack /ˈpɒlæk/ *n* abadejo *m*

pollen /ˈpɒlən/ *n* polen *m*

polling booth *n* cabina *f* de votar

pollut|e /pəˈluːt/ *vt* contaminar. **~ion** /-ʃn/ *n* contaminación *f*

polo /ˈpəʊləʊ/ *n* polo *m*. **~ neck** *n* cuello *m* vuelto

poly|styrene /pɒlɪˈstaɪriːn/ *n* poliestireno *m*. **~thene** /ˈpɒlɪθiːn/ *n* plástico, polietileno *m*

pomp /pɒmp/ *n* pompa *f*. **~ous** *adj* pomposa

pond /pɒnd/ *n* (*natural*) laguna *f*; (*artificial*) estanque *m*

ponder /ˈpɒndə(r)/ *vt* considerar. **~ous** *adj* pesado

pony /ˈpəʊnɪ/ *n* poni *m*. **~-tail** *n* cola *f* de caballo

poodle /ˈpuːdl/ *n* caniche *m*

pool /puːl/ *n* charca *f*; (*artificial*) estanque *m*; (*puddle*) charco *m*. (*common fund*) fondos *mpl* comunes; (*snooker*) billar *m* americano. **(swimming) ~** *n* piscina *f*, alberca *f* (*Mex*). **~s** *npl* quinielas *fpl*. ● *vt* aunar

poor /pʊə(r)/ *adj* (**-er**, **-est**) pobre; (quality, diet) malo. **be in ~ health** estar mal de salud. **~ly** *adj* 🅸 malito. ● *adv* mal

pop /pɒp/ *n* (*Mus*) música *f* pop; (*Amer fam, father*) papá *m*. ● *vt* (*pt* **popped**) hacer reventar; (*put*) poner. □ **~ in** *vi* (*visit*) pasar por. □ **~ out** *vi* saltar; (person) salir un rato. □ **~ up** *vi* surgir, aparecer

popcorn /ˈpɒpkɔːn/ *n* palomitas *fpl*

pope /pəʊp/ *n* papa *m*

poplar /ˈpɒplə(r)/ *n* álamo *m* (blanco)

poppy /ˈpɒpɪ/ *n* amapola *f*

popular /ˈpɒpjʊlə(r)/ *adj* popular. **~ity** /-ˈlærətɪ/ *n* popularidad *f*. **~ize** *vt* popularizar

populat|e /ˈpɒpjʊleɪt/ *vt* poblar. **~ion** /-ˈleɪʃn/ *n* población *f*

pop-up /ˈpɒpʌp/ *n* ventana *f* emergente, pop-up *m*

porcelain /ˈpɔːsəlɪn/ *n* porcelana *f*

porch /pɔːtʃ/ *n* porche *m*

porcupine /ˈpɔːkjʊpaɪn/ *n* puerco *m* espín

pore /pɔː(r)/ *n* poro *m*

pork /pɔːk/ *n* carne *f* de cerdo *m*, carne *f* de puerco *m* (*Mex*)

porn /pɔːn/ *n* 🅸 pornografía *f*. **~ographic** /-əˈgræfɪk/ *adj* pornográfico. **~ography** /pɔːˈnɒgrəfɪ/ *n* pornografía *f*

porpoise /ˈpɔːpəs/ *n* marsopa *f*
porridge /ˈpɒrɪdʒ/ *n* avena *f* (*cocida*)
port /pɔːt/ *n* puerto *m*; (*Naut*) babor *m*; (*Comp*) puerto *m*; (*Culin*) oporto *m*
portable /ˈpɔːtəbl/ *adj* portátil
porter /ˈpɔːtə(r)/ *n* (*for luggage*) maletero *m*; (*concierge*) portero *m*
porthole /ˈpɔːthəʊl/ *n* portilla *f*
portion /ˈpɔːʃn/ *n* porción *f*; (*part*) parte *f*
portrait /ˈpɔːtrɪt/ *n* retrato *m*
portray /pɔːˈtreɪ/ *vt* representar. **~al** *n* representación *f*
Portug|al /ˈpɔːtjʊgl/ *n* Portugal *m*. **~uese** /-ˈgiːz/ *adj* & *n* portugués (*m*)
pose /pəʊz/ *n* pose *f*, postura *f*. ● *vt* representar (threat); plantear (problem, question). ● *vi* posar. **~ as** hacerse pasar por
posh /pɒʃ/ *adj* 🄸 elegante
position /pəˈzɪʃn/ *n* posición *f*; (*job*) puesto *m*; (*situation*) situación *f*. ● *vt* colocar
positive /ˈpɒzətɪv/ *adj* positivo; (*real*) auténtico; (*certain*) seguro. ● *n* (*Photo*) positiva *f*. **~ly** *adv* positivamente
possess /pəˈzes/ *vt* poseer. **~ion** /-ʃn/ *n* posesión *f*; (*Jurid*) bien *m*. **~ive** *adj* posesivo
possib|ility /pɒsəˈbɪlətɪ/ *n* posibilidad *f*. **~le** /ˈpɒsəbl/ *adj* posible. **~ly** *adv* posiblemente
post /pəʊst/ *n* (*pole*) poste *m*; (*job*) puesto *m*; (*mail*) correo *m*. ● *vt* echar al correo (letter); (*send*) enviar por correo. **keep s.o. ~ed** mantener a uno al corriente
post... /pəʊst/ *pref* post, pos
post: ~age /-ɪdʒ/ *n* franqueo *m*. **~al** *adj* postal. **~al order** *n* giro *m* postal. **~ box** *n* buzón *m*. **~card** *n* (tarjeta *f*) postal *f*. **~code** *n* código *m* postal
poster /ˈpəʊstə(r)/ *n* cartel *m*, póster *m*
posterity /pɒsˈterətɪ/ *n* posteridad *f*
posthumous /ˈpɒstjʊməs/ *adj* póstumo
post: ~man /-mən/ *n* cartero *m*. **~mark** *n* matasellos *m*
post mortem /pəʊstˈmɔːtəm/ *n* autopsia *f*
post office *n* oficina *f* de correos, correos *mpl*, correo *m* (*LAm*)
postpone /pəʊstˈpəʊn/ *vt* aplazar, posponer. **~ment** *n* aplazamiento *m*
postscript /ˈpəʊstskrɪpt/ *n* posdata *f*
posture /ˈpɒstʃə(r)/ *n* postura *f*
posy /ˈpəʊzɪ/ *n* ramillete *m*
pot /pɒt/ *n* (*for cooking*) olla *f*; (*for jam, honey*) tarro *m*; (*for flowers*) tiesto *m*; (*in pottery*) vasija *f*. **~s and pans** cacharros *mpl*
potato /pəˈteɪtəʊ/ *n* (*pl* **-oes**) patata *f*, papa *f* (*LAm*)
potent /ˈpəʊtnt/ *adj* potente; (drink) fuerte
potential /pəʊˈtenʃl/ *adj* & *n* potencial (*m*). **~ly** *adv* potencialmente
pot: ~hole *n* cueva *f* subterránea; (*in road*) bache *m*. **~holing** *n* espeleología *f*
potion /ˈpəʊʃn/ *n* poción *f*
pot-shot *n* tiro *m* al azar
potter /ˈpɒtə(r)/ *n* alfarero *m*. ● *vi* hacer pequeños trabajos agradables. **~y** *n* (*pots*) cerámica *f*; (*workshop, craft*) alfarería *f*
potty /ˈpɒtɪ/ *adj* (**-ier**, **-iest**) 🄸

P

chiflado. ● *n* orinal *m*

pouch /paʊtʃ/ *n* bolsa *f* pequeña; (*for correspondence*) valija *f*

poultry /ˈpəʊltrɪ/ *n* aves *fpl* de corral

pounce /paʊns/ *vi* saltar. ~ **on** abalanzarse sobre

pound /paʊnd/ *n* (*weight*) libra *f* (= *454g*); (*money*) libra *f* (esterlina); (*for cars*) depósito *m*. ● *vt* (*crush*) machacar. ● *vi* aporrear; (heart) palpitar; (sound) retumbar

pour /pɔ:(r)/ *vt* verter; echar (salt). ~ **(out)** servir (drink). ● *vi* (blood) manar; (water) salir; (*rain*) llover a cántaros. □ ~ **out** *vi* (people) salir en tropel. ~**ing** *adj*. ~**ing rain** lluvia *f* torrencial

pout /paʊt/ *vi* hacer pucheros

poverty /ˈpɒvətɪ/ *n* pobreza *f*

powder /ˈpaʊdə(r)/ *n* polvo *m*; (*cosmetic*) polvos *mpl*. ● *vt* empolvar. ~ **one's face** ponerse polvos en la cara. ~**y** *adj* como polvo

power /ˈpaʊə(r)/ *n* poder *m*; (*energy*) energía *f*; (*electricity*) electricidad *f*; (*nation*) potencia *f*. ● *vt*. ~**ed by** impulsado por ~ **cut** *n* apagón *m*. ~**ed** *adj* con motor. ~**ful** *adj* poderoso. ~**less** *adj* impotente. ~ **plant**, ~**-station** *n* central *f* eléctrica

PR = **public relations**

practicable /ˈpræktɪkəbl/ *adj* practicable

practical /ˈpræktɪkl/ *adj* práctico. ~ **joke** *n* broma *f*. ~**ly** *adv* prácticamente

practi|ce /ˈpræktɪs/ *n* práctica *f*; (*custom*) costumbre *f*; (*exercise*) ejercicio *m*; (*Sport*) entrenamiento *m*; (*clients*) clientela *f*. **he's out of** ~**ce** le falta práctica. **in** ~**ce** (*in fact*) en la práctica. ~**se** /ˈpræktɪs/ *vt* practicar; ensayar (act); ejercer (profession). ● *vi* practicar; (professional) ejercer. ~**tioner** /-ˈtɪʃənə(r)/ *n* médico *m*

prairie /ˈpreərɪ/ *n* pradera *f*

praise /preɪz/ *vt* (*Relig*) alabar; (*compliment*) elogiar. ● *n* (*credit*) elogios *mpl*. ~**worthy** *adj* loable

pram /præm/ *n* cochecito *m*

prank /præŋk/ *n* travesura *f*

prawn /prɔ:n/ *n* gamba *f*, camarón *m* (*LAm*)

pray /preɪ/ *vi* rezar (**for** por). ~**er** /preə(r)/ *n* oración *f*

pre.. /pri:/ *pref* pre...

preach /pri:tʃ/ *vt/i* predicar. ~**er** *n* predicador *m*; (*Amer, minister*) pastor *m*

pre-arrange /pri:əˈreɪndʒ/ *vt* concertar de antemano

precarious /prɪˈkeərɪəs/ *adj* precario. ~**ly** *adv* precariamente

precaution /prɪˈkɔ:ʃn/ *n* precaución *f*

precede /prɪˈsi:d/ *vt* preceder. ~**nce** /ˈpresədəns/ *n* precedencia *f*. ~**nt** /ˈpresədənt/ *n* precedente *m*

preceding /prɪˈsi:dɪŋ/ *adj* anterior

precept /ˈpri:sept/ *n* precepto *m*

precinct /ˈpri:sɪŋkt/ *n* recinto *m*; (*Amer, police district*) distrito *m* policial; (*Amer, voting district*) circunscripción *f*. **pedestrian** ~ zona *f* peatonal. ~**s** (*of city*) límites *mpl*

precious /ˈpreʃəs/ *adj* precioso. ● *adv* [!] muy

precipice /ˈpresɪpɪs/ *n* precipicio *m*

precipitate /prɪˈsɪpɪteɪt/ *vt* precipitar. ● /prɪˈsɪpɪtət/ *n* precipitado *m*. ● /prɪˈsɪpɪtət/ *adj* precipitado

precis|e /prɪˈsaɪs/ *adj* (*accurate*)

exacto; (*specific*) preciso; (*meticulous*) minucioso. **~ely** *adv* con precisión. **~!** ¡exacto! **~ion** /-ˈsɪʒn/ *n* precisión *f*
preclude /prɪˈkluːd/ *vt* excluir
precocious /prɪˈkəʊʃəs/ *adj* precoz. **~ly** *adv* precozmente
preconce|ived /priːkənˈsiːvd/ *adj* preconcebido. **~ption** /-ˈsepʃn/ *n* preconcepción *f*
precursor /priːˈkɜːsə(r)/ *n* precursor *m*
predator /ˈpredətə(r)/ *n* depredador *m*. **~y** *adj* predador
predecessor /ˈpriːdɪsesə(r)/ *n* predecesor *m*, antecesor *m*
predicament /prɪˈdɪkəmənt/ *n* aprieto *m*
predict /prɪˈdɪkt/ *vt* predecir. **~ion** /-ʃn/ *n* predicción *f*
preen /priːn/ *vt* arreglar. **~ o.s.** atildarse
prefab /ˈpriːfæb/ *n* [!] casa *f* prefabricada. **~ricated** /-ˈfæbrɪkeɪtɪd/ *adj* prefabricado
preface /ˈprefəs/ *n* prefacio *m*; (*to event*) prólogo *m*
prefect /ˈpriːfekt/ *n* (*Schol*) monitor *m*; (*official*) prefecto *m*
prefer /prɪˈfɜː(r)/ *vt* (*pt* **preferred**) preferir. **~ sth to sth** preferir algo a algo. **~able** /ˈprefrəbl/ *adj* preferible. **~ence** /ˈprefrəns/ *n* preferencia *f*. **~ential** /-əˈrenʃl/ *adj* preferente
pregnan|cy /ˈpregnənsɪ/ *n* embarazo *m*. **~t** *adj* embarazada
prehistoric /priːhɪˈstɒrɪk/ *adj* prehistórico
prejudge /priːˈdʒʌdʒ/ *vt* prejuzgar
prejudice /ˈpredʒʊdɪs/ *n* prejuicio *m*. ● *vt* predisponer; (*harm*) perjudicar. **~d** *adj* lleno de prejuicios
preliminary /prɪˈlɪmɪnərɪ/ *adj* preliminar
prelude /ˈpreljuːd/ *n* preludio *m*
premature /ˈprematjʊə(r)/ *adj* prematuro
premeditated /priːˈmedɪteɪtɪd/ *adj* premeditado
premier /ˈpremɪə(r)/ *n* (*Pol*) primer ministro *m*
première /ˈpremɪeə(r)/ *n* estreno *m*
premise /ˈpremɪs/ *n* premisa *f*. **~s** /ˈpremɪsɪz/ *npl* local *m*. **on the ~s** en el local
premium /ˈpriːmɪəm/ *n* (*insurance ~*) prima *f* de seguro. **be at a ~** escasear
premonition /priːməˈnɪʃn/ *n* premonición *f*, presentimiento *m*
preoccup|ation /priːɒkjʊˈpeɪʃn/ *n* (*obsession*) obsesión *f*; (*concern*) preocupación *f*. **~ied** /-ˈɒkjʊpaɪd/ *adj* absorto; (*worried*) preocupado
preparat|ion /prepəˈreɪʃn/ *n* preparación *f*. **~ions** *npl* preparativos *mpl*. **~ory** /prɪˈpærətrɪ/ *adj* preparatorio
prepare /prɪˈpeə(r)/ *vt* preparar. ● *vi* prepararse. ● *adj* preparado (*willing*). **be ~d to** estar dispuesto a
preposition /prepəˈzɪʃn/ *n* preposición *f*
preposterous /prɪˈpɒstərəs/ *adj* absurdo
prerequisite /priːˈrekwɪzɪt/ *n* requisito *m* esencial
prerogative /prɪˈrɒgətɪv/ *n* prerrogativa *f*
Presbyterian /prezbɪˈtɪərɪən/ *adj* & *n* presbiteriano (*m*)
prescri|be /prɪˈskraɪb/ *vt* prescribir; (*Med*) recetar. **~ption** /-ˈɪpʃn/ *n* (*Med*) receta *f*

presence /ˈprezns/ *n* presencia *f*. **~ of mind** presencia *f* de ánimo

present /ˈpreznt/ *n* (*gift*) regalo *m*; (*current time*) presente *m*. **at ~** actualmente. **for the ~** por ahora. ● *adj* presente. ● /prɪˈzent/ *vt* presentar; (*give*) obsequiar. **~ s.o. with** obsequiar a uno con. **~able** /prɪˈzentəbl/ *adj* presentable. **~ation** /preznˈteɪʃn/ *n* presentación *f*; (*ceremony*) ceremonia *f* de entrega. **~er** /prɪˈzentə(r)/ *n* presentador *m*. **~ly** /ˈprezntlɪ/ *adv* dentro de poco

preserv|ation /prezəˈveɪʃn/ *n* conservación *f*. **~ative** /prɪˈzɜːvətɪv/ *n* conservante *m*. **~e** /prɪˈzɜːv/ *vt* conservar; (*maintain*) mantener; (*Culin*) hacer conserva de. ● *n* coto *m*; (*jam*) confitura *f*. **wildlife ~e** (*Amer*) reserva *f* de animales

preside /prɪˈzaɪd/ *vi* presidir. **~ over** presidir

presiden|cy /ˈprezɪdənsɪ/ *n* presidencia *f*. **~t** *n* presidente *m*. **~tial** /-ˈdenʃl/ *adj* presidencial

P

press /pres/ *vt* apretar; prensar (grapes); (*put pressure on*) presionar; (*iron*) planchar. **be ~ed for time** andar escaso de tiempo. ● *vi* apretar; (time) apremiar; (*fig*) urgir. ● *n* (*Mec, newspapers*) prensa *f*; (*printing*) imprenta *f*. □ **~ on** *vi* seguir adelante (**with** con). **~ conference** *n* rueda *f* de prensa. **~ cutting** *n* recorte *m* de periódico. **~ing** *adj* urgente. **~-up** *n* flexión *f*, fondo *m*

pressur|e /ˈpreʃə(r)/ *n* presión *f*. ● *vt* presionar. **~e-cooker** *n* olla *f* a presión. **~ize** *vt* presionar

prestig|e /preˈstiːʒ/ *n* prestigio *m*. **~ious** /-ˈstɪdʒəs/ *adj* prestigioso

presum|ably /prɪˈzjuːməblɪ/ *adv*. **~...** supongo que..., me imagino que... **~e** /prɪˈzjuːm/ *vt* suponer. **~ptuous** /prɪˈzʌmptʃʊəs/ *adj* impertinente

presuppose /priːsəˈpəʊz/ *vt* presuponer

preten|ce /prɪˈtens/ *n* fingimiento *m*; (*claim*) pretensión *f*; (*pretext*) pretexto *m*. **~d** /-ˈtend/ *vt/i* fingir. **~sion** /-ˈtenʃən/ *n* pretensión *f*. **~tious** /-ˈtenʃəs/ *adj* pretencioso

pretext /ˈpriːtekst/ *n* pretexto *m*

pretty /ˈprɪtɪ/ *adj* (**-ier**, **-iest**) *adv* bonito, lindo (*esp LAm*)

prevail /prɪˈveɪl/ *vi* predominar; (*win*) prevalecer. □ **~ on** *vt* persuadir

prevalen|ce /ˈprevələns/ *n* (*occurrence*) preponderancia *f*; (*predominance*) predominio *m*. **~t** *adj* extendido

prevent /prɪˈvent/ *vt* (*hinder*) impedir; (*forestall*) prevenir, evitar. **~ion** /-ʃn/ *n* prevención *f*. **~ive** *adj* preventivo

preview /ˈpriːvjuː/ *n* preestreno *m*; (*trailer*) avance *m*

previous /ˈpriːvɪəs/ *adj* anterior. **~ to** antes de. **~ly** *adv* antes

prey /preɪ/ *n* presa *f*. **bird of ~** ave *f* de rapiña

price /praɪs/ *n* precio *m*. ● *vt* fijar el precio de. **~less** *adj* inestimable; (*fam, amusing*) muy divertido. **~y** *adj* ⓘ carito

prick /prɪk/ *vt/i* pinchar. ● *n* pinchazo *m*

prickl|e /ˈprɪkl/ *n* (*thorn*) espina *f*; (*of animal*) púa *f*; (*sensation*) picor *m*. **~y** *adj* espinoso; (animal) con púas; (*touchy*) quisquilloso

pride /praɪd/ *n* orgullo *m*. ● *vr*. **~ o.s. on** enorgullecerse de

priest /priːst/ *n* sacerdote *m*. **~hood** *n* sacerdocio *m*

prim /prɪm/ *adj* (**primmer**, **primmest**) mojigato; (*affected*) remilgado

primar|ily /ˈpraɪmərɪlɪ/ *adv* en primer lugar. **~y** /ˈpraɪmərɪ/ *adj* (*principal*) primordial; (*first, basic*) primario. **~ school** *n* escuela *f* primaria

prime /praɪm/ *vt* cebar (gun); (*prepare*) preparar; aprestar (surface). ● *adj* principal; (*first rate*) excelente. **~ minister** *n* primer ministro *m*. ● *n*. **be in one's ~** estar en la flor de la vida. **~r** *n* (*paint*) imprimación *f*

primeval /praɪˈmi:vl/ *adj* primigenio

primitive /ˈprɪmɪtɪv/ *adj* primitivo

primrose /ˈprɪmrəʊz/ *n* primavera *f*

prince /prɪns/ *n* príncipe *m*. **~ss** /prɪnˈses/ *n* princesa *f*

principal /ˈprɪnsəpl/ *adj* principal. ● *n* (*of school*) director *m*; (*of university*) rector *m*. **~ly** /ˈprɪnsɪpəlɪ/ *adv* principalmente

principle /ˈprɪnsəpl/ *n* principio *m*. **in ~** en principio. **on ~** por principio

print /prɪnt/ *vt* imprimir; (*write in capitals*) escribir con letras de molde. **~ed matter** impresos *mpl*. ● *n* (*characters*) letra *f*; (*picture*) grabado *m*; (*Photo*) copia *f*; (*fabric*) estampado *m*. **in ~** (*published*) publicado; (*available*) a la venta. **out of ~** agotado. **~er** /ˈprɪntə(r)/ *n* impresor *m*; (*machine*) impresora *f*. **~ing** *n* impresión *f*; (*trade*) imprenta *f*. **~out** *n* listado *m*

prion /ˈpraɪɒn/ *n* prión *m*

prior /ˈpraɪə(r)/ *n* prior *m*. ● *adj* previo. **~ to** antes de. **~ity** /praɪˈɒrətɪ/ *n* prioridad *f*. **~y** *n* priorato *m*

prise /praɪz/ *vt*. **~ open** abrir haciendo palanca

prison /ˈprɪzn/ *n* cárcel *m*. **~er** *n* prisionero *m*; (*in prison*) preso *m*; (*under arrest*) detenido *m*. **~ officer** *n* funcionario *m* de prisiones

priva|cy /ˈprɪvəsɪ/ *n* privacidad *f*. **~te** /ˈpraɪvɪt/ *adj* privado; (*confidential*) personal; (lessons, house) particular. **in ~te** en privado; (*secretly*) en secreto. ● *n* soldado *m* raso. **~te detective** *n* detective *m* & *f* privado. **~tely** *adv* en privado. **~tion** /praɪˈveɪʃn/ *n* privación *f*

privilege /ˈprɪvəlɪdʒ/ *n* privilegio *m*. **~d** *adj* privilegiado. **be ~d to** tener el privilegio de

prize /praɪz/ *n* premio *m*. ● *adj* (idiot etc) de remate. ● *vt* estimar

pro /prəʊ/ *n*. **~s and cons** los pros *m* y los contras

probab|ility /prɒbəˈbɪlətɪ/ *n* probabilidad *f*. **~le** /ˈprɒbəbl/ *adj* probable. **~ly** *adv* probablemente

probation /prəˈbeɪʃn/ *n* período *m* de prueba; (*Jurid*) libertad *f* condicional

probe /prəʊb/ *n* sonda *f*; (*fig*) investigación *f*. ● *vt* sondar. ● *vi*. **~ into** investigar

problem /ˈprɒbləm/ *n* problema *m*. ● *adj* difícil. **~atic** /-ˈmætɪk/ *adj* problemático

procedure /prəˈsi:dʒə(r)/ *n* procedimiento *m*

proceed /prəˈsi:d/ *vi* proceder; (*move forward*) avanzar. **~ings** *npl* (*report*) actas *fpl*; (*Jurid*) proceso *m*. **~s** /ˈprəʊsi:dz/ *npl*. **the ~s** lo recaudado

process /ˈprəʊses/ *n* proceso *m*. **in the ~ of** en vías de. ● *vt* tratar; revelar (photo); tramitar (order).

P

~ion /prə'seʃn/ *n* desfile *m*; (*Relig*) procesión *f*. **~or** *n* procesador *m*. **food ~** procesador *m* de alimentos

procla|im /prə'kleɪm/ *vt* proclamar. **~mation** /prɒklə'meɪʃn/ *n* proclamación *f*

procure /prə'kjʊə(r)/ *vt* obtener

prod /prɒd/ *vt* (*pt* **prodded**) (*with sth sharp*) pinchar; (*with elbow*) darle un codazo a. ● *n* (*with sth sharp*) pinchazo *m*; (*with elbow*) codazo *m*

produc|e /prə'dju:s/ *vt* producir; surtir (effect); sacar (gun); producir (film); poner en escena (play). ● /'prɒdju:s/ *n* productos *mpl*. **~er** /prə'dju:sə(r)/ *n* (*TV, Cinema*) productor *m*; (*in theatre*) director *m*; (*manufacturer*) fabricante *m & f*. **~t** /'prɒdʌkt/ *n* producto *m*. **~tion** /prə'dʌkʃn/ *n* (*manufacture*) fabricación *f*; (*output*) producción *f*; (*of play*) producción *f*. **~tive** /prə'dʌktɪv/ *adj* productivo. **~tivity** /prɒdʌk'tɪvətɪ/ *n* productividad *f*

profess /prə'fes/ *vt* profesar; (*pretend*) pretender. **~ion** /-'feʃn/ *n* profesión *f*. **~ional** *adj & n* profesional (*m & f*). **~or** /-'fesə(r)/ *n* catedrático *m*; (*Amer*) profesor *m*

proficien|cy /prə'fɪʃənsɪ/ *n* competencia *f*. **~t** *adj* competente

profile /'prəʊfaɪl/ *n* perfil *m*

profit /'prɒfɪt/ *n* (*Com*) ganancia *f*; (*fig*) provecho *m*. ● *vi*. **~ from** sacar provecho de. **~able** *adj* provechoso

profound /prə'faʊnd/ *adj* profundo. **~ly** *adv* profundamente

profus|e /prə'fju:s/ *adj* profuso. **~ely** *adv* profusamente

prognosis /prɒg'nəʊsɪs/ *n* (*pl* **-oses**) pronóstico *m*

program /'prəʊgræm/ *n* (*Comp*) programa *m*; (*Amer, course*) curso *m*. **~me** /'prəʊgræm/ *n* programa *m*. ● *vt* (*pt* **-med**) programar. **~mer** *n* programador *m*

progress /'prəʊgres/ *n* progreso *m*; (*development*) desarrollo *m*. **make ~** hacer progresos. **in ~** en curso. ● /prə'gres/ *vi* hacer progresos; (*develop*) desarrollarse. **~ion** /prə'greʃn/ *n* progresión *f*; (*advance*) evolución *f*. **~ive** /prə'gresɪv/ *adj* progresivo; (*reforming*) progresista. **~ively** *adv* progresivamente

prohibit /prə'hɪbɪt/ *vt* prohibir; (*prevent*) impedir. **~ive** *adj* prohibitivo

project /prə'dʒekt/ *vt* proyectar. ● *vi* (*stick out*) sobresalir. ● /'prɒdʒekt/ *n* proyecto *m*; (*Schol*) trabajo *m*; (*Amer, housing ~*) complejo *m* de viviendas subvencionadas. **~or** /prə'dʒektə(r)/ *n* proyector *m*

prolific /prə'lɪfɪk/ *adj* prolífico

prologue /'prəʊlɒg/ *n* prólogo *m*

prolong /prə'lɒŋ/ *vt* prolongar

prom /prɒm/ *n* (*Amer*) baile *m* del colegio. **~enade** /prɒmə'nɑ:d/ *n* paseo *m* marítimo. ● *vi* pasearse.

> **i**
>
> **Prom** En EE.UU. un *prom* es un baile que se celebra para los estudiantes que terminan el *High School*. En Londres *the Proms* son una serie de conciertos de música clásica, durante los cuales una gran parte del público permanece de pie. Tienen lugar en el *Albert Hall* en el verano, durante ocho semanas. Oficialmente, son conocidos como los *Henry Wood Promenade Concerts*, en memoria de su fundador.

prominen|ce /'prɒmɪnəns/ *n* prominencia *f*; (*fig*) importancia *f*. **~t** *adj* prominente; (*important*) importante; (*conspicuous*) destacado

promiscu|ity /prɒmɪ'skju:ətɪ/ *n* promiscuidad *f*. **~ous** /prə'mɪskjʊəs/ *adj* promiscuo

promis|e /'prɒmɪs/ *n* promesa *f*. ● *vt/i* prometer. **~ing** *adj* prometedor; (future) halagüeño

promot|e /prə'məʊt/ *vt* promover; promocionar (product); (*in rank*) ascender. **~ion** /-'məʊʃn/ *n* promoción *f*; (*in rank*) ascenso *m*

prompt /prɒmpt/ *adj* rápido; (*punctual*) puntual. ● *adv* en punto. ● *n* (*Comp*) presto *m*. ● *vt* incitar; apuntar (actor). **~ly** *adv* puntualmente

prone /prəʊn/ *adj* (tendido) boca abajo. **be ~ to** ser propenso a

pronoun /'prəʊnaʊn/ *n* pronombre *m*

pronounc|e /prə'naʊns/ *vt* pronunciar; (*declare*) declarar. **~ement** *n* declaración *f*. **~ed** *adj* pronunciado; (*noticeable*) marcado

pronunciation /prənʌnsɪ'eɪʃn/ *n* pronunciación *f*

proof /pru:f/ *n* prueba *f*, pruebas *fpl*; (*of alcohol*) graduación *f* normal. ● *adj*. **~ against** a prueba de. **~-reading** *n* corrección *f* de pruebas

propaganda /prɒpə'gændə/ *n* propaganda *f*

propagate /'prɒpəgeɪt/ *vt* propagar. ● *vi* propagarse

propel /prə'pel/ *vt* (*pt* **propelled**) propulsar. **~ler** *n* hélice *f*

proper /'prɒpə(r)/ *adj* correcto; (*suitable*) apropiado; (*Gram*) propio; (*fam, real*) verdadero. **~ly** *adv* correctamente; (eat, work) bien

property /'prɒpətɪ/ *n* propiedad *f*; (*things owned*) bienes *mpl*. ● *adj* inmobiliario

prophe|cy /'prɒfəsɪ/ *n* profecía *f*. **~sy** /'prɒfɪsaɪ/ *vt/i* profetizar. **~t** /'prɒfɪt/ *n* profeta *m*. **~tic** /prə'fetɪk/ *adj* profético

proportion /prə'pɔ:ʃn/ *n* proporción *f*. **~al** *adj*, **~ate** /-ət/ *adj* proporcional

propos|al /prə'pəʊzl/ *n* propuesta *f*; (*of marriage*) proposición *f* matrimonial. **~e** /prə'pəʊz/ *vt* proponer. ● *vi*. **~e to s.o.** hacerle una oferta de matrimonio a una. **~ition** /prɒpə'zɪʃn/ *n* propuesta *f*; (*offer*) oferta *f*

proprietor /prə'praɪətə(r)/ *n* propietario *m*

pro rata /'prəʊ'rɑ:tə/ *adv* a prorrata

prose /prəʊz/ *n* prosa *f*

prosecut|e /'prɒsɪkju:t/ *vt* procesar (**for** por); (*carry on*) proseguir. **~ion** /-'kju:ʃn/ *n* proceso *m*. **the ~** (*side*) la acusación. **~or** *n* fiscal *m* & *f*; (*in private prosecutions*) abogado *m* de la acusación

prospect /'prɒspekt/ *n* (*possibility*) posibilidad *f* (**of** de); (*situation envisaged*) perspectiva *f*. **~s** (*chances*) perspectivas *fpl*. **~ive** /prə'spektɪv/ *adj* posible; (*future*) futuro. **~or** /prə'spektə(r)/ *n* prospector *m*. **~us** /prə'spektəs/ *n* folleto *m* informativo

prosper /'prɒspə(r)/ *vi* prosperar. **~ity** /-'sperətɪ/ *n* prosperidad *f*. **~ous** *adj* próspero

prostitut|e /'prɒstɪtju:t/ *n* prostituta *f*. **~ion** /-'tju:ʃn/ *n* prostitución *f*

prostrate /'prɒstreɪt/ *adj* postrado

protagonist /prəˈtægənɪst/ *n* protagonista *m & f*

protect /prəˈtekt/ *vt* proteger. **~ion** /-ʃn/ *n* protección *f*. **~ive** *adj* protector. **~or** *n* protector *m*

protein /ˈprəʊtiːn/ *n* proteína *f*

protest /ˈprəʊtest/ *n* protesta *f*. **in ~ (against)** en señal de protesta (contra). **under ~** bajo protesta. • /prəˈtest/ *vt/i* protestar

Protestant /ˈprɒtɪstənt/ *adj & n* protestante (*m & f*)

protester /prəˈtestə(r)/ *n* manifestante *m & f*

protocol /ˈprəʊtəkɒl/ *n* protocolo *m*

protrud|e /prəˈtruːd/ *vi* sobresalir. **~ing** *adj* (chin) prominente. **~ing eyes** ojos saltones

proud /praʊd/ *adj* orgulloso. **~ly** *adv* con orgullo; (*arrogantly*) orgullosamente

prove /pruːv/ *vt* probar; demostrar (loyalty). • *vi* resultar. **~n** *adj* probado

proverb /ˈprɒvɜːb/ *n* refrán *m*, proverbio *m*

provide /prəˈvaɪd/ *vt* proporcionar; dar (accommodation). **~ s.o. with sth** proveer a uno de algo. • *vi*. **~ for** (*allow for*) prever; mantener (person). **~d** *conj*. **~d (that)** con tal de que, siempre que

providen|ce /ˈprɒvɪdəns/ *n* providencia *f*. **~tial** /-ˈdenʃl/ *adj* providencial

providing /prəˈvaɪdɪŋ/ *conj*. **~ that** con tal de que, siempre que

provinc|e /ˈprɒvɪns/ *n* provincia *f*; (*fig*) competencia *f*. **~ial** /prəˈvɪnʃl/ *adj* provincial

provision /prəˈvɪʒn/ *n* provisión *f*; (*supply*) suministro *m*; (*stipulation*) disposición *f*. **~s** *npl* provisiones *fpl*, víveres *mpl*. **~al** *adj* provisional

provo|cation /prɒvəˈkeɪʃn/ *n* provocación *f*. **~cative** /-ˈvɒkətɪv/ *adj* provocador. **~ke** /prəˈvəʊk/ *vt* provocar

prow /praʊ/ *n* proa *f*

prowess /ˈpraʊɪs/ *n* destreza *f*; (*valour*) valor *m*

prowl /praʊl/ *vi* merodear. **~er** *n* merodeador *m*

proximity /prɒkˈsɪmətɪ/ *n* proximidad *f*

prude /pruːd/ *n* mojigato *m*

pruden|ce /ˈpruːdəns/ *n* prudencia *f*. **~t** *adj* prudente. **~tly** *adv* prudentemente

prudish /ˈpruːdɪʃ/ *adj* mojigato

prune /pruːn/ *n* ciruela *f* pasa. • *vt* podar

pry /praɪ/ *vi* curiosear. **~ into sth** entrometerse en algo. *vt* (*Amer*) see PRISE

PS *n* (*postscript*) P.D.

psalm /sɑːm/ *n* salmo *m*

psychiatr|ic /saɪkɪˈætrɪk/ *adj* psiquiátrico. **~ist** /saɪˈkaɪətrɪst/ *n* psiquiatra *m & f*. **~y** /saɪˈkaɪətrɪ/ *n* psiquiatría *f*

psychic /ˈsaɪkɪk/ *adj* para(p)sicológico

psycho|analysis /saɪkəʊəˈnæləsɪs/ *n* (p)sicoanálisis *m*. **~logical** /saɪkəˈlɒdʒɪkl/ *adj* (p)sicológico. **~logist** /saɪˈkɒlədʒɪst/ *n* (p)sicólogo *m*. **~logy** /saɪˈkɒlədʒɪ/ *n* (p)sicología *f*. **~therapy** /-ˈθerəpɪ/ *n* (p)sicoterapia *f*

pub /pʌb/ *n* bar *m*

i **pub** En Gran Bretaña, establecimiento donde se vende cerveza y otras bebidas (alcohólicas y no alcohólicas) para consumir en el local. *Pub* es la forma abreviada de *public house*. Suelen ofrecer comidas y una variedad de juegos, especialmente dardos, billar etc. Recientemente, las horas en que pueden abrir dependen de la licencia, siendo lo normal de 11 - 23 horas.

puberty /'pju:bətɪ/ *n* pubertad *f*

pubic /'pju:bɪk/ *adj* pubiano, púbico

public /'pʌblɪk/ *adj* público. **~an** *n* tabernero *m*. **~ation** /-'keɪʃn/ *n* publicación *f*. **~ holiday** *n* día *m* festivo, día *m* feriado (*LAm*). **~ house** *n* bar *m*. **~ity** /pʌb'lɪsətɪ/ *n* publicidad *f*. **~ize** /'pʌblɪsaɪz/ *vt* hacer público. **~ly** *adv* públicamente. **~ school** *n* colegio *m* privado; (*Amer*) instituto *m*, escuela *f* pública

i

public school En Inglaterra y Gales, un colegio privado para alumnos de edades comprendidas entre los 13 y 18 años. La mayoría de estos colegios tiene régimen de internado y a menudo son mixtos. En EE.UU. y Escocia, el término se utiliza para referirse a un colegio estatal.

publish /'pʌblɪʃ/ *vt* publicar. **~er** *n* editor *m*. **~ing** *n* publicación *f*. **~ing house** editorial *f*

pudding /'pʊdɪŋ/ *n* postre *m*; (*steamed*) budín *m*

puddle /'pʌdl/ *n* charco *m*

Puerto Ric|an /pwɜ:təʊ'ri:kən/ *adj & n* portorriqueño (*m*), puertorriqueño (*m*). **~o** /-əʊ/ *n* Puerto Rico *m*

puff /pʌf/ *n* (*of wind*) ráfaga *f*; (*of smoke*) nube *f*; (*action*) soplo *m*; (*on cigarette*) chupada *f*, calada *f*. ● *vt/i* soplar. **~ at** dar chupadas a (pipe). **~ out** (*swell up*) inflar, hinchar. **~ed** *adj* (*out of breath*) sin aliento. **~ paste** (*Amer*), **~ pastry** *n* hojaldre *m*. **~y** *adj* hinchado

pull /pʊl/ *vt* tirar de, jalar (*LAm*); desgarrarse (muscle). **~ a face** hacer una mueca. **~ a fast one** hacer una mala jugada. ● *vi* tirar, jalar (*LAm*). **~ at** tirar de, jalar (*LAm*). ● *n* tirón *m*, jalón *m* (*LAm*); (*pulling force*) fuerza *f*; (*influence*) influencia *f*. □ **~ away** *vi* (*Auto*) alejarse. □ **~ back** *vi* retirarse. □ **~ down** *vt* echar abajo (building); (*lower*) bajar. □ **~ in** *vi* (*Auto*) parar. □ **~ off** *vt* (*remove*) quitar; (*achieve*) conseguir. □ **~ out** *vt* sacar; retirar (team). *vi* (*Auto*) salirse. □ **~ through** *vi* recobrar la salud. □ **~ up** *vi* (*Auto*) parar. *vt* (*uproot*) arrancar; (*reprimand*) regañar

pullover /'pʊləʊvə(r)/ *n* suéter *m*, pulóver *m*, jersey *m*

pulp /pʌlp/ *n* pulpa *f*; (*for paper*) pasta *f*

pulpit /'pʊlpɪt/ *n* púlpito *m*

pulse /pʌls/ *n* (*Med*) pulso *m*; (*Culin*) legumbre *f*

pummel /'pʌml/ *vt* (*pt* **pummelled**) aporrear

pump /pʌmp/ *n* bomba *f*; (*for petrol*) surtidor *m*. ● *vt* sacar con una bomba. □ **~ up** *vt* inflar

pumpkin /'pʌmpkɪn/ *n* calabaza *f*

pun /pʌn/ *n* juego *m* de palabras

punch /pʌntʃ/ *vt* darle un puñetazo a; (*perforate*) perforar; hacer (hole). ● *n* puñetazo *m*; (*vigour*) fuerza *f*; (*device*) perforadora *f*; (*drink*) ponche *m*. **~ in** *vi* (*Amer*) fichar (*al entrar al trabajo*). **~ out** *vi* (*Amer*) fichar (*al salir del trabajo*)

punctual /ˈpʌŋktʃʊəl/ *adj* puntual. **~ity** /-ˈælətɪ/ *n* puntualidad *f*. **~ly** *adv* puntualmente

punctuat|e /ˈpʌŋkʃʊeɪt/ *vt* puntuar. **~ion** /-ˈeɪʃn/ *n* puntuación *f*

puncture /ˈpʌŋktʃə(r)/ *n* (*in tyre*) pinchazo *m*. **have a ~** pinchar. ● *vt* pinchar. ● *vi* pincharse

punish /ˈpʌnɪʃ/ *vt* castigar. **~ment** *n* castigo *m*

punk /pʌŋk/ *n* punk *m* & *f*, punki *m* & *f*; (*Music*) punk *m*; (*Amer, hoodlum*) vándalo *m*

punt /pʌnt/ *n* (*boat*) batea *f*. **~er** *n* apostante *m* & *f*

puny /ˈpju:nɪ/ *adj* (**-ier**, **-iest**) enclenque

pup /pʌp/ *n* cachorro *m*

pupil /ˈpju:pl/ *n* alumno *m*; (*of eye*) pupila *f*

puppet /ˈpʌpɪt/ *n* marioneta *f*, títere *m*; (*glove ~*) títere *m*

puppy /ˈpʌpɪ/ *n* cachorro *m*

purchase /ˈpɜ:tʃəs/ *vt* adquirir. ● *n* adquisición *f*. **~r** *n* comprador *m*

pur|e /ˈpjʊə(r)/ *adj* (**-er**, **-est**) puro. **~ity** *n* pureza *f*

purgatory /ˈpɜ:gətrɪ/ *n* purgatorio *m*

purge /pɜ:dʒ/ *vt* purgar. ● *n* purga *f*

purif|ication /pjʊərɪfɪˈkeɪʃn/ *n* purificación *f*. **~y** /ˈpjʊərɪfaɪ/ *vt* purificar

purist /ˈpjʊərɪst/ *n* purista *m* & *f*

puritan /ˈpjʊərɪtən/ *n* puritano *m*. **~ical** /-ˈtænɪkl/ *adj* puritano

purple /ˈpɜ:pl/ *adj* morado. ● *n* morado *m*, púrpura *f*

purport /pəˈpɔ:t/ *vt*. **~ to be** pretender ser

purpose /ˈpɜ:pəs/ *n* propósito *m*; (*determination*) resolución *f*. **on ~** a propósito. **serve a ~** servir de algo. **~ful** *adj* (*resolute*) resuelto. **~ly** *adv* a propósito

purr /pɜ:(r)/ *vi* ronronear

purse /pɜ:s/ *n* monedero *m*; (*Amer*) bolso *m*, cartera *f* (*LAm*), bolsa *f* (*Mex*)

pursu|e /pəˈsju:/ *vt* perseguir, continuar con (course of action). **~it** /pəˈsju:t/ *n* persecución *f*; (*pastime*) actividad *f*

pus /pʌs/ *n* pus *m*

push /pʊʃ/ *vt* empujar; apretar (*button*). ● *vi* empujar. ● *n* empujón *m*; (*effort*) esfuerzo *m*. □ **~ back** *vt* hacer retroceder. □ **~ off** *vi* ☒ largarse. **~chair** *n* sillita *f* de paseo, carreola *f* (*Mex*). **~y** *adj* (*pej*) ambicioso

pussy /ˈpʊsɪ/ (*pl* **-sies**), **pussycat** /ˈpʊsɪkæt/ *n* ☐ minino *m*

put /pʊt/ *vt* (*pt* **put**, *pres p* **putting**) poner; (*with care, precision*) colocar; (*inside sth*) meter; (*express*) decir. □ **~ across** *vt* comunicar. □ **~ away** *vt* guardar. □ **~ back** *vt* volver a poner; retrasar (clock). □ **~ by** *vt* guardar; ahorrar (money). □ **~ down** *vt* (*on a surface*) dejar; colgar (phone); (*suppress*) sofocar; (*write*) apuntar; (*kill*) sacrificar. □ **~ forward** *vt* presentar (plan); proponer (candidate); adelantar (clocks); adelantar (meeting). □ **~ in** *vt* (*instal*) poner; presentar (claim). □ **~ in for** *vt* solicitar. □ **~ off** *vt* aplazar, posponer; (*disconcert*) desconcertar. □ **~ on** *vt* (*wear*) ponerse; poner (CD, music); encender (light). □ **~ out** *vt* (*extinguish*) apagar; (*inconvenience*) incomodar; extender (hand); (*disconcert*) desconcertar. □ **~ through** *vt* (*phone*) poner, pasar (**to** con). □ **~ up** *vt* levantar; aumentar (rent); subir (price); poner (sign); alojar (guest). □ ~ **up with** *vt* aguantar, soportar

putrid /'pju:trɪd/ *adj* putrefacto

putt /pʌt/ *n* (*golf*) golpe *m* suave

puzzl|e /'pʌzl/ *n* misterio *m*; (*game*) rompecabezas *m*. ● *vt* dejar perplejo. **~ed** *adj* (expression) de desconcierto. **I'm ~ed about it** me tiene perplejo. **~ing** *adj* incomprensible; (*odd*) curioso

pygmy /'pɪgmɪ/ *n* pigmeo *m*

pyjamas /pə'dʒɑ:məz/ *npl* pijama *m*, piyama *m or f* (*LAm*)

pylon /'paɪlɒn/ *n* pilón *m*

pyramid /'pɪrəmɪd/ *n* pirámide *f*

python /'paɪθn/ *n* pitón *m*

Qq

quack /kwæk/ *n* (*of duck*) graznido *m*; (*person*) charlatán *m*. **~ doctor** *n* curandero *m*

quadrangle /'kwɒdræŋgl/ *n* cuadrilátero *m*

quadruped /'kwɒdrʊped/ *n* cuadrúpedo *m*

quadruple /'kwɒdrʊpl/ *adj & n* cuádruplo (*m*). ● *vt* cuadruplicar

quagmire /'kwægmaɪə(r)/ *n* lodazal *m*

quaint /kweɪnt/ *adj* (**-er, -est**) pintoresco; (*odd*) curioso

quake /kweɪk/ *vi* temblar. ● *n* ▣ terremoto *m*

qualif|ication /kwɒlɪfɪ'keɪʃn/ *n* título *m*; (*requirement*) requisito *m*; (*ability*) capacidad *f*; (*Sport*) clasificación *f*; (*fig*) reserva *f*. **~ied** /'kwɒlɪfaɪd/ *adj* cualificado; (*with degree, diploma*) titulado; (*competent*) capacitado. **~y** /'kwɒlɪfaɪ/ *vt* calificar; (*limit*) limitar. ● *vi* titularse; (*Sport*) clasificarse. **~y for sth** (*be entitled to*) tener derecho a algo

qualit|ative /'kwɒlɪtətɪv/ *adj* cualitativo. **~y** /'kwɒlɪtɪ/ *n* calidad *f*; (*attribute*) cualidad *f*

qualm /kwɑ:m/ *n* reparo *m*

quandary /'kwɒndrɪ/ *n* dilema *m*

quanti|fy /'kwɒntɪfaɪ/ *vt* cuantificar. **~ty** /-tɪ/ *n* cantidad *f*

quarantine /'kwɒrənti:n/ *n* cuarentena *f*. ● *vt* poner en cuarentena

quarrel /'kwɒrəl/ *n* pelea *f*. ● *vi* (*pt* **quarrelled**) pelearse, discutir. **~some** /-səm/ *adj* pendenciero

quarry /'kwɒrɪ/ *n* (*excavation*) cantera *f*; (*prey*) presa *f*

quart /kwɔ:t/ *n* cuarto *m* de galón

quarter /'kwɔ:tə(r)/ *n* cuarto *m*; (*of year*) trimestre *m*; (*district*) barrio *m*. **a ~ of an hour** un cuarto de hora. ● *vt* dividir en cuartos; (*Mil*) acuartelar. **~-final** *n* cuarto *m* de final. **~ly** *adj* trimestral. ● *adv* trimestralmente

quartz /kwɔ:ts/ *n* cuarzo *m*

quay /ki:/ *n* muelle *m*

queasy /'kwi:zɪ/ *adj* mareado

queen /kwi:n/ *n* reina *f*. **~ mother** *n* reina *f* madre

queer /kwɪə(r)/ *adj* (**-er, -est**) extraño

quench /kwentʃ/ *vt* quitar (thirst); sofocar (desire)

query /'kwɪərɪ/ *n* pregunta *f*. ● *vt* preguntar; (*doubt*) poner en duda

quest /kwest/ *n* busca *f*

question /'kwestʃən/ *n* pregunta *f*; (*for discussion*) cuestión *f*. **in ~** en cuestión. **out of the ~** imposible. **without ~** sin duda. ● *vt* hacer preguntas a; (police etc) interrogar; (*doubt*) poner en duda. **~able** *adj* discutible. **~ mark** *n* signo *m* de interrogación. **~naire** /-ˈneə(r)/ *n* cuestionario *m*

queue /kjuː/ *n* cola *f*. ● *vi* (*pres p* **queuing**) hacer cola

quibble /ˈkwɪbl/ *vi* discutir; (*split hairs*) sutilizar

quick /kwɪk/ *adj* (**-er**, **-est**) rápido. **be ~!** ¡date prisa! ● *adv* rápido. **~en** *vt* acelerar. ● *vi* acelerarse. **~ly** *adv* rápido. **~sand** *n* arena *f* movediza. **~-tempered** /-ˈtempəd/ *adj* irascible

quid /kwɪd/ *n invar* [I] libra *f* (esterlina)

quiet /ˈkwaɪət/ *adj* (**-er**, **-est**) tranquilo; (*silent*) callado; (*discreet*) discreto. ● *n* tranquilidad *f*. ● *vt/i* (*Amer*) *see* **QUIETEN**. **~en** *vt* calmar. ● *n* calmarse. **~ly** *adv* tranquilamente; (*silently*) silenciosamente; (*discreetly*) discretamente. **~ness** *n* tranquilidad *f*

quilt /kwɪlt/ *n* edredón *m*. **~ed** *adj* acolchado

quintet /kwɪnˈtet/ *n* quinteto *m*

quirk /kwɜːk/ *n* peculiaridad *f*

quit /kwɪt/ *vt* (*pt* **quitted**) dejar. **~ doing** (*Amer, cease*) dejar de hacer. ● *vi* (*give in*) abandonar; (*stop*) parar; (*resign*) dimitir

quite /kwaɪt/ *adv* bastante; (*completely*) totalmente; (*really*) verdaderamente. **~ (so!)** ¡claro! **~ a few** bastante

quits /kwɪts/ *adj*. **be ~** estar en paz. **call it ~** darlo por terminado

quiver /ˈkwɪvə(r)/ *vi* temblar

quiz /kwɪz/ *n* (*pl* **quizzes**) serie *f* de preguntas; (*game*) concurso *m*. ● *vt* (*pt* **quizzed**) interrogar. **~zical** *adj* burlón

quota /ˈkwəʊtə/ *n* cuota *f*

quot|ation /kwəʊˈteɪʃn/ *n* cita *f*; (*price*) presupuesto *m*. **~ation marks** *npl* comillas *fpl*. **~e** /kwəʊt/ *vt* citar; (*Com*) cotizar. ● *n* [I] cita *f*; (*price*) presupuesto *m*. **in ~es** *npl* entre comillas

Rr

rabbi /ˈræbaɪ/ *n* rabino *m*

rabbit /ˈræbɪt/ *n* conejo *m*

rabi|d /ˈræbɪd/ *adj* feroz; (dog) rabioso. **~es** /ˈreɪbiːz/ *n* rabia *f*

race /reɪs/ *n* (*in sport*) carrera *f*; (*ethnic group*) raza *f*. ● *vt* hacer correr (horse). ● *vi* (*run*) correr, ir corriendo; (*rush*) ir de prisa. **~course** *n* hipódromo *m*. **~horse** *n* caballo *m* de carreras. **~ relations** *npl* relaciones *fpl* raciales. **~track** *n* hipódromo *m*

racial /ˈreɪʃl/ *adj* racial

racing /ˈreɪsɪŋ/ *n* carreras *fpl*. **~ car** *n* coche *m* de carreras

racis|m /ˈreɪsɪzəm/ *n* racismo *m*. **~t** *adj & n* racista (*m & f*)

rack¹ /ræk/ *n* (*shelf*) estante *m*; (*for luggage*) rejilla *f*; (*for plates*) escurreplatos *m*. ● *vt*. **~ one's brains** devanarse los sesos

rack² /ræk/ *n*. **go to ~ and ruin** quedarse en la ruina

racket /ˈrækɪt/ *n* (*for sports*) raqueta; (*din*) alboroto *m*; (*swindle*) estafa *f*. **~eer** /-əˈtɪə(r)/ *n* estafador *m*

racy /ˈreɪsɪ/ *adj* (**-ier**, **-iest**) vivo

radar /ˈreɪdɑː(r)/ *n* radar *m*

radian|ce /ˈreɪdɪəns/ *n* resplandor *m*. **~t** *adj* radiante

radiat|e /ˈreɪdɪeɪt/ *vt* irradiar. ● *vi* divergir. **~ion** /-ˈeɪʃn/ *n* radiación *f*. **~or** *n* radiador *m*

radical /ˈrædɪkl/ *adj & n* radical (*m*)

radio /ˈreɪdɪəʊ/ *n* (*pl* **-os**) radio *f or m*. ● *vt* transmitir por radio. **~active** /reɪdɪəʊˈæktɪv/ *adj* radiactivo. **~activity** /-ˈtɪvətɪ/ *n* radiactividad *f*

radish /ˈrædɪʃ/ *n* rábano *m*

radius /ˈreɪdɪəs/ *n* (*pl* **-dii**/-dɪaɪ/) radio *m*

raffle /ˈræfl/ *n* rifa *f*

raft /rɑːft/ *n* balsa *f*

rafter /ˈrɑːftə(r)/ *n* cabrio *m*

rag /ræg/ *n* andrajo *m*; (*for wiping*) trapo *m*. **in ~s** (person) andrajoso

rage /reɪdʒ/ *n* rabia *f*; (*fashion*) moda *f*. ● *vi* estar furioso; (storm) bramar

ragged /ˈrægɪd/ *adj* (person) andrajoso; (clothes) hecho jirones

raid /reɪd/ *n* (*Mil*) incursión *f*; (*by police etc*) redada *f*; (*by thieves*) asalto *m*. ● *vt* (*Mil*) atacar; (police) hacer una redada en; (thieves) asaltar. **~er** *n* invasor *m*; (*thief*) ladrón *m*

rail /reɪl/ *n* barandilla *f*; (*for train*) riel *m*; (*rod*) barra *f*. **by ~** por ferrocarril. **~ing** *n* barandilla *f*; (*fence*) verja *f*. **~road** *n* (*Amer*), **~way** *n* ferrocarril *m*. **~way station** *n* estación *f* de ferrocarril

rain /reɪn/ *n* lluvia *f*. ● *vi* llover. **~bow** /-bəʊ/ *n* arco *m* iris. **~coat** *n* impermeable *m*. **~fall** *n* precipitación *f*. **~y** *adj* (**-ier**, **-iest**) lluvioso

raise /reɪz/ *vt* levantar; (*breed*) criar; obtener (money etc); formular (question); plantear (problem); subir (price). ● *n* (*Amer*) aumento *m*

raisin /ˈreɪzn/ *n* (uva *f*) pasa *f*

rake /reɪk/ *n* rastrillo *m*. ● *vt* rastrillar; (*search*) buscar en. □ **~ up** *vt* remover

rally /ˈrælɪ/ *vt* reunir; (*revive*) reanimar. ● *n* reunión *f*; (*Auto*) rally *m*

ram /ræm/ *n* carnero *m*. ● *vt* (*pt* **rammed**) (*thrust*) meter por la fuerza; (*crash into*) chocar con

RAM /ræm/ *n* (*Comp*) RAM *f*

rambl|e /ˈræmbl/ *n* excursión *f* a pie. ● *vi* ir de paseo; (*in speech*) divagar. □ **~e on** *vi* divagar. **~er** *n* excursionista *m & f*. **~ing** *adj* (speech) divagador

ramp /ræmp/ *n* rampa *f*

rampage /ræmˈpeɪdʒ/ *vi* alborotarse. ● /ˈræmpeɪdʒ/ *n*. **go on the ~** alborotarse

ramshackle /ˈræmʃækl/ *adj* desvencijado

ran /ræn/ *see* **RUN**

ranch /rɑːntʃ/ *n* hacienda *f*

random /ˈrændəm/ *adj* hecho al azar; (*chance*) fortuito. ● *n*. **at ~** al azar

rang /ræŋ/ *see* **RING**[2]

range /reɪndʒ/ *n* alcance *m*; (*distance*) distancia *f*; (*series*) serie *f*; (*of mountains*) cordillera *f*; (*extent*) extensión *f*; (*Com*) surtido *m*; (*stove*) cocina *f* económica. ● *vi* extenderse; (*vary*) variar. **~r** *n* guardabosque *m*

rank /ræŋk/ *n* posición *f*, categoría *f*; (*row*) fila *f*; (*for taxis*) parada *f*. **the ~ and file** la masa *f*. **~s** *npl* soldados *mpl* rasos. ● *adj* (**-er**, **-est**) (*smell*) fétido; (*fig*) completo. ● *vt* clasificar. ● *vi* clasificarse

ransack /ˈrænsæk/ *vt* registrar; (*pillage*) saquear

ransom /ˈrænsəm/ *n* rescate *m*.

hold s.o. to ~ exigir rescate por uno. ● *vt* rescatar; (*redeem*) redimir

rant /rænt/ *vi* despotricar

rap /ræp/ *n* golpe *m* seco. ● *vt/i* (*pt* **rapped**) golpear

rape /reɪp/ *vt* violar. ● *n* violación *f*

rapid /'ræpɪd/ *adj* rápido. **~s** *npl* rápidos *mpl*

rapist /'reɪpɪst/ *n* violador *m*

raptur|e /'ræptʃə(r)/ *n* éxtasis *m*. **~ous** /-rəs/ *adj* extático

rare /reə(r)/ *adj* (**-er**, **-est**) raro; (*Culin*) poco hecho. **~fied** /'reərɪfaɪd/ *adj* enrarecido. **~ly** *adv* raramente

raring /'reərɪŋ/ *adj* 🅸. ~ **to** impaciente por

rarity /'reərətɪ/ *n* rareza *f*

rascal /'rɑ:skl/ *n* granuja *m* & *f*

rash /ræʃ/ *adj* (**-er**, **-est**) precipitado, imprudente. ● *n* erupción *f*

rasher /'ræʃə(r)/ *n* loncha *f*

rashly /'ræʃlɪ/ *adv* precipitadamente, imprudentemente

rasp /rɑ:sp/ *n* (*file*) escofina *f*

raspberry /'rɑ:zbrɪ/ *n* frambuesa *f*

rat /ræt/ *n* rata *f*

rate /reɪt/ *n* (*ratio*) proporción *f*; (*speed*) velocidad *f*; (*price*) precio *m*; (*of interest*) tipo *m*. **at any** ~ de todas formas. **at this** ~ así. **~s** *npl* (*taxes*) impuestos *mpl* municipales. ● *vt* valorar; (*consider*) considerar; (*Amer, deserve*) merecer. ● *vi* ser considerado

rather /'rɑ:ðə(r)/ *adv* mejor dicho; (*fairly*) bastante; (*a little*) un poco. ● *int* claro. **I would** ~ **not** prefiero no

rating /'reɪtɪŋ/ *n* clasificación *f*; (*sailor*) marinero *m*; (*number, TV*) índice *m*

ratio /'reɪʃɪəʊ/ *n* (*pl* **-os**) proporción *f*

ration /'ræʃn/ *n* ración *f*. **~s** *npl* (*provisions*) víveres *mpl*. ● *vt* racionar

rational /'ræʃənəl/ *adj* racional. **~ize** *vt* racionalizar

rattle /'rætl/ *vi* traquetear. ● *vt* (*shake*) agitar; 🅸 desconcertar. ● *n* traqueteo *m*; (*toy*) sonajero *m*. □ ~ **off** *vt* (*fig*) decir de corrida

raucous /'rɔ:kəs/ *adj* estridente

ravage /'rævɪdʒ/ *vt* estragar

rave /reɪv/ *vi* delirar; (*in anger*) despotricar. ~ **about sth** poner a algo por las nubes

raven /'reɪvn/ *n* cuervo *m*

ravenous /'rævənəs/ *adj* voraz; (person) hambriento. **be** ~ morirse de hambre

ravine /rə'vi:n/ *n* barranco *m*

raving /'reɪvɪŋ/ *adj*. ~ **mad** loco de atar

ravishing /'rævɪʃɪŋ/ *adj* (*enchanting*) encantador

raw /rɔ:/ *adj* (**-er**, **-est**) crudo; (sugar) sin refinar; (*inexperienced*) inexperto. ~ **deal** *n* tratamiento *m* injusto, injusticia *f*. ~ **materials** *npl* materias *fpl* primas

ray /reɪ/ *n* rayo *m*

raze /reɪz/ *vt* arrasar

razor /'reɪzə(r)/ *n* navaja *f* de afeitar; (*electric*) maquinilla *f* de afeitar

Rd /rəʊd/ *abbr* (= **Road**) C/, Calle *f*

re /ri:/ *prep* con referencia a. ● *pref* re.

reach /ri:tʃ/ *vt* alcanzar; (*extend*) extender; (*arrive at*) llegar a; (*achieve*) lograr; (*hand over*) pasar, dar. ● *vi* extenderse. ● *n* alcance *m*. **within** ~ **of** al alcance de; (*close to*) a corta distancia de. □ ~ **out** *vi* alargar la mano

react /rɪ'ækt/ *vi* reaccionar. **~ion** /rɪ'ækʃn/ *n* reacción *f*. **~ionary** *adj & n* reaccionario (*m*). **~or** /rɪ'æktə(r)/ *n* reactor *m*

read /ri:d/ *vt* (*pt* **read** /red/) leer; (*study*) estudiar; (*interpret*) interpretar. ● *vi* leer; (instrument) indicar. ▫ **~ out** *vt* leer en voz alta. **~able** *adj* (*clear*) legible. **~er** *n* lector *m*

readily /'redɪlɪ/ *adv* (*willingly*) de buena gana; (*easily*) fácilmente

reading /'ri:dɪŋ/ *n* lectura *f*

readjust /ri:ə'dʒʌst/ *vt* reajustar. ● *vi* readaptarse (**to** a)

ready /'redɪ/ *adj* (**-ier**, **-iest**) listo, preparado. **get ~** prepararse. **~-made** *adj* confeccionado

real /rɪəl/ *adj* verdadero. ● *adv* (*Amer fam*) verdaderamente. **~ estate** *n* bienes *mpl* raíces, propiedad *f* inmobiliaria. **~ estate agent** *see* REALTOR. **~ism** *n* realismo *m*. **~ist** *n* realista *m & f*. **~istic** /-'lɪstɪk/ *adj* realista. **~ity** /rɪ'ælətɪ/ *n* realidad *f*. **~ization** /rɪəlaɪ'zeɪʃn/ *n* comprensión *f*. **~ize** /'rɪəlaɪz/ *vt* darse cuenta de; (*fulfil, Com*) realizar. **~ly** /'rɪəlɪ/ *adv* verdaderamente

realm /relm/ *n* reino *m*

realtor /'ri:əltə(r)/ *n* (*Amer*) agente *m* inmobiliario

reap /ri:p/ *vt* segar; (*fig*) cosechar

reappear /ri:ə'pɪə(r)/ *vi* reaparecer

rear /rɪə(r)/ *n* parte *f* de atrás. ● *adj* posterior, trasero. ● *vt* (*bring up, breed*) criar. ● *vi* **~ (up)** (horse) encabritarse

rearguard /'rɪəgɑ:d/ *n* retaguardia *f*

rearrange /ri:ə'reɪndʒ/ *vt* arreglar de otra manera

reason /'ri:zn/ *n* razón *f*, motivo *m*. **within ~** dentro de lo razonable. ● *vi* razonar. **~able** *adj* razonable. **~ing** *n* razonamiento *m*

reassur|ance /ri:ə'ʃʊərəns/ *n* promesa *f* tranquilizadora; (*guarantee*) garantía *f*. **~e** /ri:ə'ʃʊə(r)/ *vt* tranquilizar

rebate /'ri:beɪt/ *n* (*discount*) rebaja *f*

rebel /'rebl/ *n* rebelde *m & f*. ● /rɪ'bel/ *vi* (*pt* **rebelled**) rebelarse. **~lion** /rɪ'belɪən/ *n* rebelión *f*. **~lious** *adj* rebelde

rebound /rɪ'baʊnd/ *vi* rebotar; (*fig*) recaer. ● /'ri:baʊnd/ *n* rebote *m*

rebuff /rɪ'bʌf/ *vt* rechazar. ● *n* desaire *m*

rebuild /ri:'bɪld/ *vt* (*pt* **rebuilt**) reconstruir

rebuke /rɪ'bju:k/ *vt* reprender. ● *n* reprimenda *f*

recall /rɪ'kɔ:l/ *vt* (*call s.o. back*) llamar; (*remember*) recordar. ● *n* /'ri:kɔ:l/ (*of goods, ambassador*) retirada *f*; (*memory*) memoria *f*

recap /'ri:kæp/ *vt/i* (*pt* **recapped**) 🅸 resumir

recapitulate /ri:kə'pɪtʃʊleɪt/ *vt/i* resumir

recapture /ri:'kæptʃə(r)/ *vt* recobrar; (*recall*) hacer revivir

recede /rɪ'si:d/ *vi* retroceder

receipt /rɪ'si:t/ *n* recibo *m*. **~s** *npl* (*Com*) ingresos *mpl*

receive /rɪ'si:v/ *vt* recibir. **~r** *n* (*of stolen goods*) perista *m & f*; (*part of phone*) auricular *m*

recent /'ri:snt/ *adj* reciente. **~ly** *adv* recientemente

recept|ion /rɪ'sepʃn/ *n* recepción *f*; (*welcome*) acogida *f*. **~ionist** *n* recepcionista *m & f*. **~ive** /-tɪv/ *adj* receptivo

recess /rɪ'ses/ *n* hueco *m*; (*holiday*)

r

vacaciones *fpl*. **~ion** /rɪ'seʃn/ *n* recesión *f*

recharge /riː'tʃɑːdʒ/ *vt* cargar de nuevo, recargar

recipe /'resəpɪ/ *n* receta *f*. **~ book** *n* libro *m* de cocina

recipient /rɪ'sɪpɪənt/ *n* recipiente *m & f*; (*of letter*) destinatario *m*

recit|al /rɪ'saɪtl/ *n* (*Mus*) recital *m*. **~e** /rɪ'saɪt/ *vt* recitar; (*list*) enumerar

reckless /'reklɪs/ *adj* imprudente. **~ly** *adv* imprudentemente

reckon /'rekən/ *vt/i* calcular; (*consider*) considerar; (*think*) pensar. □ **~ on** *vt* (*rely*) contar con

reclaim /rɪ'kleɪm/ *vt* reclamar; recuperar (land)

reclin|e /rɪ'klaɪn/ *vi* recostarse. **~ing** *adj* acostado; (seat) reclinable

recluse /rɪ'kluːs/ *n* ermitaño *m*

recogni|tion /rekəg'nɪʃn/ *n* reconocimiento *m*. **beyond ~tion** irreconocible. **~ze** /'rekəgnaɪz/ *vt* reconocer

recoil /rɪ'kɔɪl/ *vi* retroceder. ● /'riːkɔɪl/ *n* (*of gun*) culatazo *m*

recollect /rekə'lekt/ *vt* recordar. **~ion** /-ʃn/ *n* recuerdo *m*

recommend /rekə'mend/ *vt* recomendar. **~ation** /-'deɪʃn/ *n* recomendación *f*

reconcil|e /'rekənsaɪl/ *vt* reconciliar (people); conciliar (facts). **~e o.s.** resignarse (**to** a). **~iation** /-sɪlɪ'eɪʃn/ *n* reconciliación *f*

reconnaissance /rɪ'kɒnɪsns/ *n* reconocimiento *m*

reconnoitre /rekə'nɔɪtə(r)/ *vt* (*pres p* **-tring**) (*Mil*) reconocer

re: ~consider /riːkən'sɪdə(r)/ *vt* volver a considerar. **~construct** /riːkən'strʌkt/ *vt* reconstruir

record /rɪ'kɔːd/ *vt* (*in register*) registrar; (*in diary*) apuntar; (*Mus*) grabar. ● /'rekɔːd/ *n* (*document*) documento *m*; (*of events*) registro *m*; (*Mus*) disco *m*; (*Sport*) récord *m*. **off the ~** en confianza. **~er** /rɪ'kɔːdə(r)/ *n* registrador *m*; (*Mus*) flauta *f* dulce. **~ing** /rɪ'kɔːdɪŋ/ *n* grabación *f*. **~-player** /'rekɔːd-/ *n* tocadiscos *m invar*

recount /rɪ'kaʊnt/ *vt* contar, relatar

re-count /'riːkaʊnt/ *vt* volver a contar; recontar (votes). ● /'riːkaʊnt/ *n* (*Pol*) recuento *m*

recover /rɪ'kʌvə(r)/ *vt* recuperar. ● *vi* reponerse. **~y** *n* recuperación *f*

recreation /rekrɪ'eɪʃn/ *n* recreo *m*. **~al** *adj* de recreo

recruit /rɪ'kruːt/ *n* recluta *m*. ● *vt* reclutar; contratar (staff). **~ment** *n* reclutamiento *m*

rectang|le /'rektæŋgl/ *n* rectángulo *m*. **~ular** /-'tæŋgjʊlə(r)/ *adj* rectangular

rectify /'rektɪfaɪ/ *vt* rectificar

rector /'rektə(r)/ *n* párroco *m*; (*of college*) rector *m*. **~y** *n* rectoría *f*

recuperat|e /rɪ'kuːpəreɪt/ *vt* recuperar. ● *vi* reponerse. **~ion** /-'reɪʃn/ *n* recuperación *f*

recur /rɪ'kɜː(r)/ *vi* (*pt* **recurred**) repetirse. **~rence** /rɪ'kʌrns/ *n* repetición *f*. **~rent** /rɪ'kʌrənt/ *adj* repetido

recycle /riː'saɪkl/ *vt* reciclar

red /red/ *adj* (**redder**, **reddest**) rojo. ● *n* rojo. **be in the ~** estar en números rojos. **~den** *vi* enrojecerse. **~dish** *adj* rojizo

redecorate /riː'dekəreɪt/ *vt* pintar de nuevo

rede|em /rɪ'diːm/ *vt* redimir. **~mption** /-'dempʃn/ *n* redención *f*

red: ~-handed /-'hændɪd/ *adj.* **catch s.o. ~handed** agarrar a uno con las manos en la masa. **~ herring** *n* (*fig*) pista *f* falsa. **~-hot** *adj* al rojo vivo. **~ light** *n* luz *f* roja

redo /riː'duː/ *vt* (*pt* **redid**, *pp* **redone**) rehacer

redouble /rɪ'dʌbl/ *vt* redoblar

red tape /red'teɪp/ *n* (*fig*) papeleo *m*

reduc|e /rɪ'djuːs/ *vt* reducir; aliviar (pain). ● *vi* (*Amer, slim*) adelgazar. **~tion** /rɪ'dʌkʃn/ *n* reducción *f*

redundan|cy /rɪ'dʌndənsɪ/ *n* superfluidad *f*; (*unemployment*) despido *m*. **~t** superfluo. **she was made ~t** la despidieron por reducción de plantilla

reed /riːd/ *n* caña *f*; (*Mus*) lengüeta *f*

reef /riːf/ *n* arrecife *m*

reek /riːk/ *n* mal olor *m*. ● *vi*. **~ (of)** apestar a

reel /riːl/ *n* carrete *m*. ● *vi* dar vueltas; (*stagger*) tambalearse. □ **~ off** *vt* (*fig*) enumerar

refectory /rɪ'fektərɪ/ *n* refectorio *m*

refer /rɪ'fɜː(r)/ *vt* (*pt* **referred**) remitir. ● *vi* referirse. **~ to** referirse a; (*consult*) consultar. **~ee** /refə'riː/ *n* árbitro *m*; (*for job*) referencia *f*. ● *vi* (*pt* **refereed**) arbitrar. **~ence** /'refrəns/ *n* referencia *f*. **~ence book** *n* libro *m* de consulta. **in ~ to, with ~ to** con referencia a; (*Com*) respecto a. **~endum** /refə'rendəm/ *n* (*pl* **-ums** *or* **-da**) referéndum *m*

refill /riː'fɪl/ *vt* volver a llenar. ● /'riːfɪl/ *n* recambio *m*

refine /rɪ'faɪn/ *vt* refinar. **~d** *adj* refinado. **~ry** /-ərɪ/ *n* refinería *f*

reflect /rɪ'flekt/ *vt* reflejar. ● *vi* reflejarse; (*think*) reflexionar. □ **~ badly upon** perjudicar. **~ion** /-ʃn/ *n* reflexión *f*; (*image*) reflejo *m*. **~or** *n* reflector *m*

reflex /'riːfleks/ *adj* & *n* reflejo (*m*). **~ive** /rɪ'fleksɪv/ *adj* (*Gram*) reflexivo

reform /rɪ'fɔːm/ *vt* reformar. ● *vi* reformarse. ● *n* reforma *f*

refrain /rɪ'freɪn/ *n* estribillo *m*. ● *vi* abstenerse (**from** de)

refresh /rɪ'freʃ/ *vt* refrescar. **~ing** *adj* refrescante. **~ments** *npl* (*food and drink*) refrigerio *m*

refrigerat|e /rɪ'frɪdʒəreɪt/ *vt* refrigerar. **~or** *n* frigorífico *m*, refrigerador *m* (*LAm*)

refuel /riː'fjuːəl/ *vt/i* (*pt* **refuelled**) repostar

refuge /'refjuːdʒ/ *n* refugio *m*. **take ~** refugiarse. **~e** /refjʊ'dʒiː/ *n* refugiado *m*

refund /rɪ'fʌnd/ *vt* reembolsar. ● /'riːfʌnd/ *n* reembolso *m*

refusal /rɪ'fjuːzl/ *n* negativa *f*

refuse /rɪ'fjuːz/ *vt* rehusar. ● *vi* negarse. ● /'refjuːs/ *n* residuos *mpl*

refute /rɪ'fjuːt/ *vt* refutar

regain /rɪ'geɪn/ *vt* recobrar

regal /'riːgl/ *adj* real

regard /rɪ'gɑːd/ *vt* considerar; (*look at*) contemplar. **as ~s** en lo que se refiere a. ● *n* (*consideration*) consideración *f*; (*esteem*) estima *f*. **~s** *npl* saludos *mpl*. **kind ~s** recuerdos. **~ing** *prep* en lo que se refiere a. **~less** *adv* a pesar de todo. **~less of** sin tener en cuenta

regatta /rɪ'gætə/ *n* regata *f*

regime /reɪ'ʒiːm/ *n* régimen *m*

regiment /'redʒɪmənt/ *n* regimiento *m*. **~al** /-'mentl/ *adj* del regimiento

r

region /ˈriːdʒən/ *n* región *f*. **in the ~ of** alrededor de. **~al** *adj* regional

register /ˈredʒɪstə(r)/ *n* registro *m*. ● *vt* registrar; matricular (vehicle); declarar (birth); certificar (letter); facturar (luggage). ● *vi* (*enrol*) inscribirse; (*fig*) producir impresión

registrar /redʒɪˈstrɑː(r)/ *n* secretario *m* del registro civil; (*Univ*) secretario *m* general

registration /redʒɪˈstreɪʃn/ *n* registro *m*; (*in register*) inscripción *f*. **~ number** *n* (*Auto*) (número de) matrícula *f*

registry /ˈredʒɪstrɪ/ *n*. **~ office** *n* registro *m* civil

regret /rɪˈgret/ *n* pesar *m*; (*remorse*) arrepentimiento *m*. ● *vt* (*pt* **regretted**) lamentar. **I ~ that** siento (que). **~table** *adj* lamentable

regula|r /ˈregjʊlə(r)/ *adj* regular; (*usual*) habitual. ● *n* 🄸 cliente *m* habitual. **~rity** /-ˈlærətɪ/ *n* regularidad *f*. **~rly** *adv* con regularidad. **~te** /ˈregjʊleɪt/ *vt* regular. **~tion** /-ˈleɪʃn/ *n* regulación *f*; (*rule*) regla *f*

rehears|al /rɪˈhɜːsl/ *n* ensayo *m*. **~e** /rɪˈhɜːs/ *vt* ensayar

reign /reɪn/ *n* reinado *m*. ● *vi* reinar

reindeer /ˈreɪndɪə(r)/ *n invar* reno *m*

reinforce /riːɪnˈfɔːs/ *vt* reforzar. **~ment** *n* refuerzo *m*

reins /reɪnz/ *npl* riendas *fpl*

reiterate /riːˈɪtəreɪt/ *vt* reiterar

reject /rɪˈdʒekt/ *vt* rechazar. ● /ˈriːdʒekt/ *n* producto *m* defectuoso. **~ion** /rɪˈdʒekʃn/ *n* rechazo *m*; (*after job application*) respuesta *f* negativa

rejoice /rɪˈdʒɔɪs/ *vi* regocijarse

rejoin /rɪˈdʒɔɪn/ *vt* reunirse con

rejuvenate /rɪˈdʒuːvəneɪt/ *vt* rejuvenecer

relapse /rɪˈlæps/ *n* recaída *f*. ● *vi* recaer; (*into crime*) reincidir

relat|e /rɪˈleɪt/ *vt* contar; (*connect*) relacionar. ● *vi* relacionarse (**to** con). **~ed** *adj* emparentado; (ideas etc) relacionado. **~ion** /rɪˈleɪʃn/ *n* relación *f*; (*person*) pariente *m & f*. **~ionship** *n* relación *f*; (*blood tie*) parentesco *m*; (*affair*) relaciones *fpl*. **~ive** /ˈrelətɪv/ *n* pariente *m & f*. ● *adj* relativo. **~ively** *adv* relativamente

relax /rɪˈlæks/ *vt* relajar. ● *vi* relajarse. **~ation** /-ˈseɪʃn/ *n* relajación *f*; (*rest*) descanso *m*; (*recreation*) recreo *m*. **~ing** *adj* relajante

relay /ˈriːleɪ/ *n* relevo *m*. **~ (race)** *n* carrera *f* de relevos. ● /rɪˈleɪ/ *vt* transmitir

release /rɪˈliːs/ *vt* soltar; poner en libertad (prisoner); estrenar (film); (*Mec*) soltar; publicar (news). ● *n* liberación *f*; (*of film*) estreno *m*; (*record*) disco *m* nuevo

relent /rɪˈlent/ *vi* ceder. **~less** *adj* implacable; (*continuous*) incesante

relevan|ce /ˈreləvəns/ *n* pertinencia *f*. **~t** *adj* pertinente

relia|bility /rɪlaɪəˈbɪlətɪ/ *n* fiabilidad *f*. **~ble** /rɪˈlaɪəbl/ *adj* (person) de confianza; (car) fiable. **~nce** /rɪˈlaɪəns/ *n* dependencia *f*; (*trust*) confianza *f*. **~nt** /rɪˈlaɪənt/ *adj* confiado

relic /ˈrelɪk/ *n* reliquia *f*

relie|f /rɪˈliːf/ *n* alivio *m*; (*assistance*) socorro *m*. **be on ~f** (*Amer*) recibir prestaciones de la seguridad social. **~ve** /rɪˈliːv/ *vt* aliviar; (*take over from*) relevar. **~ved** *adj* aliviado. **feel ~ved** sentir un gran alivio

religio|n /rɪ'lɪdʒən/ *n* religión *f*. **~us** /rɪ'lɪdʒəs/ *adj* religioso

relinquish /rɪ'lɪnkwɪʃ/ *vt* abandonar, renunciar

relish /'relɪʃ/ *n* gusto *m*; (*Culin*) salsa *f*. ● *vt* saborear

reluctan|ce /rɪ'lʌktəns/ *n* desgana *f*. **~t** *adj* mal dispuesto. **be ~t to** no tener ganas de. **~tly** *adv* de mala gana

rely /rɪ'laɪ/ *vi*. **~ on** contar con; (*trust*) fiarse de; (*depend*) depender

remain /rɪ'meɪn/ *vi* (*be left*) quedar; (*stay*) quedarse; (*continue to be*) seguir. **~der** *n* resto *m*. **~s** *npl* restos *mpl*; (*left-overs*) sobras *fpl*

remand /rɪ'mɑ:nd/ *vt*. **~ in custody** mantener bajo custodia. ● *n*. **on ~** en prisión preventiva

remark /rɪ'mɑ:k/ *n* observación *f*. ● *vt* observar. **~able** *adj* notable

remarry /ri:'mærɪ/ *vi* volver a casarse

remedy /'remədɪ/ *n* remedio *m*. ● *vt* remediar

remember /rɪ'membə(r)/ *vt* acordarse de, recordar. ● *vi* acordarse

remind /rɪ'maɪnd/ *vt* recordar. **~er** *n* recordatorio *m*

reminisce /remɪ'nɪs/ *vi* rememorar los viejos tiempos. **~nces** /-ənsɪz/ *npl* recuerdos *mpl*. **~nt** /-'nɪsnt/ *adj*. **be ~nt of** recordar

remnant /'remnənt/ *n* resto *m*; (*of cloth*) retazo *m*; (*trace*) vestigio *m*

remorse /rɪ'mɔ:s/ *n* remordimiento *m*. **~ful** *adj* arrepentido. **~less** *adj* implacable

remote /rɪ'məʊt/ *adj* remoto. **~ control** *n* mando *m* a distancia. **~ly** *adv* remotamente

remov|able /rɪ'mu:vəbl/ *adj* (*detachable*) de quita y pon; (handle) desmontable. **~al** *n* eliminación *f*; (*from house*) mudanza *f*. **~e** /rɪ'mu:v/ *vt* quitar; (*dismiss*) destituir; (*get rid of*) eliminar

render /'rendə(r)/ *vt* rendir (homage); prestar (help etc). **~ sth useless** hacer que algo resulte inútil

rendezvous /'rɒndɪvu:/ *n* (*pl* **-vous**/-vu:z/) cita *f*

renegade /'renɪgeɪd/ *n* renegado

renew /rɪ'nju:/ *vt* renovar; (*resume*) reanudar. **~al** *n* renovación *f*

renounce /rɪ'naʊns/ *vt* renunciar a

renovat|e /'renəveɪt/ *vt* renovar. **~ion** /-'veɪʃn/ *n* renovación *f*

renown /rɪ'naʊn/ *n* renombre *m*. **~ed** *adj* de renombre

rent /rent/ *n* alquiler *m*. ● *vt* alquilar. **~al** *n* alquiler *m*. **car ~** (*Amer*) alquiler *m* de coche

renunciation /rɪnʌnsɪ'eɪʃn/ *n* renuncia *f*

reopen /ri:'əʊpən/ *vt* volver a abrir. ● *vi* reabrirse

reorganize /ri:'ɔ:gənaɪz/ *vt* reorganizar

rep /rep/ *n* (*Com*) representante *m & f*

repair /rɪ'peə(r)/ *vt* arreglar, reparar; arreglar (clothes, shoes). ● *n* reparación *f*; (*patch*) remiendo *m*. **in good ~** en buen estado. **it's beyond ~** ya no tiene arreglo

repatriat|e /ri:'pætrɪeɪt/ *vt* repatriar

repay /ri:'peɪ/ *vt* (*pt* **repaid**) reembolsar; pagar (debt); corresponder a (kindness). **~ment** *n* pago *m*

repeal /rɪ'pi:l/ *vt* revocar. ● *n* revocación *f*

repeat /rɪ'pi:t/ *vt* repetir. ● *vi* repetir(se). ● *n* repetición *f*. **~edly** *adv* repetidas veces

repel /rɪ'pel/ *vt* (*pt* **repelled**) repeler. **~lent** *adj* repelente

repent /rɪ'pent/ *vi* arrepentirse. **~ant** *adj* arrepentido

repercussion /ri:pə'kʌʃn/ *n* repercusión *f*

repertoire /'repətwɑ:(r)/ *n* repertorio *m*

repetit|ion /repɪ'tɪʃn/ *n* repetición *f*. **~ious** /-'tɪʃəs/ *adj*, **~ive** /rɪ'petətɪv/ *adj* repetitivo

replace /rɪ'pleɪs/ *vt* reponer; cambiar (battery); (*take the place of*) sustituir. **~ment** *n* sustitución *f*; (*person*) sustituto *m*

replay /'ri:pleɪ/ *n* (*Sport*) repetición *f* del partido; (*recording*) repetición *f* inmediata

replenish /rɪ'plenɪʃ/ *vt* reponer

replica /'replɪkə/ *n* réplica *f*

reply /rɪ'plaɪ/ *vt/i* responder, contestar. **~ to sth** responder a algo, contestar algo. ● *n* respuesta *f*

report /rɪ'pɔ:t/ *vt* (reporter) informar sobre; informar de (accident); (*denounce*) denunciar. ● *vi* informar; (*present o.s.*) presentarse. ● *n* informe *m*; (*Schol*) boletín *m* de notas; (*rumour*) rumor *m*; (*in newspaper*) reportaje *m*. **~ card** (*Amer*) *n* boletín *m* de calificaciones. **~edly** *adv* según se dice. **~er** *n* periodista *m* & *f*, reportero *m*

reprehensible /reprɪ'hensəbl/ *adj* reprensible

represent /reprɪ'zent/ *vt* representar. **~ation** /-'teɪʃn/ *n* representación *f*. **~ative** *adj* representativo. ● *n* representante *m* & *f*; (*Amer, in government*) diputado *m*

repress /rɪ'pres/ *vt* reprimir. **~ion** /-ʃn/ *n* represión *f*. **~ive** *adj* represivo

reprieve /rɪ'pri:v/ *n* indulto *m*; (*fig*) respiro *m*. ● *vt* indultar

reprimand /'reprɪmɑ:nd/ *vt* reprender. ● *n* reprensión *f*

reprisal /rɪ'praɪzl/ *n* represalia *f*

reproach /rɪ'prəʊtʃ/ *vt* reprochar. ● *n* reproche *m*. **~ful** *adj* de reproche

reproduc|e /ri:prə'dju:s/ *vt* reproducir. ● *vi* reproducirse. **~tion** /-'dʌkʃn/ *n* reproducción *f*. **~tive** /-'dʌktɪv/ *adj* reproductor

reprove /rɪ'pru:v/ *vt* reprender

reptile /'reptaɪl/ *n* reptil *m*

republic /rɪ'pʌblɪk/ *n* república *f*. **~an** *adj* & *n* republicano (*m*). **R~** *a* & *n* (*in US*) republicano (*m*)

repugnan|ce /rɪ'pʌgnəns/ *n* repugnancia *f*. **~t** *adj* repugnante

repuls|e /rɪ'pʌls/ *vt* rechazar, repulsar. **~ion** /-ʃn/ *n* repulsión *f*. **~ive** *adj* repulsivo

reput|able /'repjʊtəbl/ *adj* acreditado, reputado. **~ation** /repjʊ'teɪʃn/ *n* reputación *f*

request /rɪ'kwest/ *n* petición *f*. ● *vt* pedir

require /rɪ'kwaɪə(r)/ *vt* requerir; (*need*) necesitar; (*demand*) exigir. **~d** *adj* necesario. **~ment** *n* requisito *m*

rescue /'reskju:/ *vt* rescatar, salvar. ● *n* rescate *m*. **~r** *n* salvador *m*

research /rɪ'sɜ:tʃ/ *n* investigación *f*. ● *vt* investigar. **~er** *n* investigador *m*

resembl|ance /rɪ'zembləns/ *n* parecido *m*. **~e** /rɪ'zembl/ *vt* parecerse a

resent /rɪ'zent/ *vt* guardarle rencor a (person). **she ~ed his suc-**

cess le molestaba que él tuviera éxito. **~ful** *adj* resentido. **~ment** *n* resentimiento *m*

reserv|ation /rezə'veɪʃn/ *n* reserva *f*; (*booking*) reserva *f*. **~e** /rɪ'zɜ:v/ *vt* reservar. ● *n* reserva *f*; (*in sports*) suplente *m & f*. **~ed** *adj* reservado. **~oir** /'rezəvwɑ:(r)/ *n* embalse *m*

reshuffle /ri:'ʃʌfl/ *n* (*Pol*) reorganización *f*

residen|ce /'rezɪdəns/ *n* residencia *f*. **~t** *adj & n* residente (*m & f*). **~tial** /rezɪ'denʃl/ *adj* residencial

residue /'rezɪdju:/ *n* residuo *m*

resign /rɪ'zaɪn/ *vt/i* dimitir. **~ o.s. to** resignarse a. **~ation** /rezɪg'neɪʃn/ *n* resignación *f*; (*from job*) dimisión *f*. **~ed** *adj* resignado

resilien|ce /rɪ'zɪlɪəns/ *n* elasticidad *f*; (*of person*) resistencia *f*. **~t** *adj* elástico; (person) resistente

resin /'rezɪn/ *n* resina *f*

resist /rɪ'zɪst/ *vt* resistir. ● *vi* resistirse. **~ance** *n* resistencia *f*. **~ant** *adj* resistente

resolut|e /'rezəlu:t/ *adj* resuelto. **~ion** /-'lu:ʃn/ *n* resolución *f*

resolve /rɪ'zɒlv/ *vt* resolver. **~ to do** resolver a hacer. ● *n* resolución *f*

resort /rɪ'zɔ:t/ *n* recurso *m*; (*place*) lugar *m* turístico. **in the last ~** como último recurso. □ **~ to** *vt* recurrir a.

resource /rɪ'sɔ:s/ *n* recurso *m*. **~ful** *adj* ingenioso

respect /rɪ'spekt/ *n* (*esteem*) respeto *m*; (*aspect*) respecto *m*. **with ~ to** con respecto a. ● *vt* respetar. **~able** *adj* respetable. **~ful** *adj* respetuoso. **~ive** *adj* respectivo. **~ively** *adv* respectivamente

respiration /respə'reɪʃn/ *n* respiración *f*

respite /'respaɪt/ *n* respiro *m*

respon|d /rɪ'spɒnd/ *vi* responder. **~se** /rɪ'spɒns/ *n* respuesta *f*; (*reaction*) reacción *f*

responsib|ility /rɪspɒnsə'bɪlətɪ/ *n* responsabilidad *f*. **~le** /rɪ'spɒnsəbl/ *adj* responsable; (job) de responsabilidad. **~ly** *adv* con formalidad

responsive /rɪ'spɒnsɪv/ *adj* que reacciona bien. **~ to** sensible a

rest /rest/ *vt* descansar; (*lean*) apoyar. ● *vi* descansar; (*lean*) apoyarse. ● *n* descanso *m*; (*Mus*) pausa *f*; (*remainder*) resto *m*, lo demás; (*people*) los demás, los otros *mpl*. **to have a ~** tomarse un descanso. □ **~ up** *vi* (*Amer*) descansar

restaurant /'restərɒnt/ *n* restaurante *m*

rest: ~ful *adj* sosegado. **~ive** *adj* impaciente. **~less** *adj* inquieto

restor|ation /restə'reɪʃn/ *n* restablecimiento *m*; (*of building, monarch*) restauración *f*. **~e** /rɪ'stɔ:(r)/ *vt* restablecer; restaurar (building); devolver (confidence, health)

restrain /rɪ'streɪn/ *vt* contener. **~ o.s.** contenerse. **~ed** *adj* (*moderate*) moderado; (*in control of self*) comedido. **~t** *n* restricción *f*; (*moderation*) compostura *f*

restrict /rɪ'strɪkt/ *vt* restringir. **~ion** /-ʃn/ *n* restricción *f*. **~ive** *adj* restrictivo

rest room *n* (*Amer*) baño *m*, servicio *m*

result /rɪ'zʌlt/ *n* resultado *m*. **as a ~ of** como consecuencia de. ● *vi*. **~ from** resultar de. **~ in** dar como resultado

resume /rɪ'zju:m/ *vt* reanudar. ● *vi* reanudarse

résumé /'rezjʊmeɪ/ *n* resumen *m*;

(*Amer, CV*) currículum *m*, historial *m* personal

resurrect /rezəˈrekt/ *vt* resucitar. **~ion** /-ʃn/ *n* resurrección *f*

resuscitat|e /rɪˈsʌsɪteɪt/ *vt* resucitar. **~ion** /-ˈteɪʃn/ *n* resucitación *f*

retail /ˈriːteɪl/ *n* venta *f* al por menor. ● *adj & adv* al por menor. ● *vt* vender al por menor. ● *vi* venderse al por menor. **~er** *n* minorista *m & f*

retain /rɪˈteɪn/ *vt* retener; conservar (heat)

retaliat|e /rɪˈtælɪeɪt/ *vi* desquitarse; (*Mil*) tomar represalias. **~ion** /-ˈeɪʃn/ *n* represalias *fpl*

retarded /rɪˈtɑːdɪd/ *adj* retrasado

rethink /riːˈθɪŋk/ *vt* (*pt* **rethought**) reconsiderar

reticen|ce /ˈretɪsns/ *n* reticencia *f*. **~t** *adj* reticente

retina /ˈretɪnə/ *n* retina *f*

retinue /ˈretɪnjuː/ *n* séquito *m*

retir|e /rɪˈtaɪə(r)/ *vi* (*from work*) jubilarse; (*withdraw*) retirarse; (*go to bed*) acostarse. **~ed** *adj* jubilado. **~ement** *n* jubilación *f*. **~ing** *adj* retraído

retort /rɪˈtɔːt/ *vt/i* replicar. ● *n* réplica *f*

retrace /riːˈtreɪs/ *vt*. **~ one's steps** volver sobre sus pasos

retract /rɪˈtrækt/ *vt* retirar (statement). ● *vi* retractarse

retrain /riːˈtreɪn/ *vi* hacer un curso de reciclaje

retreat /rɪˈtriːt/ *vi* retirarse. ● *n* retirada *f*; (*place*) refugio *m*

retrial /riːˈtraɪəl/ *n* nuevo juicio *m*

retriev|al /rɪˈtriːvl/ *n* recuperación *f*. **~e** /rɪˈtriːv/ *vt* recuperar. **~er** *n* (*dog*) perro *m* cobrador

retro|grade /ˈretrəgreɪd/ *adj* retrógrado. **~spect** /-spekt/ *n*. **in ~** en retrospectiva. **~spective** /-ˈspektɪv/ *adj* retrospectivo

return /rɪˈtɜːn/ *vi* volver, regresar; (symptom) reaparecer. ● *vt* devolver; corresponder a (affection). ● *n* regreso *m*, vuelta *f*; (*Com*) rendimiento *m*; (*to owner*) devolución *f*. **in ~ for** a cambio de. **many happy ~s!** ¡feliz cumpleaños! **~ ticket** *n* billete *m or* (*LAm*) boleto *m* de ida y vuelta, boleto *m* redondo (*Mex*). **~s** *npl* (*Com*) ingresos *mpl*

reun|ion /riːˈjuːnɪən/ *n* reunión *f*. **~ite** /riːjuːˈnaɪt/ *vt* reunir

rev /rev/ *n* (*Auto, fam*) revolución *f*. ● *vt/i*. **~ (up)** (*pt* **revved**) (*Auto, fam*) acelerar(se)

reveal /rɪˈviːl/ *vt* revelar. **~ing** *adj* revelador

revel /ˈrevl/ *vi* (*pt* **revelled**) tener un jolgorio. **~ in** deleitarse en. **~ry** *n* jolgorio *m*

revelation /revəˈleɪʃn/ *n* revelación *f*

revenge /rɪˈvendʒ/ *n* venganza *f*. **take ~** vengarse. ● *vt* vengar

revenue /ˈrevənjuː/ *n* ingresos *mpl*

revere /rɪˈvɪə(r)/ *vt* venerar. **~nce** /ˈrevərəns/ *n* reverencia *f*.

Reverend /ˈrevərənd/ *adj* reverendo

reverent /ˈrevərənt/ *adj* reverente

reverie /ˈrevərɪ/ *n* ensueño *m*

revers|al /rɪˈvɜːsl/ *n* inversión *f*. **~e** /rɪˈvɜːs/ *adj* inverso. ● *n* contrario *m*; (*back*) revés *m*; (*Auto*) marcha *f* atrás. ● *vt* invertir; anular (decision); (*Auto*) dar marcha atrás a. ● *vi* (*Auto*) dar marcha atrás

revert /rɪˈvɜːt/ *vi*. **~ to** volver a; (*Jurid*) revertir a

review /rɪˈvjuː/ *n* revisión *f*; (*Mil*)

revista *f*; (*of book, play, etc*) crítica *f*. ● *vt* examinar (situation); reseñar (book, play, etc); (*Amer, for exam*) repasar

revis|e /rɪˈvaɪz/ *vt* revisar; (*Schol*) repasar. **~ion** /rɪˈvɪʒn/ *n* revisión *f*; (*Schol*) repaso *m*

revive /rɪˈvaɪv/ *vt* resucitar (person)

revolt /rɪˈvəʊlt/ *vi* sublevarse. ● *n* revuelta *f*. **~ing** *adj* asqueroso

revolution /revəˈlu:ʃn/ *n* revolución *f*. **~ary** *adj & n* revolucionario (*m*). **~ize** *vt* revolucionar

revolv|e /rɪˈvɒlv/ *vi* girar. **~er** *n* revólver *m*. **~ing** /rɪˈvɒlvɪŋ/ *adj* giratorio

revue /rɪˈvju:/ *n* revista *f*

revulsion /rɪˈvʌlʃn/ *n* asco *m*

reward /rɪˈwɔ:d/ *n* recompensa *f*. ● *vt* recompensar. **~ing** *adj* gratificante

rewrite /ri:ˈraɪt/ *vt* (*pt* **rewrote**, *pp* **rewritten**) volver a escribir *or* redactar; (*copy out*) escribir otra vez

rhetoric /ˈretərɪk/ *n* retórica *f*. **~al** /rɪˈtɒrɪkl/ *adj* retórico

rheumatism /ˈru:mətɪzəm/ *n* reumatismo *m*

rhinoceros /raɪˈnɒsərəs/ *n* (*pl* **-oses** *or invar*) rinoceronte *m*

rhubarb /ˈru:bɑ:b/ *n* ruibarbo *m*

rhyme /raɪm/ *n* rima *f*; (*poem*) poesía *f*. ● *vt/i* rimar

rhythm /ˈrɪðəm/ *n* ritmo *m*. **~ic(al)** /ˈrɪðmɪk(l)/ *adj* rítmico

rib /rɪb/ *n* costilla *f*

ribbon /ˈrɪbən/ *n* cinta *f*

rice /raɪs/ *n* arroz *m*. **~ pudding** *n* arroz con leche

rich /rɪtʃ/ *adj* (**-er**, **-est**) rico. ● *n* ricos *mpl*. **~es** *npl* riquezas *fpl*

ricochet /ˈrɪkəʃeɪ/ *vi* rebotar

rid /rɪd/ *vt* (*pt* **rid**, *pres p* **ridding**) librar (**of** de). **get ~ of** deshacerse de. **~dance** /ˈrɪdns/ *n*. **good ~dance!** ¡adiós y buen viaje!

ridden /ˈrɪdn/ *see* **RIDE**

riddle /ˈrɪdl/ *n* acertijo *m*. ● *vt* acribillar. **be ~d with** estar lleno de

ride /raɪd/ *vi* (*pt* **rode**, *pp* **ridden**) (*on horseback*) montar a caballo; (*go*) ir (en bicicleta, a caballo etc). ● *vt* montar a (horse); ir en (bicycle); (*Amer*) ir en (bus, train); recorrer (distance). ● *n* (*on horse*) cabalgata *f*; (*in car*) paseo *m* en coche. **take s.o. for a ~** 🅸 engañarle a uno. **~r** *n* (*on horse*) jinete *m*; (*cyclist*) ciclista *m & f*

ridge /rɪdʒ/ *n* (*of hills*) cadena *f*; (*hilltop*) cresta *f*

ridicul|e /ˈrɪdɪkju:l/ *n* burlas *fpl*. ● *vt* ridiculizar. **~ous** /rɪˈdɪkjʊləs/ *adj* ridículo

rife /raɪf/ *adj* difundido

rifle /ˈraɪfl/ *n* fusil *m*

rift /rɪft/ *n* grieta *f*; (*fig*) ruptura *f*

rig /rɪg/ *vt* (*pt* **rigged**) (*pej*) amañar. ● *n* (*at sea*) plataforma *f* de perforación. □ **~ up** *vt* improvisar

right /raɪt/ *adj* (answer) correcto; (*morally*) bueno; (*not left*) derecho; (*suitable*) adecuado. **be ~** (person) tener razón; (clock) estar bien. **it is ~** (*just, moral*) es justo. **put ~** rectificar. **the ~ person for the job** la persona indicada para el puesto. ● *n* (*entitlement*) derecho *m*; (*not left*) derecha *f*; (*not evil*) bien *m*. **~ of way** (*Auto*) prioridad *f*. **be in the ~** tener razón. **on the ~** a la derecha. ● *vt* enderezar; (*fig*) reparar. ● *adv* a la derecha; (*directly*) derecho; (*completely*) completamente. **~ angle** *n* ángulo *m* recto.

r

~ **away** *adv* inmediatamente. **~eous** /ˈraɪtʃəs/ *adj* recto; (*cause*) justo. **~ful** /ˈraɪtfl/ *adj* legítimo. **~-handed** /-ˈhændɪd/ *adj* diestro. **~-hand man** *n* brazo *m* derecho. **~ly** *adv* justamente. ~ **wing** *adj* (*Pol*) derechista

rigid /ˈrɪdʒɪd/ *adj* rígido

rig|orous /ˈrɪgərəs/ *adj* riguroso. **~our** /ˈrɪgə(r)/ *n* rigor *m*

rim /rɪm/ *n* borde *m*; (*of wheel*) llanta *f*; (*of glasses*) montura *f*

rind /raɪnd/ *n* corteza *f*; (*of fruit*) cáscara *f*

ring[1] /rɪŋ/ *n* (*circle*) círculo *m*; (*circle of metal etc*) aro *m*; (*on finger*) anillo *m*; (*on finger with stone*) sortija *f*; (*Boxing*) cuadrilátero *m*; (*bullring*) ruedo *m*; (*for circus*) pista *f*; ● *vt* cercar

ring[2] /rɪŋ/ *n* (*of bell*) toque *m*; (*tinkle*) tintineo *m*; (*telephone call*) llamada *f*. ● *vt* (*pt* **rang**, *pp* **rung**) hacer sonar; (*telephone*) llamar por teléfono. ~ **the bell** tocar el timbre. ● *vi* sonar. ~ **back** *vt/i* volver a llamar. □ ~ **up** *vt* llamar por teléfono

ring: **~leader** /ˈrɪŋliːdə(r)/ *n* cabecilla *m* & *f*. ~ **road** *n* carretera *f* de circunvalación

rink /rɪŋk/ *n* pista *f*

rinse /rɪns/ *vt* enjuagar. ● *n* aclarado *m*; (*of dishes*) enjuague *m*; (*for hair*) tintura *f* (no permanente)

riot /ˈraɪət/ *n* disturbio *m*; (*of colours*) profusión *f*. **run** ~ desenfrenarse. ● *vi* causar disturbios

rip /rɪp/ *vt* (*pt* **ripped**) rasgar. ● *vi* rasgarse. ● *n* rasgón *m*. □ ~ **off** *vt* (*pull off*) arrancar; (☒, *cheat*) robar

ripe /raɪp/ *adj* (**-er**, **-est**) maduro. **~n** /ˈraɪpn/ *vt/i* madurar

rip-off /ˈrɪpɒf/ *n* ☒ timo *m*

ripple /ˈrɪpl/ *n* (*on water*) onda *f*

ris|e /raɪz/ *vi* (*pt* **rose**, *pp* **risen**) subir; (*sun*) salir; (*river*) crecer; (*prices*) subir; (*land*) elevarse; (*get up*) levantarse. ● *n* subida *f*; (*land*) altura *f*; (*increase*) aumento *m*; (*to power*) ascenso *m*. **give ~e to** ocasionar. **~er** *n*. **early ~er** *n* madrugador *m*. **~ing** *n*. ● *adj* (*sun*) naciente; (*number*) creciente; (*prices*) en alza

risk /rɪsk/ *n* riesgo *m*. ● *vt* arriesgar. **~y** *adj* (**-ier**, **-iest**) arriesgado

rite /raɪt/ *n* rito *m*

ritual /ˈrɪtʃʊəl/ *adj* & *n* ritual (*m*)

rival /ˈraɪvl/ *adj* & *n* rival (*m*). **~ry** *n* rivalidad *f*

river /ˈrɪvə(r)/ *n* río *m*

rivet /ˈrɪvɪt/ *n* remache *m*. **~ing** *adj* fascinante

road /rəʊd/ *n* (*in town*) calle *f*; (*between towns*) carretera *f*; (*route, way*) camino *m*. ~ **map** *n* mapa *m* de carreteras. **~side** *n* borde *m* de la carretera. **~works** *npl* obras *fpl*. **~worthy** *adj* (*vehicle*) apto para circular

roam /rəʊm/ *vi* vagar

roar /rɔː(r)/ *n* rugido *m*; (*laughter*) carcajada *f*. ● *vt/i* rugir. ~ **past** (*vehicles*) pasar con estruendo. ~ **with laughter** reírse a carcajadas. **~ing** *adj* (*trade etc*) activo

roast /rəʊst/ *vt* asar; tostar (*coffee*). ● *adj* & *n* asado (*m*). ~ **beef** *n* rosbif *m*

rob /rɒb/ *vt* (*pt* **robbed**) atracar, asaltar (*bank*); robarle a (*person*). ~ **of** (*deprive of*) privar de. **~ber** *n* ladrón *m*; (*of bank*) atracador *m*. **~bery** *n* robo *m*; (*of bank*) atraco *m*

robe /rəʊb/ *n* bata *f*; (*Univ etc*)

toga *f*
robin /ˈrɒbɪn/ *n* petirrojo *m*
robot /ˈrəʊbɒt/ *n* robot *m*
robust /rəʊˈbʌst/ *adj* robusto
rock /rɒk/ *n* roca *f*; (*crag, cliff*) peñasco *m*. ● *vt* mecer; (*shake*) sacudir. ● *vi* mecerse; (*shake*) sacudirse. ● *n* (*Mus*) música *f* rock. **~-bottom** /-ˈbɒtəm/ *adj* ! bajísimo
rocket /ˈrɒkɪt/ *n* cohete *m*
rock: ~ing-chair *n* mecedora *f*. **~y** *adj* (**-ier**, **-iest**) rocoso; (*fig, shaky*) bamboleante
rod /rɒd/ *n* vara *f*; (*for fishing*) caña *f*; (*metal*) barra *f*
rode /rəʊd/ *see* **RIDE**
rodent /ˈrəʊdnt/ *n* roedor *m*
rogue /rəʊg/ *n* pícaro *m*
role /rəʊl/ *n* papel *m*
roll /rəʊl/ *vt* hacer rodar; (*roll up*) enrollar; allanar (lawn); aplanar (pastry). ● *vi* rodar; (ship) balancearse; (*on floor*) revolcarse. **be ~ing in money** ! nadar en dinero ● *n* rollo *m*; (*of ship*) balanceo *m*; (*of drum*) redoble *m*; (*of thunder*) retumbo *m*; (*bread*) panecillo *m*, bolillo *m* (*Mex*). □ **~ over** *vi* (*turn over*) dar una vuelta. □ **~ up** *vt* enrollar; arremangar (sleeve). *vi* ! llegar. **~-call** *n* lista *f*
roller /ˈrəʊlə(r)/ *n* rodillo *m*; (*wheel*) rueda *f*; (*for hair*) rulo *m*. **R~ blades** *npl* (*P*) patines *mpl* en línea. **~-coaster** *n* montaña *f* rusa. **~-skate** *n* patín *m* de ruedas. **~-skating** patinaje *m* (*sobre ruedas*)
rolling /ˈrəʊlɪŋ/ *adj* ondulado. **~-pin** *n* rodillo *m*
ROM /rɒm/ *n* (= **read-only memory**) ROM *f*
Roman /ˈrəʊmən/ *adj & n* romano (*m*). **~ Catholic** *adj & n* católico (*m*) (romano)
romance /rəʊˈmæns/ *n* novela *f* romántica; (*love*) amor *m*; (*affair*) aventura *f*
Romania /ruːˈmeɪnɪə/ *n* Rumania *f*, Rumanía *f*. **~n** *adj & n* rumano (*m*)
romantic /rəʊˈmæntɪk/ *adj* romántico
Rome /ˈrəʊm/ *n* Roma *f*
romp /rɒmp/ *vi* retozar
roof /ruːf/ *n* techo *m*, tejado *m*; (*of mouth*) paladar *m*. ● *vt* techar. **~rack** *n* baca *f*. **~top** *n* tejado *m*
rook /rʊk/ *n* grajo *m*; (*in chess*) torre *f*
room /ruːm/ *n* cuarto *m*, habitación *f*; (*bedroom*) dormitorio *m*; (*space*) espacio *m*; (*large hall*) sala *f*. **~y** *adj* espacioso
roost /ruːst/ *vi* posarse. **~er** *n* gallo *m*
root /ruːt/ *n* raíz *f*. **take ~** echar raíces; (idea) arraigarse. ● *vi* echar raíces. **~ about** *vi* hurgar. □ **~ for** *vt* ! alentar. □ **~ out** *vt* extirpar
rope /rəʊp/ *n* cuerda *f*. **know the ~s** estar al corriente. ● *vt* atar; (*Amer, lasso*) enlazar. □ **~ in** *vt* agarrar
rose[1] /rəʊz/ *n* rosa *f*; (*nozzle*) roseta *f*
rose[2] /rəʊz/ *see* **RISE**
rosé /ˈrəʊzeɪ/ *n* (vino *m*) rosado *m*
rot /rɒt/ *vt* (*pt* **rotted**) pudrir. ● *vi* pudrirse. ● *n* putrefacción *f*
rota /ˈrəʊtə/ *n* lista *f* (de turnos)
rotary /ˈrəʊtərɪ/ *adj* rotatorio
rotat|e /rəʊˈteɪt/ *vt* girar; (*change round*) alternar. ● *vi* girar; (*change round*) alternarse. **~ion** /-ʃn/ *n* rotación *f*
rote /rəʊt/ *n*. **by ~** de memoria
rotten /ˈrɒtn/ *adj* podrido; ! pé-

r

simo ⊞; (weather) horrible

rough /rʌf/ *adj* (**-er**, **-est**) áspero; (person) tosco; (*bad*) malo; (ground) accidentado; (*violent*) brutal; (*approximate*) aproximado; (diamond) bruto. ● *adv* duro. ~ **copy**, ~ **draft** borrador *m*. ● *vt*. ~ **it** vivir sin comodidades. ~**age** /ˈrʌfɪdʒ/ *n* fibra *f*. ~**-and-ready** *adj* improvisado. ~**ly** *adv* bruscamente; (*more or less*) aproximadamente

roulette /ru:ˈlet/ *n* ruleta *f*

round /raʊnd/ *adj* (**-er**, **-est**) redondo. ● *n* círculo *m*; (*of visits, drinks*) ronda *f*; (*of competition*) vuelta *f*; (*Boxing*) asalto *m*. ● *prep* alrededor de. ● *adv* alrededor. ~ **about** (*approximately*) aproximadamente. **come** ~ **to**, **go** ~ **to** (*a friend etc*) pasar por casa de. ● *vt* doblar (corner). □ ~ **off** *vt* terminar; redondear (number). □ ~ **up** *vt* rodear (cattle); hacer una redada de (suspects). ~**about** *n* tiovivo *m*, carrusel *m* (*LAm*); (*for traffic*) glorieta *f*, rotonda *f*. ● *adj* in directo. ~ **trip** *n* viaje *m* de ida y vuelta. ~**-up** *n* resumen *m*; (*of suspects*) redada *f*

rous|e /raʊz/ *vt* despertar. ~**ing** *adj* enardecedor

route /ru:t/ *n* ruta *f*; (*Naut, Aviat*) rumbo *m*; (*of bus*) línea *f*

routine /ru:ˈti:n/ *n* rutina *f*. ● *adj* rutinario

row¹ /rəʊ/ *n* fila *f*. ● *vi* remar

row² /raʊ/ *n* (*fam, noise*) bulla *f* ⊞; (*quarrel*) pelea *f*. ● *vi* ⊞ pelearse

rowboat /ˈrəʊbəʊt/ (*Amer*) *n* bote *m* de remos

rowdy /ˈraʊdɪ/ *adj* (**-ier**, **-iest**) *n* escandaloso, alborotador

rowing /ˈrəʊɪŋ/ *n* remo *m*. ~ **boat** *n* bote *m* de remos

royal /ˈrɔɪəl/ *adj* real. ~**ist** *adj* & *n* monárquico (*m*). ~**ly** *adv* magníficamente. ~**ty** *n* realeza *f*

rub /rʌb/ *vt* (*pt* **rubbed**) frotar. □ ~ **out** *vt* borrar

rubber /ˈrʌbə(r)/ *n* goma *f*, caucho *m*, hule *m* (*Mex*); (*eraser*) goma *f* (de borrar). ~ **band** *n* goma *f* (elástica). ~**-stamp** *vt* (*fig*) autorizar. ~**y** *adj* parecido al caucho

rubbish /ˈrʌbɪʃ/ *n* basura *f*; (*junk*) trastos *mpl*; (*fig*) tonterías *fpl*. ~ **bin** *n* cubo *m* de la basura, bote *m* de la basura (*Mex*). ~**y** *adj* sin valor

rubble /ˈrʌbl/ *n* escombros *mpl*

ruby /ˈru:bɪ/ *n* rubí *m*

rucksack /ˈrʌksæk/ *n* mochila *f*

rudder /ˈrʌdə(r)/ *n* timón *m*

rude /ru:d/ *adj* (**-er**, **-est**) grosero, mal educado; (*improper*) indecente; (*brusque*) brusco. ~**ly** *adv* groseramente. ~**ness** *n* mala educación *f*

rudimentary /ru:dɪˈmentrɪ/ *adj* rudimentario

ruffian /ˈrʌfɪən/ *n* rufián *m*

ruffle /ˈrʌfl/ *vt* despeinar (hair); arrugar (clothes)

rug /rʌg/ *n* alfombra *f*, tapete *m* (*Mex*); (*blanket*) manta *f* de viaje

rugged /ˈrʌgɪd/ *adj* (coast) escarpado; (landscape) escabroso

ruin /ˈru:ɪn/ *n* ruina *f*. ● *vt* arruinar; (*spoil*) estropear

rul|e /ru:l/ *n* regla *f*; (*Pol*) dominio *m*. **as a** ~ por regla general. ● *vt* gobernar; (*master*) dominar; (*Jurid*) dictaminar. ~**e out** *vt* descartar. ~**ed paper** *n* papel *m* rayado. ~**er** *n* (*sovereign*) soberano *m*; (*leader*) gobernante *m* & *f*; (*measure*) regla *f*. ~**ing** *adj* (class) dirigente. ● *n* decisión *f*

rum /rʌm/ *n* ron *m*

rumble /ˈrʌmbl/ *vi* retumbar; (stomach) hacer ruidos

rummage /ˈrʌmɪdʒ/ *vi* hurgar

rumour /ˈruːmə(r)/ *n* rumor *m*. ● *vt*. **it is ~ed that** se rumorea que

rump steak /rʌmpsteɪk/ *n* filete *m* de cadera

run /rʌn/ *vi* (*pt* **ran**, *pp* **run**, *pres p* **running**) correr; (water) correr; (*function*) funcionar; (*melt*) derretirse; (makeup) correrse; (colour) desteñir; (bus etc) circular; (*in election*) presentarse. ● *vt* correr (race); dirigir (business); correr (risk); (*move, pass*) pasar; tender (wire); preparar (bath). **~ a temperature** tener fiebre. ● *n* corrida *f*, carrera *f*; (*outing*) paseo *m* (en coche); (*ski*) pista *f*. **in the long ~** a la larga. **be on the ~** estar prófugo. □ **~ away** *vi* huir, escaparse. □ **~ down** *vi* bajar corriendo; (battery) descargarse. *vt* (*Auto*) atropellar; (*belittle*) denigrar. □ **~ in** *vi* entrar corriendo. □ **~ into** *vt* toparse con (friend); (*hit*) chocar con. □ **~ off** *vt* sacar (copies). □ **~ out** *vi* salir corriendo; (liquid) salirse; (*fig*) agotarse. □ **~ out of** *vt* quedarse sin. □ **~ over** *vt* (*Auto*) atropellar. □ **~ through** *vt* (*review*) ensayar; (*rehearse*) repasar. □ **~ up** *vt* ir acumulando (bill). *vi* subir corriendo. **~away** *n* fugitivo *m*. **~ down** *adj* (person) agotado

rung[1] /rʌŋ/ *n* (*of ladder*) peldaño *m*

rung[2] /rʌŋ/ *see* **RING**

run: ~ner /ˈrʌnə(r)/ *n* corredor *m*; (*on sledge*) patín *m*. **~ner bean** *n* judía *f* escarlata. **~ner-up** *n*. **be ~er-up** quedar en segundo lugar. **~ning** *n*. **be in the ~ning** tener posibilidades de ganar. ● *adj* (water) corriente; (commentary) en directo. **four times ~ning** cuatro veces seguidas. **~ny** /ˈrʌnɪ/ *adj* líquido; (nose) que moquea. **~way** *n* pista *f* de aterrizaje

rupture /ˈrʌptʃə(r)/ *n* ruptura *f*. ● *vt* romper

rural /ˈrʊərəl/ *adj* rural

ruse /ruːz/ *n* ardid *m*

rush /rʌʃ/ *n* (*haste*) prisa *f*; (*crush*) bullicio *m*; (*plant*) junco *m*. ● *vi* precipitarse. ● *vt* apresurar; (*Mil*) asaltar. **~-hour** *n* hora *f* punta, hora *f* pico (*LAm*)

Russia /ˈrʌʃə/ *n* Rusia *f*. **~n** *adj & n* ruso (*m*)

rust /rʌst/ *n* orín *m*. ● *vt* oxidar. ● *vi* oxidarse

rustle /ˈrʌsl/ *vt* hacer susurrar; (*Amer*) robar. ● *vi* susurrar □ **~ up** *vt* [!] preparar.

rust: ~proof *adj* inoxidable. **~y** (**-ier**, **-iest**) oxidado

rut /rʌt/ *n* surco *m*. **be in a ~** estar anquilosado

ruthless /ˈruːθlɪs/ *adj* despiadado

rye /raɪ/ *n* centeno *m*

Ss

S *abbr* (= **south**) S

sabot|age /ˈsæbətɑːʒ/ *n* sabotaje *m*. ● *vt* sabotear. **~eur** /-ˈtɜː(r)/ *n* saboteador *m*

saccharin /ˈsækərɪn/ *n* sacarina *f*

sachet /ˈsæʃeɪ/ *n* bolsita *f*

sack /sæk/ *n* saco *m*. **get the ~** [!] ser despedido. ● *vt* [!] despedir, echar

sacrament /'sækrəmənt/ *n* sacramento *m*

sacred /'seɪkrɪd/ *adj* sagrado

sacrifice /'sækrɪfaɪs/ *n* sacrificio *m*. ● *vt* sacrificar

sacrileg|e /'sækrɪlɪdʒ/ *n* sacrilegio *m*. **~ious** /-'lɪdʒəs/ *adj* sacrílego

sad /sæd/ *adj* (**sadder**, **saddest**) triste. **~den** *vt* entristecer

saddle /'sædl/ *n* silla *f* de montar. ● *vt* ensillar (horse). **~ s.o. with sth** (*fig*) endilgarle algo a uno

sadist /'seɪdɪst/ *n* sádico *m*. **~tic** /sə'dɪstɪk/ *adj* sádico

sadly /'sædlɪ/ *adv* tristemente; (*fig*) desgraciadamente. **~ness** *n* tristeza *f*

safe /seɪf/ *adj* (**-er**, **-est**) seguro; (*out of danger*) salvo; (*cautious*) prudente. **~ and sound** sano y salvo. ● *n* caja *f* fuerte. **~ deposit** *n* caja *f* de seguridad. **~guard** *n* salvaguardia *f*. ● *vt* salvaguardar. **~ly** *adv* sin peligro; (*in safe place*) en lugar seguro. **~ty** *n* seguridad *f*. **~ty belt** *n* cinturón *m* de seguridad. **~ty pin** *n* imperdible *m*

sag /sæg/ *vi* (*pt* **sagged**) (ceiling) combarse; (bed) hundirse

saga /'sɑːgə/ *n* saga *f*

Sagittarius /sædʒɪ'teərɪəs/ *n* Sagitario *m*

said /sed/ *see* SAY

sail /seɪl/ *n* vela *f*; (*trip*) paseo *m* (en barco). **set ~** zarpar. ● *vi* navegar; (*leave*) partir; (*Sport*) practicar la vela; (*fig*) deslizarse. **go ~ing** salir a navegar. *vt* gobernar (boat). **~boat** *n* (*Amer*) barco *m* de vela. **~ing** *n* (*Sport*) vela *f*. **~ing boat** *n*, **~ing ship** *n* barco *m* de vela. **~or** *n* marinero *m*

saint /seɪnt//sənt/ *n* santo *m*. **~ly** *adj* santo

sake /seɪk/ *n*. **for the ~ of** por. **for God's ~** por el amor de Dios

salad /'sæləd/ *n* ensalada *f*. **~ bowl** *n* ensaladera *f*. **~ dressing** *n* aliño *m*

salary /'sælərɪ/ *n* sueldo *m*

sale /seɪl/ *n* venta *f*; (*at reduced prices*) liquidación *f*. **for ~** (*sign*) se vende. **be for ~** estar a la venta. **be on ~** (*Amer, reduced*) estar en liquidación. **~able** *adj* vendible. (*for sale*) estar a la venta. **~s clerk** *n* (*Amer*) dependiente *m*, dependienta *f*. **~sman** /-mən/ *n* vendedor *m*; (*in shop*) dependiente *m*. **~swoman** *n* vendedora *f*; (*in shop*) dependienta *f*

saliva /sə'laɪvə/ *n* saliva *f*

salmon /'sæmən/ *n invar* salmón *m*

saloon /sə'luːn/ *n* (*on ship*) salón *m*; (*Amer, bar*) bar *m*; (*Auto*) turismo *m*

salt /sɔːlt/ *n* sal *f*. ● *vt* salar. **~ cellar** *n* salero *m*. **~y** *adj* salado

salute /sə'luːt/ *n* saludo *m*. ● *vt* saludar. ● *vi* hacer un saludo

Salvadorean, **Salvadorian** /sælvə'dɔːrɪən/ *adj & n* salvadoreño (*m*)

salvage /'sælvɪdʒ/ *vt* salvar

salvation /sæl'veɪʃn/ *n* salvación *f*

same /seɪm/ *adj* igual (**as** que); (*before noun*) mismo (**as** que). **at the ~ time** al mismo tiempo. ● *pron*. **the ~** lo mismo. **all the ~** de todas formas. ● *adv*. **the ~** igual

sample /'sɑːmpl/ *n* muestra *f*. ● *vt* degustar (food)

sanct|ify /'sæŋktɪfaɪ/ *vt* santificar. **~ion** /'sæŋkʃn/ *n* sanción *f*. ● *vt* sancionar. **~uary** /'sæŋktʃʊərɪ/ *n* (*Relig*) santuario *m*; (*for wildlife*) reserva *f*; (*refuge*) asilo *m*

sand /sænd/ *n* arena *f.* ● *vt* pulir (floor). ◻ ~ **down** *vt* lijar (wood)

sandal /ˈsændl/ *n* sandalia *f*

sand: ~**castle** *n* castillo *m* de arena. ~**paper** *n* papel *m* de lija. ● *vt* lijar. ~**storm** *n* tormenta *f* de arena

sandwich /ˈsænwɪdʒ/ *n* bocadillo *m*, sandwich *m*. ● *vt*. **be** ~**ed between** (person) estar apretujado entre

sandy /ˈsændɪ/ *adj* arenoso

sane /seɪn/ *adj* (**-er**, **-est**) (person) cuerdo; (*sensible*) sensato

sang /sæŋ/ *see* SING

sanitary /ˈsænɪtrɪ/ *adj* higiénico; (system etc) sanitario. ~ **towel**, ~ **napkin** *n* (*Amer*) compresa *f* (higiénica)

sanitation /sænɪˈteɪʃn/ *n* higiene *f*; (*drainage*) sistema *m* sanitario

sanity /ˈsænɪtɪ/ *n* cordura *f*

sank /sæŋk/ *see* SINK

Santa (Claus) /ˈsæntə(klɔːz)/ *n* Papá *m* Noel

sap /sæp/ *n* (*in plants*) savia *f*. ● (*pt* **sapped**) minar

sapling /ˈsæplɪŋ/ *n* árbol *m* joven

sapphire /ˈsæfaɪə(r)/ *n* zafiro *m*

sarcas|m /ˈsɑːkæzəm/ *n* sarcasmo *m*. ~**tic** /-ˈkæstɪk/ *adj* sarcástico

sardine /sɑːˈdiːn/ *n* sardina *f*

sash /sæʃ/ *n* (*over shoulder*) banda *f*; (*round waist*) fajín *m*.

sat /sæt/ *see* SIT

SAT *abbr* (*Amer*) (**Scholastic Aptitude Test**); (*Brit*) (**Standard Assessment Task**)

satchel /ˈsætʃl/ *n* cartera *f*

satellite /ˈsætəlaɪt/ *n* & *a* satélite (*m*). ~ **TV** *n* televisión *f* por satélite

satin /ˈsætɪn/ *n* raso *m*. ● *adj* de raso

satir|e /ˈsætaɪə(r)/ *n* sátira *f.* ~**ical** /səˈtɪrɪkl/ *adj* satírico. ~**ize** /ˈsætəraɪz/ *vt* satirizar

satis|faction /sætɪsˈfækʃn/ *n* satisfacción *f*. ~**factorily** /-ˈfæktərɪlɪ/ *adv* satisfactoriamente. ~**factory** /-ˈfæktərɪ/ *adj* satisfactorio. ~**fy** /ˈsætɪsfaɪ/ *vt* satisfacer; (*convince*) convencer. ~**fying** *adj* satisfactorio

satphone /ˈsætfəʊn/ *n* teléfono *m* satélite

saturat|e /ˈsætʃəreɪt/ *vt* saturar. ~**ed** *adj* saturado; (*drenched*) empapado

Saturday /ˈsætədeɪ/ *n* sábado *m*

Saturn /ˈsætən/ *n* Saturno *m*

sauce /sɔːs/ *n* salsa *f*; (*cheek*) descaro *m*. ~**pan** /ˈsɔːspən/ *n* cazo *m*, cacerola *f.* ~**r** /ˈsɔːsə(r)/ *n* platillo *m*

saucy /ˈsɔːsɪ/ *adj* (**-ier**, **-iest**) descarado

Saudi /ˈsaʊdɪ/ *adj* & *n* saudita (*m* & *f*). ~ **Arabia** /-əˈreɪbɪə/ *n* Arabia *f* Saudí

sauna /ˈsɔːnə/ *n* sauna *f*

saunter /ˈsɔːntə(r)/ *vi* pasearse

sausage /ˈsɒsɪdʒ/ *n* salchicha *f*

savage /ˈsævɪdʒ/ *adj* salvaje; (*fierce*) feroz. ● *n* salvaje *m* & *f*. ● *vt* atacar. ~**ry** *n* ferocidad *f*

sav|e /seɪv/ *vt* (*rescue*) salvar; ahorrar (money, time); (*prevent*) evitar; (*Comp*) guardar. ● *n* (*football*) parada *f*. ● *prep* salvo, excepto. ◻ ~**e up** *vi/t* ahorrar. ~**er** *n* ahorrador *m*. ~**ing** *n* ahorro *m*. ~**ings** *npl* ahorros *mpl*

saviour /ˈseɪvɪə(r)/ *n* salvador *m*

savour /ˈseɪvə(r)/ *vt* saborear. ~**y** *adj* (*appetizing*) sabroso; (*not sweet*) no dulce

S

saw[1] /sɔː/ see **SEE**[1]
saw[2] /sɔː/ *n* sierra *f.* ● *vt* (*pt* **sawed**, *pp* **sawn**) serrar. **~dust** *n* serrín *m.* **~n** /sɔːn/ see **SAW**[2]
saxophone /ˈsæksəfəʊn/ *n* saxofón *m*, saxófono *m*
say /seɪ/ *vt/i* (*pt* **said** /sed/) decir; rezar (prayer). ● *n.* **have a ~** expresar una opinión; (*in decision*) tener voz en capítulo. **have no ~** no tener ni voz ni voto. **~ing** *n* refrán *m*
scab /skæb/ *n* costra *f*; (*fam*, *blackleg*) esquirol *m*
scaffolding /ˈskæfəldɪŋ/ *n* andamios *mpl*
scald /skɔːld/ *vt* escaldar
scale /skeɪl/ *n* (*also Mus*) escala *f*; (*of fish*) escama *f.* ● *vt* (*climb*) escalar. **~ down** *vt* reducir (a escala) (drawing); recortar (operation). **~s** *npl* (*for weighing*) balanza *f*, peso *m*
scallion /ˈskæljən/ *n* (*Amer*) cebolleta *f*
scalp /skælp/ *vt* quitar el cuero cabelludo a
scamper /ˈskæmpə(r)/ *vi.* **~ away** irse correteando
scan /skæn/ *vt* (*pt* **scanned**) escudriñar; (*quickly*) echar un vistazo a; (radar) explorar
scandal /ˈskændl/ *n* escándalo *m*; (*gossip*) chismorreo *m.* **~ize** *vt* escandalizar. **~ous** *adj* escandaloso
Scandinavia /skændɪˈneɪvɪə/ *n* Escandinavia *f.* **~n** *adj & n* escandinavo (*m*)
scant /skænt/ *adj* escaso. **~y** *adj* (**-ier**, **-iest**) escaso
scapegoat /ˈskeɪpgəʊt/ *n* cabeza *f* de turco
scar /skɑː(r)/ *n* cicatriz *f*
scarc|e /skeəs/ *adj* (**-er**, **-est**) escaso. **be ~e** escasear. **make o.s. ~e** ⓘ mantenerse lejos. **~ely** *adv* apenas. **~ity** *n* escasez *f*
scare /ˈskeə(r)/ *vt* asustar. **be ~d** tener miedo. **be ~d of sth** tenerle miedo a algo. ● *n* susto *m.* **~crow** *n* espantapájaros *m*
scarf /skɑːf/ *n* (*pl* **scarves**) bufanda *f*; (*over head*) pañuelo *m*
scarlet /ˈskɑːlət/ *adj* escarlata *f.* **~ fever** *n* escarlatina *f*
scarves /skɑːvz/ see **SCARF**
scary /ˈskeərɪ/ *adj* (**-ier**, **-iest**) que da miedo
scathing /ˈskeɪðɪŋ/ *adj* mordaz
scatter /ˈskætə(r)/ *vt* (*throw*) esparcir; (*disperse*) dispersar. ● *vi* dispersarse. **~ed** /ˈskætəd/ *adj* disperso; (*occasional*) esporádico
scavenge /ˈskævɪndʒ/ *vi* escarbar (en la basura)
scenario /sɪˈnɑːrɪəʊ/ *n* (*pl* **-os**) perspectiva *f*; (*of film*) guión *m*
scen|e /siːn/ *n* escena *f*; (*sight*) vista *f*; (*fuss*) lío *m.* **behind the ~es** entre bastidores. **~ery** /ˈsiːnərɪ/ *n* paisaje *m*; (*in theatre*) decorado *m.* **~ic** /ˈsiːnɪk/ *adj* pintoresco
scent /sent/ *n* olor *m*; (*perfume*) perfume *m*; (*trail*) pista *f.* ● *vt* intuir; (*make fragrant*) perfumar
sceptic /ˈskeptɪk/ *n* escéptico *m.* **~al** *adj* escéptico. **~ism** /-sɪzəm/ *n* escepticismo *m*
sceptre /ˈseptə(r)/ *n* cetro *m*
schedule /ˈʃedjuːl, ˈskedjuːl/ *n* programa *f*; (*timetable*) horario *m.* **behind ~** atrasado. **it's on ~** va de acuerdo a lo previsto. ● *vt* proyectar. **~d flight** *n* vuelo *m* regular
scheme /skiːm/ *n* proyecto *m*; (*plot*) intriga *f.* ● *vi* (*pej*) intrigar
schizophrenic /skɪtsəˈfrenɪk/ *adj & n* esquizofrénico (*m*)
scholar /ˈskɒlə(r)/ *n* erudito *m.*

~ly *adj* erudito. **~ship** *n* erudición *f*; (*grant*) beca *f*

school /sku:l/ *n* escuela *f*; (*Univ*) facultad *f*. ● *adj* (age, holidays, year) escolar. ● *vt* instruir; (*train*) capacitar. **~boy** *n* colegial *m*. **~girl** *n* colegiala *f*. **~ing** *n* instrucción *f*. **~master** *n* (*primary*) maestro *m*; (*secondary*) profesor *m*. **~mistress** *n* (*primary*) maestra *f*; (*secondary*) profesora *f*. **~teacher** *n* (*primary*) maestro *m*; (*secondary*) profesor *m*

scien|ce /ˈsaɪəns/ *n* ciencia *f*. **study ~ce** estudiar ciencias. **~ce fiction** *n* ciencia *f* ficción. **~tific** /-ˈtɪfɪk/ *adj* científico. **~tist** /ˈsaɪəntɪst/ *n* científico *m*

scissors /ˈsɪsəz/ *npl* tijeras *fpl*

scoff /skɒf/ *vt* ⓘ zamparse. ● *vi*. **~ at** mofarse de

scold /skəʊld/ *vt* regañar

scoop /sku:p/ *n* pala *f*; (*news*) primicia *f*. ▫ **~ out** *vt* sacar; excavar (hole)

scooter /ˈsku:tə(r)/ *n* escúter *m*; (*for child*) patinete *m*

scope /skəʊp/ *n* alcance *m*; (*opportunity*) oportunidad *f*

scorch /skɔ:tʃ/ *vt* chamuscar. **~ing** *adj* ⓘ de mucho calor

score /skɔ:(r)/ *n* tanteo *m*; (*Mus*) partitura *f*; (*twenty*) veintena *f*. **on that ~** en cuanto a eso. **know the ~** ⓘ saber cómo son las cosas. ● *vt* marcar (goal); anotarse (points); (*cut, mark*) rayar; conseguir (success). ● *vi* marcar

scorn /skɔ:n/ *n* desdén *m*. ● *vt* desdeñar. **~ful** *adj* desdeñoso

Scorpio /ˈskɔ:pɪəʊ/ *n* Escorpio *m*, Escorpión *m*

scorpion /ˈskɔ:pɪən/ *n* escorpión *m*

Scot /skɒt/ *n* escocés *m*. **~ch** /skɒtʃ/ *n* whisky *m*, güisqui *m*

> **Scottish Parliament** El Parlamento Escocés fue establecido en Edinburgo en 1999. Tiene competencia legislativa y ejecutiva en los asuntos internos de Escocia y poderes tributarios limitados. Los *MSPs* (*Members of the Scottish Parliament*) son 129, de los cuales 73 son elegidos directamente y el resto mediante el sistema de representación proporcional.

scotch /skɒtʃ/ *vt* frustrar; acallar (rumours)

Scotch tape *n* (*Amer*) celo *m*, cinta *f* Scotch

Scot: ~land /ˈskɒtlənd/ *n* Escocia *f*. **~s** *adj* escocés. **~tish** *adj* escocés

scoundrel /ˈskaʊndrəl/ *n* canalla *f*

scour /ˈskaʊə(r)/ *vt* fregar; (*search*) registrar. **~er** *n* estropajo *m*

scourge /skɜ:dʒ/ *n* azote *m*

scout /skaʊt/ *n* explorador *m*. **Boy S~** explorador *m*

scowl /skaʊl/ *n* ceño *m* fruncido. ● *vi* fruncir el ceño

scram /skræm/ *vi* ⓘ largarse

scramble /ˈskræmbl/ *vi* (*clamber*) gatear. ● *n* (*difficult climb*) subida *f* difícil; (*struggle*) rebatiña *f*. **~d egg** *n* huevos *mpl* revueltos

scrap /skræp/ *n* pedacito *m*; (*fam, fight*) pelea *f*. ● *vt* (*pt* **scrapped**) desechar. **~book** *n* álbum *m* de recortes. **~s** *npl* sobras *fpl*

scrape /skreɪp/ *n* (*fig*) apuro *m*. ● *vt* raspar; (*graze*) rasparse; (*rub*) rascar. ▫ **~ through** *vi/t* aprobar por los pelos (exam). ▫ **~ together** *vt* reunir. **~r** *n* rasqueta *f*

scrap: ~heap *n* montón *m* de deshechos. **~ yard** *n* chatarrería *f*

scratch /skrætʃ/ *vt* rayar (furniture, record); (*with nail etc*) arañar; rascarse (itch). ● *vi* arañar. ● *n* rayón *m*; (*from nail etc*) arañazo *m*. **start from ~** empezar desde cero. **be up to ~** dar la talla

scrawl /skrɔːl/ *n* garabato *m*. ● *vt/i* garabatear

scream /skriːm/ *vt/i* gritar. ● *n* grito *m*

screech /skriːtʃ/ *vi* chillar; (brakes etc) chirriar. ● *n* chillido *m*; (*of brakes etc*) chirrido *m*

screen /skriːn/ *n* pantalla *f*; (*folding*) biombo *m*. ● *vt* (*hide*) ocultar; (*protect*) proteger; proyectar (film)

screw /skruː/ *n* tornillo *m*. ● *vt* atornillar. □ **~ up** *vt* atornillar; entornar (eyes); torcer (face); (*sl, ruin*) fastidiar. **~driver** *n* destornillador *m*

scribble /ˈskrɪbl/ *vt/i* garrabatear. ● *n* garrabato *m*

script /skrɪpt/ *n* escritura *f*; (*of film etc*) guión *m*

scroll /skrəʊl/ *n* rollo *m* (de pergamino). □ **~ down** *vi* retroceder la pantalla. □ **~ up** *vi* avanzar la pantalla

scrounge /skraʊndʒ/ *vt/i* gorronear. **~r** *n* gorrón *m*

scrub /skrʌb/ *n* (*land*) maleza *f*. ● *vt/i* (*pt* **scrubbed**) fregar

scruff /skrʌf/ *n*. **by the ~ of the neck** por el pescuezo. **~y** *adj* (**-ier**, **-iest**) desaliñado

scrup|le /ˈskruːpl/ *n* escrúpulo *m*. **~ulous** /-jʊləs/ *adj* escrupuloso

scrutin|ize /ˈskruːtɪnaɪz/ *vt* escudriñar; inspeccionar (document). **~y** /ˈskruːtɪnɪ/ *n* examen *m* minucioso

scuffle /ˈskʌfl/ *n* refriega *f*

sculpt /skʌlpt/ *vt/i* esculpir. **~or** *n* escultor *m*. **~ure** /-tʃə(r)/ *n* escultura *f*. ● *vt/i* esculpir

scum /skʌm/ *n* espuma *f*; (*people, pej*) escoria *f*

scupper /ˈskʌpə(r)/ *vt* echar por tierra (plans)

scurry /ˈskʌrɪ/ *vi* corretear

scuttle /ˈskʌtl/ *n* cubo *m* del carbón. ● *vt* barrenar (ship). ● *vi*. **~ away** escabullirse rápidamente

scythe /saɪð/ *n* guadaña *f*

SE *abbr* (= **south-east**) SE

sea /siː/ *n* mar *m*. **at ~** en el mar; (*fig*) confuso. **by ~** por mar. **~food** *n* mariscos *mpl*. **~ front** *n* paseo *m* marítimo, malecón *m* (*LAm*). **~gull** *n* gaviota *f*. **~horse** *n* caballito *m* de mar

seal /siːl/ *n* sello *m*; (*animal*) foca *f*. ● *vt* sellar

sea level *n* nivel *m* del mar

sea lion *n* león *m* marino

seam /siːm/ *n* costura *f*; (*of coal*) veta *f*

seaman /ˈsiːmən/ *n* (*pl* **-men**) marinero *m*

seamy /ˈsiːmɪ/ *adj* sórdido

seance /ˈseɪɑːns/ *n* sesión *f* de espiritismo

search /sɜːtʃ/ *vt* registrar; buscar en (records). ● *vi* buscar. ● *n* (*for sth*) búsqueda *f*; (*of sth*) registro *m*; (*Comp*) búsqueda *f*. **in ~ of** en busca de. □ **~ for** *vt* buscar. **~ engine** *n* buscador *m*. **~ing** *adj* penetrante. **~light** *n* reflector *m*. **~ party** *n* partida *f* de rescate

sea: ~shore *n* orilla *f* del mar. **~sick** *adj* mareado. **be ~sick** marearse. **~side** *n* playa *f*

season /ˈsiːzn/ *n* estación *f*; (*period*) temporada *f*. **high/low ~**

temporada *f* alta/baja. ● *vt* (*Culin*) sazonar. **~al** *adj* estacional; (demand) de estación. **~ed** *adj* (*fig*) avezado. **~ing** *n* condimento *m*. **~ ticket** *n* abono *m* (de temporada)

seat /si:t/ *n* asiento *m*; (*place*) lugar *m*; (*in cinema, theatre*) localidad *f*; (*of trousers*) fondillos *mpl*. **take a ~** sentarse. ● *vt* sentar; (*have seats for*) (auditorium) tener capacidad para; (bus) tener asientos para. **~belt** *n* cinturón *m* de seguridad

sea: ~ trout *n* reo *m*. **~-urchin** *n* erizo *m* de mar. **~weed** *n* alga *f* marina. **~worthy** *adj* en condiciones de navegar

seclu|ded /sɪˈklu:dɪd/ *adj* aislado

second /ˈsekənd/ *adj* & *n* segundo (*m*). **on ~ thoughts** pensándolo bien. ● *adv* (*in race etc*) en segundo lugar. ● *vt* secundar. **~s** *npl* (*goods*) artículos *mpl* de segunda calidad; (*fam, more food*) **have ~s** repetir. ● /sɪˈkɒnd/ *vt* (*transfer*) trasladar temporalmente. **~ary** /ˈsekəndrɪ/ *adj* secundario. **~ary school** *n* instituto *m* (de enseñanza secundaria)

second: ~-class *adj* de segunda (clase). **~-hand** *adj* de segunda mano. **~ly** *adv* en segundo lugar. **~-rate** *adj* mediocre

secre|cy /ˈsi:krəsɪ/ *n* secreto *m*. **~t** *adj* & *n* secreto (*m*). **in ~t** en secreto

secretar|ial /sekrəˈteərɪəl/ *adj* de secretario; (course) de secretariado. **~y** /ˈsekrətrɪ/ *n* secretario *m*. **S~y of State** (*in UK*) ministro *m*; (*in US*) secretario *m* de Estado

secretive /ˈsi:krɪtɪv/ *adj* reservado

sect /sekt/ *n* secta *f*. **~arian** /-ˈteərɪən/ *adj* sectario

section /ˈsekʃn/ *n* sección *f*; (*part*) parte *f*

sector /ˈsektə(r)/ *n* sector *m*

secular /ˈsekjʊlə(r)/ *adj* secular

secur|e /sɪˈkjʊə(r)/ *adj* seguro; (shelf) firme. ● *vt* asegurar; (*obtain*) obtener. **~ely** *adv* seguramente. **~ity** *n* seguridad *f*; (*for loan*) garantía *f*

sedat|e /sɪˈdeɪt/ *adj* reposado. ● *vt* sedar. **~ion** /sɪˈdeɪʃn/ *n* sedación *f*. **~ive** /ˈsedətɪv/ *adj* & *n* sedante (*m*)

sediment /ˈsedɪmənt/ *n* sedimento *m*

seduc|e /sɪˈdju:s/ *vt* seducir. **~er** *n* seductor *m*. **~tion** /sɪˈdʌkʃn/ *n* seducción *f*. **~tive** /sɪˈdʌktɪv/ *adj* seductor

see /si:/ ● *vt* (*pt* **saw**, *pp* **seen**) ver; (*understand*) comprender; (*escort*) acompañar. **~ing that** visto que. **~ you later!** ¡hasta luego! ● *vi* ver. □ **~ off** *vt* (*say goodbye to*) despedirse de. □ **~ through** *vt* llevar a cabo; calar (person). □ **~ to** *vt* ocuparse de

seed /si:d/ *n* semilla *f*; (*fig*) germen *m*; (*Amer, pip*) pepita *f*. **go to ~** granar; (*fig*) echarse a perder. **~ling** *n* planta *f* de semillero. **~y** *adj* (**-ier, -iest**) sórdido

seek /si:k/ *vt* (*pt* **sought**) buscar; pedir (approval). □ **~ out** *vt* buscar

seem /si:m/ *vi* parecer

seen /si:n/ *see* **SEE**

seep /si:p/ *vi* filtrarse

see-saw /ˈsi:sɔ:/ *n* balancín *m*

seethe /si:ð/ *vi* (*fig*) estar furioso. **I was seething with anger** me hervía la sangre

see-through /ˈsi:θru:/ *adj* transparente

segment /ˈsegmənt/ *n* segmento

m; (*of orange*) gajo *m*

segregat|e /ˈsegrɪgeɪt/ *vt* segregar. **~ion** /-ˈgeɪʃn/ *n* segregación *f*

seiz|e /siːz/ *vt* agarrar; (*Jurid*) incautar. **~e on** *vt* aprovechar (chance). □ **~e up** *vi* (*Tec*) agarrotarse. **~ure** /ˈsiːʒə(r)/ *n* incautación *f*; (*Med*) ataque *m*

seldom /ˈseldəm/ *adv* rara vez

select /sɪˈlekt/ *vt* escoger; (*Sport*) seleccionar. ● *adj* selecto; (*exclusive*) exclusivo. **~ion** /-ʃn/ *n* selección *f*. **~ive** *adj* selectivo

self /self/ *n* (*pl* **selves**). **he's his old ~ again** vuelve a ser el de antes. **~-addressed** *adj* con el nombre y la dirección del remitente. **~-catering** *adj* con facilidades para cocinar. **~-centred** *adj* egocéntrico. **~-confidence** *n* confianza *f* en sí mismo. **~-confident** *adj* seguro de sí mismo. **~-conscious** *adj* cohibido. **~-contained** *adj* independiente. **~-control** *n* dominio *m* de sí mismo. **~-defence** *n* defensa *f* propia. **~-employed** *adj* que trabaja por cuenta propia. **~-evident** *adj* evidente. **~-important** *adj* presumido. **~-indulgent** *adj* inmoderado. **~-interest** *n* interés *m* (personal). **~ish** *adj* egoísta. **~ishness** *n* egoísmo *m*. **~-pity** *n* autocompasión. **~-portrait** *n* autorretrato *m*. **~-respect** *n* amor *m* propio. **~-righteous** *adj* santurrón. **~-sacrifice** *n* abnegación *f*. **~-satisfied** *adj* satisfecho de sí mismo. **~-serve** (*Amer*), **~-service** *adj* & *n* autoservicio (*m*). **~-sufficient** *adj* independiente

sell /sel/ *vt* (*pt* **sold**) vender. ● *vi* venderse. □ **~ off** *vt* liquidar. **~ out** *vi*. **we've sold out of gloves** los guantes están agotados. **~-by date** *n* fecha *f* límite de venta. **~er** *n* vendedor *m*

Sellotape /ˈseləteɪp/ *n* (®) celo *m*, cinta *f* Scotch

sell-out /ˈselaʊt/ *n* (*performance*) éxito *m* de taquilla; (*fam, betrayal*) capitulación *f*

semblance /ˈsembləns/ *n* apariencia *f*

semester /sɪˈmestə(r)/ *n* (*Amer*) semestre *m*

semi... /ˈsemɪ/ *pref* semi...

semi|breve /-briːv/ *n* redonda *f*. **~circle** *n* semicírculo *m*. **~colon** /-ˈkəʊlən/ *n* punto *m* y coma. **~-detached** /-dɪˈtætʃt/ *adj* (house) adosado. **~final** /-ˈfaɪnl/ *n* semifinal *f*

seminar /ˈsemɪnɑː(r)/ *n* seminario *m*

senat|e /ˈsenɪt/ *n* senado *m*. **the S~e** (*Amer*) el Senado. **~or** /-ətə(r)/ *n* senador *m*

send /send/ *vt/i* (*pt* **sent**) mandar, enviar. □ **~ away** *vt* despedir. □ **~ away for** *vt* pedir (por correo). □ **~ for** *vt* enviar a buscar. □ **~ off for** *vt* pedir (por correo). □ **~ up** *vt* 🄸 parodiar. **~er** *n* remitente *m*. **~-off** *n* despedida *f*

senile /ˈsiːnaɪl/ *adj* senil

senior /ˈsiːnɪə(r)/ *adj* mayor; (*in rank*) superior; (partner etc) principal. ● *n* mayor *m* & *f*. **~ citizen** *n* jubilado *m*. **~ high school** *n* (*Amer*) colegio *m* secundario. **~ity** /-ˈɒrətɪ/ *n* antigüedad *f*

sensation /senˈseɪʃn/ *n* sensación *f*. **~al** *adj* sensacional

sens|e /sens/ *n* sentido *m*; (*common sense*) juicio *m*; (*feeling*) sensación *f*. **make ~e** *vt* tener sentido. **make ~e of sth** entender algo. **~eless** *adj* sin sentido. **~ible**

S

/'sensəbl/ *adj* sensato; (clothing) práctico. **~itive** /'sensɪtɪv/ *adj* sensible; (*touchy*) susceptible. **~itivity** /-'tɪvətɪ/ *n* sensibilidad *f*. **~ual** /'senʃʊəl/ *adj* sensual. **~uous** /'sensʊəs/ *adj* sensual

sent /sent/ *see* **SEND**

sentence /'sentəns/ *n* frase *f*; (*judgment*) sentencia *f*; (*punishment*) condena *f*. ● *vt*. **~ to** condenar a

sentiment /'sentɪmənt/ *n* sentimiento *m*; (*opinion*) opinión *f*. **~al** /-'mentl/ *adj* sentimental. **~ality** /-'tæləti/ *n* sentimentalismo *m*

sentry /'sentrɪ/ *n* centinela *f*

separa|ble /'sepərəbl/ *adj* separable. **~te** /'sepərət/ *adj* separado; (*independent*) independiente. ● *vt* /'sepəreɪt/ separar. ● *vi* separarse. **~tely** /'sepərətlɪ/ *adv* por separado. **~tion** /-'reɪʃn/ *n* separación *f*. **~tist** /'sepərətɪst/ *n* separatista *m & f*

September /sep'tembə(r)/ *n* se(p)tiembre *m*

septic /'septɪk/ *adj* séptico

sequel /'si:kwəl/ *n* continuación *f*; (*later events*) secuela *f*

sequence /'si:kwəns/ *n* sucesión *f*; (*of film*) secuencia *f*

Serb /sɜ:b/ *adj & n see* **SERBIAN**. **~ia** /'sɜ:bɪə/ *n* Serbia *f* **~ian** *adj & n* serbio (*m*)

serenade /serə'neɪd/ *n* serenata *f*. ● *vt* dar serenata a

serene /sɪ'ri:n/ *adj* sereno

sergeant /'sɑ:dʒənt/ *n* sargento *m*

serial /'sɪərɪəl/ *n* serie *f*. **~ize** *vt* serializar

series /'sɪəri:z/ *n* serie *f*

serious /'sɪərɪəs/ *adj* serio. **~ly** *adv* seriamente; (*ill*) gravemente. **take ~ly** tomar en serio

sermon /'sɜ:mən/ *n* sermón *m*

serum /'sɪərəm/ *n* (*pl* **-a**) suero *m*

servant /'sɜ:vənt/ *n* criado *m*

serve /sɜ:v/ *vt* servir; servir a (country); cumplir (sentence). **~ as** servir de. **it ~s you right** ¡bien te lo mereces! ● *vi* servir; (*in tennis*) sacar. ● *n* (*in tennis*) saque *m*. **~r** *n* (*Comp*) servidor *m*

service /'sɜ:vɪs/ *n* servicio *m*; (*of car etc*) revisión *f*. ● *vt* revisar (car etc). **~ charge** *n* (*in restaurant*) servicio *m*. **~s** *npl* (*Mil*) fuerzas *fpl* armadas. **~ station** *n* estación *f* de servicio

serviette /sɜ:vɪ'et/ *n* servilleta *f*

servile /'sɜ:vaɪl/ *adj* servil

session /'seʃn/ *n* sesión *f*

set /set/ *vt* (*pt* **set**, *pres p* **setting**) poner; poner en hora (clock etc); fijar (limit etc); (*typeset*) componer. **~ fire to** prender fuego a. **~ free** *vt* poner en libertad. ● *vi* (sun) ponerse; (jelly) cuajarse. ● *n* serie *f*; (*of cutlery etc*) juego *m*; (*tennis*) set *m*; (*TV, Radio*) aparato *m*; (*in theatre*) decorado *m*; (*of people*) círculo *m*. ● *adj* fijo. **be ~ on** estar resuelto a. □ **~ back** *vt* (*delay*) retardar; (*fam, cost*) costar. □ **~ off** *vi* salir. *vt* hacer sonar (alarm); hacer explotar (bomb). □ **~ out** *vt* exponer (argument). *vi* (*leave*) salir. □ **~ up** *vt* establecer. **~back** *n* revés *m*

settee /se'ti:/ *n* sofá *m*

setting /'setɪŋ/ *n* (*of dial, switch*) posición *f*

settle /'setl/ *vt* (*arrange*) acordar; arreglar (matter); resolver (dispute); pagar (bill); saldar (debt). ● *vi* (*live*) establecerse. □ **~ down** *vi* calmarse; (*become more responsible*) sentar (la) cabeza. □ **~ for** *vt* aceptar. □ **~ up** *vi* arreglar cuentas. **~ment** *n* establecimiento *m*; (*agreement*) acuerdo *m*; (*of debt*) liquidación *f*; (*colony*) colonia *f*. **~r** *n* colono *m*

set: ~-to *n* pelea *f*. **~-up** *n* ⊞ sistema *m*; (*con*) tinglado *m*

seven /'sevn/ *adj & n* siete (*m*). **~teen** /sevn'ti:n/ *adj & n* diecisiete (*m*). **~teenth** *adj* decimoséptimo. ● *n* diecisietavo *m*. **~th** *adj & n* séptimo (*m*). **~tieth** /'sevəntɪɪθ/ *adj* septuagésimo. ● *n* setentavo *m*. **~ty** /'sevntɪ/ *adj & n* setenta (*m*)

sever /'sevə(r)/ *vt* cortar; (*fig*) romper

several /'sevrəl/ *adj & pron* varios

sever|e /sɪ'vɪə(r)/ *adj* (**-er**, **-est**) severo; (*serious*) grave; (weather) riguroso. **~ely** *adv* severamente. **~ity** /sɪ'verətɪ/ *n* severidad *f*; (*seriousness*) gravedad *f*

sew /səʊ/ *vt/i* (*pt* **sewed**, *pp* **sewn**, *or* **sewed**) coser. ▫ **~ up** *vt* coser

sew|age /'su:ɪdʒ/ *n* aguas *fpl* residuales. **~er** /'su:ə(r)/ *n* cloaca *f*

sewing /'səʊɪŋ/ *n* costura *f*. **~-machine** *n* máquina *f* de coser

sewn /səʊn/ *see* SEW

sex /seks/ *n* sexo *m*. **have ~** tener relaciones sexuales. ● *adj* sexual. **~ist** *adj & n* sexista (*m & f*). **~ual** /'sekʃʊəl/ *adj* sexual. **~ual intercourse** *n* relaciones *fpl* sexuales. **~uality** /-'ælətɪ/ *n* sexualidad *f*. **~y** *adj* (**-ier**, **-iest**) excitante, sexy, provocativo

shabby /'ʃæbɪ/ *adj* (**-ier**, **-iest**) (clothes) gastado; (person) pobremente vestido

shack /ʃæk/ *n* choza *f*

shade /ʃeɪd/ *n* sombra *f*; (*of colour*) tono *m*; (*for lamp*) pantalla *f*; (*nuance*) matiz *m*; (*Amer, over window*) persiana *f*

shadow /'ʃædəʊ/ *n* sombra *f*. ● *vt* (*follow*) seguir de cerca a. **~y** *adj* (*fig*) vago

shady /'ʃeɪdɪ/ *adj* (**-ier**, **-iest**) sombreado; (*fig*) turbio; (character) sospechoso

shaft /ʃɑ:ft/ *n* (*of arrow*) astil *m*; (*Mec*) eje *m*; (*of light*) rayo *m*; (*of lift, mine*) pozo *m*

shaggy /'ʃægɪ/ *adj* (**-ier**, **-iest**) peludo

shake /ʃeɪk/ *vt* (*pt* **shook**, *pp* **shaken**) sacudir; agitar (bottle); (*shock*) desconcertar. **~ hands with** estrechar la mano a. **~ one's head** negar con la cabeza; (*Amer, meaning yes*) asentir con la cabeza. ● *vi* temblar. ▫ **~ off** *vi* deshacerse de. ● *n* sacudida *f*

shaky /'ʃeɪkɪ/ *adj* (**-ier**, **-iest**) tembloroso; (table etc) inestable

shall /ʃæl/ *modal verb*. **we ~ see** veremos. **~ we go to the cinema?** ¿vamos al cine?

shallow /'ʃæləʊ/ *adj* (**-er**, **-est**) poco profundo; (*fig*) superficial

sham /ʃæm/ *n* farsa *f*. ● *adj* fingido

shambles /'ʃæmblz/ *npl* (*fam, mess*) caos *m*

shame /ʃeɪm/ *n* (*feeling*) vergüenza *f*. **what a ~!** ¡qué lástima! ● *vt* avergonzar. **~ful** *adj* vergonzoso. **~less** *adj* desvergonzado

shampoo /ʃæm'pu:/ *n* champú *m*. ● *vt* lavar

shan't /ʃɑ:nt/ = **shall not**

shape /ʃeɪp/ *n* forma *f*. ● *vt* formar; determinar (future). ● *vi* tomar forma. **~less** *adj* informe

share /ʃeə(r)/ *n* porción *f*; (*Com*) acción *f*. ● *vt* compartir; (*divide*) dividir. ● *vi* compartir. **~ in sth** participar en algo. ▫ **~ out** *vt* repartir. **~holder** *n* accionista *m & f*. **~-out**

n reparto *m*

shark /ʃɑ:k/ *n* tiburón *m*

sharp /ʃɑ:p/ *adj* (**-er**, **-est**) (knife etc) afilado; (pin etc) puntiagudo; (pain, sound) agudo; (taste) ácido; (bend) cerrado; (contrast) marcado; (*clever*) listo; (*Mus*) sostenido. ● *adv* en punto. **at seven o'clock ~** a las siete en punto. ● *n* (*Mus*) sostenido *m*. **~en** *vt* afilar; sacar punta a (pencil). **~ener** *n* (*Mec*) afilador *m*; (*for pencils*) sacapuntas *m*. **~ly** *adv* bruscamente

shatter /'ʃætə(r)/ *vt* hacer añicos. **he was ~ed by the news** la noticia lo dejó destrozado. ● *vi* hacerse añicos. **~ed** /'ʃætəd/*adj* (*exhausted*) agotado

shav|e /ʃeɪv/ *vt* afeitar, rasurar (*Mex*). ● *vi* afeitarse, rasurarse (*Mex*). ● *n* afeitada *f*, rasurada *f* (*Mex*). **have a ~e** afeitarse. **~er** *n* maquinilla *f* (de afeitar). **~ing brush** *n* brocha *f* de afeitar. **~ing cream** *n* crema *f* de afeitar

shawl /ʃɔ:l/ *n* chal *m*

she /ʃi:/ *pron* ella

sheaf /ʃi:f/ *n* (*pl* **sheaves** /ʃi:vz/) gavilla *f*

shear /ʃɪə(r)/ *vt* (*pp* **shorn** *or* **sheared**) esquilar. **~s** /ʃɪəz/ *npl* tijeras *fpl* grandes

shed /ʃed/ *n* cobertizo *m*. ● *vt* (*pt* **shed**, *pres p* **shedding**) perder; derramar (tears); despojarse de (clothes). **~ light on** arrojar luz sobre

she'd /ʃi:(ə)d/ = **she had**, **she would**

sheep /ʃi:p/ *n invar* oveja *f*. **~dog** *n* perro *m* pastor. **~ish** *adj* avergonzado

sheer /ʃɪə(r)/ *adj* (*as intensifier*) puro; (*steep*) perpendicular

sheet /ʃi:t/ *n* sábana *f*; (*of paper*) hoja *f*; (*of glass*) lámina *f*; (*of ice*) capa *f*

shelf /ʃelf/ *n* (*pl* **shelves**) estante *m*. **a set of shelves** unos estantes

shell /ʃel/ *n* concha *f*; (*of egg*) cáscara *f*; (*of crab, snail, tortoise*) caparazón *m or f*; (*explosive*) proyectil *m*, obús *m*. ● *vt* pelar (peas etc); (*Mil*) bombardear

she'll /'ʃi:(ə)l/ = **she had**, **she would**

shellfish /'ʃelfɪʃ/ *n invar* marisco *m*; (*collectively*) mariscos *mpl*

shelter /'ʃeltə(r)/ *n* refugio *m*. **take ~** refugiarse. ● *vt* darle cobijo a (fugitive); (*protect from weather*) resguardar. ● *vi* refugiarse. **~ed** /'ʃeltəd/ *adj* (spot) abrigado; (life) protegido

shelv|e /ʃelv/ *vt* (*fig*) dar carpetazo a. **~ing** *n* estantería *f*

shepherd /'ʃepəd/ *n* pastor *m*. **~ess** /-'des/ *n* pastora *f*

sherbet /'ʃɜ:bət/ *n* (*Amer, water ice*) sorbete *m*

sheriff /'ʃerɪf/ *n* (*in US*) sheriff *m*

sherry /'ʃerɪ/ *n* (vino *m* de) jerez *m*

she's /ʃi:z/ = **she is**, **she has**

shield /ʃi:ld/ *n* escudo *m*. ● *vt* proteger

shift /ʃɪft/ *vt* cambiar; correr (furniture etc). ● *vi* (wind) cambiar; (attention, opinion) pasar a; (*Amer, change gear*) cambiar de velocidad. ● *n* cambio *m*; (*work*) turno *m*; (*workers*) tanda *f*. **~y** *adj* (**-ier**, **-iest**) furtivo

shilling /'ʃɪlɪŋ/ *n* chelín *m*

shimmer /'ʃɪmə(r)/ *vi* rielar, relucir

shin /ʃɪn/ *n* espinilla *f*

shine /ʃaɪn/ *vi* (*pt* **shone**) brillar.

● *vt* sacar brillo a. ~ **a light on sth** alumbrar algo con una luz. ● *n* brillo *m*

shingle /ˈʃɪŋgl/ *n* (*pebbles*) guijarros *mpl*

shin|ing /ˈʃaɪnɪŋ/ *adj* brillante. **~y** /ˈʃaɪnɪ/ *adj* (**-ier**, **-iest**) brillante

ship /ʃɪp/ *n* barco *m*, buque *m*. ● *vt* (*pt* **shipped**) transportar; (*send*) enviar; (*load*) embarcar. **~building** *n* construcción *f* naval. **~ment** *n* envío *m*. **~ping** *n* transporte *m*; (*ships*) barcos *mpl*. **~shape** *adj* limpio y ordenado. **~wreck** *n* naufragio *m*. **~wrecked** *adj* naufragado. **be ~wrecked** naufragar. **~yard** *n* astillero *m*

shirk /ʃɜːk/ *vt* esquivar

shirt /ʃɜːt/ *n* camisa *f*. **in ~-sleeves** en mangas de camisa

shit /ʃɪt/ *n* & *int* (*vulgar*) mierda *f*. ● *vi* (*vulgar*) (*pt* **shat**, *pres p* **shitting**) cagar

shiver /ˈʃɪvə(r)/ *vi* temblar. ● *n* escalofrío *m*

shoal /ʃəʊl/ *n* banco *m*

shock /ʃɒk/ *n* (*of impact*) choque *m*; (*of earthquake*) sacudida *f*; (*surprise*) shock *m*; (*scare*) susto *m*; (*Elec*) descarga *f*; (*Med*) shock *m*. **get a ~** llevarse un shock. ● *vt* escandalizar; (*apall*) horrorizar. **~ing** *adj* escandaloso; [!] espantoso

S

shod /ʃɒd/ *see* **SHOE**

shoddy /ˈʃɒdɪ/ *adj* (**-ier**, **-iest**) mal hecho, de pacotilla

shoe /ʃuː/ *n* zapato *m*; (*of horse*) herradura *f*. ● *vt* (*pt* **shod**, *pres p* **shoeing**) herrar (horse). **~horn** *n* calzador *m*. **~lace** *n* cordón *m* (de zapato). **~ polish** *n* betún *m*

shone /ʃɒn/ *see* **SHINE**

shoo /ʃuː/ *vt* ahuyentar

shook /ʃʊk/ *see* **SHAKE**

shoot /ʃuːt/ *vt* (*pt* **shot**) disparar; rodar (film). ● *vi* (*hunt*) cazar. ● *n* (*of plant*) retoño *m*. □ **~ down** *vt* derribar. □ **~ out** *vi* (*rush*) salir disparado. □ **~ up** *vi* (prices) dispararse; (*grow*) crecer mucho

shop /ʃɒp/ *n* tienda *f*. **go to the ~s** ir de compras. **talk ~** hablar del trabajo. ● *vi* (*pt* **shopping**) hacer compras. **go ~ping** ir de compras. □ **~ around** *vi* buscar el mejor precio. **~ assistant** *n* dependiente *m*, dependienta *f*, empleado *m*, empleada *f* (*LAm*). **~keeper** *n* comerciante *m*, tendero *m*. **~lifter** *n* ladrón *m* (que roba en las tiendas). **~lifting** *n* hurto *m* (en las tiendas). **~per** *n* comprador *m*. **~ping** *n* (*purchases*) compras *fpl*. **do the ~ping** hacer la compra, hacer el mandado (*Mex*). **~ping bag** *n* bolsa *f* de la compra. **~ping cart** *n* (*Amer*) carrito *m* (de la compra). **~ping centre**, **~ping mall** (*Amer*) *n* centro *m* comercial. **~ping trolley** *n* carrito *m* de la compra. **~ steward** *n* enlace *m* sindical. **~ window** *n* escaparate *m*, vidriera *f* (*LAm*), aparador *m* (*Mex*)

shore /ʃɔː(r)/ *n* orilla *f*

shorn /ʃɔːn/ *see* **SHEAR**

short /ʃɔːt/ *adj* (**-er**, **-est**) corto; (*not lasting*) breve; (person) bajo; (*curt*) brusco. **a ~ time ago** hace poco. **be ~ of time/money** andar corto de tiempo/dinero. **Mick is ~ for Michael** Mick es el diminutivo de Michael. ● *adv* (stop) en seco. **we never went ~ of food** nunca nos faltó comida. ● *n*. **in ~** en resumen. **~age** /-ɪdʒ/ *n* escasez *f*, falta *f*. **~bread** *n* galleta *f* (de mantequilla). **~ circuit** *n* cortocircuito *m*. **~coming** *n* defecto *m*. **~ cut** *n* atajo *m*. **~en** *vt* acortar.

~hand *n* taquigrafía *f*. **~ly** *adv* (*soon*) dentro de poco. **~ly before midnight** poco antes de la medianoche. **~s** *npl* pantalones *m* cortos, shorts *mpl*; (*Amer, underwear*) calzoncillos *mpl*. **~-sighted** /-'saɪtɪd/*adj* miope

shot /ʃɒt/ *see* **SHOOT**. ● *n* (*from gun*) disparo *m*; tiro *m*; (*in soccer*) tiro *m*, disparo *m*; (*in other sports*) tiro *m*; (*Photo*) foto *f*. **be a good/poor ~** ser un buen/mal tirador. **be off like a ~** salir disparado. **~gun** *n* escopeta *f*

should /ʃʊd, ʃəd/ *modal verb*. **I ~ go** debería ir. **you ~n't have said that** no deberías haber dicho eso. **I ~ like to see her** me gustaría verla. **if he ~ come** si viniese

shoulder /'ʃəʊldə(r)/ *n* hombro *m*. ● *vt* cargar con (responsibility); ponerse al hombro (burden). **~ blade** *n* omóplato *m*

shout /ʃaʊt/ *n* grito *m*. ● *vt/i* gritar. **~ at s.o.** gritarle a uno

shove /ʃʌv/ *n* empujón *m*. ● *vt* empujar; (*fam, put*) poner. ● *vi* empujar. □ **~ off** *vi* 🅸 largarse

shovel /'ʃʌvl/ *n* pala *f*. ● *vt* (*pt* **shovelled**) palear (coal); espalar (snow)

show /ʃəʊ/ *vt* (*pt* **showed**, *pp* **shown**) mostrar; (*put on display*) exponer; poner (film). **I'll ~ you to your room** lo acompaño a su cuarto. ● *vi* (*be visible*) verse. ● *n* muestra *f*; (*exhibition*) exposición *f*; (*in theatre*) espectáculo *m*; (*on TV, radio*) programa *m*; (*ostentation*) pompa *f*. **be on ~** estar expuesto. □ **~ off** *vt* (*pej*) lucir, presumir de. *vi* presumir, lucirse. □ **~ up** *vi* (*be visible*) notarse; (*arrive*) aparecer. *vt* (*reveal*) poner de manifiesto; (*embarrass*) hacer quedar mal. **~case** *n* vitrina *f*. **~down** *n* confrontación *f*

shower /'ʃaʊə(r)/ *n* (*of rain*) chaparrón *m*; (*for washing*) ducha *f*. **have a ~, take a ~** ducharse. ● *vi* ducharse

showjumping *n* concursos *mpl* hípicos.

shown /ʃəʊn/ *see* **SHOW**

show: ~-off *n* fanfarrón *m*. **~room** *n* sala *f* de exposición *f*. **~y** *adj* (**-ier, -iest**) llamativo; (*attractive*) ostentoso

shrank /ʃræŋk/ *see* **SHRINK**

shred /ʃred/ *n* pedazo *m*; (*fig*) pizca *f*. ● *vt* (*pt* **shredded**) hacer tiras; destruir, triturar (documents). **~der** *n* (*for paper*) trituradora *f*; (*for vegetables*) cortadora *f*

shrewd /ʃru:d/ *adj* (**-er, -est**) astuto

shriek /ʃri:k/ *n* chillido *m*; (*of pain*) alarido *m*. ● *vt/i* chillar

shrift /ʃrɪft/ *n*. **give s.o. short ~** despachar a uno con brusquedad. **give sth short ~** desestimar algo de plano

shrill /ʃrɪl/ *adj* agudo

shrimp /ʃrɪmp/ *n* gamba *f*, camarón *m* (*LAm*); (*Amer, large*) langostino *m*

shrine /ʃraɪn/ *n* (*place*) santuario *m*; (*tomb*) sepulcro *m*

shrink /ʃrɪŋk/ *vt* (*pt* **shrank**, *pp* **shrunk**) encoger. ● *vi* encogerse; (amount) reducirse; retroceder (*recoil*)

shrivel /'ʃrɪvl/ *vi* (*pt* **shrivelled**). **~ (up)** (plant) marchitarse; (fruit) resecarse y arrugarse

shroud /ʃraʊd/ *n* mortaja *f*; (*fig*) velo *m*. ● *vt* envolver

Shrove /ʃrəʊv/ *n*. **~ Tuesday** *n* martes *m* de carnaval

shrub /ʃrʌb/ *n* arbusto *m*

shrug /ʃrʌg/ *vt* (*pt* **shrugged**) encogerse de hombros

shrunk /ʃrʌŋk/ *see* SHRINK. **~en** *adj* encogido

shudder /ˈʃʌdə(r)/ *vi* estremecerse. ● *n* estremecimiento *m*

shuffle /ˈʃʌfl/ *vi* andar arrastrando los pies. ● *vt* barajar (cards). **~ one's feet** arrastrar los pies

shun /ʃʌn/ *vt* (*pt* **shunned**) evitar

shunt /ʃʌnt/ *vt* cambiar de vía

shush /ʃʊʃ/ *int* ¡chitón!

shut /ʃʌt/ *vt* (*pt* **shut**, *pres p* **shutting**) cerrar. ● *vi* cerrarse. ● *adj*. **be ~** estar cerrado. □ **~ down** *vt/i* cerrar. □ **~ up** *vt* cerrar; Ⓘ hacer callar. *vi* callarse. **~ter** *n* contraventana *f*; (*Photo*) obturador *m*

shuttle /ˈʃʌtl/ *n* lanzadera *f*; (*by air*) puente *m* aéreo; (*space* **~**) transbordador *m* espacial. ● *vi*. **~ (back and forth)** ir y venir. **~cock** *n* volante *m*. **~ service** *n* servicio *m* de enlace

shy /ʃaɪ/ *adj* (**-er**, **-est**) tímido. ● *vi* (*pt* **shied**) asustarse. **~ness** *n* timidez *f*

sick /sɪk/ *adj* enfermo; (humour) negro; (*fam, fed up*) harto. **be ~** estar enfermo; (*vomit*) vomitar. **be ~ of** (*fig*) estar harto de. **feel ~** sentir náuseas. **get ~** (*Amer*) caer enfermo, enfermarse (*LAm*). **~ leave** *n* permiso *m* por enfermedad, baja *f* por enfermedad. **~ly** /ˈsɪklɪ/ *adj* (**-lier**, **-liest**) enfermizo; (taste, smell etc) nauseabundo. **~ness** /ˈsɪknɪs/ *n* enfermedad *f*

side /saɪd/ *n* lado *m*; (*of hill*) ladera *f*; (*of person*) costado *m*; (*team*) equipo *m*; (*fig*) parte *f*. **~ by ~** uno al lado del otro. **take ~s** tomar partido. ● *adj* lateral. □ **~ with** *vt* ponerse de parte de. **~board** *n* aparador *m*. **~ dish** *n* acompañamiento *m*. **~-effect** *n* efecto *m* secundario; (*fig*) consecuencia *f* indirecta. **~line** *n* actividad *f* suplementaria. **~ road** *n* calle *f* secundaria. **~-step** *vt* eludir. **~-track** *vt* desviar del tema. **~walk** *n* (*Amer*) acera *f*, vereda *f* (*LAm*), banqueta *f* (*Mex*). **~ways** *adj* & *adv* de lado

siding /ˈsaɪdɪŋ/ *n* apartadero *m*

sidle /ˈsaɪdl/ *vi*. **~ up to s.o.** acercarse furtivamente a uno

siege /siːdʒ/ *n* sitio *m*

sieve /sɪv/ *n* tamiz *m*. ● *vt* tamizar, cernir

sift /sɪft/ *vt* tamizar, cernir. ● *vi*. **~ through sth** pasar algo por el tamiz

sigh /saɪ/ *n* suspiro. ● *vi* suspirar

sight /saɪt/ *n* vista *f*; (*spectacle*) espectáculo *m*; (*on gun*) mira *f*. **at first ~** a primera vista. **catch ~ of** ver; (*in distance*) avistar. **lose ~ of** perder de vista. **see the ~s** visitar los lugares de interés. **within ~ of** (*near*) cerca de. ● *vt* ver; divisar (land). **~-seeing** *n*. **go ~** ir a visitar los lugares de interés. **~seer** /-siːə(r)/ *n* turista *m* & *f*

sign /saɪn/ *n* (*indication*) señal *f*, indicio *m*; (*gesture*) señal *f*, seña *f*; (*notice*) letrero *m*; (*astrological*) signo *m*. ● *vt* firmar. □ **~ on** *vi* (*for unemployment benefit*) anotarse para recibir el seguro de desempleo

signal /ˈsɪgnəl/ *n* señal *f*. ● *vt* (*pt* **signalled**) señalar. ● *vi*. **~ (to s.o.)** hacer señas (a uno); (*Auto*) poner el intermitente, señalizar

signature /ˈsɪgnətʃə(r)/ *n* firma *f*. **~ tune** *n* sintonía *f*

S

significan|ce /sɪgˈnɪfɪkəns/ *n* importancia *f*. **~t** *adj* (*important*) importante; (fact, remark) significativo

signify /ˈsɪgnɪfaɪ/ *vt* significar

signpost /ˈsaɪmpəʊst/ *n* señal *f*, poste *m* indicador

silen|ce /ˈsaɪləns/ *n* silencio *m*. ● *vt* hacer callar. **~cer** *n* (*on gun and on car*) silenciador *m*. **~t** *adj* silencioso; (film) mudo. **remain ~t** quedarse callado. **~tly** *adv* silenciosamente

silhouette /sɪluːˈet/ *n* silueta *f*. ● *vt*. **be ~d** perfilarse (**against** contra)

silicon /ˈsɪlɪkən/ *n* silicio *m*. **~ chip** *n* pastilla *f* de silicio

silk /sɪlk/ *n* seda *f*. **~y** *adj* (*of silk*) de seda; (*like silk*) sedoso

silly /ˈsɪlɪ/ *adj* (**-ier**, **-iest**) tonto

silt /sɪlt/ *n* cieno *m*

silver /ˈsɪlvə(r)/ *n* plata *f*. ● *adj* de plata. **~-plated** *adj* bañado en plata, plateado. **~ware** /-weə(r)/ *n* platería *f*

simil|ar /ˈsɪmɪlə(r)/ *adj* parecido, similar. **~arity** /-ˈlærətɪ/ *n* parecido *m*. **~arly** *adv* de igual manera. **~e** /ˈsɪmɪlɪ/ *n* símil *m*

simmer /ˈsɪmə(r)/ *vt/i* hervir a fuego lento. □ **~ down** *vi* calmarse

simpl|e /ˈsɪmpl/ *adj* (**-er**, **-est**) sencillo, simple; (person) (*humble*) simple; (*backward*) simple. **~e-minded** /-ˈmaɪndɪd/ *adj* ingenuo. **~icity** /-ˈplɪsetɪ/ *n* simplicidad *f*, sencillez *f*. **~ify** /ˈsɪmplɪfaɪ/ *vt* simplificar. **~y** *adv* sencillamente, simplemente; (*absolutely*) realmente

simulate /ˈsɪmjʊleɪt/ *vt* simular

simultaneous /sɪmlˈteɪnɪəs/ *adj* simultáneo. **~ly** *adv* simultáneamente

sin /sɪn/ *n* pecado *m*. ● *vi* (*pt* **sinned**) pecar

since /sɪns/

● *preposition* desde. **he's been living here ~ 1991** vive aquí desde 1991. **~ Christmas** desde Navidad. **~ then** desde entonces. **I haven't been feeling well ~ Sunday** desde el domingo que no me siento bien. **how long is it ~ your interview?** ¿cuánto (tiempo) hace de la entrevista?

● *adverb* desde entonces. **I haven't spoken to her ~** no he hablado con ella desde entonces

● *conjunction*

····▸ desde que. **I haven't seen her ~ she left** no la he visto desde que se fue. **~ coming to Manchester** desde que vine (*or* vino *etc*) a Manchester. **it's ten years ~ he died** hace diez años que se murió

····▸ (*because*) como, ya que. **~ it was quite late, I decided to stay** como *or* ya que era bastante tarde, decidí quedarme

sincer|e /sɪnˈsɪə(r)/ *adj* sincero. **~ely** *adv* sinceramente. **yours ~ely, ~ely (yours)** (*in letters*) (saluda) a usted atentamente. **~ity** /-ˈserətɪ/ *n* sinceridad *f*

sinful /ˈsɪnfl/ *adj* (person) pecador; (act) pecaminoso

sing /sɪŋ/ *vt/i* (*pt* **sang**, *pp* **sung**) cantar

singe /sɪndʒ/ *vt* (*pres p* **singeing**) chamuscar

singer /ˈsɪŋə(r)/ *n* cantante *m* & *f*

single /ˈsɪŋgl/ *adj* solo; (*not*

double) sencillo; (*unmarried*) soltero; (bed, room) individual, de una plaza (*LAm*); (ticket) de ida, sencillo. **not a ~ house** ni una sola casa. **every ~ day** todos los días sin excepción. ● *n* (*ticket*) billete *m* sencillo, boleto *m* de ida (*LAm*). □ **~ out** *vt* escoger; (*distinguish*) distinguir. **~-handed** /-ˈhændɪd/ *adj & adv* sin ayuda. **~s** *npl* (*Sport*) individuales *mpl*

singular /ˈsɪŋgjʊlə(r)/ *n* singular *f*. ● *adj* singular; (*unusual*) raro; (noun) en singular

sinister /ˈsɪnɪstə(r)/ *adj* siniestro

sink /sɪŋk/ *vt* (*pt* **sank**, *pp* **sunk**) hundir. ● *vi* hundirse. ● *n* fregadero *m* (*Amer, in bathroom*) lavabo *m*, lavamanos *m*. □ **~ in** *vi* penetrar

sinner /ˈsɪnə(r)/ *n* pecador *m*

sip /sɪp/ *n* sorbo *m*. ● *vt* (*pt* **sipped**) sorber

siphon /ˈsaɪfən/ *n* sifón *m*. **~ (out)** sacar con sifón. □ **~ off** *vt* desviar (money).

sir /sɜː(r)/ *n* señor *m*. **S~** *n* (*title*) sir *m*. **Dear S~,** (*in letters*) De mi mayor consideración:

siren /ˈsaɪərən/ *n* sirena *f*

sister /ˈsɪstə(r)/ *n* hermana *f*; (*nurse*) enfermera *f* jefe. **~-in-law** *n* (*pl* **~s-in-law**) cuñada *f*

S

sit /sɪt/ *vi* (*pt* **sat**, *pres p* **sitting**) sentarse; (committee etc) reunirse en sesión. **be ~ting** estar sentado. ● *vt* sentar; hacer (exam). □ **~ back** *vi* (*fig*) relajarse. □ **~ down** *vi* sentarse. **be ~ting down** estar sentado. □ **~ up** *vi* (*from lying*) incorporarse; (*straighten back*) ponerse derecho. **~-in** *n* (*strike*) encierro *m*, ocupación *f*

site /saɪt/ *n* emplazamiento *m*; (*piece of land*) terreno *m*; (*archaeological*) yacimiento *m*. **building ~** *n* solar *m*. ● *vt* situar

sit: ~ting *n* sesión *f*; (*in restaurant*) turno *m*. **~ting room** *n* sala *f* de estar, living *m*

situat|e /ˈsɪtjʊeɪt/ *vt* situar. **~ion** /-ˈeɪʃn/ *n* situación *f*

six /sɪks/ *adj & n* seis (*m*). **~teen** /sɪkˈstiːn/ *adj & n* dieciséis (*m*). **~teenth** *adj* decimosexto. ● *n* dieciseisavo *m*. **~th** *adj & n* sexto (*m*). **~tieth** /ˈsɪkstɪɪθ/ *adj* sexagésimo. ● *n* sesentavo *m*. **~ty** /ˈsɪkstɪ/ *adj & n* sesenta (*m*)

size /saɪz/ *n* tamaño *m*; (*of clothes*) talla *f*; (*of shoes*) número *m*; (*of problem, operation*) magnitud *f*. **what ~ do you take?** (*clothes*) ¿qué talla tiene?; (*shoes*) ¿qué número calza?. □ **~ up** *vt* [!] evaluar (problem); calar (person)

sizzle /ˈsɪzl/ *vi* crepitar

skat|e /skeɪt/ *n* patín *m*.● *vi* patinar. **~eboard** *n* monopatín *m*, patineta *f* (*Mex*). **~er** *n* patinador *m*. **~ing** *n* patinaje *m*. **~ing-rink** *n* pista *f* de patinaje

skeleton /ˈskelɪtn/ *n* esqueleto *m*. **~ key** *n* llave *f* maestra

sketch /sketʃ/ *n* (*drawing*) dibujo *m*; (*rougher*) esbozo *m*; (*TV, Theatre*) sketch *m*. ● *vt* esbozar. ● *vi* dibujar. **~y** *adj* (**-ier**, **-iest**) incompleto

ski /skiː/ *n* (*pl* **skis**) esquí *m*. ● *vi* (*pt* **skied**, *pres p* **skiing**) esquiar. **go ~ing** ir a esquiar

skid /skɪd/ *vi* (*pt* **skidded**) patinar. ● *n* patinazo *m*

ski: ~er *n* esquiador *m*. **~ing** *n* esquí *m*

skilful /ˈskɪlfl/ *adj* diestro

ski-lift /ˈskiːlɪft/ *n* telesquí *m*

skill /skɪl/ *n* habilidad *f*; (*technical*) destreza *f*. **~ed** *adj* hábil; (worker) cualificado

skim /skɪm/ *vt* (*pt* **skimmed**) espumar (soup); desnatar, descremar (milk); (*glide over*) pasar casi rozando. ~ **milk** (*Amer*), ~**med milk** *n* leche *f* desnatada, leche *f* descremada. ~ **through** *vt* leer por encima

skimp /skɪmp/ *vi*. ~ **on sth** escatimar algo. ~**y** *adj* (**-ier**, **-iest**) escaso; (skirt, dress) brevísimo

skin /skɪn/ *n* piel *f*. ● *vt* (*pt* **skinned**) despellejar. ~**-deep** *adj* superficial. ~**-diving** *n* submarinismo *m*. ~**ny** *adj* (**-ier**, **-iest**) flaco

skip /skɪp/ *vi* (*pt* **skipped**) *vi* saltar; (*with rope*) saltar a la comba, saltar a la cuerda. ● *vt* saltarse (chapter); faltar a (class). ● *n* brinco *m*; (*container*) contenedor *m* (para escombros). ~**per** *n* capitán *m*. ~**ping-rope**, ~**rope** (*Amer*) *n* comba *f*, cuerda *f* de saltar, reata *f* (*Mex*)

skirmish /'skɜ:mɪʃ/ *n* escaramuza *f*

skirt /skɜ:t/ *n* falda *f*. ● *vt* bordear; (*go round*) ladear. ~**ing-board** *n* rodapié *m*, zócalo *m*

skittle /'skɪtl/ *n* bolo *m*

skive off /skaɪv/ (*vi* 🅸, *disappear*) escurrir el bulto; (*stay away from work*) no ir a trabajar

skulk /skʌlk/ *vi* (*hide*) esconderse. ~ **around** *vi* merodear

skull /skʌl/ *n* cráneo *m*; (*remains*) calavera *f*

sky /skaɪ/ *n* cielo *m*. ~**lark** *n* alondra *f*. ~**light** *n* tragaluz *m*. ~ **marshal** *n* guardia *m* armado a bordo. ~**scraper** *n* rascacielos *m*

slab /slæb/ *n* (*of concrete*) bloque *m*; (*of stone*) losa *f*

slack /slæk/ *adj* (**-er**, **-est**) flojo; (person) poco aplicado; (period) de poca actividad. ● *vi* flojear. ~**en** *vt* aflojar. ● *vi* (person) descansar. □ ~**en off** *vt/i* aflojar

slain /sleɪn/ *see* **SLAY**

slake /sleɪk/ *vt* apagar

slam /slæm/ *vt* (*pt* **slammed**). ~ **the door** dar un portazo. ~ **the door shut** cerrar de un portazo. ~ **on the brakes** pegar un frenazo; (*sl, criticize*) atacar violentamente. ● *vi* cerrarse de un portazo

slander /'slɑ:ndə(r)/ *n* calumnia *f*. ● *vt* difamar

slang /slæŋ/ *n* argot *m*

slant /slɑ:nt/ *vt* inclinar. ● *n* inclinación *f*

slap /slæp/ *vt* (*pt* **slapped**) (*on face*) pegarle una bofetada a; (*put*) tirar. ~ **s.o. on the back** darle una palmada a uno en la espalda. ● *n* bofetada *f*; (*on back*) palmada *f*. ● *adv* de lleno. ~**dash** *adj* descuidado; (work) chapucero

slash /slæʃ/ *vt* acuchillar; (*fig*) rebajar drásticamente. ● *n* cuchillada *f*

slat /slæt/ *n* tablilla *f*

slate /sleɪt/ *n* pizarra *f*. ● *vt* 🅸 poner por los suelos

slaughter /'slɔ:tə(r)/ *vt* matar salvajemente; matar (animal). ● *n* carnicería *f*; (*of animals*) matanza *f*

slave /sleɪv/ *n* esclavo *m*. ● *vi* ~ **(away)** trabajar como un negro. ~**-driver** *n* 🅸 negrero *m*. ~**ry** /-ərɪ/ *n* esclavitud *f*

slay /sleɪ/ *vt* (*pt* **slew**, *pp* **slain**) dar muerte a

sleazy /'sli:zɪ/ *adj* (**-ier**, **-iest**) 🅸 sórdido

sled /sled/ (*Amer*), **sledge** /sledʒ/ *n* trineo *m*

sledge-hammer *n* mazo *m*, almádena *f*

S

sleek /sli:k/ *adj* (**-er**, **-est**) liso, brillante

sleep /sli:p/ *n* sueño *m*. **go to ~** dormirse. ● *vi* (*pt* **slept**) dormir. ● *vt* poder alojar. **~er** *n* (*on track*) traviesa *f*, durmiente *m*. **be a light/heavy ~er** tener el sueño ligero/pesado. **~ing bag** *n* saco *m* de dormir. **~ing pill** *n* somnífero *m*. **~less** *adj*. **have a ~less night** pasar la noche en blanco. **~walk** *vi* caminar dormido. **~y** *adj* (**-ier**, **-iest**) soñoliento. **be/feel ~y** tener sueño

sleet /sli:t/ *n* aguanieve *f*

sleeve /sli:v/ *n* manga *f*; (*for record*) funda *f*, carátula *f*. **up one's ~** en reserva. **~less** *adj* sin mangas

sleigh /sleɪ/ *n* trineo *m*

slender /ˈslendə(r)/ *adj* delgado; (*fig*) escaso

slept /slept/ *see* SLEEP

slew /slu:/ *see* SLAY

slice /slaɪs/ *n* (*of ham*) lonja *f*; (*of bread*) rebanada *f*; (*of meat*) tajada *f*; (*of cheese*) trozo *m*; (*of sth round*) rodaja *f*. ● *vt* cortar (en rebanadas, tajadas etc)

slick /slɪk/ *adj* (performance) muy pulido. ● *n*. **(oil) ~** marea *f* negra

slid|e /slaɪd/ *vt* (*pt* **slid**) deslizar. ● *vi* (*intentionally*) deslizarse; (*unintentionally*) resbalarse. ● *n* resbalón *m*; (*in playground*) tobogán *m*, resbaladilla *f* (*Mex*); (*for hair*) pasador *m*, broche *m* (*Mex*); (*Photo*) diapositiva *f*. **~ing scale** *n* escala *f* móvil

slight /slaɪt/ *adj* (**-er**, **-est**) ligero; (*slender*) delgado. ● *vt* desairar. ● *n* desaire *m*. **~est** *adj* mínimo. **not in the ~est** en absoluto. **~ly** *adv* un poco, ligeramente

slim /slɪm/ *adj* (**slimmer**, **slimmest**) delgado. ● *vi* (*pt* **slimmed**) (*become slimmer*) adelgazar; (*diet*) hacer régimen

slim|e /slaɪm/ *n* limo *m*; (*of snail, slug*) baba *f*. **~y** *adj* viscoso; (*fig*) excesivamente obsequioso

sling /slɪŋ/ *n* (*Med*) cabestrillo *m*. ● *vt* (*pt* **slung**) lanzar

slip /slɪp/ *vt* (*pt* **slipped**) deslizar. **~ s.o.'s mind** olvidársele a uno. ● *vi* resbalarse. **it ~ped out of my hands** se me resbaló de las manos. **he ~ped out the back door** se deslizó por la puerta trasera ● *n* resbalón *m*; (*mistake*) error *m*; (*petticoat*) combinación *f*; (*paper*) trozo *m*. **give s.o. the ~** lograr zafarse de uno. **~ of the tongue** *n* lapsus *m* linguae. □ **~ away** *vi* escabullirse. □ **~ up** *vi* [I] equivocarse

slipper /ˈslɪpə(r)/ *n* zapatilla *f*

slippery /ˈslɪpərɪ/ *adj* resbaladizo

slip: ~ road *n* rampa *f* de acceso. **~shod** /ˈslɪpʃɒd/ *adj* descuidado. **~-up** *n* [I] error *m*

slit /slɪt/ *n* raja *f*; (*cut*) corte *m*. ● *vt* (*pt* **slit**, *pres p* **slitting**) rajar; (*cut*) cortar

slither /ˈslɪðə(r)/ *vi* deslizarse

slobber /ˈslɒbə(r)/ *vi* babear

slog /slɒg/ *vt* (*pt* **slogged**) golpear. ● *vi* caminar trabajosamente. ● *n* golpetazo *m*; (*hard work*) trabajo *m* penoso. □ **~ away** *vi* sudar tinta [I]

slogan /ˈsləʊgən/ *n* eslogan *m*

slop /slɒp/ *vt* (*pt* **slopped**) derramar. ● *vi* derramarse

slop|e /sləʊp/ *vi* inclinarse. ● *vt* inclinar. ● *n* declive *m*, pendiente *f*. **~ing** *adj* inclinado

sloppy /ˈslɒpɪ/ *adj* (**-ier**, **-iest**) (work) descuidado; (person) des-

aliñado
slosh /slɒʃ/ *vi* 🄸 chapotear
slot /slɒt/ *n* ranura *f.* ● *vt* (*pt* **slotted**) encajar
slot-machine *n* distribuidor *m* automático; (*for gambling*) máquina *f* tragamonedas
slouch /slaʊtʃ/ *vi* andar cargado de espaldas; (*in chair*) repanchigarse
Slovak /'sləʊvæk/ *adj & n* eslovaco (*m*). **~ia** *n* Eslovaquia *f*
slovenly /'slʌvnlɪ/ *adj* (work) descuidado; (person) desaliñado
slow /sləʊ/ *adj* (**-er**, **-est**) lento. **be ~** (clock) estar atrasado. **in ~ motion** a cámara lenta. ● *adv* despacio. ● *vt* retardar. ● *vi* ir más despacio. □ **~ down**, **~ up** *vt* retardar. *vi* ir más despacio. **~ly** *adv* despacio, lentamente
sludge /slʌdʒ/ *n* fango *m*
slug /slʌg/ *n* babosa *f.* **~gish** *adj* lento
slum /slʌm/ *n* barrio *m* bajo
slumber /'slʌmbə(r)/ *vi* dormir
slump /slʌmp/ *n* baja *f* repentina; (*in business*) depresión *f.* ● *vi* desplomarse
slung /slʌŋ/ *see* **SLING**
slur /slɜː(r)/ *vt* (*pt* **slurred**). **~ one's words** arrastrar las palabras. ● *n.* **a racist ~** un comentario racista
slush /slʌʃ/ *n* nieve *f* medio derretida. **~ fund** *n* fondo *m* de reptiles
sly /slaɪ/ *adj* (**slyer**, **slyest**) (*crafty*) astuto. ● *n.* **on the ~** a hurtadillas. **~ly** *adv* astutamente
smack /smæk/ *n* manotazo *m.* ● *adv* 🄸 **~ in the middle** justo en el medio. **he went ~ into a tree** se dio contra un árbol. ● *vt* pegarle a (con la mano)
small /smɔːl/ *adj* (**-er**, **-est**) pequeño, chico (*LAm*). ● *n.* **the ~ of the back** la región lumbar. **~ ads** *npl* anuncios *mpl* (clasificados), avisos *mpl* (clasificados) (*LAm*). **~ change** *n* suelto *m.* **~pox** /-pɒks/ *n* viruela *f.* **~ talk** *n* charla *f* sobre temas triviales
smart /smɑːt/ *adj* (**-er**, **-est**) elegante; (*clever*) listo; (*brisk*) rápido. ● *vi* escocer. □ **~en up** *vt* arreglar. *vi* (person) mejorar su aspecto, arreglarse. **~ly** *adv* elegantemente; (*quickly*) rápidamente
smash /smæʃ/ *vt* romper; (*into little pieces*) hacer pedazos; batir (record). ● *vi* romperse; (*collide*) chocar (**into** con). ● *n* (*noise*) estrépito *m*; (*collision*) choque *m*; (*in sport*) smash *m.* □ **~ up** *vt* destrozar. **~ing** *adj* 🄸 estupendo
smattering /'smætərɪŋ/ *n* nociones *fpl*
smear /smɪə(r)/ *vt* untar (**with** de); (*stain*) manchar (**with** de); (*fig*) difamar.● *n* mancha *f*
smell /smel/ *n* olor *m*; (*sense*) olfato *m.* ● *vt* (*pt* **smelt**) oler; (animal) olfatear. ● *vi* oler. **~ of sth** oler a algo. **~y** *adj* maloliente. **be ~y** oler mal
smelt /smelt/ *see* **SMELL**. ● *vt* fundir
smile /smaɪl/ *n* sonrisa *f.* ● *vi* sonreír. **~ at s.o.** sonreírle a uno
smirk /smɜːk/ *n* sonrisita *f* (de suficiencia etc)
smith /smɪθ/ *n* herrero *m*
smithereens /smɪðə'riːnz/ *npl.* **smash sth to ~** hacer algo añicos
smock /smɒk/ *n* blusa *f*, bata *f*
smog /smɒg/ *n* smog *m*
smok|e /sməʊk/ *n* humo *m.* ● *vt* fumar (tobacco); ahumar (food).

● *vi* fumar. **~eless** *adj* que arde sin humo. **~er** *n* fumador *m*. **~y** *adj* (room) lleno de humo

smooth /smu:ð/ *adj* (**-er, -est**) (texture/stone) liso; (skin) suave; (movement) suave; (sea) tranquilo. ● *vt* alisar. □ **~ out** *vt* allanar (problems). **~ly** *adv* suavemente; (*without problems*) sin problemas

smother /ˈsmʌðə(r)/ *vt* asfixiar (person). **~ s.o. with kisses** cubrir a uno de besos

smoulder /ˈsməʊldə(r)/ *vi* arder sin llama

smudge /smʌdʒ/ *n* borrón *m*. ● *vi* tiznarse

smug /smʌg/ *adj* (**smugger, smuggest**) pagado de sí mismo; (expression) de suficiencia

smuggl|e /ˈsmʌgl/ *vt* pasar de contrabando. **~er** *n* contrabandista *m & f*. **~ing** *n* contrabando *m*

snack /snæk/ *n* tentempié *m*. **~ bar** *n* cafetería *f*

snag /snæg/ *n* problema *m*

snail /sneɪl/ *n* caracol *m*. **at a ~'s pace** a paso de tortuga

snake /sneɪk/ *n* culebra *f*, serpiente *f*

snap /snæp/ *vt* (*pt* **snapped**) (*break*) romper. **~ one's fingers** chasquear los dedos. ● *vi* romperse; (dog) intentar morder; (*say*) contestar bruscamente. **~ at** (dog) intentar morder; (*say*) contestar bruscamente. ● *n* chasquido *m*; (*Photo*) foto *f*. ● *adj* instantáneo. □ **~ up** *vt* no dejar escapar (offer). **~py** *adj* (**-ier, -iest**) [!] rápido. **make it ~py!** ¡date prisa! **~shot** *n* foto *f*

snare /sneə(r)/ *n* trampa *f*

snarl /snɑ:l/ *vi* gruñir

snatch /snætʃ/ *vt*. **~ sth from s.o.** arrebatarle algo a uno; (*steal*) robar. ● *n* (*short part*) fragmento *m*

sneak /sni:k/ *n* soplón *m*. ● *vi* (*past & pp* **sneaked** *or* [!] **snuck**) **~ in** entrar a hurtadillas. **~ off** escabullirse. **~ers** /ˈsni:kəz/ *npl* zapatillas *fpl* de deporte. **~y** *adj* artero

sneer /snɪə(r)/ *n* expresión *f* desdeñosa. ● *vi* hacer una mueca de desprecio. **~ at** hablar con desprecio a

sneeze /sni:z/ *n* estornudo *m*. ● *vi* estornudar

snide /snaɪd/ *adj* insidioso

sniff /snɪf/ *vt* oler. ● *vi* sorberse la nariz

snigger /ˈsnɪgə(r)/ *n* risilla *f*. ● *vi* reírse (por lo bajo)

snip /snɪp/ *vt* (*pt* **snipped**) dar un tijeretazo a. ● *n* tijeretazo *m*

sniper /ˈsnaɪpə(r)/ *n* francotirador *m*

snippet /ˈsnɪpɪt/ *n* (*of conversation*) trozo *m*. **~s of information** datos *mpl* aislados

snivel /ˈsnɪvl/ *vi* (*pt* **snivelled**) lloriquear

snob /snɒb/ *n* esnob *m & f*. **~bery** *n* esnobismo *m*. **~bish** *adj* esnob

snooker /ˈsnu:kə(r)/ *n* snooker *m*

snoop /snu:p/ *vi* [!] husmear

snooze /snu:z/ *n* sueñecito *m*. ● *vi* dormitar

snore /snɔ:(r)/ *n* ronquido *m*. ● *vi* roncar

snorkel /ˈsnɔ:kl/ *n* esnórkel *m*

snort /snɔ:t/ *n* bufido *m*. ● *vi* bufar

snout /snaʊt/ *n* hocico *m*

snow /snəʊ/ *n* nieve *f*. ● *vi* nevar. **be ~ed in** estar aislado por la nieve. **be ~ed under with work** estar agobiado de trabajo. **~ball** *n* bola *f* de nieve. **~drift** *n* nieve *f* amontonada. **~fall** *n* nevada *f*.

~**flake** *n* copo *m* de nieve. ~**man** *n* muñeco *m* de nieve. ~**plough** *n* quitanieves *m*. ~**storm** *n* tormenta *f* de nieve. ~**y** *adj* (day, weather) nevoso; (landscape) nevado

snub /snʌb/ *vt* (*pt* **snubbed**) desairar. ● *n* desaire *m*. ~**-nosed** *adj* chato

snuck /snʌk/ *see* SNEAK

snuff out /snʌf/ *vt* apagar (candle)

snug /snʌg/ *adj* (**snugger**, **snuggest**) cómodo; (*tight*) ajustado

snuggle (up) /'snʌgl/ *vi* acurrucarse

so /səʊ/ *adv* (*before a or adv*) tan; (*thus*) así; **and ~ on, and ~ forth** etcétera (etcétera). **I think ~** creo que sí. **or ~** más o menos. **~ long!** ¡hasta luego! ● *conj* (*therefore*) así que. **~ am I** yo también. **~ as to** para. **~ far** *adv* (*time*) hasta ahora. **~ far as I know** que yo sepa. **~ that** *conj* para que.

soak /səʊk/ *vt* remojar. ● *vi* remojarse. □ **~ in** *vi* penetrar. □ **~ up** *vt* absorber. ~**ing** *adj* empapado.

so-and-so /'səʊənsəʊ/ *n* fulano *m*

soap /səʊp/ *n* jabón *m*. ● *vt* enjabonar. **~ opera** *n* telenovela *f*, culebrón *m*. **~ powder** *n* jabón *m* en polvo. ~**y** *adj* jabonoso

soar /sɔ:(r)/ *vi* (bird/plane) planear; (*rise*) elevarse; (price) dispararse. ~**ing** *adj* (inflation) galopante

sob /sɒb/ *n* sollozo *m*. ● *vi* (*pt* **sobbed**) sollozar

sober /'səʊbə(r)/ *adj* (*not drunk*) sobrio

so-called /'səʊkɔ:ld/ *adj* denominado; (expert) supuesto

soccer /'sɒkə(r)/ *n* fútbol *m*, futbol *m* (*Mex*)

sociable /'səʊʃəbl/ *adj* sociable

social /'səʊʃl/ *adj* social; (*sociable*) sociable. ~**ism** *n* socialismo *m*. ~**ist** *adj & n* socialista (*m & f*). ~**ize** *vt* socializar. **~ security** *n* seguridad *f* social. **~ worker** *n* asistente *m* social

society /sə'saɪətɪ/ *n* sociedad *f*

sociolog|ical /səʊsɪə'lɒdʒɪkl/ *adj* sociológico. ~**ist** /-'ɒlədʒɪst/ *n* sociólogo *m*. ~**y** /-'ɒlədʒɪ/ *n* sociología *f*

sock /sɒk/ *n* calcetín *m*

socket /'sɒkɪt/ *n* (*of joint*) hueco *m*; (*of eye*) cuenca *f*; (*wall plug*) enchufe *m*; (*for bulb*) portalámparas *m*

soda /'səʊdə/ *n* soda *f*. ~**-water** *n* soda *f*

sodium /'səʊdɪəm/ *n* sodio *m*

sofa /'səʊfə/ *n* sofá *m*

soft /sɒft/ *adj* (**-er**, **-est**) blando; (light, colour) suave; (*gentle*) dulce, tierno; (*not strict*) blando. **~ drink** *n* refresco *m*. ~**en** /'sɒfn/ *vt* ablandar; suavizar (skin). ● *vi* ablandarse. ~**ly** *adv* dulcemente; (speak) bajito. ~**ware** /-weə(r)/ *n* software *m*

soggy /'sɒgɪ/ *adj* (**-ier**, **-iest**) empapado

soil /sɔɪl/ *n* tierra *f*; (*Amer, dirt*) suciedad *f*. ● *vt* ensuciar

solar /'səʊlə(r)/ *adj* solar

sold /səʊld/ *see* SELL

solder /'sɒldə(r)/ *vt* soldar

soldier /'səʊldʒə(r)/ *n* soldado *m*. □ **~ on** *vi* ! seguir al pie del cañon

sole /səʊl/ *n* (*of foot*) planta *f*; (*of shoe*) suela *f*. ● *adj* único, solo. ~**ly** *adv* únicamente

solemn /'sɒləm/ *adj* solemne

solicitor /sə'lɪsɪtə(r)/ *n* abogado *m*; (*notary*) notario *m*

solid /'sɒlɪd/ *adj* sólido; (gold etc)

macizo; (*unanimous*) unánime; (meal) sustancioso. ● *n* sólido *m*. **~s** *npl* alimentos *mpl* sólidos. **~arity** /sɒlɪ'dærətɪ/ *n* solidaridad *f*. **~ify** /sə'lɪdɪfaɪ/ *vi* solidificarse

solitary /'sɒlɪtrɪ/ *adj* solitario

solitude /'sɒlɪtju:d/ *n* soledad *f*

solo /'səʊləʊ/ *n* (*pl* **-os**) (*Mus*) solo *m*. **~ist** *n* solista *m & f*

solstice /'sɒlstɪs/ *n* solsticio *m*

solu|ble /'sɒljʊbl/ *adj* soluble. **~tion** /sə'lu:ʃn/ *n* solución *f*

solve /sɒlv/ *vt* solucionar (problem); resolver (mystery). **~nt** /-vənt/ *adj & n* solvente (*m*)

sombre /'sɒmbə(r)/ *adj* sombrío

some /sʌm//səm/

● *adjective*

····➤ (*unspecified number*) unos, unas. **he ate ~ olives** comió unas aceitunas

····➤ (*unspecified amount*) *not translated*. **I have to buy ~ bread** tengo que comprar pan. **would you like ~ coffee?** ¿quieres café?

····➤ (*certain, not all*) algunos, -nas. **I like ~ modern writers** algunos escritores modernos me gustan

····➤ (*a little*) algo de. **I eat ~ meat, but not much** como algo de carne, pero no mucho

····➤ (*considerable amount of*) **we've known each other for ~ time** ya hace tiempo que nos conocemos

····➤ (*expressing admiration*) **that's ~ car you've got!** ¡vaya coche que tienes!

● *pronoun*

····➤ (*a number of things or people*) algunos, -nas, unos, unas. **~ are mine and ~ aren't** algunos *or* unos son míos y otros no. **aren't there any apples? we bought ~ yesterday** ¿no hay manzanas? compramos algunas ayer

····➤ (*part of an amount*) **he wants ~** quiere un poco. **~ of what he said** parte *or* algo de lo que dijo

····➤ (*certain people*) algunos, -nas . **~ say that...** algunos dicen que...

● *adverb*

····➤ (*approximately*) unos, unas, alrededor de. **there were ~ fifty people there** había unas cincuenta personas, había alrededor de cincuenta personas

some: ~body /-bədɪ/ *pron* alguien. **~how** *adv* de algún modo. **~how or other** de una manera u otra. **~one** *pron* alguien

somersault /'sʌməsɔ:lt/ *n* salto *m* mortal. ● *vi* dar un salto mortal

some: ~thing *pron* algo *m*. **~thing like** (*approximately*) alrededor de. **~time** *adj* ex. ● *adv* algún día. **~time next week** un día de la semana que viene. **~times** *adv* a veces. **~what** *adv* un tanto. **~where** *adv* en alguna parte, en algún lado

son /sʌn/ *n* hijo *m*

sonata /sə'nɑ:tə/ *n* sonata *f*

song /sɒŋ/ *n* canción *f*

sonic /'sɒnɪk/ *adj* sónico

son-in-law /'sʌnɪnlɔ:/ *n* (*pl* **sons-in-law**) yerno *m*

sonnet /'sɒnɪt/ *n* soneto *m*

son of a bitch *n* (*pl* **sons of bitches**) (*esp Amer sl*) hijo *m* de puta

soon /suːn/ *adv* (**-er**, **-est**) pronto; (*in a short time*) dentro de poco. **~ after** poco después. **~er or later** tarde o temprano. **as ~ as** en cuanto; **as ~ as possible** lo antes posible. **the ~er the better** cuanto antes mejor

soot /sʊt/ *n* hollín *m*

sooth|e /suːð/ *vt* calmar; aliviar (pain). **~ing** *adj* (medicine) calmante; (words) tranquilizador

sooty /ˈsʊtɪ/ *adj* cubierto de hollín

sophisticated /səˈfɪstɪkeɪtɪd/ *adj* sofisticado; (*complex*) complejo

sophomore /ˈsɒfəmɔː(r)/ *n* (*Amer*) estudiante *m & f* de segundo curso (en la universidad)

sopping /ˈsɒpɪŋ/ *adj.* **~ (wet)** empapado

soppy /ˈsɒpɪ/ *adj* (**-ier**, **-iest**) [I] sentimental

soprano /səˈprɑːnəʊ/ *n* (*pl* **-os**) soprano *f*

sordid /ˈsɔːdɪd/ *adj* sórdido

sore /ˈsɔː(r)/ *adj* (**-er**, **-est**) dolorido; (*Amer fam, angry*) **be ~ at s.o.** estar picado con uno. **~ throat** *n* dolor *m* de garganta. **I've got a ~ throat** me duele la garganta. ● *n* llaga *f.*

sorrow /ˈsɒrəʊ/ *n* pena *f*, pesar *m*

sorry /ˈsɒrɪ/ *adj* (**-ier**, **-ier**) arrepentido; (*wretched*) lamentable. **I'm ~** lo siento. **be ~ for s.o.** (*pity*) compadecer a uno. **I'm ~ you can't come** siento que no puedas venir. **say ~** pedir perdón. **~!** (*apologizing*) ¡lo siento! ¡perdón!. **~?** (*asking s.o. to repeat*) ¿cómo?

sort /sɔːt/ *n* tipo *m*, clase *f*; (*fam, person*) tipo *m*. **a ~ of** una especie de. ● *vt* clasificar. □ **~ out** *vt* (*organize*) ordenar; organizar (finances); (*separate out*) separar; solucionar (problem)

so-so /ˈsəʊsəʊ/ *adj* regular

soufflé /ˈsuːfleɪ/ *n* suflé *m*

sought /sɔːt/ *see* **SEEK**

soul /səʊl/ *n* alma *f*

sound /saʊnd/ *n* sonido *m*; (*noise*) ruido *m*. ● *vt* tocar. ● *vi* sonar; (*seem*) parecer (**as if** que). **it ~s interesting** suena interesante.. ● *adj* (**-er**, **-est**) sano; (argument) lógico; (*secure*) seguro. ● *adv.* **~ asleep** profundamente dormido. **~ barrier** *n* barrera *f* del sonido. **~ly** *adv* sólidamente; (*asleep*) profundamente. **~proof** *adj* insonorizado. **~track** *n* banda *f* sonora

soup /suːp/ *n* sopa *f*

sour /ˈsaʊə(r)/ *adj* (**-er**, **-est**) agrio; (milk) cortado

source /sɔːs/ *n* fuente *f*

south /saʊθ/ *n* sur *m*. ● *adj* sur *a invar*; (wind) del sur. ● *adv* (go) hacia el sur. **it's ~ of** está al sur de. **S~ Africa** *n* Sudáfrica *f*. **S~ America** *n* América *f* (del Sur), Sudamérica *f*. **S~ American** *adj & n* sudamericano (*m*). **~-east** *n* sudeste *m*, sureste *m*. **~erly** /ˈsʌðəlɪ/ (wind) del sur. **~ern** /ˈsʌðən/ *adj* del sur, meridional. **~erner** *n* sureño *m*. **~ward** /-wəd/, **~wards** *adv* hacia el sur. **~-west** *n* sudoeste *m*, suroeste *m*

souvenir /suːvəˈnɪə(r)/ *n* recuerdo *m*

sovereign /ˈsɒvrɪn/ *n & a* soberano (*m*)

Soviet /ˈsəʊvɪət/ *adj* (*History*) soviético. **the ~ Union** *n* la Unión *f* Soviética

sow[1] /səʊ/ *vt* (*pt* **sowed**, *pp* **sowed** *or* **sown** /səʊn/) sembrar

S

sow² /saʊ/ *n* cerda *f*

soy (*esp Amer*), **soya** /'sɔɪə/ *n*. **~ bean** *n* soja *f*

spa /spɑ:/ *n* balneario *m*

space /speɪs/ *n* espacio *m*; (*room*) espacio *m*, lugar *m*. ● *adj* (research etc) espacial. ● *vt* espaciar. □ **~ out** *vt* espaciar. **~craft**, **~ship** *n* nave *f* espacial

spade /speɪd/ *n* pala *f*. **~s** *npl* (*Cards*) picas *fpl*

spaghetti /spə'getɪ/ *n* espaguetis *mpl*

Spain /speɪn/ *n* España *f*

spam /spæm/ *n* (*Comp*) correo *m* basura

span /spæn/ *n* (*of arch*) luz *f*; (*of time*) espacio *m*; (*of wings*) envergadura *f*. ● *vt* (*pt* **spanned**) extenderse sobre. ● *adj see* **SPICK**

Spaniard /'spænjəd/ *n* español *m*

spaniel /'spænjəl/ *n* spaniel *m*

Spanish /'spænɪʃ/ *adj* español; (*language*) castellano, español. ● *n* (*language*) castellano *m*, español *m*. *npl*. **the ~** (*people*) los españoles

spank /spæŋk/ *vt* pegarle a (en las nalgas)

spanner /'spænə(r)/ *n* llave *f*

spare /speə(r)/ *vt*. **if you can ~ the time** si tienes tiempo. **can you ~ me a pound?** ¿tienes una libra que me des? **~ no effort** no escatimar esfuerzos. **have money to ~** tener dinero de sobra. ● *adj* (*not in use*) de más; (*replacement*) de repuesto; (*free*) libre. **~ (part)** *n* repuesto *m*. **~ room** *n* cuarto *m* de huéspedes. **~ time** *n* tiempo *m* libre. **~ tyre** *n* neumático *m* de repuesto

sparingly /'speərɪŋlɪ/ *adv* (use) con moderación

spark /spɑ:k/ *n* chispa *f*. ● *vt* provocar (criticism); suscitar (interest). **~ing plug** *n* (*Auto*) bujía *f*

sparkl|e /'spɑ:kl/ *vi* centellear. ● *n* destello *m*. **~ing** *adj* centelleante; (wine) espumoso

spark plug *n* (*Auto*) bujía *f*

sparrow /'spærəʊ/ *n* gorrión *m*

sparse /spɑ:s/ *adj* escaso. **~ly** *adv* escasamente

spasm /'spæzəm/ *n* espasmo *m*; (*of cough*) acceso *m*. **~odic** /-'mɒdɪk/ *adj* espasmódico; (*Med*) irregular

spat /spæt/ *see* **SPIT**

spate /speɪt/ *n* racha *f*

spatial /'speɪʃl/ *adj* espacial

spatter /'spætə(r)/ *vt* salpicar (with de)

spawn /spɔ:n/ *n* huevas *fpl*. ● *vt* generar. ● *vi* desovar

speak /spi:k/ *vt/i* (*pt* **spoke**, *pp* **spoken**) hablar. **~ for s.o.** hablar en nombre de uno. □ **~ up** *vi* hablar más fuerte. **~er** *n* (*in public*) orador *m*; (*loudspeaker*) altavoz *m*; (*of language*) hablante *m & f*

spear /spɪə(r)/ *n* lanza *f*. **~head** *vt* (*lead*) encabezar

special /'speʃl/ *adj* especial. **~ist** /'speʃəlɪst/ *n* especialista *m & f*. **~ity** /-ɪ'ælətɪ/ *n* especialidad *f*. **~ization** /-əlaɪ'zeɪʃn/ *n* especialización *f*. **~ize** /-əlaɪz/ *vi* especializarse. **~ized** *adj* especializado. **~ly** *adv* especialmente. **~ty** *n* (*Amer*) especialidad *f*

species /'spi:ʃi:z/ *n* especie *f*

specif|ic /spə'sɪfɪk/ *adj* específico. **~ically** *adv* específicamente; (state) explícitamente. **~ication** /-ɪ'keɪʃn/ *n* especificación *f*. **~y** /'spesɪfaɪ/ *vt* especificar

specimen /'spesɪmɪn/ *n* muestra *f*

speck /spek/ *n* (*of dust*) mota *f*; (*in distance*) punto *m*

specs /speks/ *npl* ⓘ *see* **SPECTACLES**

spectac|le /ˈspektəkl/ *n* espectáculo *m*. **~les** *npl* gafas *fpl*, lentes *fpl* (*LAm*), anteojos *mpl* (*LAm*). **~ular** /-ˈtækjʊlə(r)/ *adj* espectacular

spectator /spekˈteɪtə(r)/ *n* espectador *m*

spectr|e /ˈspektə(r)/ *n* espectro *m*. **~um** /ˈspektrəm/ *n* (*pl* **-tra** /-trə/) espectro *m*; (*of views*) gama *f*

speculat|e /ˈspekjʊleɪt/ *vi* especular. **~ion** /-ˈleɪʃn/ *n* especulación *f*. **~or** *n* especulador *m*

sped /sped/ *see* **SPEED**

speech /spiːtʃ/ *n* (*faculty*) habla *f*; (*address*) discurso *m*. **~less** *adj* mudo

speed /spiːd/ *n* velocidad *f*; (*rapidity*) rapidez *f*. ● *vi* (*pt* **speeded**) (*drive too fast*) ir a exceso de velocidad. □ **~ off, ~ away** (*pt* **sped**) *vi* alejarse a toda velocidad. □ **~ by** (*pt* **sped**) *vi* (time) pasar volando. □ **~ up** (*pt* **speeded**) *vt* acelerar. *vi* acelerarse. **~boat** *n* lancha *f* motora. **~ camera** *n* cámara *f* de control de velocidad. **~ dating** *n* cita *f* flash, speed dating *m*. **~ limit** *n* velocidad *f* máxima. **~ometer** /spiːˈdɒmɪtə(r)/ *n* velocímetro *m*. **~way** *n* (*Amer*) autopista *f*. **~y** *adj* (**-ier**, **-iest**) rápido

spell /spel/ *n* (*magic*) hechizo *m*; (*of weather, activity*) período *m*. **go through a bad ~** pasar por una mala racha. ● *vt/i* (*pt* **spelled** *or* **spelt**) escribir. □ **~ out** *vt* deletrear; (*fig*) explicar. **~ checker** *n* corrector *m* ortográfico. **~ing** *n* ortografía *f*

spellbound /ˈspelbaʊnd/ *adj* embelesado

spelt /spelt/ *see* **SPELL**

spend /spend/ *vt* (*pt* **spent** /spent/) gastar (money); pasar (time); dedicar (care). ● *vi* gastar dinero

sperm /spɜːm/ *n* (*pl* **sperms** *or* **sperm**) esperma *f*; (*individual*) espermatozoide *m*

spew /spjuː/ *vt/i* vomitar

spher|e /sfɪə(r)/ *n* esfera *f*. **~ical** /ˈsferɪkl/ *adj* esférico

spice /spaɪs/ *n* especia *f*

spick /spɪk/ *adj*. **~ and span** limpio y ordenado

spicy /ˈspaɪsɪ/ *adj* picante

spider /ˈspaɪdə(r)/ *n* araña *f*

spik|e /spaɪk/ *n* (*of metal etc*) punta *f*. **~y** *adj* puntiagudo

spill /spɪl/ *vt* (*pt* **spilled** *or* **spilt**) derramar. ● *vi* derramarse. **~ over** *vi* (container) desbordarse; (liquid) rebosar

spin /spɪn/ *vt* (*pt* **spun**, *pres p* **spinning**) hacer girar; hilar (wool); centrifugar (washing). ● *vi* girar. ● *n*. **give sth a ~** hacer girar algo. **go for a ~** (*Auto*) ir a dar un paseo en coche

spinach /ˈspɪnɪdʒ/ *n* espinacas *fpl*

spindly /ˈspɪndlɪ/ *adj* larguirucho

spin-drier /spɪnˈdraɪə(r)/ *n* centrifugadora *f* (de ropa)

spine /spaɪn/ *n* columna *f* vertebral; (*of book*) lomo *m*; (*on animal*) púa *f*. **~less** *adj* (*fig*) sin carácter

spinning wheel /ˈspɪnɪŋ/ *n* rueca *f*

spin-off /ˈspɪnɒf/ *n* resultado *m* indirecto; (*by-product*) producto *m* derivado

spinster /ˈspɪnstə(r)/ *n* soltera *f*

spiral /ˈspaɪərəl/ *adj* espiral;

(shape) de espiral. ● *n* espiral *f.* ● *vi* (*pt* **spiralled**) (unemployment) escalar; (prices) dispararse. ~ **staircase** *n* escalera *f* de caracol

spire /'spaɪə(r)/ *n* aguja *f*

spirit /'spɪrɪt/ *n* espíritu *m.* **be in good ~s** estar animado. **in low ~s** abatido. **~ed** *adj* animado, fogoso. **~s** *npl* (*drinks*) bebidas *fpl* alcohólicas (de alta graduación). **~ual** /'spɪrɪtjʊəl/ *adj* espiritual

spit /spɪt/ *vt* (*pt* **spat** *or* (*Amer*) **spit**, *pres p* **spitting**) escupir. ● *vi* escupir. **it's ~ting** caen algunas gotas. ● *n* saliva *f*; (*for roasting*) asador *m*

spite /spaɪt/ *n* rencor *m.* **in ~ of** a pesar de. ● *vt* fastidiar. **~ful** *adj* rencoroso

spittle /'spɪtl/ *n* baba *f*

splash /splæʃ/ *vt* salpicar. ● *vi* (person) chapotear. ● *n* salpicadura *f.* **a ~ of paint** un poco de pintura. ▫ **~ about** *vi* chapotear. ▫ **~ down** *vi* (spacecraft) amerizar. ▫ **~ out** *vi* gastarse un dineral (**on** en)

splend|id /'splendɪd/ *adj* espléndido. **~our** /-ə(r)/ *n* esplendor *m*

splint /splɪnt/ *n* tablilla *f*

splinter /'splɪntə(r)/ *n* astilla *f.* ● *vi* astillarse

S

split /splɪt/ *vt* (*pt* **split**, *pres p* **splitting**) partir; fisionar (atom); reventar (trousers); (*divide*) dividir. ● *vi* partirse; (*divide*) dividirse. **a ~ting headache** un dolor de cabeza espantoso. ● *n* (*in garment*) descosido *m*; (*in wood, glass*) rajadura *f.* ▫ **~ up** *vi* separarse. ~ **second** *n* fracción *f* de segundo

splutter /'splʌtə(r)/ *vi* chisporrotear; (person) farfullar

spoil /spɔɪl/ *vt* (*pt* **spoilt** *or* **spoiled**) estropear, echar a perder; (*indulge*) consentir, malcriar. **~s** *npl* botín *m.* **~-sport** *n* aguafiestas *m & f*

spoke[1] /spəʊk/ *see* SPEAK

spoke[2] /spəʊk/ *n* (*of wheel*) rayo *m*

spoken /spəʊkən/ *see* SPEAK

spokesman /'spəʊksmən/ *n* (*pl* **-men**) portavoz *m*

sponge /spʌndʒ/ *n* esponja *f.* ● *vt* limpiar con una esponja. ~ **off**, ~ **on** *vt* vivir a costillas de. ~ **cake** *n* bizcocho *m*

sponsor /'spɒnsə(r)/ *n* patrocinador *m*; (*of the arts*) mecenas *m & f*; (*surety*) garante *m.* ● *vt* patrocinar. **~ship** *n* patrocinio *m*; (*of the arts*) mecenazgo *m*

spontaneous /spɒn'teɪmɪəs/ *adj* espontáneo. **~ously** *adv* espontáneamente

spoof /spu:f/ *n* Ⓘ parodia *f*

spooky /'spu:kɪ/ *adj* (**-ier**, **-iest**) Ⓘ espeluznante

spool /spu:l/ *n* carrete *m*

spoon /spu:n/ *n* cuchara *f.* **~ful** *n* cucharada *f*

sporadic /spə'rædɪk/ *adj* esporádico

sport /spɔ:t/ *n* deporte *m.* **~s car** *n* coche *m* deportivo. **~s centre** *n* centro *m* deportivo. **~sman** /-mən/ *n*, (*pl* **-men**), **~swoman** *n* deportista *m & f*

spot /spɒt/ *n* mancha *f*; (*pimple*) grano *m*; (*place*) lugar *m*; (*in pattern*) lunar *m.* **be in a ~** Ⓘ estar en apuros. **on the ~** allí mismo; (decide) en ese mismo momento. ● *vt* (*pt* **spotted**) manchar; (*fam, notice*) ver, divisar; descubrir (mistake). ~ **check** *n* control *m* hecho al azar. **~less** *adj* (clothes) impecable; (house) limpísimo. **~light** *n* reflector *m*; (*in theatre*) foco *m.*

~ted *adj* moteado; (material) de lunares. **~ty** *adj* (**-ier, -iest**) (skin) lleno de granos; (youth) con la cara llena de granos

spouse /spaʊz/ *n* cónyuge *m & f*

spout /spaʊt/ *n* pico *m*; (*jet*) chorro *m*

sprain /spreɪn/ *vt* hacerse un esguince en. ● *n* esguince *m*

sprang /spræŋ/ *see* **SPRING**

spray /spreɪ/ *n* (*of flowers*) ramillete *m*; (*from sea*) espuma *f*; (*liquid in spray form*) espray *m*; (*device*) rociador *m*. ● *vt* rociar

spread /spred/ *vt* (*pt* **spread**) (*stretch, extend*) extender; desplegar (wings); difundir (idea, news). **~ butter on a piece of toast** untar una tostada con mantequilla. ● *vi* extenderse; (disease) propagarse; (idea, news) difundirse. ● *n* (*of ideas*) difusión *f*; (*of disease, fire*) propagación *f*; (*fam, feast*) festín *m*. □ **~ out** *vi* (*move apart*) desplegarse

spree /spri:/ *n*. **go on a shopping ~** ir de expedición a las tiendas

sprightly /ˈspraɪtlɪ/ *adj* (**-ier, -iest**) vivo

spring /sprɪŋ/ *n* (*season*) primavera *f*; (*device*) resorte *m*; (*in mattress*) muelle *m*, resorte *m* (*LAm*); (*elasticity*) elasticidad *f*; (*water*) manantial *m*. ● *adj* primaveral. ● *vi* (*pt* **sprang**, *pp* **sprung**) saltar; (*issue*) brotar. **~ from sth** (problem) provenir de algo. □ **~ up** *vi* surgir. **~board** *n* trampolín *m*. **~-clean** /-ˈkli:n/ *vi* hacer una limpieza general. **~ onion** *n* cebolleta *f*. **~time** *n* primavera *f*. **~y** *adj* (**-ier, -iest**) (mattress, grass) mullido

sprinkle /ˈsprɪŋkl/ *vt* salpicar; (*with liquid*) rociar. ● *n* salpicadura *f*; (*of liquid*) rociada *f*. **~r** *n* regadera *f*

sprint /sprɪnt/ *n* carrera *f* corta. ● *vi* (*Sport*) esprintar; (*run fast*) correr. **~er** *n* corredor *m*

sprout /spraʊt/ *vi* brotar. ● *n* brote *m*. **(Brussels) ~s** *npl* coles *fpl* de Bruselas

sprung /sprʌŋ/ *see* **SPRING**

spud /spʌd/ *n* [!] patata *f*, papa *f* (*LAm*)

spun /spʌn/ *see* **SPIN**

spur /spɜ:(r)/ *n* espuela *f*; (*stimulus*) acicate *m*. **on the ~ of the moment** sin pensarlo. ● *vt* (*pt* **spurred**). **~ (on)** espolear; (*fig*) estimular

spurn /spɜ:n/ *vt* desdeñar; (*reject*) rechazar

spurt /spɜ:t/ *vi* (liquid) salir a chorros. ● *n* chorro *m*; (*of activity*) racha *f*

spy /spaɪ/ *n* espía *m & f*. ● *vt* descubrir, ver. ● *vi* espiar. **~ on s.o.** espiar a uno

squabble /ˈskwɒbl/ *vi* reñir

squad /skwɒd/ *n* (*Mil*) pelotón *m*; (*of police*) brigada *f*; (*Sport*) equipo *m*. **~ car** *m* coche *m* patrulla. **~ron** /ˈskwɒdrən/ *n* (*Mil, Aviat*) escuadrón *m*; (*Naut*) escuadra *f*

squalid /ˈskwɒlɪd/ *adj* miserable

squall /skwɔ:l/ *n* turbión *m*

squalor /ˈskwɒlə(r)/ *n* miseria *f*

squander /ˈskwɒndə(r)/ *vt* derrochar; desaprovechar (opportunity)

square /skweə(r)/ *n* cuadrado *m*; (*in town*) plaza *f*. ● *adj* cuadrado; (meal) decente; (*fam, old-fashioned*) chapado a la antigua. ● *vt* (*settle*) arreglar; (*Math*) elevar al cuadrado. ● *vi* (*agree*) cuadrar. □ **~ up** *vi* arreglar cuentas (**with** con). **~ly** *adv* directamente

squash /skwɒʃ/ *vt* aplastar; (*sup-*

press) acallar. ● *n*. **it was a terrible** ~ íbamos (*or* iban) terriblemente apretujados; (*drink*) **orange** ~ naranjada *f*; (*Sport*) squash *m*; (*vegetable*) calabaza *f*. **~y** *adj* blando

squat /skwɒt/ *vi* (*pt* **squatted**) ponerse en cuclillas; (*occupy illegally*) ocupar sin autorización. ● *adj* rechoncho y bajo. **~ter** *n* ocupante *m & f* ilegal, okupa *m & f*

squawk /skwɔ:k/ *n* graznido *m*. ● *vi* graznar

squeak /skwi:k/ *n* chillido *m*; (*of door*) chirrido *m*. ● *vi* chillar; (door) chirriar; (shoes) crujir. **~y** *adj* chirriante

squeal /skwi:l/ *n* chillido *m* ● *vi* chillar

squeamish /ˈskwi:mɪʃ/ *adj* impresionable, delicado

squeeze /skwi:z/ *vt* apretar; exprimir (lemon etc). ● *vi*. ~ **in** meterse. ● *n* estrujón *m*; (*of hand*) apretón *m*

squid /skwɪd/ *n* calamar *m*

squiggle /ˈskwɪgl/ *n* garabato *m*

squint /skwɪnt/ *vi* bizquear; (*trying to see*) entrecerrar los ojos. ● *n* estrabismo *m*

squirm /skwɜ:m/ *vi* retorcerse

squirrel /ˈskwɪrəl/ *n* ardilla *f*

S

squirt /skwɜ:t/ *vt* (liquid) echar un chorro de. ● *vi* salir a chorros. ● *n* chorrito *m*

St /sənt/ *abbr* (= **saint**) /sənt/ S, San(to); (= **street**) C/, Calle *f*

stab /stæb/ *vt* (*pt* **stabbed**) apuñalar. ● *n* puñalada *f*; (*pain*) punzada *f*. **have a ~ at sth** intentar algo

stabili|ty /stəˈbɪlətɪ/ *n* estabilidad *f*. **~ze** /ˈsteɪbɪlaɪz/ *vt/i* estabilizar

stable /ˈsteɪbl/ *adj* (**-er**, **-est**) estable. ● *n* caballeriza *f*, cuadra *f*

stack /stæk/ *n* montón *m*. ● *vt*. ~ (**up**) amontonar

stadium /ˈsteɪdɪəm/ *n* (*pl* **-diums** *or* **-dia** /-dɪə/) estadio *m*

staff /stɑ:f/ *n* (*stick*) palo *m*; (*employees*) personal *m*. **teaching** ~ personal *m* docente. **a member of** ~ un empleado

stag /stæg/ *n* ciervo *m*. **~-night**, **~-party** *n* (*before wedding*) fiesta *f* de despedida de soltero; (*men-only party*) fiesta *f* para hombres

stage /steɪdʒ/ *n* (*in theatre*) escenario *f*; (*platform*) plataforma *f*; (*phase*) etapa *f*. **the** ~ (*profession, medium*) el teatro. ● *vt* poner en escena (play); (*arrange*) organizar; (*pej*) orquestar. **~coach** *n* diligencia *f*

stagger /ˈstægə(r)/ *vi* tambalearse. ● *vt* dejar estupefacto; escalonar (holidays etc). **~ing** *adj* asombroso

stagna|nt /ˈstægnənt/ *adj* estancado. **~te** /stægˈneɪt/ *vi* estancarse

staid /steɪd/ *adj* serio, formal

stain /steɪn/ *vt* manchar; (*colour*) teñir. ● *n* mancha *f*; (*dye*) tintura *f*. **~ed glass window** *n* vidriera *f* de colores. **~less steel** *n* acero *m* inoxidable. ~ **remover** *n* quitamanchas *m*

stair /steə(r)/ *n* escalón *m*. **~s** *npl* escalera *f*. **~case**, **~way** *n* escalera *f*

stake /steɪk/ *n* estaca *f*; (*wager*) apuesta *f*; (*Com*) intereses *mpl*. **be at** ~ estar en juego. ● *vt* estacar; jugarse (reputation). ~ **a claim** reclamar

stala|ctite /ˈstæləktaɪt/ *n* estalactita *f*. **~gmite** /ˈstæləgmaɪt/ *n* estalagmita *f*

stale /steɪl/ *adj* (**-er**, **-est**) no fresco; (bread) duro; (smell) viciado. **~mate** *n* (*Chess*) ahogado *m*; (*deadlock*) punto *m* muerto

stalk /stɔ:k/ *n* tallo *m*. ● *vt* acechar. ● *vi* irse indignado

stall /stɔ:l/ *n* (*in stable*) compartimiento *m*; (*in market*) puesto *m*. **~s** *npl* (*in theatre*) platea *f*, patio *m* de butacas. ● *vt* parar (engine). ● *vi* (engine) pararse; (*fig*) andar con rodeos

stallion /'stæljən/ *n* semental *m*

stalwart /'stɔ:lwət/ *adj* (supporter) leal, incondicional

stamina /'stæmɪnə/ *n* resistencia *f*

stammer /'stæmə(r)/ *vi* tartamudear. ● *n* tartamudeo *m*

stamp /stæmp/ *vt* (*with feet*) patear; (*press*) estampar; (*with rubber stamp*) sellar; (*fig*) señalar. ● *vi* dar patadas en el suelo. ● *n* sello *m*, estampilla *f* (*LAm*), timbre *m* (*Mex*); (*on passport*) sello *m*; (*with foot*) patada *f*; (*mark*) marca *f*, señal *f*. □ **~ out** *vt* (*fig*) erradicar. **~ed addressed envelope** *n* sobre *m* franqueado con su dirección

stampede /stæm'pi:d/ *n* estampida *f*. ● *vi* salir en estampida

stance /stɑ:ns/ *n* postura *f*

stand /stænd/ *vi* (*pt* **stood**) estar de pie, estar parado (*LAm*); (*rise*) ponerse de pie, pararse; (*be*) encontrarse; (*Pol*) presentarse como candidato (**for** en). **the offer ~s** la oferta sigue en pie. **~ to reason** ser lógico. ● *vt* (*endure*) soportar; (*place*) colocar. **~ a chance** tener una posibilidad. ● *n* posición *f*, postura *f*; (*for lamp etc*) pie *m*, sostén *m*; (*at market*) puesto *m*; (*booth*) quiosco *m*; (*Sport*) tribuna *f*. **make a ~ against sth** oponer resistencia a algo. □ **~ back** *vi* apartarse. □ **~ by** *vi* estar preparado. *vt* (*support*) apoyar. □ **~ down** *vi* retirarse. □ **~ for** *vt* significar. □ **~ in for** *vt* suplir a. □ **~ out** *vi* destacarse. □ **~ up** *vi* ponerse de pie, pararse (*LAm*). □ **~ up for** *vt* defender. **~ up for oneself** defenderse. □ **~ up to** *vt* resistir a

standard /'stændəd/ *n* norma *f*; (*level*) nivel *m*; (*flag*) estandarte *m*. ● *adj* estándar *a invar*, normal. **~ize** *vt* estandarizar. **~ lamp** *n* lámpara *f* de pie. **~s** *npl* principios *mpl*

stand: ~-by *n* (*at airport*) standby *m*. **be on ~-by** (police) estar en estado de alerta. **~-in** *n* suplente *m & f*. **~ing** *adj* de pie, parado (*LAm*); (*permanent*) permanente *f*. ● *n* posición *f*; (*prestige*) prestigio *m*. **~off** *n* (*Amer, draw*) empate *m*; (*deadlock*) callejón *m* sin salida. **~point** *n* punto *m* de vista. **~still** *n*. **be at a ~still** estar paralizado. **come to a ~still** (vehicle) parar; (city) quedar paralizado

stank /stæŋk/ *see* STINK

staple /'steɪpl/ *adj* principal. ● *n* grapa *f*. ● *vt* sujetar con una grapa. **~r** *n* grapadora *f*

star /stɑ:(r)/ *n* (*incl Cinema, Theatre*) estrella *f*; (*asterisk*) asterisco *m*. ● *vi* (*pt* **starred**). **~ in a film** protagonizar una película. **~board** *n* estribor *m*.

starch /stɑ:tʃ/ *n* almidón *m*; (*in food*) fécula *f*. ● *vt* almidonar. **~y** (food) *adj* a base de féculas

stardom /'stɑ:dəm/ *n* estrellato *m*

stare /steə(r)/ *n* mirada *f* fija. ● *vi*. **~ (at)** mirar fijamente

starfish /'stɑ:fɪʃ/ *n* estrella *f* de mar

stark /stɑ:k/ *adj* (**-er**, **-est**) escueto. ● *adv* completamente

starling /'stɑ:lɪŋ/ *n* estornino *m*

starry /'stɑ:rɪ/ *adj* estrellado

start /stɑ:t/ *vt* empezar, comenzar; encender (engine); arrancar (car); (*cause*) provocar; abrir (business). ● *vi* empezar; (car etc) arrancar; (*jump*) dar un respingo. **to ~ with** (*as linker*) para empezar. **~ off by doing sth** empezar por hacer algo. ● *n* principio *m*; (*Sport*) ventaja *f*; (*jump*) susto *m*. **make an early ~** (*on journey*) salir temprano. **~er** *n* (*Auto*) motor *m* de arranque; (*Culin*) primer plato *m*. **~ing-point** *n* punto *m* de partida

startle /'stɑ:tl/ *vt* asustar

starv|ation /stɑ:'veɪʃn/ *n* hambre *f*, inanición *f*. **~e** /stɑ:v/ *vt* hacer morir de hambre. ● *vi* morirse de hambre. **I'm ~ing** me muero de hambre

state /steɪt/ *n* estado *m*. **be in a ~** estar agitado. **the S~** los Estados *mpl* Unidos. ● *vt* declarar; expresar (views); (*fix*) fijar. ● *adj* del Estado; (*Schol*) público; (*with ceremony*) de gala. **~ly** *adj* (**-ier**, **-iest**) majestuoso. **~ly home** *n* casa *f* solariega. **~ment** *n* declaración *f*; (*account*) informe *m*. **~sman** /-mən/ *n* estadista *m*

> **state school** En Gran Bretaña, colegio estatal de educación gratuita, financiado directa o indirectamente por el gobierno. Abarca la educación primaria y secundaria, colegios especializados, *comprehensives* etc.

static /'stætɪk/ *adj* estacionario. ● *n* (*interference*) estática *f*

station /'steɪʃn/ *n* estación *f*; (*on radio*) emisora *f*; (*TV*) canal *m*. ● *vt* colocar; (*Mil*) estacionar. **~ary** *adj* estacionario. **~er's (shop)** *n* papelería *f*. **~ery** *n* artículos *mpl* de papelería. **~ wagon** *n* (*Amer*) ranchera *f*, (coche *m*) familiar *m*, camioneta *f* (*LAm*)

statistic /stə'tɪstɪk/ *n* estadística *f*. **~al** *adj* estadístico. **~s** *n* (*science*) estadística *f*

statue /'stætʃu:/ *n* estatua *f*

stature /'stætʃə(r)/ *n* talla *f*, estatura *f*

status /'steɪtəs/ *n* posición *f* social; (*prestige*) categoría *f*; (*Jurid*) estado *m*

statut|e /'stætʃu:t/ *n* estatuto *m*. **~ory** /-ʊtrɪ/ *adj* estatutario

staunch /stɔ:nʃ/ *adj* (**-er**, **-est**) leal

stave /'steɪv/ *n* (*Mus*) pentagrama *m*. □ **~ off** *vt* evitar

stay /steɪ/ *n* (*of time*) estancia *f*, estadía *f* (*LAm*); (*Jurid*) suspensión *f*. ● *vi* quedarse; (*reside*) alojarse. **I'm ~ing in a hotel** estoy en un hotel. □ **~ in** *vi* quedarse en casa. □ **~ up** *vi* quedarse levantado

stead /sted/ *n*. **in s.o.'s ~** en lugar de uno. **stand s.o. in good ~** resultarle muy útil a uno. **~ily** *adv* firmemente; (*regularly*) regularmente. **~y** *adj* (**-ier**, **-iest**) firme; (*regular*) regular; (flow) continuo; (worker) serio

steak /steɪk/ *n*. **a ~** un filete. **some ~** carne para guisar

steal /sti:l/ *vt* (*pt* **stole**, *pp* **stolen**) robar. **~ in** *vi* entrar a hurtadillas

stealth /stelθ/ *n*. **by ~** sigilosamente. **~y** *adj* sigiloso

steam /sti:m/ *n* vapor *m*. **let off ~** (*fig*) desahogarse. ● *vt* (*cook*) cocer al vapor. ● *vi* echar vapor. □ **~ up** *vi* empañarse. **~ engine** *n* máquina *f* de vapor. **~er** *n* (*ship*) barco *m* de vapor. **~roller** *n* apisonadora *f.* **~y** *adj* lleno de vapor

steel /stiːl/ *n* acero *m.* ● *vt.* **~ o.s.** armarse de valor. **~ industry** *n* industria *f* siderúrgica

steep /stiːp/ ● *adj* (**-er**, **-est**) empinado; (increase) considerable; (price) 🅸 excesivo

steeple /ˈstiːpl/ *n* aguja *f*, campanario *m*

steeply /ˈstiːplɪ/ *adv* abruptamente; (increase) considerablemente

steer /stɪə(r)/ *vt* dirigir; gobernar (ship). ● *vi* (*in ship*) estar al timón. **~ clear of** evitar. **~ing** *n* (*Auto*) dirección *f.* **~ing wheel** *n* volante *m*

stem /stem/ *n* (*of plant*) tallo *m*; (*of glass*) pie *m*; (*of word*) raíz *f.* ● *vt* (*pt* **stemmed**) contener (bleeding). ● *vi.* **~ from** provenir de

stench /stentʃ/ *n* hedor *m*

stencil /ˈstensl/ *n* plantilla *f*

stenographer /steˈnɒgrəfə(r)/ *n* estenógrafo *m*

step /step/ *vi* (*pt* **stepped**). **~ in sth** pisar algo. ▫ **~ aside** *vi* hacerse a un lado. ▫ **~ down** *vi* retirarse. ▫ **~ in** *vi* (*fig*) intervenir.▫ **~ up** *vt* intensificar; redoblar (security). ● *n* paso *m*; (*stair*) escalón *m*; (*fig*) medida *f.* **take ~s** tomar medidas. **be in ~** llevar el paso. **be out of ~** no llevar el paso. **~brother** *n* hermanastro *m.* **~daughter** *n* hijastra *f.* **~father** *n* padrastro *m.* **~ladder** *n* escalera *f* de tijera. **~mother** *n* madrastra *f.* **~ping-stone** *n* peldaño *m.* **~sister** *n* hermanastra *f.* **~son** *n* hijastro *m*

stereo /ˈsterɪəʊ/ *n* (*pl* **-os** estéreo *m.* ● *adj* estéreo *a invar.* **~type** *n* estereotipo *m*

steril|e /ˈsteraɪl/ *adj* estéril. **~ize** /ˈsterɪlaɪz/ *vt* esterilizar

sterling /ˈstɜːlɪŋ/ *n* libras *fpl* esterlinas. ● *adj* (pound) esterlina

stern /stɜːn/ *n* (*of boat*) popa *f.* ● *adj* (**-er**, **-est**) severo

stethoscope /ˈsteθəskəʊp/ *n* estetoscopio *m*

stew /stjuː/ *vt/i* guisar. ● *n* estofado *m*, guiso *m*

steward /ˈstjʊːəd/ *n* administrador *m*; (*on ship*) camarero *m*; (*air steward*) sobrecargo *m*, aeromozo *m* (*LAm*). **~ess** /-ˈdes/ *n* camarera *f*; (*on aircraft*) auxiliar *f* de vuelo, azafata *f*

stick /stɪk/ *n* palo *m*; (*for walking*) bastón *m*; (*of celery etc*) tallo *m.* ● *vt* (*pt* **stuck**) (*glue*) pegar; (*fam, put*) poner; (*thrust*) clavar; (*fam, endure*) soportar. ● *vi* pegarse; (*jam*) atascarse. ▫ **~ out** *vi* sobresalir. ▫ **~ to** *vt* ceñirse a. ▫ **~ up for** *vt* 🅸 defender. **~er** *n* pegatina *f.* **~ing plaster** *n* esparadrapo *m*; (*individual*) tirita *f*, curita *f* (*LAm*). **~ler** /ˈstɪklə(r)/ *n.* **be a ~ler for** insistir en. **~y** /ˈstɪkɪ/ *adj* (**-ier**, **-iest**) (surface) pegajoso; (label) engomado

stiff /stɪf/ *adj* (**-er**, **-est**) rígido; (joint, fabric) tieso; (muscle) entumecido; (*difficult*) difícil; (manner) estirado; (drink) fuerte. **have a ~ neck** tener tortícolis. **~en** *vi* (*become rigid*) agarrotarse; (*become firm*) endurecerse. **~ly** *adv* rígidamente

stifl|e /ˈstaɪfl/ *vt* sofocar. **~ing** *adj* sofocante

stiletto (heel) /stɪˈletəʊ/ *n* (*pl* **-os**) tacón *m* de aguja

still /stɪl/ *adj* inmóvil; (*peaceful*) tranquilo; (drink) sin gas. **sit ~, stand ~** quedarse tranquilo. ● *adv* todavía, aún; (*nevertheless*) sin embargo. **~born** *adj* nacido muerto. **~ life** *n* (*pl* **-s**) bodegón *m*. **~ness** *n* tranquilidad *f*

stilted /'stɪltɪd/ *adj* rebuscado; (conversation) forzado

stilts /stɪlts/ *npl* zancos *mpl*

stimul|ant /'stɪmjʊlənt/ *n* estimulante *m*. **~ate** /-leɪt/ *vt* estimular. **~ation** /-'leɪʃn/ *n* estímulo *m*. **~us** /-əs/ *n* (*pl* **-li** /-laɪ/) estímulo *m*

sting /stɪŋ/ *n* picadura *f*; (*organ*) aguijón *m*. ● *vt/i* (*pt* **stung**) picar

stingy /'stɪndʒɪ/ *adj* (**-ier**, **-iest**) tacaño

stink /stɪŋk/ *n* hedor *m*. ● *vi* (*pt* **stank** *or* **stunk**, *pp* **stunk**) apestar, oler mal

stipulat|e /'stɪpjʊleɪt/ *vt/i* estipular. **~ion** /-'leɪʃn/ *n* estipulación *f*

stir /stɜ:(r)/ *vt* (*pt* **stirred**) remover, revolver; (*move*) agitar; estimular (imagination). ● *vi* moverse. **~ up trouble** armar lío 🅘. ● *n* revuelo *m*, conmoción *f*

stirrup /'stɪrəp/ *n* estribo *m*

stitch /stɪtʃ/ *n* (*in sewing*) puntada *f*; (*in knitting*) punto *m*; (*pain*) dolor *m* costado. **be in ~es** 🅘 desternillarse de risa. ● *vt* coser

S **stock** /stɒk/ *n* (*Com, supplies*) existencias *fpl*; (*Com, variety*) surtido *m*; (*livestock*) ganado *m*; (*Culin*) caldo *m*. **~s and shares**, **~s and bonds** (*Amer*) acciones *fpl*. **out of ~** agotado. **take ~ of sth** (*fig*) hacer un balance de algo. ● *adj* estándar *a invar*; (*fig*) trillado. ● *vt* surtir, abastecer (**with** de). ▫ **~ up** *vi* abastecerse (**with** de). **~broker** /-brəʊkə(r)/ *n* corredor *m* de bolsa. **S~ Exchange** *n* bolsa *f*. **~ing** *n* media *f*. **~pile** *n* reservas *fpl*. ● *vt* almacenar. **~-still** *adj* inmóvil. **~-taking** *n* (*Com*) inventario *m*. **~y** *adj* (**-ier**, **-iest**) bajo y fornido

stodgy /'stɒdʒɪ/ (**-dgier**, **-dgiest**) *adj* pesado

stoke /stəʊk/ *vt* echarle carbón (*or* leña) a

stole /stəʊl/ *see* **STEAL**

stolen /'stəʊlən/ *see* **STEAL**

stomach /'stʌmək/ *n* estómago *m*. ● *vt* soportar. **~-ache** *n* dolor *m* de estómago

ston|e /stəʊn/ *n* piedra *f*; (*in fruit*) hueso *m*; (*weight, pl* **stone**) unidad de peso equivalente a 14 libras o 6,35 kg. ● *adj* de piedra. ● *vt* apedrear. **~e-deaf** *adj* sordo como una tapia. **~y** *adj* (silence) sepulcral

stood /stʊd/ *see* **STAND**

stool /stu:l/ *n* taburete *m*

stoop /stu:p/ *vi* agacharse; (*fig*) rebajarse. ● *n*. **have a ~** ser cargado de espaldas

stop /stɒp/ *vt* (*pt* **stopped**) (*halt, switch off*) parar; (*cease*) terminar; (*prevent*) impedir; (*interrupt*) interrumpir. **~ doing sth** dejar de hacer algo. **~ it!** ¡basta ya! ● *vi* (bus) parar, detenerse; (clock) pararse. **it's ~ped raining** ha dejado de llover. ● *n* (*bus etc*) parada *f*; (*break on journey*) parada *f*. **put a ~ to sth** poner fin a algo. **come to a ~** detenerse. **~gap** *n* remedio *m* provisional. **~over** *n* escala *f*. **~page** /'stɒpɪdʒ/ *n* suspensión *f*, paradero *m* (*LAm*); (*of work*) huelga *f*, paro *m* (*LAm*); (*interruption*) interrupción *f*. **~per** *n* tapón *m*. **~watch** *n* cronómetro *m*

storage /'stɔ:rɪdʒ/ *n* almacenamiento *m*

store /stɔ:(r)/ *n* provisión *f*; (*depot*) almacén *m*; (*Amer, shop*) tienda *f*; (*fig*) reserva *f*. **in ~** en reserva. ● *vt* (*for future*) poner en reserva; (*in warehouse*) almacenar. □ **~ up** *vt* (*fig*) ir acumulando. **~keeper** *n* (*Amer*) tendero *m*, comerciante *m & f*. **~room** *n* almacén *m*; (*for food*) despensa *f*

storey /'stɔːrɪ/ *n* (*pl* **-eys**) piso *m*, planta *f*

stork /stɔːk/ *n* cigüeña *f*

storm /stɔːm/ *n* tempestad *f*. ● *vi* rabiar. ● *vt* (*Mil*) asaltar. **~y** *adj* tormentoso; (sea, relationship) tempestuoso

story /'stɔːrɪ/ *n* historia *f*; (*in newspaper*) artículo *m*; (*rumour*) rumor *m*; (🅘, *lie*) mentira *f*, cuento *m*. **~-teller** *n* cuentista *m & f*

stout /staʊt/ *adj* (**-er**, **-est**) robusto, corpulento. ● *n* cerveza *f* negra

stove /stəʊv/ *n* estufa *f*

stow /stəʊ/ *vt* guardar; (*hide*) esconder. □ **~ away** *vi* viajar de polizón. **~away** *n* polizón *m & f*

straggl|e /'strægl/ *vi* rezagarse. **~y** *adj* desordenado

straight /streɪt/ *adj* (**-er**, **-est**) recto; (*tidy*) en orden; (*frank*) franco; (hair) lacio; (🅘, *conventional*) convencional. **be ~** estar derecho. ● *adv* (sit up) derecho; (*direct*) directamente; (*without delay*) inmediatamente. **~ away** en seguida, inmediatamente. **~ on** todo recto. **~ out** sin rodeos. ● *n* recta *f*. **~en** *vt* enderezar. □ **~en up** *vt* ordenar. **~forward** /-'fɔːwəd/ *adj* franco; (*easy*) sencillo

strain /streɪn/ *n* (*tension*) tensión *f*; (*injury*) torcedura *f*. ● *vt* forzar (voice, eyesight); someter a demasiada tensión (relations); (*sieve*) colar. **~ one's back** hacerse daño en la espalda. **~ a muscle** hacerse un esguince. **~ed** *adj* forzado; (relations) tirante. **~er** *n* colador *m*. **~s** *npl* (*Mus*) acordes *mpl*

strait /streɪt/ *n* estrecho *m*. **be in dire ~s** estar en grandes apuros. **~jacket** *n* camisa *f* de fuerza

strand /strænd/ *n* (*thread*) hebra *f*. **a ~ of hair** un pelo. ● *vt*. **be ~ed** (ship) quedar encallado. **I was left ~ed** me abandonaron a mi suerte

strange /streɪndʒ/ *adj* (**-er**, **-est**) raro, extraño; (*not known*) desconocido. **~ly** *adv* de una manera rara. **~ly enough** aunque parezca mentira. **~r** *n* desconocido *m*; (*from another place*) forastero *m*

strangle /'stræŋgl/ *vt* estrangular

strap /stræp/ *n* correa *f*; (*of garment*) tirante *m*. ● *vt* (*pt* **strapped**) atar con una correa

strat|egic /strə'tiːdʒɪk/ *adj* estratégico. **~egy** /'strætədʒɪ/ *n* estrategia *f*

straw /strɔː/ *n* paja *f*; (*drinking ~*) pajita *f*, paja *f*, popote *m* (*Mex*). **the last ~** el colmo. **~berry** /-bərɪ/ *n* fresa *f*; (*large*) fresón *m*

stray /streɪ/ *vi* (*wander away*) apartarse; (*get lost*) extraviarse; (*deviate*) desviarse (**from** de). ● *adj* (animal) (*without owner*) callejero; (*lost*) perdido. ● *n* (*without owner*) perro *m*/gato *m* callejero; (*lost*) perro *m*/gato *m* perdido

streak /striːk/ *n* lista *f*, raya *f*; (*in hair*) reflejo *m*; (*in personality*) veta *f*

stream /striːm/ *n* arroyo *m*; (*current*) corriente *f*. **a ~ of abuse** una sarta de insultos. ● *vi* correr. □ **~ out** *vi* (people) salir en tropel. **~er** *n* (*paper*) serpentina *f*; (*banner*) banderín *m*. **~line** *vt* dar línea aerodinámica a; (*simplify*) racionalizar. **~lined** *adj* aerodinámico

street /striːt/ *n* calle *f*. **~car** *n* (*Amer*) tranvía *m*. **~ lamp** *n* farol *m*. **~ map**, **~ plan** *n* plano *m*

strength /streŋθ/ *n* fuerza *f*; (*of wall etc*) solidez *f*. **~en** *vt* reforzar (wall); fortalecer (muscle)

strenuous /'strenjʊəs/ *adj* enérgico; (*arduous*) arduo; (*tiring*) fatigoso

stress /stres/ *n* énfasis *f*; (*Gram*) acento *m*; (*Mec, Med, tension*) tensión *f*. ● *vt* insistir en

stretch /stretʃ/ *vt* estirar; (*extend*) extender; forzar (truth); estirar (resources). ● *vi* estirarse; (*when sleepy*) desperezarse; (*extend*) extenderse; (*be elastic*) estirarse. ● *n* (*period*) período *m*; (*of road*) tramo *m*. **at a ~** sin parar. □ **~ out** *vi* (person) tenderse. **~er** *n* camilla *f*

strict /strɪkt/ *adj* (**-er**, **-est**) estricto; (secrecy) absoluto. **~ly** *adv* con severidad; (rigorously) terminantemente. **~ly speaking** en rigor

stridden /strɪdn/ *see* **STRIDE**

stride /straɪd/ *vi* (*pt* **strode**, *pp* **stridden**) andar a zancadas. ● *n* zancada *f*. **take sth in one's ~** tomarse algo con calma. **~nt** /'straɪdnt/ *adj* estridente

strife /straɪf/ *n* conflicto *m*

strike /straɪk/ *vt* (*pt* **struck**) golpear; encender (match); encontrar (gold, oil); (clock) dar. **it ~s me as odd** me parece raro. ● *vi* golpear; (*go on strike*) declararse en huelga; (*be on strike*) estar en huelga; (*attack*) atacar; (clock) dar la hora. ● *n* (*of workers*) huelga *f*, paro *m*; (*attack*) ataque *m*. **come out on ~** ir a la huelga. □ **~ off**, **~ out** *vt* tachar. **~ up a friendship** trabar amistad. **~r** *n* huelguista *m & f*; (*Sport*) artillero *m*

striking /'straɪkɪŋ/ *adj* (resemblance) sorprendente; (colour) llamativo

string /strɪŋ/ *n* cordel *m*, mecate *m* (*Mex*); (*Mus*) cuerda *f*; (*of lies, pearls*) sarta *f*; (*of people*) sucesión *f*. □ **~ along** *vt* ⊡ engañar

stringent /'strɪndʒənt/ *adj* riguroso

strip /strɪp/ *vt* (*pt* **stripped**) desnudar (person); deshacer (bed). ● *vi* desnudarse. ● *n* tira *f*; (*of land*) franja *f*. **~ cartoon** *n* historieta *f*

stripe /straɪp/ *n* raya *f*. **~d** *adj* a rayas, rayado

strip lighting *n* luz *f* fluorescente

strive /straɪv/ *vi* (*pt* **strove**, *pp* **striven**). **~ to** esforzarse por

strode /strəʊd/ *see* **STRIDE**

stroke /strəʊk/ *n* golpe *m*; (*in swimming*) brazada *f*; (*Med*) ataque *m* de apoplejía; (*of pen etc*) trazo *m*; (*of clock*) campanada *f*; (*caress*) caricia *f*. **a ~ of luck** un golpe de suerte. ● *vt* acariciar

stroll /strəʊl/ *vi* pasearse. ● *n* paseo *m*. **~er** *n* (*Amer*) sillita *f* de paseo, cochecito *m*

strong /strɒŋ/ *adj* (**-er**, **-est**) fuerte. **~hold** *n* fortaleza *f*; (*fig*) baluarte *m*. **~ly** *adv* (*greatly*) fuertemente; (protest) enérgicamente; (*deeply*) profundamente. **~room** *n* cámara *f* acorazada

strove /strəʊv/ *see* **STRIVE**

struck /strʌk/ *see* **STRIKE**

structur|al /'strʌktʃərəl/ *adj* estructural. **~e** /'strʌktʃə(r)/ *n* estructura *f*

struggle /'strʌgl/ *vi* luchar; (*thrash around*) forcejear. ● *n* lucha *f*

strum /strʌm/ *vt* (*pt* **strummed**)

rasguear

strung /strʌŋ/ *see* **STRING**

strut /strʌt/ *n* (*in building*) puntal *m*. ● *vi* (*pt* **strutted**) pavonearse

stub /stʌb/ *n* (*of pencil, candle*) cabo *m*; (*counterfoil*) talón *m*; (*of cigarette*) colilla. □ ~ **out** (*pt* **stubbed**) *vt* apagar

stubble /ˈstʌbl/ *n* rastrojo *m*; (*beard*) barba *f* de varios días

stubborn /ˈstʌbən/ *adj* terco

stuck /stʌk/ *see* **STICK**. ● *adj*. **the drawer is** ~ el cajón se ha atascado. **the door is** ~ la puerta se ha atrancado. ~**-up** *adj* ⓘ estirado

stud /stʌd/ *n* tachuela *f*; (*for collar*) gemelo *m*.

student /ˈstju:dənt/ *n* estudiante *m & f*; (*at school*) alumno *m*. ~ **driver** *n* (*Amer*) persona que está aprendiendo a conducir

studio /ˈstju:dɪəʊ/ *n* (*pl* **-os**) estudio *m*. ~ **apartment**, ~ **flat** *n* estudio *m*

studious /ˈstju:dɪəs/ *adj* estudioso

study /ˈstʌdɪ/ *n* estudio *m*. ● *vt/i* estudiar

stuff /stʌf/ *n* ⓘ cosas *fpl*. **what's this** ~ **called?** ¿cómo se llama esta cosa?. ● *vt* rellenar; disecar (animal); (*cram*) atiborrar; (*put*) meter de prisa. ~ **o.s.** ⓘ darse un atracón. ~**ing** *n* relleno *m*. ~**y** *adj* (**-ier**, **-iest**) mal ventilado; (*old-fashioned*) acartonado. **it's** ~**y in here** está muy cargado el ambiente

stumbl|e /ˈstʌmbl/ *vi* tropezar. ~**e across**, ~**e on** *vt* dar con. ~**ing-block** *n* tropiezo *m*, impedimento *m*

stump /stʌmp/ *n* (*of limb*) muñón *m*; (*of tree*) tocón *m*

stun /stʌn/ *vt* (*pt* **stunned**) (*daze*) aturdir; (*bewilder*) dejar atónito. ~**ning** *adj* sensacional

stung /stʌŋ/ *see* **STING**

stunk /stʌŋk/ *see* **STINK**

stunt /stʌnt/ *n* ⓘ ardid *m* publicitario. ● *vt* detener, atrofiar. ~**ed** *adj* (*growth*) atrofiado; (*body*) raquítico. ~**man** *n* especialista *m*. ~**woman** *n* especialista *f*

stupendous /stju:ˈpendəs/ *adj* estupendo

stupid /ˈstju:pɪd/ *adj* (*foolish*) tonto; (*unintelligent*) estúpido. ~**ity** /-ˈpɪdətɪ/ *n* estupidez *f*. ~**ly** *adv* estúpidamente

stupor /ˈstju:pə(r)/ *n* estupor *m*

sturdy /ˈstɜ:dɪ/ *adj* (**-ier**, **-iest**) robusto

stutter /ˈstʌtə(r)/ *vi* tartamudear. ● *n* tartamudeo *m*

sty /staɪ/ *n* (*pl* **sties**) pocilga *f*; (*Med*) orzuelo *m*

styl|e /staɪl/ *n* estilo *m*; (*fashion*) moda *f*; (*design, type*) diseño *m*. **in** ~ a lo grande. ● *vt* diseñar. ~**ish** *adj* elegante. ~**ist** *n* estilista *m & f*. **hair** ~**ist** estilista *m & f*

stylus /ˈstaɪləs/ *n* (*pl* **-uses**) aguja *f* (de tocadiscos)

suave /swɑ:v/ *adj* elegante y desenvuelto

subconscious /sʌbˈkɒnʃəs/ *adj & n* subconsciente (*m*)

subdivide /sʌbdɪˈvaɪd/ *vt* subdividir

subdued /səbˈdju:d/ *adj* apagado

subject /ˈsʌbdʒɪkt/ *adj* sometido. ~ **to** sujeto a. ● *n* (*theme*) tema *m*; (*Schol*) asignatura *f*, materia *f* (*LAm*); (*Gram*) sujeto *m*; (*Pol*) súbdito *m*. ● /səbˈdʒekt/ *vt* someter. ~**ive** /səbˈdʒektɪv/ *adj* subjetivo

subjunctive /səbˈdʒʌŋktɪv/ *adj &*

n subjuntivo (*m*)
sublime /sə'blaɪm/ *adj* sublime
submarine /sʌbmə'ri:n/ *n* submarino *m*
submerge /səb'mɜ:dʒ/ *vt* sumergir. ● *vi* sumergirse
submi|ssion /səb'mɪʃn/ *n* sumisión *f*. **~t** /səb'mɪt/ *vt* (*pt* **submitted**) (*subject*) someter; presentar (application). ● *vi* rendirse
subordinate /sə'bɔ:dɪnət/ *adj & n* subordinado (*m*). ● /sə'bɔ:dɪneɪt/ *vt* subordinar
subscri|be /səb'skraɪb/ *vi* suscribir. **~be to** suscribirse a (magazine). **~ber** *n* suscriptor *m*. **~ption** /-rɪpʃn/ *n* (*to magazine*) suscripción *f*
subsequent /'sʌbsɪkwənt/ *adj* posterior, subsiguiente. **~ly** *adv* posteriormente
subside /səb'saɪd/ *vi* (land) hundirse; (flood) bajar; (storm, wind) amainar. **~nce** /'sʌbsɪdəns/ *n* hundimiento *m*
subsidiary /səb'sɪdɪərɪ/ *adj* secundario; (subject) complementario. ● *n* (*Com*) filial
subsid|ize /'sʌbsɪdaɪz/ *vt* subvencionar, subsidiar (*LAm*). **~y** /'sʌbsədɪ/ *n* subvención *f*, subsidio *m*
substance /'sʌbstəns/ *n* sustancia *f*
substandard /sʌb'stændəd/ *adj* de calidad inferior
substantial /səb'stænʃl/ *adj* (*sturdy*) sólido; (meal) sustancioso; (*considerable*) considerable
substitut|e /'sʌbstɪtju:t/ *n* (*person*) substituto *m*; (*thing*) sucedáneo *m*. ● *vt/i* sustituir. **~ion** /-'tju:ʃn/ *n* sustitución *f*
subterranean /sʌbtə'reɪmjən/ *adj* subterráneo
subtitle /'sʌbtaɪtl/ *n* subtítulo *m*
subtle /'sʌtl/ *adj* (**-er**, **-est**) sutil; (*tactful*) discreto. **~ty** *n* sutileza *f*
subtract /səb'trækt/ *vt* restar. **~ion** /-ʃn/ *n* resta *f*
suburb /'sʌbɜ:b/ *n* barrio *m* residencial de las afueras, colonia *f*. **the ~s** las afueras *fpl*. **~an** /sə'bɜ:bən/ *adj* suburbano. **~ia** /sə'bɜ:bɪə/ *n zonas residenciales de las afueras de una ciudad*
subversive /səb'vɜ:sɪv/ *adj* subversivo
subway /'sʌbweɪ/ *n* paso *m* subterráneo; (*Amer*) metro *m*
succeed /sək'si:d/ *vi* (plan) dar resultado; (person) tener éxito. **~ in doing** lograr hacer. ● *vt* suceder
success /sək'ses/ *n* éxito *m*. **~ful** *adj* (person) de éxito, exitoso (*LAm*). **the ~ful applicant** el candidato que obtenga el puesto. **~fully** *adj* satisfactoriamente. **~ion** /-ʃn/ *n* sucesión *f*. **for 3 years in ~ion** durante tres años consecutivos. **in rapid ~ion** uno tras otro. **~ive** *adj* sucesivo. **~or** *n* sucesor *m*
succulent /'sʌkjʊlənt/ *adj* suculento
succumb /sə'kʌm/ *vi* sucumbir
such /sʌtʃ/ *adj* tal (+ *noun*), tan (+ *adj*). **~ a big house** una casa tan grande. ● *pron* tal. **~ and ~** tal o cual. **~ as** como. **~ as it is** tal como es
suck /sʌk/ *vt* chupar (sweet, thumb); sorber (liquid). □ **~ up** *vt* (vacuum cleaner) aspirar; (pump) succionar. □ **~ up to** *vt* ◻ dar coba a. **~er** *n* (*plant*) chupón *m*; (*fam, person*) imbécil *m*
suckle /sʌkl/ *vt* amamantar
suction /'sʌkʃn/ *n* succión *f*

sudden /'sʌdn/ *adj* repentino. **all of a ~** de repente. **~ly** *adv* de repente

suds /sʌds/ *npl* espuma *f* de jabón

sue /su:/ *vt* (*pres p* **suing**) demandar (**for** por)

suede /sweɪd/ *n* ante *m*

suet /'su:ɪt/ *n* sebo *m*

suffer /'sʌfə(r)/ *vt* sufrir; (*tolerate*) aguantar. ● *vi* sufrir; (*be affected*) resentirse

suffic|e /sə'faɪs/ *vi* bastar. **~ient** /sə'fɪʃnt/ *adj* suficiente, bastante. **~iently** *adv* (lo) suficientemente

suffix /'sʌfɪks/ *n* (*pl* **-ixes**) sufijo *m*

suffocat|e /'sʌfəkeɪt/ *vt* asfixiar. ● *vi* asfixiarse. **~ion** /-'keɪʃn/ *n* asfixia *f*

sugar /'ʃʊgə(r)/ *n* azúcar *m* & *f*. **~ bowl** *n* azucarero *m*. **~y** *adj* azucarado.

suggest /sə'dʒest/ *vt* sugerir. **~ion** /-tʃən/ *n* sugerencia *f*

suicid|al /su:ɪ'saɪdl/ *adj* suicida. **~e** /'su:ɪsaɪd/ *n* suicidio *m*. **commit ~e** suicidarse

suit /su:t/ *n* traje *m*; (*woman's*) traje *m* de chaqueta; (*Cards*) palo *m*; (*Jurid*) pleito *m*. ● *vt* venirle bien a, convenirle a; (clothes) quedarle bien a; (*adapt*) adaptar. **be ~ed to** (thing) ser apropiado para. **I'm not ~ed to this kind of work** no sirvo para este tipo de trabajo. **~able** *adj* apropiado, adecuado. **~ably** *adv* (dressed) apropiadamente; (qualified) adecuadamente. **~case** *n* maleta *f*, valija *f* (*LAm*)

suite /swi:t/ *n* (*of furniture*) juego *m*; (*of rooms*) suite *f*

sulk /sʌlk/ *vi* enfurruñarse

sullen /'sʌlən/ *adj* hosco

sulphur /'sʌlfə(r)/ *n* azufre *m*. **~ic acid** /sʌl'fjʊərɪk/ *n* ácido *m* sulfúrico

sultan /'sʌltən/ *n* sultán *m*

sultana /sʌl'tɑ:nə/ *n* pasa *f* de Esmirna

sultry /'sʌltrɪ/ *adj* (**-ier**, **-iest**) (weather) bochornoso; (*fig*) sensual

sum /sʌm/ *n* (*of money*) suma *f*, cantidad *f*; (*Math*) suma *f*. ● □ **~ up** (*pt* **summed**) *vt* resumir. ● *vi* recapitular

summar|ily /'sʌmərɪlɪ/ *adv* sumariamente. **~ize** *vt* resumir. **~y** *n* resumen *m*

summer /'sʌmə(r)/ *n* verano *m*. **~ camp** *n* (*in US*) colonia *f* de vacaciones. **~time** *n* verano *m*. **~y** *adj* veraniego

summer camp En EE.UU., es el campamento de verano, aspecto muy importante en la vida de muchos niños. Las actividades al aire libre se practican en un ambiente natural entre las que se incluyen natación, montañismo, supervivencia al aire libre. En estos campamentos miles de estudiantes trabajan como supervisores.

summit /'sʌmɪt/ *n* (*of mountain*) cumbre *f*. **~ conference** *n* conferencia *f* cumbre

summon /'sʌmən/ *vt* llamar; convocar (meeting, s.o. to meeting); (*Jurid*) citar. □ **~ up** *vt* armarse de. **~s** *n* (*Jurid*) citación *f*. ● *vt* citar

sumptuous /'sʌmptjʊəs/ *adj* suntuoso

sun /sʌn/ *n* sol *m*. **~bathe** *vi* tomar el sol, asolearse (*LAm*). **~beam** *n* rayo *m* de sol. **~burn** *n* quemadura *f* de sol. **~burnt** *adj* quemado por el sol

Sunday /'sʌndeɪ/ *n* domingo *m*

sunflower /ˈsʌnflaʊə(r)/ *n* girasol *m*
sung /sʌŋ/ *see* **SING**
sunglasses /ˈsʌnglɑːsɪz/ *npl* gafas *fpl* de sol, lentes *mpl* de sol (*LAm*)
sunk /sʌŋk/ *see* **SINK**. **~en** /ˈsʌŋkən/ • *adj* hundido
sun: ~light *n* luz *f* del sol. **~ny** *adj* (**-ier, -iest**) (day) de sol; (*place*) soleado. **it is ~ny** hace sol. **~rise** *n*. **at ~rise** al amanecer. salida *f* del sol. **~roof** *n* techo *m* corredizo. **~set** *n* puesta *f* del sol. **~shine** *n* sol *m*. **~stroke** *n* insolación *f*. **~tan** *n* bronceado *m*. **get a ~tan** broncearse. **~tan lotion** *n* bronceador *m*
super /ˈsuːpə(r)/ *adj* [I] genial, super *a invar*
superb /suːˈpɜːb/ *adj* espléndido
supercilious /suːpəˈsɪlɪəs/ *adj* desdeñoso
superficial /suːpəˈfɪʃl/ *adj* superficial
superfluous /suːˈpɜːflʊəs/ *adj* superfluo
superhighway /ˈsuːpəhaɪweɪ/ *n* (*Amer, Auto*) autopista *f*; (*Comp*) **information ~** autopista *f* de la comunicación
superhuman /suːpəˈhjuːmən/ *adj* sobrehumano
superintendent /suːpərɪnˈtendənt/ *n* director *m*; (*Amer, of building*) portero *m*; (*of police*) comisario *m*; (*in US*) superintendente *m & f*
superior /suːˈpɪərɪə(r)/ *adj & n* superior (*m*). **~ity** /-ˈɒrətɪ/ *n* superioridad *f*
superlative /suːˈpɜːlətɪv/ *adj* inigualable. • *n* superlativo *m*
supermarket /ˈsuːpəmɑːkɪt/ *n* supermercado *m*
supernatural /suːpəˈnætʃrəl/ *adj* sobrenatural
superpower /ˈsuːpəpaʊə(r)/ *n* superpotencia *f*
supersede /suːpəˈsiːd/ *vt* reemplazar, sustituir
supersonic /suːpəˈsɒnɪk/ *adj* supersónico
superstitio|n /suːpəˈstɪʃn/ *n* superstición *f*. **~us** *adj* /-əs/ supersticioso
supervis|e /ˈsuːpəvaɪz/ *vt* supervisar. **~ion** /-ˈvɪʒn/ *n* supervisión *f*. **~or** *n* supervisor *m*
supper /ˈsʌpə(r)/ *n* cena *f* (*ligera*), comida *f* (*ligera*) (*LAm*)
supple /sʌpl/ *adj* flexible
supplement /ˈsʌplɪmənt/ *n* suplemento *m*; (*to diet, income*) complemento *m*. • *vt* complementar (diet, income). **~ary** /-ˈmentərɪ/ *adj* suplementario
suppl|ier /səˈplaɪə(r)/ *n* (*Com*) proveedor *m*. **~y** /səˈplaɪ/ *vt* suministrar; proporcionar (information). **~y s.o. with sth** (equipment) proveer a uno de algo; (*in business*) abastecer a uno de algo. • *n* suministro *m*. **~y and demand** oferta *f* y demanda. **~ies** *npl* provisiones *mpl*, víveres *mpl*; (*Mil*) pertrechos *mpl*. **office ~ies** artículos *mpl* de oficina
support /səˈpɔːt/ *vt* (*hold up*) sostener; (*back*) apoyar; mantener (family). • *n* apoyo *m*; (*Tec*) soporte *m*. **~er** *n* partidario *m*; (*Sport*) hincha *m & f*
suppos|e /səˈpəʊz/ *vt* suponer, imaginarse; (*think*) creer. **I'm ~ed to start work at nine** se supone que tengo que empezar a trabajar a las nueve. **~edly** *adv* supuestamente. **~ition** /sʌpəˈzɪʃn/ *n* su-

posición *f*

suppress /sə'pres/ *vt* reprimir (feelings); sofocar (rebellion). **~ion** /-ʃn/*n* represión *f*

suprem|acy /su:'preməsɪ/ *n* supremacía *f*. **~e** /su:'pri:m/ *adj* supremo

sure /ʃʊə(r)/ *adj* (**-er**, **-est**) seguro. **make ~ that** asegurarse de que. ● *adv* ¡claro!. **~ly** *adv* (*undoubtedly*) seguramente; (*gladly*) desde luego. **~ly you don't believe that!** ¡no te creerás eso! **~ty** /-ətɪ/ *n* garantía *f*

surf /sɜ:f/ *n* oleaje *m*; (*foam*) espuma *f*. ● *vi* hacer surf. ● *vt* (*Comp*) surfear, navegar

surface /'sɜ:fɪs/ *n* superficie *f*. ● *adj* superficial. ● *vt* recubrir (**with** de). ● *vi* salir a la superficie; (problems) aflorar

surfboard /'sɜ:fbɔ:d/ *n* tabla *f* de surf

surfeit /'sɜ:fɪt/ *n* exceso *m*

surf: ~er *n* surfista *m & f*; (*Internet*) navegador *m*. **~ing** *n* surf *m*

surge /sɜ:dʒ/ *vi* (crowd) moverse en tropel; (sea) hincharse. ● *n* oleada *f*; (*in demand, sales*) aumento *m*

surg|eon /'sɜ:dʒən/ *n* cirujano *m*. **~ery** *n* cirugía *f*; (*consulting room*) consultorio *m*; (*consulting hours*) consulta *f*. **~ical** *adj* quirúrgico

surly /'sɜ:lɪ/ *adj* (**-ier**, **-iest**) hosco

surmise /sə'maɪz/ *vt* conjeturar

surmount /sə'maʊnt/ *vt* superar

surname /'sɜ:neɪm/ *n* apellido *m*

surpass /sə'pɑ:s/ *vt* superar

surplus /'sɜ:pləs/ *adj & n* excedente (*m*)

surpris|e /sə'praɪz/ *n* sorpresa *f*. ● *vt* sorprender. **~ed** *adj* sorprendido. **~ing** *adj* sorprendente. **~ingly** *adv* sorprendentemente

surrender /sə'rendə(r)/ *vt* entregar. ● *vi* rendirse. ● *n* rendición *f*

surreptitious /sʌrəp'tɪʃəs/ *adj* furtivo

surround /sə'raʊnd/ *vt* rodear; (*Mil*) rodear, cercar. **~ing** *adj* circundante. **~ings** *npl* alrededores *mpl*; (*environment*) ambiente *m*

surveillance /sɜ:'veɪləns/ *n* vigilancia *f*

survey /'sɜ:veɪ/ *n* inspección *f*; (*report*) informe *m*; (*general view*) vista *f* general. ● /sə'veɪ/ *vt* inspeccionar; (*measure*) medir; (*look at*) contemplar. **~or** *n* topógrafo *m*, agrimensor *m*; (*of building*) perito *m*

surviv|al /sə'vaɪvl/ *n* supervivencia *f*. **~e** /sə'vaɪv/ *vt/i* sobrevivir. **~or** *n* superviviente *m & f*

susceptible /sə'septəbl/ *adj*. **~ to** propenso a

suspect /sə'spekt/ *vt* sospechar; sospechar de (person). ● /'sʌspekt/ *adj & n* sospechoso (*m*)

suspen|d /sə'spend/ *vt* suspender. **~ders** *npl* (*Amer, braces*) tirantes *mpl*. **~se** /-s/ *n* (*in film etc*) suspense *m*, suspenso *m* (*LAm*). **keep s.o. in ~se** mantener a uno sobre ascuas. **~sion** /-ʃn/ *n* suspensión *f*. **~sion bridge** *n* puente *m* colgante

suspici|on /sə'spɪʃn/ *n* (*belief*) sospecha *f*; (*mistrust*) desconfianza *f*. **~ous** /-ʃəs/ *adj* desconfiado; (*causing suspicion*) sospechoso

sustain /sə'steɪn/ *vt* sostener; mantener (conversation, interest); (*suffer*) sufrir

SW *abbr* (= **south-west**) SO

swab /swɒb/ *n* (*specimen*) muestra *f*, frotis *m*

swagger /ˈswæɡə(r)/ *vi* pavonearse

swallow /ˈswɒləʊ/ *vt/i* tragar. ● *n* trago *m*; (*bird*) golondrina *f*

swam /swæm/ *see* **SWIM**

swamp /swɒmp/ *n* pantano *m*, ciénaga *f*. ● *vt* inundar. **~y** *adj* pantanoso

swan /swɒn/ *n* cisne *m*

swap /swɒp/ *vt/i* (*pt* **swapped**) intercambiar. **~ sth for sth** cambiar algo por algo. ● *n* cambio *m*

swarm /swɔ:m/ *n* enjambre *m*. ● *vi* (bees) enjambrar; (*fig*) hormiguear

swarthy /ˈswɔ:ðɪ/ *adj* (**-ier, -iest**) moreno

swat /swɒt/ *vt* (*pt* **swatted**) matar (*con matamoscas etc*)

sway /sweɪ/ *vi* balancearse; (*gently*) mecerse. ● *vt* (*influence*) influir en

swear /sweə(r)/ *vt/i* (*pt* **swore**, *pp* **sworn**) jurar. **~word** *n* palabrota *f*

sweat /swet/ *n* sudor *m*, transpiración *f*. ● *vi* sudar

sweat|er /ˈswetə(r)/ *n* jersey *m*, suéter *m*. **~shirt** *n* sudadera *f*. **~suit** *n* (*Amer*) chándal *m*, equipo *m* de deportes

swede /swi:d/ *n* nabo *m* sueco

Swede /swi:d/ *n* sueco *m*. **~n** /ˈswi:dn/ *n* Suecia *f*. **~ish** *adj* sueco. ● *n* (*language*) sueco *m*. ● *npl*. **the ~** (*people*) los suecos

sweep /swi:p/ *vt* (*pt* **swept**) barrer; deshollinar (chimney). ● *vi* barrer. ● *n* barrido *m*. **~ away** *vt* (*carry away*) arrastrar; (*abolish*) erradicar. **~er** *n* barrendero *m*. **~ing** *adj* (gesture) amplio; (changes) radical; (statement) demasiado general

sweet /swi:t/ *adj* (**-er, -est**) dulce; (*fragrant*) fragante; (*pleasant*) agradable; (*kind, gentle*) dulce; (*cute*) rico. **have a ~ tooth** ser dulcero. ● *n* caramelo *m*, dulce *m* (*Mex*); (*dish*) postre *m*. **~en** *vt* endulzar. **~heart** *n* enamorado *m*; (*as form of address*) amor *m*. **~ly** *adv* dulcemente. **~ potato** *n* boniato *m*, batata *f*, camote *m LAm*

swell /swel/ *vt* (*pt* **swelled**, *pp* **swollen** *or* **swelled**) hinchar; (*increase*) aumentar. ● *vi* hincharse; (*increase*) aumentar. ● *adj* (*Amer fam*) fenomenal. ● *n* (*of sea*) oleaje *m*. **~ing** *n* hinchazón *m*

sweltering /ˈsweltərɪŋ/ *vi* sofocante

swept /swept/ *see* **SWEEP**

swerve /swɜ:v/ *vi* virar bruscamente

swift /swɪft/ *adj* (**-er, -est**) veloz, rápido; (reply) rápido. ● *n* (*bird*) vencejo *m*. **~ly** *adv* rápidamente

swig /swɪɡ/ *vt* (*pt* **swigged**) [!] beber a grandes tragos. ● *n* [!] trago *m*

swim /swɪm/ *vi* (*pt* **swam**, *pp* **swum**) nadar. ● *n* baño *m*. **~mer** *n* nadador *m*. **~ming** *n* natación *f*. **~ming bath(s)** *n*(*pl*) piscina *f* cubierta, alberca *f* techada (*Mex*). **~ming pool** *n* piscina *f*, alberca *f* (*Mex*). **~ming trunks** *npl* bañador *m*, traje *m* de baño **~suit** *n* traje *m* de baño, bañador *m*

swindle /ˈswɪndl/ *vt* estafar. ● *n* estafa *f*. **~r** *n* estafador *m*

swine /swaɪn/ *npl* cerdos *mpl*. ● *n* (*pl* **swine**) (*fam, person*) canalla *m* & *f*. **~ fever** *n* fiebre *f* porcina

swing /swɪŋ/ *vt* (*pt* **swung**) balancear; (*object on rope*) hacer oscilar. ● *vi* (*dangle*) balancearse; (*swing on a swing*) columpiarse; (pendulum) oscilar. ~ **open**/**shut** abrirse/ cerrarse. ● *n* oscilación *f*, vaivén *m*; (*seat*) columpio *m*; (*in opinion*) cambio *m*. **in full** ~ en plena actividad

swipe /swaɪp/ *vt* darle un golpe a; (*fam, snatch*) birlar. ● *n* golpe *m*

Swiss /swɪs/ *adj* suizo (*m*). ● *npl*. **the** ~ los suizos

switch /swɪtʃ/ *n* (*Elec*) interruptor *m*; (*exchange*) intercambio *m*; (*Amer, Rail*) agujas *fpl*. ● *vt* cambiar; (*deviate*) desviar. □ ~ **off** *vt* (*Elec*) apagar (light, TV, heating); desconectar (electricity). □ ~ **on** *vt* encender, prender (*LAm*); arrancar (engine). ~**board** *n* centralita *f*

Switzerland /'swɪtsələnd/ *n* Suiza *f*

swivel /'swɪvl/ *vi* (*pt* **swivelled**) girar. ● *vt* hacer girar

swollen /'swəʊlən/ *see* **SWELL**. ● *adj* hinchado

swoop /swu:p/ *vi* (bird) abatirse; (police) llevar a cabo una redada. ● *n* (*of bird*) descenso *m* en picado *or* (*LAm*) en picada; (*by police*) redada *f*

sword /sɔ:d/ *n* espada *f*

swore /swɔ:(r)/ *see* **SWEAR**

sworn /swɔ:n/ *see* **SWEAR**. ● *adj* (enemy) declarado; (statement) jurado

swot /swɒt/ *vt/i* (*pt* **swotted**) (*Schol, fam*) empollar, estudiar como loco. ● *n* (*Schol, fam*) empollón *m*, matado *m* (*Mex*)

swum /swʌm/ *see* **SWIM**

swung /swʌŋ/ *see* **SWING**

syllable /'sɪləbl/ *n* sílaba *f*

syllabus /'sɪləbəs/ *n* (*pl* **-buses**) plan *m* de estudios; (*of a particular subject*) programa *m*

symbol /'sɪmbl/ *n* símbolo *m*. ~**ic(al)** /-'bɒlɪk(l)/ *adj* simbólico. ~**ism** *n* simbolismo *m*. ~**ize** *vt* simbolizar

symmetr|ical /sɪ'metrɪkl/ *adj* simétrico. ~**y** /'sɪmətrɪ/ *n* simetría *f*

sympath|etic /sɪmpə'θetɪk/ *adj* comprensivo; (*showing pity*) compasivo. ~**ize** /'sɪmpəθaɪz/ *vi* comprender; (*commiserate*) ~**ize with s.o.** compadecer a uno. ~**y** /'sɪmpəθɪ/ *n* comprensión *f*; (*pity*) compasión *f*; (*condolences*) pésame *m*

symphony /'sɪmfənɪ/ *n* sinfonía *f*

symptom /'sɪmptəm/ *n* síntoma *m*. ~**atic** /-'mætɪk/ *adj* sintomático

synagogue /'sɪnəgɒg/ *n* sinagoga *f*

synchronize /'sɪŋkrənaɪz/ *vt* sincronizar

syndicate /'sɪndɪkət/ *n* agrupación *f*; (*Amer, TV*) agencia *f* de distribución periodística

synonym /'sɪnənɪm/ *n* sinónimo *m*. ~**ous** /-'nɒnɪməs/ *adj* sinónimo

syntax /'sɪntæks/ *n* sintaxis *f*

synthesi|s /'sɪnθəsɪs/ *n* (*pl* **-theses** /-si:z/) síntesis *f*. ~**ze** /-aɪz/ *vt* sintetizar

synthetic /sɪn'θetɪk/ *adj* sintético

syringe /'sɪrɪndʒ/ *n* jeringa *f*, jeringuilla *f*

syrup /'sɪrəp/ *n* (*sugar solution*) almíbar *m*; (*with other ingredients*) jarabe *m*; (*medicine*) jarabe *m*

system /'sɪstəm/ *n* sistema *m*, método *m*; (*Tec, Mec, Comp*) sistema *m*. **the digestive** ~ el aparato digestivo. ~**atic** /-ə'mætɪk/ *adj* sistemático. ~**atically** /-ə'mætɪklɪ/ *adv* sistemáticamente. ~**s analyst** *n* analista *m & f* de sistemas

Tt

tab /tæb/ *n* (*flap*) lengüeta *f*; (*label*) etiqueta *f*

table /'teɪbl/ *n* mesa *f*; (*list*) tabla *f*. **~cloth** *n* mantel *m*. **~ mat** *n* salvamanteles *m*. **~spoon** *n* cuchara *f* grande; (*measure*) cucharada *f* (grande)

tablet /'tæblɪt/ *n* pastilla *f*; (*pill*) comprimido *m*

table tennis *n* tenis *m* de mesa, ping-pong *m*

tabloid /'tæblɔɪd/ *n* tabloide *m*

taboo /tə'bu:/ *adj & n* tabú (*m*)

tacit /'tæsɪt/ *adj* tácito

taciturn /'tæsɪtɜ:n/ *adj* taciturno

tack /tæk/ *n* tachuela *f*; (*stitch*) hilván *m*. ● *vt* clavar con tachuelas; (*sew*) hilvanar. ● *vi* (*Naut*) virar ▫ **~ on** *vt* añadir.

tackle /'tækl/ *n* (*equipment*) equipo *m*; (*soccer*) entrada *f* fuerte; (*US football, Rugby*) placaje *m*. **fishing ~** aparejo *m* de pesca. ● *vt* abordar (problem); (*in soccer*) entrarle a; (*in US football, Rugby*) placar

tacky /'tækɪ/ *adj* pegajoso

tact /tækt/ *n* tacto *m*. **~ful** *adj* diplomático

tactic|al /'tæktɪkl/ *adj* táctico. **~s** *npl* táctica *f*

tactless /'tæktləs/ *adj* indiscreto

tadpole /'tædpəʊl/ *n* renacuajo *m*

tag /tæg/ *n* (*label*) etiqueta *f*. ▫ **~ along** (*pt* **tagged**) *vt* 🅸 seguir

tail /teɪl/ *n* (*of horse, fish, bird*) cola *f*; (*of dog, pig*) rabo *m*. **~s** *npl* (*tailcoat*) frac *m*; (*of coin*) cruz *f*. ● *vt* seguir. ▫ **~ off** *vi* disminuir.

tailor /'teɪlə(r)/ *n* sastre *m*. **~ed** /'teɪləd/ *adj* entallado. **~-made** *n* hecho a (la) medida

taint /teɪnt/ *vt* contaminar

take /teɪk/ *vt* (*pt* **took**, *pp* **taken**) tomar, coger (*esp Spain*), agarrar (*esp LAm*); (*capture*) capturar; (*endure*) aguantar; (*require*) requerir; llevar (time); tomar (bath); tomar (medicine); (*carry*) llevar; aceptar (cheque). **I ~ a size 10** uso la talla 14. ▫ **~ after** *vt* parecerse a. ▫ **~ away** *vt* llevarse; (*confiscate*) quitar. ▫ **~ back** *vt* retirar (statement etc). ▫ **~ in** *vt* achicar (garment); (*understand*) asimilar; (*deceive*) engañar. ▫ **~ off** *vt* (*remove*) quitar, sacar; quitarse (shoes, jacket); (*mimic*) imitar. *vi* (aircraft) despegar. ▫ **~ on** *vt* contratar (employee). ▫ **~ out** *vt* sacar. ▫ **~ over** *vt* tomar posesión de; hacerse cargo de (job). *vi* (*assume control*) asumir el poder. ▫ **~ up** *vt* empezar a hacer (hobby); aceptar (challenge); subir (hem); llevar (time); ocupar (space). ● *n* (*Cinema*) toma *f*. **~-off** *n* despegue *m*. **~-over** *n* (*Com*) absorción *f*

takings /'teɪkɪŋz/ *npl* recaudación *f*; (*at box office*) taquilla *f*

talcum powder /'tælkəm/ *n* polvos *mpl* de talco, talco *m* (*LAm*)

tale /teɪl/ *n* cuento *m*

talent /'tælənt/ *n* talento *m*. **~ed** *adj* talentoso

talk /tɔ:k/ *vt/i* hablar. **~ to s.o.** hablar con uno. **~ about** hablar de. ● *n* conversación *f*; (*lecture*) charla *f*. ▫ **~ over** *vt* discutir. **~ative** /-ətɪv/ *adj* hablador

tall /tɔ:l/ *adj* (**-er, -est**) alto. **~ story** *n* 🅸 cuento *m* chino

tally /'tælɪ/ *vi* coincidir (**with** con)

talon /'tælən/ *n* garra *f*

tambourine /tæmbəˈriːn/ *n* pandereta *f*

tame /teɪm/ *adj* (**-er**, **-est**) (animal) (*by nature*) manso; (*tamed*) domado. ● *vt* domar (wild animal)

tamper /ˈtæmpə(r)/ *vi*. ~ **with** tocar; (*alter*) alterar, falsificar

tampon /ˈtæmpɒn/ *n* tampón *m*

tan /tæn/ *vi* (*pt* **tanned**) broncearse. ● *n* bronceado *m*. **get a** ~ broncearse. ● *adj* habano

tang /tæŋ/ *n* sabor *m* fuerte

tangent /ˈtændʒənt/ *n* tangente *f*

tangerine /tændʒəˈriːn/ *n* mandarina *f*

tangible /ˈtændʒəbl/ *adj* tangible

tangle /ˈtæŋgl/ *vt* enredar. **get** ~**d (up)** enredarse. ● *n* enredo *m*, maraña *f*

tango /ˈtæŋgəʊ/ *n* (*pl* **-os**) tango *m*

tank /tæŋk/ *n* depósito *m*; (*Auto*) tanque *m*; (*Mil*) tanque *m*

tanker /ˈtæŋkə(r)/ *n* (*ship*) buque *m* cisterna; (*truck*) camión *m* cisterna

tantrum /ˈtæntrəm/ *n* berrinche *m*, rabieta *f*

tap /tæp/ *n* grifo *m*, llave *f* (*LAm*); (*knock*) golpecito *m*. ● *vt* (*pt* **tapped**) (*knock*) dar un golpecito en; interceptar (phone). ● *vi* dar golpecitos (**on** en). ~ **dancing** *n* claqué *m*

tape /teɪp/ *n* cinta *f*; (*Med*) esparadrapo *m*. ● *vt* (*record*) grabar. ~**-measure** *n* cinta *f* métrica

taper /ˈteɪpə(r)/ *vt* afilar. ● *vi* afilarse. □ ~ **off** *vi* disminuir

tape recorder *n* magnetofón *m*, magnetófono *m*

tapestry /ˈtæpɪstrɪ/ *n* tapiz *m*

tar /tɑː(r)/ *n* alquitrán *m*. ● *vt* (*pt* **tarred**) alquitranar

target /ˈtɑːgɪt/ *n* blanco *m*; (*fig*) objetivo *m*

tarmac /ˈtɑːmæk/ *n* pista *f*. **T**~ *n* (*Amer*, ®) asfalto *m*

tarnish /ˈtɑːnɪʃ/ *vt* deslustrar; empañar (reputation)

tart /tɑːt/ *n* pastel *m*; (*individual*) pastelillo *m*; (*sl, woman*) prostituta *f*, fulana *f* [!]. ● *vt*. ~ **o.s. up** [!] engalanarse. ● *adj* (**-er**, **-est**) ácido

tartan /ˈtɑːtn/ *n* tartán *m*, tela *f* escocesa

task /tɑːsk/ *n* tarea *f*. **take to** ~ reprender

tassel /ˈtæsl/ *n* borla *f*

tast|e /teɪst/ *n* sabor *m*, gusto *m*; (*liking*) gusto *m*. ● *vt* probar. ● *vi*. ~**e of** saber a. ~**eful** *adj* de buen gusto. ~**eless** *adj* soso; (*fig*) de mal gusto. ~**y** *adj* (**-ier**, **-iest**) sabroso

tat /tæt/ *see* TIT FOR TAT

tatter|ed /ˈtætəd/ *adj* hecho jirones. ~**s** /ˈtætəz/ *npl* andrajos *mpl*

tattoo /tæˈtuː/ *n* (*on body*) tatuaje *m*. ● *vt* tatuar

tatty /ˈtætɪ/ *adj* (**-ier**, **-iest**) gastado, estropeado

taught /tɔːt/ *see* TEACH

taunt /tɔːnt/ *vt* provocar mediante burlas. ● *n* pulla *f*

Taurus /ˈtɔːrəs/ *n* Tauro *m*

taut /tɔːt/ *adj* tenso

tavern /ˈtævən/ *n* taberna *f*

tax /tæks/ *n* impuesto *m*. ● *vt* imponer contribuciones a (person); gravar (thing); (*strain*) poner a prueba. ~**able** *adj* imponible. ~**ation** /-ˈseɪʃn/ *n* impuestos *mpl*; (*system*) sistema *m* tributario. ~ **collector** *n* recaudador *m* de impuestos. ~**-free** *adj* libre de impuestos

taxi /'tæksɪ/ *n* (*pl* **-is**) taxi *m*. ● *vi* (*pt* **taxied**, *pres p* **taxiing**) (aircraft) rodar por la pista

taxpayer /'tækspeɪə(r)/ *n* contribuyente *m & f*

tea /ti:/ *n* té *m*; (*afternoon tea*) merienda *f*, té *m*. ~ **bag** *n* bolsita *f* de té

teach /ti:tʃ/ *vt* (*pt* **taught**) dar clases de, enseñar (subject); dar clase a (person). ~ **school** (*Amer*) dar clase(s) en un colegio. ● *vi* dar clase(s). ~**er** *n* profesor *m*; (*primary*) maestro *m*. ~**ing** *n* enseñanza *f*. ● *adj* docente

tea: ~**cup** *n* taza *f* de té. ~ **leaf** *n* hoja *f* de té

team /ti:m/ *n* equipo *m*. □ ~ **up** *vi* asociarse (**with** con). ~ **work** *n* trabajo *m* de equipo

teapot /'ti:pɒt/ *n* tetera *f*

tear[1] /teə(r)/ *vt* (*pt* **tore**, *pp* **torn**) romper, rasgar. ● *vi* romperse, rasgarse. ● *n* rotura *f*; (*rip*) desgarrón *m*. □ ~ **along** *vi* ir a toda velocidad. □ ~ **apart** *vt* desgarrar. □ ~ **off**, ~ **out** *vt* arrancar. □ ~ **up** *vt* romper

tear[2] /tɪə(r)/ *n* lágrima *f*. **be in** ~**s** estar llorando. ~**ful** *adj* lloroso (farewell) triste. ~ **gas** *n* gas *m* lacrimógeno

tease /ti:z/ *vt* tomarle el pelo a

t

tea: ~ **set** *n* juego *m* de té. ~**spoon** *n* cucharita *f*, cucharilla *f*; (*amount*) cucharadita *f*

teat /ti:t/ *n* (*of animal*) tetilla *f*; (*for bottle*) tetina *f*

tea towel /'ti:taʊəl/ *n* paño *m* de cocina

techni|cal /'teknɪkl/ *adj* técnico. ~**cality** *n* /-'kælətɪ/ *n* detalle *m* técnico. ~**cally** *adv* técnicamente. ~**cian** /tek'nɪʃn/ *n* técnico *m*. ~**que** /tek'ni:k/ *n* técnica *f*

technolog|ical /teknə'lɒdʒɪkl/ *adj* tecnológico. ~**y** /tek'nɒlədʒɪ/ *n* tecnología *f*

teddy bear /'tedɪ/ *n* osito *m* de peluche

tedi|ous /'ti:dɪəs/ *adj* tedioso. ~**um** /'ti:dɪəm/ *n* tedio *m*

teem /ti:m/ *vi* abundar (**with** en), estar repleto (**with** de)

teen|age /'ti:neɪdʒ/ *adj* adolescente; (*for teenagers*) para jóvenes. ~**ager** *n* adolescente *m & f*. ~**s** /ti:nz/ *npl* adolescencia *f*

teeny /'ti:nɪ/ *adj* (**-ier**, **-iest**) ▣ chiquito

teeter /'ti:tə(r)/ *vi* balancearse

teeth /ti:θ/ *see* TOOTH. ~**e** /ti:ð/ *vi*. **he's** ~**ing** le están saliendo los dientes. ~**ing troubles** *npl* (*fig*) problemas *mpl* iniciales

tele|communications /telɪkəmju:nɪ'keɪʃnz/ *npl* telecomunicaciones *fpl*. ~**gram** /'telɪgræm/ *n* telegrama *m*. ~**pathic** /telɪ'pæθɪk/ *adj* telepático. ~**pathy** /tə'lepəθɪ/ *n* telepatía *f*

telephon|e /'telɪfəʊn/ *n* teléfono *m*. ● *vt* llamar por teléfono. ~**e booth**, ~**e box** *n* cabina *f* telefónica. ~**e call** *n* llamada *f* telefónica. ~ **card** *n* tarjeta *f* telefónica. ~**e directory** *n* guía *f* telefónica. ~**e exchange** *n* central *f* telefónica. ~**ist** /tɪ'lefənɪst/ *n* telefonista *m & f*

tele|sales /'telɪseɪlz/ *npl* televentas *fpl*. ~**scope** *n* telescopio *m*. ~**scopic** /-'skɒpɪk/ *adj* telescópico. ~**text** *n* teletex(to) *m*. ~**working** *n* teletrabajo *m*

televis|e /'telɪvaɪz/ *vt* televisar. ~**ion** /'telɪvɪʒn/ *n* (*medium*) televisión *f*. ~**ion (set)** *n* televisor *m*

telex /'teleks/ *n* télex *m*

tell /tel/ *vt* (*pt* **told**) decir; contar (story, joke); (*distinguish*) distinguir. ~ **the difference** notar la diferencia. ~ **the time** decir la hora. ● *vi* (*produce an effect*) tener efecto; (*know*) saber. □ ~ **off** *vt* regañar. ~**ing** *adj* revelador. ~**-tale** *n* soplón *m*. ● *adj* revelador

telly /'telɪ/ *n* 🄸 tele *f*

temp /temp/ *n* empleado *m* eventual *or* temporal

temper /'tempə(r)/ *n* (*mood*) humor *m*; (*disposition*) carácter *m*; (*fit of anger*) cólera *f*. **be in a** ~ estar furioso. **lose one's** ~ perder los estribos. ~**ament** /'temprəmənt/ *n* temperamento *m*. ~**amental** /-'mentl/ *adj* temperamental. ~**ate** /'tempərət/ *adj* templado. ~**ature** /'temprɪtʃə(r)/ *n* temperatura *f*. **have a** ~**ature** tener fiebre

tempestuous /tem'pestjʊəs/ *adj* tempestuoso

temple /'templ/ *n* templo *m*; (*of head*) sien *f*

tempo /'tempəʊ/ *n* (*pl* **-os** *or* **tempi**) ritmo *m*

temporar|ily /'tempərərəlɪ/ *adv* temporalmente, temporariamente (*LAm*). ~**y** /'tempərərɪ/ *adj* temporal, provisional; (job) eventual, temporal

tempt /tempt/ *vt* tentar. ~**ation** /-'teɪʃn/ *n* tentación *f*. ~**ing** *adj* tentador

ten /ten/ *adj & n* diez (*m*)

tenaci|ous /tɪ'neɪʃəs/ *adj* tenaz. ~**ty** /tɪ'næsətɪ/ *n* tenacidad *f*

tenan|cy /'tenənsɪ/ *n* inquilinato *m*. ~**t** *n* inquilino *m*, arrendatorio *m*

tend /tend/ *vi*. ~ **to** tender a. ● *vt* cuidar (de). ~**ency** /'tendənsɪ/ *n* tendencia *f*

tender /'tendə(r)/ *adj* tierno; (*painful*) sensible. ● *n* (*Com*) oferta *f*. **legal** ~ *n* moneda *f* de curso legal. ● *vt* ofrecer, presentar. ~**ly** *adv* tiernamente

tendon /'tendən/ *n* tendón *m*

tennis /'tenɪs/ *n* tenis *m*

tenor /'tenə(r)/ *n* tenor *m*

tens|e /tens/ *adj* (**-er**, **-est**) (*taut*) tenso, tirante; (person) tenso. ● *n* (*Gram*) tiempo *m*. ~**ion** /'tenʃn/ *n* tensión *f*; (*between two parties*) conflicto *m*

tent /tent/ *n* tienda *f* (de campaña), carpa *f* (*LAm*)

tentacle /'tentəkl/ *n* tentáculo *m*

tentative /'tentətɪv/ *adj* (plan) provisional; (offer) tentativo; (person) indeciso

tenterhooks /'tentəhʊks/ *npl*. **be on** ~ estar en ascuas

tenth /tenθ/ *adj & n* décimo (*m*)

tenuous /'tenjʊəs/ *adj* (claim) poco fundado; (link) indirecto

tenure /'tenjʊə(r)/ *n* tenencia *f*; (*period of office*) ejercicio *m*

tepid /'tepɪd/ *adj* tibio

term /tɜ:m/ *n* (*of time*) período *m*; (*Schol*) trimestre *m*; (*word etc*) término *m*. ~**s** *npl* condiciones *fpl*; (*Com*) precio *m*. **on good**/**bad** ~**s** en buenas/malas relaciones. ● *vt* calificar de

termin|al /'tɜ:mɪnl/ *adj* terminal. ● *n* (*transport*) terminal *f*; (*Comp, Elec*) terminal *m*. ~**ate** /-eɪt/ *vt* poner fin a; poner término a (contract); (*Amer, fire*) despedir. ● *vi* terminarse. ~**ology** /-'nɒlədʒɪ/ *n* terminología *f*

terrace /'terəs/ *n* terraza *f*; (*houses*) hilera *f* de casas

terrain /tə'reɪn/ *n* terreno *m*

terrestrial /tɪ'restrɪəl/ *adj* terrestre

terribl|e /'terəbl/ *adj* espantoso. **~y** *adv* terriblemente

terrif|ic /tə'rɪfɪk/ *adj* (*fam, excellent*) estupendo; (*fam, huge*) enorme. **~ied** /'terɪfaɪd/ *adj* aterrorizado. **~y** /'terɪfaɪ/ *vt* aterrorizar. **~ying** *adj* aterrador

territor|ial /terɪ'tɔ:rɪəl/ *adj* territorial. **~y** /'terɪtrɪ/ *n* territorio *m*

terror /'terə(r)/ *n* terror *m*. **~ism** *n* terrorismo *m*. **~ist** *n* terrorista *m & f*. **~ize** *vt* aterrorizar

terse /tɜ:s/ *adj* seco, lacónico

test /test/ *n* (*of machine, drug*) prueba *f*; (*exam*) prueba *f*, test *m*; (*of blood*) análisis *m*; (*for eyes, hearing*) examen *m*. ● *vt* probar, poner a prueba (product); hacerle una prueba a (student); evaluar (knowledge); examinar (sight)

testament /'testəmənt/ *n* (*will*) testamento *m*. **Old/New T~** Antiguo/Nuevo Testamento

testicle /'testɪkl/ *n* testículo *m*

testify /'testɪfaɪ/ *vt* atestiguar. ● *vi* declarar

testimon|ial /testɪ'məʊnɪəl/ *n* recomendación *f*. **~y** /'testɪmənɪ/ *n* testimonio *m*

test: ~ match *n* partido *m* internacional. **~ tube** *n* tubo *m* de ensayo, probeta *f*

t

tether /'teðə(r)/ *vt* atar. ● *n*. **be at the end of one's ~** no poder más

text /tekst/ *n* texto *m*. ● *vt* mandar un mensaje a. **~book** *n* libro *m* de texto

textile /'tekstaɪl/ *adj & n* textil (*m*)

texture /'tekstʃə(r)/ *n* textura *f*

Thames /temz/ *n* Támesis *m*

than /ðæn, ðən/ *conj* que; (*with quantity*) de

thank /θæŋk/ *vt* darle las gracias a, agradecer. **~ you** gracias. **~ful** *adj* agradecido. **~fully** *adv* (*happily*) gracias a Dios. **~less** *adj* ingrato. **~s** *npl* agradecimiento *m*. **~s!** 🅘 ¡gracias!. **~s to** gracias a

Thanksgiving (Day) /θæŋks 'gɪvɪŋ/ *n* (*in US*) el día de Acción de Gracias

that /ðæt, ðət/ *adj* (*pl* **those**) ese, aquel, esa, aquella. ● *pron* (*pl* **those**) ése, aquél, ésa, aquélla. **~ is** es decir. **~'s not true** eso no es cierto. **~'s why** por eso. **is ~ you?** ¿eres tú? **like ~** así. ● *adv* tan. ● *rel pron* que; (*with prep*) el que, la que, el cual, la cual. ● *conj* que

thatched /θætʃt/ *adj* (roof) de paja; (cottage) con techo de paja

thaw /θɔ:/ *vt* descongelar. ● *vi* descongelarse; (snow) derretirse. ● *n* deshielo *m*

the *definite article*

···➤ el (*m*), la (*f*), los (*mpl*), las (*fpl*). **~ building** el edificio. **~ windows** las ventanas

! Feminine singular nouns beginning with a stressed or accented *a* or *ha* take the article *el* instead of *la*, e.g. **~ soul** *el alma;* **~ axe** *el hacha;* **~ eagle** *el águila*

Note that when *el* follows the prepositions *de* and *a*, it combines to form *del* and *al*, e.g. **of ~ group** *del grupo*. **I went to ~ bank** *fui al banco*

···➤ (*before an ordinal number in*

names, titles) *not translated.* **Henry ~ Eighth** Enrique Octavo. **Elizabeth ~ Second** Isabel Segunda
····▸(*in abstractions*) lo. **~ impossible** lo imposible

theatr|e /ˈθɪətə(r)/ *n* teatro *m*; (*Amer, movie theater*) cine *m*. **~ical** /-ˈætrɪkl/ *adj* teatral

theft /θeft/ *n* hurto *m*

their /ðeə(r)/ *adj* su, sus *pl*. **~s** /ðeəz/ *poss pron* (el) suyo *m*, (la) suya *f*, (los) suyos *mpl*, (las) suyas *fpl*

them /ðem, ðəm/ *pron* (*accusative*) los *m*, las *f*; (*dative*) les; (*after prep*) ellos *m*, ellas *f*

theme /θi:m/ *n* tema *m*. **~ park** *n* parque *m* temático. **~ song** *n* motivo *m* principal

themselves /ðəmˈselvz/ *pron* ellos mismos *m*, ellas mismas *f*; (*reflexive*) se; (*after prep*) sí mismos *m*, sí mismas *f*

then /ðen/ *adv* entonces; (*next*) luego, después. **by ~** para entonces. **now and ~** de vez en cuando. **since ~** desde entonces. ● *adj* entonces

theology /θɪˈɒlədʒɪ/ *n* teología *f*

theor|etical /θɪəˈretɪkl/ *adj* teórico. **~y** /ˈθɪərɪ/ *n* teoría *f*

therap|eutic /θerəˈpju:tɪk/ *adj* terapéutico. **~ist** /ˈθerəpɪst/ *n* terapeuta *m & f*. **~y** /θerəpɪ/ *n* terapia *f*

there /ðeə(r)/ *adv* ahí; (*further away*) allí, ahí; (*less precise, further*) allá. **~ is, ~ are** hay. **~ it is** ahí está. **down ~** ahí abajo. **up ~** ahí arriba. ● *int*. **~! that's the last box** ¡listo! ésa es la última caja. **~, ~, don't cry!** vamos, no llores. **~abouts** *adv* por ahí. **~fore** /-fɔ:(r)/ *adv* por lo tanto.

thermometer /θəˈmɒmɪtə(r)/ *n* termómetro *m*

Thermos /ˈθɜ:məs/ *n* (®) termo *m*

thermostat /ˈθɜ:məstæt/ *n* termostato *m*

thesaurus /θɪˈsɔ:rəs/ *n* (*pl* **-ri**/-raɪ/) diccionario *m* de sinónimos

these /ði:z/ *adj* estos, estas. ● *pron* éstos, éstas

thesis /ˈθi:sɪs/ *n* (*pl* **theses**/-si:z/) tesis *f*

they /ðeɪ/ *pron* ellos *m*, ellas *f*. **~ say that** dicen *or* se dice que

they'd /ðeɪ(ə)d/ = **they had, they would**

they'll /ðeɪl/ = **they will**

they're /ðeɪə(r)/ = **they are**

they've /ðeɪv/ = **they have**

thick /θɪk/ *adj* (**-er, -est**) (layer, sweater) grueso, gordo; (sauce) espeso; (fog, smoke) espeso, denso; (fur) tupido; (*fam, stupid*) burro. ● *adv* espesamente, densamente. ● *n*. **in the ~ of** en medio de. **~en** *vt* espesar. ● *vi* espesarse. **~et** /-ɪt/ *n* matorral *m*. **~ness** *n* (*of fabric*) grosor *m*; (*of paper, wood, wall*) espesor *m*

thief /θi:f/ *n* (*pl* **thieves** /θi:vz/) ladrón *m*

thigh /θaɪ/ *n* muslo *m*

thimble /ˈθɪmbl/ *n* dedal *m*

thin /θɪn/ *adj* (**thinner, thinnest**) (person) delgado, flaco; (layer, slice) fino; (hair) ralo

thing /θɪŋ/ *n* cosa *f*. **it's a good ~ (that)...** menos mal que.... **just the ~** exactamente lo que se necesita. **poor ~!** ¡pobrecito!

think /θɪŋk/ *vt* (*pt* **thought**) pensar, creer. ● *vi* pensar (**about** en); (*carefully*) reflexionar; (*imagine*) imaginarse. **I ~ so** creo que sí. **~ of s.o.** pensar en uno. **I hadn't**

thought of that eso no se me ha ocurrido. ~ **over** *vt* pensar bien. ~ **up** *vt* idear, inventar. ~**er** *n* pensador *m*. ~**-tank** *n* gabinete *m* estratégico

third /θɜ:d/ *adj* tercero, (*before masculine singular noun*) tercer. ● *n* tercio *m*, tercera parte *f*. ~ **(gear)** *n* (*Auto*) tercera *f*. ~**-rate** *adj* muy inferior. **T~ World** *n* Tercer Mundo *m*

thirst /θɜ:st/ *n* sed *f*. ~**y** *adj* sediento. **be** ~**y** tener sed

thirt|een /θɜ:'ti:n/ *adj* & *n* trece (*m*). ~**teenth** *adj* decimotercero. ● *n* treceavo *m* ~**ieth** /'θɜ:tɪəθ/ *adj* trigésimo. ● *n* treintavo *m*. ~**y** /'θɜ:tɪ/ *adj* & *n* treinta (*m*)

this /ðɪs/ *adj* (*pl* **these**) este, esta. ~ **one** éste, ésta. ● *pron* (*pl* **these**) éste, ésta, esto. **like** ~ así

thistle /'θɪsl/ *n* cardo *m*

thong /θɒŋ/ *n* correa *f*; (*Amer, sandal*) chancla *f*

thorn /θɔ:n/ *n* espina *f*. ~**y** *adj* espinoso

thorough /'θʌrə/ *adj* (investigation) riguroso; (cleaning etc) a fondo; (person) concienzudo. ~**bred** /-bred/ *adj* de pura sangre. ~**fare** *n* vía *f* pública; (*street*) calle *f*. **no** ~**fare** prohibido el paso. ~**ly** *adv* (clean) a fondo; (examine) minuciosamente; (*completely*) perfectamente

those /ðəʊz/ *adj* esos, esas, aquellos, aquellas. ● *pron* ésos, ésas, aquéllos, aquéllas

though /ðəʊ/ *conj* aunque. ● *adv* sin embargo. **as** ~ como si

thought /θɔ:t/ *see* THINK. ● *n* pensamiento *m*; (*idea*) idea *f*. ~**ful** *adj* pensativo; (*considerate*) atento. ~**fully** *adv* pensativamente; (*considerately*) atentamente. ~**less** *adj* desconsiderado

thousand /'θaʊznd/ *adj* & *n* mil (*m*). ~**th** *adj* & *n* milésimo (*m*)

thrash /θræʃ/ *vt* azotar; (*defeat*) derrotar

thread /θred/ *n* hilo *m*; (*of screw*) rosca *f*. ● *vt* enhebrar (needle); ensartar (beads). ~**bare** *adj* gastado, raído

threat /θret/ *n* amenaza *f*. ~**en** *vt/i* amenazar. ~**ening** *adj* amenazador

three /θri:/ *adj* & *n* tres (*m*). ~**fold** *adj* triple. ● *adv* tres veces

threshold /'θreʃhəʊld/ *n* umbral *m*

threw /θru:/ *see* THROW

thrift /θrɪft/ *n* economía *f*, ahorro *m*. ~**y** *adj* frugal

thrill /θrɪl/ *n* emoción *f*. ● *vt* emocionar. ~**ed** *adj* contentísimo (**with** con). ~**er** *n* (*book*) libro *m* de suspense *or* (*LAm*) suspenso; (*film*) película *f* de suspense *or* (*LAm*) suspenso. ~**ing** *adj* emocionante

thriv|e /θraɪv/ *vi* prosperar. ~**ing** *adj* próspero

throat /θrəʊt/ *n* garganta *f*

throb /θrɒb/ *vi* (*pt* **throbbed**) palpitar; (*with pain*) dar punzadas; (engine) vibrar. ~**bing** *adj* (pain) punzante

throes /θrəʊz/ *npl*. **be in one's death** ~ estar agonizando

throne /θrəʊn/ *n* trono *m*

throng /θrɒŋ/ *n* multitud *f*

throttle /'θrɒtl/ *n* (*Auto*) acelerador *m* (*que se acciona con la mano*). ● *vt* estrangular

through /θru:/ *prep* por, a través de; (*during*) durante; (*by means of*) a través de; (*Amer, until and including*) **Monday** ~ **Friday** de lunes a

t

viernes. ● *adv* de parte a parte, de un lado a otro; (*entirely*) completamente; (*to the end*) hasta el final. **be ~** (*finished*) haber terminado. ● *adj* (train etc) directo. **no ~ road** calle sin salida. **~out** /-ˈaʊt/ *prep* por todo; (*time*) durante todo. **~out his career** a lo largo de su carrera

throve /θrəʊv/ *see* THRIVE

throw /θrəʊ/ *vt* (*pt* **threw**, *pp* **thrown**) tirar, aventar (*Mex*); lanzar (grenade, javelin); (*disconcert*) desconcertar; [!] hacer, dar (party). ● *n* (*of ball*) tiro *m*; (*of dice*) tirada *f*. □ **~ away** *vt* tirar. □ **~ up** *vi* (*vomit*) vomitar.

thrush /θrʌʃ/ *n* tordo *m*

thrust /θrʌst/ *vt* (*pt* **thrust**) empujar; (*push in*) clavar. ● *n* empujón *m*; (*of sword*) estocada *f*

thud /θʌd/ *n* ruido *m* sordo

thug /θʌg/ *n* matón *m*

thumb /θʌm/ *n* pulgar *m*. ● *vt*. **~ a lift** ir a dedo. **~tack** *n* (*Amer*) chincheta *f*, tachuela *f*, chinche *f* (*Mex*)

thump /θʌmp/ *vt* golpear. ● *vi* (heart) latir fuertemente. ● *n* golpazo *m*

thunder /ˈθʌndə(r)/ *n* truenos *mpl*, (*of traffic*) estruendo *m*. ● *vi* tronar. **~bolt** *n* rayo *m*. **~storm** *n* tormenta *f* eléctrica. **~y** *adj* con truenos

Thursday /ˈθɜːzdeɪ/ *n* jueves *m*

thus /ðʌs/ *adv* así

thwart /θwɔːt/ *vt* frustrar

tic /tɪk/ *n* tic *m*

tick /tɪk/ *n* (*sound*) tic *m*; (*insect*) garrapata *f*, (*mark*) marca *f*, visto *m*, palomita *f* (*Mex*); (*fam, instant*) momentito *m*. ● *vi* hacer tictac. ● *vt*. **~ (off)** marcar

ticket /ˈtɪkɪt/ *n* (*for bus, train*) billete *m*, boleto *m* (*LAm*); (*for plane*) pasaje *m*, billete *m*; (*for theatre, museum*) entrada *f*; (*for baggage, coat*) ticket *m*; (*fine*) multa *f*. **~ collector** *n* revisor *m*. **~ office** *n* (*transport*) mostrador *m* de venta de billetes *or* (*LAm*) boletos; (*in theatre*) taquilla *f*, boletería *f* (*LAm*)

tickl|e /ˈtɪkl/ *vt* hacerle cosquillas a. ● *n* cosquilleo *m*. **~ish** /ˈtɪklɪʃ/ *adj*. **be ~ish** tener cosquillas

tidal wave /ˈtaɪdl/ *n* maremoto *m*

tide /taɪd/ *n* marea *f*. **high/low ~** marea alta/baja. □ **~ over** *vt* ayudar a salir de un apuro

tid|ily /ˈtaɪdɪlɪ/ *adv* ordenadamente. **~iness** *n* orden *m*. **~y** *adj* (**-ier**, **-iest**) ordenado. ● *vt/i* **~y (up)** ordenar, arreglar

tie /taɪ/ *vt* (*pres p* **tying**) atar, amarrar (*LAm*); hacer (knot). ● *vi* (*Sport*) empatar. ● *n* (*constraint*) atadura *f*; (*bond*) lazo *m*; (*necktie*) corbata *f*; (*Sport*) empate *m*. **~ in with** *vt* concordar con. □ **~ up** *vt* atar. **be ~d up** (*busy*) estar ocupado

tier /tɪə(r)/ *n* hilera *f* superpuesta; (*in stadium etc*) grada *f*; (*of cake*) piso *m*

tiger /ˈtaɪgə(r)/ *n* tigre *m*

tight /taɪt/ *adj* (**-er**, **-est**) (clothes) ajustado, ceñido; (*taut*) tieso; (control) estricto; (knot, nut) apretado; (*fam, drunk*) borracho. **~en** *vt* apretar. □ **~en up** *vt* hacer más estricto. **~-fisted** /-ˈfɪstɪd/ *adj* tacaño. **~ly** *adv* bien, fuerte; (fastened) fuertemente. **~rope** *n* cuerda *f* floja. **~s** *npl* (*for ballet etc*) leotardo(s) *m(pl)*; (*pantyhose*) medias *fpl*

tile /taɪl/ *n* (*decorative*) azulejo *m*; (*on roof*) teja *f*; (*on floor*) baldosa *f*

● *vt* azulejar; tejar (roof); embaldosar (floor)

till /tɪl/ *prep* hasta. ● *conj* hasta que. ● *n* caja *f*. ● *vt* cultivar

tilt /tɪlt/ *vt* inclinar. ● *vi* inclinarse. ● *n* inclinación *f*

timber /ˈtɪmbə(r)/ *n* madera *f* (*para construcción*)

time /taɪm/ *n* tiempo *m*; (*moment*) momento *m*; (*occasion*) ocasión *f*; (*by clock*) hora *f*; (*epoch*) época *f*; (*rhythm*) compás *m*. **at ~s** a veces. **for the ~ being** por el momento. **from ~ to ~** de vez en cuando. **have a good ~** divertirse, pasarlo bien. **in a year's ~** dentro de un año. **in no ~** en un abrir y cerrar de ojos. **in ~** a tiempo; (*eventually*) con el tiempo. **arrive on ~** llegar a tiempo. **it's ~ we left** es hora de irnos. ● *vt* elegir el momento; cronometrar (race). **~ bomb** *n* bomba *f* de tiempo. **~ly** *adj* oportuno. **~r** *n* cronómetro *m*; (*Culin*) avisador *m*; (*with sand*) reloj *m* de arena; (*Elec*) interruptor *m* de reloj. **~s** /ˈtaɪmz/ *prep.* **2 ~s 4 is 8** 2 (multiplicado) por 4 son 8. **~table** *n* horario *m*

timid /ˈtɪmɪd/ *adj* tímido; (*fearful*) miedoso

tin /tɪn/ *n* estaño *m*; (*container*) lata *f*. **~ foil** *n* papel *m* de estaño

tinge /tɪndʒ/ *vt*. **be ~d with sth** estar matizado de algo. ● *n* matiz *m*

tingle /ˈtɪŋgl/ *vi* sentir un hormigueo

tinker /ˈtɪŋkə(r)/ *vi*. **~ with** juguetear con

tinkle /ˈtɪŋkl/ *vi* tintinear

tinned /tɪnd/ *adj* en lata, enlatado

tin opener *n* abrelatas *m*

tint /tɪnt/ *n* matiz *m*

tiny /ˈtaɪnɪ/ *adj* (**-ier**, **-iest**) minúsculo, diminuto

tip /tɪp/ *n* punta *f*. ● *vt* (*pt* **tipped**) (*tilt*) inclinar; (*overturn*) volcar; (*pour*) verter; (*give gratuity to*) darle (una) propina a. □ **~ off** *vt* avisar. □ **~ out** *vt* verter. □ **~ over** *vi* caerse. *n* propina *f*; (*advice*) consejo *m* (práctico); (*for rubbish*) vertedero *m*. **~ped** *adj* (cigarette) con filtro

tipsy /ˈtɪpsɪ/ *adj* achispado

tiptoe /ˈtɪptəʊ/ *n*. **on ~** de puntillas

tiptop /ˈtɪptɒp/ *adj* [I] de primera. **in ~ condition** en excelente estado

tire /ˈtaɪə(r)/ *n* (*Amer*) see **TYRE**. ● *vt* cansar. ● *vi* cansarse. **~d** /ˈtaɪəd/ *adj* cansado. **get ~d** cansarse. **~d of** harto de. **~d out** agotado. **~less** *adj* incansable; (efforts) inagotable. **~some** /-səm/ *adj* (person) pesado; (task) tedioso

tiring /ˈtaɪərɪŋ/ *adj* cansado, cansador (*LAm*)

tissue /ˈtɪʃu:/ *n* (*of bones, plants*) tejido *m*; (*paper handkerchief*) pañuelo *m* de papel. **~ paper** *n* papel *m* de seda

tit /tɪt/ *n* (*bird*) paro *m*; ([x], *breast*) teta *f*

titbit /ˈtɪtbɪt/ *n* exquisitez *f*

tit for tat *n*: **it was ~** fue ojo por ojo, diente por diente

title /ˈtaɪtl/ *n* título *m*

to /tu:, tə/ *prep* a; (*towards*) hacia; (*in order to*) para; (*as far as*) hasta; (*of*) de. **give it ~ me** dámelo. **what did you say ~ him?** ¿qué le dijiste?; **I don't want ~** no quiero. **it's twenty ~ seven** (*by clock*) son las siete menos veinte, son veinte para las siete (*LAm*). ● *adv*. **pull ~**

cerrar. ~ **and fro** *adv* de un lado a otro

toad /təʊd/ *n* sapo *m*. **~stool** *n* hongo *m* (*no comestible*)

toast /təʊst/ *n* pan *m* tostado, tostadas *fpl*; (*drink*) brindis *m*. **a piece of ~** una tostada, un pan tostado (*Mex*). **drink a ~ to** brindar por. • *vt* (*Culin*) tostar; (*drink to*) brindar por. **~er** *n* tostadora *f* (eléctrica), tostador *m*

tobacco /təˈbækəʊ/ *n* tabaco *m*. **~nist** /-ənɪst/ *n* estanquero *m*

toboggan /təˈbɒgən/ *n* tobogán *m*

today /təˈdeɪ/ *n & adv* hoy (*m*)

toddler /ˈtɒdlə(r)/ *n* niño *m* pequeño (entre un año y dos años y medio de edad)

toe /təʊ/ *n* dedo *m* (del pie); (*of shoe*) punta *f*. **big ~** dedo *m* gordo (del pie). **on one's ~s** (*fig*) alerta. • *vt*. **~ the line** acatar la disciplina

TOEFL - Test of English as a Foreign Language
Un examen que, a la hora de solicitar el ingreso a una universidad americana, evalúa el dominio del inglés de aquellos estudiantes cuya lengua materna no es este idioma.

toffee /ˈtɒfɪ/ *n* toffee *m* (golosina hecha con azúcar y mantequilla)

together /təˈgeðə(r)/ *adv* juntos; (*at same time*) a la vez. **~ with** junto con

toil /tɔɪl/ *vi* afanarse. • *n* trabajo *m* duro

toilet /ˈtɔɪlɪt/ *n* servicio *m*, baño *m* (*LAm*). **~ paper** *n* papel *m* higiénico. **~ries** /ˈtɔɪlɪtrɪz/ *npl* artículos *mpl* de tocador. **~ roll** *n* rollo *m* de papel higiénico

token /ˈtəʊkən/ *n* muestra *f*; (*voucher*) vale *m*; (*coin*) ficha *f*. • *adj* simbólico

told /təʊld/ *see* TELL

tolera|ble /ˈtɒlərəbl/ *adj* tolerable; (*not bad*) pasable. **~nce** /ˈtɒlərəns/ *n* tolerancia *f*. **~nt** *adj* tolerante. **~te** /-reɪt/ *vt* tolerar. **~tion** /-ˈreɪʃən/ *n* tolerancia *f*

toll /təʊl/ *n* (*on road*) peaje *m*, cuota *f* (*Mex*). **death ~** número *m* de muertos. **~ call** *n* (*Amer*) llamada *f* interurbana, conferencia *f*. • *vi* doblar, tocar a muerto

tomato /təˈmɑːtəʊ/ *n* (*pl* **-oes**) tomate *m*, jitomate *m* (*Mex*)

tomb /tuːm/ *n* tumba *f*, sepulcro *m*. **~stone** *n* lápida *f*

tomorrow /təˈmɒrəʊ/ *n & adv* mañana (*f*). **see you ~!** ¡hasta mañana!

ton /tʌn/ *n* tonelada *f* (= *1,016kg*). **~s of** [!] montones de. **metric ~** tonelada *f* (métrica) (= *1,000kg*)

tone /təʊn/ *n* tono *m*. □ **~ down** *vt* atenuar; moderar (language). **~-deaf** *adj* que no tiene oído (musical)

tongs /tɒŋz/ *npl* tenacillas *fpl*

tongue /tʌŋ/ *n* lengua *f*. **say sth ~ in cheek** decir algo medio burlándose. **~-tied** *adj* cohibido. **~-twister** *n* trabalenguas *m*

tonic /ˈtɒnɪk/ *adj* tónico. • *n* (*Med, fig*) tónico *m*. **~ (water)** *n* tónica *f*

tonight /təˈnaɪt/ *adv & n* esta noche (*f*); (*evening*) esta tarde (*f*)

tonne /tʌn/ *n* tonelada *f* (métrica)

tonsil /ˈtɒnsl/ *n* amígdala *f*. **~litis** /-ˈlaɪtɪs/ *n* amigdalitis *f*

too /tuː/ *adv* (*excessively*) demasiado; (*also*) también. **I'm not ~ sure** no estoy muy seguro. **~ many** demasiados. **~ much**

demasiado

took /tʊk/ *see* **TAKE**

tool /tu:l/ *n* herramienta *f*

tooth /tu:θ/ *n* (*pl* **teeth**) diente *m*; (*molar*) muela *f*. **~ache** *n* dolor *m* de muelas. **~brush** *n* cepillo *m* de dientes. **~paste** *n* pasta *f* dentífrica, pasta *f* de dientes. **~pick** *n* palillo *m* (de dientes)

top /tɒp/ *n* parte *f* superior, parte *f* de arriba; (*of mountain*) cima *f*; (*of tree*) copa *f*; (*of page*) parte *f* superior; (*lid, of bottle*) tapa *f*; (*of pen*) capuchón *m*; (*spinning* ~) trompo *m*, peonza *f*. **be ~ of the class** ser el primero de la clase. **from ~ to bottom** de arriba abajo. **on ~ of** encima de; (*besides*) además de. ● *adj* más alto; (shelf) superior; (speed) máximo; (*in rank*) superior; (*leading*) más destacado. ● *vt* (*pt* **topped**) cubrir; (*exceed*) exceder. **~ floor** *n* último piso *m*. □ **~ up** *vt* llenar. **~ hat** *n* chistera *f*. **~-heavy** /-'hevɪ/ *adj* inestable (por ser más pesado en su parte superior)

topic /'tɒpɪk/ *n* tema *m*. **~al** *adj* de actualidad

topless /tɒples/ *adj* topless

topple /'tɒpl/ *vi* (*Pol*) derribar; (*overturn*) volcar. ● *vi* caerse

top secret /tɒp'si:krɪt/ *adj* secreto, reservado

t **torch** /tɔ:tʃ/ *n* linterna *f*; (*flaming*) antorcha *f*

tore /tɔ:(r)/ *see* **TEAR**[1]

torment /'tɔ:ment/ *n* tormento *m*. ● /tɔ:'ment/ *vt* atormentar

torn /tɔ:n/ *see* **TEAR**[1]

tornado /tɔ:'neɪdəʊ/ *n* (*pl* **-oes**) tornado *m*

torpedo /tɔ:'pi:dəʊ/ *n* (*pl* **-oes**) torpedo *m*. ● *vt* torpedear

torrent /'tɒrənt/ *n* torrente *m*. **~ial** /tə'renʃl/ *adj* torrencial

torrid /'tɒrɪd/ *adj* tórrido; (affair) apasionado

tortoise /'tɔ:təs/ *n* tortuga *f*. **~shell** *n* carey *m*

tortuous /'tɔ:tjʊəs/ *adj* tortuoso

torture /'tɔ:tʃə(r)/ *n* tortura *f*. ● *vt* torturar

Tory /'tɔ:rɪ/ *adj* & *n* tory *m* & *f*

toss /tɒs/ *vt* tirar, lanzar (ball); (*shake*) sacudir. ● *vi*. **~ and turn** (*in bed*) dar vueltas

tot /tɒt/ *n* pequeño *m*; (*fam, of liquor*) trago *m*. ● *vt* (*pt* **totted**). **~ up** ⓘ sumar

total /'təʊtl/ *adj* & *n* total (*m*). ● *vt* (*pt* **totalled**) ascender a un total de; (*add up*) totalizar. **~itarian** /təʊtælɪ'teərɪən/ *adj* totalitario. **~ly** *adv* totalmente

totter /'tɒtə(r)/ *vi* tambalearse

touch /tʌtʃ/ *vt* tocar; (*move*) conmover; (*concern*) afectar. ● *vi* tocar; (wires) tocarse. ● *n* toque *m*; (*sense*) tacto *m*; (*contact*) contacto *m*. **be/get/stay in ~ with** estar/ponerse/mantenerse en contacto con. □ **~ down** *vi* (aircraft) aterrizar. □ **~ up** *vt* retocar. **~ing** *adj* enternecedor. **~y** *adj* quisquilloso

tough /tʌf/ *adj* (**-er, -est**) duro; (*strong*) fuerte, resistente; (*difficult*) difícil; (*severe*) severo. **~en**. **~ (up)** *vt* endurecer; hacer más fuerte (person)

tour /tʊə(r)/ *n* viaje *m*; (*visit*) visita *f*; (*excursion*) excursión *f*; (*by team etc*) gira *f*. **be on ~** estar de gira. ● *vt* recorrer; (*visit*) visitar. **~ guide** *n* guía de turismo

touris|m /'tʊərɪzəm/ *n* turismo *m*. **~t** /'tʊərɪst/ *n* turista *m* & *f*. ● *adj* turístico. **~t office** *n* oficina *f* de turismo

tournament /'tɔ:nəmənt/ *n* torneo *m*

tousle /'taʊzl/ *vt* despeinar

tout /taʊt/ *vi.* ~ **(for)** solicitar

tow /təʊ/ *vt* remolcar. ● *n* remolque *m*

toward(s) /tə'wɔ:d(z)/ *prep* hacia. **his attitude ~ her** su actitud para con ella

towel /'taʊəl/ *n* toalla *f*

tower /'taʊə(r)/ *n* torre *f.* ● *vi.* ~ **above** (building) descollar sobre; (person) destacar sobre. ~ **block** *n* edificio *m or* bloque *m* de apartamentos. **~ing** *adj* altísimo; (rage) violento

town /taʊn/ *n* ciudad *f*; (*smaller*) pueblo *m*. **go to ~** [!] no escatimar dinero. ~ **hall** *n* ayuntamiento *m*

toxic /'tɒksɪk/ *adj* tóxico

toy /tɔɪ/ *n* juguete *m*. □ ~ **with** *vt* juguetear con (object); darle vueltas a (idea). **~shop** *n* juguetería *f*

trac|e /treɪs/ *n* señal *f*, rastro *m*. ● *vt* trazar; (*draw*) dibujar; (*with tracing paper*) calcar; (*track down*) localizar. **~ing paper** *n* papel *m* de calcar

track /træk/ *n* pista *f*, huellas *fpl*; (*path*) sendero *m*; (*Sport*) pista *f*. **the ~(s)** la vía férrea; (*Rail*) vía *f*. **keep ~ of** seguirle la pista a (person). ● *vt* seguirle la pista a. □ ~ **down** *vt* localizar. ~ **suit** *n* equipo *m* (de deportes) chándal *m*

tract /trækt/ *n* (*land*) extensión *f*; (*pamphlet*) tratado *m* breve

traction /'trækʃn/ *n* tracción *f*

tractor /'træktə(r)/ *n* tractor *m*

trade /treɪd/ *n* comercio *m*; (*occupation*) oficio *m*; (*exchange*) cambio *m*; (*industry*) industria *f.* ● *vt.* ~ **sth for sth** cambiar algo por algo. ● *vi* comerciar. □ ~ **in** *vt* (*give in part-exchange*) entregar como parte del pago. ~ **mark** *n* marca *f* (de fábrica). **~r** *n* comerciante *m & f*. ~ **union** *n* sindicato *m*

tradition /trə'dɪʃn/ *n* tradición *f*. **~al** *adj* tradicional

traffic /'træfɪk/ *n* tráfico *m*. ● *vi* (*pt* **trafficked**) comerciar (**in** en). ~ **circle** *n* (*Amer*) glorieta *f*, rotonda *f*. ~ **island** *n* isla *f* peatonal. ~ **jam** *n* embotellamiento *m*, atasco *m*. ~ **lights** *npl* semáforo *m*. ~ **warden** *n* guardia *m*, controlador *m* de tráfico

trag|edy /'trædʒɪdɪ/ *n* tragedia *f*. **~ic** /'trædʒɪk/ *adj* trágico

trail /treɪl/ *vi* arrastrarse; (*lag*) rezagarse. ● *vt* (*track*) seguir la pista de. ● *n* (*left by animal, person*) huellas *fpl*; (*path*) sendero *m*. **be on the ~ of s.o./sth** seguir la pista de uno/algo **~er** *n* remolque *m*; (*Amer, caravan*) caravana *f*, rulot *m*; (*film*) avance *m*

train /treɪn/ *n* (*Rail*) tren *m*; (*of events*) serie *f*; (*of dress*) cola *f*. ● *vt* capacitar (employee); adiestrar (soldier); (*Sport*) entrenar; educar (voice); guiar (plant); amaestrar (animal). ● *vi* estudiar; (*Sport*) entrenarse. **~ed** *adj* (*skilled*) cualificado, calificado; (doctor) diplomado. **~ee** /treɪ'ni:/ *n* aprendiz *m*; (*Amer, Mil*) recluta *m & f*. **~er** *n* (*Sport*) entrenador *m*; (*of animals*) amaestrador *m*. **~ers** *mpl* zapatillas *fpl* de deporte. **~ing** *n* capacitación *f*; (*Sport*) entrenamiento *m*

trait /treɪ(t)/ *n* rasgo *m*

traitor /'treɪtə(r)/ *n* traidor *m*

tram /træm/ *n* tranvía *m*

tramp /træmp/ *vi.* ~ **(along)** caminar pesadamente. ● *n* vagabundo *m*

trample /'træmpl/ *vt* pisotear. ● *vi.* ~ **on** pisotear
trampoline /'træmpəli:n/ *n* trampolín *m*
trance /trɑ:ns/ *n* trance *m*
tranquil /'træŋkwɪl/ *adj* tranquilo. ~**lity** /-'kwɪlətɪ/ *n* tranquilidad *f*; (*of person*) serenidad *f*. ~**lize** /'træŋkwɪlaɪz/ *vt* sedar, dar un sedante a. ~**lizer** *n* sedante *m*, tranquilizante *m*
transaction /træn'zækʃən/ *n* transacción *f*, operación *f*
transatlantic /trænzət'læntɪk/ *adj* transatlántico
transcend /træn'send/ *vt* (*go beyond*) exceder
transcript /'trænskrɪpt/ *n* transcripción *f*
transfer /træns'fɜ:(r)/ *vt* (*pt* **transferred**) trasladar; traspasar (player); transferir (funds, property); pasar (call). ● *vi* trasladarse. ● /'trænsfɜ:(r)/ *n* traslado *m*; (*of player*) traspaso *m*; (*of funds, property*) transferencia *f*; (*paper*) calcomanía *f*
transform /træns'fɔ:m/ *vt* transformar. ~**ation** /-ə'meɪʃn/ *n* transformación *f*. ~**er** *n* transformador *m*
transfusion /træns'fju:ʒn/ *n* transfusión *f*
t
transient /'trænzɪənt/ *adj* pasajero
transistor /træn'zɪstə(r)/ *n* transistor *m*
transit /'trænsɪt/ *n* tránsito *m*. ~**ion** /træn'zɪʒn/ *n* transición *f*. ~**ive** /'trænsɪtɪv/ *adj* transitivo
translat|e /trænz'leɪt/ *vt* traducir. ~**ion** /-ʃn/ *n* traducción *f*. ~**or** *n* traductor *m*
transmission /træns'mɪʃn/ *n* transmisión *f*
transmit /trænz'mɪt/ *vt* (*pt* **transmitted**) transmitir. ~**ter** *n* transmisor *m*
transparen|cy /træns'pærənsɪ/ *n* transparencia *f*; (*Photo*) diapositiva *f*. ~**t** *adj* transparente
transplant /træns'plɑ:nt/ *vt* trasplantar. ● /'trænsplɑ:nt/ *n* trasplante *m*
transport /træn'spɔ:t/ *vt* transportar. ● /'trænspɔ:t/ *n* transporte *m*. ~**ation** /-'teɪʃn/ *n* transporte *m*
trap /træp/ *n* trampa *f*. ● *vt* (*pt* **trapped**) atrapar; (*jam*) atascar; (*cut off*) bloquear. ~**door** *n* trampilla *f*
trapeze /trə'pi:z/ *n* trapecio *m*
trash /træʃ/ *n* basura *f*; (*Amer, worthless people*) escoria *f*. ~ **can** *n* (*Amer*) cubo *m* de la basura, bote *m* de la basura (*Mex*). ~**y** *adj* (souvenir) de porquería; (magazine) malo
travel /'trævl/ *vi* (*pt* **travelled**) viajar; (vehicle) desplazarse. ● *vt* recorrer. ● *n* viajes *mpl*. ~ **agency** *n* agencia *f* de viajes. ~**ler** *n* viajero *m*. ~**ler's cheque** *n* cheque *m* de viaje *or* viajero. ~**ling expenses** *npl* gastos *mpl* de viaje
trawler /'trɔ:lə(r)/ *n* barca *f* pesquera
tray /treɪ/ *n* bandeja *f*
treacher|ous *adj* traidor; (*deceptive*) engañoso. ~**y** *n* traición *f*
treacle /'tri:kl/ *n* melaza *f*
tread /tred/ *vi* (*pt* **trod**, *pp* **trodden**) pisar. ~ **on sth** pisar algo. ~ **carefully** andarse con cuidado. ● *n* (*step*) paso *m*; (*of tyre*) banda *f* de rodamiento
treason /'tri:zn/ *n* traición *f*
treasur|e /'treʒə(r)/ *n* tesoro *m*.

~ed /'treʒəd/ *adj* (possession) preciado. **~er** /'treʒərə(r)/ *n* tesorero *m*. **~y** *n* erario *m*, tesoro *m*. **the T~y** el fisco, la hacienda pública. **Department of the T~y** (*in US*) Departamento *m* del Tesoro

treat /tri:t/ *vt* tratar; (*Med*) tratar. **~ s.o.** (*to meal etc*) invitar a uno. ● *n* placer *m*; (*present*) regalo *m*

treatise /'tri:tɪz/ *n* tratado *m*

treatment /'tri:tmənt/ *n* tratamiento *m*

treaty /'tri:tɪ/ *n* tratado *m*

treble /'trebl/ *adj* triple; (clef) de sol; (voice) de tiple. ● *vt* triplicar. ● *vi* triplicarse. ● *n* tiple *m & f*

tree /tri:/ *n* árbol *m*

trek /trek/ *n* caminata *f*. ● *vi* (*pt* **trekked**) caminar

trellis /'trelɪs/ *n* enrejado *m*

tremble /'trembl/ *vi* temblar

tremendous /trɪ'mendəs/ *adj* formidable; (*fam, huge*) tremendo. **~ly** *adv* tremendamente

tremor /'tremə(r)/ *n* temblor *m*

trench /trentʃ/ *n* zanja *f*; (*Mil*) trinchera *f*

trend /trend/ *n* tendencia *f*; (*fashion*) moda *f*. **~y** *adj* (**-ier, -iest**) ⊡ moderno

trepidation /trepɪ'deɪʃn/ *n* inquietud *f*

trespass /'trespəs/ *vi*. **~ on** entrar sin autorización (en propiedad ajena). **~er** *n* intruso *m*

trial /'traɪəl/ *n* prueba *f*; (*Jurid*) proceso *m*, juicio *m*; (*ordeal*) prueba *f* dura. **by ~ and error** por ensayo y error. **be on ~** estar a prueba; (*Jurid*) estar siendo procesado

triang|le /'traɪæŋgl/ *n* triángulo *m*. **~ular** /-'æŋgjʊlə(r)/ *adj* triangular

trib|al /'traɪbl/ *adj* tribal. **~e** /traɪb/ *n* tribu *f*

tribulation /trɪbjʊ'leɪʃn/ *n* tribulación *f*

tribunal /traɪ'bju:nl/ *n* tribunal *m*

tributary /'trɪbjʊtrɪ/ *n* (*of river*) afluente *m*

tribute /'trɪbju:t/ *n* tributo *m*; (*acknowledgement*) homenaje *m*. **pay ~ to** rendir homenaje a

trick /trɪk/ *n* trampa *f*, ardid *m*; (*joke*) broma *f*; (*feat*) truco *m*; (*in card games*) baza *f*. **play a ~ on** gastar una broma a. ● *vt* engañar. **~ery** *n* engaño *m*

trickle /'trɪkl/ *vi* gotear. **~ in** (*fig*) entrar poco a poco

trickster /'trɪkstə(r)/ *n* estafador *m*

tricky /'trɪkɪ/ *adj* delicado, difícil

tricycle /'traɪsɪkl/ *n* triciclo *m*

tried /traɪd/ *see* **TRY**

trifl|e /'traɪfl/ *n* nimiedad *f*; (*Culin*) postre de bizcocho, jerez, frutas y nata. ● *vi*. □ **~e with** *vt* jugar con. **~ing** *adj* insignificante

trigger /'trɪgə(r)/ *n* (*of gun*) gatillo *m*. ● *vt*. **~ (off)** desencadenar

trim /trɪm/ *adj* (**trimmer, trimmest**) (*slim*) esbelto; (*neat*) elegante. ● *vt* (*pt* **trimmed**) (*cut*) recortar; (*adorn*) adornar. ● *n* (*cut*) recorte *m*. **in ~** en buen estado. **~mings** *npl* recortes *mpl*

trinity /'trɪnɪtɪ/ *n*. **the (Holy) T~** la (Santísima) Trinidad

trinket /'trɪŋkɪt/ *n* chuchería *f*

trio /'tri:əʊ/ *n* (*pl* **-os**) trío *m*

trip /trɪp/ (*pt* **tripped**) *vt* **~ (up)** hacerle una zancadilla a, hacer tropezar ● *vi* tropezar. ● *n* (*journey*) viaje *m*; (*outing*) excursión *f*; (*stumble*) traspié *m*

tripe /traɪp/ *n* callos *mpl*, mon-

t

dongo *m* (*LAm*), pancita *f* (*Mex*); (*fam, nonsense*) paparruchas *fpl*

triple /'trɪpl/ *adj* triple. ● *vt* triplicar. ● *vi* triplicarse. **~t** /'trɪplɪt/ *n* trillizo *m*

triplicate /'trɪplɪkət/ *adj* triplicado. **in ~** por triplicado

tripod /'traɪpɒd/ *n* trípode *m*

trite /traɪt/ *adj* trillado

triumph /'traɪʌmf/ *n* triunfo *m*. ● *vi* triunfar (**over** sobre). **~al** /-'ʌmfl/ *adj* triunfal. **~ant** /-'ʌmfnt/ *adj* (troops) triunfador; (moment) triunfal; (smile) de triunfo

trivial /'trɪvɪəl/ *adj* insignificante; (concerns) trivial. **~ity** /-'æləti/ *n* trivialidad *f*

trod, trodden /trɒd, trɒdn/ *see* **TREAD**

trolley /'trɒlɪ/ *n* (*pl* **-eys**) carretón *m*; (*in supermarket, airport*) carrito *m*; (*for food, drink*) carrito *m*, mesa *f* rodante. **~ car** *n* (*Amer*) tranvía *f*

trombone /trɒm'bəʊn/ *n* trombón *m*

troop /tru:p/ *n* compañía *f*; (*of cavalry*) escuadrón *m*. ● *vi*. **~ in** entrar en tropel. **~ out** salir en tropel. **~er** *n* soldado *m* de caballería; (*Amer, state police officer*) agente *m* & *f*. **~s** *npl* (*Mil*) tropas *fpl*

trophy /'trəʊfɪ/ *n* trofeo *m*

tropic /'trɒpɪk/ *n* trópico *m*. **~al** *adj* tropical. **~s** *npl* trópicos *mpl*

trot /trɒt/ *n* trote *m*. ● *vi* (*pt* **trotted**) trotar

trouble /'trʌbl/ *n* problemas *mpl*; (*awkward situation*) apuro *m*; (*inconvenience*) molestia *f*. **be in ~** estar en apuros. **get into ~** meterse en problemas. **look for ~** buscar camorra. **take the ~ to do sth** molestarse en hacer algo. ● *vt* (*bother*) molestar; (*worry*) preocupar. **~-maker** *n* alborotador *m*. **~some** /-səm/ *adj* problemático. **~ spot** *n* punto *m* conflictivo

trough /trɒf/ *n* (*for drinking*) abrevadero *m*; (*for feeding*) comedero *m*

troupe /tru:p/ *n* compañía *f* teatral

trousers /'traʊzəz/ *npl* pantalón *m*, pantalones *mpl*

trout /traʊt/ *n* (*pl* **trout**) trucha *f*

trowel /'traʊəl/ *n* (*garden*) desplantador *m*; (*for mortar*) paleta *f*

truant /'tru:ənt/ *n*. **play ~** hacer novillos

truce /tru:s/ *n* tregua *f*

truck /trʌk/ *n* camión *m*; (*Rail*) vagón *m*, furgón *m*; (*Amer, vegetables, fruit*) productos *mpl* de la huerta. **~ driver**, **~er** (*Amer*) *n* camionero *m*. **~ing** *n* transporte *m* por carretera

trudge /trʌdʒ/ *vi* andar penosamente

true /tru:/ *adj* (**-er**, **-est**) verdadero; (story, account) verídico; (friend) auténtico, de verdad. **~ to sth/s.o.** fiel a algo/uno. **be ~** ser cierto. **come ~** hacerse realidad

truffle /'trʌfl/ *n* trufa *f*; (*chocolate*) trufa *f* de chocolate

truly /'tru:lɪ/ *adv* verdaderamente; (*sincerely*) sinceramente. **yours ~** (*in letters*) cordiales saludos

trump /trʌmp/ *n* (*Cards*) triunfo *m*; (*fig*) baza *f*

trumpet /'trʌmpɪt/ *n* trompeta *f*. **~er** *n* trompetista *m* & *f*, trompeta *m* & *f*

truncheon /'trʌntʃən/ *n* porra *f*

trunk /trʌŋk/ *n* (*of tree*) tronco *m*; (*box*) baúl *m*; (*of elephant*) trompa *f*; (*Amer, Auto*) maletero *m*, cajuela *f* (*Mex*). **~s** *npl* bañador *m*, traje *m* de baño

truss /trʌs/ *vt.* **truss (up)** *vt* atar

trust /trʌst/ *n* confianza *f*; (*money, property*) fondo *m* de inversiones; (*institution*) fundación *f*. **on ~** a ojos cerrados; (*Com*) al fiado. ● *vi.* **~ in s.o./sth** confiar en uno/algo. ● *vt* confiar en; (*in negative sentences*) fiarse; (*hope*) esperar. **~ed** *adj* leal. **~ee** /trʌ'sti:/ *n* fideicomisario *m*. **~ful** *adj* confiado. **~ing** *adj* confiado. **~worthy**, **~y** *adj* digno de confianza

truth /tru:θ/ *n* (*pl* **-s** /tru:ðz/) verdad *f*; (*of account, story*) veracidad *f*. **~ful** *adj* veraz.

try /traɪ/ *vt* (*pt* **tried**) intentar; probar (food, product); (*be a strain on*) poner a prueba; (*Jurid*) procesar. **~ to do sth** tratar de hacer algo, intentar hacer algo. **~ not to forget** procura no olvidarte. ● *n* tentativa *f*, prueba *f*; (*Rugby*) ensayo *m*. □ **~ on** *vt* probarse (garment). □ **~ out** *vt* probar. **~ing** *adj* duro; (*annoying*) molesto

tsar /zɑ:(r)/ *n* zar *m*

T-shirt /'ti:ʃɜ:t/ *n* camiseta *f*

tub /tʌb/ *n* cuba *f*; (*for washing clothes*) tina *f*; (*bathtub*) bañera *f*; (*for ice cream*) envase *m*, tarrina *f*

tuba /'tju:bə/ *n* tuba *f*

tubby /'tʌbɪ/ *adj* (**-ier**, **-iest**) rechoncho

tube /tju:b/ *n* tubo *m*; (*fam, Rail*) metro *m*; (*Amer fam, television*) tele *f*. **inner ~** *n* cámara *f* de aire

tuberculosis /tju:bɜ:kjʊ'ləʊsɪs/ *n* tuberculosis *f*

tub|ing /'tju:bɪŋ/ *n* tubería *f*. **~ular** /-jʊlə(r)/ *adj* tubular

tuck /tʌk/ *n* (*fold*) jareta *f*. ● *vt* plegar; (*put*) meter. □ **~ in(to)** *vi* (*fam, eat*) ponerse a comer. □ **~ up** *vt* arropar (child)

Tuesday /'tju:zdeɪ/ *n* martes *m*

tuft /tʌft/ *n* (*of hair*) mechón *m*; (*of feathers*) penacho *m*; (*of grass*) mata *f*

tug /tʌg/ *vt* (*pt* **tugged**) tirar de. ● *vi.* **~ at sth** tirar de algo. ● *n* tirón *m*; (*Naut*) remolcador *m*. **~-of-war** *n* juego de tira y afloja

tuition /tju:'ɪʃn/ *n* clases *fpl*

tulip /'tju:lɪp/ *n* tulipán *m*

tumble /'tʌmbl/ *vi* caerse. ● *n* caída *f*. **~down** *adj* en ruinas. **~-drier** *n* secadora *f*. **~r** *n* (*glass*) vaso *m* (*de lados rectos*)

tummy /'tʌmɪ/ *n* ⓘ barriga *f*

tumour /'tju:mə(r)/ *n* tumor *m*

tumult /'tju:mʌlt/ *n* tumulto *m*. **~uous** /-'mʌltjʊəs/ *adj* (applause) apoteósico

tuna /'tju:nə/ *n* (*pl* **tuna**) atún *m*

tune /tju:n/ *n* melodía *f*; (*piece*) tonada *f*. **be in ~** estar afinado. **be out of ~** estar desafinado. ● *vt* afinar, sintonizar (radio, TV); (*Mec*) poner a punto. ● *vi.* **~ in (to)** sintonizar (con). □ **~ up** *vt/i* afinar. **~ful** *adj* melodioso. **~r** *n* afinador *m*; (*Radio*) sintonizador *m*

tunic /'tju:nɪk/ *n* túnica *f*

tunnel /'tʌnl/ *n* túnel *m*. ● *vi* (*pt* **tunnelled**) abrir un túnel

turban /'tɜ:bən/ *n* turbante *m*

turbine /'tɜ:baɪn/ *n* turbina *f*

turbo /'tɜ:bəʊ/ *n* (*pl* **-os**) turbo(compresor) *m*

turbulen|ce /'tɜ:bjʊləns/ *n* turbulencia *f*. **~t** *adj* turbulento

turf /tɜ:f/ *n* (*pl* **turfs** *or* **turves**) césped *m*; (*segment of grass*) tepe *m*. □ **~ out** *vt* ⓘ echar

turgid /'tɜ:dʒɪd/ *adj* (language) ampuloso

turkey /'tɜ:kɪ/ *n* (*pl* **-eys**) pavo *m*
Turk|ey /'tɜ:kɪ/ *f* Turquía *f*. **~ish** *adj & n* turco (*m*)
turmoil /'tɜ:mɔɪl/ *n* confusión *f*
turn /tɜ:n/ *vt* hacer girar; volver (head, page); doblar (corner); (*change*) cambiar; (*deflect*) desviar. **~ sth into sth** convertir *or* transformar algo en algo. ● *vi* (handle) girar, dar vueltas; (person) volverse, darse la vuelta. **~ right** girar *or* doblar *or* torcer a la derecha. **~ red** ponerse rojo. **~ into sth** convertirse en algo. ● *n* vuelta *f*; (*in road*) curva *f*; (*change*) giro *m*; (*sequence*) turno *m*; (*fam, of illness*) ataque *m*. **good ~** favor *m*. **in ~** a su vez. □ **~ down** *vt* (*fold*) doblar; (*reduce*) bajar; (*reject*) rechazar. □ **~ off** *vt* cerrar (tap); apagar (light, TV, etc). *vi* (*from road*) doblar. □ **~ on** *vt* abrir (tap); encender, prender (*LAm*) (light etc). □ **~ out** *vt* apagar (light etc). *vi* (*result*) resultar. □ **~ round** *vi* darse la vuelta. □ **~ up** *vi* aparecer. *vt* (*find*) encontrar; levantar (collar); subir (hem); acortar (trousers); poner más fuerte (gas). **~ed-up** *adj* (nose) respingón. **~ing** *n* (*in town*) bocacalle *f*. **we've missed the ~ing** nos hemos pasado la calle (*or* carretera). **~ing-point** *n* momento *m* decisivo.
turnip /'tɜ:nɪp/ *n* nabo *m*
turn: ~over *n* (*Com*) facturación *f*; (*of staff*) movimiento *m*. **~pike** *n* (*Amer*) autopista *f* de peaje. **~stile** *n* torniquete *m*. **~table** *n* platina *f*. **~-up** *n* (*of trousers*) vuelta *f*, valenciana *f* (*Mex*)
turquoise /'tɜ:kwɔɪz/ *adj & n* turquesa (*f*)
turret /'tʌrɪt/ *n* torrecilla *f*
turtle /'tɜ:tl/ *n* tortuga *f* de mar; (*Amer, tortoise*) tortuga *f*
turves /tɜ:vz/ *see* **TURF**
tusk /tʌsk/ *n* colmillo *m*
tussle /'tʌsl/ *n* lucha *f*
tutor /'tju:tə(r)/ *n* profesor *m* particular
tuxedo /tʌk'si:dəʊ/ *n* (*pl* **-os**) (*Amer*) esmoquin *m*, smoking *m*
TV /ti:'vi:/ *n* televisión *f*, tele *f* ▣
twang /twæŋ/ *n* tañido *m*; (*in voice*) gangueo *m*
tweet /twi:t/ *n* piada *f*. ● *vi* piar
tweezers /'twi:zəz/ *npl* pinzas *fpl*
twel|fth /twelfθ/ *adj* duodécimo. ● *n* doceavo *m*. **~ve** /twelv/ *adj & n* doce (*m*)
twent|ieth /'twentɪəθ/ *adj* vigésimo. ● *n* veinteavo *m*. **~y** /'twentɪ/ *adj & n* veinte (*m*)
twice /twaɪs/ *adv* dos veces. **~ as many people** el doble de gente
twiddle /'twɪdl/ *vt* (hacer) girar
twig /twɪg/ *n* ramita *f*. ● *vi* (*pt* **twigged**) ▣ caer, darse cuenta
twilight /'twaɪlaɪt/ *n* crepúsculo *m*
twin /twɪn/ *adj & n* gemelo (*m*), mellizo (*m*) (*LAm*)
twine /twaɪn/ *n* cordel *m*, bramante *m*
twinge /twɪndʒ/ *n* punzada *f*; (*of remorse*) punzada *f*
twinkle /'twɪŋkl/ *vi* centellear. ● *n* centelleo *m*; (*in eye*) brillo *m*
twirl /twɜ:l/ *vt* (hacer) girar. ● *vi* girar. ● *n* vuelta *f*
twist /twɪst/ *vt* retorcer; (*roll*) enrollar; girar (knob); tergiversar (words); (*distort*) retorcer. **~ one's ankle** torcerse el tobillo. ● *vi* (rope, wire) enrollarse; (road, river) serpentear. ● *n* torsión *f*; (*curve*)

vuelta *f*

twit /twɪt/ *n* [!] imbécil *m*

twitch /twɪtʃ/ *vi* moverse. ● *n* tic *m*

twitter /ˈtwɪtə(r)/ *vi* gorjear

two /tuː/ *adj & n* dos (*m*). **~-bit** *adj* (*Amer*) de tres al cuarto. **~-faced** *adj* falso, insincero. **~fold** *adj* doble. ● *adv* dos veces. **~pence** /ˈtʌpəns/ *n* dos peniques *mpl*. **~-piece (suit)** *n* traje *m* de dos piezas. **~-way** *adj* (traffic) de doble sentido

tycoon /taɪˈkuːn/ *n* magnate *m*

tying /ˈtaɪɪŋ/ *see* TIE

type /taɪp/ *n* tipo *m*. ● *vt/i* escribir a máquina. **~-cast** *adj* (actor) encasillado. **~script** *n* texto *m* mecanografiado, manuscrito *m* (de una obra, novela etc). **~writer** *n* máquina *f* de escribir. **~written** *adj* escrito a máquina, mecanografiado

typhoon /taɪˈfuːn/ *n* tifón *m*

typical /ˈtɪpɪkl/ *adj* típico. **~ly** *adv* típicamente

typify /ˈtɪpɪfaɪ/ *vt* tipificar

typi|ng /ˈtaɪpɪŋ/ *n* mecanografía *f*. **~st** *n* mecanógrafo *m*

tyran|nical /tɪˈrænɪkl/ *adj* tiránico. **~ny** /ˈtɪrənɪ/ *n* tiranía *f*. **~t** /ˈtaɪərənt/ *n* tirano *m*

tyre /ˈtaɪə(r)/ *n* neumático *m*, llanta *f* (*LAm*)

Uu

udder /ˈʌdə(r)/ *n* ubre *f*

UFO /ˈjuːfəʊ/ *abbr* (= **unidentified flying object**) OVNI *m* (objeto volante no identificado)

ugly /ˈʌglɪ/ *adj* (**-ier**, **-iest**) feo

UK /juːˈkeɪ/ *abbr* (= **United Kingdom**) Reino *m* Unido

Ukraine /juːˈkreɪn/ *n* Ucrania *f*

ulcer /ˈʌlsə(r)/ *n* úlcera *f*; (*external*) llaga *f*

ultimate /ˈʌltɪmət/ *adj* (*eventual*) final; (*utmost*) máximo. **~ly** *adv* en última instancia; (*in the long run*) a la larga

ultimatum /ʌltɪˈmeɪtəm/ *n* (*pl* **-ums**) ultimátum *m*

ultra... /ˈʌltrə/ *pref* ultra... **~violet** /-ˈvaɪələt/ *adj* ultravioleta

umbilical cord /ʌmˈbɪlɪkl/ *n* cordón *m* umbilical

umbrella /ʌmˈbrelə/ *n* paraguas *m*

umpire /ˈʌmpaɪə(r)/ *n* árbitro *m*. ● *vt* arbitrar

umpteen /ˈʌmptiːn/ *adj* [!] tropecientos [!]. **~th** *adj* [!] enésimo

un... /ʌn/ *pref* in..., des..., no, poco, sin

UN /juːˈen/ *abbr* (= **United Nations**) ONU *f* (Organización de las Naciones Unidas)

unable /ʌnˈeɪbl/ *adj*. **be ~ to** no poder; (*be incapable of*) ser incapaz de

unacceptable /ʌnəkˈseptəbl/ *adj* (behaviour) inaceptable; (terms) inadmisible

t
u

unaccompanied /ʌnəˈkʌmpənɪd/ *adj* (luggage) no acompañado; (person, instrument) solo; (singing) sin acompañamiento

unaccustomed /ʌnəˈkʌstəmd/ *adj* desacostumbrado. **be ~ to** *adj* no estar acostumbrado a

unaffected /ʌnəˈfektɪd/ *adj* natural

unaided /ʌnˈeɪdɪd/ *adj* sin ayuda

unanimous /juːˈnænɪməs/ *adj* unánime. **~ly** *adv* unánimemente; (elect) por unanimidad

unarmed /ʌnˈɑːmd/ *adj* desarmado

unattended /ʌnəˈtendɪd/ *adj* sin vigilar

unattractive /ʌnəˈtræktɪv/ *adj* poco atractivo

unavoidabl|e /ʌnəˈvɔɪdəbl/ *adj* inevitable. **~y** *adv*. **I was ~y delayed** no pude evitar llegar tarde

unaware /ʌnəˈweə(r)/ *adj*. **be ~ of** ignorar, no ser consciente de. **~s** /-eəz/ *adv* desprevenido

unbearabl|e /ʌnˈbeərəbl/ *adj* insoportable, inaguantable. **~y** *adv* inaguantablemente

unbeat|able /ʌnˈbiːtəbl/ *adj* (quality) insuperable; (team) invencible. **~en** *adj* no vencido; (record) insuperado

unbelievabl|e /ʌnbɪˈliːvəbl/ *adj* increíble. **~y** *adv* increíblemente

unbiased /ʌnˈbaɪəst/ *adj* imparcial

unblock /ʌnˈblɒk/ *vt* desatascar

unbolt /ʌnˈbəʊlt/ *vt* descorrer el pestillo de

unborn /ʌnˈbɔːn/ *adj* que todavía no ha nacido

unbreakable /ʌnˈbreɪkəbl/ *adj* irrompible

unbroken /ʌnˈbrəʊkən/ *adj* (*intact*) intacto; (*continuous*) ininterrumpido

unbutton /ʌnˈbʌtn/ *vt* desabotonar, desabrochar

uncalled-for /ʌnˈkɔːldfɔː(r)/ *adj* fuera de lugar

uncanny /ʌnˈkænɪ/ *adj* (**-ier, -iest**) raro, extraño

uncertain /ʌnˈsɜːtn/ *adj* incierto; (*hesitant*) vacilante. **be ~ of/about sth** no estar seguro de algo. **~ty** *n* incertidumbre *f*

uncharitable /ʌnˈtʃærɪtəbl/ *adj* severo

uncivilized /ʌnˈsɪvɪlaɪzd/ *adj* incivilizado

uncle /ˈʌŋkl/ *n* tío *m*

> *i* **Uncle Sam** Es la típica personificación de EE.UU., en que éste es representado por un hombre de barba blanca, vestido con los colores nacionales y con un sombrero de copa adornado con estrellas. Es posible que la imagen se haya extraído del cartel de reclutamiento, en 1917, que llevaba la leyenda: "A Ud. lo necesito".

unclean /ʌnˈkliːn/ *adj* impuro

unclear /ʌnˈklɪə(r)/ *adj* poco claro

uncomfortable /ʌnˈkʌmfətəbl/ *adj* incómodo

uncommon /ʌnˈkɒmən/ *adj* poco común

uncompromising /ʌnˈkɒmprəmaɪzɪŋ/ *adj* intransigente

unconcerned /ʌnkənˈsɜːnd/ *adj* indiferente

unconditional /ʌnkənˈdɪʃənl/ *adj* incondicional

unconnected /ʌnkəˈnektɪd/ *adj* (*unrelated*) sin conexión. **the**

events are ~ estos acontecimientos no guardan ninguna relación (entre sí)

unconscious /ʌnˈkɒnʃəs/ *adj* (*Med*) inconsciente. **~ly** *adv* inconscientemente

unconventional /ʌnkənˈvenʃənl/ *adj* poco convencional

uncork /ʌnˈkɔːk/ *vt* descorchar

uncouth /ʌnˈkuːθ/ *adj* zafio

uncover /ʌnˈkʌvə(r)/ *vt* destapar; revelar (plot, scandal)

undaunted /ʌnˈdɔːntɪd/ *adj* impertérrito

undecided /ʌndɪˈsaɪdɪd/ *adj* indeciso

undeniabl|e /ʌndɪˈnaɪəbl/ *adj* innegable. **~y** *adv* sin lugar a dudas

under /ˈʌndə(r)/ *prep* debajo de; (*less than*) menos de; (heading) bajo; (*according to*) según; (*expressing movement*) por debajo de. ● *adv* debajo, abajo

under... *pref* sub...

under: ~carriage *n* tren *m* de aterrizaje. **~charge** *vt* /-ˈtʃɑːdʒ/ cobrarle de menos a. **~clothes** *npl* ropa *f* interior. **~coat**, **~coating** (*Amer*) *n* (*paint*) pintura *f* base; (*first coat*) primera mano *f* de pintura. **~cover** *adj* /-ˈkʌvə(r)/ secreto. **~current** *n* corriente *f* submarina. **~dog** *n*. **the ~dog** el que tiene menos posibilidades. **the ~dogs** *npl* los de abajo. **~done** *adj* /-ˈdʌn/ (meat) poco hecho. **~estimate** /-ˈestɪmeɪt/ *vt* (*underrate*) subestimar. **~fed** /-ˈfed/ *adj* subalimentado. **~foot** /-ˈfʊt/ *adv* debajo de los pies. **~go** *vt* (*pt* **-went**, *pp* **-gone**) sufrir. **~graduate** /-ˈgrædjʊət/ *n* estudiante *m* universitario (no licenciado). **~ground** /-ˈgraʊnd/ *adv* bajo tierra; (*in secret*) clandestinamente. ● /-graʊnd/ *adj* subterráneo; (*secret*) clandestino. ● *n* metro *m*. **~growth** *n* maleza *f*. **~hand** /-ˈhænd/ *adj* (*secret*) clandestino; (*deceptive*) fraudulento. **~lie** /-ˈlaɪ/ *vt* (*pt* **-lay**, *pp* **-lain**, *pres p* **-lying**) subyacer a. **~line** /-ˈlaɪn/ *vt* subrayar. **~lying** /-ˈlaɪɪŋ/ *adj* subyacente. **~mine** /-ˈmaɪn/ *vt* socavar. **~neath** /-ˈniːθ/ *prep* debajo de, abajo de (*LAm*). ● *adv* por debajo. **~paid** /-ˈpeɪd/ *adj* mal pagado. **~pants** *npl* calzoncillos *mpl*. **~pass** *n* paso *m* subterráneo; (*for traffic*) paso *m* inferior. **~privileged** /-ˈprɪvəlɪdʒd/ *adj* desfavorecido. **~rate** /-ˈreɪt/ *vt* subestimar. **~rated** /-ˈreɪtɪd/ *adj* no debidamente apreciado. **~shirt** *n* (*Amer*) camiseta *f* (interior).

understand /ʌndəˈstænd/ *vt* (*pt* **-stood**) entender; (*empathize with*) comprender, entender. ● *vi* entender, comprender. **~able** *adj* comprensible. **~ing** *adj* comprensivo. ● *n* (*grasp*) entendimiento *m*; (*sympathy*) comprensión *f*; (*agreement*) acuerdo *m*

under: ~statement *n* subestimación *f*. **~take** /-ˈteɪk/ (*pt* **-took**, *pp* **-taken**) emprender (task); asumir (responsibility). **~take to do sth** comprometerse a hacer algo. **~taker** *n* director *m* de pompas fúnebres. **~taking** /-ˈteɪkɪŋ/ *n* empresa *f*; (*promise*) promesa *f*. **~tone** *n*. **in an ~tone** en voz baja. **~value** /-ˈvæljuː/ *vt* subvalorar. **~water** /-ˈwɔːtə(r)/ *adj* submarino. ● *adv* debajo del agua. **~wear** *n* ropa *f* interior. **~weight** /-ˈweɪt/ *adj* de peso más bajo que el normal. **~went** /-ˈwent/ *see* UNDERGO.

~world *n* (*criminals*) hampa *f*.
~write /-'raɪt/ *vt* (*pt* **-wrote**, *pp* **-written**) (*Com*) asegurar; (*guarantee financially*) financiar

undeserved /ʌndɪ'zɜːvd/ *adj* inmerecido

undesirable /ʌndɪ'zaɪərəbl/ *adj* indeseable

undignified /ʌn'dɪgnɪfaɪd/ *adj* indecoroso

undisputed /ʌndɪs'pjuːtɪd/ *adj* (champion) indiscutido; (facts) innegable

undo /ʌn'duː/ *vt* (*pt* **-did**, *pp* **-done**) desabrochar (button, jacket); abrir (zip); desatar (knot, laces)

undoubted /ʌn'daʊtɪd/ *adj* indudable. **~ly** *adv* indudablemente, sin duda

undress /ʌn'dres/ *vt* desvestir, desnudar. • *vi* desvestirse, desnudarse

undue /ʌn'djuː/ *adj* excesivo

undulate /'ʌndjʊleɪt/ *vi* ondular

unduly /ʌn'djuːlɪ/ *adv* excesivamente

unearth /ʌn'ɜːθ/ *vt* desenterrar; descubrir (document)

unearthly /ʌn'ɜːθlɪ/ *adj* sobrenatural. **at an ~ hour** a estas horas intempestivas

uneasy /ʌn'iːzɪ/ *adj* incómodo

uneconomic /ʌniːkə'nɒmɪk/ *adj* poco económico

uneducated /ʌn'edjʊkeɪtɪd/ *adj* sin educación

unemploy|ed /ʌnɪm'plɔɪd/ *adj* desempleado, parado. **~ment** *n* desempleo *m*, paro *m*

unending /ʌn'endɪŋ/ *adj* interminable, sin fin

unequal /ʌn'iːkwəl/ *adj* desigual

unequivocal /ʌnɪ'kwɪvəkl/ *adj* inequívoco

unethical /ʌn'eθɪkl/ *adj* poco ético, inmoral

uneven /ʌn'iːvn/ *adj* desigual

unexpected /ʌnɪk'spektɪd/ *adj* inesperado; (result) imprevisto. **~ly** *adv* (arrive) de improviso; (happen) de forma imprevista

unfair /ʌn'feə(r)/ *adj* injusto; improcedente (dismissal). **~ly** *adv* injustamente

unfaithful /ʌn'feɪθfl/ *adj* infiel

unfamiliar /ʌnfə'mɪlɪə(r)/ *adj* desconocido. **be ~ with** desconocer

unfasten /ʌn'fɑːsn/ *vt* desabrochar (clothes); (*untie*) desatar

unfavourable /ʌn'feɪvərəbl/ *adj* desfavorable

unfeeling /ʌn'fiːlɪŋ/ *adj* insensible

unfit /ʌn'fɪt/ *adj*. **I'm ~** no estoy en forma. **~ for human consumption** no apto para el consumo

unfold /ʌn'fəʊld/ *vt* desdoblar; desplegar (wings); (*fig*) revelar. • *vi* (leaf) abrirse; (events) desarrollarse

unforeseen /ʌnfɔː'siːn/ *adj* imprevisto

unforgettable /ʌnfə'getəbl/ *adj* inolvidable

unforgivable /ʌnfə'gɪvəbl/ *adj* imperdonable

unfortunate /ʌn'fɔːtʃənət/ *adj* desafortunado; (*regrettable*) lamentable. **~ly** *adv* desafortunadamente; (*stronger*) por desgracia, desgraciadamente

unfounded /ʌn'faʊndɪd/ *adj* infundado

unfriendly /ʌn'frendlɪ/ *adj* poco amistoso; (*stronger*) antipático

unfurl /ʌn'fɜ:l/ *vt* desplegar

ungainly /ʌn'geɪnlɪ/ *adj* desgarbado

ungrateful /ʌn'greɪtfl/ *adj* desagradecido, ingrato

unhapp|iness /ʌn'hæpɪnes/ *n* infelicidad *f*, tristeza *f*. **~y** *adj* (**-ier**, **-iest**) infeliz, triste; (*unsuitable*) inoportuno. **be ~y about sth** no estar contento con algo

unharmed /ʌn'hɑ:md/ *adj* (person) ileso

unhealthy /ʌn'helθɪ/ *adj* (**-ier**, **-iest**) (person) de mala salud; (complexion) enfermizo; (conditions) poco saludable

unhurt /ʌn'hɜ:t/ *adj* ileso

unification /ju:nɪfɪ'keɪʃn/ *n* unificación *f*

uniform /'ju:nɪfɔ:m/ *adj & n* uniforme (*m*). **~ity** /-'fɔ:mətɪ/ *n* uniformidad *f*

unify /'ju:nɪfaɪ/ *vt* unir

unilateral /ju:nɪ'lætərəl/ *adj* unilateral

unimaginable /ʌnɪ'mædʒɪnəbl/ *adj* inimaginable

unimaginative /ʌnɪ'mædʒɪnətɪv/ *adj* (person) poco imaginativo

unimportant /ʌnɪm'pɔ:tnt/ *adj* sin importancia

uninhabited /ʌnɪn'hæbɪtɪd/ *adj* deshabitado; (island) despoblado

unintelligible /ʌnɪn'telɪdʒəbl/ *adj* ininteligible

unintentional /ʌnɪn'tenʃənl/ *adj* involuntario

union /'ju:njən/ *n* unión *f*; (*trade union*) sindicato *m*; (*student ~*) asociación *f* de estudiantes. **U~ Jack** *n* bandera *f* del Reino Unido

unique /ju:'ni:k/ *adj* único

unison /'ju:nɪsn/ *n*. **in ~** al unísono

unit /'ju:nɪt/ *n* unidad *f*; (*of furniture etc*) módulo *m*; (*in course*) módulo *m*

unite /ju:'naɪt/ *vt* unir. ● *vi* unirse. **U~d Kingdom** *n* Reino *m* Unido. **U~d Nations** *n* Organización *f* de las Naciones Unidas (ONU). **U~d States (of America)** *n* Estados *mpl* Unidos (de América)

unity /'ju:nɪtɪ/ *n* unidad *f*

univers|al /ju:nɪ'vɜ:sl/ *adj* universal. **~e** /'ju:nɪvɜ:s/ *n* universo *m*

university /ju:nɪ'vɜ:sətɪ/ *n* universidad *f*. ● *adj* universitario

unjust /ʌn'dʒʌst/ *adj* injusto. **~ified** /-ɪfaɪd/ *adj* injustificado

unkind /ʌn'kaɪnd/ *adj* poco amable; (*cruel*) cruel; (remark) hiriente

unknown /ʌn'nəʊn/ *adj* desconocido

unlawful /ʌn'lɔ:fl/ *adj* ilegal

unleaded /ʌn'ledɪd/ *adj* (fuel) sin plomo

unleash /ʌn'li:ʃ/ *vt* soltar

unless /ʌn'les, ən'les/ *conj* a menos que, a no ser que

unlike /ʌn'laɪk/ *prep* diferente de. (*in contrast to*) a diferencia de. **~ly** *adj* improbable

unlimited /ʌn'lɪmɪtɪd/ *adj* ilimitado

unlisted /ʌn'lɪstɪd/ *adj* (*Amer*) que no figura en la guía telefónica, privado (*Mex*)

unload /ʌn'ləʊd/ *vt* descargar

unlock /ʌn'lɒk/ *vt* abrir (con llave)

unluck|ily /ʌn'lʌkɪlɪ/ *adv* desgraciadamente. **~y** *adj* (**-ier**, **-iest**) (person) sin suerte, desafortunado. **be ~y** tener mala suerte; (*bring bad luck*) traer mala suerte

unmarried /ʌn'mærɪd/ *adj*

soltero
unmask /ʌn'mɑːsk/ *vt* desenmascarar
unmentionable /ʌn'menʃənəbl/ *adj* inmencionable
unmistakable /ʌnmɪ'steɪkəbl/ *adj* inconfundible
unnatural /ʌn'nætʃərəl/ *adj* poco natural; (*not normal*) anormal
unnecessar|ily /ʌn'nesəsərɪlɪ/ *adv* innecesariamente. **~y** *adj* innecesario
unnerve /ʌn'nɜːv/ *vt* desconcertar
unnoticed /ʌn'nəʊtɪst/ *adj* inadvertido
unobtainable /ʌnəb'teɪnəbl/ *adj* imposible de conseguir
unobtrusive /ʌnəb'truːsɪv/ *adj* discreto
unofficial /ʌnə'fɪʃl/ *adj* no oficial. **~ly** *adv* extraoficialmente
unpack /ʌn'pæk/ *vt* sacar las cosas de (bags); deshacer, desempacar (*LAm*) (suitcase). • *vi* deshacer las maletas, desempacar (*LAm*)
unpaid /ʌn'peɪd/ *adj* (work) no retribuido, no remunerado; (leave) sin sueldo
unperturbed /ʌnpə'tɜːbd/ *adj* impasible. **he carried on ~** siguió sin inmutarse
unpleasant /ʌn'pleznt/ *adj* desagradable
unplug /ʌn'plʌg/ *vt* desenchufar
unpopular /ʌn'pɒpjʊlə(r)/ *adj* impopular
unprecedented /ʌn'presɪdentɪd/ *adj* sin precedentes
unpredictable /ʌnprɪ'dɪktəbl/ *adj* imprevisible
unprepared /ʌnprɪ'peəd/ *adj* no preparado; (*unready*) desprevenido
unprofessional /ʌnprə'feʃənəl/ *adj* poco profesional
unprofitable /ʌn'prɒfɪtəbl/ *adj* no rentable
unprotected /ʌnprə'tektɪd/ *adj* sin protección; (sex) sin el uso de preservativos
unqualified /ʌn'kwɒlɪfaɪd/ *adj* sin título; (*fig*) absoluto
unquestion|able /ʌn'kwestʃənəbl/ *adj* incuestionable, innegable. **~ing** *adj* (obedience) ciego; (loyalty) incondicional
unravel /ʌn'rævl/ *vt* (*pt* **unravelled**) desenredar; desentrañar (mystery)
unreal /ʌn'rɪəl/ *adj* irreal. **~istic** /-'lɪstɪk/ *adj* poco realista
unreasonable /ʌn'riːzənəbl/ *adj* irrazonable
unrecognizable /ʌnrekəg'naɪzəbl/ *adj* irreconocible
unrelated /ʌnrɪ'leɪtɪd/ *adj* (facts) no relacionados (entre sí); (people) no emparentado
unreliable /ʌnrɪ'laɪəbl/ *adj* (person) informal; (machine) poco fiable; (information) poco fidedigno
unrepentant /ʌnrɪ'pentənt/ *adj* impenitente
unrest /ʌn'rest/ *n* (*discontent*) descontento *m*; (*disturbances*) disturbios *mpl*
unrivalled /ʌn'raɪvld/ *adj* incomparable
unroll /ʌn'rəʊl/ *vt* desenrollar. • *vi* desenrollarse
unruffled /ʌn'rʌfld/ (person) sereno
unruly /ʌn'ruːlɪ/ *adj* (class) indisciplinado; (child) revoltoso
unsafe /ʌn'seɪf/ *adj* inseguro
unsatisfactory /ʌnsætɪs'fæktərɪ/ *adj* insatisfactorio

unsavoury /ʌn'seɪvərɪ/ *adj* desagradable

unscathed /ʌn'skeɪðd/ *adj* ileso

unscheduled /ʌn'ʃedju:ld/ *adj* no programado, no previsto

unscrew /ʌn'skru:/ *vt* destornillar; desenroscar (lid)

unscrupulous /ʌn'skru:pjʊləs/ *adj* inescrupuloso

unseemly /ʌn'si:mlɪ/ *adj* indecoroso

unseen /ʌn'si:n/ *adj* (danger) oculto; (*unnoticed*) sin ser visto

unselfish /ʌn'selfɪʃ/ *adj* (act) desinteresado; (person) nada egoísta

unsettle /ʌn'setl/ *vt* desestabilizar (situation); alterar (plans). **~d** *adj* agitado; (weather) inestable; (*undecided*) pendiente (de resolución)

unshakeable /ʌn'ʃeɪkəbl/ *adj* inquebrantable

unshaven /ʌn'ʃeɪvn/ *adj* sin afeitar, sin rasurar (*Mex*)

unsightly /ʌn'saɪtlɪ/ *adj* feo

unskilled /ʌn'skɪld/ *adj* (work) no especializado; (worker) no cualificado, no calificado

unsociable /ʌn'səʊʃəbl/ *adj* insociable

unsolved /ʌn'sɒlvd/ *adj* no resuelto; (murder) sin esclarecerse

unsophisticated /ʌnsə'fɪstɪkeɪtɪd/ *adj* sencillo

unsound /ʌn'saʊnd/ *adj* poco sólido

unspecified /ʌn'spesɪfaɪd/ *adj* no especificado

unstable /ʌn'steɪbl/ *adj* inestable

unsteady /ʌn'stedɪ/ *adj* inestable, poco firme

unstuck /ʌn'stʌk/ *adj* despegado. **come ~** despegarse; (*fail*) fracasar

unsuccessful /ʌnsək'sesfʊl/ *adj* (attempt) infructuoso. **be ~** no tener éxito, fracasar

unsuitable /ʌn'su:təbl/ *adj* (clothing) poco apropiado, poco adecuado; (time) inconveniente. **she is ~ for the job** no es la persona indicada para el trabajo

unsure /ʌn'ʃʊə(r)/ *adj* inseguro

unthinkable /ʌn'θɪŋkəbl/ *adj* inconcebible

untid|iness /ʌn'taɪdɪnəs/ *n* desorden *m*. **~y** *adj* (**-ier**, **-iest**) desordenado; (appearance, writing) descuidado

untie /ʌn'taɪ/ *vt* desatar, desamarrar (*LAm*)

until /ən'tɪl, ʌn'tɪl/ *prep* hasta. ● *conj* hasta que

untold /ʌn'təʊld/ *adj* incalculable

untouched /ʌn'tʌtʃt/ *adj* intacto

untried /ʌn'traɪd/ *adj* no probado

untrue /ʌn'tru:/ *adj* falso

unused /ʌn'ju:zd/ *adj* nuevo. ● /ʌn'ju:st/ *adj*. **~ to** no acostumbrado a

unusual /ʌn'ju:ʒʊəl/ *adj* poco común, poco corriente. **it's ~ to see so many people** es raro ver a tanta gente. **~ly** *adv* excepcionalmente, inusitadamente

unveil /ʌn'veɪl/ *vt* descubrir

unwanted /ʌn'wɒntɪd/ *adj* superfluo; (child) no deseado

unwelcome /ʌn'welkəm/ *adj* (news) poco grato; (guest) inoportuno

unwell /ʌn'wel/ *adj* indispuesto

unwieldy /ʌn'wi:ldɪ/ *adj* pesado y difícil de manejar

unwilling /ʌn'wɪlɪŋ/ *adj* mal dispuesto. **be ~** no querer

unwind /ʌn'waɪnd/ *vt* (*pt* **unwound**) desenrollar. ● *vi* (*fam*,

U

relax) relajarse

unwise /ʌn'waɪz/ *adj* poco sensato

unworthy /ʌn'wɜ:ðɪ/ *adj* indigno

unwrap /ʌn'ræp/ *vt* (*pt* **unwrapped**) desenvolver

unwritten /ʌn'rɪtn/ *adj* no escrito; (agreement) verbal

up /ʌp/ *adv* arriba; (*upwards*) hacia arriba; (*higher*) más arriba. **~ here** aquí arriba. **~ there** allí arriba. **~ to** hasta. **he's not ~ yet** todavía no se ha levantado. **be ~ against** enfrentarse con. **come ~** subir. **go ~** subir. **he's not ~ to the job** no tiene las condiciones necesarias para el trabajo. **it's ~ to you** depende de ti. **what's ~?** ¿qué pasa? • *prep.* **go ~ the stairs** subir la escalera. **it's just ~ the road** está un poco más allá. • *vt* (*pt* **upped**) aumentar. • *n.* **~s and downs** *npl* altibajos *mpl*; (*of life*) vicisitudes *fpl*. **~bringing** /'ʌpbrɪŋɪŋ/ *n* educación *f*. **~date** /ʌp'deɪt/ *vt* poner al día. **~grade** /ʌp'greɪd/ *vt* elevar de categoría (person); mejorar (equipment). **~heaval** /ʌp'hi:vl/ *n* trastorno *m*. **~hill** /ʌp'hɪl/ *adv* cuesta arriba. **~hold** /ʌp'həʊld/ *vt* (*pt* **upheld**) mantener (principle); confirmar (decision). **~holster** /ʌp 'həʊlstə(r)/ *vt* tapizar. **~holstery** *n* tapicería *f*. **~keep** *n* mantenimiento *m*. **~-market** /ʌp'mɑ:kɪt/ *adj* de categoría

upon /ə'pɒn/ *prep* sobre. **once ~ a time** érase una vez

upper /'ʌpə(r)/ *adj* superior. **~ class** *n* clase *f* alta

up: **~right** *adj* vertical; (citizen) recto. **place sth ~right** poner algo de pie. **~rising** /'ʌpraɪzɪŋ/ *n* levantamiento *m*. **~roar** *n* tumulto *m*

upset /ʌp'set/ *vt* (*pt* **upset**, *pres p* **upsetting**) (*hurt*) disgustar; (*offend*) ofender; (*distress*) alterar; desbaratar (plans). • *adj* (*hurt*) disgustado; (*distressed*) alterado; (*offended*) ofendido; (*disappointed*) desilusionado. • /'ʌpset/ *n* trastorno *m*. **have a stomach ~** estar mal del estómago

up: **~shot** *n* resultado *m*. **~side down** /ʌpsaɪd'daʊn/ *adv* al revés (*con la parte de arriba abajo*); (*in disorder*) patas arriba. **turn sth ~side down** poner algo boca abajo. **~stairs** /ʌp'steəz/ *adv* arriba. **go ~stairs** subir. • /'ʌpsteəz/ *adj* de arriba. **~start** *n* advenedizo *m*. **~state** *adv* (*Amer*). **I live ~state** vivo en el norte del estado. **~stream** /ʌp'stri:m/ *adv* río arriba. **~take** *n*. **be quick on the ~take** agarrar las cosas al vuelo. **~-to-date** /ʌptə'deɪt/ *adj* al día; (news) de última hora. **~turn** *n* repunte *m*, mejora *f*. **~ward** /'ʌpwəd/ *adj* (movement) ascendente; (direction) hacia arriba. • *adv* hacia arriba. **~wards** *adv* hacia arriba

uranium /jʊ'reɪnɪəm/ *n* uranio *m*

Uranus /'jʊərənəs//jʊə'reɪnəs/ *n* Urano *m*

urban /'ɜ:bən/ *adj* urbano

urchin /'ɜ:tʃɪn/ *n* pilluelo *m*

urge /ɜ:dʒ/ *vt* instar. **~ s.o. to do sth** instar a uno a que haga algo. • *n* impulso *m*; (*wish, whim*) ganas *fpl*. □ **~ on** *vt* animar

urgen|cy /'ɜ:dʒənsɪ/ *n* urgencia *f*. **~t** *adj* urgente. **~tly** *adv* urgentemente, con urgencia

urin|ate /'jʊərɪmeɪt/ *vi* orinar. **~e** /'jʊərɪn/ *n* orina *f*

Uruguay /jʊərəgwaɪ/ *n* Uruguay

u

m. **~an** *adj & n* uruguayo (*m*)

us /ʌs, əs/ *pron* nos; (*after prep*) nosotros *m*, nosotras *f*

US(A) /ju:es'eɪ/ *abbr* (= **United States (of America)**) EE.UU. (*only written*), Estados *mpl* Unidos

usage /'ju:zɪdʒ/ *n* uso *m*

use /ju:z/ *vt* usar; utilizar (service, facilities); consumir (fuel). ● /ju:s/ *n* uso *m*, empleo *m*. **be of ~** servir. **it is no ~** es inútil. □ **~ up** *vt* agotar, consumir. **~d** /ju:zd/ *adj* usado. ● /ju:st/ *v mod* **~ to**. **he ~d to say** decía, solía decir. **there ~d to be** (antes) había. ● *adj*/ju:st/. **be ~d to** estar acostumbrado a. **~ful** /'ju:sfl/ *adj* útil. **~fully** *adv* útilmente. **~less** *adj* inútil; (person) incompetente. **~r** /-zə(r)/ *n* usuario *m*. **drug ~** *n* consumidor *m* de drogas

usher /'ʌʃə(r)/ *n* (*in theatre etc*) acomodador *m*. □ **~ in** *vt* hacer pasar; marcar el comienzo de (new era). **~ette** /-'ret/ *n* acomodadora *f*

USSR *abbr* (*History*) (= **Union of Soviet Socialist Republics**) URSS

usual /'ju:ʒʊəl/ *adj* usual; (*habitual*) acostumbrado, habitual; (place, route) de siempre. **as ~** como de costumbre, como siempre. **~ly** *adv* normalmente. **he ~ly wakes up early** suele despertarse temprano

utensil /ju:'tensl/ *n* utensilio *m*

utilize /'ju:tɪlaɪz/ *vt* utilizar

utmost /'ʌtməʊst/ *adj* sumo. ● *n*. **do one's ~** hacer todo lo posible (**to** para)

utter /'ʌtə(r)/ *adj* completo. ● *vt* pronunciar (word); dar (cry). **~ly** *adv* totalmente

U-turn /'ju:tɜ:n/ *n* cambio *m* de sentido

Vv

vacan|cy /'veɪkənsɪ/ *n* (*job*) vacante *f*; (*room*) habitación *f* libre. **~t** *adj* (building) desocupado; (seat) libre; (post) vacante; (look) ausente

vacate /və'keɪt/ *vt* dejar

vacation /və'keɪʃn/ *n* (*Amer*) vacaciones *fpl*. **go on ~** ir de vacaciones. **~er** *n* (*Amer*) veraneante *m & f*

vaccin|ate /'væksɪmeɪt/ *vt* vacunar. **~ation** /-'neɪʃn/ *n* vacunación *f*. **~e** /'væksi:n/ *n* vacuna *f*

vacuum /'vækjʊəm/ *n* vacío *m*. **~ cleaner** *n* aspiradora *f*

vagina /və'dʒaɪnə/ *n* vagina *f*

vague /veɪg/ *adj* (**-er**, **-est**) vago; (outline) borroso; (person, expression) despistado. **~ly** *adv* vagamente

vain /veɪn/ *adj* (**-er**, **-est**) vanidoso; (*useless*) vano. **in ~** en vano

Valentine's Day /'væləntaɪnz/ *n* el día de San Valentín

valiant /'vælɪənt/ *adj* valeroso

valid /'vælɪd/ *adj* válido. **~ate** /-eɪt/ *vt* dar validez a; validar (contract). **~ity** /-'ɪdətɪ/ *n* validez *f*

valley /'vælɪ/ *n* (*pl* **-eys**) valle *m*

valour /'vælə(r)/ *n* valor *m*

valu|able /'væljʊəbl/ *adj* valioso. **~ables** *npl* objetos *mpl* de valor. **~ation** /-'eɪʃn/ *n* valoración *f*. **~e** /'vælju:/ *n* valor *m*. ● *vt* valorar; tasar, valorar, avaluar (*LAm*) (property). **~e added tax** *n* impuesto *m* sobre el valor añadido

valve /vælv/ *n* válvula *f*

vampire /'væmpaɪə(r)/ *n*

vampiro *m*

van /væn/ *n* furgoneta *f*, camioneta *f*; (*Rail*) furgón *m*

vandal /'vændl/ *n* vándalo *m*. **~ism** *n* vandalismo *m*. **~ize** *vt* destruir

vanilla /və'nɪlə/ *n* vainilla *f*

vanish /'vænɪʃ/ *vi* desaparecer

vanity /'vænɪtɪ/ *n* vanidad *f*. **~ case** *n* neceser *m*

vapour /'veɪpə(r)/ *n* vapor *m*

varia|ble /'veərɪəbl/ *adj* variable. **~nce** /-əns/ *n*. **at ~ce** en desacuerdo. **~nt** *n* variante *f*. **~tion** /-'eɪʃn/ *n* variación *f*

vari|ed /'veərɪd/ *adj* variado. **~ety** /və'raɪətɪ/ *n* variedad *f*. **~ety show** *n* espectáculo *m* de variedades. **~ous** /'veərɪəs/ *adj* (*several*) varios; (*different*) diversos

varnish /'vɑ:nɪʃ/ *n* barniz *m*; (*for nails*) esmalte *m*. ● *vt* barnizar; pintar (nails)

vary /'veərɪ/ *vt/i* variar

vase /vɑ:z/, (*Amer*) /veɪs/ *n* (*for flowers*) florero *m*; (*ornamental*) jarrón *m*

vast /vɑ:st/ *adj* vasto, extenso; (size) inmenso. **~ly** *adv* infinitamente

vat /væt/ *n* cuba *f*

VAT /vi:eɪ'ti:/ *abbr* (= **value added tax**) IVA *m*

vault /vɔ:lt/ *n* (*roof*) bóveda *f*; (*in bank*) cámara *f* acorazada; (*tomb*) cripta *f*. ● *vt/i* saltar

VCR *n* = **videocassette recorder**

VDU *n* = **visual display unit**

veal /vi:l/ *n* ternera *f*

veer /vɪə(r)/ *vi* dar un viraje, virar

vegeta|ble /'vedʒɪtəbl/ *adj* vegetal. ● *n* verdura *f*. **~rian** /vedʒɪ'teərɪən/ *adj & n* vegetariano (*m*). **~tion** /vedʒɪ'teɪʃn/ *n* vegetación *f*

vehement /'vi:əmənt/ *adj* vehemente. **~tly** *adv* con vehemencia

vehicle /'vi:ɪkl/ *n* vehículo *m*

veil /veɪl/ *n* velo *m*

vein /veɪn/ *n* vena *f*; (*in marble*) veta *f*

velocity /vɪ'lɒsɪtɪ/ *n* velocidad *f*

velvet /'velvɪt/ *n* terciopelo *m*

vendetta /ven'detə/ *n* vendetta *f*

vend|ing machine /'vendɪŋ/ *n* distribuidor *m* automático. **~or** /'vendə(r)/ *n* vendedor *m*

veneer /və'nɪə(r)/ *n* chapa *f*, enchapado *m*; (*fig*) barniz *m*, apariencia *f*

venerate /'venəreɪt/ *vt* venerar

venereal /və'nɪərɪəl/ *adj* venéreo

Venetian blind /və'ni:ʃn/ *n* persiana *f* veneciana

Venezuela /venə'zweɪlə/ *n* Venezuela *f*. **~n** *adj & n* venezolano (*m*)

vengeance /'vendʒəns/ *n* venganza *f*. **with a ~** (*fig*) con ganas

venom /'venəm/ *n* veneno *m*. **~ous** *adj* venenoso

vent /vent/ *n* (conducto *m* de) ventilación; (*air* ~) respiradero *m*. **give ~ to** dar rienda suelta a. ● *vt* descargar

ventilat|e /'ventɪleɪt/ *vt* ventilar. **~ion** /-'leɪʃn/ *n* ventilación *f*

ventriloquist /ven'trɪləkwɪst/ *n* ventrílocuo *m*

venture /'ventʃə(r)/ *n* empresa *f*. ● *vt* aventurar. ● *vi* atreverse

venue /'venju:/ *n* (*for concert*) lugar *m* de actuación

Venus /'vi:nəs/ *n* Venus *m*

veranda /və'rændə/ *n* galería *f*

verb /vɜ:b/ *n* verbo *m*. **~al** *adj*

verbal

verdict /ˈvɜːdɪkt/ *n* veredicto *m*; (*opinion*) opinión *f*

verge /vɜːdʒ/ *n* borde *m*. □ **~ on** *vt* rayar en

verify /ˈverɪfaɪ/ *vt* (*confirm*) confirmar; (*check*) verificar

vermin /ˈvɜːmɪn/ *n* alimañas *fpl*

versatil|e /ˈvɜːsətaɪl/ *adj* versátil. **~ity** /-ˈtɪlətɪ/ *n* versatilidad *f*

verse /vɜːs/ *n* estrofa *f*; (*poetry*) poesías *fpl*. **~d** /vɜːst/ *adj*. **be well-~ed in** ser muy versado en. **~ion** /ˈvɜːʃn/ *n* versión *f*

versus /ˈvɜːsəs/ *prep* contra

vertebra /ˈvɜːtɪbrə/ *n* (*pl* **-brae** /-briː/) vértebra *f*. **~te** /-brət/ *n* vertebrado *m*

vertical /ˈvɜːtɪkl/ *adj & n* vertical (*f*). **~ly** *adv* verticalmente

vertigo /ˈvɜːtɪgəʊ/ *n* vértigo *m*

verve /vɜːv/ *n* brío *m*

very /ˈverɪ/ *adv* muy. **~ much** muchísimo. **~ well** muy bien. **the ~ first** el primero de todos. ● *adj* mismo. **the ~ thing** exactamente lo que hace falta

vessel /ˈvesl/ *n* (*receptacle*) recipiente *m*; (*ship*) navío *m*, nave *f*

vest /vest/ *n* camiseta *f*; (*Amer*) chaleco *m*.

vestige /ˈvestɪdʒ/ *n* vestigio *m*

vet /vet/ *n* veterinario *m*; (*Amer fam, veteran*) veterano *m*. ● *vt* (*pt* **vetted**) someter a investigación (applicant)

veteran /ˈvetərən/ *n* veterano *m*

veterinary /ˈvetərɪnərɪ/ *adj* veterinario. **~ surgeon** *n* veterinario *m*

veto /ˈviːtəʊ/ *n* (*pl* **-oes**) veto *m*. ● *vt* vetar

vex /veks/ *vt* fastidiar

via /ˈvaɪə/ *prep* por, por vía de

viable /ˈvaɪəbl/ *adj* viable

viaduct /ˈvaɪədʌkt/ *n* viaducto *m*

vibrat|e /vaɪˈbreɪt/ *vt/i* vibrar. **~ion** /-ʃn/ *n* vibración *f*

vicar /ˈvɪkə(r)/ *n* párroco *m*. **~age** /-rɪdʒ/ *n* casa *f* del párroco

vice /vaɪs/ *n* vicio *m*; (*Tec*) torno *m* de banco

vice versa /vaɪsɪˈvɜːsə/ *adv* viceversa

vicinity /vɪˈsɪnɪtɪ/ *n* vecindad *f*. **in the ~ of** cerca de

vicious /ˈvɪʃəs/ *adj* (attack) feroz; (dog) fiero; (rumour) malicioso. **~ circle** *n* círculo *m* vicioso

victim /ˈvɪktɪm/ *n* víctima *f*. **~ize** *vt* victimizar

victor /ˈvɪktə(r)/ *n* vencedor *m*

Victorian /vɪkˈtɔːrɪən/ *adj* victoriano

victor|ious /vɪkˈtɔːrɪəs/ *adj* (army) victorioso; (team) vencedor. **~y** /ˈvɪktərɪ/ *n* victoria *f*

video /ˈvɪdɪəʊ/*n* (*pl* **-os**) vídeo *m*, video *m* (*LAm*). **~ camera** *n* videocámara *f*. **~(cassette) recorder** *n* magnetoscopio *m*. **~tape** *n* videocassette *f*

vie /vaɪ/ *vi* (*pres p* **vying**) rivalizar

Vietnam /vjetˈnæm/ *n* Vietnam *m*. **~ese** *adj & n* vietnamita (*m & f*)

view /vjuː/ *n* vista *f*; (*mental survey*) visión *f* de conjunto; (*opinion*) opinión *f*. **in my ~** a mi juicio. **in ~ of** en vista de. **on ~** expuesto. ● *vt* ver (scene, property); (*consider*) considerar. **~er** *n* (*TV*) televidente *m & f*. **~finder** *n* visor *m*. **~point** *n* punto *m* de vista

vigil|ance *n* vigilancia *f*. **~ant** *adj* vigilante

vigo|rous /ˈvɪgərəs/ *adj* enérgico;

(growth) vigoroso. **~ur** /'vɪgə(r)/ *n* vigor *m*

vile /vaɪl/ *adj* (*base*) vil; (food) asqueroso; (weather, temper) horrible

village /'vɪlɪdʒ/ *n* pueblo *m*; (*small*) aldea *f*. **~r** *n* vecino *m* del pueblo; (*of small village*) aldeano *m*

villain /'vɪlən/ *n* maleante *m & f*; (*in story etc*) villano *m*

vindicate /'vɪndɪkeɪt/ *vt* justificar

vindictive /vɪn'dɪktɪv/ *adj* vengativo

vine /vaɪn/ *n* (*on ground*) vid *f*; (*climbing*) parra *f*

vinegar /'vɪnɪgə(r)/ *n* vinagre *m*

vineyard /'vɪnjəd/ *n* viña *f*

vintage /'vɪntɪdʒ/ *n* (*year*) cosecha *f*. ● *adj* (wine) añejo; (car) de época

vinyl /'vaɪnɪl/ *n* vinilo *m*

viola /vɪ'əʊlə/ *n* viola *f*

violat|e /'vaɪəleɪt/ *vt* violar. **~ion** /-'leɪʃn/ *n* violación *f*

violen|ce /'vaɪələns/ *n* violencia *f*. **~t** *adj* violento. **~tly** *adv* violentamente

violet /'vaɪələt/ *adj & n* violeta (*f*); (*colour*) violeta (*m*)

violin /'vaɪəlɪn/ *n* violín *m*. **~ist** *n* violinista *m & f*

VIP /vi:aɪ'pi:/ *abbr* (= **very important person**) VIP *m*

viper /'vaɪpə(r)/ *n* víbora *f*

virgin /'vɜ:dʒɪn/ *adj & n* virgen (*f*)

Virgo /'vɜ:gəʊ/ *n* Virgo *f*

virile /'vɪraɪl/ *adj* viril

virtual /'vɜ:tʃʊəl/ *adj*. **traffic is at a ~ standstill** el tráfico está prácticamente paralizado. **~ reality** *n* realidad *f* virtual. **~ly** *adv* prácticamente

virtue /'vɜ:tʃu:/ *n* virtud *f*. **by ~ of** en virtud de

virtuous /'vɜ:tʃʊəs/ *adj* virtuoso

virulent /'vɪrʊlənt/ *adj* virulento

virus /'vaɪərəs/ *n* (*pl* **-uses**) virus *m*

visa /'vi:zə/ *n* visado *m*, visa *f* (*LAm*)

vise /vaɪs/ *n* (*Amer*) torno *m* de banco

visib|ility /vɪzɪ'bɪlətɪ/ *n* visibilidad *f*. **~le** /'vɪzɪbl/ *adj* visible; (sign, improvement) evidente

vision /'vɪʒn/ *n* visión *f*; (*sight*) vista *f*

visit /'vɪzɪt/ *vt* visitar; hacer una visita a (person). ● *vi* hacer visitas. **~ with s.o.** (*Amer*) ir a ver a uno. ● *n* visita *f*. **pay s.o. a ~** hacerle una visita a uno. **~or** *n* visitante *m & f*; (*guest*) visita *f*

visor /'vaɪzə(r)/ *n* visera *f*

visual /'vɪʒʊəl/ *adj* visual. **~ize** *vt* imaginar(se); (*foresee*) prever

vital /'vaɪtl/ *adj* (*essential*) esencial; (factor) de vital importancia; (organ) vital. **~ity** /vaɪ'tælətɪ/ *n* vitalidad *f*

vitamin /'vɪtəmɪn/ *n* vitamina *f*.

vivacious /vɪ'veɪʃəs/ *adj* vivaz

vivid /'vɪvɪd/ *adj* vivo. **~ly** *adv* intensamente; (*describe*) gráficamente

vivisection /vɪvɪ'sekʃn/ *n* vivisección *f*

vocabulary /və'kæbjʊlərɪ/ *n* vocabulario *m*

vocal /'vəʊkl/ *adj* vocal. **~ist** *n* cantante *m & f*

vocation /vəʊ'keɪʃn/ *n* vocación *f*. **~al** *adj* profesional

vociferous /və'sɪfərəs/ *adj* vociferador

vogue /vəʊg/ *n* moda *f*, boga *f*

voice /vɔɪs/ *n* voz *f*. ● *vt* expresar

void /vɔɪd/ *adj* (*not valid*) nulo. ● *n* vacío *m*

volatile /ˈvɒlətaɪl/ *adj* volátil; (person) imprevisible

volcan|ic /vɒlˈkænɪk/ *adj* volcánico. **~o** /vɒlˈkeɪnəʊ/ *n* (*pl* **-oes**) volcán *m*

volley /ˈvɒlɪ/ *n* (*pl* **-eys**) (*of gunfire*) descarga *f* cerrada; (*sport*) volea *f*. **~ball** *n* vóleibol *m*

volt /vəʊlt/ *n* voltio *m*. **~age** /-ɪdʒ/ *n* voltaje *m*

volume /ˈvɒljuːm/ *n* volumen *m*; (*book*) tomo *m*

voluntar|ily /ˈvɒləntərəlɪ/ *adv* voluntariamente. **~y** *adj* voluntario; (organization) de beneficencia

volunteer /vɒlənˈtɪə(r)/ *n* voluntario *m*. ● *vt* ofrecer. ● *vi*. **~ (to)** ofrecerse (a)

vomit /ˈvɒmɪt/ *vt/i* vomitar. ● *n* vómito *m*

voracious /vəˈreɪʃəs/ *adj* voraz

vot|e /vəʊt/ *n* voto *m*; (*right*) derecho *m* al voto; (*act*) votación *f*. ● *vi* votar. **~er** *n* votante *m & f*. **~ing** *n* votación *f*

vouch /vaʊtʃ/ *vi*. **~ for s.o.** responder por uno. **~er** /-ə(r)/ *n* vale *m*

vow /vaʊ/ *n* voto *m*. ● *vi* jurar

vowel /ˈvaʊəl/ *n* vocal *f*

voyage /ˈvɔɪɪdʒ/ *n* viaje *m*; (*by sea*) travesía *f*

vulgar /ˈvʌlgə(r)/ *adj* (*coarse*) grosero, vulgar; (*tasteless*) de mal gusto. **~ity** /-ˈgærətɪ/ *n* vulgaridad *f*

vulnerable /ˈvʌlnərəbl/ *adj* vulnerable

vulture /ˈvʌltʃə(r)/ *n* buitre *m*

vying /ˈvaɪɪŋ/ *see* **VIE**

Ww

W *abbr* (= **West**) O

wad /wɒd/ *n* (*of notes*) fajo *m*; (*tied together*) lío *m*; (*papers*) montón *m*

waddle /ˈwɒdl/ *vi* contonearse

wade /weɪd/ *vi* caminar (*por el agua etc*)

wafer /ˈweɪfə(r)/ *n* galleta *f* de barquillo

waffle /ˈwɒfl/ *n* [I] palabrería *f*. ● *vi* [I] divagar; (*in essay, exam*) meter paja [I]. ● *n* (*Culin*) gofre *m*, wafle *m* (*LAm*)

waft /wɒft/ *vi* flotar

wag /wæg/ *vt* (*pt* **wagged**) menear. ● *vi* menearse

wage /weɪdʒ/ *n* sueldo *m*. **~s** *npl* salario *m*, sueldo *m*. **~r** *n* apuesta *f*

waggle /ˈwægl/ *vt* menear. ● *vi* menearse

wagon /ˈwægən/ *n* carro *m*; (*Rail*) vagón *m*; (*Amer, delivery truck*) furgoneta *f* de reparto

wail /weɪl/ *vi* llorar

waist /weɪst/ *n* cintura *f*. **~coat** *n* chaleco *m*. **~line** *n* cintura *f*

wait /weɪt/ *vi* esperar; (*at table*) servir. **~ for** esperar. **~ on s.o.** atender a uno. ● *vt* (*await*) esperar (chance, turn). **~ table** (*Amer*) servir a la mesa. **I can't ~ to see him** me muero de ganas de verlo. ● *n* espera *f*. **lie in ~** acechar

waiter /ˈweɪtə(r)/ *n* camarero *m*, mesero *m* (*LAm*)

wait: ~ing-list *n* lista *f* de espera. **~ing-room** *n* sala *f* de espera

waitress /ˈweɪtrɪs/ *n* camarera *f*,

mesera *f* (*LAm*)

waive /weɪv/ *vt* renunciar a

wake /weɪk/ *vt* (*pt* **woke**, *pp* **woken**) despertar. ● *vi* despertarse. ● *n* (*Naut*) estela *f*. **in the ~ of** como resultado de. □ **~ up** *vt* despertar. *vi* despertarse

Wales /weɪlz/ *n* (el país de) Gales

walk /wɔ:k/ *vi* andar, caminar; (*not ride*) ir a pie; (*stroll*) pasear. ● *vt* andar por (streets); llevar de paseo (dog). ● *n* paseo *m*; (*long*) caminata *f*; (*gait*) manera *f* de andar. □ **~ out** *vi* salir; (workers) declararse en huelga. □ **~ out on** *vt* abandonar. **~er** *n* excursionista *m & f*

walkie-talkie /wɔ:kɪ'tɔ:kɪ/ *n* walkie-talkie *m*

walk: ~ing-stick *n* bastón *m*. **W~man** /-mən/ *n* Walkman *m* (*P*). **~-out** *n retirada en señal de protesta*; (*strike*) abandono *m* del trabajo

wall /wɔ:l/ *n* (*interior*) pared *f*; (*exterior*) muro *m*

> **i** **Wall Street** Una calle en Manhattan, Nueva York, donde se encuentran la Bolsa neoyorquina y las sedes de muchas instituciones financieras. Cuando se habla de *Wall Street*, a menudo se está refiriendo a esas instituciones.

wallet /'wɒlɪt/ *n* cartera *f*, billetera *f*

wallop /'wɒləp/ *vt* (*pt* **walloped**) 🅘 darle un golpazo a.

wallow /'wɒləʊ/ *vi* revolcarse

wallpaper /'wɔ:lpeɪpə(r)/ *n* papel *m* pintado

walnut /'wɔ:lnʌt/ *n* nuez *f*; (*tree*) nogal *m*

walrus /'wɔ:lrəs/ *n* morsa *f*

waltz /wɔ:ls/ *n* vals *m*. ● *vi* valsar

wand /wɒnd/ *n* varita *f* (mágica)

wander /'wɒndə(r)/ *vi* vagar; (*stroll*) pasear; (*digress*) divagar. ● *n* vuelta *f*, paseo *m*. **~er** *n* trotamundos *m*

wane /weɪn/ *vi* (moon) menguar; (interest) decaer. ● *n*. **be on the ~** (popularity) estar decayendo

wangle /wæŋgl/ *vt* 🅘 agenciarse

want /wɒnt/ *vt* querer; (*need*) necesitar. ● *vi*. **~ for** carecer de. ● *n* necesidad *f*; (*lack*) falta *f*. **~ed** *adj* (criminal) buscado

war /wɔ:(r)/ *n* guerra *f*. **at ~** en guerra

warble /'wɔ:bl/ *vi* trinar, gorjear

ward /wɔ:d/ *n* (*in hospital*) sala *f*; (*child*) pupilo *m*. □ **~ off** *vt* conjurar (danger); rechazar (attack)

warden /'wɔ:dn/ *n* guarda *m*

warder /'wɔ:də(r)/ *n* celador *m* (*de una cárcel*)

wardrobe /'wɔ:drəʊb/ *n* armario *m*; (*clothes*) guardarropa *f*, vestuario *m*

warehouse /'weəhaʊs/ *n* depósito *m*, almacén *m*

wares /weəz/ *npl* mercancía(s) *f(pl)*

war: ~fare *n* guerra *f*. **~head** *n* cabeza *f*, ojiva *f*

warm /wɔ:m/ *adj* (**-er**, **-est**) (water, day) tibio, templado; (room) caliente; (climate, wind) cálido; (clothes) de abrigo; (welcome) caluroso. **be ~** (person) tener calor. **it's ~ today** hoy hace calor. ● *vt*. **~ (up)** calentar (room); recalentar (food); (*fig*) animar. ● *vi*. **~ (up)** calentarse; (*fig*) animarse. **~-blooded** /-'blʌdɪd/ *adj* de sangre caliente. **~ly** *adv* (*heartily*) calurosamente. **~th** *n* calor *m*; (*of colour, atmosphere*) calidez *f*

warn /wɔːn/ *vt* advertir. **~ing** *n* advertencia *f*; (*notice*) aviso *m*

warp /wɔːp/ *vt* alabear. **~ed** /ˈwɔːpt/ *adj* (wood) alabeado; (mind) retorcido

warrant /ˈwɒrənt/ *n* orden *f* judicial; (*search* ~) orden *f* de registro; (*for arrest*) orden *f* de arresto. ● *vt* justificar. **~y** *n* garantía *f*

warrior /ˈwɒrɪə(r)/ *n* guerrero *m*

warship /ˈwɔːʃɪp/ *n* buque *m* de guerra

wart /wɔːt/ *n* verruga *f*

wartime /ˈwɔːtaɪm/ *n* tiempo *m* de guerra

wary /ˈweərɪ/ *adj* (**-ier**, **-iest**) cauteloso. **be ~ of** recelar de

was /wəz, wɒz/ *see* **BE**

wash /wɒʃ/ *vt* lavar; fregar, lavar (*LAm*) (floor). **~ one's face** lavarse la cara. ● *vi* lavarse. ● *n* (*in washing machine*) lavado *m*. **have a ~** lavarse. **I gave the car a ~** lavé el coche. □ **~ out** *vt* (*clean*) lavar; (*rinse*) enjuagar. □ **~ up** *vi* fregar los platos, lavar los trastes (*Mex*); (*Amer, wash face and hands*) lavarse. **~able** *adj* lavable. **~basin**, **~bowl** (*Amer*) *n* lavabo *m*. **~er** *n* arandela *f*. **~ing** *n* lavado *m*; (*dirty clothes*) ropa *f* para lavar; (*wet clothes*) ropa *f* lavada. **do the ~ing** lavar la ropa, hacer la colada. **~ing-machine** *n* máquina *f* de lavar, lavadora *f*. **~ing-powder** *n* jabón *m* en polvo. **~ing-up** *n*. **do the ~ing-up** lavar los platos, fregar (los platos). **~ing-up liquid** *n* lavavajillas *m*. **~out** *n* 🅸 desastre *m*. **~room** *n* (*Amer*) baños *mpl*, servicios *mpl*

wasp /wɒsp/ *n* avispa *f*

waste /weɪst/ ● *adj* (matter) de desecho; (land) (*barren*) yermo; (*uncultivated*) baldío. ● *n* (*of materials*) desperdicio *m*; (*of time*) pérdida *f*; (*refuse*) residuos *mpl*. ● *vt* despilfarrar (electricity, money); desperdiciar (talent, effort); perder (time). ● *vi*. **~-disposal unit** *n* trituradora *f* de desperdicios. **~ful** *adj* poco económico; (person) despilfarrador. **~-paper basket** *n* papelera *f*

watch /wɒtʃ/ *vt* mirar; observar (person, expression); ver (TV); (*keep an eye on*) vigilar; (*take heed*) tener cuidado con. ● *vi* mirar. ● *n* (*observation*) vigilancia *f*; (*period of duty*) guardia *f*; (*timepiece*) reloj *m*. **~ out** *vi* (*be careful*) tener cuidado; (*look carefully*) estarse atento. **~dog** *n* perro *m* guardián. **~man** /-mən/ *n* (*pl* **-men**) vigilante *m*.

water /ˈwɔːtə(r)/ *n* agua *f*. ● *vt* regar (plants etc). ● *vi* (eyes) llorar. **make s.o.'s mouth ~** hacérsele la boca agua, hacérsele agua la boca (*LAm*). **~ down** *vt* diluir; aguar (wine). **~-colour** *n* acuarela *f*. **~cress** *n* berro *m*. **~fall** *n* cascada *f*; (*large*) catarata *f*. **~ing-can** *n* regadera *f*. **~ lily** *n* nenúfar *m*. **~logged** /-lɒgd/ *adj* anegado; (shoes) empapado. **~proof** *adj* impermeable; (watch) sumergible. **~-skiing** *n* esquí *m* acuático. **~tight** *adj* hermético; (boat) estanco; (argument) irrebatible. **~way** *n* canal *m* navegable. **~y** *adj* acuoso; (eyes) lloroso

watt /wɒt/ *n* vatio *m*

wave /weɪv/ *n* onda *f*; (*of hand*) señal *f*; (*fig*) oleada *f*. ● *vt* agitar; (*curl*) ondular (hair). ● *vi* (*signal*) hacer señales con la mano; ondear (flag). **~band** *n* banda *f* de frecuencia. **~length** *n* longitud *f* de onda

waver /'weɪvə(r)/ *vi* (*be indecisive*) vacilar; (*falter*) flaquear

wavy /'weɪvɪ/ *adj* (**-ier**, **-iest**) ondulado

wax /wæks/ *n* cera *f*. ● *vi* (moon) crecer. **~work** *n* figura *f* de cera. **~works** *npl* museo *m* de cera

way /weɪ/ *n* (*route*) camino *m*; (*manner*) manera *f*, forma *f*, modo *m*; (*direction*) dirección *f*; (*habit*) costumbre *f*. **it's a long ~ from here** queda muy lejos de aquí. **be in the ~** estorbar. **by the ~** a propósito. **either ~** de cualquier manera. **give ~** (*collapse*) ceder, romperse; (*Auto*) ceder el paso. **in a ~** en cierta manera. **in some ~s** en ciertos modos. **make ~** dejar paso a. **no ~!** ¡ni hablar! **on my ~ to** de camino a. **out of the ~** remoto; (*extraordinary*) fuera de lo común. **that ~** por allí. **this ~** por aquí. **~ in** *n* entrada *f*. **~lay** /weɪ'leɪ/ *vt* (*pt* **-laid**) abordar. **~ out** *n* salida *f*. **~-out** *adj* ultramoderno, original. **~s** *npl* costumbres *fpl*

we /wi:/ *pron* nosotros *m*, nosotras *f*

weak /wi:k/ *adj* (**-er**, **-est**) débil; (structure) poco sólido; (performance, student) flojo; (coffee) poco cargado; (solution) diluido; (beer) suave; (*pej*) aguado. **~en** *vt* debilitar. ● *vi* (resolve) flaquear. **~ling** *n* alfeñique *m*. **~ness** *n* debilidad *f*

wealth /welθ/ *n* riqueza *f*. **~y** *adj* (**-ier**, **-iest**) rico

weapon /'wepən/ *n* arma *f*. **~s of mass destruction** armas de destrucción masiva

wear /weə(r)/ *vt* (*pt* **wore**, *pp* **worn**) llevar; vestirse de (black, red, etc); (*usually*) usar. **I've got nothing to ~** no tengo nada que ponerme. ● *vi* (*through use*) gastarse; (*last*) durar. ● *n* uso *m*; (*damage*) desgaste *m*; **~ and tear** desgaste *m* natural. □ **~ out** *vt* gastar; (*tire*) agotar. *vi* gastarse

weary /'wɪərɪ/ *adj* (**-ier**, **-iest**) cansado. ● *vt* cansar. ● *vi* cansarse. **~ of** cansarse de

weather /'weðə(r)/ *n* tiempo *m*. **what's the ~ like?** ¿qué tiempo hace?. **the ~ was bad** hizo mal tiempo. **be under the ~** [!] no andar muy bien [!]. ● *vt* (*survive*) sobrellevar. **~-beaten** *adj* curtido. **~ forecast** *n* pronóstico *m* del tiempo. **~-vane** *n* veleta *f*

weave /wi:v/ *vt* (*pt* **wove**, *pp* **woven**) tejer; entretejer (threads). **~ one's way** abrirse paso. ● *vi* (person) zigzaguear; (road) serpentear. **~r** *n* tejedor *m*

web /web/ *n* (*of spider*) telaraña *f*; (*of intrigue*) red *f*. **~ page** *n* página web. **~ site** *n* sitio web *m*

wed /wed/ *vt* (*pt* **wedded**) casarse con. ● *vi* casarse.

we'd /wi:d//wɪəd/ = **we had**, **we would**

wedding /'wedɪŋ/ *n* boda *f*, casamiento *m*. **~-cake** *n* pastel *m* de boda. **~-ring** *n* anillo *m* de boda

wedge /wedʒ/ *n* cuña *f*

Wednesday /'wenzdeɪ/ *n* miércoles *m*

wee /wi:/ *adj* [!] pequeñito. ● *n*. **have a ~** [!] hacer pis [!]

weed /wi:d/ *n* mala hierba *f*. ● *vt* desherbar. □ **~ out** *vt* eliminar. **~killer** *n* herbicida *m*. **~y** *adj* (person) enclenque; (*Amer*, *lanky*) larguirucho [!]

week /wi:k/ *n* semana *f*. **~day** *n* día *m* de semana. **~end** *n* fin *m* de semana. **~ly** *adj* semanal. ● *n* semanario *m.* ● *adv* semanalmente

weep /wi:p/ *vi* (*pt* **wept**) llorar

weigh /weɪ/ *vt/i* pesar. ~ **anchor** levar anclas. □ ~ **down** *vt* (*fig*) oprimir. □ ~ **up** *vt* pesar; (*fig*) considerar

weight /weɪt/ *n* peso *m*; (*sport*) pesa *f*. **put on** ~ engordar. **lose** ~ adelgazar. ~**-lifting** *n* halterofilia *f*, levantamiento *m* de pesos

weir /wɪə(r)/ *n* presa *f*

weird /wɪəd/ *adj* (**-er**, **-est**) raro, extraño; (*unearthly*) misterioso

welcom|e /'welkəm/ *adj* bienvenido. **you're** ~**e!** (*after thank you*) ¡de nada! ● *n* bienvenida *f*; (*reception*) acogida *f*. ● *vt* dar la bienvenida a; (*appreciate*) alegrarse de. ~**ing** *adj* acogedor

weld /weld/ *vt* soldar. ● *n* soldadura *f*. ~**er** *n* soldador *m*

welfare /'welfeə(r)/ *n* bienestar *m*; (*aid*) asistencia *f* social. **W**~ **State** *n* estado *m* benefactor

well /wel/ *adv* (**better**, **best**) bien. ~ **done!** ¡muy bien!, ¡bravo! **as** ~ también. **as** ~ **as** además de. **we may as** ~ **go tomorrow** más vale que vayamos mañana. **do** ~ (*succeed*) tener éxito. **very** ~ muy bien. ● *adj* bien. **I'm very** ~ estoy muy bien. ● *int* (*introducing, continuing sentence*) bueno; (*surprise*) ¡vaya!; (*indignation, resignation*) bueno. ~ **I never!** ¡no me digas! ● *n* pozo *m*

we'll /wi:l//wɪəl/ = **we will**

well: ~**-behaved** /-bɪ'heɪvd/ *adj* que se porta bien, bueno. ~**-educated** /-'edjʊkeɪtɪd/ *adj* culto.

wellington (boot) /'welɪŋtən/ *n* bota *f* de goma *or* de agua; (*Amer, short boot*) botín *m*

well: ~**-known** /-'nəʊn/ *adj* conocido. ~ **off** *adj* adinerado. ~**-stocked** /-'stɒkt/ *adj* bien provisto. ~**-to-do** /-tə'du:/ *adj* adinerado

Welsh /welʃ/ *adj* & *n* galés (*m*). **the** ~ *n* los galeses

> *i* **Welsh Assembly** La Asamblea Nacional de Gales empezó a funcionar, en Cardiff, en 1999. Tiene poderes limitados, por lo que no puede imponer impuestos. Consta de 60 miembros o *AMs* (*Assembly Members*); 40 elegidos directamente y el resto, de las listas regionales, mediante el sistema de representación proporcional.

went /went/ *see* **GO**

wept /wept/ *see* **WEEP**

were /wɜ:(r), wə(r)/ *see* **BE**

we're /wɪə(r)/ = **we are**

west /west/ *n* oeste *m*. **the W**~ el Occidente *m*. ● *adj* oeste; (wind) del oeste. ● *adv* (go) hacia el oeste, al oeste. **it's** ~ **of York** está al oeste de York. ~**erly** /-əlɪ/ *adj* (wind) del oeste. ~**ern** /-ən/ *adj* occidental. ● *n* (*film*) película *f* del Oeste. ~**erner** *n* occidental *m* & *f*. **W**~ **Indian** *adj* & *n* antillano (*m*). **W**~ **Indies** *npl* Antillas *fpl*. ~**ward(s)** /-wəd(z)/,

wet /wet/ *adj* (**wetter**, **wettest**) mojado; (*rainy*) lluvioso; (*fam, person*) soso. '~ **paint**' pintura fresca'. **get** ~ mojarse. **he got his feet** ~ se mojó los pies. ● *vt* (*pt* **wetted**) mojar; (*dampen*) humedecer. ~ **o.s.** orinarse. ~**back** *n* espalda *f* mojada. ~ **blanket** *n* aguafiestas *m* & *f*. ~ **suit** *n* traje *m* de neopreno

we've /wiːv/ = **we have**

whack /wæk/ *vt* [!] golpear. ● *n* [!] golpe *m*.

whale /weɪl/ *n* ballena *f*. **we had a ~ of a time** [!] lo pasamos bomba [!]

wham /wæm/ *int* ¡zas!

wharf /wɔːf/ *n* (*pl* **wharves** *or* **wharfs**) muelle *m*

what /wɒt/

● *adjective*

····➤ (*in questions*) qué. **~ perfume are you wearing?** ¿qué perfume llevas?. **~ colour are the walls?** ¿de qué color son las paredes?

····➤ (*in exclamations*) qué. **~ a beautiful house!** ¡qué casa más linda!. **~ a lot of people!** ¡cuánta gente!

····➤ (*in indirect speech*) qué. **I'll ask him ~ bus to take** le preguntaré qué autobús hay que tomar. **do you know ~ time it leaves?** ¿sabes a qué hora sale?

● *pronoun*

····➤ (*in questions*) qué. **~ is it?** ¿qué es? **~ for?** ¿para qué?. **~'s the problem?** ¿cuál es el problema? **~'s he like?** ¿cómo es? **what?** (*say that again*) ¿cómo?, ¿qué?

····➤ (*in indirect questions*) qué. **I didn't know ~ to do** no sabía qué hacer

····➤ (*relative*) lo que. **I did ~ I could** hice lo que pude. **~ I need is a new car** lo que necesito es un coche nuevo

····➤ (*in phrases*) **~ about me?** ¿y yo qué? **~ if she doesn't come?** ¿y si no viene?

whatever /wɒt'evə(r)/ *adj* cualquiera. ● *pron* (todo) lo que, cualquier cosa que

whatsoever /wɒtsəʊ'evə(r)/ *adj & pron* = **whatever**

wheat /wiːt/ *n* trigo *m*

wheel /wiːl/ *n* rueda *f*. **at the ~** al volante. ● *vt* empujar (bicycle etc); llevar (en silla de ruedas etc) (person). **~barrow** *n* carretilla *f*. **~chair** *n* silla *f* de ruedas

wheeze /wiːz/ *vi* respirar con dificultad

when /wen/ *adv* cuándo. ● *conj* cuando. **~ever** /-'evə(r)/ *adv* (*every time that*) cada vez que, siempre que; (*at whatever time*) **we'll go ~ever you're ready** saldremos cuando estés listo

where /weə(r)/ *adv & conj* donde; (*interrogative*) dónde. **~ are you going?** ¿adónde vas? **~ are you from?** ¿de dónde eres?. **~abouts** /-əbaʊts/ *adv* en qué parte. ● *n* paradero *m*. **~as** /-'æz/ *conj* por cuanto; (*in contrast*) mientras (que). **~ver** /weər'evə(r)/ *adv* (*in questions*) dónde; (*no matter where*) en cualquier parte. ● *conj* donde (+ *subjunctive*), dondequiera (+ *subjunctive*)

whet /wet/ *vt* (*pt* **whetted**) abrir (appetite)

whether /'weðə(r)/ *conj* si. **I don't know ~ she will like it** no sé si le gustará. **~ you like it or not** te guste o no te guste

which /wɪtʃ/ *adj* (*in questions*) (*sing*) qué, cuál; (*pl*) qué, cuáles. **~ one** cuál. **~ one of you** cuál de ustedes. ● *pron* (*in questions*) (*sing*) cuál; (*pl*) cuáles; (*relative*) que; (*object*) el cual, la cual, lo cual, los cuales, las cuales. **~ever** /-'evə(r)/

W

adj cualquier. ● *pron* cualquiera que, el que, la que; (*in questions*) cuál; (*pl*) cuáles

while /waɪl/ *n* rato *m*. **a ~ ago** hace un rato. ● *conj* mientras; (*although*) aunque. □ **~ away** *vt* pasar (time)

whilst /waɪlst/ *conj see* **WHILE**

whim /wɪm/ *n* capricho *m*

whimper /ˈwɪmpə(r)/ *vi* gimotear. ● *n* quejido *m*

whine /waɪn/ *vi* (person) gemir; (child) lloriquear; (dog) aullar

whip /wɪp/ *n* látigo *m*; (*for punishment*) azote *m*. ● *vt* (*pt* **whipped** /wɪpt/) fustigar, pegarle a (*con la fusta*) (horse); azotar (person); (*Culin*) batir

whirl /wɜːl/ *vi* girar rápidamente. **~pool** *n* remolino *m*. **~wind** *n* torbellino *m*

whirr /wɜː(r)/ *n* zumbido *m*. ● *vi* zumbar

whisk /wɪsk/ *vt* (*Culin*) batir. ● *n* (*Culin*) batidor *m*. **~ away** llevarse

whisker /ˈwɪskə(r)/ *n* pelo *m*. **~s** *npl* (*of cat etc*) bigotes *mpl*

whisky /ˈwɪskɪ/ *n* whisky *m*, güisqui *m*

whisper /ˈwɪspə(r)/ *vt* susurrar. ● *vi* cuchichear. ● *n* susurro *m*

whistle /ˈwɪsl/ *n* silbido *m*; (*loud*) chiflado *m*; (*instrument*) silbato *m*, pito *m*. ● *vi* silbar; (*loudly*) chiflar

white /waɪt/ *adj* (**-er**, **-est**) blanco. **go ~** ponerse pálido. ● *n* blanco; (*of egg*) clara *f*. **~ coffee** *n* café *m* con leche. **~-collar worker** *n* empleado *m* de oficina. **~ elephant** *n* objeto *m* inútil y costoso. **~-hot** *adj* (metal) al rojo blanco. **~ lie** *n* mentirijilla *f*. **~n** *vt/i* blanquear. **~wash** *n* cal *f*; (*cover-up*) tapadera *f* [!]. ● *vt* blanquear, encalar

Whitsun /ˈwɪtsn/ *n* Pentecostés *m*

whiz /wɪz/ *vi* (*pt* **whizzed**). **~ by**, **~ past** pasar zumbando. **~-kid** *n* [!] lince *m* [!]

who /huː/ *pron* (*in questions*) quién; (*pl*) quiénes; (*as relative*) que; **the girl ~ lives there** la chica que vive allí. **those ~ can't come tomorrow** los que no puedan venir mañana. **~ever** /huːˈevə(r)/ *pron* quienquiera que; (*interrogative*) quién

whole /həʊl/ *adj*. **the ~ country** todo el país. **there's a ~ bottle left** queda una botella entera. ● *n* todo *m*, conjunto *m*; (*total*) total *m*. **on the ~** en general. **~-hearted** /-ˈhɑːtɪd/ *adj* (support) incondicional; (approval) sin reservar. **~meal** *adj* integral. **~sale** *n* venta *f* al por mayor. ● *adj & adv* al por mayor. **~some** /-səm/ *adj* sano

wholly /ˈhəʊlɪ/ *adv* completamente

whom /huːm/ *pron* que, a quien; (*in questions*) a quién

whooping cough /ˈhuːpɪŋ/ *n* tos *f* convulsa

whore /hɔː(r)/ *n* puta *f*

whose /huːz/ *pron* de quién; (*pl*) de quiénes. ● *adj* (*in questions*) de quién; (*pl*) de quiénes; (*relative*) cuyo; (*pl*) cuyos

why /waɪ/ *adv* por qué. **~ not?** ¿por qué no? **that's ~ I couldn't go** por eso no pude ir. ● *int* ¡vaya!

wick /wɪk/ *n* mecha *f*

wicked /ˈwɪkɪd/ *adj* malo; (*mischievous*) travieso; (*fam, very bad*) malísimo

wicker /ˈwɪkə(r)/ *n* mimbre *m & f*. ● *adj* de mimbre. **~work** *n* artícu-

W

los *mpl* de mimbre

wicket /'wɪkɪt/ *n* (*cricket*) rastrillo *m*

wide /waɪd/ *adj* (**-er**, **-est**) ancho; (range, experience) amplio; (*off target*) desviado. **it's four metres ~** tiene cuatro metros de ancho. ● *adv*. **open ~!** abra bien la boca. **~ awake** *adj* completamente despierto; (*fig*) despabilado. **I left the door ~ open** dejé la puerta abierta de par en par. **~ly** *adv* extensamente; (*believed*) generalmente; (*different*) muy. **~n** *vt* ensanchar. ● *vi* ensancharse. **~spread** *adj* extendido; (*fig*) difundido

widow /'wɪdəʊ/ *n* viuda *f*. **~er** *n* viudo *m*.

width /wɪdθ/ *n* anchura *f*. **in ~** de ancho

wield /wi:ld/ *vt* manejar; ejercer (power)

wife /waɪf/ *n* (*pl* **wives**) mujer *f*, esposa *f*

wig /wɪg/ *n* peluca *f*

wiggle /'wɪgl/ *vt* menear. ● *vi* menearse

wild /waɪld/ *adj* (**-er**, **-est**) (animal) salvaje; (flower) silvestre; (country) agreste; (*enraged*) furioso; (idea) extravagante; (*with joy*) loco. **a ~ guess** una conjetura hecha totalmente al azar. **I'm not ~ about the idea** la idea no me enloquece. ● *adv* en estado salvaje. **run ~** (children) criarse como salvajes. **~s** *npl* regiones *fpl* salvajes. **~erness** /'wɪldənɪs/ *n* páramo *m*. **~fire** *n*. **spread like ~fire** correr como un reguero de pólvora. **~-goose chase** *n* empresa *f* inútil. **~life** *n* fauna *f*. **~ly** *adv* violentamente; (*fig*) locamente

will /wɪl/

● *auxiliary verb*

past **would;** contracted forms **I'll, you'll, etc = I will, you will, etc.; won't = will not**

····➤ (*talking about the future*)

! The Spanish future tense is not always the first option for translating the English future tense. The present tense of *ir + a + verb* is commonly used instead, particularly in Latin American countries. **he'll be here on Tuesday** *estará el martes, va a estar el martes;* **she won't agree** *no va a aceptar, no aceptará*

····➤ (*in invitations and requests*) **~ you have some wine?** ¿quieres (un poco de) vino? **you'll stay for dinner, won't you?** te quedas a cenar, ¿no?

····➤ (*in tag questions*) **you ~ be back soon, won't you?** vas a volver pronto, ¿no?

····➤ (*in short answers*) **will it be ready by Monday? - yes, it ~** ¿estará listo para el lunes? - sí

● *noun*

····➤ (*mental power*) voluntad *f*

····➤ (*document*) testamento *m*

willing /'wɪlɪŋ/ *adj* complaciente. **~ to** dispuesto a. **~ly** *adv* de buena gana

willow /'wɪləʊ/ *n* sauce *m*

will-power /'wɪlpaʊə(r)/ *n* fuerza *f* de voluntad

wilt /wɪlt/ *vi* marchitarse

win /wɪn/ *vt* (*pt* **won**, *pres p* **winning**) ganar; (*achieve, obtain*) conseguir. ● *vi* ganar. ● *n* victoria *f*. □ ~ **over** *vt* ganarse a

wince /wɪns/ *vi* hacer una mueca de dolor

winch /wɪntʃ/ *n* cabrestante *m*. ● *vt* levantar con un cabrestante

wind¹ /wɪnd/ *n* viento *m*; (*in stomach*) gases *mpl*. ~ **instrument** instrumento *m* de viento. ● *vt* dejar sin aliento

wind² /waɪnd/ *vt* (*pt* **wound**) (*wrap around*) enrollar; dar cuerda a (clock etc). ● *vi* (road etc) serpentear. □ ~ **up** *vt* dar cuerda a (watch, clock); (*fig*) terminar, concluir

winding /'waɪndɪŋ/ *adj* tortuoso

windmill /'wɪndmɪl/ *n* molino *m* (de viento)

window /'wɪndəʊ/ *n* ventana *f*; (*in shop*) escaparate *m*, vitrina *f* (*LAm*), vidriera *f* (*LAm*), aparador *m* (*Mex*); (*of vehicle, booking-office*) ventanilla *f*; (*Comp*) ventana *f*, window *m*. ~ **box** *n* jardinera *f*. ~**-shop** *vi* mirar los escaparates. ~**sill** *n* alféizar *m or* repisa *f* de la ventana

wine /waɪn/ *n* vino *m*. ~**-cellar** *n* bodega *f*. ~**glass** *n* copa *f* de vino. ~**-growing** *n* vinicultura *f*. ● *adj* vinícola. ~ **list** *n* lista *f* de vinos. ~**-tasting** *n* cata *f* de vinos

wing /wɪŋ/ *n* ala *f*; (*Auto*) aleta *f*. **under one's** ~ bajo la protección de uno. ~**er** *n* (*Sport*) ala *m & f*. ~**s** *npl* (*in theatre*) bastidores *mpl*

wink /wɪŋk/ *vi* guiñar el ojo; (light etc) centellear. ● *n* guiño *m*. **not to sleep a** ~ no pegar ojo

win: ~**ner** *n* ganador *m*. ~**ning-post** *n* poste *m* de llegada. ~**nings** *npl* ganancias *fpl*

wint|er /'wɪntə(r)/ *n* invierno *m*. ● *vi* invernar. ~**ry** *adj* invernal

wipe /waɪp/ *vt* limpiar, pasarle un trapo a; (*dry*) secar. ~ **one's nose** limpiarse la nariz. ● *n*. **give sth a** ~ limpiar algo, pasarle un trapo a algo. □ ~ **out** *vt* (*cancel*) cancelar; (*destroy*) destruir; (*obliterate*) borrar. □ ~ **up** *vt* limpiar

wir|e /'waɪə(r)/ *n* alambre *m*; (*Elec*) cable *m*. ~**ing** *n* instalación *f* eléctrica

wisdom /'wɪzdəm/ *n* sabiduría *f*. ~ **tooth** *n* muela *f* del juicio

wise /waɪz/ *adj* (**-er**, **-est**) sabio; (*sensible*) prudente; (decision, choice) acertado. ~**ly** *adv* sabiamente; (*sensibly*) prudentemente

wish /wɪʃ/ *n* deseo *m*; (*greeting*) saludo *m*. **make a** ~ pedir un deseo. **best** ~**es, John** (*in letters*) saludos de John, un abrazo de John. ● *vt* desear. ~ **s.o. well** desear buena suerte a uno. **I** ~ **I were rich** ¡ojalá fuera rico! **he** ~**ed he hadn't told her** lamentó habérselo dicho. ~**ful thinking** *n* ilusiones *fpl*

wistful /'wɪstfl/ *adj* melancólico

wit /wɪt/ *n* gracia *f*; (*intelligence*) ingenio *m*. **be at one's** ~**s' end** no saber más qué hacer

witch /wɪtʃ/ *n* bruja *f*. ~**craft** *n* brujería *f*.

with /wɪð/ *prep* con; (*cause, having*) de. **come** ~ **me** ven conmigo. **take it** ~ **you** llévalo contigo; (*formal*) llévelo consigo. **the man** ~ **the beard** el hombre de la barba. **trembling** ~ **fear** temblando de miedo

withdraw /wɪð'drɔː/ *vt* (*pt* **withdrew**, *pp* **withdrawn**) retirar. ● *vi* apartarse. **~al** *n* retirada *f.* **~n** *adj* (person) retraído

wither /ˈwɪðə(r)/ *vi* marchitarse

withhold /wɪðˈhəʊld/ *vt* (*pt* **withheld**) retener; (*conceal*) ocultar (**from** a)

within /wɪðˈɪn/ *prep* dentro de. ● *adv* dentro. **~ sight** a la vista

without /wɪðˈaʊt/ *prep* sin. **~ paying** sin pagar

withstand /wɪðˈstænd/ *vt* (*pt* **-stood**) resistir

witness /ˈwɪtnɪs/ *n* testigo *m*; (*proof*) testimonio *m*. ● *vt* presenciar; atestiguar (signature). **~-box** *n* tribuna *f* de los testigos

witt|icism /ˈwɪtɪsɪzəm/ *n* ocurrencia *f.* **~y** /ˈwɪtɪ/ *adj* (**-ier**, **-iest**) gracioso

wives /waɪvz/ *see* **WIFE**

wizard /ˈwɪzəd/ *n* hechicero *m*

wizened /ˈwɪznd/ *adj* arrugado

wobbl|e /ˈwɒbl/ *vi* (chair) tambalearse; (bicycle) bambolearse; (voice, jelly, hand) temblar. **~y** *adj* (chair etc) cojo

woe /wəʊ/ *n* aflicción *f*

woke/wəʊk/, **woken** /ˈwəʊkən/ *see* **WAKE**

wolf /wʊlf/ *n* (*pl* **wolves** /wʊlvz/) lobo *m*

woman /ˈwʊmən/ *n* (*pl* **women**) mujer *f*

womb /wuːm/ *n* matriz *f*

women /ˈwɪmɪn/ *npl see* **WOMAN**

won /wʌn/ *see* **WIN**

W

wonder /ˈwʌndə(r)/ *n* maravilla *f*; (*bewilderment*) asombro *m*. **no ~** no es de extrañarse (**that** que). ● *vt* (*ask oneself*) preguntarse. **I ~ whose book this is** me pregunto de quién será este libro; (*in polite requests*) **I ~ if you could help me?** ¿me podría ayudar? **~ful** *adj* maravilloso. **~fully** *adv* maravillosamente

won't /wəʊnt/ = **will not**

wood /wʊd/ *n* madera *f*; (*for burning*) leña *f*; (*area*) bosque *m*. **~ed** *adj* poblado de árboles, boscoso. **~en** *adj* de madera. **~land** *n* bosque *m*. **~wind** /-wɪnd/ *n* instrumentos *mpl* de viento de madera. **~work** *n* carpintería *f*; (*in room etc*) maderaje *m*. **~worm** *n* carcoma *f*. **~y** *adj* leñoso

wool /wʊl/ *n* lana *f.* **pull the ~ over s.o.'s eyes** engañar a uno. **~len** *adj* de lana. **~ly** *adj* (**-ier**, **-iest**) de lana; (*unclear*) vago. ● *n* jersey *m*

word /wɜːd/ *n* palabra *f*; (*news*) noticia *f.* **by ~ of mouth** de palabra. **I didn't say a ~** yo no dije nada. **in other ~s** es decir. ● *vt* expresar. **~ing** *n* redacción *f*; (*of question*) formulación *f.* **~ processor** *n* procesador *m* de textos. **~y** *adj* prolijo

wore /wɔː(r)/ *see* **WEAR**

work /wɜːk/ *n* trabajo *m*; (*arts*) obra *f.* **be out of ~** estar sin trabajo, estar desocupado. ● *vt* hacer trabajar; manejar (machine). ● *vi* trabajar; (machine) funcionar; (student) estudiar; (drug etc) surtir efecto. □ **~ off** *vt* desahogar. □ **~ out** *vt* resolver (problem); (*calculate*) calcular; (*understand*) entender. ● *vi* (*succeed*) salir bien; (*Sport*) entrenarse. □ **~ up** *vt*. **get ~ed up** exaltarse. **~able** *adj* (project, solution) factible. **~er** *n* trabajador *m*; (*manual*) obrero *m*; (*in office, bank*) empleado *m*. **~ing** *adj* (day) laborable; (clothes etc) de trabajo. **in ~ing order** en estado de funcionamiento. **~ing class** *n* clase *f* obrera. **~ing-class** *adj* de la clase obrera. **~man** /-mən/ *n* (*pl* **-men**) obrero *m*. **~manship** *n* destreza *f*. **~s** *npl* (*building*) fábrica *f*; (*Mec*) mecanismo *m*. **~shop** *n* taller *m*

world /wɜːld/ *n* mundo *m*. **out of this ~** maravilloso. ● *adj* mundial. **W~ Cup** *n*. **the W~ Cup** la Copa del Mundo. **~ly** *adj* mundano. **~wide** *adj* universal. **W~ Wide Web** *n* World Wide Web *m*

worm /wɜːm/ *n* gusano *m*, lombriz *f*

worn /wɔːn/ *see* **WEAR**. ● *adj* gastado. **~-out** *adj* gastado; (person) rendido

worr|ied /'wʌrɪd/ *adj* preocupado. **~y** /'wʌrɪ/ *vt* preocupar; (*annoy*) molestar. ● *vi* preocuparse. ● *n* preocupación *f*. **~ying** *adj* inquietante

worse /wɜːs/ *adj* peor. **get ~** empeorar. ● *adv* peor; (*more*) más. **~n** *vt/i* empeorar

worship /'wɜːʃɪp/ *n* culto *m*; (*title*) Su Señoría. ● *vt* (*pt* **worshipped**) adorar

worst /wɜːst/ *adj* peor. **he's the ~ in the class** es el peor de la clase. ● *adv* peor. ● *n*. **the ~** lo peor

worth /wɜːθ/ *n* valor *m*. ● *adj*. **be ~** valer. **it's ~ trying** vale la pena probarlo. **it was ~ my while** (me) valió la pena. **~less** *adj* sin valor. **~while** /-'waɪl/ *adj* que vale la pena. **~y** /'wɜːðɪ/ *adj* meritorio; (*respectable*) respetable; (*laudable*) loable

would /wʊd/ *modal verb*. (*in conditional sentences*) **~ you go?** ¿irías tú? **he ~ come if he could** vendría si pudiera; (*in reported speech*) **I thought you'd forget** pensé que te olvidarías; (*in requests, invitations*) **~ you come here, please?** ¿quieres venir aquí? **~ you switch the television off?** ¿podrías apagar la televisión?; (*be prepared to*) **he ~n't listen to me** no me quería escuchar

wound¹ /wuːnd/ *n* herida *f*. ● *vt* herir

wound² /waʊnd/ *see* **WIND²**

wove, woven /wəʊv, 'wəʊvn/ *see* **WEAVE**

wow /waʊ/ *int* ¡ah!

wrangle /'ræŋgl/ *vi* reñir. ● *n* riña *f*

wrap /ræp/ *vt* (*pt* **wrapped**) envolver. ● *n* bata *f*; (*shawl*) chal *m*. **~per** *n*, **~ping** *n* envoltura *f*

wrath /rɒθ/ *n* ira *f*

wreak /riːk/ *vt* sembrar. **~ havoc** causar estragos

wreath /riːθ/ *n* (*pl* **-ths** /-ðz/) corona *f*

wreck /rek/ *n* (*ship*) restos *mpl* de un naufragio; (*vehicle*) restos *mpl* de un avión siniestrado. **be a nervous ~** tener los nervios destrozados. ● *vt* provocar el naufragio de (ship); destrozar (car); (*Amer, demolish*) demoler; (*fig*) destrozar. **~age** /-ɪdʒ/ *n* restos *mpl*; (*of building*) ruinas *fpl*

wrench /rentʃ/ *vt* arrancar; (*sprain*) desgarrarse; dislocarse (joint). ● *n* tirón *m*; (*emotional*) dolor *m* (causado por una separación); (*tool*) llave *f* inglesa

wrestl|e /'resl/ *vi* luchar. **~er** *n* luchador *m*. **~ing** *n* lucha *f*

wretch /retʃ/ *n* (*despicable person*) desgraciado *m*; (*unfortunate person*) desdichado *m* & *f*. **~ed** /-ɪd/ *adj* desdichado; (weather) horrible

wriggle /'rɪgl/ *vi* retorcerse. ~

out of escaparse de
wring /rɪŋ/ *vt* (*pt* **wrung**) retorcer (neck). **~ out of** (*obtain from*) arrancar. □ **~ out** *vt* retorcer
wrinkl|e /ˈrɪŋkl/ *n* arruga *f*. ● *vt* arrugar. ● *vi* arrugarse. **~y** *adj* arrugado
wrist /rɪst/ *n* muñeca *f*. **~watch** *n* reloj *m* de pulsera
writ /rɪt/ *n* orden *m* judicial
write /raɪt/ *vt/i* (*pt* **wrote**, *pp* **written**, *pres p* **writing**) escribir. □ **~ down** *vt* anotar. □ **~ off** *vt* cancelar (debt). **~-off** *n*. **the car was a ~-off** el coche fue declarado un siniestro total. **~r** *n* escritor *m*
writhe /raɪð/ *vi* retorcerse
writing /ˈraɪtɪŋ/ *n* (*script*) escritura *f*; (*handwriting*) letra *f*. **in ~** por escrito. **~s** *npl* obra *f*, escritos *mpl*. **~ desk** *n* escritorio *m*. **~ pad** *n* bloc *m*. **~ paper** *n* papel *m* de escribir
written /ˈrɪtn/ *see* **WRITE**
wrong /rɒŋ/ *adj* equivocado, incorrecto; (*not just*) injusto; (*mistaken*) equivocado. **be ~** no tener razón; (*be mistaken*) equivocarse. **what's ~?** ¿qué pasa? **it's ~ to steal** robar está mal. **what's ~ with that?** ¿qué hay de malo en eso?. ● *adv* mal. **go ~** equivocarse; (plan) salir mal. ● *n* injusticia *f*; (*evil*) mal *m*. **in the ~** equivocado. ● *vt* ser injusto con. **~ful** *adj* injusto. **~ly** *adv* mal; (*unfairly*) injustamente
wrote /rəʊt/ *see* **WROTE**
wrought iron /rɔːt/ *n* hierro *m* forjado
wrung /rʌŋ/ *see* **WRING**
wry /raɪ/ *adj* (**wryer**, **wryest**) irónico. **make a ~ face** torcer el gesto

W X Y

Xx

xerox /ˈzɪərɒks/ *vt* fotocopiar, xerografiar
Xmas /ˈkrɪsməs/ *n abbr* (**Christmas**) Navidad *f*
X-ray /ˈeksreɪ/ *n* (*ray*) rayo *m* X; (*photograph*) radiografía *f*. **~s** *npl* rayos *mpl*. ● *vt* hacer una radiografía de
xylophone /ˈzaɪləfəʊn/ *n* xilofón *m*, xilófono *m*

Yy

yacht /jɒt/ *n* yate *m*. **~ing** *n* navegación *f* a vela
yank /jæŋk/ *vt* [I] tirar de (*violentamente*)
Yankee /ˈjæŋkɪ/ *n* [I] yanqui *m & f*
yap /jæp/ *vi* (*pt* **yapped**) (dog) ladrar (*con ladridos agudos*)
yard /jɑːd/ *n* patio *m*; (*Amer, garden*) jardín *m*; (*measurement*) yarda *f* (*= 0.9144 metre*)
yarn /jɑːn/ *n* hilo *m*; (*fam, tale*) cuento *m*
yawn /jɔːn/ *vi* bostezar. ● *n* bostezo *m*
yeah /jeə/ *adv* [I] sí
year /jɪə(r)/ *n* año *m*. **be three ~s old** tener tres años. **~ly** *adj* anual. ● *adv* cada año
yearn /ˈjɜːn/ *vi*. **~ to do sth** anhelar hacer algo. **~ for sth** añorar

algo. **~ing** *n* anhelo *m*, ansia *f*

yeast /ji:st/ *n* levadura *f*

yell /jel/ *vi* gritar. ● *n* grito *m*

yellow /ˈjeləʊ/ *adj & n* amarillo (*m*)

yelp /jelp/ *n* gañido *m*. ● *vi* gañir

yes /jes/ *int & n* sí (*m*)

yesterday /ˈjestədeɪ/ *adv & n* ayer (*m*). **the day before ~** anteayer *m*. **~ morning** ayer por la mañana, ayer en la mañana (*LAm*)

yet /jet/ *adv* todavía, aún; (*already*) ya. **as ~** hasta ahora; (*as a linker*) sin embargo. ● *conj* pero

Yiddish /ˈjɪdɪʃ/ *n* yídish *m*

yield /ji:ld/ *vt* (*surrender*) ceder; producir (crop/mineral); dar (results). ● *vi* ceder. **'yield'** (*Amer, traffic sign*) ceda el paso. ● *n* rendimiento *m*

yoga /ˈjəʊgə/ *n* yoga *m*

yoghurt /ˈjɒgət/ *n* yogur *m*

yoke /jəʊk/ *n* (*fig also*) yugo *m*

yokel /ˈjəʊkl/ *n* palurdo *m*

yolk /jəʊk/ *n* yema *f* (de huevo)

you /ju:/ *pronoun*

····➤ (*as the subject*) (*familiar form*) (*sing*) tú, vos (*River Plate and parts of Central America*); (*pl*) vosotros, -tras (*Spain*), ustedes (*LAm*); (*formal*) (*sing*) usted; (*pl*) ustedes

> ! In Spanish the subject pronoun is usually only used to give emphasis or mark contrast.

····➤ (*as the direct object*) (*familiar form*) (*sing*) te; (*pl*) os (*Spain*), los, las (*LAm*); (*formal*) (*sing*) lo *or* (*Spain*) le, la; (*pl*) los *or* (*Spain*) les, las. **I love ~** te quiero

····➤ (*as the indirect object*) (*familiar form*) (*sing*) te; (*pl*) os (*Spain*), les (*LAm*); (*formal*) (*sing*) le; (*pl*) les. **I sent ~ the book yesterday** te mandé el libro ayer

> ! The pronoun *se* replaces the indirect object pronoun *le* or *les* when the latter is used with the direct object pronoun (*lo*, *la* etc), e.g. **I gave it to ~** *se lo di*

····➤ (*when used after a preposition*) (*familiar form*) (*sing*) ti, vos (*River Plate and parts of Central America*); (*pl*) vosotros, -tras (*Spain*), ustedes (*LAm*); (*formal*) (*sing*) usted; (*pl*) ustedes

····➤ (*generalizing*) uno, tú (*esp Spain*). **~ feel very proud** uno se siente muy orgulloso, te sientes muy orgulloso (*esp Spain*). **~ have to be patient** hay que tener paciencia

you'd/ju:d/, /jʊəd/ = **you had, you would**

you'll/ju:l/, /jʊəl/ = **you will**

young /jʌŋ/ *adj* (**-er, -est**) joven. **my ~er sister** mi hermana menor. **he's a year ~er than me** tiene un año menos que yo. **~ lady** *n* señorita *f*. **~ man** *n* joven *m*. **~ster** /-stə(r)/ *n* joven *m*

your /jɔ:(r)/ *adj* (*belonging to one person*) (*sing, familiar*) tu; (*pl, familiar*) tus; (*sing, formal*) su; (*pl, formal*) sus; (*belonging to more than one person*) (*sing, familiar*) vuestro, -tra, su (*LAm*); (*pl, familiar*) vuestros, -tras, sus (*LAm*); (*sing, formal*) su; (*pl, formal*) sus

you're/jʊə(r)/, /jɔ:(r)/ = **you are**

yours /jɔːz/ *poss pron* (*belonging to one person*) (*sing, familiar*) tuyo, -ya; (*pl, familiar*) tuyos, -yas; (*sing, formal*) suyo, -ya; (*pl, formal*) suyos, -yas. (*belonging to more than one person*) (*sing, familiar*) vuestro, -tra; (*pl, familiar*) vuestros, -tras, suyos, -yas (*LAm*); (*sing, formal*) suyo, -ya; (*pl, formal*) suyos, -yas. **an aunt of ~** una tía tuya/suya; **~ is here** el tuyo/la tuya/el suyo/la suya está aquí

yoursel|f /jɔː'self/ *pron* (*reflexive*). (*emphatic use*) ⓘ tú mismo, tú misma; (*formal*) usted mismo, usted misma. **describe ~f** descríbete; (*Ud form*) descríbase. **stop thinking about ~f** ⓘ deja de pensar en tí mismo; (*formal*) deje de pensar en sí mismo. **by ~f** solo, sola. **~ves** /jɔː'selvz/ *pron* vosotros mismos, vosotras mismas (*familiar*), ustedes mismos, ustedes mismas (*LAm familiar*), ustedes mismos, ustedes mismas (*formal*); (*reflexive*). **behave ~ves** ¡portaos bien! (*familiar*), ¡pórtense bien! (*formal, LAm familiar*). **by ~ves** solos, solas

youth /juːθ/ *n* (*pl* **youths** /juːðz/) (*early life*) juventud *f*; (*boy*) joven *m*; (*young people*) juventud *f*. **~ful** *adj* joven, juvenil. **~ hostel** *n* albergue *m* juvenil

you've/juːv/ = **you have**

Yugoslav /'juːgəslɑːv/ *adj & n* yugoslavo (*m*). **~ia** /-'slɑːvɪə/ *n* Yugoslavia *f*

Zz

zeal /ziːl/ *n* fervor *m*, celo *m*

zeal|ot /'zelət/ *n* fanático *m*. **~ous** /-əs/ *adj* ferviente; (*worker*) que pone gran celo en su trabajo

zebra /'zebrə/ *n* cebra *f*. **~ crossing** *n* paso *m* de cebra

zenith /'zenɪθ/ *n* cenit *m*

zero /'zɪərəʊ/ *n* (*pl* **-os**) cero *m*

zest /zest/ *n* entusiasmo *m*; (*peel*) cáscara *f*

zigzag /'zɪgzæg/ *n* zigzag *m*. ● *vi* (*pt* **zigzagged**) zigzaguear

zilch /zɪltʃ/ *n* ☒ nada de nada

zinc /zɪŋk/ *n* cinc *m*

zip /zɪp/ *n* cremallera *f*, cierre *m* (*LAm*), zíper *m* (*Mex*). ● *vt*. **~ (up)** cerrar (la cremallera). **Z~ code** *n* (*Amer*) código *m* postal. **~ fastener** *n* cremallera *f*. **~per** *n/vt* see **ZIP**

zodiac /'zəʊdɪæk/ *n* zodíaco *m*, zodiaco *m*

zombie /'zɒmbɪ/ *n* zombi *m & f*

zone /zəʊn/ *n* zona *f*. **time ~** *n* huso *m* horario

zoo /zuː/ *n* zoo *m*, zoológico *m*. **~logical** /zuːə'lɒdʒɪkl/ *adj* zoológico. **~logist** /zuː'ɒlədʒɪst/ *n* zoólogo *m*. **~logy** /zuː'ɒlədʒɪ/ *n* zoología *f*

zoom /zuːm/. □ **~ in** *vi* (*Photo*) hacer un zoom in (**on** sobre). □ **~ past** *vi/t* pasar zumbando. **~ lens** *n* teleobjetivo *m*, zoom *m*

zucchini /zʊ'kiːnɪ/ *n* (*invar or* **~s**) (*Amer*) calabacín *m*

Numbers/números

zero	**0**	cero
one (first)	**1**	uno (primero)
two (second)	**2**	dos (segundo)
three (third)	**3**	tres (tercero)
four (fourth)	**4**	cuatro (cuarto)
five (fifth)	**5**	cinco (quinto)
six (sixth)	**6**	seis (sexto)
seven (seventh)	**7**	siete (séptimo)
eight (eighth)	**8**	ocho (octavo)
nine (ninth)	**9**	nueve (noveno)
ten (tenth)	**10**	diez (décimo)
eleven (eleventh)	**11**	once (undécimo)
twelve (twelfth)	**12**	doce (duodécimo)
thirteen (thirteenth)	**13**	trece (decimotercero)
fourteen (fourteenth)	**14**	catorce (decimocuarto)
fifteen (fifteenth)	**15**	quince (decimoquinto)
sixteen (sixteenth)	**16**	dieciséis (decimosexto)
seventeen (seventeenth)	**17**	diecisiete (decimoséptimo)
eighteen (eighteenth)	**18**	dieciocho (decimoctavo)
nineteen (nineteenth)	**19**	diecinueve (decimonoveno)
twenty (twentieth)	**20**	veinte (vigésimo)
twenty-one (twenty-first)	**21**	veintiuno (vigésimo primero)
twenty-two (twenty-second)	**22**	veintidós (vigésimo segundo)
twenty-three (twenty-third)	**23**	veintitrés (vigésimo tercero)
twenty-four (twenty-fourth)	**24**	veinticuatro (vigésimo cuarto)
twenty-five (twenty-fifth)	**25**	veinticinco (vigésimo quinto)
twenty-six (twenty-sixth)	**26**	veintiséis (vigésimo sexto)
thirty (thirtieth)	**30**	treinta (trigésimo)

thirty-one (thirty-first)	**31**	treinta y uno (trigésimo primero)
forty (fortieth)	**40**	cuarenta (cuadragésimo)
fifty (fiftieth)	**50**	cincuenta (quincuagésimo)
sixty (sixtieth)	**60**	sesenta (sexagésimo)
seventy (seventieth)	**70**	setenta (septuagésimo)
eighty (eightieth)	**80**	ochenta (octogésimo)
ninety (ninetieth)	**90**	noventa (nonagésimo)
a/one hundred (hundredth)	**100**	cien (centésimo)
a/one hundred and one (hundred and first)	**101**	ciento uno (centésimo primero)
two hundred (two hundredth)	**200**	doscientos (ducentésimo)
three hundred (three hundredth)	**300**	trescientos (tricentésimo)
four hundred (four hundredth)	**400**	cuatrocientos (cuadringentésimo)
five hundred (five hundredth)	**500**	quinientos (quingentésimo)
six hundred (six hundredth)	**600**	seiscientos (sexcentésimo)
seven hundred (seven hundredth)	**700**	setecientos (septingentésimo)
eight hundred (eight hundredth)	**800**	ochocientos (octingentésimo)
nine hundred (nine hundredth)	**900**	novecientos (noningentésimo)
a/one thousand (thousandth)	**1000**	mil (milésimo)
two thousand (two thousandth)	**2000**	dos mil (dos milésimo)
a/one million (millionth)	**1,000,000**	un millón (millonésimo)

Verbos irregulares ingleses

Infinitivo	*Pretérito*	*Participio pasado*
be	was	been
bear	bore	borne
beat	beat	beaten
become	became	become
begin	began	begun
bend	bent	bent
bet	bet, betted	bet, betted
bid	bade, bid	bidden, bid
bind	bound	bound
bite	bit	bitten
bleed	bled	bled
blow	blew	blown
break	broke	broken
breed	bred	bred
bring	brought	brought
build	built	built
burn	burnt, burned	burnt, burned
burst	burst	burst
buy	bought	bought
catch	caught	caught
choose	chose	chosen
cling	clung	clung
come	came	come
cost	cost, costed (*vt*)	cost, costed
cut	cut	cut
deal	dealt	dealt
dig	dug	dug
do	did	done
draw	drew	drawn
dream	dreamt, dreamed	dreamt, dreamed
drink	drank	drunk

Infinitivo	*Pretérito*	*Participio pasado*
drive	drove	driven
eat	ate	eaten
fall	fell	fallen
feed	fed	fed
feel	felt	felt
fight	fought	fought
find	found	found
flee	fled	fled
fly	flew	flown
freeze	froze	frozen
get	got	got, gotten *US*
give	gave	given
go	went	gone
grow	grew	grown
hang	hung, hanged	hung, hanged
have	had	had
hear	heard	heard
hide	hid	hidden
hit	hit	hit
hold	held	held
hurt	hurt	hurt
keep	kept	kept
kneel	knelt	knelt
know	knew	known
lay	laid	laid
lead	led	led
lean	leaned, leant	leaned, leant
learn	learnt, learned	learnt, learned
leave	left	left
lend	lent	lent
let	let	let
lie	lay	lain

Infinitivo	*Pretérito*	*Participio pasado*
lose	lost	lost
make	made	made
mean	meant	meant
meet	met	met
pay	paid	paid
put	put	put
read	read	read
ride	rode	ridden
ring	rang	rung
rise	rose	risen
run	ran	run
say	said	said
see	saw	seen
seek	sought	sought
sell	sold	sold
send	sent	sent
set	set	set
sew	sewed	sewn, sewed
shake	shook	shaken
shine	shone	shone
shoe	shod	shod
shoot	shot	shot
show	showed	shown
shut	shut	shut
sing	sang	sung
sink	sank	sunk
sit	sat	sat
sleep	slept	slept
sling	slung	slung
smell	smelt, smelled	smelt, smelled
speak	spoke	spoken
spell	spelled, spelt	spelled, spelt
spend	spent	spent
spit	spat	spat
spoil	spoilt, spoiled	spoilt, spoiled
spread	spread	spread
spring	sprang	sprung
stand	stood	stood
steal	stole	stolen
stick	stuck	stuck
sting	stung	stung
stride	strode	stridden
strike	struck	struck
swear	swore	sworn
sweep	swept	swept
swell	swelled	swollen, swelled
swim	swam	swum
swing	swung	swung
take	took	taken
teach	taught	taught
tear	tore	torn
tell	told	told
think	thought	thought
throw	threw	thrown
thrust	thrust	thrust
tread	trod	trodden
understand	understood	understood
wake	woke	woken
wear	wore	worn
win	won	won
write	wrote	written

Spanish verbs

Regular verbs:

● in **-ar** (*e.g.* **comprar**)
Present; compr|o, **~as, ~a, ~amos, ~áis, ~an**
Future: comprar|é, **~ás, ~á, ~emos, ~éis, ~án**
Imperfect: compr|aba, **~abas, ~aba, ~ábamos, ~abais, ~aban**
Preterite: compr|é, **~aste, ~ó, ~amos, ~asteis, ~aron**
Present subjunctive: compr|e, **~es, ~e, ~emos, ~éis, ~en**
Imperfect subjunctive: compr|ara, **~aras, ~ara, ~áramos, ~arais, ~aran**
compr|ase, **~ases, ~ase, ~ásemos, ~aseis, ~asen**
Conditional: comprar|ía, **~ías, ~ía, ~íamos, ~íais, ~ían**
Present participle: comprando
Past participle: comprado
Imperative: compra, comprad

● in **-er** (*e.g.* **beber**)
Present: beb|o, **~es, ~e, ~emos, ~éis, ~en**
Future: beber|é, **~ás, ~á, ~emos, ~éis, ~án**
Imperfect: beb|ía, **~ías, ~ía, ~íamos, ~íais, ~ían**
Preterite: beb|í, **~iste, ~ió, ~imos, ~isteis, ~ieron**
Present subjunctive: beb|a, **~as, ~a, ~amos, ~áis, ~an**
Imperfect subjunctive: beb|iera, **~ieras, ~iera, ~iéramos, ~ierais, ~ieran**
beb|iese, **~ieses, ~iese, ~iésemos, ~ieseis, ~iesen**
Conditional: beber|ía, **~ías, ~ía, ~íamos, ~íais, ~ían**
Present participle: bebiendo
Past participle: bebido
Imperative: bebe, bebed

● in **-ir** (*e.g.* **vivir**)
Present: viv|o, **~es, ~e, ~imos, ~ís, ~en**
Future: vivir|é, **~ás, ~á, ~emos, ~éis, ~án**
Imperfect: viv|ía, **~ías, ~ía, ~íamos, íais, ~ían**
Preterite: viv|í, **~iste, ~ió, ~imos, ~isteis, ~ieron**
Present subjunctive: viv|a, **~as, ~a, ~amos, ~áis, ~an**
Imperfect subjunctive: viv|iera, **~ieras, ~iera, ~iéramos, ~ierais, ~ieran**
viv|iese, **~ieses, ~iese, ~iésemos, ~ieseis, ~iesen**
Conditional: vivir|ía, **~ías, ~ía, ~íamos, ~íais, ~ían**
Present participle: viviendo
Past participle: vivido
Imperative: vive, vivid

Irregular verbs:

[1] cerrar
Present: cierro, cierras, cierra, cerramos, cerráis, cierran
Present subjunctive: cierre, cierres, cierre, cerremos, cerréis, cierren
Imperative: cierra, cerrad

[2] contar, mover

Present: cuento, cuentas, cuenta, contamos, contáis, cuentan
muevo, mueves, mueve, movemos, movéis, mueven
Present subjunctive: cuente, cuentes, cuente, contemos, contéis, cuenten
mueva, muevas, mueva, movamos, mováis, muevan
Imperative: cuenta, contad
mueve, moved

[3] jugar

Present: juego, juegas, juega, jugamos, jugáis, juegan
Preterite: jugué, jugaste, jugó, jugamos, jugasteis, jugaron
Present subjunctive: juegue, juegues, juegue, juguemos, juguéis, jueguen

[4] sentir

Present: siento, sientes, siente, sentimos, sentís, sienten
Preterite: sentí, sentiste, sintió, sentimos, sentisteis, sintieron
Present subjunctive: sienta, sientas, sienta, sintamos, sintáis, sientan
Imperfect subjunctive: sint|iera, **~ieras, ~iera, ~iéramos, ~ierais, ~ieran**
sint|iese, **~ieses, ~iese, ~iésemos, ~ieseis, ~iesen**
Present participle: sintiendo
Imperative: siente, sentid

[5] pedir

Present: pido, pides, pide, pedimos, pedís, piden
Preterite: pedí, pediste, pidió, pedimos, pedisteis, pidieron
Present subjunctive: pid|a, **~as, ~a, ~amos, ~áis, ~an**
Imperfect subjunctive: pid|iera, **~ieras, ~iera, ~iéramos, ~ierais, ~ieran**
pid|iese, **~ieses, ~iese, ~iésemos, ~ieseis, ~iesen**
Present participle: pidiendo
Imperative: pide, pedid

[6] dormir

Present: duermo, duermes, duerme, dormimos, dormís, duermen
Preterite: dormí, dormiste, durmió, dormimos, dormisteis, durmieron
Present subjunctive: duerma, duermas, duerma, durmamos, durmáis, duerman
Imperfect subjunctive: durm|iera, **~ieras, ~iera, ~iéramos, ~ierais, ~ieran**
durm|iese, **~ieses, ~iese, ~iésemos, ~ieseis, ~iesen**
Present participle: durmiendo
Imperative: duerme, dormid

[7] dedicar

Preterite: dediqué, dedicaste, dedicó, dedicamos, dedicasteis, dedicaron
Present subjunctive: dediqu|e, **~es, ~e, ~emos, ~éis, ~en**

[8] delinquir

Present: delinco, delinques, delinque, delinquimos, delinquís, delinquen
Present subjunctive: delinc|a, **~as, ~a, ~amos, ~áis, ~an**

[9] vencer, esparcir

Present: venzo, vences, vence, vencemos, vencéis, vencen
esparzo, esparces, esparce, esparcimos, esparcís, esparcen

Present subjunctive: venz|a, **~as, ~a, ~amos, ~áis, ~an**
esparz|a, **~as, ~a, ~amos, ~áis, ~an**

[10] rechazar

Preterite: rechacé, rechazaste, rechazó, rechazamos, rechazasteis, rechazaron
Present subjunctive: rechac|e, **~es, ~e, ~emos, ~éis, ~en**

[11] conocer, lucir

Present: conozco, conoces, conoce, conocemos, conocéis, conocen
luzco, luces, luce, lucimos, lucís, lucen
Present subjunctive: conozc|a, **~as, ~a, ~amos, ~áis, ~an**
luzc|a, **~as, ~a, ~amos, ~áis, ~an**

[12] pagar

Preterite: pagué, pagaste, pagó, pagamos, pagasteis, pagaron
Present subjunctive: pagu|e, **~es, ~e, ~emos, ~éis, ~en**

[13] distinguir

Present: distingo, distingues, distingue, distinguimos, distinguís, distinguen
Present subjunctive: disting|a, **~as, ~a, ~amos, ~áis, ~an**

[14] acoger, afligir

Present: acojo, acoges, acoge, acogemos, acogéis, acogen
aflijo, afliges, aflige, afligimos, afligís, afligen
Present subjunctive: acoj|a, **~as, ~a, ~amos, ~áis, ~an**
aflij|a, **~as, ~a, ~amos, ~áis, ~an**

[15] averiguar

Preterite: averigüé, averiguaste, averiguó, averiguamos, averiguasteis, averiguaron
Present subjunctive: averigü|e, **~es, ~e, ~emos, ~éis, ~en**

[16] agorar

Present: agüero, agüeras, agüera, agoramos, agoráis, agüeran
Present subjunctive: agüere, agüeres, agüere, agoremos, agoréis, agüeren
Imperative: agüera, agorad

[17] huir

Present: huyo, huyes, huye, huimos, huís, huyen
Preterite: huí, huiste, huyó, huimos, huisteis, huyeron
Present subjunctive: huy|a, **~as, ~a, ~amos, ~áis, ~an**
Imperfect subjunctive: huy|era, **~eras, ~era, ~éramos, ~erais, ~eran**
huy|ese, **~eses, ~ese, ~ésemos, ~eseis, ~esen**
Present participle: huyendo
Imperative: huye, huid

[18] creer

Preterite: creí, creíste, creyó, creímos, creísteis, creyeron
Imperfect subjunctive: crey|era, **~eras, ~era, ~éramos, ~erais, ~eran**
crey|ese, **~eses, ~ese, ~ésemos, ~eseis, ~esen**
Present participle: creyendo
Past participle: creído

[19] argüir

Present: arguyo, arguyes, arguye, argüimos, argüís, arguyen
Preterite: argüí, argüiste, arguyó, argüimos, argüisteis, arguyeron
Present subjunctive: arguy|a, **~as, ~a, ~amos, ~áis, ~an**
Imperfect subjunctive: arguy|era, **~eras, ~era, ~éramos, ~erais, ~eran**
arguy|ese, **~eses, ~ese, ~ésemos, ~eseis, ~esen**
Present participle: arguyendo
Imperative: arguye, argüid

[20] vaciar

Present: vacío, vacías, vacía, vaciamos, vaciáis, vacían
Present subjunctive: vacíe, vacíes, vacíe, vaciemos, vaciéis, vacíen
Imperative: vacía, vaciad

[21] acentuar

Present: acentúo, acentúas, acentúa, acentuamos, acentuáis, acentúan
Present subjunctive: acentúe, acentúes, acentúe, acentuemos, acentuéis, acentúen
Imperative: acentúa, acentuad

[22] atañer, engullir

Preterite: atañ|i, **~iste, ~ó, ~imos, ~isteis, ~eron**
engull|í **~iste, ~ó, ~imos, ~isteis, ~eron**
Imperfect subjunctive: atañera, **~eras, ~era, ~éramos, ~erais, ~eran**
atañese, **~eses, ~ese, ~ésemos, ~eseis, ~esen**
engull|era, **~eras, ~era, ~éramos, ~erais, ~eran**
engull|ese, **~eses, ~ese, ~ésemos, ~eseis, ~esen**
Present participle: atañendo
engullendo

[23] aislar, aullar

Present: aíslo, aíslas, aísla, aislamos, aisláis, aíslan
aúllo, aúllas, aúlla, aullamos aulláis, aúllan
Present subjunctive: aísle, aísles, aísle, aislemos, aisléis, aíslen
aúlle, aúlles, aúlle, aullemos, aulléis, aúllen
Imperative: aísla, aislad
aúlla, aullad

[24] abolir

Present: abolimos, abolís
Present subjunctive: not used
Imperative: abolid

[25] andar

Preterite: anduv|e, **~iste, ~o, ~imos, ~isteis, ~ieron**
Imperfect subjunctive: anduv|iera, **~ieras, ~iera, ~iéramos, ~ierais, ~ieran**
anduv|iese, **~ieses, ~iese, ~iésemos, ~ieseis, ~iesen**

[26] dar

Present: doy, das, da, damos, dais, dan
Preterite: di, diste, dio, dimos, disteis, dieron
Present subjunctive: dé, des, dé, demos, deis, den
Imperfect subjunctive: diera, dieras, diera, diéramos, dierais, dieran
diese, dieses, diese, diésemos, dieseis, diesen

[27] estar

Present: estoy, estás, está, estamos, estáis, están
Preterite: estuv|e, **~iste, ~o, ~imos, ~isteis, ~ieron**
Present subjunctive: esté, estés, esté, estemos, estéis, estén
Imperfect subjunctive: estuv|iera, **~ieras, ~iera, ~iéramos, ~ierais, ~ieran**
estuv|iese, **~ieses, ~iese, ~iésemos, ~ieseis, ~iesen**
Imperative: está, estad

[28] caber

Present: quepo, cabes, cabe, cabemos, cabéis, caben
Future: cabr|é, **~ás, ~á, ~emos, ~éis, ~án**
Preterite: cup|e, **~iste, ~o, ~imos, ~isteis, ~ieron**
Present subjunctive: quep|a, **~as, ~a, ~amos, ~áis, ~an**
Imperfect subjunctive: cup|iera, **~ieras, ~iera, ~iéramos, ~ierais, ~ieran**
cup|iese, **~ieses, ~iese, ~iésemos, ~ieseis, ~iesen**
Conditional: cabr|ía, **~ías, ~ía, ~íamos, ~íais, ~ían**

[29] caer

Present: caigo, caes, cae, caemos, caéis, caen
Preterite: caí, caiste, cayó, caímos, caísteis, cayeron
Present subjunctive: caig|a, **~as, ~a, ~amos, ~áis, ~an**
Imperfect subjunctive: cay|era, **~eras, ~era, ~éramos, ~erais, ~eran**
cay|ese, **~eses, ~ese, ~ésemos, ~eseis, ~esen**
Present participle: cayendo
Past participle: caído

[30] haber

Present: he, has, ha, hemos, habéis, han
Future: habr|é **~ás, ~á, ~emos, ~éis, ~án**
Preterite: hub|e, **~iste, ~o, ~imos, ~isteis, ~ieron**
Present subjunctive: hay|a, **~as, ~a, ~amos, ~áis, ~an**
Imperfect subjunctive: hub|iera, **~ieras, ~iera, ~iéramos, ~ierais, ~ieran**
hub|iese, **~ieses, ~iese, ~iésemos, ~ieseis, ~iesen**
Conditional: habr|ía, **~ías, ~ía, ~íamos, ~íais, ~ían**
Imperative: he, habed

[31] hacer

Present: hago, haces, hace, hacemos, hacéis, hacen
Future: har|é, **~ás, ~á, ~emos, ~éis, ~án**
Preterite: hice, hiciste, hizo, hicimos, hicisteis, hicieron
Present subjunctive: hag|a, **~as, ~a, ~amos, ~áis, ~an**
Imperfect subjunctive: hic|iera, **~ieras, ~iera, ~iéramos, ~ierais, ~ieran**
hic|iese, **~ieses, ~iese, ~iésemos, ~ieseis, ~iesen**
Conditional: har|ía, **~ías, ~ía, ~íamos, ~íais, ~ían**
Past participle: hecho
Imperative: haz, haced

[32] placer

Present subjunctive: plazca
Imperfect subjunctive: placiera, placiese

[33] poder

Present: puedo, puedes, puede, podemos, podéis, pueden
Future: podr|é, **~ás, ~á, ~emos, ~éis, ~án**
Preterite: pud|e, **~iste, ~o, ~imos, ~isteis, ~ieron**
Present subjunctive: pueda, puedas, pueda, podamos, podáis, puedan
Imperfect subjunctive: pud|iera, **~ieras, ~iera, ~iéramos, ~ierais, ~ieran**
pud|iese, **~ieses, ~iese, ~iésemos, ~ieseis, ~iesen**
Conditional: podr|ía, **~ías, ~ía, ~íamos, ~íais, ~ían**
Past participle: pudiendo

[34] poner

Present: pongo, pones, pone, ponemos, ponéis, ponen
Future: pondr|é, **~ás, ~á, ~emos, ~éis, ~án**
Preterite: pus|e, **~iste, ~o, ~imos, ~isteis, ~ieron**
Present subjunctive: pong|a, **~as, ~a, ~amos, ~áis, ~an**
Imperfect subjunctive: pus|iera, **~ieras, ~iera, ~iéramos, ~ierais, ~ieran**
pus|iese, **~ieses, ~iese, ~iésemos, ~ieseis, ~iesen**
Conditional: pondr|ía, **~ías, ~ía, ~íamos, ~íais, ~ían**
Past participle: puesto
Imperative: pon, poned

[35] querer

Present: quiero, quieres, quiere, queremos, queréis, quieren
Future: querr|é, **~ás, ~á, ~emos, ~éis, ~án**
Preterite: quis|e, **~iste, ~o, ~imos, ~isteis, ~ieron**
Present subjunctive: quiera, quieras, quiera, queramos, queráis, quieran
Imperfect subjunctive: quis|iera, **~ieras, ~iera, ~iéramos, ~ierais, ~ieran**
quis|iese, **~ieses, ~iese, ~iésemos, ~ieseis, ~iesen**
Conditional: querr|ía, **~ías, ~ía, ~íamos, ~íais, ~ían**
Imperative: quiere, quered

[36] raer

Present: raigo/rayo, raes, rae, raemos, raéis, raen
Preterite: raí, raíste, rayó, raímos, raísteis, rayeron
Present subjunctive: raig|a, **~as, ~a, ~amos, ~áis, ~an** ray|a, **~as, ~a, ~amos, ~áis, ~an**
Imperfect subjunctive: ray|era, **~eras, ~era, ~éramos, ~erais, ~eran**
ray|ese, **~eses, ~ese, ~ésemos, ~eseis, ~esen**
Present participle: rayendo
Past participle: raído

[37] roer

Present: roo, roes, roe, roemos, roéis, roen
Preterite: roí, roíste, royó, roímos, roísteis, royeron
Present subjunctive: ro|a, **~as, ~a, ~amos, ~áis, ~an**
Imperfect subjunctive: roy|era, **~eras, ~era, ~éramos, ~erais, ~eran**
roy|ese, **~eses, ~ese, ~ésemos, ~eseis, ~esen**
Present participle: royendo
Past participle: roído

[38] saber

Present: sé, sabes, sabe, sabemos, sabéis, saben
Future: sabr|é, **~ás, ~á, ~emos, ~éis, ~án**
Preterite: sup|e, **~iste, ~o, ~imos, ~isteis, ~ieron**
Present subjunctive: sep|a, **~as, ~a, ~amos, ~áis, ~an**
Imperfect subjunctive: sup|iera, **~ieras, ~iera, ~iéramos, ~ierais, ~ieran** sup|iese, **~ieses, ~iese, ~iésemos, ~ieseis, ~iesen**
Conditional: sabr|ía, **~ías, ~ía, ~íamos, ~íais, ~ían**

[39] ser

Present: soy, eres, es, somos, sois, son
Imperfect: era, eras, era, éramos, erais, eran
Preterite: fui, fuiste, fue, fuimos, fuisteis, fueron
Present subjunctive: se|a, **~as, ~a, ~amos, ~áis, ~an**
Imperfect subjunctive: fu|era, **~eras, ~era, ~éramos, ~erais, ~eran** fu|ese, **~eses, ~ese, ~ésemos, ~eseis, ~esen**
Imperative: sé, sed

[40] tener

Present: tengo, tienes, tiene, tenemos, tenéis, tienen
Future: tendr|é, **~ás, ~á, ~emos, ~éis, ~án**
Preterite: tuv|e, **~iste, ~o, ~imos, ~isteis, ~ieron**
Present subjunctive: teng|a, **~as, ~a, ~amos, ~áis, ~an**
Imperfect subjunctive: tuv|iera, **~ieras, ~iera, ~iéramos, ~ierais, ~ieran** tuv|iese, **~ieses, ~iese, ~iésemos, ~ieseis, ~iesen**
Conditional: tendr|ía, **~ías, ~ía, ~íamos, ~íais, ~ían**
Imperative: ten, tened

[41] traer

Present: traigo, traes, trae, traemos, traéis, traen
Preterite: traj|e, **~iste, ~o, ~imos, ~isteis, ~eron**
Present subjunctive: traig|a, **~as, ~a, ~amos, ~áis, ~an**
Imperfect subjunctive: traj|era, **~eras, ~era, ~éramos, ~erais, ~eran** traj|ese, **~eses, ~ese, ~ésemos, ~eseis, ~esen**
Present participle: trayendo
Past participle: traído

[42] valer

Present: valgo, vales, vale, valemos, valéis, valen
Future: vald|ré, **~ás, ~á, ~emos, ~éis, ~án**
Present subjunctive: valg|a, **~as, ~a, ~amos, ~áis, ~an**
Conditional: vald|ría, **~ías, ~ía, ~íamos, ~íais, ~ían**
Imperative: vale, valed

[43] ver

Present: veo, ves, ve, vemos, veis, ven
Imperfect: ve|ía, **~ías, ~ía, ~íamos, ~íais, ~ían**
Preterite: vi, viste, vio, vimos, visteis, vieron
Present subjunctive: ve|a, **~as, ~a, ~amos, ~áis, ~an**
Past participle: visto

[44] yacer

Present: yazco, yaces, yace, yacemos, yacéis, yacen
Present subjunctive: yazc|a, **~as, ~a, ~amos, ~áis, ~an**
Imperative: yace, yaced

[45] asir

Present: asgo, ases, ase, asimos, asís, asen
Present subjunctive: asg|a, **~as, ~a, ~amos, ~áis, ~an**

[46] decir

Present: digo, dices, dice, decimos, decís, dicen
Future: dir|é, **~ás, ~á, ~emos, ~éis, ~án**
Preterite: dij|e, **~iste, ~o, ~imos, ~isteis, ~eron**
Present subjunctive: dig|a, **~as, ~a, ~amos, ~áis, ~an**
Imperfect subjunctive: dij|era, **~eras, ~era, ~éramos, ~erais, ~eran**
dij|ese, **~eses, ~ese, ~ésemos, ~eseis, ~esen**
Conditional: dir|ía, **~ías, ~ía, ~íamos, ~íais, ~ían**
Present participle: dicho
Imperative: di, decid

[47] reducir

Present: reduzco, reduces, reduce, reducimos, reducís, reducen
Preterite: reduj|e, **~iste, ~o, ~imos, ~isteis, ~eron**
Present subjunctive: reduzc|a, **~as, ~a, ~amos, ~áis, ~an**
Imperfect subjunctive: reduj|era, **~eras, ~era, ~éramos, ~erais, ~eran**
reduj|ese, **~eses, ~ese, ~ésemos, ~eseis, ~esen**

[48] erguir

Present: yergo, yergues, yergue, erguimos, erguís, yerguen
Preterite: erguí, erguiste, irguió, erguimos, erguisteis, irguieron
Present subjunctive: yerg|a, **~as, ~a, ~amos, ~áis, ~an**
Imperfect subjunctive: irgu|iera, **~ieras, ~iera, ~iéramos, ~ierais, ~ieran**
irgu|iese, **~ieses, ~iese, ~iésemos, ~ieseis, ~iesen**
Present participle: irguiendo
Imperative: yergue, erguid

[49] ir

Present: voy, vas, va, vamos, vais, van
Imperfect: iba, ibas, iba, íbamos, ibais, iban
Preterite: fui, fuiste, fue, fuimos, fuisteis, fueron
Present subjunctive: vay|a, **~as, ~a, ~amos, ~áis, ~an**
Imperfect subjunctive: fu|era, **~eras, ~era, ~éramos, ~erais, ~eran**
fu|ese, **~eses, ~ese, ~ésemos, ~eseis, ~esen**
Present participle: yendo
Imperative: ve, id

[50] oír

Present: oigo, oyes, oye, oímos, oís, oyen
Preterite: oí, oíste, oyó, oímos, oísteis, oyeron
Present subjunctive: oig|a, **~as, ~a, ~amos, ~áis, ~an**
Imperfect subjunctive: oy|era, **~eras, ~era, ~éramos, ~erais, ~eran**